MEXICO
BUSINESS

**World Trade Press
Country Business Guides**

CHINA Business
HONG KONG Business
JAPAN Business
KOREA Business
MEXICO Business
SINGAPORE Business
TAIWAN Business

MEXICO
BUSINESS

The Portable Encyclopedia
For Doing Business With Mexico

James L. Nolan, Ph.D.   Karla C. Shippey, J.D.

Alexandra Woznick   Edward G. Hinkelman

William T. LeGro   Hugo I. Vera

Dean C. Alexander, J.D., LL.M.   Manuel F. Pasero

Auerbach International • Carlsmith Ball Wichman Murray Case & Ichiki
Ernst & Young • Foreign Trade • Global Production & Transportation
J.E. Lowden & Co. International Freight Forwarders
Pasero, Martín-Sánchez y Sánchez • Reed Publishing (USA) Inc.
Porter International Freight Forwarders • The NAFTA Research Institute

Series Editor: Edward G. Hinkelman

WORLD
TRADE
PRESS ®

Resources for International Trade

1505 Fifth Avenue
San Rafael, California 94901
USA

Published by World Trade Press
1505 Fifth Avenue
San Rafael, CA 94901, USA

Cover and book design: Brad Greene
Illustrations: Eli Africa
Color maps: Magellan^{sm} Geographix
B&W maps: David Baker
Desktop Publishing: Kelly R. Krill and Gail R. Weisman
Charts and graphs: David Baker and Kelly R. Krill
Copy Editor: Michael Levy
Proofreader: Aanel Victoria

Permission to reprint copyrighted materials has been given as follows: Excerpts from *1994 Worldwide Corporate Tax Guide* and *1994 Worldwide Personal Tax Guide,* copyright © 1994 by Ernst & Young, reprinted with permission of Ernst & Young. "Effects of NAFTA on Visas," prepared by Cynthia Juarez Lange, copyright © 1994 Fragomen, Del Rey & Bernsen, P.C., reprinted with permission of the law firm and the author. Export and import statistics from *Foreign Trade,* copyright © 1994 by Defense & Diplomacy, Inc., reprinted with permission of the publisher. Articles from *Global Production & Transportation* magazine, copyright © 1993, 1994 New Hope Communications, Inc., reprinted with permission from *Global Production & Transportation* magazine and the authors. "Global Gaffe" cartoon from *Global Production & Transportation* magazine, copyright © 1994 New Hope Communications, Inc., reproduced with permission of *Global Production & Transportation* magazine, the artist, and the author. Excerpts from "NAFTA Creates Opportunity for US Companies Doing Business in Mexico," by William E. Mooz, Jr., *Holland & Hart International Update,* copyright © 1994 Holland & Hart, reprinted with permission of the law firm and the author. Discussion of industrial property rights from "Mexico's New Intellectual Property Regime," by John B. McKnight and Carlos Müggenberg R.V., *The International Lawyer* (Vol. 27, No. 1 Spring 1993), copyright © 1993 American Bar Association, reprinted by permission of the ABA and the authors. "The North American Free Trade Agreement: An Overview," by Dean C. Alexander, copyright © 1993 *International Tax and Business Lawyer,* and reprinted from *International Tax and Business Lawyer,* Vol. 11, No. 1 with permission of the journal and the author. Excerpts from *Mexico Law Digest,* Martindale-Hubbell International Law Digest, copyright © 1992, 1993, by Reed Publishing (USA) Inc., reproduced with permission of Reed Publishing (USA) Inc. *Maquila* article and selected discussions of Mexican law from materials prepared by Manuel F. Pasero of Pasero, Martín-Sánchez y Sánchez, copyright © 1994 Manuel F. Pasero, reproduced with permission of the author and the law firm. "NAFTA: Trade in Goods Boon or Boondoggle?" by Susan Kohn Ross of Ross & Associates, copyright ©1994 Susan Kohn Ross, reprinted with permission of the author. Excerpts from "New World Orders," by Geoffrey Brewer, *Sales & Marketing Management,* copyright © 1994 Bill Communications, Inc., reprinted with permission of *Sales & Marketing Management.* "NAFTA: General Provisions" and NAFTA certification checklist from *North American Free Trade Agreement Guidebook,* by Tim J. Sanford, SANFORD Tax & Customs Consulting, copyright © 1993 Tim J. Sandford, reprinted with permission of the author. Cartoon in "Business Entities & Formation" copyright © 1993 by Don Wright, *The Palm Beach Post,* reprinted with permission of artist. Cartoon by Oswaldo copyright © 1994 Oswaldo/Cartoonists & Writers Syndicate, and cartoon by Arcadio copyright © 1994 Arcadio/Cartoonists & Writers Syndicate, both reprinted by permission of the Cartoonists & Writers Syndicate. Excerpts from "Doing Business in Mexico: A Primer" by Dana I. Schiffman and R. Michael Joyce, and "No Longer a 'Pollution Haven'" by John Zebrowski, both copyright ©1994 the *Los Angeles Business Journal,* reprinted with permission of the *Los Angeles Business Journal.* "US Shipping to Mexico," *Traffic Management,* copyright © 1993 Cahners Publishing Company, reprinted with permission from *Traffic Management.* "Foreign Investment" by Timon L. Marshall and Duane H. Zobrist, copyright © 1994 Carlsmith Ball Wichman Murray Case & Ichiki, reprinted with permission of the law firm.

Library of Congress Cataloging-in-Publication Data
Nolan, James L., 1951-
   Mexico business: the portable encyclopedia for doing business with Mexico/ James L. Nolan ... [et al.].
      p. cm. — (World Trade Press country business guides)
   Includes bibliographical references and index.
   ISBN 0-9631864-0-X
    1. Mexico—Economic conditions—1982- 2. Mexico—Economic policy—1970- 3. Investments, Foreign—Government policy—Mexico. 4. International business enterprises—Mexico. I. Series.
HC135.N64 1994
658.8'48'0972—dc20   94-15696
               CIP

Printed in the United States of America

ACKNOWLEDGMENTS

We owe many leaders in the international business community a debt of gratitude. Hundreds of trade and reference experts have brought this book to life. We are indebted to numerous international business consultants, reference librarians, travel advisors, consulate, embassy, and trade mission officers, bank officers, attorneys, global shippers and insurers, and multinational investment brokers who answered our incessant inquiries and volunteered facts, figures, and expert opinions. To all these many individuals, named and unnamed, we extend our thanks.

A number of persons stepped forward with up-to-date explanations of NAFTA, making possible our comprehensive coverage of this significant treaty so soon after its historic signing. In compiling the NAFTA chapter, we crossed many faxes with author and international trade consultant Dean C. Alexander, President of Septacontinentaux Corp. and Director of The NAFTA Research Institute, as well as with customs consultant Tim Sandford, SANFORD Tax & Consulting, Sunnyvale, California, and attorney Susan Kohn Ross, Ross & Associates, Los Angeles, California.

Mil gracias a Carlos Valderrama, Director of Latin American Operations for Carlsmith Ball Wichman Murray Case & Ichiki, Los Angeles, California for his review of our dictionary and for his efforts in finding us many resources. In particular, Mr. Valderrama brought to our attention a most informative and fruitful conference on the business and financial aspects of NAFTA sponsored by the Beverly Hills Bar Association. And on that note, kudos to that association for managing to get so many first-rate international trade and law experts together in one room.

We extend sincere gratitude to the attorneys, usually absorbed in advising international traders, who have volunteered their time and efforts to consult on various portions of this book. Many legal advisors gave freely of their time, expressing concern that the international community be informed of the necessary requirements for doing cross-border business. We are especially grateful for the assistance and patience of: Timon L. Marshall, Carlsmith Ball Wichman Murray Case & Ichiki, Mexico City Branch Office; Adrian Zubikarai Arriola, Carlsmith Ball Garcia Cacho Zubikarai y Asociados, S.C., Mexico City; John Mendez, White & Case, Los Angeles, California; Kenneth R. Lee, White & Case, Mexico City Branch Office; John Liebman of Brown, Winfield & Canzoneri, Inc., Los Angeles, California; and William E. Mooz, Jr., Holland & Hart, Denver, Colorado.

A note of thanks is due those who helped track down and arrange reprint permissions, including: Kathleen Dunnewald of *Global Production & Transportation*, Boulder, Colorado, for permission granted for several reprints from that publication; Susan Monagan of Cartoonists & Writers Syndicate of New York City for assistance in researching and obtaining permission to reprint foreign political cartoons; Francis J. Quinn of *Traffic Management*; Francesca Morton of *Sales & Marketing Management*; Anne Sage of Casey & Sayre, Inc., who helped arranged for reprints from the *Los Angeles Business Journal*.

We relied heavily on the reference librarians and resources available at the libraries of Stanford University and the University of California at Berkeley, the Marin County Civic Center Library, Marin County Law Library, San Rafael Public Library, and Palo Alto Public Library. Thanks to Anita Cleary for her research skills and assistance in tracking down materials in many of these libraries.

We also acknowledge the valuable contributions of Philip B. Auerbach of Auerbach International, San Francisco, for translations; Solange Suárez-Gold for reviewing Spanish names in the "Important Addresses" chapter; all the patient folks at Desktop Publishing of Larkspur, California; Cassie Arnold of Ernst & Young, San Francisco for promptly obtaining the most current tax information from that firm's publications; to Stephen M. Sarro of the US Trade Center in Mexico City, and Patricia A. Smith of the Trade Show Bureau in Denver, Colorado, for help in pulling together elusive information regarding trade fairs; and to John Peake and Brad Nuttal of MexNET in Salt Lake City for giving us access to the network to run down information.

Special thanks to Mela Hinkelman, whose patience, understanding, generosity, and support made this project possible.

DISCLAIMER

We have diligently tried to ensure the accuracy of all of the information in this publication and to present as comprehensive a reference work as space would permit. In determining the contents, we were guided by many experts in the field, extensive hours of research, and our own experience. We did have to make choices in coverage, however, because the inclusion of everything one could ever want to know about international trade would be impossible. The fluidity and fast pace of today's business world makes the task of keeping data current and accurate an extremely difficult one. This publication is intended to give you the information that you need in order to discover the information that is most useful for your particular business. As you contact the resources within this book, you will no doubt learn of new and exciting business opportunities and of additional international trading requirements that have arisen even within the short time since we published this edition. If errors are found, we will strive to correct them in preparing future editions. The publishers take no responsibility for inaccurate or incomplete information that may have been submitted to them in the course of research for this publication. The facts published indicate the result of those inquiries and no warranty as to their accuracy is given.

Contents

Introduction

Mexico, the world's 11th largest economy, is arguably the most richly endowed with natural resources of all the nations of Latin America. It is strategically situated between Atlantic Europe and the nations of the Pacific Rim, as well as culturally and geographically between the world's largest economy—the United States—to the north and the developing economies of Central and South America. After centuries of being an isolated player with an essentially colonial economy and less than 15 years after it was declared effectively bankrupt as it struggled under the weight of the largest foreign debt in the world, Mexico has achieved a miraculous turnaround, regaining its status as one of the world's up-and-coming developing economies. For the first time in decades, the country is opening up to the outside world in an effort to secure foreign investment, upgrade its technology, and modernize its economy. At the same time it is restructuring its economy, Mexico is working to raise the standard of living of the mass of its people, who provide its low wage labor advantage.

Although growth in the economy has slowed of late, Mexico's government has managed to reduce inflation from nearly 160 percent in the mid-1980s to 8 percent in 1993 and to reduce, by more than half, the share of its gross domestic product devoted to debt service. In the process, it has: deregulated and reprivatized its financial system; sold off the vast majority of state-run firms; agreed to reduce trade barriers through membership in the General Agreement on Tariffs and Trade (GATT); signed the North American Free Trade Agreement (NAFTA); opened most sectors to increasing foreign participation; reorganized its archaic landholding system; and generally put in place free market structures and policies designed to support continued growth into the next century. Mexico has experienced more than its share of turmoil. Nevertheless, the country is expected to continue moving forward with its modernization schemes.

Mexico is an intriguing market and one well worth investigating from a number of perspectives. For buyers, Mexico can offer a wide range of medium- to higher-quality goods at competitive prices. It is a major producer of minerals, metals, and intermediate products; a growing variety of agricultural and animal products; automobiles and automotive parts; machinery and other parts; and handicrafts, among many other goods. Its businesses can handle orders ranging from the smallest to the largest. From the seller's standpoint, Mexico needs a wide range of agricultural and industrial raw materials, intermediate components, and specialty items to feed its rapidly expanding industries. Both the upgrading of its industry and its ambitious development projects require materials, capital goods, and service inputs. And rising popular demand offers an opportunity to place goods into its developing consumer markets.

For manufacturers Mexico offers a large labor pool ranging from unskilled to highly skilled workers. In addition to its low-cost and rapidly improving industrial plant, the country's *maquila* program provides an in-place framework that allows foreign producers to capitalize on Mexico's labor advantage and fill a variety of outsourcing needs. For investors, Mexico is in the process of opening up additional areas of its economy previously either off-limits or restricted to minority participation by foreigners; up to 100 percent outside ownership is no longer rare. Mexico's US and Canadian NAFTA partners will receive special consideration, but by the year 2000, most of Mexico is expected to be open to foreign investors of all nationalities.

Mexico is in the process of refocusing its economy away from the state-run monopolies and private sector oligopolies that had been protected from international competition. Mexico is caught between the fears of an old guard establishment that wants to maintain the status quo and the hopes of a new generation of internationally trained, up-and-coming leaders and businesspeople. It is backed by a hardworking and eminently pragmatic people who are willing to accept new ways of doing things in order to make a better life. Although Mexico has a long way to go, there is reason to be optimistic that it will continue to make progress toward its goals. The overall pace and level of change is expected to accelerate over the near term, making Mexico an even more complex and challenging—as well as compelling—place to do business.

MEXICO Business was designed by businesspeople experienced in international markets to give you an overview of how things actually work and what current conditions are in Mexico. It will give you the head start you need to be able to evaluate and operate in Mexican markets. It also tells you where to go to get more information in greater depth.

The next chapter discusses the main elements of the country's **Economy,** including its development, present situation, and the forces determining its future prospects. **Current Issues** explains the top concerns affecting the country and its next stage of development. The **Opportunities** chapter presents discussions of major areas of interest to importers and exporters, plus additional hot prospects. The chapter also clarifies the nature of government procurement processes. **Foreign Investment** details attitudes, policies, incentives, regulations, procedures, and restrictions, with particular reference to Mexico's new foreign investment law and its *maquila* program. **Foreign Trade** presents information on what and with whom Mexico trades. A special chapter on the **North American Free Trade Agreement** presents the latest information on this important new trading arrangement, its context, terms, and what is and isn't included—information necessary to both those affected as well as those left out of its provisions.

The **Import Policy & Procedures** and **Export Policy & Procedures** chapters delineate the nature of Mexico's trade: trade policy, and the practical information—including nuts-and-bolts procedural requirements—necessary to trade with it. The **Industry Reviews** chapter outlines Mexico's 13 most prominent industries and their competitive positions from the standpoint of a businessperson interested in taking advantage of these industries' strengths or in exploiting their competitive weaknesses. **Trade Fairs** provides a comprehensive listing of trade fairs in Mexico, complete with contact information, and spells out the best ways to maximize the benefits offered by these events.

Business Travel offers practical information on travel requirements, resources, internal travel, local customs, and ambiance, as well as comparative information on accommodations and dining in Mexico City, Guadalajara, Monterrey, and Tijuana—the main business markets in Mexico. **Business Culture** provides a user-friendly primer on local business style, mind-set, negotiating practices, and numerous other tips designed to improve your effectiveness, avoid inadvertent gaffes, and generally smooth the way in doing business with Mexicans. **Demographics** presents basic statistical data needed to assess the Mexican market, while **Marketing** outlines resources, approaches, and specific markets.

Business Entities & Formation discusses recognized business entities and registration procedures for operating in Mexico. **Labor** assembles information on the availability, capabilities, and cost of labor in Mexico, as well as terms of employment and business-labor relations. **Business Law** interprets the structure of the Mexican legal system, providing a digest of substantive points of commercial law prepared with help from international legal authorities. **Financial Institutions** outlines the workings of the financial system, including banking and financial markets, and the availability of financing and services needed by foreign businesses. **Currency & Foreign Exchange** explains the workings of Mexico's foreign exchange system. **International Payments** is an illustrated, step-by-step guide to using documentary collections and letters of credit in trade with Mexico. **Corporate Taxation** and **Personal Taxation** provide the information on tax rates, provisions, and status of foreign operations and individuals needed to evaluate a venture in the country. **Transportation** gives current information on how to physically access the country.

The **Business Dictionary** is a unique resource consisting of 550 entries focusing specifically on Mexican business and idiomatic usage to provide the businessperson with the basic means for conducting business in Mexico. More than 1,000 **Important Addresses** include contact information for Mexican official agencies; business associations; trade and industry associations; financial, professional, and service firms; transportation and shipping agencies; media outlets; and sources of additional information to enable businesspeople to locate the offices and help they need to operate in Mexico. Full-color, up-to-date **Maps** aid the business traveler in getting around in the major business venues in Mexico. The volume is cross-referenced and indexed to provide ease of access to the specific information needed by busy businesspeople.

MEXICO Business gives you the information you need, both to evaluate the prospect of doing business in Mexico and to actually begin doing it. It is your invitation to this fascinating society and market. *¡Bienvenido!*—Welcome!

Economy

Los Estados Unidos Mexicanos (the United Mexican States)—or, simply, Mexico—is the site of the oldest indigenous and European civilizations in the New World. It is the most populous Spanish-speaking nation in the world, surpassed among Latin American nations only by Brazil. Mexico, with its strong cultural identity and rapidly developing economy, is arguably the most important economy in the region. As such, it provides the model for other Latin American economies—but, being the pioneer, it also often has the dubious honor of being the first to make mistakes as its economy develops. And, as the local saying goes, poor Mexico is so far from God and so close to a much larger, dominant United States, which further complicates its situation.

Mexico, with an area of 1,967,183 square km (759,530 square miles), is the 13th largest country in the world; it occupies an area about three times that of the US state of Texas, which, prior to 1836, belonged to Mexico. In mid-1993 Mexico had an estimated population of 90.4 million, 72 percent of whom lived in urban areas and more than 50 percent of whom were less than 20 years of age. With a steep annual growth rate of more than 2 percent, Mexico's population is expected to top 100 million before the next century. Mexico's overall population density was about 45 persons per square km (119 per square mile) in 1992. However, nearly 21 million people—more than one-fifth of the country's total population—live in the greater Mexico City metropolitan area, parts of which can claim a population density of more than 15,530 per square km (40,225 per square mile). Mexico City, the center of the country's economic, political, and cultural life, is the largest city in the world; it is surpassed by Japan's greater Tokyo-Yokohama megalopolis with more than 27 million people, but this Japanese megalopolis includes separate, although contiguous, urban centers. In contrast, Mexico's least populous state, Baja California Sur, has a population density of only 4 persons per square km, and several other states are sparsely inhabited with densities of about 10 per square km.

Mexico has 10,143 km (6,339 miles) of coastline, fronting on both the Pacific Ocean to the west and the Gulf of Mexico to the east, and 4,538 km (2,836 miles) of land boundaries, including a 3,326 km (2,079 mile) northern boundary with the US and 1,212 km (757 miles) of southern boundaries with Guatemala and Belize. Its topographic and climatic zones vary from high desert in the northern and central zones to lowland tropical forest in the south and east. In the north, Mexico has two parallel northwest-to-southeast trending mountainous ridges, the Sierra Madre Occidental to the west and the Sierra Madre Oriental to the east. In the northern and central areas a broad, broken plateau—the Altiplano Central, site of Mexico's largest urban centers—separates these two ridges. The two *cordilleras* merge south of Mexico City to form the Sierra Madre del Sur, the backbone of the narrow Isthmus of Tehuantepec, where Mexico funnels into the narrow Central American Isthmus connecting North and South America. Mexico's peaks reach as high as 5,639 meters (18,500 feet)—the third highest in North America—and the zone is tectonically active, with intermittent volcanic activity and severe earthquakes. Mexico has coastal plains, which are generally narrow on the west coast but broad on the east. The eastern plains become increasingly tropical as they follow the coastline southward and extend across the low Yucatán Peninsula.

Nearly half of Mexico is classified as arid, including the northern high desert and mountains. Much of the central plateau and mountains—about 23 percent of the country—has a temperate climate accompanied by moderate rainfall. The remainder of the country—about 28 percent—is classified as warm humid or subhumid (semi-tropical or tropical), including most of the Gulf coastal plain, the Isthmus of Tehuantepec, and the Yucatán Peninsula, which are generally covered by savannah or rain forest. About 39 percent of Mexico is considered to be grasslands and 24 percent is forest. Some 13 percent is arable, and most of this is under cultivation, at least intermittently, although only 1 percent is classified as being under permanent cultivation. About 3 percent is irrigated. The remaining 24 percent of Mexico's territory is classified as "other"—a category that includes urban or otherwise developed areas, undeveloped land and bare rock, and inland waters.

Mexico is rich in natural resources, including precious and base metals—silver, lead, zinc, gold, copper, and iron—and oil, natural gas, and timber. Mexico is the world's sixth largest oil producer. Its reserves—estimated in 1991 at 51 billion barrels—are the seventh largest in the world, representing about 5 percent of proven reserves worldwide.

Mexico is also culturally rich, with a complex native heritage dating back thousands of years and compounded by more recent European additions. Some 60 percent of the population is classed as *mestizo*—or genetically and culturally mixed Indian and European, primarily Spanish—while 30 percent is Indian or predominately Indian; 9 percent are predominately of European origin, while the remaining 1 percent represent others, mostly foreign residents or those of Asian or African origin. Although there is some ambivalence about this overwhelmingly native element in a developing Mexico that looks to Europe and the US as role models, *indígenismo* (nativeness) is an important determinant of Mexican culture and national identity.

Spanish is the official language, spoken by more than 98 percent of the populace. At least 50 Indian languages and major dialects are in active use, and of the at least 6.4 million speakers for whom these represent a primary language, perhaps 1.25 million speak only a non-Spanish native tongue. And although Mexico has officially been secular since reforms in the 1860s, about 90 percent of Mexicans are at least nominally Roman Catholic. About 5 percent belong to various Protestant denominations, and the remainder are mostly unaffiliated or adherents of various native religions.

Although it is difficult to separate out and ignore Mexico's distinctive past, it is its present and its future that engage both Mexicans and foreigners who wish to do business with this rapidly changing and increasingly sophisticated nation.

HISTORY OF THE ECONOMY

The Prehistoric Period

Mesoamerica, as the Mexican culture area is known, is considered to be one of the six major world areas in which civilization developed independently (the others are Egypt, Mesopotamia, India, China, and the Peruvian Andes). Mexico has a complex prehistory. Agriculture, based on maize and beans as staples, developed independently in the area around 5000 BC.

Mexico's first noteworthy civilization was the Olmec (c.1200 to 400 BC) on the Gulf Coast. During the Classic Period (c.200 BC to AD 700), much of Mesoamerica was loosely united in an empire that reached to both coasts and as far south as Central America under the dominance of a religious and trading center at Teotihuacán, located just northeast of the current Mexico City. By AD 400, Teotihuacán, a city built around pyramids that rival some of those in Egypt in grandeur, had a population estimated at 200,000, larger than any city in Europe during the same period. Meanwhile, the Maya, living in the Yucatán, were trading with Teotihuacán; building cities in the jungle; and developing sophisticated calendars, mathematics, and notational systems. Mexico was also the location of numerous other smaller, but still substantial, rival cultures, many of which reached high levels of development and left impressive remains (which provide one of the foundation stones for Mexico's important tourism industry). However, none of these developed a surviving, decipherable written language to chronicle their achievements, as was the case among high cultures in Europe and Asia.

Mexican prehistory is perhaps best symbolized by the rise and fall of the Aztecs and their capital of Tenochtitlán, located on the site of what is now Mexico City, then a large shallow lake. The Aztecs were a small, semi-nomadic tribe from the northwest of Mexico, self-confessed barbarians who migrated to the central plateau around AD 1300. They settled on marginal islands in the lake, eventually conquering the local residents and setting up an elaborate and brutal social, political, and ritual system that involved predatory warfare and human sacrifice on a massive scale. Tenochtitlán itself eventually grew to perhaps 250,000 in population while the surrounding Valley of Mexico area supported perhaps 1 million people. At its height, the Aztec empire ruled perhaps 5 million people. Tenochtitlán's influence was even greater than this figure would indicate, because the Aztecs did not attempt to incorporate outlying groups. Rather, they demanded tribute or favorable trade access, and periodically went to war to enforce their will and gain captives to be used as sacrificial offerings to their deities.

The militaristic Aztec empire was founded on an economy based on intensive agriculture, a diverse quasi-free market economy involving complex, specialized industrial production and distribution systems and long-distance trade in commodities that reached throughout much of Mexico and beyond. The first Spanish chroniclers noted in awe that Tenochtitlán was much larger (and better organized and cleaner) than any city in Spain and that its well-stocked marketplace stretched over a vast area and was far superior to anything known in Europe at the time.

The European Conquest and the Colonial Period

If anything, Mexico's history is even more complicated than its prehistory. In 1519 an expedition with 550 men and 16 horses led by Hernán Cortés landed near Veracruz. Cortés enlisted local Indian allies, burned his ships to prevent desertion, and moved inland. Eventually, reinforced by additional Spaniards and an estimated 100,000 Indian allies, Cortés conquered the Aztecs in 1521. Cortés was aided by the advice of his Indian mistress, La Malinche, who translated and advised on local politics and strategy (and, for her traitorous behavior to her people, is still considered a villain in Mexican popular culture). Of even greater importance were the death of the Aztec ruler, Moctezuma II (which left the hierarchical Aztecs without effective leadership) and the outbreaks of European diseases (such as smallpox), to which the Indians had no immunity—all of which disrupted the Aztec system and weakened resistance.

To develop their new province, the Spanish authorities granted *encomiendas*—rights to the lands and the labor of the Indians resident on them—to the conquerors much as lords were granted lands and serfs in Europe during the Middle Ages. Large deposits of silver were discovered in Zacatecas, Guanajuato, San Luis Potosí, and Pachuca north of Mexico City in the 1540s, and Indian labor was mobilized to exploit the mines. While some clerics did oppose the rapacity of the civil authorities in exploiting Indian labor, in general, church officials were enriched by the system, thus initiating the ambivalence that most modern Mexicans still feel toward the Catholic Church—a culturally defining institution and source of comfort on the one hand and an inimical, reactionary institution on the other. Victimized by mistreatment and new diseases, Mexico's Indian population fell from an estimated 20 million in 1520 to 2 million in 1580, dropping to a low of around 1 million in the mid-1600s before native populations began to recover.

Meanwhile, the population of mixed-blood *mestizos* began to grow, and was augmented by the importation of black slaves. Also *criollos* (Mexican-born offspring of Spanish parents) began to proliferate and assume greater responsibility for the local economy, politics, and cultural affairs, although they were kept subordinate to the often inept and corrupt—but European-born—appointees from Spain (the *peninsulares* or *gachupines*), who occupied the highest stratum of society. Mexico was maintained in accord with the mercantilist economic theories of the times: it was considered to exist solely for the purpose of providing precious metals, raw materials, and other goods and services to Spain and to serve as a dumping ground for excess population,

undesirables, and overpriced manufactures from the mother country, the only country with which it was legally allowed to trade. Although it was the cultural-political focus of Spain's presence in the New World, because of such restrictions and exactions, colonial Mexico was effectively prevented from accumulating capital, developing its local industry, or setting up a separate managerial and political system.

Throughout the 17th and 18th centuries, the Spanish, who were experiencing increasing economic deterioration at home, made ever greater demands on Mexico while providing little investment and few services in return. Moreover, Spain refused to allow any autonomy or authority to the growing *criollo* population, who were beginning to identify more with local interests than with those of Spain. In the 1770s the Jesuits were expelled from the Spanish possessions as being too influential, and church property was subsequently confiscated in a desperate move by Spanish authorities to increase revenues, further alienating the locals. In 1808, when Napoleon Bonaparte of France put his own puppet ruler on the throne of Spain, many of Spain's New World colonies used this as an excuse to rebel against their overseas masters.

The struggle for Mexican independence began in 1810 and continued until 1821, when the Spanish commander, Agustín de Iturbide, defected and conspired to defeat Royalist forces with the understanding that he would become emperor of the new state. His empire fell apart rapidly, and a constitutional federal republic was established in 1824. It was not until 1829, following the expulsion of a Spanish expeditionary force by General Antonio López de Santa Anna, that Spain finally acknowledged Mexico's independence. Santa Anna became president in 1833.

The 19th Century

Santa Anna was in and out of power on 11 separate occasions over a 22-year period. He presided over a spectrum of historical phenomena: anarchy at home; the secession of Texas in 1836; the loss of New Mexico, Arizona, California, and parts of Colorado, Utah, and Nevada (about half of Mexico's national territory) to the US during what is known in Mexico as the First Northern Intervention (1846–1848); and the sale in 1853 of parts of Arizona and New Mexico to the US in the Gadsden Purchase. This final indignity caused Santa Anna to be deposed (for the last time) in 1855.

After more infighting, a reform government came to power in 1861 under Benito Juárez, a Zapotec Indian. After nearly 50 years of fighting, the country was a wreck and heavily indebted to European powers for loans that it could not repay. The Europeans took advantage of the involvement of the US in its own Civil War to challenge the Monroe Doctrine that had largely kept Europeans from intervening in American affairs;

the Europeans occupied Mexico to forcibly collect their debts. France decided to go even further—it colonized Mexico, setting up Austrian Archduke Maximilian as emperor in 1864. Once the US had finished its Civil War in 1865, it pressured France to withdraw from Mexico, which left Maximilian in an exposed position. He was defeated—and executed—in 1867, and Juárez returned to power.

Despite attempts at reform by Juárez—including declaring Mexico to be a secular polity and establishing plans for universal education—Mexico remained undeveloped economically and unsettled politically. In 1876 José de la Cruz Porfirio Díaz became president; he continued, both in and out of office, to be the power in Mexico until 1910. Díaz provided the first stability and continuity in Mexican politics in nearly 75 years. He also instituted major building and public works projects and attracted foreign investment, primarily in railway development, mining, and oil exploration. He accomplished this, however, by suppressing all political opposition, and he distributed the economic rewards of growth as patronage. The gap between the upper classes and the lower class—always wide—grew even wider. In particular, large landowners were able to build up huge estates by dispossessing peasant landholders.

The Revolution

In 1910 Francisco Madero was jailed by Díaz for attempting to run for president on a reform ticket. Madero won support from local *caudillos* (strongmen) in the north under the leadership of Francisco "Pancho" Villa. Subsequently Díaz was forced out, but Madero was unwilling to pursue radical reforms, including breaking up the large landholdings and distributing land to the peasantry, so he ran afoul of peasant leader Emiliano Zapata, whose Zapatistas held off federal troops and led other regional reformers and warlords to defy the weakened central government.

In 1913 a nephew of Porfirio Díaz started a conservative counterrevolution leading to open warfare in Mexico City. US Ambassador Henry Wilson plotted with the army to support the conservatives in order to ensure a return to stability, causing Madero's overthrow and execution by General Huerta, who seized power. Huerta then became the lightning rod for virtually all the various regional revolutionary movements; and was deposed in 1914 when the three main rebel groups under Pancho Villa, Álvaro Obregón, and Venustiano Carranza united to oppose him. During this chaotic period, the US had sent troops to occupy Veracruz in an effort to pressure Huerta into resigning; the ploy backfired, and the US Marines stayed on for several months, providing an additional reason for Mexico to distrust the US.

In 1915, the would-be allies fell out, and Villa briefly gained control, before being driven back to his stronghold in Chihuahua. Carranza gained US recognition, forced through a new constitution, and became president. Villa, angered by US recognition of the Carranza government, raided into the US, causing the US to send troops into Mexican territory, creating more ill will. Carranza, like Madero, was loath to push radical land reform and eventually had Zapata, who continued to oppose his ascent to power, assassinated (Villa was later murdered as well). Carranza was himself deposed by Obregón, who took over as president in 1920.

The bloody revolution was finally brought to an end, and the reformers seemed to have prevailed. Obregón and his successor, Plutarco Elías Calles, instituted land reform, boosted infrastructure and public works construction, expanded education, improved relations with the US, and once again encouraged foreign investment. However, Calles also organized the ancestor of a political party that later would exercise monopoly power in Mexico for at least the next 70 years. In an effort to curb the political power of the Catholic Church, Calles also closed the religious institutions, deported foreign-born priests, and banned religious processions, which led to violent popular protests—the Cristero Rebellion—that had to be put down by force.

Calles was succeeded in 1934 by Lázaro Cárdenas, who redistributed 20 million hectares (more than 77,000 square miles) of land, setting up the system of *ejidos*, by which land could be held collectively by peasant groups, thus preventing individuals from selling it off. He also improved church-state relations and helped organize labor into the Confederation of Mexican Workers (*Confederación de Trabajadores Mexicanos*, or CTM), still the main labor organization. However, Cárdenas is best remembered for standing up to the US and other foreigners by expropriating foreign rail and oil interests, nationalizing oil resources, and organizing the state-run national oil monopoly, *Petróleos Mexicanos* (Pemex). Cárdenas also reorganized and strengthened the ruling party and began the tradition of having the president name his successor during the last year of his own term.

The expropriation put an effective end to most foreign investment, although during the worldwide Great Depression of the 1930s such investment had been restrained anyway. Nevertheless, the curtailment of inflows coupled with the expense of social programs caused the Mexican economy to slow substantially. This situation was reversed during the period of World War II (1939-1946). Mexico supported the Allies to a greater extent than did many other Latin nations, providing raw materials, labor, and even a contingent of troops in the Pacific theater, thereby helping to smooth over the tensions caused by expropriations. Even more important, the war allowed Mexico to develop domestic industries to supply goods which previously were imported but which became unavailable due to wartime shortages and interrupted transport. The war also enabled Mexico to widen the range of its exports beyond the raw materials that formed the prewar core of its international trade.

The Postwar Modern Era

Mexico continued to develop its industry after the war, but with an increasing emphasis on the state sectors. Between 1945 and 1975 the government effectively took over communications, finance, and a host of other specific firms and industries, adding to its state-run oil and transportation monopolies. Although the economy continued to grow, the performance of the state-run sectors was sluggish and inefficient. Bureaucracies grew and appointments were often made based on patronage rather than on merit, while the state firms required large, ever-increasing operating subsidies. The government also spent heavily on education, social services, and infrastructure, including hydroelectric generating and power transmission grids, irrigation projects, and roadbuilding. The oil industry began to grow rapidly as well, gaining increased importance in the overall economy.

This rapid expansion led to the generation of unprecedented funds, bottlenecks, and bureaucracies; skyrocketing costs and growing graft and corruption resulted. Mexico, whose population doubled between 1935 and 1955, also began to experience social problems stemming from rural-urban migration caused by poverty. In the late 1950s and early 1960s, programs increased the redistribution of land in an attempt to keep rural migrants on the farm. These programs were bolstered by rural health and education programs. Nevertheless, rural out-migration and social problems increased, leading to internal unrest and greater tensions with the US over burgeoning illegal immigration.

To maintain order in the face of growing social problems, the administration of President Gustavo Díaz Ordaz (1964–1970) tried repressive tactics. This culminated in the violent suppression of protests preceding the 1968 Olympics in Mexico City. Despite attempts to ease up and the renewed social investment programs of the successor government of Luis Echeverría Álvarez (1970–1976), social unrest—including armed rebellion in the state of Guerrero, rising crime (including politically and economically motivated kidnappings and bank robberies), and growth of the international drug trade—increased. Some analysts trace many of these excesses to growing, endemic corruption. Again, the economy suffered as industry stagnated and the cost of social

programs designed to keep dissatisfaction under control rose astronomically.

The administration of José López Portillo (1976–1982) coincided with the jump in world oil prices following the OPEC oil boycott. Mexico suddenly found its revenues skyrocketing, and given optimistic projections for continued increases, it was able to spend and borrow based on predicted future oil revenues. This was the era of the theory of sovereign risk, under which countries were seen as being immune from going bankrupt, and international banks with petrodollars to recycle pushed loans on an eager Mexico. However, rising prices called forth rising supplies and oil prices slumped, leaving Mexico with a bloated and inefficient state-sector, social programs that served primarily to subsidize consumption rather than to invest in future production, and mountains of debt that it could not service, much less repay. This period is also seen as representing the zenith of corruption: what had been an irritant developed into a national modus operandi, fueled by the easy availability of petrodollars.

As things began to go badly wrong, the authorities hunkered down to try to exercise what little control they could and minimize the damage. Mexico declared a moratorium on payment of its staggering US$85 billion of foreign debt, demanded that the debt be restructured, and nationalized the banking system, all the while digging a figurative moat around its economy.

Recovery and Reform

The administration of President Miguel de la Madrid (1982–1988) fought a holding action against the problems inherited from its predecessor. But the Mexico City earthquake in 1985—which caused a conservatively estimated US$4 billion in damage—made things worse. Meanwhile, de la Madrid—more a technocrat than a politician—struggled to shore up Mexico's moribund economy, reschedule its massive debt, keep a lid on social problems, and manage an increasingly recalcitrant political system. Although his substantive accomplishments seemed relatively few, de la Madrid did manage to keep the roof from crashing in while giving Mexico time to recover from the various shocks it had experienced. He also put the framework in place for future economic reforms, including eased foreign investment rules, tax reform, stock market reform, and the privatization of state-run industry. Having been badly burned by its overreliance on its commodity export industry—particularly oil, which accounted for two-thirds of its exports during the early 1980s—Mexico set a goal of diversifying its economy, particularly in its foreign trade relationships. It was also during this period that Mexico began pushing its *maquila* (in-bond) program under which foreign firms were al-

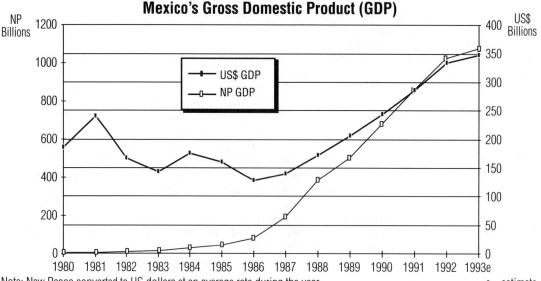

Mexico's Gross Domestic Product (GDP)

Legend: US$ GDP, NP GDP

Note: New Pesos converted to US dollars at an average rate during the year.   e = estimate
Source: International Monetary Fund

lowed to open assembly plants, employ Mexican labor and facilities, and reexport the product under favorable arrangements designed to attract business.

Although elected by a bare, and many, say suspect majority, President Carlos Salinas de Gortari (1988–1994)—a Harvard-educated technocrat—moved quickly to consolidate his hold on power. In contrast with a long list of previous executives, Salinas allowed opposition candidates to be confirmed as winners in state gubernatorial elections—a first for the monopoly central party, the *Partido Revolucionario Institucional* (Institutional Revolutionary Party, or the PRI, as it is commonly known), which had frequently resorted to fraud when bribery and intimidation had failed to seat its candidates. He has presided over the opening up of the economic system, including the welcoming of foreign participation to a greater degree in many more sectors, the privatization of numerous state-run firms and sectors, the restructuring of debt, and a campaign to reduce inflation and government spending. Salinas has also moved to promote better relations with the US. He has also been a major proponent of the North American Free Trade Agreement (NAFTA), which establishes a free trade zone and a de facto trading bloc with the US and Canada. To a somewhat lesser extent, Salinas has worked to root out corruption and drug trafficking, to institute political reform, and to work on long-neglected environmental issues. His pro-business stance and the turnaround in the global economy seem to be having a positive effect. Mexico is growing and offering many more opportunities to foreign and domestic businesspeople than has been the case for some years.

Despite its rapid rise, Mexico still has a large, often archaic system in which many functional and geographic areas have yet to catch up with the new standards and prosperity. Although many sectors have seen rapid advances and the overall economic situation has improved substantially, Mexico is a conservative land—the old guard is deeply entrenched, and the benefits of change have yet to reach many of the geographically and socially marginal elements in society. This is most evident among less-assimilated Indian populations in the underdeveloped southern states of Oaxaca and particularly Chiapas, where Indian populations are concentrated and social and economic relations are often reminiscent of the semi-feudal colonial era. A revolt broke out in Chiapas in January 1994, in which the self-styled Zapatista National Liberation Army challenged the state by kidnapping officials and taking over towns in the state. Although the Zapatistas stated that they intended to accomplish a military overthrow of the existing government and succeeded in engaging the army (which was accused of atrocities), they seemed primarily interested in trying to embarrass the government into making concessions designed to change the economic situation. As a supplementary position that gained broader national and international attention, they also demanded electoral reforms.

SIZE OF THE ECONOMY

Mexico's GDP was US$323.4 billion in 1992, up 2.6 percent in real terms from 1991's US$280 billion. During the first nine months of 1993, the economy grew at a rate of only 0.5 percent, actually contracting at a 1.5 percent rate during the third quarter; it reportedly fell below break-even in the fourth quarter as well. Preliminary figures put the 1993 GDP at about US$350 billion, representing a real growth rate of only about 0.4 percent, well below official predictions of full-year growth of 1.1 percent. Actual contractions in the third and fourth quarters suggest that by standard definitions, the Mexican economy was in recession in 1993.

Between 1984 and 1992, Mexico's GDP doubled from US$171 billion in 1984. However, in 1986 the Mexican economy experienced a sharp drop of more than 20 percent in nominal terms (or 4 percent in real terms), a loss from which it has had to recover to reach its current level. Since 1984, annual real growth has averaged about 2 percent, hitting a high of 3.9 percent for 1990 before tapering off. The official line predicts 3 percent real growth for 1994. However, few outsiders lend much credence to this optimistic forecast, although most expect to see at least the beginnings of a turnaround by mid-year, with most full-year growth predictions falling between what is still perhaps a somewhat optimistic 2 and 2.5 percent for 1994.

Official Mexican statistics—which are often delayed for extended periods and presented in a fashion apparently designed to confuse rather than reveal—are considered to be somewhat suspect by many observers. Although information is not actually falsified, it is often massaged, omitted, buried, or presented in a manner that obscures its import, calling up the recurring issue of "transparency" in official and private dealings in Mexico. Many observers note that because knowledge is power, bureaucrats often refuse to release statistical or other information without receiving some quid pro quo; some even suggest that the president himself may not always be in command of up-to-date, authoritative statistics for policymaking purposes.

Mexican statistics vary by compiler—sometimes significantly—and should be viewed primarily as a guide in assessing trends rather than as hard, absolute numbers. For instance, in an apparent attempt to smooth over evidence of slippage in economic performance in 1993, the Finance Secretariat issued its 1993 third quarter report in the nonstandard form of a nine-month summary that did not break out the figures quarter by quarter, requiring economists to back into the data using the previous quarters' documents to approximate third quarter results. Others note that the figures in question indicate—but do not explicitly state—that industrial production was down, while unemployment and bankruptcies were up, although the opaque nature of the government reports makes it difficult to assess the exact nature and degree of such phenomena. As of mid-May 1994, officials still had not released data on the performance of the economy during the first quarter.

Per capita GDP was US$3,760 in 1992, up from US$3,333 in 1991. Preliminary 1993 figures place it at US$3,872, for a modest rise of about 3 percent. The 1992 figures represent somewhat less than 15 percent of the per capita GDP of the US. Mexico's GDP—the highest in Latin America—is about the same as that of Turkey. Per capita GDP, which was US$2,224 in 1984, fell as low as US$1,537 in 1987 before recovering to more than double over the next five years. However, in a world in which trickle-down economics has generally resulted in across-the-board increases for a broad spectrum of populations, Mexico is among the few countries worldwide—most of them in Latin America—in which the gap in distribution of wealth and incomes actually increased during the period from 1960 to 1990. Inflation-adjusted wages rose 32.3 percent between 1988 and 1992, but this brought purchasing power back up only to about the level it had occupied in 1983. Meanwhile, the inflation-adjusted minimum wage fell by about 40 percent from 1988 to 1992, and the share of total wealth held by the bottom two-fifths of the population fell to 12 percent in 1992, down from 15 percent in 1988.

Overall population growth has been easing for the past 35 years, from an annual average of 3.4 percent between 1960 and 1970 to 2.3 percent between 1980 and 1990. A slower growth rate of 1.5 to 2 percent is predicted during the 1990s, despite the fact that in the early 1990s, growth appeared to be hugging the upper limits of that range. Mexico's rate of population growth has been equal to or greater than that of real economic growth during many of these years. And Mexico has experienced problems in distributing the benefits of the economic growth that it has sustained.

One index of the growing wealth and income disparity is the fact that the increase in national wealth due to the jump in the value of securities held by Mexicans (an estimated US$145 billion between 1988 and 1993) accrued primarily to the approximately 0.1 percent of the population who held brokerage accounts. There are relatively few mutual and pension funds or other national institutional investors to hold such wealth on behalf of a broader group of underlying owners, although this is changing. And the number of brokerage accounts has actually fallen from roughly 250,000 in 1988 to about 115,000 in 1993, further narrowing the concentration of such wealth.

CONTEXT OF THE ECONOMY

As recently as 10 years ago, Mexico was consigned to the ranks of the economically terminal following its declaration of a moratorium on payment of its massive foreign debt in 1982. However, not only has the country managed to hang onto life, it has also recently been held up as a model to other struggling nations in Latin American and elsewhere. Although it is making remarkable progress, and despite its politicians' proud announcements about its pending ascendancy to First World status, Mexico remains an underdeveloped, Third World economy. This is largely due to the underlying, essentially pre-19th century colonial structure of its economy and its 19th and 20th century subordination to the much larger US and European economies.

Mexico's domestic economy has suffered from a myriad of arcane and archaic restrictive regulations; corrupt and byzantine bureaucracies; and the lack of a substantial, developed middle class. This last is a function of the legacy of colonialism, in which the government monopolized most economic activity, delegating the bulk of the remainder as patronage to a handful of allied oligarchs. Business relationships in Mexico have traditionally been conducted more on a hierarchical patron-client basis than as free contractual arrangements among equals. And when it comes to needing to operate on a personal basis through introductions, intermediaries, and influence, Mexican business relationships rival those in many Asian countries.

This overall pattern was reinforced rather than weakened by economic activity during the last part of the 19th century and the first three-quarters of the 20th century. By the early 1980s, more than 50 percent of all investment in the economy was being made by the public sector, and more than half of GDP represented direct or indirect government spending, with the state reaching ever-further into the workings of the economy by such desperate actions as the 1982 nationalization of the financial system. In 1982 there were more than 1,150 government-owned enterprises (*paraestatales*), ranging from the small to the mammoth and operating in 52 out of 73 sectors of the economy. As part of the Salinas government's restructuring program, about 75 percent of these had been privatized or announced for privatization by 1991, with more scheduled to move into private hands by the end of Salinas' term of office in late 1994. Until recently, the dominance of the state sector represented a self-reinforcing situation in which government activity (or lack of it) crowded out private initiative, and private capital fled the country to avoid participating in the accelerating deterioration and general downward economic spiral.

Even before this juncture, the sectors that were not the domains of the *paraestatales* were often dominated by large, closely-held, usually family-based, industrial groups operating as oligopolies. According to *Forbes*, Mexico had 13 billionaires in 1993—up from seven the year before and more than any other country except the US, Germany, and Japan. Their personal and family empires control dominant pluralities, if not majorities, in such industries as retailing, food processing, mining, communications, agribusiness, and certain areas of finance and manufacturing. In many respects these conglomerates resemble the semi-private patriarchal *chaebol* of South Korea. Because Mexico is a less homogeneous society than Korea and lacks the ethic of consensus that characterizes traditional Asian societies, the dynamics of the operations of Mexico's personal conglomerates are considerably different from those found in Asia. Although there remains a substantial element of cooperation (some would say collusion) as well as competition among the large entities, Mexican business has (at least in the past) often resembled a *teleteatro* (soap opera) because of some of the personalities involved. However, as it has become more international, Mexican business has also become more refined, subdued, and concerned with rational economic arguments—at least on the surface.

Since the late 1930s, foreign investors have increasingly been prevented from competing with domestic state and private industry in such key areas as: finance; petroleum exploration, processing, and distribution; primary petrochemical production; forestry; media and communications; transportation; and utilities. Foreign participation in such key areas as mining, secondary petrochemicals, and auto parts, among others, has been heavily restricted. Although this situation has officially changed, foreigners have faced a less-than-welcoming reception in the recent past, and the end result has been a protected economy that has not been subjected to the influences of free market interaction. A major aspect of current policy is designed to bring Mexican business operations up to international standards, which entails reforming many of these traditionally closed practices.

Of particular importance to the recovery of the Mexican economy have been the *maquiladoras*, or in-bond assembly industries, most of which traditionally have been located near the US border. The word comes from an old practice in which millers took a portion of the flour ground from grain as a "toll" (*maquila*) in payment. Under this program—instituted in the mid-1960s but developed to its current importance during the 1980s—foreign firms could hold 100 percent ownership, import inputs duty-free, and use inexpensive Mexican labor, real estate, and raw and intermediate materials to produce goods that were then reexported, primarily to the US. In September 1993, there were 2,182 such plants (up 4.8 percent from 1992), employing a reported 552,078 Mexican workers (up 7.4 percent from the previous year). More than 85 percent of such plants are located in US-Mexican border states, although *maquilas* can be operated virtually anywhere in Mexico, and interior and other states are vying to become the home of new plants.

Prior to 1990, Mexico excluded *maquilas* from its export statistics because it officially considered their production to represent reexports rather than national products. Although they provide employment and industrial education for substantial numbers of workers, critics both at home and abroad have argued that the *maquilas* mostly pay minimum wage to unskilled, often transient workers, cause problems by concentrating masses of workers and their families in areas where infrastructure and social services are lacking, and run polluting operations that are prohibited at home but allowed in less environmentally sensitive Mexico. Changes under NAFTA as well as other new regulations have begun to deal with some of these negative issues, and new rules allowing more *maquila* production into domestic markets should serve to mainstream these operations.

As part of its attempts to shore itself up financially following its near-death experience in the early 1980s, Mexico has focused on a policy of fiscal conservatism designed to maintain a budgetary surplus that both serves as a reserve and demonstrates its probity to outside financiers. During the mid-1980s, Mexico's budget deficit reached 14 percent of GDP. In 1992 its budget surplus amounted to 0.5 percent of GDP, the first such surplus in 20 years, and the figures did not even include capital received from one-shot privatizations of major government stakes in several *paraestatales*. As of mid-1993, the government was targeting a budget surplus of 1.7 percent of GDP for the year, although weak economic performance was expected to prevent the realization of this goal. Nevertheless, most observers were expecting a budget surplus in the 1 percent range for 1993.

This policy effectively means that the government is taking resources out of the economy instead of plowing them back in via investment. In the past, a great deal of official spending and investment resulted in the protection and enlargement of bloated, inefficient, corrupt state and state-run industrial bureaucracies, as well as consumption subsidies designed to maintain social peace, rather than in productive investment. Given this background, it is easy to see the rationale behind insisting on the maintenance of such surpluses. However, the end result of focusing on fiscal control—deciding to fight inflation rather than enhance growth—has been a shortage of available investment funds and rising real interest rates even in the face of declining inflation. Borrowing costs for small- and medium-sized businesses operating in Mexico have gone as high as 40 percent, regularly reaching 30 percent, although more recent reports are that some borrowers have been able to gain access to funds for as "little" as 20 percent. Large businesses can usually avoid the main impact of such elevated rates by borrowing abroad, an option not open to smaller entities. Smaller businesses—which account for the vast majority of jobs in the Mexican economy—are under pressure due to: high interest rates and resulting costs; a decline in sales in the worldwide slow-growth, recessionary environment; and increased foreign competition now that protectionist barriers are falling. This situation argues that the Mexican economy will experience a difficult, prolonged transition, fraught with local opposition to the changes needed to upgrade it to world class status.

Some observers suggest that the remaining inflation in Mexico is due not to fiscal policy, as in the past, but to stultifyingly high interest rates; inadequate infrastructure (which makes distribution more costly); a shortage of goods and services that pushes prices up due to scarcity; and a tax policy that drives a substantial proportion of operations into the underground sector and leaves fewer and fewer licit operations to bear the burdens of funding the system. Some even argue that a policy designed to balance the Mexican budget or even to run a modest deficit—provided the excess was spent on productive infrastructure projects—would serve to actually reduce real interest rates far better than the current policy designed to produce a surplus. Some analysts even opine that the government colludes in keeping rates high as a means of attracting foreign investors to its bonds in order to remain liquid. They suggest that Mexico would be better served by allowing rates to fall, thereby freeing up foreign capital for productive direct investments (most of the money in question represents institutional funds allocated to specific overseas regional venues rather than to specific categories of investment, such as bonds).

Mexico's stock market is the quintessential emerging equities market. With a mid-1993 market value of about US$130 billion, it grew at an average annual rate of 42.9 percent between 1989 and 1992, making it one of the hottest markets worldwide. Between the end of 1984 and mid-1993, the Mexican stock market returned 1,868 percent in US dollars and 31,555 percent in pesos. It has kept Mexico on the international financial map, even during the downturn in its economy. The market is slowly turning from a speculative casino into a reliable means of raising and investing capital, although with the bulk of its activity in fewer than 30 issues and heart-stopping volatility, it has a long way to go before it hits maturity as a respected capital market.

THE UNDERGROUND ECONOMY

According to some estimates, as many as 8 million people—a number equal to nearly 30 percent of the formal workforce—operate in the underground economy. Various estimates put the value of goods and services produced by this parallel underground economy at between 20 and 40 percent of that produced in the formal economy. The underground economy is also growing at a much more rapid rate than is the official economy, having increased from an estimated 10 percent of official GDP in 1970 to more

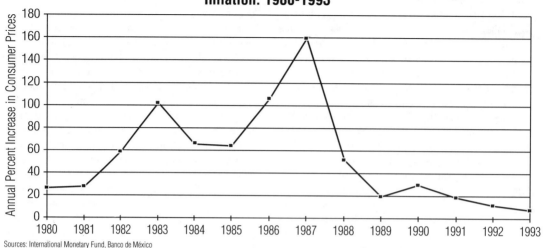

Sources: International Monetary Fund, Banco de México

elevated levels in the late 1980s and early 1990s. The size and extent of the underground economy are primarily due to the fact that it circumvents the burdens of regulation and taxation that are required of those operating within the legal framework, compounded by a shortage of jobs in the formal economic sector.

The Mexican tax system is highly progressive, and the upper brackets kick in at relatively low levels, so that common wisdom has it that one either pays at the top rate or evades taxes altogether. An ordinary worker can hit a tax bracket of 34 percent with an annual income of between US$8,000 and US$11,000. In addition to a top personal income tax rate of 35 percent (down from 60 percent as recently as 1987), individuals making more than minimum wage pay social security taxes, which are more than matched by employer contributions. Employers also make hefty required contributions toward retirement and housing benefits and must pay out 10 percent of pre-tax earnings as profit sharing to employees. In addition, a tax of 2 percent is levied on corporate assets, not profits—leading firms to understate their assets, which in turn prevents them from using their full assets to secure loans and other financing.

Although the existing tax laws do represent significant improvements over previous tax laws, many firms and workers still have substantial incentives to remain outside the formal system despite the lack of benefits, protections, and resulting inefficiencies. An estimated half of all workers in the informal sector—perhaps 4 million—could become legal relatively easily. However, at present, many can do better by staying in the informal system and cheating on taxes than they could by regularizing their situations.

The magnitude of the underground economy makes it difficult for the government to manage the formal economy. The size of the informal sector also

gives the relatively well organized participants in the underground economy considerable political clout, which has inhibited the government from cracking down on them effectively. Finally, the underground sector serves as a safety valve because the formal sector has provided inadequate and uncertain employment for Mexico's rapidly growing labor force during a period of restructuring. The goal of the current government is to bring the majority of such informal workers and enterprises within the official system, and most participants in the underground economy admit that they expect ultimately to do so. However, despite having offered some incentives to them, the government has so far balked at easing tax burdens, largely for fear that it could upset its surplus budget position by foregoing income should the number of outsiders attracted inside prove insufficient.

Joining the formal sector also subjects individuals and firms to a host of labyrinthine regulations that they are generally able to avoid while they remain outside the official economy. And no matter which side of the rules they operate on, they are generally unable to avoid the demands for bribes from bureaucrats, police, and other officials charged with enforcement. This, in turn, provides little incentive to comply with the exactions of the formal sector.

Corruption, graft, and bribery have traditionally been rampant in Mexico, a land of underpaid functionaries. In particular, *la mordida* ("the bite," as locals call bribes) has been all-pervasive. The ubiquity of petty and arbitrary regulation (known as the *pequeño poder*, or little power) and the lack of accountability of officials has made it virtually impossible to operate without encountering requests for bribes ranging from the subtle to the blatant, in amounts ranging from the trivial to the grotesquely expensive. There are indications that the current crop of technocrats have had an ameliorating effect, reducing if not eliminating corruption at the higher levels, and some small businesspeople have reported that their actual payoffs have decreased by as much as 75 percent due to new policies and vigilance regarding corruption.

Given its history, Mexico has a somewhat overstated reputation for violence, even among other Latin Americans. Although outright banditry is still occasionally reported (primarily in outlying areas) and urban street crime is common (although often less so than in some urban areas in the developed world), most offenses are likely either to be nonviolent crimes committed against property (burglary, pickpocketing) or to involve violence among acquaintances. Careful foreign travelers and businesspeople are unlikely to be directly affected. Nevertheless, some Mexican senior executives carry guns and employ armed bodyguards to protect them from criminals and political terrorists; there have been half a dozen kidnappings of Mexican executives held for multimillion dollar ransoms since 1990, including two high-profile incidents since the beginning of 1994. And a traveler's advisory was recently issued regarding road travel in certain areas of Sinaloa because of banditry.

Drug cultivation and trafficking, with their associated high levels of violence and corruption, are prominent on a large scale, primarily in border and remote areas. An estimated one-third of all illicit drugs entering the US do so through Mexico. Because of its illicit nature and the large sums of dirty money involved, the drug trade is highly organized and involves a great deal of corruption and violence.

Many Mexicans also fear the police, who they consider to be, at best, inept and venal and, at worst, active participants in crime—including violent crime.

Despite the government's efforts to clean up notorious Mexican law enforcement agencies, the police continue to be susceptible to criminal activity because of low salaries and patterns of endemic corruption. In early 1994, Federal judicial police were involved in a shoot-out with state police in Baja California Norte; the state police were allegedly involved in protecting drug traffickers. The federal police mounting the raid were found to be using vehicles stolen in the US (the vehicles still carried their US license plates). The situation is considered to have improved mightily since the López Portillo administration, although cynics argue that the record was better during the de la Madrid administration simply because there was less available to steal. De la Madrid allowed—at least tacitly—Mexico City's notoriously corrupt chief of police to flee the country, and even President Salinas—who has tried to cultivate a Mr. Clean image—stumbled when he nominated as chief of the intelligence section of the Mexico City Police Department an individual indicted in the US for running a major auto theft ring.

Intellectual Property Rights Mexico has traditionally excluded large categories of products and processes from patent protection. It has been adding more areas to its existing protections, most recently under the terms of the revised 1991 patent law, further strengthened by the terms of NAFTA. Mexico reserves the right to force patentholders to grant licenses in cases of national interest or if they have not exploited the underlying patents within three years after the granting of the patents. However, in an effort to align its policies with those of mainstream developed countries, it is offering more protections instead of arguing—as it has in the past—that innovations are the property of mankind and should be available in general, especially to under-

Mexico
Consumer Price Index (CPI)

Sources: International Monetary Fund, Banco de México

developed countries.

Trademarks are protected, but conditions have been somewhat restrictive, with foreigners being encouraged to link up with a related national entity if they wish to use overseas trademarks. Regarding copyrights, Mexico is a signatory of international conventions. Overall copyright protection is considered relatively good in most areas, and despite some loopholes that allow unauthorized exploitation under certain circumstances, penalties are a substantial deterrent. Actual enforcement, however, has been variable. Pirated computer software and audio tapes and videotapes, as well as knock-off designer clothing and cosmetics, often have underground sales estimated to be equal to, and in some cases substantially greater than, legitimate sales of the genuine articles.

INFLATION

The Mexican economy suffered from double-digit inflation in every year from 1973 through 1992; in 1993 the rise in consumer prices dipped into single-digit territory for the first time since the early 1970s. One of the key policy goals of the Salinas administration has been to control inflation, and it has done remarkably well in this area, albeit at the cost of austerity and reduced growth due to tight fiscal and monetary policies.

Preliminary figures indicate that consumer prices rose by 8 percent during 1993. This represents a drop from 11.9 percent in 1992. Although the government did not reach its target of lowering inflation to 7 percent, it came closer to doing so than it has since the 1960s. This progress on inflation was partly a result of a generally sluggish economy. For 1994, the Salinas government has called for slowing inflation to only 5 percent. Many observers expect, though, that there will actually be a modest pickup in the inflation rate in 1994 due to greater economic growth as the government—despite its promises to continue austerity policies to reduce inflation—primes the pump during an election year. And others argue that deteriorating political and economic conditions could foretell a return to substantially higher inflation. As noted, others suggest that restrictive policies are serving to keep interest rates high, far higher than they should be, given the underlying real inflation rate.

Still, those operating in Mexico would be wise to keep a weather eye on inflation. Mexico's official consumer price index was set at 100 in 1978; in November 1993 the cumulative index was an eye-popping 35,795.6. Inflation averaged more than 50 percent per annum between 1980 and 1993, but that average represents a wide range of actual annual figures: 26.4 percent for 1980; more than 50 percent in every year between 1982 and 1988; above 100 percent in 1983 and 1986; at a high of 159.2 percent in 1987; then falling to more manageable levels after 1987. Such inflation has led to a great deal of uncertainty, devaluations, and loss of purchasing power that has done substantial damage to the Mexican economy and its reputation in the not very distant past. Stubbornly high interest rates are evidence that the financial markets have neither forgotten nor forgiven the economy for its past sins.

LABOR

In 1990 Mexico's workforce officially numbered 26.2 million, of which 22.3 million were listed as being employed in civilian jobs. Some observers estimate that the unofficial workforce, consisting of those who work off the books in the underground economy, may number as many as an additional 8 million persons. Many of these are women (who make up less than one-quarter of the official workforce) and underage children, although the majority are adult males working off the books by preference or due to necessity.

Mexico nominally provides nine years of free public education and subsidizes higher education for many who elect it, although there are relatively few slots in preparatory and university programs. However, there are problems with the availability of education in many regions of the country, and given such problems, many children do not attend school regularly, especially in rural areas. Mexico estimates that more than 87 percent of its adults are literate. This figure probably overstates the actual achievement, although basic functional literacy continues to grow from what it was even a few years ago.

There is a general shortage of skilled labor, technicians, and managerial and professional personnel. Although firms are required to provide training, the workforce has primarily been oriented toward labor intensive low-skill and semi-skilled jobs. Because much labor consists of first generation workers coming from rural farming backgrounds and new to the industrial system, productivity problems exist. Such workers must learn not only their specific jobs, but more general job attitudes and skills as well. In fact, many foreign businesses report significant problems with productivity, absenteeism, turnover, and quality control issues, in some cases enough to offset the lower wage advantage. About 30 percent of the population is between the ages of 15 and 30, the prime periods for employment in such labor intensive low-skill positions. And with about half of its population younger than 20 years of age, Mexico's primary labor problem in coming years will be creation of jobs for the surge of new workers coming into its economy. In the early 1990s, official plans were calling for the annual creation of 800,000 new jobs to cope with this problem, and many observers argue that the number needed is more like one million each year.

In 1991 roughly 25.7 percent of the workforce was employed in agriculture, 23.5 percent in industry, and 49.6 percent in services.

Unemployment

Unemployment was officially 2.8 percent in 1992, up from 2.7 percent in 1991, according to the Secretariat of Labor and Social Welfare (*Secretaría de Trabajo y Previsión Social*, or STPS). Unemployment was calculated at 3.4 percent during the first quarter of 1993. Some other official sources admit to an unemployment rate of around 4 percent. However, unofficial sources place unemployment at closer to 18 percent, up from 9 percent in the early 1980s. Much of this discrepancy comes from Mexico's extremely restrictive official definition of unemployment, which only counts those with no earnings who are actively engaged in a job search and registered as such according to official guidelines and procedures.

Although officials have attempted to define away unemployment, even they balk at painting too rosy a picture, instead attributing employment woes to underemployment. They use this category to encompass not only such populations as seasonally employed rural workers and involuntarily part-time workers, but also those in the underground economy, some of whom actually make more money than many of their counterparts in the aboveground economy but just don't report it. In 1990 the official rate for such underemployment was 11.7 percent. And officials also acknowledge privately that some 3 million jobs have been lost due to restructuring during the last five years, exacerbating the situation.

As long as the economic growth rate remains at or below the population growth rate, Mexico will continue to have a substantial unemployment-underemployment problem, one which seems to be structural in nature.

The Role of Unions

Unions are quite strong in Mexico. Most estimates of participation range from 25 to 30 percent, although some estimates suggest that union membership is greater than 50 percent of the active workforce. There are even union-like labor associations among workers in the underground sector, some of which wield considerable political influence. Under federal law, any labor unit with at least 20 employees can form a company union to bargain collectively regarding working conditions and wages, and as few as two employees can choose to affiliate with an existing recognized outside union, although only one union is allowed to represent the workers of a specific company.

Collective bargaining is usually designed to extend the benefits already available under Mexico's pro-labor laws. These are explicitly designed to give the benefit of the doubt to labor in labor-management disputes. Strikes (*paros* or *huelgas*) are technically illegal unless authorized by the government (under narrowly defined conditions), although they are frequently threatened and sometimes actually occur. Work stoppages, which increased in number during the late 1980s, can turn violent, becoming a major headache for employers. However, only around 2 percent of announced strikes result in actual stoppages. In most cases, stoppages are of short duration, and only a small percentage of these cause problems beyond short-term interruptions.

About 80 to 85 percent of unionized workers belong to one of the nine nationally recognized labor organizations. The primary labor organization, the Confederation of Mexican Workers (*Confederación de Trabajadores Mexicanos*, or CTM) represents the majority of larger unions. There are a host of additional, often competing, labor organizations that make Mexico's labor situation complicated.

The CTM and the ruling PRI, have been closely linked in a symbiotic relationship since the founding of the CTM under the sponsorship of the Cárdenas government in the 1930s. However, in recent years the Salinas government has been cracking down on abuses by entrenched labor leaders, promoting fewer labor candidates for national and state offices, resulting in a lessening of clout by the CTM and its member organizations. Labor has also lost some of its influence under the terms of the Salinas government's Pact for Stability and Economic Growth (*Pacto para Estabilidad y Crecimiento Económico*, or PECE), known simply as the *pacto*. This policy—which has called for tight fiscal and monetary policies, wage and price controls, and a controlled exchange rate in order to manage the economy—has been supported uneasily by labor, which feels that it has been unfairly singled out to bear the brunt of the sacrifices needed to reorganize the economy and stimulate recovery. However, the overall positive results for the economy, despite losses, especially by minimum wage workers, have prevented labor from openly mounting an effective and open opposition.

Wages

Mexicans are paid on the basis of a seven-day week, even though actual days and hours worked varies with the job and the company according to contract provisions, making it difficult to calculate comparable wage rates. In 1992 the average hourly rate for manufacturing workers was US$2.35, up from US$2.17 in 1991 and US$1.80 in 1990 (in 1992 the average US fully loaded hourly manufacturing wage was about US$16.17). In 1989 the rate was US$2.32, higher than in either 1990 or 1991. Mexican workers have complained that on an inflation-adjusted basis, they have only just recovered from where they were in 1982. Based on 1990 official figures, the average weekly production wage was US$60.66. Wage rates for 1990 were US$12.90 in China, US$24 in Thailand, US$32.50 in the Philippines, US$149 in Brazil, and US$376 in the US.

Unofficial survey sources suggest that the average actual weekly manufacturing wage in mid-1991 was closer to US$96. Yet another source puts fully loaded labor costs at US$3.39 per hour near the US border and US$5.05 in the heavily unionized industrial interior. Most foreign businesspeople report that actual wage costs in Mexico are much higher than anticipated, although such costs remain substantially lower than they are in many other locations. Mexican wages for lower level personnel may be only 20 percent of what they are in the US and Canada. However, the cost of senior managerial personnel is even higher in Mexico than in the US or Canada, and good technical and professional people do not come cheap, either—again because of the disparity between supply and demand.

The figures given include fringe benefits that according to the 1991 survey averaged 57.1 percent of the base hourly wage. To this is added federally mandated profit sharing of 10 percent of pre-tax profits, for an all-in average added cost of nearly 70 percent. Few companies can get by with holding such costs to less than 50 percent of base payroll, while many pay 85 to 100 percent or more in benefits and profit sharing.

Many benefits are mandated by law, while others are negotiated by unions, and still others are offered by employers in hopes of attracting and retaining a higher caliber workforce. Most employers provide: life and health insurance; savings schemes; an on-site subsidized cafeteria if larger, or meal allowances (if smaller); discount coupons redeemable at local stores; at least two weeks' paid vacation (one week is required by law after one year, with additional increments with each additional year of service) plus a required minimum 25 percent vacation bonus above the base pay rate; holidays (seven official plus additional negotiated holidays); and a year-end (Christmas) bonus equal to one month's wages (two weeks' wages is the required minimum). Many contracts formerly required employers to gross up workers' pay to cover social security taxes as well, but this practice is fading. Workers can be dismissed for cause or at will, and there is no unemployment insurance, although dismissed workers must usually be given a minimum payment ranging from three to six months' wages as severance, depending on length of service and type of position. In general, the lower the hourly rate paid, the higher the cost of the benefits package in percentage terms.

Mexico has a three-tiered legal minimum daily wage that is usually reset annually. In 1991 the legal minimum was US$4.01 per day for Mexico City and other higher-cost locales; US$3.65 for Guadalajara, Monterrey, and certain other large cities; and US$3.30 in other areas of the country. In 1992 the top-tier rate increased to US$4.30 and in 1993 to US$4.65, while in early 1994 the top rate had risen to about US$4.93. Although most Mexican workers make at or near the minimum wage, in practice, employers regularly pay substantially more for higher skilled, experienced workers.

Many employers report that they would like to pay even higher wages in order to attract better workers with greater skills, but government strictures and taxes effectively prevent them from offering higher wages. Others point out that such limitations prevent them from competing effectively with the informal sector for scarce skilled labor, because some workers can make substantially more in the underground economy—despite the hefty benefits that accrue from having aboveground jobs.

Workweek

The maximum legal workweek in Mexico consists of six eight-hour days, for a total of 48 hours. A day of rest—usually Sunday—must be provided. In recent years, 44- and 40-hour weeks have become far more common, especially in office settings, mainly due to negotiated contractual arrangements. Unofficial survey figures put the average workweek at 42.5 hours for 1991, up from the official 33.7-hour workweek in 1990. The first nine hours of overtime in any given week must be paid at double the regular rate, while any additional overtime is paid at triple the usual rate, with Sunday work commanding a 25 percent premium.

ELEMENTS OF THE ECONOMY

In 1991, 59.7 percent of the official GDP came from the Mexican services sector, while the industrial sector accounted for 32.8 percent and the agricultural sector for 7.5 percent. These percentages have changed relatively little during the late 1980s and early 1990s. However, they are substantially different from the situation in the 1960s and 1970s, when the agricultural sector was much larger and the service and industrial sectors less developed.

Agriculture

Mexico has historically been an agricultural country. However, this tradition has served to inhibit the modernization of Mexico's agricultural economy; many rural residents have strong ties with the land and the traditional means of using it. Archaic land-holding rules dating from the Revolution of 1910 have further served to retard development in the sector, but reforms are changing this situation to some extent. Although in 1991 agriculture (including ranching, forestry, hunting, and fishing) accounted for only 7.5 percent of total official GDP, the sector still employed 22.6 percent of the official workforce—mostly on family subsistence farmsteads. Virtually all of the 28 percent of Mexicans who lived in rural areas depended directly or indirectly on agricultural pursuits for their livelihood.

The dominant small-scale traditional agriculture is inefficient. It adds little to the national economy because it often does not even support those who practice it, much less produce a marketable surplus at a competitive price. This in turn means that government intervention, subsidies, and services are required to support those engaged in it. The government's stated policy is to cut the proportion of the population dependent on agriculture in half over the next 15 years, while supporting the development of more modern, large-scale, specialized, and mechanized agribusiness.

The contribution of agriculture is down from 15.6 percent of GDP in 1960 and 39.4 percent of the workforce employed in the sector as recently as 1970. Between 1970 and 1990, employment in the sector grew slightly by an annual average of 0.2 percent in absolute numbers, but shrank in percentage terms at an annual average rate of 2.75 percent. If the underground economy is taken into account, agriculture's contribution in employment shrinks even further, to perhaps 17 percent of the total workforce and 6 percent of effective GDP.

Production in the sector grew 3.4 percent in 1990 and 4.2 percent in 1991 after shrinking at similar rates during 1988 and 1989. Production is still below the average 6.7 percent growth experienced between

1948 and 1965, but better than the anemic 2.9 percent average growth between 1966 and 1979.

Much of Mexico is arid, requiring irrigation to ensure agricultural production. The country has about 20.2 million hectares of cultivated land (about 78,000 square miles). Some 67 percent of this is dedicated to grain crops (mostly maize and wheat, and virtually all for domestic consumption), 12 percent is in forage crops that primarily support the livestock industry, 5 percent in oilseed crops, and the remaining 16 percent in other specialty crops (which are responsible for the majority of Mexico's food exports). Despite inefficiency in the sector—due mainly to holdings being too small to be amenable to modern mechanized farming techniques, plus poor storage and distribution systems—and variability in the weather, Mexico has been basically self-sufficient in food production in good years. However, in recent years, a small but steadily growing structural deficit has developed, particularly in grain and dairy production, requiring imports to satisfy growing domestic demand.

In 1990 Mexico's main agricultural sector exports were fresh tomatoes, other fresh vegetables, coffee, cattle, processed fruits and vegetables, beer, melons, and orange juice. In the same year, the major agricultural imports were powdered milk, maize, sorghum, fats, meat, soybeans, oilseeds, animal feed, hides and skins, and live cattle. In 1990 total agricultural exports represented US$1.95 billion, while imports were US$2.09 billion. In 1991 basic grains were the major import (27 percent), followed by powdered milk (15 percent), sugar (12 percent), and other items (46 percent). In 1991 the major exports were vegetables (47 percent, 20.3 percent of which were tomatoes), fruits (12 percent), orange juice (8 percent), coffee (2 percent), and other items (31 percent alto-

Structure of the Mexican Economy - 1991

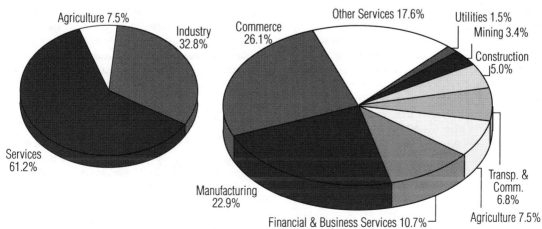

Note: Totals exceed 100 percent due to inclusion of financial transfer adjustments. Source: Instituto Nacional de Estadística Geografiá y Información (INEGI)

gether, each representing less than 2 percent of the total). Recent trends of note include the development of a cut flower export industry and a growing import market for processed foods.

Given Mexico's history and the importance of agriculture in the iconography of the revolution (its main slogan: *tierra y libertad*—land and liberty), the government remains concerned with supporting the rural agricultural sector, especially in improving sectoral production and the welfare of the largely poor rural agricultural population. Goals include improved production of grains, root crops, and oilseeds, and advances in forestry and livestock raising. In particular, it is encouraging development in the dairy and poultry industries. The government is also involved in agronomic research and irrigation, flood control, conservation, and reforestation projects.

As part of its privatization program, the government has effectively gotten rid of many of the sector's state-run agricultural monopolies (for example, Tabamex and Azúcar S.A., respectively the state tobacco and sugar monopolies) or reduced the monopoly to being a marketing intermediary (Conasupo, the former agricultural commodities distribution monopoly), a research, development, and promotion organization (Inmecafé, the former coffee monopoly), or as merely one among several competing firms (Fertimex and Pronase, respectively the former fertilizer and seed monopolies).

The government has also reduced subsidies to rural agricultural credit, making such credit available on a prime-plus basis that more closely approximates market rates. This action led to a rash of foreclosures in 1993 and a storm of political protest, although it remains to be seen who will be the first to back down on this issue—the peasants or the government. At the end of 1993, as part of its new *pacto*, the Salinas government announced that it would reduce overall crop subsidies and institute a smaller per-hectare subsidy program designed to wean marginal farmers away from the inefficient production of traditional staples that had been encouraged by the previous subsidy structure. Authorities have also reduced the need for import permits on agricultural products. However, foreign importers argue that due to the idiosyncratic way in which the government manages imports, they still need permits on goods valued at 59 percent of total agricultural imports rather than the 43 percent the government claims. Nevertheless, either figure is down from 79 percent of the total that required such permits in 1984. Liberalization under NAFTA is likely to open up this area even more in the near future.

As a relic of the revolution, Mexico had forbidden ownership of productive land by corporations—domestic or foreign—and limited private landholdings to no more than 100 hectares (about 250 acres)

of prime irrigated land, although loopholes and gentlemen's agreements have allowed the buildup of new large landed estates, albeit mostly for ranching rather than farming per se. More than half (53 percent) of all land in Mexico is held as part of an *ejido*, a plot held in common to support a local peasant community. These could not be sold, bought, or even rented, which further tied up and complicated the use of land. The government retains title to much of the rest of the land, although little of what it holds is economically useful.

Under the new agrarian law of 1992, the government agreed to halt further land distribution, removing the threat of government intervention in private landholding arrangements in order to stabilize the market in productive land. *Ejidatarios*—those participating in *ejidos*—are now also allowed to actually own, lease, and sell the lands representing their share of the total. They can also use their land as capital to form contracts with other parties. The new rules also permit corporations to hold title to such land, up to an amount equal to 25 times the amount that an individual could own. This means that agribusiness entities can own up to: 2,500 hectares (about 6,250 acres) of irrigated land; 3,750 hectares (about 9,375 acres) of land dedicated to cotton farming; 7,500 hectares (about 18,750 acres) dedicated to sugarcane, coffee, fruit trees, and similar multiyear investment production crops; and 20,000 hectares (about 50,000 acres) for forestry purposes. Foreigners, who were previously severely limited in the amounts of land they could gain access to, are now eligible to hold up to 49 percent of the stock in such agribusiness firms.

There are active, albeit mostly small- to medium-scale operations in fishing and forestry. Both have been subject to recent limitations due to environmental concerns, reducing their contribution to the economy, especially in terms of foreign exchange. Although much of Mexico is forested with potentially exploitable wood resources, the forestry industry is relatively undeveloped and primarily supplies local industries such as paper and furniture-making. There have been many attempts to develop fisheries, and the overall commercial catch and sport fishing are both growing. However, overfishing is expected to limit growth in these areas over the intermediate term.

Manufacturing and Industry

Manufacturing and industry—which includes mining, construction, and utilities—accounted for 32.8 percent of the official GDP in 1991. It employed 27.8 percent of the official workforce, up from a 22.9 percent share in 1970. Growth in employment in the sector between 1970 and 1990 was an average 4 percent per annum in absolute terms, or 1 percent in share terms. If the underground economy, which involves a great deal of informal light manufacturing and assembly operations, is taken into account, the sector could account for perhaps 25 percent of the total workforce and perhaps 27 percent of real GDP.

Although it accounts for only about one-third of the official economy, this sector—which includes the dominant petroleum industry—has been the engine that has fueled the main growth in the Mexican economy since before World War II. It has also driven Mexico's recent recovery, with industrial production growing by 3 percent in 1991. Official projections call for average growth of 6 percent during the period 1992 through 1995. In 1991 the manufacturing segment alone accounted for 22.9 percent of official GDP, while construction represented 5 percent, mining 3.4 percent, and utilities 1.5 percent.

Mexico's economy has been closed to a large degree and local industries have been highly protected, with most past industrialization being focused on import substitution. Recent developments—including, but not limited to, NAFTA (which is more a symptom than a cause)—are changing this situation. Due to the new competition, several Mexican industries are expected to either become more streamlined or fade. Among the industries at risk are electronics (assembly of generally less sophisticated consumer items such as radio, audio, and television equipment), furniture, and textiles. However, others argue that access to wider markets could revitalize some industries, such as textiles, that have been limited in their development by relatively small domestic markets that neither required nor supported investment or economies of scale.

The *maquiladora* sector has been strong as Mexico developed an export industry. However, growth in this segment—accounting for nearly half of exports—is actually expected to ease under NAFTA as the Mexican economy opens up. *Maquiladoras*—factories which import inputs on a temporary duty-free basis, assemble products using cheap Mexican labor, and reexport the results—are scheduled to lose their import protection edge as tariff and other barriers fall, although they will be allowed to sell more of their products in the domestic market.

Further rationalization of the industrial sector is anticipated due to radical privatization, which has resulted in the sell-off of the vast majority of previously state-run operations, ranging from sugar mills to major iron and steel mills and certain areas of pharmaceutical, petrochemical, and mining production.

Manufacturing In 1991 food, beverage, and tobacco processing was the largest segment in manufacturing, accounting for 25.2 percent of production, most of it for the domestic market. This was closely followed by metal products, machinery, and equipment (including the automotive industry), accounting for a 23.2 percent share of manufacturing; metal-

working was also the fastest growing segment of manufacturing, increasing by 12.9 percent in 1991. Chemicals, petroleum by-products, and plastics was third, with an 18.2 percent share, followed by textiles and leather, with a 10 percent share of manufacturing. Together, these four segments accounted for more than three-quarters of manufactures. Nonmetallic mineral products (6.7 percent); basic metals (5.7 percent, with a 1991 growth rate of 8 percent); paper, printing, and publishing (5.5 percent, with a 1991 growth rate of 7 percent); and miscellaneous manufactures (2.5 percent) round out the Mexican manufacturing sector.

Mining In 1990 Mexico was the world's largest producer of silver, bismuth, and celestite; third in antimony and fluorite; fourth in arsenic, cadmium, and graphite; and fifth in barite. The country also produces major amounts of gold, lead, copper, and zinc, among other metals and minerals. Natural gas production also falls under the heading of mining, and there has been major interest in exploration and development of natural gas reserves in the Gulf of Mexico.

However, in general Mexico's mining industry has languished due to flagging world commodity prices, lack of investment, and restrictions on foreign participation which have exacerbated investment problems. The recent liberalization of foreign investment designed to give greater control to overseas investors should prove reinvigorating the mining sector.

Oil and Primary Petrochemicals Oil production and downstream operations are restricted to the federal government, which operates through the gigantic Petróleos Mexicanos (Pemex) monopoly, the country's largest single firm. Mexico got into trouble by relying too heavily on oil revenues in the early 1980s; in 1984, oil sales accounted for nearly 70 percent of its exports, while by 1991 oil was down to about 25 percent of exports. Subsequently, Mexico has worked hard to diversify its economy and husband its resources. Except for the spike caused by the Persian Gulf crisis in 1990 and 1991, sluggish oil prices have largely forced the country to look elsewhere for revenues, a problem that has been exacerbated by continued weakness in oil prices in early 1994. At current production rates, Mexico could become a net importer of oil by 1997, according to some experts.

Mexico's oil industry has suffered from inadequate investment and maintenance since the early 1980s. Mexico has reorganized the ponderous Pemex monopoly into smaller, specialized, and hopefully more nimble and efficient companies. It is planning major new exploration and development projects that will allow some foreign participation, mainly in the financial and oilfield service areas. And there are persistent rumors that some or all of Pemex will be privatized and that at least some oil operations will be opened to foreigners. However, this is considered unlikely—especially in the near term—because it would require a change in the constitution, which reserves exploitation of all hydrocarbons for the state.

Construction Construction has been the fastest-growing segment of the industrial sector, increasing overall by about 4 percent in 1991. A great deal of activity has resulted from government infrastructure projects in port and highway construction, although there has been substantial demand for building in the private sector. Housing, hotel, manufacturing, and commercial space have been coming on-line at a rapid rate. In fact, some observers are worried because they see a glut of office, commercial, and manufacturing space coming onto the market, the result of over-optimistic projections of the needs of NAFTA-based business. Unlike most other places in the world, real estate investment in Mexico is neither highly leveraged nor primarily financed by banks or the government, so real estate represents somewhat less of a financial time bomb in Mexico.

Several port, highway, and other infrastructure projects have been undertaken by the private sector on a concession basis under which the builders are allowed to operate the facilities on a toll or royalty basis. The verdict is still out, but many of these projects have run way over budget, inflating the fees that must be charged and extending the period before they are turned over to the state, making them less of a help than was anticipated. The new privately developed Cuernavaca-Acapulco toll road, for instance, costs about US$150 per car round-trip. Despite plans for additional public works construction (the government plans to boost public sector infrastructure construction by 24 percent to nearly US$5 billion in 1994) and private construction (set to rise by 17 percent to more than US$11 billion) many observers worry that the sector is set to enter a slump.

Services

The service sector—including commerce (wholesale, retail, hotels, and restaurants); transportation and communication, financial and business services; and other services—accounted for about 59.7 percent of official GDP in 1991 (nearly three-fifths). In 1990, about 49.6 percent of the official workforce was employed in the service sector, up from about 37.7 percent in 1970. This represented an average annual growth rate of 3.8 percent in the actual number of persons, or 1.4 percent as a proportion of the workforce—a faster rate of growth than was found in the burgeoning industrial sector. Official figures also understate the dominance of the service sector, because the bulk of the participants in the underground economy are involved in service activities, which could place the real total participation in the sector at close to 58 percent of the total workforce. The service sector may well account for

nearly two-thirds of real GDP if activity in the underground economy is factored in.

In 1991 commerce accounted for about 26.1 percent of total official GDP, followed by other services with a 17.6 percent share; financial and business services (10.7 percent); and transportation and communications (6.8 percent). Growth in specific service areas has been somewhat erratic, although the service sector—especially if the informal sector is taken into account—is the most complex and dynamic in the economy as a whole.

Commerce Retailing and wholesaling in Mexico is somewhat anarchic, consisting not so much of layers of intermediaries (the way it is intentionally in some other countries, such as Japan) as it does of ad hoc arrangements that serve to get around a lack of infrastructure and formal organization. As such, these activities offer a wide range of niche opportunities, especially as the economy opens up to outside goods and operators. Consumer demand exists, and one of the government's policy goals for revitalized economic growth is to provide the means to satisfy this demand. Goals notwithstanding, except for some specific tourist-oriented investments, the government has been slow to allow foreigners to participate in these areas of the domestic economy.

Financial and Business Services Financial and business services have been heavily restricted in the past, but they are opening up to foreign participation and in the process becoming more professional and conversant with international standards. The privatization of Mexican banks in 1991 is expected to go a long way toward reversing the damage done by nationalization of the financial system in 1982, as is the newly independent status accorded to the Banco de México (the central bank), which had previously been relegated largely to the role of a dependent government policy tool. Although foreigners still must operate as junior partners and with minority positions in Mexican financial affairs, they can now participate in a much freer fashion than was previously allowed. And even many authorities privately acknowledge that although Mexico may be able to maintain its limits on foreign participation in commercial banking as it has insisted in the past, under NAFTA it must allow a phase-in of majority (and eventually 100 percent) foreign participation in areas such as investment banking, securities operations, funds management, and insurance.

Tourism Although it is not of major importance in the national budget, tourism is an economic mainstay in many areas of the country, providing an important and steadily growing stream of foreign exchange (as a source of foreign exchange, it is generally ranked third behind oil and *maquila* exports). New hotel and resort construction has been enhancing the country's natural and historic attractions. Development has been uneven, however, with the provision of infrastructure, transport, and subsidiary amenities such as golf courses, marinas, convention centers, parks, and other entertainment facilities lagging behind the basic ability to house a larger contingent of tourists. Mexico's tourist industry must also adjust to the fact that many of these new tourists are more demanding. They are more interested in a full-service experience than they are in roughing it in exotic locales—as was often the case in the past.

Transportation and Communications and Other Services These areas are in flux. Mexico has privatized its national air carriers and its national communications monopoly, and it is allowing greater foreign as well as domestic participation in certain aspects of these heavily regulated operations. This is generating new investment and the development of new organizational structures. In particular, the anticipated reorganization of the trucking industry is causing a revolution in the way business is going to be done in Mexico, where most freight moves by road.

TRADE

During much of the modern era, Mexico's economy has been focused inward, although it has relied on exports to generate foreign exchange to pay for technology and other goods that it needed as enhancements. The inward focus spawned some of the make-do inefficiencies that now plague its economy as it attempts to reorganize and open up its operations. Exports and imports are now seen as a corrective to this situation; the need to earn foreign exchange to service debt and acquire the capital goods necessary to upgrade the economy—not to mention support the consumer demand that accompanies a more open economy—makes the issue even more pressing. In 1985 the Mexican government began a fairly wide-ranging relaxation of its trade policy and exports, and imports have begun to grow both in volume and strategic importance. With the passage of NAFTA, foreign trade is expected to become even freer and take on even greater importance.

The share of imports into Mexico requiring prior licensing approval fell from virtually 100 percent in 1984 to about 20 percent in 1990, with only about 3 percent of products being quantitatively restricted by 1991. Essentially all prior approval licensing is scheduled to be phased out under NAFTA, at least for imports from NAFTA member nations. Import tariffs have also been lowered, with the highest tariffs being set at 20 percent and the majority falling to around 10 percent, down from averages greater than 50 percent in the mid-1980s. Remaining tariffs will be reduced to zero under NAFTA. Although NAFTA allows for phaseout periods of as long as 15 years for some product categories, most remaining duties that are not eliminated immediately will be gone after periods of between five and 10 years. This liberalization of import regulations has served to lower prices and make the Mexican operations that are exposed to competition more efficient. However, it has carried a cost: disruption of the Mexican economy and a rapidly growing trade deficit.

Total foreign trade was an estimated US$77.2 billion in 1993, up marginally from US$75.7 billion in 1992. Trade surged from about US$9.5 billion in 1976 to US$65.1 billion in 1991, growing at an annual average rate of about 13 percent between 1976 and 1993. This includes a period between 1981 and 1988 during which trade generally contracted due to Mexico's general economic woes.

Mexico's Foreign Trade

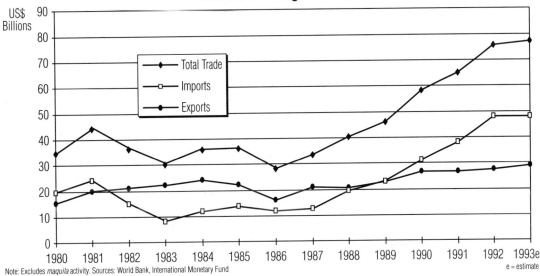

Note: Excludes *maquila* activity. Sources: World Bank, International Monetary Fund

e = estimate

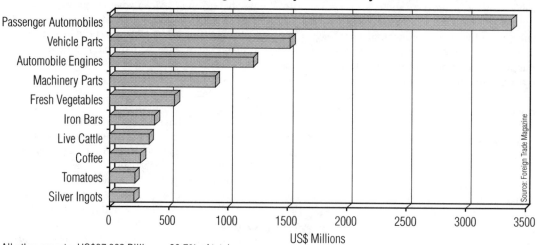

Mexico's Leading Exports By Commodity - 1992

Passenger Automobiles
Vehicle Parts
Automobile Engines
Machinery Parts
Fresh Vegetables
Iron Bars
Live Cattle
Coffee
Tomatoes
Silver Ingots

0   500   1000   1500   2000   2500   3000   3500

US$ Millions

Source: Foreign Trade Magazine

All other exports: US$37.262 Billion or 80.7% of total
Total 1992 Exports: US$46.198 Billion (includes *maquila* exports)

It is important to note that different sources within Mexico—not to mention in the US and elsewhere—report varying trade statistics. Thus the Secretariat of Commerce and Industry, the Bank of Mexico, and the Geography and Information Institute (*Instituto Nacional de Estadística, Geografía y Información*, or INEGI)—the official statistical branch—often report figures that differ by amounts that cannot be explained by simple rounding error. One particular problem is that Mexico historically excluded figures derived from *maquiladora* production from its trade statistics on the grounds that such production represented basically foreign production for reexport rather than national production. Because of this, exports (and, on occasion, imports of inputs as well) were often understated, compounding the disagreement among sources. But official Mexican statistics were changed in 1990 to account explicitly for the *maquila* contribution, giving a somewhat artificial boost to trade figures. Thus trade grew by nearly 17 percent in nominal terms in 1989, but jumped by an exaggerated 26 percent in 1990, before again settling down to 12 to 13 percent growth in 1991 and 1992. However, the US Department of Commerce continued to filter out *maquila* production from bilateral trade statistics, adding to the confusion. As *maquila* production becomes increasingly more integrated into Mexico's domestic economy, more agencies—including all of those noted above—have begun to include *maquila* sector output in their trade and production statistics, although they have done so on different schedules and discrepancies persist.

From the mid-1970s until the early 1980s, when oil was presumed to be Mexico's ticket to the good life and officials felt that the country could afford to be a big spender, Mexico ran a trade deficit amount-

ing to about 13.5 percent of total trade. As the oil mirage faded and Mexico was forced to conserve foreign exchange to service its massive external debt, it reined in imports and attempted to boost exports. This resulted in a merchandise trade surplus, which in 1984 reached as high as 36 percent of total trade. This situation continued even when total trade contracted during the mid-1980s; it began to reverse itself only after reforms began to open the economy in the late 1980s. In 1989, Mexico sustained a merchandise trade deficit equal to 1.5 percent of total trade. This deficit has increased steadily, reaching an estimated 24.4 percent of total trade in 1993. Such deficits are expected to continue to rise due to the effects of NAFTA. They should stabilize in the next few years, although they will continue to be a structural factor for some time. In recent years, inflows of foreign investment capital have served to offset the deficits, at least to some extent.

Exports

That Mexico's exports are generally categorized as petroleum or non-petroleum indicates the importance of the role played by oil in the Mexican economy. As noted, this role has been decreasing as Mexico's economy develops. In 1980 the products of extractive industries—predominately oil, but including mining—accounted for 67.8 percent of total exports. By 1991 exports in this figure had fallen to 28.8 percent, with non-petroleum minerals representing the larger portion instead of oil. In 1985 petroleum exports alone reached a high of 68.2 percent of the total, but by 1990 they had dropped to 37.6 percent of the total, despite a spike in prices due to the Persian Gulf crisis. Petroleum prices were destined to fall even further in subsequent years.

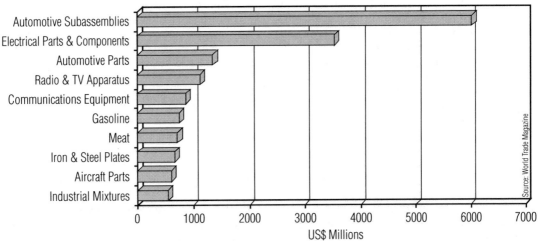

Mexico's Leading Imports By Commodity - 1992

Source: World Trade Magazine

All other imports: US$46.035 Billion or 74.1% of total

Total 1992 Imports: US$62.129 Billion (includes *maquila* input)

Of the less than one-third of total exports represented by non-extractive export products in 1980, manufactured goods represented 22.1 percent, with agricultural products (including exports of animal and forestry products) accounting for 10.1 percent. Other exports were negligible, representing less than 0.01 percent of the total. By 1991 non-extractive exports accounted for 71.2 percent of all exports—manufactured goods represented 61.9 percent of the total; agricultural products 8.7 percent (animal products grew to a 1.8 percent share of total exports, up from 0.8 percent in 1980); and other exports accounted for 0.6 percent of the total. The 1985 figures show non-petroleum exports at 31.8 percent—manufactured goods accounted for 23.4 percent of total exports; agricultural and animal products 5.4 percent; and mining products 3 percent. By 1990, manufactured goods accounted for 52 percent of the total, agricultural and animal products for 8.1 percent, and mining products for 2.3 percent.

In 1992, Mexico's top 10 exports—including *maquila* exports, but excluding oil—accounted for 19.3 percent of total exports. These exports consisted of: automobiles (7.3 percent); automotive parts (3.3 percent); automotive engines (2.6 percent); machinery parts (1.9 percent); fresh vegetables (1.2 percent); iron bars (0.8 percent); live cattle (0.7 percent); coffee (0.6 percent); tomatoes (0.5 percent); and silver ingots (0.5 percent). Remaining exports represented less than 0.5 percent of the total per category.

Imports

Although the volume of Mexico's imports has grown radically during the last several years, the composition of imports has remained fairly stable: Mexicans are primarily buying more of what they were buying before, at least according to some categorizations. In 1980, manufactured items accounted for 86.6 percent of imports, while agricultural and animal products represented 10.8 percent, extractive materials 1.4 percent, and other miscellaneous products 1.2 percent. By 1991, manufactured goods represented 92.9 percent of all imports, agricultural and animal products 5.4 percent, extractive materials 1 percent, and other items 0.7 percent.

In 1985, using a different categorization system, goods classified as raw materials—a residual category including essentially all inputs not specifically categorized as either capital or consumer goods—accounted for 81.7 percent of imports, while capital goods represented 13.6 percent and consumer goods 4.7 percent. By 1991, raw materials had fallen to 63 percent, with capital goods rising to 22.2 percent and consumer goods to 14.8 percent. Prior to 1985, government import restrictions designed to conserve foreign exchange would have been expected to severely reduce consumer goods imports and to put a brake on big-ticket capital goods items. The 1991 figures show a rebound in consumer goods imports and a refocusing on the capital goods needed to build the economy.

Imports are highly diversified. In 1992 the top ten import categories (including *maquila* inputs) accounted for only 26 percent of total imports, with remaining categories each representing less than 1 percent of the total. The top import categories were: automotive subassemblies (9.7 percent); electrical parts and components (5.7 percent); automotive parts (2.2 percent); radio and television apparatus (1.8 percent); communications equipment (1.4 percent); gasoline (1.2 percent); meat (1.1 percent); iron and steel plates (1.1 percent); aircraft parts (1 percent); and industrial mixtures (0.9 percent).

Trading Partners

Mexico's dominant trading partner is the US, which regularly takes almost 70 percent of Mexico's exports and provides more than 60 percent of its imports. Again, differing methods of calculating exports and imports result in variant figures. In 1992 the US took 68.7 percent of Mexican exports and provided 63 percent of the country's imports. Mexican exports were also bought by Spain (4.4 percent), Japan (3.2 percent), Canada (2.8 percent), France (2 percent), Germany (1.8 percent), Brazil (1.6 percent), the Benelux countries (1 percent), the UK (0.9 percent), Venezuela (0.7 percent), Colombia (0.7 percent), and Argentina (0.6 percent) in 1992. The remaining 11.6 percent of exports were taken by other countries, none of which took more than 0.5 percent of the total.

Besides its purchases from the US, in 1992 Mexico bought imports from Japan (6.3 percent), Germany (5.1 percent), France (2.7 percent), Brazil (2.3 percent), Canada (2.2 percent), Italy (2 percent), Spain (1.8 percent), the UK (1.3 percent), China (1.1 percent), the Benelux countries (0.6 percent), and Argentina (0.5 percent). The remaining 11.1 percent of imports were purchased from other countries, none of which provided more than 0.5 percent of the total.

With its heavy historic dependence on the US, Mexico is striving to diversify its trading relationships. It has signed a framework trading agreement with the European Community as well as bilateral agreements with individual European countries. Mexico is a member of the Latin American Integration Association (LAIA in English and ALADI, for *Asociación Latinoamericana de Integración*, in Spanish), has signed bilateral agreements with many individual Latin countries, and in early 1994 concluded a trilateral trade agreement with Colombia and Venezuela. It is also negotiating trade agreements with Caribbean, Eastern European, and, in particular, Asian nations, and, upon endorsing NAFTA in late 1993, was granted membership in the Asia Pacific Economic Cooperation group (APEC).

FOREIGN PARTICIPATION IN THE ECONOMY

Mexico's basic stance since the 1930s has been one that sought to limit foreign participation in its economy. Mexicans are extremely sensitive to any hint of outside interference, and their history is replete with examples of such intervention and slights, both the very real and injurious and the merely perceived. The act of standing up to foreigners through the expropriation and nationalization of the petroleum industry in the 1930s made Lázaro Cárdenas a national hero, a fact that continues to resonate within the Mexican political and cultural milieu, and the focus on import substitution and strict limits on foreign ownership has guided much of Mexico's economic policy since the 1940s.

However, this situation is changing rapidly. Since the early 1980s, Mexico has recognized that its success in the world economy requires it to upgrade its operations to international standards by participating more openly in the global arena, and it has seen its need for outside inputs in order to do so. Both require that it more freely open its economy to greater outside scrutiny and participation. However, old habits die hard; it behooves outsiders to tread lightly with respect to Mexican sensibilities and to expect setbacks and informal limits. But in general, Mexico is moving both rapidly and across a broad front to incorporate outsiders into its growing economy to an unprecedented extent.

Until the passage of the new Foreign Investment Law in December 1993, foreign investment in Mexico was governed by the restrictive 1973 Foreign Investment Law. The 1973 law had prevented outsiders from participating in a variety of industries and operations and—in an effort to ensure national control—generally limited their participation even in approved areas to a maximum 49 percent equity position. However, beginning in 1989, the regulations implementing the law were eased substantially. Foreigners were allowed a radically expanded role; all but a relatively few sectors were opened to direct foreign participation and many of the other sectors that remain restricted were opened to indirect participation. The allowable proportion of foreign ownership increased to as much as 100 percent, depending on the particular industry and case. The relaxed regulations allow the initiation of nonrestricted investments without prior approval. The repeal of foreign exchange controls in late 1991 has also served to make foreign investment considerably easier. Efforts by Mexico to liberalize its traditionally somewhat restrictive international trade regime as a condition of its membership in the General Agreement on Tariffs and Trade (GATT) have further opened up its economy to foreign trading participation, as has the recent passage of NAFTA.

Mexican bureaucrats do not generally exercise the effective veto power over executive initiatives that can be seen in some other countries—particularly in Asia. But the traditional hierarchical, personalized, and opaque way of doing business in Mexico means that implementation of these liberalizing changes is being accomplished in a torturous, nontransparent way. Closely positioned observers of the Mexican economic and political scene stress that while the foreign investment climate is greatly improved and, on balance, more highly favorable to outsiders than at any time in living memory, it is necessary to have expert, well connected, local help in order to penetrate the bureaucratic thicket that has grown up around doing business in the country even for locals.

Even under its more welcoming rules, Mexico offers few incentives to foreign investors. As noted, Mexico has opened up more sectors to greater foreign participation, and investments in about two-thirds of all sectors can be 100 percent foreign owned, with such investments usually requiring no prior approval. Procedures have also been streamlined for investments in the remaining areas that do require official approval. Even where prohibitions continue to exist, there has been a tendency to loosen up some of the rules. For instance, although the state retains its monopoly on primary petrochemical production, it has recently reclassified 14 major product groups as secondary products, making them eligible for foreign investment. New rules allow either direct or trust foreign investment in real estate, even in the previously restricted border and coastal zones and in agricultural lands.

At the end of 1993 the Salinas administration sent a package of reforms to congress designed to make Mexican law conform to provisions of NAFTA and to codify some of the regulatory changes that have been made in recent years by fiat. Provisions of this new Foreign Investment Law not only include the opening up of additional sectors to foreign investment and increased percentages of foreign ownership, but also extend many of the benefits negotiated under NAFTA to foreign investors at large.

Size of Foreign Participation

During the first three-quarters of 1993, about US$10 billion in direct foreign investment flowed into Mexico. However, about half of that amount consisted of investments in the volatile Mexican financial markets, much of it representing temporary "hot" money allocations rather than long-term investment. It should also be noted that again actual figures are somewhat suspect, with official agencies such as the Foreign Investment Commission and the Bank of Mexico issuing differing numbers. Some of this discrepancy may be accounted for by contrasting authorized (or planned investment) versus actual (or paid-up) investment within a given period, but as with many Mexican statistics, the figures should be taken to establish a trend rather than to be an absolute level. Repatriation of Mexican flight capital has also traditionally caused a problem in accounting for foreign investment, although a great deal of the capital that fled the country during the dark days of the mid-1980s has been returned, making this less of an issue than it was even a few years ago.

The Salinas government set a goal of attracting US$5 billion per year in foreign investment for the five-year period 1990–1994, to reach a total of US$25 billion in new direct foreign investment during its administration. This figure would equal the total cumulative registered direct foreign investment in Mexico between 1940 and 1990; represent twice the amount received between 1982 and 1988; and bring the overall foreign participation in the Mexican economy to a 20 to 25 percent level by the beginning of 1995, up from roughly 10 percent in 1990 (which already represented an increase from approximately 5 percent in 1985).

The amount of foreign investment recorded in 1993 (preliminary figures suggest that full-year investment was about US$15 billion) represented an increase of more than 50 percent over the US$9.9 billion in direct foreign investment received in 1991 and the US$4.4 billion in 1990. Between 1989 and 1991, direct foreign investment was US$17.8 billion, and as of the end of 1991, cumulative direct foreign investment was US$33.9 billion. This figure rises to US$41.9 billion if financial market investments are included. An additional US$16.5 billion was invested in 1992. By the end of 1993, total cumulative direct foreign investment was estimated at about US$56.75 billion. Thus at the end of 1993, direct foreign investment had already reached a level 60 percent higher than had been targeted for the entire period from 1990 through 1994 by the Salinas administration, and observers predict that at least an additional US$15 billion will be invested during 1994.

In terms of dollar value, the bulk of foreign investment comes from a relatively few big multinational firms with large investments in such areas as the automotive and other manufacturing industries (in 1993, 87 percent of Fortune 500 firms had a presence in Mexico). Nevertheless, an increasing number of investments represent relatively modest commitments by small, entrepreneurial foreign firms coming into Mexico under its newly liberalized investment rules.

Origin of Foreign Investment

As is not unreasonable to expect, given its size and proximity, the US has consistently accounted for more than three-fifths of foreign investment in Mexico. At the end of 1990, US investment totaled US$16.7 billion, representing 62.1 percent of total foreign investment made since records have been kept. By the end of 1991, this share had grown to 63.4 percent and US$21.5 billion, an increase in value of more than 30 percent. As of mid-1993, US investment had risen to about 72 percent of the total.

Following the dominant US, foreign investors in Mexico in 1990 included: Germany (6.4 percent); the UK (6.3 percent); Japan (4.8 percent); Switzerland (4.4 percent); France (3.1 percent); Spain (2.3 percent); and other countries, each representing less than a 2 percent share (combining to 9.4 percent). Cumulative foreign investment at the end of 1990 was US$26.5 billion, of which UK investment represented

US$1.8 billion; German, US$1.7 billion; Japanese, US$1.3 billion; Swiss, US$1.2 billion; and other countries, US$3.8 billion.

The balance shifted slightly in 1991. The US maintained an even more dominant share, followed by: Germany (US$2 billion, 6 percent); the UK (US$2 billion, 5.9 percent); Japan (US$1.5 billion, 4.5 percent); France (US$1.4 billion, 4.3 percent); and Switzerland (US$1.4 billion, 4.2 percent). Together, these six countries represented 88.3 percent of all foreign investment, with remaining investment being made by countries which each represented less than a 4 percent share.

Areas of Foreign Investment

Since the mid-1980s, foreign investment has progressively been shifting from the industrial to the service sector. In 1986, 77.9 percent of foreign investment went into industry, while 12.7 percent was made in service enterprises. By 1991, industrial investment had shrunk to 58.6 percent of the total, while service investment had grown to 32.2 percent, a change from roughly one-eighth to one-third of the total.

At the end of 1990, 60.2 percent of total cumulative foreign investment had been made in the industrial sector, followed by 31 percent in services; an additional 7.1 percent represented investment in commerce, a sub-sector of services; and 1.7 percent in mining, a sub-sector of industry. As of the end of 1991, industry was listed as having received a cumulative US$19.9 billion in foreign investment (for a 58.9 percent share); services received US$10.9 billion (32.2 percent); commerce, US$2.4 billion (7.1 percent); mining, US$0.5 billion (1.5 percent); and agriculture and ranching, US$0.1 billion (0.3 percent).

An alternative partial-year reckoning from the *Secretaría de Comercio y Fomento Industrial* (SECOFI) based on slightly different numbers and a somewhat different breakdown listed manufacturing as having a 59.4 percent cumulative share of foreign investment, services a 32 percent share, commerce 6.6 percent, mining 1.6 percent, and agriculture, forestry, and fishing 0.4 percent. As of mid-1993, the manufacturing sector had received 53.3 percent of foreign investment, followed by services with a 27.3 percent share. Commerce, mining, and, to a lesser degree, agriculture received greater shares under liberalized regulations. Another partial-year 1993 report listed manufacturing as garnering roughly 50 percent, while services captured 30 percent and commerce a much larger 15 percent share.

GOVERNMENT ECONOMIC DEVELOPMENT STRATEGY

Given the degree of discretion allotted to the Mexican president, each successive administration largely gets to set its own social and economic policies. Al-though it usually must deal with the fallout from its predecessor and must also deal with the almost ritualized expectations of the electorate, it generally sets the tone, the format, and, to a great degree, the substance of its policies. After the near-disaster of the López Portillo administration (1976–1982) and the finger-in-the-dike posture of the de la Madrid administration (1982–1988), the Salinas government has taken the initiative in a variety of areas.

President Carlos Salinas de Gortari has focused on reducing inflation by curbing government spending and reforming policy as it relates to business, including the privatization of large portions of the burdensome state-run sector. This has included keeping the demands of labor on a relatively short leash to combat inflation and retain what is one of Mexico's main competitive advantages: its low labor costs. He has also worked to decentralize the Mexican economy and upgrade it, largely by opening it up to outside competition through investment and trade initiatives. In the process, Salinas has roiled traditionally placid waters by taking on powerful special interests. On balance, he is winning the economic fight, and the local assessment is that "macro looks good, although micro still needs work." However, Salinas has experienced major setbacks in the areas of political and social reform, neither of which have been among the strong points of this hardly charismatic technocrat (local wags have compared the president to the Tin Man in the Wizard of Oz: stalwart, but without a heart).

Mexican presidents customarily issue a National Development Plan (*Plan Nacional de Desarrollo*, or PND), a document that is *conceptuoso* (conceptual): long on revolutionary rhetoric and catchphrases, but short on substance and specifics. More specific proposals have involved greater regional integration, as evidenced by renewed hemispheric activity—including the signing of a trade accord with Venezuela and Colombia and Salinas' strong espousal of NAFTA. Salinas also built on the Economic Solidarity Pact (*Pacto por Solidaridad Económico*, or PSE) inherited from his predecessor, which had represented a pro-business, market-oriented, outward-looking change from the traditional inward-looking, control-oriented, pro-labor status quo official posture toward the Mexican economy. Salinas' PECE, which succeeded the PSE, elaborated on this theme. It called for stabilization of the economy, recovery through market-led growth, and the most radical restructuring of the economy in more than 50 years, including privatization and reorganization. It also put labor on notice that it would be held accountable for helping to get the economy on track. Many in labor argue that this *pacto* effectively funded its reforms at the expense of labor by calling on that sector to bear a disproportionate share of the sacrifice while opening up the prospect of market-based profits to entice the private sector into supporting the plan.

In October 1993, Salinas announced the outline of a new *pacto* designed to guide the economy through the end of his term in December 1994. Now that he has achieved most of what he set out to do—and what is doable, given constraints on resources and time—he has, in keeping with past practice, added something for just about everyone who has felt left out of previous policies in order to smooth the way for the election of his successor. For farmers suffering from the phaseout of crop subsidies, the plan adds a per hectare subsidy designed to ease the burden on the small producers while removing the crop subsidies that had resulted in inefficient production of staple items. For labor, which has seen its purchasing power erode, there are low-income tax credits that will boost the effective earnings of affected low-end workers by 10 to 11 percent. For big business, there is a drop in the corporate tax rate from 35 percent to 34 percent, coupled with a reduction in the withholding tax on overseas payments.

Some free market critics argue that the new plan does not go far enough in revising counterproductive taxes, such as the capital gains tax, although others complain that it sweetens the pot for too many without instituting any means of recovering the lost revenues that will fund the giveaways. Generally the only major group to feel left out of the *pacto* in a major way consists of people in small- and medium-sized businesses, who argue that none of its provisions benefit them and that the plan ignores their needs for more available, cheaper credit.

The Salinas administration also has: signed Mexico on as the first formal adherent of the so-called Brady Plan, which was designed to stabilize and ultimately reduce Mexico's massive foreign debt problem; strengthened the in-bond *maquila* program to promote foreign trade and investment; and taken on the sacred cow of the archaic *ejido* agricultural system, providing a framework for breaking up the communal landholdings and subsidies that have largely served to keep Mexican agribusiness in a permanent state of underdevelopment.

Salinas has used his broad discretionary powers to effect substantial change. He also has been seen as using them during the final two years of his term to put reforms in place that will reduce the leeway available to his successors in reversing his policies. Previous administrations have generally left those who followed the freedom to do as they pleased. However, perhaps no administration since the political system was put in place in the 1920s has made such sweeping changes. As more of these changes get codified as the Salinas term winds down, it will become increasingly difficult for future presidents to alter them substantially, much less reverse them. Nevertheless, things do change, and the personality of or the conditions faced by subsequent presidents could dictate radically different approaches.

POLITICAL OUTLOOK FOR THE ECONOMY

The Mexican economy is facing its brightest prospects in more than a dozen years. Many would argue that given the fact that the prospects of 12 years ago were largely illusory in nature, it is now seeing the brightest prospects of the entire modern era.

During much of recent Mexican history, the last year of an outgoing administration has been one of turmoil. But for the last 60 years the transfer of power in Mexico has at least been anticlimactic, because the monopoly party political system has been designed—for good or for ill—to make the transition certain. Even though the assassination of ruling party candidate Luis Donaldo Colosio Murrieta in March 1994 disrupted the routine transition, Mexico still seems far from slipping into anarchy.

Inside the ruling PRI, transitions have tended to be less placid, as various factions jockey for position. For the factions that back the right candidate, the subsequent coronation of the party's standard bearer has meant that they are set for the next six years, and often for life. For those who guessed wrong, there was often exile from the seat of power and a deaf ear turned toward their concerns and those of their constituents. Nevertheless, that is the way the game had come to be played.

That changed with the last election, when the excesses of the López Portillo and the austerity of the de la Madrid administrations prompted a popular outcry and the rise of surprisingly strong outsider candidates. Whereas de la Madrid had been elected by a better than a 70 percent majority (with the leading opposition candidate gaining less than 16 percent of the vote), Salinas won only a 50.74 percent official share of the vote, the barest of majorities. The leading opposition candidate, Cuauhtémoc Cárdenas—son of folk hero Lázaro Cárdenas and a left-of-center populist—gained an official 31 percent of the vote amid strident charges of electoral fraud. The next candidate, Manuel Clouthier of the rightist opposition *Partido de Acción Nacional* (PAN), polled an official 16.8 percent. Most observers doubt that the opposition candidates could actually have beaten Salinas, even in a wholly fair contest. However, given the closeness of the vote and past tactics, it is likely that Salinas' majority may really have been only a plurality. At any rate, he did not come to power with a clear popular mandate.

Many observers also note that the vote for Cárdenas was more in the nature of a protest against austerity and a perception of ruling party business-as-usual than it was an actual endorsement of his left-leaning politics. And Salinas' ability to distance himself from the dirty tricks of the campaign, his staking out of an independent position with respect to traditional power blocs, his acquiescence to off-year losses in state elections, and his basic success in turning the economy around led most people to give him the benefit of the doubt.

In fact, as time drew near for Salinas to name his successor, opposition candidacies—although strong in certain states and local areas—were fading fast at the national level. The right-wing PAN, the vocal Number Two opposition party in 1988, had fallen by the wayside, its pro-business support having been largely co-opted by Salinas. Meanwhile, Cárdenas' leftist Democratic Revolutionary Party (*Partido Revolucionario Decomcrático*, or PRD) was having trouble getting noticed—much less taken seriously—in the context of a recovering economy.

The main hope for the opposition lay in the generally unexciting nature of the PRI designate for the presidency, Luis Donaldo Colosio. Colosio was the former head of the PRI's executive committee, a former senator from the state of Sonora, and head of Solidarity, the semi-official popular front pork barrel operation. He was also a technocratic protégé of Salinas who had served as the president's campaign manager in 1988. What little interest there was resulted from the resignation of Manuel Camacho Solís, the appointed mayor of Mexico City, who resigned in a huff at having been passed over. Even this small drama was not considered important, although some thought Camacho might break party ranks and challenge Colosio as a third party candidate.

This was considered idle speculation until the uprising in Chiapas in January 1994. Protesting the social and political inequities in the country and the unevenness of the economic miracle that left them outside the recovery, the self-styled Zapatista rebels embarrassed the government and, to some extent, revived the moribund candidacy of Cárdenas. And although the Zapatistas were primarily interested in local economic and political concerns, they also called for national political and social reform.

The Zapatistas won many of their points in the negotiations (further incensing hardliners who wanted to use force to simply crush the insurgency and considered it anathema to dignify their demands by talking to them). The points raised included renewed promises of greater economic aid, plus assurances of both local and national level political reforms, that would provide for free elections with outside observers—something Mexico has previously refused to allow. How well the implementation will actually work remains to be seen, but the issue has been made into a mainstream one and accepted as such by the ruling party.

Then on March 23, 1994, candidate Colosio was assassinated while on a campaign stop in Tijuana. Although the assassin was apprehended and confessed to acting alone, wild conspiracy theories immediately surfaced, blaming hardliners within the PRI, drug lords, Camacho, Salinas, Los Angeles gangs, or just about anyone else except—surprisingly—the CIA and space aliens. Preliminary investigations did give some credibility to a conspiracy by disaffected bureaucrats, but all but the lowest-level suspects were quickly released for lack of evidence. Many observers doubt that there will ever be a satisfactory resolution of the assassination.

The Salinas administration was thrown into a crisis as it searched frantically for a replacement candidate. Camacho, the obvious candidate, quickly withdrew his name from consideration, although most observers doubt that he would have been tapped, because he was considered to have committed too many political sins in his independent near-run for the presidency. The Mexican constitution further limited the search because it requires candidates to have been out of the government for six months prior to the election, which was scheduled within five months of the assassination. The government briefly floated proposals to either change the constitution or postpone the election, but met resistance both from the opposition forces and internally from the party organization. With most potential candidates ineligible because of recent active government service, Salinas passed over the head of the PRI and, within a week, named Ernesto Zedillo Ponce de León, Colosio's 42-year-old campaign manager.

Zedillo holds a PhD from Yale University (Colosio had an MA from the University of Pennsylvania, and Salinas is a Harvard man), and had served as Secretary of Education and Secretary of Budget and Planning. Although Zedillo comes from a lower middle class background—he noted that as a boy he had once worked a church shoeshine concession that he had wangled by agreeing to split the take with the priest—he is considered inexperienced and stiff in public.

Although the polls, not surprisingly, gave Zedillo the lead—after all, no PRI candidate for national office has ever lost—the candidate was on shaky ground. After initially wrapping himself in the cloak of the fallen Colosio, Zedillo moved to establish himself as a separate independent entity as he proceeded with his crash course in electoral politics. He stated—many think primarily for foreign consumption—that not only is he a firm supporter of Salinas' reform policies, but Mexico cannot afford a radical shift away from the reforms, and his policy would be to stay the course. Nevertheless, Zedillo and his supporters were frantically trying to mend fences with the less-than-enthusiastic party faithful, making what many fear are substantial concessions that could undermine the Salinas reforms to the old guard in return for their support.

On May 11, 1994, the three major candidates held Mexico's first-ever presidential debate. The earnest but deadpan Cárdenas lost momentum—as did the inexperienced Zedillo—in the face of pyrotechnics from the PAN candidate Fernandez de Cevallos, a noted debater. Zedillo is also considered to be at a disadvantage because heavy security in the wake of the assassination is hindering him from meeting the people close up. One of the main functions of Mexican political campaigning is to introduce the often sheltered candidate to the people and vice versa, allowing the electorate to become comfortable with the candidate and the candidate to get a feel for the range of conditions within the country, before he disappears into the artificial environment of the imperial Mexican presidency.

There is considerable concern, both at home and abroad, over the Zedillo candidacy. It is virtually inconceivable that the PRI's candidate could lose the election, especially when the opposition is so relatively weak. There is real concern that a minority party victory would lead to chaos, because only the PRI has the infrastructure in place to manage the government, especially at this delicate economic juncture. However, others are quietly voicing concern that the election of an unprepared and dependent Zedillo could lead to domination by party reactionaries, who could do considerable damage as well.

There are any number of wild cards in Mexico as well as in the world economy. Nevertheless, it is likely that Mexico has come too far along the road of restructuring for it to be able to slip back into the old patterns to any significant degree. There will be ups and downs, but it seems certain that Mexico is on the road to greater economic openness and growth, and any political administration is more likely to advance this general trajectory than it is to retard—much less reverse—it.

MEXICO'S INTERNATIONAL ROLE

Mexico has long been a member of a variety of international associations. Recently it has taken the lead in applying for membership in additional ones as well as initiating new ones, mostly regional in nature. Mexico is a member of the United Nations and most of its agencies, GATT (since 1986), the International Bank for Reconstruction and Development (the IBRD, usually called the World Bank), the International Monetary Fund (IMF), and various international commodities agreements. It is also a charter member of the Organization of American States (OAS, or the *Organización de los Estados Americanas*, or OEA in Spanish), LAIA (ALADI in Spanish), and the Latin American Economic System, as well as various bilateral and multilateral regional trading agreements, including NAFTA. As a Pacific Rim nation, it has also joined APEC.

In late March 1994, Mexico was admitted to membership in the Organization for Economic Cooperation and Development (OECD). This association of the largest, most developed economies in the world extended membership to Mexico—its first Third World member—in recognition of Mexico's growing modernization.

In the past, Mexico often joined international organizations out of a sense of its own importance as much as anything else. It is now, however, seeking to use such memberships primarily as a means of integrating itself into the international community.

Current Issues

POLITICAL REFORM— WHITHER THE PRI?

Changing Conditions Like many other governments during the late 1980s and early 1990s, the authorities in Mexico are striving to implement reforms designed to introduce a more open economic system. As is the case with other regimes, these officials have simultaneously been trying to retain control, keeping the brakes on reform in the social and political spheres as much as possible, even as they promote change in the economic arena.

For Mexico this means that the ruling *Partido Revolucionario Institucional* (Institutional Revolutionary Party), or PRI, must learn to adapt to a new set of circumstances that require it to be more open-ended and consultative. Observers ask not only whether it can adapt with good grace, but whether it can adapt at all, and if not, what will follow. This question is of more than merely local interest because PRI dominance has allowed Mexico to maintain political stability since the late 1920s, a prerequisite for economic reform and especially for foreign investment.

Political Evolution Although it is organized as a constitutional federal republic, Mexico is not a democracy in the sense understood by most Westerners. The theoretically independent judiciary and legislature defer to a strong executive branch headed by a president who exercises seemingly unlimited power. Despite his broad powers, the president must in reality integrate a wide range of constituencies, any of which can be snubbed temporarily, but not ignored indefinitely. The trappings of power are absolute, but the reality is considerably more constrained.

The Evolution of the Ruling Party President Calles organized the first monopoly political party, the *Partido Nacional Revolucionario*, or PNR—the forerunner of today's PRI—in 1929. From the beginning, Calles controlled the new party, imposing his own handpicked candidate on the first convention. However, when the candidate attempted to exercise

independent power following his election, Calles deposed him, substituting a more pliable interim official.

This high-handed *caudillismo* (or chieftanship, in the sense of independent, unchecked personalized authority, backed by coercive force; *caudillo, cacique*, and *jefe* all have similar meanings) led to increased unrest. As the 1934 elections approached, Calles and the PNR searched for a more popular candidate, settling on General Lázaro Cárdenas del Rio. However, once in office, Cárdenas began acting against the interests of the elites who had reached accommodation with Calles. When Calles began to make noises about disposing of the upstart, Cárdenas responded forcefully by removing Calles' supporters from the military and the government. When Calles mounted a renewed assault in 1936, Cárdenas summarily deported him and his inner circle.

Cárdenas removed party, government, and outside officials, most of whom were appointees who held their positions through personal loyalty to Calles. He reformed organized labor, helping to set up the *Confederación de Trabajadores Mexicanos* (CTM)—which represents labor to this day—and the *Confederación Nacional de Campesinos* (CNC) to bring the peasantry into the political sphere in a formal manner. Cárdenas also organized a body to represent the important civil service; and he provided for an association to represent the interests of the military (this agency was subsequently dropped). Formal representation of the private business sector was omitted, but business interests have been able to gain access to the government, even when it is publicly excoriating them. Finally, in 1938, Cárdenas set up an executive council to integrate these sectors into a new party machine, renamed the Mexican Revolutionary Party (*Partido Revolucionario Mexicano*, or PRM).

The Cárdenas Legacy Besides organizing the ruling party into a functioning entity responsive to one man but formalized enough so that it neither depends on nor expires with that individual, Cárdenas set the policy, followed by every subsequent president, of personally selecting his successor with at best only a nominal bow toward broader consultation. Cárdenas also showed himself to be ruthless in summarily dismissing rivals and exiling Calles. Cárdenas the populist also showed himself to be a willful, idiosyncratic manager and policymaker, pursuing on his own authority economic policies—expropriation and nationalization—that nearly resulted in the ruin of the economy.

Although Cárdenas set in motion those changes that would determine the shape of modern Mexico politically and economically, it remained for President Miguel Alemán Valdés to set the format that would apply for the next several decades. It was largely at Alemán's behest that the PRM changed its name to the *Partido Revolucionario Institucional* in 1946. This new concept, institutionalized revolution, served to designate the party and its bureaucracy as the sole heir to the revolution, vesting it with the responsibility for determining what would be legitimate and authorized politically. By extension, outsiders were deprived of significance, of any legitimacy to influence the pronouncements of the party and hence the governance of the country. Thus, a pattern was set in place: Mexico would be governed largely by a clique of insiders supported by a growing bureaucracy for the next 25 years.

The Technocrat's Mexico Many observers see 1970 and the accession of Luis Echeverría as representing the beginnings of a further stage in Mexico's political evolution. Echeverría was a more bureaucrat and a technician than a traditional politician. He changed the tone of political discourse, dropping some of the hackneyed revolutionary rhetoric in favor of more modern material, opening discussion with outside interests (although continuing to keep the lid on substantive dissent or opposition), and filling his administration with young, post-revolutionary technocrats.

Echeverría's successor, José López Portillo, was another technocrat lacking a traditional political background. López Portillo presided over the discovery of major oil reserves in 1976. But borrowing soon outstripped oil revenues; inflation began to rise sharply; and with all that money floating around, the *sexenio* (or six-year term) of López Portillo is generally seen as the most corrupt in Mexican history.

When oil prices began to slip in 1981, the economy deteriorated as rapidly as it had risen just a few years before. López Portillo went from being wildly popular to openly reviled. His successor, Miguel de la Madrid, was Mexico's third nonpolitical technocratic president in a row. De la Madrid faced tough, unpopular choices. He chose to focus on restoring international confidence, at the expense of shoring up things at home. The poor suffered the

most, with labor seeing its standard of living recede. Whereas the standard of living of the middle class had previously risen the most sharply, it now fell just as steeply; the middle class formed the core of a protest movement that for the first time began to seek legitimate alternatives at the polls. There was less patronage to go around, and many of the party faithful were also left out in the cold. Nevertheless, the party's old guard continued to support the system, using their skills to prevent the middle class backlash from undermining the president, although many suspect that they had to stretch things pretty far to keep PRI candidates on the winning side of the ledger in a host of local elections during the mid-1980s.

To the growing dismay of the old guard, the selection of Carlos Salinas de Gortari to succeed de la Madrid in 1988 continued the trend of nonpolitical technocrats as president. Salinas firmly established the *técnicos*, at the expense of the party faithful. An increasing number of *técnicos* are using their expertise to bypass party membership as they advance up a parallel ladder to positions of influence previously restricted to party members. Such party old-timers sneer that Salinas was never elected to any office prior to becoming president, although by this they generally mean that he was insufficiently beholden to them.

This tension between technicians and populists (old-style supporters of the political status quo, which includes isolationism and a statist economy), has been growing since the Echeverría years. The main battleground has been within the PRI, but struggles have also spilled over into outside, public forums.

The Threat of Dissent There have always been competing interests and political dissent in Mexico, but since the consolidation of national power under the control of the PRI, outside dissent has been minor, relatively quiet, and generally seen as being of a fringe nature, outside the mainstream and lacking in legitimacy.

The president's choice of officeholders—especially of his successor—is preceded by an elaborate ritual of non-campaigning in which aspirants must promote themselves and denigrate their opponents, all without being seen to do so. During the de la Madrid administration, the president leaked a list of names of potential candidates to the press to allow for comment, but previous presidents ignored even this minimal level of outside—especially public—input.

The procedure is potentially disruptive, because it involves not only the prospective candidates, but all their supporters and protégés all the way down the line. Backing the wrong horse can mean exile from the seat of power, and the party has had to develop some means of rewarding losers in order to prevent schisms. Above all, it has had to maintain public unity and a high level of discipline. Those on the inside have learned to be subtle, indirect, and patient; any departure from this norm is cause for comment, concern, and punishment.

In 1986, Cuauhtémoc Cárdenas broke the rules by announcing that he wanted to be the presidential candidate in 1988. Cárdenas—the son of Lázaro Cárdenas—had generally served the PRI with distinction, although some party bigwigs considered him to be too independent. Cárdenas proceeded to organize a PRI splinter group called *Corriente Democrática* (Democratic Current) to push for reform of the electoral process. The PRI allowed the rebellion to proceed, even allowing coverage by the tightly controlled press. According to some observers, PRI officials let the movement go on just to give the appearance of dynamism and free debate within the party.

After Salinas was named as the PRI candidate, Cárdenas accepted the presidential nomination of the minority *Partido Auténtico de la Revolución Mexicano* (Authentic Party of the Mexican Revolution, or PARM) instead of fading into the background and supporting the mainstream candidate. Cárdenas also garnered nominations from other minority parties, including the *Partido Mexicano Socialista* (Mexican Socialist Party, or PMS), Mexico's main leftist party, and began to mount a serious opposition campaign.

Cárdenas campaigned on populist issues based on the 1917 constitution: guaranteed employment, education, housing, and health care for all Mexicans; forgiveness of Mexico's foreign debt; greater state involvement in the economy through state-run industry; less foreign participation; reduced oil sales; and greater social spending. In addition to leftist, nationalistic rhetoric, he also espoused the idea of open primaries with effective suffrage to select candidates for office at all levels. The message found a receptive audience among segments of the rural poor, some unionized urban workers, and the middle class. Even those who did not support the platform saw Cárdenas' campaign as a means of sending a message of disapproval to the ruling PRI.

Salinas, the PRI's candidate, won a majority by a margin of less than 1 percent, the smallest majority in Mexican history. Cárdenas was given an official 31 percent of the vote, with various other minority party candidates receiving 18.2 percent. The official computer system "broke down" for several hours and some final counts were never released, resulting in the widespread belief that the PRI falsified the numbers to steal the election. Many observers consider that Salinas probably won a plurality rather than a majority. Some diehards continue to argue that the PRI stole an actual majority from Cárdenas, but most doubt that, even in a totally free election, the minority candidate was in a position to win an outright majority.

Subsequently, Cárdenas organized a separate party, the *Partido Revolucionario Democrático* (Democratic Revolutionary Party, or PRD), which has presented a variety of candidates in local, state, and national elections since 1989. Cárdenas is again the PRD's candidate in 1994. However, he has attracted relatively little interest during the current campaign. Despite being given a new lease on life by a flagging economy, the popular uprising in Chiapas, and the Colosio assassination, his leftist message resonates less now that a changed economy is improving prospects for the urban middle class.

The other main source of organized political dissent in Mexico comes from the right-of-center, avowedly pro-business *Partido de Acción Nacional* (National Action Party, or PAN). Strongest in the northern tier states (which have traditionally been somewhat more independent and US-influenced), the PAN got only 16.8 percent of the vote in the 1988 election. However, it won recognition for itself—and for Salinas as well—when its candidate was actually allowed to take office after winning the election for governor in Baja California Norte in 1989, the first non-PRI opposition gubernatorial candidate to actually be confirmed by the electoral process since the PRI was formed.

Between 1979 and 1988, minority parties almost doubled their representation in the legislature, from 25.6 to 47.6 percent of legislative seats. In 1990, 30 of the 31 state governors belonged to the PRI, as did 60 of the 64 senators, 91 percent of the municipal presidents, and 70 percent of the local deputies. New rules, passed in 1993, call for limiting the majority party to 315 of the 500 seats in the lower house, while expanding the upper house and guaranteeing that minority parties hold at least 25 percent of such seats. However, many minority representatives habitually vote with the PRI, and the legislature operates primarily as a rubber stamp for the PRI executive branch anyway, so such "advances" are seen as window dressing by most observers.

Preparing for the 1994 Presidential Campaign
Despite his limited prior political experience, Salinas has received generally good marks as president. Although acceding to the victory of the PAN in three governor's races between 1988 and 1992, the PRI is generally considered to have stolen a gubernatorial election in Michoacán and interfered in a number of other elections. In 1990 Salinas pushed through a reform package that created an elections commission and elections tribunal designed to make the process more fair and open. In 1993 he sponsored constitutional amendments that are supposed to reduce fraud, and he issued regulations requiring officials to submit to an audit of personal assets and income as a deterrent to corruption.

Other reforms allow minority candidates greater

access to television and newspaper coverage. Newspapers play a relatively minor role in Mexico: the government largely controls the press through its control over official advertising, its "subsidies" to friendly journalists, and its purchased feature articles *(gacetillas)* that look exactly like news items. Television is somewhat more influential, although relatively few people have access to television sets. Some critics argue that while television is generally subservient to the government and airs little formal commentary or analysis, it has propagated the conservative slant of the media moguls who run it. Even though its sound bite format provides for little analysis or editorialization, radio remains Mexico's primary source of information. In 1993 the government was accused of threatening radio stations with the loss of their licenses for giving too much exposure to minority candidates and to opponents of the official pro-NAFTA party line.

The PRI has had a virtually unlimited budget (some reports suggest that its 1994 campaign budget is greater than the total that the two major US parties spent on the 1992 US presidential campaign). However, new regulations limit campaign contributions to a maximum of NP1 million (about US$285,000); contributions must come from individuals or social organizations (corporations, religious groups, and foreign organizations cannot legally contribute). These reforms came as fallout from an attempt by PRI officials to solicit large contributions from wealthy businesspeople. Although this attempt was ostensibly conceived to develop a source of funding clearly separate from public monies, it provoked charges of influence peddling and caused the officials to return contributions and back off from their plan. The head of the PRI was subsequently replaced over the flap. Another less touted "reform" prohibits the running of coalition candidates. This would prevent multiple parties from naming the same candidate, the tactic that helped give Cárdenas his large vote in 1988.

The opposition, which is generally poorly organized, customarily files complaints about voting irregularities. Recently, the reported instances have appeared to be relatively minor in nature, and even opposition protesters grudgingly acknowledge that they are often soundly beaten and would be even in a perfectly clean election. However, the long-term dominance of the PRI has created a climate in which irregularities occur due to force of habit, and the bulk of voters continue to vote for the PRI candidates simply because they have no other real choice. The touchiness of the government also points up the fact that in the newly charged atmosphere, any protest of substance by opposition candidates could serve to call even relatively open elections into question. Indeed, as of late May 1994, several Mexican commentators were arguing that because of its past record, it would be virtually impossible for the PRI to convince the populace that elections were fair unless the PRI presidential candidate actually lost to an opposition candidate. Even last-minute reforms providing for new identification documents and updated, audited voter lists have failed to placate critics, who continue to insist that the IDs are faked and the lists padded with phantom PRI voters. For the first time, the government agreed to allow independent monitoring of elections, although it has continued to resist international monitors as an invasion of national sovereignty.

A major PRI defeat is still considered virtually impossible, even in a completely free election: the opposition candidates simply do not have the broad-based support needed to successfully challenge even a relatively weak PRI candidate on a nationwide basis. However, it will be difficult to justify a PRI win, which could cause either an unraveling of majority party control or increased rigidity on the part of the ruling party operatives.

Part of this newfound sensitivity on the part of the government about such past and continuing embarrassments is due to the greater international scrutiny to which it has been subjected during the debate over NAFTA and its own attempts to make itself seem more cosmopolitan, international, and sophisticated. In the past, the PRI simply didn't care. The fact that it now does, say some of the hard-liners, is the problem. According to this viewpoint, the new technocrats, while skilled at speaking the language of international agencies and businesspeople, are out of touch with their own roots and people. Because of their own political ineptitude they have failed at damage control, allowing such incidents to be blown out of proportion; they have surrendered important prerogatives (and political positions, patronage, and influence) that they should have been able to hang onto; and they have generally failed to maintain the system. Old timers argue that the new breed sees the PRI organization merely as a necessary evil: a sort of "Ministry of Elections" that gets trotted out to do the dirty work as needed, but otherwise gets no respect. And they darkly mutter that they and the country won't stand for such disorganization indefinitely.

The 1994 Campaign The chosen candidate for president is known as the *tapado* (the veiled one) or *el bueno* (the good one). When the president considers that the time is right, the *destape* (unveiling) takes place. In November 1993, Salinas announced that Luis Donaldo Colosio Murrieta, 44, his Secretary of Social Development and Environment and the campaign manager of Salinas' 1982 campaign, would be the PRI's candidate. Colosio, a US-educated (MA in Economics from the University of Pennsylvania) politician from

Sonora who had served as a senator, headed the PRI (and conceded the PAN's victory in the Baja governor's race), negotiated the environmental side-accords to NAFTA, and been the head of Solidarity (Mexico's US$3 billion social welfare program), was also considered relatively charismatic and popular. He was considered too much of a new style technocrat by many within the party, but more acceptable than some others. His platform was based on the continuation of the economic policies of Salinas and—secondarily—opening up the political process. He was also the internal front-runner, challenged primarily by Manuel Camacho Solís, the appointed Mayor of Mexico City and former environmental minister.

Camacho resigned in a huff after being passed over. Also US-educated (MPA, Princeton) and a former head of the PRI, the 47-year-old Camacho was even more popular and charismatic than Colosio. His lack of good grace at being passed over was noteworthy, and there was speculation that he would mount an independent candidacy. This speculation received enough publicity to suggest that officials were willing to let him to provide a little excitement in what was shaping up to be a boring campaign.

This situation held through the early weeks of the announcement as Colosio's campaign got off to a creaky start (PRI old-timers attributed this to Colosio's appointment of Ernesto Zedillo, another inexperienced whiz kid, as his campaign manager). This lack of energy came despite Colosio's offer to decentralize government to the extent that gubernatorial nominees would be selected from among local candidates, rather than having the statehouses used as dumping grounds for central government of-

ficials either on the way up or down. He also made an unprecedented offer to debate minority party candidates (he later reneged, offering to send a substitute to debate Cárdenas and claiming scheduling conflicts).

With the attack by Zapatista rebels in Chiapas on January 1, 1994, the situation changed dramatically. First, Colosio's already slow-to-ignite campaign was overshadowed to an even greater degree. This was followed by Salinas' appointment of Camacho as chief negotiator with the rebels, who listed national political reform as one of their demands among the more standard economic local concerns.

Camacho gained renewed national prominence. He negotiated a cease-fire with the rebels, who had demanded the resignation of Salinas. At the end of February 1994, the government agreed to name a commission to audit voter rolls; to set up an office under the attorney general to prosecute election irregularities; to open the polls to independent observers; to change the format of voter registration cards to prevent fraud; to increase public financing available to minority parties; and to stiffen the penalties for fraud.

After making noises about mounting an independent campaign, Camacho announced in late March 1994 that he would not run. Just as the country, its politicians, and its foreign investors were breathing a sigh of relief at the removal of this potential conflict, candidate Colosio was assassinated at a campaign stop in Tijuana on March 23, 1994. Authorities initially produced evidence accusing a deranged, lone gunman; then they announced a conspiracy. However, within a week, many of those detained as suspects were released for lack of evidence, and the

Cartoonists & Writers Syndicate

Artist: Oswaldo. Originally published in Excelsior, Mexico City. Copyright © 1984 Oswaldo/Cartoonist & Writers Syndicate.

government began edging back toward the lone gunman theory. Most observers doubt that there will be a satisfactory resolution regarding the assassination.

Although no hard evidence was advanced to support the theory, many adherents claimed that PRI hard-liners were behind the assassination of the increasingly independent candidate who was becoming more convinced of the need to institute real democratic reforms that would displace many old-style party functionaries.

Selecting a Backup Candidate In the immediate aftermath of Colosio's assassination, the president's job was to keep the lid on and pick a new candidate. In addition to keeping things under control and the difficulties of again realigning factions and personalities that had been so recently reconciled, Salinas was hampered by a constitutional provision banning any serving member of the government from being elected until he or she had been out of the government for 180 days (the August 21st election was then only 150 days off). To distance himself, Camacho—who was potentially eligible and had previously advertised his interest—withdrew his name from consideration almost immediately after the assassination.

Speculation had it that the choice would be between Fernando Ortiz Arana, the head of the PRI and a veteran political operative (albeit one without economic training or public experience), and Ernesto Zedillo Ponce de León, Colosio's campaign manager. Zedillo, 42, was named as the replacement candidate on March 30. He has a PhD in Economics from Yale and has served as Education Minister and Minister of Budget and Planning. Unfortunately for someone thrust into the situation in which he needs to act decisively and quickly, the inexperienced Zedillo is generally considered to have little warmth and public personality.

Zedillo's main credentials are his free market orientation and ability to deal with foreign corporate interests, and he immediately said that he would continue the policies of Salinas and Colosio. Outside fairly narrow areas of the bureaucracy, Zedillo is known primarily for his run-ins with those on both the left and the right: as Secretary of Education, he tried to adopt new history textbooks that criticized the military for the 1968 massacre at Tlatelolco, while at the same time offending the left by dumping Marxist rhetoric and portraying the private sector in a somewhat more favorable light. Historians were offended by the number of basic factual errors that found their way into the books. The texts were withdrawn, and analysts hope that this exposure to the realities of policy will have made an impression on the candidate.

Because of his low recognition factor, his inexperience in public presentation, and the short time before the election—exacerbated by tight security

that limits his ability to circulate and meet the public—many fear that Zedillo will be particularly dependent on the PRI machine to work its magic for him. He quickly began trying to mend fences with traditional party and labor leaders, packing his campaign with inside operators. Although still the front-runner at this writing, Zedillo personifies the tensions within the Mexican body politic.

Although the PRI was stumbling in the polls in mid-April 1994, and despite dire predictions that this could be the election that the PRI could actually lose, resulting in economic chaos, several factors argue against degeneration into such anarchy. In the first place, there appears to be no opposition candidate with the strength to seriously challenge the party nominee. In the second place, it would be exceedingly difficult for even a left-leaning, nationalistic president such as Cárdenas to reverse Mexico's current trajectory toward economic reform, especially over the near term. And finally, the incompatibility of economic reform without political reform and vice versa is likely to ensure that change will continue, although it is just as likely that it will occur in fits and starts.

Prospects for August and Beyond Mexico's first-ever presidential debate was held on May 12, 1994. The initial results showed Zedillo to have lost ground, dropping marginally from a 45 percent to a 38 percent approval rating. The clear winner was Diego Fernández de Cevallos, the aggressive PAN candidate, who at least temporarily doubled his approval rating to around 30 percent. Cárdenas was the clear loser, falling to third with a loss from 15 percent to only 11 percent. However, most observers see little lasting benefit to Fernandez, who hasn't differentiated himself from the PRI on substance, yet lacks the backing of the PRI organization. Only one more debate was scheduled before the election, and this second and final debate was to include minority candidates, leaving reduced opportunities for a standout performance.

As of late May 1994, it still appeared that, barring further unforeseen disruptions, the PRI would win in a fairer—if hardly pristine—election, if for no other reason than the opposition is as yet unable to provide a coherent alternate. Cárdenas seems to have been neutralized as a viable alternative, although his place in history is assured as the force that pried open the modern Mexican political system. The PAN—under Fernandez de Cevallos—seems to be on the rise, although it is heavily committed to a position somewhat to the right of that generally considered acceptable to most Mexicans. It is still too soon to expect the PAN to assume a dominant position.

Many observers worry that a premature victory by an unready outside party could do more damage to the Mexican political system than a temporary return to a less open system dominated by PRI insiders. However, many of these same observers worry that despite the objective lack of the necessary heft on the part of the opposition, popular disillusionment will lead to unrest if and when the PRI wins.

Some observers have expressed concern that the general weakness of the PRI—as symbolized by the haphazard and weak Zedillo candidacy—could cause a resurgence of the hard-liners ("the dinosaurs," as they are known). This scenario holds that the supporters of old-style politics will use manipulation to steal the election and then force a reversal of reforms on a candidate beholden to them. Although there is some danger of this happening, barring some additional blow to the system, it will remain relatively small.

The Mexican system has already absorbed more than its share of such blows. A weakening economy, the Chiapas uprising, high-profile kidnappings, and the assassination of the front-runner have all contributed to a seemingly non-random, ostensibly insupportable pattern of disasters. However, while most observers expect the Mexican system to buckle, few expect it to break, even under this load. Mexico also has an advantage over some other modernizing nations. Unlike China, where the ruling party is attempting to deny any linkage between economic and social and political change, Mexico is not officially opposed to such social and political change. The remaining elements determined to suppress all such change are in the minority and are fighting a losing battle that can delay, but not reverse, change. And Mexico is unlike Russia, where there is no extant business infrastructure from which to launch economic reform, no matter how extensive the instituted social and political reforms may be; Mexico has a narrow, but fully functioning business community, one that has received a significant boost from NAFTA. From most perspectives, Mexico's political outlook is cautiously optimistic.

SOCIAL REFORM

Poverty and the Failed Social Revolution Economically, Mexico is one of the most polarized societies in the world. As its government and business community work to prepare it for the 21st century, much of the country outside the larger cities is still struggling to enter the 20th century. There are also substantial portions of Mexico that are still effectively mired in the colonial era. Although the country's overall wealth is increasing at a rapid pace, distribution of the wealth being created is extremely unequal and growing more so. Trickle-down economics has not worked in Mexico.

About 28 percent of Mexicans—about 25 million—are classified as poor, and an additional 16 percent—a minimum of 14 million people—are classified as extremely poor. Some private sector economists estimate actual unemployment at 25 to 30 percent (although most put it in the 15 to 20 percent range), and even most officials acknowledge that the minimum wage—the actual level of earnings realized by nearly half of those employed—is adequate to satisfy only about one-third of real needs. Although the situation has improved somewhat along with the general economy, the increasing divergence of incomes and the failure of wages to keep up with inflation in terms of real purchasing power means that substantial portions of the population remain in a desperate situation.

Mexico's real economic growth has seldom exceeded population growth. Although the rate of population growth has slowed, the demographic bulge—more than half of the population is under 20 years of age—and the vast amount of catching up needed to provide those already in or on the verge of entering the workforce with adequate employment opportunities means that rapid and even significant improvement will be difficult under the best of conditions. And although the delivery of public health and medical services to the majority of Mexicans remains poor, improvements in health care have placed additional pressures on this demographic situation by lowering mortality rates. Life expectancy rose from 58 years in 1960 to 70 years in 1990, and infant mortality was cut in half between 1970 and 1991.

Although the Salinas administration has increased mandatory schooling from six to nine years, a sizable number of children throughout the country are unable to avail themselves of more than a token education. People in many areas report that facilities are substandard, as are teacher pay and training. Even in areas where educational opportunities are available, many parents are forced to pull their children out of school in order to have them work illegally to help support the family.

The situation is perhaps most critical among traditional Indian populations in Mexico. About 10 percent of the population identifies itself as Indian, and observers argue that nearly 30 percent are primarily culturally and genetically Indian. Mexico is a country in which the Indian past is praised, but the Indian present is considered somewhat of an embarrassment. Mexico's Indians occupy the lowest rung of the socioeconomic ladder, usually inhabiting its most marginal lands.

The Zapatistas Attack The inequities of the system and the desperation of many of the people within it were demonstrated graphically when the self-styled Zapatista National Liberation Army (*Ejército Zapatista de la Liberación Nacional*, or EZNL, named after the early 20th century revolutionary peasant hero Emiliano Zapata), seized several towns in the southernmost state of Chiapas on January 1, 1994. The Zapatistas—a makeshift, poorly armed force—took the army and the authorities by surprise. They attacked the army garrison at San Cristóbal de las Casas and held several towns in the area for limited periods, even threatening to march on Mexico City. However, when their military efforts bogged down within two weeks of the start of hostilities, they readily agreed to a cease-fire.

Officials listed 145 deaths during the initial period of the revolt, although church spokespeople argue that casualties were closer to 400. Although the Zapatistas appeared to be reasonably well-trained, organized, and controlled, they were not a militarily impressive force. Nevertheless, the Chiapas incident constitutes the most serious outbreak of armed revolt in Mexico in at least 50 years, and the Mexican army began a rapid buildup in the area, blockading the guerrilla-controlled zone.

Responding to the Threat The decision of the government to negotiate surprised many observers. The rebels called for the resignation of the "dictator" Salinas, vilifying and threatening the president personally. Nevertheless, Salinas chose to deal nonviolently with the group, showing a flexibility and statesmanship that is unwonted in Mexican precedents (or presidents). In doing so, Salinas took a calculated risk that may yet backfire. His quick offer to negotiate rather than suppress enabled the government to regain the initiative, but it enraged hard-liners within the PRI and made the military restive. Although generally supported at home and abroad, Salinas' actions seem weak to a substantial portion of his home audience; there are others who wonder whether, as a lame duck, he will be able to retain enough authority to pursue prolonged negotiations or deliver on promises made.

The army has remained remarkably subdued, pulling back and resisting the urge to scorch the earth and root out the rebels. Mexico's military, which as recently as the 1920s regularly intervened—often violently—in political affairs, has been largely co-opted by the government. Given Mexico's past history of coups, there always remains the possibility of a barracks-led takeover. However, the army has quietly remained under the direction of civilian policymakers.

After arranging the cease-fire, Salinas appointed Manuel Camacho Solís (who had recently broken ranks over Salinas' failure to name him as the PRI candidate for president) as his chief negotiator. Camacho was also out of favor with the party's old guard, who saw him as a too-liberal reformer. As if to make things even less palatable to the hard-liners, the negotiations proceeded with the mediation of

Catholic Bishop Samuel Ruiz (a proponent of liberation theology who has been calling for popular reforms in Chiapas since the 1970s).

The Zapatistas submitted a list of 34 demands, most of which had to do with improved local economic conditions, but which also included the demand that Salinas step down, that electoral procedures be radically overhauled, and that NAFTA be canceled. By mid-February, Camacho had worked out agreements on all but these last three items. Most elements of the agreement had to do with assuring that government agencies would be more responsive to local needs—government bureaucracies are seen most often as responding to local party rather than popular needs. The talks recessed while the Zapatistas reportedly polled the local people on the tentative agreement.

Intervening events have made the situation more precarious. The assassination of candidate Colosio at the end of March made the hard-liners scream louder for blood. And since the January rebellion, other peasants in Chiapas have taken the opportunity to squat on an estimated 40,000 hectares (about 100,000 acres), leading the reactionary local landowners to threaten to revive the *guardias blancas*—death squads—that operated to keep peasants in line as recently as the early 1980s. Observers worry that a cease-fire violation or another unrelated incident elsewhere in the country could set off a conflagration that could be difficult to stop.

The Intransigent Underlying Situation Several elements suggest how hard it will be to substantively alter the conditions that led to the impasse. The largely conservative landowners have operated as traditional *caciques* since the colonial period. Many Indian peasants were effectively tied to the landed estates, living as serfs, until freed by the landowners in the 1940s—only 50 years ago. Many landowners subsequently expelled their former retainers and deforested the area to make way for cattle raising operations. These landowners retained a monopolistic stranglehold on local power, working out a tacit arrangement with the national authorities by which they delivered votes to the PRI, kept things under control, and in turn received the funds allocated for the area and were largely left alone by the authorities.

The conflict between the traditional landowning elite and the predominately Mayan peasants heated up in the early 1980s, when the Indians ran out of land and tried to claim hacienda lands. Death squads—purportedly sponsored by the landowners—sprang up to enforce the status quo, but the real blow was economic and largely unrelated to this attempted takeover. Chiapas grows one-third of Mexico's coffee, and when the producer cartel—the International Coffee Organization—decided to let the world price of coffee float in 1989, prices plummeted, wiping out many small peasant growers. Finally, in an attempt to modernize Mexico's archaic landholding and agricultural regime, the Salinas government repealed Article 27 of the constitution in 1991. This provision had allowed peasant communities to petition the government for land, and although it had never worked very well in practice, the article served as a safety valve for the downtrodden. Its loss was the final blow for many of the Chiapas peasants, who then began to support the idea of armed insurrection.

Some of these conditions are unique to Chiapas—or are found there in a much aggravated form—but most can be duplicated elsewhere in Mexico. Part of the problem lies with the difference between the ruling party's revolutionary rhetoric and its traditionally reactionary deeds. The PRI built a sociopolitical system that functioned remarkably well, at least on the surface, for 50 years. However, the system became inflexible and increasingly less able to deal with changing conditions. In particular, it fell out of step with the needs of an open economy and developing international standards.

Salinas has worked to change the system both symbolically and pragmatically. He brought into his government not only technocrats, but also a broader spectrum of outsiders, including liberals who had previously been excluded from the inner circle. His appointees have worked to rein in the repressive and corrupt Attorney General's Office and Secretariat of the Interior. And although many see the Solidarity program as a PRI pork barrel and vote-buying operation, it has been designed to deliver funding directly to those at the bottom, who need it most. Salinas has given prominence to reformers within the PRI and has faced down the most conservative elements in the party, in labor, and in the military.

Although Salinas' stature has grown far more than virtually any observer predicted when he became the candidate six years ago, his performance has still been less than dazzling personally. And policies designed to reorganize and open the Mexican economy have undoubtedly hurt many Mexicans badly. They have also allowed the effective concentration of wealth in the hands of perhaps 20 families in Mexico, mimicking the situation that prevailed at the beginning of the Revolution of 1910. Thus, the Zapatista's call for Salinas' resignation struck a chord throughout the country, and gave voice to a largely unarticulated, but very real, concern.

The View from the Bottom Although the Zapatistas called for national level reforms, the rank-and-file rebels have seemed to echo the sentiments of the man on the street elsewhere in Mexico: they are interested in nuts-and-bolts economic issues, not broader political issues. In truth, the average Zapatista wants more and better access to land in small quantities, better farm equipment and financing, and better access to basic education. Most deny any familiarity with or interest in who is or isn't the candidate or in international economic relations. These larger issues seem to have been added by the more politically conditioned leadership to gain broader recognition. And while it is likely that the Zapatistas—and many Mexicans—might fight for land, tractors, and schools, it is less certain that they will fight to the death for electoral reform.

In the mid-1980s, the US intelligence community reportedly studied the Mexican situation, and—citing rampant corruption, economic disruption, a lack of central control, and popular unrest—predicted the likelihood of a political collapse of major proportions. Other analysts with greater local experience downgraded the dire risk assessment to no more than a 20 percent probability. The final report further noted that the real probability of a major blowup in Mexico was actually substantially lower.

Mexicans by and large are not ideologues. They are extremely pragmatic, capitalists at heart despite the revolutionary rhetoric and their communalistic background. Mexican cultural expectations are also much lower than are often found elsewhere, and much more divergent. Historically, popular revolutions usually occur not when conditions are at their worst, but after they have begun to improve, however marginally. Nevertheless, Mexico's cultural context involving centuries of direction from the top alongside a pragmatism conditioned by limited options among the masses seems to suggest that while it certainly won't have an easy time of it, Mexico will continue to pursue the path toward internationalization and modern economic development.

The Prospects As of the end of May 1994, the Zapatistas were reportedly voting on the terms of the agreement negotiated back in February. Talks have been at a standstill since then. Following the Colosio assassination, negotiators and intermediaries warned the rebels that they could not expect further concessions from the government, which was already under pressure for allegedly coddling the insurgents. It is also questionable whether the bulk of the populace—most of whom have bought into the system—would support radical reform that would benefit the least progressive elements of the economy at the cost of additional setbacks to those who are committed to new ways and who are just now beginning to see some of the benefits. Populism continues to play well in Mexico, but pragmatism is expected to win out.

Although few observers suggest that there will be a reversal of the current direction over the long term, many warn that Mexican politicians can be expected to retrench, funneling Mexico's budget surplus and international reserve positions into social programs in an attempt to buy peace. This could upset international investors and reduce Mexico's already anemic growth over the near term, especially if it is accompanied by anti-foreign rhetoric and pull-backs from announced liberalized positions. However, unless additional unforeseen disruptions occur, it is unlikely that Mexico would—or even could—reverse its chosen direction, especially not over the near term. Still, Mexico's social problems are and will remain massive, retarding progress and requiring major, long-term commitments of funds and attention before the country can begin to think about assuming First World status.

Opportunities

OPPORTUNITIES FOR IMPORTING FROM MEXICO

Steady diversification has been the rule for Mexico's exports since the early 1980s when the country's oil-dependent economy was devastated by the drastic price drops that affected petroleum markets worldwide. Spurred in particular by the *maquila* industry, exports of assembled items have grown most rapidly, with the greatest export increases in automotive parts and electronic equipment. Agricultural products—particularly shrimp, fruits, vegetables, and cut flowers—also have played a significant role in the diversification process.

Mexico's ability to diversify its exports reveals the nation's competitive strength and spirit. The following section describes both exports and reexports as areas of opportunity for importing from Mexico.

AGRICULTURAL PRODUCTS

Opportunities in agricultural products are heavily dependent on worldwide weather, insect or similar invasions, and political conditions, which can cause immediate and unforeseen shortages, excesses, and resultant price fluctuations. This market also fluctuates with consumer trends—health fads, cultural tastes, and fast-paced lifestyles. To remain competitive in world markets, many Mexican producers of agricultural products are seeking joint arrangements with foreign firms aimed at cutting costs, promoting production efficiency, improving technology, and expanding distribution channels.

Some Hot Items:

- beer
- broccoli
- cattle
- cauliflower
- cereals
- chicken soup flavoring
- coffee
- confectionery products
- cookies and crackers
- flowers
- fruits
- honey
- margarita mixes
- molasses
- orange juice
- poultry
- seafood—frozen shrimp
- spices, herbs, seasoning blends
- sugar
- tequila
- tobacco
- tomatoes
- traditional foods—*mole poblano* and *pipian* preparations
- vegetables (fresh)

ARTS AND HANDICRAFTS

Traditional and contemporary arts and handicrafts—*artesanias*—flourish throughout Mexico. Often flavored with humor and brilliant with color, Mexican arts and handicrafts are popular worldwide. The emphasis on the marketing of these items has largely been internal—primarily on a retail level, to the tourist trade. Although they have been seen largely as novelty items, there is a growing market for them as decorative folk art. Most arts and handi-crafts are made by small, family-owned operations, and supplies are often available in relatively small quantities that change frequently at the whim of the artists. Central and southern Mexico are especially famous for a large variety of handicrafts.

Some Hot Items:
- Aztec calendars (carved wood or stone)
- baskets
- ceramics
- glass (hand-blown)
- hammocks
- hats (cowboy, Panama, *sombrero*)
- *huichol* yarn paintings
- jewelry (silver, semiprecious stone mounted)
- lacquerware
- leather goods (handbags, sandals, saddles)
- *majolica* dishware
- masks (carved wood, painted, unpainted, decorated)
- mats (henequen)
- metalwork (iron, tin, brass, copper)
- musical instruments
- woolen and cotton weavings and embroidered items (rugs, serapes, blankets)

COMPUTER, ELECTRICAL, AND ELECTRONIC PRODUCTS

Mexican manufacturers are expending immense efforts to modernize computer, electrical, and elec-tronics production and to develop an array of value-added items. Several international firms in Mexico are producing vast quantities of computers and com-puter parts for export. Computers are shipped from Mexico to more than 50 countries, and computer manufacturing firms are among Mexico's top export-ers. These firms have also branched into computer-related areas and now offer software and consulting services for other manufacturers. Consumer elec-tronic products are manufactured in Mexico for re-export by foreign-invested companies—mainly *maquilas*. Foreign investors are being invited to join with established Mexican companies to provide new technology and set up specialized production lines. High-tech overseas firms are beginning snap up the incentives being offered, resulting in the availability for export from Mexico of a wider variety of higher quality electrical and electronic products.

Some Hot Items:
- actuators for hard disks
- air conditioning units
- audio equipment
- computer products
- diskettes
- electrical switching apparatuses
- keyboards
- network boards
- operative software
- office machines and parts
- personal computers
- television sets, components, chassis assemblies
- television tuners
- videocassette recorders (VCRs)

FURNITURE AND WOOD PRODUCTS

Mexican handmade furniture is a popular import item. In hotels, restaurants, and homes worldwide one can find *equipal* chairs and tables, wrought iron items, and carved stone and wood furnishings made in Mexico. Most handcrafted furniture is made in small family shops, and therefore quality, quantity, availability, cost, and styles are determined at the whim of the artisans. A careful importer can find unique and valuable opportunities in this area. In several of Mexico's northern states, manufactured wood products—doors, plywood, and paper prod-ucts—are produced in large quantities for export.

Some Hot Items:
- cantara stone furniture
- cardboard and packaging papers
- distressed wood furniture
- doors
- infant furniture
- iron tables, lamps, chairs, clothesracks, and candelabras
- marble tables and benches
- wooden carved furniture

HOUSEHOLD PRODUCTS

Most household products available for import from Mexico are assembled items that are reexported by *maquilas*. The exceptions are ceramic tile and table, kitchen, and bath products. The Mexican state of Chi-huahua is the site of the largest manufacturer of ce-ramic tile in North America, and this company pro-duces substantial amounts of tile and plumbing fix-tures for export. The largest Mexican producers of household products have formed joint ventures with (or have bought out) US companies to improve tech-nology and gain international marketing channels.

Some Hot Items:
- baby bottles
- baby carriages
- blenders
- ceramic tile
- electric fans
- glassware
- irons

- ovenware
- plumbing fixtures
- tableware—china, silverware, decorative items

RAW AND INDUSTRIAL MATERIALS

The Mexican industries that mine and extract raw materials are among the nation's leading exporters. The number one export is oil, but chemicals, rubber, plastics, cement, and silver all hover near the top of the list. The world's fourth largest cement producer, Mexico is shipping its products to markets in Europe, the US, Central and South America, and Asia. And Mexico is a top world producer of silver, strontium, and sodium sulfate. It is also home to the world's third largest salt mine. The 1993 Foreign Investment Act has opened many mining activities to foreign companies, and this sector promises lucrative opportunities—with an estimated three-quarters of its stones yet unturned. Of particular interest to foreign investors, a number of Mexican firms are seeking joint ventures in order to modify their operations to take advantage of modern, efficient methods for exploring and extracting Mexico's immense raw material resources.

Some Hot Items:

- aluminum
- cement
- copper
- crude oil
- gold
- iron bars
- lumber and plywood
- marble
- petrochemicals
- polystyrene polyethylene terephthalate
- polyvinyl chloride (PVC)
- salt
- silver bars
- sodium sulfate
- steel
- strontium

TEXTILES AND APPAREL

Textile and apparel exports from Mexico have more than tripled since 1985, and exports of these products are expected to rise further, to more than US$2.5 billion by 1997. Tremendous opportunity exists in this sector for foreign investors who are willing to become joint venturers with Mexican textile and apparel firms. Mexican textile and apparel companies are discovering that they are in serious need of automated and modern machinery, production systems, and designers. Many are actively seeking foreign investment. With the continued availability of relatively low-cost Mexican labor, apparel manufacturing—a labor intensive enterprise—remains an inviting proposition.

Some Hot Items:

- blankets
- blouses (cotton and acrylic)
- dresses (cotton and acrylic)
- hats (palm)
- hosiery
- shoes
- sweaters (acrylic)
- towels
- vests (acrylic)

VEHICLES AND PARTS

Trade in vehicles and vehicle parts flows both ways across the Mexican border, but exports of completed vehicles have far surpassed imports during the past decade. Passenger cars are Mexico's second largest export, followed closely by vehicle parts and car engines. The primary exporters of vehicles are international companies: six of the world's largest automobile, bus, and truck manufacturers are operating plants in Mexico. Exporters of vehicle parts are mainly Mexican companies, many of which are associated with, or are seeking to associate with, international firms.

Some Hot Items:

- axles
- batteries
- bearing covers
- brakes
- car engines, fully assembled
- chassis
- diesel engine machined parts
- directional signals
- lights
- mirrors
- monoblocks
- motor heads
- motor mounts
- passenger cars
- seats
- springs
- stamped body parts
- tires
- transmissions, transmission blocks
- truck cabins
- wiring

OPPORTUNITIES FOR EXPORTING TO MEXICO

With a population of more than 90.4 million, Mexico holds vast potential for exporters. Imports have a strong, growing share in many domestic market sectors, and a large number of foreign, brand names are already well established. Between 1983 and 1993, exports to Mexico grew sixfold. Mexico's government continues to eliminate trade barriers, creating more openings for foreign firms to introduce their products and services to public and private industrial, business, and individual consumers. Progressive government policies are promoting the modernization, automation, and computerization of Mexico's financial, commercial, industrial, and transportation infrastructures. The purchasing power of Mexican consumers is on the rise, and they often show a marked preference for imported goods.

AGRICULTURAL AND FORESTRY PRODUCTS

Although agricultural products are among its top exports, Mexico does not always meet its own demands for some products. Substantial opportunities exist for exporting agricultural products to Mexico, particularly items that are difficult to grow in Mexico or that have a tremendous domestic demand. Mexico's tourist hotels and restaurants are major end users of imported foods, catering to the tastes and fads of international travelers. Consumers are hot for prepackaged and fast foods; ice cream bars, frozen pizzas, frozen pancakes, and corn-dogs are a sampling of the items meeting with success. Exports of processed food to Mexico amounted to nearly US$314 million in 1992, and these exports are expected to increase by at least 10 percent annually over the next several years.

Some Hot Items:
- almonds
- animal feeds
- bottled water
- frozen processed foods
- maize (corn)
- meat—pork, beef
- lumber
- pulp, paper, and newsprint
- seafood, particularly lobster and scallops
- sesame seeds
- soybeans
- tobacco
- tomatoes
- wheat
- woods for furniture production

AIRCRAFT AND AIRCRAFT PARTS

Improvements in air transportation and air terminals are creating a growing demand for aircraft and parts, primarily in the commercial and tourist centers. Foreign investors can now own substantial interests in Mexican companies that administer and manage operations at the terminals of commercial airports. These include firms that provide airplane refueling, cargo handling, reservations and ticketing, vehicle rental, and food services. Air transport companies—primarily involved in commercial cargo and express package transport, air ambulance services, and air taxi routes—are also now open to foreign investment.

Some Hot Items:
- aircraft parts
- cargo handling equipment
- forklifts
- fuel handling equipment

COMPUTERS AND PERIPHERALS

Computers are in high demand in the Mexican market. This industry has been spurred by a modernization program instituted in the early 1990s by the Mexican government. An estimated 450,000 computers are purchased every year. In 1991, the Mexican market for computer peripherals alone grew 63 percent. Although growth slowed to 14 percent in 1992—primarily because of weak economic conditions and reduced government contracts—the computer peripherals industry is expected to grow at an annual average rate of 15 percent over the next several years. Prime end users include banks, Pemex, retail chain stores, brokerage houses, and the *Comisión Federal de Electricidad* (Mexican Electricity Commission, or CFE). The quest for software is taking on enormous proportions. Businesses are diversifying from basic word processing software, discovering the wonders of database and spreadsheet applications, networks, and computer-aided design systems. With each new program introduced, the market for upgrades and improvements also grows.

Some Hot Items:
- computer-aided design systems
- computer security consulting services
- continuity testers
- information systems (IS) software
- integrated circuit testers
- laptop computers
- massive storage devices
- modems
- monitors
- multimeters

- network management software
- parts—repair and upgrade
- personal computers
- printers (laser or matrix)
- routers
- servers
- support services
- telecommunication software
- test equipment

ELECTRIC AND ELECTRONIC PRODUCTS

Electrical power systems are rated the second best prospect for exports to Mexico in 1994, with a market in Mexico estimated at US$6.2 million. Mexican industries—principally *maquilas*—also import substantial quantities of high-tech electronic components for assembly into computers, telecommunications equipment, consumer products, and office machines. Electronic equipment is in great demand in the Mexican business community. Established Mexican and foreign companies are in an expansion mode, and a multitude of new firms are taking root. The increasing demand for electrical and electronic products is, in turn, creating a demand for installation, parts, upgrades, replacement parts, and repair service.

Some Hot Items:

- capacitors
- copy machines
- electrical installation parts
- electrical power systems
- electronic calculators, cash registers, and components
- electronic typewriters and word processors
- integrated circuits and memory circuits
- logic devices
- mimeograph machines
- printed circuit boards
- relays
- security, safety, and fire alarm systems
- semiconductors
- time recorders
- x-ray detection devices

HOUSEWARES AND CONSUMER PRODUCTS

Imports of household appliances are on the rise, encouraged by improving economic conditions among many Mexican consumers. A parallel increase is being seen in imports of components for household appliances, needed not only for local manufacture, but also for repair and after-sales service. Increasing affluence has created an expanding demand for household chemicals and cleaners. Leisure prod-

ucts are also becoming hot items among Mexico's growing middle class.

Some Hot Items:

- cleansers and cleaning chemicals
- clothes washing machines and dryers
- compact discs and players
- freezers
- plastic and rubber kitchenware
- records and stereo components
- refrigerators
- small appliances
- videotapes

HEALTH AND COSMETIC PRODUCTS

As economic conditions improve, Mexican consumers are purchasing more cosmetic products, most of which are imports. They are also seeking improved and increased medical services. More than 1,500 hospitals operate in Mexico, employing some 32,000 doctors. Mexican law mandates that employees be enrolled with the *Instituto Mexicano del Seguro Social* (IMSS)—the state health care provider. Nearly 40 million people are registered with the IMSS, and enrollment increases at an average rate of 5 percent annually. In past few years, the IMSS health services have been decentralized, and construction and modernization of health facilities has been a government priority. The growing demand for high-tech medical equipment is being met by imports.

Some Hot Items:

- blood donor kits
- capillary products
- cystoscopes
- dental acrylic resins and cement
- dental equipment, instruments, and apparatus
- electro-diagnostic apparatus
- makeup products
- medical instruments and apparatuses
- medical monitoring systems
- opthalmoscopes
- perfumes
- respiratory and respiratory analysis equipment
- skincare creams and other products
- x-ray equipment—dental and medical

GASOLINE STATION EQUIPMENT AND PRODUCTS

Plans are underway to modernize the more than 3,200 gasoline stations now located throughout Mexico and to erect another 3,000 or so. Retail outlets are franchised by Pemex, the national oil monopoly, but station operators are directly responsible for equipment purchases. Domestic suppliers of this equipment are for the most part nonexistent, and therefore nearly all of it must be imported. Each station in Mexico supplies on average three times the number of vehicles as US stations, or two times the number of vehicles as European stations. However, many stations are operating with outmoded and inefficient equipment; they require upgrades for environmental, safety, and improved service reasons.

Some Hot Items:

- computerized control systems
- electrical current shut-off systems
- electronic counters
- electronic systems (sealed for fire danger areas)
- fire extinguishing equipment
- fuel storage tanks (double-wall steel or fiberglass)
- gas recovery systems
- grounding systems
- hoses
- oil products
- pump dispensers
- shut-off valves
- station signs—illuminated or other
- uniforms for employees
- venting pipes

INDUSTRIAL MACHINERY

The growth in manufacturing in Mexico is creating a demand for high-tech mechanized systems. Established facilities are modernizing, automating, and expanding production capacity. Projects in the steel fabrication and automotive sectors are increasing the demand for machine tools and metalworking machinery. Government programs have been established to encourage textile design and manufacturing centers, which will require substantial investments in automated textile machinery. The plastics processing industry has also shown dynamic growth in recent years. Manufacturers in Mexico are investing in automation to remain afloat despite the avalanche of competing imported plastic products that have hit the Mexican markets since deregulation. The growth of industry has brought environmental concerns to the fore, and the Mexican government is demanding that private firms comply with strict anti-pollution regulations. Federal, state, and municipal governments have spent substantial funds in this sector.

Some Hot Items:

- agricultural machinery and equipment
- automatic auto emission control analyzers
- backhoes
- beam, warp, warp tying, drawing in, and slashing machinery
- bleaching, dyeing, and finishing equipment
- blow molding machines
- catalytic converters
- centrifugal dryers
- chain saws
- chemical production machinery
- circular saws
- computer numerically controlled machine tools
- concrete and asphalt mixers and pavers
- construction equipment
- cranes
- cultivators
- dairy equipment
- dies
- dishwashers and parts
- dust control equipment and components
- electronic photocomposition equipment
- environmental control equipment
- evaporative coolers
- exploration equipment
- extrusion machines
- farm implements and hand tools
- fertilizing equipment
- filtration units
- flexographic presses
- food processing and packaging equipment
- forestry and woodworking machinery
- grinding machines, parts, and accessories
- harvesters
- heliographic presses
- hoists
- hydraulic excavators
- incinerator plants
- injection molding machines
- inorganic waste treatment plants
- knitting machines
- lathes
- looms and spindles
- meat and fish processing equipment
- metal presses
- metalworking equipment, particularly for automotive manufacturing
- milling machines
- mining equipment
- mining machinery
- numerically controlled machine tools
- offset printing presses
- organic waste treatment plants
- packing, packaging, and bottling machinery
- parts for machinery
- planers, joiners, shapers, lathes
- planing and surfacing machines
- plastics production machinery
- pollution control equipment
- printing and graphic arts equipment
- process controls for food processing
- processing machine parts and attachments
- quality control equipment
- refrigerators and parts

- restaurant china and cutlery
- road graders
- saws
- scales and parts
- serigraphic equipment
- single-color rotating printing presses
- skein, bobbin, quill, and cone machinery
- textile machinery
- timbering and sawmill equipment
- tractors
- vacuum distillation units
- water coolers
- water purifiers
- web paper winding machines
- winding machines
- yogurt machines

INDUSTRIAL MATERIALS

Large quantities of industrial materials are imported to support production at *maquila* and other manufacturing facilities throughout Mexico. Annual consumption of raw materials alone averages more than US$10 billion. Materials in demand include a variety of chemicals, plastics and resins, and building and construction products. Demand for secondary petrochemicals is growing rapidly, particularly with the opening of this industry to foreign investors.

Some Hot Items:

- acrylic
- alkyd resins
- amides
- amino acids and peptides
- anti-smoke agents
- anti-static agents
- aromatic acids and salts
- bricks and bricklaying tools
- builders' hoists
- building and construction materials
- cement
- chemicals
- coal
- coupling agents—titanatos, silanos, zirconatos
- epoxic
- epoxy resins
- fluorine-containing compounds
- fluropolymers
- fuels
- gasoline
- heat and flame retardants
- high-density polyethylene
- impact and flow modifiers
- inorganic chemicals for food processing
- iron—scrap, pig, bars, and plates
- ladders
- low-density polyethylene
- masonry bonds

- melamine
- nylon
- organic chemicals for basic foods
- perfuming and flavoring agents
- pigments
- plastics and resins
- polyacetal resins
- polyamide
- polycarbonate teflon
- polyesters
- polypropylene
- polyurethane
- preservatives
- propane
- steel plates
- synthetic rubber
- thioamides
- ultraviolet light stabilizers
- urea resins

TOYS, GAMES, AND SPORTING GOODS

The popularity of sports and fitness programs is on the rise in Mexico. Resorts, gyms, exercise, and recreational centers are opening in many areas; the weekend getaway is becoming a national pastime. Sailing, golf, scuba diving, fishing, and tennis are a few of the favorite activities. Mexico's domestic toy industry has suffered greatly from deregulation and a flood of imports. In 1991 the Mexican toy market—heavily supplied by imports—was estimated at US$611.3 million, and it was expected to grow to US$703 million by 1994.

Some Hot Items:

- battery-operated toys
- boats
- dolls, doll clothing, doll accessories
- fishing tackle
- golf clubs, bags, balls, and other supplies
- hobby kits
- mechanical toys
- motorcycles
- motors
- plastic toys
- plush toys
- remote-control toys
- scale models
- sporting shotguns
- video and computer games

TELECOMMUNICATION EQUIPMENT

Mexico's telecommunications sector is one of the country's most promising areas of opportunity. Improvements are rapidly being made to Mexico's general telephone and communication systems. Private companies are now allowed to invest in this sector, and concessions have been granted to companies offering advanced services, including satellite pagers, trucking radio services, and radiotelephones. Cellular phone service is available in the largest business centers, including Mexico City, Monterrey, Guadalajara, and the larger Mexican-US border towns. Spurred by opportunities under NAFTA, US-based long-distance companies that already operate in North America have plans to connect their systems and provide identical services—including voice, data, and video communications—to customers throughout North and Central America.

Some Hot Items:
- local area network (LAN) systems
- microwave transmitters and receivers
- multiplexors
- radio receivers and transmitters
- radiophonic sets
- telegraphic sets
- television receivers and transmitters
- satellite communications equipment
- wide area network (WAN) systems

TEXTILES AND APPAREL

Apparel and accessories from overseas are popular among Mexico's middle and upper economic classes. Consumer appreciation for innovative designs and high quality fabrics is apparent from the large quantity of imports from foreign suppliers. A significant influx of imported textiles have been welcomed into Mexico's markets, reflecting the near elimination of trade barriers in this industry and demand by local manufacturers for more modern materials to compete with the imports.

Some Hot Items:
- belts, scarves, and other accessories
- children's apparel
- drapery cotton and synthetic fabrics
- industrial fabrics
- lingerie
- lycra fabrics
- men's shirts, suits, and slacks
- purses and wallets
- sweaters
- upholstery cotton and synthetic fabrics
- women's dresses
- women's skirts, slacks, and blouses

VEHICLES AND VEHICLE PARTS

Foreign vehicle manufacturers control nearly 90 percent of Mexico's total automotive production, creating a significant market in Mexico for automotive parts. Six of the world's largest automobile, bus, and truck manufacturers—Chrysler, General Motors, Ford, Volkswagen, Nissan, and Dina—operate about 20 plants in Mexico. Most assembled vehicles are exported from Mexico, but a growing number of passenger cars—both assembled in Mexico and elsewhere—are being sold in domestic markets. By 1996, car and truck exports to Mexico are expected to top 50,000 units from Canadian and US producers alone. On the average, the more than 5.5 million vehicles being driven in Mexico are 10 years old, and these aging vehicles are driven over roads that are often in poor condition. Mechanics and automotive parts are sorely needed by those who cannot afford to replace their cars. Imports of automotive parts into Mexico have topped US$5.4 billion annually.

A significant opportunity lies on the horizon for firms to provide modern public buses that run on propane or electricity: modernization is being considered for city bus fleets, the interstate bus system, and the interstate trucking fleet. Nationwide, an estimated 60,000 public transit buses need replacement, offering an opportunity for between US$5 billion and US$10 billion in sales, depending on whether new or remanufactured vehicles are purchased; domestic production has typically supplied only about 25 percent of this market. Of the multimillion dollar market for trucking cargo rigs, foreign-made vehicles are likely to account for about 50 percent. Opportunities also exist for companies that can provide dependable, centralized maintenance and repair services for public transportation systems.

Some Hot Items:
- air conditioning hose assemblies
- analyzers and test equipment for motors
- automotive and truck chassis
- automotive servicing equipment
- axles and bearings
- batteries
- brakes
- buses
- clutches
- defoggers and defroster systems
- parts
- pistons and piston rings
- propane fuel conversion kits
- pumps—water or oil
- radiators
- repair equipment
- shafts
- spark plugs
- springs, suspensions, and shocks
- starters
- transmissions
- trucks—cargo rigs, tanker rigs, liquefied gas rigs
- wheels
- wheel alignment equipment
- vehicles and passenger cars

OPPORTUNITIES FOR GROWTH

MANUFACTURING

Mexico is among the world's major low-cost manufacturing nations, and opportunities in its manufacturing sector continue to grow under government policies to encourage foreign trade: tariff cuts, enhanced industrial and intellectual property protections, reforms in import licensing, and elimination of foreign investment barriers. Low-cost labor remains a significant incentive to businesses that are considering locating labor-intensive operations in Mexico. Mexican firms are actively seeking foreign investors to share new technologies and assist in modernizing production facilities. The elimination and reduction of tariffs under NAFTA has added to the growth potential of Canadian and US companies manufacturing in Mexico: now they are expanding heavily into domestic markets in addition to reexporting products.

MINING

Mexico has privatized and opened up its mining industry to increased domestic and foreign investment. Foreign companies are rushing to lay claims to the vast resources buried in Mexico's mountains. Investors are particularly being sought for gold, silver, and copper exploration and mining projects. Opportunities also exist to exploit immense untapped resources of sulfur, potassium, phosphorous, iron, and coal. In 1993 and 1994, the industry anticipates investment of US$1 billion for expansion and modernization of existing mining facilities.

FINANCIAL SERVICES

Mexico estimates that it has one bank for every 19,000 Mexican citizens. And during the past three decades, the only foreign bank operating in the country has been Citibank, which has a special waiver because it established its presence in Mexico before the government restricted foreign bank operations. The 1993 Foreign Investment Law, in combination with NAFTA, has opened up financial institutions in Mexico to substantial foreign participation, creating a tremendous growth opportunity in this sector. To protect Mexican banks from the sudden impact of the expected intense competition, restrictions on foreign investment will continue to be in effect during phase-in periods. Mexican banks are accelerating their efforts to modernize computer networks and to offer new types of deposits and services, including improved automated teller systems. They are reshaping loan portfolios to raise the volume of credits offered to private sector borrowers while decreasing financing available to the public sector. In par-

ticular, Mexican banks are targeting industry sectors and foreign trade, offering financing for land acquisition, construction, importation of equipment, and working capital. In 1993, Mexican banks posted historic gains, with profits rising 26.9 percent in real terms to reach NP9.1 billion (about US$2.9 billion). Foreign-invested institutions offering diverse services—credit, multiple banking, and investment banking—will find significant growth potential in the Mexican market. At least 20 to 30 foreign-owned banks are currently preparing plans for doing business in Mexico.

INSURANCE SERVICES

Mexico's 1993 Foreign Investment Law has opened up the nation's insurance business to international companies, allowing substantial foreign investment in bonding and insurance companies. Opportunities exist for companies to form joint ventures in individual and group insurance and pension and other such benefit plan provision. Several foreign firms have already struck deals to provide life insurance and underwriting services in combination with Mexican companies.

ARCHITECTURAL, CONSTRUCTION, AND ENGINEERING SERVICES

Government and private entities have major ongoing and future projects for construction of hospitals, schools, dams, transportation, electricity generation and electrical co-generation plants, and other infrastructure items. More than US$16 billion has been earmarked by public and private entities for transportation and communication infrastructure improvement projects in 1994. Mexico has a critical housing shortage, and with low-cost housing in high demand, companies that offer and construct prefabricated housing should enjoy enormous success in border zones and other areas of heavy population concentration. Many of these services are provided through joint ventures undertaken by multiple private companies, because several small firms can combine resources to undertake these large projects. Industrial plant design and construction is one area of demand, and major modernization projects are underway or proposed at many ports, border crossings, railroad facilities, and airports to sustain Mexico's gigantic leap into international business and trade. The construction industry and providers of raw materials to this industry are expected to lead economic growth in Mexico during the next several years.

EDUCATIONAL AND EMPLOYMENT TRAINING SERVICES

With modernization and automation of industries, Mexican workers are being asked to perform technical tasks and are being promoted into management and supervisory capacities for which they have not been trained. Trade associations and corporations throughout the nation are promoting programs to provide the necessary education and training. Several of the nation's development banks have also set up programs for businesses in sectors targeted for financial support, and these banks often seek alliances with international firms that provide management and technical training programs for these businesses. Foreign investment of up to 49 percent is allowed in private companies that provide educational services. Services that offer training in personal improvement, time management skills, worker retraining skills, technical courses, and other similar courses are expected to thrive. Technical training is needed at journeyman levels—such as for mechanics, plumbers, masons, industrial machine operators—at higher skill levels (particularly for computer operators)—and at professional levels—such as in bookkeeping, accounting, foreign languages, economics, and law.

ENVIRONMENTAL CONSULTING AND SERVICES

Companies that are now entering Mexico or seeking to expand already existing facilities are coming up against new environmental requirements and tougher regulators, which in turn creates an opportunity for consultants who specialize in advising companies on how to clean up their environmental acts. Mexico has stepped up enforcement of its tough environmental laws, closing and suspending operations at plants that do not meet government standards. Experts are needed to assist in evaluating environmental impacts, finding low-cost environmental solutions, and carrying out the solutions with permissible adaptations as needed. Major emphasis is being placed on automotive pollution controls, recycling, toxic waste disposal, and sanitary services. Some of the best opportunities for foreign environmental service firms are in joint ventures and similar arrangements with Mexican firms, who already have the contacts and cultural knowledge needed in an area that is replete with sensitive and complex public and political issues.

MEDIA

Marketing distribution channels in Mexico are still in the initial stages of development. Radio advertising reaches the largest population, mail services are undependable, newspapers are mistrusted, and—while it is growing—television is still beyond the means of most Mexicans. Cable networks are expanding, but continue to be concentrated in the largest urban centers. Whether the emergence of foreign-invested newspapers—49 percent foreign ownership is now allowed under the 1993 Foreign Investment Law—will change the readership patterns in Mexico remains to be seen. Advertising consultants who understand the limitations and the culture are important to any business that intends to succeed in the Mexican market. Services can expect to generate great demand if they can offer creative advertising ideas that reach the targeted audience and allow for follow-up to promote a high rate of retention.

AIR CARGO SERVICES

Mexico's sheer size, coupled with rising levels of both domestic and international business, has created a demand for fast and reliable air transport services. Much of the demand is being filled by the largest international air carrier firms, with more than a dozen large American and European carriers currently operating air cargo services in and out of Mexico. However, smaller firms are also finding opportunities by specializing in serving particular companies or countries. Mexico's own air carriers are expanding their domestic cargo services and are actively seeking import business, mainly from the US.

BUSINESS SERVICES

Business services—such as marketing, public relations, staff education, automation and computerization assistance, and quality control consulting—are in great demand in Mexico's largest commercial centers. The demand for these services promises to expand even more rapidly with the passage of NAFTA, the completion of industry privatization, and increasing efforts to promote foreign trade and international investment in general. Opportunities for growth exist particularly in data processing, market research, office support, and brand testing. Mexico's business community is in the midst of a technology revolution, creating high sales potential for retailers of state-of-the-art personal computers, facsimile equipment, copiers, and telephone systems, as well as for business service centers that would offer the use of such equipment.

LEGAL, ACCOUNTING, AND REAL ESTATE CONSULTANTS

Multinational firms that are entering the Mexican market are demanding expertise in the legal, accounting, and property aspects of their transactions. They need to know both the local and international requirements and considerations. As a result, real estate, law, and accounting professionals are discovering significant business opportunities in Mexico. Government restrictions have eased, allowing foreign professionals and their firms to establish consulting firms and form joint ventures and other arrangements with local firms, many of which—although they already participate successfully in local markets—are looking to upgrade their operations to international standards and attract an international clientele.

FRANCHISING

Opportunities for franchising are wide open in Mexico. Growth in franchising has been particularly strong since the removal of government restrictions, the streamlining of the registration process, and the increased protections now offered for industrial property rights. In the course of a decade, franchising activity has risen from zero to nearly 200 franchisers operating 760 franchises with more than 5,200 individual franchise outlets in 1993. Total annual sales by franchise operations have reached nearly US$2.2 billion. Franchises are attractive to operators because of the financial and training support offered by the parent company in all aspects of establishing the business, hiring and training personnel, and managing and operating the franchise. And the consumer market in Mexico is just what a franchiser would order: high demand and concentrated populations with growing incomes to support frequent consumption of mostly low-ticket franchise products. The international and domestic tourist industry is booming, and more than half of Mexico's population is under 20, more than 70 percent live in urban areas, and more than a one-third are able to afford products offered through franchises. Fast food restaurants and tourist service outlets are still among the fastest growing franchise sectors, but a variety of others are in hot demand—athletic shoes, gasoline stations, video rental stores, theaters, copy centers, real estate services, consulting and business services, and weight control and exercise centers.

RETAILING SERVICES

Giant retail chain stores and warehousing discount outlets are expanding into Mexico, carefully choosing strategic locations in a few areas to begin warming up the Mexican working class to the notion of one-stop shopping at warehouse-size outlets. So far, most stores have been located in and around Mexico City, the country's largest consumer market. Pricing strategies based on volume purchases allow the large retailers to offer substantial discounts, and current indicators project success for these ventures. A few specialized high-volume discount stores—toy stores, drugstores, office supply outlets—offering substantial price discounts are beginning to enter the market, and their appeal is growing rapidly among consumers. In several urban areas, Mexican consumers are also being introduced to the concept of shopping centers. US-style shopping centers are extremely popular among Mexico's growing middle class, offering upscale department stores, movie theaters, restaurants, professional offices, specialty shops, and franchise outlets, all in a single location. Companies that establish warehousing outlets and shopping centers are creating additional downstream opportunities: most are in need of computer equipment and services, bar code and scanner equipment, and distribution centers.

ENTERTAINMENT INDUSTRY

Mexico's entertainment market is ripe for the plucking. The implementation of tariff cuts and increased enforcement of intellectual property protections combined with rising affluence among consumers is creating a promising music scene that is capturing the interest of major international record companies. In 1992, Mexico was the source of 46 percent of the total music sales in Latin America, and it has become the world's 10th largest record market. Wholesale record sales have nearly doubled over the past four years, to nearly US$295 million. Concert venues are being developed, particularly in the Mexico City area. Several international movie theater chains are undertaking projects, concentrating on the urban areas and the new retail centers being built to target Mexico's middle class shoppers. The production of Spanish-language movies and television programs has been stepped up to meet growing demands for quality foreign-made product.

PUBLIC PROCUREMENT

OPPORTUNITIES

Purchases by Mexican government agencies and state-owned (parastatal) enterprises have accounted for more than 15 percent of Mexico's total imports in recent years. However, many government-owned industries have now been privatized and decentralized, offering significant opportunities to private sector firms, but at the same time eliminating substantial government procurement budgets. Decentralization has also exacerbated the multiplication of agencies and procedures which must be dealt with in order to sell to official Mexican entities. Government procurement opportunities continue to exist in several areas, including:

- airport facilities
- electricity generation plants
- marine ports
- medical and testing laboratories, educational facilities, and health care institutions
- petroleum facilities
- transportation systems
- water systems

Among the top prospects for foreign suppliers:

- airport facility construction equipment and materials for building terminals, parking facilities, runways, and fueling operations
- cargo handling equipment at airports
- cargo wharf construction equipment and materials
- cranes—gantry, container, multipurpose, and mobile—for marine ports
- cranes—jib, boom jib, rotating—for oil and gas fields
- cooling towers for oil and gas production
- dredging equipment
- electric public transit buses (trolleys)
- hazardous waste management equipment, including incinerators, solid and liquid storage facilities, drummed waste storage facilities, decontamination equipment, waste disposal cells, ash disposal cells, and power supplies
- generators—steam and turbo
- geological analytical equipment for oil, gas, and mineral exploration
- laboratory balances
- laboratory centrifuges
- laboratory filters and calorimeters
- laboratory shakers, stirrers, diluters, and dispensers
- laboratory sterilizers and autoclaves
- measuring equipment for power generation
- mechanized cargo handling systems, including conveyor belts, pipelines, forklifts, yard tractors, front-handlers, yard chassis, roll-on, roll-off (RoRo) equipment, and rail connections for marine ports
- natural gas vehicle conversion kits, compressor stations, mobile natural gas tube trailers, test equipment, distribution centers, and emission labs
- oil and gas boring and drilling rigs and machinery
- oil and gas extraction process controls
- oil and gas pipes for extraction
- oil and gas pumps
- railroad cars—doublestack container trains
- railroad construction equipment, switching systems, track, and supplies
- refractometers, spectrophotometers, and spectrometers
- road and bridge construction equipment and materials
- seamless steel tubes
- storage facilities at ports—refrigeration equipment, tanks, reefer plugs, warehouse construction materials
- supervision control equipment for power generating plants and networks
- tank trucks for ports
- trucks for garbage collection
- tug boats
- vaccines (for a nationwide immunization program)
- valves
- waste water treatment equipment—lake restoration equipment, waste water collection and treatment systems, potable water supply facilities, flood control and irrigation systems, elevated storage tanks, lift stations, pumps, meters, concrete pipe, sewer collection systems, and design and engineering services

PUBLIC PROCUREMENT PROCESS

Mexican government and parastatal entities buy through their purchasing offices from prequalified domestic and foreign suppliers. Most of the entities divide their procurement responsibilities among several offices, each of which follows a somewhat different procedure. Every entity also has a separate procurement committee responsible for formulating procedures for the entity's purchases. Most will furnish a manual of procurement procedures on request. A sampling of the varied requirements is included at the end of this section, organized by government agency. Other agencies that offer procurement contracts include: the *Comisión Federal de Electricidad* (Federal Electricity Commission, or CFE);

Secretaría de Desarrollo Social (Secretariat of Social Development, or SEDESOL); and *Secretaría de Comunicaciones y Transportes* (Secretariat of Communications and Transportation, or SCT). (Refer to the "Important Addresses" chapter for contact information for government agencies.)

Approval or Registration of Supplier

A company must be approved as a supplier before it is eligible for a procurement contract. Factors that are taken into account in the approval process are the financial solvency of the company, its technical capability, and its reputation. Application is made to the particular entity with responsibility for the area of procurement, and each entity has, or is developing, its own review and approval procedures. A few entities require advance registration, which will remain effective for all subsequent bids submitted. Others do not maintain a central registry, requiring bidders to submit information with each bid.

If an entity maintains a central registry, registration is usually accomplished by sending the entity a letter, on company stationery, requesting registration. In addition, the supplier must enclose the following original documents and certified copies:

- Power of attorney—this document must appoint one or more individuals as company representatives in Mexico and must authorize them to submit and receive legal documents, sign contracts on behalf of the company, and subject themselves to legal process and liability on behalf of the company. The power of attorney must be in Spanish and must be notarized by a Mexican consul in the applicant's home country.
- Copy of the contract—signed by the local company representative, translated into Spanish, and notarized by a Mexican consul in the applicant's home country.
- Information on the company's local representative, if that representative registers on behalf of the company—the information required includes a copy of the representative's contract with the company (in Spanish and notarized), federal tax registration, legal business formation documents, records of membership in the appropriate Mexican organization, and the representative's photograph (signed or stamped).

Local Presence

Under Mexican law, a contractor with any government or parastatal entity must establish some legal presence in Mexico so that it is subject to Mexican authority. Essentially, this requirement simply means that the contractor must designate someone—such as a sales agent or representative, joint venture partner, or subsidiary company—located in Mexico to submit and receive legal documents and sign contracts on the contractor's behalf. Something that is difficult for the designee is that he or she is subject to personal liability for charges incurred by or on behalf of the company.

Advertisement of Tenders

Bid solicitation is typically accomplished through government tenders, direct advertising, or (rarely) by invitation to registered suppliers. In the past, no single journal or central office has been established for this purpose, and tenders have commonly been announced in a variety of Mexican newspapers, although being large circulation dailies, *El Universal* and *Excelsior* have been frequently used.

However, this practice is changing under NAFTA, which requires the publication of public tender announcements in a single journal of record. (Refer to the "Important Addresses" chapter for Mexican newspaper contact information.) A private company in Mexico is now printing a weekly Spanish publication that lists Mexican government tender announcements by bid number, entity, and product. For information, contact:

Resumen de Convocatorias
(Summary of Government Tender Announcements)
Editorial Grupo Miranova
Moras 736
Col. del Valle
México, DF, México
Tel: [52] (5) 524-3752, 575-5348, 404-5386

Many entities also advertise public tenders in international media, particularly those with substantial circulation in business circles. These include the *Journal of Commerce, Wall Street Journal, New York Times, Washington Post,* and *Business Development* (published by the Office of Business Development, Small Business Administration).

Lead Times

Mexican law mandates a 10-day minimum lead time for bids on supplies and a 20-day minimum lead time for bids on projects. Lead time is defined as the period between the first day that the tender is announced and the first date bids are accepted. Under NAFTA, minimum lead times will be doubled. Many entities allow for significantly longer lead times on most tenders except those for administrative supplies. Nevertheless, lead times are relatively short, and companies without active on-site representation may be hard-pressed to prepare a bid within the time allotted.

Contract Awards

Procurement contracts are normally awarded to the lowest bidder that meets the specifications of the government or parastatal entity. With respect to awarding contracts to foreign firms, most of the entities have established informal policies. In general, preferences are given to domestic companies, provided the goods or services they offer meet the quality requirements, are available in the quantities needed, and are priced competitively. Products are considered to be produced domestically and eligible for preference if the Mexican content is more than 50 percent.

If only a few Mexican nationals bid on a tender, the government and parastatal entities may attempt to ensure competitive pricing by comparing the bids to information compiled on international pricing on comparable goods and services. If international prices are lower than the local prices by a certain percentage—often 10 percent—or if local bids exceed a maximum price set by the entity, the bidding will then opened to international firms, even if it was previously restricted.

PROCUREMENT SPECIFICS

Instituto de Seguridad y Servicios Sociales de los Trabajadores del Estado (ISSSTE)— Mexican Federal Employee Health System

Areas of Procurement Medical equipment and supplies; drugs and pharmaceuticals; administrative supplies.

Registration Not required, but unregistered supplier must submit information about the bidder's company with each bid. Central registry is maintained and is recommended for companies doing ongoing business with ISSSTE. Registration is free and should be renewed annually to ensure that information—new products, prices, models, and other catalog information, and corporate or business documentation—is current.

Product Requirements If laboratory testing is required, the procedure and criteria will be outlined in the bid package. Pharmaceuticals must be registered with the General Director of Sanitation Control of Goods and Services:

Director General de Control Sanitario de Bienes y Servicios, Secretaría de Salud (SS)
Donceles 39, Piso 1
Col. Centro
06010 México, DF, México
Tel: [52] (5) 521-3050, 521-9134

Local Representative Not required, but helpful. For controlled substances and pharmaceuticals, a local laboratory or a relationship with a local laboratory is required.

Tender Information Often combined into one bid package. A bid package that totals at least US$225,000 must be opened for public bidding. Medical supply tenders are primarily made between November and January.

Lead Times For medical equipment tenders, 90 days on average; for tenders of drugs, pharmaceuticals, and administrative supplies and services, 10 to 15 days.

Bid Package Fees Varies depending on size of contract tendered. Average range is NP200 (about US$60) to NP1,000 (US$300).

Bid Requirements For a combined bid package, bidders must specify the tender on which they are bidding.

New Products New medical equipment and supplies are best introduced through contacts with doctors at "level three" facilities—these doctors wield the most influence in the purchasing decisions made in the rest of the system.

Supplier's Bond For medical equipment and medical and administrative supplies, supplier may be required to post a one-year surety bond of 10 percent of the contract price; for drugs and pharmaceuticals, a one-year surety bond of 2 to 5 percent of the contract price.

In 1993, ISSSTE budgeted an estimated US$20 million for spending on medical equipment, US$30 million on medical supplies, and US$30 million on drug and pharmaceutical products. A significant percentage of ISSSTE tenders for medical equipment and supplies, drugs, and pharmaceuticals are offered internationally. The largest overseas suppliers of these products to Mexico are Japan, Germany, and the US. By contrast, only about 5 percent of tendered administrative services and supplies are purchased from international sources; these are mainly in the area of computer equipment, software, and supplies.

For information on registration and specific tenders with the ISSSTE, contact the Subdirector of Procurement:

Subdirector de Adquisiciones
Instituto de Seguridad y Servicios Sociales de los
Trabajadores del Estado (ISSTE)
Callejón Via San Fernando 12, Piso 4
Col. Barrio San Fernando Tlalpan
14070 México, DF, México
Tel: [52] (5) 606-2121, 606-2101, 606-2271
Fax: [52] (5) 606-5766

For information on medical equipment and supply tenders, contact the Chief of Procurement for Medical Instruments and Equipment:

Jefe de Servicios de Adquisiciones de
Instrumentales y Equipo Medico
Instituto de Seguridad y Servicios Sociales de los
Trabajadores del Estado (ISSTE)
Callejón Via San Fernando 12, Piso 3
Col. Barrio San Fernando Tlalpan
14070 México, DF, México
Tel: [52] (5) 606-8016, 606-2121, 606-2143
Fax: [52] (5) 606-5766

Instituto Mexicano del Seguro Social (IMSS)—Mexican Institute of Social Security

Areas of Procurement Medical equipment and instruments; pharmaceuticals and medical supplies; administrative supplies.

Registration Not required, but an unregistered supplier must submit information about the company with each bid. Central registry is maintained and is recommended for companies doing ongoing business with IMSS. Registration is free and need not be renewed annually, although it may be updated as needed for new products, price, model, or other such information.

Product Requirements If laboratory testing is required, the procedure and criteria will be outlined in the bid package. Pharmaceuticals must be registered with the General Director of Public Health Goods and Services at:

Director General de Control Sanitario de Bienes y
Servicios, Secretaría de Salud (SS)
Donceles 39, Piso 1
Col. Centro
06010 México, DF, México
Tel: [52] (5) 521-3050, 521-9134

Local Representative Not required, but helpful. For controlled substances and pharmaceuticals, a local laboratory or a relationship with a local laboratory is required.

Tender Information Often combined into one bid package. Tenders of more than NP750,000 (about US$225,000) must be made public. Tenders for pharmaceuticals and medical supplies are primarily made around October. Local offices of the IMSS are authorized to make administrative supply purchases of less than NP280 (about US$85). Purchases of such supplies in excess of that amount are made through the central office.

Lead Times For medical equipment and instrument tenders, 60 days on average; for pharmaceuticals and medical supplies, 15 days; for administrative supplies, 10 days.

Bid Package Fees For medical equipment and instrument, average NP1,000 (about US$300); for pharmaceutical and medical supply bid packages, NP250 (about US$75) on average, and rarely exceed NP1,500 (about US$450); for administrative supplies, from NP500 (about US$150) to NP2,000 (about US$600).

Bid Requirements For a combined bid package, bidders must specify the tender on which they are bidding.

New Products All new products are best introduced by approaching the appropriate board responsible for making final purchasing decisions for the type of product. The board may request product tests, additional information, or a presentation.

Supplier's Bond Suppliers must usually furnish a letter of credit or post a one-year surety bond of 10 percent of the contract price. This practice ensures that the IMSS will have legal recourse in case of a supplier's failure to fulfill a procurement contract.

Mexican health authorities are promoting the strengthening and modernizing of local health systems, including IMSS. For 1993, IMSS anticipated that its purchases of medical equipment and instruments would total about US$100 million; plans include buying new equipment for its National Health Center. A high percentage of acquisitions have been made from firms primarily in Japan, Germany, and the US.

For information on medical equipment and instrument purchases, contact the Procurement Manager for Medical Equipment and Instruments at:

Sub-Jefe de Adquisiciones de Equipos y
Instrumentos Medicos
Instituto Mexicano del Seguro Social (IMSS)
Durango No. 323, Planta Baja, México
Tel: [52] (5) 211-4873, 211-0592, x269

For information on registration with the IMSS, contact Coordinator of Companies for Development and Pricing at:

Coordinadora de Empresas de Precios y Desarrollo
Instituto Mexicano del Seguro Social (IMSS)
Shakespeare 157
Col. Anzures
México, DF, México
Tel: [52] (5) 545-1861

For information on administrative supply tenders, contact the Procurement Manager for Supplies:

Sub-Jefe de Adquisiciones de Bienes de Consumo
Instituto Mexicano del Seguro Social (IMSS)
Durango No. 323, Planta Baja
México, DF, México
Tel: [52] (5) 286-0497

Petróleos Mexicanos (Pemex)—Mexican Petroleum Company

Areas of Procurement Equipment and supplies for gas and petroleum exploration, extraction, primary and secondary refining, and transport.

Registration Advance registration not required, but contractor must register at time of submitting the bid. Central registry is maintained by parent company. Each registered contractor is assigned an identification number for product and company tracking purposes. Contractors who anticipate being onsite at a Pemex facility must apply for a building pass and must supply personal identification information, including a photograph, when submitting registration materials. Registration is free. It must be renewed annually and requires resubmission of the application and updated documentation. The applications must be submitted to the Department of Supplier Liaison:

El Departmento de Atención a Proveedores
Avenida Marina Nacional 329
Edificio B-2, Piso 9
Col. Anahuac
11311 México, DF, México
Tel: [52] (5) 531-6217 Fax: [52] (5) 531-6017

Houston/Pemex
Vendor Affairs
Office of the Pemex Representative
3600 S. Gessner
Houston, TX 77063, USA
Tel: [1] (713) 978-7974 Fax: [1] (713) 975-4951

Local Representative Minimal local presence required in accordance with Mexican law. A Mexican business owner or entity that represents a foreign contractor must submit the Mexican license and proof of the most recent property tax filing for the business with the contractor's registration application. If the Mexican business is not a sole proprietorship, it must additionally include Mexican papers authorizing the formation of the entity, a list of company principals, any recent modifications of its Mexican business registration, and proof of its current membership in an appropriate Mexican business association.

Tender Information All tenders are open to public bidding. Pemex sometimes extends invitations to bid to selected contractors to encourage their participation.

Lead Times Rarely extend beyond minimums required by Mexican law (10 to 20 days).

Bid Package Fees US$100 on average.

For Pemex registration information, contact:

Acquisitions Department
Petróleos Mexicanos Oficinas Generales
Marina Nacional 329
Edificio B-2, Piso 11
Col. Huasteca
11311 México, DF, México
Tel: [52] (5) 254-2044, 250-2611
Fax: [52] (5) 531-6017

As the fifth largest oil company in the world and the largest domestic company and top exporter in Mexico, Pemex continues to be the most significant source of foreign currency for Mexico. In recent years, the company has been reorganized into well defined divisions and is actively seeking foreign investment in many areas to promote further growth and to modernize its facilities—despite a constitutional prohibition on direct investment by foreign nationals. Oil and gas exploration are high priorities, and the development of newly discovered fields is a top concern.

Under NAFTA, 50 percent of Pemex's multimillion dollar procurement contracts have been opened to Canadian and US suppliers, and this percentage will increase over the next 10 years until all service contracts valued at more than US$250,000 and all construction contracts of more than US$8 million are open to Canadian and US suppliers. Moreover, Mexico's 1993 Foreign Investment Law authorizes 100 percent foreign investment by 1995 in exploration and refining infrastructure—including exploration (test, but not production) wells, refining plants, and related machinery and equipment—and by 2001 in other areas—including construction of pipelines and pumping stations.

For information on tenders for exploration and production equipment and supplies, contact:

Pemex Exploración y Producción
Avenida Marina Nacional 329
Edificio B-1, Piso 7
Col. Anahuac
11311 México, DF, México
Tel: [52] (5) 254-0440

For information on tenders for refining equipment and materials, contact:

Pemex Refinación
Avenida Ejército Nacional 216, Piso 17
Col. Polanco
México, DF, México
Tel: [52] (5) 531-9927 Fax: [52] (5) 531-6262

For information on tenders for equipment and supplies related to primary petrochemical production, contact the Chief of Material Resources at:

Gerente de Recursos Materiales
Pemex Gas y Petroquimica Basica
Avenida Marina Nacional 329
Torre Ejecutiva, Piso 18
Col. Huasteca
México, DF, México
Tel: [52] (5) 203-0283, 250-2611)

For information on tenders for equipment and supplies related to secondary petrochemical production, contact:

Pemex Petroquimica Segundaria
Avenida Marina Nacional 329
Edificio B-1, Piso 9
Col. Anahuac
México, DF, México
Tel: [52] (5) 250-2611 Fax: 531-6221

Comisión Nacional del Agua (CNA)— National Water Commission

Areas of Procurement Drainage and irrigation (canals, dams, and irrigation systems); potable water (water treatment systems); and equipment and materials (heavy equipment, motors, piping, pumps, and supplies).

Registration No advance registration required. All registration information—such as incorporation papers, statements of technical capacity, and declarations of capital—must be submitted as part of a bid. If awarded a bid, a company must register its activities with:

Cámara Nacional de la Industria de la
Construcción
(National Chamber of the Construction Industry)
Periférico Sur 4839
Col. del Pedregal
14010 México, DF, México
Tel: [52] (5) 665-2167, 665-1500, 665-2167
Fax: [52] (5) 606-6720, 606-8329

Local Representative Not required, but CNA recommends that foreign companies appoint someone in Mexico to: respond to questions from the decision panel; visit the construction site; submit the bid; be present when the decision is made; sign the contract; and receive any advance payment. The person designated must be given a duly notarized power of attorney that establishes his or her authority to act on the company's behalf.

Bid and Tender Information Tenders available to foreign bidding are designated as international, but foreign companies can bid on national projects as well. Projects exceeding US$5 million or funded by the World Bank must be open to international bidding. A few tenders are offered by invitation to select suppliers. For equipment and supplies, all tenders that exceed US$700,000 are designated international. If tenders for less than that amount fail to attract a sufficient number of local bidders, the central office will also offer those tenders to international bidders. Bid packages usually give escalation information for costs subject to inflation—labor, equipment, and materials. Moreover, some bid packages include information on future projects (usually related or staged projects). They will also contain specifications or laboratory testing criteria and procedures, if testing is required. Equipment and machinery tenders are made through the central CNA office, while supplies and services are handled directly through the specific office involved—a state office, the Distrito Federal office, or any of the five regional offices.

Lead Times Lead times vary depending on the institution providing the project financing. For most of the drainage, irrigation, and potable water projects, the average is 45 working days, but for projects under US$5 million, lead times may be as short as 30 working days. For equipment and materials tenders, the average is 10 to 15 days.

Bid Package Fees For drainage and irrigation projects, fees range between NP$1,000 (about US$300) and NP$2,000 (about US$600); for potable water projects, US$300 on average; for equipment or material tenders, from NP$1,000 (about US$300) to NP$1,500 (about US$450).

Bid Requirements Bids must be in Spanish, and all documents submitted with them must be translated into Spanish and notarized by a Mexican consul in the supplier's country. The institution financing the project may have specific bid requirements, as stated in the bid package. For potable water projects, final bid decisions are made by state and municipal water commissions, although project and bid criteria are set by the *Gerencia de Construcciones* (Office of Construction Management), which also announces the tender and may intervene if problems with the bidding or contracting process arise

Supplier's Bond May be required. For drainage or irrigation projects, a one-year surety bond in the amount of 10 percent of contract price; for potable water projects, a one-year surety bond in the amount of 2 to 5 percent of contract price; for equipment and supplies, a one-year surety bond in the amount of 10 to 15 percent of contract price.

The CNA division responsible for drainage and irrigation projects—primarily canals, dams, and irrigation systems—publishes an average 120 tender announcements each year, of which 15 to 20 are specifically open to international firms. In 1993, the CNA planned to offer potable water projects—such as water treatment plants—totaling an estimated US$1 billion, at least 50 percent of which would be open to international bidding. Most of the CNA projects are funded through financing from the World Bank or the Inter-American Development Bank (IADB). The CNA division devoted to equipment and materials—heavy equipment, motors, piping, pumps, and supplies—estimated its 1993 procurement budget at US$100 million.

For information on specific tenders, contact:

Gerente de Construcción (Construction Manager)
Comisión Nacional del Agua
Infr. Hica. Urbana E. Ind.
Cda. J. Sanchez Azcona 1723, Piso 4
Col. del Valle
03100 México, DF, México
Tel: [52] (5) 524-6985, 524-2650
Fax: [52](5)524-1129

Jefe de Proyecto de Concursos Contratos y
Estimaciones
(Project Chief of Bids, Contracts, and Estimates)
Comisión Nacional del Agua
Balderas 94, Piso 2
Col. Centro
06070 México, DF, México
Tel: [52] (5) 512-7927, 512-5561
Fax: [52] (5) 518-6960

Gerente de Recursos Materiales
(Resource Material Manager)
Comisión Nacional de Agua
Avenida Insurgentes Sur no. 2140
Col. Ermita
01070 México, DF, México
Tel: [52] (5) 661-3680, 662-4715

Portuarios—Mexican Marine Ports

Areas of Procurement Materials, projects, and concessions (mainly low-value service contracts).

Registration Advance registration is not required. If contractor is unregistered, information—such as incorporation documents, statement of capital, and declaration of technical capacity—must be submitted as part of the bid. If awarded a bid, a company must register its activities with the National Chamber of the Construction Industry at:

Cámara Nacional de la Industria de la
Construcción
Periférico Sur 4839
Col. del Pedregal
14010 México, DF, México
Tel: [52] (5) 665-2167, 665-1500, 665-2167
Fax: [52] (5) 606-6720, 606-8329

Local Representative Not required, but local presence is advised.

Bid and Tender Information Material purchases are centralized, and all published bids are open to international bidding. For material tenders of less than NP9,000 (about US$2,700), direct purchases are allowed; for material tenders of NP9,000 to NP25,000 (up to about US$7,500), at least three bids must be reviewed, and these may be solicited by invitation. For material tenders of NP25,000 to NP270,000 (about US$7,500 to US$80,000), at least eight bids must be reviewed, bidding is open to international firms, and bids are sometimes solicited by invitation. Material tenders of more than NP270,000 (about US$80,000) must be publicized. All public tenders for projects are open to international participation. Tenders for

NAFTA CREATES OPPORTUNITY FOR
US COMPANIES DOING BUSINESS IN MEXICO*

MANUFACTURING

Mexico's tariffs on US exports have averaged 10 percent in recent years. NAFTA's reduction of this Mexican trade barrier is providing a tremendous boost for US companies doing business in Mexico. Half of all US exports in Mexico—including semiconductors, certain computer products, telecommunications equipment, and electronic equipment—have been receiving duty-free treatment since NAFTA took effect on January 1, 1994. Within five years of NAFTA's implementation, Mexican tariffs on 65 percent of US industrial exports will be removed, while tariffs in certain sensitive sectors will be phased out over 10 to 15 years. Key economic sectors that promise to benefit from NAFTA are the following:

Automotive Industry Under NAFTA, Mexico immediately reduced by 50 percent (from 20 to 10 percent) its tariffs on US passenger automobiles and light trucks. Seventy-five percent of Mexican tariffs on US auto parts will be phased out in five years. Tariffs on the remaining 25 percent will be eliminated over 10 years.

Chemicals, Rubber, and Plastics Industry Before NAFTA, 27 percent of all US exports to Mexico in this industry received duty-free treatment. Upon implementation, NAFTA immediately eliminated all tariffs on another 31 percent of the exports in this industry. The remaining tariffs will be phased out over five to 10 years.

Computer and Software Industry NAFTA immediately eliminated Mexican tariffs, which ranged from 10 to 20 percent, on 70 percent of US exports of computer equipment and software. Mexican duties on the remaining products, which include CPUs, impact printers, and certain other peripheral devices, will be eliminated over five years.

Electronics Industry NAFTA immediately eliminated tariffs on 49 percent of US electronics exports to Mexico, including capacitors, BV connectors, switches, piezoelectric crystals, and some categories of resistors and tubes. The remaining tariffs will be eliminated within five to 10 years.

Processed Foods and Beverages Industry

Before NAFTA, 12 percent of US exports to Mexico in this industry—including certain meat products, butter, and malts—received duty-free treatment. Tariffs on another 2.5 percent of US exports were lifted immediately under NAFTA. Tariffs will be eliminated over a five-year period for an additional 3.5 percent of US processed foods exports and over a 10-year period for 46 percent of such US exports. Tariffs on remaining exports in this sector will be eliminated through the mechanism of tariff rate quotas and a phase-out of tariffs. Thus, a certain volume of processed foods will receive duty-free treatment, with exports above this volume being subject to a tariff that will be phased out over 15 years.

Telecommunications Industry Under NAFTA, more than 80 percent of present US telecommunications equipment exports to Mexico, including most telecommunications line equipment, private branch exchanges, cellular phones, modems, and telecommunications equipment parts, receive immediate duty-free treatment. Tariffs on the remaining telecommunications exports to Mexico will be eliminated over a five-year period. However, tariffs on paging alert devices (tone only), certain coaxial cables, and antennae will be phased out over 10 years.

SERVICES

NAFTA also relaxes Mexico's restrictions on service exports. NAFTA extends the benefits of national treatment and most—favored nation treatment to US service providers. In addition, NAFTA prohibits Mexico from conditioning the ability of US service providers to do business in Mexico on the establishment of a Mexican residence, office, or branch. Service sectors benefiting from the liberalization of trade barriers under NAFTA include the following:

Trucking Services Three years after NAFTA takes effect, US truck operators will be allowed to deliver and pick up international cargo in Mexican border states. After six years, US trucking firms will be allowed cross-border access to all of Mexico. However, Mexico will

*By William E. Mooz, Jr., of the law firm of Holland & Hart, Denver, Colorado. Reprinted from the law firm's publication, Holland & Hart International Update. Reprinted with permission of the author and the law firm. Copyright © 1994 Holland & Hart.

NAFTA OPPORTUNITIES (cont'd.)

not be required to remove restrictions regarding domestic cargo.

Banking and Securities US banks can establish or own up to 8 percent of the Mexican banking market in the first year, increasing annually to 15 percent in the sixth year. The market share limit for US firms in the Mexican securities market will increase from 10 to 20 percent over the first six years. Individual market share caps of 1.5 percent for banks and 4 percent for securities dealers will apply during this time. Even after the initial phase-in period of six years, a 4 percent market share limitation will be applied to bank acquisitions.

Finance Companies US finance companies may establish separate subsidiaries in Mexico for the purpose of providing consumer, commercial, or mortgage lending and credit card services. The size of such subsidiaries will be limited until the year 2000.

Insurance US insurers that form joint ventures with Mexican insurers may own all the equity in such a venture after a phase-in period of six years. US firms currently owning an interest in a Mexican insurer may increase their levels of equity participation to 100 percent by January 1, 1996. Subject to certain market share limits that expire in the year 2000, US insurers may establish subsidiaries in Mexico.

sion of *Portuarios* had a 1993 budget of approximately NP54,000,000 (about US$17.3 million).

In the past, the office that handles concessions and service contracts has generally offered only low-value service contracts. Competition for these contracts has been negligible in comparison to the other procurement divisions of *Portuarios*. But this office is currently being reorganized to handle the substantial anticipated port management contracts recently allowed under new legislation. The intention is to attract private sector investment to modernize the nation's ports with the introduction of port mechanization and modern management methods. Regulations are being formulated, and no clear or final registration or bidding policies were available at press time. Final regulations will be published in *Diario Oficial*—Mexico's journal of government proceedings—and each port authority should be able to provide information on its current procedures. (Refer to the "Transportation" chapter for contact information on individual port authorities.)

For information on procurement procedures and current tenders, contact the Mexican Port Authority at:

Puertos Mexicanos
Municipio Libre No. 377
Col. Santa Cruz Atoyac
03310 México, DF, México
Tel: [52] (5) 604-3070, 604-3829, 604-4249
Fax: [52] (5) 688-9368, 688-9243

concessions are made by each local port authority as services are needed.

Lead Times for material tenders, the average is 30 days; for project tenders, the average is 20 days.

Bid Package Fees for material bid packages, the average is NP300 (about US$90); for project bid packages, NP300 to NP500 (about US$90 to US$150).

Bid Requirements bids and all documents submitted with them must be in Spanish and notarized by Mexican consul in supplier's country.

Supplier's Bond for material contracts, a one-year surety bond in the amount of 5 percent of contract price. For specialty materials, the amount of the bond is usually higher, often 15 percent of the contract price. For projects, a one-year surety bond in the amount of 10 percent of the contract price.

The 1993 budget for materials included NP56,427,000 (about US$18.1 million) for capital goods, NP6,000,000 (about US$1.9 million) for general services, and NP2,870,000 (about US$921,000) for general supplies. The projects procurement divi-

Foreign Investment

INVESTMENT CLIMATE AND TRENDS

Historically, Mexico has shifted back and forth in its attitudes toward and regulation of foreign investment, swinging from periods of greater or lesser openness to periods of closed isolation. The country is currently entering a cycle in which foreign investment is largely being welcomed, even actively encouraged and facilitated, certainly to a greater extent than has been the case since the 1920s. Mexico has determined that it needs external capital, technology, job creation, and innovative marketing and management techniques, and is determined to do what it can to acquire them.

After a period in which foreign investment faced barriers consisting of outright bans and complicated, discretionary, and discriminatory approval procedures by which investment was nominally allowed but effectively denied, Mexico has technically become one of the more open economies in the world today. Despite continued sensitivities and reservations, the country is making a genuine effort to modernize itself and enter the world economic mainstream. Part of this favorable posture is due to the general trend toward internationalization of the world economy and the free market technocratic orientation of recent governments, and part is due to a certain swallowing of pride and acknowledgment that the country needs outside inputs if it is to advance. At any rate, Mexico currently feels that its best interests would be served by enabling foreigners to invest in its national economy.

Such opportunities come infrequently and can be withdrawn on relatively short notice. Virtually all of Mexico's national heroes are those who have resisted the foreign invader: militarily, in the cases of the last Aztec emperor Cuauhtémoc, the hapless Santa Anna, Benito Juárez, and Pancho Villa, or economically, as with Lázaro Cárdenas, who sent foreign oil and railroad interests packing in the 1930s. The current crop of leaders is trying to convince its people that growth and integration can be heroic as

well, even if it involves accepting suspect foreigners as part of the price that must be paid. And with Mexico still hamstrung by its massive foreign debt and experiencing a brittle recovery, it needs foreign goodwill, expertise, and investment funds to sustain its advance.

Throughout the 1970s and most of the 1980s, Mexico effectively excluded foreigners from significant participation in its economy, which had become progressively more state-directed and oligarchic. The 1973 Law for the Promotion of Mexican Investment and Regulation of Foreign Investment, with its focus on promoting national investment and controlling foreign investment, codified existing administrative rules, set additional limits on new investment, and restricted the expansion of existing foreign operations. The law limited foreign ownership to a maximum of 49 percent in virtually all areas, barred foreign participation even on a minority basis in a variety of others, including some of the most crucial national industries, and established cumbersome bureaucratic approval processes that kept foreigners at arm's length in an attempt to reserve the economy for nationals. Inefficiency and corruption were exacerbated as an indirect result.

This skewing of the economy led to a variety of distortions, including: a lack of access to imported goods; high domestic prices coupled with low quality and limited variety; a deteriorating domestic industry starved for investment, technology, or even basic maintenance; and a growing inability to compete in world markets. The relatively few successful domestic businesses in this protected environment became accustomed to subsidizing inefficiency, obtaining artificially high margins, and operating with a lack of competitive pressure. The national economy sagged, unable to support its populace and falling further behind rapidly improving international markets.

Yet Mexico has a wealth of riches—its strategic location (fronting on two oceans and linking North America geographically and culturally with Latin America), its abundant natural resources, and its hardworking, affordable labor force. Although still underdeveloped, Mexico is fast reaching the income threshold at which it can become a significant consumer of a wide range of goods and services as well as a competitive producer of desirable products. Its infrastructure, although rudimentary, is basically in place, and its leadership is oriented toward supporting its transition to become a player of substance on the modern world scene.

The de la Madrid administration (1982–1988) stopped the slide of the national economy and promoted openings for foreign investors through the *maquila* program. Although dating to 1964, the program did not begin to grow until the mid-1970s. The Salinas administration (1988–1994) has put in place many of the prerequisites for internal growth and stability and taken the first steps in opening Mexico up to foreign investment. In 1989 the government rewrote the implementing regulations for the restrictive 1973 foreign investment law, expanding the number of sectors, activities, and geographic areas open to foreign participation; increasing the level of foreign participation allowed to as much as 100 percent for many investments; and reducing the approvals needed to invest in Mexico. The new rules freed up foreigners at least potentially to fully own operations in about two-thirds of all economic sectors. The new regulations also eliminated the requirements that foreign operations maintain a positive foreign exchange balance, commit to making additional fixed asset investments, or export a certain volume of products.

Since then, the administration has proceeded to deregulate and reorganize the economy, privatizing a raft of state-run operations, massively restructuring the agricultural and landholding systems, removing foreign exchange controls and many tariff barriers, and generally promoting freer economic activity.

The Mexican government has strongly supported the North American Free Trade Agreement (NAFTA), and under its terms has pledged to remove most remaining barriers to foreign participation in its economy by nationals of cosignatories the US and Canada. In late 1993 Mexico went beyond the mandated treaty conditions to rewrite its foreign investment law, confirming and broadening the liberalization of the regulations espoused in 1989. This new foreign investment law, which went into effect on January 1, 1994, supersedes existing foreign investment regulations. It eliminates performance requirements (except those included as part of narrowly defined incentives), expands the scope of neutral investments (trusts that allow greater foreign participation in otherwise closed or limited areas), and reduces the need for notifications and authorizations. In addition, Mexico has been negotiating agreements with other Latin American, Asian, and European nations designed to open up new economic relationships outside North America. It is widely anticipated that the same privileges allotted to US and Canadian investors through NAFTA will in large part be made available to investors from other countries as well, following a lag for NAFTA implementation, resulting in an open, level playing field. However, investors from other countries must operate under the somewhat less favorable existing rules for the present.

LEADING FOREIGN INVESTORS

Size of Foreign Investment Cumulative recorded direct nonfinancial foreign investment (that is, other than portfolio investment in financial instruments like stocks and bonds) in Mexico as of August 1993 amounted to US$49.2 billion. During the 1970s, foreign investment trickled into a largely closed Mexico, averaging only about US$300 million annually. As of 1986, when Mexico began easing its foreign investment posture to the degree that it allowed outsiders to cancel external dollar-denominated debt to swap for pesos destined for investment in the country, foreign investment rose to US$2.4 billion. It reached US$3.9 billion in 1987 and US$3.2 billion in 1988, about one-quarter of which came from debt swaps.

At the beginning of 1989, cumulative foreign investment had been only US$16.1 billion, rising to US$16.7 billion by year's end, an indication of how relatively closed Mexico had been before the recent change in attitudes and regulations. At the end of 1991, total foreign investment was US$33.9 billion—double the 1989 figure—and totaled US$41.9 billion if stock market investments are included. Between 1989 and mid-1993 (the first four and a half years under the new liberalized investment rules), direct foreign investment was US$33.1 billion, representing more than two-thirds of all recorded direct foreign investment. Preliminary figures for 1993 indicate that the full year foreign direct investment was about US$15 billion, and based on results during the first two months of 1994, observers expect to see at least an additional US$15 billion invested during all of 1994. However, during January 1994, 75 percent of all foreign investment was in securities, while only 23 percent was in other registered foreign investments (the remaining 2 percent was made in approved government projects).

A further complication involves differences between direct foreign investment contracted and direct foreign investment actually received, a more conservative measure. Based on the paid up direct foreign investment, the Banco de México listed a total of US$4.4 billion for 1992 and US$4.9 billion for 1993. This represented 19.6 percent of total foreign investment (including US$18 billion in portfolio investment) in 1992 and 14.7 percent of the total (including US$28.4

billion in portfolio investment) in 1993.

Origin of Foreign Investment The US is the largest investor in Mexico, accounting for more than 60 percent of all foreign investment both past and present. As of 1993, 87 percent of all US Fortune 500 firms already had operations of one sort or another in Mexico. At the end of 1991, cumulative US investment was nearly US$21.5 billion, or 63.4 percent of all direct foreign investment registered since such records have been kept, up about 30 percent in nominal dollar terms from the 1990 level. As of mid-1993 US investment accounted for about 72 percent of total cumulative foreign investment.

As of December 1990, the US accounted for 63 percent of total cumulative direct nonfinancial foreign investment, followed by Germany with 6.4 percent, the UK with 6.3 percent, Japan (4.8 percent), Switzerland (4.4 percent), France (3.1 percent), and Spain (2.3 percent); these seven countries accounted for more than 90 percent of all foreign investment. At the end of 1991, the positions of major cumulative foreign investors had shifted slightly, with the US rising to US$21.466 billion (63.4 percent), followed by Germany (US$2.041 billion, 6 percent), the UK (US$1.988 billion, 5.9 percent), Japan (US$1.529 billion, 4.5 percent), France (US$1.446 billion, 4.3 percent), and Switzerland (US$1.415 billion, 4.2 percent). Together, these top six investor countries still accounted for more than 88 percent of all cumulative recorded nonfinancial direct foreign investment.

The remaining US$3.962 billion (11.7 percent) was made by various countries, each of which accounted for much less than a cumulative 4 percent share of total investment. Other countries with significant but lower per period and cumulative investments include Spain, Italy, and the Netherlands. Canadian investment in Mexico surged on the prospects of NAFTA, reaching a reported cumulative total of US$854 million at the end of 1993. Although this represents less than 1.75 percent of total foreign investment, it does represent a sharp increase from the relatively minor estimated cumulative US$156 million invested by Canadians as of the end of 1992.

Given the terms of NAFTA that they consider to be unfavorable to nonparticipant investors such as themselves, investors from countries like Japan have expressed doubts about increased investment. As of the end of 1993, Japan had roughly 230 operations in Mexico, but about 60 of them were *maquilas* that counted on special tariff exemptions that are scheduled to be phased out by the year 2000. However, most tariffs are scheduled to be phased out over the same period, so *maquila* investors are not so much losing special treatment on tariffs as they are losing artificial protection. Although *maquila* owners from the US and Canada are somewhat buffered from the effects of this phaseout, essentially all those who have relied on special import-export treatment to ensure the margins for their *maquila* operations will be faced with deciding whether to continue their operations under the new, unprotected conditions. To offset losses, *maquilas* will be allowed to direct ever-greater portions of their production to the Mexican domestic market over the same period during which their import privileges are being phased out.

Sectors of Foreign Investment As of the end of 1991, investments in industry accounted for 58.6 percent of total cumulative direct foreign nonfinancial investment, with a total of US$19.874 billion. Service sector investments followed with a 32.2 percent share (US$10.920 billion). Commerce (7.2 percent, US$2.447 billion), extractive industries (1.5 percent, US$515 million), and agriculture and ranching (0.4 percent, US$135 million) rounded out the picture of foreign investments.

The trend has been away from investment by foreigners in manufacturing and toward greater concentration in services and, more recently, in commerce and other activities. In 1986, when foreign investment except in the *maquilas* was still heavily restricted 77.9 percent of such investment as there was went into manufacturing, 12.7 percent went into services, and 9.4 percent went into other activities. Manufacturing's share of investment has dropped steadily since then, falling to 58.6 percent in 1991 as compared to service sector investments of 32.2 percent and investments in other activities of 9.2 percent. In the first quarter of 1993, 53.3 percent of foreign investment was in manufacturing, 27.3 percent in services, and 19.4 percent in other activities, and figures for August 1993 showed roughly 50 percent of foreign investment dedicated to manufacturing, 30 percent to services, and 20 percent to other activities. During January 1994, 38.2 percent of foreign investment went into industry (primarily into the food, beverage, and tobacco sector), 50 percent into retail and services, 10.3 percent into construction, and 0.4 percent into the mining sector.

This trend mirrors the shift within the domestic economy to a greater role for the service sector. It reflects, as well, growth in the attractiveness of other activities, including commerce, mining, and agriculture and ranching, all of which are being opened up to foreign investment for the first time in decades.

INVESTMENT POLICY AND CHANGES

Definition of Foreign Investment Foreign investment is legally defined as investment made by foreign individuals, companies, or unincorporated entities, as well as by Mexican companies with primarily foreign ownership or in which foreigners have the right to appoint and control the management of the entity. Foreign investors may not have representation on the board of directors greater than that which is strictly proportional to their share of the equity ownership in the venture. Indirect ownership through the extension of financing, technology transfer, or shares held in trust is not considered foreign investment unless it results in managerial control of the Mexican entity.

Investments made by foreign individuals with permanent resident, or *inmigrado*, status are usually treated as domestic investments. However, investments made by such individuals can be considered to be either national or foreign, depending on the circumstances and, to some extent, location.

Investment Authorization and Procedures The National Foreign Investment Commission (*Comisión Nacional de Inversión Extranjera*), or FIC, is the official entity charged with approving and regulating foreign investment in Mexico. The FIC is administered through the Secretariat of Commerce and Industrial Development (*Secretaría de Comercio y Fomento Industrial*, or SECOFI) and is chaired by the secretary or, more usually, his designate. The FIC includes cabinet level representatives or designates from the Secretariats of the Interior; Foreign Relations; Finance; Social Development; Energy, Mines, and Parastatal Industries; Communications and Transportation; Labor and Social Security; and Tourism. The FIC is charged with setting guidelines and procedures, ruling on specific applications, consulting with other agencies, and issuing regulations governing foreign investment.

New investments valued at less than US$100 million in sectors that do not otherwise require approval have not required FIC approval under the regulations established in 1989. This level was not stipulated in the 1993 foreign investment law, and new numerical levels are expected to be set by the FIC. However, according to the 1993 law, investments in existing Mexican companies valued at less than NP85 million (about US$25.25 million) in activities not otherwise reserved or limited are eligible to proceed without prior authorization.

Specific guidelines are not included in the 1993 foreign investment law. Under the revised investment regulations in effect since 1989, foreign investments in approved areas have not been required to submit to formal review by the FIC provided they met certain criteria. Such authorization has been automatic for new investments valued at less than US$100 million that fall within the following parameters:

- The investment is funded using resources brought in from abroad, with paid-in capital equal to at least 20 percent of the value of the total proposed fixed asset investment having been received and invested prior to the commencement of operations.

- Industrial investments are located outside of Mexico City, Guadalajara, Monterrey, and certain areas of Hidalgo designated Zone III-A. (Commercial and service investments are exempted from this locational restriction.)
- Cumulative foreign exchange flows are scheduled to at least be in balance during the first three years of operations.
- The investment is scheduled to create permanent new jobs, and has plans for formal ongoing worker training and development.
- The investment involves appropriate technology and complies with all environmental requirements.

The FIC is authorized by the 1993 law to rewrite these guidelines, although it has given no indication to date whether it intends to alter them materially. Until new regulations are issued, these preexisting guidelines are expected to continue to govern foreign investment authorization.

Projects that do not unequivocally meet all of these requirements or that involve other gray areas require full FIC review and authorization. The FIC has fairly broad discretionary powers to authorize foreign investment if it finds that the investment will be economically beneficial because it complements domestic operations, increases employment and wages, or improves access to technology. The FIC is expressly forbidden from imposing requirements or making determinations that distort international trade. Proposed investments cannot result in a monopoly, which in Mexico is defined as the use of tactics to reduce competition, an issue addressed in some detail through Mexico's new antitrust law. (Elsewhere, monopolies are usually defined in terms of excessive market share.)

According to the 1993 foreign investment law (which confirms the preexisting rules), approval is automatic if the FIC fails to act on a formal application within 45 working days. The interested party can subsequently request an official notification of non-objection (which is tantamount to a formal authorization) if such is the case. In practice, the FIC can get around this through a partial action, such as sending the application back for clarification or additional information, which would allow it to restart the clock.

Existing regulations that made it difficult for foreigners to expand their activities, initiate new products or lines of business, or increase their ownership in existing investments were eased under the 1989 regulations, although the 1993 law does not address these issues specifically. No authorization was required for the expansion of *maquila* and certain other export-oriented enterprises; for formal mergers accomplished through tender offers or negotiated arrangements; or for expansions that involve investment in new fixed assets valued at a minimum of 10 percent of existing fixed assets. These rules are unlikely to be made more restrictive by any new regulations.

Foreign investors are officially accorded national status, implying that they are ineligible to receive special consideration as foreigners. This is known in Mexico as the Calvo rule, after its author. Because of this equivalent status, the right to request intervention on behalf of a foreign investor by a home country government to obtain special treatment or as an avenue of appeal is considered to have been waived.

The joint venture agreement (*asociación en participación*, or A. en P.) represents something of a gray area. These contractual arrangements usually cover limited term cooperative projects between Mexican and foreign firms and do not result in the formation of a separate entity. However, depending on the activity engaged in, such agreements could technically be considered subject to foreign investment law if the foreign participant has rights to more than 49 percent of the profits or serves as the manager of the venture. Many legal consultants recommend that the FIC be notified of such agreements, although others argue that such agreements lie outside the letter and intent of the foreign investment rules and that notification is neither necessary nor in fact advisable. Foreigners involved in such agreements should consult local legal professionals to determine whether the nature of the specific investment is likely to require any such action.

Reserved, Restricted, and Unrestricted Investment Activities Under the new foreign investment law passed in December 1993 and effective as of 1994, foreign investments are classified by sector and activity as: reserved to the state; reserved to Mexican resident nationals; open to foreign investment of up to 10 percent, 25 percent, 30 percent, or 49 percent; or open to foreign investment of up to 100 percent with prior FIC approval. All other activities not specifically dealt with by the law—constituting about two-thirds of all sectors—are approved for foreign investment with up to 100 percent ownership without prior formal approval. For activities with percentage limits on foreign participation of less than 50 percent, foreigners can be approved to hold effective ownership on a temporary basis through investment trust funds.

Interpretation and assignments of specific activities have been in a state of flux since 1989 and, despite the apparent specificity of the categories established by the 1993 law, remain so to a certain degree. Potential investors are advised to contact the authorities regarding specific projects. Some activities that are restricted are actually being opened to foreign investment on a subcontractor or partial basis with national entities retaining only nominal official oversight. Because the law is so new, and be-

cause implementing regulations have yet to be written for many items contained in it, it will take months and perhaps years to see exactly how its provisions will be interpreted in practice. Nevertheless, the provisions of the law are fairly straightforward, especially when compared to the situation in the past.

Article Five of the foreign investment law lists the following activities as reserved exclusively to the Mexican state:

- Petroleum and other hydrocarbons;
- Basic petrochemicals;
- Electricity generation;
- Generation of nuclear energy;
- Radioactive minerals;
- Satellite communications;
- Telegraphy;
- Radiotelegraphy;
- Mail Service;
- Railways;
- Issuance of banknotes;
- Minting of coins;
- Control, supervision, and oversight of ports, airports, heliports; and
- Any other activities that may be expressly limited by other laws.

The 1993 law codifies several modifications that have come into practice since the change in the implementing regulations made in 1989. Although the Mexican constitution reserves petroleum rights and operations explicitly for the state, the responsible state-run monopoly, Pemex, has been reorganized to allow greater leeway for its subsidiary units to operate. Many of these units have increasingly sought bids from outside—that is, foreign—firms that are potential subcontractors for specific projects in exploration, construction, supply, and various services. Pemex has also reclassified all but the most basic petrochemicals as secondary petrochemicals, reducing the number of reserved chemicals from 34 to 20, thus opening up their production to foreign investors. (The number of secondary petrochemicals previously reserved for national operators had been reduced from 800 to 66, and even these are not exclusively reserved by the new law.) In 1989 the financial system was reserved to the state. But it has been reprivatized through the sale of commercial banks in 1991 and 1992, opening that sector to private and—to a greater extent—foreign investment. The communications monopoly, Teléfonos de México, or Telmex, has been largely privatized (with the government scheduled to dispose of its remaining stock holdings in spring 1994) and is available for foreign stock ownership. Foreigners have explicitly been allowed to invest in high-tech communications. There has been talk of further deregulation and privatization involving aspects of the utilities, railway, and basic communications industries.

Article Six lists the following activities as reserved to Mexican resident nationals:

- National land transportation of passengers, tourists, and cargo (excluding messenger and parcel delivery services);
- Retail distribution and sale of gasoline and liquid petroleum gas;
- Radio broadcasting and other radio and television services and activities, except for cable television;
- Credit union operations;
- Development bank operations;
- Professional and technical services as noted in specific laws (primarily quasi-official functions such as customs inspectors).

Many specific areas which were previously limited to nationals have changed since 1989. The national airlines have been privatized and are open to foreign investment on a portfolio basis, although foreigners are still restricted from providing domestic air service (although they can now own a minority position in some related areas). Financial services, except for the smallest retail and largest quasi-official development banking activities, have been opened up to foreign participation. To a growing degree, professional and other services are also being opened up to outside investors. Even the national mass media have been opened up to the extent that consortia with foreign participants were allowed to bid during privatization (although they lost out to national buyers). In general, national reservations are falling by the wayside; they can be sidestepped at least to some extent through neutral trust holdings of stock, even when direct participation is denied.

The list of activities in which foreign participation is limited to various percentages—all less than 50 percent—has been modified extensively by Article Seven of the 1993 law. Even the percentages themselves have been changed. Under the previous rules, the limits were set at 34 percent, 40 percent, or 49 percent. In a substantial shift, the new law distinguishes activities limited to 10 percent, 25 percent, 30 percent, or 49 percent foreign participation.

Activities limited to 10 percent foreign participation involve:

- Production cooperatives.

Activities limited to 25 percent foreign participation include:

- Internal domestic air transportation;
- Air taxi transportation;
- Specialized air transportation.

Activities limited to 30 percent foreign participation include:

- Companies controlling financial groups;
- Multiple (nationwide commercial) banking institutions;
- Securities firms;
- Stock exchange specialists.

Activities limited to 49 percent foreign participation include:

- Insurance companies;
- Bonding companies;
- Foreign exchange houses (casas de cambio);
- Bonded warehouses (arrendadoras);
- Leasing companies;
- Factoring companies;
- Limited-purpose financial firms that issue securities;
- Certain other securities firms;
- Capital stock of investment companies and investment operating companies;
- Manufacture and sale of explosives, firearms, munitions, and fireworks (except purchase and use of explosives in industrial and mining applications), or intermediate processing of explosives for such activities;
- Printing and publication of periodicals for exclusive national distribution;
- Series T shares for holding companies of agricultural, ranching, and forestry enterprises;
- Cable television operations;
- Basic telephone service;
- Freshwater and coastal fishing in national waters, excluding aquaculture;
- Port authority administration;
- Piloting in domestic waters;
- Domestic shipping (except tourist cruise operations, dredging, and naval services involving construction, conservation, and port operations);
- Ancillary railway services, such as passenger services, maintenance and rehabilitation of rail systems, loading and unloading services, engine and car repairs, trading and making up of trains, operation of terminals, and operations communications;
- Supply of fuel and oil for maritime, air, and rail transport.

Mining activity, which made up a large portion of the previous restricted list is conspicuous by its absence in the new law, leaving it open to foreign investment. Of particular interest in implementing the opening of the mining sector is the allowance for the use of explosives in such activity. Previous activity had been delayed because foreigners were prohibited from acquiring and using explosives without special permission from the Mexican army, which had been uncooperative in approving applications.

Although the law specifies that limitations cannot

be generally modified through the use of vehicles designed to evade restrictions, it establishes procedures for doing so through the use of authorized neutral trusts (Title Five). It is also worth noting that under the terms of NAFTA, most financial firms listed in the restricted list will be eligible by the year 2000 to have up to 100 percent foreign ownership without limitation on domestic market share. The anticipated trend is that non-NAFTA nations will be accorded foreign participation privileges comparable to those extended under NAFTA after the NAFTA provisions are implemented for its signatories.

Activities eligible for 100 percent foreign ownership with FIC approval (Article Eight) include:

- Services that are ancillary to domestic maritime operations, such as towing, lighterage, and mooring;
- Transoceanic (international) shipping operations;
- Air terminal administration;
- Private education activities (preschool through high school);
- Legal services;
- Credit information services;
- Securities rating services;
- Insurance agents;
- Cellular telephone services;
- Petroleum and byproduct pipeline construction;
- Petroleum drilling.

This new list is considerably shorter than the old list, although several activities previously eligible for as much as 100 percent foreign participation with approval have apparently been shifted to the 49 percent participation list. Nevertheless, the restricted areas are much more specific and narrow than was the case under previous rules, and several new areas have been opened up as well. For instance, earlier restrictions effectively limited insurance activity to national firms and individuals. Foreigners are now explicitly allowed to operate in the insurance business in Mexico (provided, of course, that they pass professional qualifications tests—which no longer specify that they must be nationals). A variety of services, including industrial services involving the previously tightly closed petroleum sector, have also been opened up via the new law.

Under Article Nine of the new foreign investment law, prior FIC approval is required for a total foreign investment of greater than 49 percent in the stock of a Mexican firm. However, the law specifies that this will apply only to cases in which the total assets of the Mexican company exceed a limit that is set administratively by the FIC. Thus, portfolio investment and acquisition through market tender are made potentially somewhat uncertain—either easier or more difficult according to the shifting policy position of the government. Most observers see the policy as limiting foreign ownership only in cases of particularly large firms of national significance rather than as a means of effectively restricting foreign stock ownership across the board.

The 1993 foreign investment law provides that business activities involving the international ground transport of passengers, tourists, and freight inside Mexico, administrative services related to trucking, and ancillary services, which are currently reserved for Mexican nationals, will be opened to foreign participation of up to 49 percent as of December 1995, 51 percent as of January 2110, and 100 percent as of January 2004, without prior FIC approval. As of the date the 1993 foreign investment law goes into effect (January 1, 1994), foreign firms can acquire without prior approval up to 49 percent of national firms involved in the manufacture and assembly of automotive parts, equipment, and accessories. This authorization expands to up to 100 percent ownership of such firms in January 1999. Videotext and telephone switching activities can be entered by foreigners on a 49 percent basis immediately, with the authorization rising to 100 percent as of July 1995.

Specific prior FIC approval is required for more than 49 percent foreign participation in building, construction, and installation services; construction of pipelines and transport of petroleum products and derivatives; and the drilling of oil or gas wells. General construction activities can be 100 percent foreign-owned after January 1999, although majority ownership of petroleum-related construction activities will continue to require authorization. However, participation below 49 percent does not require such authorization.

Temporary and Other Special Arrangement Foreign Investments Foreigners have long been allowed to invest in some activities reserved for Mexican nationals or to exceed the percent of ownership limits prescribed for them through the use of trusts (*fideicomisos*). For instance, in the 1980s foreigners were allowed to purchase proxy holdings with a limited duration of 20 years by capitalizing an existing foreign currency liability or by making a fresh cash investment in a company that needed it to remain viable. Such an entity had to demonstrate that it was unable to find national investors and that current shareholders had waived their preferential rights to acquire such ownership before foreign investment was allowed. Specific activities eligible for this kind of investment included: gas distribution; air and maritime transport; some mining activities; secondary petrochemicals production; automotive parts manufacturing; certain aspects of fishing; telecommunications; leasing; insurance; river, lake, and harbor transport; and explosives and firearms production—all activities that were otherwise off-limits to foreigners. These emergency provisions have largely been superseded by more recent liberalization rules that allow greater general foreign access in most of these areas. Moreover, the urgent nature of the need for such exemptions has also receded.

Although generally allowed to own real estate directly in most of Mexico (within the limits imposed on all owners, whether national and foreign, with respect to the amount of allowable ownership according to the type of land held), foreign investors have been limited in their ability to own Mexican property located within 100 km (62 miles) of a border or 50 km (31 miles) of the coast. Under the liberalized 1993 foreign investment law, foreign investors are now allowed to hold such real estate directly for industrial or touristic purposes within these so-called restricted zones. Previously, foreigners could only hold such property through a 30-year bank trust, renewable for a maximum term of 30 years.

Foreign ownership or control over residential real estate in the restricted zones, which was completely barred, is now allowed for individuals and corporations through 50-year investment trusts. Such trusts are eligible to be renegotiated and renewed indefinitely on a case-by-case basis. Outright purchases must be registered with the Secretariat of Foreign Relations (*Secretaría de Relaciones Exteriores*, or SRE), which must officially acknowledge or challenge the purchase within 15 business days. The SRE must also approve residential trusts within 30 business days. In either case, failure by the SRE to act within the stipulated periods constitutes approval. The new regulations specifically allow the SRE to audit, intervene, and cancel authorization for such trust holdings at any time. Subsequent beneficial transfers do not require government approval, although trust assets can only be disposed of to a Mexican national or entity entitled to own such real estate. Trusts are administered by a Mexican bank, which holds actual title to residential land.

Similarly, the government has authorized the issue of "N" (Neutral) shares by Mexican corporations, allowing foreigners to purchase holdings in Mexican firms that would otherwise be unavailable for foreign ownership. These neutral holdings represent either a portion of ownership greater than would otherwise be allowed (usually more than 49 percent of equity), or proxy ownership in companies in which foreign ownership is barred due to the nature of the activities of the firm. Such N shares represent a specially issued class of shares that are held in trust by a brokerage house. Investors receive all the economic rights of ownership—proportional ownership of corporate assets and rights to earnings—but do not have the right to vote on corporate governance.

Specific classes of neutral shares include "C" shares, which allow no participation in corporate

NAFTA-SPECIFIC FOREIGN INVESTMENT PROVISIONS

The 1993 foreign investment law codifies most of the investment guarantees specified in NAFTA, making them available to all foreign investors. However, NAFTA does offer certain advantages available only to US and Canadian investors. Most involve accelerated and enhanced opportunities to operate in financial services areas for investors from these nations. NAFTA also provides for US and Canadian investors to receive market value reimbursement for any operations that are officially expropriated by Mexico and to submit claims to international arbitration, an avenue denied to most other investors, who must accept national treatment and agree to internal adjudication of claims without recourse.

NAFTA also removes performance requirements, including domestic sales requirements, export quotas, local content rules, domestic sourcing requirements, and trade balancing requirements. It deregulates technology transfers, making them a contractual issue rather than one requiring government approval. NAFTA stipulates that repatriation of capital and earnings will be freely available through market rate access to foreign exchange; this had been instituted prior to NAFTA, but the agreement further reinforces Mexico's commitment to such open-market policies. In short, many of the NAFTA provisions codify existing liberalized rules. In fact, many of the provisions of the 1993 foreign investment law, which passed after NAFTA and which applies to investors of whatever nationality, are even more liberal than those found in NAFTA.

Truckers from NAFTA countries will be allowed to cross the border and operate in Mexican border states beginning in 1997 and throughout the entire country by 2000, although they will be restricted from competing for domestic internal business. Foreign firms can own 49 percent of domestic transport companies in 1997, 51 percent in 2001, and 100 percent in 2004. They can own 100 percent of facilities in Mexico that are required to handle their own international cargoes. Also 100 percent ownership of the cargo handling facilities of outside companies is technically open to foreign investors with prior FIC approval. Foreign ships cannot serve domestic routes—although they can serve international routes—and foreign ownership of air service is limited to a 25 percent share in all NAFTA countries.

governance, and "L" shares, which allow holders to vote only on major issues, such as mergers and liquidations. An additional class of "T" shares, allows investors to hold ownership proxies in agricultural, ranching, and forestry properties and operations which would otherwise be prohibited. "N" shares are usually limited to no more than 30 percent of the total capitalization of a corporation. Under the terms of the 1993 foreign investment law, shares held as neutral investments are legally separate and are not considered to constitute foreign investments for the purpose of calculating percentage of ownership.

Foreign governments and their agencies, as well as international agencies, are barred from investing in Mexico either directly or through securities—particularly government securities—due to concerns over potential control and sovereignty issues. The neutral shares provision allows agencies such as the International Development Bank (IDB) to take a position in Mexican firms as a condition of providing them with necessary funding. The liberalized provisions extend the maximum period for holding such stakes from 10 years to 20 years.

National Registry of Foreign Investment All businesses with any foreign ownership that operate within Mexico, all foreign branch offices, all national firms with any degree of foreign ownership, and all trusts with foreign participation—that is, any entity in which a foreigner holds an equity position—must register with the National Registry of Foreign Investment (*Registro Nacional de Inversión Extranjera*) which is maintained by SECOFI. All such entities must file notice of ownership within 40 days of investment. Any change in the information submitted in the original registration application requires an update of the registration. In any case, registrations must be renewed annually. The registry is not part of the public record. Because no exchange controls exist, there is no requirement to register actual investment funds.

Foreign-invested companies that fail to register can have their authorizations withdrawn, and actions of entities which fail to register in accordance with the law are declared null. The registrar also reserves the right to levy substantial fines (calculated as a multiple of total payroll) on the entity and its officers for various classes of violation. Fines can also be assessed against persons who fraudulently obtain or aid others in obtaining for foreign interests any benefits reserved for nationals.

Other Regulatory Changes The foreign investment law allows immediate foreign investment (pending approval of implementing regulations) of from 30 to 50 percent in a variety of Mexican financial institutions. Effective January 1, 1994, revisions of the credit institutions law and the financial groups law provide for an entity known as a treaty bank—that is, a bank organized in a country with which Mexico has a treaty that allows the establishment of a foreign-owned commercial bank—to be established in Mexico. (This specifically implements the provisions of NAFTA that call for the three signatory countries to permit banking by the nationals of each in the territories of the others.) Currently, only US and Canadian banks would technically be allowed to set up such an institution in Mexico. To date, none has filed to do so, and observers expect that it will be some time before any licenses are actually issued. However, the way the Mexican law was phrased would allow other countries to negotiate similar treaty provisions to enable their home country banks to participate in a similar fashion.

The revision of the financial group law also offers the potential for a treaty bank to operate a financial group with a variety of financial institution subsidiaries. This would theoretically be of interest not only because it offers a broad-based entree into the Mexican financial market, but also because the US in particular maintains a somewhat more rigid separation between commercial banking and other forms of financial activity.

Mexico's Technology Transfer Law was superseded by the 1991 Law for Development and Protection of Industrial Property which provides broader protections and regulations. Technology transfers no longer require government approval or registration and can be freely negotiated between principals.

Services Some foreign ownership already exists in the service sector. But although foreigners can legally operate in most services, some barriers remain—such as the difficulty in obtaining visas for foreigners to engage in such businesses. Foreigners are hoping that the government will create new business visa categories and streamlined procedures that will enable foreign businesspeople to work in Mexico on an expedited basis.

Foreign attorneys are allowed to consult in Mexico, although they cannot practice Mexican law. Many foreign law firms that are interested in doing business in Mexico have formed some type of strategic alliance with Mexican law firms. Accounting and consulting firms in Mexico are often foreign-owned or affiliated. Financial services have been opened up, with initial stakes of up to 30 percent allowed under the new regulations, although many foreign financial institutions have expressed doubts about taking a minority ownership position. However, the allowable ownership position under NAFTA rises in most cases to 100 percent during a phase-in period that will culminate in the year 2000. Foreign brokerages are in the process of opening representative offices, and the authorizations—although in most cases not the mechanisms—are in place for additional foreign investment and operation. For instance, foreign insurance firms can now legally own up to 49 percent of

Mexican operations, although as of early 1994 no authorizations had been received for more than a 30 percent stake. Data processing services are mostly delivered through the personnel of foreign manufacturers.

The new 1993 foreign investment law provides for a gradual easing of limits on foreign investment in transport-related activities, although the implementing regulations have yet to be determined. As a preliminary, restrictive limits to new domestic competition have been reduced or abolished.

Some foreign presence has been established in the retail and wholesale areas, mostly through either small individual operations or joint ventures between large Mexican and foreign firms, primarily in the US. Foreign tourism investment has been growing for some years, and development of facilities and management is being encouraged.

Foreign participation has opened up in mining, agriculture, ranching, forestry, and aquaculture—all areas that had been heavily restricted or banned previously.

INVESTMENT INCENTIVES

Mexico offers relatively few investment incentives. Investment policy is based on the concept of national treatment for all investors, that is, treatment that is technically no different for foreigners than it is for nationals. In practice, incentives are almost never extended to primarily foreign-owned firms. Moreover, in the 1980s, the few incentives that had been established were largely dumped because they were considered too expensive. There are no tax concessions or treaties that provide favorable treatment for foreign firms that establish offshore operations located in Mexico, and as a consequence, Mexico has not become a center for offshore operations. In general, Mexico has done little to attract investment through the use of incentives.

Tax Incentives In an effort to encourage the decentralization of industrial development, marginal federal tax incentives exist for establishing new industrial plant outside the already heavily industrialized zones of Mexico City, Guadalajara, and Monterrey. No general personal or corporate tax investment incentives are available. Limited accelerated depreciation is available for some plant modernization expenditures. Some state governments have periodically offered incentive packages to attract new industry. These have consisted mainly of reduced property taxes. (There are no state or local income taxes.)

Mexico does offer some general industry-based tax incentives. Publishing is generally eligible for a 50 percent income tax reduction. Publishers that are no more than 40 percent foreign-owned and that plow their profits back into operations can receive a 100 percent waiver of taxes owed. Manufacturing firms are eligible for an exemption from value-added taxes (VAT) for imported inputs normally paid for through reinvestment of profits. Enterprises operating in agriculture, ranching, forestry, and fishing are eligible for a 50 percent tax reduction if they qualify as small private entities (this status, in effect, applies only to nationals). Corporate, commercial producers engaged in these activities can be eligible for a 25 percent reduction, which could have an effect on foreign investors. Low-income rental housing construction remains technically eligible for tax breaks, although this 1987 program has been suspended indefinitely.

Non-Tax Incentives The major non-tax incentives involve investments in tourism and pollution. FONATUR, the government tourism agency, develops and sells rights to approved tourist location facilities at subsidized rates. The agency also provides consulting support. Foreigners are allowed to own and develop tourist properties.

Accelerated depreciation—of up to 35 percent per year—is available for investments in approved pollution control equipment.

Some state governments have on occasion offered land for industrial development at reduced rates to attract investors.

The *Maquila* Program Some, including some within the government, consider the entire in-bond processing program to be an investment incentive. At a time when foreign investment was generally discouraged, *maquilas* were not only allowed to operate, but could also be 100 percent foreign-owned. Under the program, components could be imported duty-free, assembled or processed in Mexico, and reexported. The US—the primary target market for such goods—has usually levied import duties only on the added value of the reexport. Following a period during which such operations could only be located near the US-Mexican border, *maquilas* can now be operated nationwide. Mexican suppliers to *maquilas* have been considered to be exporters and are thus relieved of paying value-added tax (VAT) on their inputs. As import duties are reduced under the terms of NAFTA, the *maquila* advantage will become less pronounced, and this category of operations is expected to lose its favored status. (*See* the *Maquiladoras* section of this chapter).

In addition the states of Baja California Norte and Baja California Sur and parts of the state of Sonora have declared duty-free zones where goods can be imported, moved within the zone, and utilized, as long as they are not exported to other locations in Mexico.

Debt-Equity Swaps Although not currently operative, Mexico has had a formal debt swap program that allowed foreign investors to purchase external Mexican government debt denominated in dollars at a discount, deliver it to the Secretariat of Finance

(*Hacienda*) for cancellation, and receive pesos equivalent to a predetermined portion of the face value for approved fixed asset investments in Mexico. This mechanism, the descendent of previous debt-swap programs, was established as part of the 1990 foreign debt renegotiation. Using this procedure, Mexico has been able to reduce its external debt to some extent and to induce some additional foreign investment at a relatively low cost. Meanwhile, foreign investors have been able to receive some discounted funds and sometimes apparently gain approval for projects that might have faced greater hurdles had they not been financed through the debt-swap program (although the FIC has hotly denied that debt-swap funded projects receive any special considerations). Some foreign banks have also been able to use the sale of such debt held in their portfolios as an exit mechanism.

Under the program, interested firms had to submit bids for a quota of the amount of debt to be authorized for exchange. Minimum bid levels were specified—for instance, bids had to be at least 65 percent of face value on par bonds and new money bonds—but these minimums were below the market value of debt, enabling investors to arbitrage their investments. The government accepted the most favorable bids, authorizing the investors to acquire the bonds in question (which generally cannot be held except by financial institutions). Peso accounts were established, from which investors could draw to fund their investments.

Although the program has run its course and the more open investment and financing climate makes it less necessary, the debt-equity swap program or a similar scheme could be revived if future conditions were to make it attractive again.

AVAILABILITY OF LOANS AND CREDIT

Foreigners are allowed to borrow in both US dollars and pesos from domestic financial institutions, and they often are in a position to get somewhat better terms than domestic firms. However, credit has been scarce, and such borrowing has been extremely expensive—far more so than in US and other international markets. Foreigners have also been discouraged from offering debt or equity securities in Mexico. Although no laws or regulations ban foreign entities from issuing securities in Mexico, the country has given preferential access to limited national investment capital only to domestic firms, fearing that stronger external firms would soak up a disproportionate amount of this scarce resource. (Refer to the "Financial Institutions" chapter.)

REAL ESTATE PRICES IN MEXICO

During the first quarter of 1994, rental rates in desirable urban areas of Mexico City were reported to be running around US$41 per square meter. This reflects a slight decrease in rental costs due to lower inflation and interest rates, greater availability of capital—especially from foreign sources—and overcapacity (although locals argue that overcapacity has been greatly overstated and that little excess space actually exists). Nevertheless, the supply of high-end locations and properties is finite, and construction and replacement costs continue to rise. In recent years, construction costs in downtown Mexico City have surged from around US$150 per square meter to up to US$600. Some observers argue that these costs could go to US$2,500 to US$3,000 per square meter for upper-end buildings in the not-too-distant future. Many firms are already finding that their Mexico City realty costs can approach those in such high-cost venues as Hong Kong.

These high costs are yet another reason to decentralize operations away from Mexico City. Property costs considerably less in secondary centers and less developed areas. However, outside the capital there is less availability, and construction from scratch can be an expensive proposition, especially where there may be a dearth of builders experienced in up-to-date construction. Many foreign operations are trying to hold down their real estate costs by shifting back-office and other non-essential operations out of core, high-cost areas.

Observers note that foreigners often get taken by failing to do their homework and by not retaining a broker versed in local ways. There is no developed arm's-length real property market, and special features, services, and terms make it difficult to directly compare the effective rates on specific properties; therefore local brokers are far better equipped to cut favorable deals than are outsiders. Foreigners should also be aware of the frequent need to pay what is known as a *guante*—an extra or "charity" payment—to a previous tenant or owner to secure the space. For instance, the *guante* to obtain high-end Mexico City retail space was reportedly running around US$525 per square meter or a flat fee of between US$10,000 and US$12,000 (a bargain for anything larger than a few square meters) during the first quarter of 1994.

REAL ESTATE—COMMERCIAL AND INDUSTRIAL SPACE*

Foreign business firms locating in Mexico should be prepared to assemble an effective team of consultants capable of creating a workable business plan, identify an appropriate site, design and construct the required facility, and prepare a plan for operations.

The "Mexico Team" should involve input from an accountant with knowledge of both home country and Mexican tax law, assistance from one of the many excellent Mexican law firms with expertise in areas spanning immigration, corporate formation, tax, and real estate, and most important for the initial stages, a foreign-based brokerage and real estate service firm with on-the-ground experience and ability to either provide or arrange for the multiple services required to get a business operating in Mexico.

The services of these brokers can range from providing all of the required pre-planning information and analysis to assisting with post-construction operational issues. It is critical to choose a broker with enough in-house capabilities, or which has aligned itself with sufficient professional expertise so that day-to-day professional monitoring of all the planning disciplines can be achieved. Several excellent and well known foreign-based brokerage companies are filling this role in Mexico.

However, a real estate "market" as such has never existed in Mexico as in the US, nor has there been to date a complete database on real estate opportunities in Mexico. Therefore, it is all the more important to select a broker who can provide or arrange (under his own supervision) the numerous professional services that will be required to select a site and complete a facility. In particular, these "consultants" should demonstrate a working knowledge of all of the major and lesser markets in Mexico so that the prospective foreign business can pinpoint the appropriate location based on distribution, labor, and marketing factors.

Site Selection In many regards, site selection in Mexico is substantially similar to the same process elsewhere. There are, however, certain critical differences: foreign firms expanding in Mexico should have available to them the services of an industrial specialist with in-depth knowledge of the relevant markets and with general contractors, architects, engineers, and soil and environmental consultants. There are excellent Mexican professionals in all these areas, and the industrial specialist can play a key role in coordinating the work of the various disciplines to assure that the client's requirements are properly translated, communicated, and implemented in the final product. Where technology gaps

exist, the industrial specialist can coordinate with required foreign professionals.

As noted above, another critical difference is that unlike other countries where brokers maintain detailed and widespread data, market information in Mexico is more limited. Each consulting group gathers much of its own market data on a proprietary basis. Foreign users should also recognize that a multiple listing service or its equivalent does not yet exist in Mexico. Consequently, a foreign firm seeking core brokerage services from one broker may be introduced only to properties which represent a potential commission to that particular broker. Such an approach may not provide the foreign user with a full understanding of the options offered by the marketplace.

Industrial Sites Users seeking to expand or relocate in Mexico should also be aware of fundamental differences between foreign and Mexican markets for industrial sites. For instance, unlike various regions in the United States, the market for single user facilities in Mexico is thin at best. This is due, in part, to the general absence of speculative development in Mexico, reflecting the fact that construction and permanent financing as known abroad has not historically existed in Mexico. The banking industry has traditionally stayed away from real estate based lending, and the government has shown little interest in promoting a real estate finance industry. Thus, developers in Mexico have typically developed with their own cash and have raised additional funds necessary by sales or by forming condominiums, especially for office projects. Accordingly, to date, foreign corporations that have established manufacturing, warehousing, or distribution facilities in Mexico have largely relied on internal financing. As discussed below, however, third party financing sources are expected to emerge over time.

Key to the site selection process in Mexico will be a careful consideration given to the underlying entitlements, and equally important, the availability of infrastructure and utilities. Paying a premium for the inherent assurances provided by a well established industrial park, with guarantees of utilities, access to labor pools, and transportation, is not a mistake.

The phaseout of pre-NAFTA local content requirements and restrictions on the *maquiladora* industry in Mexico should result in increased border zone industrial activity. Furthermore, there should be additional development in the centrally located Bajío region of Mexico due to a migration of industrial facilities from Mexico City where developable sites with complete infrastructure can fetch from US$12 to US$20 per square foot and where polluting industries are

*This material on real estate is excerpted from "Doing Business in Mexico: A Primer" by Dana I. Schiffman and R. Michael Joyce, supplement to both the Los Angeles Business Journal and Orange County Business Journal. Reprinted with permission of the Los Angeles Business Journal. Copyright © 1994 the Los Angeles Business Journal.

being "forced" by local government to relocate. A further consideration for the foreign executive will be a location that can provide a springboard for trade with rapidly developing South American economies.

The user will need to consider many fundamental issues in deciding whether to lease or own and finance its facility. In some locations, such as the state-owned industrial parks more commonly found in the interior of Mexico, the decision will be simplified by the fact that industrial sites can only be purchased and not leased. Where leases are feasible, the lease can either be structured as a ground lease with the tenant arranging for the construction and most likely financing of its own facility or a build-to-suit lease.

Fee Ownership Under Mexico's Foreign Investment Law of 1993 ("New Foreign Investment Law"), fee ownership of Mexican land by foreigners has been greatly simplified. Mexican corporations which are wholly or partially owned by foreigners can now acquire title in fee simple anywhere in Mexico, including the "Restricted Zones," that is, areas within 100 km of Mexico's international borders and 50 km from any coast.

Although foreign individuals and business entities which are not Mexican corporations are still barred from fee ownership in the Restricted Zones, the benefits of fee ownership can nevertheless be obtained through the use of a renewable 50-year land trust arrangement known as *fideicomiso*.

Under a *fideicomiso*, a Mexican bank serves as the trustee and acquires fiduciary title to the property. The foreign investor is the beneficiary of the trust and has the exclusive right to use, control, and enjoy the benefits of the property during the term of the trust, including the right to all proceeds from any sale of the property. The New Foreign Investment Law also offers streamlined procedures for securing required permits.

Leasing Property While the general principles of leasing are much the same in Mexico as elsewhere, there are many issues, variations, and subtleties with which prudent foreign landlords and tenants should be familiar.

Mexico utilizes a civil code legal system, in which all laws are drafted and codified by legislative bodies, rather than a common law system, in which judge-made law complements statutory law. Under Mexican law, a lease of real property is considered a civil act and is therefore governed and regulated by the Civil Code of each state or the Federal District of the Republic of Mexico.

Unlike the United States, in which two states may regulate an activity quite differently, all of the Mexican states have patterned their civil codes on the Civil Code of the Federal District (Mexico City) and are therefore quite similar. While no civil codes regulate leases per se, they do recognize and uphold the legal principle that parties to an agreement may bind themselves as they like so long as such agreement does not compromise the public interest or the rights of third parties. The Mexican Civil Codes are also distinctly pro-tenant in many important respects.

The Mexican Civil Codes provide maximum terms for various leases depending on the contemplated use of the property, that is residential (10 years) and commercial and industrial (20 years); however, parties may add stipulations and lease extension options to provide for longer overall tenancies.

Lease Differences Mexican leases rarely contain rights and remedies provisions that match the coverage of their foreign counterparts. For example, landlords may have trouble evicting tenants because Mexican law does not provide summary remedies for landlords to secure possession of leased premises from defaulting tenants. One of the major tasks of home country counsel will be to work with Mexican lawyers in an effort to achieve a set of workable and understandable remedies that both parties to the lease can rely on in the event of defaults or disputes. Most Mexican Civil Codes also grant tenants a right of first refusal to either purchase the leased premises or to enter into a new lease if certain conditions are met, that is the tenant is current in its lease payments, the tenant has made significant improvements and has leased the premises for more than five years. A waiver of these provisions should be anticipated by foreign tenants under a Mexican lease.

Although the Mexican government has been enormously successful in slowing the inflation of the peso, many foreigners (and many Mexicans as well) prefer the security of rent streams or revenues in dollars as an extra hedge against currency fluctuation. However, many states deem foreign currency exchange in domestic transactions to be contrary to the public interest and consequently prohibit the payment of rent in foreign currency. Moreover, many civil codes make this prohibition unwaivable. When confronting such a restriction, the parties must transact in pesos, but in the lease language they can agree to peg their peso transaction amounts to the US dollar (or any other foreign currency such as the Japanese yen or the Deutsche mark). Mexican leases typically provide for rent adjustments in accordance with consumer price indexing.

The Mexican Civil Codes often include various provisions assigning rights and duties to the leasing parties in connection with maintenance, repairs, and alterations. However, all of the maintenance, repair, defect, and improvement-related provisions generally can be waived with carefully drafted language, thereby allowing a "net" lease relationship to be structured. Landlords are frequently obligated by statute to maintain the premises in the same condition throughout the term of the lease and to make all necessary repairs to that effect and are also held fully liable for all of the tenant's damages arising from any defects hidden or apparent, existing prior to the lease. Should the landlord fail to fulfill the aforementioned duties, the tenant may terminate the lease. Alternatively, the tenant may appear before a court, through an established summary procedure, to compel the landlord's compliance and recover any damages caused by the landlord's untimely repairs. Following repair by the landlord, if the tenant remains "inconvenienced" from the defects, the tenant may request a rent reduction reflecting its continued inconvenience or may terminate the lease. Landlords will often be required to compensate the tenant for improvements effected by the tenant on the premises if the landlord authorized such improvements and agreed to pay for them; the improvements are "useful" and the lease is terminated for reasons attributable to the landlord; where the lease term is undetermined, if the landlord authorized the improvements and then terminates the lease before the tenant has fully amortized the use of the improvements. Again, foreign tenants should anticipate in most cases carefully structured waivers of the foregoing tenant remedies.

Unlike in the United States, it is very uncommon in Mexico for a lease to contain "pass-through" provisions whereby the property taxes are paid by the tenant. Although it is a negotiable item, the landlord usually is responsible for all property tax payments. However, the tenant pays the Value Added Tax of 10 percent to which lease agreements are subject.

Secured Loans A full-scale real estate finance industry in Mexico for the numerous build-to-suits that will be required by foreign manufacturers seeking to establish facilities in Mexico may take some time to emerge. Conventional construction and permanent financing for Mexican real estate to date has been practically non-existent. In years to come real estate finance in Mexico will be truly a pioneer area and a traditional US-type finance industry may well require additional changes to statutory law to accommodate traditional lender concerns. The following discussion highlights some of the issues and structures that should be considered in creating a security interest in Mexican real property under today's laws.

The legal aspects of real property secured financing are largely governed by the individual 3l Mexican state laws and the laws of the Federal District. Recourse liability is the rule, with no "security first" or anti-deficiency rules. Similarly, there are no usury limits applicable to commercial loans in Mexico. Due on sale provisions are enforceable and prepayment penalties can also be structured to ensure enforceability.

Because there will always be a certain amount of uncertainty for a foreign-based lender in connection with a Mexican real estate loan, a foreign lender and its home country counsel will generally try to structure loans to foreign-based borrowers in Mexico based upon foreign loan documents, governed by the applicable foreign law. However, the lender would still have to determine whether or not a security interest in Mexican real estate will also be used to buttress the lender's position in the event of a default, and in that event Mexican real property security laws will apply.

Historically, financings on Mexican real property have taken the form of a "straight" mortgage; a mortgage with a foreclosure letter; or a trust or trust and pledge structure. The "straight" mortgage is not a favorite means of creating a security interest in Mexican real property. Although the Mexican mortgage creates the same type of security interest as would a deed of trust or mortgage, the problem of the Mexican mortgage is the difficulty of foreclosure. Summary procedures are allowed under Mexican law, but resolution can be frustrated by multiple appeals sought by the borrower so that the process can be strung out over a period of years. Due to the difficulty of foreclosure, Mexican lawyers have developed a number of alternative structures to ensure a more certain recovery by the lender in the event of default. The most common alternative structures involve the use of a "foreclosure letter" or a trust or trust and pledge arrangement known as a "guaranty trust." The "foreclosure letter" is not a complete mortgage substitute but rather is used in connection with the mortgage or loan agreement as a means to supplement the foreclosure procedure. The "foreclosure letter" can best be identified by foreign counsel by its similarity to a deed in lieu of foreclosure agreement.

Title Insurance Although the methods of recording and determining title to property in Mexico are very similar to those elsewhere, title insurance as it is known in the United States does not exist in Mexico. The parties to a Mexican property transaction instead normally rely upon a title opinion prepared by a Mexican attorney. Nevertheless, in anticipation that foreign investors and lenders will wish to deal with title insurance on familiar terms and may seek greater assurances than provided by a title opinion backed only by a law firm's net worth and malpractice insurance, a few title companies have begun to offer both owner's and lender's policies of title insurance on Mexican real property which are very similar in form to the policies offered in the United States. There are important price and coverage distinctions between the title insurance products offered on Mexican real property and analogous US policies of title insurance.

Transaction Costs A tax is imposed upon the transfer of any real property in Mexico, including the transfer of real property into a land trust and the transfer of a beneficial trust interest from one entity to another. After several reductions in transfer tax pursuant to national legislation, effective January l, 1994 the federal transfer tax may be no more than 2 percent of the appraised value of the real estate.

Role of Notaries A final item of note is the role of notary publics in Mexican real estate transactions. In Mexico the notary not only authenticates the signature of the person signing the documents, but also drafts documents to make sure that taxes are collected, verifies the facts in the notarized documents, and records them in the public record. The notary charges a fee for the purpose of recording real estate documents, usually equal to 1 to 2 percent of the value of the real estate. In addition, there is a registration fee paid to the real estate registrar. Although it varies from city to city and is generally in the range of 0.001 percent of the purchase price, in some states the registration fee is substantial.

MAQUILADORAS*

Maquiladora *Industry Background*

During World War II the US and Mexico signed a labor agreement that sent thousands of Mexican laborers north to work over the next decades. The so-called Bracero Program (from the Spanish word *brazo*, or arm) initially filled jobs left vacant in the US by the war. The program survived after the war because both US agribusiness and the Mexican government had a vested interest in it—the former to keep labor costs down, the latter because Mexico had no jobs to offer.

During this time, the Mexican population expanded, but industry did not. In many ways, the Mexican border region had closer ties to the US than to Mexico. Goods and services were easier to acquire from the US than from Mexican suppliers far to the south, given poor communication and transportation infrastructures.

In 1964 the Bracero Program was canceled, making Mexico's need for border development critical. There had been northern border "free trade zones" since the 1930s, primarily established to supplement insufficient supplies sent north by manufacturers in central Mexico. Recognizing the potential in the then-emerging oriental concept of production sharing, Mexico adopted free zone elements in 1963, creating the *maquiladora*, its own version of production sharing.

The first appearance of the *maquiladora* export industry was a part of the "National Program of Unemployment Abatement in the North." The idea behind it was to attract US companies that could profit from the combination of Mexico's low labor costs

and the proximity of the US. The program allowed 100 percent foreign ownership of companies producing entirely for export, then a privilege not readily available in other sectors of the Mexican economy. It also offered duty-free temporary import of machinery, equipment, and materials needed for the production process. These imports were subject to the posting of a bond as guarantee to later reexport.

Then US tariff sections 806.30 and 807.00 (today: 9802.00.60 and 9802.00.80) allowed return of "fabricated" metal products and reimport of assembled products, respectively, to the US. Under these tariff sections, duty was paid only on the foreign value added.

The combination of Mexican temporary import provisions and US special duty provisions combined into an attractive package when added to low Mexican labor costs.

The heart of the *maquiladora* system is still temporary guaranteed (in-bond or otherwise) import for assembly and reexport. But the industry has matured and increased in sophistication over its 30 years of operation. Beginning in the 1980s, soaring labor costs and dwindling labor pools in developed nations further stimulated the program. With the increasing integration of the world economy and the proximity to the lucrative US market, manufacturers from not only the US, but also from the Pacific Rim and Europe, have discovered the exciting possibilities of Mexico's *maquiladora* program.

The law defines a *maquiladora* as "the enterprise, individual or corporate, for which a *maquiladora* operation program is approved, and which exports its production." This is a deceptively simple statement.

What makes a company a *maquiladora* is the *maquila* program. The *maquila* program allows the duty-free temporary import of materials for the production process. Typically a *maquila* program provides that all production will be exported, either directly or indirectly, through sale to another *maquiladora* or exporter. The type of production may be simple assembly of temporarily imported parts, processing of temporarily imported materials, start-to-finish manufacture of a product using materials from various countries (including Mexico), or any other conceivable combination of the various production phases.

However, there are also subjective definitions of what a *maquiladora* is, depending on the interests involved. For example, to Mexican policymakers a *maquiladora* is a launch pad for domestic industrial development and an important source of foreign (hard) currency, jobs, technology, and training. For a community where a *maquiladora* is established, it

---

*This material on the maquiladora industry is taken from "Maquiladora Industry Framework" and "The Maquiladora Decree," by Manuel F. Pasero, managing partner of Pasero, Martín-Sánchez y Sánchez, a Tijuana-based business-oriented law firm. Reprinted by permission of the author. Copyright © 1994 Manuel F. Pasero.

CHANGES IN THE
MAQUILADORA DECREE

The main changes of the *Maquiladora* Decree deal with sales into Mexico by in-bond manufacturing corporations and with the assimilation of the operations of corporations operating under the Program for Temporary Importations to Manufacture Exportation Products (PITEX).

With respect to sales into Mexico, the schedule provided by the North American Free Trade Agreement (NAFTA) for sales into Mexico is incorporated in the Decree. Such percentages will be based on the prior year's production.

Year	Percentage
1994	55
1995	60
1996	65
1997	70
1998	75
1999	80
2000	85
2001	100

means employment, economic stimulation, and changes in culture and lifestyle. For investors, it initially represents a survival strategy in a competitive world; when it succeeds, it creates new perceptions about management, production and business cultures in general. In short, the *maquiladora* is a reflection of our increasingly interdependent world. It is a crossroads where cultural, economic, and political differences meet and must be resolved.

The Maquiladora *Industry Today*

Some 30 years ago, northern Mexico was mostly ranching and farming country. During this brief time, the region has seen the development of a large blue-collar population develop and the emergence of an industrial work ethic. This, of course, is due largely to the *maquiladora* industry.

At the beginning of 1990, statistics showed about 1,700 *maquiladora* plants in Mexico, directly employing more than 430,000 workers. An estimated one out of every six Mexican workers in the US-Mexican border region was directly or indirectly dependent on the *maquiladora* industry. Growing at an average rate of around 20 percent per year, the *maquiladora* industry is Mexico's second most important source of foreign currency, after oil products.

The industry's impact on the US is also impres-

sive. A Pan-American University study estimates that 10,000 US border jobs in Texas resulted from *maquiladora* industry development in 1986. The estimated payroll for these jobs ranged between US$80 and US$100 million. A Ciudad Juárez study showed that in 1987, some 20,743 US companies in 1,200 US cities manufactured parts sent to Mexico for processing of some kind.

Local monetary impact was considerable. The study found some US$9.6 million flowing through El Paso banks due to Juárez manufacturing, with US$15.4 million directly entering El Paso's economy through leases, mortgage, and other real estate-related payments to pay for US *maquiladora* support facilities.

Recent economic studies for San Diego found that imports to the *maquiladora* industry flowing through San Diego in 1987 exceeded US$900 million dollars. About 15 percent of the manufacturers responding to surveys reported a connection to the industry, noting that 12 percent of their total employment is due to the *maquiladoras*. Sixty-one percent of San Diego professional firms responding said they were involved in the industry, reporting 14 percent of their total employees to be in *maquiladora*-related jobs.

Studies in Arizona show that in 1986, US$110,814,300 (20.8 percent) of Sonora *maquiladora* supply spending went directly into Arizona. Arizona US Representative Jim Kolbe, speaking of a joint analysis done by the US Department of Labor and the Wharton Institute in 1988, noted that the *maquila* industry not only preserves US jobs but also creates new US jobs.

Evidence of the program's mutual benefits to both sides of the border, and beyond, continues to mount. Once an industry engaged in simple assembly, today it has expanded to include all kinds of industrial processes. Amendments to the *maquiladora* legal framework recently adopted by Mexico further open opportunities for *maquiladoras*, promising continued success for the program.

Types of Maquiladora *Operation*

There are three general approaches to *maquiladora* operation in Mexico. Depending on its experience with offshore production sharing and its size and resources, a company can customize one or a combination of these designs to fit its specific circumstances.

Subcontracting Subcontracting works well for inexperienced companies that are uncertain about Mexican start-up and that use processes involving fairly simple tasks. In these cases, the foreign company contracts with a company already operating in Mexico (either foreign- or Mexican-owned) to assemble the product. The foreign company provides supplies, materials, and parts from abroad. Here the company's investment in Mexico, and its exposure to labor and tax liability, is minimal. The entire processing operation is the Mexican company's responsibility. Subcontracting prices are ordinarily based on piecework or lots.

Shelter Smaller companies and companies new to offshore production often opt for a shelter. The shelter concept divides operations in the Mexican facility between production functions and administrative functions. The shelter company typically supplies the physical plant, undertakes hiring of the work force, handles all internal administrative tasks, and deals with all governmental agencies involved. The manufacturer supplies working capital, equipment, technical know-how, testing, quality control, materials, and parts. This type of operation affords the foreign company total control over production without the aggravations of management issues in a foreign business environment. The shelter company in effect runs the plant. Shelter fees are usually based on plant size and the number of hours worked by the direct labor force.

One advantage of a shelter operation is that administration with the necessary experience and facilities is usually in place from the outset. Another advantage is that a shelter allows the foreign company to "ease into" Mexico, gaining experience it can later incorporate into running its own operations. The disadvantage is that if the shelter team fails, serious disruption on the production line may occur from issues over which the foreign company has little or no control. This can cause the foreign company considerable damage, a risk for which few options other than canceling the shelter contract may be available.

Subsidiary Sooner or later, most corporations with experience in Mexico prefer to set up a wholly owned and controlled subsidiary. This form has the obvious advantage of affording the owner complete control over all administrative and productive aspects of the operation. The foreign company can handle any problems that surface directly on the basis of both local circumstances and overall corporate strategy.

Applicable Mexican Law

The *maquiladora* program is essentially a Mexican legal concept. As such, Mexican law and policy govern it. US law does not make special provision for *maquiladoras*; even the tariff sections that have encouraged *maquiladora* growth predate the program.

The Mexican legal system differs from the US system; Mexican statutes tend to be extremely comprehensive. Matters left vague in the US which are later defined by court interpretation or the legislative process are regularly included in the underlying statute in Mexico. Executive regulations or decrees work much like US administrative regulations in describing how specific legal provisions should be implemented. However, the Mexican system traditionally has given considerable discretion to officials for interpretation of administrative provisions. This gives administrative law a more prominent place in Mexico than in the US.

Mexico, like the US, has a federal system. The following discussion concentrates on Mexican Federal Law. However, in any given location, there may be state laws as well as federal laws that affect operations. Also, interpretation of federal law by enforcement officials may vary from region to region, or even within the same state, depending on regional concerns and values.

General Law of Commercial Corporations *Maquiladoras* are, first and foremost, Mexican corporations. Therefore, they must meet requirements for incorporation as a Mexican company. They must also observe provisions that govern such matters as corporate structure, capital, and record-keeping.

Foreign Investment Law The foreign investment aspects of *maquiladoras* are regulated by the Foreign Investments Law, enacted in late 1993, which superseded the Law to Promote Mexican Investment and to Regulate Foreign Investment of 1973, and its 1989 Regulations. Aside from allowing 100 percent foreign ownership, the Foreign Investments Law deals with such matters as registrations with the National Foreign Investment Registry and acquisition of real estate by foreigners.

The *Maquiladora* Decree In December 1989 an entirely new Decree for Development and Operation of the *Maquila* Industry was put into effect, reflecting industry development and its priority position in Mexico's economic policy. The decree is the "nuts and bolts" legislation governing operation of the industry. It describes application procedures and requirements to obtain approval of a *maquila* program—the basis for the special in-bond temporary imports—and other specifics that apply only to companies with approved *maquila* programs. The decree has recently been amended to allow *maquiladoras* to sell a percentage of their production in Mexico instead of exporting it.

Labor Law Provisions Mexico's Constitution protects workers' rights as fundamental. The Federal Labor Law provides the statutory framework for observing the Constitution's commands. The Federal Labor Law is intended to regulate all aspects of labor relationships, whether individual or collective. *Maquiladora* operations are responsible for observing all relevant portions of Mexican labor law and receive no special waivers from any of its provisions.

Taxes There are several federal tax laws that apply to *maquiladoras*, the most important being the Income Tax Law and the Asset Tax Law. Although the situation is being rationalized to a greater degree, tax provisions are frequently changed, and substantial revision is given to tax laws at the end of each calendar year. Because of the changing character of Mexican tax law, only the broadest generalities can be discussed.

The Income Tax Law provides both assessment on corporate profits and employee withholding, requiring monthly payments on an estimated basis. The corporate income tax rate is 34 percent. Since the law provides deductions similar to those available under US tax laws, adjustments are available for overpayments or underpayments of these taxes. Dividend payments abroad are basically subject to income tax withholding. However, if the payer of the dividends maintains a so-called Net Fiscal Profits Account and the dividends are paid from said account, then there is no additional taxation once corporate taxes have been paid. The tax on assets (2 percent on the average value of assets) must also be paid each month on the basis of estimates, but it can be offset by income tax paid.

Mexico also has a value-added tax (VAT) which is payable at the rate of 10 percent for purchases and for definitive imports of goods or services. Since imports made by *maquiladoras* are not definitive but temporary, they are not taxable under VAT. Also, value-added tax is paid only by the end user. Via a tax accreditation procedure, all tax paid by a *maquiladora* on purchases or definitive imports of goods is subtracted from the tax paid on exports and the tax payable on sales by the *maquiladora* in Mexico. This results in the calculation of an amount due or refundable that nets out the value-added taxes on exempt transactions. Exports are not taxed under VAT, which gives most *maquiladoras* the right to a refund of all tax paid on purchases or definitive imports of goods or services. However, if the *maquiladora* makes sales in Mexico, taxes due in connection with said sales will be deducted from the refundable amount.

The Federal Tax Code governs application of specific tax laws. The Code includes the 1989 agreement with the US which promotes better enforcement and cooperation between the two countries.

Foreign Employees All foreigners hired by *maquiladoras* to work in Mexico must obtain temporary working visas (FM3). Their families must also obtain visas as dependents of the employee. This type of visa is easily obtained, is effective for six months, and may be renewed as often as necessary. The *maquiladora* company files an application showing the basis for employing the foreigner consisting of a job description together with evidence of the employee's qualifications. It must also file evidence demonstrating its corporate existence and show that the percentage of foreign employees does not exceed 10 percent of the company's total workforce. Certification that the employee has no criminal record and

a certificate of good health for the employee and his family may be required as well.

Directors entering Mexico for occasional board meetings or routine visits will be issued a special temporary visa for the specific visit.

Environmental Concerns In Baja California, all new companies must file an preventive environmental report with the State Directorate of Ecology (SDE) to set up and begin operations. The SDE will determine if an environmental impact statement is required. Most states have a similar agency, and the federal government operates the Agency for the Protection of the Environment within the Secretariat of Social Development (SEDESOL). If an environmental impact statement or specific tests are required, the company must use the services of duly authorized professionals for the preparation of the documents. Companies undertaking significant new activities such as construction or the use of a different process are also subject to this requirement. Once the SDE approves the preventive report or the environmental impact statement, the company must apply for an operating license which entails a similar type of filing.

Mexico's Environmental Law and Regulations now require observance of certain ecological technical standards for wastewater discharge, air emissions, and hazardous waste handling. Facilities near the coast are subject to additional requirements concerning ocean and estuary quality. Most Mexican states now have specific additional state environmental legislation. Companies should make sure that they meet all applicable state as well as federal requirements. Local government units can also write their own ordinances, and many municipalities are taking action on environmental issues within their areas.

Environmental quality enforcement is relatively new in Mexico. Due to severe environmental problems in Mexico City and concern about the environmental situation along the US-Mexican border, joint agreements on border environmental quality and enforcement are being taken seriously. There is an unusual degree of mutual cooperation and coordination between the US Environmental Protection Agency and SEDESOL. This cooperation includes information sharing and cross-border training inspections of personnel.

All of these factors suggest that planners should become familiar with Mexico's environmental requirements as early as a company's preoperational phase, working with the SDE and, if necessary, with SEDESOL to comply with them.

Government Agencies

United States government agencies involved in the *maquiladora* industry are the same ones involved in any import or export operation. They include primarily the Department of Commerce, the Environ-

NAFTA ON THE SHOP FLOOR*

After last year's NAFTA debate between US Vice President Al Gore and billionaire Ross Perot, Lawrence Bossidy held up a spark plug. "We make 18 million of them," the chairman and CEO of Allied Signal Inc. said. "We're going to make 25 million of them. The question is, where are we going to make them? Right now you can't sell these in Mexico, because there's a 15 percent tariff. If this NAFTA is passed, and that tariff is removed, we'll make these in Fostoria, Ohio."

That NAFTA, the North American Free Trade Agreement, went into effect on January 1. Since then, US producers have been rethinking their regional manufacturing strategies. Toymaker Lego Systems Inc., for instance, is considering expanding its Enfield, Connecticut plant in order to supply the Mexican market from there, instead of from plants in Switzerland and Denmark. And, in anticipation of NAFTA, General Motors last year announced plans to increase production of Cavaliers in the United States for the North American market, rather than in Mexico.

Then there's Ford. Consistent with NAFTA, the US automaker has begun rationalizing production in North America and increasing US and Canadian exports to Mexico. In 1994 the company will retool its Cuautitlan plant in Mexico to produce Ford Contour and Mercury Mystique models. At the same time, Ford will add a second production source for those vehicles in Mexico to serve the domestic market, while it moves production of the Thunderbird and Cougar models for the Mexican market to its assembly plant in Lorain, Ohio. Finally, Ford will export Lincoln Mark VIII luxury coupes and Ford Escorts from Michigan to Mexico.

Going for Market Proximity

Others are planning to shift production to Mexico to serve its expanding market. Last fall, Mattel Inc. revealed "likely" plans to move production from Asia to Mexico under NAFTA to take advantage of cost and marketing benefits presented by the pact. And Woods Wire Products Inc., a Cannel, Indiana-based producer of electrical devices, predicts it will increase investment in Mexico as the consumer market grows and absorbs the company's current capacity there.

William Farley, chairman and CEO of Chicago, Illinois-based apparel maker Fruit of the Loom, says companies in his industry will become "both export-oriented back to the United States (which they have been under the US 807 program eliminating tariffs on US content assembled abroad) and market-oriented towards the countries that they're serving (a new approach for many producers who have used Mexican assembly plants primarily to serve the US market)." Fruit of the Loom, which has two plants in Mexico and two in Honduras, is looking at new investment in Mexico, Central America, and the Caribbean.

Maquiladoras Transformed

Mexico's *maquiladoras* are likely to feel NAFTA's biggest impact. In seven years, they will lose their tariff advantages over other manufacturing companies in Mexico. Not only that, but those using supplies from outside of North America will begin to pay duties on them as they enter Mexico. The result will be a movement by Asian firms to North America, especially by apparel and electronics companies to Mexico, in order to supply both industry and consumers.

"The *maquiladora* stands as an anachronism in the new world of the Mexican economy," says Dr. Herbert Schuette, professor at the Babcock School of Management at Wake Forest University in Winston-Salem, North Carolina. He foresees a movement of manufacturing to the interior of Mexico as producers (including *maquiladoras*) focus on supplying the growing Mexican market; as Mexico's roads improve; and as US trucks gain access beyond Mexico's borders in six years, under NAFTA's provisions. Companies anticipating Central American accession to the agreement may even locate south of Mexico City, Schuette says, in order to serve that market. What that means for the border region, he adds, is higher wages to attract workers. Laborers finding manufacturing jobs in the interior no longer will be interested in leaving their families for work on the border.

Preparing for a Technology Infusion

But *maquiladora* operators are more optimistic. They

By Kathleen Dunnewald. Reprinted with permission from Global Production & Transportation magazine. Copyright © 1994 New Hope Communications Inc.

NAFTA ON THE SHOP FLOOR (cont'd.)

expect an infusion of US technology previously blocked by high tariffs and local sourcing restrictions. And they expect to convert their plants from assembly operations to full-blown manufacturing businesses, as the percentage of product they can sell to the Mexican market rises under NAFTA. In essence, they will convert from cost centers to profit centers.

Cameron Clark, president of consulting firm Production Sharing International Ltd., based in Southport, Connecticut, explains: "NAFTA means you can send a roll of aluminum south [to Mexico], cut it, punch it, drill it. Today you can't do that to get the advantage under 807." In the apparel industry, he says, NAFTA enables producers to have fabric cut in Mexico (previously done in the United States under the 807 program), assuming it meets NAFTA's rules of origin. (North American fabric content must be from yarn forward or fiber forward, depending on the fabric.)

Prices Down, Margins Up

NAFTA's most obvious impact is on cost: as tariffs come down, either prices will come down or profit margins will rise.

International law firm Holland & Hart, based in Denver, Colorado, reports immediate gains for several industries. Duties on about half of all US products entering Mexico ended on January 1. Among NAFTA's first beneficiaries were makers of some computer products, semiconductors, telecommunications equipment, and electronic goods. Within five years, the firm reports, 65 percent of US industrial exports to Mexico will be free of tariffs. And duties on remaining products will disappear in 10 to 15 years.

That, combined with NAFTA's elimination of performance requirements for companies that want to invest in and sell to the Mexican market, means manufacturers will be free to produce where it makes the most sense. They will no longer be hampered by local content, export, foreign exchange, and local sales limit requirements. For some, as Ford's case suggests, this translates into a regional manufacturing strategy supplanting a national strategy—an approach aligned with the single North American market and based on economies of scale.

NAFTA Unleashes Competition

"We looked at [NAFTA] much more as a marketing issue," says Nancy Young, spokeswoman for apparel maker Sara Lee, which has operations and contractors in Mexico and the Caribbean Basin. When customers like retail giant WalMart began penetrating the Mexican market, Sara Lee found itself at a disadvantage, facing tariffs averaging 17 percent. Now the company ships product from automated plants in North Carolina to Mexico, as well as from Mexican plants, such as those of Mexico's No. 2 underwear and hosiery makers, which Sara Lee acquired in December 1992. Through them, the apparel maker is broadening its Mexican product line.

NAFTA also is a marketing issue for Cummins Engine Co., which has operations in Mexico under Cummins, S.A. de C.V. The engine maker experienced the positive investment effects of free trade with Mexico's 1989 Automotive Decree; with NAFTA it will feel free trade's competitive impact. "The engine that we produce in Mexico we now have to produce at a lower cost and better quality and deliver with shorter lead times," says Steve Knaebel, president and general manager of Cummins, S.A. de C.V. "We're competing against giant people who have production levels 10 and 15 times what we have in terms of volume. We have to have as good or better quality than they are able to supply from plants outside of Mexico." "We also have to have a very strong distribution system for comparative advantage against our competitors," he adds. That, he says, requires distributor support—information, training, warranty, parts availability, and service shops to support products in the field.

Remaking Management

Knaebel says per-capita disposable income in Mexico has grown 2-1/2 times since 1987. And Woods Wire Products, which makes devices ranging from extension cords to surge suppressors and telephone accessories, has felt the results. "Already (due to the arrival of WalMart and other major chains in Mexico), we've sold more in the last month than we have in a year and a half in the Mexican market," says Tom Cook, the company's vice president of manufacturing. "Our market down there will grow tenfold in the next two years." What that will demand of his company, he says, is stronger coordination.

"Before, delivery on time was not as important. Now, when you've got a WalMart in Mexico who's used to US service in three days, and our Mexicans are saying, 'Well, we'll get it to you in a couple of weeks—plus or minus a week,' that's not good enough. So there will be a change in management philosophy as performance levels go up." Cook also expects Mexico's high distributor margins (now running 25 to 40 percent, in his experience) to come down, thanks to discount chains that won't tolerate them and manufacturers who will bypass them by supplying merchandise directly.

IPR Agreement Confers Confidence

NAFTA intellectual property rights (IPR) provisions are giving software maker Microsoft Corp. the confidence to outsource more in Mexico, should the need arise. This as Mexico's demand for technology grows with the infusion of capital and the development of the financial sector.

"Most of Mexico's intellectual property rights changes came in the 1991 IPR bill," says Jeffrey Steinhardt, Microsoft's attorney for Latin America." As Mexico's attorney general told me," he adds, "now, with NAFTA, there exists the political will to enforce IPR." NAFTA's international tribunals, Steinhardt explains, give manufacturers extra leverage to settle piracy disputes, although Steinhardt points out that, for his company, the government-to-government route is a last resort.

A Hemispheric Issue

North America is just one chapter of the integration tale. "The big story," says Wake Forest's Herb Schuette, "is the change outside of Mexico because of NAFTA. To what degree and how fast other countries line up with the terms of the agreement could shift the investment picture." Cameron Clark, of Production Sharing International, elaborates: "The tariff advantages that have existed in Central America and the Caribbean with the Caribbean Basin Initiative will be mitigated by NAFTA, creating temporary confusion on the part of investors as to whether to go there or to Mexico."

New investment may go to Mexico rather than the Caribbean, but, asked if he expects disinvestment from companies already operating in the Caribbean, Clark says not yet. "There won't be disinvestment immediately, but, if parity with NAFTA (for the Caribbean) were not to exist five or six years down the road, the answer is yes." The urgency to protect their assets in the Caribbean has apparel makers lobbying Congress for passage of a NAFTA parity bill this year, perhaps, if nothing else, one that addresses only textiles and apparel.

Internal Implications

The expectation of free trade's spread through the Americas, via NAFTA accession or bilateral free trade pacts, turns the agreement into a hemispheric issue. For companies like Fruit of the Loom, this could have internal repercussions. "In the last three years, we've set up sort of a Mexican management group that manages Mexico and reports directly to the president of Fruit of the Loom in the United States," says chairman and CEO Farley. "But it's really a very contained structure for Mexico. And I think what we're looking at is perhaps creating a new manufacturing/sourcing/marketing combination that will integrate operations and deal with this hemisphere."

mental Protection Agency, where applicable, and the Department of the Treasury. In specific instances, state or local agencies also participate, particularly in environmental areas. From the US perspective, a *maquiladora* import or export is just like any other import or export, and a *maquiladora* is just another foreign subsidiary.

In Mexico, where the physical plant is located, the situation becomes more complex. This is a Mexican company subject to Mexican corporate, environmental, tax, and other laws that govern doing business in Mexico. In addition, the entity is subject to the special provisions for *maquiladoras*.

On the federal level, the Secretariat of Foreign Relations will have to give the company initial approval to incorporate. The Secretariat of Commerce and Industrial Development (SECOFI) approves *maquila* programs and oversees compliance with them. *Maquiladoras* with foreign investment must register with the National Foreign Investment Registry, also within SECOFI's jurisdiction. The Secretariat of Finance and Public Credit is responsible for customs and also for tax issues. The Secretariat of Social Development (SEDESOL) oversees environmental issues and requires certain filings to assure that plants meet environmental standards. The Secretariat of Labor is responsible for assuring that companies follow labor requirements. The Secretariat of the Interior handles non-Mexican employee work visas. The Secretariat of Communications and Transportation deals with such questions involving approval of communications systems and trucking regulations. The Social Security Institute records all workers, requires a salary assessment for all employees, and provides employee health care.

Most of these agencies handle routine matters through regional offices strategically located around the country. In an attempt to simplify administrative procedures, some offices have been adapted to serve as clearing houses for several permits and authorizations and often handle a number of matters that formerly required separate processing.

On the state and local levels, a plant will work with the local public works agencies and with local environmental officials, if any, on construction and pollution control issues. The State Labor Board approves employee training programs and hears ordinary labor disputes. The city government (the *municipio*) approves land use. A soil use license is generally required before starting any industrial operation. Additionally, the Public Registry of Property and Commerce must record certain corporate documents such as articles of incorporation and bylaws, and property deeds. All title search tasks should be carried out through this office. Many corporate documents will need to be formally notarized by a notary public to have full legal effect.

Steps in Setting Up a Maquiladora

The bureaucratic procedures involved in establishing a *maquiladora* may seem confusing. Yet setting up a *maquiladora* is actually quite simple, with proper planning. Essentially, there are four steps: incorporating, preparing to operate, securing the *maquila* program authorization, and registering with the necessary agencies.

Incorporation A permit from the Secretariat of Foreign Relations is necessary to incorporate any company in Mexico. To obtain this permit, the secretariat only needs the proposed corporate name (preferably at least three options). The incorporators should then draft the company's articles of incorporation. Once the Secretariat of Foreign Relations gives its approval for incorporation, the articles of incorporation must be notarized. A notary public will then release a provisional charter, for purposes of registration of the company with the Federal Taxpayers Registry. Registration with the tax and customs authorities as an importer and exporter is indispensable at this time.

Preparation for Operations After incorporating, the company should find out from the local land zoning and public works authority if the site selected is suitable for the planned operation. If it is, negotiations for an option, a lease, or purchase agreements

can begin, with drafting of the needed texts. Once the location is settled, an inter-company (assembly) contract can be drawn up to cover whatever arrangement the foreign or parent company will have with the new *maquiladora* company. Such arrangements usually include technical assistance, financing, and other essential elements for the working relationship between the parties.

Application for a *Maquila* Export Program Once these preliminaries have been taken care of, a company that wants to operate as a *maquiladora* is ready to apply for the *maquila* export program approval from SECOFI. To fill out the application form properly, the applicant needs all relevant data available. The corporate information is what one might expect it to be: name and address, capital and structure, annual investment, and value of machinery to be used in the *maquila* program. The applicant must also supply product information, including description of the product and its use, with whom *maquila* contracts have been signed, export destination of the product, and whether the business involves textiles. SECOFI also requires considerable operational data: the process, value of materials (both Mexican and imported), the amount of Mexican value added, the number and types of jobs involved, and annual production capacity. On imports, SECOFI requests a list of materials to be imported, how long they will be in Mexico, quantity, and unit and total costs. It also wants the same kind of information for machinery and equipment. The applicant should also indicate which port of entry it will use.

As attachments to the application, the petitioner should provide the relevant agreements and documents, such as inter-company *maquila* (assembly) and technical assistance contract, articles of incorporation, and any required permits and authorizations. Draft agreements related to lease, purchase, or trust arrangements on facilities should also be filed. A draft format prepared for individual or collective labor agreement should be submitted as well.

SECOFI will approve the program and issue the permits for temporary imports based on these materials. SECOFI also issues the permanent *maquiladora* identification code.

Registrations SECOFI does not process all registrations, and there remain several additional required filings. The company must also register separately with the National Industry Chamber, the National Foreign Investment Registry, the National Workers Housing Fund Institute, the Social Security Institute, and the Health Department.

The company must also register with the State Directorate of Ecology and, if necessary, with SEDESOL. On the state and local levels, it must register with the Public Registry of Property and Commerce in the city where it has corporate domicile, and must obtain registrations and licenses from the municipal revenue department and other operating authorities. The company must also obtain a permit from the local public works authority covering land use and construction as well.

After completing these four steps, operations can begin. However, immediately upon start-up the company should make sure the following licenses and registrations are obtained and steps taken, if they have not already been:

- Operating license from the local authorities;
- Sanitary license from the Secretariat of Health (this license must be renewed annually);
- Secretariat of Health license if there is to be a dining room or cafeteria (to be obtained by the food service concessionaire);
- Registration with the Secretariat of Finance and Public Credit as an exporter and importer;
- Registration with the Secretariat of Planning and Budget's Department of Statistics;
- Operation permit from the SDE, together with any special permits needed for waste water discharge, hazardous materials handling, air emissions, or other environmental concerns;
- Create a formal employee training program and register it with the State Labor Authority;
- Register with the Federal Joint Safety and Health Commission;
- When applicable, get authorizations for operating mechanical energy transformers from the Secretariat of Labor; authorizations from the Secretariat of Communications and Transportation to operate communications system; and authorization to operate gas furnaces from SECOFI;
- Obtain immigration visas from the Secretariat of Interior for all foreign employees so they can work legally in Mexico; and
- File individual labor contracts and submit the internal work regulations to the State Labor Board.

Incorporation should take roughly three weeks after receipt of the Secretariat of Foreign Relations approval. The additional permits and registrations should all be issued within another 30 days. The key is proper preparation of all preliminary documents.

The Maquila *Program*

The *maquila* program entitles a company to register with the National *Maquiladora* Industry Registry and to receive the special customs treatment available for temporary in-bond imports. The company develops the program's content, within the parameters of the *Maquiladora* Decree's provisions.

The imports allowed under a *maquila* program include all inputs the plant will need for its intended

production: raw materials; parts; containers, packing materials, and labels; literature related to production; tools; equipment for production, health and safety, and pollution control; work manuals; industrial plans; computers and communication equipment; and quality control and testing equipment. The *maquiladora* may also bring in "administrative development equipment" and trailer bodies and containers.

The temporary import authorization for materials used in production or shipping is good for one year. Once any item is imported, it may remain in Mexico for one year from the import date. Machinery and equipment can remain in Mexico as long as the *maquila* program remains in effect, but trailers and containers may not remain for more than 20 years.

Maquila programs have indefinite duration with no requirement to renew or update the authorization. However, if processes change or operations expand, the program must be amended using the same procedure as for initial approval.

Following the amendments to the regulatory framework introduced as of January 1, 1994, a *maquiladora* is authorized to sell in the Mexican market part and eventually all of its production, in accordance with the schedule indicated. (*See* Changes in the *Maquiladora* Decree in this chapter.)

Finally, a *maquila* program imposes certain requirements on the *maquiladora*. The company must make every effort to create jobs, help Mexico's trade balance through net foreign currency contributions, and improve linkage with Mexican industry. As must all other Mexican manufacturing companies, a *maquiladora* should also provide employee training and technological development. Additionally, the decree expressly requires *maquiladoras* to strictly comply with environmental laws and regulations.

A *maquiladora* can manufacture, assemble, or produce all or part of; process; or rebuild any product it wishes. Only firearms, explosives, or the manufacture of articles containing radioactive material are restricted. Firearms and explosives cannot be produced without authorization from the Secretariat of Defense, and companies that use radioactive materials in their processes must get authorization from the Mexican Nuclear Regulatory Agency.

What a *maquiladora* will produce depends on parent company business considerations such as available markets and duties on imports into those markets. Additionally, NAFTA provisions may have an impact on what a company decides to produce or where it sources its parts.

Real Estate

Following the new Foreign Investments Law, in effect from January 1, 1994, Mexican companies with foreign investment may purchase and obtain direct ownership of real estate located within the so-called "restricted zone," the 50 km strip along the coast and the 100 km strip along the borders of Mexico. In those areas, foreign individuals or companies may not hold direct ownership over real estate. However, use rights are available to them through purchase of trust rights. To buy rights to a trust in the forbidden zone, foreigners need a permit from the Secretariat of Foreign Affairs.

Under a trust, a Mexican bank holds title to the real estate and acts as trustee. The foreign company has use and enjoyment of the land as beneficiary of the trust. For its services as trustee, the bank charges a fee. A trust may now have a duration of up to 50 years, which term is extendible without limitation. Other than in the forbidden zones, *maquiladoras* may directly buy real estate anywhere in Mexico. In the past, Mexican companies had to seek a permit for land purchase from the Secretariat of Foreign Relations. Today, this requirement no longer exists. However, foreign individuals must obtain authorization from both the Secretariat of Foreign Relations and the Secretariat of the Interior to buy real estate in Mexico.

A one-time title transfer tax of 2 percent of the value of the property is due upon execution of either the purchase or the trust agreement. There is also an annual property tax, but the amount is negligible and varies depending on the type of improvements made in and around the property. Leases on real estate may not have a term of more than 20 years, and no permit nor registration is required.

Before buying either land or trust rights to land, it is advisable to invest in a careful title search. There is no title insurance in Mexico, and a thorough title search performed by reputable professionals is the sole means of making sure that title is clear. It is also advisable to have an environmental analysis done for the land under consideration to ensure that it has no use history that could result in environmental liability. This is important because, once acquired, liability for hazardous waste found on the property is the responsibility of the owner or possessor.

At closing, the buyer must register the title transfer (or the trust agreement) with the Public Registry of Property.

Customs

The US may classify *maquiladora* products under any of four categories:

- The United States' Generalized System of Preferences, or GSP, applicable (if 35 percent or more of the product is found to be of Mexican content, it may enter the US duty-free);
- US tariff sections 9802.00.60 or 9802.00.40 applicable (duty will be assessed only on the value added in Mexico);
- NAFTA rules of origin applicable (if the product is deemed to be of Mexican origin, no duties will be payable); or
- Full duty applicable (US originated material is low in comparison to parts imported from countries that do not qualify for GSP treatment).

Usually, the importer will need a Certificate of Registration with US Customs on the exports to Mexico, as well as a US commercial invoice on the Mexican processing cost. It is advisable to seek the assistance of a US customs broker in determining the specific requirements for a given situation. Many *maquiladora* operations use free trade zones to further reduce duty costs in the US.

Mexican law requires that hazardous waste generated by processing temporarily imported materials be returned to the country of the materials' origin. This requirement stems from a bilateral agreement between Mexico and the US. The return of *maquiladora* hazardous waste to the US will need EPA manifests on the shipment for US Customs to accept its entry.

The *maquiladora* should obtain any necessary rulings from the US Customs authorities during pre-operational planning to avoid production transfer problems. US Customs is as important as Mexican Customs to *maquiladora* operations.

Mexican Customs requires SECOFI approval of the specific *maquila* program before it will allow the *maquiladora* duty-free temporary import of machinery, equipment, and materials for its production process.

The *maquiladora* must guarantee payment of applicable duties and fines in case it fails to observe the temporary import requirements. Once the guarantee is posted, customs will allow import of the items needed. Bonding requirements for such guarantees vary from place to place. For example, posting bond at the Baja California–California border is not the norm. However, at the Chihuahua–Texas border posting of bond is standard operating procedure. Even when the bond requirement is observed, the cost is negligible.

Import to or export from Mexico of hazardous materials requires a special manifest for hazardous materials in addition to the ordinary customs manifests. The importer or exporter must also have approval for the movement from the Secretariat of Social Development (SEDESOL).

Foreigners with proper immigration visas may bring their household items to Mexico duty-free.

Customs procedures at the border have recently undergone simplification and streamlining through adoption of a random inspection system, and additional simplification and synchronization by both countries will be implemented as NAFTA is put into place. Import documents are fed through a computer, which signals whether the shipment can go through without inspection. If the computer selects a cargo for inspection, customs officials must complete the procedure within three hours, examining only 10 percent of the freight. If the computer does not call for inspection, the customs inspector will only make sure that the proper documents are submitted. Once out of the port of entry, there is no further inspection for freight carriers.

Banking and Finance

Maquiladoras have received such favorable treatment in part due to their contribution to the economic recovery of Mexico, not only as a source of employment, but also as a source of fresh financial resources for the country.

At the time of incorporation, the company must declare its intended initial capital. Other filings during the *maquiladora* application process show the government authorities involved whether or not the project is financially feasible. The company must clearly show that it has sufficient financial support for the planned operation. There will, of course, be a reduction in initial costs, and thus in committed capital, if the company subcontracts or works through a shelter.

The company must post bonds for all of its temporary imports. The bond contract must be with a federally authorized bonding firm. The amount of the bond must be equal to the total amount of duty payable on the temporary imports because the purpose is to guarantee that if the merchandise remains in Mexico, all duty owed on it will be paid. Movement of hazardous materials or waste is also subject to bonding to pay off potential damages if an accident occurs.

If a *maquiladora* is working with a Mexican domestic company on supply development, financing for the Mexican company can come from Mexico's financial establishment. The Mexican economic development system has designed several mechanisms for financing increased Mexican access to the *maquiladora* market.

Sales to the Mexican Market

Originally, *maquiladoras* had to export all of their production. Over the years this has gradually changed, culminating with the amendments to the *Maquiladora* Decree of 1989, which came into effect on January 1, 1994. This greatly enhances access to the Mexican market for *maquiladora* production. (*See* Changes in the *Maquiladora* Decree in this chapter.)

Maquiladoras now may sell in Mexico in one of two ways. A *maquiladora* can supply other *maquiladoras*, in what is still an export operation in the eyes of the Mexican government. However, *maquiladoras* are now permitted to sell part or all of their production directly into the Mexican domestic market on a phased-in basis beginning with 55 percent of the previous year's production in 1994, rising to 100 percent of produc-

tion for the year 2000 in 2001.

All duties due in connection with the definitive import of goods which were originally imported under a temporary basis must be paid at the time of the sale in Mexico according to the tariff classification of the foreign content. The company must maintain at least a break-even foreign currency position. Also, products sold in Mexico must meet the same quality standards as those exported and meet Mexican product standards. Another consideration in the decision to enter the Mexican market is the potential income tax liability because earnings from domestic sales will be considered taxable income in Mexico.

The explosive growth of the *maquiladora* industry has created a growing market for sales to the *maquiladora* industry itself. In recent years, *maquiladoras* have incorporated specifically for indirect export; that is, they supply parts to other *maquiladoras* for use in their export products. The arrival in Mexico of *maquiladoras* from abroad who are traditional suppliers of existing *maquiladoras* reflects this trend, as does an increase in Mexican firms dedicating a part of their production to *maquiladora* supply.

Other Related Issues

Labor Normally, if a product is labor intensive, a Mexican *maquiladora* may be useful in holding or increasing a manufacturer's competitive edge. However, if the main goal is to lower labor costs, it is advisable to do a thorough cost analysis before making a decision to move the operation to Mexico. For instance, factors such as company size and production processes should be reviewed. Labor force required and programmed savings should outweigh shipping and Mexican business costs. The company should make special efforts to evaluate brokerage fees, import and export costs, along with all indirect labor costs.

The minimum wage is an insufficient guide to justify the establishment of a *maquiladora*. Companies need to consider the cost of statutory benefits such as social security, the National Worker Housing Fund, vacation premiums, length of employment premiums, and various other mandated benefit costs. Costs can also vary according to the particular labor market. Where strong competition for labor exists, increased benefits are needed to attract workers. These include bonuses for attendance and punctuality, subsidized meals, subsidized transportation, and several variations of these benefits.

The Mexican constitution guarantees many worker rights. These rights are not subject to waiver. However, the particular way in which employees exercise constitutional rights is negotiable. In some cases the authorities will recognize mutual agreements between employer and employees.

The right to unionize is a constitutional right. On

the other hand, interest in unionizing varies from region to region. The main concern in the industrial union movements has been the improvement of working conditions. Since *maquiladoras* usually provide benefits above those required by law, employee interest in organizing is minimal unless the region has a strong historical union tradition. This interest may change if personnel policies and communication with management are inadequate, leaving employees no alternative but to organize.

The tradition among *maquiladora* unions is to cooperate with management, and management assumes many labor-related chores. Unions often provide lines of communication between labor and management and participate in tasks such as hiring, benefit distribution, vacation schedules, and, of course, contract negotiation.

Markets If the US market is the primary target market, and if the parent company is European, Japanese, or otherwise distant from that market, Mexico's advantages go beyond low labor costs. However, Mexican trade relationship and the domestic market may argue for direct foreign investment rather than *maquiladora* export production. Companies should explore the options available before deciding how to set up Mexican operations.

Characteristics of Operation The size of a company, the operations it wishes to undertake in Mexico, and its previous experience with offshore production all enter into the decision on how to operate in Mexico. Discovering whether subcontracting, shelter, or subsidiary status best fits the company's goals requires careful analysis. Companies subcontracting in Mexico should take special care to select someone reliable to assure quality control. Another concern when deciding on the type of operation is the implied liability involved. Although there is widespread belief that subcontracting and shelters protect the foreign company from liability, this is true only where the subcontractor or shelter is financially secure.

If a labor dispute results in a significant award to the workers, the possibility exists that an insolvent subcontractor or shelter would be unable to pay the award. Liability would then pass to anyone who received benefit from the labor in proportion to the benefit. Basically, whoever makes the contract or uses the shelter shares liability with the direct employer for obligations to workers.

Personnel Available for Foreign Service If a company does not have top people available, it should invest in finding individuals appropriate for foreign service. Companies should support this investment by providing adequate cultural and business orientation for the Mexican operation to their expatriate personnel, and, ideally, for their families as well.

In today's internationally competitive markets, the former practice of using a Mexican operation to avoid retooling may be short sighted. State-of-the-art equipment run by trained personnel under competent management goes a long way toward assuring success for a Mexican *maquiladora*.

Location The factors to be considered in deciding whether to locate on the Mexican border or in the interior include company size, available infrastructure, the technology involved, and transportation costs.

Labor cost in the interior tends to be less than on the border. In addition, some nontraditional industrial locations offer certain advantages to companies that choose them. For example, the state of Quintana Roo offers certain tax exemptions for a period of time to companies that locate there.

Border locations experience higher turnover among employees. If investment in training is costly, the company may find Mexico's interior more attractive than the border. Since many interior locations have less competition for labor, turnover rates are lower and wages are more stable, even among skilled workers and technicians.

Quality of life is an often overlooked but significant factor in location decisions. A company should try to locate where good management people will be willing to serve.

Transportation Materials have to get from the company warehouse or supplier to the plant, and products from the plant have to get to the market. Truck transportation is the most efficient way to ship freight in Mexico. Mexican law reserves freight service to Mexican nationals. However, companies are allowed to operate their own trucking fleets to carry their own products. The only legal restriction is that it must buy its tractors in Mexico.

In hiring a trucking company, companies should carefully examine the trucker's equipment and safety record. Government regulation of trucking rates no longer exists, so companies need to compare rates. Another issue is the ability of the carrier to keep to schedules.

Communications International voice and data transmission systems are in place and operating for *maquiladoras* in border areas. Experienced international enterprises (AT&T, MCI) have entered the Mexican arena to offer international communications services. Expansion of communications infrastructure is ongoing, but the level of sophistication varies from region to region. Companies should explore the availability of the services they require in the area they are considering as a site.

Foreign Trade

Mexico is a large country endowed with a wide variety of natural resources. As a legacy of its colonial heritage, it relied for centuries on the export of raw materials and other commodity products and the import of manufactured and finished goods to sustain its economy. In the 1950s Mexico explicitly began closing its borders to most imports in order to protect import substitution production by nascent national industries. Unfortunately few of these domestic firms took advantage of this opportunity to improve their operations. Instead they relied on their closed markets to reap high margins and subsidize inefficient, low-quality production, failing to upgrade technology or—in many cases—even adequately maintain existing plant, while slipping further behind international standards and becoming less competitive. This situation also led Mexican consumers to crave foreign goods at virtually any price whenever and however they could get them, creating huge pent-up demand. At the same time, Mexico was able to avoid having to upgrade its domestic production of exports to compete in international markets because it could obtain sufficient foreign exchange through international sales of oil, further cushioning domestic producers. As an indicator of the lack of emphasis placed on export development, as late as 1988 a Mexican business source reported that only 150 domestic firms accounted for 80 percent of all exports from the country.

This cozy situation was undermined by the collapse of world oil prices in the early 1980s, leaving Mexico with reduced ability to earn foreign exchange, massive external debt to service, and nearly moribund national industries, many of them run by the state. In 1982 petroleum accounted for 78 percent of exports, with other commodities and manufactures representing the remainder. Mexico was faced with a steepening decline in the value of its primary foreign exchange earner, oil, and an uncompetitive and undeveloped position in alternative exports. Even after the initial oil and debt shock of 1982 the government attempted to maintain its import substitu-

tion-based closed economic model. However, a renewed drop in oil prices in 1985–1986 jolted the government out of any remaining hopes that it could maintain the status quo by tinkering within the framework of the existing system.

To address this dangerously out-of-balance situation the government of President de la Madrid took the desperate and courageous step of opening up the economy by lowering protective tariff and nontariff barriers. Initially this move was allowed with the idea of letting in only the capital goods needed to upgrade export-oriented industries. However, it proved to be difficult to filter out other imports, and the government ended by opening the overall system to a greater degree than had been seen in decades. This revolution took concrete shape in 1986, when Mexico joined the General Agreement on Tariffs and Trade (GATT), pledging itself to the ideal of free trade.

In 1982 virtually all imports into Mexico were limited by quotas. By 1990 only about 3 percent of all items, representing 13.8 percent of the value of all imports, were subject to quotas. As of 1982 virtually all imports also required prior licensing, a figure that fell to about 20 percent by 1990, a level which had not been seen since the mid-1950s. By 1993 items requiring such licenses had been reduced to 30, down from 12,000. Remaining prior import licensing is scheduled to be phased out completely under the terms of the North American Free Trade Agreement (NAFTA).

Tariff barriers have also been reduced radically. In 1987 the tariff system was restructured and simplified, reducing the number of tariff categories from 16 to five. During the early 1980s maximum tariff rates were 100 percent. Beginning in 1986, when Mexico joined GATT, these fell sharply to 45 percent over roughly a six-month period and were down to 20 percent by the beginning of 1988. Average tariffs have always been much lower than the maximum, tending to fluctuate in the 15 to 30 percent range from 1982 (when the average was 27.7 percent) through

NAFTA: IMPLICATIONS FOR TRADE

NAFTA is first and foremost a trade agreement. As such it is designed to open up trade among the signatory nations: the United States, Canada, and Mexico. Under the terms of the agreement, all tariffs on eligible goods are to be eliminated no later than 15 years after the effective date of January 1, 1994. As of January 1994 about half of all US goods will be able to enter Mexico on a duty-free basis. As of the end of 1993, prior to implementation of NAFTA, average Mexican duties on US goods were in the neighborhood of 10 percent, while US duties on Mexican goods averaged 3 percent.

With regard to specific key sectors, certain agricultural items will remain subject to Mexican tariffs for up to 15 years, although duties on 94 percent of all such trade will be eliminated within the first 10 years in which the treaty is in force. Mexican import licensing of agricultural commodities is scheduled to be phased out after 10 years, with all remaining such license requirements expiring by the end of 15 years. Mexico retains the right to restrict the import of certain agricultural products by using tariff-linked quotas to protect its national producers against international commodities price instability.

Mexico has agreed to phase out its duties on auto and auto parts imports over a 10 year period. NAFTA requires Mexico to remove limits on foreign (non-Mexican) auto sales in its domestic market, although under the terms of the agreement origin rules require a minimum of 62.5 percent of the total content to be North American to qualify for sale in the Mexican national market.

Although the Mexican energy sector remains closed to foreigners, NAFTA allows greater opportunities for US and Canadian businesses to bid on contracts to provide services and equipment to Pemex, the state oil company, and its subsidiaries and to the national electric power company, CFE. Reclassification of broad categories of petrochemicals from primary—whose production is reserved to nationals—to secondary—open to foreign participation—allows greater opportunity for trade in goods and services in this industry.

Tariffs on about 50 percent of pharmaceutical products entering Mexico will be eliminated immediately under NAFTA, with tariffs on 90 percent of all such products scheduled to be removed within 10 years. Revisions in intellectual property laws provide increased protection, specifying a minimum patent term of 20 years and allowing "pipeline" protection for drugs patented elsewhere as of July 1991. NAFTA also prohibits signatories from using compulsory national licensing requirements that serve to discriminate against foreign ethical drug products. Some US and Canadian firms remain concerned about unresolved issues involving the protections accorded to biotechnology and patentable procedural innovations.

Tariffs on many foreign telecommunications and electronic products will be eliminated immediately, with tariffs on central switching and most mobile communications equipment being phased out over five years. Foreign firms are to be given access to national networks on a nondiscriminatory basis.

In the textiles area, roughly 20 percent of foreign exports to Mexico by value will be allowed in on a duty-free basis immediately, with tariffs being removed on an additional 60 percent after six years. All duties on textiles are scheduled to be eliminated after 10 years. Rules of origin are designed to restrict entry benefits to items of North American origin.

Rules of origin restrictions are designed to limit agreement benefits to goods produced by the signatory nations. Such North American origin can be determined based on regional value content (usually a minimum of 60 percent of customs assessed value must originate within North America) or on a net cost basis (usually a minimum of 50 percent of net cost must represent North American value added). Provisions in the agreement allow for cumulative value-added origin determinations and establish specific content requirements for certain products, including autos, computers, and textiles.

Other NAFTA provisions call for the Mexican government to open up its procurement procedures so as to allow foreign firms to bid more freely on official national contracts for supplying goods and services. Open procurement is currently available only from specified Mexican agencies and is limited to contracts valued at more than US$50,000 for goods and services and US$6.5 million for construction projects. Oil industry and electric power generation monopoly projects must be valued at a minimum of US$250,000 for goods and services and US$8 million for construction projects to be eligible.

A final addition to NAFTA is the provision for a trilateral commission to adjudicate trade disputes. NAFTA calls for prompt decisions on cases, which must be ruled on within eight months from filing, and institutes mechanisms to avoid national bias. Authorized penalties include trade compensation levies against the responsible country. The commission is also empowered to deal with the issues of dumping and subsidies.

Although NAFTA forms an exclusive regional trade bloc, providing special terms that favor the national firms of the signatories with respect to those of other nations, the general impetus of Mexican trade policy calls for negotiation of bi- and multilateral trade pacts with other countries to extend the same or similar benefits on a broad basis. Canadian and US national firms may have a temporary edge due to NAFTA, but it is anticipated that firms from other countries can expect the extension of similar treatment in the not so distant future after a lag.

given by Mexican authorities. The frequency of such instances is expected to decline, and ultimately most barriers are expected to fall as a result of NAFTA. However, observers note that importing to Mexico still requires delicate negotiations largely conducted through experts rather than simply following an explicit and open cookbook procedure.

SIZE OF MEXICO'S FOREIGN TRADE

Mexico's foreign trade has grown from a relatively small US$3.7 billion in 1970—about 10 percent of its gross domestic product (GDP) in that year—to an estimated US$72.2 billion in 1993, representing about 22 percent of GDP. In 1992 Mexican trade was equal to 23.4 percent of GDP (this figure rises to approximately 33.7 percent when *maquila* exports and imports are included). This level of trade as a percent of GDP in 1992 compares with 15 percent for Brazil, 15.2 percent for Japan, 17.5 percent for the United States, 40.2 percent for China, 43.8 percent for Great Britain, 46.2 percent for France, 60 percent for Germany, and 76.9 percent for Taiwan.

This points up the fact that between three-quarters and two-thirds (depending on the measure used) of Mexico's economy remains focused on domestic markets. This emphasis is a function of two factors. First, Mexico is relatively undeveloped economically as compared to more highly developed economies such as the UK, France, and Germany, which depend on foreign trade for a much greater proportion of their overall economic activity. Second, Mexico's large and important domestic markets constitute the core of its economy, as is the case with Brazil, the US, and Japan. And, in common with China, Mexico has a large, developing domestic economy, but has recently begun to focus more of its energies on the important international trade sector.

Mexico's foreign trade grew at an average annual rate of 14.1 percent in nominal terms, or by a factor of about 20 between 1970 and 1993 from a low initial base at the beginning of the period. Between 1980 and 1993, the growth rate averaged only 5.9 percent despite Mexico's greater focus on trade, but this slower growth was largely the result of economic problems. During this period, total trade fell in four years—1982, 1983, 1985, and 1986, all of which represented periods of economic crisis in Mexico—by as much as 22 percent in 1986. During the years in which trade increased, annual growth averaged 20 percent in nominal terms, surging by as much as 52 percent in 1984. However, total trade increased by only about 2 percent (8.3 percent if *maquila* trade is included) in 1993 as the Mexican economy faltered.

The growth of total trade camouflages the important differential in the growth in its component parts.

1988. By 1990 the average was down to 13.1 percent and had fallen to 11 percent by the end of 1993. Most remaining tariffs are scheduled to fall to zero under NAFTA, although the phaseout period for duties on specific items ranges up to 15 years. As it now stands, 98 percent of imports are duty-free and require no import licenses, a remarkable change from the situation even a few years ago. Mexico also dropped its 5 percent export development tax on imports as well as its use of official pricing in calculating customs valuation.

Despite this official opening up of the economy, practical difficulties remain. Some domestic importers have reported that months after new tariffs and regulations are promulgated, customs agents still profess to have received no notification of the new arrangements and insist on either applying the old rules or holding up the shipments. And foreign importers note that the apparently idiosyncratic way in which items are actually classified and valued has meant that, for instance, as of the early 1990s import licenses were still being required on agricultural imports accounting for 59 percent of the value of all such imports, as opposed to the 43 percent figure

Mexico's Exports by Commodity
(in US$ millions)

Commodity	1992	1991	% Change
Passenger cars	$3,379	$3,263	4
Vehicle parts	1,523	1,210	26
Car engines	1,207	1,199	1
Machinery parts	890	820	9
Fresh vegetables	552	489	13
Iron in bars	378	330	15
Cattle	330	357	-8
Coffee	258	369	-30
Tomatoes	211	261	-19
Silver in bars	208	232	-10
Total, Incl. Others	$46,198	$42,688	8%

Source: National Institute of Statistics

During the period 1980 through 1993 exports grew at an annual rate of 4.75 percent, while imports grew at 6.6 percent. Exports increased in absolute numbers in every year except 1985 and 1986, when they fell by 33 percent, and 1988, when they dropped by only 0.5 percent from the previous year's level. All in all, exports rose by 91 percent between 1980 and 1993, while imports rose by 146 percent, nearly two-thirds faster. Much of the sluggishness in the growth of exports relative to that of imports is due to the continuing weakness in oil prices, and the need to develop competitive export products while at the same time having to import expensive capital goods in order to upgrade lagging export industries.

EXPORTS

Petroleum Versus Non-Petroleum Exports

During the late 1970s and early 1980s in the atmosphere of the Middle Eastern oil shocks, Mexico's oil producing capacity was coming on line in a major way. Policymakers and foreign observers as well thought that Mexico had it made, needing only to tap into its oil reserves to cover its expenses virtually forever. In 1982 petroleum exports accounted for 78 percent of total Mexican exports, while all other commodity and manufacturing exports represented only 22 percent. In 1985 oil exports still represented 67.4 percent—fully two-thirds—of exports. Oil plunged to a 38.3 percent share of exports the following year, reflecting the second stage in the 1980s drop in energy prices that finally convinced Mexico that it had to restructure its economy. The vast majority of the nearly US$6 billion—almost 27

percent—drop in total exports in 1986 was attributable to lower prices received for oil exports.

Petroleum exports recovered slightly to a 41 percent share in 1987 before weakening again. The Persian Gulf crisis in late 1989 and early 1990 resulted in a worldwide oil price spike that caused oil's share of Mexican exports to jump to 37.4 percent in 1990, adding US$2.2 billion to exports and driving the dollar value contribution of foreign oil sales above US$10 billion for the first time since 1985. However, oil exports fell back US$2.75 billion to below the 1989 level and to a new low of 26 percent of total exports in 1991. Although total exports barely eked out a gain—from US$26.8 billion in 1990 to US$26.9 billion in 1991—this was the first time that the export economy was able to hold its own without the prop of oil revenues. Non-oil exports were actually able to offset the drop in the oil contribution. Between 1982 and 1992 the percentage contributions of oil and non-oil exports reversed themselves, from a greater than three-quarters oil and less than one-quarter non-oil share to a more than three-fourths non-oil and less than one-fourth oil ratio. Mexico still has some of the largest petroleum reserves in the world that it can draw on, but it has, first, learned not to rely so heavily on them and, second, it has enhanced its non-

Mexico's Imports by Commodity
(in US$ millions)

Commodity	1992	1991	% Change
Automobile assembled parts	$6,007	$5,025	20
Electrical installation parts/pieces	3,524	2,874	23
Parts for automobiles, buses, trucks	1,343	1,100	22
Radio/TV receivers & transmitters	1,111	860	29
Radiophonic & telegraphic sets	856	1,376	-38
Gasoline	748	736	2
Meat	709	631	12
Iron & steel plates	656	615	7
Aircraft parts	596	455	31
Industrial mixtures	544	496	10
Total, including Others	$62,129	$52,938	17%

Source: National Institute of Statistics

oil export capacity so as to lessen its reliance on oil in the future.

Agricultural and Other Commodity Exports

In 1991 Mexico's exports of agricultural, ranching, fishery, forestry, mineral, and other related products accounted for 10.9 percent of total exports.

Mining production and exports have been relatively stagnant since the 1950s, fluctuating little on a constant value basis. Although Mexico is the world's largest producer of silver (in 1992 Mexico reported US$208 million in silver exports) and a major producer of several other metals and minerals, lack of investment has kept production down and costs up, limiting exports. Some materials are also processed to a greater or lesser degree and therefore included in other categories as manufactured items. New rules making it easier for foreigners to invest in the mining industry should boost production and exports.

In the pre-oil, pre-manufacturing days of 1970 agricultural exports accounted for 54.2 percent of total exports from Mexico. By 1975 this share had declined to 34 percent, falling to 11.2 percent in 1980 as the importance of the oil industry exports kicked in. By 1985 agriculture was providing 7.9 percent of exports, a figure that continues to shrink, reaching 6.9 percent in 1991. In dollar value terms, agricultural exports increased from US$1.545 billion in 1980 to US$2.372 billion in 1991, a rise of 53 percent overall, with average annual growth of 4 percent. Overall agricultural production has been relatively stagnant due to structural problems. As the sector modernizes under new regulations and begins to receive more foreign investment, production—especially of cash crops for export markets—should begin to rise.

In 1991 major food exports included vegetables (47 percent of agricultural exports; the largest single vegetable product is tomatoes at 20.3 percent of the total), fruits (12 percent), orange juice (8 percent), coffee (2 percent), and other items (31 percent, each of which represented less than 2 percent of the total). Beef is a significant export, both as live animals and as fresh, chilled, frozen, and processed meat products.

Industrial and Manufactured Exports

Mexico's manufacturing exports have grown significantly since the early 1980s. Between 1982 and 1989 Mexico's manufacturing exports grew a total of 450 percent, compared with growth in that category of 330 percent in Hong Kong, 290 percent in Singapore and Taiwan, and 280 percent in South Korea, all manufacturing export powerhouses. It should be noted that Mexico's growth came off of a low base and statistically includes some intermediate commodity products not generally lumped under the manufactured goods heading. As recently as 1985 manufacturing exports accounted for less than one-quarter (23.4 percent) of total exports. By 1987 they had risen to half (50.7 percent), and they rose to 62.5 percent by 1991. Mexico counts as manufactures all items that have received some intermediate processing, including foods, beverages, tobacco (which in 1991 accounted for 7.6 percent of manufacturing exports and ranked third among categories of manufactured exports), and mining products (for which the combined categories accounted for 8.7 percent of manufacturing exports).

In 1991 manufacturing exports were led by metal products, machinery, and equipment (US$8.7 billion, 54.3 percent of all manufacturing exports and up nearly 20 percent in value from 1990). Chemicals were next (12.3 percent of manufacturing exports and up 17.6 percent from the previous year), followed by foods, beverages, and tobacco (7.6 percent share and up 11 percent); iron and steel (6.4 percent share, up 6.2 percent); textiles and leather goods (4.7 percent share, up 20.8 percent); mining and metallurgical manufactures (4.7 percent share, down 22.1 percent); nonmetallic mineral products (4 percent share, up 23.4 percent); paper, printing, and publishing (1.4 percent share, up 14.5 percent); woodworking products (1.2 percent share, up 13.4 percent); plastics and rubber products (1.1 percent share, up 36.5 percent—the highest percentage gain by category in 1991); and other miscellaneous products (2.3 percent share, down 22.1 percent).

Since 1991 several of these areas, such as textiles and leather goods, woodworking products, and plastics and rubber products, have come under pressure due to more efficient foreign competition and lower tariff barriers. For instance, Mexico has lost 40 percent of its textile manufacturing capacity since 1986, and 20 percent of the capacity in the leather industry center of León closed down between 1991 and 1993. Additional loss of protection under the terms of NAFTA is expected to further injure some of these industries and their export competitiveness. Conversely, loss of tariff barriers and international investment and integration is expected to give an added boost to such areas as metal products, chemicals, and mining.

Maquiladoras

Mexico's *maquila* program was designed to allow the temporary import on a duty-free basis of equipment and inputs for processing in Mexico and the subsequent export of the products created. The program, which until relatively recently offered the only way for foreigners to invest as majority owners in Mexican ventures, has boosted manufacturing exports considerably. However, it is somewhat difficult

THE WORLD ACCORDING TO GATT*

On December 15, 1993, after seven years of bargaining, more than 100 nations set aside their differences long enough to strike a deal and end the latest round of the General Agreement on Tariffs and Trade (GATT). The deal they struck paves the way for tariffs across all product categories to be cut by at least one-third. It's an agreement that President Clinton wants the US Congress to ratify by April 15, 1994, when the world's trade ministers meet to approve the accord. [Note: 109 of the 125 GATT member nations signed the treaty on April 15, 1994. The treaty must still be ratified by the individual member states. The goal is to have the treaty ratified and go into effect on January 1, 1995.]

In several product categories, negotiators cut tariffs to zero, at least for the major trading nations. The result for the United States is, in part, a more level playing field. Before the zero-tariff deal, US duties on these products tended to be low (3 to 5 percent) compared to foreign tariffs of 7 to 15 percent. The wholesale elimination of tariffs on products such as pharmaceuticals, medical equipment, construction equipment, agricultural equipment, steel, beer, distilled spirits, paper, pulp, printed matter, and toys primarily covers the United States, the European Union, Australia, and New Zealand. But, in some cases, fast-growing Asian countries such as Korea, Hong Kong, and Singapore signed on. Japan, which has relatively low tariffs but some impossible non-tariff barriers, has agreed to most of these cuts but continues to balk at reducing tariffs on cut lumber and plywood.

Zero Tariffs Double World Trade

The zero-tariff collection of goods represents about US$1.6 trillion in trade (the 1993 total) and is forecast to represent a market worth more than US$3.2 trillion by the year 2000. Trade in these products is growing at a rate 1 to 1.5 percent faster than the overall rate for all products traded. What this means is that, from 1993 to 2000, real growth in GATT-sensitive products will be on the order of 6.6 percent, compared to 5.7 percent for all traded products.

For nearly all products outside the zero-tariff group, countries have committed to lowering duties by one-third. In some Latin American countries this is a significant concession, since some of their tariffs approach 50 percent in order to protect inefficient and technology-starved local industries. For those countries, cutting duties doesn't assure that their imports will grow, since, for many, the bigger problem is finding enough hard currency to pay for imports.

Non-Tariff Measures

GATT's deepest impact is on tariffs. But other negotiated items have significant implications.

- The World Trade Organization, or WTO (GATT's new moniker), will live under new rules opening the door to greater enforcement against unfair trade practices.
- Strong antidumping and countervailing-duty rules will be maintained.
- US companies will have more opportunities to bid on government projects overseas.
- More consistent health and safety standards will allow US firms more access to overseas markets and greater ability to compete against local firms.

GATT's Economic Impact

There is no simple, foolproof measurement of GATT's value to the world economy. Rough estimates have been made on the high and the low side. One oft-quoted estimate from the OECD (Organization for Economic Cooperation and Development) suggests that GATT will add between US$213 billion and US$275 billion to the world Gross Domestic Product (GDP) over the next 10 years. This is probably on the low end, since the US Special Trade Representative estimates that the net gain for the 67 countries alone by 2005 will be about 4 percent of real output (about a one-half of 1 percent increase in real output growth per year).

If this scenario plays out, GATT will add about US$1.2 trillion to G7 output by 2005 and US$2.1 trillion to the world economy. Over a 10 year phase-in period, the aggregate gain will be about US$12 trillion. DRI/McGraw-Hill's analysis suggests that the actual impact may be a net increase in world output of about 3

*By David L. Blond, principal and director of international trade forecasting and analysis for DRI/McGraw-Hill. Reprinted with permission from Global Production & Transportation magazine. Copyright © 1994 New Hope Communications Inc.

percent by 2005, which, while substantial, is small by the standards of the global market.

Implications for NAFTA

One question looming over participants in the GATT is the agreement's effect on regional trade pacts. In fact, the North American Free Trade Agreement (NAFTA), which grants trade preferences to North American nations, goes against the intent of GATT. The reason is that GATT is structured to eliminate preferential treatment among trading partners. But GATT provides only general guidelines on allowable tariffs, while other trade pacts, such as NAFTA, are specific. The reality is that many such trade pacts are in existence, and all of them likely will remain in force under GATT.

GATT and Latin America

For Latin America, GATT represents a new opportunity to significantly reduce tariff barriers in hopes of realizing greater trade within and outside the continent. Traditionally, Latin America has tended to lag behind when it comes to tariff reduction, despite bold moves towards developing regional trading communities in Mexico and Central and South America. This is because the "infant industries" argument, which allowed governments to protect local markets behind high tariff walls, dies hard in Latin America, where the idea was born.

Nonetheless, in spite of starts and stops since the 1960s, some of the region's markets are on a faster track toward open economies. It's a direction that translates into expected annual growth rates exceeding 10 percent for trade in key products in some Latin American countries. For foreign producers selling zero-tariff products into those markets, that means thriving business—especially for US exporters of pharmaceuticals, computers, and miscellaneous consumer products to Mexico. Brazil promises to become a substantial market for textile fabrics, while other countries in eastern South America will become leading markets for heavy transportation equipment.

A Vote of Confidence for Global Integration

The ties that bind the world economy today are far stronger than at any time in the past decade. The United Nations estimates that, by 1992, the stock of foreign-owned investments worldwide topped US$2 trillion and that these companies did more than US$5.5 trillion in business. Both large and small firms have participated in this boom, and the results show up in a web of worldwide interconnections that is impossible to unravel.

More than the numbers, then, the significance of this GATT treaty is its effect on business confidence. It's an assurance that the world trading system will not break apart and that the rapid integration of world economies will continue. This is not to say that managing in a new, more open system will be without problems. Undoubtedly, displacement of workers and industry will occur, and temporary trade barriers will be erected. But, by agreeing to GATT's tariff reductions, most nations are agreeing with mainstream economic theory, which suggests that the fastest way to more growth is through open markets.

GATT sets the course for a world trade boom of about 6 percent annual economic growth in the 1990s—a continuation of the fast growth rate achieved during the 1980s. The net result in the years to come is an upward trend in the world's standard of living.

to track these developments because prior to 1990 Mexico did not tabulate them as such (US Department of Commerce statistics did not begin counting them in total exports and imports until recently). Trade statistics increasingly include *maquila* production, but it remains difficult to sort out exactly what is and is not included, because reporting agencies seldom note it explicitly. As increasing amounts of *maquila* production are allowed into domestic markets, assessing the trade contribution could become even more difficult.

Because the main national input was labor, the government chose to exclude *maquila* production from statistics on national production, imports, and exports, counting only the sales of labor and ancillary inputs. As the scope of *maquilas* has grown in importance and the production becomes more integrated into the total economy, this statistical anomaly has taken on greater importance. In 1980 *maquilas* earned US$771.6 million in foreign exchange, slightly less than was earned by the tourism industry, Mexico's second largest foreign exchange earner after oil sales. This figure rose to US$3.6 billion in 1990, surpassing tourism as an earner of foreign exchange. During the first half of 1992 the more than 2,000 *maquila* operations employed 455,000 Mexican workers and accounted for US$3.1 billion in foreign exchange, more than 85 percent of the full year's take in 1990. At the end of the third quarter of 1993, there were 2,182 *maquilas* in operation, employing 552,078 workers (more than 20 percent of total national employment in the manufacturing sector).

The Secretariat of Trade and Industrial Development (SECOFI) calculated that *maquila* production was equal to 78 percent of domestic manufacturing exports in 1974. This figure had risen to 85.3 percent in 1982, and averaged 90.8 percent between 1985 and 1990. During this period it never fell below 72.6 percent (in 1987) and rose as high as 103.4 percent of domestic export manufacturing production (in 1990). In gross dollar value terms, such *maquila* production grew from US$870 million in 1974 to US$14.4 billion in 1990 (compared to US$13.9 billion of domestic manufacturing exports and US$26.8 billion of total exports; *maquila* production was equivalent to 53.7 percent of total exports).

The majority of *maquila* operations have been involved in the assembly of finished goods such as consumer electronics and industrial subassemblies. Although most of these ventures have tended to involve fairly low-grade labor intensive operations, some firms have invested in sophisticated hi-tech operations as well. *Maquilas* are expected to change substantially in the post-NAFTA era. In the first place, they will be allowed to direct an increasingly large proportion of their production to Mexican domestic markets, beginning in 1994 with an amount equivalent to 55 percent of their 1993 production and rising to 100 percent of 2000's production in the year 2001. Secondly, they will gradually lose their privileged duty-free status as overall tariffs are reduced to zero, removing their cost advantage and causing them to restructure to serve the domestic market directly and the export market on a fully competitive basis, or to close down entirely. *Maquilas* operated by non-NAFTA nations will lose their comparative advantage because they are not expected to receive the same preferential treatment as NAFTA-based operations with respect to duties on *maquila* production that is either exported abroad (primarily to the US) from a Mexican base or sold into the Mexican domestic market.

Export Products

In 1991 Mexico's top 15 export product categories together accounted for 60.1 percent of total exports, with remaining export categories each representing less than 0.9 percent of total exports. The top five export product categories were led by petroleum products with a 27 percent share of total exports, down 27.4 percent from the value of such exports in the preceding year. The second largest export product category was automobiles, with a 13.5 percent share, up 45.7 percent. Automobile motors were the next largest export, with a 4.4 percent share, although value of these exports fell by 21 percent from the previous year. The fourth largest export category was fresh vegetables, with a 1.8 percent share, up 13.7 percent from 1990. The fifth largest category was automobile parts, with a 1.7 percent share, up 9.1 percent.

The next 10 largest exports were machinery parts (1.5 percent share, up 37.6 percent, the largest percentage gain after automobiles), computer equipment (1.5 percent share, up 10.1 percent), coffee (1.4 percent share, up 10.5 percent), cattle (1.3 percent, up 2.6 percent), pig iron (1.2 percent, down 1.6 percent), glass and related products (1.1 percent, up 18.2 percent), steel tubing (1 percent, up 16.7 percent), plastics and synthetic resins (0.9 percent, down 5.9 percent), silver ingots (0.9 percent, down 23.2 percent, the largest percentage drop for a major product category other than oil), and steel plates and sheets (0.9 percent, down 7.7 percent).

In 1992 exports of automobiles rose by about 4 percent, while automobile engines rose by a marginal 1 percent, but other automotive parts jumped by 26 percent. Machinery parts exports rose by 9 percent. Vegetable exports rose by 13 percent overall, but were hurt by a nearly 20 percent drop in the sale of tomatoes. Cattle exports eased by 8 percent, while the value of coffee shipments plunged by 30 percent. Exports of pig iron grew by 15 percent, but exports of silver continued to drop by an additional 10 percent.

IMPORTS

Manufacturing and Industrial Imports

Mexico categorizes the bulk of its imports as manufacturing imports because they are destined for use in its manufacturing industries. Thus Mexico subsumes raw material imports—including foodstuffs which will receive any form of subsequent intermediate processing and packaging—under the heading of manufacturing imports, along with capital goods and other manufactured items, excluding only consumer goods (which in turn include foods, such as canned and other packaged foods that receive no further processing). This means that most imports are classified as industrial in nature. In 1985 91.8 percent of all imports were considered to be industrial. Between 1987 and 1991 industrial imports constituted an average of 87.7 percent of total imports, ranging from a low of 85 percent in 1987 and growing steadily to a high of 93.2 percent in 1991. Even given this inclusive definition of industrial imports, capital goods imports have been growing as a percent of total imports. In 1990 imports of capital goods grew by 43 percent to almost

Mexico's Imports by Country (in US$ millions)			
Commodity	**1992**	**1991**	**% Change**
United States	$30,384	$24,750	23%
Japan	3,025	2,030	49
Germany	2,464	2,319	6
France	1,297	967	34
Brazil	1,106	753	47
Canada	1,041	784	33
Italy	975	622	57
Spain	869	572	52
United Kingdom	615	499	23
China	538	428	26
Belgium/Luxembourg	303	328	-8
Argentina	239	364	-34
Source: Foreign Trade Magazine			

Mexico's Exports by Country (in US$ millions)			
Commodity	**1992**	**1991**	**% Change**
United States	$18,911	$18,951	0
Spain	1,217	1,149	6
Japan	879	1,240	-29
Canada	779	575	36
France	549	599	-8
Germany	489	570	-14
Brazil	430	187	130
Belgium/Luxembourg	282	321	-12
United Kingdom	240	219	10
Venezuela	199	126	57
Colombia	183	155	18
Argentina	178	185	-4
Source: Foreign Trade Magazine			

double the level in 1989 as Mexico struggled to upgrade its industry.

Traditionally imports destined for processing in *maquilas* have not been included in official tallies of imports on the grounds that they are not destined for internal consumption. However, some statistics have begun to include such imports. For instance, in 1991 total imports including *maquila* imports were listed at US$52.9 billion, 38.2 percent higher than the US$38.2 billion generally listed for the year. In 1992 total imports including *maquila* imports were US$62.1 billion versus US$48.2 billion, a difference of US$13.9 billion, or 28.8 percent of the total.

Import Products

In 1990 the top 10 categories of imports (excluding *maquila* inputs) accounted for 41.1 percent of imports. These included automobile parts (8.6 percent); machinery (6.2 percent); staple foodstuffs (corn, beans, soybeans, and sorghum—4.5 percent); radio and television equipment and parts (4.3 percent); airplanes and airplane parts, auto and truck assembly parts and subassemblies (3.8 percent); electrical motors, parts, and apparatus (3.4 percent); sugar and powdered and condensed milk (3.3 percent); computers and parts (3 percent); paper, paper products, and books (2.7 percent); and apparel (1.3 percent).

The next largest category was pharmaceuticals at 1.2 percent. Remaining products accounted for 57.7 percent of imports, each category representing less than 1.2 percent of the total.

In 1991 the top 10 categories (including *maquila*

inputs) accounted for only 26.8 percent of imports. The top import was automobile subassemblies, with a 9.5 percent share. From there the categories shift from the previous year so that automotive subassemblies were followed by electrical apparatus and parts (5.4 percent); telephone apparatus (2.6 percent); automobile, truck, and bus parts (2.1 percent); radio and television apparatus (1.6 percent); gasoline (1.4 percent—Mexico has large supplies of oil, but limited refining capacity); meat (1.2 percent); iron and steel plates (1.2 percent); aircraft parts (0.9 percent); and industrial mixtures (primarily industrial chemicals and intermediate inputs—0.9 percent). The remaining 73.2 percent of imports represent categories that each account for less than 0.9 percent of the total. The inclusion of *maquila* imports serves to reduce the share of given product categories, making import trade seem more highly diversified.

In 1992 the top 10 imports (including *maquila* inputs) accounted for slightly less of the total—26.1 percent. These included automotive subassemblies (9.7 percent share, up 19.5 percent in dollar value); electrical apparatus and parts (5.7 percent, up 22.6 percent); automobile, truck, and bus parts (2.2 percent, up 22.1 percent); radio and television apparatus (1.8 percent, up 29.2 percent); telephone apparatus (1.4 percent, down 37.8 percent); meat (1.1 percent, up 12.4 percent); iron and steel plates (1.1 percent, up 6.7 percent); aircraft parts (1 percent, up 19.6 percent); and industrial mixtures (0.9 percent, up 9.7 percent). Remaining import categories each account for less than 0.9 percent of the total.

TRADE PARTNERS

Mexico's primary trade partner has been and continues to be the United States, a situation that has prevailed since the late 1800s. Despite concerns among some in the US that Mexico's comparatively small economy prevents it from buying substantial amounts of US goods, Mexico is the US's third largest trade partner, behind Canada and Japan. The United States regularly takes about 70 percent of Mexico's exports and provides more than 60 percent of its imports, although differences in defining what constitutes exports and imports (due largely to varying ways of treating *maquila* activity) makes it difficult to assess the exact figures. In 1992 the US took 76.2 percent of Mexico's exports, including *maquila* exports, while in 1993 it bought 76.9 percent— slightly more. In 1992 the US provided 65.4 percent of Mexico's imports, including *maquila* imports, while in 1993 it sold 63.6 percent, somewhat less and an indication of a marginal trend toward diversification of suppliers.

In 1992 Japan was Mexico's second largest trade partner, taking 3.2 percent of exports and providing 6.3 percent of imports. Collectively the nations of the European Community—primarily the United Kingdom, Germany, France, Italy, and Spain—take about 12 percent of Mexican exports and provide about 14.7 percent of imports, while Latin American and Caribbean countries take 7 percent of exports and provide 4.5 percent of imports. Canada has historically taken only about 1 percent of Mexico's exports and provided 2.1 percent of its imports.

In 1991 the US was the leading buyer of Mexican exports with a 70.4 percent share of the market. The US was followed by Japan with 4.6 percent. Spain was third with 4.3 percent, followed by France (2.2 percent), Canada (2.2 percent), Germany (2.1 percent), the Benelux countries (1.2 percent), the UK (0.8 percent), Brazil (0.7 percent), Argentina (0.7 percent), Colombia (0.6 percent), and Venezuela (0.5 percent). Together these top 12 buyers accounted for 90.2 percent of total exports (excluding *maquila* exports). The remaining 9.8 percent was taken by countries each of which bought less than 0.5 percent of the total.

Trade patterns shifted somewhat in 1992, although the US remained the top buyer of Mexican goods with a 68.8 percent share, down slightly by 2.25 percent (the percentage is higher when *maquila* exports are included). Spain rose to second place with a 4.4 percent share, up 5.9 percent in dollar value and up 2.3 percent in overall share. Japan slipped to third (3.2 percent, down 30.4 percent), followed by Canada (2.8 percent, up 33.3 percent), France (2 percent, down 9 percent), Germany (1.8 percent, down 14.3 percent), Brazil (1.6 percent, up 128.6 percent in share and 46.9 percent in dollar value of purchases), Benelux (1 percent, down 16.7 percent), the UK (0.9 percent, up 12.5 percent), Venezuela (0.7 percent, up 40 percent from a low base), Colombia (0.7 percent, up 16.7 percent), and Argentina 0.6 percent, down 14.3 percent). These top 12 buyers of Mexican exports accounted for 88.5 percent of total exports, excluding *maquila* exports. The remaining 11.5 percent was accounted for by countries which individually took less than 0.6 percent of total exports. In general there has been a shift away from European and Asian buyers and with greater participation by Canadian and Latin American buyers, although it may be premature to assess any real secular change in trade patterns.

In 1991 the United States provided 64.8 percent of

Mexico's Leading Trade Partners

Exports - 1992

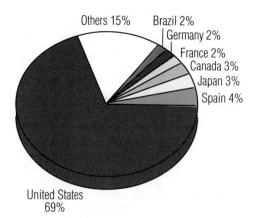

Others 15%   Brazil 2%
Germany 2%
France 2%
Canada 3%
Japan 3%
Spain 4%

United States
69%

Total 1992 Exports: US$27.5 Billion (excludes *maquila* exports)
Note: Figures rounded to nearest whole percent. Source: Foreign Trade Magazine

Imports - 1992

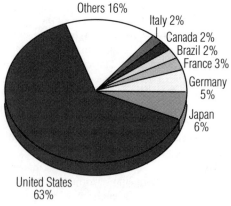

Others 16%
Italy 2%
Canada 2%
Brazil 2%
France 3%
Germany 5%
Japan 6%

United States
63%

Total 1992 Imports: US$48.2 Billion (excludes *maquila* imports)

Mexico's imports. Germany was second with a 6.1 percent share, followed by Japan with a 5.3 percent share. These top three sellers were followed by France (2.5 percent share), Canada (2.1 percent), Brazil (2 percent), Italy (1.6 percent), Spain (1.5 percent), the United Kingdom 1.3 percent), China (1.1 percent), Argentina (1 percent), and the Benelux countries (0.9 percent). Together these 12 countries accounted for 90.2 percent of Mexico's non-*maquila* imports. The remaining 9.8 percent was provided by other countries, each selling less than 0.9 percent of the total.

In 1992 the US continued to provide the majority of imports, although its share fell 2.75 percent to 63 percent (the percentage stays about the same even when *maquila* imports are included). Japan replaced Germany in the number two position with a 6.3 percent share, up 18.9 percent in share terms and 49 percent in dollar value. Germany was third with a 5.1 percent share (down 16.4 percent in share terms and 6.25 percent in dollar terms). These were followed by France (2.7 percent share, up 8 percent), Brazil (2.3 percent, up 15 percent), Canada (2.2 percent, up 4.75 percent), Italy (2 percent, up 25 percent), Spain (1.8 percent, up 20 percent), the UK (1.3 percent, up 23.2 percent in dollar terms but even with 1991 in percentage share terms), China (1.1 percent, up 25.7 percent in dollar terms but even with 1991 in percentage share terms), the Benelux countries (0.6 percent, down 33.3 percent), and Argentina (0.5 percent, down 34.3 percent in dollar terms and 50 percent in share terms). Together these 12 countries provided 88.9 percent of total exports, excluding *maquila* imports. The remaining 11.1 percent was provided by other countries, each of which sold Mexico less than 0.5 percent of its imports.

Mexico has a policy of diversifying its trade, although to date it has shown relatively few results. The country's goal is to increase trade with other nations, particularly with other Latin nations as well as with those in Asia and Eastern Europe.

BALANCE OF TRADE

Because Mexico traditionally has needed to import higher priced finished goods while selling primarily low priced commodity raw materials and intermediate goods, its merchandise balance of trade has historically been negative. In 1970 its balance of trade deficit amounted to 35.1 percent of total trade, while in 1975 it had increased to 37.5 percent of total trade. During the 14 years from 1980 through 1993 Mexico had surpluses in seven years and deficits in seven years. The surpluses were the result of explicit government policies between 1982 and 1988 that restricted imports to avoid the expenditure of scarce foreign exchange. During the period the surplus averaged 2.3 percent of total trade, soaring as high as

47.2 percent of trade in 1983 and falling to 3 percent in 1988 as the crackdown on imports began to fade. At the beginning of the period, Mexico had its usual trade deficits, which returned again in 1989 and have continued since then as Mexico has boosted its imports in an effort to bring in capital goods to build up its export economy. During this period the trade deficit has averaged 14.2 percent of total trade, falling to a low of 1.3 percent in 1989 during the transition from surplus to deficit and rising to a high of 27.3 percent in 1992.

Although Mexico seems to have what is essentially a structural merchandise trade deficit, that deficit did ease somewhat to an estimated 24.4 percent of total trade in 1993. This appears to be the result of a more conscious effort to rein in imports while boosting exports. Since the low point in 1986, Mexico's imports have been growing at an average annual rate of 18.9 percent, two-and-a-half times as fast as exports, which during the same period have grown at an average annual rate of 7.6 percent (in 1993 imports grew at a 5.3 percent rate while exports grew by a healthier 12.3 percent). And despite the influx of capital into financial and fixed asset investments experienced by Mexico in recent years (Mexico's intangibles' balance tends to be negative as well, due to the imbalance between the services it needs and the services it can offer), this still does not represent the level of favorable trade in intangibles necessary to offset the net outflows in its merchandise balance.

Mexico has been able to sustain this situation recently because of an austerity program designed to produce a budgetary surplus as well as because of liquid funds generated by foreign investments. In 1970 Mexico's foreign currency reserves were US$568 million, a figure that grew steadily at a 13.8 percent rate until the upheavals of the 1980s. Under the influence of oil sales, foreign reserves jumped to US$4.1 billion in 1981 (from just under US$3 billion in 1980) before plunging to US$834 million in 1982. Afterwards international reserves fluctuated wildly before beginning another steady climb to nearly US$27 billion at the end of 1993. In the period of post-NAFTA passage euphoria, international reserves reached nearly US$30 billion in February 1994, much of it the result of inflows of speculative financial market investment capital. By the end of the first quarter of 1994, an estimated US$6.5 billion had flowed out again.

Observers note that Mexico's ability to continue to absorb a trade deficit amounting to one-quarter of its total trade is limited, especially given the brittle nature of its political and economic equilibrium. At some point Mexico's export economy will have to begin to produce at a higher level. Many expect that Mexico will have to devalue the peso, making imports more expensive and exports more competitive, especially if the government has to backpedal on its austerity program and spend its budgetary surplus and more on social programs to deliver more benefits to the vast majority of the populace that has yet to benefit from the economic turnaround.

Despite Mexico's history as a buyer of a broad range of goods and services, there is a persistent concern that the country's relatively low per capita income presents a barrier to the ability of Mexicans to buy in international markets. Although this is patently true for many big-ticket consumer items (and the definition of "big" kicks in at a relatively low level because the average worker makes little more than minimum wage), Mexico is nevertheless a purchaser of a vast array of goods. As noted above, Mexico is the third largest trading partner for the US. While this position is unlikely to improve in terms of share, the median value of goods purchased is likely to rise significantly as Mexico's markets open.

MEXICAN TRADE POLICY

Since its accession to GATT in 1986 Mexico has bravely pursued a free trade stance. Despite the practical limits placed on the implementation of this policy, the fact that such a policy exists at all and that any significant progress has been made in this direction are noteworthy in this previously closed economy.

The official policy on trade is contained in President Salinas' report of 1990, which states that Mexico stands for overall tariff reduction nationally and internationally, with the reservation that there should be equalizing protective tariffs to prevent predatory economic behavior. This policy is supplemented by one of reduction of non-tariff barriers as long as such lowering of barriers is reciprocal and allows Mexico to fairly enhance its own ability to export. Both reforms should be carried out within a framework that allows for long term stable access rather than arbitrary short-term fluctuation of policy on access. Mexico further calls for balanced bilateral and multilateral dispute resolution mechanisms, specifically objecting to any mechanisms that permit unilateral national action to resolve international trade disputes. Finally, Mexico professes to seek rational economic complementarity based on comparative advantage rather than the development of redundant competing national industries in areas other than those related to national security.

MEMBERSHIP IN INTERNATIONAL ORGANIZATIONS

In the past a more isolationist Mexico participated in international organizations largely out of national pride—because it felt it should in order to validate its national importance. Now Mexico is looking to activity within such forums to promote its trade and economic development, with a view that national status is more likely to flow from such participation and development than from mere assertion.

Mexico has been a member of the United Nations (or in Spanish, *Organización de Naciones Unidas* or ONU) and most of its agencies since its founding in 1945. It is a member of the World Bank, the International Monetary Fund (IMF), the International Finance Corporation (IFC), and the Inter-American Development Bank (IADB). In March 1994 Mexico joined the Organization for Economic Cooperation and Development (OECD), which was considered to represent a recognition of its rising international stature. The country participates in international agreements covering commodities such as coffee, sugar, cotton, lead, zinc, and wool. Regionally, it is active in the Organization of American States (OAS, or in Spanish, *Organización de Estados Americanos* or OEA), the Latin American Integration Association (LAIA, or in Spanish *Asociación Latinoamericana de Integración* or ALADI), and the Latin American Economic System. It is also a participant in agreements establishing negotiating frameworks for trade agreements with the European Community and members of the Central American Economic Zone.

Mexico has a policy of signing trade agreements with its neighbors. It has such bilateral agreements with Chile, and recently signed one with Costa Rica. It has some limited agreements with neighboring Guatemala, and in early 1994 signed a trilateral trade pact with Colombia and Venezuela and announced the opening of negotiations with Nicaragua. Mexico's most ambitious agreement is the North American Free Trade Agreement (NAFTA, known in Spanish as the *Tratado Libre Comercial* or TLC) signed with the United States and Canada at the end of 1993. In consideration of Mexico's participation in NAFTA, the US proposed the country for membership in the Asia Pacific Economic Cooperation group (APEC), which focuses on Pacific Rim economic issues.

The North American Free Trade Agreement

NAFTA: AN OVERVIEW*

INTRODUCTION

The North American Free Trade Agreement (NAFTA) has created a powerful economic bloc consisting of 360 million consumers in the United States, Mexico, and Canada. The combined Gross National Products of these countries is over US$6.3 trillion. NAFTA will provide numerous opportunities to business, industry, and workers. The agreement is designed to lead to a more efficient use of North American resources—capital, land, labor, and technology—while heightening competitive market forces. NAFTA should stimulate trade and investment in North America beyond current levels. In 1991, the levels of North American trade were as follows: US–Canada, US$143 billion; Mexico–US, US$64 billion, and Mexico-Canada, US$3 billion. US direct investment in Canada and Mexico in 1991 totaled US$68.5 billion and US$11.6 billion, respectively. During the same period, Canadian and Mexican direct investment in the United States reached US$30 billion and US$0.6 billion, respectively. These trade and investment figures should increase once the investment framework and trade provisions of NAFTA are implemented.

NAFTA's goals are several-fold. Increased trade and investment will be accomplished under the Agreement by the gradual elimination of tariff and non-tariff barriers to trade in areas as diverse as automobiles, agriculture, electronics, textiles, and apparel. NAFTA also removes numerous impediments to investment, such as performance requirements and investment screenings.

Implementation of NAFTA should also create economic opportunities in various service sectors, including the financial, telecommunications, construc-tion, tourism, transportation, and environmental areas. In addition, the Agreement covers other sub-jects that will affect business in the region, such as intellectual property rights, technical standards, and environmental issues.

RULES AND PRINCIPLES

Competition Policy, Monopolies, and State Enterprises The Agreement provides that the parties to NAFTA will maintain or adopt rules against anti-competitive business practices, while pledging to co-operate on enforcing competition law. Government enterprises—federal, state, or provincial—will be re-quired to abide by general NAFTA principles of non-discrimination when exercising administrative, gov-ernmental, or regulatory authority, including grant-ing of licenses. Specific rules on government and pri-vate monopolies are included in NAFTA, including the use of commercial considerations for assessing the sale of monopolies, and the prohibition of discrimi-nation by monopolies. Moreover, a trilateral trade and competition committee will review competition law with respect to the principle of free trade.

Dispute Resolution NAFTA provides several methods for the resolution of disputes under the Agreement. The NAFTA Trilateral Trade Commission will regularly review trade relations among the NAFTA governments and will discuss the general implemen-tation of NAFTA. The Commission may also establish bi-national or tri-national panels of private sector trade experts to resolve NAFTA disputes. If the recommen-dations regarding the resolution of particular disputes are not complied with, the aggrieved nation may with-draw "equivalent trade concessions."

NAFTA also contains special provisions for re-

*"The North American Free Trade Agreement: An Overview," by Dean C. Alexander, LL.M., J.D., Director, The NAFTA Research Institute, Washington, DC; Co-editor, NAFTA Law and Policy Series, Martinus Nijhoff Publishers; President, Septacontinentaux Corp., Bethesda, Maryland. Copyright © 1993 by International Tax and Business Lawyer. Reprinted from International Tax and Business Lawyer, Vol. 11, No. 1, by permission.

NAFTA: GENERAL PROVISIONS*

The following provisions establish rules governing trade in goods with respect to customs duties, restrictions, fees, origin, and tariffs. They improve and make the access for goods produced and traded within the NAFTA territory more secure.

Trade Restrictions

The three NAFTA Parties will eliminate prohibitions and quantitative restrictions currently applied at the borders, such as quotas and import licenses. However, each NAFTA territory retains the right to impose border restrictions in some circumstances, for example, to protect plant, animal, or human life, or the environment. Special rules apply to trade in agriculture, autos, energy, and textiles.

Customs User Fees

The three countries agreed not to impose any new customs user fees, for example, the United States merchandise processing fee or the Mexican customs processing fee. By June 30, 1999, Mexico will eliminate its current customs processing fee on NAFTA goods. Additionally, the United States will eliminate its current merchandise processing fee on goods originating in Mexico by June 30, 1999. For goods originating in Canada, the United States is currently lowering and will eliminate this fee by January 1, 1994, as agreed upon in the Canada-United States Free Trade Agreement.

De Minimis Rule

The *De Minimis* rule prevents goods from losing eligibility for NAFTA preferential treatment solely because they contain some small fixed percentage of "non-originating" material. Under this rule, a good that would otherwise fall to meet a specific rule of origin will be considered to be of NAFTA origin if the value of non-originating materials is no greater than 7 percent of the customs appraised value.

Drawback

NAFTA establishes rules on the use of "drawback" or similar programs that provide for the refund or waiver of customs duties on materials used in the production of goods subsequently exported from one NAFTA Party to another.

Existing drawback programs will terminate by January 1, 2001, for Mexico–United States, and Canada–Mexico trade; the Agreement will extend the deadline established in the Canada–United States Free Trade Agreement for the elimination of drawback programs to January 1, 1996. When these programs are eliminated, each NAFTA Party will adopt a procedure for goods subject to duties in the free trade area to avoid dual taxation of the payment of duties between the two NAFTA Parties.

Under the new procedures, the amount of customs duties that a NAFTA Party may waive or refund will be less than: (a) duties owed or paid on imported, non-originating materials used in the production of a good which will later be exported to another NAFTA Party; or (b) duties paid to that NAFTA Party on the importation of such good.

Duty-Free Temporary Admission of Goods

The Agreement allows business the authority to bring into a NAFTA Party professional equipment or tools of the trade duty-free for a temporary period. These rules also cover commercial samples, some advertising films, goods imported for sporting events, and displays or demonstrations. By 1998 all goods that are returned from one NAFTA Party to another after repair or alteration will reenter duty-free. The United States also establishes a provision for ship repairs done in other NAFTA territories on United States flagged vessels.

General Rules of Origin

Rules of origin are necessary to define which goods are eligible for NAFTA preferential treatment. They are designed to ensure that NAFTA preference is accorded only to goods determined as originating within the NAFTA territory.

The NAFTA rules of origin specify that goods may be considered originating in the NAFTA territory if they are wholly produced or obtained within the NAFTA territory; or goods containing non-regional materials can be considered to be originating in the NAFTA territory if the non-regional materials undergo an HS tariff change in the NAFTA territory. In some cases, goods must pass a regional value content test which confirms a specified

---

Reprinted from North American Free Trade Agreement Guidebook, SANDFORD, Tax & Customs Consulting with permission of author, Tim J. Sanford. Copyright © 1993 SANDFORD.

percentage of originating materials and labor.

Marking Goods for NAFTA Treatment

To promote market accessibility among the NAFTA Parties country of origin, marking rules will be developed. The reason for establishing marking rules for NAFTA is to secure both objectivity and predictability in country of origin determination. The marking rules will be designed to be less stringent than the NAFTA rules of origin for preferential treatment. However, it stands to reason that an article which qualifies under the NAFTA rules of origin will be marked as such. The marking rule will not include a value content requirement, but will prescribe specific tariff classification changes.

Tariff Elimination

The NAFTA provides for the progressive elimination of all tariffs on goods qualifying under its rules of origin. For most goods, existing customs duties will either be eliminated immediately or phased out in five or 10 equal annual stages. For certain sensitive items, tariffs will be phased out over a period of up to 15 years.

The staging categories are as follows:

- Duties on goods provided for in the items in staging category A in a Party's Schedule shall be eliminated entirely and such goods shall be duty-free, effective January 1, 1994;
- Duties on goods provided for in the items in staging category B in a Party's Schedule shall be removed in five equal annual stages commencing on January 1, 1994, and such goods shall be duty-free, effective January 1, 1998;
- Duties on goods provided for in the items in staging category C in a Party's Schedule shall be removed in 10 equal annual stages commencing on January 1, 1994, and such goods shall be duty-free, effective January 1, 2003;
- Duties on goods provided for in the items in staging category C+ in a Party's Schedule shall be removed in 15 equal annual stages commencing on January 1, 1994, and such goods shall be duty-free, effective January 1, 2008; and
- Goods provided for in the items in staging category D in a Party's Schedule shall continue to receive duty-free treatment. (Other staging categories will be displayed in the tariff schedules of each Party and may be incorporated here.)

Other tariffs will be phased out from the applied rates in effect on July 1, 1991, including the United States Generalized System of Preferences (GSP) and the Canadian General Preferential Tariff (GPT) rates. Tariff phaseouts under the Canada-United States Free Trade Agreement will continue as scheduled under that Agreement. The NAFTA provides that the three countries may consult and agree on a more rapid phaseout of tariffs.

Tariff elimination schedule for selected sensitive goods:

A. Immediate Elimination on 1/1/94

- Cattle
- Computers
- Jewelry
- Microwave Ovens
- Passenger Cars
- Telephones
- Televisions

B. Elimination over five years beginning on 1/1/94

- Baseball Caps
- Cotton Yarns
- Men's Pajamas
- Table Cloths
- Women's Cotton Dresses

C. Elimination over 10 years beginning on 1/1/94

- Cigarettes
- Cotton
- Footwear
- Glassware
- Luggage
- Rum

D. Elimination over 15 years beginning on 1/1/94

- Dry Beans
- Most Fresh Vegetables
- Orange Juice
- Peanuts
- Sugar

solving disputes involving environmental and health issues. The Agreement also provides for the establishment of special panels to review antidumping and countervailing duty cases. These panels will analyze whether actions taken by the United States, Mexico, or Canada were consistent with the actor's domestic law. In addition, NAFTA encourages resolution of private commercial disputes through alternative dispute settlement procedures.

NAFTA also provides for the resolution of investment disputes through international arbitration and other means of alternative dispute resolution.

Government Procurement In the United States, government procurement amounts to approximately US$30 billion yearly. Mexican government procurement of petroleum and electricity alone is over US$8 billion. The Agreement eliminates the discriminatory practice of requiring the use of domestic purchasers or suppliers in government procurement. NAFTA opens a significant portion of the government procurement market, including various goods and construction services, to non-discriminatory bidding. The mechanisms for the liberalization of this area are NAFTA's national treatment principle, most-favored-nation treatment, and pre-determined procedural disciplines.

NAFTA covers federal government agencies, departments, and enterprises in each contracting State. The Agreement applies to federal government agencies' and departments' procurements of goods and services if the amount exceeds US$50,000 and to federal government agencies' and departments' procurements of construction services of US$6.5 million or more. Similarly, NAFTA is applicable to procurements by federal government enterprises exceeding US$250,000 in goods and services, and US$8 million in construction services. Mexico will phase in its obligations under this section of NAFTA over a transition period. The dollar thresholds established by the Canadian Free Trade Agreement (CFTA) will remain in effect. To facilitate the process of government procurement, NAFTA also specifically provides for the exchange of technical information on the subject. Finally, NAFTA recognizes that some modifications of government procurement rules are necessary, particularly in the application of this subject to state and provincial governments.

Intellectual Property Rights NAFTA provides a high standard of protection for copyrights (including sound recordings), patents, trademarks, trade secrets, plant breeders' rights, industrial designs, and integrated circuits (semiconductor chip). NAFTA's copyright provisions will provide protection for 50 years. The Agreement's patent protection provisions will safeguard inventions in areas as diverse as pharmaceuticals and agricultural chemicals. NAFTA establishes strong enforcement procedures in this area,

including provisions on damages, injunctive relief, and due process.

Investment NAFTA's coverage of investment issues includes all forms of ownership and interests in a business: tangible property, intangible property, and contractual rights. More specifically, NAFTA regulates minority as well as majority interests in business and other types of investment such as bonds, real estate, and stocks. NAFTA significantly reduces the need for approval of investments by foreign governments. The Agreement also provides for the elimination of various investment distortions, including the requirements that foreign investors use domestic goods or services, export a given level (or percentage) of goods or services, limit imports to a certain percentage of exports, or transfer technology to competitors. Furthermore, NAFTA prohibits discrimination against US investors who seek to acquire, establish, or operate a business in Mexico. Under NAFTA, Mexico will eliminate the screening of new foreign investments in most sectors and will severely curtail its review of takeovers of existing enterprises.

Investments in a NAFTA country by a party in another NAFTA country are protected from unjust expropriation. NAFTA establishes procedural guidelines for the resolution of investment disputes through arbitration, which include provisions for binding international arbitration. If a country has expropriated, the Agreement provides for the full repatriation in foreign currencies of the investors' profits, royalties, and capital as well as for fair compensation to the injured party.

Despite its comprehensive scope with regard to investment, the Agreement contains some country-specific exceptions to the principle of national treatment, most-favored-nation treatment and certain performance requirements. In addition, NAFTA does not cover investment issues related to maritime concerns and government sponsored technology consortia and research and development programs.

Market Access NAFTA covers numerous principles relevant to market access, including tariffs, quotas, and import licenses. Significantly, the NAFTA countries agreed to prohibit the use of import and export restrictions. Nevertheless, each NAFTA nation may, under limited circumstances, establish certain border restrictions such as those relating to health, safety, and welfare. In addition, NAFTA addresses the topic of drawbacks and duty referral programs. Under the NAFTA drawback provision, refunds or waivers of customs duties are granted on materials that are used in the production of goods subsequently exported to another NAFTA member. The Agreement provides for the elimination of these drawback programs for Mexico–US and Mexico–Canada trade by January 1, 2001. The time-frame for the elimination of the drawback programs under the

CFTA was, however, extended by two years. Once these programs are eliminated, the NAFTA parties will use new procedures for items that remain subject to duties in the free trade area in order "to avoid the 'double taxation' effects of the payment of duties in two countries."

The NAFTA parties also agreed not to impose additional customs user fees (customs merchandise fees and processing fees). The United States is gradually reducing customs user fees on items of Canadian origin, and their complete elimination was expected by January 1, 1994. Moreover, the United States and Mexico agreed to eliminate merchandise processing fees on goods originating from their respective countries by June 30, 1999. Along similar lines, NAFTA provides that Mexico will eliminate its performance-based customs duty waiver program or duty remission program. In accordance with the CFTA, Canada will eliminate its existing duty remission programs by January 1, 1998. Finally, NAFTA discusses various other issues such as export taxes, other export measures, and duty-free temporary admission of goods.

Tariffs and Rules of Origin NAFTA provides for the gradual elimination of tariffs on US, Mexican, and Canadian products by the Member States. Tariff reductions are referred to in NAFTA according to the Harmonized Commodity Description and Coding System (HS) classification. The reduction in tariffs will occur at different stages on a variety of products. Some tariffs will be completely removed as soon as the Agreement enters into force. Tariffs on other products will be removed after five or 10 years, while tariffs on some sensitive products will not be fully removed for 15 years. Tariffs on US–Canadian trade will be controlled according to the provisions of the US–Canada Free Trade Agreement.

Under NAFTA, two rules of origin mechanisms are utilized: tariff-shift rules and value-content rules. Tariff-shift rules require that all non-NAFTA inputs must be in a different tariff classification than the final product. More specifically, these rules require that the non-NAFTA input be in a different HS chapter heading or tariff item number.

Under NAFTA's value-content rules, a set percentage of the value of the good must be North American (often in conjunction with a tariff-shift requirement). Some goods are subject to the value-content rule only when they fail to pass the tariff-shift test because of non-NAFTA inputs.

NAFTA establishes tough rules of origin, which require that products contain substantial North American content in order to obtain duty-free status under the Agreement. These provisions are intended to prevent non-Member States from using a NAFTA nation as a minor processing, transshipment center, or export platform.

NAFTA provides specific rules of origin for various trade sectors. For example, light trucks and passenger vehicles ultimately will be subject to a 62.5 percent North American content requirement in order to obtain preferential treatment under NAFTA. NAFTA also provides for the imposition of a 60 percent North American content requirement on other vehicles after a phase-in period. In the textiles sector, NAFTA requires as a condition of preferential treatment that garments must be made from North American fabric and yarn. Finally, in order for computers to qualify for duty-free treatment under NAFTA, the motherboard (a key component which generally accounts for between 20 to 40 percent of the value of a computer) must be made in North America.

Technical Standards NAFTA affirms the right of the parties to adopt, apply, and enforce standards-related measures to promote safety and protect people, animals and plants, and the environment. In addition, NAFTA stipulates that standards-related measures must provide both national treatment and

Cartoonists & Writers Syndicate
Artist: Arcadio. Originally published in La Nacion, San José, Costa Rica. Copyright © 1994 Arcadio/Cartoonists & Writers Syndicate.

most-favored-nation treatment. The Agreement establishes conformity assessment procedures for determining whether the requirements set out in technical regulations or standards are being complied with. Moreover, NAFTA encourages agreements between governments and private standards organizations for mutual acceptance of test results and certification procedures. Finally, NAFTA generally requires that changes in standards-related measures be subject to a public notice procedure.

GOODS AND SERVICE SECTOR OVERVIEW

Agriculture When NAFTA enters into force, one-half of US agricultural exports to Mexico will become duty-free. Most of the remaining Mexican tariffs on US items will be eliminated within five years of the initiation of the Agreement. By the 10th year, nearly 95 percent of US agricultural exports will enter Mexico duty-free. In addition, Mexican tariffs on certain import-sensitive products originating from the United States and Canada will be phased out after 15 years. At the outset, Mexican import licenses will be eliminated on a large proportion of the US agricultural exports which are currently licensed. All US and Mexican non-tariff barriers will be converted to either tariff-rate quotas or ordinary tariffs. The CFTA will continue to be operative for US–Canadian agricultural trade.

Mexico and Canada negotiated a separate arrangement in the agricultural area. This Mexican-Canadian arrangement gradually eliminates all tariff and non-tariff barriers on agricultural goods, with the exception of dairy products, eggs, poultry, and sugar. Also, Mexican import licenses on Canadian agricultural exports will be converted to tariffs, and the latter will be eliminated on most items in 10 years. These changes will give Canadian exporters of pork, apples, and potato products greater access to Mexican markets.

Automotive NAFTA will further liberalize and integrate the North American automotive sector by increasing competitiveness, creating employment opportunities, and reducing prices for North American consumers. Another important effect of the implementation of NAFTA will be the termination of the Mexican Auto Decree at the end of NAFTA's transition period. During this transition period, the restrictions under the Mexican Auto Decree will be modified by the elimination of limits on the sale of imported vehicles in Mexico, by amendments to trade balancing requirements, and by changes to the national value-added rules. Mexican tariffs on autos and light trucks from Canada and the United States will be reduced by 50 percent when NAFTA enters into force. The remaining Mexican tariffs on autos will be

eliminated in 10 years, and those on light trucks in five years. In addition, US sales of medium and heavy trucks to Mexico, although subject to a large quota during the first five years of NAFTA, will become duty-free after that period. Similarly, Mexican tariffs on almost 75 percent of US auto parts will be removed within five years of NAFTA's entry into force. Restrictions on the importation of used motor vehicles will be phased out. NAFTA provides for the elimination of investment restrictions on the aforementioned automotive sectors over a 10 year period. In addition, Mexico will allow US and Canadian investors to make investments of up to 100 percent in Mexican "national suppliers" of parts, as well as up to 49 percent in other automotive parts enterprises—reaching 100 percent after five years. Moreover, adjustments to the United States Corporate Fuel Economy rules will enable Mexican-produced parts and vehicles exported to the United States to be classified as domestic products.

US–Canadian automotive issues will remain covered by automotive provisions of the US–Canada Free Trade Agreement.

Energy NAFTA provides US and Canadian firms greater access to Mexico's electricity, gas, petrochemical, energy services, and equipment markets. For instance, NAFTA provides opportunities for US and Canadian firms to sell to the Mexican state-owned oil company (Pemex) and the State Electricity Commission (CFE) through open and competitive bidding rules. The Agreement also permits private foreign ownership and operation of electric generating plants for self-generation, co-generation, and independent power plants in Mexico. Implementation of NAFTA will immediately reduce trade and investment restrictions on most Mexican petrochemicals, lifting investment restrictions on 14 of the 19 previously restricted basic petrochemicals and 66 secondary petrochemicals. Moreover, NAFTA permits firms to negotiate supply contracts directly with Mexican buyers of natural gas and basic petrochemicals. The Agreement also provides for performance incentives in service contracts, which might be used for such activities as oil drilling.

In addition, NAFTA permits barrier-free trade in Mexican non-energy refinery products, including asphalt, greases, lubricating oils, and waxes. Also, CFE and electric utilities in the United States and Canada will have the right to negotiate power purchase and sales contracts.

The US–Canadian energy sector will continue to be covered by the US–Canada Free Trade Agreement.

Environment NAFTA will create numerous opportunities for environmental equipment firms and services, including companies in the following areas: solid waste disposal technology, hazardous and non-hazardous waste engineering consulting, sewage treatment, water treatment, wastewater treatment, environmental rehabilitation, and specialized monitoring services. NAFTA's trade liberalization should increase US exports to Mexico in air pollution control technology. US exports in control technology for Canadian paper and mining firms should also increase.

NAFTA provides that existing environmental accords, such as the Montreal Protocol on Substances that Deplete the Ozone layer, have primacy over conflicting NAFTA provisions. NAFTA also encourages an upward harmonization of environmental standards in the three Member States. Even as the Agreement promotes investment in various sectors, it requires the maintenance of stringent health, safety, and environmental standards. It requires national treatment for environmental standards on investments, and requires that environmental impact assessments be made on investments. Under the Agreement's dispute settlement section, a NAFTA member may buttress its complaint concerning another party's environmental and health standards by calling on scientific and environmental experts. The NAFTA parties established the North American Commission on Environmental Cooperation in September, 1992, to "set in motion a process for sustained, long-term effective trilateral environmental cooperation."

Financial Services NAFTA provides a comprehensive approach to the regulation of providers of various financial services, including banks, securities firms, finance companies, leasing companies, and insurance companies. The Agreement contains definitive liberalization commitments and transition periods for compliance. NAFTA permits members of the Agreement to accord national treatment and most-favored-nation treatment to the various financial services. A key benefit of the Agreement is that those involved in trade transactions in Mexico will be able to use "one-stop shopping," which permits the use of the same financial service providers for both domestic and international operations. NAFTA also stipulates the need for procedural transparency for applications relating to the creation of financial institutions. Finally, the financial services sector will be subject to NAFTA's dispute settlement mechanism.

US–Canadian financial services commitments made under CFFA are incorporated into NAFTA. In addition, Mexico will be exempt from Canada's prohibition against non-residents acquiring more than 25 percent of the shares of federally-regulated Canadian financial institutions. Mexican banks will not be subject to Canada's combined 12 percent asset ceiling, which will still apply to non-NAFTA banks.

Furthermore, Mexican banks will not need the approval of Canada's Ministry of Finance as a condition of opening multiple branches in Canada.

Mexico will permit financial firms organized according to NAFTA's requirements to be established in Mexico under certain market share limits, which will be eliminated by the year 2000. Even after implementation, various aggregate market share limits will continue to apply to US and Canadian firms in the Mexican banking and securities area., Mexico will also permit US and Canadian finance companies to establish separate subsidiaries to engage in consumer lending, commercial lending, mortgage lending, and the provision of credit cards. During the transition period, aggregate assets of such subsidiaries will be restricted. Leasing companies and factoring firms will be subject to aggregate market share limits in Mexico (as securities firms), but not individual market share limits. NAFTA foreign exchange houses, mutual fund management companies, warehousing companies, and bonding companies will be allowed to establish subsidiaries without ownership or market share limits when the Agreement goes into effect.

Mexican financial groups that have acquired a Mexican bank with operations in the United States will be allowed to continue to operate a securities firm in the United States for five years after the acquisition. However, the acquisition must occur prior to the date on which NAFTA goes into effect. Moreover, under these rules the acquired banks must have been operating in the US market on January 1, 1992, and the acquired securities firm must have been operating in the US market on June 30, 1992. The securities firms may not expand the scope of their activities or acquire other securities firms in the United States, and will be subject to nondiscriminatory restrictions on transactions between parent and affiliate.

Insurance NAFTA enables US and Canadian firms to penetrate Mexico's US$3.5 billion insurance market. Currently, foreign ownership in a Mexican insurance firm is limited to 49 percent. Under NAFTA, US and Canadian firms that form joint ventures with Mexican insurers may increase, at set intervals, their stakes in such firms with the possibility of ultimately owning 100 percent by the year 2000. Also, US and Canadian insurers may establish subsidiaries in Mexico, subject to aggregate limits of 6 percent market share, gradually increasing to 12 percent in 1999, and subject to individual market caps of 1.5 percent. These restrictions will ultimately be eliminated by 2000. US and Canadian firms that have already established an ownership interest in Mexican insurers may raise their equity participation to 100 percent by 1996. Auxiliary and intermediary insurance service companies will be permitted to form subsidiaries without ownership or market share limits when NAFTA goes into effect.

Pharmaceuticals In 1991 US exports of pharmaceutical products to Mexico and Canada reached US$645 million and US$121 million, respectively. Under NAFTA, Mexico will remove its import licenses on pharmaceutical products, and will eliminate tariffs on these products over ten years. Currently, Mexican tariffs on pharmaceuticals range between 10 percent and 20 percent. NAFTA will also eliminate compulsory licensing for pharmaceuticals and will extend patent protection to at least 20 years. Under the Agreement, Mexico will greatly open its government procurement market for pharmaceuticals.

Sanitary and Phytosanitary Measures This section of NAFTA focuses on the establishment and enforcement of standards for the protection of human, animal, and plant life, as well as standards for health risks due to animal pests or plant diseases, food additives, or food contaminants. While providing that each NAFTA country may establish its own sanitary and phytosanitary rules, the Agreement stipulates that such measures must be based on scientific principle and risk assessment and must be applied only to the extent necessary to meet the country's chosen level of protection. They must not be established to promote unfair discrimination, or to serve as disguised restrictions on trade. In addition, NAFTA calls for member nations to strive toward the establishment of harmonized standards. The Agreement furthers procedural transparency by generally requiring public notice prior to the adoption or modification of sanitary and phytosanitary measures that may affect North American trade.

Services NAFTA improves access to Canada's US$250 billion services market and opens Mexico's US$146 billion services market. The Agreement liberalizes trade-related services by extending the basic principles of national treatment and most-favored-nation treatment to this sector. NAFTA also eliminates the requirement that a service provider establish a local presence. Nevertheless, some restrictions on services will remain, including various state, provincial, or federal reservations, non-discriminatory quantitative restrictions, licensing and certification requirements, denial of benefits to specific firms, and exclusions. Among the key service sectors affected by NAFTA are: accounting, advertising, architecture, consulting/management, construction, engineering, enhanced telecommunications, environmental services, health care management, land management, law, medicine, and tourism. While NAFTA does not address basic telecommunications services, such as local and long-distance telephone services, enhanced services such as advanced data-processing services are covered. Similarly, although domestic maritime services are not covered by NAFTA, reference is made to the desire to maintain relatively open international shipping markets. NAFTA also covers specialty air services such as aerial mapping and surveying.

Telecommunications NAFTA reduces barriers to Mexico's US$6 billion market for telecommunications equipment and services. Mexico's demand for im-

ported telecommunications products is expected to grow by 42 percent by the year 2000. These projected changes increase the possibility that US exports of telecommunications equipment and enhanced services, which reached US$750 million and US$22 million, respectively, in 1991, will grow significantly under NAFTA. This will in part be due to provisions in NAFTA that will streamline testing and certification requirements of telecommunications equipment while eliminating over 80 percent of tariffs on US telecommunications equipment exports to Mexico. Moreover, under NAFTA, Mexico will immediately remove all tariffs on telecommunications equipment, with the exception of central switching apparatus and telephone sets. Tariffs on these products will gradually be phased out by 1998. Trade in enhanced telecommunications services will be liberalized when NAFTA enters into force. To complement this general trade liberalization, NAFTA provides that public telecommunications transport networks and services are to be made available on reasonable, non-discriminatory terms and conditions.

Specific rules on access to and use of public networks are set out under the Agreement. Of critical importance is the movement toward future compatibility of interoperable telecommunications services in the United States, Mexico, and Canada. NAFTA does not require contracting parties to provide or operate telecommunications transport networks or services for other contracting parties.

Textiles and Apparel NAFTA covers a wide range of products—fibers, yarns, textiles, and clothing. The three Member States have agreed that NAFTA should have primacy over other textile agreements. The NAFTA nations will immediately remove, or phase out over a maximum period of 10 years, their customs duties on textile and apparel goods that satisfy NAFTA rules of origin. Under NAFTA, the United States will initially remove import quotas on such goods produced in Mexico, and will gradually remove import quotas on Mexican textile and apparel goods that do not meet NAFTA rules of origin. Also, NAFTA establishes new rules of origin under which yarns, as well as fabrics in a garment, must be produced in the United States, Canada, or Mexico.

NAFTA opens the US$6.4 billion Mexican textile and apparel market, of which US exports comprised US$1.1 billion in 1991. For example, NAFTA will immediately remove Mexican barriers on over 20 percent (US$250 million) of US textile and apparel exports to Mexico. Six years after NAFTA enters into force, Mexican barriers on another US$700 million worth of US textile exports will be removed. Both Canada and Mexico will phase out tariffs on apparel over 10 years and tariffs on textile products over eight years.

NAFTA increases most quotas on textiles and apparel by 2 percent per year for five years. Such quotas may be raised in the future. In addition, NAFTA permits the use of safeguards, such as increased tariffs or the imposition of quotas when serious damage to the domestic market results from a greater volume of imports. NAFTA provides strict rules of origin, including provisions covering yarn content, fiber content, and tariff rate quotas. Finally, various textile and apparel labeling requirements are applicable under NAFTA.

Transportation NAFTA removes barriers to various land transportation services and sets forth rules for the establishment of compatible land transport technical and safety standards. In the bus and trucking services area, the United States will amend its moratorium on granting operating authority to Mexican trucks and buses by allowing Mexican charter and tour bus operators full access to the US cross-border market. Canadian truck and bus companies are not subject to the US moratorium. Mexico will in turn grant equivalent rights to US and Canadian charter and tour bus operators and will also accord them full access to regular bus routes by the end of 1996. By the end of 1995, Mexico will permit US and Canadian truck operators to make cross-border deliveries to and pick up cargo in Mexican border states. Similarly, by the end of 1995, the United States will permit such services to Mexican companies. Under the Agreement, Mexico will permit US and Canadian bus and trucking firms to establish international cargo subsidiaries or new companies in Mexico. Mexico will allow Canadian and US bus and trucking firms to obtain the following levels of ownership in Mexican firms: minority ownership by the end of 1995; majority ownership by 2000; and 100 percent ownership by 2003. US and Canadian firms will permit Mexican trucking firms to distribute international cargo. Yet, the Agreement does not obligate NAFTA countries to remove restrictions on truck carriage of domestic cargo. By the end of 1996, Mexico will permit cross-border bus service to and from any part of Mexico and by the end of 1999 this will be extended to truck service as well. Under the same guidelines, the United States will provide reciprocal privileges to Mexican firms. Finally, NAFTA provides for the harmonization of operating and safety standards within a three- to six-year period, including drivers' licenses, equipment standards, and the standards relevant to the transport of dangerous goods.

In the area of rail service, NAFTA does not affect US or Canadian capacity to market their services in Mexico, operate unit trains with their own locomotives, construct and own terminals, or finance the construction of rail infrastructure. Mexico will continue to enjoy full access to the US and Canadian railroad systems.

In the marine transport area, Mexico will allow US and Canadian firms to be the sole owners and operators of various port facilities used by firms handling their own cargo or firms handling other companies' cargo.

NAFTA SUPPLEMENTAL AGREEMENTS

On August 13, 1993, the US, Mexico, and Canada announced that they had reached agreement on supplemental accords to NAFTA on labor, environment, and import surges. Completion of the parallel agreements will enable the Clinton Administration to draft implementing legislation, which must be passed by the US Congress.

The benefits of the parallel agreements are several-fold. More specifically, the supplemental accords will help ensure that enforcement of domestic environmental laws and workplace standards and requirements are strengthened. The accords also provide that no nation can lower labor or environmental standards, only raise them, and all states or provinces can enact even more stringent measures. In addition, the process of consultation, evaluation, and dispute settlement will be opened to the public. Furthermore, access to justice and due process rights are extended to environmental and labor issues, and administrative remedies as well as court procedures are available.

The accords provide for the establishment of commissions to evaluate and settle disputes on labor and environmental issues. Moreover, enforcement proceedings have real "teeth," assuring compliance. At the same time, the agreements strengthen border clean up and infrastructure development. They establish a new mechanism for consultations among the NAFTA nations and for examining economic factors in the region. Although not formally part of the NAFTA supplemental agreements, the funding of US-Mexico infrastructure was also discussed.

Labor Issues

The Agreement on Labor Cooperation will promote improved labor conditions and strong enforcement of national labor laws in the US, Mexico, and Canada.

Labor Commission The Agreement creates a new Commission on Labor Cooperation, with each country represented on a Council by its top, cabinet-level labor official. The Council has a broad mandate to work cooperatively on labor issues, including occupational health and safety, child labor, minimum wages, benefits for workers, industrial relations, legislation on formation and operation of unions, and the resolution of labor disputes. The Council will be able to obtain public advice and assistance in these activities.

An independent International Coordinating Secretariat will provide technical support to the Council, and will itself report periodically to the Council on a wide range of labor issues. Each nation will also appoint a National Administrative Office that will be a point of contact between other Commission entities and national governments.

Labor Principles and Objectives The objectives of the Agreement include promotion of improved labor laws and standards, effective enforcement of these laws, encouraging competition based on rising productivity and quality, and the promotion of such key labor principles as the protection against child labor, the right to strike and to bargain collectively, freedom of association, and minimum employment standards.

Transparency and Domestic Enforcement Each country undertakes to ensure the transparency of its laws and to enforce those laws through special means, including the publication of laws, regulations, and procedures and the promotion of public awareness of these laws and regulations. The goal is to ensure that workers and employers know their rights and responsibilities. The involvement of the employers and workers in this process is expected to better ensure the promotion of, and compliance with, the laws, as well as enforcement of the provisions.

Access to Fair Domestic Procedures The Agreement establishes detailed requirements that are consistent with US law and process, assuring fair administrative and judicial review. These include the following commitments: to provide effective means for binding domestic enforcement of rights granted under a country's labor laws; to maintain domestic administrative and judicial processes that are independent and impartial; to provide a right to seek independent review; and to provide a right for the parties to a proceeding to seek remedies for the enforcement of labor rights.

Encouraging Effective Enforcement by Governments The Independent Coordinating Secretariat will be reporting periodically on labor laws and their enforcement in each country. On the next level, the National Administrative Office can consult and exchange information on enforcement, and the Council can also consult on any labor matter. In addition, an Evaluation Committee of Experts, composed of independent experts, will be convened at the request of any party to examine a matter involving a pattern of practice. Provisions have been made for dispute settlement panels, backed ultimately by fines and trade sanctions. These provisions can be invoked if a party believes that another is persistently failing to enforce labor laws effectively.

Environmental Issues

The Agreement on Environmental Cooperation will ensure that economic growth is consistent with the goals of sustainable development.

New Independent Organization The Agreement creates a new Commission on Environmental Cooperation. The top environmental officials of the three nations will comprise the Commission's Council.

Environmental Obligations The NAFTA partners have committed to undertake important environmental policies regarding the development, implementation, and enforcement of their environmental laws. These nations will guarantee their citizens access to national courts to petition governments to undertake enforcement actions and to seek redress of harm. In addition, the nations will ensure the openness of judicial and administrative proceedings and transparent procedures for the creation of environmental laws. The NAFTA members have pledged to ensure that their laws and standards will continue to provide high levels of environmental protection, and they will work cooperatively in enhancing protections. In addition, the NAFTA nations have agreed to effectively enforce those laws, a commitment backed by a dispute settlement process. Furthermore, the Agreement does not affect the rights of states and provinces under NAFTA to maintain standards at levels higher than the federal governments. The nations are obligated to report on the state of their environments and to promote environmental education, scientific research, and technological development. Furthermore, they will work toward limiting trade in toxic substances that they have banned domestically.

Commission's Agenda A major goal of the Commission is to broaden cooperative activities among the NAFTA partners. The Commission will have an aggressive and important workplan. It will consider the environmental implications of process and production methods. Also, it will promote greater public access to information about hazardous substances. Among its tasks, the Commission will consider ways to promote the assessment and mitigation of transboundary environmental problems. It will serve as a point of inquiry for public concerns about NAFTA's effect on the environment.

Public Participation and Dispute Settlement Transparency is the hallmark of the Agreement. Citizens of all three nations will be free to make submissions to the Commission on their concerns related to the full range of environmental issues.

Scope of Environmental Agreement Any environmental or natural resource may be addressed through the work program, and any environmental concern or obligation of the Agreement may be the subject of consultations between parties.

Import Surges

The understanding on import surges establishes a new mechanism for consultations among the NAFTA nations and for examining economic factors,

NAFTA REFERENCES AND RESOURCES

Publications

"Annual Symposium: The North American Free Trade Agreement," International Lawyer, Vol. 27, page 589 (1993).

Mexico & NAFTA Report Available from: Latin American Newsletters, 61 Old St., London EC1V 9HX, UK; Tel: [44] (71) 251-0012 Fax: [44] (71) 253-8193.

NAFTA Business Manual Available from: Business and International Trade Editorial, 405 Harvard Avenue West, Winnipeg, MB R2C 1Y8, Canada; Tel: (204) 222-9038.

"NAFTA Dispute Resolution," "NAFTA Environment," "NAFTA Intellectual Property Rights," "NAFTA Investment," "NAFTA Market Access: Goods," "NAFTA Services" Published by the Office of the US Trade Representative, 600 17th Street NW, Washington, DC 20506, USA; Tel: [1] (202) 395-3204.

NAFTA Facts Flash Facts Delivers a wide range of short documents on NAFTA via an automated fax retrieval system. Available from: US Department of Commerce; Tel: [1] (202) 482-4464.

NAFTA Implementation Act Public Law Number 12,889. Available in: 58 Fed. Reg. 69,681 (1993).

NAFTA Law Reporter Available from: WorldTrade Executive, PO Box 761, Concord, MA 01742, USA; Tel: [1] (508) 287-0302 Fax: [1] (508) 287-0301.

NAFTA Made Simple Available from: SANDFORD Tax & Customs Consulting, PO Box 60186, Sunnyvale, CA 94088, USA; Tel: [1] (408) 720-0577.

North American Free Trade Agreement (NAFTA), Vols. I & II. US$41.00. Stock number 041-001-00376-2. Available from: US Government Printing Office, Washington, DC 20402-9328, USA; Tel: [1] (202) 783-3238.

"Planning for the North American Free Trade Agreement," by Merriam Mashatt, Business America (October 19, 1992). Available on the National Trade Data Bank or from: US Government Printing Office, Washington, DC 20402-9328, USA; Tel: [1] (202) 783-3238.

"Sector-by-Sector: Key Provisions of Trade Agreement," Journal of Commerce (August 13, 1992), p. 5A.

Understanding the North American Free Trade Agreement Available from: Kluwer Law and Taxation Publishers, 675 Massachusetts Avenue, Cambridge, MA 01239, USA; Tel: [1] (617) 354-0140 Fax: [1] (617) 354-8595.

US–Mexico Law Journal Available from: University of New Mexico, School of Law, 1117 Stanford NE, Albuquerque, NM 87131, USA; Tel: [1] (505) 227-2146.

Agencies & Organizations

Info Export
External Affairs and International Trade Canada
125 Sussex Drive
Ottawa, ON K1A 0G2, Canada
Tel: [1] (613) 944-4000 Fax: [1] (613) 996-9709

NAFTA Help Desk
US Customs Service
1301 Constitution Ave NW, Room 1325
Washington, DC 20229, USA
Tel: [1] (202) 927-0066 Fax: [1] (202) 927-0097

NAFTA Information Desk
Revenue Canada Customs, Excise and Tax
555 MacKenzie Avenue
Ottawa, ON K1A 0L5, Canada
Tel: [1] (613) 941-0965 Fax: [1] (613) 941-8138

NAFTA Research Institute
4410 Massachusetts Ave. NW, Suite 324
Washington, DC 20016, USA
Tel: [1] (202) 298-4574 Fax: [1] (202) 686-2828

NAFTA Secretariat, Canadian Section
90 Sparks Street, Suite 705
Ottawa, ON K1P 5B4, Canada
Tel: [1] (613) 992-9380 Fax: [1] (613) 992-9392

US Department of Commerce
Trade Information Center
14th St. and Constitution Ave. NW
Washington, DC 20229, USA
Tel: (800) USA-TRADE (Toll-free in the US only)

including employment.

NAFTA Safeguard Provisions NAFTA itself contains several key provisions to safeguard a country's industry and workforce against import surges. A bilateral safeguard mechanism permits a "snap-back" to pre-NAFTA or most-favored-nation tariff rates for up to three years (or four years for extremely sensitive products) if increased imports from Mexico are a substantial cause of, or threaten serious injury, to a domestic industry.

Also, a global safeguard mechanism allows the imposition of tariffs or quotas on imports from Mexico or Canada, or both, as part of a multilateral safeguard action when imports from either or both countries are a substantial cause of, or threaten serious injury to, a domestic industry. In addition, sensitive agricultural products are handled specially in the form of tariff-rate quotas, under which high most-favored-nation tariffs become effective above a specified quantity of imports. Sensitive textile and apparel products also have special provisions to respond to those industries needs.

Changing NAFTA'S Provisions The Working Group established under the Agreement will consider how well NAFTA's safeguard provisions are working and make recommendations for revisions, as appropriate.

Funding Environmental Infrastructure Projects in the US–Mexico Border Region

New Institutional Developments A basic agreement was reached on a new institutional structure to promote effective coordination of infrastructure projects. A hallmark of the institution will be transparent process, which incorporates the views of local residents and nongovernment organizations. Initially, the institution will focus on projects addressing the serious wastewater treatment and water pollution problems along the border. Also, the institution will provide assistance on both the technical and financial aspects of the projects.

Financing Options Although the institution will not itself offer bonds initially, it will work to mobilize multiple sources of financing, depending on the nature of the individual projects. As appropriate, it could turn to the private sector, direct government support (loans, grants, or guarantees at the federal, state, and local level), and a border environmental financing facility. Subject to future agreement, the institution could raise capital directly. Furthermore, the US and Mexico are pursuing the capitalization of a new financing mechanism to serve the border institution as one source of direct loans and partial guarantees.

CONCLUSION

NAFTA will clearly lead to greater economic integration in North America. As the Agreement enters into force, North American businesses and consumers will be presented with new opportunities and challenges for trade and investment.

The creation of NAFTA represents, in a sense, a continuation of the efforts by several groups such as the European Community, the Association of Southeast Asian Nations, and the Caribbean Community Common Market to accelerate trade through regional trade agreements. The success of regional frameworks should be contrasted with the continued obstacles in the multilateral General Agreement on Tariffs and Trade. In the face of such multilateral difficulties, regional frameworks such as NAFTA may become an increasingly attractive means of expanding international trade.

NAFTA: TRADE IN GOODS BOON OR BOONDOGGLE?*

NAFTA CERTIFICATE OF ORIGIN

There are two steps every shipper and consignee will have to undertake in order to take advantage of NAFTA's trade in goods benefits (see Chapter 4, North American Free Trade Agreement; HR 3450; 19 CFR Part 181). All items in a product line should be reviewed to determine the impact of the NAFTA rules of origin. Having done the analysis and decided that the products qualify, the second step is to secure a Certificate of Origin issued by the exporter to his importer *before* making any NAFTA claim. If you do not have the Certificate, then you may make a NAFTA claim retroactively.

If your analysis finds that your product is not NAFTA eligible, then you are faced with the question of sourcing your components and raw materials in the territory (US, Canada, and/or Mexico). Part of any such decision-making process will be to take a look at whether there is a satisfactory alternative source within the territory. If so, you then need an analysis of whether the quality of the replacement raw materials and components is similar or better than the quality of the components or raw materials from the original source. If so, then you get into the question of whether the cost of the goods from the source within the territory is more or less than the cost from the original source. In the end, all companies that find their goods not eligible for NAFTA will have to do a cost–benefit analysis to ascertain how much more it will cost to source and manufacture within the territory versus how much duty will be saved.

A new Certificate of Origin (CF 434) form was created and is now available for sale through the US Customs Service. It must be used for all imports into the US, unless the Mexican or Canadian versions are used.

The exporter's Certificate may cover one shipment, a caravan, or a series of shipments. If the latter, then the time span (Blanket Period) must be indicated on the Certificate (maximum 12 months). Whether the Certificate covers one or many shipments, both the importer and the exporter (to the same transaction) must amend their claims within 30 days whenever either has "reason to believe" that the original claim is incorrect.

If you are a related party, you must have the completed Certificate signed by your sister plant (the exporter) to make your NAFTA claim. In turn, they will need one from you for the materials and components you send them in order to prepare yours.

If you are not the manufacturer but rather source

By Susan Kohn Ross, Ross & Associates, Los Angeles, California. Reprinted with permission of author and law firm. Copyright © 1994 Susan Kohn Ross.

components or materials from others (producers), to make a NAFTA claim, you must state on the Certificate the basis for NAFTA eligibility. As a result, it will be necessary for you to obtain written information from your suppliers about the origin of their components or materials. One of the bases for a non-producer NAFTA claim is reliance on written assurances from the actual producer, similar to manufacturers' affidavits and American goods returned. However, one must review each product's rule of origin to determine the detail required in the assurance.

Certificates may only be signed by an individual who can bind the corporation, so managers, officers, or directors will have to be involved, not clerks. A Certificate for an individual shipment is valid for four years from date of signature but there are exceptions when the Certificate is not required (usually low value or noncommercial transactions). The original Certificate is retained in the importer's files until production is demanded by the importer's home country Customs Service.

NAFTA RULES OF ORIGIN

North American Free Trade Agreement Article 401

To determine whether a product is eligible for NAFTA benefits requires an understanding of the rules of origin. There are four basic rules: A) wholly obtained or produced; B) not wholly obtained or produced; C) produced entirely from originating materials; and D) unassembled or disassembled components and parts provided for in the same tariff provision as the finished product. The rules are applied in order.

Rule A—Wholly Obtained or Produced Covers natural resources such as agricultural products, mineral goods, items taken from the ocean or air, and waste and scrap produced in the territory. Examples for this rule would be flowers grown from seeds, shellfish, other forms of marine life, motor oil made in Mexico from Mexican crude, and silver jewelry made in the US from Mexican silver.

Rule B—Not Wholly Obtained or Produced Arises when foreign materials and components are imported into the territory and become originating due to further manufacturing. An example would be plastic boxes made from foreign resins. To qualify under this and the remaining rules of origin, one needs to be familiar with two concepts: tariff shift and regional value content.

Tariff shift results when the change in tariff classification occurs as dictated by Article 401. The individual rule of origin must be consulted as the amount of change necessary varies by rule, sometimes the change needs to be only at the two digit (chapter) level, other times to the four (subchapter),

six (subheading), or eight (tariff provision) digit level. In addition, for import sensitive goods there are exceptions to be concerned about. The key to qualifying is that the necessary manufacturing steps are undertaken in the region.

Regional value content (RVC) requires that a certain percentage of value be added in the region for the product to qualify. For many products only a tariff shift is required. For others, there may only be an RVC requirement. But for many others, they may qualify *either* by tariff shift or RVC. There are two formulas for RVC: transaction value and net cost. The formula that applies depends on the product and the parties involved.

RVC transaction value is not the same as transaction value for dutiable calculation (GATT value). While the concepts are similar, GATT value calls for the value of the item in its condition for export to the US. RVC transaction value calls for the price paid or payable to the *producer* (who may not be the exporter).

Net cost is the required computation if you are importing footwear, certain word processing equipment, and certain autos and auto parts. It is also required where the transaction is between related parties. However, the definition of "related" is somewhat different. The US Customs and US Internal Revenue Service (IRS) definition of "related" calls for certain types of familial, business (partnership, common directors, officers, etc.), or shareholder (5 percent) relationships. NAFTA "related" builds on those principles, leaving the existing provisions as they are except as to the shareholder definition (which is raised to 25 percent) *and* a quantitative sales requirement: 85 percent or more of the sales between the parties must be of identical or similar merchandise.

Net cost is defined as the total cost of production less sales promotion, royalties (there is a new definition), shipping and packing costs, and nonallowable interest (also a new concept). "Usual" profits are also excluded.

Royalties are defined as payment for the "use or right to use" the copyright, patent, or trademark. The current distinction in US Customs law between right to manufacture versus right to sell (royalty versus subsequent proceeds, see 19 USC 1401a) is eliminated in NAFTA.

Nonallowable interest arises if the party pays more than 7 percent above the interest rate set in the Uniform Regulations or the debt rate to the IRS or its Mexican or Canadian equivalent.

Rule C—A Good Produced in the Territory Exclusively from Originating Materials Results when raw materials are imported and become originating due to further processing. Those intermediate materials are then further manufactured into finished products. For example, a desk made in Canada from Canadian wood with metal hardware qualifies under

FOUR STEPS TO PRODUCT CERTIFICATION UNDER NAFTA*

The process for determining whether the NAFTA duty-savings provisions apply to your products when importing or exporting goods to Canada, Mexico, or the United States is as follows:

1. Determine the tariff classification of your goods from the Harmonized Tariff Schedule. (This step is required for all goods, regardless of whether NAFTA certification is sought.)
2. Determine whether the goods are subject to duties or are free of duties. If the goods are free of duties, you can stop at this step. (This step is required for all goods, regardless of whether NAFTA certification is sought.)
3. Compile a bill of materials or other listing of all materials used in manufacturing your product, including information on cost, description, and quantity.
4. Determine whether the goods qualify under NAFTA rules of origin by reviewing the bill of materials to determine the country of origin of the goods.
   - Are the goods wholly obtained entirely within Canada, Mexico, or the United States?
   - For goods not wholly obtained, have they been processed entirely within Canada, Mexico, or the United States such that they are significantly transformed and their tariff classification is changed, qualifying the goods for NAFTA treatment?
   - If the goods are not transformed, does a NAFTA *de minimis* rule exception apply?

Further Reading

North American Free Trade Agreement Guidebook provides a detailed, concise explanation, complete with examples, checklists, and forms, on how to determine whether a product qualifies for treatment under NAFTA and how to obtain NAFTA certification. Available from: SANDFORD, Tax & Customs Consulting, PO Box 60186, Sunnyvale, CA 94088 USA; Tel: [1] (408) 720-0577.

this rule if the imported metal was manufactured into the hardware in Canada.

Rule D—For Parts and Components This rule of origin arises in those circumstances where the imported item is disassembled or unassembled but complete. It also includes the circumstance in which the parts are classified in the same provision as the finished item—for example, projector parts are classified under 9007.92, as is the projector itself. If your product falls into any of these categories, then there is an RVC requirement.

In addition to the four basic rules of origin described above, there are two special ones.

Rule E—Deals with Computer Products Guided by the provisions of NAFTA Annex 308.1, the principle here is that between years five and 10 of the phase-in period, and when the rates of duty are the same in all three countries for the prescribed computer and related parts, a customs union will be formed in effect. An imported part will be duty-paid once at the time of its original importation into the territory. Thereafter, it may move from one country to the next within the territory without the payment of additional duties.

Rule F—Governs Agricultural Products (See also NAFTA Annex 703.2.) For all purposes but duty phase-outs and US–Canada agricultural issues, NAFTA supersedes the US–Canada Free Trade Agreement (CFTA). NAFTA governs US–Mexican relations regarding agriculture.

Although there is no separate rule of origin for textile products (unlike Annex 703.2 for agriculture), textiles and agriculture share the concept that quotas are to be eliminated. In their place, we will be dealing with tariff preference levels (TPLs). Many of us are used to this being called tariff rate quotas. A certain quantity is allowed importation at a lower (preferential) rate of duty. Once that level is reached, importations continue but the most favored nation rate of duty applies. Of course, TPLs apply primarily to originating goods.

Complexities and Applications While we have addressed the rules of origin in a general way, it is important to remember that these rules were written by all three countries, in part, to protect certain import sensitive industries. The rules were also written with an eye towards returning to North America certain manufacturing that is thought to represent the industries of the future. As a result, the most complicated rules arise for textiles, agriculture, footwear, autos, and high technology equipment. For example, for certain television sets to qualify as originating (for NAFTA benefits), the cathode ray tube (CRT) must originate. When you consult the CRT rule of origin, you quickly find that exceptions include all sorts of glass. As a result, the CRT must be manufactured from glass made within the territory for the television set to qualify.

In the textile context, for example, most imported cotton and man-made-fiber fabric will not qualify, nor will the garments manufactured from it. For agriculture, the complication comes primarily from the tariff preference levels and the resulting new tariff numbers. Overall some 1,800 new numbers were added to the Harmonized Tariff Schedule of the United States (HTS) with the enactment of NAFTA.

One shortcoming of the CFTA was rectified in NAFTA. Under the CFTA, even one foreign bolt could disqualify an otherwise fully US piece of machinery. As a result, NAFTA includes a *de minimus* rule. Up to 7 percent of the value of an item (7 percent by weight for textiles, and check for further exceptions) may be foreign, but the product will nonetheless qualify for NAFTA benefits.

To determine how the rules of origin apply requires us to start with the item in its condition as imported. What is its classification? What are the requirements of the applicable rule of origin? Where do the components or raw materials used in production come from? And if RVC is required, you value breakdown. Only once you have all that information, can you begin to determine the application of the rules of origin.

NAFTA MARKING RULES

North American Free Trade Agreement Annex 311

Adding to the changes that importers and exporters face as the result of NAFTA are the new country-of-origin marking rules. Although the customs procedures in the three countries were supposed to be the same, each country has issued its own set of marking rules. The estimation is that the requirements coincide about 85 percent of the time.

The principles for marking are similar to the ones for rules of origin: 1) wholly obtained or produced; 2) produced exclusively from domestic materials (raw materials manufactured in the region thereby becoming originating); and 3) tariff shift.

If you are unable to establish origin using these rules, you must establish essential character. If essential character comes from goods that are fungible and commingled, then origin is determined based on the type/quality of the inventory system.

Regarding sets, mixtures, or composite goods (General Rule of Interpretation 3), you again must determine essential character. If there are components that co-equally impart essential character but are from one origin, that origin applies. If there are several sources, you may have to establish the last country where processing (excluding simple assembly and minor processing) or assembly (if there are

multiple origins of co-equal parts) occurred. Failing that, multiple origins may apply.

The marking rules include a *de minimus* provision that allows no more than 7 percent of the materials (10 percent for goods of Chapter 22 HTS; 7 percent by weight for Chapters 50-63; and again check for exceptions) to be of foreign origin and not undergo tariff shift. When determining marking, you are allowed to disregard retail and export packaging materials and containers; accessories, spare parts and tools, and indirect materials.

Perhaps the most complicated part of the marking rules deals with parts. If the final product is shipped in an unassembled or disassembled condition, origin comes from the country of production. Where the HTS provision includes the parts in the same provision as the finished product, origin is conferred by the country of production *but only if* a substantial transformation occurs, that is, if a product with a new name, character, and use results.

It is possible to qualify for NAFTA benefits under the rules of origin but fail to qualify under the marking rules. If so there is a NAFTA override provision: you may claim US, Mexico, or Canada as the originating country anyway.

These marking rules are intended by US Customs to include all goods shipped from Canada or Mexico *regardless* of whether NAFTA benefits are claimed. Also US Customs has stated its intention to apply these marking rules to *all* products regardless of the country in which the import originates. Comments are due to US Customs by July 5, 1994, to the NAFTA marking rules and the concept of applying these rules to all imports.

To comply, companies will now routinely have to obtain information from their suppliers (all along the production chain) about the origin of all the parts, components, and mixtures used in the final product, adding yet another costly record-keeping obligation to insure compliance with the law.

CONCLUSION

In the interest of brevity, this article has only touched on the main points that will impact importers and exporters. It is important to remember that exporters will be as affected by NAFTA as importers in that for a Canadian or Mexican importer to take advantage of NAFTA, that company will have to have a Certificate of Origin from a US exporter. NAFTA is a drastic departure from what exporters have been used to because, in the past, they have simply shipped their goods. Now US exporters will be required to undergo an extensive analysis to determine whether or not the goods being shipped qualify.

The use of the Certificate of Origin is such that the original of the form remains in the importer's file until such time as his or her home country's Customs Service requests its production. In Mexico, this production is being requested routinely at time of clearance because of reasons having to do with certain dumping cases involving Chinese imports into Mexico. In the US and Canada, the form is not required proforma to be produced at time of entry.

What has also occurred is that each of the three countries has strengthened its penalty provisions. In fact, in the US the second part of the North American Free Trade Agreement bill (HR 3450) included what is referred to as the Customs Modernization and Informed Compliance Act (The Mod Act). It contains in it penalties of up to US$100,000 or 75 percent of the value of the imported goods per transaction as the fine to be imposed in the event that the record-keeping requirements are not complied with. One can quickly understand that accuracy will be at a premium.

Beyond the technical issues raised in this brief article, there are a couple of other trade issues that are impacted by NAFTA and so are worth mentioning. First of all, whether dealing with *maquiladoras* in Mexico or Foreign Trade Zones or bonded warehouses in the US and Canada, there have been programs that allow for the deferral or elimination of duties. These programs will be eliminated under NAFTA effective between the US and Canada on January 1, 1996, and between the US and Mexico on January l, 2001. On those effective dates what will transpire is that duty will have to be paid when the goods are withdrawn from either the bonded warehouse, Foreign Trade Zone, or *maquiladora* even though they are intended for export. What has been developed to offset the potential of having to pay the duty twice (for example, once coming into the US domestic economy and once going into the Canadian or Mexican economy) is a new type of drawback. In its simplest form, what will occur is that goods will be duty-paid as though coming into the US domestic market and will then be subject to an offset for the amount of duty paid in the second country. There is a set period of time in the proposed regulations (19 CFR Part 181), which delays the accounting and payment periods.

In addition, for the first time, US exporters are subject to the jurisdiction of the US Customs Service for record-keeping and similar purposes, all with the goal of confirming that when NAFTA benefits are claimed, the claim is valid.

Hopefully it is clear from this brief article that claiming NAFTA benefits can be (depending upon the product) a fairly complicated and certainly a record-keeping intensive process. It is not something that should be undertaken lightly. It should also be clear that many times it will not be possible to obtain the necessary information. If so, prudence dictates that the company not make the NAFTA claim until that documentation can be obtained. If it cannot be obtained, one should not make the NAFTA claim. It is clear that all three Customs Services are concerned that NAFTA claims will be made that are invalid and, therefore, good business judgment dictates that claims only be made when full documentation is available for subsequent production and proof of qualification.

While NAFTA was touted as increasing trade between the three countries, at least in part due to its rules of origin, in fact we may find the same phenomenon that arose with the CFTA. The US certainly has enjoyed an increase in trade with Canada (some 25 percent since 1989), but the increase is attributed to the elimination of nontariff barriers. The rules of origin and record-keeping requirements of the CFTA were so complicated that many companies chose not to take advantage of them. Perhaps the same will be true with NAFTA. Only time will tell.

Import Policy & Procedures

As a result of major changes in its previously restrictive import policies since the late 1980s, Mexico has become one of the world's top import markets. Many protectionist tariff and non-tariff barriers have been dismantled, foreign exchange controls have been eliminated, and restrictions on importation of many services have been removed. In a significant break with past policies, Mexico's government now is officially encouraging imports from advanced, industrialized countries and from newly developing ones.

The encouragement of imports is critical to the survival of Mexico's exploding economy. To support rapid expansion of its manufacturing industries, Mexico has been compelled to import more and more foreign goods and services—continued restrictions would soon starve its industries of needed raw and industrial materials, capital equipment, transportation services and equipment, and business support services. Imports must be available and affordable to Mexico's agricultural sector for its producers to modernize their methods, expand their operations, and remain competitive in world markets. Technical advances are essential to Mexican industries supplying domestic consumer markets with products—from toys to household appliances to clothing—and alliances with foreign manufacturers anxious to expand into Mexico's markets are a prime means of gaining technology transfers. (Refer to the "Opportunities" chapter for export and import prospects.)

This section discusses Mexico's policies and procedures for importing into the country. Such information is useful to persons seeking to sell goods and services to Mexico, firms that decide to establish a manufacturing facility or other operation in Mexico, foreign investors who are considering an interest in an entity located in Mexico, and persons in Mexico who are seeking to import from sources outside the country. (Refer to the "Marketing" chapter for a discussion of sales channels in Mexico and the "Business Entities" chapter for information on establishing a company in Mexico.)

IMPORT POLICIES

Government Regulation

Importing into Mexico is controlled by a web of regulations woven by multiple ministries and agencies and applied somewhat at the whim of customs agents. If the importer or exporter overlooks a requirement or fails to complete a form, trade can come to a screeching halt at the border. The Mexican government is taking steps to modernize the process, cut corruption, and smooth out the obstructions, but the system is still not user-friendly and the best way to facilitate the process is to hire professionals—freight forwarders and customs brokers. At least 90 percent of the goods that cross the Mexican border are cleared through customs by such freight forwarders and customs brokers (refer to the "Important Addresses" chapter for a list of customs brokers.)

Although the North American Free Trade Agreement (NAFTA) is expected to enhance trading relations between Canada, Mexico, and the US, it does not create a common market. That is, NAFTA does not authorize the unfettered movement of goods between these countries. Customs administrations still exist, customs officers are still enforcing each country's import and export laws and regulations, and exporters and importers still have to comply with the full array of laws and regulations of both the exporting and importing countries.

The agency with primary responsibility for the administration of foreign trade in Mexico is the *Secretaría de Comercio y Fomento Industrial* (SECOFI). In addition to implementing Mexico's international

This chapter was reviewed by Ross E. Porter, Sales and Marketing Manager, Porter International, Inc., a customhouse brokerage and international freight forwarding firm in San Diego, California; and Jim Fitzgerald, Vice President, J.E. Lowden & Co., a customhouse brokerage and international freight forwarding firm in San Francisco, California.

IMPORTING GLOSSARY

ad valorem tariff A tariff assessed as a percentage rate on the value of the imported merchandise.

agente aduanal A Mexican customs broker or agent, who is hired by an importer in Mexico to assist in clearing goods through Mexican Customs. The *agente aduanal* usually coordinates with a US (or other national) customs broker and with US and Mexican freight forwarders in order to ship goods to Mexico with minimal delays.

aviso A notice of importation required for bringing into Mexico food, cosmetics, toiletry articles, alcoholic beverages, or other nontoxic agricultural items that do not require prior SS (*Secretaría de Salud*) authorization. The *agente aduanal* will submit the *aviso* to a Mexican Customs or other authorized official at the time of importation.

consular visa Any one of several official endorsements by a consul of a country. A consular visa can be issued for travel, consular invoices, certificates of origin, shipping documents, and other legal documents.

devolución (CUDD) A Mexican importer's commitment to use foreign exchange. If an importer must send advance payment for goods to a foreign supplier, the importer must register a *devolución*.

FOB value The free-on-board value of goods at a designated point, which includes the value of the goods plus all costs related to shipping—insurance, packaging, loading, transport, and other charges. FOB value at a Mexican port of entry refers to the FOB value of goods at the time they reach the Mexican port of entry.

General Agreement on Tariffs and Trade (GATT) A multilateral trade agreement aimed at expanding international trade. GATT's main goals are to liberalize world trade and place it on a secure, stable regulatory basis. GATT is the only multilateral instrument that lays down agreed-upon rules for international trade. The organization that oversees the agreement—formerly also known as GATT, but now called the World Trade Organization (WTO)—is the principal international body concerned with negotiating the reduction of trade barriers and improving international trade relations.

Harmonized System (HS) A multipurpose international goods classification system designed to be used by manufacturers, transporters, exporters, importers, customs officials, statisticians, and others in classifying goods that move in international trade under a single commodity code. The system contains approximately 5,000 headings and subheadings of goods generally organized by industry.

legal kilo *See* legal weight.

legal weight The total weight of the merchandise and its own packaging, but excluding exterior containers or packing materials. The legal weight of canned vegetables would include the vegetables and the can, but not the crate and wrappings for shipping.

NOM certification Official Mexican Standards— *Normas Oficial Mexicanas* (NOM)—are technical regulations adopted by Mexican governmental agencies to impose standards of health, quality, and safety on products sold in Mexico. Products that are subject to NOM regulations must be tested by Mexican laboratories and approved by SECOFI, which will issue a NOM certificate for the products, before sale in Mexico.

North American Free Trade Agreement (NAFTA) A free trade agreement that comprises Canada, the US, and Mexico. The objectives of NAFTA are to eliminate barriers to trade, promote conditions of fair competition, increase investment opportunities, provide protection for intellectual and industrial property rights, and establish procedures for the resolution of disputes.

Organization for Economic Cooperation and Development (OECD) The primary forum for the discussion of common economic and social issues confronting the developed countries. Its fundamental objective is to achieve the highest sustainable economic growth and employment and a rising standard of living in member countries while maintaining financial stability, and thus contributing to the world economy. Members include Australia, Austria, Belgium, Luxembourg, Canada, Denmark, Finland, France, Germany, Greece, Iceland, Ireland, Italy,

Japan, the Netherlands, New Zealand, Norway, Portugal, Spain, Sweden, Switzerland, Turkey, the UK, and the US. Mexico joined the OECD in March 1994.

Secretaría de Comercio y Fomento Industrial (SECOFI) The Secretariat of Commerce and Industrial Development in Mexico, responsible for adopting and administering commercial regulations generally, including those governing business enterprises, imports, exports, product safety and quality standards, and business licensing.

Secretaría de Hacienda y Crédito Público (Hacienda) Mexico's Secretariat of Finance and Public Credit, which is the government authority primarily responsible for administering and regulating financial matters, such as taxes, license and registration fees, financial institutions, and export and import tariffs.

Secretaría de Salud (SS) Mexico's Secretariat of Health, which oversees many product health and quality standards and approves the importation of medical, agricultural, and toxic products.

value-added tax (VAT) An indirect tax on consumption that is assessed on the increased value of goods at each discrete point in the chain of production and distribution, from the raw material stage to final consumption. The tax on processors or merchants is levied on the amount by which they increase the value of the items they purchase and resell.

trade policies, SECOFI specifically administers imports and exports, issues licenses, conducts inspections, and monitors import and export operations. Other agencies which are vital to the importing process include the *Secretaría de Hacienda y Crédito Público* (or *Hacienda*), *Hacienda's Subsecretaría de Ingresos,* the *Secretaría de Salud* (SS), the *Secretaría de Agricultura y Recursos Hidráulicos* (SARH), and the *Secretaría de Comunicaciones y Transportes* (SCT). *See* Useful Addresses at the end of this chapter for contact information.

Tariffs

Mexican importers are required to pay customs tariffs, if any, in order for goods to clear customs. Mexico's import tariffs are assessed against goods that are classified based on the Harmonized Commodity Description and Coding System (HS). Of the 11,951 tariff categories, duties are imposed on about

83 percent, 16 percent are duty-free, 0.1 percent are prohibited imports, and nearly 3 percent can be imported only with an advance permit.

Rate of Tariffs Mexico assesses an ad valorem tariff against the free-on-board (FOB) value of the goods at the Mexican port of entry, as shown on the commercial invoice. The FOB value at the port of entry refers to the value of the goods, including all costs related to shipping—insurance, freight, and other charges—up to the Mexican port of entry. Tariffs range from 5 to 20 percent, although most effective tariffs are between 10 and 20 percent. The general rules for application of tariffs are as follows:

Duty-free Consumption goods in short supply in Mexico, raw materials in short supply in Mexico and needed by priority industries, and capital goods not produced in Mexico.

5 percent Partially processed raw materials and products not made in Mexico.

10 percent Intermediate goods used by manufacturers in Mexico.

15 percent High value-added intermediate goods used to produce final products in Mexico.

20 percent Consumer goods and food products for final consumption in Mexico.

Declarations and Guarantees of Value Proof of value is usually made by a declaration signed under oath by the Mexican importer and based on a declaration of value made by the foreign supplier, often contained in the commercial invoice. If the foreign supplier's country is a member of the Organization for Economic Cooperation and Development (OECD), Mexican Customs will accept as evidence of value an invoice certified by an industry association or chamber of commerce in that country. In an effort to keep the valuation system fair, uniform, and neutral, Mexico follows the Customs Valuation Agreement created during the Tokyo Round of GATT, which provides for the use of alternative valuation methods in a prescribed sequence.

To import into Mexico, the importer is usually required to post a bond or other guarantee for payment of additional tariff amounts assessed in case the *Secretaría de Hacienda y Crédito Público* decides that the goods were undervalued and establishes a higher value for them. After posting the bond, the importer can then obtain release of the goods from customs. Under regulations effective September 21, 1993, importers can post term bonds, which cover a number of transactions over time, even further reducing trade disruptions. Mexican Customs is required to lift a tariff guarantee requirement for a shipment within seven days after an *agente aduanal* submits a certified invoice and a request for such removal.

Preferential Tariff Treatment With the excep-

NAFTA: TARIFF REDUCTION AND ELIMINATION

For most of the trade among Canada, Mexico, and the US, the North American Free Trade Agreement (NAFTA) either eliminates customs duties immediately or phases them out over a period of between five and 10 years (with the phaseout of tariffs on a few sensitive articles set to occur over 15 years), and special provisions continue the import tariff restrictions on used industrial and construction equipment and materials. The NAFTA countries may agree to a faster tariff phaseout on any particular goods. (For an explanation of the provisions of this treaty, refer to the "NAFTA" chapter.)

In general, tariffs are eliminated or reduced only on goods that originate in a NAFTA country, as defined under NAFTA. An understanding of the NAFTA rules of origin is therefore essential for determining whether goods will qualify for non-tariff or reduced tariff treatment.

The NAFTA rules of origin are intended to reserve maximum benefits for goods that originate in a NAFTA country and to preclude benefits for goods that originate in other countries and merely pass through a NAFTA country. Even if goods are made of materials or parts that were produced in another country, the rules allow for NAFTA qualification if goods are in fact processed to a certain extent in a NAFTA country. Thus, products can qualify for NAFTA tariff benefits under one of the following rules:

(1) The goods are wholly obtained or produced in a NAFTA country.

(2) The goods are produced in a NAFTA country entirely from originating materials.

(3) The goods contain materials from other countries, but meet the Annex 401 rules as follows:

- All nonoriginating materials are processed in a NAFTA country such that their HS tariff number changes to the extent required by the treaty.

- The goods have a certain minimum regional value-content, which means a certain percentage of the value of the goods is derived from a NAFTA country.

- The goods are produced in a NAFTA country from parts imported from another country under special circumstances and meet a regional value-content test.

- The goods include materials from another country that are not changed in processing, but the value-content of the foreign materials is small enough to meet NAFTA's *de minimis* rule.

- The goods are made of a company's self-produced intermediate materials that the company has designated as originating materials, a NAFTA rule mainly aimed at vertically integrated companies that could otherwise be precluded from taking advantage of NAFTA benefits merely because they do not use independent suppliers.

Special rules of origin apply to certain sectors—textiles, automotive goods, electronic products, and agricultural products. These rules replace or limit the general rules of origin applicable to most products.

(Refer to the "NAFTA" chapter for a further explanation of the rules of origin.)

tion of preferential duties available through specific treaties, Mexico applies its tariffs on a nondiscriminatory basis. By treaty, tariffs are lowered or eliminated on certain imports from members of the Latin American Integration Association (ALADI)—Argentina, Bolivia, Brazil, Chile, Columbia, Ecuador, Mexico, Paraguay, Peru, Uruguay, and Venezuela—and parties to the North American Free Trade Agreement (NAFTA)—Canada and the US. Mexico also has various free trade agreements with Colombia, Venezuela, Chile, Guatemala, and certain Central American countries.

Special tariff treatment is accorded to *maquiladora* companies, which can import raw materials, machinery, and spare parts duty-free or in-bond, provided the majority of their production is reexported in accordance with rules established by SECOFI. (Refer to the "Foreign Investment" chapter for a more detailed discussion of *maquila* operations.) Mexico also has a number of duty-free zones in the states of Baja California Norte, Baja California Sur, Sonora, and Quintana Roo, where certain goods can be imported duty-free or at reduced rates. Merchandise sold in these zones cannot be transported to other parts of Mexico without payment of duties and, if required, the acquisition of an import license. Many of these products are sold to tourists or reexported, although local consumers derive considerable direct and indirect benefits from the arrangements.

Antidumping and Countervailing Duties Additional duties will be assessed against goods that the Mexican authorities determine have been dumped on the domestic market. The government investigates antidumping charges made against foreign companies that sell a mass quantity of products at prices far below local market value. Assessment of extra duties is a means of equalizing foreign and domestic competition and reducing unfair competition from foreign merchandise traded in Mexico. Mexico has levied countervailing duties against a variety of goods from the People's Republic of China.

Used Equipment Value To determine the customs duties on used equipment, the fair market value is computed on a standard basis by reducing the invoice price of a new item of the same kind by a certain percentage for each year of age. For equipment that is less than six years old, the price may be discounted only 10 to 20 percent, as determined by the customs official. For older equipment, the customs inspector selects the discount, which in any case cannot exceed 70 percent of the original price. Imports of used equipment are restricted, as noted below.

Other Fees and Taxes

Customs Processing Fee (CPF) At the time of its entry, each shipment is subject to a customs processing fee. This fee is determined as 0.8 percent of the FOB value of the goods at the port of entry, as shown on the commercial invoice. (For an explanation of FOB value, see the "Rate of Tariffs" section earlier in this chapter.)

Value-Added Tax (VAT) Most imports are subject to a 10 percent value-added tax, which is assessed against the cumulative value of the ad valorem tariff, the customs processing fee, and the FOB value of the goods at the port of entry. This tax is reduced to 6 percent for imported medicines, while basic food products are exempt.

Restrictions and Prohibitions on Imports

Before certain goods may be imported, the importer or exporter must obtain the prior approval of a government agency in Mexico. Some items that are considered to adversely affect public security, health, or morality cannot be imported at all. In addition, the importer or exporter may be required to obtain advance government permission to use certain shipping methods for the delivery of particular goods.

Quotas and Import Permits Fewer than 200 products are controlled by import quota and permit requirements in Mexico. These products are in trade-sensitive industry sectors, such as agriculture, petrochemicals, footwear, vehicles, and electronic equipment. Information on the specific products controlled is available from the American Chamber of Commerce or the US Embassy in Mexico City, the Mexico Desk at the US Department of Commerce, or

the *Dirección General de Asuntos Fronterizos* at SECOFI. (*See* Where US Exporters Can Get Advice and Useful Addresses at the end of this chapter for contact information.)

Restrictions on Specific Products All imports sold to public entities and governmental agencies require prior approval from SECOFI. Other restrictions and prohibitions are as follows.

- Imports subject to quotas and permits: agricultural commodities; automobiles and automotive parts; chemical products; heavy construction equipment; heavy farm equipment; and pharmaceuticals. (Microfilm and microfiche imports require permits, but are not subject to quotas.)
- Imports which cannot be shipped by mail or US parcel post: ammunition, firing caps, and loaded metal cartridges for portable firearms; banknotes; coins; perishable confections; currency (paper money); perishable fruit; gold; jewelry; meat; pastries; pistols; platinum; pork products; securities payable to bearer; silver; precious stones; tear gas emitting devices; traveler's checks; vegetables.
- Imports which require prior authorization by the *Secretaría de Salud* (SS): beauty products; cosmetics; medicines; and toilet articles.

SECOFI must authorize shipment by regular mail service of chocolate and chocolate products.

Imports of used equipment are restricted to equipment that is in good condition, less than 10 years old, and manufactured outside Mexico; entry is usually denied for projects that are receiving investment incentives.

Carnets

Mexico has not joined the Admission Temporair/Temporary Admission (ATA) Convention, which established the use of an international customs document known as the ATA Carnet. A carnet allows a person to bring merchandise temporarily into a member country for demonstration, show, and similar purposes without paying duties on it.

Admission of Sample Merchandise

Products for use as samples or demonstrations may be temporarily imported into Mexico for six months under bond. The bond must be arranged with Mexican Customs in advance, a process that usually take a minimum of several days. If no bond has been arranged when the goods arrive at a port of entry, Mexican Customs will hold the goods until a bond is furnished.

The importation is duty-free only if:
- the goods have no commercial value;
- the goods are testing samples delivered to a

Mexican laboratory; or
- the goods are destined for exhibit use in a specified convention or trade fair.

For most other commercial samples, the product will be taxed at a monthly rate of 2 percent of the full customs duty amount during the period it is present in Mexico. There are two exceptions. First, if the samples are consumed during the demonstration, and therefore are not reexported, the usual tariff and import permit requirements will apply. Second, special regulations are imposed on processed foods and beverages. Samples of such products may be brought into Mexico only under a temporary import clearance permit, which is valid for 20 days from the date of issuance; for information on this type of permit, contact the *Director General de Control Sanitario de Bienes y Servicios* at the *Sub-Dirección de Sanidad Internacional y Consultoria.* (*See* Useful Addresses at the end of this chapter for contact information.)

All samples should be shipped with the same commercial, shipping, and customs documentation as would be required for importation of the product generally. If goods are brought into Mexico for a particular trade fair, the foreign company must be certain to label all containers of sample products with the number that has been issued to the Mexican trade fair organizers. Mexican Customs may hold goods that are not so labeled, releasing them only after the foreign company pays a fine. Such release may not come until after the exhibit closes.

Admission of Advertising Materials

Catalogs and similar materials are free of duty and value-added tax only if they are not printed in Spanish and if no more than three copies are shipped per consignment to the importer in Mexico. In all other cases, the importer must have an import license and must pay a 50 percent ad valorem duty assessed against the greater of the invoice value or NP25 (about US$7.50) per legal kilo. The importer may also be liable for a value-added tax (VAT).

For lithographed or printed advertising circulars, the importer must pay a duty of NP5 (about US$1.50) per legal kilo. Additionally, a 100 percent ad valorem duty is levied on the greater of the invoice value or NP58 (about US$17.25) per legal kilo.

Advertising materials that are being brought to a particular convention or exhibition can enter duty-free. However, the exporter must obtain an exemption for such materials from the *Director de Convenciones* at:

Consejo Nacional de Turismo
Mariano Escobedo No. 726
México, DF, México
Tel: [52] (5) 531-0949

To obtain an exemption, the exporter must submit details of the convention and copies of the materials to be admitted. An exporter should allow at least two months' lead time. Failure to comply with customs entry regulations is grounds for impoundment of convention materials by Mexican Customs at the port of entry. To ensure compliance, an exporter may find that working through a reliable freight forwarder is the safest practice.

Mandatory Technical Standards

More than 80 classes of products sold in Mexico, whether foreign- or domestic-made, are subject to government-imposed standards of quality and safety. All Mexican government technical regulations have the prefix NOM (for *Normas Oficial Mexicanas*) regardless of which agency issues them. A person who imports into Mexico any product that is subject to any of the more than 300 mandatory standards must first obtain NOM certification showing that the product conforms to the standards. NOM certification is evidenced by a certificate of quality—also known as a certificate of compliance—which must be presented with the merchandise at the time of entry into Mexico.

As of August 1992, the products requiring NOM certification included the following:

- Ceramic products
- Containers
- Electric household appliances
- Electronic products
- Glass products
- Industrial instruments
- Liquors and wines
- Medical appliances and instruments
- Plastic articles
- Photocopying equipment
- Plumbing items
- Pumps and valves
- Radio and television products
- Rubber goods
- Safety and security devices
- Silver objects
- Stoves and ovens that are gas-fueled.

Exemptions are allowed for raw materials and industrial inputs, and no certification is required for textiles and apparel, although proper labeling is required upon entry.

Mexico is currently modifying its quality and safety standards, and the products that are subject to technical standards are therefore changing frequently. As part of these changes, Mexican authorities are classifying products for standardization using HS numbers, adding them gradually to the list of products subject to testing and certification. For this reason, the exporter should check with SECOFI to find out whether a particular product must be NOM certified.

An exporter should request the designating NOM number and the regulations that govern a certain product from SECOFI. With the NOM number at hand, the exporter may easily access information on the mandatory standards for a particular product by requesting a copy of the standards for that number from either the *Dirección General de Normas* at SECOFI or *Información Tecnologica y Consultoria* (INFOTEC). (*See* Useful Addresses at the end of this chapter for contact information.) Allow one to four weeks processing time.

Marking

A manufacturer that marks goods with a trademark and exports the goods to Mexico should register the trademark in Mexico. (Refer to the "Business Law" chapter for an explanation of trademark registration and protection.) While there is no requirement to register a trademark in Mexico, registration is wise because it is the best legal protection against piracy. If the trademark is registered in Mexico, any goods that bear the trademark should include the following: the words *"marca registrada"* or "MR"; the factory location; and the country of manufacture. This information may be placed on the label if the products themselves are too small to accommodate it.

Labeling

All products must be labeled in Spanish before they are allowed to be sold in Mexico. Such labels may be applied using a sticker or tag, and may be added to an existing English-language label. For most products, Spanish labels can be affixed after importation to Mexico (that is, such labeling is not a condition of import, but only of subsequent sale).

However, there are certain products for which the law requires that Spanish labels be affixed prior to entry as a condition of importation . These products include drugs, cosmetics, food products, refrigerators, textiles and apparel items, and leather products. Until recently, Mexican authorities often failed to enforce this law, allowing importers and distributors of these foreign products to attach Spanish-language labels after the products arrive in Mexico. This policy has now changed, and enforcement is becoming more stringent. Foreign companies exporting to Mexico, as well as importers and distributors in Mexico, should note that if such products do not bear Spanish-language labels, they may be turned back at the border. Foreign companies that export these types of products to Mexico must comply with Spanish labeling requirements in advance because they can expect to be inspected.

The requirements for the precise contents of labels differ somewhat for each type of product. For the most part, all labels must contain the following information:

- Name of product;
- The name of the country of origin; .
- The name and address of the national manufacturer or importer;
- The trademark or commercial name brand of the manufacturer;
- A list of raw materials used, in declining quantitative order (although specific percentages are not required);
- Additional country of origin information, including a description of all raw materials not produced in the exporting country and the name of each such material's country of origin;
- The product size, if applicable (weights and measures must be in the metric system);
- Date of manufacture;
- Instructions for use and care, if applicable;
- A product description (but only if the packaging is such that the actual product is not visible).

Additional requirements are imposed on such products as silver, silver-plated and nickel-plated items, wearing apparel, leather goods, packaged foods, beverages, pharmaceutical and veterinary products, prepared feeds, fertilizers, and insecticides. Labels on imported refrigerators must comply with Mexico's energy laws, specifying the cubic meter capacity, estimated average energy consumption, and annual energy consumption costs of the model. A special stamp must be affixed to cigarettes. For products that require SS (*Secretária de Salud—* Secretariat of Health) import authorization, the label must state the following: "*Aceptado S.S.A. No.* (license number here)." For hazardous materials, special labeling requirements apply and vary depending on the mode of transportation. (*See* the Documentation at Shipping section in this chapter for an explanation of the required documents for each mode of transport.)

Mexico frequently revises and updates its labeling regulations. The most current requirements related to a specific product can be obtained from the following offices (*see* Useful Addresses at the end of this chapter for contact information):

- *Departamento de Certificaciones e Información Comercial Dirección General de Normas* (General information on marking and labeling requirements)
- *Control Sanitario de Bienes y Servicios* (Requirements for food, beverages, cosmetics, and toiletries)
- *Dirección de Control de Insumos para la Salud* (Requirements for medicines, medical equipment, and medical supplies)
- *Dirección General de Prevención y Control de la Contaminación Ambiental*

(Requirements for pesticides, fertilizers, and other toxic substances)

Credit and Payment Conditions

Normal credit terms apply in transactions with Mexican companies. Transfers of payment typically occur without difficulty, provided the parties adhere to the procedures required by their contracts and financial institutions. Drafts and open accounts are sometimes used, although payments using a letter of credit (L/C) are recommended for a new customer in the private sector. (Refer to the "International Payments" chapter for more detailed information on means of payment). The credit term is negotiable, with most deals allowing for 90- to 180-day payment terms. In contracts with government agencies and government-owned companies, credit terms are sometimes extended to 360 days.

Countertrade

Mexico does not encourage countertrade, but regulations in Mexico do allow for countertrade and barter transactions, particularly for the export and import of commodities, including crude oil, oil products, coffee, cotton, shrimp, and engines. For a countertrade transaction, traders must obtain the advance permission of SECOFI and the Banco de México.

IMPORT PROCEDURES

In an international transaction, the seller and buyer must comply with two sets of requirements: the export regulations of the country from which the goods are shipped, and the import regulations of the country to which the goods are delivered. This discussion focuses on the second step: bringing the goods into Mexico. A shipper of goods must also abide by the export regulations of his or her own country, which may include export documentation, declarations, and licenses. (*See* An Illustration: US Export Regulations and Procedures in this chapter.)

For many transactions, importing into Mexico is a straightforward process. It often begins with a request from a Mexican buyer for a quote on products, including shipping to a Mexican port of entry. After the terms of the sale are set, the Mexican buyer will arrange for payment. The foreign supplier will receive confirmation of payment and then ship the goods to the Mexican port or border point of entry, often through a common carrier. In most countries, customs documentation may be submitted in advance—sometimes electronically—to avoid delays in leaving one country and entering the another. At the border, the freight forwarder takes over, arranging clearance through Mexican Customs in conjunction with the importer and

the importer's *agente aduanal* (customs broker). The goods go to a Mexican transport service arranged for by the importer's *agente aduanal*, the exporter's freight forwarder, or a contracted US carrier that offers through bill of lading direct service for delivery to the Mexican destination.

Import Registrations and Licenses

Registry of Importers and Exporters All importing companies located in Mexico are required to register with *Hacienda*, which maintains a National Registry of Importers and Exporters. This Registry was established as a means of reducing illegal imports and tax evasion. (*See* Useful Addresses at the end of this chapter for contact information.)

Goods Requiring Import Permits For most goods, no import permit is required; permits are needed to import only about 200 of the 11,951 items subject to Mexico's general tariff. Exceptions to the permit requirements are made for temporary imports of raw materials and intermediate goods for export industries. The following are among the materials for which an import permit is needed:

- Agricultural commodities
- Automobiles and automotive parts
- Chemical products
- Construction equipment (heavy)
- Farm equipment (heavy)
- Microfilm, microfiche, and computer data
- Pharmaceutical products.

Application for Permit If an import permit is required, the importer in Mexico is responsible for obtaining it. A foreign supplier should request confirmation that the importer has received a license before shipping the merchandise to Mexico. In a contract for merchandise that requires an import license, the parties often agree that the date of shipment will be within a certain number of days after the supplier receives confirmation that the importer has been licensed to import the goods. Application for an import license is made to SECOFI, where the request is referred to one or more committees. (*See* Useful Addresses at the end of this chapter for contact information.)

The applicant must be registered in the National Registry of Importers and Exporters maintained by *Hacienda*. License requests are commonly refused if a product, or a close substitute, is readily available in Mexico. To support the license application, an applicant may need the foreign supplier to furnish a pro forma invoice with a detailed product description. The foreign supplier should provide such an invoice in accordance with the importer's instructions.

A license application usually takes at least one or two months to process, and further delays are not uncommon. Importers and exporters must allow adequate time to obtain an initial permit, as well as any extensions that may be needed.

Restrictions on License Two restrictions are placed on import licenses: time and quantity. An import license is typically issued effective for an average time of up to nine months, and can be extended for another three months. The license is also issued based on an estimated quantity of imports—usually for an amount 20 percent higher than prior actual imports. The quantity may be increased if the importer can justify a greater amount. A licensed importer who has used up at least 70 percent of the quantities authorized in any earlier licenses can obtain a new license.

Penalties for Importing Without a Permit An importer who fails to obtain a required permit and who imports the articles anyway is subject to a fine ranging from NP100 (about US$30) to NP20,000 (US$5,950), plus an additional penalty equal to twice the value of the goods imported. Government authorities may require the importer to remove the articles from Mexico at the importer's expense. Alternatively, the authorities may direct that the merchandise be delivered, at cost plus duties, transport charges, and handling fees, to distributors or consumers designated by SECOFI. An importer who fails to comply with a government directive to remove or deliver merchandise is subject to a further fine ranging from NP100 (about US$30) to NP10,000 (US$2,975).

Registration for Foreign Exchange

Advance Payment by a Party in Mexico An importer in Mexico who agrees by contract to send an advance payment to an exporter of goods must apply to obtain foreign currency. The importer applies by registering a commitment of use—or *devolución*—of foreign exchange (CUDD). The importer then has 180 days to show that the foreign currency was in fact used to pay for imports and associated expenses or the importer must return the foreign currency. For payments made through a letter of credit, the time limit is reduced to 60 days.

If payment is made through a letter of credit or if the merchandise value does not exceed US$10,000 (about US$2,975), full advance payment is permitted. Otherwise, the importer is permitted to advance only 20 percent of the price. Maximum limits are also placed on advance payments of associated expenses: 6 percent of free-on-board (FOB) value for North American imports or 8 percent of FOB value for imports from other regions.

Acknowledgment by a Foreign Supplier The foreign supplier is required to confirm the receipt of advance payment for any individual transaction that exceeds US$10,000 (about NP36,000).

Preshipment Stage

Advance Classification for Tariffs Before importing a product, a foreign company should determine the Harmonized System (HS) classification number for the product. This number is used to determine the tariffs that apply to exporting and importing the product, and it must be included on several forms submitted to customs. If the goods will be valued by an appraiser at the time they reach the Mexican port of entry, the foreign exporter may provide catalogs and descriptive materials for the product to the appraiser in advance to facilitate product classification and allow for an estimate of tariffs before shipping.

A foreign company may also request an advisory, nonbinding opinion on the HS classification of the product from the Mexican Customs Service in advance for purposes of estimating the import tariff. These requests are usually made through a customs broker. The application is submitted to the *Departamento de Consulta, Dirección General de Aduanas. (See* Useful Addresses at the end of this chapter for contact information.)

An application should be accompanied by a detailed description and sample of the product. If a sample cannot be submitted because of the nature of the product, the foreign seller may instead provide photographs, drawings, and other data that fully describe the product and its use. Advance arrangements must be made with the *Departamento de Consulta* before sending the product. The product should be presented in the same packaging and with the same labels, brochures, and pamphlets as it will have when imported.

Preshipment Inspection Shipments of certain imports to the public sector must be monitored by an agency designated by Mexican authorities, currently the *Société Generale de Surveillance S.A.* (SEG). For information on the products subject to preshipment inspection and the process generally, contact:

Société Generale de Surveillance S.A.
Miami Office
8120 NW 53rd Street, Suite 200
Miami, FL 33166, USA
Tel: [1] (305) 592-0410

Insurance Arrangements At the time the merchandise is shipped, a seller or importer may be required to present a certificate of insurance to the shipping company. Under Mexican law, goods transported from a foreign country to Mexico cannot be insured with a foreign company if the risks are to be borne by persons or firms domiciled in Mexico. Thus, companies that ship merchandise to Mexico for payment by letter of credit drawn on a Mexican financial institution cannot insure the goods with a foreign company,

AN ILLUSTRATION: US EXPORT REGULATIONS AND PROCEDURES

Before US merchandise can reach a Mexican importer, it must first be transported to a Mexican port of entry and pass through US Customs, a process fraught with rules and which can involve frustrating pitfalls for even the most knowledgeable exporter. The simple fact is that merchandise not in compliance with US laws and regulations cannot be exported to Mexico. Among the complications: there are lots of "X's"—exceptions, exclusions, exemptions—and even some ways to bend rules (just a little, of course). The advice given by experienced exporters—large and small—is to hire a professional freight forwarder and customs broker. Many firms offer both services. These are the people who are paid to know the rules and resolve the difficulties.

A freight forwarder can: help the exporter ensure that the merchandise is packed properly, labeled and documented correctly, and insured against damage, loss, and even delay; advise on fees and costs for freight, authorizations, ports, insurance, and handling; and arrange to have the merchandise placed in a container or packed at the port. This process begins before the goods are shipped so that by the time the merchandise reaches the border, all requirements for shipping and export have been met; the goods can ease through customs with minimal delays. A freight forwarder will often coordinate with the persons who come in contact with the goods—US and Mexican customs brokers, customs officials, transporters, inspectors, appraisers, and importers. The cost of freight forwarding services is a legitimate export expense that may be passed on to a customer.

If the freight forwarder does not also handle customs arrangements, the US exporter should consider finding a US licensed customs broker. The broker will advise on export requirements, pass the goods through US Customs, and hand all necessary documentation over to the Mexican customs broker.

The US export process requires the following:

Acquisition of export license

An export license is required for all articles exported to Mexico. Most products can be exported under a general license, which requires no application with any agency. Some may be exported only under an individually validated license (ILV), which requires at least an application and sometimes a number of supporting documents. A few articles require special export licenses.

Whether an ILV or special license is needed depends on three factors: (1) the ultimate destination; (2) the type of merchandise; and (3) the value of the merchandise. The basic rule is that an ILV or a special license is required to export military products or products that have both military and civilian uses. To find out what the requirements are for a specific product, an exporter must learn a new language: the EAR contains ECCN listings for all dual-use items, and if the CGN for the destination country is under the ECCN listing, then an IVL is required unless an exception applies. Or at least get a translation: a set of government regulations (Export Administration Regulations—EAR) classifies worldwide export destinations by country group number (CGN). The regulations also index all products that could be used for military purposes under export control commodity numbers (ECCNs). For each product that has an ECCN, the regulations list the country group numbers (CGNs) for the destinations for which a validated export license must be obtained.

The easy way to determine whether an IVL is needed to export a particular product is to make a telephone call to a local Bureau of Export Administration (BXA) Office and ask, or hire a customs broker or freight forwarder to advise in the export process. To find the nearest BXA office, call the US Department of Commerce help line at (800) USA-TRADE.

The hard way would be to look up the export licensing rules contained in the Export Administration Regulations (EAR), which are published in Title 15, Code of Federal Regulations (CFR). An exporter who truly yearns to scan the EAR can probably find the regulations in a local law library. The more committed can subscribe to them (not free, of course) from:

Superintendent of Documents
US Government Printing Office
Washington, DC 20402, USA
Tel: [1] (202) 783-3238 (order line),
512-0000 (main number)
(Note: There are also 21 GPO bookstores outside Washington, DC.)

Subscription forms are available at any local Commerce Department district office or from:

Office of Export Licensing
Exporter Counseling Division, Room 1099D
US Department of Commerce
Washington, DC 20230, USA
Tel: [1] (202) 377-4811

For most products that require an IVL for export, the exporter must apply (on form BXA-622P) to:

Bureau of Export Administration
US Department of Commerce
14th St. and Constitution Ave. NW
Washington, DC 20230, USA
Tel: [1] (202) 482-1455, 482-2721
Fax: [1] (202) 482-2387

Exceptions are made for products that are controlled by other government agencies, such as exports of munitions, which require approval from the Department of State:

US Department of State
2201 C Street NW
Washington, DC 20520, USA
Tel: [1] (202) 647-4000

Compliance with health and environmental regulations

A limited number of exporters must be certain that their products are in compliance with regulations of the Food and Drug Administration (FDA)—prohibiting adulteration and misbranding—and the Environmental Protection Agency (EPA)—controlling hazardous wastes, pesticides, and toxic chemicals. If a product might be covered by any of these regulations, the exporter should contact the following agencies, as appropriate:

Public Health Service
Food and Drug Administration
200 Independence Ave SW
Washington, DC 20201, USA
Tel: [1] (202) 690-6867 Fax: [1] (202) 690-6274

Office of International Activities
US Environmental Protection Agency
401 M Street SW
Washington, DC 20460, USA
Tel: [1] (202) 260-4870, 382-4880
Fax: [1] (202) 260-9653

Use of accepted marking and labeling on exterior shipping containers

Labels and markings must meet rules for shipping and cargo handling, comply with customs regulations, and allow for quick identification of the shipment by the recipient. Markings usually must include a shipper's mark, country of origin, weight, number of packages, size of cases, handling and cautionary notations, port of entry, and any hazardous material warnings. Many of these must be in more than one language and unit of weight or measure (English and metric). Customs regulations regarding freight labeling are often strictly enforced. Freight forwarders and customs brokers can supply necessary information on the specific regulations.

Submission of proper documentation to US Customs officials

To export merchandise from the US, a formidable mass of documents must be properly filled out and submitted to US Customs. The documents required will vary depending on the US and Mexican regulations affecting the particular merchandise at any one time. Freight forwarders and customs brokers are the best resource for ensuring proper customs documentation. The most common documents required at US Customs are as follows:

- **Commercial invoice** Customs will refer to this to identify the goods, the exporter, the country of destination, the value of the goods, the shipper, and the importer.
- **Bill of lading** Customs may request to see the bill of lading to verify the goods shipped and the arrangements for transport.
- **Export license** Customs will deny export permission unless the proper license has been obtained.
- **Export packing list** Customs may use this detailed listing of all package contents to verify the cargo.
- **Shipper's Export Declaration (SED)** Customs requires this form for all shipments destined for a free world country and valued at more than US$2,500, and for all shipments needing an individually validated license (IVL). If an IVL is needed, the IVL export authorization number must be shown on line 21 of the SED. If a general license is sufficient, line 21 should be filled in with the term "G DEST."
- **Special documents** Customs will usually verify that the exporter has obtained all necessary certificates or origin; health, sanitary, and quality certificates; consular invoices and visas; and other legalization documents required for transporting the goods across the border.

WHERE US EXPORTERS CAN GET ADVICE

In Washington DC

Bureau of Alcohol, Tobacco and Firearms
Tel: [1] (202) 927-8500, 927-7777

Export-Import Bank
Tel: [1] (202) 566-8860, 566-8944, 566-8234

Small Business Administration
Office of International Trade
Tel: [1] (202) 205-6720 Fax: [1] (202) 205-7272

United States-Mexico Chamber of Commerce
Tel: [1] (202) 296-5198 Fax: [1] (202) 728-0768

US Department of Agriculture
AgExport Connections
Tel: [1] (202) 447-7103

US Department of Agriculture
Animal and Plant Health Inspection Service (APHIS)
Tel: [1] (202) 720-2511 Fax: [1] (202) 720-3054

US Department of Agriculture
Foreign Agricultural Service
Tel: [1] (202) 720-3448

US Department of Commerce
Bureau of Export Administration
Tel: [1] (202) 482-1455, 482-2721
Fax: [1] (202) 482-2387

US Department of Commerce
Exporter Counseling Division
Tel: [1] (202) 377-4811

US Department of Commerce
Flash Facts
Tel: [1] (202) 482-4464

US Department of Commerce
Mexico Desk
Tel: [1] (202) 482-4464

US Department of Commerce
Office of Technology Administration
Tel: [1] (202) 482-5150 Fax: [1] (202) 482-4826

US Food and Drug Administration
Center for Food Safety and Applied Nutrition
Tel: [1] (202) 205-4850 Fax: [1] (202) 205-5025

US Food and Drug Administration
Health & Human Services Dept.
Tel: [1] (301) 443-6143 Fax: [1] (301) 443-1309

In Mexico City

American Chamber of Commerce
Lucerna 78-4
Col. Juárez
06500 México, DF, México
Tel: [52] (5) 705-0995, 724-3800
Fax: [52] (5) 703-9980

US Trade Center, US & Foreign Commercial Service
Liverpool 31
06600 México, DF, México
Tel: [52] (5) 591-0155 Fax: [52] (5) 566-1115

From computer databases

Electronic Bulletin Board (EBB)
Tel: [1] (703) 487-4650 Fax: [1] (703) 321-8547

National Trade Data Bank (NTDB)
Tel: [1] (202) 482-1986

Trade Opportunity Program (TOP)
US Department of Commerce
Tel: [1] (202) 377-4203

World Trade Centers Association
Tel: [1] (212) 313-4600

In Publications

A Basic Guide to Exporting, available from: World Trade Press, 1505 Fifth Avenue, San Rafael, CA 94901, USA; Tel: [1] (415) 454-9934 Fax: [1] (415) 453-7980.

Commerce Business Daily, available from: US Government Printing Office, Washington, DC 20402, USA; Tel: [1] (202) 783-3238.

Export Shipping Manual, available from: Bureau of National Affairs, 1231 25th Street NW, Washington, DC 20037, USA, Tel: [1] (202) 452-4200.

Journal of Commerce, available from: Two World Trade Center, 27th Fl. New York, NY 10048-0203, USA; Tel: [1] (212) 837-7000, (908) 859-1300 (subscriptions) Fax: [1] (212) 837-7035.

National Council on International Trade Documentation (NCITD), 350 Broadway, Suite 1200, New York, NY 10013, USA; Tel: [1] (212) 925-1400. Provides a variety of publications on trade documentation.

South of the Border: US Trucking in Mexico, available from: American Trucking Association, 2200 Mill Road, Alexandria, VA 22314, USA; Tel: [1] (703) 838-1996.

because the risk of loss or damage falls to a Mexican domiciliary. Goods may be insured with a foreign company up until the risks pass to the Mexican importer. If the importer in Mexico bears the risk, the foreign supplier may arrange for insurance with a Mexican company or for contingent insurance in the supplier's own country. Companies selling goods to Mexico should note that there are dangers in transferring coverage from one insurer to another while goods are in transit due to the potential for disputes over responsibility for coverage, especially if a through bill of lading is used. A growing number of US–Mexican insurance alliances can now write a single policy to cover the cargo over the entire route to avoid such issues of specific responsibility.

NOM Certification If a product is subject to the Mexican technical standards noted in the first part of this chapter, an exporter cannot ship it to Mexico until it has been NOM certified. The SECOFI regulations provide that the importer must seek NOM certification, but foreign companies are not precluded from obtaining the certificate and then sharing it with their importers. The advantage of letting the importer in Mexico handle the certification process is that the importer will undertake the testing, bear the costs, and give the application a local flavor—which may serve to facilitate its approval. However, there is a major disadvantage: the certificate will be issued in the importer's name and cannot be transferred without the importer's consent. A not-totally-amicable parting of the ways between an importer and a foreign supplier can interrupt importation by a new importer of the product until SECOFI recertifies it, despite having previously passed the same product under the name of the first importer.

Another disadvantage is that the person to whom the certificate is issued has a right to license or lease it. Thus, an importer could license or lease the certificate to another importer without the approval of the foreign supplier, potentially blocking cross-border trading until the parties work out their relationship or until the product is recertified with yet another importer.

Unless otherwise requested, a certificate of compliance—or certificate of quality—is issued for each model or prototype of a product. The certificate is usually issued without time or quantity limits, in which case it remains valid as long as that model of the product is sold in Mexico. Thus, NOM certification need be sought only once for a particular model. The applicant should avoid requesting NOM certification for only a particular shipment or lot, because SECOFI will then issue only a limited certificate, requiring the importer or foreign company to apply for new NOM certification for every future importation of a different shipment or lot of the same product.

To be NOM certified, a product will probably have to be tested in a laboratory in Mexico. The lab must be accredited by *Sistema Nacional de Calibración* (SNC) or *Sistema Nacional de Acreditamiento de Laboratorios De Prueba* (SINALP) of SECOFI. While more than 100 accredited Mexican labs are currently available for testing various products, certified labs are still nonexistent (or barely existent) for many products. To relieve backlogs, SECOFI has implemented a crash accreditation program for some products.

The testing procedure involves sending an application to an accredited Mexican lab, together with a few samples of the product. For testing purposes, an exporter may usually ship three samples into Mexico without a NOM certificate. Tests are performed on products in the order received. Each lab is permitted to set its own prices. Complaints about a particular lab, including inordinate delays, excessive charges, or refusals to test, should be referred to the *Dirección General de Normas* of SECOFI, by fax or letter explaining the particulars in either Spanish or English (but preferably in Spanish).

To facilitate customs clearance, the importer should have a copy (at least) of the NOM certificate—the original is preferable. The person to whom the original certificate of compliance was issued can obtain duplicate originals upon request—these are helpful to distributors and agents throughout the marketing chain (allow at least four weeks for SECOFI to process a request for duplicates). Such requests must be made in writing to the *Dirección General de Normas.* (*See* Useful Addresses at the end of this chapter for contact information.)

Sanitary Certificates Before being allowed to export certain products into Mexico, a foreign supplier may need to obtain a sanitary certificate—or its equivalent—from the home country government authorities. A sanitary certificate states that the products were produced in an environment that complies with standards imposed by the government of the country of origin. These certificates are typically required for livestock, animal products, seeds, plants, and plant products. For example, a sanitary certificate may declare that a particular plant product was grown outside a region that has been quarantined for pest infestation. (No sanitary certificate is required for processed foods.)

An exporter must allow adequate time to obtain a sanitary certificate. The usual procedure is to apply in the exporting country to a national, state, county, or other local government authority that is responsible for inspecting or controlling the product. In the US, these certificates are issued at the place of origin by the Animal and Plant Health Inspection Service of the US Department of Agriculture, by local state authorities, or by an accredited veterinarian. Once that authority has issued the certificate, the exporter must submit it in quadruplicate to a Mexican Consul for notarization. Finally, when the goods are shipped, the exporter must include four copies of it with the other documents.

Health Certificates A health certificate attests to the physical condition of a live animal or animal by-product. A shipper who wants to export an animal or animal by-product into Mexico will need a health certificate, which must also specify the country of origin. To authenticate the country of origin, the certificate usually must be signed by a licensed veterinarian and preferably countersigned and attested by a government agricultural inspector or other such official with authority to do so.

Phytosanitary Certificates To import agricultural seeds or any products intended for sowing and propagation, or any fresh fruits and vegetables into Mexico, the exporter must obtain a phytosanitary certificate. This certificate declares that the shipment has been inspected and is free from harmful pests and plant diseases. The certificate also shows the country of origin. It must be issued by an authorized government inspector and then submitted to a Mexican Consul to obtain a consular visa.

Authorization of the *Secretaría de Salud* (SS) Before importation of certain medical, agricultural, or toxic products, the importer or foreign company must obtain approval from the SS. Products that fall into this category include pharmaceuticals, medical equipment and supplies, pesticides, fertilizers, products containing toxic substances, and some food items (specifically seafood, dairy products, animal fats, vegetable oils, and alcoholic beverages). Processed foods do not require prior SS import authorization. For information on the procedures for authorization, contact the *Dirección General de Control Sanitario de Bienes y Servicios* or the *Dirección General de Control de Insumos Para la Salud. (See* Useful Addresses at the end of this chapter for contact information.)

Medical Device Registration

The procedure for obtaining prior SS import authorization requires product testing and the submission of a packet of documents, including the original and one copy of the following:

- Application form (available from the SS).
- Certificate of origin or sanitary certificate issued by the country of origin and showing the geographic origin and the quantity of the product for which it is valid.
- Original label and back label of product in Spanish and in the form to be used when marketed in Mexico.
- Commercial or pro forma invoice.
- Certificate of free sale, valid for one year and issued by an authority in the exporting country that is responsible for ensuring that the product complies with the legal requirements and is used, sold, or consumed without restriction in the country of origin. This certificate must be translated into Spanish, notarized in the exporting country, and also notarized by a Mexican Consul. In the US, free sale certificates are issued by the Bureau of Alcohol, Tobacco, and Firearms (alcohol products) or the Food and Drug Administration's Center for Food Safety and Applied Nutrition (non-alcohol products). A request for a certificate should be designated

"Request for Certificate of Free Sale" and should include the company name, the product's generic and proprietary brand names, and model numbers or other identifying information. Such applications need not be accompanied by a sample. For information and policies on issuing free sale certificates, contact the Bureau of Alcohol, Tobacco, and Firearms.

- Physio-chemical analysis of the chemical and physical contents of a product provided by the manufacturer, a national laboratory, or an authorized and reputable foreign entity in the country of origin or source. The analysis must state the specific product, configuration, and quantity for which the analysis is valid. It must be in Spanish and notarized by a Mexican Consul. The analysis may be written on a form or letterhead stationery, and it should include the name, signature, and position of the chemist authorized to make the analysis. In the US, this analysis must be made by a laboratory of—or authorized by—the Heath and Human Services Department of the US Food and Drug Administration.
- Microbiological analysis report from an authorized organization in the country of origin or source showing microorganisms found in the product and the quantity of the product covered by the analysis. This analysis may also be written on a form or letterhead stationery and should include the name, signature, and position of the chemist authorized to make it.

Once it grants authorization based on the aforementioned documents, the SS will issue the applicant a registration number. The SS registration number must be shown on the product when marketed in Mexico.

If a product is not on the prior SS authorization list, but is a food item, cosmetic or toiletry, alcoholic beverage, or another agricultural article not containing toxic substances, the *agente aduanal* must submit a notice of importation—an *aviso*—to an authorized Mexican representative at the time of importation. (For an explanation of this procedure, see Customs Clearance Requirements in this chapter.)

Authorization of the *Secretaría de Agricultura y Recursos Hidráulicos* (SARH) An import permit and health import authorization must be obtained from the *Secretaría de Agricultura y Recursos Hidráulicos* (SARH) for the import of agricultural products, animals, animal products, and unprocessed food not otherwise licensed for import by SECOFI. The SARH health authorization indicates that the products meet Mexico's plant and animal health standards. The authorization will specify any

US SHIPPING TO MEXICO*

The Mexican government might as well put up a sign at the border that says "Welcome to Mexico: Land of Golden Opportunity." Judging from the number of shipments crossing the border, that's clearly how US exporters see our neighbor to the south.

They have good reason to do so. Now that President Salinas' economic reforms have stabilized inflation and spurred domestic growth, US–Mexican trade has skyrocketed, nearly doubling since 1987. In fact, at US$33.3 billion, Mexico was the United States' third largest export market in 1991.

This rapid growth means more and more US companies are exporting to Mexico for the first time. The process of shipping to Mexico can be frustrating not only to novices, but to experienced exporters as well. To help US exporters know what to expect, here's a brief guide to documentation and customs procedures, along with advice from forwarders and shippers on how to cross the border successfully.

Bilingual is Best

You may have heard that exports move on paper as well as on ships and airplanes. That's certainly true for Mexico, where customs inspectors pay excruciatingly close attention to documentation. There's no room for error in terms of accuracy and timing on any of the papers that the exporter must prepare: the bill of lading, the commercial invoice, and the Shipper's Export Declaration. What follows is a brief discussion of how these documents should be completed:

- *Bill of lading* The standard form US bill of lading for whichever mode of transport is being used is acceptable. It's important to include names and telephone numbers of the US freight forwarder and the Mexican customs broker. It's also a help if the information is listed on the bill of lading in both Spanish and English.
- *Commercial invoice* This crucial document must be bilingual. Some manufacturers of export forms offer Spanish/English versions, or you can create your own. In either case, be sure to have your freight forwarder at the border check the invoice for accu-

racy. Many of them offer a translation service for a reasonable fee.

In addition to the usual information contained on a commercial invoice, you must include the full name and address of the Mexican customs broker and of the Mexican consignee, as well as the consignee's Mexican tax identification number, or *registro federal de causantes* (RFC). If you do not provide this number, your shipment will not be allowed through customs. The reason is that Mexico requires importers to be current on their tax payments. At the time of entry, the ID number on your invoice is entered into a computerized central tax registry. If the importer is not on that list or shows up as delinquent in paying taxes, then customs will refuse entry to the goods.

Merchandise descriptions in both languages should be clear and detailed, and should include the Harmonized System number that identifies the commodity. "Use plain English in your invoice descriptions," advises Ross Porter, sales and marketing manager for freight forwarder Porter International in San Diego. "Computerized inventory and documentation systems are great, but they don't always have room for the kind of description needed for an international shipment. Just giving a product code and model name are not enough to get through Mexican Customs!"

- *Shipper's Export Declaration* Use the standard US form, but be sure to include the merchandise description in Spanish.
- *Other documents* In addition to the forms mentioned above, shippers of certain commodities may have to provide other, specialized documents. For example, some items require a certificate stating that they meet Mexican product-quality standards, says Joe Alcantar Jr., vice president of El Paso, Texas-based forwarder Brown, Alcantar & Brown Inc. Furthermore, phytosanitary certificates (which attest that the contents are clear of insect and bacterial contamination) and certificates of origin are required for most foodstuffs, Alcantar says. "But be aware that [when NAFTA goes] into effect, nearly every-

US SHIPPING TO MEXICO (cont'd.)

thing will require a certificate of origin," he adds.

Crossing the Border

The border-crossing scene is quite complicated because there are so many parties involved. To illustrate how it works, we'll follow an export shipment as it moves through customs. We've chosen a truck shipment since about 80 percent of commerce between the US and Mexico moves by motor carrier.

Well before the shipment leaves the manufacturer's plant, all export documentation should be in order. Freight forwarders recommend faxing them copies as early as possible so they can get the process started before the shipment arrives at the border. (You should send original documents along immediately after.) The forwarder checks the papers for accuracy and sends them to the Mexican customs broker.

After receiving copies of the import documents, the broker prepares a quote that includes duties, a customs user fee, a value-added tax, and its own handling charge. All of this adds up to quite a sum: duties range from zero to 20 percent of the stated value; the Mexican customs user fee is 0.8 percent of the invoice value; and the value-added tax represents 10 percent of the value of the goods plus the duty. The broker sends the quote with a request for payment to the paying party (usually the consignee) and to the US freight forwarder.

Because all taxes and fees must be paid before the shipment can enter the country, nothing can happen until the broker receives payment. Waiting for the appropriate party to pay can slow a shipment down; as Alcantar notes, Mexican brokers rarely extend credit to their customers. Once it has received the money, the broker prepares the *pedimento de importación,* which is the customs entry document. It states the tariff classification, the importer of record, and the duty owed. The broker then goes to customs to pay the amount due and submit the *pedimento,* the invoice, and any other necessary documents.

Once the Mexican Customs inspector has approved the documentation, the broker has three days to import the merchandise. He notifies the US freight forwarder to release the freight to the Mexican cartage agent. This local trucker takes the freight and the Shipper's Export Declaration through US Customs, then meets the Mexican broker's representative at Mexican Customs. If the trucker's documents match up with the already approved broker's documents, the trucker goes to a red and green stoplight and pushes a button. If the light is green, he is given a copy of the *pedimento* and may proceed into Mexico. If it turns red, he must pull over into a special yard so the goods may be physically inspected. According to the American Trucking Associations, about 10 percent of trailers are inspected under this system.

In the final step, the cartage agent turns the trailer over to the Mexican carrier designated by the original US trucker. Mexican law does not allow foreign carriers to enter the country, thus the Mexican carrier is responsible for delivering the goods to the consignee and returning the trailer to the border.

Given the complexity of the system and the current growth in trade, it's not surprising that there can be delays getting through certain customs checkpoints. For example, both the crossings at Laredo and El Paso, Texas, which see the vast majority of US-Mexico truck traffic, are plagued with endless lines of idling trucks that may take most of a work day to inch up to the customs window. Other border crossings are less crowded, but still may take several hours.

Breaking Down Barriers

Congestion at customs checkpoints is just one of many problems that US shippers must deal with. The Mexican Customs Service itself is seen by many as a barrier to trade. Sally Essex, purchasing manager for Printline Products of San Francisco, tells the story of a truckload of computer and printer parts that was stopped for inspection. Every time the inspection was completed and the truck reloaded, the inspector would find something else he had "missed" and demand that the trailer be unloaded again.

Essex is hopeful, though, that those days are over. In an attempt to eliminate corruption, President Salinas in 1990 fired 90 percent of his country's customs employees and transferred their responsibilities to the treasury department. "I give Salinas a lot of credit for bringing a degree of professionalism to customs that wasn't there.

He's done everything he could to eliminate bribery," she says. That's not to say that Mexican Customs is trouble-free, however. "Things have definitely shaped up, but if I had to criticize Mexican Customs, I'd criticize the degree of rigidity," Essex adds. "They have a tendency to concentrate on the letter, not the spirit, of the law."

Another problem US shippers should be prepared for is the scarcity of specialized transportation equipment in Mexico. "If you need a flatbed, a lowboy, or a refrigerated trailer, you should let the Mexican broker know that well in advance," says Ross Porter. "You can't always get them in Mexico when you need them, and it can be especially difficult if the delivery point will be far from a major city."

The transportation system in Mexico has other limitations, adds Celina Mier, general manager of Cal-Tex Spice Co. in Anthony, Texas. For example, shippers should recognize that "the logistics of the rail system in Mexico is still in the development stage. Sometimes your shipment may get to its destination a lot later than you had planned," she warns.

Cargo insurance is a murky area that can give US exporters a headache, too, says Alcantar. He recommends having your US freight forwarder ensure there is sufficient coverage in line with US commercial practice. Mexican brokers and carriers don't automatically offer the kind of insurance protection US companies expect. Furthermore, settling insurance claims is difficult enough here, let alone in a foreign country.

Many shippers are intimidated by the need to present documentation and communicate in Spanish. For most, it pays to choose a freight forwarder that has a bilingual, bicultural staff. "Even if you're very fluent in Spanish, it might not be enough. They'll always see you as a foreigner and you may not have the same access to information as a native does," believes Essex.

Have a Good Team

The most important thing you can do to ensure success, the experts agree, is to develop a close working relationship with an experienced US freight forwarder and Mexican customs broker. "It's more than a matter of being trustworthy, it's also being accurate and reliable because of all the parties they have to collaborate with," believes Ross Porter of Porter International.

Celina Mier says her best advice to new exporters is to have a good border broker. "Now more than ever it's important to have a good broker, since the Mexican government is putting in place new (import) regulations.... A well-informed broker can save you a lot of time, money, and headaches!"

Finally, says Alcantar, be prepared for anything to happen and be willing to follow up on details. "When shipping to Mexico, it's important not to assume anything," he warns. "And there's no such thing as a dumb question!"

---

additional documentation—possibly including health certificates and tests results—that must accompany the authorization when it is presented to Mexican Customs. The authorization is valid for a specific time or volume, whichever is reached first. These authorizations are issued by:

- *Departamento de Autorizaciones Zoosanitarias Dirección General de Salud Animal, SARH* (For livestock and products, except processed meat, animal feed, and feed ingredients)
- *Dirección General de Sanidad Vegetal, SARH* (For fresh vegetables, fruits, selected grains and oilseeds, planting seeds, tobacco leaf, and live plants)
- *Dirección General de Sanidad Forestal, SARH* (For forest products, logs, lumber, and panel products)

Authorization of the *Secretaría de Desarrollo Social* (SEDESOL) Import authorizations are needed for products that contain materials—such as toxic materials—that may adversely affect the environment. For information and import authorization procedures, contact *Dirección General de Prevención y Control de la Contaminación Ambiental,* at the *Secretaría de Desarrollo Social.* (*See* Useful Addresses at the end of this chapter for contact information.)

Documentation at Packing

Packaging represents an extremely important stage in the import transaction. The goods should be packed in such a manner as to allow for easy loading and unloading—at one or more customs inspections, for storage at a port of exit or entry, and for transfer among freight companies. To avoid delays in transport, at the packaging stage, goods must be properly inspected, marked, and labeled in accordance with shipping and customs requirements.

Accuracy and completeness of documents are extremely important because of an emphasis on formalities at Mexican Customs. This emphasis has been increased by the efforts of Mexican governmental authorities to eliminate corruption, which requires customs inspectors to go "by the book." An exporter may now be charged with tax evasion and fined if a customs officer cannot locate a required document. Consultation with the importer, freight forwarder, and customs broker is recommended at the packing stage to ensure that all current documentary requirements are met. The wisest course is to send an invoice by fax to the US forwarder and importer in advance to make corrections.

The following documents are required regardless of the mode of transport used to deliver goods to Mexico.

Commercial Invoice All commercial shipments and all goods with commercial value should be shipped with a commercial invoice. Exceptions are made for imports: delivered to foreign embassies and consulates, their employees, and officials; related to electric energy, crude petroleum, natural gas, and their derivatives when received by pipeline; or brought in as personal effects by authorized persons.

The exporter should insert one original and at least two copies—all signed—of a commercial invoice into the package. Additional copies of the invoice may be requested by the freight forwarder, by the *agente aduanal,* or by the importer in Mexico. A signed copy should be sent directly to the importer in Mexico.

If the same shipment consists of several packages, the exporter may number the packages consecutively and enclose the commercial invoices in only one of them. The exporter must then clearly label the package containing the invoice and endorse the other packages with the statement: *"Facturas incluido en paquete número X…"* (Invoices included in package no. X).

No special format is required for a commercial invoice. It must be translated into Spanish or be accompanied by an equivalent Spanish translation, and the translation must be signed by the shipper, addressee, or consignee.

The mandatory requirements for commercial invoices are as follows:

- The foreign supplier must sign each copy of the enclosed invoices, preferably below a declaration of the truth and accuracy of the values and other data included in the invoice.
- The invoice must state:
  - The place and date of its issuance—the date must be within 90 days of the time the goods arrive in Mexican Customs.
  - The name and complete street address of the foreign supplier (a post office box alone is unacceptable), consignee and importer (if different), and the RFC (*registro federal de causantes*—the consignees's Mexican tax ID number).
  - A separate description of each product, including any identifying numbers (such as model or serial numbers engraved on the products), manufacturer's imprints, trade names, brand names, the quantity sold, the unit price, the total price, and the country of origin. A trademark, a patent name, or an abbreviated designation alone will not meet this requirement.
  - The total number of goods shipped.
  - Gross and net weights.
  - Free-on-board (FOB) value of goods at port of entry.
  - Itemized charges for all costs related to shipping, including cost of insurance and freight handling.
  - Any marks or numbers on the packages.
  - The type of package—that is, box, barrel, bundle, or other.
- The invoice must not be altered by any corrections, erasures, or notations, except that packaging information may be added.

A foreign supplier should seek the advice of the importer or a freight forwarder in filling out a commercial invoice because requirements often change. One of the important questions to ask is whether to include on the invoice the intended point of entry for the goods into Mexico. The importer or freight forwarder should be able to instruct on which product weight—gross, legal, net—should be declared in the invoice. If corrections must be made, the exporter should also consult the importer or a freight forwarder as to the best procedure.

Failure to comply with mandatory invoice content requirements will cause delays in shipping. If the information might be ascertained by inspecting the product, a customs officer may open the cases or packages. Otherwise, the invoice will be returned to the shipper for conformance. Only in rare instances will Mexican customs allow the *agente aduanal* to fill in missing information, such as an incomplete address for a *maquila* shipment.

To avoid being subject to contraband charges, the foreign supplier must be certain that the invoice description of goods sold conforms exactly to the actual goods shipped. If a Mexican customs officer finds goods in a quantity exceeding the amount shown on the invoice by more than 10 percent, the excess may be confiscated and the foreign supplier fined. A similar disposition is made of any merchandise included in the shipment but not listed (in any amount) on the invoice.

Packing List The foreign supplier must usually enclose at least three copies of the packing list for a shipment, although the list may not be needed for a shipment by mail or US parcel post, as per the importer's instruction. The packing list should be translated into Spanish and must specify: the gross, legal, and net weights of each item shipped as well as of the entire shipment; the total number of packages shipped; and the type and capacity of the packaging containers. If the seller could not fit a complete description of each product onto the commercial invoice, the packing list must show all of the required descriptive information and be attached to the invoice copies.

The packing list should indicate the type of package being shipped, unless this information is already stated in the commercial invoice. If a shipper has formed a single package from several boxes, bundles, or other items that each contain the same type of goods, the packing list must state the total number of items in the package, the gross and legal weight of each, and the gross weight of the total. Exceptions to this requirement are allowed for products that are commonly bound together in packages, including pipes, iron bars, and machinery.

Certificates of Origin or Certifications of Origin Certain goods must be accompanied by an original certificate or certification that attests to the country where the goods were manufactured, assembled, or finished. For this purpose, the country of origin is considered to be wherever the last substantial transformation of the goods took place, providing the transformation resulted in the final merchandise being classified under an HS tariff number different from the HS number of the inputs used to make the goods. An example: if goods are imported into the US under one HS tariff classification, assembled or altered in a US factory so that a change in the HS classification takes place, then exported to Mexico under the different HS classification, the US is considered the country of origin regardless of where the original materials came from.

A certificate or certification of origin is required mainly for goods being imported under NAFTA tariff preferences or those that have been the subject of antidumping actions. For goods subject to the origin requirements, a notation of the country of origin on the commercial invoice will not suffice. Instead, an attested declaration is necessary. This type of certificate or certification of origin should not be confused with a NAFTA certificate of origin, which is only needed to qualify for preferential treatment under NAFTA. (*See* NAFTA Certificate of Origin in this chapter.)

The major distinction between a certificate or origin and certification of origin is in the person who uses it: a reseller of goods uses a certificate of origin, whereas a producer of goods completes a certification of origin. However, this distinction has become somewhat blurred, in that producers may present either a certificate or certification of origin. Moreover, government authorities have mandated that Mexican customs officers should accept either of these documents when clearing shipments.

A certificate of origin is a statement that is signed by a reseller or producer of goods who attests to the origin of the goods. The certificate must be separate from any other documentation and must not be included on the commercial invoice. It must be submitted to Mexican customs on a separate form at the same time as the other import documents. A certification of origin is similar in content to a certificate of origin, but it may be used only by the producer of the goods and may be included on the commercial invoice. The certificate or certification may be in English; but in either case, the importer (or the importer's representative or consignee), must sign and submit to Mexican Customs the following additional written declaration in Spanish:

Declaro bajo protesta de decir verdad que la mercancía que ampara ___ (if declaration is on the invoice, use: esta factura; if declaration is not on the invoice, use: la factura número ___) es originaria de ___ (Spanish name of country); manifiesto conocer las sanciones previstas por la legislación penal aplicable a quienes incurren en falsedad de declaraciones o informes ante una autoridad.

(I declare below as truth that the product cited on ___ [if declaration is on the invoice: this invoice; if declaration is not on the invoice: invoice number ___] originated in ___ [name of country]; in doing so, I am aware of the sanctions in the penal legislation applicable to those who make false declarations or testimonials to an authority.)

A single certificate or certification of origin may cover goods sent in multiple shipments, provided that the certificate or certification, first, refers to the *pedimento de importación* (customs import declaration) for each shipment, and, second, identifies the products individually.

The products that require certificates or certifications of origin change frequently, and the exporter should request information with regard to the specific product from a freight forwarder, customs broker, the importer, or a government customs office.

Goods requiring a certificate of origin for import into Mexico—primarily because of antidumping concerns—have recently included the following:

- Bicycles and bicycle tires and seats,
- Clothing and textiles,
- Electrical machines and parts,
- Flouric acid,

- Malleable iron products,
- Organic chemical products,
- Shoes,
- Steel products,
- Tools and cutting implements, and
- Toys.

Some goods are specifically exempt from the certificate of origin requirement—including charitable donations, household effects belonging to those with *inmigrante* (authorized permanent resident) status, inputs for government-owned enterprises, and various noncommercial imports. If the value of the goods imported does not exceed US$1,000 (about NP3,360), Mexican customs will generally not require a certificate or certification of origin, although if the goods are subject to antidumping duties, these amounts must nevertheless be paid. Special treatment is also afforded to goods earmarked for *maquila* companies, unless the goods are to be resold in the Mexican market.

Documentation at Shipping

The documentation requirements for shipping goods to Mexico vary depending on the mode of transport: land (truck or rail), sea, air, or mail. In addition to the bill of lading documents described below, a shipper may request to see insurance, health, and other certificates. The importer or the bank handling payment for the goods may have further documentary requirements that must be met before the shipper will accept the load. When the product is wrapped, secured, documented, and waiting on a loading dock, be certain that the freight forwarder knows of the imminent departure. Never ship without advance notice to the forwarder.

Air Freight Cargo transported by airlines must be accompanied by an air waybill. The importer and airline will furnish information about specific requirements for the contents of this bill and the number of copies to be enclosed. The commercial invoice should indicate the number of the air waybill. Special rules are applicable to the transport of dangerous and restricted goods. Most freight airlines will supply information on these rules, which may include national and international regulations (found in the International Air Transport Association (IATA) rules and the International Civil Aviation Organization (ICAO) rules).

Mail Service Mexico imposes no documentary requirements on regular mail shipments valued at less than NP5,000 (about US$1,490). For such items, the shipper should comply with any instructions from the importer.

For shipments valued at NP5,000 or more, the exporter must mark the package on the outside with one of the following, as appropriate: "Addressee does not require Mexican import license" or "Addressee possesses Mexican import license" (*include issued license number*).

The exporter must additionally comply with customs requirements for mailing from the exporting country. An explanation of these requirements should be obtained in the home country from a local post office or customs office.

An example: a US exporter must complete and attach US Customs labels and forms to send any of the following by regular mail to Mexico:

- A letter or letter package of dutiable merchandise,
- A package of dutiable prints, or
- A small packet.

For each of the listed items, the US exporter must fill in a green customs label C1—Form 2976 (Authorization for Customs to Open International Mail) and attach it to the address side. If the contents are valued at more than US$400 (about NP1,350) or if the US exporter does not want the contents to be described on the outside of the mailed item, the US exporter should attach the upper portion of the label on the outside, and enclose a completed US Customs declaration C2—Form 2976 (Customs Declaration) in the package. Special customs forms are also required for shipping goods from the US by parcel post or using an express mail service. The US exporter should follow the advice of the US Postal Service with regard to the required forms and labels.

Shipments by Sea For shipments by sea, the exporter must furnish a bill of lading, which should indicate the marks, serial numbers, quantity and kinds of packages, and the gross weight in metric units. A shipping company or freight forwarder will provide advice and information on the documentation needed before, during, and after the voyage.

Overland Transport An exporter may send goods to Mexico from the US by either of two methods: a local bill of lading or a through bill of lading.

A local bill of lading conducts the shipment to the border of the exporting country (usually the US), where the goods must be reshipped to the importer in Mexico, usually by an *agente aduanal* or freight forwarder at the point of entry into Mexico. The original local bill of lading must be sent either directly or via a bank, to the *agente aduanal* or freight forwarder at the border. That agent will then take possession of the goods and will arrange reshipment and customs formalities for transport into Mexico. A local bill of lading has the distinct advantage of placing the goods in the hands of an agent who is knowledgeable about tariff and customs requirements and who can, if necessary, revise, repack, or otherwise change the shipment to secure the most favorable customs treatment.

Using a through bill of lading, the seller delivers

NAFTA: CERTIFICATE OF ORIGIN

An importer in Mexico may claim NAFTA benefits for imported goods. Goods that qualify for NAFTA treatment can be exported to Mexico either duty-free or at a reduced tariff rate. (Refer to the "NAFTA" chapter for a discussion of the provisions of this treaty.) To qualify goods for NAFTA treatment, the importer makes a declaration directly on the import documentation, requesting NAFTA treatment based on a valid NAFTA Certificate of Origin. The actual certificate must be presented to Mexican Customs on request. If, however, the certificate is found to contain inaccurate information, the importer will be required to submit a corrected declaration and pay any additional duties as required.

A NAFTA Certificate of Origin is a uniform, printed form used in all NAFTA countries. A NAFTA Certificate of Origin is completed and signed by the exporter, who must then provide it to the importer (and customs officials of the exporting country, if requested). An exporter who is not also the producer of the goods may nevertheless complete a NAFTA Certificate of Origin on the basis of any of the following:

1. The exporter's knowledge that the goods meet the origination rules.
2. The exporter's reasonable reliance on the written statement of the producer that the goods meet the origination rules.
3. The producer's completed NAFTA Certificate of Origin for the goods, signed and voluntarily provided to the exporter.

A NAFTA Certificate of Origin may be completed in the language of either the importing or exporting country, but Mexican Customs requires, in case of a NAFTA Certificate of Origin in English or French, that an importer in Mexico submit a Spanish translation.

A NAFTA certificate might cover a single importation of goods, or multiple importations of identical goods, or multiple shipments of more than one type of goods. The last of these three, the NAFTA Certificate of Origin for multiple shipments, is a blanket certificate; it applies to the various goods specified in the certificate imported within a designated 12-month period. The blanket certificate will remain valid for NAFTA preference claims made up to four years from the date the certificate was signed. This delayed date of validity allows a person who initially imports goods into Mexico within the 12-month period—but then fails to enter them for use in Mexico within that time—to nevertheless claim NAFTA treatment after the 12-month expires period but within the four-year period.

Even if NAFTA treatment is not requested at the time of importation, it may still be requested up to one year after that date. The importer and exporter must provide copies of the NAFTA certificate to their respective customs administrations on request.

the shipment to a carrier in the US, which then undertakes delivery, transferring the goods to one or more additional carriers under the same bill of lading until the shipment reaches its destination. The original through bill of lading is sent, generally by means of a bank, to the importer, who will need the bill in order to take possession of the goods on arrival. A signed copy of the bill of lading must be marked "For customhouse purposes only" and given to the agent who handles customs formalities at the border.

There are several advantages to using a through bill. Freight charges to the point of destination can be fixed in advance and billed to the Mexican importer. Cargo handling expenses at the border are also lower, because the shipment simply continues in transit. Delays for repacking, rebilling, reshipping arrangements, and other manipulations at the border can be kept to a minimum, and the goods can keep on moving after clearing customs. The risk of

theft is also reduced. Traditionally, local bills have predominated, but with improved shipping and customs efficiency, the advantages are tempting more firms to ship under a through bill of lading.

Mexican Customs

At the port of entry, documents are presented and reviewed and duties and other charges are paid. The paperwork must be completed in advance, then the tariffs and fees can be calculated; payment funds should be ready so that transfer can take place immediately. Mexico is modernizing its customs procedures, allowing, at some ports of entry, for electronic transmission to speed the process. Nevertheless, the lack of a customs bond system requires that duties and value-added taxes be paid at the time of clearance in order to process the goods through Mexican customs. The importer in Mexico is usually responsible for getting the goods through Mexican customs; this task is customarily assigned to a Mexican *agente aduanal*, or customs broker.

For the goods to enter Mexican customs, the agent will require copies of many of the documents discussed above. Customs entry typically requires the following:

- A commercial invoice for merchandise exceeding US$300 (about NP1,000) in value.
- A written declaration of value signed by the importer, stating the value of the goods based on the information provided in the shipping documents. Mexican customs officials will use this declaration in determining customs duties on the imports.
- A written declaration signed by the exporter on a form available from customs. A US shipper's export declaration is required for goods shipped from the US, but only if a validated export license is needed or if the value exceeds US$2,500 (about NP8,400). For shipments through the US Postal Service, however, this upper limit drops to US$500 (about NP1,680).
- A bill of lading or air waybill endorsed by the carrier.
- All required documents showing compliance with import restrictions and non-tariff import regulations.
- A notice of importation—*aviso*—for food products, alcoholic beverages, cosmetics, toiletries, and agricultural products not containing toxic substances. This notice is required for each shipment of such products and is usually given by the *agente aduanal* to the Mexican representative, who then forwards it to the SS. The notice should be given on an application form or by a letter provided to the *agente aduanal* containing the following information (preferably in tabular format): the name of the exporter; the country of origin; the name of the importers; the port of entry; the name and address of the warehouse where the products will be stored; the HS number for the products; a declaration, if appropriate, that this shipment is the first to Mexico of this product; and the quantity and value of the products. To the extent applicable, the notice must be accompanied by a sanitary certificate, certificate of origin, certificate of free sale, and physiochemical or microbiological analysis. Information on notification procedures may be obtained from the following agencies, preferably by fax requests (*see* Useful Addresses at the end of this chapter for contact information):
  - *Control Sanitario de Bienes y Servicios*
    (For food, beverages, cosmetics, and toiletries)
  - *Dirección General de Control de Insumos Para la Salud*
    (For medicines, medical equipment, and medical supplies)
  - *Dirección General de Prevención y Control de la Contaminación Ambiental*
    (For pesticides, fertilizers, and other toxic substances)
- If necessary, proof of the country of origin and the country of export.
- Documentation of a bond or guarantee for the payment of additional duties on merchandise that may be deemed undervalued on the invoice.

The importer in Mexico must pay all customs duties, fees, and other taxes before the goods can be released from Mexican customs. To make payment, the agent presents to customs a declaration—*pedimento de importación*—which is valid when stamped *pagado* (paid) by customs. No merchandise will be released until this form has been completed and stamped.

After customs is satisfied with the documents and payments, the merchandise is presented to a stoplight—a *semáforo fiscal*—that randomly indicates whether an inspection will be required. If the shipment gets a green light, it is not selected for inspection, is released immediately, and may proceed into Mexico. A shipment is designated for examination if it encounters a red light; then it will be subject to the review by customs officials. Barring the discovery of discrepancies, inspection should be accomplished within three hours.

In the case of unloading, goods should be cleared by Mexican customs within 15 days after such unloading; warehouse storage charges begin to accrue thereafter. If a problem develops and the goods cannot be cleared, the foreign supplier or Mexican importer may be able to have the goods transferred to a private, bonded warehouse until customs is satisfied.

If a shipment remains in Mexican customs for more than 60 days and no *pedimento de importación* has been officially presented, the products can usually be returned to the freight forwarder without penalty. Mexican customs typically allows a two-week grace period. This time is reduced to 30 days for shipments arriving by air.

Once a *pedimento* has been presented, goods must be retrieved within 60 days. After that time, the goods will be considered to have been abandoned and will become the property of Mexican customs.

Requirements After Customs Clearance

After the goods have cleared customs, they are transferred for transport into Mexico in accordance with the arrangements stipulated on the bill of lading.

If an importer registered a *devolución* to make an advance payment of foreign currency for the merchandise, the importer must present to SECOFI proper documentation showing that the imported goods have cleared customs. This documentation must be presented within 30 days from the date of clearance. (*See* Registration for Foreign Exchange in this chapter for a discussion of advance payment requirements.)

Exporters and importers must retain documentation showing legal importation, in case the government authorities require clarification after the goods have cleared customs.

USEFUL ADDRESSES

Control Sanitario de Bienes y Servicios
Lieja 7, Piso 7
Col. Juárez
06600 México, DF, México
Tel: [52] (5) 518-3696 Fax: [52] (5) 512-9628

Departamento de Autorizaciones Zoosanitarias
Dirección General de Salud Animal, SARH
Recreo 51
México, DF, México
Tel: [52] (5) 534-1131/8 Fax: [52] (5) 534-3985

Departamento de Certificaciones e Información
Comercial Dirección General de Normas, SECOFI
Av. Puente de Tecamachalco No. 6
Lomas de Tecamachalco
53950 Naucalpan, Edo. de Méx., México
Tel: [52] (5) 540-2620 Fax: [52] (5) 520-9715

Departmento de Consulta
Dirección General de Aduanas
Secretaría de Hacienda y Crédito Público
Av. 20 de Noviembre 195
06090 México, DF, México
Tel: [52] (5) 709-6365

Dirección General de Control de Insumos Para la Salud
Secretaría de Salud (SS)
Insurgentes Sur 1397, Piso 3
Col. Guadalupe Inn
01020 México, DF, México
Tel: [52] (5) 598-9029

Dirección de Control de Insumos para la Salud
Insurgentes Sur 1397, Piso 3
Col. Guadalupe Inn
01020 México, DF, México
Tel: (5) 254-2538 Fax: (5) 250-6962

Dirección General de Asuntos Fronterizos, SECOFI
Periférico Sur 3025, Piso 7
Col. Héroes de Padierna
Deleg. Magdalena Contreras
México, DF, México
Tel: [52] (5) 683-4394, 683-7005 x2706

Dirección General de Control Sanitario de Bienes y Servicios
Sub-Dirección de Sanidad Internacional y Consultoria
Secretaría de Salud (SS)
Donceles 39
Col. Centro
06000 México, DF, México
Tel: [52] (5) 521-3050

Dirección General de Normas (DGN), SECOFI
Av. Puente de Tecamachalco No. 6, Piso 3
Lomas de Tecamachalco
53950 Naucalpan, Edo. de Méx., México
Tel: [52] (5) 540-2620, 589-9877
Fax: [52] (5) 606-0386

Dirección General de Prevencion y Control de la Contaminacion Ambiental
Río Elba 20
Col. Cuauhetémoc
06500 México, DF, México
Tel: [52] (5) 553-2977, 553-9481
Fax: [52] (5) 658-6059, 289-8559

Dirección General de Sanidad Forestal, SARH
Progreso 5, Piso 2
Col. Viveros de Coyoacan
México, DF, México
Tel: [52] (5) 658-8974, 658-8438

Dirección General de Sanidad Vegetal, SARH
Guillermo Perez Valenzuela No. 127
México, DF, México
Tel: [52] (5) 554-0512, 658-1671
Fax: [52] (5) 554-0529

Dirección General de Servicios al Comercio Exterior, SECOFI
Blvd. Adolfo Lopez Mateos 3025
Col. Héroes de Padierna
00700 México, DF, México
Tel: [52] (5) 683-5066, 683-4344
Fax: [52] (5) 595-5881/3

Director General de Control Sanitario de Bienes y Servicios
Sub-Dirección de Sanidad Internacional y Consultoria, SS
Donceles 39
Col. Centro
06000 México, DF, México
Tel: [52] (5) 521-3050

Información Tecnológica y Consultoria (INFOTEC)
Apdo. Postal 22-860
Tlalpan
14060 México, DF, México
Tel: [52] (5) 606-0011, 606-1620
Fax: [52] (5) 606-0386

Secretaría de Agricultura y Recursos Hidráulicos
(SARH)
Avda. Insurgentes Sur No. 476, Piso 13
Col. Roma Sur
06038 México, DF, México
Tel: [52] (5) 584-0066, 584-0096, 584-0271

Secretaría de Comercio y Fomento Industrial
(SECOFI)
Calle Alfonso Reyes No. 30
Col. Condesa
06140 México, DF, México
Tel: [52] (5) 211-0036, 286-1757, 286-1823, 286-1461
Fax: [52] (5) 224-3000, 286-0804, 286-1551, 286-1543

Secretaría de Comunicaciones y Transportes (SCT)
Avda. Universidad y Xola
Col. Navarte
03028 México, DF, México
Tel: [52] (5) 519-7456, 519-1319, 530-9203, 530-1074
Fax: [52] (5) 519-9748, 530-1074

Secretaría de Hacienda y Crédito Público
(Hacienda)
Palacio Nacional
1 Patio Mariano
06066 México, DF, México
Tel: [52] (5) 518-2060, 518-2711
Fax: [52] (5) 542-2821, 510-3796

Secretaría de Salud (SS)
Lieja 7, Piso 7
Col. Juárez
06600 México, DF, México
Tel: [52] (5) 553-0758 Fax: [52] (5) 286-5497

Subsecretaría de Ingresos, Hacienda
Avenida Hidalgo 77, Módulo 1, P.B.
Col. Guerrero
Deleg. Cuauhtemoc
06300 México, DF, México

Export Policy & Procedures

In the past decade, Mexico's international trading policies have emphasized deregulation, promotion of exports and imports, and simplification of exporting and importing procedures. The government has dealt substantial blows to corruption in Mexican Customs, including the firing of 90 percent of its customs employees in 1990 and the transfer of their responsibilities to the *Secretaría de Hacienda y Crédito Público (Hacienda)*—Mexico's Secretariat of Finance.

The following section discusses Mexico's export policy and the procedures for exporting from the country. This information is useful if you want to purchase goods and services from Mexico, expand your current operations in Mexico to export markets, establish an enterprise in Mexico that will supply foreign markets, or invest in an export business located in Mexico.

EXPORT POLICIES

Government Agencies

The administration of foreign trade is primarily the responsibility of the *Secretaría de Comercio y Fomento Industrial* (SECOFI). In addition to implementing Mexico's international trade policies, SECOFI specifically administers imports and exports, issues licenses, conducts inspections, monitors import and export operations, and classifies products.

The other agency of particular importance to the exporting process is the *Subsecretaría de Ingresos* at the *Secretaría de Hacienda y Crédito Público*, which is responsible for evaluation of export value, collection of fees and taxes, administration of Customs, and licensing of *agentes aduanal. See* Useful Addresses at the end of this chapter for contact information.

Exports Requiring Permits

Of the more than 5,200 categories of goods on the export tariff schedule, only about 360 require prior export permits. In general, export permits are required for products that are important to state security, must comply with international conventions, must adhere to sanitary and safety standards, or are subject to environmental regulations. Examples include petrochemical products, some raw materials, blood derivatives and other pharmaceutical articles, and weapons.

Export Tariffs

Less than 30 of the 5,200 categories of exports on the tariff schedule are taxed. Tariffs are applied to products produced by industries that are under special government control, primarily because of military or other national security interests.

Quality Standards

Only a few Mexican exports must be certified for quality under the *Normas Oficiales Mexicanas* (NOM)—Mexican Official Standards. Products subject to an international convention may need to be NOM certified, such as tequila, which must be sourced as required under the Lisbon Agreement on Denomination of Origin. For other products, NOM certification is optional. Information on quality standards for exports can be obtained from the *Dirección General de Normas. See* Useful Addresses at the end of this chapter for contact information.

Import Preferences for Mexican Exports

Trading Privileges Mexico is a signatory to a number of international treaties and conventions, under which the members are accorded special tariff treatment and trading preferences.

This chapter was reviewed by Ross E. Porter, Sales and Marketing Manager, Porter International, Inc., a customhouse brokerage and international freight forwarding firm in San Diego, California; and Jim Fitzgerald, Vice President, J.E. Lowden & Co., a customhouse brokerage and international freight forwarding firm in San Francisco, California.

EXPORTING GLOSSARY

agente aduanal A Mexican customs broker or agent, who is hired by an exporter in Mexico to assist in clearing goods through Mexican customs. The *agente aduanal* usually coordinates with a US customs broker and with US and Mexican freight forwarders to ship goods from Mexico with minimal delays.

General Agreement on Tariffs and Trade (GATT) A multilateral trade agreement aimed at expanding international trade. Its main goals are to liberalize world trade and place it on a secure basis thereby contributing to economic growth and development. GATT is the only multilateral instrument that lays down agreed-upon rules for international trade. The organization that oversees the agreement—formerly also known as GATT, but now called the World Trade Organization (WTO)—is the principal international body concerned with negotiating the reduction of trade barriers and improving international trade relations.

Generalized System of Preferences (GSP) An international program under which the members allow, as a means of encouraging economic growth, imports of merchandise from developing countries to enter duty-free or at reduced tariff rates.

Harmonized System (HS) A multipurpose international goods classification system designed to be used by manufacturers, transporters, exporters, importers, customs officials, statisticians, and others in classifying goods that move in international trade under a single commodity code. The system contains approximately 5,000 headings and subheadings of goods generally organized by industry.

legal kilo *See* legal weight.

legal weight The total weight of the merchandise and its own packaging, but excluding exterior containers or packing materials. The legal weight of canned vegetables would include the vegetables and the can, but not the crate and wrappings for shipping.

NOM Certification Official Mexican Standards—*Normas Oficial Mexicanas* (NOM)—are technical regulations adopted by Mexican governmental agencies to impose standards of health, quality, and safety on products sold in Mexico. Products that are exported from Mexico may also be NOM certified to show compliance with Mexican standards and with standards required by the importing country.

North American Free Trade Agreement (NAFTA) A free trade agreement among Canada, the US, and Mexico. The objectives of NAFTA are to eliminate barriers to trade, promote conditions of fair competition, increase investment opportunities, provide protection for intellectual and industrial property rights, and establish procedures for the resolution of disputes.

Secretaría de Comercio y Fomento Industrial (SECOFI) The Secretariat of Commerce and Industrial Development in Mexico, responsible for adopting and administering commercial regulations generally, including those governing business enterprises, imports, exports, safety and product quality standards, and business licensing.

Secretaría de Hacienda y Crédito Público (Hacienda) Mexico's Secretariat of Finance and Public Credit, which is the government authority primarily responsible for administering and regulating financial matters, such as taxes, license and registration fees, financial institutions, and export and import tariffs.

- **GATT Trading Status** Mexico holds most-favored nation (MFN) status under GATT. Among GATT members, MFN status requires nondiscriminatory trade treatment. However, Mexico is also recognized as a developing country, and therefore receives favorable tariff treatment for some exports under the Generalized System of Preferences (GSP) established under GATT for developing countries. The GSP allows certain Mexican products to enter an importing country free of tariffs and others to enter on payment of a tariff assessed against only the value added in Mexico. Products are accorded GSP treatment only if at least 35 percent of their customs value is derived from Mexico. Nearly 40 percent of Mexican exports to Europe and 70 percent to Japan are accorded GSP benefits. However, GSP status is reviewed and changed regularly; it is phased out as a country rises to a certain level of development—one which Mexico is fast approaching.

- **North American Free Trade Agreement (NAFTA)** Provides for the elimination of tariff and nontariff barriers in trading among Canada, Mexico, and the US.
- **Latin American Integration Association (ALADI)** Provides for preferential trade treatment among Argentina, Bolivia, Brazil, Colombia, Chile, Ecuador, Mexico, Paraguay, Peru, Uruguay, and Venezuela.
- **Pacific Basin Economic Council** Promotes trade among Pacific Basin countries that are members of the Council.
- **Global System of Commercial Preferences** Provides for nondiscriminatory trading practices among the developing nations that are members.

Reduced Duties for Reexports to US Goods that are assembled in Mexico from US inputs and then reexported to the US can qualify for reduced tariffs. This special duty preference, designed to promote the *maquila* industry in Mexico, permits a company to ship unassembled parts and materials to Mexico, employ Mexican labor to assemble products, and then export the finished goods back to the US. A company need not, however, formally be established as a *maquila* to claim these duty preferences. As tariffs are reduced and eliminated under NAFTA, these duty preferences will become less and less important. (*See* NAFTA: Impacts on Exporting to Canada and the US on this page and refer to the "NAFTA" chapter for a general discussion.)

Import Barriers to Mexican Exports

Unfair Competition Restrictions An importing country may assess antidumping and countervailing tariffs against Mexican exports that are found to have unfairly flooded the market in the importing country with goods priced below market. These tariffs vary depending on the antidumping charges brought at any one time against Mexican exports. European countries have imposed antidumping tariffs against Mexican exports of steel and synthetic fibers in recent years, and the United States has placed similar tariffs on Mexican exports of cement and some steel products.

Export Quotas Products that are particularly competitive often face quotas that limit the amount of sales to foreign countries. Quotas are usually fixed by the importing country or by multilateral and bilateral trade restraint agreements with other countries.

NAFTA: IMPACTS ON EXPORTING TO CANADA AND THE US

For most trade among Canada, Mexico, and the US, the 1994 North American Free Trade Agreement (NAFTA) either eliminates customs duties immediately or phases them out over five to 10 years, with the phaseout of tariffs on a few sensitive articles will occur over 15 years. Subsequent to ratification of the treaty, the NAFTA countries may agree to a faster tariff phaseout on any particular goods. (Refer to the "NAFTA" chapter for an explanation of the provisions of this treaty.)

In general, tariffs are eliminated or reduced only on goods defined as originating in a NAFTA country. Duty rates also vary depending on where the goods were produced. An understanding of the NAFTA rules of origin is therefore essential to determining whether goods will qualify for non-tariff or reduced tariff treatment. The rules of origin are the same whether goods are transported into or out of Mexico. (Refer to the "Import Policies & Procedures" chapter for a brief discussion on these rules.)

An importer in Canada or the US may claim NAFTA benefits for goods imported from Mexico. Goods that qualify for NAFTA treatment can be imported from Mexico duty-free or at a reduced tariff. To qualify goods for NAFTA treatment, the importer makes a declaration directly on the import documentation that requests NAFTA treatment based on a valid NAFTA Certificate of Origin (a uniform, printed form used in all NAFTA countries). It must be completed and signed by the exporter, who must then provide it to the importer (and to customs officials in the exporting country, if requested). The importer must present the certificate to customs of the importing country. If the certificate is found to contain inaccurate information, the importer will be required to submit a corrected declaration and pay any additional duties as required.

- **GSP Quotas** A GSP quota is established by an importing country on the basis of the Generalized System of Preferences (GSP) established under GATT. An importing country may limit the number of items that can be brought into the country with favorable GSP tariff treatment. Once that number has been admitted, tariffs on additional imports of the product rise to the rates set under GATT. Products that often exceed GSP quotas include petrochemicals shipped to Europe.
- **Quota Treaties** Mexico is a party to the following treaties that place quotas on its exports:
  - **Multifiber Agreement on International Textile Trade** Limiting apparel, acrylan fiber, and cotton fiber exports to the United States.
  - **Voluntary Restriction Agreement** Restricting steel exports to the United States.

EXPORT PROCEDURES

Parties to an export-import transaction must comply with two sets of requirements: the export regulations of Mexico and the import regulations of the country to which the goods will be delivered. This discussion focuses on the first step: sending the goods out of Mexico. Once the goods clear Mexican Customs, the foreign buyer must meet the import regulations of his or her own country, which may include import documentation, declarations, and licenses. (Refer to "An Illustration: US Import Regulations and Procedures" in this chapter.)

As a rule, export procedures are less complicated than those for importing. Financial and shipping procedures for exporting are similar to those for importing, but government controls on trade coming into a country are generally greater than on products leaving the country. The exceptions to this general rule include products that are controlled for purposes of national security, environmental restrictions, and worldwide health and safety reasons. For most products, exporters simply make a contract, confirm payment, ship the products to the Mexican port or border point of exit, and complete minimal customs forms for Mexican authorities. The foreign importer then takes possession of the goods and is responsible for clearing customs in the importing country and transporting the goods to the final destination.

The Mexican supplier is usually responsible for making sure that the merchandise clears Mexican Customs, and the exporter will most likely contract this job to a licensed customs broker, or *agente aduanal*. In past years, government regulations required most exporters to use such licensed customs brokers to facilitate the export process. Although this restriction has been lifted, at least 90 percent of Mexican exports are still handled by *agentes aduanal*.

In some situations, a foreign buyer will need to know the Mexican export procedures. This need arises particularly if a Mexican supplier prefers free-on-board (FOB) transactions, in which the foreign buyer becomes responsible for transport of the goods from the time of transfer to a carrier in Mexico. In such an event, the foreign importer usually contracts with a licensed customs broker to handle transportation as well. Even if the Mexican supplier is responsible for customs compliance, the foreign importer should be aware of the export requirements and should be prepared to offer assistance to resolve problems and get the goods released and moving to their destination as quickly as possible.

Export Registrations and Licenses

Registry of Importers and Exporters All exporting companies located in Mexico are required to register with *Hacienda*, which maintains a National Registry of Importers and Exporters. The Registry was established as a means of reducing illegal imports and tax evasion.

Export Licenses If an export license is required, the exporter must apply to SECOFI on preprinted form 320-006. The application may be sent to any regional office of SECOFI or to SECOFI's Mexico City center. (Refer to the "Important Addresses" chapter for a listing of regional office contact information.)

An export license is usually valid for the value of exports requested in the application, plus an additional 50 percent of that value. However, some applications are issued only for the value requested.

Preshipment Stage

Preshipment Customs Clearance An exporter may avoid delays at a port or border by requesting advance clearance from a local customs office. This process requires advance registration with *Hacienda* in Mexico City. The exporter must include a tax registration number and records of tax payments with the application. On approval of the application, the exporter's company name will appear on a list that *Hacienda* issues monthly. The exporter must then complete all of the customs documentation regularly required for export at a port or border. In addition, the exporter must file documents showing that the goods are traveling through Mexico in-bond. Once approval is received from the local customs office, the goods are then handed over to a transport company, which is responsible for taking them out of Mexico.

Insurance Arrangements An exporter should consider insuring the goods until the risk of damage or loss passes to the importer. By law, insurance covering risks in Mexico must be obtained from a

AN ILLUSTRATION: US IMPORT REGULATIONS AND PROCEDURES

Merchandise that has been cleared through Mexican Customs on its way into the US must pass stringent US Customs requirements before being released into the US. Until US Customs authorizes importation, the goods must be held at the port of arrival or transported in-bond and held at another port of entry. Compliance with US Customs requirements usually falls on the US importer, a task that is complex at best. Most US importers approach US Customs through professionals—freight forwarders and customs brokers—who are familiar with the ever-changing regulations and who are experts at handling the extensive documentation needed. Customs brokers can be found through local telephone directories, or through references available from local broker associations or the national association:

National Customs Broker and Forwarders Association
1 World Trade Center, Suite 1153
New York City, NY 10048, USA
Tel: [1] (212) 432-0050 Fax: [1] (212) 432-5709

The typical US import process through at a port of entry requires the following steps:

- **Comply with quotas and other restrictions.** Certain types of merchandise are prohibited or restricted from entering the US to protect the US economy, ensure national security, safeguard consumers, and preserve the environment. Some articles are subject to import quotas and restraints under trade agreements or other similar arrangements. Customs clearance will be given only if importation is not restricted or prohibited by these laws and regulations. Products that are subject to quotas, restrictions, and prohibitions generally include certain categories of agricultural commodities, weapons, radioactive materials, consumer products, electronic products, alcoholic beverages, processed foods, drugs, cosmetics, medical devices, gold, silver, currency, stamps, pesticides, toxic and hazardous substances, textiles, furs, wildlife and pets, and petroleum products. Importers of such products should seek advice from a customs broker or the government agency responsible for regulating the product for requirements on importation.

- **Use accepted marking and labeling on exterior shipping containers.** Labels and markings must meet rules for shipping and cargo handling, comply with customs regulations, and allow for quick identification of the shipment by the recipient. Markings usually must include a shipper's mark, country of origin (in English), weight, number of packages, size of cases, handling and cautionary notations, port of entry, and hazardous material warnings. Customs regulations regarding freight labeling are strictly enforced. Freight forwarders and customs brokers can supply necessary information on the specific regulations and on exceptions to marking requirements.

- **Arrange for surety.** The US importer is required to post a bond with US Customs to cover any potential duties, taxes, and penalties that may accrue. The bond may be posted in the form of US cash funds or designated US government obligations. A US customs broker can advise the importer on bond requirements. Some US customs brokers also offer bonds that provide the required coverage.

- **Submit entry documents to US Customs.** A US importer (or agent) must file entry documents with US Customs at the port of entry within five working days (or within any extension period granted) of the date the goods arrive. The entry documents include:

    Form for merchandise release Typically an Entry Manifest (Customs Form 7533) or Application and Special Permit for Immediate Delivery (Customs Form 3461).

    Proof of right to make entry Goods may be imported into the US only by the owner, purchaser, or licensed customs broker. US Customs will request to see proof that the person presenting the goods has a right to bring them into the country. Such proof may be in the form of a bill of lading, air waybill, or a carrier's certificate.

    Commercial invoice Customs will refer to this to identify the goods, the exporter, the value of the goods, the shipper, and the importer. A pro forma invoice may be provided if the commercial invoice cannot be produced.

AN ILLUSTRATION: US IMPORT REGULATIONS AND PROCEDURES (cont'd.)

Packing list Customs may use this detailed listing of all package contents to verify the cargo.

Special documents Customs will usually verify that the exporter has obtained all necessary certificates or origin; health, sanitary, and quality certificates; and other documents required for transporting and selling the goods in the US.

Proof of surety Customs will verify that the importer has posted a satisfactory bond for payment of any additional assessments after release of the goods.

- **Present goods for inspection.** A shipment may be inspected before importation is permitted, or the US Customs officer may waive examination.

- **Pay duties.** If duties are assessed on the goods imported from Mexico, the estimated duties must be paid within 10 working days after US Customs releases the merchandise for import. Payment should be forwarded to the customhouse designated in the import documentation.

- **File entry summary documentation.** After the goods are released for import into the US, the importer must comply with further documentation requirements. These documents must be filed at the customhouse designated in the documents within 10 working days of the release of the merchandise. The entry summary documentation consists of:

Entry package After merchandise is released, the entry package is returned to the importer (or agent), and a copy of it must be submitted to US Customs.

Entry summary This form (US Customs Form 7501) contains detailed information on the exporter, importer, and the goods imported.

Other invoices and documents Customs may request other documents to complete assessment of duties, collect statistics, or determine that all import requirements have been met.

Special import procedures have been developed for expediting the process with respect to certain items: imports valued at less than US$1,250, agricultural products, trade fair items, and merchandise imported from Mexico. Customs will expeditiously release these articles on arrival at the port of entry, and they can then be immediately delivered to the US importer. The immediate delivery procedure requires advance application for a special permit (US Customs Form 3461), which must be approved before the merchandise arrives at the port of entry.

There are also special procedures for importing by US mail or parcel post. Mail entry is permissible for merchandise that is not under quota or other restrictions and that is less than US$1,250 in value. The forms and requirements for shipping by mail can be obtained from the US Postal Service.

Mexican insurance company, not a foreign company. Once the risk of damage or loss passes from the Mexican domicilliary, the prohibition on foreign insurance no longer applies, and the foreign importer may insure the goods with a foreign company from the time the importer assumes the risk. However, transferring coverage in mid-shipment can introduce additional problems; shippers may wish to retain the same insurer throughout the process to avoid potential problems concerning assessing responsibility for a claim where there are multiple insurers.

NOM Certification For products that must meet sanitary or safety standards before being exported, the exporter must apply to SECOFI for NOM certification. Only a few products—those subject to standards pursuant to a convention or other agreement with the importing country—require NOM certification. Information on quality standards for exports can be obtained from the *Dirección General de*

Normas. See Useful Addresses at the end of this chapter for contact information.

Unless otherwise requested, NOM certification is issued for each model or prototype of a product, without time or quantity limits. Thus, NOM certification need be sought only once for exportation of a particular model. The applicant should avoid requesting NOM certification for only a particular shipment or lot, because SECOFI will instead issue a limited certificate, requiring the exporter to apply for a new NOM certification for the same product in each future shipment or lot. To facilitate customs clearance, the exporter should present the original of the NOM certificate to the Mexican Customs official.

To be NOM certified, a product will probably have to be tested in a Mexican laboratory accredited by *Sistema Nacional de Calibración* (SNC) or *Sistema Nacional de Acreditamiento de Laboratorios De Prueba* (SINALP) of SECOFI. The procedure involves sending an application for testing to an accredited Mexican testing lab, together with a few samples of the product. Tests are performed on products in the order received. The cost for testing differs among labs, since each is permitted to set its own prices.

More than 100 accredited labs are available for testing various products. However, accredited testing labs are still nonexistant (or barely existant) in Mexico for many categories of product. To relieve backlogs, SECOFI has implemented a crash accreditation program for labs that would handle some products.

Documentation at Packing

Clearance through customs will be more efficient if the exporter makes certain that all the necessary documents are completed and properly attached during the packaging stage. The following documents are required regardless of the mode of transport chosen for exporting the goods from Mexico.

Commercial Invoice All commercial shipments require a commercial invoice. The exporter should insert one signed original into the package and should provide further signed copies as advised by the *agente aduanal* or the importer. A signed copy should be sent directly to the importer, as well.

No special format is required for a commercial invoice. It must be in Spanish, and it may be accompanied by a translation into any other language appropriate to the destination of the goods—particularly if regulations of the importing country require such a translation. For purposes of clearing Mexican Customs, there are fewer requirements for the contents of commercial invoices for exports than for such invoices for imports. (Refer to the "Import Policies & Procedures" chapter for a description of invoice contents.) However, the importing country may have additional requirements, and the *agente aduanal* should be consulted in preparing the invoice. Mexican Customs will require the exporter's commercial invoice to state the following:

- The name and address of the exporter and importer, who must be unrelated persons or entities, except in the case of *maquila* companies;
- The name and address of the consignee who will receive the goods for the foreign importer;
- A description of each product, including the quantity sold and the value of the goods in the currency in which they were sold;
- The product weight; and
- The dimensions of the package.

An exporter should seek the advice of an *agente aduanal* in filling out the commercial invoice because the specifics of the requirements often change. The *agente aduanal* should be able to instruct on which product weight—gross, legal, net—should be declared in the invoice.

Failure to comply with the mandatory invoice content requirements will cause delays in shipping. If the information might be ascertained by inspecting the product, a customs officer may open the cases or packages. Otherwise, the invoice will be returned to the shipper for conformance. In rare instances, Mexican Customs will allow the *agente aduanal* to fill in missing information, such as an incomplete address for a *maquila* shipment.

Packing List The exporter should ask the *agente aduanal* and the importer whether a packing list should be enclosed with the shipment. Usually, a packing list specifies the weight of each item shipped, the total weight of the shipment, the total number of packages shipped, the type of packages shipped, and the description of each product, if not included on the commercial invoice.

Certificates of Origin If a claim for GSP or NAFTA preferences will be made with respect to the goods, the exporter should complete a certificate of origin showing the country of origin. (Refer to NAFTA Certificates of Origin in the "Import Policy & Procedures" chapter.) A certificate of origin is a document that proves, separately from other documentation, the origin of the goods. It consists of the foreign supplier's statement of where the goods originated.

Documentation at Shipping

The documentary requirements for shipping goods from Mexico vary depending on the mode of transport: land (truck or rail), sea, air, or mail. In addition to the bill of lading documents described below, a shipper may request to see insurance, health, and other certificates. The foreign importer or the bank handling payment for the goods may have additional documentary requirements that must be met before the shipper will accept the load. The shipping documentation for exports is similar to the documents for shipping goods into Mexico.

Air Freight Cargo transported by airlines must be accompanied by an air waybill. The foreign importer and airline will furnish information about their specific requirements for the contents of this bill and the number of copies to be enclosed. The commercial invoice should indicate the number of the air waybill. Special rules are applicable to the transport of dangerous and restricted goods. Most freight airlines will supply information on these rules, which may include national and international regulations, the International Air Transport Association (IATA) rules, and the International Civil Aviation Organization (ICAO) rules.

Shipments by Sea For shipments by sea, the exporter must furnish a bill of lading, which should indicate the marks, serial numbers, quantity and kinds

WHERE US IMPORTERS CAN GET ADVICE

Agencies and Organizations

American Chamber of Commerce of Mexico
Lucerna 78-7
Col. Juárez, Deleg. Cuauhtémoc
06600 México, DF, México
Tel: [52] (5) 705-0995, 724-3800, 703-3908
Fax: [52] (5) 703-2911 Tlx: 1777609
US mailing address: PO Box 60326, Apdo. 113,
Houston, TX 77205-1794
(Publishes the Mexican Exporter's Manual)

Export-Import Bank
811 Vermont Ave., NW
Washington, DC 20571
Tel: (202) 566-8860
(Small business assistance hotline)

Small Business Administration
Office of International Trade
409 Third Street SW, 6th floor
Washington, DC 20416
Tel: (202) 205-6605

US Customs Service
1301 Constitution Ave. NW
Washington, DC 20229
Tel: (202) 927-1000

Publications and databases

Custom House Guide
North American Publishing Company
401 Broad Street
Philadelphia, PA 19108
Tel: (215) 238-5357

Customs Law and Administration
American Association of Exporters and Importers
11 West 42nd Street
New York, NY 10036
Tel: (212) 944-2230

Customs Regulations of the United States
Superintendent of Documents
US Government Printing Office
Washington, DC 20402
Tel: (202) 275-3054

Doing Business in Mexico
Transnational Juris Publications
1 Bridge Street
Irvington, NY 10533
Tel: (800) 914-8186 (orders) Fax: (941) 591-2688

Flash Facts
US Department of Commerce
Washington, DC 20230
Tel: (202) 482-4464
(Fax service with documents on duties, taxes, customs procedures, and other trade information)

Importers Manual USA
World Trade Press
1505 Fifth Avenue
San Rafael, CA 94901
Tel: (415) 454-9934 Fax: (415) 453-7980

National Council on International Trade Documentation (NCITD)
350 Broadway, Suite 1200
New York, NY 10013
Tel: (212) 925-1400
(Provides low-cost publications on specific documentation commonly used in international trade)

National Trade Data Bank (NTDB)
US Department of Commerce
Office of Business Analysis
Room 4885 HCHB
Washington, DC 20230
Tel: (202) 482-1986
(CD-ROM database with wide range of information)

US Customs Tariffs and Trade
Bureau of National Affairs
1231 25th Street, NW
Washington, DC 20037
Tel: (202) 452-4200

World Trade Centers Association
One World Trade Center, Suite 7701
New York, NY 10048
Tel: (212) 313-4600
(Bulletin board database for trade leads; local networking programs)

---

of packages, and the gross weight in metric units.

Overland Transport An exporter may send goods overland (truck or rail) to Central America or the US by either of two methods: a local bill of lading or a through bill of lading. Through bills have been used relatively infrequently, but are becoming more prevalent.

A local bill of lading allows shipment to the Mexican border, where the goods must be reshipped to the foreign importer, usually through a customs broker at the point of entry. The original local bill of lading must be sent directly or through a bank to

the freight forwarder at the border. That agent will then take possession of the goods and will arrange reshipment and customs formalities for the goods to be transported to the foreign destination. A local bill of lading has a distinct advantage—it places the goods in the hands of an agent or freight forwarder who is knowledgeable in tariff and customs requirements and who can, if necessary, revise, repack, or otherwise change the shipment to secure the most favorable customs treatment.

A through bill of lading allows the seller to deliver the goods to a carrier in Mexico, and it allows the goods to be transferred to one or more additional carriers using the same bill of lading until reaching their destination. The original through bill of lading is sent—generally by means of a bank—to the importer, who will need the bill to take possession of the goods on arrival.

There are several advantages to using a through bill. Freight charges to the point of destination can be fixed in advance and billed to the foreign importer. Cargo handling expenses at the border can be less because the shipment simply continues in transit. Delays for repacking, rebilling, reshipping arrangements, and other manipulations at the border can be kept to a minimum, and the goods can be kept moving after clearing customs.

Clearing Mexican Customs

A smooth passage through Mexican Customs often depends on the reputation of the *agente aduanal* selected. For this reason, the selection of such a broker should be made with care, based on recommendations from other exporters, the facilities offered at the ports where the goods will be exported, and financial references.

The exporter should provide a separate letter of instruction to the *agente aduanal* to cover each individual shipment. Sometimes this letter will include instructions from the foreign importer as well. The letter should include such details as the name of the freight forwarder in the importing country, the port of exit, and the transport companies involved.

Documentation Mexican Customs will request the exporter to provide some of the documents discussed earlier and some additional ones, as follows:

- Commercial invoice in Spanish—customs will use the invoice to verify the goods shipped and determine whether any export tariffs are owed.
- *Pedimento de exportación*—an export declaration by the Mexican exporter, although it may be completed by the *agente aduanal* either at the border or on computer for electronic transmission to Mexican Customs. This *pedimento* states: the names of the buyer and seller; the tax registration number of the *agente aduanal*; the Harmonized System (HS) tariff code for the goods; details about the value of the goods; the number of goods shipped; the mode of transport; the conditions of sale; and the applicable tariffs. The tax registration number declared on the *pedimento de exportación* will be checked against state records for delinquencies in tax payments. The clearance of goods through customs will be delayed if a tax delinquency is found, so choose an *agente aduanal* who pays on time.
- Bill of lading or other shipping documenta-

tion—customs may also use this documentation when inspecting the goods and verifying the goods shipped.
- *Compromiso de Venta de Divisas* (CVD)—this form is submitted to a Mexican bank. It constitutes a commitment by the exporter to exchange at that bank the foreign currency earned in the sale. The exchange is guaranteed at a controlled rate within 90 days of the export.
- Export license, if required.
- Certificate of origin, if required to qualify for GSP or NAFTA preferential tariff treatment—For shipments to the US, the exporter can issue this certificate. For exports to other countries, SECOFI must issue it.
- Packing list, if requested.

To speed the customs process, most documents can be submitted in advance. In addition, not all shipments are inspected. The merchandise is presented before a stoplight—*semáforo fiscal*—that randomly indicates whether an inspection will be required. A shipment that gets a green light—about one out of 10—may leave the country without further delay. A shipment stopped by a red light is be subject to the examination of customs officials. At least two officers must be present during the inspection, which should be accomplished within three hours, barring the discovery of discrepancies.

USEFUL ADDRESSES

Dirección General de Normas (DGN)
(Directorate General of Standards)
Puente de Tecamachalco No. 6
Col. Lomas de Tecamachalco, Sec. Fuentes
53950 Naucalpan, Edo. de Méx., México
Tel: [52] (5) 520-8493/4 Fax: [52] (5) 540-5153

Dirección General de Servicios del Comercio
Exterior, SECOFI
(Directorate General of Foreign Trade Services)
Col. Héroes de Padierna
00700 México, DF, México
Tel: [52] (5) 683-5066, 683-4344
Fax: [52] (5) 595-5881/3

Secretaría de Comercio y Fomento Industrial
(SECOFI)
(Secretariat of Commerce and Industrial
Development)
Calle Alfonso Reyes No. 30
Col. Condesa
06140 México, DF, México
Tel: [52] (5) 211-0036, 286-1757, 286-1823, 286-1461
Fax: [52] (5) 224-3000, 286-0804, 286-1551, 286-1543

Subsecretaría de Ingresos, Hacienda
Av. Hidalgo 77, Módulo 1, P.B.
Col. Guerrero, Deleg. Cuauhtémoc
06300 México, DF, México

Industry Reviews

This chapter describes the status of and trends in major Mexican industries. It also lists key contacts for finding sources of supply, developing sales leads, and conducting economic research. We have grouped industries into the 13 categories discussed in the chapter. Some smaller sectors of commerce are not detailed here, while others may overlap into more than one area. If your business even remotely fits into a category, don't hesitate to contact several of the organizations listed; they should be able to assist you further in gathering the information you need. We have included industry-specific contacts only. General trade organizations, which may also be very helpful (particularly if your business is in an industry not directly covered), are listed in the "Important Addresses" chapter at the end of this book.

Each section has two segments: an industry summary and a list of useful contacts. The summary gives an overview of the range of products available in a certain industry and that industry's ability to compete in worldwide markets. The contacts include government departments, trade associations, publications, and trade fairs that can provide information specific to the industry. Addresses and telephone and fax numbers for each are listed in the "Important Addresses" chapter, in the sections indicated. An entire volume could likely be devoted to each area, but such in-depth coverage is beyond the scope of this book; our intent is to give you a basis for your own research.

We highly recommend that you peruse the "Trade Fairs" and "Important Addresses" chapters, where you will find additional resources including a variety of trade promotion organizations, chambers of commerce, business services, and media.

AGRICULTURAL PRODUCTS, PROCESSED FOODS, AND BEVERAGES

Mexico's agriculture and food processing industries are among the nation's top 10 producers and exporters. Agricultural products account for about 7.5 percent of Mexico's Gross Domestic Product (GDP), while the category of processed foods and beverages represent 7.6 percent of total manufacturing exports.

Mexican exports of agricultural, livestock, food, and beverage products have posted steady growth over the past decade, increasing by nearly 50 percent since 1985. Much of this increase is due to exports of fresh produce—Mexico is now one of the world's largest exporters of these products. Principal exports include tomatoes, fresh fruits, coffee, onions, pickles, rubber and rubber products, fresh flowers, and wood and wood products. The US absorbs nearly 90 percent of Mexico's agricultural exports.

Farm and Ranch Products

About 13 percent of Mexico's land is considered suitable for farming, of which only 3 percent are irrigated. From 40 to 50 percent of Mexico's land can potentially be used for ranching. About 40 percent of total agricultural output is grown in central Mexico, primarily in the states of Jalisco, Zacatecas, Puebla, Oaxaca, and Michoacán, and at least an additional 35 percent is grown in the northern states of Sinaloa, Chihuahua, Durango, Sonora, and Tamaulipas. Production in the southwest and peninsula zones—including the states of Veracruz, Guanajuato, and Chiapas—tends to be at a subsistence rather than a commercial level. These areas depend on rainfall rather than irrigation, and most farmers work small parcels.

Products Mexico's principal agricultural export is tomatoes; it is the second largest tomato exporter in the world. Tomatoes account for more than 30 percent of vegetable production and as much as 50 percent of total vegetable exports. At least 30 percent of domestically grown tomatoes are shipped to the US, supplying 80 percent of US tomato imports. Other important vegetable exports are onions, pumpkins, chickpeas, and eggplants. Mexican farmers additionally produce cauliflower, broccoli, cabbage, carrots, peas, corn, beans, and green peppers for domestic and export markets.

Mexico is a large producer of nearly every type of fruit. Grapes, guavas, pineapples, bananas, tangerines, lemons, limes, oranges, apples, mangoes, apricots, strawberries, coconuts, cantaloupes, watermelons, avocados, papayas, pears, peaches, and plums are supplied to domestic markets and exported fresh, primarily to the US.

Coffee is another leading export, and Mexico is one of the largest suppliers of unroasted coffee to the US. Mexico is the world's fourth largest producer of honey, and the second largest honey exporter, with most exports going to Germany and other European countries. Other major Mexican crops include tobacco, sorghum, wheat, soybeans, oats, safflower, rice, and sugarcane; substantial amounts of cotton are supplied to textile manufacturers in both export and domestic markets. Mexican farmers also produce substantial amounts of such commercial crops as sesame, barley, alfalfa, henequen, garlic, sunflower seeds, walnuts, peanuts, cocoa, chilis, potatoes, and turnips.

Cattle are among Mexico's top five agricultural exports. Millions of head of cattle are raised annually, primarily in the northern states of Chihuahua, Sonora, and Coahuila. The ranching industry also raises pigs, sheep, chicken, and horses for domestic and export markets.

Competitive Situation Mexico's land tenure system and water shortages have contributed to stagnation and decline in agricultural productivity since the early 1980s, and particularly since 1987. Investment and expansion in this sector have been lower than the rate of population growth. Most agricultural production remains labor intensive, with minimal levels of mechanization. In some areas, production is at subsistence levels and yields no income.

Since the 1910 revolution, Mexico's agricultural industry has operated under an outdated system of limited land rights. About half of all cultivated land is owned through *ejidos* (communally owned holdings to which individual members of the community are allowed access for cultivation), and much of the remainder consists of private land holdings averaging around 12.5 hectares (about 31 acres); median plots are much smaller. This system was originally designed to break up large landed estates (*latifundias*) and redistribute land to small farmers. However, most farmers were not allowed to acquire direct legal title to the land they cultivated, and an overwhelming majority of farms are too small to support the costs of or to profit from modernization of machinery and farming techniques.

Lack of water is another major obstacle to agriculture in Mexico. Nearly two-thirds of the land is arid or semi-arid, limiting expansion of cultivated lands and causing production to rise and fall with weather patterns. In some areas, farmers can drill wells—often at least 125 meters (more than 400 feet) deep—to find water, but they must be able to afford not only the cost of drilling, but also the cost of pumping and irrigating. Most farms depend on annual rainfall because irrigation is available only in a few areas. Precipitation is unevenly distributed geographically and seasonally. Barely one-fourth of Mexico's total land area normally receives rain sufficient for spring and summer crops, and less than 5 percent for winter crops. Moreover, Mexico has no continental rivers or mountains with snow-packs to augment reservoir levels and provide water for irrigation.

In the past decade, Mexican agriculture has been in transition. Since 1990 it has shown a strong economic recovery, with production growing each year and surpluses occurring regularly in the country's agricultural trade balance. This recovery is attributed in part to good weather, but primarily to government initiatives that are intended to develop Mexican industries generally and agriculture in particular. In a major undertaking aimed largely at reforming farming practices in rural Mexico, the government is instituting land tenure reforms that allow for both private ownership of *ejido* lands and corporate investment and joint ventures in the *ejidos*. Unfortunately, these land reforms are slow to take hold, for a number of reasons. First, the process of issuing titles to rural and isolated areas is an imposing and continuing task. Second, approximately 20 percent of the communal lands are agriculturally marginal in the first place, making them unattractive to investors. Third, investment is constrained by a lack of available credit, which in turn is hindered by inadequate financial resources and lack of development of a real property market throughout rural Mexico. Fourth, new land courts have been created, and many investors are waiting to see how they will rule in some early cases involving problems with the land reforms before they invest heavily in such communal lands. Nevertheless, a few Mexican companies have taken advantage of the reforms by investing in communal lands and arranging exclusive contracts with those farmers to receive their output of particular products.

For a number of years, the government has been encouraging farmers through financial programs to substitute income-producing crops for staples that are heavily subsidized and uncompetitive. In an effort to speed up rural land reform programs, the Mexican government has amended its subsidy program. Additional funds have been allocated to the agriculture sector, and a program has been set up to provide direct federal aid to food producers based on size of the area cultivated rather than the specific crop—with the intent of discouraging the production of certain over-subsidized and over-produced crops and encouraging the substitution of other crops that are more competitive in international markets.

The primary obstacle for rural farmers is inability to obtain financing for machinery needed to modernize production. In past years, government subsidies were available for the purchase of new machinery, including resale of state-purchased machinery at below-market prices or below-market interest rates. However, these subsidies have been eliminated in favor of direct financing programs. To this end, the government is working with the agricultural development bank to restructure the latter's loan portfolio, and the agricultural insurance system is also being revamped. These changes are expected to improve the availability of credit to rural farmers. In addition, import duties have been removed on agricultural machinery, making this equipment more accessible and affordable.

Aquatic Products

Local coastal fishing still supplies the majority of Mexico's domestic market for fresh and processed fish. However, several states now support significant aquacultural industries, and 95 percent of the farmed fish are supplied fresh to domestic markets. Some fresh fish is exported, but most exports are processed.

With few exploitable freshwater resources in Mexico, the fishing industry is seafood-oriented. The Mexican states notable for their fishing therefore lie on the coasts: Baja California Norte, Baja California Sur, Campeche, Colima, Guerrero, Jalisco, Quintana Roo, Sinaloa, Sonora, Tabasco, Tamaulipas, Veracruz, and Yucatán. In the past decade, aquafarms for freshwater fish have been promoted in several states, particularly Chihuahua.

Products Significant products include shrimp and turtles. Mexico is one of the world's top 10 shrimp farming nations, and it ranks fifth in production of mollusks, primarily Gulf oysters. Other shellfish include lobster, crab, crayfish, and clams. The boats bring in large quantities of sardines, anchovies, tuna, shark, sea bass, sole, and bonito, and a few octopus. Mexico now ranks among the top five world producers of carp, tilapia, and channel catfish. Aquafarms in Chihuahua also raise significant numbers of rainbow trout.

Competitive Situation Coastal fishing has largely been either a sporting-tourist or a subsistence level activity in Mexico. Over the past decade fishing has begun developing into a commercial industry, with several fleets now operating out of Gulf and Pacific Coast ports. The infrastructure of many of these ports is still being developed.

As a relatively new sector, Mexico's aquacultural industry is still expanding its production capacities. The industry has tended to concentrate on a limited number of fish species, and it has not been fully integrated with such areas as processing, packing, storage, transportation, and distribution. The industry's efforts at R&D have been occasional and minimal, hampering the technological development of fish farms.

The government allows several incentives to investors in aquafarms, including long-term licenses, no fee on water usage, and tax benefits. In addition, Mexican authorities are promoting several programs to assist the aquatic farming industry in mastering technology for raising specific commercially valuable species, diversifying production into species that are less affected by changing market demands, establishing a modernized infrastructure, and integrating processing and distribution systems. Under NAFTA, tariffs on many species of live, fresh, and processed fish—including trout, carp, black bass, lobster, and shrimp—are being phased out, creating a frenzy in Mexico's aquatic food trade with the US and Canada.

Flowers

Commercial flower production is a relatively new industry in Mexico, but it has burst into full bloom in the past decade with an increase of nearly 80 percent in areas cultivated for flower crops. Mexico has the world's second highest yield in millions of stems per hectare. Exports of roses, carnations, and chrysanthemums are shipped primarily to the US. Mexico holds at least 3 percent of the US imported flower market.

Mexican flower growers do most of their export trade during winter months, when production is more costly in the major flower importing countries. Further development of this sector is promising, especially in view of Mexico's excellent climate for these crops and increasing world demand for fresh flowers.

Growers are currently undertaking 40 new flower production projects, which will place an additional 720 hectares into use for flower growing as of 1994.

Food and Beverage Processors

Mexico's food and beverage processing industry includes approximately 1,100 companies. These processors are concentrated in the northwestern states of Sinaloa and Sonora and the central states of Guanajuato, Querétaro, and Michoacán, which are also the major agricultural states. Other states that produce significant amounts of processed food include Colima (fruit and fish); Guerrero (coffee); Hidalgo (grains and fruit); México (vegetables, grains and fruit); Morelos (tomatoes, rice, and sugar); Nuevo León (beer); Oaxaca (canned food and sugar); San Luis Potosí (grains, sugar, and coffee); Tamaulipas (seafood canning); and Yucatán (citrus, vegetable, poultry, and seafood).

Products Mexico's principal processed food exports are fruits, vegetables, and frozen shrimp. Most items are available in canned, dried, or frozen form. Various fruit extracts are also made. Food processors supply substantial amounts of grain products, including flour, cereals, breads, and cookies. Other products include pickles, cigarettes, cigars, spices, sauces, and chocolate.

The major processed beverage export is beer. Small and large Mexican companies offer potable, mineral, and flavored waters, mainly supplying domestic markets. Several large franchise and foreign-invested operations in Mexico produce significant quantities of soft drinks for domestic and export markets. Other significant beverage products that are sold domestically and overseas are fruit juices, tequila, mescal, coffee liqueur, and margarita mixes.

Rubber and Rubber Products

Rubber production, processing, and fabrication has long been one of Mexico's top 10 industries. At least 35 rubber manufacturing plants operate in Mexico, many in the state of Tabasco, the primary source of rubber. Most plants are foreign-invested.

Products Mexico's rubber industry is a major producer and exporter of tires and rubber household products and is a prime supplier to its automotive parts factories.

Wood and Paper Products

Substantial natural resources are available to Mexican manufacturers of wood and paper products. Forests occupy more than 45 million hectares, but only about 20 million are considered suitable for commercial use, and only about 7 million are now being exploited. Mixed coniferous and broadleaf forests cover the mountain ranges that run north and south through the center of the country, and tropical rainforests are found over much of the southern and peninsula regions.

Primary timber producing states are Chiapas, Chihuahua, Michoacán, Morelos, and Oaxaca, plus Quintana Roo for tropical woods. Wood processing plants are largely centered in Chihuahua and Durango. Paper, pulp, and cellulose are among the primary products of Durango, Jalisco, Nuevo León, Puebla, and Veracruz. Oaxaca is well known for its semi-precious wood carvings and products.

Products Significant wood exports include plywood, doors, and furniture. The lumber industry provides large amounts of fir, pine, white cedar, and oak to domestic manufacturers and the construction industry. Some tropical woods are harvested, although in relatively low volume compared to industrial needs. Paper processing plants export cardboard, packaging paper, crepe paper, and sterilized, heliographic, and impregnated papers.

Competitive Situation Mexico's forestry production has tapped very few of its resources, leaving enormous potential for growth. Much of the industry lacks modern technology, and forestry management techniques have yet to be used countrywide. Many lumber companies continue to rely on unmanaged natural timber stands, rather than on reseeded and improved resources, resulting in extremely low yields from harvested areas. In the paper and pulp industry, a number of plants have increased their use of secondary and recycled fibers while reducing reliance on virgin fibers.

Recent legal reforms have created incentives for investment in forestry by providing for land tenure security and eliminating bureaucratic administrative requirements. Commercial plantations of trees are being promoted in several states, including Tabasco, Veracruz, and Campeche. To increase productivity while maintaining sound environmental protections, government measures have been implemented to improve technology and introduce advanced forestry management techniques.

Government Agencies & Entities

Refer to listings under Mexican Government Agencies and Entities in the "Important Addresses" chapter for complete contact information.

Comisión Nacional del Agua (National Water Commission)
Comisión Nacional del Cacao (National Cocoa Commission)
Instituto Mexicano del Café (Mexican Coffee Institute)
Secretaría de Agricultura y Recursos Hidráulicos (Secretariat of Agriculture and Water Resources)
Secretaría de la Reforma Agraria (Secretariat of Agrarian Reform)
Secretaría de Pesca (Secretariat of Fisheries)

Trade Associations

Refer to listings under Industry-Specific Trade and Professional Associations in the "Important Addresses" chapter for complete contact information.

Bakery Industry National Chamber (Cámara Nacional de la Industria Panificadora)

Beer Manufacturing National Chamber (Asociación de Fabricantes de la Cerveza)

Beverage and Carbonated Water Producers National Association (Asociación Nacional de Productores de Refrescos y Aguas Carbonadas)

Bottled Water Producers National Chamber (Asociación Nacional de Productores de Aguas Envasados)

Canned Goods Industry National Chamber (Cámara Nacional de la Industria de Conservas Alimenticias)

Cardboard Box and Packaging Manufacturers National Association (Asociación Nacional de Fabricantes de Cajas y Empaques de Cartón)

Chocolate and Candy Manufacturers National Association (Asociación Nacional de Fabricantes de Chocolate, Dulces y Similares)

Coconut Product Manufacturers National Confederation (Confederación Nacional de Productores de Coco y Sus Derivados)

Coffee Exporters Association (Asociación Mexicana de Exportadores de Café)

Coffee Industry National Chamber (Asociación Nacional de la Industria del Café)

Corn Industry National Chamber (Cámara Nacional de Maíz Industrializado)

Cotton Growers Associations Confederation (Confederación de Asociaciones Algodoneras)

Fishing Industry National Chamber (Cámara Nacional de la Industria de la Pesca)

Floriculturist and Nursery National Confederation (Confederación Nacional de Floricultores y Viveristas)

Food and Restaurant Industry National Chamber (Cámara Nacional de la Industria de Restaurantes y Alimentos Condimentados)

Food Processors Industry of Jalisco Chamber (Cámara de la Industria Alimenticia de Jalisco)

Forest Industry National Chamber (Cámara Nacional de la Industria Forestal)

Forest Products and Derivatives Industries National Chamber (Cámara Nacional de las Industrias de la Silvicultura)

Grape Growers and Wine Producers National Association (Asociación Nacional de Vitivinicultores)

Lumber Industry National Chamber (Cámara Nacional de la Industria Maderera y Similares)

Lumber Manufacturers National Association (Asociación Nacional de Fabricantes de Tableros de Madera)

Milk Products Industry National Chamber (Cámara Nacional de Industriales de la Leche)

Oils and Foodstuffs Industries National Association (Asociación Nacional de Industriales de Aceites y Comestibles)

Packing Association (Asociación Mexicana de Envase y Embalaje)

Paper and Cellulose Industries National Chamber (Cámara Nacional de las Industrias de la Celulosa y el Papel)

Paper Bag Manufacturers National Association (Asociación Nacional de Fabricantes de Sacos de Papel)

Rubber Industry National Chamber (Cámara Nacional de la Industria Hulera)

Salt Producers Association (Asociación Mexicana de Productores de Sal)

Sugar and Alcohol Industry National Chamber (Cámara Nacional de la Industria Azucarera y Alcoholera)

Swiss Registered Cattle Breeders Association (Asociación Mexicana de Criadores de Ganado Suizo)

Tequila Industry Regional Chamber (Cámara Regional de la Industria Tequilera)

Tuna Producers National Association (Asociación Nacional de Productores de Atún)

Directories & Periodicals

Refer to listings under Directories, Annuals and Surveys; and Industry-Specific Periodicals in the "Important Addresses" chapter for contact information.

Agricultura Técnica en México (Agricultural technology)

Agro-Cultura (Agriculture)

Agro-Síntesis: Agricultura-Ganadería-Avicultura (Agriculture, livestock and poultry)

Agromundo

Agronegocios en México (Cattle, finance, forestry, poultry and industry)

ATCP Revista (Pulp and paper trade industry)

Confección (Confectionary industry)

Dulcelandia: Industrias Alimenticias (Baking and confection indutries)

El Campo: Revista Mensual Agrícola y Ganadera (Agriculture and livestock)

Gaceta Agrícola (Agriculture)

Ganadero/Rancher (Livestock)

Guía de la Industria Alimentaria (Food industry)

Guía de la Industria: Hule, Plásticos y Resinas (Plastics, rubber, and resins)

Guía Del Envase y Embalaje (Packaging industry)

Hule Mexicano y Plásticos: Revista Técnica Industrial (Rubber and plastics)

Hulequipo (Rubber)

Industria Alimentaria (Food industry)

Informador: Noticias y Comentarios de la Industria Mueblera y Maderera (Lumber and furniture)

International Green Book Directory (Cottonseed, soybean, linseed, and peanuts processors)

Mexico Holstein (Dairy industry)

Pan Directorio De Proveedores (Bread suppliers)

Pastizales (Range management, cattle production)

Prontuario Agroquímico (Agricultural chemicals)

Tecnología de Alimentos (Food industry)

Trade Fairs

Refer to the "Trade Fairs" chapter for complete listings, including contact information, dates, and venues. Trade fairs with particular relevance to this industry include the following, which are listed in that chapter under the headings given below:

Agriculture & Fishing
- AFIA Mexico
- Agroindustrial
- Expo Lacteos
- PESCA

Construction & Housing
- Constructo
- Construexpo
- Cuarta Muestra de la Industria de la Construcción
- Expo CIHAC
- T.M.I.: Techno Mueble Internacional

Food, Restaurants & Hotels
- Alimentos y Bebidas
- Confitexpo
- Expo Conacca
- Expo Natura
- Expo Pan
- Expoalimentos
- Hostal
- Mexi-Pan
- Mexico Restaurant, Food Service and Hospitality Expo
- Rest-O-Mex Restaurant, Food Service and Hospitality Expo
- Restaurant, Hotels And Food Show

Packing
- Mex Pack

Paper & Stationery
- Converflex
- Expo Papel Latino Americana
- Fipamex

Plastics and Rubber
- Expo Hulera Internacional

ELECTRICAL, ELECTRONIC, TELECOMMUNICATIONS, AND COMPUTER PRODUCTS

Mexico's electrical and electronics industries—including manufacture of computer and telecommunication products—consist of *maquila* and non-*maquila* operations. The *maquilas* dominate exports, while the non-*maquila* companies produce goods for domestic consumption. Only 5 percent of the companies are classified as large, while 10 percent are medium-sized; the remainder are small or extremely small. Most *maquilas* are centered in the northern Mexico border areas and in the states of Jalisco and Aguascalientes and in the Federal District (Mexico City).

Maquila-assembled electrical and electronic products account for a substantial share of Mexican exports. Approximately 530 *maquilas*—nearly 35 percent of the total number of these operations—are involved in manufacturing electrical and electronic products. Producers of computers account for 19 percent of these operations, components for 16 percent, and telecommunications equipment for 9 percent. More than 60 percent of *maquila* exports represent computer and electronic products. Due to its *maquilas*, Mexico is one of the largest suppliers of color televisions and computer keyboards to the US market.

Computers

Maquilas and other foreign-invested companies are the main manufacturers of computers in Mexico. This industry is still small, and production tends to concentrate on particular components.

Products Mexican companies currently produce printers, minicomputers, personal computers, mainframes, computer parts, diskettes, and network boards. Computer keyboards are major export items produced by *maquilas*.

Competitive Situation A government program to encourage the modernization of Mexico's computer industry was begun in 1990. Participating companies were required to meet certain standards with regard to annual sales, assets, and R&D investment. In return they received a discount on import duties. Ten Mexican firms took advantage of this program to begin manufacturing printers, personal computers, and minicomputers. With the ratification of NAFTA and the elimination of import duties on these products, this program ended.

The marketing and manufacturing of computer equipment in Mexico is expected to grow rapidly under NAFTA. Demand for computer products will increase the need for local servicing and custom software development. Stricter enforcement of intellectual and industrial property rights in Mexico is reassuring to many foreign firms that had been reluctant to enter Mexican markets, and NAFTA requirements related to these rights are expected to boost foreign investment in Mexico's computer industry.

Electrical and Electronic Components

An estimated 95 percent of the electronic components used in Mexico's domestic market are imported from Japan, Sweden, and the US, with components used in *maquila* production accounting for nearly 80 percent of these imports. A large number of components produced by *maquila* plants are used by other *maquiladoras* that manufacture such items as computers, telecommunication devices, consumer electronic products, office machines, and entertainment equipment. Value-added reexports of *maquila* companies have shown particularly high growth in recent years.

Products Electronic components made in Mexico include integrated circuits, semiconductors, diodes, thyristors, and transistors. Several companies supply electrical switch boxes, primarily to manufacturers and assemblers of products in Mexico.

Competitive Situation The end users of electronic components demand technical improvements, quality, and reliability. These end users—primarily the computer, telecommunications, consumer electronics, office machine, and entertainment industries—tend to grow and change rapidly on a continuing basis. Mexican electronic component manufacturers have traditionally been unsuccessful in meeting these requirements and in keeping pace with the intense competition from imports. Many non-*maquila* operations have closed down as a result of trade liberalization policies and an inability to keep up with technological advances.

Electronic component producers in Mexico are seeking to expand and integrate their operations. They are looking for ways to improve technology, with the intent of producing competitive high-tech products for applications in various industries, including aerospace, avionics, communications, computer, automobile, industrial design, and machinery tool and die operations. Of all the electrical and electronic industries, the components industry is expected to benefit the most from ratification of NAFTA, because it is the primary supplier to producers of computer, electronic consumer, and telecommunication products.

Electronic Consumer Products

With the exception of *maquila* production, only a few electronic consumer products are manufactured in Mexico. *Maquiladoras* export huge quantities of these products to the US.

Products Mexico's major export is color television sets. *Maquilas* in Chihuahua alone have the capacity to produce seven million units annually. A few Mexican firms assemble imported parts to produce relatively low-tech consumer items such as amplifiers and 12-inch black and white televisions sets for local markets.

Competitive Situation By opening its borders to imports and lowering duties on electronic products, Mexico has nearly crushed its domestic industry; local manufacture of electronic consumer products has all but ceased. Many producers of these products have become importers and distributors of foreign electronic consumer products. A few companies have reverted to assembling products from imported parts, but they have been hard-pressed to compete with more technologically advanced imports.

Office Machines

Mexico's production of office machines supplies about 30 percent of total domestic demand, and exports are limited. The primary exports are photocopiers, which are produced by foreign-owned companies and shipped to Central America and the US. Of the nine manufacturers of office equipment registered as operating in Mexico, six are foreign-invested.

Products Two companies are producing photocopiers in Mexico, and three currently make electronic typewriters. One company manufacturers cash registers, while another produces electronic calculators for Mexico's domestic market.

Competitive Situation This industry has faced difficult times because of a sluggish domestic market, coupled with a growing consumer preference for imported items and Mexico's new open-market policies. Domestic markets were opened to foreign trade in 1986, at which time half of the producers of adding machines and cash registers disappeared. Some former manufacturers switched to wholesaling and distributing.

Demand for office machines from Mexico's government remains a significant factor in this market, but it has decreased somewhat as the government reduces its workforce and streamlines its operations by liquidating, merging, and privatizing numerous state-controlled firms. Other end users of office machinery—mainly financial and banking institutions, financial leasing firms, insurance companies, and advertising enterprises—have been privatized and deregulated since 1990. These industries are now beginning to recover and are investing in expanding and modernizing their operations and equipment to create an increase in domestic demand. Retail outlets and home office workers account for a small but growing market, which is expected to rise as the government imposes stricter accountability on retail sales in an effort to limit tax evasion.

Telecommunications Equipment

Production of telecommunications equipment in Mexico is limited to the assembly of foreign components, and most of the 69 companies that operate in the country are subsidiaries of foreign businesses. Imports have risen sharply because of the increasing need for high-tech equipment, which is unavailable from local producers.

Products Telecommunication equipment made in Mexico includes central office switches, telephone switchboards, transmission equipment, cables, and radio systems and receivers.

Competitive Situation A telecommunications revolution is underway in Mexico. This country is rapidly acquiring the largest, most comprehensive, and modern telecommunications network in Latin America. The major provider of telecommunications services in Mexico, *Teléfonos de México*, or Telmex, is installing new telephone lines, rural telephones, fiber-optic networks, and integrated digital networks. It is also trying to improve long-distance service and upgrade overall quality.

Seven networks and 115 cable networks control Mexico's television market. Mexico's government plans to launch two new satellites to replace its existing satellite system. It has designated two of the four state-owned television networks for sale to private operators. The important national radio industry has more than 750 AM, 260 FM, and 29 shortwave broadcasting stations.

Several companies are providing cellular telephone service in 85 cities, and paging services are available in many locales. Over the past several years, market penetration of cellular telephones has increased, and Mexico now has more than 1 million cellular users. Mexico ranks third in Latin America in the number of cellular telephone users, exceeded only by Chile and Venezuela.

Mexican end users of telecommunications equipment have primarily turned to imports for the high-tech quality products they need. In this highly competitive field, a number of Mexican manufacturers of components used in telecommunications equipment have ceased operations because of inability to compete with foreign products.

Government Agencies & Entities

Refer to listings under Mexican Government Agencies and Entities in the "Important Addresses" chapter for complete contact information.

Dirección General de Telecomunicaciones
(Directorate General of Telecommunications)
Información Tecnologiá y Consultoría (Office of Information Technology)

Trade Associations

Refer to listings under Industry-Specific Trade and Professional Associations in the "Important Addresses" chapter for complete contact information.

Cable Television Industry National Chamber (Cámara Nacional de la Industria de Televisión por Cable)
Communications and Transportation National Chamber (Cámara Nacional de Transportes y Comunicaciones)
Electric Manufacturers National Chamber (Cámara Nacional de las Manufacturas Eléctricas)
Electronics and Communications Industry National Chamber (Cámara Nacional de la Industria Electronica y de Comunicaciones Eléctricas)
Household Electric Appliance Manufacturers National Association (Asociación Nacional de Fabricantes de Aparatos Electrodomésticos)

Directories & Periodicals

Refer to listings under Directories, Annuals and Surveys; and Industry-Specific Periodicals in the "Important Addresses" chapter for contact information.

Ciencia y Desarrollo (Science and technology)
Comunicaciones (Telecommunications)
Desarrollo Tecnológico (Electronics and computer sciences)
Informe Anual: Instituto de Investigaciones Eléctricas (Electric industry)
Información: Imagen Nacional e Internacional de Comunicaciones y Transportes (Communications and transportation)
Ingenieria Mecánica y Eléctrica (Mechanical and electrical engineering)
PC-TIPS: Ideas y Recomendaciones Para Optimizar el Uso de Su Computadora Personal (Personal computers)
Revista Mexicana de Comunicación (Communications)
Tecno Industria (Technology and industry)

Trade Fairs

Refer to the "Trade Fairs" chapter for complete listings, including contact information, dates, and venues. Trade fairs with particular relevance to this industry include the following, which are listed in that chapter under the headings given below:

Comprehensive
- Exposición y Conferencias Tecnos
- USATECH

Computers, Electronics & Communications
- Banking, Insurance and Tech
- C.E.S. Mexico
- Comdex/ComExpo Mexico
- Compuexpo
- Compumundo
- Electronica
- ExpoComm Mexico
- Expo Electronica
- Exposición y Conferencias Tecnos

- Identimex
- Latin American Imaging & Information Technology Exhibition & Conference
- MacWorld Expo
- MexCom
- Software
- TelNets

Construction & Housing
- Expo Ferrelectrica

Office Equipment
- Ofisistemas

Safety & Security
- Expo Seguridad
- Seguridad
- Seguritech

FURNITURE

Compared with other industry sectors, Mexico's furniture industry is relatively small and fragmented. It contributes less than 0.5 percent to Mexico's GDP. Household and office furniture is produced primarily for domestic markets, although exports are rising because Mexico's furniture makers have been forced to seek foreign markets as domestic demand has faltered. The principal furniture export markets are the US and Central America.

Official statistics indicate that there are no more than 2,400 furniture manufacturers in Mexico. This data is contradicted by trade experts, who estimate that between 6,000 and 8,000 firms, including family businesses, are currently in operation. Small (and very small) firms represent 95 percent of the total number of furniture makers, and fewer than 2 percent are considered large companies. Geographically, this industry is widely dispersed throughout the country. About 36 percent of the companies are concentrated in the Federal District and its surrounding metropolitan area. Other important centers are in the states of Jalisco, Chihuahua, Michoacán, Nuevo León, and San Luis Potosí.

Household Furniture and Lighting Fixtures

More than 70 percent of the furniture produced in Mexico is for household use. Manufacturers of household furniture and lighting fixtures supply more than 80 percent of Mexico's domestic market for these items. Infant furniture and baby carriages have become the leading exports of this industry. Only a small percentage of other Mexican-made household furniture and lighting fixtures are exported.

Products Agglomerate furniture accounts for 60 percent of the total household furniture produced, wood furniture represents 20 percent, and metal furniture about 20 percent. Most of this furniture is for living rooms and kitchens (55 percent). Dining room furniture accounts for an additional 30 percent of total production, and bedroom furniture makes up the remainder. Mattresses and lighting fixtures, including fluorescent and incandescent lamps, are also significant products.

Small shops offer hand-crafted furniture of cantara stone—stoneworkers in Chiapas are considered to be among the best—and raw marble, wrought iron, and *equipal* (leather with reed or wooden bases). Most outlets for *equipal* are centered in Guadalajara, Jalisco. Other small shops—particularly around San Miguel de Allende, Guanajuato—carve ornate wooden furniture and make antiqued wooden furniture from weathered or distressed wood, usually treated pine.

Office Furniture

Local production of office furniture still commands more than 80 percent of Mexico's domestic market, but its share has been slowly slipping as imports capture more of the market each year. Exports constitute only about 11 percent of total production. Approximately 190 firms manufacture office and institutional furniture in Mexico.

Products Domestic production consists primarily of wooden office furniture, including desks, cabinets, chairs, file drawers, and panels. The most common woods used are fir, pine, white cedar, and oak. Some metal furniture is also available. Mexican companies supply general office furniture, as well as special items for schools, hospitals, and hotels.

Competitive Situation

With the opening of Mexico's economy to foreign trade in the late 1980s, 65 percent of the local furniture makers (about 2,700 firms) closed down and 50 percent of the industry's production capacity was idled. Companies could not compete with many imported products because raw materials available in Mexico for furniture manufacture were not equal to materials offered by foreign countries in either quality or price. Some former manufacturers became distributors of imports. In recent years, demand in domestic markets has been somewhat slow because of Mexico's sluggish economy, and an influx of relatively inexpensive furniture from such countries as Taiwan and Korea has caused another 200 companies to cease operations since 1991.

To produce at full capacity, some Mexican furniture makers have begun to seek foreign markets. This strategy has been hindered by sluggish demand due to the worldwide recession, but international markets are beginning to improve as the economies of major importing countries stabilize. In an attempt to defend their markets against foreign competition, Mexican manufacturers have begun reinvesting profits into their operations. In particular, they are concentrating on raising quality standards, expanding product lines, and improving prices. A laboratory for measuring furniture quality has been established in Jalisco. In some production areas, the furniture industry has started to recover. Producers of infant furniture have found a niche in export markets, and competition in wooden kitchen furniture has become intense because a large number of small carpentry workshops with lower overhead have been able to produce quality kitchen furniture at lower prices than larger firms.

Despite these efforts, Mexico's furniture industry has made minimal inroads into export markets and continues to lose its share of domestic markets to fierce foreign competition. Automation levels remain low, production is on a relatively small scale, and qualified skilled labor is in short supply. Furniture manufacturers are small and widely dispersed, capital investment is minimal, and R&D in new designs and processes is essentially nonexistent. Small suppliers frequently have financial problems, quality varies from worker to worker, and delivery times are often delayed. To make matters worse, Mexican suppliers of raw materials—woods, adhesives, enamels, resins, wood laminates, textiles, metal fittings and hardware, and sandpaper—are often undependable with respect to quality of product and delivery schedules.

Growth in the furniture industry is expected to be spurred over the next few years due to substantial investments by the Mexican government in the infrastructure of the industry and in planned new construction that should give a boost to the building industry. Companies in this sector are also taking advantage of the open-market policies, and especially NAFTA, to procure higher-quality raw materials and accessories from more stable foreign sources. In an effort to expand into export markets and take advantage of improving domestic and worldwide economies, a number of Mexican companies are seeking investment arrangements with foreign firms.

Trade Associations

Refer to listings under Industry-Specific Trade and Professional Associations in the "Important Addresses" chapter for complete contact information.

Cámara Nacional de la Industria de la Transformación (National Chamber of the Manufacturing Industry, Furniture Coordinating Council)
Furniture Makers of Jalisco Association (Asociación de Fabricantes de Muebles de Jalisco)
Gift, Decoration, and Craft Manufactures Association of Mexico (Asociación Mexicana de Fabricantes de Artículos para Regalo, Decoración y Artesanías)
Lumber Industry National Chamber (Cámara Nacional de la Industria Maderera y Similares)
Lumber Manufacturers National Association (Asociación Nacional de Fabricantes de Tableros de Madera)
Plastic Industries National Association (Asociación Nacional de Industrias del Plástico)
Tannery Industry National Chamber (Cámara Nacional de la Industria de la Curtiduría)
Textile Industry National Chamber (Cámara Nacional de la Industria Textil)

Directories & Publications

Refer to listings under Directories, Annuals and Surveys; and Industry-Specific Periodicals in the "Important Addresses" chapter for contact information.

Cámara Nacional de la Industria de Transformación: Boletín Informativo (Manufacturing industry)
Informador: Noticias y Comentarios de la Industria Mueblera y Maderera (Lumber and furniture)
Intermueble (Furniture)
Mueble Equipo (Furniture manufacturing equipment)

Trade Fairs

Refer to the "Trade Fairs" chapter for complete listings, including contact information, dates, and venues. Trade fairs with particular relevance to this industry include the following, which are listed in that chapter under the headings given below:

Furniture & Housewares
- Expo Mueble
- Exposición Provi Mueble
- Ofisistemas
- T.M.I.: Techno Mueble Internacional

Gifts & Crafts
- AMFAR Expo Regalo
- Artesanias Mexicanas de Toda la República
- Expo Arte
- Expo Joven
- Exposición Nacional de Artesanias
- Manualidades: 1er Salon Nacional de las Artes Manuales
- Sede del Regalo y Salon de la Importación

GIFTS, HANDICRAFTS, AND JEWELRY

Mexican giftware, handicrafts, and jewelry are world famous. Artists and artisans in Mexico offer products made of pottery, silver, gold, copper, wood, yarn, straw, reeds, and lacquerware. Many objects considered to be folk art have evolved from items used in daily life or in festivals or other special occasions. Once made for domestic use, now these items are produced largely for sale to tourists and galleries as decorative items.

Products Mexican potters, mainly from the states of Puebla, Oaxaca, Chiapas, Jalisco, and Michoacán, offer both simple unglazed and glazed ware and brightly painted or glazed plates, cups, tiles, and decorative items. Distinctive among Mexican pottery is the tree of life (made primarily in Puebla), unglazed black pottery and green glazed ware from Oaxaca, and earthenware from Chiapas fired in the open.

The woodcarvers of Oaxaca are known for their ceremonial masks and intricate, often whimsical carvings, often of animals; fine guitars are produced in Michoacán; and artisans in Guerrero and Michoacán specialize in lacquerware boxes, trays, and other items. Unique to Mexico are the intricate yarn paintings of the Huichol Indians of Jalisco.

Silversmiths work in several areas of Mexico, but the most famous center is in Taxco, Guerrero. Important centers for gold jewelry are in Guanajuato and Oaxaca. Silver and gold jewelry set with turquoise and other semiprecious stones is made in Puebla and Querétaro. In the copper mining state of Michoacán, more than 50 workshops offer a wide variety of hammered and finely worked copper bowls, candlesticks, lamps, and plates. Tin is hammered, painted, and finely worked into a large variety of ornamental items in many areas, but a prime center is San Miguel de Allende in Guanajuato.

Oaxaca is a large producer of palm mats, baskets, and string bags. For sisal and henequen baskets, mats, bags, hammocks, hats, and other woven products, Mérida, Yucatán, is the place to go. The Tarascan Indians of Tzintzuntzan, Michoacán, weave reed figurines and mats.

Competitive Situation The works of Mexico's artists and artisans tend to be original, varied, and inexpensive. Native handicrafts are widely sought after, but are generally made by single artists and small family groups, resulting in low production rates, low volume of production, and considerable variability in the quality of production and supplier reliability. Distribution is still largely through informal market channels—street markets and tourist shops are major outlets. With increasing demand, mass-produced imitations of native handicrafts are becoming increasingly common.

Trade Associations

Refer to listings under Industry-Specific Trade and Professional Associations in the "Important Addresses" chapter for complete contact information.

Gift, Decoration, and Craft Manufacturers Association of Mexico (Asociación Mexicana de Fabricantes de Artículos para Regalo, Decoración y Artesanías)

Graphic Arts Industry National Chamber (Cámara Nacional de la Industria de Artes Gráficas)

Household Appliance Manufacturers National Association (Asociación Nacional de Fabricantes de Aparatos Domésticos)

Household Appliance Suppliers National Association (Asociación Nacional de Distribuidores de Aparatos Domésticos)

Silver and Jewelry Exporters and Importers Association (Asociación Nacional de Exportadores e Importadores de Platería y Joyería)

Silver and Jewelry Industry National Chamber (Cámara Nacional de la Industria de la Platería y la Joyería)

Periodicals

Refer to listings under Industry-Specific Periodicals in the "Important Addresses" chapter for complete contact information.

Impresor: Al Servicio de las Artes Gráficas (Graphic arts industry)
Pequeña Diana (Arts and handicrafts)
Ultima Moda (Apparel and fashion industry)

Trade Fairs

Refer to the "Trade Fairs" chapter for complete listings, including contact information, dates, and venues. Trade fairs with particular relevance to this industry include the following, which are listed in that chapter under the headings given below:

Gifts & Crafts
• AMFAR Expo Regalo
• Artesanias Mexicanas de Toda la República
• Expo Arte
• Expo Joven
• Exposición Nacional de Artesanias
• Feria Navidad
• Manualidades: 1er Salon Nacional de las Artes Manuales
• Sede del Regalo y Salon de la Importación

Jewelry
• Expo Joya
• Expo Joyería
• Expo Regio Joya
• Exposición Oro y Plata

HEALTH PRODUCTS AND EQUIPMENT

Mexico's health-related industries supply three types of products: drugs and pharmaceuticals, cosmetics and toiletries, and fitness equipment. Drug and pharmaceutical manufacturing is the most developed and largest exporter, but it is facing difficult economic times. The cosmetics and toiletries industry has recovered following the opening of Mexican markets to foreign products and is expected to begin increasing its exports. The fitness equipment industry, which is extremely small, manufactures some low-end equipment for domestic markets, but primarily distributes imports. Most exports go to US markets, but a substantial proportion is sent to Latin American countries.

Cosmetics

The 20 largest Mexican manufacturers of cosmetics and toiletries control about 85 percent of the domestic market for these items. Exports account for only about 10 percent of production. Most major manufacturers are subsidiaries of foreign companies.

Products Cosmetics and toiletries made in Mexico include hair products (shampoos, conditioners, dyes, hair treatments, and hair sprays), fragrances, makeup (face, eye, and lip products), nail polish and polish remover, creams and other skin care products (masks, cleansers, and eye creams), deodorants, bath products, powders, shaving foam and cream, children's products (fragrances, powders, oils, creams, and shampoos), and suntan and sun protection products.

Competitive Situation When trade was deregulated in 1986, domestic manufacturers were faced with a huge influx of imports, which gained more than one-half of the domestic market for cosmetics and toiletries. In response, most foreign-invested companies located in Mexico imported finished products from their parent foreign corporations as a strategy to compete locally. At the same time, the opening of the markets in Mexico allowed domestic producers to more readily obtain lower-cost raw materials from abroad. With improved access to raw materials, Mexican companies were able to manufacture a greater variety of higher-quality products locally. Many seized the opportunity, gearing up to supply the same products that they were importing from abroad from local facilities. As a result, domestic production has increased by 88 percent each year since 1990. Mexican companies have succeeded in regaining a substantial share (85 percent) of their domestic market and in slowing imports. Because of heavy concentration on domestic markets, exports of Mexican-made cosmetics and toiletries have actually decreased since 1991, but many domestic companies are expected to begin focusing on exports as domestic markets become saturated.

Drugs and Pharmaceuticals

Mexico exports more than 60 percent of its locally produced drugs and pharmaceuticals, and exports have continued to rise marginally each year. The Mexican pharmaceutical industry is divided into two sectors: the pharmachemical sector, and a sector comprised of manufacturers of medicines and makers of surgical products.

Pharmachemical Sector The pharmachemical sector consists of 56 companies, 18 of which are large, 23 of which are medium-sized, and 15 of which are small (having fewer than 100 employees). These companies process raw materials, such as chemical substances and plants, to obtain the compounds used for manufacturing medicines. Thus, they are dedicated to industrial development; synthesis, extraction, and fermentation processes; and sales promotion of the active ingredients used in medicines. This sector produces approximately 150 products and serves as the major supplier to Mexican manufacturers of medicines.

Drug and Surgical Products Manufacturing Sector The second sector of this industry consists of approximately 350 companies, which contribute about 0.6 percent to Mexico's GDP. These companies offer nearly 7,000 medicines, including vitamin and mineral supplements for human and veterinary use. They also make low-tech surgical products and supplies, including catheters.

Nearly 80 pharmaceutical products are exported to foreign markets. The two leading exports are steroids—nearly the entire production of which is dedicated for export—and antibiotics.

Competitive Situation Mexico's pharmaceutical industry has performed erratically during recent decades because of difficult economic conditions. In 1984 the government established a program designed to promote this industry. Under this program, manufacturers focused on import substitution and experienced slow growth through 1988. In 1989 deregulation began, import duties were reduced, and competition from foreign suppliers intensified, resulting in large fluctuations in the number of pharmaceutical companies and products produced each year. In 1992 domestic production dropped by about 70 percent, in part because domestic demand fell sharply, reflecting a sluggish Mexican economy, and in part because a large number of companies simply ceased operations.

As Mexican currency has appreciated inexorably against the US dollar, imports have become progressively more affordable. In fact, the prices are lower for some foreign products than for some domestically produced items. Several foreign-made products have displaced locally manufactured ones entirely. Local manufacturers have begun to claim unfair competition on the part of importers, particularly from China and India, where the governments are said to be subsidizing products.

A major problem for the industry is its lack of infrastructure for basic and clinical research. Most companies expend only minimal resources on R&D, and they have a poor record of integrating available research into production processes. The industry tends to be oriented toward domestic markets, and it is having to expend greater sums to comply with pollution control laws. The troubles pharmaceutical companies face have been magnified by limited availability of credit.

Mexico's pharmaceutical industry is expected to recover and resume its growth over the next few years. In part, the industry is relying on income from exports. The federal government and banking authorities are trying to devise ways to solve the credit problems. In addition, government programs are emphasizing the construction of rural medical units, construction and refurbishing of health care centers, modernization of hospital emergency rooms and remote outpatient clinics, and the vaccination of all Mexican children, all of which should create greater domestic demand for drug and pharmaceutical products.

Fitness Equipment

Approximately 15 percent of Mexico's market for fitness equipment is supplied by local manufacturers; the rest is imported. A small percentage of Mexican-made fitness equipment is exported. Four major companies are currently producing fitness equipment in Mexico, and all of these serve as distributors of imported products as well.

Products In comparison with imports, Mexican fitness equipment is of lower quality but also of lower price. Products are solid, designed to last longer than imports, but generally lack aesthetic appeal. For the most part, they are mechanical and lack computer controls, although some companies are now importing computer controls to enhance their equipment. Mexican-made items include stationary bicycles, some rowing machines, benches, weights, and general equipment for professional gyms.

Competitive Situation The fitness equipment market in Mexico is small but expanding rapidly. In addition to professional gymnasiums, hotels and household consumers have become significant end users. Much of this growth is attributed to greater consumer awareness of the importance of physical fitness, limitations on outdoor exercise because of rising pollution levels, and government campaigns stressing the benefits of exercise. Mexican firms are anxious to capture more of the domestic and export markets, to which end they are seeking investment and distribution arrangements with foreign companies.

Government Agencies

Refer to listings under Mexican Government Agencies and Entities in the "Important Addresses" chapter for complete contact information.

Comisión del Cuadro Básico de Medicamentos y Equipo (National Commission for Medicines and Equipment)

Dirección General de Control de Insumos Para la Salud (Directorate General of Control of Medical Products)

Dirección General de Control Sanitario de Bienes y Servicios (Directorate General of Sanitary Control of Works and Services)

Instituto de Seguridad y Servicios Sociales de los Trabajadores del Estado (Institute of Federal Employees' Insurance and Social Services)

Instituto Mexicano del Seguro Social (Mexican Institute of Social Security)

Secretaría de Salud (Secretariat of Health)

Trade Associations

Refer to listings under Industry-Specific Trade and Professional Associations in the "Important Addresses" chapter for complete contact information.

Chemical and Pharmaceutical Industry National Chamber (Cámara Nacional de la Industria Química y Farmacéutica)

Hospital National Chamber (Cámara Nacional de Hospitales)

Hygiene and Safety Association (Asociación Mexicana de Higiene y Seguridad)

Medicine Distributors National Association (Asociación Nacional de Distribuidores de Medicinas)

Perfumery and Cosmetics Industry National Chamber (Cámara Nacional de la Industria de Perfumería y Cosméticos)

Pharmaceutical Association (Asociación Farmacéutica Mexicana)

Pharmaceutical Manufacturers National Association (Asociación Nacional de Fabricantes de Medicamentos)

Physical Fitness Industry National Chamber (Cámara Nacional de la Industria del Embellecimiento Físico)

Directories & Publications

Refer to listings under Directories, Annuals and Surveys; and Industry-Specific Periodicals in the "Important Addresses" chapter for contact information.

ADM (Dentistry)

Alto Peinado (Beauty industry)

Atención Médica (For doctors in general practice)

Farmacia Actual (Pharmaceuticals)

Gaceta Médica de México (Medical sciences)

Hair Fashion de México: Sólo Moda en Peinados y Belleza (Beauty industry)

Hombre y Trabajo: Boletín de Medicina, Seguridad e Higiene (Occupational health and general medicine)

Mundo Médico (Medical science)

Perfumería Moderna/Modern Perfuming (Suppliers' guide to perfumes, cosmetics, aerosols, detergents, insecticides, pharmaceuticals, and chemical products)

Trade Fairs

Refer to the "Trade Fairs" chapter for complete listings, including contact information, dates, and venues. Trade fairs with particular relevance to this industry include the following, which are listed in that chapter under the headings given below:

Health & Beauty
- Belleza y Salud
- Congreso de Estetica y Cosmetologia de Occidente
- Expo Belleza
- Expo-Belleza y Salud

Medical & Dental
- Congreso y Exposicion de Traumatologia
- Expo ARIC Dental
- Expo Farma
- Expo Hospital
- Medical Congress
- Medi-Lab

Sporting Goods & Recreation
- Deporte
- Deportexpo
- Expo Deporte
- Mexiplast
- Sede del Deporte

HOUSEHOLD APPLIANCES AND PRODUCTS

Domestic production of household appliances and products tends to be limited in variety and modern technical features, and because of this rudimentary nature exports have remained at a low level and have experienced little growth. A substantial portion of the products made for exports come from *maquiladoras*, most of which reship assembled goods to the US. *Maquilas* have become the largest suppliers to the US of air conditioners and household refrigerators.

Household goods include durable appliances, small appliances, ceramic tiles and fixtures, and table, kitchen, and bath accessories.

Durable Appliances

The consumer durable appliance industry supplies less than 4 percent of the Mexican manufacturing GDP, but this percentage has grown slightly every year since 1987. It is comprised of about 23 companies. Five of these are large corporations, four are medium-sized, and the remainder are small firms located mainly in the states of San Luis Potosí and Nuevo León.

Products Consumer durable appliances include air conditioners, refrigerators, freezers, stoves, ovens, clothes washing machines, and dishwashers. In addition, manufacturers make filters, motors, generators, and other parts for these appliances.

Competitive Situation The durable appliance industry in Mexico, and Mexican manufacturers in particular, are facing difficult financial problems. Production of durable appliances remains largely labor intensive, and domestic consumer demand is declining because of a sluggish economy. In addition, foreign products are penetrating the Mexican market at an increasing rate.

To remain in operation, Mexican producers have been forced to look abroad for markets. As a result, exports of durable appliances continue to increase gradually each year. Similarly, companies with co-invested Mexican and foreign interests have expanded exports to counteract the effect of the slowing trend in domestic Mexican markets. Appliance manufacturers have also managed to keep their assembly processes competitive with those of the US, Canada, and Asian countries, even though automation is used minimally.

To boost domestic markets, the industry is counting on the effect of the government's current economic plans. Confidence in these plans is expected to increase business investment, reduce unemployment, and raise the income levels of the Mexican working class, which in turn should increase domestic demand for consumer durable appliances.

Small Appliances

Manufacturers of small appliances in Mexico primarily supply domestic markets. Most exports of these appliances are from *maquiladoras*.

Products Mexican companies make a large variety of small appliances for household use. The best-selling items are irons, blenders, and fans. In addition, Mexican appliance manufactures offer mixers, food processors, extractors, juicers, coffee makers, coffee mills, toasters and toaster ovens, fryers, and vacuum cleaners.

Competitive Situation Consumer demand for small appliances has slowed in the Mexican market, affecting the levels of imports as well as domestic production. In response, Mexican producers have reduced both the number of models made for each product and the overall levels of production. These reductions are expected to be maintained for some time because the purchasing power of Mexican consumers is showing a continuous, but slow, recovery. To remain competitive with foreign products in the domestic market, Mexican manufacturers of small appliances are concentrating on offering a limited number of higher-quality products and attempting to deliver better service to consumers.

The confidence of investors in Mexico's small

appliance industry is showing an increase, primarily because of the ratification of NAFTA and the signing of bilateral treaties with Chile, Colombia, Venezuela, and other Latin American countries. With increasing investments in this industry, the level of export capacity is also rising.

Personal Security Devices

A small percentage of Mexico's domestic production of personal security equipment is exported. Approximately 70 percent of domestic production consists of padlocks and closed circuit television systems. The latter are manufactured under the *maquila* program and exported from Mexico. Other products include fire extinguishers, smoke detectors, and gas masks.

Ceramic Tiles and Fixtures

The state of Chihuahua is the site of the largest manufacturer of ceramic floor tile in North America. Through joint ventures with foreign—mainly US—companies, Mexico's ceramic tile producers are exporting substantial quantities of ceramic floor and wall tile and plumbing fixtures. The major export market is the US.

Table, Kitchen, Infant, and Bath Items

Seven large companies and many small ones manufacture a variety of housewares for table, kitchen, and bath use. Approximately one-third of these products are exported, of which a large percentage are glass items. Mexico is also a strong exporter of infant products, which are made by five large firms and several small ones. About 70 percent of the infant items produced are exported, primarily to Central America and the US.

Products Glass products manufactured in Mexico include glass tableware, containers, furniture, and ovenware. Major products for infants include nursing bottles and baby carriages. Other houseware products include china and tableware, knives, silverware, kitchenware, and bath accessories.

Competitive Situation Local production continues to hold most of the domestic market, but import levels are increasing dramatically and are expected to take close to half of the market. Faced with an import boom, Mexican producers have had to look to foreign markets to maintain their sales. They have become major exporters of glass, glass articles, and tableware.

Trade Associations

Refer to listings under Industry-Specific Trade and Professional Associations in the "Important Addresses" chapter for complete contact information.

Construction Industry National Chamber (Cámara Nacional de la Industria de la Construcción)
Electric Manufacturers National Chamber (Cámara Nacional de las Manufacturas Eléctricas)
Gift, Decoration, and Craft Manufactures Association of Mexico (Asociación Mexicana de Fabricantes de Artículos para Regalo, Decoración y Artesanías)
Household Appliance Manufacturers National Association (Asociación Nacional de Fabricantes de Aparatos Domésticos)
Household Appliance Suppliers National Association (Asociación Nacional de Distribuidores de Aparatos Domésticos)
Household Electric Appliance Manufacturers National Association (Asociación Nacional de Fabricantes de Aparatos Electrodomésticos)

Directories & Periodicals

Refer to listings under Directories, Annuals and Surveys; and Industry-Specific Periodicals in the "Important Addresses" chapter for contact information.

Cámara Nacional de la Industria de Transformación: Boletín Informativo (Manufacturing industry)
Glass Factory Directory and US Industry Factbook (Glass factories in the US, Canada, and Mexico)
Intermueble (Furniture)
Obras (Housing and urban planning)
Pequeña Diana (Arts and handicrafts)
Promacasa (Building and construction)

Trade Fairs

Refer to the "Trade Fairs" chapter for complete listings, including contact information, dates, and venues. Trade fairs with particular relevance to this industry include the following, which are listed in that chapter under the headings given below:

Construction & Housing
- Expo Cocina
- Triexpo CBR: Cocinas, Banos y Recubrimentos

Furniture & Housewares
- Expo Mueble
- Exposición Provi Mueble
- Ofisistemas
- T.M.I.: Techno Mueble Internacional

Machines, Tools & Instruments
- CME Mexico
- Expo Nacional Ferretera
- Mexico Hardware Show
- USA/Mexico Industrial Expo

Safety & Security
- Expo Seguridad
- Seguridad
- Seguritech

INDUSTRIAL MACHINERY

Machinery and equipment manufactured in Mexico for industrial purposes tend to be limited in technology and variety. Most of the firms that export are *maquila* companies, which supply their parent companies in the US. As a result, imports of industrial machinery and equipment hold a large, and growing, share of Mexico's domestic market.

Estimates indicate that between 50 and 60 percent of the purchases of industrial machinery and equipment in Mexico are made by the petrochemical industry. The remainder is supplied to other Mexican process industries, the most important of which are the chemical, pharmaceutical, metallurgy, cement, food processing, agriculture, and pulp processing industries.

Agricultural Machinery

Domestic production of agricultural machinery supplies just over half of the local market. About 20 percent of Mexican-made machinery is exported, excluding machinery produced by *maquiladoras*. The largest Mexican market for agricultural machinery and equipment is in the northern states of Sinaloa, Chihuahua, Durango, Sonora, and Tamaulipas, where more than 35 percent of Mexico's total agricultural production and virtually all of its large-scale agricultural production is generated.

At least 200 local producers make, sell, and service agricultural machinery and equipment in Mexico. Most are small workshops that simply assemble or repair machines. The few large companies are foreign-invested, including the larger tractor manufacturing companies, which are held by US, Rumanian, Russian, Japanese, and Italian interests.

Products Tractors are the major product of Mexico's agricultural equipment industry. Tractors of 70 HP to 180 HP are manufactured and assembled in Mexico. Domestic production supplies more than half of the Mexican market for tractors, and fewer than 20 percent of Mexican-made tractors are exported.

A large percentage of the plowing, cultivating, planting, and fertilizing machinery used in Mexico is domestically assembled. Products are limited to relatively basic planters, seeders, self-propelled mowers, hay forks, baling presses, potato diggers, fertilizers, rotary cutting machines, crushers, mixers, and subsoilers. Mexican companies also produce machines for grading fruit and other produce. Several Mexican companies furnish accessories for these machines. A few companies make agricultural dryers, self-propelled spraying units for irrigation, and self-propelled mowers and harvesters, combined harvester-threshers, and sugarcane harvesters.

Competitive Situation The low domestic production of agricultural machinery and equipment reflects the difficulties faced by Mexico's agribusiness. Agricultural production in Mexico suffers from the limits imposed by the system of small communal and private farms, coupled with its limited water resources. Most farmers have no capital to invest in modern machinery, have insufficient assets to secure the financing needed to purchase machinery, and basically are unable to mechanize in an economically advantageous fashion given their relatively small plots (the average holding is about 12.5 hectares).

In an effort to modernize Mexico's agribusiness, the Mexican government has instituted a program of land reforms. The reforms are primarily aimed at increasing private ownership of farms and allowing corporate investment and joint ventures in agriculture. Although slow to take hold, these reforms should increase the domestic demand for agricultural machinery, which in turn is expected to boost local production of such machinery. To further encourage these reforms, the Mexican government has worked with the agricultural development bank to restructure loan programs for the purchase of machinery to better accommodate small farmers.

Materials Handling Equipment

The production of materials handling equipment in Mexico is limited to low-tech machinery. Other equipment—such as cranes, mining and hydraulic cement trucks, and containers—are imported. Domestic production has increased significantly since 1991 because exports have risen substantially, amounting to about 90 percent of domestic production in 1992 compared to only about 40 percent in 1990.

Primary end users of materials handling equipment are food processing companies, transportation and cargo handling firms, mining companies, and construction companies. Other purchasers of materials handling equipment include automotive, pharmaceutical, petrochemical, and chemical, tool and instrument fabrication, and steel manufacturers.

Products The production of materials handling equipment in Mexico is limited to such items as conveyor belts and specialized trucks, such as tankers, trailers, and garbage collecting vehicles.

Competitive Situation The advent of NAFTA is expected to boost sales of materials handling equipment as companies improve, modernize, and expand their operations to handle increased trade and competition. This industry has also benefited greatly from the recovery of the Mexican economy.

Petrochemical Processing Equipment

Mexico's production of petrochemical machinery and equipment is limited and is on a decline. This type of machinery and equipment is not exported. Several US firms have assembly operations in Mexico for products such as thermocouples, pneumatic transmitters, controls, and registering equipment. However, these firms have reduced their assembly operations, and most exist primarily as importers of these products. Other local producers—mainly of manual non-electronic instruments and related equipment, such as temperature indicators, alarm signals, flow meters, thermocouples, control valves, manometers, and graphic controllers—supply 45 to 50 percent of the domestic market. Local market demands for pumps, taps, tubing, cocks, containers, small ovens, and similar equipment is met by Mexican companies.

Process Controls Devices

Nearly all types of Mexican industries use process controls, whether for pollution-related or production processes. Process controls include measurement and control devices. Applications for such devices are as varied as water treatment systems, drinking water systems, sewage processors, and recycling systems. Industries that need these systems include food and food processing, mining, and chemical, petrochemical, cement, beverage, sugar, and paper manufacturers.

Products Mexican manufacturers of process control devices have concentrated on low-tech products, such as manometers, thermometers, and valves. Manufacturers of valves constitute the largest sector of the Mexican process control industry. These companies produce iron, steel, and bronze valves, as well as valves for special applications and connections for them. Available valves include Christmas-tree, globe, gate, angle, poppet, ball or spherical, retention, needle, diaphragm, safety, relief, butterfly, solenoid, burst prevention, thermostatic, quick closing, control, diaphragm-operated, escape, mud-regulating or -reducing, filling, air elimination, air trap, steam trap, faucet, and level valves. Valve sizes range from 3.2 mm (1/8 inch) to 1.8 m (72 inches), and pressures range from 7.031 kg/cm (100 psi) to 703.10 kg/cm (10,000 psi). In general, the products comply with the standards issued by Mexico's General Bureau of Standards, the American Petroleum Institute (API), the American Standards Association (ASA), the American Society of Test Materials (ASTM), the American Society of Metals Engineering (ASME), and the American National Standards Institute (ANSI).

Competitive Situation The Mexican valve industry has a high level of domestic integration; 85 percent of the value of the component parts are estimated to be of domestic origin, in part because of the significant development in Mexico of the steel and copper industries. However, the rest of the Mexican process control industry is highly dependent on imports to satisfy demand. Domestic production in the rest of this industry has decreased significantly, primarily because of a lack of demand from end users caused by budget cuts in federal government investments and general economic recession. As domestic production has declined, imports have risen, particularly from the US.

Although the decrease in demand is expected to turn around as Mexican industries begin to deal with efficiency and productivity concerns, the anticipated increase in demand will probably be met by imports because the trend has been toward purchasing high-tech control instruments not manufactured in Mexico. Mexican producers lack the advanced technology needed to manufacture more advanced process control devices. Production capacity remains limited, and protectionist labor unions and federal labor laws have made it difficult to raise worker productivity. The size of the domestic market is too small to make local manufacturing economically feasible, and Mexican companies cannot compete with US manufacturers on price because of the high cost of upgrading. In addition, a foreign company that grants a manufacturing license for a particular device often restricts the markets to which it may be exported. Importation of these devices, and of technical assistance, are essential for the foreseeable future. A higher fiscal burden in Mexico reduces the purchasing power of individuals and, of corporations, increases the cost of the product. Product liability, which is imposed by law, has had an adverse effect as well, and protectionist legislation in the US has further limited exports.

Government Agencies

Refer to listings under Mexican Government Agencies and Entities in the "Important Addresses" chapter for complete contact information.

Comisión Federal de Electricidad (Federal Electricity Commission)

Comisión Nacional del Agua (National Water Commission)

Instituto Mexicano de Control de Calidad (Mexican Institute of Quality Control)

Petróleos Mexicanos (Pemex) (Mexican National Oil Company)

Secretaría de Agricultura y Recursos Hidráulicos (Secretariat of Agriculture and Water Resources, Department of Agricultural Machinery)

Secretaría de Agricultura y Recursos Hidráulicos (Secretariat of Agriculture and Water Resources, Department of Science and Technology)

Secretaría de Comunicaciones y Transportes (Secretariat of Communications and Transportation)

Trade Associations

Refer to listings under Industry-Specific Trade and Professional Associations in the "Important Addresses" chapter for complete contact information.

Automatic Meter and Control Equipment Manufacturers Association (Asociación Mexicana de Fabricantes de Equipo de Medición y Control Automático)

Construction Industry National Chamber (Cámara Nacional de la Industria de la Construcción)

Machinery Distributors Association (Asociación Mexicana de Distribuidores de Maquinaria)

Manufacturing Industry National Chamber (Cámara Nacional de la Industria de la Transformación)

Valves Manufacturers National Association (Asociación Mexicana de Fabricantes de Valvulas)

Directories & Periodicals

Refer to listings under Directories, Annuals and Surveys; and Industry-Specific Periodicals in the "Important Addresses" chapter for contact information.

Agricultura Técnica en México (Agricultural technology)

Autoindustria (Automotive industry)

Cámara Nacional de la Industria de Transformación: Boletín Informativo (Manufacturing industry)

Ciencia y Desarrollo (Science and technology)

Constru-Noticias (Building and construction)

Guía de la Industria: Equipo y Materiales (Machinery and materials)

Hule Mexicano y Plásticos: Revista Técnica Industrial (Rubber and plastics)

Ingenieria Civil/Civil Engineering

Ingenieria Mecánica y Eléctrica (Mechanical and electrical engineering)

Ingenieria Petrolera (Petroleum engineering)

Más Caminos: Por un Sistema Integral de Transportes (Transportation)

Minero-Noticias (Mining)

Mueble Equipo (Furniture manufacturing equipment)

Revista Mexicana del Petróleo (Oil, gas, and petrochemical industries)

Tecno Industria (Technology and industry)

Trade Fairs

Refer to the "Trade Fairs" chapter for complete listings, including contact information, dates, and venues. Trade fairs with particular relevance to this industry include the following, which are listed in that chapter under the headings given below:

Construction & Housing
- Constructo
- Construexpo
- Cuarta Muestra de la Industria de la Construcción
- Expo CIHAC

Machines, Tools & Instruments

- Agroindustrial
- Ambientec
- Analitica y Control 94
- APICE
- CME Mexico
- Converflex
- Expo Clean
- Expo Lacteos
- Expo Metal Mecanica
- Exposición de Máquinas de Herramientas
- Manejomat
- Maquinamex and Metalmex
- Materials Handling
- Mexico Hardware Show
- Mineria
- PEMEX-Po. Plantas
- Platicos
- T.M.I.: Techno Mueble Internacional
- Tecnos
- Urbanismos
- USA/Mexico Industrial Expo

INDUSTRIAL MINERALS, CHEMICALS, AND MATERIALS

Mexico's mining and chemical industries are leading producers and exporters. In 1992 the Mexican chemical, petrochemical, rubber, and plastics sectors accounted for 18.2 percent of manufacturing GDP and 4.1 percent of Mexico's overall GDP. The petrochemical sector is Mexico's largest producer and exporter, although the economy is becoming less oil-dependent through aggressive steps by Mexico's government and private industries to encourage other manufacturing sectors. Mexico is also a top world supplier of cement and a large number of minerals, particularly silver, and it has a long-established, dynamic plastics industry.

Biotechnology Products

Although biotechnology activity in Mexico is not as developed as in the US, Europe, or Japan, Mexico leads Latin America in biotechnology R&D. About 40 private firms and 30 to 35 R&D groups are engaged in biotechnology production. Many of the private companies have been well established for several decades and have recently added biotechnology laboratories as the technology and markets have developed. The groups in R&D centers work in traditional university laboratories or government-supported facilities, which tend to engage in primary research rather than applied technological development.

Products Private firms have been engaged in biotechnology development in three areas: pharmaceuticals, food processing, and plant and flower propagation. Products include antibiotics, amino acids, baking yeast, enzymes, citric acid, aspartame, edible mushrooms, and alcoholic beverages.

Competitive Situation Biotechnology research is on the rise in Mexico, primarily because of increased funding from government agencies and private sector contracts. Firms are expanding their R&D beyond health care and food products to such areas as environmental pollution, industrial microbiology, agriculture, and livestock.

Cement

Monterrey is the headquarters of the world's fourth largest cement producer, which supplies nearly 65 percent of the cement used in Mexico. Mexico's domestic consumption is on the rise, with heavy investments designed to improve the country's transportation, housing, and environmental treatment facilities. The largest export markets for cement have been the US and Central and South America. However, exports are being promoted to Asian markets, and operations have been extended to Europe as well.

Minerals

Mexico has substantial reserves of nearly every mineral sought in world markets. Production has risen in almost all sectors of Mexico's mining industry, sometimes dramatically. The leading mining states are Sonora (gold, silver, and copper), Chihuahua (lead, zinc, silver, and copper) and Zacatecas (silver, lead, copper, and zinc). Durango is also notable for its silver and gold production.

Products Mexico is the world's leading producer of silver, strontium, and sodium sulfate. Other minerals mined in Mexico include bismuth, cadmium, stibnite, graphite (carbon), coal, mercury, arsenic, barite, sulfur, molybdenum, phosphorous, potassium, salt, feldspar, gypsum, gold, copper, zinc, lead, and iron.

Competitive Situation Mexico's mining sector has been adversely affected by the low international prices for silver and gold. In addition, a scarcity of credit has forced many small mining companies to restrict operations because of the extremely high costs of exploration and extraction, both of which require high front-end investments. To remain operational, Mexican mining companies have reduced costs and implemented a series of evolutionary, rather than revolutionary, innovations.

An estimated three-quarters of the country's mineral resources have not been exploited. The potential for this industry is therefore quite promising. Increased access through privatization of the remaining mineral holdings and implementation of NAFTA should enhance prospects in this industry.

New incentives have been created under recent mining legislation, which substantially deregulates this industry. New laws have been enacted that open to exploration 9.6 million mineral reserve acres in previously unexploited areas. This legislation also increases the amount of land that a single enterprise may claim, allowing companies to consolidate the small holdings of their subsidiaries and eliminate the added cost structure represented by those subsidiaries. Foreign investment is now permitted in the exploitation of minerals previously reserved to the state. The new mining laws also double the time allowed for exploration and exploitation of mineral lands, and permit renewal of mineral rights. The result affords substantial protection for investors, who must make enormous infrastructural investments to develop a mine.

Petrochemicals

Mexico's petrochemical industry has shown impressive growth in recent decades. This industry accounts for nearly 3 percent of Mexico's GDP, and now supplies about 3 percent of the world's petrochemicals, ranking 15th among nations that produce petrochemicals. Mexico is the largest producer in Latin America.

Mexico's economy remains heavily reliant on petroleum. Private and public oil companies can satisfy less than half of the domestic demand for petrochemicals, and less than 20 percent of local production is exported (excluding exports to *maquila* companies). This industry provides more than 30 percent of Mexico's export earnings. Some 60 percent of petrochemical exports go to the US.

More than 400 private firms operate about 700 plants for manufacturing petrochemicals in Mexico. Production is fairly evenly divided between the private producers and the state-owned Petróleos Mexicanos (Pemex), which is Mexico's largest company and the largest single source of income and foreign revenue to the Mexican government. Pemex is one of the top 10 oil producers in the world, operating eight refineries and nearly 110 petrochemical plants, including the world's fourth largest facility. In addition, Pemex has about 40 plants that produce complementary products.

Products Products of Mexico's petrochemical companies include basic petrochemicals such as ethane, propane, butanes, raw materials for carbon black, naphthas, hexane, haptene, and pentanes; and intermediate petrochemicals such as acetylene, ethylenes, benzene, butadiene, butylenes, toluene, xylenes, ammonia, polypropylene, acrylonitrile, acetaldehyde, methanol, n-paraffins, paraxylene, orthooxylene, propylene, styrene, and ethylene oxide.

Petrochemicals are processed into gasoline, kerosene, diesel, asphalt, fibers, and plastic resins. Processors of petrochemicals supply such products as adhesives, food additives, lubricant and combustion additives, tensoactive agents, colorants, elastomers and carbon black, explosives, pharmochemicals, chemical fibers, fiber polymers, rubber chemicals, catalysts, pesticides, plastifiers, propellants and refrigeration chemicals, synthetic resins, flavors and fragrances, and automotive lubricants and formulators.

Competitive Situation Petrochemical plants in Mexico are almost completely dependent on imports of high-tech equipment and instruments. Local manufacturing of this production machinery and equipment is minimal, and its share of the market is decreasing. Expansion and modernization of Mexico's petrochemical industry relies on the availability of this equipment from foreign countries, particularly the US.

In anticipation of increasing competition from foreign countries under NAFTA, Mexico's petrochemical producers are expanding and modernizing their plants. Substantial investments are being made in exploration and drilling. The discovery of new reserves is critical because new findings have not kept up with the rate of oil extraction. With NAFTA incentives, foreign investors are looking to the integration of Mexico's petrochemical industry as an important step toward creating one of the world's largest supply regions.

Restrictions on Mexico's private petrochemical industry have been loosened. The number of petrochemicals over which the state held a monopoly has been reduced from 34 to eight. About 60 of the state-owned plants are to be sold in an attempt to promote private sector capital investment, to gain funds from international and domestic investors, and, specifically, to develop production of ethylene and its derivatives. In addition, the state-owned company has been restructured into a parent company with four subsidiaries, and private investment is being allowed in the subsidiary responsible for producing intermediate petrochemicals.

Plastics

Mexico has been producing plastic materials and resins for more than four decades. This industry's production growth rate has generally exceeded the general rate of growth of the GDP. It supplies most of the domestic demand for plastic resins, although high-density polyethylene and special application and engineering resins are imported. More than 20 percent of total production is exported, compensating for insufficient domestic absorption of supply in some areas.

Mexico's plastics industry is composed of more than 3,100 extremely diverse primary petrochemical producers, raw materials manufacturers, plastics processing companies, machinery suppliers, and recycling companies. Firms that produce high-tech products coexist with small family-owned businesses. More than 60 percent of the firms employ fewer than 20 workers, while only 3 percent are classified as large companies. The highest concentra-

tion of firms is in Mexico City and the surrounding area. Additionally, a large number of *maquila* firms are located along the Mexico–US border.

Products Principal exports of Mexican-made plastics are polyvinyl chloride, polystyrene, and polyethylene terephtalate. Other plastic materials and resins manufactured in Mexico include low-density polyethylene, urea and phenol resins, urea formaldehyde, polyurethanes, unsaturated polyester, melamines, and polymethyl methacrylate. Processed plastic products available include toys and packaging materials (cellophane or polypropylene). Some firms offer design services for companies that need custom packaging materials.

Competitive Situation On average, the production rate in Mexico's plastics industry has increased at a rate greater than Mexico's economy as a whole. During the 1980s, the plastics industry continued to register overall growth primarily due to increased production of polyvinyl chloride products. However, the smaller plastics firms remain technically and managerially unsophisticated, and many of them are wilting in the face increasing imports.

The types of resins available in Mexico are limited to commodity resins and materials. Mexican firms are interested in exploring new materials and novel applications in the plastics industry. Domestic production of high-tech engineering resins and plastics additives is not yet economically feasible because demand is low and production costs high.

Mexican companies primarily use injection, extrusion, and blow molding production processes. Many firms have begun replacing basic injection processes with more sophisticated methods, such as laminating, rotational molding, foaming, compression, thermoforming, coating, metalizing, and electrochrome decorating and finishing processes.

Soaps and Detergents

As one of the oldest sectors of the chemical industry in Mexico, soap and detergent manufacturers supply practically all of the domestic market needs. Two of the largest soap and detergent plants in the world are located in Mexico. However, exports are minimal, representing only about 1 percent of total production. Most exports are sent to the US, where sales in Hispanic communities account for 90 percent of total exports.

More than 90 firms produce laundry soaps, personal care soaps, and detergents. About two-thirds of the firms produce 96 percent of the soaps and nearly all of the detergents. Soap and detergent plants are located mainly in the Federal District and in the states of Jalisco and México.

Products Mexican soap manufacturers produce 130 brands of laundry soap in 314 presentations. More than 41 brands of personal care soaps are available in 131 presentations, and nearly 20 brands of detergents are supplied in 98 presentations.

Competitive Situation The major Mexican manufacturers of soaps and detergents use advance technology in production. All of the subsectors are currently producing below their installed capacity. This industry tends to be dependent on imports of raw materials from the US, but it also purchases raw materials from suppliers in 40 other countries.

Steel

Five fully integrated Mexican firms and a large number of smaller ones supply more than 90 percent of Mexico's domestic steel market. The five large firms operate seven plants. In addition, there are 20 semi-integrated mini-mills and more than 100 smaller manufacturers that specialize in particular items.

Products Products include forged and milled steel sheets, pipes and tubings, containers, and wires, as well as steel and iron structures. Most products are sold to local automotive, rail, and other manufacturers.

Competitive Situation Mexico's steel industry is being reorganized, beginning with the privatization of 55 companies between 1982 and 1991. Another 56 firms have been sold, 15 closed, four merged, and four converted to other uses. The remaining firms are now undertaking new projects, and 5 percent annual growth is being predicted through 1996.

In 1992 Mexico's steel industry suffered from deregulation, with a heavy influx of imported steel products taking a large share of the domestic market. Since then, antidumping charges have been brought against many foreign companies as the industry struggles to survive. It appears to be in recovery, spurred by increasing national demand for steel as a result of the push to modernize Mexico's transportation, communication, and housing infrastructures.

Government Agencies & Entities

Refer to listings under Mexican Government Agencies and Entities in the "Important Addresses" chapter for complete contact information.

Instituto Mexicano del Plástico Industrial (Mexican Institute of Industrial Plastics)
Dirección General de Prevención y Control de la Contaminación Ambiental (Directorate General of Environmental Contamination, Prevention and Control)
Petróleos Mexicanos—Pemex (Mexican National Oil Company)
Secretaría de Energía, Minas y Industria Paraestatal (Secretariat of Energy, Mine and Parastatal Industry)
Siderúrgica Nacional (National Iron and Steel Company)

Trade Associations

Refer to listings under Industry-Specific Trade and Professional Associations in the "Important Addresses" chapter for complete contact information.

Aluminum Institute (Instituto del Aluminio)
Cement National Chamber (Cámara Nacional del Cemento)
Chemical Industry National Association (Asociación Nacional de la Industria Química)
Chemicals and Pharmaceutical Industry National Chamber (Cámara Nacional de la Industria Química y Farmacéutica)
Construction Industry National Chamber (Cámara Nacional de la Industria de la Construcción)
Copper Association (Asociación Mexicana del Cobre)
Detergent Manufacturers Association (Asociación de Fabricantes de Detergentes de la República Mexicana)
Gas Distributors Association (Asociación Mexicana de Distribuidores de Gas Licuado y Empresas Conexas)
Iron and Steel Industry National Chamber (Cámara Nacional de la Industria del Hierro y del Acero)
Laundry Industry National Chamber (Cámara Nacional de la Industria de Lavanderías)
Match Industry National Chamber (Cámara Nacional de la Industria Cerillera)
Mining Chamber of Mexico (Cámara Minera de México)
Mining Engineers, Metallurgists and Geologists Association (Asociación de Ingenieros de Minas, Metalurgistas y Geólogos de México)
Oil, Grease and Soap Industry National Chamber (Cámara Nacional de la Industria de Aceites, Grasa y Jabones)
Paint and Ink Manufacturers National Association (Asociación Nacional de Fabricantes de Pinturas y Tintas)
Pesticides and Fertilizer Industry Association (Asociación Mexicana de la Industria de Plaguicidas y Fertilizantes)
Plastic Industries National Association (Asociación Nacional de Industrias del Plástico)
Plastic Pipes National Institute (Instituto Nacional de Tuberías Plásticas)
Zinc and Lead Institute (Instituto Mexicano del Zinc, Plomo y Coproductos)

Directories & Periodicals

Refer to listings under Directories, Annuals and Surveys; and Industry-Specific Periodicals in the "Important Addresses" chapter for contact information.

Anuario Latinoamericano de los Plásticos (Plastics industry)

Cámara Nacional de la Industria del Hierro y del Acero: Informe del Presidente (Iron and steel industry)

Ciencia y Desarrollo (Science and technology)

Directory of Steel Foundries in the United States, Canada and Mexico)

Environment Watch Latin America

Ferretecnic - FYT: La Revista de la Industria Ferretera (Metallurgy)

Geomimet (Energy resources sector of Mexico.)

Guía de la Industria: Hule, Plásticos y Resinas (Plastics, rubber and resins)

Guía de la Industria Química: Productos Químicos (Chemical engineering)

Hule Mexicano y Plásticos: Revista Técnica Industrial (Rubber and plastics)

Ingeniería Civil (Civil engineering)

Ingeniería Mecánica y Eléctrica (Mechanical and electrical engineering)

Ingeniería Petrolera (Petroleum engineering)

Instituto Mexicano del Petróleo: Revista (Petroleum and gas)

La Minería en México (Mining)

Minero-Noticias (Mining)

Panorama Plástico: La Revista Mexicana del Plástico (Technical information on plastics industry)

Pemex: Boletín Bibliográfico (Abstracts from scientific and technical journals.)

Perfumería Moderna/Modern Perfuming (Suppliers' guide to perfumes, cosmetics, aerosols, detergents, insecticides, pharmaceuticals, and chemical products)

Plasti-Noticias (Plastics)

Prontuario Agroquímico (Agricultural chemicals)

Producción Química Mexicana (Chemical engineering)

Revista Mexicana del Petróleo (Oil, gas and petrochemical industries)

Tecno Industria (Technology and industry)

Trade Fairs

Refer to the "Trade Fairs" chapter for complete listings, including contact information, dates, and venues. Trade fairs with particular relevance to this industry include the following, which are listed in that chapter under the headings given below:

Cleaning
- Expo Clean
- Expo Tintoreria y Lavanderia

Construction & Housing
- Concreto
- Constructo
- Construexpo
- Cuarta Muestra de la Industria de la Construcción

- Expo CIHAC

Environmental & Energy
- Control Ambiental Expo
- Ecologia
- Environmex
- Enviropro Mexico
- Pro Eco
- T&D World Expo Mexico

Machines, Tools & Instruments
- PEMEX-Po. Plantas
- Plasticos
- T.M.I.: Techno Mueble Internacional

Petroleum, Gas & Mining
- American Gas Association International Conference
- Expo Petro y Chem
- International Petroleum Exhibition and Conference of Mexico
- Minería
- Petro y Chem Mexico

Plastics & Rubber
- Expo Hulera Internacional
- Plast Imagen
- Plásticos

SERVICE INDUSTRIES

Service industries are leading the economic expansion in Mexico. They account for nearly 60 percent of Mexico's GDP. Retail outlets, franchises, and joint ventures with foreign investors, corporations, and entrepreneurs are springing up throughout the country.

Business Support Services

The rapidly growing industrial and service industries are spawning necessary support services, including air, land, and sea transport services, packaging and freight forwarding companies, and computer sales and service centers. Legal, insurance, public relations, and other professional services are available from Mexican and foreign firms, mainly in the business centers of Mexico City, Monterrey, and Guadalajara.

A wide variety of consulting services are available to international business owners. The largest companies—including owners and operators of industrial parks—can advise clients on existing and potential markets; assist customers in establishing or expanding operations in Mexico; consult and oversee the development of a business, from choosing a site and erecting a building to hiring and training a labor force and installing high-tech computer and other equipment. Some will even provide the plant, labor, and training. Many specialize in particular business channels, such as industrial park developers and border marketing firms.

Financial Services

Financing has been, and continues to be, a significant barrier to establishing, expanding, or modernizing an enterprise in Mexico. Major strides have been taken, however, to increase available financial services and to extend them outside Mexico's main commercial centers. With privatization of banks and the formation of financial investment groups, Mexico's financial services sector is being transformed. The advent of open trade policies and NAFTA has created opportunities for foreign banks and brokerage firms to enter Mexico—by acquiring an interest in a Mexican institution or by establishing local offices. Regional banks are being promoted, and the government has allowed several private conglomerates with multiple commercial interests to buy into financial institutions. However, the government is closely regulating this industry during the conversion, controversy over reforms is high, and many programs have yet to be implemented.

Real Estate

Industrial and corporate real estate services are being offered on a local and national basis. Several joint ventures have been formed—many with US brokers—to provide real estate brokerage services to international companies seeking to invest in and establish Mexican-based operations. Some of these brokers have extended their range to Central and South America as well.

Developers are also operating in Mexico, building industrial parks, warehouses, offices, and commercial spaces. The largest companies have joint arrangements with US and other foreign firms and provide construction, engineering, environmental, and security services. Of the service industries, Mexico's construction industry has shown the fastest growth in recent years. Extensive public housing, transportation, and communication projects have been undertaken through the sponsorship of both public and private entities.

Retail Services

Retail space in Mexico is generally at a premium because of the concentration in a few urban centers of the groups with the greatest purchasing power. Overhead on large stores tends to be high, and large tracts of land are seldom available in commercially attractive areas. A significant and growing proportion of retail sales are made through large discount outlets, but nearly one-third are accomplished through such informal channels as flea markets, street markets, and door-to-door sales. Perhaps another third of retail sales are split among department, specialty, and government-owned stores.

Regional outlets have had more success than national ones because of the isolation of Mexico's population clusters. Most retail outlets prefer to receive deliveries directly from suppliers, and distribution centers have not been developed to any great degree. Automated and computerized inventory, pricing, and other systems have made few inroads into traditional practices.

Retail outlets are on the rise, reflecting Mexico's improving economy. A number of malls are being developed in and around the commercial centers, and large foreign retailers—particularly representing US chains—are opening outlets in various locations around the country. Several retail chains have adapted to space restrictions in urban areas by opening warehouse-style, volume discount stores—*bodegas*—for the sale of general merchandise to working-class and low-income markets. A few high-volume discount stores that specialize in a product area, such as toys, furniture, or drugs (the so-called "category killers"), have plans to open in a few cities, but these types of stores are generally unfamiliar to Mexican consumers and are expected to require extensive promotion and adaptation in order to succeed in Mexican culture.

Tourist Services

Tourism has long been one of Mexico's largest service industry sectors. In some states—particularly Baja California Sur, Guerrero, and Quintana Roo—tourists at luxury seaside resorts have been a major source of revenue for decades. With travel statistics showing Mexico as one of the most popular vacation destinations for US tourists, international hotel chains continue to pour substantial investment funds into these resort areas. Developers are constructing vacation homes, golf courses, tennis facilities, and conference centers to accommodate business and pleasure travelers.

However, profits at the luxury coastal resorts are beginning to slow. Overdevelopment is one reason that luxury resorts have become less attractive to investors, but profit margins are being more severely affected by two other factors: the trend of vacationers preferring family, close-to-home outings and the stability of the Mexican peso. Devaluations of the peso were profitable to hotel investors because of the gap between hotel rates (paid in US dollars) and expenses (paid in pesos). With the stabilization of the peso, hotel rates have also stabilized, although expenses remain subject to inflation. Another factor has been the lack of support services beyond the resort facilities themselves.

Strategies in Mexico's tourism industry are changing with the trends. Many states are promoting their inland attractions, generally centering around natural (waterfalls, beaches, spas, canyons, rock formations, forests, and lakes) and cultural (historical and archaeological sites, museums, colonial architecture, artist colonies) resources. Popular recreational resorts are being developed in areas within driving distance of Mexico's largest commercial centers, catering to increasing crowds of nationals who are seeking quick weekend retreats. Some enterprises are focusing on business travelers, expanding their operations to new cities and seeking to offer chain hotels and recreational centers that can provide the same recognizable facilities and services at each site. Private and state organizations are also diversifying their promotions—nearly 85 percent of resort vacationers are US tourists—to other markets, particularly those in Canada and Asia.

Competitive Situation

The rapid growth of Mexico's service industries has been especially spurred by private and government spending on the country's infrastructure. In most areas of the country, transportation, housing, water treatment, and electrical facilities have not been modernized and are now being severely overtaxed. Extensive investments are being made to improve transportation and communication systems, provide public housing, and introduce environmental controls. Mexico's recent changes in foreign investment laws have opened areas previously closed to foreign investors, creating a phenomenal growth in the number companies offering services in nearly every sector. Government programs are offered to travel agents in Canada and the US to promote Mexico's tourist locales.

Government Agencies

Refer to listings under Mexican Government Agencies and Entities in the "Important Addresses" chapter for complete contact information.

Comisión Nacional Bancaria (National Banking Commission)
Comisión Nacional de Valores (National Securities Commission)
Consejo Nacional de Turismo (National Council of Tourism)
Secretaría de Hacienda y Crédito Público (Secretariat of Finance and Public Credit)
Secretaría de Turismo (Secretariat of Tourism)

Trade Associations

Refer to listings under Industry-Specific Trade and Professional Associations in the "Important Addresses" chapter for complete contact information.

Advertising Agency Association (Asociación Mexicana de Agencias de Publicidad)
Air Transport National Chamber (Cámara Nacional del Aerotransporte)
Bank Association (Asociación Mexicana de Bancos)

Communications and Transportation National Chamber (Cámara Nacional de Transportes y Comunicaciones)
Construction Industry National Chamber (Cámara Nacional de la Industria de la Construcción)
Consulting Firms National Chamber (Cámara Nacional de Empresas de Consultoria)
Fair, Exposition and Conference Professionals Association (Asociación Mexicana de Profesionales en Ferias, Exposiciones y Convenciones)
Food and Restaurant Industry National Chamber (Cámara Nacional de la Industria de Restaurantes y Alimentos Condimentados)
General Counsel National Association (Asociación Nacional de Abogados de Empresas)
Graphic Arts Industry National Chamber (Cámara Nacional de la Industria de Artes Gráficas)
Guarantee Companies of Mexico Association (Asociación de Compañías Afianzadoras de México)
Hotel and Motel Association (Asociación Mexicana de Hoteles y Moteles de la República)
Hotel Association (Asociación Nacional Hotelera)
Insurance and Guarantee Agents of Mexico Association (Asociación Mexicana de Agentes de Seguros y Fianzas)
Insurance Institutions Association (Asociación Mexicana de Instituciones de Seguros)
International Transport and Commerce Industries Association (Asociación de Industriales de Transporte y Comercio Internacional)
Lawyers National Association (Asociación Nacional de Abogados de México)
Restaurant Association of Mexico (Asociación Mexicana de Restaurantes)
Roads Association (Asociación Mexicana de Caminos)
Stock Brokers Association (Asociación Mexicana de Casas de Bolsa)
Tourist Transportation National Chamber (Cámara Nacional de Autotransporte de Pasaje y Turismo)
Touristic Development Association (Asociación Mexicana de Desarrolladores Turísticos)
Travel Agents of Mexico Association (Asociación Mexicana de Agencias de Viajes)

Directories & Periodicals

Refer to listings under Directories, Annuals and Surveys; Newspapers; and Industry-Specific Periodicals in the "Important Addresses" chapter for contact information.

Actualidad en Seguros y Fianzas (Insurance and surety bonds sector)
Mexican Stock Exchange Trading Report
Communicator (Credit bureaus, collection

agencies and related services throughout the US, Canada, and Mexico)

Comportamiento Del Sistema Asegurador Mexicano (Financial information about groups of companies of the insurance sector)

Constru-Noticias (Building and construction)

Directorio MPM—Agencias y Anunciantes (Advertising agency directory)

Directorio MPM—Medios Audiovisuales (Audiovisual media rates and data)

Directorio MPM—Medios Impresos Tarifas y Datos (Print media rates and data)

Directory of Executive Recruiters (More than 2,700 executive recruiting offices in the United States, Canada and Mexico)

El Financiero (National financial paper)

El Financiero Internacional (Weekly English-language version of El Financiero)

Guía Aérea de México y Centro-America (Air transport industry)

Inversionista Mexicano (Investment business newsletter)

Laws of Mexico in English

Más Caminos: Por un Sistema Integral de Transportes (Transportation)

Mayoreo y Distribución (Grocery industry)

Mercado de Valores (Investments)

Negocios y Bancos (Negobancos) (Important banking and finance journal)

Progreso: Comercio-Industria-Finanzas-Desarrollo)

Prontuario Internacional (Banking and finance)

Revista Mexicana de Seguros y Finanzas (Insurance and finance)

Trade Fairs

Refer to the "Trade Fairs" chapter for complete listings, including contact information, dates, and venues. Trade fairs with particular relevance to this industry include the following, which are listed in that chapter under the headings given below:

Business Services
- Banking, Insurance and Tech
- Credi Expo
- Expo Publicitas
- Expo Servicios
- Expo Servicios al Comercio Exterior
- Shopping Center Developments in Mexico

Franchising
- Conferencia Internacional de Franquicias
- Feria de Oportunidades de Franquicias en México
- Shopping Center Developments in Mexico
- USA/Mexico Franchise Expo

Office Equipment
- Expo Comm Mexico
- Ofisistemas

Representation

- Border Buyer Industrial Show
- Monterrey Show
- Rep-Com
- Representaciones Guadalajara
- Representaciones Monterrey

Retail
- ANTAD

Sporting Goods & Recreation
- Expo Fonatur

Transportation
- Warehousing, Development & Distribution in Mexico

TEXTILES AND LEATHER PRODUCTS

Mexico's textile industry is among the country's top five manufacturing sectors. However, it accounts for less than 1 percent of Mexico's overall GDP and less than 5 percent of the manufacturing GDP. Production has been increasing steadily, but at a gradual pace. An extremely small proportion of total production is exported.

Mexican-made apparel supplied approximately 95 percent of the domestic market in 1992, but that percentage is expected to decrease with imports taking a larger share. The Mexican apparel industry is estimated to consist of roughly 17,000 companies, of which 77 percent are small, with up to 15 employees producing from 5,000 to 20,000 garments each month. The smaller companies tend to be family enterprises, while most of the larger ones are foreign-operated. Large companies account for approximately 4 percent of Mexican apparel production.

Textile firms are concentrated in Mexico City. Secondary centers are located in the states of México, Puebla, Guanajuato, Nuevo León, and Jalisco.

Apparel

Most of the apparel produced in Mexico is for women and girls, with about 40 percent made for men and boys. Cotton garments are the primary output, reflecting Mexican weather conditions. Garments of man-made fibers are second in popularity and production. Mexican firms produce clothing of all sorts, from casual to dressy, pants to skirts, shirts to dresses, nightwear to underwear, swimwear to overcoats. Woolen garments and acrylic sweaters are primarily made for export and are known internationally for their high quality.

Carpets and Decorative Fabrics

Two major Mexican producers export carpets, and many smaller firms weave carpets and decorative fabrics. Textile products for home use include wall coverings, curtains and blinds, and decorative hangings. Small local producers play a key role in the Mexican market, but exports are important because of generally low domestic demand for carpets and decorative fabrics.

Much of the carpet produced is exported, with more than 50 percent of total carpet exports going to the United States. Use of carpets in Mexico is relatively low compared to other countries (only 20 percent of the European, US, and Canadian average) because of the low per capita income, cultural factors, and the hot climate in many areas. In rural areas, which represent the majority of the country, carpets are considered an unnecessary luxury. Domestic carpet purchases are concentrated in the major urban areas—Mexico City, Monterrey, and Guadalajara.

Leather Products

A large number of small Mexican businesses produce a wide variety of leather products, including sandals, sports shoes, boots, work shoes, dress shoes, vests, jackets, handbags, and luggage.

Linens

Mexican manufacturers of linens produce a significant number of products. Product include sheets, blankets, bedspreads, pillows, tablecloths, placemats, and towels. Mexico exports about one-third of its production. Domestic consumers tend to prefer imported linens, which are usually of higher quality and better design.

Textiles

The bulk of domestic fabric consumption is still satisfied by domestic producers. Synthetic fibers, including acrylics, polyesters, and nylons, are the leading products, followed by cotton. Wool textiles constitute less than 2 percent of total domestic consumption.

Competitive Situation

A majority of Mexican textile and apparel producers lack advanced technology and modern manufacturing equipment. Because of their size and limited production, they are unable to achieve economies of scale or obtain financial support. For these reasons, they are unable to upgrade machinery, purchase fashion designs, or train employees. Their efforts to expand into export markets are hampered by inability to change their designs and production to accommodate the tastes of consumers elsewhere.

Small apparel manufacturers tend to copy designs from clothing found in prestigious stores, making their own adaptations with cheaper materials and hand labor. These companies lack quality control and standardization for size, style, and finishing details. The medium-sized companies, which do have greater management depth, are nevertheless faced with many of the same problems because they have been unable to obtain necessary financial support.

After years of protectionism, Mexico's fabric and apparel firms face intense competition from imports now that trade barriers have largely been eliminated. Producers of men's clothing have a stronger position in the market than makers of women's apparel, primarily because the former are not as affected by fashion changes. With the influx of imports, Mexican producers of women's clothes are having to compete with innovative and constantly changing designs and fabrics that offer greater variety and quality at competitive prices. This industry has neglected to replace equipment, maintain quality and fashion, improve efficiency, and become competitive in price and quality. Mexican products are losing their market position to imports because Mexican consumers have an often justified preference for foreign items.

The larger companies are surviving foreign competition because they have strong financial support and access to internationally prestigious fashion specialists and designers. They also have advanced technology for cutting, designing, and manufacturing clothes; have been able to fund technology upgrades; and have developed good quality control. Many have been able to locate export markets to compensate for decreasing domestic demand.

Many medium and small apparel enterprises are facing outright bankruptcy. In an attempt to retain some competitive edge, domestic producers are emphasizing services, such as the return or exchange of merchandise not sold. Factory representatives are available to assist stores in arranging and promoting products, pricing merchandise, and cutting prices on items not sold. They will quickly supply additional merchandise if a previous order sells out too quickly, and they offer special bonuses if prices have to be cut.

Mexico's government is promoting foreign investment in the textile and apparel industries. Also, commercial chambers and business associations are encouraging Mexican apparel firms to enter into joint ventures with foreign companies in an effort to gain the technical and financial support required to compete in world markets. Such arrangements would allow domestic companies to produce higher-quality garments and retain the services now offered.

The clear consensus in the textile and apparel industry is that in order to compete domestically and internationally, Mexican companies must invest in plant automation and modernization, product quality, and product design. To survive, Mexican textile companies will need to lower their operating and materials costs and improve productivity. Some companies have taken the lead in investing in computer-aided design and manufacturing processes, but most of this industry still lags behind world-class levels. With the elimination of tariffs among Canada, Mexico, and the US under NAFTA, Mexican textile companies have an opportunity to develop their capacity to export lower-grade, labor intensive products, buying time while they modernize their operations to regain a greater share of domestic markets. However, they also face even greater assaults on what remains of their protected domestic position. Many companies are attempting to find specialized niche markets, such as for cotton goods.

Trade Associations

Refer to listings under Industry-Specific Trade and Professional Associations in the "Important Addresses" chapter for complete contact information.

Garment Industry National Chamber (Cámara Nacional de la Industria del Vestido)

Rubber Industry National Chamber (Cámara Nacional de la Industria Hulera)

Shoe Industry National Chamber (Cámara Nacional de la Industria del Calzado)

Tannery Industry National Chamber (Cámara Nacional de la Industria de la Curtiduría)

Textile Industry National Chamber (Cámara Nacional de la Industria Textil)

Directories & Periodicals

Refer to listings under Directories, Annuals and Surveys; and Industry-Specific Periodicals in the "Important Addresses" chapter for contact information.

Apparel Industry Magazine (Apparel manufacturing in the USA, Canada, and Latin America)

Apparel: Latin American Industrial Report (Available for each of 22 Latin American countries)

Davison's Textile Blue Book (Mills, dyers and finishers in the US, Canada, and Mexico)

Pequeña Diana (Arts and handicrafts)

Textil Vestido (Apparel industry)

Ultima Moda (Apparel and fashion industry)

Vesti-Noticias (Apparel industry)

Trade Fairs

Refer to the "Trade Fairs" chapter for complete listings, including contact information, dates, and venues. Trade fairs with particular relevance to this industry include the following, which are listed in that chapter under the headings given below:

Footwear & Leather
- APICE
- Expo Piel
- Exposición Nacional Del Calzado
- Sapica
- Selec Moda Primavera/Verano

Sporting Goods & Recreation
- Deporte
- Deportexpo
- Mexiplast
- Sede del Deporte

Textiles & Apparel
- Articulos Para Niños
- Encuentro con la Moda
- Exhimoda Otoño-Invierno
- Exhimoda Primavera-Verano
- Exomtex
- Expo Boda
- Expo Fashion
- Expo Textil
- Expotela
- Sede de la Moda
- Semana Internacional de la Moda
- Textiles

TOOLS AND INSTRUMENTS

Mexican manufacturers supply low-tech laboratory and machine tools, primarily to domestic markets. In some fields, such as glass laboratory equipment, exports are relatively high. However, most exporting is done by *maquila* companies.

Laboratory Instruments

Laboratory analytic instruments are primarily imported, mainly from the US, with local production capturing less than 20 percent of the Mexican market. Mexico exports more than 45 percent of its locally produced laboratory instruments.

Laboratory analytic instruments are manufactured mainly for the chemical, petrochemical, pharmaceutical, and medical industries. The chemical and petrochemical industries alone account for about 27 percent of the total demand for these instruments, while the pharmaceutical and medical industries each account for about 22 percent of total demand. Other industry sectors, such as food and beverage processing, education, and research, also use substantial numbers of these instruments.

Products Domestic production focuses on glassware, a few models of electric measurement equipment, and laboratory furniture. A significant portion of this equipment is at the assembly level under the in-bond program.

Competitive Situation The opportunity exists for Mexico's production of laboratory instruments to expand through concentration on its own domestic markets. Interest in quality control systems, analysis of the environment, limitation of pollution and industrial waste, and life sciences programs is rising in Mexico. Strict enforcement of product standards—*Normas Oficial Mexicana* (Mexican Official Standards)—by the *Secretaría de Comercio y Fomento Industrial* (Secretariat of Commerce and Industrial Development) is expected to boost sales of laboratory instruments in the Mexican market.

Moreover, imported products are not always

suited to Mexican requirements. Imported electric instruments with small tolerances may be damaged by the wider fluctuations that are characteristic of Mexican electric power. Imports may not even be usable with the electric wiring available in many parts of Mexico, and use of US instruments, which are generally calibrated in the English system, is frequently inappropriate because Mexico uses the metric system. These discrepancies leave a gap in market demand that could be captured by domestically designed and produced instruments.

Despite these opportunities, the lack of technological development and skilled labor are major handicaps that Mexico's laboratory instruments industry is not likely to overcome in the near future. Significant technology transfers will be needed for this industry to develop in Mexico to the point at which it can compete in international markets. Foreign companies are optimistic about the Mexican market, partly because of the lack of competition from local producers for technologically advanced products. Mexico's dependence on imports of these instruments is likely to continue to increase.

Machine Tools

Mexico imports more than 80 percent of the grinding machines and other machine tools required by its domestic industries. Only two firms are producing machine tools in Mexico. Local production meets only about 10 percent of total domestic market demand, and exports have dropped significantly since 1991. Many exports are believed to be imported into Mexico for subsequent reexport to other countries, especially in Latin America.

Products Mexican-made machine tools include numerically controlled (NC) grinding machines, high-production cylindrical grinders, interior and flat universal grinding machines, and sharpening tools.

Competitive Situation Low technology and unskilled labor has plagued the Mexican machine tool industry. Moreover, these companies are facing increased foreign competition in their own domestic markets with the ratification of NAFTA and the elimination of ad valorem duties on grinding machines. At the same time, demand in domestic markets is rapidly accelerating, particularly in the automotive, steel, and mining sectors, which need machine tools to manufacture equipment, to make spare parts, and to repair and maintain equipment in use.

Mexican machine tool firms are intensifying their efforts to modernize. New plants and production facilities are being built and older ones refurbished. Changes in production processes are being made so as to enhance efficiency, and product quality is being emphasized.

Significant transfers of technology are needed to make this industry competitive in domestic and foreign markets. To this end, the Mexican government has amended the Foreign Investment Law to allow direct foreign investment of up to 100 percent in machine tool companies. With this incentive, it is hoped that more US producers will enter joint ventures or licensing agreements with Mexican companies to penetrate the Mexican market, bringing much-needed upgrades in technology, automation, and job training.

Government Agencies

Refer to listings under Mexican Government Agencies and Entities in the "Important Addresses" chapter for complete contact information.

Dirección General de Desarrollo Tecnológico (Directorate General of Technology Development)

Dirección General de Normas (Directorate General of Standards)

Instituto Mexicano de Control de Calidad (Mexican Institute of Quality Control)

Laboratorios Nacionales de Fomento Industrial (Industrial Promotion National Laboratories)

Trade Associations

Refer to listings under Industry-Specific Trade and Professional Associations in the "Important Addresses" chapter for complete contact information.

Aluminum Institute (Instituto del Aluminio)

Auto Parts Industry National Association (Asociación de la Industria Nacional de Autopartes)

Auto Parts Wholesalers National Association (Asociación Nacional de Mayoristas de Partes para Automóviles)

Automatic Meter and Control Equipment Manufacturers Association (Asociación Mexicana de Fabricantes de Equipo de Medición y Control Automático)

Automobile Repair Shops Association (Asociación de Talleres Automotrices)

Chemical Industry National Association (Asociación Nacional de la Industria Química)

Chemicals and Pharmaceutical Industry National Chamber (Cámara Nacional de la Industria Química y Farmacéutica)

Construction Industry National Chamber (Cámara Nacional de la Industria de la Construcción)

Copper Association (Asociación Mexicana del Cobre)

Hospital National Chamber (Cámara Nacional de Hospitales)

Household Appliance Manufacturers National Association (Asociación Nacional de Fabricantes de Aparatos Domésticos)

Iron and Steel Industry National Chamber (Cámara Nacional de la Industria del Hierro y del Acero)

Machinery Distributors Association (Asociación Mexicana de Distribuidores de Maquinaria)

Mining Chamber of Mexico (Cámara Minera de México)

Pharmaceutical Association (Asociación Farmacéutica Mexicana)

Pharmaceutical Industry National Chamber (Cámara Nacional de la Industria Farmacéutical)

Pharmaceutical Manufacturers National Association (Asociación Nacional de Fabricantes de Medicamentos)

Valves Manufacturers National Association (Asociación Mexicana de Fabricantes de Valvulas)

Zinc and Lead Institute (Instituto Mexicano del Zinc, Plomo y Coproductos)

Directories & Publications

Refer to listings under Directories, Annuals and Surveys; and Industry-Specific Periodicals in the "Important Addresses" chapter for contact information.

Guía de la Industria: Equipo y Aparatos (Para Laboratorios y Plantas) (Machinery for laboratories and plants)

Guía de la Industria: Laboratorios de Especialades y Control (Laboratory instruments)

Producción Química Mexicana (Chemical engineering)

Agricultura Técnica en México (Agricultural technology)

Constru-Noticias (Building and construction)

Farmacia Actual (Pharmaceuticals)

Ferretecnic—FYT: La Revista de la Industria Ferretera (Metallurgy)

Mercado de las Artes Gráficas (Graphic arts and printing)

Mueble Equipo (Furniture manufacturing equipment)

Tecno Industria (Technology and industry)

Trade Fairs

Refer to the "Trade Fairs" chapter for complete listings, including contact information, dates, and venues. Trade fairs with particular relevance to this industry include the following, which are listed in that chapter under the headings given below:

Automotive
- Auto Show
- Automex
- Autoparts Show
- Expo Internacional RUJAC
- Expo Promoata
- PAACE

Construction & Housing
- Constructo

- Construexpo
- Cuarta Muestra de la Industria de la Construcción
- Expo CIHAC

Machines, Tools & Instruments
- Agroindustrial
- Ambientec
- Analitica y Control 94
- APICE
- CME Mexico
- Expo Metal Mecanica
- Expo Nacional Ferretera
- Exposition de Maquinas de Herramientas
- Maquinamex and Metalmex
- Medi-Lab
- Mexico Hardware Show
- T.M.I.: Techno Mueble Internacional
- USA/Mexico Industrial Expo

TOYS

Toymakers in Mexico primarily supply the domestic markets. Exports of Mexican-made toys are minimal and are made mostly to Central and South America, with a few going to the southern United States. Fewer than 100 companies produce toys in Mexico. Except for a few large plastic toy manufacturers, most Mexican toymakers are small family operations.

Products Mexican toy production still consists primarily of low-technology, traditional handmade wooden toys and games and mass-produced plastic toys and games. These goods are sold primarily in street markets to low-income consumers. Larger manufacturers offer high-quality stuffed animals and inflatable toys, and Mexico is the world's leading manufacturer of plastic balls. Mexico imports most of its electronic games, parts, and components from Japan, Taiwan, Korea, and the US, but some items such as pin-ball machines are assembled in Mexico from US designs.

Competitive Situation

The opening of Mexico's domestic markets to imports in 1986 caused a huge influx of foreign toys, drastically reducing the sales of Mexican-made toys and causing many toy manufacturers to close. Of the nearly 400 toymakers producing goods in Mexico in 1987, nearly three-quarters have ceased operations, and the number of toy companies continues to dwindle. Only about 80 companies remain, and Mexican-made toys now claim only a minute fraction of domestic markets. Remaining Mexican toy manufacturers are fighting for survival.

The years of protectionism gave Mexican toy producers a captive market. Improvements in technology and design were not required and, therefore, not made. Many companies could not afford to modernize after the difficult economic times of the early 1980s. Since trade deregulation, toymakers have been further hurt by tax increases that have effectively reduced their margins, costly financing that has often proved unavailable at any price, and rapidly multiplying government regulations that have forced companies to hire lawyers and consultants to handle compliance and noncompliance claims. As a result, a large number of Mexican toy manufacturers have been unable to invest the funds and time needed to create innovative designs that can compete in novelty-oriented international and domestic toy markets.

Toy manufacturers are under siege from low-priced, illegally imported toys being sold in street markets. Most toymakers in Mexico have been unable to compete with these imports, and they have lost at least 70 percent of the domestic market. Nevertheless, Mexican toymakers are finding ways to avoid total destruction of their industry, and some experts claim that the industry is beginning to stabilize and show signs of new growth.

The larger toy companies are pressuring Mexican authorities to enforce laws against smugglers and to adopt toy safety standards. In response, the Mexican government is investigating dumping charges, increasing tariffs on Chinese-made toys as it drafts the requested standards.

Some toy manufacturers have cut production costs and are modernizing their plants. Others are specializing in certain types of toys; switching from manufacturing to assembling products; or producing high-quality products. A few manufacturers are considering forming joint ventures. Mexican toymakers are also looking beyond Mexico's borders, focusing on export markets and seeking foreign investors for the capital they need to continue and expand operations. In domestic markets, they are promoting the quality of their products and the availability of fast local service.

Trade Associations

Refer to listings under Industry-Specific Trade and Professional Associations in the "Important Addresses" chapter for full contact information.

Electric Manufacturers National Chamber (Cámara Nacional de las Manufacturas Eléctricas (CANAME)

Electronics and Communications Industry National Chamber (Cámara Nacional de la Industria Electronica y de Comunicaciones Eléctricas

Gift, Decoration, and Craft Manufacturers Association of Mexico (Asociación Mexicana de Fabricantes de Artículos para Regalo, Decoración y Artesanías)

Plastic Industries National Association (Asociación Nacional de Industrias del Plástico)

Periodicals

Refer to listings under Industry-Specific Periodicals in the "Important Addresses" chapter for complete contact information.

Energia y Movimiento (Electric toys)
Pequeña Diana (Arts and Handicrafts)
Plasti-Noticias (Plastics)

Trade Fairs

Refer to the "Trade Fairs" chapter for complete listings, including contact information, dates, and venues. Trade fairs with particular relevance to this industry include the following, which are listed in that chapter under the headings given below:

Comprehensive
- Expo Niños

Books & Education
- Feria Internacional del Libro Infantil y Juvenil

Gift & Crafts
- Artesanias Mexicanas de Toda la República

Plastics & Rubber
- Expo Hulera Internacional
- Plast Imagen
- Plásticos

Sporting Goods & Recreation
- Expo Diversiones
- Jugueti Expo

VEHICLES AND VEHICLE PARTS

Automobile and parts assembly plants are among the largest of Mexico's top five manufacturing industries and exporters. Automobiles, engines, and automobile parts represent 30 percent of total manufacturing exports. This industry generates almost 3 percent of Mexico's GDP, and it has been growing at a rate far in excess of Mexico's general economy.

Two-thirds of the vehicles produced are sold domestically, but demand for exports is growing faster than domestic demand. In 1993 Mexico's export of cars and light trucks continued to climb, and spurred by NAFTA, exports are expected to take a giant leap in 1994. The US is the major export market, and Mexico is the fourth leading vehicle supplier and third leading automotive parts supplier to the United States.

An overwhelming share of automobile exports are supplied by *maquila* companies, which have tended to cluster in the border state of Chihuahua. Three foreign-owned vehicle manufacturers dominate Mexico's automobile industry, producing and selling 98 percent of all vehicles and accounting for nearly all vehicle exports. Vehicle parts manufacturers supply these companies, and they supply other domestic and international consumer and industrial markets.

Vehicles

The automobile industry is divided into three sectors: automobiles and light-to-medium trucks, heavy trucks, and buses. Of the 16 automobile plants operating in Mexico, ten are US-owned, two German, three Japanese, and one Mexican. Manufacturing plants that are wholly owned by foreign corporations account for 90 percent of Mexico's production of automobiles, trucks, and motors. The plants that are primarily Mexican-owned manufacture truck trailers, agricultural tractors, and buses. Tractors and trucks of less than 20 tons are produced or assembled by foreign-invested companies in Mexico to supply Mexico's road construction industry.

Vehicle Parts

More than 540 companies manufacture automotive parts in Mexico. Domestic production accounts for less than 30 percent of the market in Mexico. Many parts are imported by *maquila* plants for assembly into reexported vehicles. Vehicle parts made in Mexico include axles, carburetors, clutches, pumps, radiators, aluminum car wheels, shafts, shock absorbers, batteries, mufflers, exhaust pipes, filters, hoses, and transmissions. Mexican vehicle parts manufacturers also supply higher-end components—wire harnesses, upholstery, electrical systems, ABS brakes, windshields, instruments, controls, air bags, safety belts, vehicle bodies, aluminum injection molding, and stereos—to component-assembly plants.

Competitive Situation

All of the major automobile companies in Mexico have expanded their manufacturing facilities in anticipation of increased production and demand under NAFTA. Mexican motor vehicle producers are expected to handle exclusively at least 6 models of cars for foreign-based companies. To meet skyrocketing demands for automobile parts, substantial foreign investment ownership is being permitted under NAFTA.

Vehicle parts manufacturers are attempting to expand and integrate their operations into final assembly plants so as to become direct suppliers of the *maquila* vehicle producers. They are also moving into production of higher-end components, including electrical and electronic components, instruments, high-tech upholstery, plastic and aluminum injection molding, and metal stamped and machined parts.

Government Agencies

Refer to listings under Mexican Government Agencies and Entities in the "Important Addresses" chapter for complete contact information.

Dirección General de Prevención y Control de la Contaminación Ambiental (Directorate General of Environmental Contamination, Prevention and Control)
Secretaría de Comunicaciones y Transportes (Secretariat of Communications and Transportation)

Trade Associations

Refer to listings under Industry-Specific Trade and Professional Associations in the "Important Addresses" chapter for complete contact information.

Auto Parts Industry National Association (Asociación de la Industria Nacional de Autopartes)
Auto Parts Wholesalers National Association (Asociación Nacional de Mayoristas de Partes para Automóviles)
Automobile Repair and Reconstruction Association (Asociación de Rectificadores y Reconstructores Automotrices)
Automobile Repair Shops Association (Asociación de Talleres Automotrices)
Automotive Industry Association (Asociación Mexicana de la Industria Automotriz)
Battery Manufacturers National Association (Asociación Nacional de Fabricantes de Acumuladores)
Iron and Steel Industry National Chamber (Cámara Nacional de la Industria del Hierro y del Acero)
Rubber Industry National Chamber (Cámara Nacional de la Industria Hulera)
Valves Manufacturers National Association (Asociación Mexicana de Fabricantes de Valvulas)

Directories & Periodicals

Refer to listings under Directories, Annuals and Surveys; and Industry-Specific Periodicals in the "Important Addresses" chapter for contact information.

Guía de la Industria: Automotriz (Automotive industry)
Autoindustria (Automotive industry)
Cámara Nacional de la Industria de Transformación: Boletín Informativo (Manufacturing industry)
Más Caminos: Por un Sistema Integral de Transportes (Transportation)

Trade Fairs

Refer to the "Trade Fairs" chapter for complete listings, including contact information, dates, and venues. Trade fairs with particular relevance to this industry include the following, which are listed in that chapter under the headings given below:

Agriculture & Fishing
• AFIA Mexico

- Agroindustrial

Automotive

- AMDA
- Auto Show
- Auto Show Monterrey
- Automechanica
- Automex
- Autoparts Show
- Expo Internacional RUJAC
- Expo Promoata
- PAACE

Transportation

- TransExpo

Trade Fairs

Mexico hosts a wide range of trade fairs and expositions that should interest anyone seeking to do business in the country's dynamic, expanding economy. Whether the aim is to buy Mexican goods or offer your own goods and services for sale in the Mexican market, you will almost undoubtedly find several trade fairs that suit your purposes. Mexico is also a major site for international trade fairs for companies from Latin American nations, attracting exhibitors and buyers from many other countries as well.

The listing of trade fairs in this section is designed to acquaint you with the scope, size, frequency, and length of the events held in Mexico and to give you contact information for the organizers. While every effort has been made to ensure that this information is correct and complete as of press time, the scheduling of such events is in constant flux. Announced exhibitions may be canceled; dates and venues are often shifted. If you are interested in attending or exhibiting at a show listed here, we urge you to contact the organizer well in advance to confirm the venue and dates and to ascertain whether the event is appropriate for you. (*See* Tips for Attending a Trade Fair, following this introduction, for further suggestions on selecting, attending, and exhibiting at trade fairs.) When you are deciding whether to participate in a trade fair—as an exhibitor or as an attendee—the information in this chapter will give a significant head start.

In order to give you the easiest possible access to this information, fairs have been grouped alphabetically by product category, and within product category, alphabetically by name. Product categories, with cross-references, are given in a table of contents following the introduction. Note that the first heading listed is out of alphabetical order—trade fairs listed under *Comprehensive* do not focus on a single type of product, but instead showcase a broad range of goods, perhaps from one geographic area or centered around a particular theme. When appropriate, fairs have been listed in more than one category. The breadth of products on display at a given

fair means that you may want to investigate categories that are not immediately obvious. Many exhibits include the machinery, tools, and raw materials used to produce the products associated with the central theme of a fair. Anyone interested in such items should consider a wide range of the listings.

The list gives the names and dates of both recent and upcoming events, together with site and contact information and a description of the products featured. Many shows take place on a regular basis—annual or biennial schedules are common. When we were able to confirm the frequency of a show through independent sources, it has been indicated. Many others on the list may also be regular events, although some are one-time events. Because specifics on frequency are sometimes difficult to ascertain and because schedules for a few 1994 and many 1995 shows were not available at press time, we have given both recent and future dates. It is quite possible that a fair listed for 1993 will be held again in 1994 or 1995, so it would be worthwhile getting in touch with the contact listed for any show that looks interesting. Even if we were unable to confirm the frequency, you can infer a likely time cycle if several dates are given for a fair.

As you gather further information on fairs that appeal to you, do not be surprised if the names are slightly different from those listed here. Some large trade fairs include several smaller exhibits, and some use short names or acronyms, and Spanish names may have been translated or transcribed in a variety of ways. Dates and venues, of course, are always subject to change.

TRADE FAIR VENUES IN MEXICO

There are now nearly 200 established trade fairs in Mexico, a number that is expected to grow quickly during the next few years. One interesting aspect of the country's trade show industry is that Mexico City is not the primary location for exhibits. A third of the major shows in 1993 were held at Expo

Guadalajara, Mexico's largest facility, and nearly as many were held at Cintermex in Monterrey. If you are exporting out of Mexico, it may also be helpful to contact Cintermex about their Permanent Business Center, which displays and promotes Mexican goods, with an emphasis on those from the state of Nuevo León.

Mexico City does not have one dominant venue. Exhibimex, a converted supermarket, is currently the major exhibit facility in Mexico City, although the 1995 renovation of the World Trade Center is expected to boost the attractiveness of that site. The Palacio Mundial de las Ferias and the US Trade Center are the next most popular venues, while the larger hotels host most of the remaining shows.

US exporters are well served by the US Trade Center. In operation since 1972, it hosts a wide range of events, including about a dozen trade shows annually for US manufacturers looking for buyers or distributors. Any exhibitor at one of these shows may take advantage of their RepFind service, which arranges at no extra charge several meetings with potential Mexican representatives, distributors, or agents. Catalog shows, seminars, conferences, trade missions, and other US trade-related events are held at the Trade Center as well. Facilities and services include four exhibit halls, seminar rooms, a meeting room, simultaneous translation equipment, and the services of bilingual Trade Aides. Occasionally there are US pavilions set up by the Trade Center at large international exhibits. The Trade Center is also involved in events in Guadalajara, Monterrey, and other cities, often sharing the coordination with the local US consulates.

Expo Guadalajara
Centro de Exposiciones
Av. Mariano Otero 1499
44550 Guadalajara, Jal., México
Tel: [52] (3) 671-0555, 671-0099
Fax: [52] (3) 671-0044

Centro Internacional de Negocios Monterrey, A.C.
(Cintermex)
Av. Fundidora 501
64010 Monterrey, NL, México
Tel: [52] (83) 69-6944, 69-6969
Fax: [52] (83) 69-6911, 69-6932

Exhibimex Salon de Exposiciones
Av. Cuauhtémoc frente al Centro Medico
06700 México, DF, México
Tel: [52] (5) 520-6824 Fax: [52] (5) 584-1710

World Trade Center Mexico City
Montecito 38, Piso 34
Col. Nápoles
03810 México, DF, México
Tel: [52] (5) 660-3917 x4796, 682-9822
Fax: [52] (5) 682-1067, 543-1324

Palacio Mundial de las Ferias
La Fragua No. 4
Col. Centro Historico
México, DF, México
Tel: [52] (5) 705-6341 Fax: [52] (5) 592-6748

US Trade Center Mexico
Liverpool 31
Col. Juárez
06600 México, DF, México
Tel: [52] (5) 591-0155 Fax: [52] (5) 566-1115
US mailing address: PO Box 3087, Laredo, TX 78044-3087, USA

EXHIBITING IN MEXICO

Facilities and procedures are not as standardized in Mexico as they are in the US, Japan, or Europe. Take special care to read whatever literature you receive and to talk to the organizers as well as people who have exhibited at the same facility or trade show. Booth sizes are metric, and the types of displays commonly used are different than those in the US. Consider renting an exhibit in Mexico rather than importing one. This will not only give greater assurance that dimensions and other specifications will be appropriate, but will also reduce the amount of material which must clear customs. While you can bring in exhibits and other materials as temporary imports, which reduces your customs duties, plenty of paperwork is still involved. The US Trade Center offers in-bond facilities that permit temporary importation of display equipment without prior licensing or payment of duties, but certain Mexican government and customs broker fees will still be required. In most cases it is easier to import as little as possible and pay the applicable duties on what you do bring in. In some cases it will be cheaper to leave items in Mexico than to ship them back.

Whether you bring in your own exhibit or rent one, keep in mind that once you get it to the hall, it will have to be set up. Mexico does not have the overbearing union rules (and charges) governing the setup and breakdown of booths commonly found elsewhere, but neither will you find a cadre of workers ready to whisk your goods into the exhibit hall when you arrive—unless you've arranged for them in advance. Be sure to communicate with the show organizers about the appropriate arrangements to make for hiring laborers.

FOR FURTHER INFORMATION

The Trade Commission of Mexico's 24-hour Information Service in Los Angeles is a good place to start. Call [1] (213) 628-8966 from your handset-equipped fax machine, listen to the recorded message, and request the complete menu of information, which will be sent to your fax machine at the end of the call. One of the menu items will be a current list of upcoming trade shows in Mexico. This number can be called from outside the US, but non-US residents may want to contact a Trade Commission of Mexico office in their country first. (Refer to the "Important Addresses" chapter for a complete listing of offices worldwide.) US businesspeople, particularly those who are selling or looking for Mexican representatives, should contact the US Trade Center in Mexico City. The Trade Center keeps an updated list of trade fairs in Mexico, both events that they sponsor directly and others of which they are aware or in which they are involved more peripherally. In addition, the Trade Center sponsors trade missions, catalog shows, and other events that help promote exports from the US. Note that the mailing address is in the US (to circumvent the notoriously slow Mexican postal system), although the office itself is located in Mexico City. If you reside outside the US, contact the commercial section of your country's embassy in Mexico City for details about trade show and trade mission sponsorships available to you.

Trade Commission of Mexico
World Trade Center
350 S Figueroa St., Suite 296
Los Angeles, CA 90071, USA
Tel: [1] (213) 628-1220 Fax: [1] (213) 628-8466
24-hour Information Service
Tel/Fax: [1] (213) 628-8966
Note: You must call this number from a fax machine equipped with a handset.

US Trade Center Mexico
Mailing address:
PO Box 3087
Laredo, TX 78044-3087, USA
Tel: [52] (5) 591-0155 Fax: [52] (5) 566-1115

If you are looking for US and international listings in general, the quarterly publication *The Exhibit Review* is a valuable resource; it also provides a custom report service with updated listings of trade fairs in any country the periodical covers. While the majority of listings are for US events, *The Exhibit Review* has been expanding its international coverage and is well worth consulting. In addition, the Trade Show Bureau is a research and promotion organization for the exposition industry and has a wide range of publications and reports available which can help increase the efficacy of a trade fair for both attendees and exhibitors.

The Exhibit Review
4620 SW Beaverton-Hillsdale Hwy., Suite B-1
Portland, OR 97221, USA
Tel: [1] (503) 244-8677 Fax: [1] (503) 244-8745

The Trade Show Bureau
1660 Lincoln St., Suite 2080
Denver, CO 80264, USA
Tel: [1] (303) 860-7626 Fax: [1] (303) 860-7479

Contacting the major trade show venues directly is another good strategy, particularly if you are already traveling to a particular area. (See the list of the primary venues above.) Other valuable sources of information include the commercial sections of Mexico's overseas diplomatic missions, chambers of commerce in Mexico, other business organizations dedicated to trade between your country and Mexico, and the embassy or consulates of your own country located in Mexico. Professional and trade organizations in Mexico involved in your area of interest may also be worth contacting. (Refer to the "Important Addresses" chapter for Mexican embassies, consulates, chambers of commerce and business organizations, diplomatic missions located in Mexico, and trade organizations.)

FURTHER READING

Mexico's Exposition Industry, Trade Show Bureau, 1660 Lincoln Street, Suite 2080, Denver, CO 80264, USA; Tel: [1] (303) 860-7626 Fax: [1] (303) 860-7479.

Exhibitor's Handbook: Mexico, by Wendell R. Deaton. Available from: Proteus Publishing, PO Box 2940, Ann Arbor, MI 48106, USA; Tel: [1] (313) 668-2734.

The Exhibit Manager's Companion: Exhibiting in Mexico, available from Marketech, Inc., 8532 S. Florence Ave., Tulsa, OK 74137, USA; Tel: [1] (918) 481-0607.

Marketing by Exhibiting in the Global Market: A Complete Handbook to International Exhibiting, by Michael S. Muribi and Carol A. Fojtik. Available from: Expressions International, Inc., 330 N. Garfield, Suite 110, Lombard, IL 60148, USA; Tel: [1] (708) 495-8740.

TIPS FOR ATTENDING TRADE FAIRS

Overseas trade fairs can be extremely effective for making face-to-face contacts and sales or purchases, identifying suppliers, checking out competitors, and finding out how business really works in the host country. However, the cost of attending such fairs can be high. To maximize the return on your investment of time, money, and energy, you should be very clear about your goals for the trip and give yourself plenty of time for advance research and preparation.

You should also be aware of the limitations of trade fairs. The products on display probably do not represent the full range of goods available on the market. In fact, some of the latest product designs may still be under wraps. And while trade fairs give you an opportunity to make face-to-face contacts with many people, both exhibitors and buyers are rushed, which makes meaningful discussions and negotiations difficult.

These drawbacks can easily be minimized if you have sufficient preparation and background information. Allow several months for preparation—more if you first need to identify the fair that you will attend. Even under ideal circumstances, you should begin laying the groundwork a year in advance. Don't forget that exhibiting at or attending a fair in a foreign country means more complex logistics: numerous faxes and phone calls involving you, the show operator, and local support people, plus customs and transportation delays.

Participating in international trade fairs, particularly at the outset, should be considered a means of fulfilling long-term goals. At domestic fairs, you may exhibit on a regular basis with short-term sales and marketing goals. But at a foreign fair, it is often best to participate as a way to establish your company, make contacts for the future, and learn more about a market, its consumers, and products. New exporters may not generate high sales, but they often come away with information that assists them with future marketing and product development.

Selecting an appropriate trade fair

Consult the listings of trade fairs in this book to find some that interest you. Note the suggestions in this chapter for finding the most current calendars of upcoming fairs. Once you have identified some fairs, contact the organizers for literature, including a show prospectus, attendee list, and exhibitor list. Ask plenty of questions! Be sure not to neglect trade organizations in the host country, independent show-auditing firms, and recent attendees. Find out whether there are "must attend" fairs for your particular product group. Fairs that concentrate on other, but related, commodities might also be a good match. Be aware that there may be preferred seasons for trade in certain products.

Your research needs to cover a number of points:

Audience • Who is the intended audience? Is the fair open to the public or to trade professionals only? Are the exhibitors primarily foreigners looking for local buyers or locals looking for foreign buyers? (Many trade fairs are heavily weighted to one or the other.) Decide whether you are looking for an exposition of general merchandise produced in one region, a commodity-specific trade show, or both.

Statistics • How many people attended the fair the last time it was held? What were the demographics? What volume of business was done? How many exhibitors were there? How big is the exhibition space? What was the ratio of foreign to domestic attendees and exhibitors?

Specifics • Who are the major exhibitors? Are any particular publications or organizations associated with the fair? On what categories of products does the fair focus? Does the fair have a theme that changes each time? How long has the fair been in existence? How often is it held? Is it always in the same location, or does it move each time? How much does it cost to attend? Are there any separate or special programs connected with the event, and do they require additional entrance fees? What does it cost to rent space?

Before you go

• If you have not already spoken with someone who attended the fair in the past, be sure to find someone who will give you advice, tips, and general information.

- Make your reservations and travel arrangements well in advance, and figure out how you are going to get around once you get there. Even if the fair takes place in a large city, do not assume that getting around will be easy during a major trade fair. If the site is in a small city or a less-developed area, the transportation and accommodation systems are likely to become overburdened sooner than in metropolitan areas.
- Will you need an interpreter for face-to-face business negotiations? A translation service to handle documents? Try to line up providers well in advance of your need for their services.
- For printed materials, pay attention to language barriers and make preparations that will help you overcome them. Assess your literature and decide what should be available in translation or in bilingual editions. Have the translation work done by a true professional, particularly if technical terms are used. Consider having a bilingual business card, and add the country and international dialing code information to the address and telephone number. Find out from the show organizers which countries will be represented, and prepare information in the languages of those countries as well, if necessary.
- Do you need hospitality suites and/or conference rooms? Reserve them as soon as you can.
- Contact people you would like to meet before you go. Organize your appointments around the fair.
- Familiarize yourself with the show's hours, locations (if exhibits and events are staged at multiple venues), and the schedule of events. Then prioritize.

While you are there

- Wear businesslike clothes that are comfortable. Find out what the norm is for the area and the season.
- Immediately after each contact, write down as much information as you can. Do not depend on remembering it. Several companies now make inexpensive portable business card scanners with optical character recognition (OCR) software to read the information into a contact management program.
- Be sensitive to the selling styles of the country you are in. Are hard-sell approaches taboo? Are you dealing with the right person? Status within one's company is often very important; someone may want to be clear about your position, and you will want to be sure your aren't causing offense by going to the wrong level.
- Consider arriving a day early to get fully oriented, confirm appointments, and rest up.
- It's common sense: make sure you take breaks, even if you have to schedule them. You'll end up having far more energy and being more effective.

After the fair

- Within a week after the fair, write letters to new contacts and follow up on requests for literature. If you have press releases and questionnaires, send them out quickly as well.
- Write a report evaluating your experiences while they are still fresh in your mind. Even if you don't have to prepare a formal report, spend some time organizing your thoughts on paper for future reference. Aim to quantify the results. Did you meet your goals? Why or why not? What would you do differently? What unforeseen costs or problems arose?
- With your new contacts and your experiences in mind, start preparing for your next trade fair.

If you are selling

- Familiarize yourself with import regulations for products that you wish to exhibit at the fair.
- Set specific goals for sales leads, developing product awareness, selling and positioning current customers, and gathering industry information. For example, target the numbers of contacts made, orders written, leads converted into sales, visitors at presentations, brochures or samples distributed, customers entertained, and seminars attended. You can also set goals for total revenue from sales, cost-to-return benefit ratio, amount of media coverage, and amount of competitor information obtained.

- Review your exhibitor kit. Is there a show theme that you can tie into? Pay particular attention to the show's hours and regulations, payment policies, shipping instructions and dates, telephone installation policies, security, fire regulations, and extra-cost services.
- Find out about the labor situation. Is it unionized, and what are the regulations? Will you have to hire your own workers to set up and break down the booth, or can the organizer or showcase facility provide them for you?
- Gear your advertising and product demonstrations to the expected target audience. Should you stress certain aspects of your product line? Will you need brochures and banners in different languages? Even if you do not need to translate the materials currently in use into another language, will you need to rewrite them for a different culture? Consider advertising in publications that will be distributed at the fair.
- Plan the display in your booth carefully; you will have only a few seconds to grab the viewer's attention. Secure a location in a high-traffic area—for example, near a door, a restroom, a refreshment area, or a major exhibitor. For banners use copy that is brief and effective. Focus on the product and its benefits. Place promotional materials and giveaways near the back wall so that people have to enter your area, but make sure that they do not feel trapped. If you plan to use videotapes or other multimedia, make sure that you have enough space. Remember to ascertain whether you will need special equipment or equipment for different current. Such presentations are often better suited to hospitality suites, because lights are bright and noise levels high in exhibition halls.
- Attend to the details. Order office supplies and printed materials that you will need for the booth. Have all your paperwork—order forms, business cards, exhibitor kit and contract, copies of advance orders and checks, travel documents, and so on—in order and at hand. If you ordered a telephone line, obtain your own host-country compatible telephone or arrange to rent one. Draw up a schedule for staffing the booth.
- Plan and rehearse your sales pitch in advance, preferably in a space similar to the size of your booth.
- Do not sit, eat, drink, or smoke while you are in the booth.
- If you plan to return to the next show, reserve space while you are still on-site.

If you are buying

- Familiarize yourself with customs regulations on the products that you seek to purchase and import into your own country or elsewhere. Be sure to get such information on any and all products that you might be interested in.
- Set specific goals for supplier leads and for gathering industry information. For example, target the numbers of contacts made, leads converted to purchases, seminars and presentations attended, and booths visited. Other goals might be cost-to-return benefit ratio, amount of competitor information gathered, and percentage of projected purchases actually made.
- List all the products that you seek to purchase, their specifications, and the number of units you plan to purchase of each.
- Know the retail and wholesale market prices for the goods in your home country and in the country where you will be buying. List the highest price you can afford to pay for each item and still get a worthwhile return.
- List the established and probable suppliers for each of the products or product lines that you plan to import. Include addresses and telephone numbers and note your source for the information. Before you go, contact suppliers to confirm who will attend and to make appointments.

TRADE FAIRS
TABLE OF CONTENTS

Trade Fair	Site/Date	Contact

COMPREHENSIVE   Trade fairs exhibiting a wide range of goods

Trade Fair	Site/Date	Contact
Arte Nupcial Wedding articles exhibition	Monterrey Cintermex May 11–16, 1994	Cintermex Ave. Fundidora 501 64010 Monterrey, NL, México Tel: [52] (83) 69-6944, 69-6969 Fax: [52] (83) 69-6911 Contact: Alejandro Monroy
Canaexpo Commercial trade show from Canada	Mexico City April 12–18, 1994	Canadian Embassy Schiller 529 Col. Polanco 11000 México, DF, México Tel: [52] (5) 254-3288 Fax: [52] (5) 545-1764
Commercial Fair of the Americas Wide variety of consumer goods and services including food products, banking, travel, gifts, import-export, automobiles, franchise and business opportunities. Size: 5,000 attendees; 110 exhibitors.	Guadalajara Carlton Hotel Annual Nov. 30–Dec. 1, 1994	Commercial Fair of the Americas 106 W. 32nd St., 6th Floor New York, NY 10001, USA Tel: [1] (212) 279-3737 Fax: [1] (212) 279-3846 Contact: Dave Gonzales, VP of International Marketing
Expo Merceria Beauty and health equipment, supplies, services exhibition and seminar. Manufacturers, distributors and buyers of sewing supplies, fabrics, needlework, knitting, and crafts.	Mexico City World Trade Center March 8–11, 1994	Tradex Exposiciones Internacionales Río Churubusco No. 422 Col. Del Carmen Coyoacán 04100 México, DF, México Tel: [52] (5) 659-1631 Fax: [52] (5) 554-3616
Expo Niños Apparel, toys, games, educational materials for young children	Monterrey Cintermex November 18–20, 1994	Cintermex Ave. Fundidora 501 64010 Monterrey, NL, México Tel: [52] (83) 69-6944, 69-6969 Fax: [52] (83) 69-6911 Contact: Alejandro Monroy
Exposición y Conferencias Tecnos International technological development show	Monterrey Cintermex October 20–23, 1993	Cintermex Ave. Fundidora 501 64010 Monterrey, NL, México Tel: [52] (83) 69-6944, 69-6969 Fax: [52] (83) 69-6911 Contact: Alejandro Monroy
Mercatodo/General Merchandise Show of Mexico	Guadalajara Expo Guadalajara May 12–14, 1994	Cámara Nacional de Comercio de Guadalajara Avenida Vallarta No. 4095 Col. Don Bosco Vallarta Guadalajara, Jal., México Tel: [52] (3) 647-3300 Fax: [52] (3) 647-8111

AEROSPACE

Trade Fair	Site/Date	Contact
AERO Aeronautic industry exhibition	Guadalajara Expo Guadalajara April 20–22, 1994	Universal de Servicios, S.A. de C.V. Lerdo de Tejada No. 2339, Int. 8 Col. Americana Guadalajara, Jal., México Tel: [52] (3) 615-4279 Fax: [52] (3) 615-4279

AGRICULTURE & FISHING   *See also:* Food, Restaurants & Hotels

Trade Fair	Site/Date	Contact
AFIA Mexico Agroindustry and livestock exhibition	Guadalajara Expo Guadalajara June 16–18, 1994	Organización de Promociones y Exposiciones, S.A. de C.V. Aviacion Comercial No. 42 Fracc. Industrial Puerto Aereo 15710 México, DF, México Tel: [52] (5) 785-7553 Fax: [52] (5) 785-7638

Trade Fair	Site/Date	Contact
Agroindustrial Exhibition and seminar of agricultural machinery, equipment and supplies. Size: 4,000 attendees; 60 exhibitors.	Mexico City US Trade Center Annual January 25–29, 1995 1996 dates TBA	US Trade Center Mexico PO Box 3087 Laredo, TX 78044-3087, USA Tel: [52] (5) 591-0155 Fax: [52] (5) 566-1115
Agroindustrial Exhibition and seminar of agricultural machinery, equipment and supplies	Guadalajara Expo Guadalajara January 27–30, 1994	Grupo Gefecc, S.A. de C.V. Av. Baja California No. 32-A Col. Roma Sur 06760 México, DF, México Tel: [52] (5) 564-0329, 264-7029 Fax: [52] (5) 574-5696, 564-7040
Expo Lacteos International machinery, equipment and dairy products fair	Guadalajara Expo Guadalajara February 3–6, 1994	Grupo Gefecc, S.A. de C.V. Av. Baja California No. 32-A Col. Roma Sur 06760 México, DF, México Tel: [52] (5) 564-0329, 264-7029 Fax: [52] (5) 574-5696, 564-7040
PESCA International commercial fishing and aquaculture exhibition and conference	Veracruz ExpoVer June 8–12, 1994	Expoavance One Liberty Square Boston, MA 02109, USA Tel: [1] (617) 426-6440 Fax: [1] (617) 426-6441 Contact: Kerry Mott

AUTOMOTIVE

Trade Fair	Site/Date	Contact
AMDA Automobile distributors' exhibition	Monterrey Cintermex October 7–10, 1993	Cintermex Ave. Fundidora 501 64010 Monterrey, NL, México Tel: [52] (83) 69-6944, 69-6969 Fax: [52] (83) 69-6911 Contact: Alejandro Monroy
Auto Show Trade show for auto parts, components, accessories, dealers and conversions	Monterrey Cintermex November 17–21, 1993 November 9–13, 1994	Organización y Promoción de Eventos Especializados Rayón No. 675 Col. Moderna Guadalajara, Jal., México Tel: [52] (3) 625-6350 Fax: [52] (3) 625-6350
Auto Show Monterrey In association with the Automobile Dealers Association in Monterrey	Monterrey Cintermex December 1–4, 1994	Source Mexico Consultants, L.C. 118 Broadway, Suite 634 San Antonio, TX 78205, USA Tel: [1] (210) 227-2502 Fax: [1] (210) 229-9761
Automechanica Open to US manufacturers of auto parts, maintenance and repair equipment and car accessories. Sponsored by the US Trade Center.	Mexico City US Trade Center March 9–11, 1993 February 7–9, 1995	US Trade Center Mexico PO Box 3087 Laredo, TX 78044-3087, USA Tel: [52] (5) 591-0155 Fax: [52] (5) 566-1115 Contact: Raquel Polo
Automex Automotive and related industries	Puebla Expo Puebla March 5–13, 1994	PROFEI, S.A. de C.V. Av. Insurgentes Centro No. 132, Desp. 212 Col. Tabacalera 06030 México, DF, México Tel: [52] (5) 592-8105 Fax: [52] (5) 546-6336
Autoparts Show	Monterrey Cintermex August 25–27, 1994	APEX, A.C. Av. Parque Fundidora No. 501-22 Col. Obrera 64010 Monterrey, NL, México Tel: [52] (83) 69-6660 Fax: [52] (83) 69-6660

Trade Fair	Site/Date	Contact
Expo Internacional RUJAC Autoparts exhibition	Guadalajara Expo Guadalajara August 24–26, 1994	Refacciones Unidas de Jalisco General Coronado No. 132 Guadalajara, Jal., México Tel: [52] (3) 625-4202 Fax: [52] (3) 625-4202
Expo Promoata Autoparts and after-market accessories	Mexico City Palacio Mundial de las Ferias April 13–15, 1994	Promoata Oaxaca No. 12-4 Col. Roma 05600 México, DF, México Tel: [52] (5) 525-0012 Fax: [52] (5) 208-2254
PAACE Pan-American auto components and accessories exposition	Mexico City Annual July 26–28, 1994	William T. Glasgow, Inc. 16066 S. Park Ave. South Holland, IL 60473, USA Tel: [1] (708) 333-9292 Fax: [1] (708) 333-4086

BOOKS & EDUCATION

Trade Fair	Site/Date	Contact
Expo Didactica Educational materials	Mexico City Exhibimex February 22–25, 1994	Reed Exhibition Companies Prolongación Calle 18 No. 205 Col. San Pedro de los Pinos 01180 México, DF, México Tel: [52] (5) 515-2610 Fax: [52] (5) 273-0312
Expo Educación Cultural and educational exposition	Monterrey Cintermex April 21–24, 1994	Cintermex Ave. Fundidora 501 64010 Monterrey, NL, México Tel: [52] (83) 69-6944, 69-6969 Fax: [52] (83) 69-6911 Contact: Alejandro Monroy
Expo Esco Educational materials	Monterrey Cintermex May 25–29, 1994	Expo Monfer Av. Fundidora No. 501 Local 14 Col. Obrera 64010 Monterrey, NL, México Tel: [52] (83) 69-6961 Fax: [52] (83) 69-6962
Feria Internacional del Libro International book fair	Monterrey Cintermex October 8–16, 1994	ITESM Av. Garza Sada No. 2501 Col. Tecnologico Monterrey, NL, México Tel: [52] (83) 58-2000 x4025 Fax: [52] (83) 59-2000
Feria Internacional del Libro International book fair	Guadalajara Expo Guadalajara Nov. 26–Dec. 4, 1994	Universidad de Guadalajara Avenida Hidalgo No. 1417 Col. Artesanos Guadalajara, Jal., México Tel: [52] (3) 625-2817, 625-8662 Fax: [52] (3) 625-7359
Feria Internacional del Libro **Infantil y Juvenil** International children's book fair	Mexico City December 3–19, 1993	Consejo Nacional Para la Cultura y Las Artes Tel: [52] (5) 548-2908
Feria International del Libro International book fair	Mexico City Palacio de Mineria Feb. 26–Mar. 3, 1994	Universidad Nacional Autonoma de Mexico Tacuba No. 5 06000 México, DF, México Tel: [52] (5) 512-8723 Fax: [52] (5) 512-8956

BUSINESS SERVICES

Trade Fair	Site/Date	Contact
Banking, Insurance and Tech	Mexico City January 1, 1994	US Trade Center Mexico PO Box 3087 Laredo, TX 78044-3087, USA Tel: [52] (5) 591-0155 Fax: [52] (5) 566-1115

Trade Fair	Site/Date	Contact
Credi Expo Bank and credit institutions	Monterrey Cintermex October 13–16, 1994	Cintermex Ave. Fundidora 501 64010 Monterrey, NL, México Tel: [52] (83) 69-6944, 69-6969 Fax: [52] (83) 69-6911 Contact: Alejandro Monroy
Expo Publicitas Advertising and publicity exhibition	Guadalajara Expo Guadalajara March 9–11, 1994	Exposición Publicitaria Guadalajara Francisco Rojas No. 453 Col. Ladron de Guervara 44600 Guadalajara, Jal., México Tel: [52] (3) 615-2663 Fax: [52] (3) 630-0797
Expo Servicios Services exhibition	Mexico City World Trade Center April 26–29, 1994	Tradex Exposiciones Internationales Río Churubusco No. 422 Col. Del Carmen Coyoacán 04100 México, DF, México Tel: [52] (5) 659-1631 Fax: [52] (5) 554-3616
Expo Servicios al Comercio Exterior Export-import agents and services	Monterrey Cintermex April 14–16, 1994	Cintermex Ave. Fundidora 501 64010 Monterrey, NL, México Tel: [52] (83) 69-6944, 69-6969 Fax: [52] (83) 69-6911 Contact: Alejandro Monroy
Shopping Center Developments in Mexico Opportunities in Mexico for US chain stores, franchisers, real estate development firms, and investors	Mexico City Presidente Hotel Annual April 25–27, 1994	Colchester Group 1220 4th St., Suite D Santa Rosa, CA 95404, USA Tel: [1] (707) 573-0583 Fax: [1] (707) 573-1082 Contact: Richard Abel

CLEANING

Trade Fair	Site/Date	Contact
Expo Clean Cleaning machinery and products	Guadalajara Expo Guadalajara April 14–16, 1994	Grupo Direxa Alvaro Obregón No. 541 Norte Monterrey, NL, México Tel: [52] (83) 746-418, 746-428 Fax: [52] (83) 722-191
Expo Tintoreria y Lavanderia Dry cleaner and laundry equipment exhibition	Mexico City June 24–26, 1994	Luis Quest, S.A. de C.V. Tel: [52] (5) 256-3399 Fax: [52] (5) 256-2958

COMPUTERS, ELECTRONICS & COMMUNICATIONS

Trade Fair	Site/Date	Contact
Banking, Insurance and Tech	Mexico City January 1, 1994	US Trade Center Mexico PO Box 3087 Laredo, TX 78044-3087, USA Tel: [52] (5) 591-0155 Fax: [52] (5) 566-1115
C.E.S. Mexico Consumer electronics show	Mexico City Palacio de los Desportes October 4–6, 1994	International Trade Information, Inc. 21031 Ventura Blvd., Suite 405 Woodland Hills, CA 91364, USA Tel: [1] (818) 340-8864 Fax: [1] (818) 340-7017
Comdex/ComExpo Mexico Worldwide manufacturers of small computer systems, peripherals, multimedia, networks, software, accessories, services and supplies which are resold to the end user. Size: 38,000+ attendees.	Mexico City World Trade Center March 8–11, 1994 March 7–10, 1995	The Interface Group 300 First Ave. Needham, MA 02194-2722, USA Tel: [1] (617) 449-6600 Fax: [1] (617) 449-6953 Contact: Cathy Selvatella
Compuexpo Electronics exhibition	Guadalajara Expo Guadalajara January 26–29, 1994	Compuexpo, A.C. Justo Sierra No. 2786-9 Col. Ladron de Guevara 44690 Guadalajara, Jal., México Tel: [52] (3) 616-3166 Fax: [52] (3) 616-6455

Trade Fair	Site/Date	Contact
Compumundo Computers	Mexico City October 19–22, 1993 October 18–21, 1994	Compu-Com Internacional González de Cosio 334 Col. del Valle 03100 México, DF, México Tel: [52] (5) 669-4672, 563-7507 Fax: [52] (5) 664-1140
Electronica Electronic components, production and test equipment for the electronics industry and electrical equipment. Size: 2,500 attendees; 65 exhibitors.	Mexico City US Trade Center Every 2 years June 7-9, 1994 1996 dates TBA	US Trade Center Mexico PO Box 3087 Laredo, TX 78044-3087, USA Tel: [52] (5) 591-0155 Fax: [52] (5) 566-1115
ExpoComm Mexico International telecommunications, computer and office automation exhibition and conference for Latin America. Size: 10,500 attendees; 350 booths.	Mexico City Camino Real Hotel Annual February 17–20, 1995	E.J. Krause & Associates, Inc. 7315 Wisconsin Ave., Suite 450 North Bethesda, MD 20814, USA Tel: [1] (301) 986-7800 Fax: [1] (301) 986-4538 Contact: Billi Famiglietti
Expo Electronica Consumer electronics show for dealers and distributors, organized with the Cámara Nacional de la Industria Electronica y de Comunicaciones Electricas	Mexico City World Trade Center April 19–22, 1994 May, 1995	Reed Exhibition Companies Prolongación Calle 18 No. 205 Col. San Pedro de los Pinos 01180 México, DF, México Tel: [52] (5) 515-2610 Fax: [52] (5) 273-0312
Exposición y Conferencias Tecnos International technological development show	Monterrey Cintermex October 20–23, 1993 October 19–21, 1994	Cintermex Ave. Fundidora 501 64010 Monterrey, NL, México Tel: [52] (83) 69-6944, 69-6969 Fax: [52] (83) 69-6911 Contact: Alejandro Monroy
Identimex International exhibition and conference of bar coding and automated data collection technologies. Size: 2,500 attendees; 60 exhibitors.	Mexico City Camino Real Hotel Annual February 22–24, 1995	Expocon Management Associates, Inc. 7 Cambridge Dr., PO Box 1019 Trumbull, CT 06611, USA Tel: [1] (203) 374-1411 Fax: [1] (203) 374-9667 Contact: Peter Nathan, x104
Latin American Imaging & Information Technology Exhibition & Conference Networking, open systems, work station exhibition	Mexico City Maria Isabel Sheraton October 25–27, 1994	Hoffman Business Connections, Inc. 345 Woodcliff Dr. Fairport, NY 11450, USA Tel: [1] (716) 383-8330 Fax: [1] (716) 383-8442
MacWorld Expo For business, professional, governmental and general users of Macintosh computers, their products and services	Mexico City September 21–23, 1993	World Expo Corp. PO Box 9107 Framingham, MA 01701-9107, USA Tel: [1] (508) 879-6700 Fax: [1] (508) 872-8237
MexCom Communications equipment including VSAT, multimedia, cable and wiring	Mexico City Maria Isabel Sheraton January 25–27, 1995	Latcom, Inc. 9200 S. Dadeland Blvd., Suite 309 Miami, FL 33156-2703, USA Tel: [1] (305) 670-9444 Fax: [1] (305) 670-9459
Software Packaged and custom software products exhibition and seminar	Mexico City US Trade Center August 3–5, 1993	US Trade Center Mexico PO Box 3087 Laredo, TX 78044-3087, USA Tel: [52] (5) 591-0155 Fax: [52] (5) 566-1115
TelNets Telecom, computer, and data-com networks for the end user, focusing on data networks, hardware/software, and business services	Monterrey Cintermex May 18–20, 1994	Latcom, Inc. 9200 S. Dadeland Blvd., Suite 309 Miami, FL 33156-2703, USA Tel: [1] (305) 670-9444 Fax: [1] (305) 670-9459

CONSTRUCTION & HOUSING *See also:* Furniture & Housewares

Concreto Exposition of concrete	Acapulco April 25–29, 1994	Lic. Carlos Calvillo Tel: [52] (5) 662-6356 Fax: [52] (5) 661-3282, 661-4659

Trade Fair	Site/Date	Contact
Constructo Building materials and construction industry trade show	Monterrey Cintermex October 13–16, 1993 October 26–29, 1994	APEX, A.C. Av. Parque Fundidora No. 501 Local 22 Col. Obrera 64010 Monterrey, NL, México Tel: [52] (83) 69-6660 Fax: [52] (83) 69-6665
Construexpo Exhibition of construction materials, equipment and technology	Guadalajara Expo Guadalajara November 12–14, 1993 November 18–20, 1994	Cámara de la Industria de la Construcción de Jalisco Lerdo de Tejada No. 2151 Col. Obrera 44140 Guadalajara, Jal., México Tel: [52] (3) 615-0352 Fax: [52] (3) 615-7212
Cuarta Muestra de la Industria de la Construcción Construction industry	Mexico City May 2–6, 1994	Conex Calz. de las Aguilas 101, Desp. 302 01710 México, DF, México Tel: [52] (5) 593-9500
Expo CIHAC Building materials and construction industry	Mexico City Exhibimex October 3–9, 1994	Centro Impulsor de la Construcción y la Habitación Empresa 165 Col. Extremadura-Insurgentes 03740 México, DF, México Tel: [52] (5) 661-0844 Fax: [52] (5) 661-0600
Expo Cocina Kitchen equipment	Mexico City May 28–June 5, 1994	ANFAMECI Tel: [52] (5) 563-3400
Expo Ferrelectrica Electrical components and materials for the construction industry	Mexico City Auditorio Nacional June 23–25, 1994	EIFESA Baja California No. 206-503 Col. Roma Sur 06760 México, DF, México Tel: [52] (5) 574-4846 Fax: [52] (5) 574-8687
Triexopo CBR: Cocinas, Banos y Recubrimentos Kitchen and bathroom fixtures and tile manufacturers and dealers trade show	Monterrey Cintermex December 1–5, 1993	Cintermex Ave. Fundidora 501 64010 Monterrey, NL, México Tel: [52] (83) 69-6944, 69-6969 Fax: [52] (83) 69-6911 Contact: Alejandro Monroy

ENVIRONMENTAL & ENERGY *See also:* Petroleum, Gas & Mining

Trade Fair	Site/Date	Contact
Control Ambiental Expo Products and services for hazardous materials management, pollution abatement and control, hazardous waste disposal, environmental management, emergency response and environmental remediation.	Mexico City Annual September 12–14, 1994	Advanstar Exhibitions 800 Roosevelt Rd. Bldg. E, Suite 408 Glen Ellyn, IL 60137, USA Tel: [1] (708) 469-3373 Fax: [1] (708) 469-7477
Ecologia Pollution control and hazardous waste management exhibition and seminar	Mexico City US Trade Center November 16–18, 1993	US Trade Center Mexico PO Box 3087 Laredo, TX 78044-3087, USA Tel: [52] (5) 591-0155 Fax: [52] (5) 566-1115 Contact: Raquel Polo
Ecologia Pollution control and hazardous waste management exhibition and seminar	Guadalajara Expo Guadalajara November 11–13, 1993	Expo Guadalajara Centro de Exposiciones Av. Mariano Otero 1499 44550 Guadalajara, Jal., México Tel: [52] (3) 671-0555, 671-0099 Fax: [52] (3) 671-0044 Contact: Rebeca L. Garcia Siordia
Environmex Held in conjunction with USATECH (*See* Comprehensive category)	Monterrey September 21–23, 1993 1995 dates TBA	International Exhibitions 1635 W. Alabama Houston, TX 77006, USA Tel: [1] (713) 529-1616 Fax: [1] (713) 529-0936 Contact: Richard Jennings

Trade Fair	Site/Date	Contact
Enviropro Mexico Environmental conference and exhibition addressing Mexico's environmental hazards. Supported by the regulatory agency of the Mexican government. Size: 125 booths.	Mexico City Annual September 7–9, 1994	E.J. Krause & Associates, Inc. 7315 Wisconsin Ave., Suite 450 North Bethesda, MD 20814, USA Tel: [1] (301) 986-7800 Fax: [1] (301) 986-4538 Contact: John Gallagher
Pro Eco Environmental products and services exhibition	Monterrey Cintermex May 3–5, 1994	Instituto para la Protección Ambiental Ocampo No. 250 Pte., Desp. 1010 Monterrey, NL, México Tel: [52] (83) 69-0200, 446-887 Fax: [52] (83) 448-575
T&D World Expo Mexico Electric power delivery expo and conference. Products include the latest developments in electrical transmission and distribution.	Mexico City March 2–4, 1994	Marketing International Corp. 200 McGlebe Rd., Suite 900 Arlington, VA 22203, USA Tel: [1] (703) 527-8000 Fax: [1] (703) 527-8006

FOOD, RESTAURANTS & HOTELS

Alimentos y Bebidas Festival of food and beverages	Mexico City American Embassy September 6–8, 1994	American Embassy in Mexico Paseo de la Reforma 305 06500 México, DF, México Tel: [52] (5) 211-0042 Fax: [52] (5) 202-0528
Confitexpo Candy industry manufacturers and distributors confectionery industry	Guadalajara Expo Guadalajara September 10–13, 1993 August 25–28, 1994	Grupo Gefecc, S.A. de C.V. Av. Baja California No. 32-A Col. Roma Sur 06760 México, DF, México Tel: [52] (5) 564-0329, 264-7029 Fax: [52] (5) 574-5696, 564-7040
Expo Conacca Fruit and vegetable suppliers	Guadalajara Expo Guadalajara July 28–30, 1994	Expo Guadalajara Centro de Exposiciones Av. Mariano Otero 1499 44550 Guadalajara, Jal., México Tel: [52] (3) 671-0555, 671-0099 Fax: [52] (3) 671-0044 Contact: Rebeca L. Garcia Siordia
Expo Natura Vegetarian and health products retail show	Guadalajara Expo Guadalajara December 10–12, 1993 November 11–13, 1994	Del Hexagono Productos Apicolas Río Nilo No. 603 Guadalajara, Jal., México Tel: [52] (3) 619-4482 Fax: [52] (3) 619-2176
Expo Pan Baking industry machinery and raw materials	Mexico City Palacio de los Deportes September 22–26, 1994	Conexpro S.A. de C.V. José Maria Bustillos No. 49 México, DF, México Tel: [52] (5) 530-6062 Fax: [52] (5) 538-8679
Expoalimentos Food and beverage industry exhibition	Monterrey Cintermex September 12–13, 1994	APEX, A.C. Av. Parque Fundidora No. 501 Local 22 Col. Obrera 64010 Monterrey, NL, México Tel: [52] (83) 69-6660 Fax: [52] (83) 69-6665
Hostal Suppliers to the hotel and restaurant industry	Guadalajara Expo Guadalajara June 30–July 2, 1994	Expo Guadalajara Centro de Exposiciones Av. Mariano Otero 1499 44550 Guadalajara, Jal., México Tel: [52] (3) 671-0555, 671-0099 Fax: [52] (3) 671-0044 Contact: Rebeca L. Garcia Siordia
Hotel & Restaurant Exhibition of equipment systems and services for hotels and restaurants. Size: 2,000 attendees; 105 exhibitors.	Mexico City US Trade Center Every 2 years July 19–21, 1994 1996 dates TBA	US Trade Center Mexico PO Box 3087 Laredo, TX 78044-0155, USA Tel: [52] (5) 591-0155 Fax: [52] (5) 566-1115

Trade Fair	Site/Date	Contact
Mexi-Pan Bread industry exhibition	Mexico City October 25–28, 1994	AMPROPAN Tel: [52] (5) 665-4892 Fax: [52] (5) 606-9092
Mexico Restaurant, Food Service and Hospitality Expo	Mexico World Trade Center October 3–5, 1994	Reed Exhibition Companies Prolongación Calle 18 No. 205 San Pedro de los Pinos México, DF, México Tel: [52] (5) 515-2610 Fax: [52] (5) 273-0312
Rest-o-Mex Restaurant, Food Service and Hospitality Expo	Mexico City Exhibimex Aug. 31–Sept. 2, 1994	Exhibimex Operadora Expomex Av. Cuauhtémoc s/n Col. Roma Sur 06700 México, DF, México Tel: [52] (5) 564-0055 Fax: [52] (5) 584-1710
Restaurant, Hotels and Food Show Equipment and supplies exhibition	Monterrey Cintermex November 11–13, 1993 November 3–5, 1994	Restaurantes y Licencias, S.A. Av. Constitutión No. 1257 Poniente Monterrey, NL, México Tel: [52] (83) 42-2987 Fax: [52] (83) 43-8210

FOOTWEAR & LEATHER *See also:* Textiles & Apparel

APICE Footwear industry machinery, components, and raw materials	Guadalajara Expo Guadalajara September 10–12, 1994	Asociación de Proveedores de la Industria del Calzado Efrain Gonzalez Luna No. 2481-104 Guadalajara, Jal., México Tel: [52] (3) 616-4224 Fax: [52] (3) 616-5806
Expo Piel Leather articles and apparel	León Centro de Exposiciones September 10–13, 1994	Asociación Nacional de Fabricantes de Ropa y Articulos de Piel, A.C. Blvd. Lopez Mateos No. 3401 Oriente Leon, Gua., México Tel: [52] (47) 11-7871 Fax: [52] (47) 11-7801
Exposición Nacional Del Calzado National wholesale footwear show	Guadalajara Expo Guadalajara May 21–24, 1994 October 16–19, 1994	Cámara de la Industria del Calzado de Jalisco Prolongación Av. Alcade No. 1918 44270 Guadalajara, Jal., México Tel: [52] (3) 624-9596 Fax: [52] (3) 653-4983
Sapica Footwear and leather items	León Centro Exposiciones May 21–24, 1994	Cámara de la Industria del Calzado Blvd. Lopez Mateos No. 3401 Ote. León, Gua., México Tel: [52] (47) 11-7517 Fax: [52] (47) 11-4120
Selec Moda Primavera/Verano Spring-summer footwear	Mexico City Exhibimex Sept. 28–Oct. 1, 1993 Sept. 29–Oct. 1, 1994	Cámara Nacional de la Industria del Calzado Durango No. 245 Col. Roma 06700 México, DF, México Tel: [52] (5) 533-6255, 525-4960 Fax: [52] (5) 511-5054

FRANCHISING

Conferencia Internacional de Franquicias Franchise conference	Mexico City November 23–24, 1994	A.M.F. Tel: [52] (5) 661-0655
Feria de Oportunidades de Franquicias en México Franchises in Mexico City	Mexico City June 8–10, 1994	A.M.F. Tel: [52] (5) 661-0655

Trade Fair	Site/Date	Contact
Shopping Center Developments in Mexico Opportunities in Mexico for US chain stores, franchisers, real estate development firms, and investors. Mexican companies seeking US partners will be in attendance.	Mexico City Presidente Hotel Annual April 25–27, 1994	Colchester Group 1220 4th St., Suite D Santa Rosa, CA 95404, USA Tel: [1] (707) 573-0583 Fax: [1] (707) 573-1082 Contact: Richard Abel
USA/Mexico Franchise Expo	Guadalajara Annual November 9–10, 1994	Source Mexico Consultants, L.C. 118 Broadway, Suite 634 San Antonio, TX 78205, USA Tel: [1] (210) 227-2502 Fax: [1] (210) 229-9761
USA/Mexico Franchise Expo	Mexico City Maria Isabel Sheraton Annual March 15–16, 1995	Source Mexico Consultants, L.C. 118 Broadway, Suite 634 San Antonio, TX 78205, USA Tel: [1] (210) 227-2502 Fax: [1] (210) 229-9761
USA/Mexico Franchise Expo	Monterrey Cintermex Annual May 11–12, 1994	Source Mexico Consultants, L.C. 118 Broadway, Suite 634 San Antonio, TX 78205, USA Tel: [1] (210) 227-2502 Fax: [1] (210) 229-9761

FURNITURE & HOUSEWARES

Trade Fair	Site/Date	Contact
Expo Mueble Furniture exhibition	Monterrey Cintermex September 1–4, 1994	INTERSO, S.A. Av. Fundidora No. 501 Local 94 Col. Obrera 64010 Monterrey, NL, México Tel: [52] (83) 69-6569 Fax: [52] (83) 69-6574
Expo Mueble Furniture products including beds, chairs, tables and gifts.	Guadalajara Expo Guadalajara Twice a year August 4–7, 1994 February 23–26, 1995	Asociación de Fabricantes de Muebles de Jalisco, A.C. Av. Niños Héroes 2663 Jardines del Bosque Guadalajara, Jal., México Tel: [52] (3) 621-1949, 622-7178 Fax: [52] (3) 622-7103, 621-4977
Exposición Provi Mueble Furniture exhibition	Monterrey Cintermex March 18–20, 1994	Interso Avenida Fundidora No. 501, Primer Nivel Ofna. 94 64010 Monterrey, NL, México Tel: [52] (83) 69-6569 Fax: [52] (83) 69-6574
Ofisistemas Office furniture, automation equipment, and services exhibition and seminar Size: 1,500 attendees; 50 exhibitors.	Mexico City US Trade Center Every 3 years June 21–23, 1994 1997 dates TBA	US Trade Center Mexico PO Box 3087 Laredo, TX 78044-3087, USA Tel: [52] (5) 591-0155 Fax: [52] (5) 566-1115 Contact: Charles Crowley
T.M.I. **Techno Mueble Internacional** Machinery, tooling, supplies and services for the furniture, cabinet, casegoods, millwork and industrial wood products industries. Size: 3,000 attendees; 600 booths.	Guadalajara Expo Guadalajara Annual July 8–10, 1994 July 7–9, 1995	Asociación de Fabricantes de Muebles de Jalisco, A.C. Av. Niños Héroes 2663 Jardines del Bosque Guadalajara, Jal., México Tel: [52] (3) 621-1949, 622-7178 Fax: [52] (3) 622-7103

GIFTS & CRAFTS *See also:* Jewelry

Trade Fair	Site/Date	Contact
AMFAR Expo Regalo Decoration, handicrafts, and gifts	Guadalajara Expo Guadalajara September 8–11, 1994	AMFAR, A.C. Monterrey No. 149 06700 México, DF, México Tel: [52] (5) 564-8961, 564-4564 Fax: [52] (5) 774-9709

Trade Fair	Site/Date	Contact
Artesanias Mexicanas de Toda la República Handicrafts from all over the Mexican Republic	Mexico City Annual November 12–20, 1993	D.I.F. Tel: [52] (5) 688-6691, 588-6691
Expo Arte International and contemporary art	Guadalajara Expo Guadalajara June 15–19, 1994	Ges Arte y Cultura Circunvalacion Providencia No. 1210-A Fracc. Lomas Country Guadalajara, Jal., México Tel: [52] (3) 623-7814 Fax: [52] (3) 653-1192
Expo Joven Exposition of art and design	Mexico City World Trade Center May 3–6, 1994	World Trade Center Montecito No. 38 Col. Nápoles 03810 México, DF, México Tel: [52] (5) 682-9822 Fax: [52] (5) 682-1067, 543-1324
Exposición Nacional de Artesanias Handicrafts exhibition	Tlaquepaque El Refugio Cultural Center August 4–7, 1994	Cámara Nacional de Comercio de Tlaquepaque Independencia 321 Tlaquepaque, Jal., México Tel: [52] (3) 635-4035 Fax: [52] (3) 635-2162
Feria Navidad International Christmas decoration show	Monterrey Cintermex December 12–24, 1993 December 10–24, 1994	Bostos Vega y Asociados Av. Fundidora No. 501 Local 3 Col. Obrera 64010 Monterrey, NL, México Tel: [52] (83) 69-6527 Fax: [52] (83) 69-5474
Manualidades: 1er Salon Nacional de las Artes Manuales Handicrafts exhibition	Guadalajara Centro de Exposiciones October 1–3, 1993	Expo Guadalajara Centro de Exposiciones Av. Mariano Otero 1499 44550 Guadalajara, Jal., México Tel: [52] (3) 671-0555, 671-0099 Fax: [52] (3) 671-0044 Contact: Rebeca L. Garcia Siordia
Sede del Regalo y Salon de la Importacion Gift items and home furnishings	Mexico City Exhibimex January 23–28, 1994 August 21–26, 1994	Grupo Salones Promocionales Benjamin Hill No. 185 Col. Hipódromo Condesa 06170 México, DF, México Tel: [52] (5) 271-0503, 271-0531 Fax: [52] (5) 273-1681, 516-2729

GRAPHIC ARTS

Trade Fair	Site/Date	Contact
Artes Graficas Graphic arts industry equipment and systems exhibition and seminar. Size: 2,500 attendees; 55 exhibitors.	Mexico City US Trade Center Every 2 years August 16–18, 1994 1996 dates TBA	US Trade Center Mexico PO Box 3087 Laredo, TX 78044-3087, USA Tel: [52] (5) 591-0155 Fax: [52] (5) 566-1115 Contact: Charles Crowley
Imprexpo Graphic arts industry exhibition	Guadalajara Expo Guadalajara March 20–23, 1994	Grupo Industrial El Vod, S.A. Jésus García No. 185 Col. Mezquitan Country 44260 Guadalajara, Jal., México Tel: [52] (3) 642-1792 Fax: [52] (3) 640-2186

HEALTH & BEAUTY *See also:* Medical & Dental

Trade Fair	Site/Date	Contact
Belleza y Salud Beauty and health equipment, supplies and services exhibition and seminar	Mexico City US Trade Center March 15–17, 1994	US Trade Center Mexico PO Box 3087 Laredo, TX 78044-3087, USA Tel: [52] (5) 591-0155 Fax: [52] (5) 566-1115

Trade Fair	Site/Date	Contact
Congreso de Estetica y Cosmetologia de Occidente Beauty congress and trade show	Guadalajara Annual September 11–12, 1993	Expo Guadalajara Centro de Exposiciones Col. Verde Vallo 44550 Guadalajara, Jal., México Tel: [52] (3) 671-0555, 671-0099 Fax: [52] (3) 671-0044 Contact: Rebeca L. Garcia Siordia
Expo Belleza Beauty products show for both men and women	Monterrey December 2–5, 1993	Cintermex Ave. Fundidora 501 64010 Monterrey, NL, México Tel: [52] (83) 69-6944, 69-6969 Fax: [52] (83) 69-6911 Contact: Alejandro Monroy
Expo-Belleza y Salud Beauty and health exhibition	Mexico City World Trade Center October 19–22, 1993	World Trade Center Montecito No. 38 Col. Nápoles 03810 México, DF, México Tel: [52] (5) 682-9822 Fax: [52] (5) 682-1067, 543-1324

JEWELRY *See also:* Gifts & Crafts

Trade Fair	Site/Date	Contact
Expo Joya Jewelry exhibition	Guadalajara Expo Guadalajara Sept. 28–Oct. 2, 1993 Sept. 27–Oct. 1, 1994	Cámara Regional de la Industria de la Plateria y Joyeria Avenida Topacio No. 2485 Guadalajara, Jal., México Tel: [52] (3) 621-9238 Fax: [52] (3) 647-0039
Expo Joyeria Jeweler's exhibition	Mexico City World Trade Center February 2–6, 1994	AMEFJO, A.C. Río Marne No. 19 P.H. Col. Cuauhtémoc México, DF, México Tel: [52] (5) 703-2483 Fax: [52] (5) 703-2560
Expo Regio Joya Jewelry industry show	Monterrey November 25–28, 1993	Cintermex Ave. Fundidora 501 64010 Monterrey, NL, México Tel: [52] (83) 69-6944, 69-6969 Fax: [52] (83) 69-6911 Contact: Alejandro Monroy
Exposición Oro y Plata Gold and silver jewelry exhibition	Guadalajara Expo Guadalajara April 19–23, 1994	Union de Plateros y Joyeros Rivas Guillen No. 817 Sector Libertad Guadalajara, Jal., México Tel: [52] (3) 649-1403 Fax: [52] (3) 655-6744

MACHINES, TOOLS & INSTRUMENTS
See also: Categories including exhibitions with machines and tools specific to those industries

Trade Fair	Site/Date	Contact
Agroindustrial Exhibition and seminar of agricultural machinery, equipment and supplies. Size: 4,000 attendees; 60 exhibitors.	Mexico City US Trade Center Annual January 25–29, 1995 1996 dates TBA	US Trade Center Mexico PO Box 3087 Laredo, TX 78044-3087, USA Tel: [52] (5) 591-0155 Fax: [52] (5) 566-1115
Ambientec Control, measure and safety equipment	Guadalajara Expo Guadalajara November 11–13, 1994	Diseno Expositor Av. Mariano Otero No. 1332 Fracc. Jardines del Bosque 44560 Guadalajara, Jal., México Tel: [52] (3) 647-5908 Fax: [52] (3) 647-5911
Analitica y Control 94 Analytical process and quality control instruments, systems and services exhibition and seminar. Size: 2,000 attendees; 55 exhibitors.	Mexico City US Trade Center September 6–8, 1994	US Trade Center Mexico PO Box 3087 Laredo, TX 78044-3087, USA Tel: [52] (5) 591-0155 Fax: [52] (5) 566-1115

Trade Fair	Site/Date	Contact
APICE Footwear industry machinery, components, and raw materials	Guadalajara Expo Guadalajara September 10–12, 1994	Asociación de Proveedores de la Industria del Calzado Efrain Gonzalez Luna No. 2481-104 Guadalajara, Jal., México Tel: [52] (3) 616-4224 Fax: [52] (3) 616-5806
CME Mexico Machinery, equipment and products for electronic textile, metal working and many other industries	Guadalajara 1994 dates TBA	Contract Manufacturers Expos 3310 W. Big Beaver Rd., Suite 403 Troy, MI 48084-2807, USA Tel: [1] (313) 643-6807 Fax: [1] (313) 643-0856
CME Mexico Machinery, equipment and products for appliance, electronic, automotive, metal working and many other industries	Monterrey Cintermex 1995 dates TBA	Contract Manufacturers Expos 3310 W. Big Beaver Rd., Suite 403 Troy, MI 48084-2807, USA Tel: [1] (313) 643-6807 Fax: [1] (313) 643-0856
Converflex Machinery and equipment for the paper industry	Mexico City World Trade Center October 25–28, 1994	Organización de Promociones y Exposiciones, S.A. de C.V. Aviacion Comercial No. 42 Fracc. Industrial Puerto Aereo 15710 México, DF, México Tel: [52] (5) 785-7553 Fax: [52] (5) 785-7638
Expo Clean Cleaning machinery and products	Guadalajara Expo Guadalajara April 14–16, 1994	Grupo Direxa Alvaro Obregón No. 541 Norte Monterrey, NL, México Tel: [52] (83) 746-418, 746-428 Fax: [52] (83) 722-191
Expo Lacteos International machinery, equipment and dairy products fair	Guadalajara Expo Guadalajara February 3–6, 1994	Grupo Gefecc, S.A. de C.V. Av. Baja California No. 32-A Col. Roma Sur 06760 México, DF, México Tel: [52] (5) 564-0329, 264-7029 Fax: [52] (5) 574-5696, 564-7040
Expo Metal Mecanica Tools, compressors, machinery for metal mechanic industry	Guadalajara Expo Guadalajara September 1–3, 1994	Diseno Expositor, S.A. de C.V. Av. Mariano Otero No. 1332 Fracc. Jardines del Bosque 44560 Guadalajara, Jal., México Tel: [52] (3) 647-5908 Fax: [52] (3) 647-5911
Expo Nacional Ferretera National hardware show	Guadalajara Expo Guadalajara September 19–21, 1993 September 18–20, 1994	Expo Nacional Ferretera, A.C. Adolfo Prieto No. 623-801 Col. del Valle 03100 México, DF, México Tel: [52] (5) 682-1470, 669-4447 Fax: [52] (5) 669-4532
Exposition de Maquinas de Herramientas Tool and machinery distributors	Mexico City World Trade Center April 19–22, 1994	World Trade Center Montecito No. 38 Col. Nápoles 03810 México, DF, México Tel: [52] (5) 682-9822 Fax: [52] (5) 682-1067, 543-1324 Asociación Mexicana de Maquinaria Tel: [52] (5) 604-8807 Fax: [52] (5) 604-6328
Manejomat Materials handling equipment and systems	Mexico City US Trade Center February 15–17, 1994	US Trade Center Mexico PO Box 3087 Laredo, TX 78044-3087, USA Tel: [52] (5) 591-0155 Fax: [52] (5) 566-1115
Maquinamex and Metalmex Tools and metal mechanic industry exhibition	Mexico City World Trade Center June 28–July 1, 1994	Reed Exhibition Companies Prolongación Calle 18 No. 205 Col. San Pedro de los Pinos 01180 México, DF, México Tel: [52] (5) 515-2610 Fax: [52] (5) 273-0312

Trade Fair	Site/Date	Contact
Materials Handling Materials handling equipment and systems	Mexico City March 8–10, 1994	US Trade Center Mexico PO Box 3087 Laredo, TX 78044-3087, USA Tel: [52] (5) 591-0155 Fax: [52] (5) 566-1115 Contact: Charles Crowley
Medi-Lab Medical and scientific equipment and material exhibition and seminar	Mexico City US Trade Center July 13–15, 1993 September 5–7, 1995	US Trade Center Mexico PO Box 3087 Laredo, TX 78044-3087, USA Tel: [52] (5) 591-0155 Fax: [52] (5) 566-1115
Mexico Hardware Show	Monterrey Cintermex April 21–23, 1994	Oprex Avenida de las Palmas No. 751 Col. Lomas de Chapultepec 11000 México, DF, México Tel: [52] (5) 520-7588 Fax: [52] (5) 520-7388
Mineria Mexican Mining Congress equipment and services exhibition	Acapulco October 27–30, 1993	US Trade Center Mexico PO Box 3087 Laredo, TX 78044-3087, USA Tel: [52] (5) 591-0155 Fax: [52] (5) 566-1115 Contact: Charles Crowley
PEMEX-Po. Plantas Plant engineering and maintenance	Mexico City Annual May 25–27, 1994	Advanstar Exhibitions 800 Roosevelt Rd. Bldg. E, Suite 408 Glen Ellyn, IL 60137, USA Tel: [1] (708) 469-3373 Fax: [1] (708) 469-7477
Plasticos Plastics materials, production equipment, and technology	Mexico City US Trade Center February 9–12, 1993 August 15–17, 1995	US Trade Center Mexico PO Box 3087 Laredo, TX 78044-3087, USA Tel: [52] (5) 591-0155 Fax: [52] (5) 566-1115
T.M.I. **Techno Mueble Internacional** Machinery, tooling, supplies and services for the furniture, cabinet, casegoods, millwork and industrial wood products industries. Size: 3,000 attendees; 600 booths.	Guadalajara Expo Guadalajara Annual July 8–10, 1994 July 7–9, 1995	Asociación de Fabricantes de Muebles de Jalisco, A.C. Av. Niños Héroes 2663 Jardines del Bosque Guadalajara, Jal., México Tel: [52] (3) 621-1949, 622-7178 Fax: [52] (3) 622-7103
Tecnos Industrial machinery and equipment	Monterrey Cintermex October 19–21, 1994	APEX, A.C. Av. Fundidora No. 501 Col. Obrera Monterrey, NL, México Tel: [52] (83) 69-6660 Fax: [52] (83) 69-6660
Urbanismos Machinery, equipment, services, municipal supplies	Guadalajara Expo Guadalajara June 2–4, 1994	EIFESA Baja California No. 206-503 Col. Roma Sur 06760 México, DF, México Tel: [52] (5) 574-4846 Fax: [52] (5) 574-8687
USA/Mexico Industrial Expo Broad-based industrial trade show	Guadalajara Expo Guadalajara Annual February 2–4, 1994 1995 dates TBA	Source Mexico Consultants, L.C. 118 Broadway, Suite 634 San Antonio, TX 78205, USA Tel: [1] (210) 227-2502 Fax: [1] (210) 229-9761
USA/Mexico Industrial Expo Broad-based industrial trade show	Monterrey Cintermex Annual June 14–16, 1994	Source Mexico Consultants, L.C. 118 Broadway, Suite 634 San Antonio, TX 78205, USA Tel: [1] (210) 227-2502 Fax: [1] (210) 229-9761

Trade Fair	Site/Date	Contact
USA/Mexico Industrial Expo Broad-based industrial trade show	Mexico City World Trade Center November 2–4, 1993 1995 TBA	Source Mexico Consultants, L.C. 118 Broadway, Suite 634 San Antonio, TX 78205, USA Tel: [1] (210) 227-2502 Fax: [1] (210) 229-9761

MEDICAL & DENTAL

Trade Fair	Site/Date	Contact
Congreso y Exposición **de Traumatologia** International traumatology show	Monterrey October 28–November 2, 1993	Cintermex Ave. Fundidora 501 64010 Monterrey, NL, México Tel: [52] (83) 69-6944, 69-6969 Fax: [52] (83) 69-6911 Contact: Alejandro Monroy
Expo ARIC Dental Dental industry exhibition	Guadalajara Expo Guadalajara September 9–12, 1994	Asociación Regional de la Industria Dental de Occidente Av. Lázaro Cárdenas No. 3260-6 45050 Guadalajara, Jal., México Tel: [52] (3) 621-3169 Fax: [52] (3) 621-3169
Expo Farma Pharmaceutical exhibition	Mexico City Exhibimex April 11–13, 1994	Asociación Farmacéutica Mexicana Adolfo Prieto No. 1649 Col. del Valle 03100 México, DF, México Tel: (5) 524-5685 Fax: [52] (5) 534-5098
Expo Hospital	Mexico City Exhibimex February 22–25, 1994	Reed Exhibition Companies Prolongación Calle 18 No. 205 Col. San Pedro de los Pinos 01180 México, DF, México Tel: [52] (5) 515-2343, 515-2408 Fax: [52] (5) 273-0312
Medical Congress Medical equipment and supplies	Monterrey Cintermex October 30–November 5, 1994	Cintermex Ave. Fundidora 501 64010 Monterrey, NL, México Tel: [52] (83) 69-6944, 69-6969 Fax: [52] (83) 69-6911 Contact: Alejandro Monroy
Medi-Lab Medical and scientific equipment and material exhibition and seminar	Mexico City US Trade Center July 13–15, 1993 September 5–7, 1995	US Trade Center Mexico PO Box 3087 Laredo, TX 78044-3087, USA Tel: [52] (5) 591-0155 Fax: [52] (5) 566-1115

OFFICE EQUIPMENT

Trade Fair	Site/Date	Contact
Expo Comm Mexico International telecommunications, computer and office automation exhibition and conference. Size: 10,500 attendees; 350 booths.	Mexico City Camino Real Hotel Annual February 15–18, 1994 February 17–20, 1995	E.J. Krause & Associates, Inc. 7315 Wisconsin Ave., Suite 450 North Bethesda, MD 20814, USA Tel: [1] (301) 986-7800 Fax: [1] (301) 986-4538 Contact: Billi Famiglietti
Ofisistemas Office automation equipment, furniture and services exhibition and seminar. Size: 1,500 attendees; 50 exhibitors.	Mexico City US Trade Center Every 3 years June 21–23, 1994 1997 dates TBA	US Trade Center Mexico PO Box 3087 Laredo, TX 78044-3087, USA Tel: [52] (5) 591-0155 Fax: [52] (5) 566-1115 Contact: Charles Crowley

PACKING

Trade Fair	Site/Date	Contact
Expopak de las Americas Packing industry exhibition	Mexico City Exhibimex May 17–20, 1994	Organización de Promociones y Exposiciones, S.A. de C.V. Aviacion Comercial No. 42 Fracc. Industrial Puerto Aereo México, DF, México Tel: [52] (5) 785-7553 Fax: [52] (5) 785-7638

Trade Fair	Site/Date	Contact
Mex Pack Packing and food processing industries exhibition	Mexico City World Trade Center May 24–27, 1994	Reed Exhibition Companies Prolongación Calle 18 No. 205 Col. San Pedro de los Pinos 01180 México, DF, México Tel: [52] (5) 515-2343, 515-2408 Fax: [52] (5) 273-0312

PAPER & STATIONERY

Trade Fair	Site/Date	Contact
Converflex Machinery and equipment for the paper industry	Mexico City World Trade Center October 25-28, 1994	Organización de Promociones y Exposiciones, S.A. de C.V. Aviacion Comercial No. 42 Fracc. Industrial Puerto Aereo 15710 México, DF, México Tel: [52] (5) 785-7553 Fax: [52] (5) 785-7638
Expo Papel Latino Americana Comprehensive international pulp and paper exhibition and conference for Latin America	Mexico City Exhibimex June 1–3, 1994	E.J. Krause & Associates, Inc. 7315 Wisconsin Ave., Suite 450 North Bethesda, MD 20814, USA Tel: [1] (301) 986-7800 Fax: [1] (301) 986-4538 Contact: Steven Douglas
Expo Papeleria Stationery and office supplies	Mexico City World Trade Center February 22–24, 1994	Feria Nacional de la Papeleria, A.C. Av. Revolución No. 1657 México, DF, México Tel: [52] (5) 550-7010 Fax: [52] (5) 550-7152
Fipamex Stationery industry	Guadalajara Expo Guadalajara March 9–12, 1994	Internacional de Exposiciones Presa Falcon No. 176 Col. Irrigación 11500 México, DF, México Tel: [52] (5) 557-1033 Fax: [52] (5) 395-0010

PETROLEUM, GAS & MINING *See also:* Environmental & Energy

Trade Fair	Site/Date	Contact
American Gas Association **International Conference**	Mexico City January 10–12, 1994 February, 1996	Exhibit Promotions Plus 11620 Vixens Path Ellicott City, MD 21042, USA Tel: [1] (410) 997-0763 Fax: [1] (410) 997-0764
Expo Petro y Chem Oil and gas field machinery: onshore and offshore equipment, including geophysical instruments, specialized pumps, oils and gas separating equipment	Mexico City November 3–5, 1993 November 9–11, 1994	E.J. Krause & Associates, Inc. 7315 Wisconsin Ave., Suite 450 North Bethesda, MD 20814, USA Tel: [1] (301) 986-7800 Fax: [1] (301) 986-4538 Contact: Billi Famiglietti
International Petroleum Exhibition **and Conference of Mexico**	Veracruz ExpoVer October 10–13, 1994	International Exhibitions 1635 W. Alabama Houston, TX 77006, USA Tel: [1] (713) 529-1616 Fax: [1] (713) 529-0936 Contact: Richard Jennnings
Mineria Mexican Mining Congress equipment and services exhibition	Acapulco October 27–30, 1993	US Trade Center Mexico PO Box 3087 Laredo, TX 78044-3087, USA Tel: [52] (5) 591-0155 Fax: [52] (5) 566-1115 Contact: Charles Crowley
Petro y Chem Mexico Petroleum and petrochemical equipment. Size: 8,500 attendees, 250 booths.	Mexico City Every 2 years December, 1994 December, 1996	Marketing International Corp. 200 McGlebe Rd., Suite 900 Arlington, VA 22203, USA Tel: [1] (703) 527-8000 Fax: [1] (703) 527-8006

Trade Fair	Site/Date	Contact

PLASTICS & RUBBER

Trade Fair	Site/Date	Contact
Expo Hulera Internacional International rubber exhibition	Mexico City September 22–24, 1993	Asormex Río Marne 19-403 Col. Cuauhtémoc México, DF, México Tel: [52] (5) 822-3714 Fax: [52] (5) 824-3262
Plast Imagen Plastic industry exhibition	Guadalajara Expo Guadalajara February 7–11, 1994	Organización de Promociones y Exposiciones, S.A. de C.V. Av. Paseo de las Palmas 751, Piso 4 Lomas de Chapultepec 11000 México, DF, México Tel: [52] (5) 282-5995 Fax: [52] (5) 520-7388
Plasticos Plastics materials, production equipment, and technology.	Mexico City February 9–12, 1993	US Trade Center Mexico PO Box 3087 Laredo, TX 78044-3087, USA Tel: [52] (5) 591-0155 Fax: [52] (5) 566-1115

REPRESENTATION

Trade Fair	Site/Date	Contact
Border Buyer Industrial Show All-purpose trade show for US and Mexican industrial purchasers and distributors to locate sources, markets and partners	San Luis Potosí October, 1994	Border Buyer Industrial Trade Shows 52 Medical Drive Brownsville, TX 78520, USA Tel: [1] (210) 542-5101 Fax: [1] (210) 546-5003
Monterrey Show All-purpose trade show for US and Mexican industrial purchasers and distributors to locate sources, markets and partners	Monterrey November, 1994	Border Buyer Industrial Trade Shows 52 Medical Drive Brownsville, TX 78520, USA Tel: [1] (210) 542-5101 Fax: [1] (210) 546-5003
Rep-Com Exhibition of US firms seeking Mexican representatives, agents, distributors, licensees or joint ventures. Size: 5,000 attendees; 200 exhibitors.	Mexico City US Trade Center Annual December 6–8, 1994	US Trade Center Mexico PO Box 3087 Laredo, TX 78044-3087, USA Tel: [52] (5) 591-0155 Fax: [52] (5) 566-1115
Representaciones Guadalajara Exhibition of US firms seeking Mexican representatives, agents, distributors, licensees or joint ventures. Size: 4,000 attendees;150 exhibitors.	Guadalajara American Consulate Annual September 27–29, 1994 September 19–24, 1995	US Trade Center Mexico PO Box 3087 Laredo, TX 78044-3087, USA Tel: [52] (5) 591-0155 Fax: [52] (5) 566-1115 Contact: Raquel Polo
Representaciones Monterrey Exhibition for US firms seeking Mexican representatives, agents, distributors, licensees or joint-venture partners. Includes a seminar for Mexican representatives on how to represent US firms.	Monterrey Cintermex Annual April 4–6, 1995	US Trade Center Mexico PO Box 3087 Laredo, TX 78044-3087, USA Tel: [52] (5) 591-0155 Fax: [52] (5) 566-1115 Contact: Stephen Sarro

RETAIL

Trade Fair	Site/Date	Contact
ANTAD Store fittings exhibition	Guadalajara Expo Guadalajara Feb. 26–March 1, 1994	Asociación Nacional de Tiendas de Autoservicio Homero No. 109, Piso 11 Col. Polanco 11560 México, DF, México Tel: [52] (5) 254-6220 Fax: [52] (5) 203-4495

Trade Fair	Site/Date	Contact

SAFETY & SECURITY

Trade Fair	Site/Date	Contact
Expo Seguridad Distributors of public, industrial, and personal security	Guadalajara Expo Guadalajara July 8–10, 1994	Expo Guadalajara Centro de Exposiciones Av. Mariano Otero 1499 44550 Guadalajara, Jal., México Tel: [52] (3) 671-0555, 671-0099 Fax: [52] (3) 671-0044 Contact: Rebeca L. Garcia Siordia
Seguridad Exhibition of public, industrial, and personal security equipment. Size: 2,500 attendees; 60 exhibitors.	Mexico City US Trade Center Every 2 years October 25–27, 1994	US Trade Center Mexico PO Box 3087 Laredo, TX 78044-3087, USA Tel: [52] (5) 591-0155 Fax: [52] (5) 566-1115
Seguritech Security equipment	Monterrey Cintermex June 23–25, 1994	Cintermex Ave. Fundidora 501 64010 Monterrey, NL, México Tel: [52] (83) 69-6944, 69-6969 Fax: [52] (83) 69-6911 Contact: Alejandro Monroy

SPORTING GOODS & RECREATION

Trade Fair	Site/Date	Contact
Deporte Sporting goods exhibition	Guadalajara Expo Guadalajara July 28–30, 1994	Expo Fair Santa Maria No. 219 Col. Chapalita 45000 Guadalajara, Jal., México Tel: [52] (3) 621-6582 Fax: [52] (3) 621-6583
Deportexpo Sporting goods and sportswear exhibition	Guadalajara May 12–14, 1994	World Trade Center Guadalajara Av. de las Rosas No. 2965 Col. Miravalle 44640 Guadalajara, Jal., México Tel: [52] (3) 671-0000 Fax: [52] (3) 671-0017
EXIME International exposition for amusement machines; attendees are amusement store owners and operators and vending machine retailers. Size: 2,500 attendees; 150 booths.	Mexico City Annual July 20–21, 1994	William T. Glasgow, Inc. 16066 S. Park Ave. South Holland, IL 60473, USA Tel: [1] (708) 333-9292 Fax: [1] (708) 333-4086
Expo Deporte Exhibition on sports	Mexico City World Trade Center Dates TBA	Tradex Exposiciones Internationales Río Churubusco No. 422 Col. Del Carmen Coyoacán 04100 México, DF, México Tel: [52] (5) 659-1631 Fax: [52] (5) 554-3616
Expo Diversiones Children's fairground exhibition	Guadalajara Expo Guadalajara June 8–13, 1994	Chain de Mexico S.A. Ave. La Paz No. 920 Altos Sector Juárez Guadalajara, Jal., México Tel: [52] (3) 614-3015 Fax: [52] (3) 647-8839
Expo Fonatur Tourism exposition	Mexico City World Trade Center April 15–18, 1994	World Trade Center Montecito No. 38 Col. Nápoles 03810 México, DF, México Tel: [52] (5) 682-9822 Fax: [52] (5) 682-1067, 543-1324 Fonatur Tel: [52] (5) 582-5311 Fax: [52] (5) 682-4500

Trade Fair	Site/Date	Contact
Jugueti Expo Toy exhibition	Mexico City World Trade Center May 24–27, 1994	World Trade Center Montecito No. 38 Col. Nápoles 03810 México, DF, México Tel: [52] (5) 682-9822 Fax: [52] (5) 682-1067, 543-1324 Mario Delgado Tel: [52] (5) 611-3899
Mexiplast Sporting goods	Mexico City Palacio de Deportes November 8–13, 1993	Tel: [52] (5) 553-1172, 553-0559 Fax: [52] (5) 256-3354
Sede del Delporte Manufacturers of sporting goods	Mexico City August 11–14, 1994	Grupo Salones Promocionales Benjamin Hill No. 185 Col. Hipódromo Condesa 06170 México, DF, México Tel: [52] (5) 271-0503, 271-0531 Fax: [52] (5) 273-1681, 516-2729
Show-Mexico Exhibition of production equipment and materials for the entertainment industry	Mexico City Aug. 31–Sept. 2, 1993	US Trade Center Mexico PO Box 3087 Laredo, TX 78044-3087, USA Tel: [52] (5) 591-0155 Fax: [52] (5) 566-1115

TEXTILES & APPAREL *See also:* Footwear & Leather

Trade Fair	Site/Date	Contact
Articulos Para Niños Children's clothing	Mexico City October 27–29, 1993	Grupo Industria Elvod Tel: [52] (5) 561-4825
Encuentro con la Moda Fashion designers' international show	Guadalajara Expo Guadalajara October 15–16, 1993	Expo Guadalajara Centro de Exposiciones Av. Mariano Otero 1499 44550 Guadalajara, Jal., México Tel: [52] (3) 671-0555, 671-0099 Fax: [52] (3) 671-0044 Contact: Rebeca L. Garcia Siordia
Exhimoda Otono-Invierno Dress show	Monterrey Dates TBA	Cintermex Ave. Fundidora 501 64010 Monterrey, NL, México Tel: [52] (83) 69-6944, 69-6969 Fax: [52] (83) 69-6911 Contact: Alejandro Monroy
Exhimoda Primavera-Verano **Exhimoda Otono-Invierno** Wholesale apparel trade show	Guadalajara Expo Guadalajara Twice a year (spring- summer and autumn- winter) January 18–21, 1994 July 20–23, 1994	Cámara Nacional de la Industria del Vestido Av. Circunvalacion Providencia 1264 Col. Lomas del Country Guadalajara, Jal., México Tel: [52] (3) 624-2615, 653-6893 Fax: [52] (3) 653-6656
Exomtex Fabrics, machinery, accessories for the textile industry	Puebla November 8–11, 1994	Cámara de la Industria de Puebla y Tlaxcala Depto. de Comercio Exterior 11 Sur No. 2104, Piso 1 72000 Puebla, Pue., México Tel: [52] (22) 43-4200 Fax: [52] (22) 37-3876
Expo Boda Wedding exhibition	Guadalajara Expo Guadalajara March 13–15, 1994	Producciones y Convenciones Sagitario No. 5061-4 Col. La Calma Guadalajara, Jal., México Tel: [52] (8) 634-6726 Fax: [52] (8) 634-6726
Expo Fashion Apparel exhibition	Mexico City World Trade Center October 26–29, 1993 May 17–20, 1994	Imagen de Exposiciones Mexico Viaducto Miguel Alemán No. 165 Col. Roma 06760 México, DF, México Tel: [52] (5) 564-7571 Fax: [52] (5) 574-9481

Trade Fair	Site/Date	Contact
Expo Textil Textile industry exhibition	Guadalajara Expo Guadalajara April 28–May 1, 1994	Cámara Textil de Occidente Mexicaltingo No. 2208 Col. Moderna 44150 Guadalajara, Jal., México Tel: [52] (3) 615-6646, 616-4483 Fax: [52] (3) 615-6656, 616-0009
Expotela Apparel industry exhibition	Mexico City March 15–17, 1993 Feb. 28–Mar. 2, 1994	Bobbin Blenheim, Inc. PO Box 1986 Columbia, SC 29202, USA Tel: [1] (803) 771-7500 Fax: [1] (803) 799-1461
Sede de la Moda Clothing manufacturers	Mexico City August, 1994	Grupo Salones Promocionales Benjamin Hill No. 185 Col. Hipódromo Condesa 06170 México, DF, México Tel: [52] (5) 271-0503, 271-0531 Fax: [52] (5) 273-1681, 516-2729
Semana Internacional de la Moda Fashion apparel show	Monterrey Cintermex Twice a year (spring-summer and autumn-winter) January 23–28, 1994 June 22–25, 1994	Cámara del Vestido de Nuevo Leon Modesto Arreola No. 905 Col. Centro Monterrey, NL, México Tel: [52] (83) 42-3937 Fax: [52] (83) 42-2633
Textiles Exhibit of textiles and materials primarily for commercial and industrial use. Size: 3,000 attendees; 75 exhibitors.	Mexico City US Trade Center May 24–26, 1994 May 9–11, 1995	US Trade Center Mexico PO Box 3087 Laredo, TX 78044-3087, USA Tel: [52] (5) 591-0155 Fax: [52] (5) 566-1115

TRANSPORTATION

TransExpo International trucking exhibition and conference	Monterrey Cintermex Sept. 28–Oct. 1, 1993 September 27–30, 1994	Expoavance One Liberty Square Boston, MA 02109, USA Tel: [1] (617) 426-6440 Fax: [1] (617) 426-6441 Contact: Kerry Mott
TransExpo International trucking exhibition and conference	Mexico City Sports Palace November 7–10, 1994	Expoavance One Liberty Square Boston, MA 02109, USA Tel: [1] (617) 426-6440 Fax: [1] (617) 426-6441 Contact: Kerry Mott
Warehousing, Development & Distribution in Mexico	Mexico City Nikko Hotel February 17–18, 1994	Colchester Group 1220 4th St., Suite D Santa Rosa, CA 95404, USA Tel: [1] (707) 573-0583 Fax: [1] (707) 573-1082 Contact: Richard Abel

Business Travel

The business traveler will find Mexico a land of extreme contrasts. There is the speed—and sometimes even the efficiency—of Mexico City's metro and the rough, potholed roads of the countryside; ostentatious displays of wealth alongside incredible poverty; sophisticated high-value international business transactions and beggars on the streets; friendly, hospitable citizens; surly, seemingly threatening police; daring thieves; attentive hotel staff and do-nothing hotel staff. Mexico is a nation in rapid transition, and because it is a very big, very populous nation, change doesn't occur everywhere at every level with equal speed and magnitude. It all makes for a business trip full of ups and downs, with every level of comfort and discomfort, and gratifyingly smooth service matched by inefficiency and intense frustration. The key to your adaptation and success may well be to relax when things aren't working well, while remembering to appreciate it to the fullest when things happen the way you want them to.

NATIONAL TRAVEL OFFICES WORLDWIDE

Despite hosting millions of visitors every year and depending on tourism for substantial amounts of foreign exchange and employment, Mexico still lacks an efficient travel bureaucracy. In testing the responsiveness of various branches of the Mexican Government Tourism Office in the United States, we found the full gamut of attitudes, from friendly in Houston to suspicious in Los Angeles. The offices don't seem to have any information specific to business travel. However, travelers will be able to get some general tourist information and brochures. Your best bets are travel agents and travel books—as the staff in the Los Angeles office advised us. (*See* Best Travel Books in this chapter.)

Europe

France 4 rue Notre-Dame-des-Victoires, 4, 75002 Paris, France; Tel: [33] (1) 40-20-07-34 Fax: [33] (1) 42-86-05-80.

Germany Wiesenhuettenplatz 26, 06000 Frankfurt-am-Main 1, Germany; Tel: [49] (69) 25-3413 Fax: [49] (69) 25-3755.

Italy Via Barberini 3, 00187 Roma, Italy; Tel: [39] (6) 482-7160 Fax: [39] (6) 482-3630.

Japan 2-15-1 Nagata-Cho, Chiyoda-ku, Tokyo 100, Japan; Tel: [81] (3) 3581-2110 Fax: [81] (3) 3503-5643.

Spain Calle de Velázquez 126, Madrid 28006, Spain; Tel: [34] (1) 261-1827 Fax: [34] (1) 411-0759.

United Kingdom 60-61 Trafalgar Square, 3rd Floor, London WC2 N5DS, UK; Tel: [44] (71) 734-1058 Fax: [44] (71) 930-9202.

United States

Chicago 70 East Lake Street, Suite 1413, Chicago, IL 60601, USA; Tel: [1] (312) 606-9015 Fax: [1] (312) 606-9012.

Florida 128 Aragon Avenue, Coral Gables, FL 33134, USA; Tel: [1] (305) 443-9160 Fax: [1] (305) 443-1186.

Houston 2707 North Loop West, Suite 450, Houston, TX 77008, USA; Tel: [1] (713) 880-5153 Fax: [1] (713) 880-1833.

Los Angeles 10100 Santa Monica Boulevard, Suite 224, Los Angeles, CA 90067, USA; Tel: [1] (310) 203-8191 Fax: [1] (310) 203-8316.

New York City 405 Park Avenue, 14th Floor, New York, NY 10022, USA; Tel: [1] (212) 755-7261 Fax: [1] (212) 753-1758.

Washington, DC 1911 Pennsylvania Avenue NW, Washington, DC 20006, USA; Tel: [1] (202)728-1750.

Canada

Montréal 1 Place Ville-Marie, Suite 1526. Montréal, PQ H3B 2B5, Canada; Tel: [1] (514) 871-1052 Fax: [1] (514) 871-3825.

Toronto 2 Bloor Street West, Suite 1801, Toronto, ON M4W 3E2, Canada; Tel: [1] (416) 925-0704 Fax: [1] (416) 925-6061.

Vancouver 1610-999 W. Hastings St., Vancouver, BC V6C 2W2, Canada; Tel: [1] (604) 669-2845 Fax: [1]

(604) 669-3498.

In the US, you can also try calling the toll-free Mexico Hotline for brochures and questions at (800) 446-3942, although the service is heavily over-worked. Consulates, similarly overburdened, are not a very good source of business travel information, although it is necessary to deal with them to obtain specific documents. They usually provide only recorded messages.

In Texas, five Mexican states maintain their own tourism and trade development offices:

Casa Guerrero State Promotion Office 5075 Westheimer, Suite 980, Houston, TX 77056, USA; Tel: [1] (713) 552-0930 Fax: [1] (713) 552-0207.

Casa Jalisco State Promotion Office 418 Villita, San Antonio, TX 78205, USA; Tel: [1] (210) 227-2887 Fax: [1] (210) 227-2889.

Casa Morelos State Promotion Office 45 NE Loop 410, Suite 240, San Antonio, TX 78216, USA; Tel: [1] (210) 366-0992.

Casa Nuevo Léon State Promotion Office 100 West Houston Street, Suite 1400, San Antonio, TX 78205, USA; Tel: [1] (210) 225-7032, (800) 872-3350 (toll-free in the US).

Casa Tamaulipas State Promotion Office World Trade Center, 118 Broadway, Suite 628, San Antonio, TX 78205, USA; Tel: [1] (210) 225-0204 Fax: [1] (210) 225-0206.

VISA AND PASSPORT REQUIREMENTS

Mexico allows foreigners into its territory under three separate classifications: non-immigrant (*no-inmigrante*), immigrant (*inmigrante*), and immigrated (*inmigrado*). Non-immigrants are temporary visitors such as tourists, transients, and visitors; they represent the lowest-grade commercial visa category. Immigrants are long-term residents and include those stationed in Mexico by their companies for extended periods. Immigrated persons are full-time permanent foreign residents.

US and Canadian citizens only need proof of citizenship to get Mexican tourist cards, which they can get from a travel agent, a Mexican consulate, an airline agent at the airport, or—most commonly—from a flight attendant on the plane. Proof of citizenship can be either a valid passport or an original birth certificate along with a photo ID. It is a good idea to bring your passport with you when you travel in Mexico—keep the original in your hotel safe, but make copies of the salient pages to carry with you.

A tourist card is good for six months; if you are planning to stay longer than three months, you should get permission at the border or the consulate nearest you. Keep the tourist card in a secure place, such as a hotel safe, and carry a copy with

EFFECTS OF NAFTA ON VISAS*

The North American Free Trade Agreement (NAFTA), which went into effect on January 1, 1994, was designed to liberalize the ability of businesspersons to conduct business, invest, and trade between Mexico, the US, and Canada.

NAFTA created four new non-immigrant visa classifications which are available on a reciprocal basis to nationals of the three signatory countries:

- **Business Visitor**—visas for business trips of short duration (for Mexico, trips must be of less than 30 days, and the business visitors must be paid from a source outside of Mexico);

- **Professional**—visas for employment assignments of up to one year for qualified professionals in occupations enumerated by NAFTA (most of the listed occupations require completion of a baccalaureate or *Licenciatura* degree);

- **Intracompany Transferee**—visas for managerial, executive, or "specialized knowledge" employees of multinational companies who have been employed for at least one out of the preceding three years with a qualifying affiliated organization outside Mexico; and

- **Investor/Trader**—visas for persons engaged in supervisory, executive, or "essential skills" capacities within an investment or trading enterprise.

The Mexican government has begun establishing procedures for implementing the business visitor visa category. This visa will be called an "FMN" visa, and it will be available at no cost at ports of entry and Mexican consulates abroad. The Mexican government is further expected to establish procedures for the remaining visa categories in the near future.

As the specific requirements and availability of the new non-immigrant visas has not been finalized, competent legal counsel should be contacted to obtain more specific information.

By Cynthia Juarez Lange of the law offices of Fragomen, Del Rey & Bernsen, P.C., Los Angeles, California. Reprinted with permission of the authors and of the firm. Copyright © 1994 Fragomen, Del Rey & Bernsen, P.C.

you. Upon your departure, Mexican authorities will require that the card be returned. Loss of or failure to produce the card sets in motion a complicated, time-consuming bureaucratic hassle that will fray your patience and possibly delay your departure as you attempt to document and justify your presence in the country.

The only time you don't need a tourist card to enter Mexico is if you're visiting US–Mexico border towns, or Baja California as far south as Ensenada, for a period of less than three days.

Citizens of the UK need valid passports and tourist cards, while citizens of other countries need passports, visas, and tourist cards.

Although many foreigners can get by with conducting limited business in Mexico using only a tourist card or tourist visa, Mexico technically requires those visiting the country on business to have a business visa. Failure to procure one can result in legal difficulties. This requirement is satisfied by obtaining a six-month *visitante* (business visitor) visa. Other specialized temporary visa categories include those for: foreign directors of Mexican companies, who are allowed to enter for board meetings; aliens seeking political asylum; students; distinguished visitors; local visitors; and provisional visitors. Of these, only the business visitor and director visas will be of interest for business travelers, and the latter only if they are board members.

Immigrant visas are granted for periods of one year and are renewable on an annual basis. Categories include those for: *rentistas*—those interested in residing in Mexico and living on the income from outside sources; investors who plan to bring in significant capital for investment in the country; professionals desiring to practice in Mexico (infrequently issued); confidential personnel—managers who are necessary because of their skills or relationship to the company such that they cannot be replaced by Mexican personnel; scientists who are teaching or doing research; technicians who have skills unavailable from Mexican citizens; and family members of persons eligible to be in Mexico under another visa category.

Persons who have maintained immigrant status for five years are eligible to receive visas indicating immigrated status. Such visa holders can be out of the country for up to 24 months at a time, but must not be out of the country for more than five years on a cumulative basis during any 10-year period. Such status allows holders to import personal effects on a duty-free basis.

Those who are in the country to buy goods, research the market, hire agents, inspect goods, arrange shipments, make repairs as a technician, or conduct business meetings—in other words, for any activities that do not result in direct payment by a

Mexican company for your work—can obtain a basic business visitor visa good for six months by submitting a letter on company letterhead explaining the purpose of the trip and guaranteeing that the company is responsible for expenses. The business visa requires two color photos. This type of business visa costs about US$75 to US$115 and requires about two to four weeks to process. If the trip is going to result in a foreign firm earning money from a Mexican company—or involves assorted other business activities—an advanced type of visitor business visa is needed. Because of special requirements and the ongoing changes in the visa situation in Mexico, businesspeople should check with local Mexican consulates or legal firms with expertise in Mexico for updates and specific requirements. (Refer to the "Important Addresses" chapter.)

IMMUNIZATION

Required No proof of vaccination is needed unless you are arriving in Mexico from an infected area, such as tropical South and Central America (cholera and yellow fever) or tropical Africa (yellow fever).

Recommended Hepatitis A and tetanus; plus typhoid, diphtheria, and polio immunizations for travel in the tropical zones; antimalarial drugs for travel in a malarial area (the Yucatán and undeveloped coastal areas away from resorts).

CLIMATE

Mexico is a vast country of mountains, valleys, plateaus, deserts, jungles, and seacoasts. It has many distinct regional climates—plus microclimates within them—to match these varied terrains and altitudes. The northern half of the country—including the states of Sonora, Chihuahua, Nuevo León, Coahuila, Durango, and Sinaloa, and parts of Zacatecas, San Luis Potosí, Tamaulipas, and Baja California—has the aridity and temperature extremes of the southwestern US. The central plateau's altitude in the north averages around 1,500 meters (about 4,750 feet), increasing toward the south. At an elevation of 538 meters (about 1,750 feet), Monterrey has temperatures that range from blistering days in August (although the nights are cool) to freezing nights in January (although the days are usually pleasant).

The southern half of the country lies within the tropics, but only the southeast and southwest coasts and low-lying parts of the interior have tropical climates (marked by high temperature, humidity, and rainfall); nevertheless, the southeast coast can be hit by "Arctic Express" winter winds. Acapulco, on the southwest coast, has January temperatures ranging from 22°C to 31°C (72°F to 88°F) and an August temperature range of 25°C to 33°C (77°F to 91°F). Even at tropical latitudes, the altitude of the central plateau creates year-round temperate springlike conditions, including a June-through-September wet season and an October-through-May dry season. Mexico City, at 2,240 meters (7,250 feet) elevation, has a January temperature range of 5°C to 21°C (41°F to 70°F), while April, the warmest month, ranges from 10°C to 27°C (50°F to 81°F). Guadalajara, at 1,590 meters (5,150 feet) elevation, is slightly warmer than Mexico City.

Baja California has a climate all its own: the Pacific coast, including Tijuana, has generally warm temperatures moderated by the ocean and summertime fog; the low-lying area around Mexicali and the coast along the Sea of Cortés is largely a desert with hot days and cool nights in summer, and mild temperatures in winter.

AIR TRAVEL TIME TO MEXICO CITY

- From Chicago nonstop on United Airlines: 4 hours 22 minutes
- From Frankfurt nonstop on Lufthansa: 12 hours 15 minutes
- From Houston nonstop on Continental Airlines: 2 hours 15 minutes
- From London nonstop on British Airways: 11 hours 50 minutes
- From Los Angeles nonstop on United Airlines: 3 hours 32 minutes
- From New York City nonstop on Delta Airlines: 5 hours 24 minutes
- From Paris direct via Houston on Air France: 14 hours 40 minutes
- From San Francisco nonstop on United Airlines: 4 hours 22 minutes
- From Tokyo via Vancouver on Japan Airlines: 13 hours 20 minutes, plus overnight in Vancouver

---

BUSINESS ATTIRE

Business attire in Mexico is the same as that in most Western and Pacific Rim countries: for men, conservative business suits in dark colors, with expensive but understated accessories and for women, conservative hemlines, necklines, sleeve lengths, accessories, and makeup (pantsuits are not appropriate). Dress for the climate of the area to be visited—tropical weight fabrics for the coasts and the secondary cities; year-round temperate weight fabrics for the central plateau in summer, and somewhat warmer clothing during winter (a medium weight coat, especially a raincoat, will be welcome, although heavy overcoats or tweeds are not needed). You will need an umbrella and raincoat for the wet season, which, along with the altitude, keeps the plateau at springlike—that is, brisk—temperatures; cool nights persist in the central plateau even during the summer.

AIRLINES

One would expect more airlines to offer a variety of flights to a nation as geographically large and economically important as Mexico. But although several US carriers serve Mexico City well, most European- and Asian-based airlines require their passengers to take connecting flights from the US. Moreover, only a few cities other than the capital (primarily tourism centers) receive international flights, and service is relatively infrequent, so the best bet may be to fly to Mexico City and transfer to a domestic flight. Mexicana and Aeroméxico provide the vast majority of flights within Mexico. Aero California,

Aero Guadalajara, Aeromar, Aviacsa, Servicio Leo López, SARO and TAESA are the main regional carriers. It is feasible to drive yourself in the US–Mexico border towns, although you will need to use your private car or rent one in Mexico, because US car rental companies generally do not permit their cars to be taken into Mexico. (*See* Domestic Transportation in this chapter.)

TIME CHANGES

All of Mexico except for the northwest is six hours behind Greenwich Mean Time (GMT) and located in the Central Standard Time Zone, which matches it with corresponding zones in the US and Canada, as well as all the nations of Central America except Panama. The exceptions include the states of Baja California Sur, Sinaloa, and Sonora, and parts of Nayarit; these are on Mountain Standard Time, seven hours behind GMT, which they share with their counterparts in the US and Canada. The remaining exception is the state of Baja California Norte, which is always on Pacific Time and is the only state to observe daylight savings time. It is always on the same time as California.

Plans were announced to put the rest of Mexico on daylight savings time in 1994 in order to save energy, but at press time the changeover had not taken place, and it appears unlikely that daylight savings time will actually go into effect. During daylight savings time (in the US, from the last Sunday in October to the first Sunday in April), which most of Mexico doesn't observe, its time zones fall one hour behind their counterparts in the US and Canada. This means that during daylight savings time, Mexico's Central Standard Time becomes the same as US and Canadian Mountain Daylight Savings Time, while Mexico's Mountain Standard Time becomes the same as the north's Pacific Daylight Savings Time.

When in Mexico City, you can determine what time it is in any of the cities listed here by adding

(+) or subtracting (−) the number of hours shown to or from Mexico City time. If it is daylight savings time in the city you are calling, add one more hour to the number shown.

Auckland	+18
Athens	+8
Bangkok	+13
Beijing	+14
Caracas	+2
Chicago	0
Denver	+1
Frankfurt	+7
Hong Kong	+14
Houston	0
Kansas City	0
London	+6
Madrid	+7
Manila	+14
New York City	+1
Rio de Janiero	+3
San Francisco	−2
Santiago	+2
Seattle	−2
Sydney	+16
Taipei	+14
Toronto	−1
Tokyo	+15

CUSTOMS ENTRY (PERSONAL)

Going through customs in Mexico—whether you're entering or leaving the country—can be either a breeze or considerably more difficult. Mexican Customs officials at the airports and border crossings usually don't search luggage very carefully, if at all. At some heavily used entry points, such as the Mexico City airport, customs is run on something like a lottery basis: you give your customs declaration to an inspector, who has you push a button that makes either a green or a red light flash. A green light means you enter without an inspection; a red light means your bags are inspected to a greater or lesser degree. The odds are usually about 15 to 1 in your favor. However, customs authorities can always require an intensive search for any reason they deem appropriate.

Mexican Customs agents have a somewhat spotty history of at times overzealous and exclusionary enforcement of regulations leading to the blockage of entry of items or the levying of heavy duties and fees, as well as for soliciting bribes—*la mordida* (the bite). The duty or fee charged may well be genuine. You'll know you've been bitten if you ask for *un recibo* (a receipt) and don't get one. The people most at

risk are those who look like wealthy tourists headed for the plush resorts, carrying such expensive items as cameras, jewelry, and designer clothes, or those dressed in what in Mexico is considered outlandish fashion (there is still a prejudice against "hippies"). Run-of-the-mill tourists and those dressed for business are less likely to be subjected to extensive searches or solicited for bribes.

Should you encounter a request for a bribe, follow this advice:

- No matter what happens, always hold your temper, remaining cool, formal, and polite. You don't want to be held up indefinitely or tossed out of the country or into *la cárcel* (jail).
- Frown and ignore the request; say that you don't speak Spanish. If you can drag it out long enough, the official may give up and move on to others waiting in line behind you.
- Ask for a receipt before you pay. If the fee is legitimate, the official will show you the receipt book when he asks for the fee.

The Salinas administration reorganized customs in 1990 and businespeople are now less likely to meet up with discourteous or dishonest customs officials.

Travelers are allowed to bring in the following items in the stated amounts. Other items or greater amounts are dutiable.

Duty-free
- 2 liters of wine or alcohol for personal use;
- 200 cigarettes, 50 cigars, or 250 grams (about 8 1/2 ounces) of tobacco;
- Perfume for personal use;
- One movie or video camera and one still camera, plus 12 rolls of film or tape for each (rarely enforced);
- Gifts with a total value of up to US$300;
- ATA carnet items—Mexico has not signed the ATA convention but generally accepts its practices, which include duty-free temporary importation of professional equipment, commercial samples, and advertising material.
- Cash—No limit on foreign currency.

Prohibited or restricted
- Firearms;
- Illegal drugs.

FOREIGN EXCHANGE (PERSONAL)

The *nuevo peso*, or new peso, went into circulation on January 1, 1993, when Mexico dropped three zeros from the old peso, multiplying the value a thousandfold. The exchange rate at the end of the first quarter of 1994 was NP3.3565 per US dollar. This is

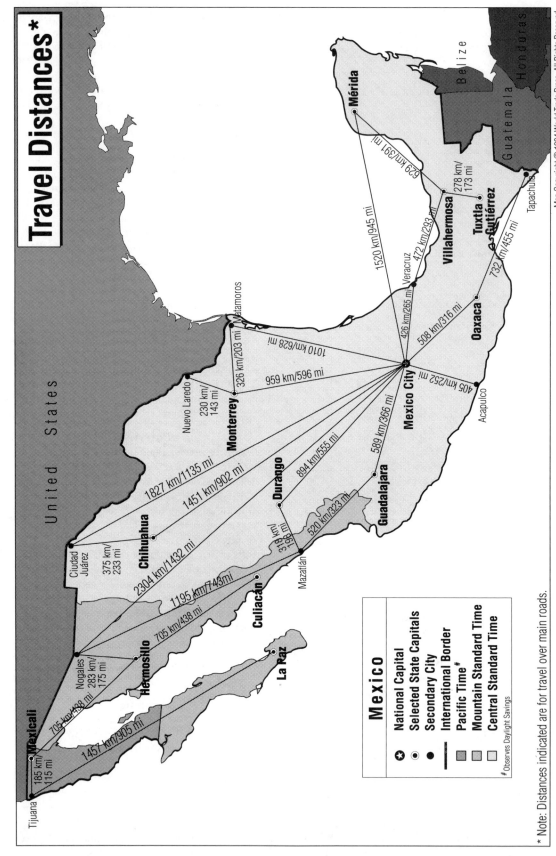

Travel Distances*

Mexico

- ✪ National Capital
- ⊙ Selected State Capitals
- ● Secondary City
- —— International Border
- Pacific Time#
- Mountain Standard Time
- Central Standard Time

Observes Daylight Savings

United States

Tijuana
185 km/115 mi
Mexicali
705 km/438 mi
1457 km/905 mi
La Paz
Nogales
283 km/175 mi
Hermosillo
705 km/438 mi
Culiacán
1195 km/743 mi
Mazatlán
319 km/198 mi
Ciudad Juárez
375 km/233 mi
Chihuahua
2304 km/1432 mi
1451 km/902 mi
1827 km/1135 mi
Durango
520 km/323 mi
Guadalajara
894 km/555 mi
589 km/366 mi
Nuevo Laredo
230 km/143 mi
Monterrey
959 km/596 mi
1010 km/628 mi
326 km/203 mi
Matamoros
Mexico City
405 km/252 mi
Acapulco
508 km/316 mi
Oaxaca
426 km/265 mi
Veracruz
472 km/293 mi
Villahermosa
278 km/173 mi
Tuxtla Gutiérrez
732 km/455 mi
Tapachula
629 km/391 mi
1520 km/945 mi
Mérida

Belize
Guatemala
Honduras

Map Copyright © 1994 World Trade Press. All Rights Reserved.

* Note: Distances indicated are for travel over main roads.

down somewhat from approximately 3 to 1 at the beginning of 1993. Although the peso is losing value against the dollar, Mexico has largely brought its huge inflation problem—averaging 8 percent in 1993—under control, so the current loss trend is marginal compared to the mid-1980s, when inflation ran as high as 159 percent.

The new peso is divided into 100 *centavos*. The new money circulates in coin denominations of 1, 2, 5, or 10 pesos and 5, 10, 20, or 50 centavos and in notes of 10, 20, 50, or 100 pesos. All old pesos are to be withdrawn from circulation by January 1, 1996, and there are still plenty of them floating around (many public phones and vending machines accept only the old peso coins), representing a source of confusion. When you receive change in pesos, examine the coins and notes closely to be sure you're getting the correct amounts. It will become increasingly more difficult to use old pesos as circulation of the new peso becomes more general.

The coins were redesigned; the new face denominations are much smaller. You can tell if you have old peso coins if there is more than one zero on the value of the coin. Although the new peso notes are the same color as the old, you can again distinguish between the two by looking at the denominations, which began at 10,000 in the old notes but do not rise above 100 for the new notes. Because the values are close enough to US and Canadian dollars that some unscrupulous vendors are known to take advantage of the confusion, make sure before you get a written bill whether the price is in pesos or dollars. And be aware of the fact that the symbol "$" is used for both dollars and pesos (new peso prices are supposed to be designated by "N$", but this is not always the case).

Another problem is small change, or rather the lack of it. Shopkeepers and taxi drivers are chronically out of change or use the excuse to "round up" the amount of a purchase. When it comes your way, hang onto small change to avoid the problem in future transactions. When paying with cash, the bill is supposed to be rounded to the nearest 5 centavos. However, for commercial and credit card purchases, charges can be to the nearest centavo or even fraction thereof. Note: Mexico has a value-added tax (VAT) of 10 percent, which must by law be included in any price quoted to you. Thus, you usually won't see the VAT itemized as a separate amount on your bills.

US dollars are widely accepted, especially in major cities, border towns, and resort areas, although the exchange rate used in retail purchases is usually lower than the official rate for more formal exchanges. Acceptance is far from universal, and some areas have had experience with counterfeit US dollars; other areas are so remote that they are unfamiliar with US currency. Other foreign currencies are not used. Mexico has many automated teller machines (ATMs), especially in urban and tourist areas, that are part of such international systems as Cirrus and Plus. US banks should have a directory of Plus ATMs in Mexico. For Cirrus locations, call (800) 4-CIRRUS in the US.

Major brands of traveler's checks and credit cards (VISA, MasterCard, and American Express) are generally accepted in Mexico, especially in cities and tourist areas. However, small shops and restaurants usually take only cash, and credit cards are unfamiliar to merchants off the beaten path. Now that interest rates have fallen, merchants are less likely to demand surcharges on credit card purchases as was the practice in the recent past.

Banks give better rates on traveler's checks than on cash, but money exchange houses do just the opposite. And some banks and exchange houses charge commissions of up to 5 percent. Travelers may wish to convert a small amount of money into pesos at a home country bank before leaving for Mexico in order to avoid the long lines at airport money exchange counters. Mexican banks and airport counters offer the best retail exchange rates; remember that hotels give the worst rates.

TIPPING

Tipping is expected in Mexico. Service people, especially in the big hotels and restaurants, know how much their counterparts in the US receive, and they often seem to expect the same from foreign travelers, although they expect less from Mexican travelers. This situation, combined with Mexico's current daily minimum wage of about US$5 and the poverty that the vast majority of Mexicans endure, makes it difficult for foreigners to decide what is fair and what is overtipping.

Some restaurants add a 10 to 15 percent service charge to the bill, and this is the amount you should tip if there is no service charge (assuming the service merits it). It is sometimes difficult to determine if a service charge is included, and you may wish to enquire to be sure. It is common, but not necessary, to tip a taxi driver 10 percent, especially if assistance with luggage has been given, in which case it is expected. A moderate tip for a porter or bellboy would be about NP2 (about US$0.60) per bag, or at more expensive hotels NP3 to NP4 (about US$0.90 to US$1.20). Tip room service waiters NP1 at expensive hotels or 50 centavos at lesser hotels (about US$0.30 to US$0.15). Tip your maid NP2 (about US$0.60) per day, no matter what class of hotel. You are not expected to tip in cheap hotels and restaurants, although you may choose to do so.

ACCESS TO CITIES FROM AIRPORT

Mexico City Benito Juárez International Airport is only 6 km (3.75 miles) east of the city center, an area that includes the Alameda Central, El Zócalo, and Zona Rosa areas, where most businesspeople are likely to congregate. Because the Mexico City Metro (subway) prohibits any luggage bigger than a shoulder bag, a taxi is the best way to get to the city center. There are many official taxis, most of which are reasonably large and comfortable, give good service, and are fairly priced. Buy a fixed-price ticket from the taxi ticket counters (*transportación terrestre*) near the baggage carousels or outside at the curb. Fares are priced according to the zone of your destination; you can either find your zone on the map near the counters or tell the ticket agent the name of your hotel (usually the agent will know the zone). Fares to most hotels are less than US$10 for a ride averaging 35 minutes. There are no private limos or bus companies that come into the airport, but if you take a taxi from just outside the airport, the cost is about half.

Guadalajara Miguel Hidalgo International Airport is 19 km (12 miles) southeast of the city's center. You can get to your hotel by VW minibus (*combi*), taxi, or limousine. The *combis*, run by Autotransportes Aeropuerto (Tel: (3) 689-0032), take several passengers and their luggage to hotels for fares based on distance—the fare is usually US$8 to US$14 per person, which is cheaper than taxis. However, the *combi* fare from the city's center to the airport is about the same as the taxi fare if you call for the *combi* to pick you up.

In theory, taxis charge fixed rates; in reality, you should settle with the driver before you get in. The fare should run about US$12 to US$18, depending on the distance to your hotel and your bargaining prowess. The average trip takes about 45 minutes.

Monterrey Mariano Escobedo International Airport is 22 km (14 miles) northeast of city's center. Aeropuerto Transportaciones (Tel: (83) 45-3330) runs *combis*: if you share the ride, is about US$7, and for a few dollars more, you have it to yourself. The 35-minute taxi ride costs about US$15.

ACCOMMODATIONS

Travelers accustomed to the exorbitant hotel room rates in the US, Canada, or East Asia will be pleased to see what they get for their money in Mexico. Although Mexico City has a few top-end hotels that charge US$150 a day and up, the city's 17,000 hotel rooms come in a wide range of prices—most are reasonably priced and located in compact districts, which are close to each other. Hotels add a 10 percent sales tax, and many of the more expensive ones also tack on a service charge, which varies with the hotel.

Getting a hotel reservation should be no problem for the business traveler, who is presumably going to business areas rather than to resorts, which do tend to fill up. Hotel reservations are difficult to obtain during holidays—particularly around Christmas and Easter—but few foreign businesspeople should expect to do serious business during these periods anyway. Even those arriving in Mexico City without a reservation can expect to get one through the Mexican Hotel and Motel Association's airport booth (Tel: (5) 286-5455).

Expensive and moderately priced Mexican hotels offer international standards of amenities and service, as well as some examples of spectacular architecture and painstaking historical preservation. However, many of the most enticing hotels are located on extremely busy city streets, so you may want to insist on a room that is away from the street. Being far from a busy lobby is also a good idea, because Mexicans frequently entertain in hotel lobbies until very late into the night—often with live *mariachi* music that wafts up through towering atriums directly to the rooms, even those that have *no molestar* (do not disturb) signs hanging on the doorknobs.

All the more expensive and moderately priced hotels accept major international credit cards, as do many of the cheaper lodgings. The rates posted in hotels may or may not include the 10 percent value-added tax; be sure to ask. The rates quoted here are for single occupancy (although some hotels charge the same for single or double occupancy) and, because they are subject to change, are given only to establish the order of magnitude of costs. Among the confusion factors: many higher-end hotels offer corporate rates which are substantially lower than standard rates; at these hotels, weekday rates are often much higher than weekend rates, when demand is lower. Hotels frequently drop or raise their rates, offer special package deals, and reverse the weekend–weekday differentials, depending on the season or on how business has been lately. Hence the wide range and all-too-frequent unreliability of the stated rates.

Rooms usually have air conditioning, telephones, television, and radios; many have refrigerators and minibars. Most hotels have restaurants, bars, or nightclubs. Those intent on economizing may wish to search out hotels normally used by Mexican tourists and businesspeople. They usually lack the frills of the hostelries that cater to the international traveler, but they are comfortable, clean, and generally much easier on the budget. Budget hotels listed usually have such amenities as phones and TVs. All have private baths; and all are clean, comfortable, and safe. Their main problem may be noise. Note that references to "the Zócalo" in hotel descriptions refer to the central plaza in each city.

US Government Per Diem Allowances as of May 1994

	LODGING	FOOD & INCIDENTALS	TOTAL
Mexico City	US$135	US$61	US$196
Guadalajara	US$116	US$59	US$175
Monterrey	US$120	US$79	US$199
Tijuana	US$63	US$78	US$141

MEXICO CITY

The main hotel area in Mexico City runs from the government district (near the National Cathedral and the National Palace on the Zócalo) to downtown (the Alameda Park) and down Paseo de la Reforma to the financial district, which is near the Zona Rosa entertainment and shopping district. The five-digit number which follows the street address is the postal code.

Top-end

Camino Real Mariano Escobedo 700, 11590; near business and financial districts. Striking architecture and art; considered by many to be the best hotel in the city; favored by heads of state, celebrities, executives. Bilingual business center (computers available), secretarial service, executive floor, health club, pools, tennis, restaurants. Rates: US$195 to US$245. Tel: (5) 203-2121 or (800) 722-6466 (toll-free in the US) Fax: (5) 250-6897.

Galería Plaza Hamburgo 195 at Varsovia, 06600; Zona Rosa district (Pink Zone, entertainment and shopping). A Westin hotel. Business center, secretarial service, pool, shops, restaurants, airport transfer. Rates: US$155 to US$250. Tel: (5) 211-0014 or (800) 228-3000 (toll-free in the US) Fax: (5) 207-5867.

Krystal Rosa Liverpool 155, 06600; in the Zona Rosa. Business center (computers available), convention facilities, restaurant, pool, airport transfer. Rates: US$155 to US$265. Tel: (5) 211-0092 or (800) 231-9860 (toll-free in the US); Fax: (5) 511-3490.

Marquis Reforma Paseo de la Reforma 465, 06500; in financial district. Business center, computer services, in-room fax and modem hookups, health club, restaurants, shops, airport transfer. Rates: US$175 and up. Tel: (5) 211-3600 Fax: (5) 211-5561.

Stouffer Presidente Mexico Campos Elíseos 218, 11560; across from Chapultepec Park, near financial district; business/convention hotel. Business center, conference facilities, meeting rooms, restaurants, shops, airport transfer. Rates: US$165 to US$205. Tel: (5) 327-7700 or (800) HOTELS-1 (toll-free in the US) Fax: (5) 327-7730, 250-9130.

Expensive

Aristos Paseo de la Reforma 276, 06600; in financial district, across from US Embassy and Mexican Stock Exchange. Bilingual business center (computers available), secretarial service, message service, gymnasium, pool, travel agency, dining room. Rates: US$80 to US$110. Tel: (5) 211-0112 or (800) 5-ARISTO (toll-free in the US) Fax: (5) 525-6783, 514-8005.

Calinda Geneve Londres 130, 06600; in Zona Rosa. A Quality Inn. Refined, Old World style. Restaurant, business center (computers available), secretarial service, travel agency. Rates: US$80 to US$109. Tel: (5) 211-0071 or (800) 228-5151 (toll-free in the US) Fax: (5) 208-7422.

Gran Hotel Howard Johnson 16 de Setiembre 82, 06000; downtown, adjacent to the Zócalo. In 19th century former department store with striking Belle Epoque lobby and modern rooms. Restaurants, travel agency. Rates: US$80 to US$110. Tel: (5) 510-4040 or (800) 654-2000 (toll-free in the US) Fax: (5) 512-2085.

Marco Polo Amberes 27, 06600; in heart of Zona Rosa; boutique hotel, all-suite, small (60 suites and 4 penthouses), ultramodern, posh. Multilingual secretarial service, business center (computers available), restaurant, airport transfer. Rates: US$100 to US$160. Tel: (5) 207-1893 Fax: (5) 533-3727.

Plaza Florencia Florencia 61, 06600; in Zona Rosa. Small (140 rooms). Restaurant. Rates: US$105. Tel: (5) 211-0064 Fax: (5) 511-1542.

Moderate

Best Western Hotel de Cortés Avenida Hidalgo 85, 06000; downtown, corner of Paseo de la Reforma, opposite the Alameda. An 18th century Augustinian monks' hospice, a national monument. Small (29 modern rooms and suites). Courtyard, restaurant. Rates: US$76 to US$86. Tel: (5) 518-2181 or (800) 528-1234 (toll-free in the US) Fax: (5) 518-1863.

Best Western Majestic Madero 73, 06030; downtown, near Zócalo. Colonial style, built 1937. Courtyard, rooftop restaurant. Rates: US$64 to US$86. Tel: (5) 521-8600 or (800) 528-1234 (toll-free in the US) Fax: (5) 518-3466.

Days Inn Mexico Río Lerma 237, 06500; downtown, near Zócalo. Restaurant, airport transfer. Rates: US$70 to US$77. Tel: (5) 211-0109 Fax: (5) 208-2014, 511-0693.

Emporio Mexico Paseo de la Reforma 124, 06600; midtown. European atmosphere. Restaurant, airport transfer. Rates: US$58 to US$123. Tel: (5) 566-7766

Fax: (5) 703-1424.

María Cristina Río Lerma 31, 06500; quiet residential section near Zona Rosa. Colonial style, circa 1937; courtyard, modern rooms; popular, so reserve in advance. Restaurant, travel agency. Rates: US$60. Tel: (5) 566-9688.

Budget

Casa González Río Sena 69, 06500; near Zona Rosa. Formerly two mansions; small (21 rooms), pleasant. Rates: US$16 to US$25. Tel: (5) 514-3302.

Corinto Vallarta 24, 06030; midtown, near Revolución Monument. Restaurant, small rooftop pool, purified tap water. Rates: US$35. Tel: (5) 566-6555, 566-9711 Fax: (5) 546-6888.

Montecarlo Uruguay 69, 06000; near Zócalo. Augustinian monastery built 1772, later became home of D.H. Lawrence. Slightly odd, very popular (book ahead). Rates: US$20. Tel: (5) 518-1418, (5) 521-2559 Fax: (5) 510-0081.

GUADALAJARA

Most first class hotels in Guadalajara are in commercial, residential, and shopping areas 3 to 4 km (1.8 to 2.5 miles) west or southwest of downtown, a taxi ride of 15 to 20 minutes. Downtown hotels are cheaper, have fewer amenities, and are often subject to traffic and nightlife noise, but they offer comfort, cleanliness, convenience, and savings.

Top-end

Camino Real Avenida Vallarta 5005, 45040; 15 minutes by cab from downtown. A Westin hotel; avoid rooms in rear wing, which is on a noisy street. Full business center (computers available), secretarial and translation services, computers, tennis, pools, restaurants, purified water system. Rates: US$140 to US$200. Tel: (3) 647-8000 or (800) 228-3000 (toll-free in the US) Fax: (3) 647-6781.

Fiesta Americana Aurelio Aceves 225, 44100; Minerva Circle at junction of Vallarta and López Mateos, near downtown. Part of largest hotel chain in Latin America; popular with business travelers. Business center, executive floors, health club, pool, tennis, purified water system, restaurants, shopping center. Rates: US$170 to US$190. Tel: (3) 625-3434 or (800) 223-2332 (toll-free in the US) Fax: (3) 630-3725.

Quinta Real Avenida México 2727, 44680; near Minerva Circle at intersection with López Mateos, near downtown. Small (79 units, mostly suites), luxurious, in residential neighborhood. Secretarial service, small pool, restaurant, airport transfer, purified water system. Rates: US$180 to US$220. Tel: (3) 615-0000 Fax: (3) 630-1797.

Expensive

Carlton Avenida Niños Héroes 105, 44100; the only first class downtown hotel. Caters to business travelers; take upper room, away from noise. Business center, health club, pool, restaurant. Rates: US$120. Tel: (3) 614-7272 Fax: (3) 613-5539.

Hyatt Regency Guadalajara Avenida López Mateos Sur and Moctezuma, 45050; in residential area. Business center (computers available) with bilingual staff, voicemail system, fax and computer data ports in each room, VIP club, health club, shopping arcade, ice skating rink, restaurants, purified water system. Rates: US$135 to US$175. Tel: (3) 678-1234, 622-7778 or (800) 228-9000 (toll-free in the US) Fax: (3) 678-1222, 622-9877.

Moderate

Best Western Fénix Avenida Corona 160, 44100; downtown. Convenient location; popular nightspot; choose room away from noisy streets. Restaurant, shops. Rates: US$50 to US$65. Tel: (3) 614-5714 or (800) 528-1234 (toll-free in the US) Fax: (3) 613-4005.

De Mendoza Venustiano Carranza 16, 44100; downtown, convenient side street location. Small (100 rooms), quiet, period architecture (former convent). Pool, restaurant, some balconies. Rates: US$66 to US$73 (walk-in rates cheaper than call-in). Tel: (3) 613-4646, 614-5714 Fax: (3) 613-7310.

Frances Calle Maestranza 35, 45050; downtown. Guadalajara's oldest hotel, dating from 1610; a national monument, restored and renovated. Small (60 rooms), exquisite. Restaurants. Rates: US$60. Tel: (3) 613-1190.

Quality Inn Calinda Roma Avenida Juárez 170, 44100; downtown. Best downtown hotel, completely renovated in 1993. Restaurant, rooftop garden with pool and putting green. Rates: US$40 to US$80. Tel: (3) 614-8650 or (800) 228-5151 (toll-free in the US) Fax: (3) 613-0557.

Suites Bernini Avenida Vallarta 1881, 44140; 15-minute taxi ride west of downtown. Small (15 suites), elegant, spotless. Rates: US$60 to US$90. Tel: (3) 616-6736.

Budget

Las Américas Avenida Hidalgo 76, 45120; downtown, opposite Plaza Tapatía. One of the best deals in the city; quiet despite noisy street, clean, well kept. Rates: US$20. Tel: (3) 613-9622 or 614-1604.

San Francisco Plaza Avenida Degollado 267, 44100; downtown; 60 rooms. Highly recommended; courtyards, large rooms, restaurant. Rates: US$35. Tel: (3) 613-8954 or 613-8971.

MONTERREY

Most of Monterrey's better hotels are downtown near the Gran Plaza in the Zona Rosa entertainment and shopping district. Cheaper hotels cluster inconveniently around the city's enormous bus station

North America

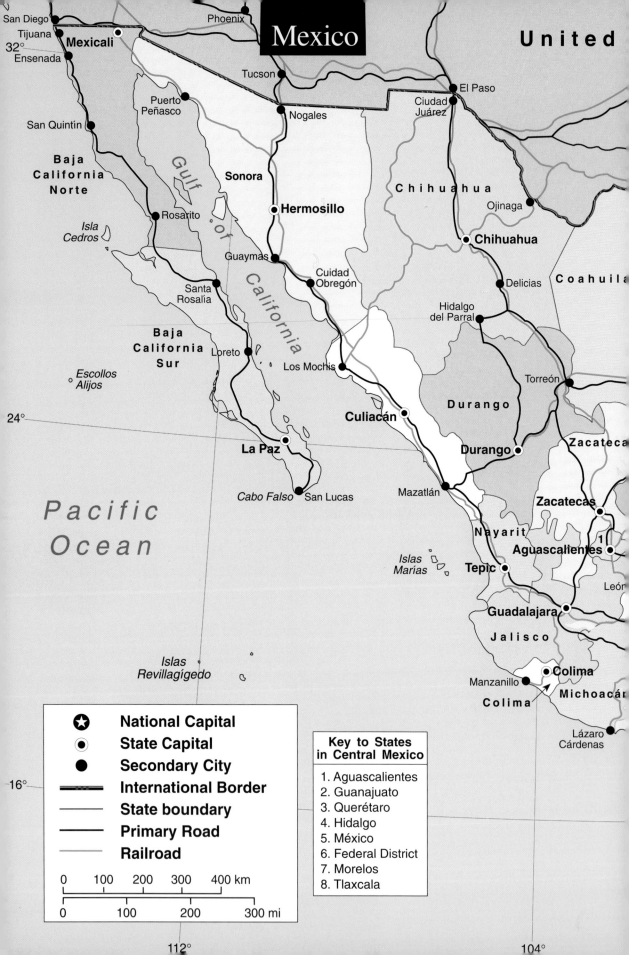

Mexico

United

San Diego
Tijuana
Mexicali
Ensenada
32°
Phoenix
Tucson
El Paso
Ciudad Juárez
Nogales

San Quintín

Baja California Norte

Puerto Peñasco

Sonora

Chihuahua

Ojinaga

Chihuahua

Isla Cedros

Rosarito

Hermosillo

Guaymas

Cuidad Obregón

Delicias

Coahuila

Escollos Alijos

Baja California Sur

Loreto

Santa Rosalía

Los Mochis

Hidalgo del Parral

Torreón

Durango

24°

Culiacán

La Paz

Cabo Falso San Lucas

Durango

Zacateca

Mazatlán

Pacific Ocean

Nayarit

Zacatecas

1

Aguascalientes

León

Islas Marías

Tepic

Islas Revillagígedo

Guadalajara

Jalisco

Manzanillo

Colima

Colima

Michoacán

Lázaro Cárdenas

Legend

✪	**National Capital**
⊙	**State Capital**
●	**Secondary City**
▬▬	**International Border**
—	**State boundary**
▬▬	**Primary Road**
▬▬	**Railroad**

Key to States in Central Mexico

1. Aguascalientes
2. Guanajuato
3. Querétaro
4. Hidalgo
5. México
6. Federal District
7. Morelos
8. Tlaxcala

16°

0   100   200   300   400 km

0   100   200   300 mi

Gulf of California

112°   104°

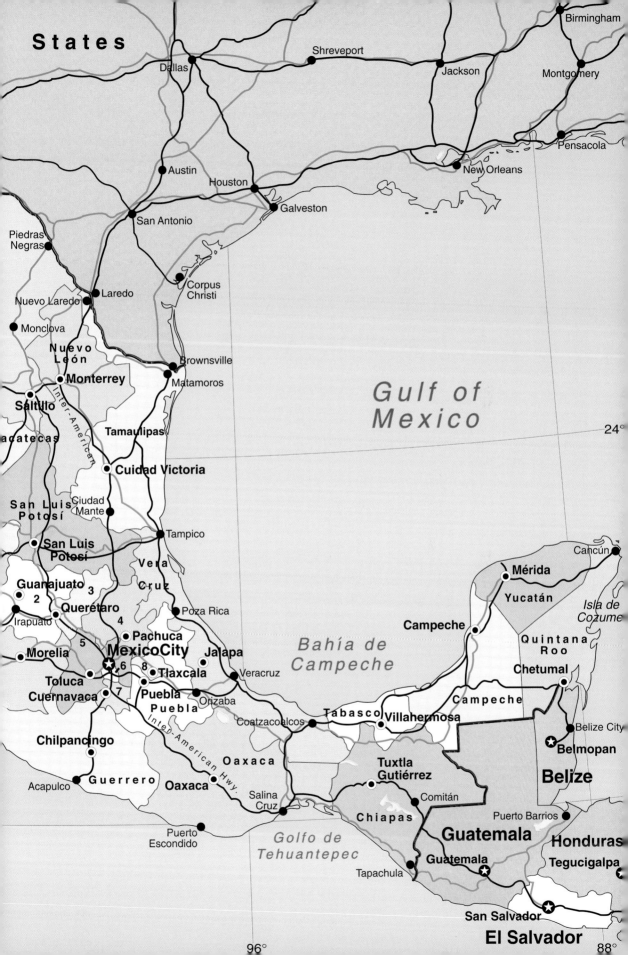

States

Shreveport
Birmingham
Dallas
Jackson
Montgomery
Pensacola
Austin
Houston
New Orleans
San Antonio
Galveston
Piedras Negras
Corpus Christi
Nuevo Laredo **Laredo**
Monclova

Nuevo León
Monterrey
Brownsville
Matamoros
Saltillo
Zacatecas
Tamaulipas

Gulf of Mexico

24°

Cuidad Victoria

San Luis Potosí
Ciudad Mante

Tampico

San Luis Potosí

Vera Cruz

Cancún

Mérida

Guanajuato 3
2
Querétaro
Irapuato
4

Poza Rica

Yucatán
Isla de Cozumel

Campeche

Quintana Roo

5
Pachuca
Morelia
MexicoCity **Jalapa**
6
8
Chetumal

Bahía de Campeche

Toluca
7
Tlaxcala
Veracruz
Cuernavaca
Puebla
Puebla
Orizaba

Campeche

Chilpancingo

Inter-American Hwy.

Coatzacoalcos
Tabasco
Villahermosa
Belize City
Belmopan

Oaxaca

Guerrero
Acapulco
Oaxaca

Tuxtla Gutiérrez
Belize

Salina Cruz

Comitán
Puerto Barrios

Chiapas

Puerto Escondido

Golfo de Tehuantepec

Guatemala
Honduras

Guatemala
Tegucigalpa

Tapachula

San Salvador
El Salvador

96°
88°

Inter-American

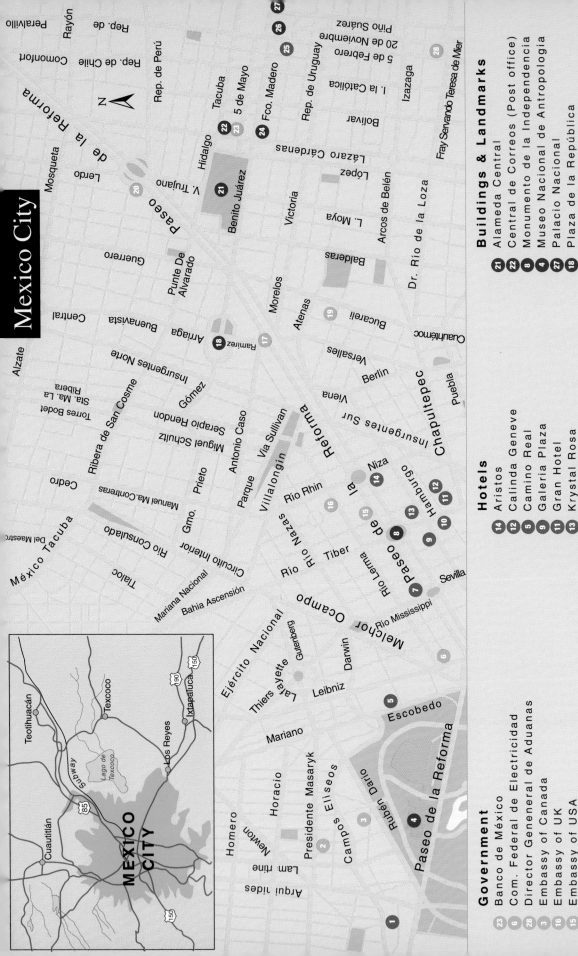

Mexico City

Buildings & Landmarks

- Alameda Central
- Central de Correos (Post office)
- Monumento de la Independencia
- Museo Nacional de Antropologia
- Palacio Nacional
- Plaza de la República
- Torre Latinoamericana
- Zócalo (Plaza de la Constitución)

㉑ ㉒ ⑧ ④ ㉗ ⑱ ㉔ ㉖

Hotels

- Aristos
- Calinda Geneve
- Camino Real
- Galeria Plaza
- Gran Hotel
- Krystal Rosa
- Marco Polo
- Marquis Reforma
- Plaza Florencia

⑭ ⑫ ⑤ ⑨ ⑪ ⑬ ⑦ ⑩ ①

Government

- Banco de México
- Com. Federal de Electricidad
- Director Gen eneral de Aduanas
- Embassy of Canada
- Embassy of UK
- Embassy of USA
- Procuraduría General
- Sec. de Agricultura y Recursos Hidráulicos
- Sec. de Gobernacion

㉓ ⑥ ㉘ ③ ⑯ ⑮ ⑳ ⑰ ⑲

northwest of downtown. When it comes to room rates, Monterrey doesn't have many bargains.

Expensive

Ambassador–Camino Real Calle Hidalgo 310 Oriente, 64000; downtown. Generally considered the best hotel in the region; restored landmark building. Business center (computers available), health club, pool, tennis, travel desk, restaurants, shops, airport transfer. Rates: US$108 to US$148. Tel: (83) 40-6390, 42-2040 or (800) 722-6466 (toll-free in the US) Fax: (83) 45-1984.

Gran Hotel Ancira Radisson Plaza Calle Hidalgo y Escobedo, 64000; downtown. Neoclassic landmark, circa 1912, beautifully maintained; large rooms. Business center, secretarial service, meeting rooms, gym, restaurants, shops. Rates: US$160 and up. Tel: (83) 45-7575 or (800) 333-3333 (toll-free in the US) Fax: (83) 44-5226.

Holiday Inn Crowne Plaza Avenida Constitución Oriente 300, 64000; near downtown. Business center (computers available), health club, pool, tennis, restaurants, airport transfer. Rates: US$88 to US$230. Tel: (83) 43-5120, 19-6000 or (800) HOLIDAY (toll-free in the US) Fax: (83) 44-30-07.

Monterrey Clarion Morelos 574 Oriente, 64000; downtown, overlooks Plaza Zaragoza and Gran Plaza (try to get room in front). Recent renovation. Business center, secretarial service, restaurant, airport transfer. Rates: US$65 to US$130. Tel: (83) 43-5120, 43-8820 Fax: (83) 44-73-78.

Moderate and Budget

Best Western Royal Courts Avenida Universidad 314, 66450; 9 km north of downtown on Highway 85. Business center (computers available), restaurant, pool, airport transfer. Rates: US$59 to US$80. Tel: (83) 76-2010/7 or (800) 528-1234 (toll-free in the US) Fax: (83) 76-2017, 76-292.

Colonial Calle Hidalgo Oriente 475, 64000; downtown, opposite Hotel Ancira. Convenient, recently redecorated; small rooms. Rates: US$43. Tel: (83) 43-6791.

Jolet Padre Mier 201 Pte., 64000; near downtown. Modern. Rates: US$70 to US$79. Tel: (83) 40-5500 Fax: (83) 45-3731.

Nuevo Léon Amado Nervo Norte 1007, 64000; near bus station. Clean, modern, small. Rates: US$22. Tel: (83) 74-1900.

Royalty Calle Hidalgo Oriente 402, 64000; downtown. Opposite Hotel Ancira. Restaurant. Rates: US$65 to US$75. Tel: (83) 40-2800 Fax: (83) 40-5812..

TIJUANA

The hotel room count in Tijuana has not kept pace with the city's explosive growth, and there is a deficit of acceptable and affordable accommoda-tions. Most hotels are downtown on Avenida Revolución, south of downtown on Boulevard Agua Caliente near the country club, and east of downtown on Paseo de los Héroes in the Río Tijuana area, which is the city's Zona Rosa entertainment and shopping district.

Top-end

Gran Hotel Tijuana Boulevard Agua Caliente 4558, 22420; near golf course. Formerly Fiesta Americana Hotel; highrise with good views. Health club, pool, tennis, travel agency, restaurants. Rates: US$130 and up. Tel: (66) 81-7000 Fax: (66) 81-7016.

Expensive

Lucerna Boulevard Paseo de los Héroes and Avenida Rodríguez; in Río Tijuana. Gardens, pool, tennis, restaurant. Rates: US$74. Tel: (66) 34-2000 or (800) LUCERNA (toll-free in the US) Fax: (66) 34-2400.

Radisson Paraiso Tijuana Boulevard Agua Caliente 1; overlooking golf course. Business services, meeting rooms, pool, exercise room, balconies, restaurant. Rates: US$65 to US$99. Tel: (66) 81-7200 or (800) 333-3333 (toll-free in the US) Fax: (66) 86-36-39.

Moderate

Best Western–Country Club Tapachula 1, 22000; near golf course and racetrack. Restaurant, banquet facilities, Fax: service. Rates: US$53 to US$66. Tel: (66) 81-7733 or (800) 528-1234 (toll-free in the US) Fax: (66) 81-7066.

Best Western–Hacienda del Río Boulevard General Rodolfo Sánchez Tabaoda 10606, 22000; in Zona Río. Restaurant, pool, Fax: service. Rates: US$68 to US$78. Tel: (66) 84-8644 or (800) 528-1234 (toll-free in the US) Fax: (66) 84-8620.

Best Western–Hotel Plaza de Oro Avenida Miguel Martínez 539, 22700; near downtown. Fax service. Rates: US$34 to US$62. Tel: (66) 85-3776 or (800) 528-1234 (toll-free in the US) Fax: (66) 85-6703.

Corona Plaza Boulevard Agua Caliente 1426; near bullring. Pool, restaurant. Rates: US$60. Tel: (66) 81-8183.

La Villa de Zaragoza Avenida Madero 1120; downtown near El Palacio Frontón (Jai Alai). Restaurant. Rates: US$55. Tel: (66) 85-1832.

Otay Bugambilias Boulevard Industrial and Carretera Aeropuerto; near airport. Convenient for business in the Otay Mesa industrial area. Meeting rooms, pool, gym, restaurant. Rates: US$57. Tel: (66) 23-8411 or (800) 472-1153 (toll-free in the US) Fax: (66) 23-76-00 x358.

Budget

Hotel Nelson Avenida Revolución 503; downtown. Rates: US$28. Tel: (66) 85-4302.

EATING

Mexico's ethnic heritage and eventful history have given it a unique cuisine that is becoming internationally known for its flavor, creativity, and variety. For the most part, it is based on the traditional Indian staple diet of beans, corn, and chilis, which staples still form the diet of the nation's poor. The country is also the original source of chocolate, vanilla, and avocados, adding complexity to classic Mexico cooking. Rice, garlic, onions, tomatoes, and coriander and cumin are also prominently featured. Spanish nuns and French invaders made their own additions to an elaborate Aztec court cuisine, all of which filtered down to the distinctive everyday *comida popular.*

Visitors from the US, Canada, and Europe are probably most familiar with the *tortilla,* the flat, round, unleavened bread made from corn or wheat. Mexicans fill *tortillas* with rice, beans, cheese, various meats or seafood, spices, and sauces, rolling them into *burritos,* folding them into *tacos,* frying them flat and serve them spread or heaped with ingredients to make *tostadas,* making them into cheese turnovers called *quesadillas,* filling them with potato, sausage, beans or fruit and frying them to make *empanadas,* rolling them with ingredients and smothering them with sauce to make *enchiladas.* And that is just the beginning—Mexicans also eat *tortillas* plain as bread and use them as edible utensils to scoop up other food. Leftover *tortillas* are layered with cheese, sausage, onions, and sauces to make a casserole called *chilaquiles,* often served as a traditional breakfast. Corn *tortillas* are used throughout Mexico, but asking for flour *tortillas* marks one as being from the northern part of the country.

Mexican cuisine is also famous for *mole*—a rich, complex sauce often made with dozens of ingredients, with regional variations that include spices, sesame seeds, chilis, ground peanuts, squash seeds, and chocolate—and for *salsa*—a ubiquitous sauce or condiment usually based on tomatoes, onions, and chilis, but which can be made in any number of ways using an unending variety of ingredients. *Tamales* are corn dough stuffed with meat, beans, and chilis, or with fruit and sweet dough as a dessert. *Tortas* are the Mexican sandwich, made with a French-style bread called *telera* or *bolillo.*

Mexicans eat many vegetables (*verduras*), but usually mix them into other dishes. Because of problems with water purity, it is usually unwise for visitors to eat raw, unpeeled fruits or vegetables and salads. Seafood, such as *huachinango* (red snapper), crab, swordfish, and shrimp, is also popular. Try *ceviche,* a seafood cocktail of raw fish and shellfish (make sure it's fresh), marinated in lime juice and topped with cilantro (coriander leaves), onion, and chilis. Mexico has many varieties of fruit, including bananas, papayas, melons, mangoes, and a variety of other tropical and more familiar fruits. Soups (*sopas*) include *gazpacho* (tomato), *pozole* (hominy and meat, usually pork), *sopa de flor de calabaza* (squashflower), *sopa azteca* (broth with *tortilla* and avocado), *menudo* (tripe stew), *sopa de lentejas* (lentil soup), *sopa de chícharos* (pea soup), and *sopa de cebolla* (onion soup), among many others.

Except for the poor, who cannot afford it, Mexicans tend to eat a lot of meat, mainly beef, chicken, pork, and lamb. And the Mexican national alcoholic beverages are justifiably famous. They can be made from any of several varieties of the *maguey* cactus, which is the source of *pulque, mezcal,* and *tequila,* the form in which most outsiders will find it. Mexican beers, many of which have an international reputation, are brewed in the German style courtesy of Teutonic immigrants, and national vintners—the heirs to an early Spanish industry—are producing good wines in Baja California Norte and Querétaro.

Drink only bottled or purified water; your body probably would reject the unfamiliar bacteria in untreated Mexican water, much to your discomfort. You're safe drinking beer, wine, or other alcoholic drinks, or sodas, as long as they are not served with ice (ask for them *helado pero sin hielo*—chilled but without ice).

Mexican businesspeople often have just coffee or tea and a roll or pastry before going to work, then break for a hearty breakfast at mid-morning, which often becomes the basis for a business meeting. Dinner (*comida*), the main meal, is served around 2 to 4 pm, often as a fixed-price, daily set menu called *comida corrida.* Supper is similar to *comida,* but usually lighter, and is eaten around 9 or 10 pm. Dinner prices quoted refer to *comida;* other meals will be less expensive and elaborate. Expect restaurant service to be slower in Mexico than at home; the whole attitude is more leisurely and formally ceremonial. Get the waiter's attention by waving or raising your hand (pointing with the index finger is considered demeaning). If you don't want your food spicy, tell the waiter, *no picante.* Ask for the check by saying, *la cuenta, por favor,* or just smile and make a scribbling motion on your palm as if writing up the bill.

The restaurants listed in this section have been recommended by travel writers and restaurant critics. Of course, there are literally thousands of places to eat, although some carry more cachet than others for impressing local business contacts. Most of the pricier restaurants have cosmopolitan offerings, but also prepare gourmet Mexican dishes. Your best bet for sampling genuine regional dishes and real Mexican food would be the smaller establishments catering to local people, such as *cenadurías, taquerías,* and *merenderos* that bear the sign "*Antojitos Mexicanos,*" indicating that authentic Mexican food is served. The larger restaurants often accept credit cards, but be sure to bring cash to the smaller ones.

Mexico City

Most major restaurants in Mexico City have á la carte menus. Entrees usually include a vegetable and a starch (often a *sopa seca*—"dry soup"—consisting of a rice dish served before the main course, or *tortillas*, French-style bread, or fried potatoes). Salads, soups, desserts, and beverages will be extra. The prices quoted here are for entrees only.

Ambassadeurs Continental cuisine. *Comida*: US$12 and up. No breakfast. Jacket and tie. Reservations advised. Paseo de la Reforma 12. Tel: (5) 566-9400.

Cafe El Popular Mexican cuisine. *Comida*: Less than US$8. Serves breakfast. Casual. Open 24 hours. No reservations. Cinco de Mayo 52, Zócalo. Tel: (5) 518-6081.

El Buen Comer French cuisine. *Comida*: Less than US$15. No breakfast. Casual. Reservations required. Edgar Allen Poe 50, Polanco; Tel: (5) 203-5337 or (5) 545-8057.

Estoril International cuisine and traditional Mexican. *Comida*: US$35 and up. No breakfast. Jacket and tie. Reservations advised. Polanco location: Alejandro Dumas 24; Tel: (5) 531-4896. Zona Rosa location: Génova 75; Tel: (5) 511-3421.

Fonda El Refugio Regional Mexican cuisine. *Comida*: US$20 and up. No breakfast. Dressy casual. Reservations advised. Liverpool 166, Zona Rosa; Tel: (5) 528-5823.

Honfleur French cuisine. First class. *Comida*: US$35 and up. No breakfast. Jacket and tie. Reservations advised. Amberes 14-A, Zona Rosa. Tel: (5) 533-1181.

Isadora Mexican cuisine. *Comida*: US$35 and up. No breakfast. Jacket and tie. Reservations required. Molière 50; Tel: (5) 520-7901.

Las Cazuelas Traditional Mexican cuisine. *Comida*: Less than US$15. No breakfast. Casual. No reservations. República de Colombia 69; Tel: (5) 522-0689.

Restaurante Vegetariano y Dietético Vegetarian cuisine. *Comida*: Less than US$6. Serves breakfast. Casual. No reservations. Madero 56, Zócalo; Tel: (5) 521-6880; and Filomata 13, Zócalo; Tel: (5) 521-1895.

Restaurante y Cafeteria del Rhin Mexican cuisine. *Comida*: Less than US$9. Serves breakfast. Casual. No reservations. Río Rhin 49, Zona Rosa, around corner from British Embassy. Tel: (5) 571-9452.

Guadalajara

Acuarius Vegetarian cuisine. *Comida*: Less than US$10. Serves breakfast. Casual. No reservations. Prisciliano Sánchez 416, near Plaza de Armas; Tel: (3) 613-6277.

Dainzu Oaxacan cuisine. *Comida*: Less than US$15. No breakfast. Casual. No reservations. Avenida Diamante 2598, between Plaza del Sol and Plaza Arboledas; Tel: (3) 647-5086.

La Vianda International cuisine, with emphasis on Mexican and New Orleans Creole. *Comida*: US$35 and up. No breakfast. Jacket and tie. Reservations advised. Avenida Chapalita 120; Tel: (3) 622-5926.

Place de la Concorde French cuisine. *Comida*: US$35 and up. Evenings only. Formal attire. Reservations advised on weekends. In Fiesta Americana Hotel; Tel: (3) 625-3434.

Rio Viejo Mexican cuisine. *Comida*: US$20 and up. No breakfast. Jacket and tie. Reservations advised. Avenida de Las Americas 302; Tel: (3) 616-5321.

Monterrey

The regional cuisine of Nuevo León features *cabrito* (baby goat), barbequed over coals.

El Pastor Regional Mexican cuisine. *Comida*: US$15 to US$25. No breakfast. Casual. No reservations. Madero Poniente 1067, Zona Rosa; Tel: (83) 46-8954.

El Rey del Cabrito Regional Mexican cuisine. *Comida*: Less than US$15. Casual. No reservations. Corner of José Coss and Constitución; Tel: (83) 45-3232.

Luisiana Continental cuisine. *Comida*: US$25 and up. No breakfast. Jacket and tie. Reservations advised. Plaza Hidalgo, Zona Rosa; Tel: (83) 43-1561, 40-2185, 40-3753.

Residence Mexican and Continental cuisines. *Comida*: US$30 and up. No breakfast. Jacket and tie. Reservations advised. Delgollado and Matamoros; Tel: (83) 45-5418, 45-5040, 45-5478.

Taquería las Monjitas Mexican cuisine. *Comida*: Less than US$7. Serves breakfast. Casual. No reservations. Escobedo 913; Tel: (83) 44-6713.

Tijuana

If you want to sample the range of food available in Tijuana, take a stroll down Avenida Revolución— a Mexican version of a Singaporean hawker's center, with restaurants and stalls offering food for every palate and budget. Try seafood prepared Mexican style, or pheasant, quail, rabbit, and duck, in addition to the more mundane beef, chicken, and pork.

Alcázar del Río International cuisine. *Comida*: US$20 and up. No breakfast. Jacket and tie. Reservations advised. Boulevard Paseo de los Héroes 56-5, opposite Sears Shopping Center; Tel: (66) 84-2672.

La Especial Home-style Mexican. *Comida*: Less than US$8. Casual. No reservations. Avenida Revolución 718; Tel: (66) 85-6654.

La Fonda Roberto's Regional Mexican cuisine. *Comida*: Less than US$15. Casual. No reservations. In Siesta Motel, Old Ensenada Highway near

Boulvevard Agua Caliente; Tel: (66) 86-1601.

Señor Frog's International cuisine. Part of the Carlos Anderson chain. *Comida*: Less than US$8. Casual. No reservations. In Pueblo Amigo Center, Paseo Tijuana; no phone.

Tía Juana Tilly's Mexican food. *Comida*: Less than US$15. Casual. No reservations. Avenida Revolución at Calle 7; Tel: (66) 85-6024.

LOCAL CUSTOMS OVERVIEW

In many ways, business etiquette in Mexico is similar to that in many Asian nations. There's a premium on formality, politeness, and graciousness, as well as on personal relationships. This emphasis on form, and the almost choreographic nature of interactions, means that business negotiations take on a subtlety that is easily lost on visitors from outside the culture. This is less of a factor in northern Mexico—for example, in Monterrey, Tijuana, or Ciudad Juárez—where the pace is faster and businesspeople have been heavily influenced by the more blunt business style of their *gringo* neighbors.

Intrinsic to the emphasis on politeness is the prohibition on saying "no," a prohibition that could cost you time and money if you are unable to read between the lines. Like Asians, Mexicans go to great lengths to avoid delivering bad news; they are taught to please people, to give them what they want. Thus, if they don't know the answer to a question, don't want to give you what you want during negotiations, or want to tell you what you want to hear, they may answer yes—and you'll find out later that they didn't mean what they said. When confronted, their excuse will be, "Something came up (*algo sucédio*)." This national trait has given Mexico a reputation for unreliability, difficulty, and interminable delay, although a lack of understanding of the local context on the part of foreigners contributes mightily to this situation.

It is important to ask for specific answers. This can be a true test of patience, which you must never abandon. Just keep pressing your point—politely—until you've narrowed the answer down as much as you can. This tactic can ensure neither the quality of a product or service, nor on-time delivery, but it can give you a better idea of what to expect and thus save you time, money, and worry. You may also want to employ the services of a consultant whose sole duty it is to track the production and delivery performance of Mexican firms.

As Mexico modernizes and expands its international trade, especially under pressure from the North American Free Trade Agreement (NAFTA) and the General Agreement on Tariffs and Trade (GATT), Mexican businesspeople will have to adopt international standards of reliability and straightforwardness; those who don't will face bankruptcy.

The personal relationship that is developed through negotiations and business dealings is as important to Mexicans as the negotiations or dealings themselves. Every economic transaction is also a social transaction, a fact that many Western businesspeople tend to forget. Indeed, relationships lay the foundation for business; without a solid personal relationship, negotiations can founder and business can fail to get off the ground. Of course, building a personal relationship takes time, and Mexicans seem to have plenty of time to talk about everything (especially family) except business. Don't expect to begin serious negotiations until you've made several trips to meet your prospective partner, supplier, distributor, or agent. When conversations about family, the weather, food, and sports have waned, you can try gently to steer things around to a discussion of business. Once your relationship has blossomed, you'll find you can do deals with a handshake. However, don't trust a handshake alone. Be sure to get it in writing and in detail—in Spanish with an English (or other appropriate language) translation.

The personal nature of business in Mexico also means that introductions and connections are invaluable. People in high places and with good contacts can act as matchmakers. Because Mexicans have deep respect for position, status, and power, the grander the matchmaker's title and more exalted the position, the better. That person can refer you to someone else, and so on down the line, until you meet the person you want. In Mexico, it is who you know and whose name you can drop that count as much as—if not more than—anything else.

Give some serious thought to what your policy towards bribery is before you go to Mexico. Demands for bribes aren't as common or blatant as they once were, but businesspeople at virtually all levels are likely to encounter them somewhere along the line. Because bribery is endemic in Mexico, it is difficult to avoid the issue altogether. It may be necessary to pay to get products into or out of the country. On the other hand, if you deal through a Mexican agent or distributor, it may not be necessary to become directly involved.

Finally, a few points on business etiquette:

- The handshake is the standard greeting.
- Your attempts to speak Spanish will be much appreciated and endear you to your Mexican contacts; even if you speak Spanish poorly and they laugh at you (usually not to your face), they will appreciate your efforts.
- Address your contact by his title, both in speaking and writing—for example, *Ingeniero* or *Arquitecto*. If you don't know the title, use *Licenciado* instead of *Señor*. Abbreviate the titles when you write them—for example, *Ing,*

Arq, or *Lic.*

- Most Mexicans use both patronymic and matronymic surnames, such as López García— the father's name precedes the mother's maiden name. Drop the mother's name in conversation, but include it in writing and formal or legal address. For example, say "Ingeniero López" but write "Ing. López García."
- Be prepared to wait for your appointment beyond the scheduled time. Mexicans often deliberately schedule business appointments during siesta time (between 2 and 5 pm), when they will be at lunch or effectively off-duty. They may also schedule several appointments at the same time, knowing that many people won't show up at all. On the other hand, a few may show up, causing others to run behind. In Mexico, it is generally considered acceptable— in some cases preferable—to be late. It is also a sign of power to make others wait. Just relax; they'll understand your explanation that "something came up."
- It is good to engage in chitchat as you build your relationship, but certain topics should be avoided. Such topics include, first and foremost, the Mexican War of 1846 (known in Mexico as the Northern Intervention), corruption, illegal immigration to the US, and many areas of religion and politics. Don't refer to your traveler's diarrhea as Montezuma's Revenge; in fact, don't refer to it at all more than to mildly excuse yourself for *un mal del estómago* (an upset stomach).
- Mexico is a country of *machismo*—aggressive maleness—and women in business can be at a real disadvantage. Mexican men unfairly regard lone women as potential prey—although often the leers and remarks are little more than a game which is engaged in because it is expected. However, do not merely assume this. If a foreign woman must do business with a Mexican man, she should make every effort to dress and behave in a conservative, strong, businesslike manner, walking the fine line between brooking no nonsense while at the same time not threatening the Mexican male's ego.

DOMESTIC TRANSPORTATION

Metro Both Mexico City and Guadalajara have well thought out public underground rail (Metro) systems. Businesspeople may want to consider using them, especially given the congested nature of surface traffic. Monterrey's Metro has only a single line, which runs east-west and serves mainly the suburbs and residential areas; a north-south line is supposed to open in 1994, which may make the Monterrey Metro useful for the business visitor.

Some five million people crowd onto Mexico City's Metro trains every working day. You can't carry luggage onto the Metro, and you can easily have your pocket picked. In fact, the likelihood of losing your wallet, purse, money, and documents to clever thieves—often working in tandem—belies the cheapness of the ride, a mere 40 centavos (about US$0.12). Otherwise, the Metro is very safe. A key preventative is to avoid rush hours, when the uninitiated find it difficult to even get down the stairs and into the stations; stick to middays and Sundays. Women (and men) should note that during rush hours, some cars are reserved for women and children, ostensibly to protect them from harassment and thievery.

Mexico City's Metro stations are clean and well lighted; some even have artwork or preserved Aztec temples discovered during construction. The trains are modern and quiet, running on rubber tires. There are eight ever-expanding lines with stations — some of them quite elaborate, such as Insurgentes, which is a major below-ground shopping complex— throughout the city and the metropolitan area. Use the color-keyed signs and maps, or ask at the information counters to determine which train you should take. Head for the boarding platform (*andenes*), buy a ticket (*boleto*) at a ticket booth, slip it into the turnstile, and board the train. When you get off, look for the exit (*salida*) sign.

Guadalajara's Metro is less elaborate. It has only two lines, but they go to just about all the important places for only about US$0.25.

Taxi Taxis are by far the most convenient way to get around Mexican cities. If convenience has monetary value to you, they're also the cheapest conveyance. Nevertheless, because of the chaotic nature of street traffic, you can usually count on spending extended periods in any cab you take, so you might consider walking the shorter distances.

Some taxis are metered, some are not; some are metered in the daytime but not at night; some have broken meters; and some drivers charge fixed fares. Before you get in a taxi, ask the driver if the meter is working: *"¿Funciona el taxímetro?"* If the meter isn't working, bargain with the driver to set the fare before going anywhere. You don't have to tip the driver unless he helps with your luggage, in which case 10 percent is the going rate. Don't plan on just being able to give the driver the address of your destination. The Mexican system confuses even the taxi drivers. Instead, give him the name of the hotel, building, or place and what it is near.

Bus Government-owned city buses in Mexico City are a good and cheap way to get around—if you avoid rush hours and the routes most used by tourists, especially Paseo de la Reforma and around the Zócalo, Alameda, and Zona Rosa (which are likely to be the places you most want to go). More than 15 million riders daily use the city's buses and mini-buses; that means crowds, and crowds mean pickpockets and thieves, as well as delays and discomfort. Fares are only a few centavos. Privately owned microbuses are less likely to harbor pickpockets. They also run along major streets; hold out your hand when the one you want comes by; each has a route sign on the windshield. Tell the driver where you want to get off—shout *"baja,"* (for "down")—or push the button near the door. The fares begin at about US$0.20.

Guadalajara also has an excellent bus system that provides comprehensive service throughout the city. Monterrey's system is not as easy to use, and a taxi is a better choice there. Taxis are also the best way to get around Tijuana.

Intercity buses cover the nation, and can be a good way to see the countryside provided you choose well. The only long-distance buses that can compare with standard US or European long-distance buses are the *de lujo* (deluxe, also called *ejecutivo* or *plus*) buses. These are big, modern, and comfortable. And they can get you from city to city at a fraction of the cost of air travel, although, of course, the bus takes more time. The better class buses usually have reclining seats, video monitors, toilets, and stewards serving snacks and beverages. However, note that smoking is permitted on Mexican buses, so the air is often thick; you should bring your own toilet paper just in case; and you should also pack a lunch in the event that the restaurant where the bus stops doesn't appeal to you. Very often the air conditioning—assuming it is working at all—is turned to the "glacier" setting, so bring a sweater. Reserve your seat a day in advance for these buses. Oddly enough, they tend to keep to their schedules, so be on time.

Private Car Driving in Mexico is primarily for the truly adventurous. In many areas of the country, driving takes on the characteristics of a frontier trek. In Mexico City, the world's largest and most polluted urban center, it can be a nightmare. The only exception to the general rule dictating that outsiders refrain from driving in Mexico involves the towns near the US border—Tijuana, Ensenada, and Mexicali in Baja California Norte; Nogales and Agua Prieta in Sonora; Ciudad Juárez in Chihuahua; and Nuevo Laredo, Reynosa, and Matamoros in Tamaulipas. Travelers can also generally include Monterrey on this list of places where it is reasonable for them to drive, because the city has new four-lane toll roads connecting it to Nuevo Laredo and Reynosa, making it a straightforward three-hour drive from the border. The distances are short enough, the roads in good enough repair, the law enforcement and services availability good enough—and the alternatives poor enough—to make driving to these bustling industrial and commer-

cial centers a reasonable proposition.

If you drive your own car into Mexico, you need Mexican auto insurance, which you can buy at crossings on either side of the border for about US$10 to US$20 a day. Be sure to get sufficient coverage for the length of your stay and the distance into Mexico you expect to drive. If you get into an accident and don't have Mexican insurance, you will probably end up in jail while the authorities decide what to do about you—under Mexico's Napoleonic Code legal system, you are basically guilty until proven innocent.

If you are driving your car from the US into Mexico and will be traveling outside the border zone or free trade zone (including the Baja California Peninsula and the Sonora Free Trade Zone) you will need to obtain a permit for temporary importation of the car. The permit is valid for periods of up to six months and is good for multiple crossings during that time. Be certain to carry the permit with you at all times, but do not leave it in the car, since you will need it if the car is stolen or damaged. If you are stopped and are unable to present valid documents, the car can be confiscated immediately.

To obtain the permit at the border, it is necessary to present:

- A valid state registration certificate for the car or a document that certifies the legal ownership of the vehicle;
- The leasing contract (if the vehicle is leased or rented), which must be in the name of the person importing the car; if the vehicle belongs to a company, present documentation certifying that the employee works for the company;
- A valid driver's license, issued outside Mexico; and
- An international credit card (American Express, Diner's Club, MasterCard or VISA), also issued outside Mexico.

The credit card will be charged in an amount equivalent to US$10. If you do not possess an international credit card, you will be asked instead to post a bond, payable to the Mexican Federal Treasury, issued by an authorized bonding company in Mexico. As an alternative to posting a bond, you may make a cash deposit at the Banco del Ejército in an amount based on the value of your vehicle, ranging from US$500 to US$20,000 on an official sliding scale according to the type and age of the vehicle. For this purpose, there are Banjército (Banco del Ejército) "banking modules" at 18 border points, many of them open 24 hours a day and seven days a week. Your deposit, whether made through Banco del Ejército or a bonding company, plus any interest it may have earned, will be returned to you when you leave Mexico. Bonding companies assess taxes and processing costs for their services. For more information on temporary importation of vehicles, contact the nearest Mexican consulate (refer to the "Important Addresses" chapter) or Mexico Information, 355 Palermo, Coral Gables, FL 33134, USA; Tel: (800) 446-8277 (in the US only).

US car rental companies have varying restrictions on their cars being taken into Mexico from the US. Depending on the city you drive in from, the distance you can drive into Mexico may be as much as 400 miles or as little as 25 miles. Or you can rent a car at exorbitant rates from the Mexican branches of US-based auto rental firms, such as Avis, National, Budget, and Hertz, in which case you can expect to pay upwards of US$80 a day (US$400 per week) for a Volkswagen Beetle, including insurance. Neither your personal auto insurance nor your credit card car rental insurance coverage will be in force in Mexico. Carefully check the car you're renting—it is common to get one with bald tires, dents, scratches, and missing parts. In addition to the safety issues these conditions suggest, you can be charged for them upon return unless you have noted them in writing before signing the contract and accepting the vehicle. Despite the hassle, renting a car can be a convenient way to make short day trips into the countryside.

Never park illegally in Mexico: the police will either confiscate your license plates—which means a trip to the police station to pay a fine—or confiscate the car should the license plates be welded to the car (as many car rental companies are doing these days). Always obey the speed limits in the cities and towns to avoid a "fine" that seems to be payable directly to the police officer. Use only premium fuel: *sin* at the Pemex stations. It is only 87 octane, but it is the highest grade available in Mexico. Despite attempts to curb auto emissions pollution, it is still difficult to obtain unleaded fuel in Mexico. Never plan to drive at night in Mexico, because road hazards increase seemingly geometrically after dark.

If you run into road trouble—have a breakdown or an accident, run out of fuel, need a tow, or seek protection from criminals—the Green Angels can come to your aid. The Mexican Tourism Administration operates the *Angeles Verdes*, a radio-dispatched fleet of 250 trucks with bilingual drivers who patrol certain sections of highway from 8 am to 8 pm. Within their patrol areas are roadside phones for calling them—the 24-hour toll-free number is 250-4817. Their services are free, and they sell parts and fuel at cost. (They do appreciate tips.)

Air Air travel is the only real option for getting around this huge country with anything resembling a schedule and comfort. Mexicana and Aeroméxico are the main domestic carriers, while Aero California and Aeromar also offer domestic flights. Call the airlines directly to book a flight. Arrive an hour early to keep from getting bumped off the chronically overbooked

HOLIDAYS	
New Year's Day	January 1
Constitution Day	February 5
Benito Juárez's Birthday	March 21
Good Friday and Easter	Late March or April
Labor Day	May 1
Battle of Puebla Day *(Cinco de Mayo)*	May 5
President's Annual Message	September 1
Declaration of Independence Day	September 15
Independence Day	September 16
Day of the Race (Columbus Day)	October 12
All Saints/All Souls Day	November 1-2
Anniversary of the Mexican Revolution	November 20
Day of Our Lady of Guadalupe	December 12
Christmas	December 25

flights, and collect and recheck your luggage between connecting flights. Expect to pay as much for air travel within Mexico as you would for domestic flights in the US or any Western country.

Train For anyone but the most rough and ready traveler, train travel in Mexico is not an option for business purposes, and when cost is factored in, it can't even compete with the deluxe buses. In general, Mexico's state-run train system is for those with lots of time, lots of personal padding, and lots of patience—and for those who bring their own food, water, and toilet paper. Under these conditions, even a short haul—for example, the 12-hour trip from Mexico City to Guadalajara—can seem endless. The single exception is *El Regiomontaño*, a train which runs between Nuevo Laredo and Mexico City, with stops in Monterrey, Saltillo, and San Luis Potosí. The sleeper fare is about US$90. For information and schedules, call Mexico By Train (Tel: (800) 321-1699) in the US.

HOLIDAYS/BANK HOLIDAYS

Mexico's many holidays and festivals represent religious observation, Indian lore, or political or historical remembrance. In addition to the holidays listed here—during which most banks, businesses, and government agencies are closed—there are many regional festivals that also close down regular business for a day or two. Business slows to crawl around Christmas and New Year's and at Easter (*semana santa*, or holy week).

BUSINESS HOURS

Commerce adjusts to the *siesta* (midday nap), which in Mexico usually lasts from 2 pm to 4 pm. Most banks are open from 9 am to 1:30 pm weekdays (although some in the larger cities reopen after *siesta* from 4 pm to 6 pm), on Saturdays from 10 am to 1:30 pm and 4 pm to 6 pm, and even on Sundays from 10 am to 1:30 pm. Businesses and shops are generally open from 9 am to 2 pm and 4 pm to 7 pm. Government offices operate from 8 am to 3 pm, and do not reopen.

COMMUNICATIONS

Telephones If Mexico has serious plans to join the modern world, it will have to modernize its antiquated and overpriced telephone system. If you plan to get your own phone in Mexico, plan six months ahead, because that is generally how long you will have to wait. There aren't enough lines; switching equipment is archaic and overworked; connections are often scratchy; the number of digits in phone numbers varies from city to city; and public phones are out of order more often than not. Area codes range from one digit to three, and, along with city exchanges, are being changed all over the country. For example, Guadalajara's city code changed recently from 36 to 3; the 6 was added to the beginning of the local numbers, which thus increased from six digits to seven —and so every Guadalajara phone number begins with a 6. The same thing could have happened to poor six digit Monterrey by the time you read these words. All this confusion can add up to trouble when you make a phone call—and that is when you will discover that operators are not exactly founts of information. To add insult to injury, Mexico recently raised local rates, while lowering long-distance rates marginally.

Local Calls Because public phones are so often broken, it is much easier—but also much more expensive—to make local calls from your hotel room or lobby. You can also use phones in telephone company offices and in certain shops (usually those with a telephone symbol in the window or on a sign).

Long-Distance Calls Call long-distance within Mexico on Ladatel: (short for *larga distancia telefono*) phones, which are located in *caseta de larga distancia* (long-distance telephone offices), hotels, airports, railway stations, and bus terminals, as well as on major streets. You will find calling instructions in English and French as well as Spanish. You can use coins, tokens or cards—either major credit cards or telephone company debit cards, which you can buy at telephone company offices, hotel reception desks, or pharmacies. Some Ladatel phones tick off the minutes as you talk (at about US$1 per minute). Always direct-dial your long-distance call; operator-assisted calls are not only expensive, but frustrating. First dial 91 for station-to-station calls (or 92 for person-to-person or collect calls), then the area code, then the local number. To save money, call during evenings (after 5 pm) or on weekends.*

International Calls International calls are especially expensive: Mexico's phone tariffs are so high that, even from the US, it is still cheaper to call Europe than to call most places in Mexico for the first minute, and additional minute charges are greater than those to Ethiopia, Singapore, Saudi Arabia, or Brazil. It's even worse if you use the Mexican phone system: a half-hour operator-assisted call from Mexico City to the US could cost US$100 when you include hotel surcharges. With such a cash cow in its barn, Mexico so far has refused to join World Connect, the international affiliation of major phone companies that allows visitors in foreign countries to call their home countries, or other countries, by dialing an access code that bypasses the local phone system—and bills the call to their home phone number, saving a lot of money in the process.

NAFTA tariff-cutting rules say that phone rates must reflect economic costs, so Mexico may eventually be forced to lower its international calling rates. But for now there are few ways to reduce your international calling costs:

- Have people in the US or other countries call you in Mexico, rather than calling them from Mexico.
- Use AT&T USADirect (dial 95 (800) 462-4240) or MCI USA Service (dial 95 (800) 674-7000). You can use either service with your regional phone company calling card or your major credit card; each also accepts its own calling card. Or you can call collect.
- Use AT&T's Message Service, which will leave a message up to one minute long for anyone with access to a phone anywhere in the world. Call the USADirect access number (dial 95 (800) 462-4240) and ask for the Message Service. The attendant will ask for your calling card or major credit card number, and then for the phone number your message is going to. You'll record your name for the greeting, and the attendant will ask if you want the recipient to record a one-minute reply for no additional charge. You then specify whether the message is for a specific person or for anyone who picks up the phone. Record your message. Because it is only one minute long, put your hotel room number or phone number where you can be reached early in the message. Tell the attendant what time and date you want the message to go out—you can

---

Refer to the "Important Addresses" chapter for a listing of city codes within Mexico.

arrange it up to a week in advance. AT&T will try to reach that number every 15 minutes for four hours. If the message isn't delivered within that time frame, there is no charge. Afterwards, you can call the Message Service again to find out if the message got through.

If for some reason you cannot use these services, you can direct-dial internationally from Ladatel phones by pressing 95 (or 96 for person-to-person or collect calls) to reach the US and Canada; you do not need to press 1 for the country code. Press 98 (or 99 for person-to-person or collect calls) to reach other countries; then dial the country code, area code, and local phone number.

Fax Services Most first class hotels have fax services, at the front desk, in a business center, or in individual hotel rooms. You can also find fax machines at major post offices.

Post Office Mexico's mail service is notorious for delays and poor service. Whenever possible, use fax and courier services instead.

USEFUL TELEPHONE NUMBERS

AT&T USADirect 95 (800) 462-4240
MCI USA Service 95 (800) 674-7000
Mexico long-distance station-to-station 91
Mexico long-distance person-to-person or collect 92
USA and Canada station-to-station 95
USA and Canada person-to-person or collect 96
Other countries station-to-station 98
Other countries person-to-person or collect 99
International operator 09
Long-distance operator 02
Local directory assistance 04
Long-distance directory assistance 01
Angeles Verdes (Green Angels emergency road service)
    24-hour toll-free 250-4817
Mexico tourist information hotlines, 24-hour
    (call collect by dialing 91 first) .... (5) 250-0123,
    .... 250-8419, 250-8601
Mexico City tourist information .... (5) 525-9380/3
Tourist legal advice, 24-hour .. (5) 625-8618, 250-0151,
    .... 250-0493, 250-0589, 250-0123
Mexico City Consumer Protection .... (5) 761-3811/3801
Mexican National Railways .... (5) 547-1084
Central de Autobuses
    (fee-for-service bus reservations) .... (5) 533-2047
Mexico Hotel and Motel Association
    (reservations) .... (5) 286-5455
Taxis, Mexico City .... (5) 516-6020, 566-0077

English-Language Media The leading English-language newspaper is *The Mexico City News*, which you can find throughout the country in the larger cities. You can find smaller papers or newsletters in cities and towns that have large numbers of English-speaking tourists and retirees. Most hotels have TV and radios that receive US broadcasts, such as CNN and ESPN.

Courier Services Mexico has a great many courier services, among them Federal Express, DHL, and UPS.

Federal Express

Mexico City Calzada de la Viga 1975, 11590; Tel: (5) 258-9904 Fax: (5) 524-5340. Francisco Sarabia 17, 02440; Tel: (5) 785-6144 Fax: (5) 785-1569. Insurgentes Sur 899, Col. Ampliacíon Nápoles, 02810; Tel: (5) 255-4140 Fax: (5) 254-5340, 203-4066.

Guadalajara Calzada Independencia Sur 1065, Col. Moderna, Sec. Reforma XP, 44100; Tel: (3) 619-6441, 619-0071 Fax: (3) 619-0100.

Monterrey Calle B No. 506, 64860 Apodcaca; Tel: (83) 69-3659 Fax: (83) 69-3654.

DHL

Mexico City Paseo de la Reforma 76, Col. Juárez, 06600; Tel: (5) 546-5302 Fax: (5) 546-5939.

Guadalajara Lázaro Cárdenas 1299, Fracc. Industrial Alamo, 44900; Tel: (3) 670-1885 Fax: (3) 670-2141.

Monterrey Carretera Miguel Alemán Valdez No. 205, Col. Lindavista, 67130 Guadalupe; Tel: (83) 77-1672 Fax: (83) 34-4624.

UPS

Mexico City Calle 2 No. 284, esq. Calle Unión, Col. Pantitlan, 08100; Tel: (5) 756-6590, 756-8122; Fax: (5) 758-5104.

Guadalajara Río Obi 1781, Col. Alamo Industrial, 44910; Tel: (3) 657-2390, 657-2490 Fax: (3) 639-7677.

Monterrey Millimex, Carretera Miguel Alemán km 16.5, Apodaca Bodega 15; Tel: (83) 69-3548/9 Fax: (83) 86-2217.

LOCAL SERVICES

Mexico's big business cities—Mexico City, Guadalajara, Monterrey, Tijuana—have all the business services one would expect. First class hotels often have business centers; if yours doesn't, ask the concierge or the desk to direct you. Whether you need secretarial and translation services, printers, or office rentals, you can find them through your hotel, your Mexican business contacts, or in the phone book. Here we list a few such services in Mexico City.

Secretarial Services

Alto Nivel Secretarial y Administrativo S.A., Boulevard Miguel Avila Camacho 1994-102; Tel: 398-3011/7650.

Manpower S.A., Miguel Laurent 15; Tel: (5) 559-9702, 559-5161, 559-5480, 575-3764.

Secretarías Temporales S.A., Rio Danubio 69; Tel: (5) 514-7844.

Servicios Secretariales Ejecutivos A.P., Baja California 245-404; Tel: (5) 584-7865.

Temporary Office Rentals

A few Mexico City companies specialize in temporary office rentals and services, supplying offices, receptionists, telephone answering services, word processing, private telephone lines (something to consider seriously, given the wait for one you'd otherwise have), phone-in dictation, conference rooms, and fax services.

Headquarters Companies, Presidente Masaryk 61-20, near Paseo de la Reforma; Tel: (5) 203-1749 Fax: (5) 531-9659.

Servicios Ejecutivos Mexicanos, Avenida Insurgentes Sur 2388; Tel: (5) 550-4657.

Servicios Integrales Ejecutivos, Presidente Masaryk 61; Tel: (5) 203-1740, 203-2178, 254-2328, 531-9564.

Translation Services

Translation services provide not only translations of documents, but simultaneous translation interpreter service, computer printouts, audio and video equipment rentals, conference organization services, and bilingual aides (*edecanes*).

Berlitz, E. Nacional 530 PB, Col. Polanco; Tel: (5) 255-3341 Fax: (5) 255-3817.

CITI, Avenida Chapultepec 471, Desp. 403; Tel: (5) 286-9192, 286-8832 Fax: (5) 538-0421.

Lanser de México, Durango 247, Piso 4, 06700; Tel: (5) 208-5735, 514-0605.

Sittco, Melchor Ocampo 193, Desp. A, Plaza Galerias; Tel/Fax: (5) 260-0676.

STAYING SAFE AND HEALTHY

Turista Traveler's diarrhea is common for foreigners in Mexico as it is for foreigners anywhere else, including the US. Your digestive system isn't ready for the foreign intestinal flora it encounters and tries to expel them, at great inconvenience, discomfort, occasional embarrassment, and some slight risk to you and your busy schedule.

To minimize the problem, drink only boiled or bottled water, which is available everywhere. If you're not sure about the water, have a cup of coffee or tea, or a soda or beer. Never drink tap water; don't even use it to brush your teeth. Don't use ice cubes, since they are usually made from tap water. Don't eat raw fruits or vegetables unless you can wash them in boiled or bottled water and peel them yourself. If you are traveling for three weeks or less, you may want to take Pepto Bismol or an antibiotic (doxycycline or trimethoprim/sulfamethoxazole) as a preventive. There is also a grapefruit-based antibacterial product called NutriBiotic that is available in health food stores as drops that can be used to purify water. But be careful: sometimes there are side-effects, and antibiotics in particular increase the risk that your body will develop resistant bacteria.

Even with such precautions, it is likely that you will have a bout with diarrhea. The best treatment is to ride it out as your body adapts and heals itself. The main danger is dehydration, especially in a warm climate like Mexico's. Keep yourself well hydrated by drinking plenty of water (again boiled or bottled is best, but any is better than none), carbonated drinks, herbal teas, fruit juices, and clear broth soups. Drink at least two glasses of liquid after each trip to the bathroom. Avoid solid foods for the first 24 hours, and then begin eating bland foods—bananas, rice, crackers, plain toast or bread, potatoes, fish, lean meat, beans, and lentils. Avoid dairy products, raw fruits (except bananas) and vegetables, fats, greasy foods, colas, and spicy foods. Also avoid caffeine and alcohol: both are diuretics, which cause your body to lose water.

If severe nausea or vomiting accompanies your diarrhea, don't try to eat anything, but focus on rehydration. Take small, frequent sips of liquid. If the vomiting doesn't stop within a day, take an anti-nausea drug such as promethizine, which you can get from your hotel doctor or a pharmacy without a prescription.

If you must travel with traveler's diarrhea, take a plane, a deluxe train, or a bus, all of which have bathrooms. If the bathroom just can't meet your needs, Pepto Bismol can usually handle mild to moderate diarrhea. If you have heavy-duty diarrhea, you'll need over-the-counter Immodium or Lomotil. Be aware that while these drugs are very good at stopping you up, they treat only the symptoms, not the cause, so take them only when absolutely necessary. Otherwise, follow the treatment regimen above and allow your body to heal itself.

Altitude Sickness Most of your business in Mexico will be conducted on the central plateau. Mexico City is near the 2,300 meter mark (7,500 feet), while Guadalajara is at 1,590 meters (5,150 feet). If you plunge right into business as soon as you arrive from a low elevation, you'll probably notice shortness of breath, headache, fatigue, and maybe nausea—the symptoms of altitude sickness. Your body could take up to a week to adjust completely, but if you take it easy for a couple of days, you should be able to function reasonably well. In Mexico City your rate and ability to adapt depends a great deal on the air pollution level, which is highest during winter air inversions. Drink plenty of fluids (but not alcohol), don't exercise, and avoid inhaling motor vehicle exhaust.

Bronchitis Lowered resistance from colds or flu plus the world class smog, dust, and other particulates in Mexico City (some studies have rated breathing Mexico City's air as the equivalent of smoking two packs of cigarettes per day) often add up to bronchitis, which can be either viral or bacterial. The main danger of bronchitis is that it can set you up for pneumonia.

If you get a cold or the flu, you can fend off bronchitis by getting out of the city to a place with fresh air and a relaxing pace; one of the many beach or mountain resorts will do just fine. If you can't get away, don't hang around the streets too much, always travel in air conditioned taxis and buses, and avoid cigarette smoke. Treatment includes steam inhalation and hot drinks to loosen phlegm, plus a balanced and varied diet with plenty of liquids. If yours is a severe case of bacterial bronchitis—marked by greenish phlegm—you may need to see a doctor for antibiotics. Viral bronchitis produces a clear phlegm. There's no medicine to directly combat viral infections; you can take medicines for the symptoms, but the only treatment is rest, liquids, good nutrition, and the avoidance of irritants.

Crime Travel in Mexico, even in the cities, is safer than in many places in the US. However, pickpockets and purse-snatchers are common, especially in the teeming crowds of Mexico City, but less so in other large cities. Thieves consider tourists to be prime targets, and look for prey in places tourists frequent, such as in a city's Zona Rosa (entertainment and shopping district), or the Mexico City Metro, on buses, inside pedestrian underpasses, and in crowded plazas. Follow these tips to protect your person and valuables:

- Check in with your embassy or consulate when you arrive in Mexico. Ask about street crime and precautions.
- Ask at your hotel about the safety of the surrounding streets.
- Avoid flashy displays of wealth—gold, jewelry, and clothes. Dress and behave conservatively.
- Leave most of your cash and traveler's checks, your passport and other documents, jewelry, and camera in your hotel safe unless you absolutely need to take them with you. Be sure to get a receipt from the desk clerk.
- Make several photocopies of your passport's salient pages and of other travel documents, and carry them with you instead of the original items.

- Place the money that you carry with you in a moneybelt; carry only small amounts of cash in your pockets.
- Use credit cards or traveler's checks for most of your transactions.
- Behave and walk confidently as if you know where you are, where you are going, and what you are doing. Muggers are known to be drawn to the lost, confused, or tentative as they are to designer logos, Rolex watches, or wads of cash.
- Walk with your briefcase or shoulder bag to the side away from the street to keep motorcycling thieves from grabbing it.
- Carry your own baggage whenever possible. Always keep it within sight unless you've entrusted it to a first class hotel porter; a uniformed airport porter; or an airline, deluxe bus (not a village or second class bus) or first class train baggage check-in.

Personal Care Products Bring your own prescription medicines, vitamins, women's sanitary products, deodorant, shaving lotion, and the like. The kinds of products you're used to are in short supply and very expensive, if they're available at all. Film is readily available, but imported film is very expensive. Make sure your prescription medicines are properly labeled and that you don't have excessive amounts, or you could run into trouble at the border, both upon entering and leaving Mexico.

EMERGENCY INFORMATION

Police

While some Mexican police officers are friendly, helpful, and competent, they are generally of little help in emergency situations. Your best bet is always to contact your consulate or a tourist hotline for help. The attorney general of each state has an aide just to help tourists in legal trouble with officials or businesspeople. (*See* also Useful Telephone Numbers in this chapter.)

Mexico City:
- Emergency (fire police, ambulance, etc.) 06
- Police (non-emergency) 08
  (5) 625-8008
  (5) 625-7490
- Fire .... (5) 768-3700
- Federal Highway Police .... (5) 684-2142
  (5) 684-9512
- Red Cross .... (5) 557-5757

Guadalajara:
- State police .... (3) 617-5838
- Highway patrol .... (3) 612-7194
- Tourist office (days only) .... (3) 614-0606 x114

Doctors and Hospitals

Mexico has generally good medical care, but be careful about entrusting your health to any but the better big city hospitals. All major hotels have doctors on call. Your consulate, or in some cases your hotel, can refer you to trusted doctors.

Mexico City American British Cowdray Hospital, Calle Sur 136-201; Tel: (5) 277-5000; for emergencies: (5) 516-8077, 515-8359.

Hospital Angeles del Pedregal, Camino de Santa Teresa 1055, Col. Héroes de Padierna; Tel: 652-1188.

Mexican Red Cross; Tel: (5) 557-5757 or 393-1111.

Guadalajara Mexico-American Hospital, Colomos 2110; Tel: (3) 641-3141, 641-0089, 642-4520, 642-4510.

DEPARTURE FORMALITIES

Leaving Mexico is uncharacteristically simple. If you are flying out, you hand in your tourist card and pay a US$12 departure tax at the airport before boarding the plane (the tax may already have been included in the price of your ticket). If you are driving your car back to the US, the US border guards will ask to see your registration and title. Your car may be searched cursorily for fruit, drugs, or illegal aliens, but long lines at the border crossings mostly preclude the guards devoting their efforts to any but the most suspicious-looking people and vehicles.

BEST TRAVEL BOOKS

For any country, the best travel books will not only give you much practical information for surviving, but will enlighten you about the people, history, and culture. Remember that Mexico is changing fast, and telephone numbers, street addresses, and prices lead the way, so be prepared. We've found that a few books on Mexico stand out from the crowd, although none are especially directed toward the business traveler.

Fodor's 94 Mexico, edited by Paula Consolo. New York: Fodor's Travel Publications, 1993. ISBN 0-679-02528-6. 572 pages, US$18.00. Oriented towards the tourist and shopper, but strong on transportation, hotels, and restaurants. 67 pages of maps of fair quality. Needs more on Monterrey and other major cities outside Mexico City and Guadalajara.

Mexico '94 on $45 a Day: Frommer's Budget Travel Guide, by Marita Adair. New York: Prentice Hall Travel, 1994. ISBN 0-671-84908-5. 778 pages, US$19.00. As up-to-date as you can get in a travel book of this scope. Huge amounts of information on money-saving hotels and restaurants. Good on background and on transportation and communications. Lots of extra tips. Inexplicably ignores Baja California Norte (Tijuana, Mexicali, and Ensenada), as if it weren't even there. 52 pages of maps, which could be much better.

Frommer's also has guides for several cities in Mexico which are less focused on budget travel, giving a wider range of hotels and restaurants, as well as bit more detail on the sights. *Frommer's Puerto Vallarta, Manzanillo & Guadalajara '94-95* and *Frommer's Acapulco, Ixtapa, & Taxco '93-94* are both fairly current, but unfortunately, *Frommer's Mexico City & Acapulco '91-92* has not been revised.

Mexico: A Travel Survival Kit, by Tom Brosnahan, John Noble, Nancy Keller, Mark Balla, and Scott Wayne. Hawthorn, Victoria, Australia: Lonely Planet Publications, 1992. ISBN 0-86442-166-4. 924 pages, US$19.95. The usual Lonely Planet guide for the independent, budget-minded traveler: fat, thorough, insightful, irreverent, practical, especially for backpacking wanderers and those who want to spend like them—but still, the best travel book on Mexico, whatever the budget. Very good maps—174 of them.

Baedeker's Mexico, New York: Prentice Hall Travel 1993. ISBN 0-671-87478-0. US$24.00. Little practical travel information, but lots of background: sights, history, and culture, with many color illustrations and maps. The alphabetical encyclopedia style of the bulk of the book means that some smaller towns not covered in other guides are included here. Another major bonus is the large, detailed foldout road map of the entire country.

Mexico: An American Express Travel Guide, by James and Oliver Tickell. New York: Prentice Hall Travel, 1993. 4th edition. US$15.00. Organized state-by-state, with good color maps of the country and Mexico City. The presentation is somewhat dry, but the book is packed with practical information on hotels, restaurants, entertainment, and shopping.

Business Culture

Understanding Mexico's cultural heritage and traditional power relationships is the first and most important step in understanding its people and how business is done in the country. Mexico has a long, rich heritage of not only glory and triumph, but also of struggle and defeat. Although free trade and modernization are current buzzwords in Mexico's business sectors, the country is steeped in history, tradition, and custom, to such an extent that not being aware of these elements constitutes a definite obstacle to operating successfully there.

The Living Past and Its Present Legacy

A highly developed civilization, the Aztec empire was glorious, colorful, brutal, and highly organized. The Spanish chroniclers make it clear that they were in awe of the grandeur of Aztec society. However, the society was divided: the privileged few governed the many. Local *caciques* (chiefs) made all decisions and ritually administered—if they did not actually handle—all transactions, making for a highly centralized system of trade, taxation and tribute, and social and political control. Social status was determined by birth, yet every person felt that he or she had a vital, ordained role to play in society, and thus steadfastly identified with the body politic.

The Spanish conquest of Mexico was relatively rapid and remarkably easy, primarily because the Spanish simply removed the Aztec leadership and took over the existing system. By retaining much of the preexisting authoritarian structure, the *conquistadores*, despite being heavily outnumbered, were able to assure stability in their new colony. The Spanish introduced not so much fundamental change as a new cultural layer, dominating the Indians, who had no tradition of self-government.

The Spanish did add some new cultural elements to Mexican society: stratification based on race, the attendant idea of racial mixing, and Catholicism. The encounter between the two alien cultures led to some interesting results. For example, Mexico's Virgin of Guadalupe, the national patroness, has Indian features and dark skin—a striking adaptation of a European icon to a New World context; the basilica of the Virgin of Guadalupe is even built on the ruins of an Aztec shrine dedicated to a native goddess. The willingness of the Spanish to take Indian wives and mistresses resulted in a tricultural society consisting of Europeans, Indians, and *mestizos* (a mixture of the other two) all three united within a common, if often uncomfortable, identity as Mexicans.

In Mexico City, the *Plaza de las Tres Culturas* (Plaza of the Three Cultures) at Tlatelolco—the site of the main Aztec market and of the final battle in which Cortés defeated Cuauhtémoc, the last Aztec emperor—is a striking reminder of this blending and layering of disparate cultural elements. Here the modern Foreign Secretariat building stands directly behind a church built out of stone salvaged from the destroyed Tlatelolco pyramid whose ruins stand in front of it. The contrasting styles of these buildings symbolize the divided but interlinked cultures that account for the makeup of contemporary Mexico.

It is important to note that although Mexicans take great pride in the native past, they are somewhat more ambivalent about the present. Because Indians generally occupy the bottom rung of this highly class-conscious, largely mixed-race society, there are few Mexicans who proclaim their Indian heritage. It is considered inappropriate and potentially insulting to refer to someone's Indian features.

Events in the 19th century added additional elements to the Mexican heritage: independence from a faltering Spain in 1821 after more than 10 years of chaos and violence; the struggle to build an independent nation by a people ill prepared for self-determination after 3,000 years of autocratic indigenous rule and 300 years of colonial exploitation; and humiliating foreign interventions, primarily by France and the US. In 1848 in its worst defeat, Mexico lost half its territory to the "colossus of the North." This event still raises the ire of Mexicans, and foreigners should not allude to it. These events are not seen as having occurred in some hazy, distant past, but are viewed as immediate insults, having a continuing impact. Thus, foreigners—especially those from the US—are viewed with suspicion and must expect to overcome such attitudes through behavior that is sensitive to Mexican concerns.

Mexico's initial attempts at modernization echoed these foreign adventures all too closely. In the 1870s, President Porfirio Díaz invited foreign capital to participate freely in the rapid industrialization of the country. By the end of his rule, Mexico had developed the underpinnings of an industrial infrastructure. Yet virtually all of these improvements were owned by foreign enterprises and their local allies, and little of the wealth generated had benefited the poverty-stricken, rural, predominately Indian communities.

The result was the Revolution of 1910, which engulfed Mexico in civil war. The revolution was nominally over in 1917, but order was not truly restored until the ascendancy of Mexico's most important political figure of the modern era, General Lázaro Cárdenas. The populist Cárdenas took office in 1934 and defied the power-brokers who effectively controlled the country, distributing land to communally held *ejidos*, organizing labor, reducing the power of business interests, and, finally, nationalizing foreign-held rail and oil interests. For perhaps the first time in its long history, the nation was truly united, albeit under the banner of anti-foreign nationalism. It was also at this time that the forerunner of the all-powerful *Partido Revolucionario Institucional* (PRI) came to power. For the next 50 years, the country would largely seek to isolate itself from the rest of the world.

The PRI was able build a political machine that co-opted competing alliances by being responsible for distribution of resources. This was accomplished by establishing a nationwide network of PRI-affiliated officials and bureaucrats who were able to obtain political favors from the federal government—a system not all that different from the traditional *cacique* system of the Aztecs. Although the PRI-dominated system has become creaky with age, it remains largely responsible for the way things operate in Mexico.

Mexico's initial attempts to reenter the modern world through the vehicle of its huge oil wealth in the 1980s again led to near-disaster. Oil prices collapsed and Mexico was left a debtor nation and international pariah in 1982. Political administrations since then have been involved in trying to turn around the country's archaic economy and convince its people that its hope lies in modernization and internationalism rather than in isolation. It has been a hard sell, but the technocrats have finally made progress toward opening Mexico up to the outside. However, this opening is still somewhat fragile and dependent upon outsiders making the effort to meet the Mexicans more than halfway.

Regional Differences: Cultural Cleavages

Generalizations about a country as diverse as Mexico are akin to saying that all apples are red. In reality, there are many varieties of apple—and a multitude of Mexican national identities, many of which depend on the region, social class, and experience of the particular person. The country can be divided into five regions, each with its particular traditions, customs, and ways of doing business.

First, there is the northern region, of which Monterrey is the center. The *Norteños* are known for their strong work ethic, penny-pinching frugality, and a generally aggressive, straightforward approach to problem-solving. The region is rich in mineral resources, but the rough terrain and harsh climate have demanded that its settlers be tough and industrious. *Norteños* see themselves as the heirs to this hardy pioneer tradition.

The second region is the west central area, with Guadalajara as its center. This is the land of the *mariachi*, the best and the worst of the Mexican stereotype as known by outsiders. The business environment has traditionally been dominated by family enterprises and agriculture. However, the area has undergone a spurt of growth that has changed it substantially, and Guadalajara—Mexico's second largest city—bustles with activity, particularly among dynamic, medium-sized firms and the subsidiaries of multinational companies. This has resulted in the transformation of the traditional *siesta* ambiance (which was always largely a means of fooling the unwary by getting them to let down their guard) by increasingly Westernized and sophisticated managers and executives. Nevertheless, the business atmosphere remains generally relaxed, and the *Tapatios*—as the locals are known—are still considered to be easygoing, fun-loving characters.

The third area—the southern region—seems to be caught in a time warp in comparison with the rest of the country. The dominant faction—conservative landowners in Oaxaca, Yucatán, and Chiapas—still maintain an almost colonial mind-set, bolstered by archaic social, political, and economic institutions. Business is based on paternalistic ties and entrenched, class-influenced relationships; there is relatively little developed modern business infrastructure or activity. The people of the region tend to be much more relaxed and easygoing than those elsewhere in Mexico. Nevertheless, class tensions and an even more than usual skewing of wealth and income distributions mar what otherwise appears to be an idyllic scene (the world was reminded of this most recently by the outbreak of violence in Chiapas in January 1994). The isolated mountainous jungles have allowed the survival of indigenous communities in the area, and many inhabitants speak only their native language, venturing into the mainstream economy only to sell coffee, maize, and crafts in local markets.

The fourth region is the bustling, highly urbanized zone in and around Mexico City, where business is modern, dynamic, and internationally oriented. Here power is most visible and tangible, and the contrasts between rich and poor are the most blatant. The business mentality of *la Capital* is much more in tune with that of Mexico's neighbors to the north. Although Mexico City is quintessentially Mexican, it has much in common with New York, London, and Tokyo in terms of international business ambiance. It is here in the Distrito Federal, or *el DF* (pronounced ell deh eff-ay), that the most traditional and tangible nodes of business, politics, and culture are to be found. And although Mexico's economy is increasingly decentralized, many decisions must still be cleared one way or another through *la Ciudad de México*.

Finally, Mexico's fifth region is the US-Mexico border area, where Mexican and US cultures have had much more direct interaction than has been the case elsewhere. The major cities of the zone—Ciudad Juárez and Tijuana—have grown along with the foreign-owned *maquiladoras*. Much of the population in this region consists of laborers who are migrants from elsewhere in Mexico. Because of US economic and cultural dominance and the mixture of the many more-or-less displaced and transient persons found in the border zone, acculturation (some would say "deculturation") has proceeded much more rapidly here than elsewhere in Mexico. The business style adopted has been strongly influenced by US managers and executives, and the business ambiance is most

reminiscent of the expansive mix of sophistication and down-home horse-trading that would be familiar in business suites and barbecue joints in Houston.

Foreign businesspeople might also wish to distinguish a sixth region, one somewhat less geographic in nature, but growing in importance: the emerging provincial cities throughout Mexico. These might include such cities as Puebla, Veracruz, Tampico, León, Aguascalientes, Zacatecas, Durango, and Culiacán. Each of these centers could be classified within one of the geographic regions already noted. However, they also share similarities with each other that cut across regional lines. All are comparatively large, rapidly growing centers that serve the people in the surrounding hinterlands. Because they have been overshadowed by the major centers in the country, all remain relatively underdeveloped, having achieved their current levels of development largely through their own efforts. Their relative isolation in the past has kept them in a secondary position, and their business communities and infrastructures are rather poorly developed. Nevertheless, they are eager to move to the next level and are anxious to compete with more established centers, making them areas well worth investigating.

UNDERSTANDING THE MEXICAN PSYCHE

The Mexican mentality has been shaped by its long history of imperialism, colonial subjugation, foreign intervention, and revolution. The Mexican perspective of the world is profoundly different from

Art: C. A. Boyer; Content: Gary M. Wederspahn, MS&B International, a unit of Prudential Relocation Management. Reprinted with permission from Global Production & Transportation magazine. © 1993 New Hope Communications Inc.

that of other Western European- or Asian-influenced cultures because Mexico's history is so different. The fusion of European and Indian cultures in Mexico has also deeply affected the moral values and traditional concepts around which every social—and economic—transaction and interaction takes place. Therein lies the importance to the foreigner of understanding the psychology of the Mexicans.

Dignity and Respect

The Mexican character is complex, as is the history of the nation. The mystique and despair that surrounds the tragic clash of cultures in Mexico's history extends to the individuals who inhabit the country today. Accordingly, Mexicans are defined both consciously or unconsciously by an exaggerated need to protect their dignity, uphold their honor, and defend themselves from any assault on their character or good name. Extremes of what is manifested as megalomania and what appears to be a world-class paranoia are constantly at war within the Mexican psyche, as Mexicans try to comprehend their history and get through their challenging present.

The uniqueness of the individual is honored in Mexico. Each person is judged and accorded respect not so much on his or her achievements as on the merits of his or her demeanor, trustworthiness, and "character." The concepts of *personalidad* (personhood, or individuality) and *dignidad* (dignity) are extremely important to Mexicans, and although they may not fully explain Mexican behavior, they go a long way toward making it comprehensible to an outsider.

Respect becomes one of the most important elements of a Mexican's relationship with those with whom he comes in contact. The sensitivity (or, as it often appears to those from other cultural backgrounds, bewildering hypersensitivity) of Mexicans to the most insignificant action or remark made in what they interpret as a negative or deprecating manner can destroy the trust that has previously been established. This is particularly true when the Mexican feels he has been slighted publicly, especially in front of friends or associates. Because of this sensitivity, Mexicans are often thought of as suffering from an inferiority complex, but this assertion overlooks the importance of saving face in a very close-knit society in which relationships and respect are the most important values for individuals.

Conversely, Mexicans are fond of displaying their outward, individual personalities, demanding respect for and validation of their self-concept and opinions. Conversation and personal interchange is therefore crucial when cultivating relationships. A Mexican should never be cut off or dismissed when he or she is making a statement or revealing some personal belief or thought because such will be seen as a devaluation of the individual.

Foreigners should be prepared to give such respect, as well as demand it in return. However, they walk a fine line in that they must be confident and strong without appearing to be aggressive or arrogant.

Status and Power Relations

The highly complex web of political and economic relations in Mexico is difficult for outsiders to understand, but it determines power and status relations. For instance, foreigners will notice that new business acquaintances behave in an overly polite, almost obsequious manner toward each other, going to great lengths to show their admiration and respect in what may strike outsiders as an overdone and insincere fashion. While Mexicans are generally punctiliously polite in formal business situations, much of this exaggerated behavior disappears once the parties have established their relative positions within the hierarchy and with respect to each other. It is extremely important to Mexicans that relative positions be clearly understood. For this reason, it is crucial to determine and acknowledge the status of the person you are dealing with when preparing for a face-to-face meeting as well as to convey as clearly and realistically as possible your own position.

Although all Mexicans desire to be treated with respect as individuals (as, of course, people everywhere do), they recognize that Mexico is a land of unequal relationships. Because of this, there exists a whole set of prescribed relationships, designed to acknowledge the subordinate-superordinate (or patron-client) nature of most interactions.

If for some reason a foreign businessperson cannot approach a Mexican contact as an equal or is patently in the client position, there may nevertheless be certain advantages. Patrons have a right to make decisions and to receive their due. However, they also have an obligation to provide for their clients once the relationship is acknowledged. It may well be, then, to the outsider's advantage to adopt the client position, because it allows the Mexican party to behave as a patron and—more importantly—allows the outsider a means of entry and a role which might otherwise be denied to him or her.

Foreigners should note that they will also be evaluated on their outward displays, their *imagen* (image). Foreign businesspeople should dress well; stay at the best hotel they can afford; and, when reciprocating hospitality, do so at top-notch restaurants. Offering Mexican guests a choice of fancy restaurants can win even more points. However, always remember not to be overly ostentatious. Dignified understatement is appreciated, while crassness is not.

Names and titles Mexicans are extremely fond of titles that grant respect and authority and define or enhance status. *Señor, Señorita,* or *Señora* (used, respectively, for a man, an unmarried woman, and a married woman) are the equivalents of the English Mr., Miss, and Mrs. (There is no equivalent for Ms. in Spanish.) These titles are used to bestow general individual dignity and respect and set off the family name. Their use conveys a relatively low level of respect. However, not to use them can convey a snub.

In more formal settings, such as business and government, the title *Licenciado* (*Licienciada* for a woman) is a catch-all title that acknowledges that person's qualifications. Although technically it means that the person holds a baccalaureate or other formal degree, there are many more *licenciados* in Mexico than there are university graduates. It is safe to use this title to imply respect when inquiring about or addressing a new business acquaintance. The person will correct you if she or he doesn't feel entitled. Usually, however, the person will just enjoy being thus acknowledged (or promoted).

It is appropriate and preferable to use other titles such as *Doctor* (*Doctora* in the feminine; it means Doctor, either medical or PhD, but it should represent an actual degree), *Ingeniero* (*Ingeniera* in the feminine; it means Engineer, again implying a formal technical degree), *Arquitecto* (Architect), or other formal title when the person's profession and credentials make it appropriate. Foreigners should be sure to use any similar designations to which they themselves are entitled.

Don and *Doña* are everyday nontechnical terms used to dignify age or status outside of a professional setting. These forms of address are used less frequently and carry less weight in Mexico—which lacks a formal nobility such as that of Spain, which these titles mimic—than they do in some other Spanish-speaking countries.

It is also worth noting that in general, unless you have positive personal knowledge that a woman is married (that is, she has been introduced to you as *Señora*), any woman is usually addressed as *Señorita*, whatever her age. The term *Señora* does not in and of itself convey a status that makes it preferable to the more general *Señorita*. In general, all female secretarial and office personnel are addressed as *Señorita*.

Given the importance of names in determining social position and status, a Mexican normally retains both the mother's and father's last names in his or her own formal name. Attention to such genealogical information can be helpful in figuring out power relationships in a country where many businesses are still family controlled and nepotism is an accepted fact of life. The father's name is the surname (or *apellido*, the name requested when filling out documents) and always comes first in this patriarchal culture. The mother's maiden name follows as the last name in the list, although it is generally found only in formal and legal usage and not in ordinary address. Those unfa-

miliar with the practice may make an embarrassing mistake by incorrectly using this name as a form of address. For example, in the name Juan Miguel González Rodriguez, Juan and Miguel are given names, while González represents the father's name and Rodriguez the mother's maiden name. In the example noted, the individual may be addressed as *Señor* or *Licenciado* González, and not as *Sr.* or *Lic.* Rodriguez. When corresponding, or in formal or legal usage, always use the person's full name.

Married women usually retain their father's name and add their husband's *apellido* with the preposition *de* (of). For example, if Maria Elena Vásquez Ramirez marries Juan Miguel González Rodriguez, she becomes Maria Elena Vásquez Ramirez de González. In practice, this is shortened to Maria Vásquez de González, or, simply, *Señora* González. In certain instances, the formal name can use the term *de* or *de la* to point up the importance of an ancestor, a collateral relationship, or a point of geographic origin.

Forms of Address   Provided the people involved in the relationship are of equal professional or social standing, they will try to personalize the relationship by inquiring about each others' families or about their personal affairs, reaching the point at which they address each other using the informal *tu* construction instead of the formal *usted*. However, the foreigner should always wait to receive permission to *tutear*—that is, to use the informal pronoun *tu*—from his or her Mexican counterpart to avoid offending that person. The same is true of the use of given names: an outsider should continue to use a Mexican's title and last name until the Mexican specifically requests that the relationship be put on a first name basis.

Although Mexicans can be extremely warm friends, Mexico is a formal society in which undue familiarity is deemed inappropriate. Worse, uninvited familiarity can imply that the person so addressed is a subordinate, since the familiar *tu* or a first name is customarily used only by mutual agreement with close associates or to address those of lower status—such as children or obvious social inferiors. However, if the relationship is of an established unequal nature, the less powerful person—that is, the one in a support position—is always expected to address the other using the formal *usted* or by title and last name, regardless of age or seniority in the organization, and irrespective of how the more powerful person addresses him or her.

Loyalty   The highly structured nature of professional relationships is defined by a system of personalized patronage rather than by any strict code of conduct or clearly drawn boundaries of formal do's and don'ts. Therefore, the person who is able to show his respect, admiration, and loyalty to the boss or to a person in a pivotal position in the most visible manner will generally be able to conduct business more quickly and efficiently than the rest. Establishing oneself as the client of the right person can avoid enormous amounts of red tape. Nevertheless, care must be taken not to overdo it, since an overly aggressive fascination with pleasing the *patrón* or *jefe*—boss, in Mexico—can call one's sincerity into question. It is always difficult for outsiders to get the nuances right, and words and actions that are appropriate from a native may ring false or even be in poor taste when coming from an outsider not well versed in the unwritten rules of the game. Equally important, providing favors to a business counterpart that demonstrate your own position of power will enable you to cultivate the respect and loyalty of your *socios* (business associates).

Religion

The Catholic Church is a powerful force in Mexican society and it is difficult to overestimate the role it plays in Mexican psychology. Although many Mexicans are only nominally Catholic, the church permeates Mexican life, and most Mexicans consider that its influence provides the strong moral underpinnings that distinguish them from many other nations. In general, men are less involved in church activities than women, and religious displays are more prevalent outside of the large cities. In more modern urban settings, religious expressions are acknowledged, but do not play a visible role in business or government dealings. Nevertheless, many factories and offices prominently feature religious images. It may also be standard local practice to have new premises, equipment, or ventures blessed by a priest, a gesture that is considered to improve worker morale. Because religion is such a loaded subject, foreigners are well advised to avoid it and related topics. However, they should be aware of the relative importance of religion in Mexico as compared with the more private role played by religion in many other societies.

Although the Revolution of 1910 banned public religious displays and imposed a strict separation between church and state—the liberal reforms of the 1860s had already declared Mexico to be a secular republic—the law is often ignored. In the 1940s, President Avila Camacho ended years of church-state tension by declaring that he was a believer, and the Salinas administration's resumption of diplomatic ties with the Vatican in 1993 endeared it to a Catholic population that looks to papal authority.

Despite the strong undercurrent of faith, there is considerable ambivalence toward the Catholic church in Mexico, largely the result of the circumstances of history. Although some priests took the side of the Indians during the colonial period, the church hierarchy is generally seen to have operated in tandem with secular authorities in the exploitation of the Indian masses. During the 19th century, the struggle between the liberals—who espoused greater popular participation in government and a more equitable distribution of wealth—and the conservatives usually found the church hierarchy on the side of conservative privilege, leading to distrust of the church by reformers. More recently, the rise of so-called liberation theology, in which social reformers within the clergy have called for the church to become involved in radical politics as a means of improving the lot of the masses has also led to unrest of a different sort.

On a more general, spiritual level, Mexicans tend to believe that fate is determined by a mystical, all-powerful force. Whereas other cultures tend to believe that personal effort and hard work produce results, Mexicans are highly fatalistic, believing that they have only limited direct control over outcomes. They thus resign themselves to negative results and attribute success to luck more than to effort, not an unrealistic outlook given the fact that effort and merit often go unrewarded. This belief can be traced back to the fatalism of the conquered tribes that suffered under Aztec rule. It is especially evident among the lower classes, who find it a convenient means of rationalizing their plight.

In work situations, this sense of powerlessness may translate into a lack of effort, initiative, or belief in the importance of the enterprise at hand. The foreign executive or manager must be careful not to label such attitudes as laziness and would do well to find ways to reinforce the personal initiative of employees or partners in order to gain their loyalty, trust, and consistent effort. Attempts to make Mexican counterparts and employees feel appreciated in the workplace can also work wonders in changing such entrenched fatalistic attitudes.

The Family

The family is probably the single most important entity for Mexicans. It commands the individual's highest loyalty. For both economic as well as traditional reasons, offspring may live with their parents until they marry, often well into their mid-30s. Family obligations usually take precedence over business or other outside matters, and to behave otherwise is generally considered to exhibit a warped sense of priorities. Foreign businesspeople will find that taking an avid—and genuine rather than cursory and insincere—interest in the families of their Mexican associates is important in establishing relationships. Such interest is an effective and acceptable means of extending a relationship to encompass the personal as well as the business sphere.

Accomplishment in the professional sphere is

important to Mexicans. However, it plays less of a defining role in Mexican society—where it occupies a relatively minor position in establishing a person's overall social worth—than it does in many Western and Asian cultures, where it often becomes the primary element of one's identity. Mexicans tend to see such overly focused individuals as incomplete and as having priorities that lack perspective. Mexicans may admire such outwardly focused people, but they are unlikely to identify with or truly trust them.

The foreigner should be prepared to be asked about family and friends, because Mexicans tend to use family relationships to gauge a person's values and integrity. The non-Mexican manager should also be prepared to accept absences and excuses for missed appointments related to illness in the family or another family matter. This is especially true given the traditional lack of external social welfare programs, which places the burden for care of children and the elderly entirely upon the family unit. As the *patrón*, the employer often becomes at least indirectly responsible for the family of the employee and can expect to be called upon to render moral and material assistance. It is necessary to be aware of this social—and often financial—obligation and to understand the role it plays in the culture.

The personal and the professional are fused to a greater degree in Mexico than is the case in many other societies, requiring adjustments by outsiders. This is not to say that there are no limits between the business and the personal, but that identifying such limits requires careful and sympathetic evaluation.

Nationalism

Mexicans are extremely proud of their country, their city, and their region. A deep sense of patriotism is instilled in every Mexican through the highly regulated and extremely nationalistic public school system. This sense of national pride carries over into every sphere of professional activity. While modernization, with its attendant lessening of localism, is taking hold in many parts of the country, Mexicans—regardless of their class or status—jealously guard their national traditions and values.

Foreigners should be extremely careful to avoid making any disparaging remarks about Mexico's policies, government, or traditions when in a group, with a business partner, or in any similar situation; a perceived derogatory opinion might get back to one's associates. Anyone who commits such a faux pas—however inadvertently—risks being considered a pompous snob, a boorish "ugly American" with no respect for Mexico and Mexicans, or even an outright enemy looking to undermine the sanctity of the nation. Mexicans generally expect outsiders to neither appreciate nor make any real effort to understand their unique culture. Because of this, they can

be extremely touchy. By the same token, they can also respond well to sincere attempts by outsiders to learn something about Mexico's heritage.

Attitudes Toward Foreigners

The corollary to this deep sense of national pride is a long-standing suspicion of (and at times outright hatred for) outsiders, particularly the money-grubbing *gringos* to the north. While the official policy has been to welcome foreign investors and businesspeople, Mexicans still carry centuries of hurt pride and long-standing grievances against the US in particular and toward outsiders in general.

Mexicans tend to view outsiders as uncultured and boorish, wasteful and precipitate, and as having poor morals and values. They feel that foreigners do not take the trouble to study Mexican history and culture, which is long, complex, glorious, and rich in exemplary lessons on how to persevere and prevail with grace under pressure. Foreigners are materialistic and profligate. Lacking as they are in feelings for the social niceties and nuances in which Mexicans are steeped, foreigners inappropriately try to push things too far too fast. They simply don't understand the sense of the individual and of social relationships that are central to Mexican culture. Foreigners generally are also seen as lacking the deep religious faith, commitment to family, and sense of morality that the Mexicans see as their strongest points. Not only are foreigners generally lacking in these qualities, but they are also inexplicably successful despite their shortcomings, leading Mexicans to envy them their material success, while at the same time making them feel disloyal for doing so.

Most Mexicans are quick to point out that even their neighbors' adoption of the name "America" is presumptuous and insulting because Mexico is also part of America. When speaking about the US, it is preferable to say *los Estados Unidos* (the United States) or *Estadounidense* (one from the US). Even this is potentially difficult, because Mexico is also the United Mexican States. However, most Mexicans are willing to cede the designation US to those to the north. Elsewhere in Latin America, *Norteamericano* is acceptable usage, and this is generally true in Mexico. However, even this can be somewhat suspect, because Mexico is also part of North America.

The term *gringo* also requires care. Its origins are obscure, but it is applied to outsiders, particularly to those of US and European origin. It may be used to describe a light-complected or blond person or as a term of mild affection, denoting a positive relationship between a Mexican and an outsider. However, it generally has negative connotations and can be a "fighting word," equivalent to a curse.

The antidote to Mexicans' harsh views of foreigners is to calm their fears as much as possible by contradicting the negative stereotypes. This requires work and conscious effort. You must try to win them over—to you, not to your superior way of doing things. This in turn means that you must learn their ways and adhere to them as much as possible. Mexico is the Mexicans' country, and you are responsible for going the extra mile to conform to their way of doing things.

First, outsiders must do their homework to become conversant with Mexican history and culture. Awareness helps in avoiding the unintentional, ignorance-based slight. Next, foreigners must learn to be patient, flexible, and, above all, sensitive to Mexican concerns. Do not seem to condescend, but always be respectful, as befits a guest in someone else's home. Do not insist on having it your own way; especially avoid insisting that your way is somehow better. In fact, it may not be better in the Mexican context, and even if it is, pointing that out to your hosts will not win you their thanks but rather their enmity. Go along as much as is possible.

Finally, Mexicans expect, from long, hard experience, that foreigners are in their country to use them economically to their own detriment, take the profits, and get out. Although Mexican business also normally goes for the high-margin, short-term deal and then moves on to something else (foreigners should note that few Mexican businesses will be interested in extended paybacks or low margins, no matter what the long-term returns), the difference is that Mexican businesses do so within the context of a commitment to Mexico. They expect and want to be there, operating in their own milieu, forever. Foreign businesspersons must be sensitive to this expectation of transience and rapacity on their part and do their best to counter it. Business will work in Mexico only if it is seen to represent a win-win rather than a win-lose situation, and the best way for it to be seen as such is for it to be so.

Attitudes Toward Women

Women are at the same time the most venerated and the most oppressed members of Mexican society. The Mexican woman is honored for her role at the center of the all-important family, where she tends to occupy an elevated position and on a practical level to be in charge of everything from child rearing to the spending and investment of household funds. Nevertheless, the legacy of the Spanish male conqueror's abuse of native women has tainted Mexican society with a very strong male chauvinistic bent, and women operating outside the household are often considered to be fair game by males.

Women, although afforded equal legal rights at all levels under law, are still far behind men in Mexican social and economic spheres. They have by and large been kept out of decision-making roles and executive positions. In behavior and treatment, men and women are clearly separate in this largely patriarchal country. Women in Mexico are expected to display their femininity by using appropriate amounts of makeup, wearing dresses, and not appearing overly aggressive in the company of a man. Foreign women will have a difficult time gaining the respect of Mexican executives, managers, and employees. They are clearly at a disadvantage because it is extremely difficult for women to be accepted into the "men's club" mentality that dominates business networks in Mexico.

In general, foreign businesswomen must behave very circumspectly to be effective. However, the consensus is that women can in fact do business successfully in Mexico, unlike some other countries in which they cannot expect to operate independently at all. Nevertheless, foreign companies and women should be aware of the difficulties they can expect to face in doing business in Mexico. Younger, more cosmopolitan Mexican businesspeople are adapting to women who are assuming responsibility in the workplace, but many—especially those with lower-class backgrounds, and older, executive level men—remain uncomfortable with (or even unwilling to do business with) women. However, some observers argue that foreign businesswomen may have at least some initial advantage because senior managers are such old-school gentlemen that they will extend courtesies to women that they might not offer to similarly placed men.

One of the most important sources of cultural misunderstanding between Mexicans and foreign women lies in the more restricted sphere allotted to women in Mexico. This is particularly open to misinterpretation in matters of dress. Clothing which is perfectly respectable in her home cultural context may signify sexual availability in Mexico. Shorts, pants, and anything considered too revealing can fall into this category. Thus, foreign women are advised to dress more conservatively than normal, especially if traveling alone or with another woman. Women must also be careful not to do anything to offend the spouse of a Mexican businessman, lest their business relationship be precluded because of jealously or dislike. Foreign businesswomen should not attend a social occasion or meal unless the female spouse of her Mexican counterpart is invited and expected to attend. A foreign businesswoman hosting a business meeting, lunch, or other event should arrange to hold it in her hotel in order that it may be billed directly to her account. Otherwise the arrival of the check can be expected to provoke a fight over her not being allowed to pay. In general, women do not go to bars, certainly not alone (the exception to this rule is the cocktail lounge of a first class hotel).

Mexican men often consider all women—and especially foreign women—as fair game. Many Mexican men consider it de riguer to make comments—known as *piropos* ("jewels" or "compliments")—which can range from the mildly appreciative to the witty, through the double entendre-laced to the blatant and sexually crude. In most cases the comments are pro forma in nature, and some women may even be gratified by the attention. However, outsiders unfamiliar with the local rules of the game can quickly find themselves out of their depth. Even if a situation does not become dangerous to the woman, it can destroy her business credibility and thus should be avoided. Perhaps the best way to handle the situation is to avoid making eye contact, ignore the comment, and coolly act as if the incident did not occur. If the male acquaintance does not take the hint or becomes overly aggressive, it may be necessary to issue a clear and curt response to the effect that additional similar behavior is inappropriate and unwelcome. Unfortunately, women must often walk a fine line, being careful to avoid wounding the egos of an overeager male, which can also result in bad feelings that could damage a business relationship.

Machismo

Machismo—behavior associated with an exaggerated sense of maleness—has its roots in the conquistador mentality of the Spanish, who simply took what they wanted, justifying their behavior by the fact that they were willing to risk their lives to do so. The term *macho* conjures up an image of a domineering male; *macho* is most often associated with sexual prowess, mastery over women, and a tendency to resort to violence. Yet these elements are secondary to what is, in essence, an expression of the Mexican male's struggle to prove his competence and his ability to exercise control in a given situation. The emphasis on exerting control belies the stereotype: out-of-control passions. The generally derogatory, somewhat Neanderthal connotation that the term carries outside of Mexico also fails to take into account its subsidiary meaning—related to that of *dignidad*—which refers to the idea of accepting responsibility for oneself and others.

In business or professional settings, a Mexican man will tend to display his power and authority visibly. This is particularly true of higher level executives and managers. Such behavior is also common among lower level aspirants intent on enhancing their own image, although they will generally shrink before real authority from those above. Maintaining a high degree of authority and control is crucial for the Mexican businessperson, and the outsider must be extremely cautious in bringing up what may be a thorny issue in a fashion that is too direct or abrasive. Always keep in mind the eggshell sensitivity of the Mexi-

can ego. Mexicans place great value on word choice and attitude, and will take an overly aggressive approach to be a personal affront. While Anglos, in particular, value directness and tend to want to get right to the point, Mexican business dealings demand heavy doses of tact, diplomacy, indirectness, and the smoothing of ruffled feathers to resolve problems without making things worse or creating enemies.

Foreigners must be careful to project a confident, strong, and assertive—but not aggressive—image. They must be careful not force a Mexican, either intentionally or unintentionally, into any position in which the Mexican feels he must defend his honor.

THE MEXICAN WORK ENVIRONMENT

Connections and Clientism

Using *palancas* (levers) to procure contracts or new customers is crucial in Mexico, especially for a new business. Therefore, cultivating personal relationships with those who may be in a position to benefit you in the future should be a permanent part of your agenda. This is not as cynical and manipulative as it may sound to an outsider, because it involves the development of genuine relationships, not merely short-term opportunistic contacts.

Mexican businesspeople, government officials, and others in advantageous positions tend to form a loose network of friends, relatives, and colleagues who constantly turn to each other for information, advice, and potential business contacts. These relationships, like all others in Mexico, are built on complex personal ties rather than simply on dry business calculations. Although it is often painstakingly difficult to accomplish, once a foreigner has been accepted into this system—referred to as clientism by many outside observers—his or her chances of establishing a lasting and successful business in Mexico will increase exponentially. Being accepted as part of a network also entails reciprocity: you will be expected to use your own *palancas* to help others when called upon for assistance.

Ethical Issues

Virtually any transaction in Mexico may involve some unofficial, informal transfer of money or other consideration. While many outsiders view such practices with moral outrage or at least distaste, it is imperative that a foreigner doing business in Mexico understand the culturally-based economic realities of the country as distinct from moral codes imposed from the outside. From the tribute system of the Aztecs to the entrenched economic stratification of contemporary Mexican society, *la mordida*—the bite—has long been the lubricant that has kept the wheels of the economy turning.

In a country where incomes are often grossly inadequate, the bite is viewed by many as an instantaneous form of income redistribution and by many others as simply a cost of doing business. Although the government periodically attempts to curb this practice, it continues to be widely accepted out of fear that a complete crackdown on what appears to be extortion could result in social upheaval and total failure of the society to function. Nevertheless, even Mexicans inured to the practice acknowledge that it got out of hand during the oil boom years. And although it is deeply ingrained in the culture and economy, many observers expect that such activity will fade at least somewhat as international business standards become more accepted in Mexico.

Foreign businesspeople must learn to downplay their culturally biased ethics if they hope to accomplish tasks quickly and with a minimum of hassle. Whether procuring government licenses, acquiring signatures for business permits, or concluding a business agreement, the foreigner must be prepared to bend the rules just enough to get the task done. Any plans to initiate business dealings in Mexico must include a careful evaluation of the uncertainty of what the added costs will be. There should also be a clear-cut understanding regarding *la mordida* between top management and on-site personnel. Foreign negotiators must have the flexibility necessary to conclude a deal if the terms are favorable and the conditions are right.

As a practical matter, most outsiders choose to delegate at least some operating authority to local consultants, who can negotiate the backwaters of the Mexican system. If you end up dealing directly with such uncomfortable situations, some observers suggest that you try to brazen it out, acting as if you do not understand or are too important to be bothered. If it becomes clear that the obstacle cannot be removed without an accommodation, you should be the one to make an offer as circumspectly as possible (Mexicans will not ask directly). Remain impassive and never lose your temper or raise your voice. (Refer to the section on the US Foreign Corrupt Practices Act in the "Business Law" chapter.)

Work ethic

The Mexican work ethic follows the traditional Latin American tenet that one works to live rather than lives to work (the latter being emphasized by many Western and Asian societies). Mexicans generally approach work as a necessary evil that must be submitted to in order to enjoy the more important things in life—family, friends, and other earthly pleasures for which work provides the wherewithal. Those who are too eager to spend long hours at work or overly preoccupied about their careers or mate-

rial wealth are perceived as being a bit odd and outside the accepted norm.

Nevertheless, with the introduction of economic policies that stress competitiveness and efficiency, these perceptions have recently undergone dramatic changes. For this reason, foreign managers may find employees and business partners more willing to accept new management and productivity regimes. Yet, old habits are difficult to change, and foreigners must be aware of differences found in the Mexican workplace.

Decision Making

Mexican businessmen have a great respect and need for authority. The *patrón* does not accept questioning, and his managers normally are not delegated important decision-making roles or authority. Instead, they are given a variety of relatively limited tasks to carry out independently with minimal supervision. However, it is understood that despite this delegation, the boss has the final say. In medium-sized and larger firms where increased distribution of authority is necessary, there are a larger number of mid-level managers and administrators, but final authority remains narrowly concentrated in the hands of the few at the top. Decisions are not made by committee, although specialists do have necessary input. Nor are final decisions made based strictly on a cost-benefit basis, as in many modern enterprises. Instead, senior executives often decide by the feel they have developed for the project and their counterparts, on context more than on content. Most subordinates willingly submit to this highly centralized process because it is the norm as well as out of the fear of making a mistake or of being punished for being too independent. The general understanding has been that jobs are relatively secure and that there may be a possibility of future advancement—provided the subordinates play the game and don't rock the boat.

Nevertheless, a new generation of mostly US-educated managers who are beginning to gain prominence in larger Mexican firms do believe in the decentralization of the decision-making process and in the increased delegation of authority. As this approach becomes increasingly successful, the general trend will gradually begin to change. So far, this is true only in the larger cities and enterprises. The business environment in the rest of the country remains extremely autocratic.

Implementation Foreign businesspeople entering into a contract or venture in Mexico should be aware that Mexicans tend to enjoy the big-picture excitement of developing projects, but often have limited interest in the detail work needed to implement and administer operations. The lack of delegated authority contributes to the difficulties in completing business projects. Implementing such projects necessitates a knowledge of sophisticated management tools and broad authority, which are rarely available to Mexican mid-level managers. The result is often unmet goals and frustration, apathy, and dissatisfaction among those facing such unresolved problems with few means at hand for resolving them.

For a foreign businessperson accustomed to dealing with active, results-oriented executives and managers, bridging the gap between concept and application may appear to be a simple affair. However, in Mexico it often becomes a virtually insurmountable problem. When entering into a business venture in Mexico, the foreign businessperson might well suggest that there be built-in bilateral cooperation between mid-level managers and technicians to ensure the successful progress of the venture. If the suggestion is presented tactfully, the foreign managers may be in a position to monitor progress and influence outcomes. Another possible approach would be to build rigorous progress reporting into the arrangement.

Communication and Control Communication between superiors and subordinates tends to be rigidly stylized and often ineffective. Because trust, loyalty, and respect are highly valued, the Mexican worker or manager will attempt to guard his or her limited pocket of autonomy, carrying out tasks independently and with little communication or control from above. Likewise, once having delegated a task, the executive generally does not believe it to be appropriate to oversee the execution. What is seen as monitoring in other systems is seen as meddling in the Mexican business environment, and Mexicans will tend to become worried that the *patrón* doesn't trust them; they may become ineffective or even balky as a result.

For the foreign businessperson, this lack of communication and thus of effective control—no matter how much nominal control exists in theory—is frustrating. However, an aggressive attempt to implement foreign communication and control procedures runs the risk of destroying the loyalty and trust of Mexican employees and managers. As noted, tact and diplomacy are crucial. A more appropriate and effective approach is the gradual introduction of such management tools, along with the training of new staff and gradual retraining of those already in place to accept the new standards and procedures (which, after all, are not part of the existing business culture).

Foreign managers can expect that their authority and their ideas will be resisted due to the ingrained suspicion and hostility of Mexicans towards outsiders. The best advice is: have trusted Mexican managers who have been thoroughly coached in how to implement the new procedures carry out as many as the changes as possible, while you make a concerted effort to personalize your relations with your employees and business partners in Mexico, soothing them past the trauma of change.

Time

In Mexico, people tend to take precedence over schedules. It is considered insultingly rude to cut a conversation short by announcing that you have other obligations. There are more subtle ways of getting the point across. Your attention should always be clearly and exclusively focused on the person in front of you. The level of attention increases with the status and importance of the person or persons you are meeting with. However, be aware that many meetings will include interruptions; such interruptions should be borne with good grace.

Mexicans may schedule several meetings at the same time, counting on some people not to show up. They may also schedule meetings at a time when they know that they will not be available, or at odd hours. Foreigners should try to get appointments between 10 am and 1 pm or between 4 pm and 6 pm. Although outsiders should be prompt, they should recognize that they will generally be kept waiting, often for 30 minutes to one hour. It is a loss of face to be made to wait, and a gain in face to make others wait. However, this is seldom malicious, and foreigners should not make an issue of it. Instead bring a book or some work. Chances are that you will be late for some appointments. Although there always exists the potential that someone will be offended, it is generally accepted that appointment times are somewhat fluid. It is usually acceptable to politely and apologetically state that *algo sucedio*—something came up.

Social occasions also usually begin 30 minutes to one hour after the stated time. Those arriving on time may find that the host is not ready, causing embarrassment all around. If a specific time is required, the hour should be specified as *a la gringa*; otherwise it will be understood to be *a la mexicana*.

Mexicans have been vilified by outsiders because of the *mañana* syndrome: the idea that there is always another day to complete today's business. This is a basic tenet of Mexican business. However, it is incorrect to equate it with laziness or a lackadaisical or unprofessional attitude. Rather it represents a different approach to doing business, one that seeks to prioritize effort given scarce resources that seldom allow rapid advances to be made on many fronts simultaneously. Mexicans recognize that there are other priorities in life and that conditions often conspire to prevent the realization of plans as envisioned. Thus, *mañana* represents an adaptation that allows for general progress and flexibility without overcommitting to unreasonable specific goals. Foreigners should recognize it for what it is and accommodate themselves as much as possible to it.

When trying to set deadlines, foreigners should be aware that when Mexicans promise something will be done by a certain time or date, they are most likely saying it to please the person they are dealing with rather than giving an honest and straightforward appraisal of when the work will be done, much less making a contractual statement. Time commitments are more likely made out of politeness and the need for having a ballpark idea of when the work will be completed. Therefore, foreigners should not expect that work will actually be finished when promised and plan accordingly.

This approach is most prevalent in rural areas, public sector enterprises, and government bureaucracies, where activity tends to occur at what seems like an excruciatingly slow pace. When doing business that requires government approvals, forms, and special licenses, foreigners should consider using a local Mexican intermediary or attorney who is familiar with procedures and personalities and has control over the *palancas* necessary to get tasks accomplished as efficiently as possible.

Personnel

Jobs in Mexico are usually filled with friends, colleagues, or relatives through the old-boy network. There is little experience with either the concept or the use of open competition to fill positions, although some of the larger cities now offer executive placement agencies catering to larger firms and corporations. Promotions usually occur when an employee has carried out his or her assigned tasks faithfully—but not necessarily effectively—and has proved to be cooperative, courteous, and trustworthy over a period of time. Nepotism is still a fact of life in Mexico, where family is of consummate importance. Often, the person skilled in political maneuvering and diplomacy will rise in the ranks faster than the person who has achieved quantifiable gains for the company in the field.

Competition

Mexican businesspeople do not possess the cutthroat business mentality attributed to their neighbors to the north. Rather, open conflict or even direct opposition of viewpoints is to be avoided, while as many alliances as possible are to be created. It is considered distasteful to blatantly undercut competitors or to push fellow workers aside while trying to gain the notice of one's superiors. While profits remain the overriding goal, growth is achieved not by a "get there first with the most" approach, but rather by slowly and methodically amassing the tools and the relationships necessary to get a contract or enter a new market.

Getting Started

Cultivating Relationships For the foreign businessperson, the difficulties in cultivating solid relationships can be the biggest obstacle to success in Mexico; Mexicans seldom do business with strangers. They need an opportunity to get acquainted and size up the potential associate's character and intentions to their own satisfaction. Foreigners will be evaluated on whether they are *simpático* (sympathetic) and *buena gente* (good folks) as much as, if not more than, on what they can bring to the venture in terms of resources and expertise. The goal for an outsider is to have trust (*tener confianza*) with a Mexican counterpart, a difficult, time-consuming process, but one that can be both personally and professionally rewarding.

Find a Matchmaker One of the best ways to make contacts with potential Mexican business associates is to have a mutual friend serve as an intermediary and make an introduction. If the third party has close relationships with both sides, that alone may constitute a basis for initiating business negotiations. Finding this third party may be as simple as asking a local businessperson who has done business in Mexico. Anyone who has worked in Mexico or who has cooperated with Mexican authorities is a possible source of contacts. There are also many business consultants who provide assistance for a fee. Chambers of commerce, small business associations, and the Trade Commission of Mexico are valuable resources that should be consulted. In addition, some US states (the border states of California, Texas, Arizona, and New Mexico, among others) have offices that promote trade in cities such as Monterrey, Mexico City, and Guadalajara.

Go to the Source If finding a third party for introductions in your home country doesn't work, consider making a fact-finding trip to Mexico. Try to schedule your trip when there is a trade show in one of the major cities that allows you to display goods or services and gauge your business prospects. Or you can simply spend your time meeting potential contacts in your area of business. Before leaving for Mexico, telephone, write, or fax businesses in the area that you are interested in and try to arrange a meeting or short visit. Because of economic deregulation, Mexican businesses are eager to enter into investment, trade, and cooperative ventures with the outside world, and initial meetings are an excellent way of starting your own network of potential rainmakers.

Another productive way of making contacts and becoming familiar with commercial possibilities in Mexico is to arrange a visit one of the many foreign-owned *maquiladoras* (most are located along the US–Mexican border). Executives at these enterprises tend to be more than happy to share their experiences.

Patience Mexican business managers and executives spend a considerable part of each day cultivating business relationships, particularly when they do not know the persons they are dealing with. Thus foreigners investigating the Mexican business scene should plan on several trips, realizing that they probably will not be able to accomplish anything concrete during the initial visit. During the first set of meetings with your Mexican counterparts, expect to spend considerably more time socializing than discussing substantive business issues. Mexican executives and managers want and need to get to know you as a person in order to evaluate your credibility.

Always remember that in Mexico, trust and personal relationships tend to win out over lower prices or a technically better deal. Conversely, if you convey impatience and express irritation over what may appear to be time wasted in "pointless" conversations and social events, you will risk alienating your potential counterparts and lose the opportunity to gain their trust. Mexicans tend to view foreigners as somewhat uncouth, largely because they seem to lack the manners required to develop relationships at an appropriately civilized pace.

Maintain Your Perspective Finally, foreign businesspeople will benefit from the process of cultivating personal connections by keeping in mind that it gives them an opportunity to learn about the people with whom they are dealing; getting to know your business associates would be a smart move in any culture. Learning about the personality of an associate can make communication and understanding smoother, and the resulting knowledge can be critical when it comes time to decide how far to take the business relationship. Even if you do not end up doing business with them, you can count on the contacts you have made when a future need arises.

Social Customs and Behavior

A knowledge of Mexican etiquette and rules of acceptable social behavior is a major asset for foreigners doing business in Mexico. Nuances of body language, facial expressions, and clothing will often tell you more about a person or situation than direct verbal communication. In contrast to those from the US or other Westerners who value straight, unambiguous dialogue, Mexicans are masters at intricate wordplay and behavior that is rich in meaning and potential to the initiate.

Conversation Cultural, political, and linguistic differences can result in difficulties between Mexicans and foreigners over such seemingly harmless matters as small talk. Mexicans are fond of entering into elaborate philosophical, political, and economic discussions with foreigners, pitting Mexican viewpoints against those of an outsider and giving free rein to the participants to engage in wordplay and to bond as they get to know each other better. Although this sort of behavior is a national pastime for Mexicans, it can be intimidating and uncomfortable for foreigners who are uncertain about the rules of the game.

The foreigner may also find himself subject to interrogations about family, financial position, or opinions on the latest political crisis. The basic rule of thumb in conversation is to steer a middle-of-the-road course. Avoid saying anything that Mexicans might consider offensive or insulting. Family, hometown, school, or some established mutual interest are fair and usually safe topics that allow you to establish your individuality as well as your common humanity.

Formal Spanish is often extremely elaborate, convoluted, overly polite, and stilted. Lavish praise and exaggerated emotion are part of the Mexican persona. Where an outsider might say "pleased to meet you," a Mexican would tend to say "I am very enchanted to make your acquaintance." Foreigners may find this awkward and somewhat insincere, but it is imperative to understand the social importance attached to such formal conventions.

Mexicans are very adept at inserting double entendres, soaring turns of phrase, traditional sayings (*dichos*), and clever word play into an otherwise dry conversation. Spanish is an excellent language for such byplay. It is not absolutely necessary to learn Spanish to operate in Mexico—most cosmopolitan Mexicans (especially senior level personnel) are fluent in English and sometimes in French or German as well—and it is difficult to develop colloquial fluency. However, Mexicans appreciate any sincere attempts by foreigners to speak their language. Foreigners who are able to learn a few Mexican idioms and use them in conversation will be admired for trying, and will be considered in a positive light.

Humor is another means by which Mexicans build personal   connections. Their *charritas* (short jokes) are plentiful and tend to come up in the course of any informal social event. Among males, sexual jokes are common, but these are usually not proper in mixed company and are never told in formal or family settings. Remember that humor often does not translate well, and, in general, the non-Mexican should be wary of engaging in joke-telling unless it is absolutely certain that the offering will work in a cross-cultural setting.

Conversation about money and personal finances is common outside of the office, although as a rule you should not be the one to initiate it. Except for private sector executives and high government officials who are very well paid, most Mexicans earn much less than their counterparts in the developed world and are curious to find out how big the discrepancy really is. You may choose to avoid the question through generalities such as "not enough" or "not as much as I would like to earn." If you choose to answer specifically, be prepared to experience some resentment. It may help somewhat to go on about the high cost of living at home that offsets your apparently high salary. Mexicans are fond of talking about their own financial situation, either validating their status through references to their wealth, or complaining about the unfairness and inadequacy of their wages. In every case, the foreigner should listen carefully and react with understanding, appreciation, commiseration, or admiration, as appropriate.

Discussions about religion or politics should be avoided when dealing with people with whom you are seeking to do business. Concepts such as democracy and equality have very different meanings in Mexico than in many other cultures. Virtually any comment on Mexico's political system can be perceived as being disrespectful of the country's long history and rich cultural and political traditions. While lower and middle class Mexicans are very fond of political discussions, controversial topics including political corruption, the treatment of Indians, or historical incidents such as the 1968 Tlatelolco massacre are to be avoided with businesspeople, who often have close ties with the ruling PRI.

Greetings and Contact Greetings always require acknowledgment with a respectful smile. It is considered polite to greet every member of a group individually. The same applies when leaving. Foreigners should carry an ample supply of business cards and should exchange them immediately during the greeting. It is not strictly necessary to translate them into Spanish because most Mexican businesspeople can at least read basic English even if they cannot speak it (after all, the alphabets are essentially the same), but doing so would leave a good impression with your Mexican contacts. You may want to have bilingual cards printed up before leaving home, because there can be delays in getting them in Mexico. Be sure to include your official title and any degrees, because they carry weight in Mexico.

The normal greeting is a handshake or a nod of the head. Women may greet each other with a kiss on the cheek. Men should wait for a woman to initiate a handshake; otherwise they should confine themselves to a small, polite bow. A Mexican business associate will signal that you have begun to gain his trust by greeting you or saying goodbye with an *abrazo* (hug), by placing his arm around your shoulder, patting you on the back, or shaking your hand while simultaneously holding you forearm firmly with his left hand. Women will usually offer a light hug or kiss on the cheek to show their affection and trust for established acquaintances. All of these maneuvers are an indication of acceptance and are executed with appropriate warmth, but they do not carry the same connotations of physical intimacy implied by similar contacts in some other parts of the world.

Eye contact between equals in Mexico tends to be much more direct and prolonged than it is in the US. Foreigners who appear to be uncomfortable with or avoid such contact may be perceived as suspicious characters with something to hide, thus not to be trusted. Yet, subordinates in Mexico are not supposed to maintain prolonged eye contact with their superiors; doing so would be disrespectful, challenging, and inappropriate.

Physical Distance The spacing between people in conversation is closer in Mexico than in the rest of North America. This may make those from the US or Canada so uncomfortable that they instinctively pull away or step back. Such a withdrawal may unintentionally communicate a lack of trust in or dislike of the speaker or a distaste for the topic being discussed. Although the unaccustomed physical closeness of the Mexican may seem pushy or aggressive and thus uncomfortable, foreigners must learn to accept this form of body language in order to avoid sending the wrong message.

Gestures The use of the hands is more expressive in Mexico than in the rest of North America. However, outsiders should be careful, because some gestures that are common elsewhere might have a negative (or even an obscene) import in Mexico and Latin America; forming a circle with the index finger and the thumb—the "okay" sign in the US—is an example of a gesture that becomes extremely offensive. Men should not keep their hands in their pockets. Standing with the hands on the hips is tantamount to issuing a challenge. Shaking the hand from side to side with the index finger extended and the palm outward means "no." However, as in the rest of North America, the "thumbs up" signal means approval or agreement. Pointing at someone with the index finger is considered accusatory and provocative and should be avoided. When pointing, use either the entire hand or two fingers in the direction desired. Throwing anything to a person is considered ill mannered and offensive. Always hand such items directly to the person. Payment should usually be placed directly in the hand of the collector rather than on a counter. Hissing "psst" is an accepted way of getting someone's attention, although it is considered undignified to summon a waiter in this fashion. When someone sneezes, you may say *salud* (health), which is also used in making a toast.

Laughter is well accepted in the appropriate context, but overly raucous guffaws will call undue and undesired attention to the foreigner. The elongated expression *ay*—phonetically pronounced "ayeeee," with more than one syllable—is extremely versatile, and is used to give emphasis when expressing surprise, pain, or admiration. A flip of the head upwards along with an exaggerated raising of the eyebrows signals a passing informal greeting or goodbye. Mexicans also often cross their legs at the knee and close together, a posture that in the US tends to be acceptable only for women.

Meetings, Visits, and Executive Lunches

Mexicans are very hospitable people. Unannounced as well as expected visitors at home or in the office are normally offered coffee or refreshments as a prelude to a short chat before getting to the business at hand. While the husband or boss may offer, it is the female secretary or wife who will be responsible for bringing the drinks, cookies, or a light snack. It is considered rude to refuse anything offered. It is, however, considered appropriate to accept and make a pretense of tasting the item offered. You don't have to clean your plate. In larger corporations and in more cosmopolitan areas, this tradition of non-optional hospitality is beginning to change as more modern business practices take hold and schedules get tighter.

Meals are generally considered to be social rather than business occasions. Although they are important to business relationships, specific business deals are usually not broached over food. General business and economic conditions are appropriate topics of conversation, but specific mutual business interests should not be brought up unless your Mexican host introduces the topic. Although the person who issues the invitation usually expects to pick up the check, it is considered good form to fight over it in more than just a token manner.

Lunch—the main meal (*comida*) of the day—usually occurs sometime between 1 pm and 4 pm. When taking part in a business lunch in Mexico with a Mexican associate, be prepared for a three- to four-hour feast. The event may begin as late as 3 pm and may include martinis, wine, cognac, several courses, and a heavy dessert. This tradition is particularly important in Mexico City, where it is often used to finalize deals and strengthen the personal bonds of a business relationship. The event often is extended into the evening in a celebratory fashion if a business deal has been concluded satisfactorily.

Although somewhat less frequent and elaborate, breakfast meetings are also common. Most Mexican businesspeople have coffee or tea and a roll before beginning the day, but may schedule a substantial mid-morning breakfast. Such meetings are considered somewhat more intimate—a plus for the outsider invited—but are also usually reserved for lesser obligations that do not merit the full lunch treatment.

Evening business meals are less common and usually connote a more personal contact, which can be important for cementing a relationship. Such events seldom begin before 9 pm and can extend until quite late. Some Mexicans have a snack around 5 pm to tide them over and drinks around 7 pm.

Although it is usually up to the Mexican businessperson to extend the initial invitation to dine, the foreigner will be expected to reciprocate and should do so in an appropriate manner. While one should offer one's guests a first class experience, it is not appropriate to try to upstage them. Nor is it appropriate to share with them the great little *taqueria* you found around the corner from your hotel. Business meals are generally single gender; do not invite spouses unless yours is attending. If you are the host at a cocktail party, be sure to arrange for plenty of finger foods to be served to avoid the embarrassment of running out.

You should also be aware that Mexicans are generally rather heavy social drinkers. However, drunkenness is usually frowned upon, and Mexicans will usually try to drink companionably rather than competitively with a business associate. If you don't want to drink, make this clear at the beginning. Medical advice is usually an acceptable excuse for not joining in the fun; you can say you have liver problems (*problemas del higado*) or simply that your doctor says no (*mi medico me dijo que no*). This advice also holds for foods that disagree with you: never risk offending someone by saying you don't like something. Always blame your doctor instead.

Invitations to Social Occasions

Mexicans are very proud of their hospitality and will interpret a refusal to an invitation to their home, to a meal at a restaurant, or even for a beer at a local bar as a slap in the face. If you value the person's relationship, do not refuse.

Being invited to a Mexican home is usually a signal that you have been accepted by an associate. Business attire is appropriate unless you are told otherwise. It is appropriate to send flowers to the hostess beforehand, but avoid marigolds (associated with death) or red flowers (associated by some with witchcraft). You may bring imported wine or champagne, chocolates, or pastries. Toys—especially imported electronic toys—for children will also earn you high marks. You should admire the host's house and furnishings, but not too volubly, or he may feel obligated to give you the item you admire, resulting in embarrassment for both.

When invited to a Mexican home for a social occasion, the guest is not permitted to lift a finger or enter the kitchen. You will be expected to sample and praise everything served. Also, it is considered rude to arrive at the exact time specified verbally or in the formal invitation; it is normal and polite for guests to arrive 30 minutes to an hour after the stated time. If everything goes well, you may end up staying until all hours engaged in some deep philosophical or personal discussion, although it is considered proper to offer to leave about 30 minutes after the meal is over.

You will have to gauge the sincerity of your host's insistence that you stay longer.

Appropriate Attire

What you wear indicates your respect towards the people you meet with and the importance that you attach to the meeting and your job. Because status is very important in Mexico, upper class Mexicans take appearance very seriously. Businesspeople, especially in metropolitan areas and particularly in Mexico City, keep abreast of the latest European fashions, wear expensive jewelry, and are always well groomed. They generally prefer an understated, formal style to flashier dressing. Women who dress well—including jewelry, heels, and makeup—are appreciated, although they should avoid overly flashy, faddish, or revealing clothing or accessories. Mexican women do tend to use makeup that is heavier and more vivid than is often common elsewhere. Also note that you should not remove your jacket or loosen your tie unless invited to do so by your host (he should do the same himself).

Formal business attire is not necessarily the norm in smaller towns and rural areas; in fact, it is often considered pretentious. Mexicans in these less well-to-do areas do not appreciate blatant displays of wealth, and can be expected to feel resentment toward "city types" in expensive suits. In these situations, dark slacks, dress shoes, and a sport coat without a tie is preferable for men. Women should dress conservatively and avoid excessive makeup or gaudy jewelry.

Men can sometimes get away with wearing *guayaberas*—loose-fitting, light shirts that are not tucked inside the pants and that are popular in Latin America, especially in the summer in provincial areas. Be sure to check out what Mexicans are wearing, especially those of the class and professional level that you need to associate with, before attempting to make a fashion statement. Outside resort areas, bathing suits, shorts, and jeans are considered in poor taste, and should be avoided. Although required infrequently, tuxedos and tasteful, long black dresses are the norm for strictly formal occasions. Invitations will not normally specify black tie, so if there is any doubt, ask.

Gifts

Gift-giving does not play the critical role in Mexico that it does in some other cultures. It is seen more as a way to strengthen existing relationships than it is to get them off the ground. In fact, a gift given prematurely would be viewed as inappropriate and could be seen as an attempt to short-circuit elaborate business courtship behavior or even as an attempt to bribe the potential associate.

However, once the relationship has been estab-lished, small tokens can become appropriate. Because many Mexicans smoke, foreign cigarettes or cigarette lighters may be appropriate gifts. However, the gift should be presented as offering the novelty of an imported alternative rather than relieving the recipient of having to smoke an inferior Mexican product. Imported liquor, calculators, gold pen and pencil sets, and coffee table art books are also acceptable gifts. Perfume for the secretarial staff—"my wife sent this to you"—is also a welcome gesture. Do not give silver items to Mexicans, who generally consider silver to be for tourists. Electronic gadgets are also possibilities, as are electronic toys or logo-imprinted items for the associate's children. This reinforces your interest in the family. However, it is usually wiser not to offer gifts, especially personal gifts, to an associate's spouse because of the potential for misunderstanding and offense.

Gauge the gift to the level of the recipient and the relationship. For example, a cigarette lighter could be either disposable and imprinted with your company logo or solid gold and suitably engraved, although the latter item would only be appropriate for a very narrow range of senior level associates in a very narrow range of business circumstances. Remember that Mexicans are sensitive to the appropriateness of such gifts, and overdoing it may be seen as gauche or even insulting.

BUSINESS NEGOTIATIONS

Once you have cultivated the necessary contacts, attended the necessary lunches and dinners, and decided on the venture you wish to pursue, the next step is putting together a negotiating team for a formal presentation. Ideally, your team will include someone with an excellent knowledge and understanding of Mexican Spanish. If this is not possible, it is essential that you have a competent interpreter present at all times during a trade mission or negotiation session. An interpreter may be of benefit while negotiating even if your negotiating team includes fluent speakers of Spanish or your Mexican counterparts seem fluent in your language. This may be used as a tactic on your part to make the Mexican negotiating team feel that you are playing by their rules, that is, using their language. It also prevents them from using a "secret" language that you don't understand for side discussions during negotiations. Nevertheless, your team members should preferably have at least a working knowledge of Spanish, and definitely have a solid understanding of the business culture they will be operating in. Ideally, the people you choose to accompany you will be the ones possessing the best people skills and management acumen.

Procedure When arranging negotiations with Mexicans, it is normal etiquette to give them as much detail as possible on the issues to be discussed, as well as a list of the delegation members attending. Their titles and positions should be clearly stated in order that the Mexican team may respond with reciprocal information. You should also communicate, in writing, the format you wish to follow during the negotiations. If there is any resistance from your negotiating counterparts, you may be able to come to an agreement on structure even before you reach the table, thereby providing more time for the discussion of substantive issues.

Another issue that should be clarified before coming to the table is that of authority. It is important that you be aware of the discretionary power to enter into a contract of the persons with whom you are negotiating. Because of the centralized nature of decision making in Mexican firms, you want to be absolutely sure that an agreed-upon contract draft can be immediately approved and signed. At the very least, you should be aware of which Mexican team member will be communicating with the top and how quickly approval can be obtained.

Formulating an Approach In business negotiations in Mexico, a positional bargaining approach is usually not the most effective method of dealing. You should be aware that if you enter into a contract that is too good to be true, it probably is. Because your Mexican counterparts will have carefully assessed your character and interests before deciding even to enter into negotiations, it will prove to be that much more difficult for you to take an unreasonably hard-nosed positional approach. If you do pressure your Mexican counterparts into accepting an agreement on your terms because of your company's size or powerful financial position, you run the risk that the agreement will backfire. If you notice weaknesses on the other side, taking undue advantage of it is likely to result either in the withdrawal of the Mexican team or in the nonperformance of the contract agreed to, in which case you will have lost much valuable time and other resources. However, be aware that the other side may feel free to attempt to pressure you if it senses that it holds the advantage.

Instead, it is advisable to use a more mutually beneficial, win-win approach that takes into account the satisfactory fulfillment of the interests on both sides. Due to the Mexican emphasis on human relations and the personal approach to business, proving your goodwill throughout the negotiating process will go a long way toward ensuring a positive relationship with your Mexican colleagues, leading perhaps to greater benefits and more lucrative business deals in the future. At the same time, you will go far in dispelling the notion of the aggressive foreign businessperson who only cares about short-term profits without regard for people and long-term relationships. Bear in mind that all economic transactions are also social transactions.

Failure to cultivate the social aspects of the transaction will leave you unprotected: if the other party has no reason to accept you as a person, they will be under no obligation to treat you well or fairly, and will even take pleasure in taking advantage of you. Playing the game is absolutely necessary.

Beginning the Meeting Negotiations are likely to be held in a hotel, conference center, or meeting room near the Mexican place of business, but usually not at the Mexican place of business. In accordance with the idea of Mexican hospitality, the negotiating venues are usually comfortable and well equipped. If you have been in the area before and have a preference for a particular location, it is acceptable to request that your counterparts make the meeting arrangements at that location. Subordinates usually arrive early to attend to seating arrangements and see to other details. A higher status executive will arrive later with a personal secretary, interpreter, bodyguard, and any other necessary members of the entourage, although it is considered bad form to pack the gallery with nonessential retainers. This grand entrance will give both teams an indication of who the power-brokers are.

After a round of handshaking and smiles, the host seats the visitors at the negotiating table. Spend the next few minutes exchanging pleasantries and getting a feel for those present. The senior people will take the lead in this, and subordinates may join in, although they should take their cues from the Mexican junior people, matching their level of involvement. Efforts to begin dealing immediately with substantive issues will be construed as rude and suspicious behavior. Remember that Mexicans consider impatience one of the main cultural failings of non-Mexicans. Easing into substantive talks gives you and your counterparts time to settle down and get comfortable with each other.

Entering Into Substantive Talks Following the initial courtesies—which can be relatively prolonged—the head of the host delegation usually opens the meeting by making formal, general welcoming remarks and then turns the floor over to the head of the guest delegation. As noted, most often the structure of the session will have been decided earlier. Thus, the foreign delegation's head speaker should begin by reiterating the format and structure of the meeting to make sure that there are no unforeseen disagreements about the proposed agenda. Distributing an outline or using an overhead transparency may also aid in clarifying the issues to be dealt with, their order, and any specific procedural matters.

When speaking, the visiting delegation leader should look toward the head of the Mexican team, not at the interpreter. If your Mexican counterparts are not proficient in English (a rarity these days among larger firms, at least in Mexico City), the speaker should make every effort to speak slowly and clearly. However, speakers should resist the tendency to talk down or speak more loudly than necessary. The use of interpreters can stretch a meeting to three times its normal length, so make sure to build plenty of breaks and rest periods into the schedule. Remember that the necessity of concentrating on cross-cultural and linguistic differences on top of the tensions of negotiating is also more tiring than usual and plan accordingly.

After the visitor outlines the team's position, the Mexican team leader takes the floor and answers item by item, proposing and making any needed changes to the agenda. From this point on, the negotiations will take on a life of their own, and it is up to each delegation to stay on track and address each issue thoroughly as disagreements arise. However, be aware that discussions often take a nonlinear form, jumping from issue to issue. Negotiators should be flexible and not insist on slavishly following the agenda, as long as they make sure that all the relevant substantive points do get covered. Decisions in Mexico are made based on context as much, as if not more than, on content. Mexicans also expect to *regatear* (bargain). This give-and-take is part of the social interaction. Mexicans tend to look down on those who don't play the game as being naive, lacking in social skills, and perhaps undeserving of their full trust.

Responsible parties will not allow negotiations to reach the stage of confrontation. It is important to keep lines of escape open. Negotiations should be allowed to stay open-ended, and if it becomes apparent that agreement cannot be reached on key issues, it is important to allow the talks to fade away rather than reach a dramatic conclusion. This allows everyone to save face and leaves open the possibility of future talks.

Mexican Negotiating Tactics Mexican negotiating teams present a united front, making it virtually impossible to exploit differences among their members, who dutifully defer to the principal negotiator. This person is usually the main spokesperson. The rest of the team members may not even be allowed to discuss issues; they may perhaps not even be allowed to address your team except on very narrow technical grounds in which they possess specific expertise. The senior person present, in turn, defers to the president or executive vice president for periodic advice on the phone if necessary. As noted, it is crucial that you understand the chain of command and who is ultimately responsible for signing the deal.

The Mexican emphasis on people skills means that most principal negotiators are very experienced, adept, and persuasive. They will often try to play on friendship to obtain concessions. It is up to your team to separate the personalities from the economic issues. Mexican negotiators may also use temper as a tool in an attempt to soften you up. Look for and recognize these age-old negotiating tricks, and prepare an appropriate counterplan to get the negotiations back on a principled and fair footing should these detours occur.

Mexican negotiators usually do not resort to threats such as suggesting that they have other interested competitors or breaking off talks abruptly over a point of contention. They will try to gauge how badly your side wants the agreement and exert the pressure they feel is appropriate according to the situation. Many outsiders are inclined to want to rush through an agreement so they can get on with their business; Mexicans will readily exploit this weakness if you exhibit impatience or a sense of urgency. It is more effective to take matters slowly and methodically, suggesting to your Mexican counterparts that you are willing to postpone your return home in order to finalize the deal or perhaps make a second trip if the differences cannot be settled this time around.

Tips for Foreign Negotiators

A number of tactics may be helpful to foreign negotiators dealing with Mexican businesspeople.

- Preparation is an essential part of the negotiation process. The successful negotiator will have a thorough knowledge of the Mexican personnel involved. Interview other businesspeople who have dealt with the company you are negotiating with, research and study any existing contracts they may have with other companies, and know the professional history of as many of the negotiators on the other side as possible.
- Put yourself in their shoes. Ask yourself, "If I were representing their team, what would I ask for? What would represent a fair agreement?" Such an exercise will give you fresh insight into their interests, strengths, and weaknesses.
- Prepare a list of possible positions the other side may take and develop alternatives to these before coming to the negotiating table.
- Use objective criteria in setting your standards and formulating your agreement proposals, such as independent market studies, government price indexes, and other independent objective measures. This will make it more difficult for the other side to contest your position by using more emotional and anecdotal grounds.
- Develop and keep in mind your best alternative position throughout the course of the negotiations. This represents your bottom line. Do not let your counterparts know what your best alternative is up front. If turns out to be stronger, use the alternative as a tool to

improve the terms of a possible agreement. Always give yourself the freedom to believe that you can walk out if you feel you aren't getting what you need.

- Don't put all your cards on the table, but play them one at a time. This fits in well with the Mexican viewpoint of negotiation as a social transaction. It also avoids a take-it-or-leave-it approach, which is seen as insulting, a challenge, and not playing the game.
- Use silence. Be prepared to sit quietly and impassively for what seems like an eternity to see what will ensue. This gives the appearance of deliberate consideration, avoids the appearance of overly hasty response, and may result in additional concessions or information from the other side.
- Listen carefully and take copious notes. To dispel any confusion, repeat important points after they are stated. This also lets the other team know that you have been listening to them. You will thus flag points of contention and eliminate extraneous misunderstandings and keep the talks on target. Use every occasion possible to assure the Mexican team that you are thinking long-term and therefore are interested in satisfying mutual concerns.
- Never force your opposites into making closed-ended, yes-no declarations. The cultural tendency in Mexico is to always answer yes, due to politeness and the assumption that a negative answer implies that the respondent lacks control. In reality, compliance may be either highly unlikely or downright impossible. To outsiders, this is maddening; they expect a straightforward answer and equate such a culturally conditioned response with a lack of truthfulness. Therefore, always phrase your question to allow your Mexican counterpart to indicate a tendency rather than a direct answer and follow up by eliciting additional information to help you determine how strong the tendency is.
- Build into the accords contingent agreements stipulating enforcement mechanisms and penalties for nonperformance. If the Mexican team objects, tell them that you in no way doubt their goodwill, but that such addenda are mere formalities demanded by your lawyers.
- Be prepared to walk away from the deal. Bad business is worse than no business, and if the terms and the all-important chemistry aren't right, it will be bad business. However, don't stalk out in a huff or tie up the loose ends too tightly. You have invested a considerable amount of time, money, and effort to get this far, and you don't want to burn any bridges. Besides, in the highly personalized world of Mexican business, if you leave those on the other side of the table with a bad impression, word will get around, thus closing off other potential avenues of business. Leave them with a good impression—that you are *muy simpático y buena gente*—and it may open other doors in the future. One observer estimates that in the tightly knit Mexican business community, every one-on-one contact you have influences a potential network of 30 to 40 other Mexican businesspeople who are the *socios* of the person with whom you are dealing.

The Mexican Approach to Contracts

Foreign businesspeople entering into contracts with Mexican enterprises or individuals should be aware of the ever-present difference between what may seem an honest verbal promise and the actual intention or ability of the contracting party to perform. Mexico has only recently begun to institute the rule of law in business. This means that many, if not most, Mexican executives view written contracts as less important when compared to personal commitments between associates. You are therefore advised to consult with a local attorney about the legally binding nature and enforceability of any written or verbal agreements you enter into. Also, be aware that judicial relief is particularly time-consuming, costly, and uncertain in Mexico, reason enough to work out as many issues as possible ahead of time.

While negotiating a detailed contract is important, keep in mind that you have not only entered into a given quantifiable and tangible agreement, but have also become part of a larger, ongoing relationship that needs to be nurtured if you are to benefit from it. Mexicans see an agreement in this context, and therefore consider you part of their close, personal network of business associates through which bigger and better things can be achieved in the future. You should therefore be comfortable with what may prove to be an extremely positive and beneficial affair.

FURTHER READING

The preceding discussion of Mexican business culture and etiquette is by no means a comprehensive presentation. The following sources may be consulted for additional insights.

Distant Neighbors, by Alan Riding. New York: Alfred A. Knopf, 1985. A modern near-classic on Mexico's past, politics and psychology.

Hippocrene Language & Travel Guide to Mexico, by Ila Warner. New York: Hippocrene, 1992. An interesting blend of basic language guide and cultural guide, giving real-life situations and the appropriate phrases for them.

Interact: Guidelines for Mexicans and North Americans, by John C. Condon and George W. Renwick. Chicago, Illinois: Intercultural Press, Inc., 1980. This study focuses on cultural differences between Mexicans and natives of the US, and how these differences affect style, mutual perceptions, and misunderstandings.

La Capital: *The Biography of Mexico City,* by Jonathan Kandell. New York: Random House, 1988. A recent discussion of Mexican history that uses the development of Mexico City as the means of approaching that of the country.

Management in Two Cultures: Bridging the Gap Between US and Mexican Managers, by Eva S. Kras. Chicago, Illinois: Intercultural Press, Inc., 1988. A small volume that uses a case study approach to flag cultural and management style differences between Mexican and US operators.

The Mexicans: A Personal Portrait of a People, by Patrick Oster. New York: Harper & Row, 1989. A fact-packed discussion of a variety of Mexican "types" that assesses the Mexican situation for outsiders.

Demographics

AT A GLANCE

These statistics are compiled from a variety of authoritative sources, including the United Nations, the World Bank, the International Monetary Fund, the United States Department of State, the International Labor Organization, and the government of Mexico.

POPULATION GROWTH RATE AND PROJECTIONS

Average annual growth rate (percent)

1960–70	1970–80	1980–91	1991–2000
3.4%	3.2%	2.3%	1.9%

Age structure of population (percent)

	1990	2025
Under 15 years old	38.5%	23.3%
15–64 years old	57.1%	68.3%
Over 64 years old	4.4%	8.4%

POPULATION BY AGE AND SEX, 1990

AGE	TOTAL	MALE	FEMALE
All ages	81,249,645	39,893,969	41,355,676
0–9	20,757,412	10,498,287	10,259,125
10–14	10,389,092	5,230,658	5,158,434
15–19	9,664,403	4,759,892	4,904,511
20–24	7,829,163	3,738,128	4,091,035
25–29	6,404,512	3,050,595	3,353,917
30–34	5,387,619	2,578,736	2,808,883
35–39	4,579,116	2,210,565	2,368,551
40–44	3,497,770	1,705,013	1,792,757
45–49	2,971,860	1,452,573	1,519,287
50–54	2,393,791	1,161,875	1,231,916
55–59	1,894,484	918,864	975,620
60–64	1,611,317	769,917	841,400
65 +	3,376,841	1,578,808	1,798,033
Unknown	492,265	240,058	252,207
15 +	49,610,876	23,924,966	25,685,910

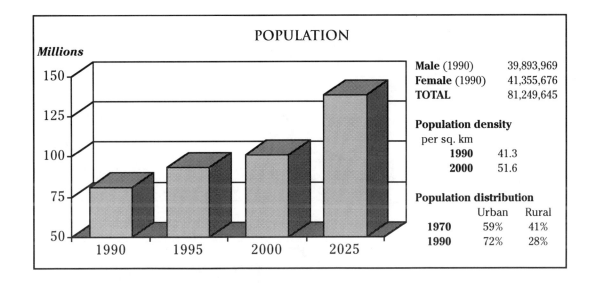

POPULATION

Millions

Male (1990)   39,893,969
Female (1990)   41,355,676
TOTAL   81,249,645

Population density
per sq. km
| 1990 | 41.3 |
| 2000 | 51.6 |

Population distribution
	Urban	Rural
1970	59%	41%
1990	72%	28%

VITAL STATISTICS

Live births	**1990**	2,710,573

Birth rate (per 1,000 persons)
	1982	32.8
	1990	31.5

Infant mortality rate (per 1,000 births)
	1970	72
	1991	36

Child mortality rate (per 1,000 births)
	1960	148
	1975	95
	1990	38

Registered deaths	**1990**	456,366

Death rate (per 1,000 persons)
	1982	5.7
	1990	5.3

Life expectancy at birth (years)
Overall	**1960**	56
Overall	**1990**	70
Male	**1990**	68
Female	**1990**	76

Fertility rate (children born per women)
	1970	6.5
	1991	3.2
	2000	2.4

Women of child–bearing age
(% of all women)
	1965	43
	1991	51

PRINCIPAL CITIES
(1990 census)

Mexico City	15,473,200
Guadalajara	2,884,000
Monterrey	2,549,400
Mexico City incorporated suburbs:	
Nezahualcoyótl Ecatepec Naucalpan	2,479,486
Puebla	1,454,500
León	956,000
Torreón	876,400
Toluca	827,300
Ciudad Juárez	797,600
Tijuana	742,700
San Luis Potosí	658,700
Mexicali	602,300
Culiacán	602,100
Mérida	595,300
Acapulco	592,200
Tampico	559,000
Chihuahua	534,300
Coatzacoalcos	515,300
Aguascalientes	506,300
Morelia	489,700
Querétaro	454,000
Veracruz	451,300
Hermosillo	449,400
Durango	414,000
Villahermosa	390,100
Irapuato	362,500
Jalapa	349,900
Cuernavaca	348,900
Celaya	315,600
Mazatlan	314,200
Los Mochis	305,500
Matamoras	303,400

Mexico
Consumer Price Index (CPI)

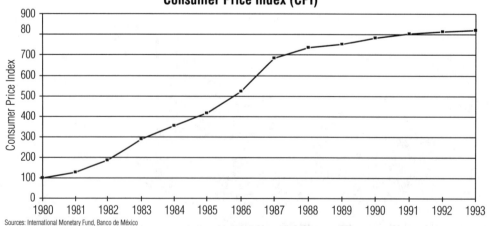

Sources: International Monetary Fund, Banco de México

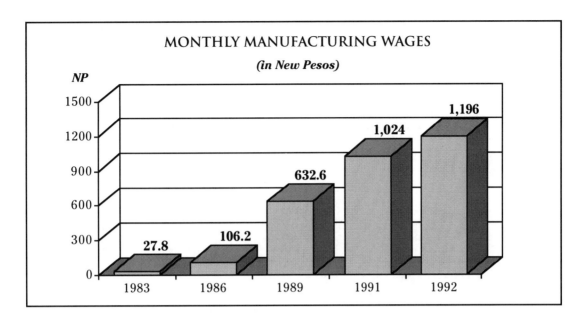

NATIONAL INCOME

GNP per capita (1991): US$3,030

Average annual growth rate 1980–91: -0.5%

Income Distribution
(Percent share of income, 1984)

Lowest	20%	4.1
Second	20%	7.8
Third	20%	12.3
Fourth	20%	19.9
Top	20%	55.9
Top	10%	39.5

PRICE INDEX BY CATEGORY

(1980 = 100)

Category	1989	1990	1991
Food	11,192	14,034	16,855
Rent/utilities	9,565	13,737	17,988
Clothing	11,470	13,036	15,274
Other	11,889	15,058	18,470

AVERAGE ANNUAL RATE OF INFLATION

1970–80	1980–90	1992	1993
18.1%	66.5%	11.9%	8.0%

HEALTH

**Health Expenditures
as a percentage of GDP**

1987	2.7%
1988	2.8%
1989	2.5%
1990	2.9%

Tobacco Consumption

(kilos per capita in adult population)

1974–76	1.4
1990	1.0
2000	1.1

Mexican Nutrition Individual Daily Average Consumption					
Calories			% of Calorie Requirements		
1980	1986	1990	1967–70	1980	1984–86
3,101.2	3,098.0	2,985.7	116%	120%	135%

COMMUNICATION CHANNELS

Daily newspapers

	Circulation (thousands)	Number of dailies
1975	5,499	216
1979	8,322	317
1986	10,356	308
1988	10,539	286

Televisions and Radios (thousands of sets in use)

	Televisions	Radios
1975	2,700	6,900
1980	3,820	9,000
1985	8,500	15,000
1990	12,350	21,500

Telephones (sets in use)

	Number (thousands)	Per 100 persons
1980	4,992	7.2
1987	8,016	9.7
1989	9,359	11.1
1990	10,103	11.8

MOTOR VEHICLES

Type	1988	1989	1990
Cars	5,806,984	6,201,018	6,754,096
Trucks	2,435,952	2,685,203	2,892,848
Motorcycles	218,207	225,403	231,503
Buses	86,566	91,267	94,004

ENERGY CONSUMPTION PER CAPITA

(kg of oil equivalent)

1970	1990
786	1,383

EDUCATION

Level	1988–89	1989–90	1990–91
Initial	100,817	104,397	105,201
Preschool	2,688,561	2,662,588	2,734,054
Primary	14,656,357	14,493,763	14,401,588
Secondary	4,355,334	4,267,156	4,190,190
Intermediate	427,686	413,481	378,894
High school	1,642,785	1,678,839	1,721,626
Bachelor college	126,676	118,501	108,978
Undergraduate	1,085,164	1,095,325	1,097,141
Graduate	45,102	45,889	45,899
Subtotal	25,128,482	24,879,945	24,783,588
Other training	439,958	436,168	413,587
Total	25,568,440	25,616,117	25,197,167

Marketing

Selling a product in Mexico can be as simple as signing a contract with a local retailer or as complex as establishing a company or chain of companies in the country. Mexico's markets are opening to imports, many trade barriers are being lifted, and many Mexican businesses are seeking alliances and trade relationships with foreign firms. Of course, horror stories abound, from lengthy delays at customs to inadequate remedies for the collection of unpaid bills, and even imprisonment for alleged misuse of government-backed development loans. However, most problems can usually be avoided with proper advance planning.

It isn't necessary to spend a fortune on research to learn whether there is a market. It's easy to find that out from a variety of sources. This book is one. Your own embassy's commercial services and Mexican trade associations are others. All along the way, you will find knowledgeable, experienced people whose job it is to help you wend your way through the mazes constructed by knowledgeable, experienced people whose job it is to get you lost. One key is to keep initial costs as low as possible—probably through direct sales—until you have established a toehold. Another key is to go overboard in servicing orders *immediately* and answering inquiries *immediately.* Above all, your firm must make a genuine and explicit commitment to exporting, because otherwise the worst problems will come from within, not from the competition or the market. Export sales generate a momentum of their own that is difficult to stop, and they pull repeat business, new accounts, and offers from persons eager to serve as your local representatives, but not before you have laid the groundwork.

Virtually everything is changing in Mexico these days, and marketing is no exception. Although the North American Free Trade Agreement (NAFTA) does not directly address marketing issues, it alters the existing rules regarding market access in many sectors and is expected to have a substantial effect on how goods and services are sold in Mexico. In fact,

some observers argue that NAFTA largely represents an after-the-fact acknowledgment of existing realities: there has already been a rush by companies—particularly those from the US—to do business in Mexico. For example, one need only to look to the gains made by franchisers in Mexico in recent years.

In the near term, NAFTA-inspired interest is likely to swamp Mexico's relatively rudimentary, undeveloped marketing channels. Over time, the increasing volume of foreign business is sure to introduce international practices and standards and call forth greater capacity and new ways of approaching markets. However, in the interim, pioneering marketers are largely going to have to solve their problems on an ad hoc basis. This makes for both huge frustration and opportunity. On the one hand, marketers won't be able to rely on standard operating procedure, nor will they be able to count on the support systems to which they probably have become accustomed. On the other hand, they won't be trapped by the straitjacket of traditional perceptions and ways of doing things and will have the chance to create a new way of doing business.

Marketing in Mexico requires that you:

- Learn the geographic markets,
- Discover the best marketing channels for your product,
- Find the right means of advertising—remember cost and coverage,
- Overcome the trade barriers, and
- Commit to exporting.

WHERE IS THE MARKET?

Mexico is a country of more than 90 million people. Its markets are extremely diverse, with demands that range from the most basic to the most sophisticated high technology. Manufacturing, agriculture, forestry, mining, tourism, and services are but a few of the prominent sectors. Indeed, the question to ask is not: "Is there a market?" but "What is the best market in Mexico?" The great expanses of farmlands and ranches are potential markets for makers of heavy and light agricultural equipment, fertilizers, pesticides, and many other items, while Mexico's largest commercial centers—Mexico City, Guadalajara, Monterrey—hold outstanding promise for companies offering consumer products and services.

The trick to finding a market in Mexico is identifying the primary users of the product and where they are concentrated. Begin by reviewing the information on the Mexican states included in this chapter, as well as in the "Opportunities" and "Industry Reviews" chapters. Many find it helpful to contact Mexican trade associations and government agencies listed in the "Important Addresses" chapter. And don't forget services offered by foreign governments. For example, the US Department of Commerce offers a Customized Sales Survey (CSS) containing information on potential markets and distribution channels for a specific product and gold/silver key reports that review a particular market, potential representatives, and related business services. The Trade Opportunity Program (TOP) offered by the US and Foreign Commercial Service (US&FCS) offers research on some of the current private and public import opportunities in Mexico.

In researching Mexico's markets, keep in mind

that its economy is still in a relatively early stage of development. Without a doubt, Mexicans have less purchasing power, different income groupings, and different priorities compared to buyers in more developed economies. Statistical data are often lacking, and sellers may need to conduct special surveys if they require detailed information for their sales programs. A number of market research firms have sprung up to cater to growing Mexican demand.

With 22 percent of Mexico's population and 40 percent of its total consumption focused in the Mexico City metropolitan area, there is no doubt that *la Capital* leads the country in terms of purchasing power. However, suppliers of foreign goods also need to investigate other major centers of business activity, including Guadalajara, Monterrey, and the larger Mexican-US border towns. Guadalajara accounts for 8 percent and Monterrey for 7 percent of Mexico's consumption, followed by important and growing secondary commercial centers. A growing number of provincial cities have populations of greater than 500,000, increasing countrywide opportunities for selling in Mexico. Companies from many countries—Japan, Germany, England, Canada, and the US, to name a few—are investing in the Mexican market, some merely through representative offices and others through more substantial establishments, including manufacturing facilities, retail outlets, and distribution chains. To have any hope of meeting the competitive challenge, a marketer will have to visit Mexico's commercial centers and explore its formidable industries.

THE STATES OF MEXICO

Aguascalientes

(Population: 720,000; cities: Aguascalientes, Rincon de Romos) Centrally-located Aguascalientes is a major road, rail, and communications hub. Nearly one-third of the state is cultivated, growing mostly fruits and vegetables (it is number one nationally in guavas and number two in grapes). Mines produce lead, silver, zinc, and fluorite. The capital city has grown into a medium-sized metropolis, with five industrial parks, focusing on automation. Products include textiles, apparel, footwear, wine, brandy, and processed foods. Foreign-invested operations produce automobiles, locomotives, metal and mechanical products, and electronic and computer equipment.

Baja California Norte

(Population: 1.7 million; cities: Mexicali, Ensenada, Tecate, Tijuana) This state is one of Mexico's most urbanized. Baja Norte ranks first nationwide in industrial parks with at least 50. Numerous organizations promote industrial development, which is based primarily on *maquiladora* production, tourism, and trade with the US. Manufacturers produce garments, machine tools, trucks, agricultural tools and machinery, furniture, and metal and plastic products. Tecate is famous for beer and wine and Ensenada for tourism and vacation and retirement development. Cross-border day tourists are a specialty in Tijuana and Mexicali. In recent years, Baja California Norte has sought to diversify its economy through agriculture, fishing, aquaculture, and wine and beer production. Baja Norte produces grapes, olives, cotton, alfalfa, barley, dates, sorghum, and citrus fruits. Wheat milling and livestock feed are also prominent.

Baja California Sur

(Population: 320,000; cities: La Paz) Mexico's least populous state, Baja Sur focuses on fishing and tourism. The rugged, undeveloped state relies on airports more than roads. Government and foreign investment in tourism and retirement resort development have driven the economy. Baja Sur has huge potential for commercial fishing, which has gone from a subsistence activity to become a substantial sportfishing industry with several small seaports, an industrial fishing park in Pichilingue, and port facilities in the capital of La Paz. Baja California Sur's easy access to the Pacific Rim has attracted a growing *maquiladora* industry, primarily producing textiles and electronics. The state has many untapped natural resources. Baja Sur has one of the world's largest salt mines and produces gypsum, phosphorus, and magnetite. Modern irrigated agricultural operations produce sorghum, cotton, wheat, chickpeas, grapes, dates, citrus fruits, and peaches. Wheat milling, cotton processing, and food canning also are prominent.

Campeche

(Population: 530,000; cities: Campeche, Ciudad del Carmen) The tropical state of Campeche focuses on the oil industry. The state accounts for a large share of Mexico's oil production and more than one-fourth of its natural gas production. Government funds have resulted in well developed seaports at Ciudad del Carmen and the city of Campeche that support fishing and seafood processing. A fleet of more than 5,000 vessels has allowed the state to become a prime frozen seafood exporter. Campeche's agricultural sector produces honey, rice, fruit, corn, and sugarcane. Tropical forests cover more than half of Campeche, although production of wood products is still at an early stage.

Chiapas

(Population: 3.2 million; cities: Tuxtla Gutiérrez, Tapachula, San Cristóbal de las Casas) Located on Mexico's southern border with Guatemala, Chiapas

---

CONFRONTING CORRUPTION*

Seller beware. The new Mexican economy may be more open and modern. But there's still the same old graft.

"You're most likely to see corruption in areas that are more rural, and less supervised by the federal government and federal authorities," says David Oskandy, an attorney with G.M.&A. International Attorneys and Business Counselors, a Chicago law firm specializing in Latin American trade affairs. "Let's say your company is building a warehouse in Mexico. You might need all kinds of permits: a construction permit, environmental permits, that sort of thing. It's possible you'll encounter someone who says you have to pay him to get that permit. But I'd hate to leave the impression that graft is typical, or more common than in the US."

The attorney offers this advice: don't get sucked in. Hire a good lawyer. "There are established procedures and, let's face it, the law is the law," he says. "If you pay off one person, the word will get around, and everyone will play that game with you. Besides, you could get into legal trouble."

Another form of graft is payola to middlemen before companies can sell to end users. "Business can be done through relationships in which you can sell to company X, only if you go through dealer Y," says H. Philip Welt, general manager of Microsoft Mexico, in Mexico City. (He notes that Microsoft refuses to pay anyone off.) "I don't know why this arrangement exists, but I can only imagine."

How can companies win at this corrupt game? By offering a superior product. "If you've got a great product, one that company X has to have, then you can get around the middleman," Welt says. "I don't think you can legislate an end to corruption, but the more competitive the Mexican economy gets, the less graft there will be."

*Excerpted from article entitled "New World Orders" by Geoffrey Brewer. Reprinted by permission of Sales & Marketing Management. Copyright © 1994 Bill Communications, Inc.

---

is the country's primary gateway to Central America. With nearly a quarter of Mexico's water supply located within its borders, Chiapas is home to Mexico's three largest dams and generates almost 20 percent of the nation's electricity. The state has many natural resources, including gold, silver, marble, amianthus, sulfur and sulfates, and oil. Developed during the 1980s, oil fields are among Mexico's top five suppliers of crude oil and natural gas. The state is one of the top Mexican producers of coffee, bananas, cocoa, soybeans, and corn. Much of Chiapas is devoted to cattle raising, and the harvest of tropical woods supports a woodcarving industry. Contemporary Indian cultures and Mayan ruins attract tourists. Industrial development is in an early phase, with little infrastructure or trained labor. However, natural resources and location offer great potential for development.

Chihuahua

(Population: 2.4 million; cities: Chihuahua, Ciudad Juárez, Ciudad Camargo) The border state of Chihuahua is Mexico's fastest-growing. *Maquiladoras* are the most dynamic sector and the mainstay of the economy, producing electronic components, automotive parts, and textile goods. Many related industries in the various industrial parks support the *maquiladoras.* Chihuahua also produces timber and related goods and cattle. Major local groups have invested in cellulose, pulp, wood moldings, plywood, furniture, and beer, as well as in *maquila* production. The state is a major producer of corn, beans, wheat, cotton, and alfalfa. Apples, peaches, and nuts are exported, and more than 60 percent of Mexico's total fruit production comes from Chihuahua. The state leads in zinc mining and also produces iron, copper, lead, and silver. Chihuahua's natural attractions—particularly the Cañón de Cobre—hold potential for the development of a substantial tourist industry.

Coahuila

(Population: 2 million; cities: Saltillo, Monclova, Torreón, Piedras Negras) This northern state is noted for its fluorite, coal, barium, feldspar, oxide, dolomite, titanium, lead, and tin mines; the foundries that process their ores; and the *maquiladora* production has contributed to the diversification of Coahuila's economy. Monclova is the site of one of Mexico's leading iron and steel producers and several large automobile assembly plants have been established in Saltillo. Coahuila's agricultural sector is supported by a well developed irrigation infrastructure. The Laguna region is one of Mexico's largest producers of agricultural products—particularly wheat, corn, oats, safflower, and cotton—and livestock, including sheep, cattle, and goats.

Colima

(Population: 425,000; cities: Colima, Manzanillo) Because of its location and its well-established network of roads, railways, and airports, plus the large seaport at Manzanillo, the small Pacific Coast state of Colima has great potential for business investment. Manzanillo is the location of important freight and transport companies, fisheries, seafood processors, and industrial parks. Also famous as a resort, it caters to more affluent tourists; foreign investment is substantial in Colima's tourist industry. Major irrigation projects are under construction, and agricultural products include peanuts, sorghum, coffee, lime extract, lemons, bananas, coconuts, mangoes, and palm oil. Processed food products include lemon, coconut-copra, and marine products. Mines produce iron ore pellets for iron and steel works in other parts of Mexico.

Distrito Federal

(Population: 19.9 million; Mexico City) The Federal District is the country's political, financial, commercial, industrial, and cultural center. Although smaller in area than any other political unit in the country, the DF offers an immense market: nearly one-fourth of the country's population lives in the metropolitan area, and it ranks as the largest city in the world. Recent emphasis has been on the development of regions outside the Federal District, but the city continues to be the major player in the modernization of the Mexican economy. Infrastructure here is more highly developed than in any region in Mexico. The DF has the best communications, financial, and business infrastructure, and a wide variety of business support services. Many multinational companies have located either their entire operations or at least their headquarters here, even in the face of Mexico's decentralization policy that seeks to move investment into other areas. Nevertheless, the Federal District holds considerable potential for future growth, particularly for utilities and service-oriented businesses.

Durango

(Population: 1.3 million; cities: Durango, Gómez Palacio) The interior state of Durango has established industrial parks, and foreign-invested companies are on the rise, including firms involved in metallurgy, engineering, textiles, and food processing. The mountainous state is known for mining and forestry resources, producing more than one-third of Mexico's timber and timber products (cellulose, plywood, railroad ties, and pine and oak lumber). Mines produce gold, uranium, silver, lead, iron ores, and high quality marble. One-third of Durango's gross domestic product (GDP) consists of agricultural goods—corn, beans, cotton, wheat, alfalfa, grapes, apples, apricots, peaches, and nuts—and livestock.

Guanajuato

(Population: 3.9 million; cities: Guanajuato, Celaya, Irapuato, León) Located in Mexico's central Bajío region, Guanajuato's highway and railway infrastructure is extensive, and airports service the cities of León and Celaya. Guanajuato's economy has strong agricultural, mining, industrial, and tourist sectors. This state produces asparagus, strawberries, broccoli, livestock, and other agricultural products. Guanajuato remains a leading producer of silver, gold, lead, and tin. At least eleven industrial parks have been built, and its cities are centers of such diverse industries as leather (León), electrical equipment and textiles (Irapuato), oil refining (Salamanca), and agribusiness (Celaya). Tourists flock to San Miguel de Allende and the capital city of Guanajuato for colonial architecture and local artist colonies.

Guerrero

(Population: 2.6 million; cities: Chilpancingo, Acapulco, Zihuatanejo, Iguala, Taxco) Often referred to as "the Mexican Riviera," Guerrero relies on tourism, fishing, and agriculture. Agriculture involves the production of corn, beans, and sorghum, and fruits, sugarcane, and coffee are also cultivated. Livestock and forestry exploitation is being encouraged. However, the tourist industry is the driving force behind the state's economy. Many tourists visit Taxco, which is famous for its colonial architecture and silversmiths and lies within day-trip distance from Mexico City. Many more vacation at the booming international resorts of Acapulco and Ixtapa. Guerrero's less developed industries include food processing, metal product manufacturing, gold and silver finishing, and oil and soap production.

Hidalgo

(Population: 1.9 million; cities: Pachuca, Tulancingo) Hidalgo has benefited from its proximity to Mexico City. It sports 11 industrial parks in Pachuca, Tulancingo, Tepeji, Tula, and Tizayuca. One of Mexico's first industrial parks was developed at Ciudad Sahagún, known for its subway and rail car production. The state's industrial facilities attract primarily small- and medium-scale enterprises that wish to remain near Mexico City. Manufactures include textiles, automotive parts, processed foods, petrochemicals, footwear materials, and electronic products. Agricultural products include corn, barley, coffee, and alfalfa. Since colonial times, this state has supported a healthy silver and gold mining industry. Visitors flock to the archaeological site of Tula and relax in Hidalgo's many colonial cities and spas.

Jalisco

(Population: 5.3 million; cities: Guadalajara, Puerto Vallarta) The state of Jalisco extends from the Pacific Coast into Mexico's mountainous interior. Guadalajara, with around 3 million people, is the most important financial and commercial center outside Mexico City. More than 50 percent of Jalisco's workforce is employed in commerce and service industries while fewer than 15 percent work in agriculture. Nevertheless, the state is Mexico's top food producer, growing corn, sorghum, wheat, fruit, vegetables, fodder, meat, milk, and eggs. Mining continues to offer potential for future development. Jalisco's industries produce processed foods; animal feeds; metal products; textiles, synthetic fibers, and garments; footwear; chemicals; glassware; and photographic supplies. Major foreign-invested electronics companies are located around Guadalajara. Jalisco's coastline has prime development potential for tourist and fishing ventures. Puerto Vallarta is a major stop for cruise ships.

Estado de México

(Population: 11.6 million; cities: Toluca, Tlalnepantla) Long a major producer of staple crops, the Estado de México's closeness to the Federal District has made it a key player in the industrial development of the country. Industrial parks, originally clustered in the areas closest to Mexico City, have now spread into more distant areas. Many of the more than 30 parks are home to foreign-invested automobile and electronic production and assembly facilities. The chief industries are food processing, construction, vehicle assembly, chemical production, textiles, paper, machinery, and electric and electronic equipment and appliances production. Tourism is also an important industry, with many visitors particularly attracted by the world renowned archaeological complex at Teotihuacán with its massive pyramids.

Michoacán

(Population: 3.5 million; cities: Morelia, Uruapan, Zitácuaro, Lázaro Cárdenas) An important producer of agricultural staples, Michoacán also grows tropical fruits—mangoes, papayas, limes, and avocados. Pig farming is important, and more than one-third of the farmed land is irrigated, a high proportion for Mexico. Forests provide a rich variety of tropical and other woods, and Michoacán is Mexico's third largest timber producer. Iron deposits supply ore to the works at the port of Lázaro Cárdenas. Steel, food processing, forestry-related products, and capital goods are the most important industries. Tourists are drawn to this state for its Tarascan Indian culture, although tourist resources are relatively undeveloped.

Morelos

(Population: 1.2 million; cities: Cuernavaca, Cuautla) Because of its warm weather, abundant water supply, and proximity to the Federal District, Morelos is a popular resort getaway. Tourism contributes substantially to the state's economy. Morelos has two industrial parks and a high-tech facility. A third industrial park is located in Cuautla. Morelos is most famous as a major agricultural region, and high-value horticulture—such as of exotic flowers for export—is replacing sugarcane growing. Morelos also caters to many foreign-invested companies that produce a variety of products, from pharmaceuticals to tires and automobiles.

Nayarit

(Population: 850,000; cities: Tepic) Nayarit's economy is still largely based on agriculture, and the northern part of the state is linked to the intensive agribusiness development in neighboring Sinaloa. Crops include sugarcane, rice, coffee, and various fruits. Tobacco growers supply cigarette factories in the capital of Tepic. Industry has primarily focused on agriculture and food processing, wood products, and textiles. However, the economy is undergoing change with the recent establishment of *maquiladora* plants funded largely by Japanese interests. The state has developed a beach resort at Nuevo Vallarta. Nayarit offers opportunities for investors who seek a relatively undeveloped area with convenient access to the Pacific Rim.

Nuevo León

(Population: 3.2 million; cities: Monterrey) The third largest center in Mexico, Monterrey, is the capital of the northern state of Nuevo León. This industrial and commercial city, lying only 150 miles from the US border, is well known for its institutions of higher learning. In general, the workforce in Nuevo León is relatively highly skilled in traditional industrial activities, commercial services, and technical applications. Numerous enterprises of every size, the smaller ones often working as subcontractors to the larger ones, have roots in this state. Operations produce iron, steel, glass, textiles, petrochemicals, beer, chemicals, paper, and cardboard. *Maquiladoras* are abundant. This state is an attractive market for modern machinery and equipment, industrial raw materials, and high-tech products. Agriculture plays a relatively minor role in Nueva León's economy.

Oaxaca

(Population: 3 million; cities: Oaxaca, Salina Cruz) Oaxaca is the hub for the roads and railways that connect the coast and the inland regions of this large Pacific coast state. Oaxaca is primarily involved in agriculture—fruit production—and livestock raising. Industry is centered in the Tuxtepec region and around the port of Salina Cruz, with its large oil refinery, that supplies petroleum products consumed in the domestic Pacific coastal markets and most of the crude oil shipped to Japan. Tourism is important to Oaxaca's economy. This state has striking pre-Columbian ruins, a charming colonial capital, and a number of contemporary Indian groups. Huatulco has been developed as a beach resort, and Oaxaca is promoting further tourist development. The state's port cities are potential strategic locations for export to the Pacific Rim, and prospects for development are good.

Puebla

(Population: 4.1 million; cities: Puebla, Huachinango, Tehuacán) Puebla's strong private sector is highly diversified, with agriculture, industry, and tourism each contributing large shares. Puebla's major crops include corn, potatoes, coffee, avocados, beans, sugarcane, and barley. It also has some high-grade specialized agricultural operations and is noted for the production of apples in particular. Long-established foreign-invested operations produce automobiles and textiles. The state is known for its substantial bottled mineral water industry. Colonial architecture, pre-Columbian archaeological sites, and the area's renowned cuisine draw international tourists.

Querétaro

(Population: 1.1 million; cities: Querétaro, San Juan del Rio, Jalpan del Sierra) This state is a crossroads linking western Mexico and the interior Bajío region. Querétaro has 11 industrial parks, and its capital city is one of Mexico's burgeoning secondary commercial centers. More than half of Querétaro's GDP comes from agriculture. However, the state has attracted considerable foreign investment, and industrial plants have been established in the capital and in San Juan del Rio, producing such diverse products as chemicals, photographic supplies, machinery, electronic equipment, paper products, and processed foods.

Quintana Roo

(Population: 495,000; cities: Chetumal, Cancún) Quintana Roo is largely dependent on the tourist industry. Other substantial economic contributions are made by the state's production of corn and its forestry industry, which specializes in tropical and precious woods. Quintana Roo also has a sizable fishing fleet and good potential for further development of its fishery and seafood processing industries.

San Luis Potosí

(Population: 2 million; cities: San Luis Potosí, Matehuala, Ciudad Valles) Historically, this state has been a mining center, and mining continues to play an important economic role through the production and processing of gold, silver, zinc, copper, fluorite, lead, manganese, and mercury. Nearly half of the state's workforce is active in agriculture—growing such products as coffee, citrus and tropical fruits, and vegetables—and cattle raising, particularly in the Huasteca region. However, industry is now the most important economic sector. The state capital is home to such diverse manufacturing industries as automobile and auto parts factories, mineral processors, chemical and pharmaceutical firms, food and beverage processors, machinery makers, and textile companies.

Sinaloa

(Population: 2.4 million; cities: Culiacán, Mazatlán, Los Mochis) The western state of Sinaloa has substantial trade potential, with major highways that connect it to Nogales on the US border and two major seaports. A third industrial seaport, geared to exports for the Pacific Rim, is being created at Topolobampo. Agriculture is still the main economic activity, and plans are underway for further expansion of its irrigation infrastructure. Sinaloa produces rice, vegetables, wheat, and beans. Fishing is the second most important activity, and Sinaloa is Mexico's top producer in terms of value. Substantial investments are being made to develop aquaculture, particularly shrimp production. Sinaloa has several industrial parks and development areas, mostly canning, packing, and frozen food processing plants related to the state's agricultural and fish production. Tourism is most developed along Sinaloa's southern coast, where international cruise ships enter port at Mazatlán.

Sonora

(Population: 1.8 million; cities: Hermosillo, Guaymas, Ciudad Obregón) Many of Sonorans live along the US border (in the area of Nogales) and to the south (around the state capital of Hermosillo). Extensive irrigation systems support agricultural zones producing wheat, soybeans, safflower, cotton, sesame seeds, grapes, citrus fruit, and vegetables and top-quality beef. Mexico's largest fishing fleet operates out of Guaymas. Mining also makes a significant contribution to Sonora's economy through the production of copper, graphite, silver, tin, lead, gold, and tungsten, among other minerals. Foreign-invested manufacturing facilities, including substantial numbers of *maquiladoras* along the US border and in the state capital, produce automobiles, cement, and electronic equipment.

Tabasco

(Population: 1.5 million; cities: Villahermosa, Cárdenas) In the past, this tropical Gulf Coastal state depended on the production of bananas. In recent years, flood control has allowed the agriculture sector to diversify into beef and dairy cattle production as well as into a number of other crops. Tabasco is also Mexico's leading producer of rubber and cocoa. Most of Tabasco's industry is still in a relatively early

FOLLOW THE RULES*

Doing business in Mexico requires more than learning Spanish. Companies must absorb the culture, too, as they do when dealing with any foreign country. For two decades, Jeffrey Peters, CEO of the US Mexican Development Corp., in New York, has been giving advice to top US executives on how to enter the Mexican market. Here are some of his rules:

Rule No. 1 Be patient, persistent, and maintain a good sense of humor. "It often takes longer than expected to consummate successful business transactions in Mexico, so be prepared," Peters says.

Rule No. 2 Start selling at the top; close sales at the top. "Mexicans are more hierarchical, so don't 'spin your wheels' with underlings."

Rule No. 3 Throw away the corporate handbook, or your normal ways of doing business in the US. "They won't work in Mexico, and they'll only serve to frustrate your potential Mexican partner. Relax your rigid schedule, leave the handbook at home, and let yourself enjoy the flexibility of doing business the 'Mexican way'—over a long business luncheon."

Rule No. 4 In the joint-venture courtship, get engaged before you get married. "Once you have identified your best prospective partner, begin with a first project under a one- to two-year contract. Remember that joint ventures are more difficult than marriage."

Rule No. 5 Consult with a trusted third party before forming a partnership with a Mexican company. "You need to know the difference between an interesting acquaintance and a good partner. A trusted third party can best provide that insight. The wrong partner can be the worst mistake you will make, so be careful."

Rule No. 6 Consider second-tier Mexican companies as joint-venture partners. "They are often more flexible and more aggressive in pursuing and winning business."

*Excerpted from article entitled "New World Orders" by Geoffrey Brewer. Reprinted by permission of Sales & Marketing Management. Copyright © 1994 Bill Communications, Inc.

developmental stage. The state is promoting diversification and has established several industrial parks in its major cities to move it away from its dependence on oil production and refining. Much recent industrial investment is concentrated in food processing, but cement production is also important.

Tamaulipas

(Population: 2.3 million; cities: Ciudad Victoria, Reynosa, Matamoros, Nuevo Laredo, Tampico) Mexico's northeasternmost state of Tamaulipas extends from the US state of Texas to Veracruz. The busy international ports of Altamira and Tampico are located at the southern end of the state. With substantial irrigation systems, this state is an important producer of such staple crops as sorghum, wheat, and corn. Shrimp, crayfish, oysters, and crabs are among its major seafood products. Industry has developed primarily from oil and *maquiladora* production. Extensive oil and petrochemical production are found in Tampico, Ciudad Madero, and Reynosa, while most of the *maquiladoras* are located along the US border.

Tlaxcala

(Population: 765,000; cities: Tlaxcala, Huamantla) Mexico's smallest state, Tlaxcala, boasts 17 industrial parks and an extensive highway and railway system linking it to Mexico City and the international port of Veracruz. Traditionally based on agricultural and livestock production, Tlaxcala grows wheat, barley, potatoes, and alfalfa. Industry now claims the major share of Tlaxcala's production. Long-established textile mills in the region of Santa Ana Chiauhtempan supply thread, fabrics, and finished garments. In an effort to diversify, Tlaxcala is actively encouraging foreign-invested factories to locate in the state. Its success is seen in the thriving production of metal manufactured goods, machinery and equipment, automotive parts, chemicals, pharmaceuticals, petrochemicals, wood products, cellulose, paper, and cardboard. Tlaxcala has a significant tourist industry, based on well preserved colonial towns and resorts.

Veracruz

(Population: 6.7 million; cities: Jalapa, Veracruz, Tuxpan, Coatzacoalcos) The state of Veracruz is Mexico's primary gateway to Europe and remains Mexico's leading state in terms of the amount of cargo handled. It is also Mexico's third most populous state, with a network of highways and railways. Oil is the major industry in northern Veracruz, with much of the production shipped to the petrochemical and industrial centers of Ciudad Madero and Tampico in neighboring Tamaulipas. Growers in the

---

THE SERVICE EDGE*

Doing business in Mexico might require learning a new language and culture. But the formula for success is written in plain English. In fact, it's spelled out in just about any textbook on total quality management. "If you want to win in Mexico, you've got to get the service edge," says Brian Brison, an assistant commercial attaché with the US Embassy in Mexico. "Mexicans tend to rank service, the personal touch, right up there with price. They want attention before, during, and after the sale."

Just ask John Lopez, who manages Mexican accounts for Houston-based Vista Chemical Company's Latin American division. He spends 60 percent of his time in Mexico, keeping in touch with customers and trying to attract new accounts. "There are plenty of flights from Houston, so I get down there all the time," says the bilingual Lopez, who was born in Colombia. "We're not selling a commodity, we're selling a product that requires a lot of technical support. That means I need to be as close to the customer as possible. You treat Mexican customers just as you would treat a US customer."

That may come as a surprise to some US companies, the Ugly Americans who over the years have dumped cheap goods on unwitting customers across the border, raked in a few pesos, then headed north, never to be seen again. "Mexican businesses have been burned all too often by poor product coming across the border," says Joe Martorelli, president of American Machinery Services, Inc. of Bedford Park, Illinois. "There's also been very little follow-up."

But Lopez thinks the days of Mexicans accepting any old product from the north are long gone. "Many of the businesspeople you deal with were educated at the best schools in Europe and the US," he says. "Standards in Mexico are much higher than people think. If you underestimate the Mexicans, you won't be very successful there."

Dave Noelken, engine group manager for Caterpillar America, in Peoria, Illinois, agrees. "We sell through our Mexican dealer network to a very fast-growing trucking industry, and our customers there aren't asking about yesterday's products," he says. "They want to know what you're going to offer tomorrow. They want technologically advanced products. In no way is this a substandard marketplace."

*Excerpted from article entitled "New World Orders" by Geoffrey Brewer. Reprinted by permission of Sales & Marketing Management. Copyright © 1994 Bill Communications, Inc.

Jalapa area supply a major share of Mexico's coffee exports, the state's most important crop. Textile production is dominant in the industrial centers of Córdoba, Orizaba, and Río Blanco. Coatzacoalcos in southern Veracruz is the site of one of Mexico's largest petrochemical complexes, and ranching dominates the inland Acayucan region. The tourist industry is a specialty of Veracruz, known for its climate, cuisine, and archaeological sites.

Yucatán

(Population: 1.4 million; cities: Mérida) Yucatán's primary economic sector is agriculture, and it is Mexico's top producer of sisal and an important supplier of corn, beans, sorghum, oranges, mangoes, and lemons. This state has a substantial seaport infrastructure, with five principal and four subsidiary shelter ports. With numerous important Mayan ruins, Yucatán attracts worldwide attention, and tourism is a major industry. Industrialization is in an early phase of development, consisting mainly of the production of consumer goods. Several *maquiladoras* have located here in recent years, and their production is expected to grow in future years.

Zacatecas

(Population: 1.3 million; cities: Zacatecas, Fresnillo, Sombrete) The economy of Zacatecas has traditionally been based on agriculture and mining. The state is a major producer of fruit—guavas, grapes, peaches, and apples—while cattle and sheep ranching take up more than half of its area. Zacatecas ranks first in silver, second in lead, third in tin, and fourth in gold production nationally. Economic diversification is an important theme, and the state is constructing new hotels and inviting investment in associated services. The sights in Zacatecas are primarily aimed at culturally-oriented tourists who come to discover its colonial architecture. In addition, several foreign-invested companies have located in the state, primarily to take advantage of the close proximity of the raw materials produced there.

FROM A TOEHOLD TO AN ESTABLISHED PRESENCE: ELEVEN STEPS INTO MEXICO'S MARKETS

Most exporters enter Mexico's markets in three stages. They usually start by seeking a few orders through the major marketing channels already established in the country. Three channels dominate marketing in Mexico, and it is through these that most international businesses establish footholds in the market:

- Private Mexican traders—these are direct importers, distributors, and sales agents.

- Public and private Mexican-owned end users—these include manufacturers, utilities, hospitals, schools, and other institutional buyers.
- Foreign-owned companies in Mexico—these are branches or subsidiaries of foreign firms that buy and sell parts to incorporate into their own products or completed products that complement their own products.

The second phase is to open a sales office to handle increasing volume and enhance market reputation by offering local service. Once the volume of sales warrants a more permanent presence, the exporter is ready for the third phase: investing in a business or organizing a new domestic distribution system, either through an arrangement with a Mexican firm or as a foreign subsidiary in Mexico.

At each stage, businesspeople must evaluate which of the following steps will best accomplish the goal of successful penetration of the market. Depending on the product involved, some businesses may find that it is feasible to bypass an entire stage.

1. Use an established distribution channel.

An established distribution channel can be used to test whether Mexican markets are receptive to your product. Steps 2 through 6 that follow involve distribution channels already available in Mexico. Of the channels available, the one chosen depends on the product. The goal is to determine which channel is most likely to effectively reach the primary users of the product.

Advantages By using one or more of these existing distribution channels, marketers can define, before they invest heavily in exporting, the nature of the market for the product in Mexico, such as: the location and size of the market; the best means of reaching it; and the need to modify the product to fit market demands.

Disadvantages Marketing occurs through and under the name of another business. The reputation of that business will reflect on the product placed in the Mexican market, and the wise choice of a distributor is critical. Moreover, the product will not stand on its merit alone, but will be sold with the backing of another business. As a result, it may become necessary to establish, or at least reconfirm, the independent reputation of the product and of your firm in the market should you later switch to direct marketing.

2. Exhibit at trade or regional fairs.

Fairs are particularly useful for introducing a product to Mexico's private and public commercial entities, as distinct from direct consumers, who generally do not attend such fairs. Consider not only trade fairs, but also state, regional, and national fairs, where agricultural and industrial displays are increasingly common.

Advantages Products and new technology can actually be demonstrated to potential customers. Hands-on testing by buyers increases product awareness, and a favorable perception and can result in a competitive edge. It is also possible to make contact with smaller buyers, as well as with large firms, distributors and agents, and foreign and local industry representatives.

Disadvantages It is often necessary to wait before an appropriate fair is scheduled, which can delay entry. Competition is also likely to be intense because many producers at the fair are targeting the same set of buyers.

3. Do direct marketing.

Firms that prefer to avoid the cost of a distributor or other intermediary, may contact local importers, warehousers, chain outlets, and end users directly. This method is often chosen by firms that supply consumer products or specialized items for a small niche market. Small retailers and sole proprietorships still predominate, at least in numerical terms, but discount stores and regional chains are taking an increasingly large share of the market. Be sure to consider large-scale stores, which often have their own transportation and distribution systems as well, transportation and distribution being among the major hurdles in Mexico.

Contractual terms and conditions are similar to those used in other developed nations. The contract need not be in Spanish, unless it must be filed with a government registry. Nor are any special signature procedures required.

Advantages Allows direct access to large consumer and end user markets, and each sale will establish the reputation of the seller, not that of an intermediary.

Disadvantages Direct marketing can be extremely difficult for those unfamiliar with the language or culture. Direct marketing also is often expensive in terms of the advertising and labor required to obtain orders. If a local distributor is used, these costs are usually the concern of that party. Sales to warehouses and chain outlets are usually made with slim profit margins because of intense competition from producers of similar products and the market power exercised by such outlets.

4. Enter bids on public projects or procurement contracts.

More than 15 percent of all imports are purchased by government agencies and state-owned enterprises. Sales of products and services to public institutions are typically made through bidding procedures. Bids are solicited through government tenders, direct advertising, or invitations to qualified and registered government suppliers. Even public hospitals purchase drugs and pharmaceuticals through bidding procedures. The Mexican government also promotes some products—such as automotive emissions control equipment—through a bidding process. Bidders should be sure to target persons who advise the bidding review boards with promotional material that clearly explains the features, quality, and benefits of the firm's product. Don't forget the state and local governments when seeking bidding opportunities.

Advantages Successful bids can advance a product's reputation in domestic markets, and once a firm becomes a registered government supplier, it gains access to future bidding opportunities more easily.

Disadvantages Price concessions may be required in order to be chosen over other bidders. Some preferences for Mexican bidders may be allowed, and foreign companies may be further hampered by having to show that they can meet registration and import requirements, offer strict product guarantees, post bonds, and provide costly on-site, follow-up services. All suppliers must register and be approved by the government agency or branch responsible for the procurement tender. Registration procedures vary among agencies: some require fees to register, some periodically demand renewals, and most require that bidders have a permanent representative in Mexico. (Refer to the "Opportunities" chapter for a discussion of procurement opportunities and procedures.)

5. Hire a local distributor or wholesaler.

Exporters of consumer goods, light industrial equipment, and products aimed particularly at public institutional buyers often enter a market through a local, non-exclusive distributor or wholesaler. A distributor or wholesaler purchases the product and resells it for his or her own account. Domestic manufacturers of many products are often wholesalers as well, accounting for a significant portion of imports. Larger distributors will operate countrywide, while medium- and small-scale operations limit their activities to particular cities or regions.

Advantages For products with well established competitors, or for specialty and high-tech products, a distributor who knows local needs and customs may be essential. The use of a local distributor eliminates the need to create a marketing structure from scratch. In addition, local distributors are often aware of opportunities before they are made public. A distributor will also know the best methods for negotiating and advertising and will be familiar with bidding requirements. Being local, a distributor can efficiently promote and handle many small sales, which can add up over time. Compensation for a distributor is paid indirectly; usually it is derived from whatever profit margin that the distributor is able to obtain. Distributor arrangements can be terminated for any reason without legal penalty, because Mexico has no distributor indemnity laws.

Disadvantages A distributor will charge a fee for services provided, often based on a percentage of sales, and the costs for a distributor are usually greater than those for a sales agent (because the distributor takes more risk in fronting the money for the product before a sale is assured). Many distributors will purchase only the cheaper products for their own account, preferring to market expensive, specialized items as sales agents instead. Suppliers have little or no control over a distributor's marketing methods, and your distributor's reputation will reflect on the products handled, so it is important to choose a distributor wisely.

6. Hire a local independent sales agent.

A local sales agent generally works on commission, and often becomes an exclusive representative in Mexico. Sales agents often work in companies that have representatives in different states. Sales agents do not purchase goods, but only solicit sales. Once they have found a willing buyer, it is up to the provider to complete the sale and deliver the product.

Advantages Local talent knows local customs, easing the entry of your product past the cultural and language barriers inherent in the Mexican market. Greater control over sales methods used is possible because the agent is a direct representative. However, giving an agent authority to act on a firm's behalf can also become a problem, because the firm can be legally bound by an agent operating with such authority. Mexico has no indemnity laws on terminating agents, and minimum performance clauses in contracts are permissible.

Disadvantages Responsibility for completing a sale, and taking a credit risk, fall on the provider. Instead of shipping all products to one distributor, shipping will be direct to any number of customers. Mexican law may also treat a sales agent as an employee and require the contracting firm to comply with burdensome and expensive tax and labor laws.

TIPS FOR CHOOSING AN AGENT

Seek out an agent through various leads:

Government services Contact services available from your own government as well as those in Mexico. For example, the United States and Foreign Commercial Service offers the Agent/Distributor Service at district offices of the US Department of Commerce. The US Trade Center in Mexico provides the Repfind service.

Trade associations Learn from the trade associations who the largest distributors are in a particular industry and region in Mexico.

Trade fair contacts More than 3,000 independent agents and distributors attend the annual Repcom exhibition sponsored by the US Trade Center in Mexico City. Many are also attendees of industry-specific fairs.

Trade and telephone directories Search the listings in the industries and regions that seem to be the most appropriate markets for your product.

Newspaper and magazine listings Research the services offered by reviewing the advertisements of those who promote themselves.

End users, retailers, wholesalers, and industry experts Consult with your contacts in the industry. Ask customers and potential clients for references to the agents they use most often.

Investigate your prospective agent's:

Experience Find an agent who is in the business of distributing, selling, or servicing foreign goods in general, and who is knowledgeable about your type of product and about the region you want to target in particular. If you want to sell laboratory analytical instruments, find an agent who promotes medical, chemical, or educational products, not one who deals primarily in textiles. No matter how good their reputation is in that field, it won't help you in yours.

Financial status Get an independent analysis from trade or bank references.

Reputation Check with the agent's references, both those of other clients and bankers.

Strength Find out whether your agent's company is well established. An impressive name may represent only a new and struggling mom-and-pop operation.

Goals Query your agent's intentions. You want an agent with long-term objectives and a commitment to your product, not a take-the-money-and-run type.

Conflicts of interest Be certain your agent isn't involved with other companies or organizations that have interests adverse to or in competition with yours.

It is therefore important that any contract with the agent clearly establish that the agent is an independent contractor.

7. Establish a local representative office.

After sales have increased to the point that a presence in Mexico would prove useful in building a reputation with customers through an on-site presence, consider opening a local representative office. Representative offices are often effective in providing after-sales service for high-tech products or large-scale equipment and for cultivating close relationships with clients.

Advantages The ability to offer prompt, high-touch quality service adds a competitive edge, showing commitment to customers. It also allows the firm to provide personal—possibly even on-site—consulting and to steer existing and potential buyers toward additional products. A local office suggests a more permanent presence in domestic markets, giving the appearance of greater stability and long-term availability. Local representatives work exclusively for the outfit they represent, not for an independent company that may also represent other products.

Disadvantages Added costs of establishing and operating a representative office must be spread over larger volumes of business to justify the expense, necessitating larger sales and reducing the overall profit margin. A representative presence can also result in additional costs through the customization of products to suit the expressed needs of clients, further reducing the take on sales made.

8. Negotiate a joint arrangement with a local company.

Once the volume and nature of business conducted in Mexico has gone beyond that which can be readily serviced through a representative office, firms will need to consider establishing a larger, more permanent presence in Mexico. Many products need to be customized for the Mexican market—perhaps even for each customer, or at least for each group or category of customers. Sales volume is on the rise, market demand is growing, and products are holding up well against the competition. Products have been protected against copyright, patent, or trademark infringements. A joint arrangement—corporation, partnership, technology transfer agreement, or most probably, joint venture—with a local company is one major avenue for deepening a business presence in Mexico without going all the way to a wholly-owned company. (Refer to the "Business Entities & Formation" chapter for a description of the formalities and details of joint arrangement structures.)

Advantages A joint arrangement takes advantage of the strengths that a Mexican ally has to offer, such as its local distribution network and contacts, lower labor costs, and an understanding of how to make the product fit the needs of the Mexican market. It also can allow the homegrown control necessary to address such concerns as superior product quality, technological sophistication, and customer service.

Disadvantages Joint arrangements typically allow for technology transfer and worker and management training. As in any marriage, difficulties between the parties must be constantly worked out, and honesty and fairness are at a premium. A tightly framed contract is essential to protect against potential damages from infringement of property rights, unfair competition, and disruption or dissolution of the arrangement. Consider a trial period of sufficient length—such as a year or two—before agreeing to any permanent investment.

9. Open your own distributorship or retail store.

For companies with large arrays of products, opening one or more distributorships or retail stores may be appropriate.

Advantages Direct market access to consumers allows providers to keep prices low and competitive by eliminating intermediaries. The ability to control the sales environment and the training of personnel can improve quality and service, reducing the gap between supplier and consumer.

Disadvantages Having an independent operation also means incurring the costs necessary to establish, maintain, and staff it. It will also become necessary to overcome possible bias among consumers who are already accustomed to local merchants, in addition to language and cultural barriers.

10. Establish a franchise.

Franchising is one of the most effective marketing systems in Mexico. In 1992, 4,100 franchise outlets were operated by more than 170 franchisers. By the end of 1993, about 200 franchisers operating 5,200 outlets had entered the Mexican market. Franchising has a key role in helping medium- and small-sized companies modernize and acquire new technology. For this reason, new financing support systems are being developed for local franchisees. The most promising economy subsectors for franchising have been those oriented toward tourist services, including fast food restaurants, retail stores, hotels, and car rental agencies. However, real estate agencies, video rental outlets, shoe retailers, and computer stores are but a few of the other ventures now joining the franchise gold rush.

Advantages For a small- to medium-scale operation, a franchise may be preferable to a joint venture involving two or more parties. In a franchise, there is a single investor, trained and supported by a national or multinational chain.

Disadvantages The disadvantages of franchising are similar to those that occur when establishing any business in Mexico. Because it operates as a separate business entity, a franchise is required to comply with the full range of local labor, tax, registration, and other commercial and foreign investment requirements and restrictions.

11. Build local manufacturing facilities.

Foreign companies have made significant inroads into the Mexican market by producing goods in Mexico, thereby relying on lower-cost local labor and transportation costs to allow them to remain competitive with local companies that lack design, technology, financing, and other advantages.

Advantages Labor costs are usually lower, which helps keep the prices of foreign-invested goods competitive with products made by local manufacturers. Incentives offered by federal, state, and local governments to entice foreign investors, particularly in the less commercially developed regions, can make the difference in establishing a competitive local facility. Building a dedicated plant can enable a volume manufacturer to avoid the need to license rights to foreign companies.

Disadvantages Operations in Mexico will be subject to Mexican labor, tax, and commercial laws. Management and technology will generally have to be imported into Mexico, and training programs for local workers are not only required, but necessary, and they represent only the first of a host of ancillary expenses.

CHANNELS OF ADVERTISING

Mexico is not as dependent on television advertising as are more industrially developed nations, although radio remains an important advertising channel. Telecommunications is fairly well developed in the commercial centers of the country, but often does not reach into many of the less developed regions. Thus, to tap into many Mexican markets, it is necessary to explore Mexico's less technologically advanced channels of advertising. If a local distributor or agent is retained, the chore of choosing advertising media is usually delegated to that person. Print and broadcast media are listed in a directory, *Radio and T.V.*, published quarterly by:

Medios Publicitarios Mexicanos, S.A. de C.V.
Avda. México 99-303
Col. Hipódromo Condesa
06170 México, DF, México
Tel: [52] (5) 574-2604, 574-2858
Fax: [52] (5) 574-26-68

Print Media

Newspapers One of the advertising channels available in Mexico is newspapers. The 15 daily newspapers printed in Mexico City and more than 320 other regional newspapers combine for a claimed daily circulation of more than 20 million copies. However, many observers scoff at such numbers and note that each paper generally has a fairly small readership. Advertising costs can run high—as much as US$3,000 per page—and Mexico's populace reads far more comic books than newspapers anyway. All in all, relatively few people read Mexican newspapers, which have a generally poor reputation for editorial independence. The government provides much of the advertising support—although with privatization of state-run operations, this is lessening—and thus indirectly controls editorial freedom and content. Many journalists receive unofficial "subsidies" to keep them friendly to the powers that be, and periodicals are usually open to printing *gacetillas*, or paid articles, that are seldom identified as such. Nevertheless, newspapers are one means to reach opinion leaders, although low-ticket consumer items are better advertised through other media.

Mexico's major dailies are *Excelsior, El Universal, El Sol De México,* and *La Prensa.* Many papers feature color advertisements. Government procurement notices are published in several of these papers, primarily *Excelsior* and *El Universal.*

Magazines Trade and industry magazines offer large circulation to commercial enterprises throughout the country. More than 200 major magazines are published in Mexico, and many of these are specialized business publications.

Directories Telephone and trade directories are the preferred media for advertising specialty products intended for a limited, nonconsumer market.

Television

More than 9.5 million Mexican households receive television. Seven networks located in Mexico City broadcast in Spanish nationwide, although reception and availability vary. Some areas—particularly Mexico City, Monterrey, Guadalajara, and the US-Mexican border towns—also receive transmissions from the United States. In addition, a large number of cable systems are operating in Mexico; more than 70,000 subscribers receive Cablevision in Mexico City.

Radio

Most of the more than 900 radio stations in Mexico are commercial. Mexico City alone has 25 FM and 35 AM radio stations, broadcasting in Spanish. English programs are broadcast on a growing number of stations. Although not as expensive as television, radio advertising can be costly. For maximum benefit, advertising must be carefully targeted

ELEVEN TIPS TO BOOST YOUR SALES

1. Make frequent visits to Mexico to support your local contacts.

Personal contact—whether with customers, agents, importers, or business associates—is critical to building your commercial relationships. Without it, no amount of effort can produce success in Mexico. Keep in mind that your competitors are also paying personal visits to their agents, traders, and customers. Reciprocate this hospitality by inviting your important counterparts to visit you, which will also serve to familiarize them with your country and company.

2. Offer numerous demonstrations and exhibits of your products.

If you supply to Mexican manufacturers, the value of sales presentations at factories cannot be overemphasized. Factory engineers and managers are directly responsible for the equipment and machinery to be purchased, and they have considerable influence over the decision to buy. This is such a highly effective—and cheap—sales booster that it would be irresponsible for an exporter to fail to implement it along with the more usual approaches to higher-ups.

3. Increase the distribution of promotional brochures and technical data to potential buyers, libraries, and industry associations.

When you or your agent makes an initial personal sales call, potential customers who have seen your literature won't be completely in the dark. Follow-up promotional materials, catalogs, and telephone calls will maintain your presence in the market. Information should be disseminated in Spanish and should focus on the quality of existing products and new releases.

4. Respect language and cultural differences, and adapt your product and marketing as needed.

The profit motive generally operates cross-culturally, and the nationals of most countries—especially within a given region—have much in common with one another. However, there are substantial differences, enough to cause a generic marketing program to fall flat on its face and even build ill will in the process. You may have some success with a one-size-fits-all approach, but you won't be able to build a solid operation or maximize profits with it. What works in your country won't necessarily work in Mexico.

Markets are individual, and you may well need to tailor your products to suit individual needs. A foreign country has official regulations and cultural preferences that differ from those of your own and even from those within the region. Avoid multimillion dollar mistakes by eliminating culturally-biased thinking. Learn about these differences, respect them, and adapt your product accordingly. Your sales, service, and warranty information may contain a wealth of information, but if it's not in their language, you leave foreign distributors, sales and service personnel, and consumers out in the cold. Sure it's expensive to translate everything into Spanish, but it's a necessity, not merely an expendable courtesy.

5. Aim your product promotion at a specific geographical region and market segment.

To avoid wasteful spending, focus your marketing efforts. A lack of focus means that you will be likely to waste your money, time, and energies. Without specificity, your foreign operations may get too big too fast. Not only does this cost more than the local business can justify or support, it also can translate into an impersonal attitude towards sales and service and the relationships you are working so hard to build. Instead, concentrate your time, money, and efforts on a specific market or region, and work on building the all-important business relationships that will carry you past the many obstacles to successful export marketing.

Your product will determine the size and scope of your sales market. Thus, products geared to high-income customers are generally sought in lower volume by smaller chains and individual stores; products aimed at low-income consumers can be sold in higher volume to larger outlets; specialty and high-tech products are marketed to industrial manufacturers and firms offering financial and commercial services. Play the percentages. After you have successfully penetrated the most likely markets, you can consider expanding distribution into new areas from an established base.

6. Improve follow-up on initial sales leads.

Do whatever is necessary to pursue a lead, and if your agent in Mexico requests support, give it. Establish a liaison for major accounts—someone who will work with the client from the start of the transaction, continue to address the client's needs through installation, and provide after-sales support.

7. Don't get greedy.

Price your product to match the market you're entering. Don't try to generate maximum profits in the first year: take the long-term view. It's what your competitors are doing, and they're in it for the long haul. Mexicans are very price-conscious. When you're pricing your product, include in your calculations the demand for spare parts, components, auxiliary equipment, and follow-up sales. Add-on profits from these sources can help keep the primary product price down and therefore more attractive.

8. Demand quality.

A poor-quality product can ambush the best-laid marketing plans. Mexicans may look at price first, but they want value and won't buy junk, regardless of how cheap it is. The competition is getting too tough to ignore quality. Any market you gain initially will rapidly fall apart if you have a casual attitude towards quality. And it is hard to come back from an initial quality-based flop. On the other hand, a product with a justified reputation for high quality and good value creates its own potential for market and price expansions.

9. Deliver on time.

If you don't, you can believe that someone else will. Failure to deliver on time can destroy your carefully built reputation. Moreover, your local agent will be embarrassed, undermining your relationship and jeopardizing future sales. There's not much you can do to make

ships go faster or airlines schedule more flights, but you can stockpile products in Mexico to ensure that your agent has a steady supply. Do your best to avoid nasty interruptions at customs by finding the best possible freight forwarder and customs broker. When you must (and when possible), forget the expense and deliver your product by air. The extra effort will go a long way toward establishing, fortifying, and expanding your reputation in the market.

10. Train your representatives and personnel comprehensively, from sales to installation to after-sales requirements.

The treatment of your customers is as important as the quality of your product. Your representatives and personnel must be able to explain your product: what it will do, and how it operates. Technicians who install and service equipment and high-tech machinery must be able to deal not only with the product, but also with the customer.

11. Emphasize excellent after-sales service.

Some products demand more work than others—more sales effort, more after-sales service, more hand-holding of the distributor, and more contact with the end user. The channel you select is crucial. Paradoxically, in this age of ubiquitous and lightning-fast communications and saturation advertising, people rely more than ever on word of mouth to sort out the truth from hyperbole. Nothing will sink your product faster than a reputation for poor or nonexistent service and after-sales support.

Consider establishing a local office or service facility, or at the least provide an international toll-free number for customer service. If possible, maintain a properly trained service person or staff in Mexico, and stock a reasonable selection of spare parts there. For major accounts, assign a particular person to handle after-sales service to create more of a personal and permanent relationship with the customer, and make sure that your representative knows that serving the customer is as important as fixing the machine.

through stations that broadcast to the regions where the product is most likely to sell and to the audience segments most likely to purchase it. Mexican listeners tune in on an estimated 25 million radios.

Premiums and Catalogues

Many firms promote their products using small giveaway items such as stationary products—pens, calendars, and paperweights. Catalogues, preferably printed in Spanish, are a means of presenting a company's entire product line to a customer, often bringing in repeat and new business. In some industries, such as pharmaceuticals, products may be promoted by offering free samples to end users. Promotions of various kinds are common.

Advertising Agencies

Dozens of advertising agencies, most of which are located in Mexico City, can assist in preparing and placing advertisements in various media. Many of these are foreign agencies that have opened offices in Mexico to cater to existing clients who are entering the market there. A list of Mexican advertising agencies is compiled by the US Embassy in Mexico City. (Refer to the "Important Addresses" chapter.)

Public Relations Firms

Often overlooked as marketing resources, the use of public relations firms can sometimes yield more than traditional advertising. Decent television commercials and four-color plates in newspapers and magazines can cost many thousands of dollars, while a skillful PR agency can turn a US$10,000 investment into a million dollars' worth of publicity. Sometimes all that is needed is a well timed, well placed news release. If an advertising budget is limited, a PR agency may be the best choice.

A number of Mexican agencies are springing up to take advantage of increasing import markets. They can help establish a company's name in this competitive market, build reputation through such means as corporate sponsorships and community betterment projects, spread the word about products, help with labor relations, and even lay the groundwork for obtaining financial assistance. However, be sure to check the credentials and past performance of the agency: bad PR is worse than none, and there is little recourse for firms burned by inept practitioners.

OVERCOMING THE TRADE BARRIERS

At least in theory, marketing in Mexico isn't so difficult. The general climate is favorable to imports and foreign investment. Since Mexico joined the General Agreement on Tariffs and Trade (GATT) in 1986,

a number of economic policies have been implemented to encourage international trade, including the reduction of the maximum import duty from 100 to 20 percent and a general opening of domestic markets to foreign goods. With the implementation of NAFTA, importation of products from Canada and the US into Mexico will become even easier, and access is also expected to increase for firms of other nations as well.

Nevertheless, foreign businesses will encounter trade barriers—tariffs and fees, language and cultural differences, obstructive bureaucrats, nontransparent laws and regulations that are hidden from foreigners just in case they're thinking of violating them—that can overwhelm all but the most determined. Plan ahead, be aware that there are hurdles, and practice patience. Virtually all foreign businesspeople are likely to come up against these barriers at one time or in one form or another.

Import Fees and Taxes Products are usually subject to an Ad Valorem Duty (AVD) percentage, applied to the Cost, Insurance, and Freight (CIF) invoice value. In addition, there is a customs processing fee (CPF), which is a percentage of the CIF invoice value. Finally, a percentage Value Added Tax (IVA tax) is assessed on the cumulative values of the AVD, the CPF, and the CIF invoice. The IVA tax is recoverable in the sales transaction.

Language and Cultural Differences It is not absolutely necessary to learn Spanish, but it certainly helps. It is also necessary to take into account the cultural nuances that make Mexico a little different from your country. (Refer to the "Business Culture" chapter.) For these reasons, local agents and distributors can become important facilitators, and the fastest access into Mexico's markets may be through such local representatives.

Registration In August 1992, the *Secretaría de Hacienda y Crédito Público* (the Finance Secretariat, or *Hacienda*) introduced a mandatory national registry for importers. Companies that seek to import into Mexico are required to meet certain requirements and enroll in this registry. To be included, a company must prove that it has paid any taxes owed during the previous four years. Each registered company must also obtain a Mexican tax identification number. Imports may be temporarily delayed until registration is completed.

Product Labeling and Certification There are Spanish-language label requirements for many products, particularly those intended for consumer markets, and some products must be accompanied by a certificate of quality before they are allowed to be sold in Mexico. (Refer to the "Import Policies & Procedures" chapter.)

Metric and Other Measurements The government does not officially require that products imported into Mexico use the metric system. However, the metric system is the official and exclusive accepted Mexican standard of weights and measures, so importers usually demand metric labeling for packaged goods. Dual labeling is acceptable. Mexico adheres to the International System of Units in both official and common practice. Electrical standards are the same as those in the United States (electrical power operates at 60 cycles per second, with normal voltage being 110, 200 and 400; three phase and single phase 230 volt current is also available.)

Government Red Tape Special paperwork requirements are imposed on firms wishing to do business with Mexican government agencies and state-run enterprises. (Refer to the "Opportunities" chapter for a discussion of official procurement policies and procedures.)

Lack of Financial Resources In some markets, financing difficulties will inhibit sales. Many private businesses lack the financial resources needed to modernize and upgrade their facilities or even to finance current imports, materials purchases, and operations. The vast majority are unable to offer adequate guarantees to banks for the needed financing. To begin or extend participation in the Mexican market, a foreign company must often be willing to offer attractive financing terms, such as extended payment terms and discounts for large-volume purchases and prompt or early payment. However, be sure to run a credit check through private or public financial institutions before extending credit.

As an alternative to financing large machinery purchases, consider offering a lease program. Cross-border leasing has become more available in Mexico and is fairly common in the *maquiladora* and freight transport industries. Leased equipment is subject to Mexican customs procedures, and the lessee usually must post a bond with customs for the amount of the import duties plus an additional percentage. A temporary import permit is then issued, designating the length of time that the equipment may be kept in Mexico. The lessor should be certain that the lease terms specify removal arrangements and clearly show the lessor's ownership rights. Purchase of leased equipment at the end of the lease term requires that applicable duties be paid on the original value.

Substandard Transport and Communications Infrastructure In many areas of Mexico, road and air transportation remain unreliable. Warehouse space and loading docks are often unsuitable, rail transport is not always dependable, and electric power generation isn't what it ought to be. But special deals can be made with transport companies, and some companies have built their own facilities. The government is making major investments in the transport and communications infrastructures, developing an interstate highway system, satellite communications, new port facilities, a world-class telecommunications system, much of it through public-private partnerships or private enterprise incentives. (Refer to the "Transportation" chapter.)

HELPING YOUR COMPANY LEARN TO LOVE EXPORTING

FIVE IN-HOUSE RULES

1. Eliminate as much guesswork as possible.

You cannot get into successful exporting by accident. You need a well thought out marketing plan, and the use of expert consultants usually represents time and money well spent. It's not simply a matter of saying, "Let's sell our product in Mexico." You need to know where and how you're going to sell it. First, do you need to make obvious changes to your product? Who is your buyer, or how are you going to find one? How will your buyer find you? Do you need to advertise or exhibit at a trade fair? How much can you expect to sell? How many different products can you sell? A plan is the best way to uncover hidden traps and costs before you get overly involved in a fiasco. While you may see an opportunity, knowing how to exploit it isn't necessarily a simple matter. You must plot, plan, and prepare.

2. Just go for it.

We're not suggesting that you forget the planning, but sometimes the best "plan" is to use a shotgun approach—just blast away to see if you hit anything. You can narrow things down later. If your product is new to the market, there may be precious little marketing information, and you may essentially have no other choice.

3. Get your bosses to support you, and stick with the program.

Whether your company consists of 10, 50, 500, or 5,000 people—or just you—and whether you're the head of the company, the chief financial officer, or the person leading the exporting charge, there must be an explicit commitment to weathering the initial setbacks and financial requirements of export marketing. You must be sure that the firm is committed to the long term: don't waste money by abandoning the project too early.

International marketing consultants report that because results don't show up in the first few months, the international marketing and advertising budget is *invariably* the first to be cut in any company that doesn't have money to burn. Such short-sighted budgetary decisions are responsible for innumerable premature failures in exporting.

The hard fact is that exports don't bring in money as quickly as domestic sales. It takes time and persistence for an international marketing effort to succeed. There are many hurdles to overcome—personal, political, cultural, and legal, among others. It will be at least six to nine months before you and your foreign associates can even begin to expect glimmers of success—and it may take even longer. Be patient, keep a close but not suffocating watch on your international marketing efforts, and give the venture a chance to develop.

4. Avoid an internal tug-of-war.

Consultants report that one of the biggest obstacles to successful export marketing in larger companies is internal conflict among divisions within a company. Domestic marketing battles international marketing, while each is also warring with engineering—and everybody fights with the bean counters. All the complex strategies, relationship building, and legal and cultural accommodations that export marketing requires mean that support and teamwork are crucial to the success of the venture.

5. Stick with export marketing even when business booms at home.

While exporting isn't something to fall back on when your domestic market falters, neither is it something to put on the back burner when business is booming at home. It is difficult to ease your way into exporting. All the investment in relationships and financial and management resources, and just plain blood, sweat, and tears that export marketing requires means that a clear commitment is necessary from the beginning. Any other attitude essentially dooms the venture right from the start; you might as well forget it. We can't overstress this aspect: take the long-range view or don't play at all. Decide that you're going to export and that you're in it for the long haul as a viable, money-making, full-fledged division within your company.

Business Entities & Formation

TYPES OF BUSINESS ENTERPRISES

Commercial and civil codes in Mexico offer Mexican and foreign nationals a variety of recognized options for establishing a business. These include corporations, partnerships, joint ventures, branch offices, and sole proprietorships. Investors can also form agent, distributor, or licensing—such as for transfer of technical assistance—agreements. (Refer to the "Marketing" chapter for discussion of such arrangements.) The specific type of business entity selected depends on the objectives, circumstances, degree of control desired, preferred tax treatment, and anticipated duration of the investment, as well as other personal and business circumstances and preferences. (Refer to the "Corporate Taxation" and "Personal Taxation" chapters for a discussion of tax treatment.)

Of particular interest to foreign investors are corporations (*sociedad anónima*, or S.A.), corporations with variable capital *(sociedad anónima de capital variable*, or S.A. de C.V.), in-bond companies *(maquiladoras)*, and joint ventures *(asociación en participación*, or A. en P.). Although businesses may be structured in other ways, these are the most common forms for Mexican private enterprises. Other business forms—including sole proprietorships and most partnerships—are less desirable because they fail to offer the owners limits on liability or because they are designed for non-commercial—such as the civil society *(sociedad civil,* or C.V.)—Or nonprofit—such as the civil association *(asociación civil,* or A.C.) entities.

Corporations

A corporation is an entity that is organized for profit-seeking purposes and is owned by shareholders having limited liability. Each shareholder is liable only up to the amount of capital for which that shareholder subscribed. A corporation is formed under Mexico's federal corporate law—the General Law of Commercial Companies, which applies throughout the country. Each corporation has legal status as a juristic person separate from its owners. Mexican law recognizes two types of corporations, which are designated *sociedad anónima* (corporation) and *sociedad anónima de capital variable* (corporation with variable capital). The two types are distinguished by their corporate names, which must include the appropriate Mexican designation or its abbreviation—"S.A." or "S.A. de C.V." In practice, the S.A. de C.V. is the most common form used to incorporate a business in Mexico.

***Sociedad Anónima de Capital Variable* (S.A. de C.V.)** Large- and medium-sized foreign and domestic firms tend to prefer the form of the corporation with variable capital, designated *sociedad anónima de capital variable* (S.A. de C.V.) in Mexico, when incorporating as a Mexican company. An S.A. de C.V. is capitalized with two distinct funds: fixed capital in the minimum amount required by law and additional variable capital in an amount designated in the corporate charter. Most S.A. de C.V. charters provide for an unlimited amount of variable capital, without specifying any maximum.

The advantage of the variable capital structure is that the corporation can issue additional capital with a minimum of formalities. With respect to fixed capital, the *Secretaría de Relaciones Exteriores* (Secretariat of Foreign Relations, or SRE), and in certain cases the *Comisión Nacional de Inversión Extranjera* (National Foreign Investment Commission, or FIC as it is generally referred to in English), must authorize all reductions of minimum capital and must approve any increases in maximum capital for firms with foreign participation. Domestic corporations without foreign participation require similar authorizations from the *Secretaría de Comercio y Fomento Industrial* (the Secretariat of Commerce and Industrial Development, or SECOFI). In contrast, a corporation's variable capital is authorized and registered on an open-ended basis at its creation, and therefore in many cases—such as when no increase is made in the proportion of foreign investment or when no change is made in the proportions held by individual foreign investors—variable capital can be modified through

KEY CONTACTS AND REGULATORS

Mexican Investment Board (MIB)

A government office, designated the Mexican Investment Board, was established in 1990 to assist investors interested in Mexico and to promote Mexican industries overseas. The MIB provides information to prospective investors regarding business opportunities and requirements for doing business in the country. After a company has received the required authorizations to do business in Mexico, the MIB will further assist the company with understanding tax, labor, utility, and other similar requirements.

National Commission on Foreign Investment (FIC)

As the centralized agency for approval of foreign investment in Mexican companies, the FIC is responsible for authorizing the organization of new enterprises and the use of existing foreign investment in new economic activities or product lines.

National Registry of Foreign Investment

The National Registry of Foreign Investment is an office of the *Secretaría de Comercio y Fomento Industrial* (SECOFI) that maintains a register of financial and other information on foreign individuals or corporations conducting business in Mexico, Mexican companies with foreign-owned capital stock, and trusts with foreign participation. Registration is mandatory, even for operations that do not require formal authorization.

Secretaría de Comercio y Fomento Industrial (SECOFI)

The Secretariat of Commercial and Industrial Development regulates trade and industry in Mexico and approves the formation of domestic Mexican companies.

Secretaría de Hacienda y Crédito Público

The Secretariat of Public Finance—or *Hacienda* as it is generally known—is Mexico's financial and tax regulatory agency. Most companies are required to file certain financial information and periodic updates with this agency.

which may be as simple as passage of a resolution by the board of directors or the shareholders. By law, an S.A. de C.V. must make any such increases in capital stock available to the existing shareholders through a rights offering before extending the offer to outsiders. The current shareholders are entitled to purchase the same proportion of the additional capital stock as that which they hold in the existing capital stock.

***Sociedad Anónima* (S.A.)** The capital structure of a basic corporation, designated *sociedad anónima* (S.A.) in Mexico, distinguishes it from an S.A. de C.V. An S.A. has only legal minimum fixed paid-in capital. No amount of variable capital stock is permitted, and therefore an S.A. that desires to issue additional shares beyond the maximum fixed capital amount designated in its charter must obtain prior authorization from the SRE and sometimes from the FIC if foreign invested, or from SECOFI if wholly domestically owned.

Common Capital Requirements With the exception of the capital structures discussed above, the S.A. and S.A. de C.V. are nearly identical. Ownership interests are represented by shares. At least two shareholders are required in order to form a Mexican corporation, but the law imposes no maximum limit. The minimum actual paid-in capital required to establish a Mexican corporation is NP$50,000 (about US$15,000), which amount may be increased by Mexican authorities with respect to a particular corporation. If the shareholders pay cash for their shares, a minimum of 20 percent of the capital value must be paid in immediately on formation. A shareholder whose contribution is made in equipment or other property must pay in the total value of the shares at the time of formation.

For purposes of raising capital, a corporation may issue debentures convertible into shares, mortgage obligations, and unsecured debentures, any of which may be listed on the stock exchange for public sale. It may also contract loans with or without guarantees, although loans may not be secured by corporate shares. In addition, a corporation is allowed to capitalize surplus that arises from the revaluation of its assets, provided that the corporation complies with three requirements. First, the corporation must have the assets revalued by a professional appraiser recognized by the National Securities Commission (the revaluation cannot exceed the value obtained in such an independent appraisal). To the extent that the surplus relates to investments in shares or commodities, the revaluation amount must be derived from certified market quotations. Second, before the surplus is capitalized, the corporation must disclose the revaluation surplus on a balance sheet approved by the shareholders. Third, if the corporation is listed on the Mexican Stock Exchange, it must comply with

internal procedures without prior government approval. Mexican corporations are not allowed to hold their own shares and must issue them as capital is required, so the S.A. de C.V. allows some flexibility in expanding or contracting capital to reflect the changing needs of the corporation.

The corporate charter of an S.A. de C.V. should provide procedures for increasing and decreasing the variable capital stock. An S.A. de C.V. has considerable discretion in establishing these procedures, certain limitations on the amount of revaluation surplus that can be capitalized.

Share Characteristics Shares may have a stated par value or no par value. They are equal in value and confer equal rights on the shareholders unless the corporate charter authorizes the issuance of different classes of shares. Corporate shares may be issued in classes of preferred and common stock and, within classes, in series. Preferred shares may have, for example, limited voting or preferred dividend rights. If Mexican nationals must hold a minimum percentage of the shares, the corporation is required to issue two separate series of shares. The first series ("A" shares) may legally be owned only by Mexican nationals, with the exception of certain permanent immigrants in particular circumstances. It carries full rights to the appropriate proportional share of corporate assets and to participate in corporate governance. The second series ("B" shares) may be owned by any person and usually carries identical rights to the first series. Additional classes of neutral ("N" shares), similar to preferred shares, can be issued to allow limited investments by foreigners. Usually no class of "N" shares can constitute more than 30 percent of the total equity capitalization of the company.

Issuance, Transfer, and Reacquisition of Shares Within one year from the date on which the SRE or SECOFI approves the corporate charter, all subscribed capital must be completely paid-in. The corporation may not issue additional capital stock until all existing shares are paid in full. No shares may be issued at a discount to their face value. If the corporation issues any shares in exchange for property, the transaction is referred to as "in-kind." The corporation keeps such shares for two years, at the end of which time the value of the assets is formally assessed. If the value of the assets has decreased by 25 percent or more of the nominal value, the shareholder must remit the difference to the corporation.

Unless otherwise provided for in the corporate charter, shares are freely transferable. However, a transfer becomes valid only when it has been recorded in the corporation's share register. If a shareholder sells shares that were only partially paid into the corporation, the shareholder remains jointly liable with the buyer for five years for any unpaid balance.

No Mexican corporation is permitted to acquire its own shares, except through a court judgment or in payment of corporate credits. A corporation that reacquires shares must sell them within three months or cancel the shares and reduce its capital stock by a proportional amount. No treasury shares are allowed.

Modification of Authorized Shares An increase or reduction in fixed capital shares is considered to be an amendment to the corporate charter. Thus a corporation that seeks to modify the number of authorized fixed capital shares must obtain prior approval of the SRE or SECOFI. Foreign-invested corporations may also need prior authorization from the FIC. If authorized shares are increased, existing shareholders are entitled to subscribe to the additional shares before the corporation offers them to outsiders. If capital is reduced, each shareholder has a right to redeem shares in proportion to the number of shares held, and the shares canceled must be withdrawn before a notary public or broker. Any reduction in authorized capital must be published three times in the government's official newspaper—*Diario Oficial*—to give notice to creditors.

Shareholders may vote to pay share premiums, which constitute additional capital contributions for which shares are not received. Share premiums are often authorized when the corporation needs to cover a loss. They may also be approved to require new share subscribers to pay more than the price of the original issue. Any such share premiums are to be distributed later—usually upon liquidation of the corporation—to the shareholders in proportion to the number of shares they own.

Management The corporate charter sets forth the management structure of the corporation. Any change in management structure is deemed an amendment of the corporate charter, requiring prior government approval. Therefore, to the extent possible, the management structure should be determined at the outset.

Shareholders Shareholders wield ultimate authority in a Mexican corporation, electing corporate management, setting overall corporate policies, and authorizing or approving corporate operations. The shareholders have exclusive authority to amend the corporate bylaws, declare dividends, and make other allocations of profits.

Actions by the shareholders are taken at an annual or special meeting, referred to as a general assembly. Holders of at least half of the outstanding capital stock must be represented at the annual general meeting before the shareholders may take action; the needed quorum is increased to three-fourths for extraordinary meetings. A general meeting of shareholders must be called in advance in compliance with established notice procedures. However, if all outstanding shares are present or represented at the time a vote is taken, compliance with the prior call rules is not required for a valid vote.

A general meeting of the shareholders must be held at the corporation's official domicile annually within four months of the end of the year. Annual meetings are held for such purposes as approving the annual financial statements, distributing annual profits, electing directors, and selecting a statutory auditor. Certain matters can be determined only at extraordinary shareholder meetings, which are

SIZING UP YOUR FINANCING OPTIONS IN MEXICO*

Mexican tax law may dictate your choices.

If you're eyeing Mexico for a manufacturing venture, one of your first questions likely will be how to pay for it. Your options as a US manufacturer operating in Mexico depend in part on your marketing plans and the tax burden you can shoulder.

If you are going to produce and sell your product in the Mexican market, local commercial banks, such as *Bancomer* and *Banca Serfin,* may be your best bets, since they can make loans either in Mexican pesos or in foreign currencies. In the case of Mexican subsidiaries of US companies, if the banks follow tradition, they will negotiate the line of credit with the parent company and require the parent to guarantee the direct loan to the subsidiary.

Choose Your Currency with Care

If you decide to take out a loan in pesos, proceed with caution. Interest rates on peso-denominated loans have not been stable. Mexico has been trying to attract and retain capital and, at the same time, lower inflation, so interest rates on loans in Mexican pesos have not been competitive. In fact, they have run as many as 20 points above the rate of inflation compared to 5 or 6 points above inflation for loans made in foreign currencies.

Exporters, though, may receive preferential loans from Mexican banks, since the country counts on exports to furnish foreign currency and help improve Mexico's balance of trade. For its exporters, Mexico's Foreign Trade Bank (Bancomext) makes loans in US dollars and helps companies find local financing. Loans in US dollars also are available from foreign banks. And, although Mexican law requires borrowers to pay taxes on loans, you may qualify for an exemption if you meet three conditions:

1. You export product;
2. The term of your loan is three years or more;
3. Your loan is registered with Mexico's tax authorities.

Alternatives for Subsidiaries

US subsidiaries in Mexico frequently turn to their parent or sister companies for financing. However, if the subsidiaries pay interest on those loans, this route can be expensive. The reason is that Mexican law requires the parent company to pay tax on the interest payment it receives from Mexico, since that amount represents Mexican resources repatriated to the United States.

The tax rate is 35 percent, paid on the full amount of the interest payment. The only deductible portion is the amount over and above Mexico's inflation rate. Therefore,

if a subsidiary's interest payment to its parent company is 12 percent and the Mexican inflation rate is 10 percent, the parent company has to pay tax on the full 12 percent (calculated on a monthly basis) and can deduct only 2 percent. In practice, these deductions have been rare, since Mexico's inflation rate has tended to exceed the interest rate charged on loans.

To avoid this tax impact, parent companies may want to make interest-free loans to their subsidiaries. In this case, only the subsidiary pays a tax, this time on the entire loan (rather than the interest payment), but only on the portion equal to the inflation rate. Therefore, if your parent company lends you US$100, and Mexico's inflation rate is 10 percent, you'll pay a 35 percent tax on US$10.

When to Convert to Equity

If the parent company plans to grant its Mexican subsidiary a loan for a term of more than two years, it is advisable to convert that loan to equity. In this case, the parent company, rather than extending a loan, would buy capital stock in the subsidiary, and both parties would avoid the 35 percent tax. To accomplish the transaction, Mexican law requires foreign investors to obtain approval at a stockholders' meeting. The stockholders adopt a resolution and issue stock certificates to the parent company, whereupon a notary certifies the minutes of the meeting.

Besides the tax advantage, this alternative is a good deal for the parent company, because, when the parent decides to withdraw its capital contribution, the subsidiary can reimburse the parent at an amount adjusted for inflation, with no tax assessed on the difference. That would not be true in the case of a direct loan.

While this scheme works with parent companies, it doesn't work with financial institutions, because Mexican banks generally do not participate as stockholders of manufacturing companies in Mexico. But it does work with other unrelated companies. In fact, you may find it cheaper and more practical to arrange equity purchases by unrelated businesses, as long as you can retain your desired level of control over your company. This route is more practical because both the parent and subsidiary avoid the financial and tax burdens associated with intracompany loans and stock purchases, as well as those associated with loans from financial institutions.

Increasing Your Standing with Foreign Investors

As a foreign company operating in Mexico, one of your selling points to potential investors is that Mexico no

By Gabriel Amante, partner, Ernst & Young. Reprinted with permission from Global Production & Transportation magazine. Copyright © 1993 New Hope Communications Inc.

longer restricts the repatriation of earnings or the repayment of loans obtained from abroad. Mexican authorities also no longer require that you obtain their approval to send that money out of the country. This means that foreign investors can pump capital into your company and expect to receive their return on your schedule, rather than the government's.

called as required. These matters include any proposed merger, issuance of debentures, modification of the corporate charter or bylaws, or another action for which an extraordinary meeting is specifically required by the corporate charter.

Each share represented at a meeting has a single vote, unless voting rights are limited by the corporate charter. Shares with limited voting rights may be permitted, for example, to vote only at extraordinary meetings or on designated matters. Shareholder resolutions and decisions are usually passed by a majority vote of the outstanding capital stock entitled to vote, although the charter may require a greater-than-majority vote. Unfortunately, a dissatisfied minority shareholder has little legal recourse to challenge the majority's lawful decision. The corporate charter may give some protection to minority shareholders, particularly when the minority represents a substantial ownership interest in the corporation, if it specifies that a more than simple majority vote be required to carry important matters. Thus, two-thirds of the total outstanding shares may be required for such actions as the approval of an amendment to the corporate charter, a contract for substantial indebtedness secured against corporate assets, the appointment of board members and officers, the salaries and benefits of high-level employees, or an extraordinary dividend to a particular class or series of shares.

Administrator or Directors At the first organizational meeting, the shareholders may elect, in accordance with the corporate charter, a sole administrator or a board of directors to manage corporate affairs. The corporate charter must specify whether a sole administrator or board of directors is to be elected, describes the powers and duties of the administrator or directors, and restricts certain management actions over which the shareholders retain control. The charter may also provide for a sole administrator while the corporation is being formed and a later election of directors after organization has been completed.

If a board of directors is created, the charter should specify the term of office—usually one year or until replacement—and require election of alternate directors. A provision for alternates is especially useful if any of the regular members reside outside Mexico, allowing meeting quorum requirements to be met and making board action possible even if a nonresident director cannot attend. Board meetings may be held at any location, regardless of where the corporation is domiciled.

Officers The board of directors usually designates a general manager to undertake daily business operations. Authority to appoint a general manager must be stated in the corporate charter, which should also specify the powers and duties of the general manager and the management powers of the board that cannot be delegated.

Dividends Regardless of whether shares are issued in classes and series, all shareholders must be permitted to participate in profits. For shares with limited voting rights, Mexican law requires the corporation to pay a cumulative annual dividend of at least 5 percent before any dividends are paid on other shares. The shareholders may declare a valid dividend from only those funds shown on the corporation's balance sheet as accumulated profits available for distribution. Every Mexican corporation is required to set aside 5 percent of its annual net profits in a statutory reserve account until an amount equal to one-fifth of the capital stock has accumulated; such reserves are not available for dividends. No dividends may be declared until the corporation has provided for losses incurred in prior years. Shareholders, administrators, and directors who authorize dividends before these conditions are satisfied may be held jointly liable for reimbursement of all funds on the demand of a shareholder or creditor.

Books, Records, and Statutory Auditors Corporations must keep bound books of the minutes of shareholder and director meetings, a register of shares, and financial accounts. These records must be kept at the official domicile of the corporation. Financial records must be kept in pesos and in Spanish, although they may be kept in other currencies or languages in addition.

All Mexican corporations must appoint at least one statutory auditor, known as a *comisario*. The auditor acts as an independent representative of the shareholders, attends board of directors meetings, demands monthly financial reports from the board, and reports to the shareholders at least annually with regard to whether proper financial policies are being implemented and applied and whether management's information honestly represents the corporation's financial status.

Liquidation The circumstances under which a Mexican corporation must be dissolved by law include the expiration of its legal term, the completion of its objective, the occurrence of an event that makes it impossible for the corporation to carry on its principal purpose, a reduction in the number of shareholders to less than the statutory minimum, or a loss equal to more than two-thirds of the corporation's capital stock. The corporate charter may specify other circumstances under which dissolution will occur, such as by resolution of the shareholders. On dissolution, the corporation must be liquidated. However, no legal penalties can be assessed against a corporation that continues operations after an event requiring dissolution has occurred, although a creditor or minority shareholder may file a legal action to force liquidation in such an event.

The corporate charter usually describes the procedures for liquidating the corporation. It should set forth a process for naming at least one liquidator. No shares may be fully redeemed until all creditors are paid. Partial redemption is permissible, provided notice of it appears in the official newspaper three times in 30 days, and provided no creditors object. Unless otherwise provided for in the corporate charter, all shareholders have an equal right of redemption—that is, one shareholder's right is not preferred over that of another and all are to be compensated on a pro rata basis—with the exception of any outstanding shares with limited voting rights, which must be redeemed before common shares. The amounts distributed for redemption of shares are apportioned based on the paid-in contributions of the shareholders.

Liquidators are required to retain the corporation's books and records for ten years after liquidation.

Partnerships

Mexican law recognizes four types of partnerships: partnerships in which all members have limited liability—*sociedades de responsabilidad limitada* (S. de R.L.); general partnerships—*sociedades en nombre colectivo* (S. en N.C.); partnerships of limited and general investors—*sociedades en comandita* (S. en C.); and civil partnerships—*sociedades civiles* (S.C.). Of these organizations, the S. en N.C. and S. en C. resemble the concept of partnership under US law. The S. de R.L. is similar to a corporation in its operation, but resembles a US partnership in its organizational structure.

The S. de R.L. and S. en N.C. forms are occasionally used by foreign investors who desire to have their home country tax income from the Mexican entity as being derived from a foreign partnership. Business owners tend to form limited liability partnerships more often than general partnerships because only the former offer some limitation of liability. Partnerships of limited and general investors are rarely established, and civil partnerships are used only for noncommercial purposes, such as for administrative service units of affiliated corporations, educational institutions, and organizations that offer professional services.

Sociedad de Responsabilidad Limitada (S. de R.L.) The Mexican limited liability partnership—the *sociedad de responsabilidad limitada*—is a business

Reprinted with permission from Don Wright. © 1993 Don Wright, Palm Beach Post.

organization in which all of the members are liable only up to the amount for which they have subscribed. In some respects, the S. de R.L. is operated like a corporation, but it also has many characteristics of a partnership. From as few as two to as many as 50 individuals or entities may organize an S. de R.L., which must be capitalized with a minimum of NP$3,000 (about US$900).

Members hold a proportional share of the partnership's capital account, although no share certificates are issued out. Ownership interests are referred to as participations—*participaciónes*—which cannot be issued as negotiable certificates and cannot be transferred except as prescribed by law. A member may own only one *participación*, the value of which may be increased proportionally if the member makes a further contribution. No new members are admissible without unanimous consent of the other members, unless otherwise provided for in the company agreement. Members have a right of first refusal over any capital account that is to be sold to a new investor. An S. de R.L. may not commence operations until all capital is subscribed and at least 50 percent of each participation is actually paid into the company.

Management The members are the highest authority in a S. de R.L. They may select one or more managers to operate the partnership or, alternatively, conduct business without central management. A manager need not be a member.

A general meeting of the members must be held at least once a year. Each member is entitled to vote at the meetings, and votes are counted and profits shared in proportion to the amount of each member's contribution to the capital account. Actions are usually taken by majority vote, unless the company agreement requires a unanimous decision. However, unanimous approval is necessary for a change in the company's purpose or for an increase in the obligation of the members, and modification of the company agreement requires approval by holders of at least three-quarters of the capital. Only the members may authorize a distribution of profits.

Bound records of partnership meetings and transactions must be maintained in similar fashion to the requirements for Mexican corporations, except that an S. de R.L. keeps a register of capital accounts instead of shares. The partnership charter may require the members to elect a board of examiners—*consejo de vigilancia*—to perform duties comparable to those performed by the statutory auditor of a corporation.

Liquidation Requirements and procedures for the liquidation of an S. de R.L. are generally the same as for a Mexican corporation. The partnership charter should also provide for the effect on the S. de R.L. of the death of a member. For example, it may allow a transfer of the deceased's interest by inheritance without consent of the other members, or it may require dissolution of the company.

***Sociedad en Nombre Colectivo* (S. en N.C.)** All partners who belong to a Mexican general partnership—*Sociedad en Nombre Colectivo*—have unlimited, joint liability to third persons. Partnership capital may be fixed or variable, but may not be reduced to less than 20 percent of the original capital. Unless otherwise stated in the partnership agreement, capital may be distributed only on dissolution and liquidation of the partnership.

Management Unless the partners designate an administrator to manage the partnership, all partners may participate in management directly. The person selected as administrator need not be a partner, but any dissenting partner has a right to leave the enterprise if a nonpartner is appointed over the partner's objection. Partners who are not administering the firm are entitled to appoint an inspector and to examine partnership books and accounts.

Most decisions of the partners are made by simple majority vote. However, if a single partner holds the majority interest, the supporting vote of another partner is required to carry the action. In general, minority partners who dissent to a partnership action have a right to withdraw from the enterprise. Modification of the partnership agreement, admission of new partners, and assignment of partnership rights requires unanimous consent, unless the partnership agreement reduces this requirement.

***Sociedades en Comandita* (S. en C.)** are similar to limited partnerships in the US, although such forms are used infrequently by foreign investors. The *sociedad en comandita en simple* consists of one or more general partners who bear joint and several liability for all debts and limited partners who bear liability that is usually limited by the amount of their respective contributions of capital. Within the similar *sociedades en comandita por acciones* partnership holdings are divided into shares. The shares of limited partners are readily transferable, but transfer of the shares of general partners can only take place with the consent of all general partners and a two-thirds vote of the limited partners.

***Sociedad Civil* (S.C.),** or civil partnership, is a partnership form used by professionals such as accountants, attorneys, and architects. Because of general liability issues and limits on the ability of foreign professionals to do business directly in Mexico, this form of organization is not expected to be of interest to foreign investors.

Joint Ventures

Joint ventures are popular arrangements for foreign investors, particularly small- and medium-sized enterprises, which seek to conduct specific projects with Mexican enterprises that have preexisting operations, infrastructure, and contacts in Mexico. A joint venture—an *asociación en participación* (A. en P.)—Is a contractual arrangement by which two or more individuals or entities agree to combine financial resources, property, and labor or other contributions for the purpose of conducting certain business activities and to share in the profits and losses. Such agreements must be in written form. Mexican law imposes no minimum capital requirement on joint ventures. No shares are issued to the venturers. In general the rights and responsibilities of joint venture participants are similar to those of formal partners. An A. en P. does not have to be entered in the commercial register.

The contract does not create a separate legal entity, and therefore the managing joint venturer—the *asociante*—is liable to third parties. Limited liability is available to the silent joint venturers—the *asociados*. They are liable for losses only to the extent of the amount that they agreed to contribute to the venture, unless the contract expressly requires them to cover any excess losses.

Joint venture operations are usually conducted by the *asociante,* although in large ventures, the parties may delegate the responsibility for controlling the venture to a committee. Such a committee is similar in function to a corporate board of directors. It represents the interests of the nonmanaging or silent venturers and is headed by a representative of the managing venturer. The requirements for operation and dissolution are primarily the same as for partnerships, except when contrary to specific rules for joint ventures. A joint venture contract may impose conditions or procedures specific and unique to the particular venture. Joint ventures terminate upon the death of a venturer.

Franchises

Companies that have established franchises in Mexico have become increasingly common, particularly in tourist-oriented services, such as hotels, car rental agencies, and fast food outlets. Since 1991 a growing number of franchising operations have taken advantage of the government's elimination of technology-transfer impediments. Franchising operations are expected to expand further under NAFTA as import duties are eliminated and demand swells in Mexican markets for products from franchise chains. Some observers predict that under current free trade policies, a growing number of Mexican nationals will also become financially able to buy foreign franchises.

Foreign franchising in Mexico is regulated under foreign investment, trademark, and tax laws. A franchise agreement is subject to a simple registration process with minimum disclosure requirements for the franchisee. No government approval is required.

Branch Offices

In practice, a foreign corporation may register to operate a branch office, or *sucursal de sociedad extranjera*, in Mexico. However, the foreign corporation must comply with the formalities required by the Mexican government and must obtain government approval, including authorization from the SRE and FIC largely as if it were incorporating as a Mexican corporation. Historically, the government has not encouraged branch office operations, preferring that foreign investors set up wholly or partially owned national entities. The FIC has tended to authorize temporary branch offices mainly when operations are limited to contracts with government agencies. However, Mexico's policies toward foreign capital have changed, and the changes are expected to facilitate the establishment of branch offices in the country by foreign companies in the future. Some foreign investors may find that use of a branch office format can allow them to reduce Mexican income taxes on service fees by allocating some operating costs to parent units located outside the country.

Sole Proprietorships

A sole proprietorship—an *empresa de persona física*—is generally neither an acceptable nor a feasible vehicle for a foreign investor seeking to operate a business in Mexico. However, it is one of the most common forms of business enterprise for small- and medium-sized Mexican operations. A business owner who operates a sole proprietorship bears unlimited personal liability because this form of organization is not recognized as a separate legal entity. Although the sole proprietorship is popular for small businesses because formation and operational requirements and costs are minimal, the fact that liability is unlimited generally deters owners of larger organizations from using this form. Moreover, sole proprietorships may be operated only by Mexican nationals or permanent residents, and therefore a foreigner may do business in this form only if the foreigner has permanent resident—*inmigrado*—status, which is usually not available unless the foreigner has already been in the country on business for an extended period.

FORMATION AND REGISTRATION

Formation and Registration of Business Operations

At a minimum, businesses in Mexico must register with the appropriate authorities before commencing business operations. In addition, the formation of most business entities requires prior government authorization. Private businesses, whether national or foreign are barred from certain activities altogether, and foreign-invested companies are prohibited from conducting certain other operations either entirely or are limited to a minority participation. Moreover, no enterprise may conduct business in areas or activities beyond the scope allowed by the terms of its registration, although these restrictions are easing under the terms of the North American Free Trade Agreement (NAFTA) and the new Foreign Investment Law passed in December 1993. This section outlines the procedures and documentation required to form and register a business in Mexico. Most entities are formed and registered under Mexican commercial laws, but foreign entities also need to comply with the provisions governing foreign investments.

Business entities created in Mexico are regulated by state and federal laws and rules relating to companies generally. Foreign-owned entities operating in Mexico are also subject to the Foreign Investment Law. In theory, an investor or owner may handle business formation and registration in Mexico without professional assistance. However, the investor or owner will face an intricate legal and bureaucratic maze fraught with limitations, regulations, and opaque required procedures and will be compelled to deal with various government authorities. Setting up a business in Mexico often requires not only approval, but also rulings on the practical application and interpretation of Mexican laws and regulations that require the applicant to go beyond mere compliance with stated procedures. Even Mexican nationals are often unaware of or confused by the various requirements of doing business in their country, and a foreigner who is considering a business arrangement with a local partner should not rely solely on the Mexican national to raise and handle all possible issues.

It is essential to obtain legal and accounting advice at an early stage of the formation process from professionals in the country who know the federal and local government structures and who are familiar with the myriad of regulatory requirements and procedures. With such assistance, business owners may be able to structure their companies in such a way as to maximize compliance while minimizing exposure to regulatory agencies. In addition, the investor or owner should continually monitor the progress and status of agency approvals and all subsequent registration procedures to ensure that the process does not become sidetracked and that additional requirements are clearly identified in a timely manner. (Refer to the "Important Addresses" chapter for partial listings of government agencies and legal and accounting firms.)

Formation Without Government Approval

An enterprise that does not engage in any classified activity may be wholly foreign-owned. Such an enterprise may commence operations without prior government approval, provided it complies with the business registration procedures and with certain conditions. These conditions include the investment of a minimum amount (currently 20 percent of the proposed amount) of foreign funds in fixed assets prior to the beginning of operations, selection of a location for the company's facilities outside designated high-density industrial areas, maintenance of an overall favorable foreign exchange balance during the first three years of operation, creation of permanent jobs and employee training programs, use of appropriate technology, and adherence to environmental regulations. (Refer to the "Foreign Investment" chapter for a discussion of allowed foreign investments and conditions.)

Formation With Government Approval

A business owner must seek government approval before forming a Mexican company, commencing operations in a classified activity, or putting in place foreign investment that exceeds otherwise allowable levels. With respect to a foreign-invested company, approval must be obtained from the FIC. Approval will depend on such factors as the extent to which the company will complement domestic investment, show a positive balance of payments, promote exports, create jobs, improve employee earnings, contribute to the development of zones or regions where economic improvement is of high priority, bring in new technology, and contribute to the development of local technological research.

Special Considerations—*Maquiladoras* Since the 1960s, foreign firms have benefited from Mexico's *maquiladora* (in-bond processing company) program under which a foreign enterprise may arrange to conduct 100 percent foreign-owned operations in Mexico. *Maquiladoras* produce sub-assemblies, assemblies, semi-finished goods, and finished goods for export, primarily to their affiliated foreign companies. Thus, they serve as a means for foreign companies to take advantage of Mexico's comparatively lower labor costs by moving labor intensive production there. This program was originally established to promote exports, provide employment, and generate foreign exchange. It has been highly successful, now employing more than 500,000 Mexicans and ranking as the country's second largest foreign exchange earner after petroleum exports. Manufacturers of automobile and automotive parts, electronics, and textiles in particular have established thriving *maquiladora* operations.

A *maquiladora* operation may be set up as one of the following: a Mexican subsidiary, which is wholly

REPORTING REQUIREMENTS*

All Mexican corporations in which foreigners have participation, foreign individuals or corporations, and real estate or neutral investment trusts must be registered with the Foreign Investment Registry within 40 working days from the date of incorporation, notarization of the documents evidencing the operation of a branch, or creation of a trust. Any amendments to the data provided on registration must also be reported to the Foreign Investment Registry, and the registration must be renewed every year.

All applications for rulings from the Foreign Investment Commission must be granted or denied by that agency within 45 working days from the date a complete application is filed. Otherwise an approval ruling will be deemed as granted.

In order to issue a ruling, the Foreign Investment Commission will consider the impact in employment, the technological contributions, the environmental impact, and the possibility of increasing competitiveness of Mexico. The Foreign Investment Commission may deny access to foreign investment for national security reasons.

The corporations that have commitments under the prior legal framework can request an exemption to the new requirements, and the General Directorate of Foreign Investments of the Ministry of Commerce and Industrial Development (SECOFI) must respond within 45 working days of the date of the application.

There is a penalty section under which actions can be rendered invalid and fines can be imposed for violations of the reporting requirements. This section also provides the right to a hearing before any penalties are imposed.

*By Manuel F. Pasero, managing partner of Pasero, Martín-Sánchez y Sánchez, a Tijuana-based business-oriented law firm. Reprinted with permission of the author. Copyright © 1994 Pasero, Martín-Sánchez y Sánchez.

a fee equal to actual costs—primarily wage and fringe benefits, building occupancy overhead, and administrative expenses—plus a percentage.

In a shelter operation, the foreign owner supplies the equipment and materials needed for production and a production manager to an established Mexican company, the shelter firm. The Mexican company invests in the facility, hires employees, and runs all aspects of the operation—including customs, labor, legal, and accounting requirements—for a fee calculated on the basis of the labor hours spent. The foreign owner has no direct Mexican labor or tax liabilities.

A subcontracting arrangement is similar to a shelter operation, except that the foreign owner generally does not provide a production supervisor and the fee is based on unit cost. Therefore costs are usually higher because the subcontractor's financial risk is greater. The fee often includes the use of standard manufacturing equipment.

A foreign company may set up a *maquiladora* after obtaining government approval of the arrangement or the formation of the Mexican subsidiary. Relatively few restrictions are imposed on *maquila* operations, although they must comply with all national laws. A simplified procedure has been implemented to handle requests for information about and approval of *maquiladoras*, and government approval for a *maquiladora* project takes about three weeks.

Maquiladora companies are in a transitional phase under the NAFTA provisions that gradually eliminate tariffs, deregulate restrictions on sales to Mexico's domestic market, and create new rules of origin. These companies have seven years during which they may operate essentially as they have under prior regulations while adjusting to the NAFTA provisions. Thereafter, *maquiladoras* will become an integral part of Mexico's economy on the same footing as other industrial sectors. *Maquiladoras* that adjust to the rules of origin during the transitional period will benefit as tariffs are gradually eliminated on the added value generated in Mexico. The timing of these benefits will vary depending on the schedule of tariff elimination, which varies from product to product. *Maquiladoras* that fail to adjust will be subject to a duty-drawback, which is a new tariff system under which the company must pay the larger of the export or import tariff on nonregional (that is, Mexican, Canadian, and US) inputs incorporated into export products. (Refer to the "Foreign Investment" chapter for a detailed discussion of *maquiladoras*.)

Procedures—Publicly Traded Mexican Corporations A publicly traded corporation is established through public subscription. The promoters of such a corporation must complete the following steps:

owned by a foreign entity; a shelter operation; or a subcontract arrangement. Of these three, the Mexican subsidiary arrangement is favored by industries with complex manufacturing processes that involve considerable engineering or R&D support.

The usual Mexican subsidiary arrangement requires the foreign company to furnish the machinery, equipment, raw materials, and components required for assembly, all of which are under bond and remain the property of the foreign company. In addition, the foreign company authorizes the use of necessary patents and provides training, management, and technical assistance. The Mexican company arranges for the factory premises and labor, receiving

- Prepare and sign a prospectus that sets forth the proposed bylaws and the statements required by Mexican statutes and regulations. (Refer to the "Business Law" chapter for a description of prospectus contents.)
- File a prospectus with the Commercial Registry and obtain approval from the *Secretaría de Relaciones Exteriores* (Secretariat of Foreign Relations).
- File required financial details about the corporation with the *Secretaría de Hacienda y Crédito Público* (Finance Secretariat).
- Obtain written public subscriptions to capital stock.
- Open an account with the credit institution designated in the prospectus where cash payments for subscriptions will be deposited and held until the corporation is formed.
- Have subscribers who are paying by an exchange of property deed the property to the corporation, effective as of the time of formation.
- Once capital is subscribed and 20 percent is paid into the corporate account, call and hold the initial shareholder meeting, at which the shareholders approve the capital values received, appoint corporate management, and designate persons authorized to act on the corporation's behalf.
- Have the minutes of the initial shareholder meeting protocolized (notarized) and registered.

Procedures—Private Mexican Corporations A person who seeks to form a private Mexican corporation must obtain certain government authorizations and file notarized documents. These same procedures must be followed to modify bylaws. The procedures are as follows:

- Negotiate the terms of the business ownership and prepare and sign a written pre-incorporation or other contract, such as a *maquiladora* agreement, for a wholly owned Mexican subsidiary.
- Prepare the application for authorization, which must state all required information, including the following:
  - The purpose of the corporation.
  - If shares may be owned by foreigners, a Calvo Clause, which provides that, with respect to their stock interests, all foreign shareholders must consider themselves to be Mexican nationals, must not invoke the protection of their own governments concerning ownership issues, and are subject to the forfeiture of their holdings to Mexico as a penalty for violation of this clause.
  - If restricted, the minimum percentage of the capital stock that must be held by Mexican nationals.

- Any types of activities in which the corporation is not allowed to participate.
- Details of the organizational meeting of shareholders, including the names and identification of the founding shareholders, the amount of capital paid in by each, and the payment terms for any amounts owed.
- The names of the initial officers—president, secretary, treasurer—of the corporation, members of the board of directors, and statutory auditors.
- Apply for authorization from the *Secretaría de Comercio y Fomento Industrial* (SECOFI).
- If the corporation is subject to the Foreign Investment Law, request authorization from the *Secretaría de Relaciones Exteriores* (Secretariat of Foreign Relations) and the FIC, if required.
- After approvals are secured, have the charter and bylaws of the corporation entered into a formal document.
- Have the document notarized and entered in the commercial registry of the political entity where the corporation is domiciled.
- File required financial details about the corporation with the *Secretaría de Hacienda y Crédito Público* (Finance Secretariat).

Corporate existence is deemed to commence as of the date of the notarized deed. Formation should take about three to four weeks to complete, although some observers suggest that in practice it usually requires about six weeks. In an effort to ensure quick processing of applications for authorization, the regulations under the 1993 Foreign Investment Law include time standards for processing. All cases are supposed to be resolved within 45 business days. The regulations also provide for automatic approval of the application if the government agency fails to reply within that period. However, the term "reply" is not defined; it could include, for example, a communication acknowledging the agency's receipt of the application without indicating the action taken. Also, any request for additional information could technically serve as an acknowledgment while restarting the clock. Even though a company representative has received some communication from the agency, automatic approval should not be assumed, and representatives may wish to obtain positive confirmation. For companies that supply products solely to *maquiladoras*, the required approvals from the FIC are usually given quickly.

Costs of incorporation typically include legal and notarial fees. The fee for incorporating is based on the amount of the beginning capital stock.

Procedures—Partnerships Persons who desire to form a Mexican partnership should complete the following steps:

- Prepare a partnership agreement, or, for an S. de R.L., a charter.
- File an application for authorization from SECOFI.
- If the partnership is subject to the Foreign Investment Law, request authorization from the FIC, as needed.
- After approvals are secured, file the necessary partnership papers with the public commercial register of the political entity where the partnership is domiciled.
- File required financial details about the corporation with the Finance Secretariat.

Organization costs and time necessary to form a partnership are approximately the same as for a Mexican corporation.

Procedures—Joint Ventures Parties who desire to enter into a joint venture should proceed as follows:

- Negotiate and prepare a written joint venture contract, which should include:
  - A designation of the joint venture parties.
  - The contributions and obligations of each joint venturer.
  - The purpose of the joint venture.
  - The term of the venture.
  - The process for distribution of profits and losses.
- Have all joint venturers sign a written contract.
- If foreign investors in joint ventures operating in sectors in which restrictions exist are to receive more than the allotted percentage of the profits, FIC approval may be required before operations can begin (local experts should be consulted before signing any such agreements.)

Additional Registration Requirements All foreign individuals or companies that intend to conduct business in Mexico must register with the National Registry of Foreign Investment, regardless of whether they form a separate Mexican company, including foreign individuals or corporations that invest in a company operating in Mexico; Mexican companies with any foreign-owned capital stock; and trusts with foreign participation. These persons must file an application to register within 40 business days after they become subject to registration. In addition, registered Mexican corporations that are wholly or partially foreign owned must periodically file forms that contain detailed economic, financial, and balance-of-payments information.

By law, Mexican companies are required to join the regional or national trade association that pertains to its business. In addition, several registers are maintained for special industries—such as the Register of Technological Industries—and companies that are classified within those industries must comply with those registration requirements as well.

Almost every business must file with the tax authorities, which operate through the Finance Secretariat. Each taxpayer will be assigned a federal tax registration number. (Refer to the "Corporate Taxation" and "Personal Taxation" chapters for a discussion of tax liabilities.)

TEN REMINDERS, RECOMMENDATIONS, AND RULES

1. The S.A. de C.V., *maquiladora,* and joint venture are the most popular types of business entities used by local and foreign investors. These are the business formats encouraged by Mexican authorities.
2. Establishing and fostering personal relationships with individuals in the Mexican governmental agencies and business enterprises are of the utmost importance to succeed in business in Mexico.
3. Mexico has privatized and is deregulating its industries at a rapid pace, and rules, interpretation, and conditions are in flux.
4. Mexican laws and regulations remain a bureaucratic maze, making professional assistance from consulting, legal, and accounting firms essential for gaining initial approval of a business operation and continuing freedom to operate with minimal government interference.
5. Any foreign individual or entity that conducts business in Mexico is required to obtain all necessary permissions and registrations prior to undertaking any business.
6. Companies are generally regulated by the General Law of Commercial Companies; foreign companies are also subject to the Foreign Investment Law; additional legal requirements may be imposed under various Civil Codes operating at the state level.
7. Mexico is encouraging the establishment of businesses, and to this end is streamlining its approval and registration systems by designating single government offices to be responsible for certain types of entities and by allowing for automatic approvals.
8. Foreign entities that are not operating within classified activities can obtain quick approval and registration by agreeing to the technological, labor, location, and environmental conditions established by the Foreign Investment Commission (FIC).
9. Foreign individuals and companies can generally own land and immovable fixtures in compliance with Mexican law.

10. The *Secretaría de Comercio y Fomento Industrial* (SECOFI) is the main regulatory agency for manufacturing industries, while the FIC regulates foreign persons doing business in Mexico. An approval from one of these agencies does not constitute approval from the other, and the requirements of both must often be met before business operations commence in Mexico.

USEFUL ADDRESSES

In addition to the government agencies listed here, individuals or firms should contact chambers of commerce, embassies, banks and other financial service firms, local consultants, legal and accounting firms, and resident foreign businesses for assistance and information. (Refer to the "Important Addresses" chapter for more complete listings.)

American Chamber of Commerce of Mexico
Lucerna 78-4
Col. Juárez, Deleg. Cuauhtémoc
06600 México, DF, México
Tel: [52] (5) 705-0995, 724-3800, 703-3908
Fax: [52] (5) 703-2911 Tlx: 1777609

Banco Nacional de Comercio Exterior S.N.C.
(Bancomext)
(National Foreign Trade Bank)
Camino Santa Teresa No. 1679, Piso 12 Ala Norte
Col. Jardines del Pedregal
01900 México, DF, México
Tel: [52] (5) 652-4022, 227-9000 x3394, 568-2122
Fax: [52] (5) 652-7255, 652-4235

Mexican Investment Board (MIB)
Paseo de la Reforma 915
Lomas de Chapultepec
México, DF, México
Tel: [52] (5) 328-9929, 202-7804
Fax: [52] (5) 328-9930, 202-7925

Nacional Financiera (Nafin)
(National Development Bank)
Insurgentes Sur No. 1971, Torre IV, Piso 8
Col. Guadalupe Inn
Deleg. Alvaro Obregón
01020 México, DF, México
Tel: [52] (5) 325-7050, 325-7051 Fax: [52] (5) 325-7249

Secretaría de Agricultura y Recursos Hidráulicos
(SARH)
(Secretariat of Agriculture and Water Resources)
Avda. Insurgentes Sur No. 476, Piso 13
Col. Roma Sur
06038 México, DF, México
Tel: (5) 584-0066, 584-0096, 584-0271 Tlx: 1775890

Secretaría de Comercio y Fomento Industrial
(SECOFI)
Dirección General de Inversion Extranjera
(Directorate General of Foreign Investment)
Blvd. M. Avila Camacho No. 1, Piso 11
Lomas de Chapultepec
11000 México, DF, México
Tel: [52] (5) 540-1331, 540-1426, 540-2766
Fax: [52] (5) 540-2749 Tlx: 1763158 SCME

Secretaría de Energía, Minas y Industria Paraestatal
(Secretariat of Energy, Mines and Parestatal Industry)
Avda. Insurgentes Sur No. 552, Piso 3
Col. Roma Sur
06769 México, DF, México
Tel: [52] (5) 564-9789, 564-9790, 584-4304
Fax: [52] (5) 574-3396 Tlx: 1775690

Secretaría de Hacienda y Crédito Público
(Hacienda)
Dirección General de Politica de Ingresos
Palacio Nacional, Patio de la Emperatriz
Edificio 5, Piso 5
Col. Centro
México, DF, México
Tel: [52] (5) 521-7237, 512-5309
Fax: [52] (5) 510-3796

FURTHER READING

The preceding discussion is provided as a basic guide for those interested in doing business in Mexico. The resources described in this section provide additional information on business law, investment, taxation, accounting, and procedural requirements.

Doing Business in Mexico, Ernst & Young. New York: Ernst & Young International, Ltd., 1991. Available in the US from: Ernst & Young, 787 Seventh Avenue, New York, NY, USA; Tel: [1] (212) 773-3000. Available in Mexico from: Mancera y Freyssinier, S.C., Plaza Polanco, Jaime Balmes No. 11, Torre "D", Pisos 4 y 5, Col. Los Morales Polanco, 11510 México, DF, México; Tel: [52] (5) 557-9511. Provides an overview of the investment environment in Mexico together with information about taxation, business organizational structures, business practices, and accounting requirements.

Doing Business in Mexico, Price Waterhouse. Los Angeles: Price Waterhouse World Firm Limited, 1993. Available in the US from: Price Waterhouse, 400 South Hope Street, Los Angeles, CA 90071-2889, USA; Tel: [1] (213) 236-3000. Available in Mexico from: Price Waterhouse, Apdo. Postal 1403, 06000 México, DF, México; Tel: [52] (5) 211-7883. Covers the investment and business environment in Mexico and audit, accounting, and taxation requirements.

Business Operations in Mexico, Bureau of National Affairs, Foreign Income Portfolio 972. Available in the US from: Bureau of National Affairs, 1231 25th St. NW, Washington DC 20037, USA; Tel: [1] (202) 833-7480. Describes the legal aspects of forming business entities in Mexico and business relationships with Mexican nationals.

Labor

THE LABOR ECONOMY

Although Mexico's general economy has experienced massive and radical change during recent years, its labor economy has altered to a far lesser degree. Mexico remains basically a low-skill, low-wage labor market that suffers from having a level of development that has not kept pace with that in other sectors of its economy. At the same time, Mexico's available, cheap labor is one of its most important resources and one of the chief attractions for foreign investors interested in operations in the country. Mexico also has pockets of remarkably sophisticated, skilled production operations, mostly run by large multinational manufacturers who have made major investment commitments—ranking alongside any in the world—although these remain in the minority.

Labor relations are governed primarily by the 1970 federal labor law (*Ley Federal de Trabajo*), which largely serves to codify the provisions of the 1917 constitution. It is explicitly designed to give the benefit of the doubt to labor instead of management in disputes. This has been seen as necessary to protect labor, given its often minimal effective bargaining power in the face of much stronger business and government interests. Besides, as in many other areas, although the revolutionary rhetoric is strong, Mexican actions are often considerably more conservative, with the government paying lip service to labor, but often supporting management. Mexican labor has been relatively nonmilitant in practice—although not in words—because it largely recognizes this fact of life. The recent explicit tilt by the Salinas government away from the traditional labor allies of his Institutional Revolutionary Party (PRI) toward business has caused concern in labor circles. However, to date there has been no effective action plan by labor to try to alter the changing balance of power. However, with the assassination of PRI presidential candidate Luis Donaldo Colosio in March 1994 and the selection of the relatively inexperienced Ernesto Zedillo as his replacement with just a short time to

go until the election, many observers suspect that old-line labor leaders will be in a position to demand concessions in return for their help in pushing through the new candidate.

Jurisdiction Federal law is administered primarily through state labor departments, which can also add local requirements to the federal rules, although federal regulations have priority. Most enterprises come under state jurisdiction. Although this is true in terms of actual numbers of enterprises supervised, there is a lengthy list of key industries that are subject to direct, original federal regulation. These include: textiles; electricity generation; cinematography; rubber; sugar; metals; basic minerals exploration, extraction, smelting, and processing; steel smelting and fabrication; hydrocarbons; chemicals and petrochemicals; cement; lime; the automotive industry; pharmaceuticals; cellulose and paper; edible oils; food and beverage processing; railroads; wood products; glass; and tobacco, as well as any other state-run operations. The federal government also exercises direct supervision over activities carried out under federal contracts, in federal zones, or in territorial waters. Cross-border disputes (both interstate and international) and issues involving education and occupational safety are handled at the federal level as well.

The Labor Secretariat has broad discretionary powers to mediate labor issues, adjudicate disputes (there is no formal appeal to its rulings), and levy penalties on both unions and employers to enforce its rulings. Unions have a long tradition of being extremely cozy with ruling party politicians, who have usually given labor (or at least labor leaders) wide latitude to run their own operations in order to be assured of the votes the labor leaders can deliver. Such familiarity and effective immunity has emboldened some union leaders to overstep their bounds and engage in irregular and corrupt behavior. During the Salinas administration, authorities have cracked down on at least some of the more blatant abuses. In fact, one of the first acts of the Salinas government designed to establish itself as being fully in command despite its minuscule margin of electoral victory was to take on the notoriously corrupt, previously untouchable oil workers' union chief Joaquín Hernández Galicia. Salinas actually sent federal troops into a pitched gun battle to capture Hernández' fortified estate. Despite this forceful action, which won plaudits for the new administration and did result in real change within the union, the organization remained in the hands of Hernández' loyal henchmen. Union dissidents have also attempted to depose leaders who are considered to be out of touch with the membership, although this has mostly occurred at the local level. The government has been eager to exploit such internal warfare for its own benefit.

The Salinas government has focused on restructuring and opening Mexico's economy. Labor policy has played a crucial—although secondary—role in these efforts. Labor has been called on to limit its demands (some, and not just among labor sympathizers, have argued that labor has been asked to do too much in this area) in order to allow the general economy to strengthen. Specific labor policies have emphasized improving quality control and productivity, and both labor and management have been pressured into avenues that support these goals. There have been some noteworthy results: between 1989 and 1992 Mexican worker productivity rose by a total of about 20 percent, or about 6.5 percent each year on average, more than double the roughly 3 percent annual growth for US workers during the same period. True, this rise was highly localized in specific industries and operations, came off of a very low base, and still left US workers ahead in productivity by a factor of 10 overall. Nevertheless, this represented a significant improvement. It also came at the cost of substantial structural upheaval and higher unemployment, especially among the lower skilled workers who make up the bulk of Mexico's labor force.

The PECE and NAFTA Mexican union leaders also acquiesced to the government's "voluntary" Pact for Economic Stability and Growth (*Pacto para Estabilidad y Crecimiento Económico*, or PECE), which severely limited labor's demands and maneuvering room. The *pacto*, as it is known, called for tight fiscal and monetary policies, wage and price controls, and careful foreign exchange management. Although business howled over the tight credit policy, many argue that it was less affected than was labor. With wages held in check, business was able to make up some of the difference. And observers note that although wages were held closely to the terms of the *pacto*, prices generally were allowed to creep up to a greater degree. The program has been highly successful in reducing inflation and reviving the Mexi-

can economy. However, workers have lost purchasing power, jobs, and influence during the period. The major labor groups have become increasingly restive with each annual extension of the PECE. However, they have not felt able to challenge it directly and, from their perspective, the damage has already been done.

In 1992 the Salinas administration also pushed through the National Accord for Raising Productivity and Quality (*Acuerdo Nacional para la Elevación de Producción y Calidad*, or ANEPC). Another "voluntary" agreement among government, business, and labor, this plan called for federal and state governments and businesses to underwrite increased worker training and investment in return for union flexibility on work rules and quality and productivity issues. Again labor was a less than eager participant and delayed the accord until it could insert language designed to prevent it from being used as an end-run around the now archaic federal labor law, which business and government would like to revise. Many in labor feel that they again received short shrift, because the government has used this framework as a mechanism to allow business to push through work rule changes opposed by labor.

The North American Free Trade Agreement (NAFTA), which was originally scheduled to bypass labor issues, became caught up in US domestic politics and almost stalled over a number of subsidiary labor concerns. A labor side agreement dealing with transition periods, rules of origin, and safeguards was incorporated. Transition accords call for phase-in periods of up to 15 years, during which protections will continue to be in effect on a gradually reduced scale, ostensibly giving labor time to adjust. Safeguards are designed to ease the effect of the anticipated restructuring that is expected to occur due to tariff reductions and increases of imports into Mexico. By and large, Mexican unions have supported NAFTA, figuring to gain additional jobs as US and Canadian firms moved their high-cost operations to low-cost Mexico, although following passage, this mass exodus appears to be a much less certain outcome. Some analysts suggest that the main effect of NAFTA will be to speed the transition in Mexico from its traditional labor system—in which a paternalistic management pays low wages, but provides a high level of benefits—to a more modern one in which management pays higher wages, but offers fewer specific benefits.

Despite the traditional benefit of the doubt given to labor by the authorities, heavy unionization, and huge benefits and rigid work and seniority rules (not to mention the often antibusiness rhetoric enshrined by the revolution), those who know Mexican labor argue that it is actually much easier to deal with and more accommodating than labor in many other parts of the Western world. Although hidebound to a large extent, unions are used to working with management and generally want the enterprise to succeed. They also value their positions and need only look over their shoulders to see the horde of other workers eager to replace them should they prove too intransigent.

Population

Official figures listed Mexico's population as 82.4 million in 1990, the date of its last full-scale census. About 49.1 percent were males and 50.9 percent were females, while slightly more than half were 20 years of age or younger. Outside estimates placed the country's population at 90.4 million as of mid-1993. Mexico's population grew at an annual average rate of 2.3 percent between 1980 and 1990, and although growth is expected to ease to between 1.5 to 2 percent during the rest of the 1990s, the placement of new workers in jobs is expected to remain a major concern for the foreseeable future.

About 72 percent of the populace lives in urban areas, with about 22 percent—about 20 million—living in the Mexico City metropolitan area. Mexico is ethnically diverse, with about 60 percent of its population being classified as *mestizo*, that is of mixed Indian and European descent. Some 30 percent are described as culturally and genetically Indian, 9 percent as of European (predominately Spanish, although there are large German, Italian, English, and French, not to mention US, contingents) origin, and the remaining 1 percent represent other groups, mainly of African and Asian origin.

Labor Force Population

In 1990 the Mexican National Institute of Statistics, Geography, and Information *(Instituto Nacional de Estadística, Geografía, y Información,* or INEGI) listed the domestic labor force as 26.2 million, 76.5 percent of whom were males and 23.5 percent females. This would result in a workforce representing 31.8 percent of the total population, or 56.6 percent of citizens between the ages of 15 and 64. Mexico actually counted everyone 12 years of age and older as being in the workforce, an acknowledgment that underage workers were common and that few workers were actually able to retire (some estimates put the proportion of those 60 years of age or older still in the work force at 80 percent). Some estimates place the underground workforce—which includes underage and overage workers as well as women excluded from ordinary workforce calculations—as high as 8 million. This is up from 6 million in the late 1980s, partially the result of differing assumptions, but also partially due to an increasing lack of employment opportunities in the official sector. According to the US State Department, the Mexican labor force was growing at an average annual rate of 2.4

percent during the late 1980s and early 1990s, about as fast or even slightly faster than the overall growth in the general population.

Labor Availability and Distribution by Sector

Competitive—that is, low-priced—labor has been one of Mexico's major selling points. The country has a surplus of labor, with more persons officially and unofficially seeking work than there are available positions. Despite the creation of an estimated 2 million new jobs between 1988 and 1993, restructuring resulted in the loss of an estimated 3 million jobs through 1993, giving Mexico a net loss of about 1 million positions. Mexico has estimated that it needs to see the creation of at least 800,000 new jobs annually to accommodate new entrants into the workforce through at least the mid-1990s. Other observers put the annual jobs needed figure at one million or more.

Up until the mid-1970s, Mexico encouraged population growth, resulting in a demographic bulge in which minimally skilled young workers continue to come onto a largely saturated labor market in great numbers. The problem has worsened as population growth has resulted in a surplus in rural areas at the same time that fewer people find they are able to make a living through traditional agricultural pursuits. This has led to massive migration from depressed rural areas to overcrowded cities and to illegal emigration, primarily to the US. The flood of illegal immigrants has led to chronic tensions between Mexico and the US. Despite the resulting international political tensions, this tide of illegal emigrants serves as an important safety valve for the overstressed Mexican labor economy. In the late 1980s and early 1990s, it was further estimated that transfer payments to Mexico from the hundreds of thousands of such undocumented workers in the US accounted for more than US$1 billion annually, a source of foreign exchange just behind tourism, itself (at US$2 billion a year), the third largest source of foreign exchange in the economy behind oil and *maquila* exports.

Mexico's labor force consists of about two-thirds unskilled and one-third semi-skilled or skilled labor. There is a great demand for those in the skilled and semi-skilled categories, where virtually all of the newly created jobs have centered, while the demand for unskilled labor continues to ebb, especially as the economy has been reorganized to make it more competitive internationally. This shift has resulted in a surplus of often essentially unemployable unskilled labor, while creating a shortage of skilled and semi-skilled workers. Mexico already has some pockets of highly skilled, hi-tech, high-quality production that experts rank as the equal of any in the world.

As more production shifts from lower-skilled sub-assembly to the production of finished goods both for export and the domestic market, this level is expected to increase. This development is also expected to put further pressure on labor costs. The supply and demand imbalance is also leading to a rise in costs for such desirable labor, reducing the country's labor market competitiveness on the margin. There also exist such reported disjunctions as instances of overqualified university engineering graduates taking basic factory jobs in order to get in the door during periods of localized oversupply, only to have employers subsequently bemoan the lack of trained technicians at a somewhat later date or in different functional or geographic areas. Despite a focus on national education and employer-supplied worker training, the demand generally has yet to call forth an effective increase in the supply. This is at least partially due to the scope and rapidity of the changes in the economy.

Because of this need to provide employment and despite shortages of qualified personnel, Mexico has been reluctant to admit foreign employees. However, it has been relatively easy to justify the need for and obtain permission and visas for technicians with specific skills. Nevertheless, the authorities have sought to keep such foreign workers to a minimum and have been even less accommodating as regards the admission of managerial and professional staff. With the rather minor exception of refugees from Central and South America who find their way to Mexico and may try to work, illegal alien labor has not been a consideration in the country.

In 1991, 22.6 percent of the workforce was listed as employed in the agricultural sector, 27.8 percent in the industrial sector, and 49.6 percent in the service sector. If the underground economy is included, agriculture and industry are estimated to employ less of the total workforce—perhaps 17 percent and 25 percent, respectively—while services employ more, perhaps as much as 58 percent.

As recently as 1970, 39.4 percent of the official workforce was employed in agriculture. Between 1970 and 1990 agriculture employment grew at an average rate of 0.2 percent per year in absolute numbers, but its share of total employment shrank at an annual average rate of 2.75 percent. The industrial sector accounted for 22.9 percent of employment in 1970, growing at an average annual rate of 4 percent in absolute numbers between 1970 and 1990 and gaining at an annual average rate of 1 percent in its share of the total workforce. The service sector accounted for 37.7 percent of employment in 1970. Service employment grew at 3.8 percent annually between 1970 and 1990 in absolute numbers and by 1.4 percent as a percent of the total workforce. Agriculture is expected to continue to lose ground to industry and services as a source of employment in Mexico, with the service sector accounting for an increasingly large percentage of all employment in future years.

Foreign Workers

As noted, Mexico promotes the employment of nationals, even when there is an insufficient pool of such candidates for many specialized jobs. Mexico's federal labor law requires that a minimum of 90 per-

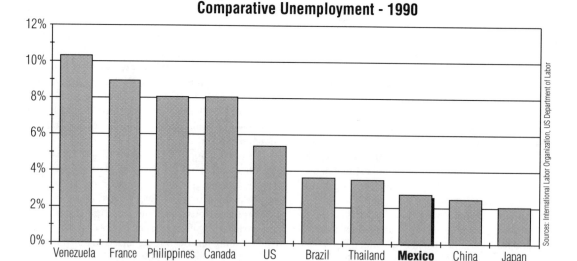

Comparative Unemployment - 1990

Sources: International Labor Organization, US Department of Labor

Note: In virtually all cases actual unemployment is substantially greater than official figures. This is particularly true in Mexico which has an extremely restrictive definition of unemployment. Outside organizations such as the United Nations Economic Commission on Latin America, the US embassy, the Cámara Nacional de la Industria de Transformación (Canacintra), and the Mexican Secretariat of Planning and Budget estimated real unemployment in Mexico of around 18 percent in the late 1980s. Observers believe it continues to be in that range.

NAFTA: IMPLICATIONS FOR LABOR

The North American Free Trade Agreement (NAFTA) does not deal directly with issues of labor and contains no specific provisions regarding labor. As a trade pact, it is not required to do so. However, a number of understandings regarding labor have become attached to the treaty. Although it is less of a problem for Canada, separated as it is from Mexico by more than 1,000 miles of US territory, illegal Mexican immigrant labor is a major concern for the US and an embarrassment for Mexico. The agreement does not deal with the issue directly, but the understanding is that Mexico has undertaken to improve its own economy and wages in an effort to raise the national standard of living. This is important because it will keep more of its citizens at home by increasing domestic opportunities and wages for them. In particular, US labor groups fought what they saw as a license for low-wage seeking US corporations to export US jobs to low-wage Mexico, arguing that Mexico did not pay a living wage to its workers. These groups also lobbied to raise Mexican wages as an offset. The argument was also advanced that low wage Mexicans would be unable to purchase US goods, which was somewhat of a red herring, given the fact that Mexico is already the US's third largest trade partner.

In essence, the labor side agreement to NAFTA called on parties to respect the provisions of each others' labor laws. Mexico in particular agreed to work to raise the standard of living for its workers in order to bring them closer in line with those of the other NAFTA signatories. In return it was given a 10 year grace period before it will be required to liberalize its policies allowing foreign participation in its labor force.

To begin to counteract these concerns, the Salinas government agreed to boost wages in 1994, which it did by raising official minimum wages by 7 percent to largely cover the previous year's inflation rather than by the initially announced 5 percent designed to cover the anticipated coming year's targeted inflation rate. The government's *pacto* also boosted wages at the bottom by a tax credit designed to increase effective earnings by about 10 percent.

The US (and Canada) remain technically closed to most Mexican labor, and the pact does nothing to resolve this issue. Nor does it point toward a borderless free labor market, as is the goal in the European Community and, as at one point, some negotiators wished to make a goal of NAFTA. Mexico, for its part, won agreement for it to retain its relatively restrictive policies on foreign labor. Although it is in the process of liberalizing its visa arrangements for at least some foreign businesspeople (largely through the institution of a special automatic 30 day business visa for US and Canadian citizens), it is keeping its rules limiting foreign workers to no more than 10 percent of total labor in any firm, even though it allows foreigners the right to own up to 100 percent of many such firms. It also continues to require a determination that no comparable domestic labor is available before it will admit technical and managerial personnel into the country. Mexican authorities also make it a condition for approving the required training program that nationals must be prepared to take over virtually all functions filled by foreigners. Mexico also continues to make it difficult for outside professionals to practice in the country, although this, too, is under review.

---

cent of all employees of any enterprise be nationals. Foreign technicians with required skills are usually allowed in to fill specific positions, but the authorities have generally kept tight control over professional positions, making it difficult for foreign practitioners to operate in Mexico except in limited capacities.

Professionals and those in the service sector have also had difficulties obtaining visas to work in the country. Generally foreigners are admitted on a temporary basis on visitors (*visitante*) visas. Those seeking to remain for a longer term must obtain *inmigrante* visas (provisional permanent resident visas that allow them to work in Mexico). Those holding such visas can engage in only the activities specified in their permissions and are allowed to spend no more than 18 months total outside the country during their first five years. The initial authorization runs for one year and can be renewed annually for a total of five years. After this period, the holder may be granted permanent residence (*inmigrado*) status, allowing freer entry and exit.

Unemployment Trends

Unemployment is a major problem, as evidenced by the large numbers of the mostly unskilled, mostly illegal migrants surging into the United States and the huge role played by the underground economy in Mexico as it attempts to absorb the large number of potential workers unable to be placed within the formal system. Nevertheless, Mexico's official unemployment figures are only slightly above those published by many essentially full-employment Asian countries that have seldom suffered unemployment of greater than 3 percent in recent years.

Mexican unemployment is defined very narrowly, with anyone who had any earnings at all in the period prior to that used in the calculation being counted as employed. Only those meeting extremely narrow established criteria are considered to be officially unemployed, leading locals to joke that being unemployed is a full-time job. Thus, urban unemployment was officially calculated at 2.8 percent in 1990, 2.7 percent in 1991, 2.8 percent in 1992, and 3.4 percent in the first quarter of 1993. During this period, male unemployment averaged 2.75 percent while female unemployment averaged 3.1 percent. The high point of official unemployment during this span was 3.6 percent, the low point 2.1 percent. Open unemployment—the difference between the total workforce and total employment—averaged 4 percent between 1989 and 1991. It should be noted that these figures are for urban unemployment and ignore rural unemployment, for which there are even fewer statistics but which is estimated to be substantially higher.

Independent sources (including the United Nations and the US Embassy, as well as CANACINTRA, a Mexican business group, and even the Secretariat of Planning and Budget) estimate that actual Mexican unemployment was about 9 percent in 1982, rising into double digits thereafter. It reached an estimated 18 percent in 1987 and has remained at about that level since then. Some even worry that it was edging even higher as the economy slowed in 1993 and early 1994.

While insisting on an artificially low unemployment rate, based largely on definitional issues, Mexican authorities acknowledge a substantially higher underemployment rate. One measure, which focuses on those who work fewer than 15 hours per week in formal jobs, listed the underemployed at 6 percent of the workforce in 1990, 6.1 percent in 1991, 6.5 percent in 1992, and 7.6 percent during the first quarter of 1993. Nevertheless, other government sources reported a much higher underemployment rate of 17 percent for 1992. Yet another indicator lists the percentage of workers earning more than the minimum wage as 81.5 percent in 1990, 85.75 percent in 1991, 84.6 percent in 1992, and 82.4 percent in the first quarter of 1993. Even these numbers are considered to be ridiculously high by many, with some observers arguing that underemployment regularly reaches 40 percent with nearly half of all Mexican workers earning only the minimum wage.

As part of Mexico's austerity program, economic restructuring, and—primarily—the privatization of many state-run firms, government employment has fallen significantly since the mid-1980s. Pemex (the state-run oil monopoly) alone dropped an estimated 100,000 positions between 1989 and 1993. Except in cases of bankruptcy, private firms have resisted massive layoffs. However, many have cut back on new hires, reduced head count through attrition, and reduced the number of shifts and hours worked, all of which has added to the unemployment and underemployment problem.

HUMAN RESOURCES

Throughout most of its history, Mexico's human capital has been relatively undervalued, with the country placing greater reliance on its abundant natural resources than on its human resources. The country's 19th century liberal reformers lobbied for public education, but funding and delivery have traditionally lagged behind intentions, falling in priority behind other economic and social investments. Mexico is now showing greater interest in developing its human resources as it seeks to enter the global economy, where quality is increasingly being valued over quantity as far as labor is concerned. One indication of this is that Mexico places great importance on worker training, requiring foreign investors to provide such training as a precondition of investment approval. Most companies, both foreign and domestic, have been willing to provide at least some training because of two factors. First, the labor is inexpensive enough that they can afford to do so, and, second, the labor generally has such rudimentary skills that they must do so to meet their operational goals.

Education and Attitudes Toward Learning

In general, Mexicans have placed a relatively low value on education, seeing it as being of limited importance. This has largely been a realistic assessment because traditionally there has been little access to education, making it relatively futile to aspire to it. Moreover, the patron-client structure of the society and the economic system traditionally meant that who you knew was often more important than what you knew. This situation has left a legacy that has been difficult to overcome. Nevertheless, conditions and attitudes are changing, with both the government and the populace at large becoming more aware of the importance of education as a necessity for building an internationally competitive labor force and economy.

Tuition for basic education is so nominal as to be essentially free for all but the poorest of the poor, although such subsidiary expenses as clothing, books, and supplies effectively place it out of the reach of many. Education is supposed to be mandatory for a period of nine years for ages six through 14, and students are expected to be able to reach basic competency levels before they are graduated from the system. During the late 1980s the median level of educational accomplishment among the adult population was sixth grade, or completion of primary school, which was the maximum required level until education reform in 1992 extended the required years of schooling to include middle school. In 1989 Mexico boasted of a literacy rate of 92 percent for those over age 15, although some other official sources put literacy at closer to 87 percent, still an optimistic figure. These statistics almost certainly overstate actual functional literacy by a substantial amount, especially in rural areas.

Education has been a relatively low-priority item, although expenditures increased from 6 percent of the federal budget in 1989 to 13.5 percent in 1991. Aside from funding issues, delivery has been a problem, with many more marginal groups—particularly those in more remote areas—having limited access, especially on a full-time basis. And the level of literacy achieved is in many cases fairly marginal. Nevertheless, Mexico has made great strides in providing a basic education for a much larger proportion of its population (literacy was calculated at only 57.8 percent during the 1940s).

There is a fairly wide range of public and private advanced secondary, preparatory, university, and technical programs available, and the government has been increasing financial aid for those wishing to pursue more than a basic education. Historically the government has allocated considerable resources to higher levels of education designed to create a cadre of *licenciados* (or degree holders), such as professionals, managers, researchers, intellectuals, and other leaders. Mexico City's National Autonomous University of Mexico (*Universidad Nacional Autónomo de México*, or UNAM) is the primary institution of higher education in the country. It is also the primary research center in the country, accounting for about 50 percent of academic research conducted in Mexico, mostly in engineering and the social sciences. Although the quality of many Mexican institutions is high and the standards of the rest are improving, much of Mexican higher education has been highly politicized in the past. Large numbers of Mexicans who can afford it and aspire to do so seek higher education abroad. (Many of the senior members of the Salinas administration, including the president and virtually all those within the ruling party seriously considered as presidential candidates, hold advanced degrees from US Ivy League institutions).

Total national enrollment for all educational levels was 25.2 million during the 1990-1991 school year, representing about 30 percent of the population. Of this total, 21.4 million (84.9 percent) were enrolled in preschool through secondary grades, 2.1 million (8.3 percent) were in high school, 1.2 million (4.8 percent) were in undergraduate programs, 46,000 (0.2 percent) were in graduate programs, and 414,000 (1.6 percent) were in formal vocational training programs.

Training

Mexico is recognizing the need for worker training, and federal labor law places much of the onus for delivering this training on the employer. Specific company training plans must be approved by the Secretariat of Labor and monitored by a company-based Mixed Commission for Training and Instruction consisting of representatives of both labor and management. The regulations do not specify numerical requirements for minimum training standards, but they clearly indicate that workers are expected to receive training that is adequate to produce results: measurably improved skills, improved productivity, reduced accidents, and advancement. In general, companies are expected to promote internally and to train workers to be able to fill such positions as become available. Although very large, very small, and highly specialized companies usually provide their own training, companies are allowed to hire outside training firms to comply with the regulations. Companies are allowed to deduct the cost of approved training programs as a business expense. Because of this formal training requirement, with the necessity for government approvals, training costs in Mexico are considered to be roughly double what they are in the United States, on average about 4 percent versus 2 percent of payroll.

For years, training provisions were generally ignored by employers, usually with the collusion of their unions, which preferred to see resources put into wages and other benefits. This has changed, with the government putting greater emphasis on worker training to improve competitiveness and productivity. This is especially so because the authorities can use this legal mandate to pass on much of the upfront cost and responsibility for such front line training to companies as part of compliance enforcement.

Women in the Workforce

Since the 1970s the Mexican constitution has prohibited discrimination on the basis of race, religion, or sex. Nevertheless, Mexico is a traditionally patriarchal society with strictly prescribed roles for men and women. Generally men still operate outside the household in the public and work spheres, while women are expected to confine themselves to the domestic sphere. As noted, the official Mexican workforce is overwhelmingly male (76.5 percent versus 23.5 percent). According to official statistics, the highest participation by women in the workforce occurs between the ages of 20 and 24, when 29.1 percent of women are listed as being economically active as compared to 77.1 percent of the male population. After the age of 24 the percentage declines as women get married, have children, and exit the workforce, although participation remains greater than 20 percent until women reach age 40 (the male participation level, however, reaching as high as 92.2 percent during this period).

The general shortage of entry level positions along with relatively lower educational levels have further prevented women from entering the formal labor market. However, economic necessity has also served to inject more women into the informal sector as well as into service industries, and, increasingly, manufacturing and other less traditional jobs. Educated women have also made some advances in penetrating the business world. However, the personalized and formal nature of business interaction has largely kept women from making substantial advances there. Although foreign businesswomen can usually expect to be treated with impeccable courtesy, they may find that they are not taken seriously. Although attitudes are changing, many Mexican businessmen remain uncomfortable dealing with women and may actually be somewhat insulted if a foreign firm chooses to send a woman as its representative.

CONDITIONS OF EMPLOYMENT

Working conditions in Mexico are controlled by federal labor law and its subsequently issued regulations. The law sets fairly strict and extensive minimum conditions covering most aspects of labor. Conditions apply whether the workforce is unionized or not. Employers cannot obtain waivers of any legally stipulated conditions, and any contractual arrangement that fails to meet the provisions of the law can be declared null and void. Even if no union or formal contract exists, labor law provides an enforceable minimum set of standards, benefits, and conditions. Even in the absence of a union, most businesses execute a formal contract to establish credibility with the authorities in case of a dispute, which is otherwise likely to go against them given the pro-labor bias written into the law.

Working Hours, Overtime, Holidays, and Vacations

Workweek and Hours By law the maximum regular workweek is 48 work hours, consisting of six eight-hour days, plus one paid day of rest, usually Sunday. In recent years, shorter weeks have become increasingly common. A 40-hour workweek is prevalent for white collar jobs, especially in urban areas. Workweeks of five-and-a-half eight-hour days (44-hour week) and five nine-hour days (45-hour week) are also relatively common arrangements. Regular day shifts are eight hours long. Night shifts are seven hours, for a 42-hour standard workweek, while split shifts are seven and a half hours (a 45-hour workweek).

In 1988 the average actual number of hours worked per week was 50.9. The figure eased to 48.4 in 1989, and plummeted to 33.7 in 1990, the latest year for which official statistics are available. According to an unofficial survey source, the average number of hours worked rose to 42.5 in 1991.

Workers must receive twice their regular hourly wage for the first nine hours of overtime worked in a given week. They receive triple time for any overtime beyond nine hours and for work performed on their designated rest day or on a legal holiday. Employers cannot legally require employees to work more than nine hours of overtime per week as a condition of employment. Because Sunday is usually the designated day of rest, Sunday work commands a 25 percent premium over the regular hourly rate for workers who work on that day, even when they do so as part of their regular schedule and have an alternate day designated as their day of rest.

Holidays Mexican law establishes seven legal paid holidays annually: New Year's Day (January 1), Constitution Day (February 5), Juárez's Birthday (March 21), Labor Day (May 1), Independence Day (September 16), Revolution Day (November 20), and Christmas Day (December 25). In addition, Inauguration Day (December 1) is a national holiday in years in which a presidential installation occurs (once every six years, with one scheduled in 1994).

Many banks, offices, and stores also close on major secondary holidays even though such days are not designated legal national holidays. Most labor contracts call for at least four or five such days to be declared paid company holidays, and other firms find that they cannot count on conducting business during these periods because of absenteeism and the closure of so many other businesses. Although some such holidays are secular in nature—Flag Day (February 24), the anniversary of the Battle of Puebla (May 5), and Columbus Day (October 12)—many others are religious in nature, including Holy Week (especially Good Friday and Easter); All Saints' and All Souls' Days (November 1 and 2); the feast of Our Lady of Guadalupe (December 12), the national saint's day; plus a raft of other saint's days. Generally, holidays that fall on a Tuesday or Thursday result in a semi-official Monday or Friday holiday as well, and major festivals tend to get stretched out over an entire week. Garden-variety absenteeism (often referred to as observing *el día de San Lunes,* or Saint Monday's day) is also common, as are *días feriados de ganas* (time taken off because the worker feels like it). Many employers report that such absenteeism is a significant labor problem.

Vacations Workers must be given six days (one workweek) of paid vacation after one year of service. Two additional days are given for each of the next three years of service, for a total of 12 paid vacation days (two work weeks) that accrue at the end of four years of service. After five years of employment, two more days of vacation must be allotted for each additional five-year block of service. And these are the minimum requirements, with many contracts providing for even more liberal vacation policies. Employers are also required to pay vacation time at full salary plus a 25 percent vacation premium. Some firms have negotiated bonus payments in lieu of accumulated vacation time (the 125 percent vacation pay plus an additional buyback bonus is fairly common) to avoid losing critical personnel for extended periods.

Special Leave

Special leave is usually not granted, although it can be negotiated to cover specific needs and circumstances. Employers are legally required to give 12 weeks of paid maternity leave to women, with 90 days of mandatory unpaid leave—45 days before and 45 days after delivery. Many companies offer combinations of paid and partially paid leave during this period.

Employment of Minors

Individuals are generally considered ready to enter the workforce upon completion of required education at about age 15. Children through age 14 are supposed to be in school on a full-time basis and are not legally available for work, although many in fact do. The government included persons older than 12 years of age in its calculations of total potential labor force in the 1990 census, counting 4.4 percent of the population between the ages of 10 and 14 and 32.3 percent of those between 15 and 19 as being economically active (this predated the official extension of required education to cover those between the ages of 12 and 15).

The only explicit federal labor provisions governing the employment of minors apply to 14- and 15-year-olds. Such minors are not allowed to work more than six hours per day, and their work must be divided into two shifts of no more than three hours with a minimum one-hour rest break separating them. They are not allowed to work overtime, on holidays, or on rest days, nor can they work during the night shift in industrial jobs or after 10 pm in non-industrial jobs. Those 16 or older are subject to the standard adult employment regulations.

Hiring Policies

In theory, firms are allowed to hire whomever they want. However, there exist government and union labor policies that serve to limit this freedom to a greater or lesser extent. The somewhat restrictive prescriptive federal regulations can be superseded by an executed union contract specifying hiring policies. And many firms find that unions are willing to allow greater managerial leeway on a case-by-case basis in return for other considerations.

Article 159 of the federal labor law specifies that promotion is to be based on seniority. This provision is not quite as hard and fast as the language of the statute indicates, because those with union contracts can negotiate provisions for merit-based promotion arrangements as long as the employer provides a training program designed to ensure that internal candidates receive the training necessary to improve their chances for advancement. With the current emphasis on competitiveness, these limitations are becoming less restrictive in practice.

Termination of Employment

Mexican law allows employers to dismiss workers virtually at will. However—and this is a large qualification—it also requires employers to pay extremely hefty severance benefits in all but the narrowest and most flagrant examples of dismissal for cause, with the onus for demonstrating cause resting with the employer. Aside from dismissal for cause, head count can be reduced in the event of mutual consent, death of a worker, completion of the job for which a worker was hired, physical or mental disability preventing a worker from fulfilling his or her duties, acts of God or other circumstances beyond the control of the employer, demonstrated cost inefficiency of an operation that allows it to close regardless of any labor contract in force, bankruptcy, or upgrading of equipment resulting in elimination of the position.

Employees with more than 20 years of seniority generally can be dismissed only for serious cause, and in practice it may prove virtually impossible to fire such individuals. Dismissed employees can sue for reinstatement, and, if successful, are entitled to full back pay and may receive punitive damages as well. Reinstatement is not available for employees dismissed after less than two years of service with the firm or employees classified as confidential employees, that is, members of management such as executives, inspectors, supervisors, and auditors. However, both categories are eligible for severance pay. Most dismissed employees opt to accept their generous severance packages, and many companies find that they prefer to pay rather than go through procedures to justify dismissal for cause.

THE REAL LABOR COSTS OF DOING BUSINESS IN MEXICO

The noisy debate over NAFTA in the United States hinged largely on its opponents' contentions that US labor was being sold out to cheap Mexican labor earning a substandard US$0.55 per hour, only about one-eighth of the US minimum wage of US$4.25 per hour. To cost conscious businesspeople looking for low-cost outsourcing options, this figure looks too good to be true—and it is. Just as few US firms can reasonably expect to get an adequate and appropriate supply of labor for US$4.25 an hour, those who expect to be able to hire Mexican workers for 55 cents an hour are deceiving themselves. Base salary is merely a starting point. Many US and other national firms assume that they can offer the same type of benefits in Mexico that they offer at home and calculate their labor costs accordingly. But in reality most required Mexican benefits represent thinly disguised additional cash payouts, not benefits that can be bought at a discount. Such cash benefits include the following federally mandated items:

- Christmas bonus: minimum of 14 days' pay in cash, due by December 20th (the average contract calls for 25 days' pay; many call for even more);
- Vacation: vacation time is paid at a 25 percent premium above regular pay (many contracts require larger premiums of more than 75 percent; vacations accrue beginning with six vacation days after the first year and two more each year thereafter to year five, when accrual slows to two additional days for each additional five years of service);
- Profit sharing: 10 percent of all pre-tax profits must be paid out to employees annually in cash;
- Days off and holidays: seven annual national holidays and additional contractual holidays (average total of 18);
- Overtime, Sunday, and holiday rates: the first nine hours of weekly overtime are paid at double time; any additional overtime is paid at triple time; work scheduled on a holiday or regular day off is paid at triple time; Sunday work, even on a regularly scheduled basis, is paid at a 25 percent premium;
- Social Security (IMSS): employers contribute a minimum of 17.42 percent of individual workers'

salaries to fund extensive social security benefits (the government is raising the maximum levels and including additional benefits as taxable income to raise its social security take);

- Retirement account: employers contribute 2 percent of wages to fund a self-directed individual retirement account for each employee; and
- Housing benefits (INFONAVIT): employers contribute 5 percent of individual workers' salaries to fund housing benefits.

In addition, most larger Mexican and virtually all foreign firms offer matching contribution qualified savings plans designed to give employees an amount equal to 13 percent of their salary on a tax free basis. Nearly 90 percent of firms offer some form of scrip or discount coupons to subsidize food and other purchases at local grocery and department stores. Subsidized on-site cafeterias and transportation, attendance and punctuality bonuses, uniform or clothing allowances, and other benefits are considered de rigeur by employers interested in keeping their turnover down to 10 percent—per month. All in all, employers pay 40 to 80 percent above the nominal salary in such expenses, with the average package running just over 60 percent.

Foreign employers also must recognize that although they may be able to get ample unskilled labor at the minimum wage, they are in competition for a scarce resource when it comes to skilled or even semi-skilled labor. Skilled personnel at lower and medium levels may cost only 50 to 75 percent of what they do in the United States, with costs moving up to parity for middle level executives and technicians. However, upper level executive personnel are even more expensive, by perhaps 15 percent on average. And such people expect benefits that are big (and often unusual) by stateside firm standards: 70 percent get either company cars (often chauffeured) or a US$1,000 to US$3,000 monthly transportation allowance in lieu of a car. And headhunters and competitors actively try to lure away just the people companies are most interested in keeping, so labor turns out not to be the place to try to save money on operating expenses.

Because of lower overall skill levels—even in sectors where there is a relatively high level of development—and high turnover, effective labor costs are a multiple of nominal labor costs. One US firm estimated that it took three times as much labor to accomplish a given operation in Mexico as it did in the US. Another study reported a consistent average rate of return of 6 percent for skilled operations performed in plants in high-wage home countries versus an average loss of 3 percent in low-wage outsourced venues. Firms regularly find their training costs doubled in Mexico. Training is not only rigidly mandated by the government, it is absolutely necessary for firms wishing to accomplish their goals.

All in all, one source calculates the fully loaded average hourly Mexican wage at US$5.38, nearly 10 times the 55-cent-an-hour, largely fictitious rate. However, the same source calculates that the comparable US figure is about US$13.70, two-and-a-half times as much as the Mexican wage, making it a close call for a lot of firms.

Employers must notify an employee of termination in writing, including the effective date and the reasons. Although the law does not explicitly require firms to pay severance to workers with less than one year's service, many firms establish a contractual policy that entails severance payments to govern this period. Explicit 30-day probationary periods, during which no separation benefits, are payable are common written policy among firms. However, once a worker has a minimum of one year's service, he or she is automatically eligible for severance payments.

For involuntary terminations without cause, basic payments (the *cesantia*) consist of a legal minimum of three months' salary. This amount increases by 20 days' pay per year of service. For voluntary terminations, these payments consist of a seniority premium (the *antiguedad*) of 12 days' pay per year of service. Such payments are owed to virtually anyone who leaves, regardless of the reason, if the employer initiates the separation.

The seniority premium is payable for personnel who leave for whatever reason (including voluntary resignation) after 15 years of service or for persons who die while employed. In cases of dismissals, whether for cause or not, the period covered by seniority premiums cannot extend prior to May 1970, when the law went into effect, even if the worker was hired prior to that date. The seniority premium is calculated from a maximum base of double the current minimum wage.

Acceptable reasons for dismissal for cause include: submission of false references and documentation to obtain employment (in which case dismissal must usually be within 30 days of employment); violence in the workplace that affects production; damage to premises, products, equipment, or other materials due to gross negligence; more than three unauthorized absences within a 30-day period; gross insubordination; careless or reckless endangerment of personnel or premises; the commission of immoral acts in or outside of the workplace; revealing trade secrets, resulting in harm to the firm; flagrantly neglecting safety procedures so as to endanger others; or working under the influence of drugs or alcohol. Employees can also be dismissed for cause if they are convicted of a crime and sentenced to prison. Dismissals are supposed to take place within 20 business days of the offense, so that it is difficult for management to use the threat of dismissal to punish infractions discovered after the fact.

Companies are allowed to set up a reserve for this contingent liability. However, the reserve is not a deductible expense except under very narrow circumstances, and few companies maintain such a fund. A company can defer payouts for a period of one year if more than 10 percent of its staff leaves within a given year, resulting in cash flow problems.

Employees are allowed to resign at will. However, those with less than 15 years service can be denied severance benefits unless they can argue that there was breach of contract on the part of the employer, or that the employer did not live up to the contract by providing a safe workplace, did not make required payments, did not provide stipulated training, or some other similar reason. In practice, unless the employee simply waives all recourse by failing to file a complaint (and some employees simply walk off the job without even applying for back pay due), the parties usually negotiate some arrangement. All such arrangements must be in writing and submitted to the Federal Labor Conciliation and Arbitration Board (*Junta de Conciliación y Arbitraje*, or JFCA) for approval.

WAGES AND BENEFITS

Mexico's low-wage labor has been one of its primary attractions. However, its low basic wage rates are offset by several factors, including mandated benefits that increase the effective cost and lower productivity and high turnover that require the use of more inputs of labor. Benefits alone can add 60 to 80 percent or more to the basic cost of labor. By comparison, average benefits are reported to be in the range of 37 percent of actual earnings in the United States, with actual mandated benefits costing less than 10 percent of payroll.

Mexican workers often prefer to work for foreign

companies because they generally consider foreign companies to be both somewhat more likely to have greater financial staying power and also less adamant in resisting labor demands than are domestic firms. Some foreign employers have even complained that government attempts to hold down costs have artificially kept wages too low and that they would prefer to be able to pay higher wages in order to attract better workers. Some lament that official wage constraints prevent them from competing for desirable laborers who remain in the underground economy because they can earn more there. On the other hand, it is generally acknowledged that major foreign *maquila* employers have often acted in concert to set wages at or near the minimum level in order to avoid costly wage-based competition for basic unskilled and some semi-skilled labor. They have justified this apparently anti-competitive practice by pointing out that their average turnover can reach 30 percent per month. Even in more stable work situations, employers note that monthly turnover often averages 10 percent per month.

Wages, Salaries, Allowances, and Bonuses

Labor Costs Mexico's workers are technically paid on the basis of a seven-day week, so real hourly wages involve a variety of assumptions based on actual hours worked as well as those not worked. In fact, federal labor law technically bars payment on an hourly basis, although pay can be based on a per day, per week, per month, or other basis. Such sums are then prorated to account for such items as hourly overtime. Lump sum and commission compensation arrangements are also allowed, although piecework compensation has not been approved.

In 1992 the average prorated hourly manufacturing rate in Mexico was US$2.35, up from US$2.17 in 1991, US$1.80 in 1990, US$2.32 in 1989, and US$1.99 in 1988 (the 1988 and 1989 wages represent an artificially high peso exchange rate relative to the US dollar). From 1986 through 1992, earnings rose about 125 percent in nominal dollar terms, or about an average of 12 percent per year. Mexican workers complain that on an inflation-adjusted and purchasing power basis they are only now recovering to where they were in 1983 and that effective real wages during much of the 1980s were no better than they were in the 1960s. The PECE, or *pacto*, negotiated by the government in the fall of 1993 sought to placate labor to some extent, not by raising wages, but by adjusting low-income tax credits to give those at the bottom an effective 10 to 11 percent boost in wages and purchasing power in 1994.

Based on official figures, the average weekly production worker's wage was US$60.66 in 1990. Rates were US$12.90 in China, US$24 in Thailand, US$32.50 in the Philippines, US$149 in Brazil, and US$376 in the United States. Average hourly rates in 1991 were US$2.17 in Mexico, US$3.59 in Hong Kong, US$4.32 in South Korea, US$4.38 in Singapore, and US$4.42 in Taiwan. One US company with parallel operations calculated all-in average labor costs at US$5.38 per hour in Mexico versus US$13.70 in the United States (however, the firm, which moved its production back to the US, noted that its US workers were three times as productive).

Unofficial survey sources suggest that the average actual manufacturing wage paid by foreign invested firms in mid-1991 was about US$96, only slightly above the US$2.17 hourly average for the

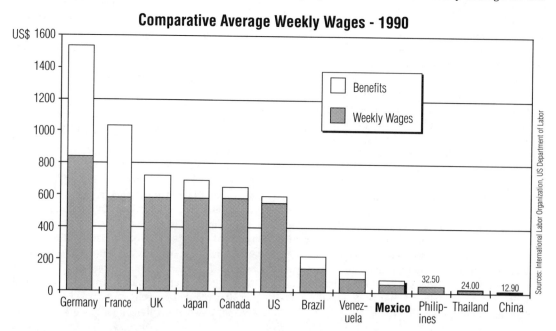

Comparative Average Weekly Wages - 1990

Sources: International Labor Organization, US Department of Labor

average 42.5-hour workweek recorded in 1991. Yet another source put 1993 fully loaded labor costs at US$3.39 per hour near the US border and US$5.05 in the heavily unionized industrial interior. In early 1994 Mexico City region factory workers expected to earn NP30 per day (about US$8.95), roughly twice the legal minimum wage. The figures noted include fringe benefits, many of which represent negotiated items above the level of the already generous officially mandated benefits.

Fully loaded Mexican wages increased at an average annual rate of about 20 percent on a nominal basis between 1988 and 1992. Noting the drop in inflation in the Mexican economy, some observers expect increases to decline to around 10 percent per year over the next several years.

Most foreign businesspeople report that actual wage costs in Mexico are much higher than anticipated, although such costs remain substantially lower than they are in many other locations worldwide. Mexican wages for lower-level personnel may be only 20 percent of what they are in the US and Canada. However, the cost of senior management personnel—those who are knowledgeable and educated, have connections and a track record, and are bilingual—can often command rates higher than are usually paid in the US because of limited supply and growing demand. And good technical and professional people do not come cheap either, again because of supply and demand. For instance, a survey conducted by the American Chamber of Commerce in 1993 listed average annual salaries (exclusive of benefits) for finance directors at US$89,934, marketing managers at US$51,519, bilingual secretaries at US$17,272, accountants at US$16,834, and data processors at US$7,030. Those operating in Mexico also note that because of the scarcity of specific categories of personnel, there is constant competition and raiding by rival firms.

Mandatory Profit Sharing Mexican law mandates a wide range of employer provided benefits. In addition to the mandated holiday, vacation, and overtime payments already noted, firms are generally required to set up a profit sharing account equal to 10 percent of their taxable profits for annual distribution to their employees. The taxable income figure includes pre-tax profits plus certain add-backs, such as prior-year loss deductions and special charges. Earnings subject to such provisions include only those attributable to a company's Mexican operations. Attempts to minimize earnings subject to profit sharing, such as splitting operations into separate legal entities in an attempt to book inordinate profits in one division (usually vested with the firm's capital) while presenting another (usually containing the labor component) as a cost center to reduce profits—a common ploy—can result in fines.

Average Hourly Earnings by Occupation
(in US$)

Occupation	1989	1990	1991
Laborer	1.89	2.20	2.70
Clerical	2.97	3.90	4.90
Semi-skilled workers	2.38	2.80	3.40
Professional/managerial	13.99	18.20	22.70

Source: US Department of Labor

Average Hourly Earnings by Industry—1990
(in US$)

Industry	Mexico	US
Textiles	1.94	10.31
Food and tobacco	1.67	13.42
Electronic equipment	1.54	13.96
Industrial and office machinery	2.02	15.97
Chemicals	2.61	18.96
Autos and parts	2.75	21.93
Iron and steel	3.20	24.26

Sources: US Department of Labor; Instituto Nacional de Estadística, Geografía, y Información

The profit sharing provision, in effect since 1963, covers virtually all enterprises, from sole proprietorships up through large corporations, and all employees except senior management. Distributions must be made within five months after the close of the books for the year, and the employees must be given access to the enterprise's tax return in order to be able to challenge it if they suspect that tax status has been manipulated to result in lower payments to them. Such challenges are rare in practice.

Half of the total amount is distributed on a pro-rated basis calculated on the number of days worked by a given employee (usually the employee must work a minimum of 60 days to be eligible to participate), with the remainder being parceled out in proportion to the individual employee's base salary. For professional and personal service firms, small firms that do not normally compute an adjusted gross business income (such as sole proprietorships), and certain other special situations, the payout can be limited to one month's base pay. Confidential employees (usually middle to upper level eligible managers and professional staff) are limited to payments equal to 120 percent of the wage used for computing the payment to the highest-paid nonconfidential employee.

Exemptions from profit sharing are available for newly formed entities during their first year of existence: new firms involved in manufacturing new products for two years; mining and related firms during their exploration period; recognized public and private not-for-profit entities; and for small entities with invested capital and profits below a certain threshold level established by the Labor Department.

Annual Bonus In addition to profit sharing, entities are required to pay a year-end (Christmas) bonus (the *aguinaldo*) consisting of at least 15 days' pay to all employees. Payments are prorated for employees who have worked less than the full year. This sum must be paid out in cash prior to December 20. Many contracts call for payouts of a full month's base pay, and some firms offer even more, although the average seems to be around 25 days' worth. In the past, many firms have dismissed employees at the end of November in order to avoid having them on the books and eligible for year-end payouts, although this tactic is only semi-legal and self-defeating at best.

Social Security Employers are charged hefty payroll taxes to support the social security system (run by the *Instituto Mexicano del Seguro Social*, or IMSS), that provides health, retirement, survivors', and other benefits for dependents as well as employees. Other separate agencies cover government employees and those of Pemex, the state oil monopoly. All employers with even a single worker—including nonprofit and tax exempt employers, but excluding those in remote areas not covered by the system—are required to contribute. There are special provisions to cover the self-employed, domestic help, and certain farm workers. Failure to register and participate leaves an employer open to liability in the event of work-related illness or accident and can result in a fine as well.

Social security provides benefits that include day care, sickness, maternity, hospitalization, old age, death, disability, and basic and supplementary retirement benefits. IMSS also provides some indirect unemployment and life insurance benefits. In theory, covered workers need no additional insurance. In practice, those who can afford to sometimes buy private insurance and seek private medical treatment because of the basic level of and long waits for most care provided by social security system doctors. Non-work-related illnesses of greater than three days' duration are treated by IMSS, with the agency paying a benefit of between 60 and 80 percent of the regular wage while the employee is not working. The employer is not obligated to pay anything during the time the worker is receiving such social security wage replacement payments, although some companies will pay the differential for full-time employees under contract provisions. In cases of permanent disability, IMSS pays 50 percent of the covered salary. Survivor benefits are payable in cases of work-related deaths.

The base rates are computed as a percentage of the individual worker's wage and adjusted for industry risk categories. Such risk premiums run from a nominal 0.34 percent to as much as 10.035 percent. Traditionally, IMSS has set the rate for the entire firm at a level matching that of the highest-risk individual worker or operation, leading many firms to set up separate subsidiaries for their higher-risk operations, thereby insulating the rest of the business from higher levies. Beginning in 1995, companies are scheduled to begin rating themselves based on actual experience; thus individual firms will have an incentive to reduce claims. Under the old system, negotiation and maneuvering to get a more favorable classification was common, and many expect this maneuvering to continue even under the new, supposedly more straightforward scheme. Observers also note that the change makes the employer responsible for more of the administrative costs of the program.

Although actual amounts and percentages paid vary widely, employers generally pay about 80 percent of the total required contribution; employees earning more than the minimum wage pick up the remaining 20 percent (minimum wage employees owe nothing, with employers being responsible for the entire contribution). In the past, companies have been pressured to gross up pay to cover the employees' social security contribution, but this practice seems to be on the way out as labor becomes more cost conscious and more concerned with stability of employment than with the extension of benefits. Most employers are scheduled to pay a base amount of 17.42 percent of wages in 1994: 8.75 percent for medical, 5.67 for old age benefits, 2 percent for pension benefits, and 1 percent for childcare assistance. This base amount is adjusted upwards for risk categories, but can equal less than the base percent of gross payroll because of caps on amounts contributed for medical (capped at 25 times the minimum wage) and old age benefits (capped at 10 times minimum wage). Most employers pay between 13 and 27 percent of gross payroll (in most cases between 14 and 18 percent) for social security, with employees paying an additional 2.6 to 5.4 percent (the statutory amount is 5.24 percent, but as noted, adjustments can raise or lower the actual amount paid).

In mid-1993 the government announced a 1.5 percent increase in the social security tax (1.2 percent to be paid by employers, 0.25 percent by employees, and 0.05 percent by the government). In order to raise its collections, IMSS also expanded the definition of what compensation is to be included in basic wages used for calculating the payment. Such items as overtime pay; employer contributions to

EIGHT ESSENTIALS FOR EFFECTIVE LABOR RELATIONS*

The first step to successful labor relations in Mexico is to, in the words of Richard Sinkin, "Leave all your preconceptions behind." Sinkin is managing director of Inter-American Holdings Co., a company based in San Diego that helps US businesses set up operations in Mexico. "When coming to Mexico for the first time, it is critical not to take the US model of labor relations and apply it to Mexico." Instead, labor consultants advise the following:

1. Know Mexico's labor laws.

The Federal Labor Law, a 3-1/2-inch-thick document, regulates labor contracts, minimum wages, benefits, and all union activity in Mexico. Unlike in the United States, for instance, Mexican workers are paid by the day, not by the hour. When a business signs a labor agreement, the contract states that the worker will be paid for seven days a week.

Manufacturers also pay employees on their days off. Most manufacturing employees normally work nine hours a day for five days a week, or eight hours a day for six days a week. In addition, overtime (at a rate of either double or triple normal pay, depending on the hours worked) must be paid for any hours worked over the normal work week of 48 hours.

2. Know what labor confederation you are dealing with.

About 9.5 million Mexican workers are unionized, although, in recent years, unions have lost some of their traditional influence. Still, they command considerable power. Furthermore, union activity in Mexico is regional. For instance, in northeastern Mexico, especially the city of Matamoros, more than 90 percent of workers are unionized, while, in Tijuana and Ciudad Juárez, less than 20 percent of workers belong to labor organizations.

The largest and most powerful labor organization in Mexico is the Mexican Labor Confederation, known as the CTM in Spanish, which has more than 5 million members. The CTM, which is affiliated with the ruling Revolutionary Institutional Party (PRI), is headed by Fidel Velázquez, its 94-year-old leader who for years has made labor a pillar of support for the institutional party.

3. Understand standard employee benefits.

A Price Waterhouse report shows that loading factors on wages (including payroll taxes, social security contributions, and other statutory and commonly granted benefits) are generally 100 percent of wages. A study by Intergamma shows that the average base minimum wage in Mexico is 39 pesos per day (about US$13 a day). But the actual labor cost per working day shoots up to 93 pesos (about US$31), when benefits, vacation time, Christmas bonuses, and rest days are factored in. (Minimum and average wages vary by region in Mexico.)

Among the benefits mandated by law are social security (employers pay almost 9 percent of covered salaries), a federal housing program (employers must pay 5 percent of covered salaries), and payments into a federal retirement fund (employers must pay 2 percent of employees' wages into a designated retirement account). In addition, the Federal Labor Law mandates a profit-sharing program, a Christmas bonus of at least half-a-month's pay (although most manufacturers pay a full month's wage) and paid holidays and vacations.

Besides the legally prescribed benefits, others are commonly provided: transportation to plants (most Mexican workers do not own cars), on-site cafeterias that serve free food, and shopping coupons for local supermarkets. Bob Craig, a customs consultant based in McAllen, Texas says these kinds of benefits have increased productivity and reduced absenteeism.

4. Hire a Mexican to oversee union relations.

Most labor experts say companies should hire someone who is keenly knowledgeable not only of Mexico's labor law, but of its culture and its unions. "You need to have a Mexican national involved who will know how to deal with the people," says Daniel Cavazos, a partner with the law firm Dyer, Cavazos and Kimbell, based in McAllen, Texas.

5. Make contact with industry chambers and unions as early as possible.

Months before beginning operations, manufacturers should meet with industry officials and labor leaders. "The first meeting with labor leaders shouldn't be

Excerpted from "At the Negotiating Table with Mexico's Labor Unions," by Paul Sherman. Reprinted with permission from Global Production & Transportation magazine. Copyright © 1994 New Hope Communications Inc.

EIGHT ESSENTIALS (cont'd.)

one to get to the specifics of negotiation. You should introduce your company. You need to educate the union about what you will be doing," says Craig.

There are hundreds of regional and sectoral chambers that can provide assistance and background information on regions and industries. The main chambers involved with foreign manufacturing are the Association of Importers and Exporters of the Mexican Republic (ANIERM) and the National Chamber of Industrial Transformation (CANACINTRA). Also, the American Chamber of Commerce has offices in Mexico City, Monterrey, and Guadalajara.

6. Study other manufacturers in the region.

Generally, unions will negotiate contracts similar to agreements they have with other plants in the area. In regions where unions are not strong, wages and benefits should be kept on a par with those in the area and with unionized plants elsewhere. During the first years of operation, unions often will be more lenient in contract negotiations.

7. Understand cultural differences.

It is important to be flexible. There are many benefits that might seem unnecessary in the United States but that are important in Mexico. The celebration of local festivals and religious holidays, in addition to cafeterias and transportation, all need to be taken into account.

8. Reexamine human-resource management.

The old top-down management style is beginning to change in Mexican manufacturing. Luis Manuel Guaida, chairman of the labor committee for the American Chamber of Commerce in Mexico, has stressed that companies need to do more than simply adjust salaries to increase productivity. He says international competition mandates new management styles that give workers a sense of belonging to their company.

Also, with more high-tech companies manufacturing in Mexico, firms need to give more time and resources to training. Says Guaida, who spoke at a recent labor-relations conference sponsored by AIC Conferencias, "Productivity is not only achieved with technology and new methods of production. Rather, it is the way people function in an organization."

welfare funds (except contractual union or pension fund contributions); excess withdrawals from company-provided savings funds; food and housing allowances valued at greater than 20 percent of the minimum wage; *dispensas* (discount coupons) valued at more than 40 percent of the minimum wage; and on-time and attendance incentive bonuses valued at more than 10 percent of regular salary—all of which were previously excluded—now have become part of the wage base on which social security contributions are calculated. In addition, the maximum base wage on which such contributions are calculated was upped from 10 times the minimum wage to 25 times the minimum wage for the portions of the contribution charged for workplace hazard, maternity leave, and childcare programs. Percentage contributions for workplace hazard, illness, maternity, disability, and retirement programs were also raised. The new rules were imposed by executive fiat, and have been roundly denounced by private sector businesses for raising their costs and making them less competitive. However, businesspeople recognize that they have no recourse in the matter.

Pensions and Retirement Because the current costs to provide its relatively generous benefits have spiraled upward, the social security system has had relatively few funds left over to provide retirement benefits and virtually none avialable to accrue for future liabilities. There is no mandatory retirement age, although covered workers with a minimum of 500 weeks of paid-up service can retire at age 65 with full benefits or at age 60 with partial benefits. Calculation of benefits is based on covered earnings during the most recent 250 weeks of employment.

In practice, few Mexican workers actually retire (an estimated 80 percent continue to work past age 60) because benefits are relatively meager and have not been effectively indexed to keep up with the rising cost of living. In fact, one of the arguments advanced by private firms instituting private pension plans is that they can serve as an incentive to induce older workers to retire and make way for younger, more flexible, and technologically skilled workers. (As noted, most promotions are made on the basis of seniority, and it is nearly impossible to dismiss workers with seniority.) Also, because of the relative youth of the workforce, this has not been an issue pushed by workers or their unions. Nevertheless, in 1992 the government, with a nervous eye toward future liabilities, instituted a mandatory supplementary retirement scheme known as the SAR (*Sistema de Ahorro para el Retiro*). This scheme required employers to contribute 2 percent of social security wages up to 25 times the minimum wage to an individual retirement bank account vested in the employee's name.

In the first year of the program, the funds in these retirement accounts could only be placed with banks in interest-bearing accounts holding government bonds to back them. In subsequent years, employees were allowed to manage their own retirement accounts, investing them in bank accounts or mutual funds. Securities firms and insurance companies were also allowed to sponsor and administer such retirement investment plans, leading to an expected surge in business to provide investment services.

Funds can be withdrawn only at age 65 or upon other retirement or permanent disability. Employees are also allowed to make additional voluntary contributions on their own. It is too soon to evaluate the effect of this program in terms of providing actual retirement benefits. However, it may serve to relieve somewhat the limited pressure that had been building for private firms to offer pension benefits. Employers are also allowed a tax deduction for all such social welfare funds paid directly to or on behalf of an employee.

Housing Payments Because of a constitutional requirement that workers be entitled to what is somewhat vaguely defined as "adequate" housing, employers have been required to pay 5 percent of each employee's eligible wages (capped at 10 times the minimum wage) to the National Workers' Housing Fund Institute (INFONAVIT) since 1972. Employees were allowed to borrow from INFONAVIT for home purchase, construction, renovation, or retirement of existing mortgage debt, but not for rent subsidies. The employer, as the agent of INFONAVIT, became responsible for deducting repayments of such loans from the employee's pay.

Employer payments for housing are now being redirected from INFONAVIT directly to a sub-account of the individual employee's SAR. Under the new plan, employees will draw directly on their own accounts (rather than apply to a general account operated by a bureaucracy) for such approved expenses; they will be able to accumulate as additional retirement funds whatever balances are not used for housing. Now that it is no longer the primary agency responsible for administering housing funds, INFONAVIT is scheduled to become a separate quasi-official entity offering financing for housing construction and mortgage guarantees.

Work Place Safety Employers are charged with providing a safe workplace according to the standards established by the IMSS and the Labor Secretariat. Companies must: set up a labor management committee to monitor such concerns; develop safety procedures and training in them; and investigate any work-related accidents, hazards, or illnesses. The authorities can impose fines and other sanctions, including indefinite closure for failure to correct gross hazards. In the past, industrial safety was a low-priority item. However, standards and enforcement are becoming tighter. The same is true with regard to environ-

mental issues affecting business and the workplace. This trend is expected to accelerate under the scrutiny of NAFTA, which was held up while an environmental side agreement was negotiated to cover such issues. These environmental side agreements require active enforcement of existing regulations, which have often been ignored in the past.

Additional Benefits The preceding items represent the established legal minimum for employer provided benefits for full-time workers. Many companies—especially most foreign companies—offer a wide range of additional benefits. Such benefits can include private supplementary pension plans; early retirement plans; additional paid holidays and vacation time; enhanced Christmas and vacation bonuses; general savings funds with employer matching contributions; coupons or other discounts (*dispensas*) for meals, food, or other goods; subsidized on-site meals; additional private medical and life insurance coverage; transportation allowances; uniform and clothing allowances; punctuality and attendance bonuses; and various other incentive, productivity, and benefit schemes. Some firms offer bonuses to employees who marry or have children, and some offer scholarships available to the children of employees.

Most firms offer lunch—the main meal in Mexico—to their workers with subsidies that cover more than 80 percent of the cost. Most firms with attendance bonuses have settled by trial and error on an amount equal to between two and four weeks' pay yearly to provide an adequate incentive to keep workers showing up every Monday morning. Qualified savings plans are provided for by Mexican tax law. Employers and employees can make tax-advantaged equal contributions totaling up to 13 percent of an amount equal to 10 times the minimum wage. These amounts must be funded on a monthly basis and paid out annually to the worker; workers can borrow against their accumulated balances during the year.

Many companies also offer such additional benefits as facilities for employee use, employee outings, Christmas parties, summer picnics, raffles, movies or other entertainment, and company-sponsored sports teams. On an individual level, employees often look to employers to provide additional benefits, such as interest-free loans, help in emergencies, and other sponsorship—the legacy of the patron-client social and economic system that has been so highly developed in Mexico.

In hopes of improving their operations, employers have offered additional benefits in order to placate unions and workers; to attract and retain a stable, higher caliber workforce; and to transfer as much income on a tax-free basis as possible (this goal is facing greater limits as the government looks for more sources of revenue). While Mexico's level of employer-provided benefits falls short of that generally required of employers in a socialist country (such as China), it is much higher and implies a far greater degree of paternalism and involvement than that which employers in the West are accustomed to providing. Observers also caution that employers in Mexico should be exceedingly careful in instituting any benefits above the required level because granting such voluntary benefits usually serves to set a precedent. It is likely that labor will come to see such benefits as a right and expect such benefits to be extended indefinitely in the future. Nor has labor traditionally been amenable to the alteration of terms of a benefit or the substitution of one benefit for another, holding out instead for additional benefits.

Minimum Wage

Unlike many countries in which the legal minimum wage is set at levels far below the prevailing wage, the Mexican minimum wage represents the effective wage for a broad spectrum of the working populace. Although official statistics indicate that more than 80 percent of the workforce earns more than the minimum wage, some outside observers argue that close to half of all workers actually earn little or no more than minimum wage.

Federal labor law requires that the official minimum daily wage represent a living wage that will provide a basic standard of living. Most officials privately—and sometimes publicly—acknowledge that, at best, the minimum wage covers little more than half to one-third of such needs. It is slipping even further behind the rising cost of living as the government has kept labor on a tight leash in its efforts to get a grip on inflation.

The National Minimum Wage Commission—which is composed of representatives from labor, management, and government and which operates through local committees—is authorized to revise the minimum wage at its discretion "as needed" based on inflation and general economic conditions. In practice, it executes the policy of the central government. In 1987, when inflation neared 160 percent, the minimum wage was revised upward five times during the year. In recent years as inflation has slowed and the government has tried to impose stability and restraint, revision has been on an annual basis. Revisions usually come at the beginning of the year, although in 1989 the government waited until November to raise the minimum wage.

The commission actually sets a series of minimum wages based on geographic location and, increasingly, on occupational categories. The three main geographic zones include high-cost Mexico City, the states of Baja California and certain other areas along the US border, as well as the center of the oil industry (Zone A); the second zone (Zone B), including the large cities of Monterrey and Guadalajara as well as a few other larger, more heavily industrialized urbanized areas (such as parts of Sonora, Tamaulipas, and Veracruz); and a third zone (Zone C) covering the remainder of the country, including rural areas. Although the gap in average wages set in the three zones has narrowed, the commission, through its local committees, has established a growing number of region-specific occupation-based supplementary minimum wages. In 1993 there were 86 separate semi-skilled, skilled, and office worker categories in Mexico City, each with its own separate minimum wage. These represented a wide range of specialties, with some of the higher skilled occupations calling for a compensation premium of more than two-thirds above the standard minimum wage.

In 1991 the minimum daily wage was US$4.01 per day for the Mexico City zone (up from US$3.92 in 1990 and US$3.00 in 1989), US$3.65 in the second zone, and US$3.30 in the rest of the country. In 1992 the top tier rate rose to US$4.30, while in 1993 the minimum wage ranged between US$4.65 and US$4.15.

In early 1994 the commission upped the minimum wage by 7 percent to NP15.27 (about US$4.93 at the beginning of the year, but down to about US$4.55 by the end of the first quarter due to the deterioration of the peso) for Mexico City, NP14.19 (about US$4.22) for Zone B, and NP12.89 (about US$3.84) for Zone C.

LABOR RELATIONS

Worker rights are guaranteed under the constitution. These include the right of association, the right to bargain collectively, and the right to strike. In theory, these rights may be extended through contract, as they often are, but not reduced. In practice, rights are selectively ignored according to the specific circumstances and current policy requirements.

Federal labor law provides that a minimum of 20 employees of an enterprise can form a company union that the employer must recognize. As few as two employees may choose to affiliate with a recognized outside union, and the employer will be required to recognize and deal with that organization. And despite accusations of union-busting and blacklisting by some employers—primarily foreign *maquila* operators—most eligible work units are unionized. Participation varies by industry and location, but in general a minimum of between 25 and 30 percent of workers are union members, although some observers argue that union membership runs as high as 50 percent. Unions even represent some sectors of the underground economy and have grown to wield considerable political clout based on the votes they can deliver.

Unions are divided into: company unions, that

is, those that represent a specific company; industrial unions, which represent workers of several companies in the same industry; and national unions, representing workers in state agencies or across several related areas and jurisdictions. Company unions are considered to be the most unpredictable because they are often founded by people with no union experience and no affiliation with the government or the established labor movement.

Conversely, large industrial unions are usually represented by union professionals who have little exposure to the problems of the shop floor and are more inclined to work with management to reach a compromise. In fact many employers find that with the help of such professionals they can get around certain provisions of labor law that can only be altered through a union contract. And the union can sometimes be persuaded to certify that some of the more vague requirements have been met by an employer who might be hard-pressed to demonstrate this objectively on his own.

Although all but a few narrowly defined confidential (management) personnel are eligible to belong, Mexican unions have traditionally been blue collar. Although government bureaucrats are well organized in their own unions, white collar, technical, and professional personnel have generally been slow to unionize. Bargaining about working conditions is undertaken every two years, while negotiations over wages are an annual event.

Unions and the Labor Movement

About 80 percent of unionized workers belong to one of the nine largest national labor confederations, while the remaining 20 percent are covered by single-firm company unions. There is some competition among unions, and jurisdictional disputes between different unions can cause headaches for employers caught in the middle. Nevertheless, unions are usually relatively well disciplined and keep to their own turf.

By law, companies can only deal with a single union, although different subsidiaries and even separately organized operations can deal with different unions, especially if the divisions are functionally separate. Nevertheless, there is generally a requirement that a given unit deal only with one union. Workers can institute proceedings to change unions. This action, which entails filing a lawsuit, is not to be taken lightly. Federal referees attempt to determine which union the employees actually favor, make their determination, and turn the company over to that union as of the next scheduled negotiating session. Workers who lose such a contest usually end up being fired, because most union contracts have exclusivity clauses. Thus the entrenched union can be expected to call on the company to fire any dissi-

dents attempting to affiliate with a rival union, while winners in a challenge invariably call upon the company to get rid of the losers.

The main labor organization is a loose labor umbrella organization known as the Congress of Labor (*Congreso de Trabajo*, or CT). Formed in the mid-1960s, the CT represents 37 PRI-affiliated labor confederations and independent unions. It has claimed to represent as many as 10 million union members, about 105 percent of total estimated union membership at the time, as some observers have wryly pointed out. Although this organization is the official voice for a more conservatively estimated 85 percent of organized labor, it has relatively little real function or influence.

Of far greater importance is the Confederation of Mexican Workers (*Confederación de Trabajadores Mexicanos*, or CTM), the dominant labor union confederation, with between 5 and 6 million members. Established during the Cárdenas administration in the late 1930s, the CTM has been closely linked with the PRI throughout the history of both. The CTM is generally considered to be the most politically powerful labor organization in Mexico. Its nonagenarian leader, the stridently anti-communist Fidel Velázquez, is one of the original CTM organizers and one of the most powerful individuals in Mexico. An adherent of the old-line PRI way of doing things, Velázquez and the CTM have been losing ground to the new party technocrats, who have gradually gone farther in ignoring and defying him. Nevertheless, one of the main considerations in Mexican labor politics and Mexican politics at large is how Velázquez will react to any given issue and what the plans are for his succession. Some observers suggest that, in effect, many politicians are simply waiting for Velázquez to pass from the scene before attempting to institute major—and most likely pro-business—labor reforms. However, the wily Velázquez has fended off every attempt to retire him and remains firmly in control. Despite the fact that at least some of the younger technocrats don't expect him to live forever, his own plans seem to call for such, and he is considered necessary because he represents the voice of labor and delivers much-needed votes.

The Federation of Government Employees (*Federación de Sindicatos de Trabajadores al Servicio del Estado*, or FSTSE), with between 1.5 and 1.8 million members, represents public sector employees. Despite its size and key insider position, this union is generally seen as being on the defensive, the victim of austerity and privatizations.

The Revolutionary Workers and Peasants Confederation (*Confederación Revolucionaria de Obreros y Campesinos*, or CROC), with perhaps 500,000 to 600,000 members (it claims as many as 3 million members, 10 times its estimated strength), is the main rival of the CTM. Some observers contend that, although strong in certain geographic areas, the CROC would have died out long ago were it not quietly encouraged and supported by the government, which looks to the CROC to counterbalance the dominant CTM and keep the latter from becoming all-powerful.

There exist a host of other smaller labor confederations, including the Regional Confederation of Mexican Workers (*Confederación Regional Obrera Mexicana*, or CROM), which, with a membership estimated between 250,000 and 350,000 (it claims as many as 2 million members), has been gaining strength at the expense of the larger confederations, as well as the General Confederation of Workers (*Confederación General de Trabajadores*, or CGT), the Revolutionary Confederation of Workers (*Confederación Revolucionaria de Trabajadores*, or CRT), and the Revolutionary Workers Confederation (*Confederación de Obrera Revolucionaria*, or COR), all of which boast 30,000 to 50,000 members. The National Federation of Independent Unions (*Federación Nacional de Sindicatos Indepiendentes*, or FNSI), with about 200,000 members, is composed of independent unions and is dominant in the state of Nuevo León and its capital of Monterrey, where it represents an estimated 70 percent of organized labor.

One of the more recent entries into the confederation sweepstakes is the Federation of Unions in Business Providing Goods and Services (*Federación de Sindicatos de Empresas de Bienes y Servicios*, or FESEBES), formed in 1990 by workers at the newly privatized, formerly state-run communications monopoly, Telmex. This somewhat more forward-looking confederation of telephone workers, electricians, airline pilots, flight attendants, and cinematographers—all of whom are involved in high-tech or service businesses—has actively supported the opening of the economy and, with about 120,000 members, is considered to be an up-and-coming power on the labor scene. The small (7,000 member) *Frente Auténtico de Trabajo* (the Authentic Labor Front) is another new body, consisting of a half-dozen small unions run by a council rather than by an autocratic leader. It is one of the few domestic labor entities that has cooperated actively with US unions in an attempt to organize Mexican workers.

In addition, Mexico has a number of single unions that, due either to their size or sectoral influence, represent forces to be reckoned with. These include: SNTE, or national teachers union, with an estimated 1.2 million members; the 150,000-member national railroad workers union; the 100,000-strong National Union of Mining and Metallurgical Workers; the bank employees union, or FENASIB; the 100,000-member oil workers union; and SUTIN, the generally far-left

nuclear power workers union.

A variety of other smaller unions and confederations are also active to a greater or lesser degree, ranging from those that represent a particular political ideology to those that are old-style, garden variety local unions concerned with improving working conditions on the factory floor.

Strikes and Disputes

Although Mexico has enshrined the right to strike in its constitution, labor statutes, and implementing regulations, in practice it limits such labor disputes. At least part of this is due to the legacy of long-time Secretary of Labor Arsenio Farell Cubillas, who represents a hard line with both labor and management in attempts to settle labor disputes and avoid strikes. The government has been willing to crack heads—usually figuratively rather than literally, although the latter is not unknown—and dictate settlements to both labor and management. Nevertheless, collective bargaining is slowly beginning to take on the character of an open negotiation determined by competitive forces rather than by government policy. Management has been emboldened by a somewhat more favorable government posture. Having lost considerable influence and purchasing power over the past 12 years, labor is facing pressure from the rank and file to resist the government's edicts to keep costs down, and disputes and strikes have risen in number, frequency, and intensity, as has management's willingness to provoke and endure them.

To be legal, strikes must be approved by the government. In 1991 some 7,006 formal notices of intent to strike were filed with the Federal Labor Arbitration and Conciliation Board (JFCA), which, however, approved only 136 actual strikes. This represented about a 10 percent increase in threatened labor actions from the year before, although about 10 percent fewer actual strikes were sanctioned in 1991 than in 1990. In general, the JFCA fails to authorize most strikes, and those that are allowed are usually of short duration. Few represent more than a minor disruption, although strikes in Mexico have the potential to be both prolonged and violent. Despite labor's frustration and sense that it has been made to absorb a disproportionate share of the burden for restructuring the economy, its militancy has been counterbalanced by the obvious fact that the economy has relatively little maneuvering room and vast legions of the unemployed and underemployed are waiting in the wings to pick up any jobs that organized labor finds beneath its standards.

Recent Examples In a sampling of recent labor disputes with implications for future labor policy, management seems to be gaining the upper hand to some extent, at least with reference to its former position. In 1991 a dissident faction of the large national teachers union staged wildcat strikes in protest over the pitiful state of teachers' pay. In this dispute both the government and the union leadership held firm, forcing the protesters back to work. The government made some efforts to placate the teachers, giving them a larger-than-average raise (although only about one-quarter of what they were demanding). However, it also reorganized the education system, turning responsibility over to the states, so that the union will now have to negotiate 31 separate state contracts as well as the federal district contract, weakening its national position through a divide-and-conquer maneuver.

The government has also apparently forced the powerful oil workers union to knuckle under. Shortly after assuming office in 1989, President Salinas sent federal troops after the corrupt head of the oil workers union, slapping him in jail and replacing him with a more manageable successor. Since then Pemex has seen the loss of an estimated 100,000 jobs as well as the restructuring of the monolithic oil monopoly into smaller specialized operating units, each with its own labor contract, which further reduces the power of the union.

In 1991 dissidents of the more militant COR finally were allowed to hold an election in an attempt to unseat the reigning CTM-affiliated union representing workers at Ford's Mexico City plant. They narrowly lost, charged fraud, and were again defeated in a hearing before the JFCA, which upheld the CTM union. Ford remained officially neutral, although the US AFL-CIO supported the COR, and its influence was thought to have prevented the wholesale dismissal of the dissidents following the election. Incidentally, despite a long-term relationship with the US American Federation of Labor (AFL), the CTM has resisted entreaties from the northern labor federation to take a more activist stance. And the AFL was chagrined when the CTM came out in support of NAFTA.

Of special interest was the strike against Volkswagen's Puebla plant in 1992, in which the company proposed a radical restructuring of its operations in the name of raising productivity. Although the majority of workers accepted the proposal, a minority of dissidents pressed for a strike. After examining the issues, the JFCA refused it permission to strike, leading the dissidents to start a wildcat strike. Volkswagen, with the tacit consent of the government, fired its entire workforce and then promptly rehired all but the dissidents under a new contract that incorporated the proposed changes.

This has become a tactic used with greater frequency. Some managers have found that it is ultimately cheaper and easier to fire the workforce and hire either new or the same labor under a different contract that incorporates the desired changes than

it is to go through the fights involved in negotiating changes in work rules. Such firings invariably obligate the firm to pay severance benefits to all those dismissed, but even so, many consider there to be a net gain in many instances despite the up-front costs. Observers also note that this procedure restarts the clock on seniority, which plays an inordinate role in most Mexican labor contracts.

The *Maquila* Labor Situation One area of increased union activity has been in *maquila* industries. Workers in these industries have complained that employers have banded together in unfair and illegal ways to prevent them from exercising their rights and obtaining fair wages and benefits. There have been accusations of collusive wage setting, blacklisting, and union busting by employers. Employers respond that they have had to limit their costs because they have had to provide training for laborers that are ill equipped to function in a factory environment, have an astronomical absentee and turnover rate, and display an abysmal quality and productivity record.

Nevertheless, as *maquila* operations have become better established and as they face greater integration into the mainstream under NAFTA, there has been an effort on the parts of both labor and management to build a more constructive base for long-term relationships. Labor has lobbied for benefits more in line with those of regular employees elsewhere. And has seen benefits double until they were almost equivalent in value to base salary during the early 1990s. The workweek has also been reduced from 48 hours to an average of 40 hours. Labor has continued to press employers on the issues of higher pay, larger year-end bonuses, higher vacation bonuses, higher profit sharing, and the provision of supermarket vouchers as a standard benefit. At least some employers have begun to respond, and average *maquila* wages, which actually lagged behind the minimum wage during the early 1980s, have surged ahead of it during the late 1980s and early 1990s as employers have attempted to build a more stable workforce.

The Productivity Hurdle In recent years government policy has stressed increases in productivity. The JFCA has been either explicitly or quietly evaluating the record of productivity improvement of companies which are the targets of strike threats. If productivity falls below the norm, strikes may be authorized. If, as was the case with Volkswagen, productivity is above the norm, the JFCA is more likely to turn a deaf ear to the union demands.

Of import for future labor developments, the 1994 PECE also allows firms to negotiate contracts based on productivity instead of offering an across-the-board percentage increase. The main component of the salary increase will continue to be based on a straight percentage change linked to inflation. However, the remaining component will be linked to productivity gains, allowing labor to share in any gains so generated, but also making it at least somewhat liable if such gains fail to materialize. Several large foreign industrial firms operating in Mexico have already negotiated labor contracts involving productivity goals.

Employer Organizations

A variety of management organizations exist in Mexico to lobby the government concerning labor issues, represent their members before government and labor groups, and advise members about various labor issues. Major organizations include: the Importers and Exporters of the Mexican Republic (ANIERM), Corporate Coordinating Council (CCE), Confederation of Industrial Chambers of Commerce of the United Mexican States (CONCAMIN), the Employers' Confederation of the Mexican Republic (COPARMEX), National Chamber of the Manufacturing Industry (CANACINTRA), the Confederation of National Chambers of Commerce (CONCANACO), and the American Chamber of Commerce of Mexico (AMCHAM of Mexico). The largest US chamber of commerce outside the United States, the Mexican AMCHAM unit represents roughly 85 percent of US companies doing business in Mexico. It operates special committees on *maquilas* and on labor issues.

Future Trends for Organized Labor

Despite the close relationship between the ruling party and organized labor, the government has been attempting to wean itself away from its previous dependence on labor and, in the opinion of many, reducing its special relationship with labor in its efforts to restructure the economy. The government, which used to cater to labor and anoint labor candidates in local, state, and national elections, has been more aloof in recent years. The new technocratic political leadership is more pro-business and middle class oriented than before. It is also more likely to require that labor justify its demands on rational rather than emotional grounds and that organized labor clean up its act and stay within its legitimate sphere of influence.

Some observers wonder if organized labor hasn't already lost the war. Traditional union leaders, many of whom have relatively recently been confirmed for multiyear terms despite advanced age (including the 94-year-old Fidel Velázquez, none is younger than 70), are openly referred to by some both inside and outside the labor movement as "dinosaurs." They are viewed as unlikely to be able to adapt to the new circumstances. Through its autocratic leadership, labor has been coopted into supporting government austerity and reorganization plans despite reservations. Some observers consider that the unions, having acquiesced this long, may have lost the initiative in regaining lost ground. There is also concern that NAFTA will expose the weakened Mexican unions to unfavorable international scrutiny. Both the government and the young turks of labor have essentially been biding their time, waiting for the passing of the current old guard before attempting to renegotiate the role that labor plays in Mexican affairs.

This situation could change if union leadership seizes the opportunity to make its weight felt in the 1994 presidential election. Many credit organized labor, through both its overt and covert support, with providing President Salinas with his suspiciously thin margin of victory in the 1988 election, although, based on the limited role played by labor during his administration, many see him as having been inadequately grateful. And although the PRI relies heavily on the unions to do a lot of legwork and deliver votes around election time, labor was expected to play a lesser role in electing Luis Colosio in 1994.

Colosio's assassination in March 1994 and the PRI's scramble to find a substitute candidate radically altered the prevailing balance. Colosio had proved to be a relatively effective campaigner and had largely succeeded in becoming known and accepted on his own. Given the PRI's preponderant influence and the lack of a truly organized opposition, the campaign revolves around allowing voters to reach a comfort level with the candidate, and Colosio seemed to be well on his way toward election.

The new candidate, Ernesto Zedillo, has a lower recognition factor and less charisma than his predecessor, not to mention little time in which to establish himself and attain the requisite comfort level. He also lacks the support of many within the party, especially among the old guard. As a former Secretary of Education, Zedillo is also associated with the weakening of the national teacher's union, which is unlikely to endear him to organized labor. Some observers argue that without labor's active support and intervention, Zedillo could well become the first PRI candidate to lose the presidency. And labor could be in a position to demand major concessions as the price of backing the candidate.

The trend in Mexico has been away from the old-style way of doing business, and this shift has left traditional organized labor behind. However, things can and do change, and circumstances have given labor the opportunity to perhaps cut a deal to get back some of what it has lost.

Business Law

INTRODUCTION*

Mexico has revised many of its commercial laws and regulations, particularly as they relate to foreign business activities and investments. Many industries have been privatized and deregulated, and Mexico is now encouraging foreign investment through the provisions of a newly liberalized foreign investment law. Numerous government agencies impose a system of rules and regulations on trade within Mexico, many of which affect foreign businesses operating in the country. It is necessary to carefully investigate all current legal requirements that apply to your particular business activities, no matter how tangential they seem.

The information in this chapter is intended to emphasize the important issues in Mexican commercial law. It does not constitute legal advice, nor should it replace legal advice from a licensed attorney. As a civil code country, Mexico has a legal system based on statutes and regulations that are often highly specific. Be certain to review your business activities with an attorney familiar with international transactions, the laws of Mexico, and the laws of your own country. (Refer to the "Important Addresses" chapter for a list of law offices in Mexico.)

BASIS OF THE LEGAL SYSTEM

Mexico is a civil code country, which means that its legal system is founded on codified laws. Judicial decisions are based primarily on code provisions, not on precedent set by past decisions. A decision of Mexico's Supreme Court becomes binding on lower courts only after the Supreme Court has issued five opinions with the same finding on a point of law.

Mexico's legal system was originally derived from the Napoleonic Code. Until independence in 1821, Mexico was ruled by Spain, and therefore has a legal system heavily influenced by Spanish law.

The Introduction section is based on interviews with Timon L. Marshall, Carlsmith Ball Wichman Murray Case & Ichiki, Mexico City Branch Office; Adrian Zubikarai Arriola, Carlsmith Ball García Cacho Zubikarai y Asociados, S.C., Mexico City; Carlos Valderrama, Director of Latin American Operations for Carlsmith Ball Wichman Murray Case & Ichiki, Los Angeles, California; Manuel F. Pasero, Pasero, Martín-Sánchez y Sánchez, Tijuana, BC; John Mendez, White & Case, Los Angeles, California; and Kenneth R. Lee, White & Case, Mexico City Branch Office.

STRUCTURE OF GOVERNMENT AND LAWS

Mexico is a federal democratic republic, politically divided into the Federal District (Mexico City) plus 31 states. The government has three branches: the executive branch led by the president, a bicameral legislature consisting of an upper house (the Senate) and a lower house (the Chamber of Deputies), and a judiciary. Its highest federal court is the Supreme Court of Justice. Separate state governments are organized in a similar fashion, with a governor, legislature, and judiciary. A mayor, appointed by the President, presides over the Federal District.

Mexico's constitution is the supreme law of the land. Pursuant to constitutional authority, Mexico's federal and state legislatures enact and amend various civil, commercial, and other codes. Those codes are supplemented by regulations issued by various government departments and agencies. Mexico has also ratified numerous bilateral and multilateral international treaties and conventions. (*See* Treaties entry in the Law Digest in this chapter.)

LAWS GOVERNING BUSINESS

Foreign Investment and Companies Before doing business in Mexico, foreign corporations must register in the National Registry of Foreign Investment, as required by the 1993 Foreign Investment Law. Non-Mexican citizens who travel to Mexico on business, even on a temporary and informal basis, must comply with the Mexican Immigration Code, which requires them to obtain visas and other documents that legalize their presence in the country for purposes of conducting business.

Foreign investment in Mexico is restricted by Mexico's constitution, and is further regulated by the 1993 Foreign Investment Law. Mexico's constitution and laws also impose some limits on foreign ownership of real property.

Local and Foreign Companies The formation and operation of companies in Mexico are controlled primarily by the General Law of Commercial Companies. Government approval for formation is required, and most requests to open manufacturing operations in metropolitan areas are now being denied under policies designed to force industrial activity into less developed areas. Specific aspects of business operation are also governed by such laws as the Federal Fiscal Code, which mandates certain accounting procedures; the Law of Investment Companies, which regulates certain financial companies; and the Federal Labor Code, which sets forth requirements for labor relations, workplace safety, job training, and social security issues.

The Civil Code and General Law of Commercial Companies mandate that all individuals and entities involved in certain activities or transactions in Mexico must file with various registries, as appropriate. The general registry is the National Commercial Registry, maintained by the *Secretaría de Comercio y Fomento Industrial* (SECOFI). Other registries include the Importers and Exporters Registry and the Technological Entities Registry.

Commercial Activities Business transactions are governed generally by contract, agency, and remedy laws contained in the Civil Code. For commercial contracts between merchants, the Commercial Code applies, and its provisions are controlling whenever they conflict with the those of the Civil Code. Financial aspects of a transaction are regulated by decrees and regulations on foreign exchange, and by such specific laws as the Law of Credit Instruments and Transactions.

Mexico has some of the most advanced legislation in the world for protection of the environment. All new businesses that emit gases, odors, and solid or liquid particles into the atmosphere must file an environmental impact study (EIS) and demonstrate compliance with these laws. All firms currently operating in Mexico must conform as well. Mandatory treatment and recycling programs are being instituted. Enforcement and inspection measures are being beefed up. In Mexico, failure to comply with environmental laws and regulations results in closure or partial closure of a facility until the requirements are met. In 1992, 2,000 enforcement actions were pending; this number had risen to 20,000 by August of 1993, with nearly 2,000 plants shut down completely and 3,400 suffering partial closure.

The Mexican constitution prohibits monopolies, a provision that has been implemented through numerous laws and regulations, including the Organic Law on Monopolies, the Law on Economic Competition, and the Federal Law on Consumer Protection. In addition, Mexico's Foreign Trade Law prohibits unfair foreign trade practices. One of the government's key aims in enacting the Law on Economic Competition was to foster fair competition among businesses operating in Mexico, while preventing monopolistic and other anti-trust practices.

Legal methods for the collection of property include attachment (governed by the Commercial Code and Code of Civil Procedure) and execution (regulated by the Code of Civil Procedure). Mexico is a party to the UN Convention on Recognition and Enforcement of Foreign Arbitral Awards. A pledge of property as a means of securing a debt is allowed under the Civil Code, and foreclosure procedures are provided for in the Code of Civil Procedure. For commercial matters, prescriptive periods within which actions must be brought are defined in the Commercial Code, and for other matters, such periods are fixed by the civil code of the federal or state court having jurisdiction over the action.

Intellectual and Industrial Property Mexico offers considerable protection to foreigners and Mexican nationals for intellectual property under its copyright law. Patents, trademarks, and trade names are protected under the Law to Promote and Protect Industrial Property. In addition, Mexico has signed and ratified many international treaties affording protection for foreign-registered copyrights, patents, trademarks, and trade names.

GEOGRAPHICAL SCOPE OF LAWS

This chapter describes Mexican federal laws, which are national in scope and govern both the Federal District and all of the Mexican states. Each state also has its own laws, including a civil code, penal code, code of civil procedure, and a code of Criminal Procedure. The state codes are generally similar to the federal ones, but may vary in details. Therefore, the laws of the particular state in which you are doing business must always be checked for deviations from the federal requirements. Federal codes take precedence in instances of conflict.

PRACTICAL APPLICATION

Significant Legal Considerations Foreign business owners face primarily two legal barriers in conducting business in Mexico: government regulations and undeveloped areas of law.

As a civil law country, Mexico relies on statutes and regulations to govern persons doing business within its jurisdiction. As a result, knowledge of these statutes and regulations is essential. Mexico often requires authorizations and approvals from different agencies, each of which has its own established procedures and requirements, and which may overlap in areas of specific jurisdiction. To conduct commercial transactions in the country, nearly all business owners must file applications and registrations with several government agencies. Until they have received the proper certificates, licenses, permits, and other authorizing documents, businesspeople will generally be unable to undertake such activities as opening a business bank account or entering into a lease in Mexico. Knowledge of the rules and regulations is crucial; hiring a Mexican lawyer at an early stage of a business transaction can ease and accelerate the process considerably.

Mexico's commercial law is still developing in many areas. To conduct certain activities or make particular arrangements, you may need to rely on the opinions of various government agencies with respect to how a law or regulation may be applied or what may be the outcome of a proposed action. Your request for an opinion or approval of a particular action may need to be supported by authoritative legal arguments indicating that the question has not yet been addressed by Mexican law and further suggesting what the outcome would be under the laws of another country and why such an outcome would be appropriate in Mexico. For this reason, you can increase the chances of having a favorable outcome by consulting an attorney who has contacts with various agencies, who is knowledgeable international law, and who knows the procedures of the Mexican administration.

Role of Legal Counsel A remarkable transformation of the role of legal counsel in Mexican business transactions is underway. Although a large number of attorneys were in practice prior to the 1980s, few firms handled commercial transactions. During the past two decades, attorneys have played an increasingly significant role in Mexico's business community. Today commercial companies usually seek legal counsel in the early stages of a transaction, not just for opinions and advice, but for assistance in actually structuring, negotiating, and consummating the deal. The role of legal counsel has rapidly expanded as Mexican industries are privatized and deregulated, and has been further spurred by the passage of NAFTA. That treaty creates new opportunities for expanding the role of attorneys—particularly for law firms with Mexican, Canadian, and US clients—by reducing restrictions on foreign service firms, mandating the creation of a dispute arbitration system, and increasing protection for intellectual and industrial property rights.

Mexico has many licensed attorneys, and the overall quality of legal services is on a par with those available in most of the developed world. Firms are generally small in size, even in the major business venues. Companies involved in international trade with Mexico should retain at least one attorney who is knowledgeable in Mexican law and commercial transactions and who has bicultural or multicultural experience. Firms that deal with such transactions are located primarily in Mexico's commercial centers—Mexico City, Monterrey, and Guadalajara—and in Mexico–US border areas. Attorneys can often be contacted through referrals from foreign law firms with local offices in Mexico, the Mexico listings in Martindale-Hubbell's *International Lawyers*, embassies, and chambers of commerce. (Refer to the "Important Addresses" chapter.)

Many foreign companies operating in Mexico use both foreign and Mexican attorneys. Foreign attorneys are permitted to act as consultants in Mexico, but they may not practice law there; the practice of Mexican law is restricted to attorneys licensed in Mexico. A growing number of foreign law firms are establishing local offices in Mexico, some as consulting firms with branch offices, others as correspondents or joint ven-

LEGAL GLOSSARY

acceptance An unconditional assent to an offer or one conditioned on minor changes that do not affect material terms of the offer. *See* Counteroffer, Offer.

acknowledgment *See* Authentication.

agency The relationship between an agent and a principal. The agent represents and acts on behalf of the principal, who instructs and authorizes the agent to so act.

after sight A term in a financial instrument making the instrument payable a specified number of days after presentation or demand. Example: a bill of exchange payable 30 days after sight matures and becomes payable 30 days after the person for whom the bill is drawn (the drawee) presents it to a bank (the payee).

at sight A term in a financial instrument under which the instrument is payable on presentation or demand. Example: a bill of exchange that is payable at sight is payable at the time the person for whom the bill is drawn (the drawee) presents it to a bank (the payee).

attachment The legal process for seizing property before a judgment to secure the payment of damages if awarded. Attachment may be sought before commencing a court action or during the action. This process is also referred to as sequestration. Example: a party who claims damages for breach of contract may request a court to issue an order freezing all transfers of specific property owned by the breaching party pending resolution of the dispute.

authentication The act of conferring legal authenticity on a written document, typically made by a notary public, who attests and certifies that the document is in proper legal form and that it is executed by a person identified as having authority to do so. Authentication is also referred to as acknowledgment.

bill of exchange A written instrument signed by a person (the drawer) and addressed to another person (the drawee), typically a bank, ordering the drawee to pay unconditionally a stated sum of money to yet another person (the payee) on demand or at a future time.

counteroffer A reply to an offer that materially alters the terms of the offer. Example: a seller who accepts a buyer's offer on condition that the goods will be made of a different material has made a counteroffer. *See* Acceptance, Offer.

crossed check A check that bears on its face two parallel transverse lines, indicating that it cannot be presented for cash. A bank that accepts such a check will pay the proceeds only to another bank, which will credit the money to the account of the payee of the check.

execution The legal process for enforcing a judgment for damages, usually by seizure and sale of the debtor's personal property. Example: if a court awards damages in a breach of contract action and the breaching party fails to remit them, the party awarded damages may request the court to order seizure and sale of the breaching party's inventory to satisfy the award.

juridical act An action intended to have, and capable of having, a legal effect, such as the creation, termination, or modification of a legal right. Example: The signing of a power of attorney is a juridical act because it gives legal authority to an agent.

juridical person An individual or entity recognized under law as having legal rights and obligations. Example: limited liability companies, corporations, and partnerships are entities recognized as juridical persons.

negotiable instrument A written document transferable merely by endorsement or delivery. Example: a check or bill of exchange is a negotiable instrument.

offer A proposal that is made to a specific individual or entity to enter into a contract. The proposal must contain definite terms and must indicate the offeror's intent to be bound by an acceptance. Example: a buyer's order to purchase designated goods on certain delivery and payment terms is an offer. *See* Acceptance, Counteroffer.

power of attorney A written document by which one individual or entity (the principal) authorizes another individual or entity (the agent) to perform stated acts on the principal's behalf. Example: a principal may execute a special power of attorney (authorizing an agent to sign a specific contract) or a general power of attorney (authorizing the agent to sign all contracts for the principal). *See* Agency.

promoter of corporation The individual or entity that organizes a corporation.

rescind A contracting party's right to cancel the contract. Example: a contract may allow one party to rescind if the other party fails to perform within a reasonable time.

sequestration *See* Attachment.

statute of Frauds A law that requires designated documents to be in writing in order to be enforced by a court. Example: contracting parties may orally agree to transfer ownership of immovable property, but a court might not enforce that contract, and might not award damages for breach, unless the contract was written.

tures with Mexican law firms. These firms typically have alliance, referral, or other arrangements with Mexican law firms for work that requires local expertise and licenses. Such combined efforts are beneficial to clients in that a foreign attorney can advise on the international aspects of commercial and investment transactions, while a Mexican attorney, who knows the specific statutory and regulatory procedures and has contacts in various government agencies, can expedite the process in Mexico.

Contracts Historically, written contracts in a civil law country are short and contain few detailed provisions, because the business relationship is largely established by the nation's laws and regulations. Instead of emphasizing a single transaction, contracts in Mexico often define a general, continuing relationship between the parties. Accordingly, these contracts could be negotiated by the parties to the transaction, with perhaps some guidance from attorneys should an explanation of certain legal aspects be needed.

With the onslaught of international trade, business relationships in Mexico are beginning to display new facets. Contracts are becoming more complex in order to cover the needs of multicultural transactions that are not completely provided for in the nation's own legal system. Mexican business owners have become more adept at negotiating the details of transactions as they learn about protections that exacting contractual terms can offer when dealing in international markets.

Each party to a business contract should retain separate legal counsel as needed to complete the transaction. An attorney will very rarely advise both parties, because to do so raises concerns over conflict of interest.

Role of Notaries The notarial profession is an extremely important one in Mexican business circles, largely due to the tendency in Mexico's government and commercial community to emphasize formality. Verification by a *notario publico*—public notary—is needed for many documents, including agreements and deeds relating to the sale and purchase of property, corporate records, business registration applications, and documents that must be recorded or registered with a public agency. The *notario publico* is an attorney who is specially licensed to retranscribe, approve, and register such documents with appropriate government agencies.

Mexico also licenses *corredores públicos*, who are authorized to verify certain documents related to a more limited number of activities, such as maritime liens.

Dispute Resolution Parties involved in business disputes in Mexico are advised to avoid bringing lawsuits whenever possible. Despite increasing reliance on Mexico's legal system to settle disputes, the general belief is that a dispute is best resolved privately and unofficially, not in a public courtroom. Few summary remedies are available to give immediate relief pending resolution of a dispute. The Mexican legal system tends to favor defendants, in that many procedures for delaying the proceedings are available to defendants at little cost or effort to them. The resulting litigation can be costly, protracted, and unsatisfying for the plaintiff. Moreover, if a dispute is made public, the Mexican government may choose to become involved, creating additional delays, expenses, and burdens for both parties, and ultimately may encourage the parties to settle their own differences without official interference.

When entering into any transaction, the parties should structure their agreement to provide for private dispute resolution. The agreement should be clear and precise with regard to: what each party's rights and obligations will be if the contract becomes impossible to perform; what happens if either or both parties breach the agreement; and whether either party can exercise a right to terminate. Such provisions should define such issues as how goods will be stored or returned, whether equipment and machinery can be dismantled and retrieved, and whether business operations must be suspended during a dispute.

Businesspeople must recognize that alternative dispute resolution (ADR) processes, such as mediation and arbitration, are new to Mexico. These are not yet well established, and parties to commercial transactions usually prefer to agree to strict contract clauses for private dispute resolution, to use private guarantee or insurance arrangements, or to litigate. Although ADR is being promoted in some circles and is used by some of the largest companies, the general legal and business community remains reluctant to submit disputes to ADR.

The parties may be able to agree to take unresolvable conflicts to an international arbitration board, although such procedures are costly. Mexico has accepted the UN Convention on Recognition and Enforcement of Foreign Arbitral Awards and various of the Inter-American Conventions, and the courts will recognize foreign judgments and arbitral awards, but authentication and litigation for recognition and enforcement can become a lengthy process in and of itself. Arbitration is being encouraged under NAFTA, which mandates the establishment of an arbitration system to deal with NAFTA-related issues, and a new mediation program is being implemented by Bancomext, the quasi-official national foreign trade development bank. In line with NAFTA, Mexico's president has introduced an initiative proposing statutory amendments that would set up a framework for arbitration of international commercial disputes outside the federal court system. However, we emphasize that the acceptance of ADR is expected to spread slowly.

THE INTERNATIONAL TRANSACTION: BASICS OF A ONE-TIME SALE*

When dealing internationally, you must consider the business practices and legal requirements of the country where the buyer or seller is located. Parties generally have the freedom to agree to any contract terms that they desire, but the laws of your country or the foreign country may require a written contract. In some transactions, the laws may even specify all or some of the contract terms. Whether a contract term is valid in a particular country is mainly of concern if you may have to seek enforcement. Otherwise, you have fairly broad flexibility in negotiating contract provisions. However, you should always be certain to come to a definite understanding with the other party on four basic issues: the goods (quantity, type, and quality); the time of delivery; the price; and the time and means of payment.

For a small, one-time sale, an invoice or a simple contract may be acceptable. For a more involved business transaction or an ongoing relationship, a formal written contract is preferable in order to define clearly the rights, responsibilities, and remedies of all parties. Contracts that involve capital goods, high credit risks, or industrial or intellectual property rights will require special protective clauses. In preparing such contracts, it is essential to obtain legal advice from a professional who is familiar with the laws and practices of both countries.

For a simple, one-time deal you need to consider at least the following clauses:

Contract date

Specify the date when the contract is signed. This date is particularly important if payment or delivery times are fixed in reference to it—for example, "shipment within 30 days of the contract date."

Identification of parties

Name the parties, describe their relation to each other, and designate the persons who are authorized to act for each party. The persons designated should also be the ones who sign the contract. If performance of the agreement extends beyond a single transaction, the person's authority to act for the Mexican company will have to be established additionally by a copy of a statement of capacity certified by a government official in the Mexican state of the Mexican party and by a corporate resolution of the Mexican company's board of directors. The Mexican company may require similar certified proof of authority on the part of the person acting for the foreign company. The parties should agree at the beginning on the documents that will be considered satisfactory evidence of authority.

Goods

Description Describe the type and quality of the goods. You may simply indicate a model number, or you may have to attach detailed lists, plans, drawings, or other specifications. This clause should be clear enough that both parties fully understand the specifications and have no discretion in interpreting them.

Quantity Specify the number of units, or other measure of quantity, of the goods. If the goods are measured by weight, you should specify net weight, dry weight, or drained weight. If the goods are prepackaged and are subject to weight restrictions in the end market, you may want to ensure that the seller will provide goods packaged to comply with those restrictions.

Price Indicate the price per unit or other measure, such as per pound or ton, and the extended price.

Packaging arrangements

Set forth packaging specifications, especially for goods that can be damaged in transit. At a minimum, this provision should require the seller to package the goods in such a way as to withstand transportation. If special packaging requirements are necessary to meet consumer and product liability standards in the end market, you should specify them also.

Transportation arrangements

Carrier Name a preferred carrier for transporting the goods. You should designate a particular carrier if, for example, a carrier offers you special pricing or is better able than others to transport the product.

Storage Specify any particular requirements for storage of the goods before or during shipment, such as security arrangements, special climate demands, and weather protection needs.

Notice provisions Require the seller to notify the buyer when the goods are ready for delivery or pickup, particularly if the goods are perishable or fluctuate in value. If your transaction is time-sensitive, you could even provide for several notices to allow the buyer to track the goods and take steps to minimize damages if delivery is delayed.

Shipping time State the exact date for shipping or provide for shipment within a reasonable time from the contract date. If this clause is included and the seller fails to ship on time, the buyer may claim a right to cancel the contract, even if the goods have been shipped, provided

*Reviewed by John R. Liebman, a member of the law firm of Brown, Winfield & Canzoneri, Incorporated, Los Angeles, California.

that the buyer has not yet accepted delivery.

Costs and charges

Specify which party is to pay any additional costs and charges related to the sale.

Duties and taxes Designate the party that will be responsible for import, export, and other fees and taxes and for obtaining all required licenses. For example, a party may be made responsible for paying the duties, taxes, and charges imposed by that party's own country, since that party is best situated to know the legal requirements of that country.

Insurance costs Identify the party that will pay costs of insuring the goods in transit. This is a critical provision because the party responsible bears the risk if the goods are lost during transit. A seller is typically responsible for insurance until title to the goods passes to the buyer, at which time the buyer becomes responsible for insurance or becomes the named beneficiary under the seller's insurance policy.

Handling and transport Specify the party that will pay shipping, handling, packaging, security, and any other costs related to transportation, which should be specified.

Terms defined Contracts for the sale of goods most commonly use Incoterms—as defined by the International Chamber of Commerce in Paris—to assign responsibility for the risks and cost of transport. (Refer to the "International Payments" chapter for explanations of the Incoterms.)

Insurance or risk of loss protection

Specify the insurance required, the beneficiary of the policy, the party who will obtain the insurance, and the date by which it will have been obtained.

Payment provisions

In a one-time transaction, the seller will typically seek the most secure form of payment before committing to shipment, while a buyer will want the goods cleared through customs and delivered in satisfactory condition before remitting full payment. If payments cannot be made in advance, parties most often agree to use documentary credits. (Refer to the "International Payments" chapter for an explanation of such payments.)

Method of payment State the means by which payment will be tendered—for example, delivery of a documentary letter of credit or documents against payment; prepayment in cash or traveler's checks; or credit for a specified number of days.

Medium of exchange Designate the currency to be used—for example, US currency, currency of the country

of origin, or currency of a third country.

Exchange rate Specify a fixed exchange rate for the price stated in the contract. You may use this clause to lock in a specific price and ensure against fluctuating currency values.

Import documentation

Designate the documents for exporting and importing that each party will be responsible for obtaining, completing, and presenting to customs. Shipment of the goods, and even the contract itself, may be made contingent on a party's having obtained in advance the proper licenses, inspection certificates, and other authorizations. (Refer to the chapters "Import Policies & Procedures" and "Export Policies & Procedures" for further discussion of these requirements.)

Inspection rights

Provide that the buyer has a right to inspect goods before taking delivery to determine whether the goods meet the contract specifications. This clause should specify the person who will do the inspection—for example, the buyer, a third party, or a licensed inspector; the location where the inspection will occur—for example, at the seller's plant, the buyer's warehouse, or a receiving dock; the time at which the inspection will occur; the presentation of a certified document of inspection, if needed; and any requirements related to the return of nonconforming goods, such as payment of return freight by the seller.

Warranty provisions

Limit or extend any implied warranties, and define any express warranties on property fitness and quality. The contract may, for example, state that the seller warrants that the goods are of merchantable quality, are fit for any purpose for which they would ordinarily be used, or are fit for a particular purpose requested by the buyer. The seller may also warrant that the goods will be of the same quality as any sample or model that the seller has furnished as representative of the goods. Finally, the seller may warrant that the goods will be packaged in a specific way or in a way that will adequately preserve and protect the goods.

Indemnity

Agree that one party will hold the other harmless from damages that arise from specific causes, such as the design or manufacture of a product.

Enforcement and Remedies

Time is of the essence Stipulate that timely performance of the contract is essential. In the US, inclusion of this clause allows a party to claim breach merely because

THE INTERNATIONAL TRANSACTION: BASICS OF A ONE-TIME SALE (cont'd.)

the other party fails to perform within the time prescribed in the contract. Although common in US contracts, a clause of this type is considered less important in other countries.

Modification Require the parties to make all changes to the contract in advance and in a signed written modification.

Cancellation State the reasons for which either party may cancel the contract and the notice required for cancellation.

Contingencies Specify any events that must occur before a party is obligated to perform the contract. For example, you may agree that the seller has no duty to ship goods until the buyer forwards documents that secure the payment for the goods.

Governing law Choose the law of a specific jurisdiction to control any interpretation of the contract terms. The law that you choose will usually affect where you can sue or enforce a judgment and what rules and procedures will be applied.

Choice of forum Identify the place where a dispute may be settled—for example, the country of origin of the goods, the country of destination, or a third country that is convenient to both parties.

Arbitration provisions Although not yet a common remedy in Mexico, arbitration can be used as an alternative to litigation for the resolution of disputes that arise. You should

agree to arbitrate only if you seriously intend to settle disputes in this way. If you agree to arbitrate but later file suit, the court is likely to uphold the arbitration clause and force you to settle your dispute as you agreed under the contract.

An arbitration clause should specify whether arbitration is binding or nonbinding on the parties; the country where arbitration will be conducted (which should be Mexico or another country that has adopted the UN Convention on Recognition and Enforcement of Foreign Awards or a similar convention); the procedure for enforcement of an award; the rules governing the arbitration, such as the UN Commission on International Trade Law Model Rules; the institute that will administer the arbitration, such as the International Chamber of Commerce (Paris); the law that will govern procedural issues or the merits of the dispute; any limitations on the selection of arbitrators (for example, a national of a disputing party may be excluded from being an arbitrator); the qualifications or expertise of the arbitrators; the language in which the arbitration will be conducted; and the availability of translations and translators if needed.

Severability Provide that individual clauses can be removed from the contract without affecting the validity of the contract as a whole. This clause is important because it provides that, if one clause is declared invalid and unenforceable for any reason, the rest of the contract remains in force.

Property Infringement Concerns Mexico has long recognized the need for property protection rights as an incentive to encourage foreign investment. Strong federal laws protect intellectual and industrial property rights—including patents, copyrights, trademarks, and trade names—and it is a signatory to many international treaties that secure these rights.

Mexico has no copyright filing requirements. Automatic copyright protection is extended once copyrightable material is published in any nation that is a member of the Berne Copyright Convention. However, a person who files for copyright protection in Mexico enjoys more legal protection and the right to damages for infringement under Mexican law. Copyrights are filed with the *Dirección de Derechos de Autor*—the Copyright Department—of the Secretariat of Public Education.

Patents may be registered in Mexico, but only if the invention is still secret when the application is filed. Filing a patent application for a simple invention will usually cost much less—in the range of US$3,000 to US$5,000—than for complex ones, such

as pharmaceuticals, which may cost US$10,000 or more. These figures include government filing fees, official translation and notary fees, and attorney fees.

A trademark or trade name must be registered with the Secretariat of Industrial Products in Mexico before it is used there. Registration requires filing a form with the Secretariat, which is best accomplished through an attorney. Filing and attorney fees can run in the thousands of US dollars because of required formalities, such as the need to obtain notarized documents, authentication from home country officials, and approval from the Mexican consulate. The registration procedure can take as long as a year and a half.

Protections are being extended to trade secrets and strengthened for manufacturing process, pharmaceutical, and medical patents. Enforcement of these laws is becoming stricter, particularly since the advent of NAFTA, which requires better enforcement and allows for injunctions as a means of relief during infringement claims. A separate agency has been created to focus solely on these rights. Even

THE US FOREIGN CORRUPT PRACTICES ACT

US business owners are subject to the Foreign Corrupt Practices Act (FCPA). The FCPA makes it unlawful for any US citizen or firm (or any person who acts on behalf of a US citizen or firm) to use a means of US interstate commerce (examples: mail, telephone, telegram, or electronic mail) to offer, pay, transfer, promise to pay or transfer, or authorize a payment, transfer, or promise of money or anything of value to any foreign appointed or elected official, foreign political party, or candidate for a foreign political office for a corrupt purpose (that is, to influence a discretionary act or decision of the official) for the purpose of obtaining or retaining business.

It is also unlawful for a US business owner to make such an offer, promise, payment, or transfer to any person if the US business owner knows, or has reason to know, that the person will give, offer, or promise directly or indirectly all or part of the payment to a foreign government official, political party, or candidate. For purposes of the FCPA, the term "knowledge" means both "actual knowledge"—the business owner in fact knew that the offer, payment, or transfer was included in the transaction—and "implied knowledge"—the business owner should have known from the facts and circumstances of a transaction that the agent paid a bribe, but failed to carry out a reasonable investigation into the transaction. A business owner should make a reasonable investigation into the transaction if, for example, the sales representative requests a higher commission on a particular deal for no apparent reason, the buyer is a foreign government, the product has a military use, or the buyer's country is one in which bribes are considered customary in business relationships.

The FCPA also contains provisions applicable to US publicly held companies concerning financial recordkeeping and internal accounting controls.

Legal Payments

The provisions of the FCPA do not prohibit payments made to facilitate routine government action; a facilitating payment is one made in connection with an action that a foreign official must perform as part of the job. In comparison, a corrupt payment is made to influence an official's discretionary decision. For example, payments would not generally be considered corrupt if made to cover an official's overtime if such overtime is necessary to expedite the processing of export documentation for a legal shipment of merchandise or to cover the expense of additional crew to handle a shipment.

A person charged with violating FCPA provisions may assert as a defense that the payment was lawful under the written laws and regulations of the foreign country and therefore was not for a corrupt purpose. Alternatively, a person may contend that the payment was associated with demonstrating a product or performing a pre-existing contractual obligation and therefore was not for obtaining or retaining business.

Enforcing Agencies and Penalties

Criminal Proceedings The US Department of Justice prosecutes criminal proceedings for FCPA violations. Firms are subject to a fine of up to US$2 million. Officers, directors, employees, agents, and stockholders are subject to fines of up to US$100,000, imprisonment for up to five years, or both.

A US business owner may also be charged under other federal criminal laws. On conviction, the owner may be liable for one of the following: (1) a fine of up to US$250,000; or (2) if the owner derived pecuniary gain from the offense or caused a pecuniary loss to another person, a fine of up to twice the amount of the gross gain or loss.

Civil Proceedings Two agencies are responsible for enforcing civil provisions of the FCPA: the Department of Justice handles actions against domestic concerns, and the Securities and Exchange Commission (SEC) files actions against issuers. Civil fines of up to US$100,000 may be imposed on a firm, or on any officer, director, employee, agent, or stockholder acting for a firm. In addition, the appropriate government agency may seek an injunction against a person or firm that has violated or is about to violate FCPA provisions.

Conduct that constitutes a violation of FCPA provisions may also give rise to a cause of action under the federal Racketeer-Influenced and Corrupt Organizations Act (RICO), as well as under similar state statutes if such exist in a state with jurisdiction over the US business.

Administrative Penalties A person or firm that is held to have violated any FCPA provisions may be barred from doing business with the US government. Indictment alone may result in suspension of the right to do business with the government.

Department of Justice Proceedings

Any person may request the Department of Justice to issue a statement of opinion on whether specific proposed business conduct would be considered a violation of the FCPA. The opinion procedure is detailed in 28 CFR Part 77. If the Department of Justice issues an opinion stating that certain conduct conforms with current enforcement policy, conduct in accordance with that opinion is presumed to comply with FCPA provisions.

with all these protections, businesspeople should insist on protective contractual provisions that clearly establish ownership of such rights and set forth private remedies a party may pursue for enforcing those rights before resorting to litigation or other means of government enforcement.

RELATED SECTIONS

Refer to the chapters "Personal Taxation" and "Corporate Taxation" for a discussion of tax issues in Mexico; "Business Entities & Formation" for a description of the business forms recognized in Mexico and organizational procedures; "Foreign Investment" for a discussion of provisions and regulations; "Labor" for employment rules and standards; and "Import Policy & Procedures" and "Export Policy & Procedures" for discussions of rules involved in trade.

LAW DIGEST*

(Abbreviations used are: C.C., Civil Code of Federal District; Com. C., Commercial Code; C.C.P., Code of Civil Procedure of Federal District. References are to articles of these Codes.)

ACKNOWLEDGMENTS

Certificates of acknowledgment are unknown in Mexican law, since all documents which in the United States would ordinarily require a certificate of acknowledgment are executed before a notary public who certifies in the instrument itself to the facts which, in the United States, are usually expressed in a certificate of acknowledgment.

Documents executed in the United States should be acknowledged in the usual manner if they are to be used in Mexico. A certificate of the county clerk or other competent official as to the power of the notary to take the acknowledgment should be attached and a certificate of a Mexican consular or diplomatic officer should then be obtained to the effect that the signature of the county clerk or other official is authentic and that he is qualified to act. When the Minister of Foreign Relations of Mexico has attached a certificate regarding the qualifications of the consular or diplomatic officer the document may be recorded in the protocol of a Mexican notary by order of a competent court and is then duly recognized.

ALIENS

According to Constitution of 1917 aliens have same individual guarantees as citizens.

Legal Rights for Foreigners to Reside in Mexico Under Mexican Constitution and laws enacted in accordance with it, every person is accorded right to enter and depart from Mexico, to travel in its territory, and to make changes of residence without need for authorization or documentation of any kind.

In practice, however, exercise of these rights is subordinated to limitations imposed by immigration, population, and public health laws of Republic as well as to authority of Federal Executive summarily to ban or eject from country any foreigner whom government considers to be "persona non grata."

Migration to Mexico or entry for any purpose other than tourism is fraught with restrictions arising from statutes, administrative regulations, and internal policy. Latter, as fixed by Secretariat of Interior (*Secretaría de Gobernación*), General Bureau of Population (*Dirección General de Población*), and Department of Immigration (*Departamento de Migración*), is not always written.

Mexican Immigration Code is federal [and] administered and enforced through Secretariat of Interior (*Gobernación*), which also is charged with responsibility for civil peace and tranquillity of nation.

Another important power relating to foreigners stems from Art. 33 of Constitution under which President of United Mexican States is clothed with exclusive authority to deport summarily any alien from national territory without hearing if in judgment of Federal Executive his presence in Mexico is deemed disadvantageous ("*inconveniente*") for nation.

In contrast, Ministry of Interior in moving to expel alien must act on finding of fact and one that falls within causes for expulsion set out in General Law of Population (*Ley General de Población*). These are that alien has entered country illegally; hidden his previous expulsion (if any); failed to obey previous order from Ministry to leave country; committed illicit or dishonest act; concealed or been accomplice to concealment of alien who has committed any of previously described acts; claimed immigration status different from that actually possessed; or made false declaration in order to enter or remain in Mexico.

Immigration Categories Fact that alien is subject to these administrative proceedings points to differences between status of foreigner and that of citizen.

General Law of Population establishes three general categories under which aliens may enter Mexico temporarily, or reside here as case may be, namely: (a) Nonimmigrant (*"no-inmigrante"*), (b) immigrant (*"inmigrante"*), and (c) one who has immigrated (*"inmigrado"*).

Letters and numbers following Spanish designation of each sub-category is pertinent form number used to document status.

Nonimmigrant Status ("No-Inmigrante")* Nine sub-categories included under this general heading are following:

[1. Tourist (*"Turista"* F.M.T.) status.]

[2. Individual in Transit (*"Transmigrante"* F.M. 6) status.]

3. Visitor (*"Visitante"* F.M. 3) status is provided for individual whose purpose is to enter Mexico temporarily to engage in licit and honest activity for which he may be remunerated from source in Mexico or abroad. Such permit is granted for six months, and is renewable for another six months. However, if holder depends upon his own resources with which to live and which he has brought with him from outside of Mexico or from invested income generated by assets brought in and invested here or from any other income which has foreign origin; or if his activity in Mexico is of scientific, technical, or artistic nature; or if it pertains to sports (professional athlete is usually documented as *visitante*), or similar activity, then his *visitante* status pursuant to strict interpretation of law may be extended for two renewals of six months each. Therefore, visitor status has potential for 12 to 18 months.

However, immigration authorities have been regularly extending *visitante* permits described in this paragraph for three periods of six months each without distinction, which augments holder's potential stay here to 24 months under same immigration papers.

4. Foreign Members of board of directors (*"Consejero"* F.M. 3) of Mexican corporation entering to participate in board meeting may be granted visitors permit useful for attendance at such meeting or for purpose of rendering services in advisory capacity as well as to carry out temporary functions which are peculiar to his particular capabilities. This temporary authorization is good only for six months; it may not be extended. It may also provide for multiple entries and departures but no given sojourn in Mexico by holder of this status may exceed 30 days nor may document have life longer than six months. Similar document under like condition may be issued to shareholder in Mexican corporation desiring to attend shareholders meeting here.

[5. Political Asylum status.]

[6. Student status.]

7. Distinguished Visitor (*"Visitante Distinguido"* F.M. 3) status is granted in special cases and in exceptional instances as matter of courtesy enabling recipient to enter and reside in Mexico; and its validity may run up to six months. This status may also be granted to those who are internationally recognized for their work in research or science, or in humanities, or to journalists or other prominent individuals. Secretariat of Interior may extend life of such permit where it is deemed advisable.

[8. Local Visitor (*"Visitante Local"* F.M. 3) status.]

[9. Provisional Visitor (*"Visitante Provisional"* F.M. 3) status.]

Immigrant Status ("Inmigrante") Under this category [the] following six sub-categories fall:

1. Individual Alien Sustained by Unearned Income (*"Rentista"* F.M. 2) sub-category is available to individual alien who is immigrating—intending to live permanently and to be domiciled in Mexico—who will rely for support upon resources brought with him into Mexico from outside country; from interest produced by investment here in certificates of deposit, credit instruments, and/or bonds issued by government or by national banking institution or other sources which may be approved by Secretariat of Interior or finally, other permanent income from foreign source. Ministry of Interior may authorize *"Inmigrante Rentista"* to render personal services as professor or as scientist or to engage in scientific research and to function as technician where it deems such activity to be beneficial to country.

2. Investor (*"Inversionista"* F.M. 2) sub-category is available to person immigrating to Mexico with intention to take up permanent domicile here bringing with him capital for investment in industry pursuant to Federal laws applicable to foreign investment and provided that investment contributes to economic and social development of nation and therefore is approved by Ministry.

3. Professional (*"Profesional"* F.M. 2) status is granted only in exceptional cases for purpose of permitting given individual to practice his profession here. However, he must first register his professional degree or diploma with Bureau of Professions, Secretariat of Public Education, which must find it acceptable and approve it.

4. Confidential Personnel (*"Cargos de Confianza"* F.M. 2) is classification applied to those individuals who are to serve in high level management capacity or other positions of trust and/or confidence in enterprise or institution established in Mexico, provided that in judgment of Secretariat of Interior there

---

*The North America Free Trade Agreement (NAFTA) has created four new nonimmigrant visa categories. Refer to the "Business Travel" chapter for discussion.

is no duplication in position or responsibility on staff of employer and that service which will be extended by given candidate for this status merits his being permitted to immigrate to Mexico.

Enterprise sponsoring individual seeking permit such as "*Inmigrante*" must have at least two-year operating history to qualify as such. *Gobernación* is empowered to make exemptions although seldom does so.

5. Scientist ("*Cientifico*" F.M. 2) status is granted to person who will direct or conduct scientific research, impart his scientific knowledge to others, prepare research personnel, and do some teaching provided such activities are being conducted in interest of national development, in judgment of Ministry of Interior.

6. Technician ("*Técnico*" F.M. 2) category is available to individual who is capable of carrying out applied research in field of production engaged in by his employer here or who is engaged to assume technical or special position provided capability required is not in judgment of Ministry of Interior available among current residents in country.

7. Family Members ("*Familiares*" F.M. 2) This status may be granted to dependent spouse of "*inmigrante*" or "*inmigrado*". Sons, daughters, nephews, grandchildren and brothers of "*inmigrante*" or "*inmigrado*" may also be admitted as "*inmigrante familiares*" as long as they are minors, unless they are students or if they are physically handicapped making it impossible for them to earn their livelihood.

One Who Has Immigrated ("*Inmigrado*" F.M. 2) Each immigrant must renew his status at Ministry of Interior annually. At end of fifth year "*inmigrante*" is eligible to become "*inmigrado*" (one who has immigrated and acquired right to reside permanently in Mexico). In each case, however, applicant's situation is subject to review and appraisal by Ministry and every applicant must be specifically approved for this change in status. Neither annual renewals of "*inmigrante*" status nor final move to become "*inmigrado*" is automatically granted.

Under category "*inmigrado*" there are no sub-categories. "*Inmigrado*" is permitted to engage in any licit vocational activity anywhere in Republic (usually with exception of working as bartender).

"*Inmigrado*" may be absent from Mexico during 24 consecutive months without losing his or her status. Physical absence from Mexico in excess of 24 consecutive months results in forfeiture of said status; furthermore, accumulated absences in excess of five years over 10-year period also cause extinction of status.

Immigration Status for Business Purposes—Foreign businessman may be documented in one of three ways pursuant to Immigration Code. First two are both in "*visitante*" sub-category and they differ not

so much in defined legal status as in nature of business activity that they authorize holder to carry out. Third is "*inmigrante*."

Visitante Permit First Type (F.M. 3): In general activity permitted under this first "*visitante*" type is more ephemeral and of simpler nature than that in second to be described subsequently.

This type of permit should be petitioned for when individual is entering Mexico for any of following purposes: (a) to engage in conversations and conferences of business nature; (b) to inspect commodities or merchandise being purchased here; (c) to arrange for shipment of merchandise from Mexico; (d) to study possibility and/or availability of making investment in Mexico; (e) to carry out technical assignment such as adjustment, repair, or installation of equipment; (f) to attend meeting of shareholders of Mexican corporation.

"*Visitante*" permit for all above purposes with exception of purpose (e) is valid for six months. Such permits are no longer renewable, however, as was previously possible except in case of purpose (e). An (e) permit is issued initially for only 30 days but it may be amplified to run for six months.

No one holding "*visitante*" permit under any of above situations may execute contracts or negotiate orders for foreign principal. Nor may any of them render services directly to Mexican enterprise. Their remuneration must be sourced outside of Mexico and they may not perform any activity in Mexico other than that described in their immigration document.

This type of permit is most frequently used in case of foreign business representatives entering Mexico to confer with actual or intended Mexican associates to conduct preliminary market survey, or to visit subsidiary or affiliate company. It is extremely convenient that such permit can be issued by career Consuls of Mexico abroad without necessity of referring application to Ministry of Interior in Mexico City for approval, thus making it usually quite readily available.

Form F.M. 3 which is issued to document this "*visitante*" status describes in its body, when properly prepared by issuing official, precise activity permitted to holder once in Mexico. Document may be issued for multiple entries and departures, and this should be requested in application; otherwise it may be issued for single entry and departure only. No limit is imposed on time that may be spent outside of Mexico during period for which permit is valid.

Visitante Permit Second Type (F.M. 3): Application for "visitante" permit of second type must be petitioned for directly to Mexico City. In theory application can be lodged with Mexican career Consul abroad who is expected to forward it to Ministry of Foreign Relations for transmittal to Bureau of Immigration, Ministry of Interior for processing. As practical matter proceeding in that manner seldom produces requisite documentation for admission to Mexico.

This second category permit is appropriate when intended activity is more continuing than in first type and of such nature that it would normally be remunerative in Mexico, whether or not payment is actually made from Mexican source. There is no possibility of immigrating to Mexico on permanent basis, or of accepting specific position or of becoming functionary in Mexican business enterprise with this documentation. This F.M. 3 is renewable for two successive periods of six months but again as matter of policy such permits are being renewed by authorities three times for six-month period each. In effect it enables holder to remain in Mexico for as much as two years. Holder must be physically in Mexico at time each renewal is processed.

Three purposes illustrate kind of business visit for which this document is appropriate: (a) to carry out business activity, industrial or technical in nature, not limited to simple conversations or studies, and including negotiation and/or execution of contracts; (b) to enter direct employment of Mexican enterprise for limited time in any field, with provision that holder is strictly limited to engage only in activity authorized by his official immigration document; (c) to attend board of directors and/or shareholders' meeting of Mexican corporation.

Only holder of "*visitante*" permit of second type who is head of family may obtain documentation for his wife and minor children et al., to enter as "*visitantes familiares.*" Law no longer makes specific provision for "*visitantes familiares*" as it previously did.

Juridical persons (companies or corporations) and individual entrepreneurs sponsoring application for "*visitante*" permit to enable holder to render personal services to sponsor should as practical matter have capital subscribed and paid-in or investment in business concerned, of not less than 150,000 pesos. Neither statutes nor regulations state any such minimum, but lesser amount gives Bureau of Immigration pause in reviewing case for approval and raises question of bona fide nature of sponsor.

In neither of two types of "*visitante*" permits, to repeat, will holder be granted authority to carry corporate title or to accept particular position (unless it be as member of board of directors of Mexican corporation). In case of need, however, even though holder has no title he may receive and act under general or special power of attorney from his Mexican employer authorizing performance of administrative acts. Secretariat of Interior resists documenting "*visitante*" with title in his immigration papers because to do so, it is reasoned, would not be consistent with fact that permit (and consequently stay in Mexico of permit holder) is of temporary nature.

Immigrant Status ("Inmigrante" F.M. 2) Only subcategory No. 4 (*Cargos de Confianza*), No. 5 (*Científico*),

and No. 6 (*Técnico*) of seven enumerated above are relevant to this detailed consideration. These are subcategories that should be sought by foreigners intending to take up residence in Mexico for extended period of time to act: (a) in position of confidence or particular trust, (b) in principal executive capacity, (c) in directing or conducting research or instructing and in preparing research personnel, or (d) in permanent or semi-permanent technical capacity.

Conditions under which permit will be granted and renewed vary as between types of activity. For example, to act in technical capacity, applicant must possess capability not readily available in Mexico and services of applicant must be demonstrably needed for long term.

Furthermore, as condition for annual renewal of "*inmigrante*" papers of technician, he must be training at least three Mexicans in his specialty (same condition for renewal may be imposed on technicians documented as "*visitante*"). Differences also exist as between technical personnel and other two categories in granting permits for employment in newly-established companies with less than two-year operating record. While *tecnico* will probably be issued "*inmigrante*" documentation, executives and confidential personnel may have to resort to "*visitante*" status during first two years.

Sponsoring employer company in Mexico of "*inmigrante*" must satisfy more onerous conditions than sponsors of "*visitantes.*"

Administration of Immigration Law Granting of any immigration status, and issue of relevant documentation, are within discretion of Secretariat of Interior; they are not issued as matter of right. *Gobernación* may deny aliens entry into Mexico or change of immigration status after entry when: (1) no reciprocity exists in matters of immigration between Mexico and country of applicant; (2) demographic interchange between Mexico and country of applicant is not in equilibrium; (3) quotas based on nationality, immigration category, or vocational activities as fixed by Ministry of Interior have been filled; (4) granting of permit is deemed not to be in national interest; (5) conduct of applicant has not been in keeping with "morality and good customs"; (6) applicant has infringed Mexican law or regulation.

Given this discretionary element, kinship with Mexican citizen, whether by birth or marriage, lends significant weight to application for "*inmigrante*" status.

ATTACHMENT

Attachments may be granted either before commencing an action or during the course of the same, in the following cases: (1) when there is reason to fear the defendant will abscond or conceal himself; (2) in an action in rem when it is feared that the defendant will conceal or injure the property; (3) in an action in personam when the defendant has no property other than that which is to be attached and it is feared that he will conceal or alienate it.

The plaintiff must prove his right to and the necessity for the attachment.

If the attachment is granted before the action is commenced, the plaintiff must give bond and the action must be begun within three days if the action is brought in the same place as the attachment is levied, plus an additional day for every 20 kilometers if brought in another place. (Com. C. 1168-93).

Certain documents entitle the holder to bring what is termed an executive action, in which case the plaintiff is entitled, as a matter of right, to attach the defendant's property. He may also be entitled to this right as a precautionary measure, as noted above. The following entitle the holder to executive action and consequently to attachment: (1) an executive judgment or nonappealable award; (2) public instruments (*see* Public Instruments); (3) judicial confession of the debtor; (4) bills of exchange, drafts, notes, orders, and other commercial paper, providing, however, that such instruments are properly executed (*see* Bills and Notes); (5) policies of insurance; (6) awards of experts designated in insurance matters if given before a notary, if not so given, a judicial declaration of the experts, acknowledging their signatures and genuineness of the award, must first be had; (7) invoices, current accounts, and any other commercial contract signed and judicially recognized by the debtor. (Com. C. 1391; C.C.P., art. 443).

CONTRACTS

In area of contracts as in other branches of civil law distinction between commercial and civil transactions must be continually borne in mind. Commercial Code contains special rules governing commercial contracts, principal purpose of which is to simplify procedure. Commercial Code provides that in mercantile transactions parties are bound in manner and terms upon which they appear to have obligated themselves and that validity of commercial transactions does not depend upon observance of definite formalities and requisites except: (1) in cases where code requires an agreement to be in form of a public document (for example, articles of association of a corporation or partnership) or where special formality or solemnity is required to render it effective (as, for example, bills of exchange); and (2) that in case of agreements executed in foreign countries they must comply with formalities required in country of execution regardless of whether or not such formalities are required in Mexico. (Com. C. 78, 79). Commercial contracts may be evidenced by correspondence, contract being complete from time offer is accepted and by

telegrams if that class of document has been agreed upon in writing between parties and if telegrams conform with conditions and conventional signs, if any, previously agreed upon. (Com. C. 80). Certain classes of commercial contracts are not perfected until a record of them is made before registered broker who is a sort of commercial notary (*corredor*). (Com. C. 82).

With modifications and restrictions established by Commercial Code, provisions of civil law governing civil contracts as they relate to capacity of parties, exceptions and causes which rescind or invalidate contracts, are applicable to commercial contracts. (Com. C. 81).

If contract consists of offer and acceptance made at different places, and time within which acceptance must take place is not stated in offer, offer is considered as remaining open and offerer bound for three days in addition to time necessary for regular passage of mail between two places or time deemed sufficient in case there are no public mails taking into account distances and facility or difficulty of communication, unless there is a mistake relating to fundamental motive of one of parties. If an acceptance is not absolute it is considered as a new offer. Contracts are void for mistake of law. Mistake of arithmetic is only subject to correction. (C.C. 1803-1823).

Certain contracts must be in writing, such as contracts agreeing to make a future contract, sales of real estate, leases, pledges, mortgages, etc. Writing must be in form of public instrument depending on value of real property sold or mortgaged calculated according to formula set forth in C.C. Also public instrument is required in lease of rural property when lease exceeds value set forth in C.C. (C.C. 1832, 2317-2320, 2406, 2407, 2860, 2917. *See* Public Instruments). Reference is made to Civil Code of various jurisdictions for provisions of law with regard to interpretation of contracts, classes of obligations, performance, extinction of obligations, rescission, etc., and special classes of contracts such as suretyship, pledge, bailments, loans, insurance, sales, leases, etc.

CORPORATIONS (SOCIEDADES ANÓNIMAS)

Caveat: as to corporations which have foreign participation, certain special requirements must be met.

Provisions relating to corporations are found largely in General Law of Commercial Companies, of July 28, 1934 as amended.

Special permit from Department of Foreign Relations is required to organize any corporation. (Law of Dec. 31, 1925, and Regulations of Mar. 22, 1926, as amended by Decree of June 29, 1944).

Name of Mexican corporation may be freely chosen, but words "*Sociedad Anónima*" or abbreviation "S.A." must appear at end of corporate name.

Organization Corporations are formed either by public subscription or by articles of incorporation.

Public Subscription In case of formation by public subscription, the promoters must file in Public Registry of Commerce a prospectus signed by them, all shares must be subscribed within one year from date of prospectus unless shorter period is fixed therein, [and if] capital stock is not subscribed, or for any other reason constitution of company is not concluded, subscribers are released and entitled to recover amounts paid in.

Articles of Incorporation When public subscription is not resorted to, it is sufficient that articles of incorporation be executed as a public document by incorporators. Articles of incorporation and amendments must be recorded in Commercial Registry on judicial order; petition must be filed before competent judge and summary proceeding follows.

Shares of Stock are generally of equal value and confer equal rights; but articles of incorporation may provide for different classes of shares with special rights for each class. Each share has one vote; but it may be agreed that some of the shares can be voted only at special meetings called for extraordinary purposes stated in law, such as increase or reduction of capital, changes of object, bond issues, etc.

Shares with limited voting power must be reimbursed in preference to common shares in case of liquidation of company, and their holders have right to oppose resolutions of stockholders' meetings and to examine balance sheets and books of company.

No shares may be offered for sale to public without an authorization from Federal Government, unless shares are listed in a stock exchange.

Corporations are allowed, when articles of incorporation so authorize, to issue "workers' shares" (*acciones de trabajo*) and "participating shares" (*acciones de goce*). Former may be issued to employees of company under special conditions and restrictions. Latter share in net profits after dividends have been paid on common shares.

Corporations cannot grant loans or advances on their own shares. Shares issued for property other than cash must be deposited with company during two years; if value of property then appears to be 25 percent less than its estimated value, shareholder is liable for difference and company has a preferred lien on deposited shares.

Management may be in hands of sole administrator or of board of directors elected by stockholders but who need not be stockholders. Law calls them *mandatorios*. There may also be managers appointed by stockholders or board of directors or sole administrator and removable by them at any time. Administrators, directors, and managers must furnish bond as determined in bylaws or by stockholders: administrators and directors are liable as agents and in manner provided by law and in bylaws; they are also responsible to company for faithful performance of their duties.

Supervision of affairs of company is in hands of one or more inspectors called "*comisarios*," who may, but need not, be shareholders and who are appointed by shareholders; they must give bond and their responsibility is similar to that of directors. *Comisarios* shall demand from board or managers financial monthly report.

Shareholders' Meetings are regular or special and are known as general assembly. They must be held at corporate domicile. Regular meetings are held at least once a year within four months after close of fiscal year. Special meetings may be held at any time to decide on matters specially enumerated by law, such as modification of articles of incorporation, bond issues, etc. At least half capital must be represented, and resolutions adopted by meeting are valid when taken by a majority of shares represented. At special meetings at least three-fourths of capital stock must be represented and resolutions must be approved by shareholders representing at least half capital stock.

Dividends may not be paid on common shares unless a dividend of 5 percent has been paid on shares having limited voting power. Articles of incorporation may provide that dividend on shares having limited voting power be larger than that on common shares. When shares are not fully paid, dividends may be paid only in proportion to part paid in. Bylaws may provide for payment, during a period not exceeding three years from date of respective issue, of interest not exceeding 9 percent per annum on shares; this interest is charged to general expenses.

Reserve Funds At least 5 percent of net earnings must be set aside each year as a legal reserve fund until such fund amounts to one-fifth of capital of company. Reserve fund must be built up in same manner if depleted.

Stockholders at general meeting are authorized to set aside not more than 10 percent of net earnings as a further reserve fund for reinvestment in improvements or for promotion of corporate purposes.

Bonds and Other Obligations issued by corporations are payable to designated person. Holders of obligations of same series must have equal rights. No issue may be made for an amount greater than net assets of corporation as shown in balance sheet specially prepared for that purpose, unless issue is intended to provide value or price of property for whose acquisition or construction corporation has contracted.

Law permits corporations to issue convertible bonds or debentures and then they may issue treasury stock to cover issue. This stock is not subject to preemptive rights.

In connection with issue corporation must execute an instrument before a notary public, which must be recorded at registry office of place where property mortgaged, if any, is located, and also at registry office of domicile of corporation.

Obligation-holders may sue corporation for payment of coupons, obligations due or drawn, or amortizations or reimbursements due or ordered, provided that no action by common representative is pending to same effect. Actions for payment of coupons and obligations prescribe in three and five years respectively. (Law of Aug. 26, 1932, arts. 208-228 as amended by Law of Dec. 28, 1963 and by Decree of Dec. 22, 1982).

The Annual Balance must be completed within three months after close of fiscal year and submitted to inspectors at least one month before date of stockholders meeting in which it is to be discussed. Annual balance with inspector's annual report must be at stockholders' disposition at least 15 days before meeting. Annual balance must show amount of capital, amount paid in and to be paid in, cash assets and accounts constituting assets, and liabilities of company. It must be published in official newspaper of state in which company is domiciled, and certified copy must be deposited in Public Registry of Commerce.

Fiscal Obligations (Law of Dec. 30, 1981 as amended). Accounting must be performed in accordance with Federal Fiscal Code. Business reflected in foreign money must be registered and converted into Mexican pesos according to official foreign exchange rate on that business day.

Dissolution may be effected: (1) on expiration of legal term; (2) by impossibility of carrying on principal object of company or when such object has been consummated; (3) by resolution of stockholders, taken in accordance with articles of incorporation and law; (4) when number of shareholders is reduced to less than minimum provided by law or when all shares are owned by one person; or (5) on loss of two-thirds of capital stock. On dissolution of company, it must be liquidated by one or more liquidators.

Government Supervision In order to obtain authorization of Federal Government to offer shares for sale to public, company must consent that its investments and business be supervised by a committee representing Government, with power to call meetings of shareholders. This supervision is carried on through a permanent auditor appointed by committee and paid by company. (Law of Dec. 30, 1939, and Regulations of July 16, 1940, amended by Decrees of June 20, 1945, and Feb. 11, 1946).

Organization and Registration Fees Tax payable on execution of the corporate papers of a domestic civil (noncommercial) corporation or upon protocolization of those of a foreign corporation, is 2 pesos for each 1,000 pesos of capital or fraction thereof. (Law of Federal Fees of Dec. 28, 1982 as amended).

DEEDS AND REGISTRATION

Sales of real property may be made by private documents signed by parties before two witnesses. If value of real property exceeds value set forth in C.C. sale must be in form of public document. (*See* Contracts; Public Instruments). All contracts transferring or modifying ownership, possession, or enjoyment of real property or rights in rem must be recorded in Public Registry of Property. Otherwise they do not affect third persons. On execution of deed involving such contract, notary advises registrar, who makes annotation, and if deed is filed for record within one month after execution, registration is effective from date of such annotation, otherwise it takes effect from date of filing deed. Since registration fees are based on amount involved, actual and not nominal consideration must be stated in contract. (C.C. 2317-2320, 3002, 3003, 3018; Regulations of June 21, 1940 and Decree of Dec. 26, 1973).

Deeds executed in foreign countries may be recorded if authenticated by Mexican Consul and Ministry of Foreign Relations of Republic and protocolized. *See* Acknowledgments.

FOREIGN JUDGMENTS

(C.C.P. 604-608; UN Convention on Recognition and Enforcement of Foreign Arbitral Awards 1958).

Judgments and other judicial decisions emanating from foreign courts have such force in Mexico as treaties may provide. In absence of treaty they have same force as are given Mexican judgments and decrees in country of origin. Foreign judgments and decrees will be enforced only if: (a) they comply with regulations relating to letters rogatory; (b) they were given in personal action; (c) obligation on which they are based is legal in Mexico; (d) defendant was personally summoned in action; (e) they are final judgments according to law of country of origin; and (f) they are properly authenticated. Such judgments are enforced by court which would have had jurisdiction if judgments had been rendered in Mexico. Judgment must be duly translated, and both parties are heard as well as Government attorney. Appeal lies from decision of court. Court does not inquire into merits of judgment but merely determines its authenticity and whether it is enforceable under Mexican law.

FOREIGN INVESTMENT*

Mexico's foreign investment regime is primarily set forth in the Constitution of the United Mexican States (the "Constitution"); the recently enacted Foreign Investment Law (the "FIL") and the Regulations to the law to Promote Mexican Investment and to Regulate Foreign Investment (the "Regulations"); the law for the Promotion and Protection of Industrial Property (the "Industrial Property Law"); the Federal law of Author's Rights (the "Copyright law"); the Credit Institutions law (the "CIL"); and the law to Regulate Financial Groups (the "Financial Groups Law").

The Foreign Investment Law   The FIL was passed in December 1993 as part of Mexico's NAFTA implementation package. The FIL replaces the 1973 law to Promote Mexican Investment and to Regulate Foreign Investment (the "LPMI") and essentially codifies most of the Regulations instituted in 1989, which were promulgated by the Salinas administration to liberalize the restrictive LPMI. Pursuant to the transitional provisions of the FIL, the Regulations will remain in force (to the extent not inconsistent with the FIL) until new regulations are prepared.

Among other things, the FIL (i) eliminates all performance requirements (except where certain investment incentives are involved and those that are not prejudicial to international trade); (ii) expands the scope of the neutral investment provisions introduced in the Regulations; and (iii) reduces or eliminates many of the notifications and authorizations previously required for foreign investments under the LPMI.

The FIL defines "foreign investment" as an investment made by (i) foreign individuals or corporations, (ii) foreign economic entities with no legal status, or (iii) Mexican companies in which foreigners hold a majority interest. In general, the FIL allows up to 100 percent foreign investment in most economic sectors without requiring that such investments be screened and authorized by the Ministry of Trade and Industrial Development (*Secretaría de Comercio y Fomento Industrial*, or SECOFI) through the National Foreign Investment Commission (*Comisión Nacional de Inversión Extranjera*, or CNIE), as was previously the case under the LPMI.

Despite the liberalization of foreign investment under the FIL, some investment is still significantly restricted. Direct investment by non-Mexicans is generally either prohibited or limited with respect to the following categories of investment:

- **Activities Reserved to the Mexican State**   Article 5 of the FIL lists the following activities as being reserved exclusively to the Mexican state: the minting or printing of currency; postal services; telegraph and radio-telegraph services; satellite communications; petroleum and other hydrocarbons; basic petrochemicals; radioactive minerals; generation of nuclear energy and electricity; railways; control and supervision of ports, airports, and heliports; and any other areas that may be expressly reserved to the Mexican state by specific legislation.

- **Activities Reserved to Mexican Nationals**   Under Article 6 of the FIL, foreign participation is excluded from the domestic land transportation of passengers and cargo (excluding messenger and parcel services), the retail distribution and sale of gasoline and liquid gas fuel, radio broadcasting and other radio and television services (with the exception of cable television), credit unions, development banking institutions, and professional and technical services expressly reserved to Mexican nationals by specific legislation.

- **Activities in which Foreign Investment is Limited to a Specified Equity Percentage**   Under Article 7 of the FIL, foreign ownership is allowed up to 10 percent in production cooperatives; 25 percent in domestic air transportation, air taxi services, and specialized air transportation; 30 percent in financial group holding companies, multiple banking institutions, securities firms, and stock exchange specialists; 49 percent in insurance companies; bonding companies; foreign exchange companies; bonded warehouses; financial leasing companies; financial factoring companies; limited-purpose financial companies; investment management companies; arms manufacturers; companies engaged in the printing and publication of periodicals for domestic distribution; basic telephone services; series "T" shares of companies holding agricultural, ranching, and forestry properties; fresh water and coastal fishing within the exclusive economic zone (with the exception of aquaculture); harbor administration; shipping dedicated exclusively to domestic commercial transports; services related to railways; and the supply of fuel and lubricants to ships, airplanes, and railroad equipment.

- **Activities Requiring CNIE Approval for Foreign Investment to Exceed 49 Percent**   Under Article 8 of the FIL, the following economic activities require

---

*Reprinted with permission of the law firm of Carlsmith Ball Wichman Murray Case & Ichiki and the authors, Duane H. Zobrist of the Los Angeles office, and Timon L. Marshall of the Mexico City Branch Office. Copyright © 1994 by Carlsmith Ball Wichman Murray Case & Ichiki.

the prior approval of the CNIE for foreign investment to exceed 49 percent: harbor services for piloting, towing, mooring, and lighterage; shipping companies engaged in transoceanic transportation; the administration of air terminals; private educational services; legal services; credit information companies; insurance agents; cellular telephone services; securities rating companies; construction of pipelines for oil and oil derivatives; and drilling of oil and natural gas wells.

In addition to the industry-specific restrictions set forth in Articles 5 through 8 of the FIL, the CNIE has also reserved the right to review and approve proposed acquisitions by foreign investors of more than 49 percent of the capital stock of Mexican companies engaged in economic activities other than those mentioned above when the total value of the assets of the targeted company exceeds a threshold amount established by the CNIE on an annual basis. Moreover, even though only a small percentage of foreign investments require the approval of the CNIE, all foreign investments (with the exception of neutral investments, which are discussed below) must be recorded in the National Foreign Investment Registry (*Registro Nacional de Inversiones Extranjeras*).

Neutral Investments The Regulations introduced, and the FIL codifies, the concept of allowing foreigners to participate in certain Mexican companies by acquiring certificates of participation. These certificates of participation are issued by Mexican banks acting as trustees whose assets are composed of shares of the capital stock of the targeted Mexican company. These certificates only provide economic rights to the shares held by the trust, and not voting rights. For this purpose, special series of shares designated as class "N"—or neutral shares—are issued specifically for the placement, which may only be acquired by the trust. Under both the Regulations and the FIL, investments in neutral shares are not considered to be foreign investments in Mexico and thus are not subject to the restrictions of Articles 5 through 9 of the FIL.

The Effect of NAFTA Chapter 11 of NAFTA provides comprehensive protection for tangible and intangible investments in the industrial, service, and energy sectors in each of the three countries. Although the FIL—which applies to all foreign investors and not just those from the US and Canada—codifies most of the investment guarantees stipulated in the NAFTA text, there are certain additional assurances provided for under NAFTA which are not found in the FIL. Among other things, NAFTA creates for US and Canadian investors the right to receive prompt payment of market value for their investments in the event of expropriation and to submit investment related claims against the Mexican government to binding international arbitration. NAFTA also carves out certain investment opportunities in Mexico for treaty members that are not otherwise available to other foreign investors.

In sum, even though certain Mexican economic sectors remain as restricted as before, the FIL represents a significant opening of Mexico's economy to foreign investment. Agriculture, banking, cable television, forestry, insurance, mining, and telephone services are just a few of the economic sectors which have become more accessible to foreign investors as a result of the FIL.

The Credit Institutions Law and the Financial Groups Law In addition to the FIL, which permits up to 30 percent foreign investment (regardless of the foreign investor's country of origin) in multiple banking institutions and companies controlling financial groups, certain amendments to the CIL and the Financial Groups Law entered into force on January 1, 1994, to give effect to Mexico's commitments under NAFTA with respect to financial services.

Pursuant to Articles 45-A through 45-N of the CIL, a "treaty bank" may establish a wholly-owned subsidiary in Mexico. A treaty bank is a bank that is organized in a country with which Mexico "has entered into a treaty or international agreement by virtue of which the establishment in national territory of [foreign-owned commercial banks] is permitted." Thus, because the only treaty or international agreement that is currently covered by this provision is NAFTA, qualifying US and Canadian banks are currently the only ones that may set up wholly-owned subsidiaries in Mexico.

Furthermore, amendments to the Financial Groups Law now allow a treaty bank to apply for authorization to operate a financial group. A financial group holding company may own a controlling interest in a commercial bank, a securities firm, an insurance company, a financial leasing company, a factoring company, a bonding company, a foreign exchange company, a limited-purpose financial company, a warehousing company and/or an investment management company. The prospect of a treaty bank owning not only a Mexican subsidiary bank but an entire Mexican financial group is quite inviting to some US banks because it could give them an opportunity to experiment with a method of operation that is forbidden to them in the US. The US Glass-Steagall Act prohibits a commercial bank from affiliating with a full-fledged securities firm; and bank/insurance company affiliations are also generally prohibited. In addition, some of the other types of financial service companies permitted to be affiliated with banks in Mexico are rarely used by US commercial banks.

ENVIRONMENTAL LAWS: NO LONGER A "POLLUTION HAVEN"*

US companies who think of Mexico as a "pollution haven" will be in for a rude awakening when they discover the impact its environmental laws can have on their plans to expand or relocate south of the border.

A "pollution haven" needs two components: lenient or nonexistent environmental laws and regulations and little or no enforcement of existing laws. Contrary to popular belief, Mexico has had a comprehensive environmental program in place since 1988. However, until recently, poor enforcement was admittedly a serious threat to environmental conditions throughout the country. Yet it was not a lack of concern, but rather a scarcity of funds, that prevented adequate enforcement and resulted in Mexico's widely publicized pollution problems. Now with a new influx of funds from the Mexican government and from World Bank loans, with the leverage of NAFTA itself as well as its Supplemental Agreements on the environment, and with binational cooperation and training from US federal and state environmental agencies, Mexico has received an enormous boost to its enforcement capabilities.

The comprehensive scheme of environmental laws and regulations Mexico enacted in 1988 is called the General Law of Ecological Equilibrium and the Protection of the Environment, or the "Ecology Law." The Ecology Law is an umbrella statute which contains dozens of laws, regulations, and standards modeled principally after US environmental laws and regulations. In 1992 Mexico further enhanced the Ecology Law by reevaluating and reissuing all of its existing 83 environmental standards (the functional equivalent of US regulations) and by the end of this year it is expected to release an additional 125 new environmental standards. Meanwhile, Mexican states also have been appointing delegations to establish regional environmental policies in coordination with Mexico's federal agencies. Today all but a few Mexican states have such delegations.

Mexico also restructured the administration and enforcement of its federal environmental program in 1992. The program is now a major component of Mexico's Secretariat of Social Development (*Secretaría de Desarrollo Social*, or SEDESOL). A new semi-independent office for environmental enforcement, the Federal Attorney General for Environmental Protection, was also created in 1992, reflecting a significant change in Mexico's attitude toward the enforcement of its updated environmental laws and standards. Mexico made a major effort to improve its environmental regulation

and enforcement image to get NAFTA passed. Now it is hoping that improved environmental conditions will attract new investors and minimize the long-term impact of environmental problems on Mexico's economy.

Existing Facilities

Purchasers of existing manufacturing facilities in Mexico should be aware that until recently, loopholes in Mexico's hazardous waste regulations and enforcement practices allowed widespread environmental abuses which could seriously impair the facility. For example, unlike the US Resource Conservation and Recovery Act (RCRA), which prohibits on-site storage of hazardous wastes longer than 90 days, waste generators in Mexico could (and still can) store such wastes at their facilities indefinitely. This has allowed companies to stockpile or even bury waste at their facilities, leading to widespread soil and ground water contamination.

Stockpiling (or burying) hazardous wastes at facilities may have been common for several other reasons. First, until recently, enforcement of environmental laws in Mexico was largely a matter of self-regulation. Second, even at those facilities which tried to follow existing laws, compliance was difficult and expensive. For example, Mexico still has only one landfill authorized to accept hazardous waste. (Applications are presently pending for the development of several new landfills.) Third, since 1988 hazardous wastes generated from raw materials imported into Mexico had to be exported to the country of origin. Until very recently, this law was extraordinarily difficult to enforce, and its complexity did little to encourage compliance. These problems now are being addressed by such technological innovations as a computerized binational hazardous waste tracking system making available to US and Mexican inspectors a computerized inventory of all chemicals and wastes moving across the border. Nonetheless, prospective buyers of facilities should be aware that hazardous wastes still may be buried or stockpiled on site and that most facilities will not have systems in place to properly control or dispose of their waste streams.

Voluntary Audits

SEDESOL recently initiated an innovative voluntary audit program which can be beneficial to prospective purchasers of existing facilities. The program is intended to promote compliance by allowing facilities to conduct their own environmental audits under SEDESOL guidelines and to correct problems in cooperation with SEDESOL to avoid

* "No Longer a 'Pollution Haven'" by John R. Zebrowski, partner and Chair of the Compliance Section of the Environmental Law Department at the Los Angeles, California law firm of Allen, Matkins, Leck, Gamble & Mallory. Reprinted with permission of the Los Angeles Business Journal. Copyright © 1994 Los Angeles Business Journal.

ENVIRONMENTAL LAWS: NO LONGER A "POLLUTION HAVEN" (cont'd.)

future surprise inspections, shutdowns, or fines.

While SEDESOL to date has been targeting the petroleum, petrochemical, and textile industries for participation in the program, any company can voluntarily participate and is welcomed by SEDESOL. A prospective buyer should consider requiring voluntary participation in the program as a condition to purchase, as this would identify existing environmental problems, establish a baseline respecting the facility, put the new owner in good standing with SEDESOL, and virtually assure the new owner that its facility will not soon be inspected.

The voluntary audit program entails a comprehensive plant survey by an approved private consultant. There presently are approximately 200 approved consultants, many of whom are based in the US. The audit itself has three phases: pre-audit, audit, and post-audit. During pre-audit the auditor examines facility data including hazardous materials handling records and health and safety records, and develops an audit work plan. During the audit the auditor evaluates plant management, including environmental policy, hazardous waste handling practices, and other factors pertaining to controlling pollution or contamination. In post-audit the audit results are evaluated, an action plan is developed for problems identified, the action plan is negotiated with SEDESOL and the plan becomes legally binding.

New Facilities

Since 1988 anyone wishing to conduct activities in Mexico that could cause an "ecological imbalance" or surpass limits established in the Ecology Law environmental standards has had to seek prior approval of federal and state authorities by filing an environmental impact statement (EIS). Any major development project undertaken in Mexico probably will trigger this requirement, which, until recently, had been largely ignored.

Since 1992 the filing of an EIS, including the requirement that it be prepared by a licensed consultant, has been rigorously enforced. In fact, the EIS requirement is so rigorously enforced today that some developers with poor environmental "track records" are not being allowed to operate in Mexico.

SEDESOL has started using computer networks to track environmental problem sites in the US and to identify whether the EIS applicant has a poor track record of environmental compliance. Also, as part of the EIS process, SEDESOL routinely requests records of the applicant's US operations. If the agency finds that the applicant is involved in any US environmental problem sites, this may be used as a basis to deny the project.

If an applicant wants to construct a facility which will generate, store, or dispose of hazardous wastes, it will also have to comply with a number of other newly-enacted regulations. First, it must seek authorization for the project from Mexico's National Institute for Ecology. Second, waste generators must have a plan to reduce or minimize their hazardous wastes and periodically report their progress to SEDESOL. Third, if the activity is considered "high risk," the applicant must prepare a risk study and comply with detailed location standards.

Toxic or Hazardous Wastes

While most major Mexican industrial facilities have operating permits, it is estimated that more than 90 percent of all industrial facilities presently operating in Mexico, particularly smaller ones, are operating without permits. As Mexico's inspection and enforcement capabilities increase, more and more of these unpermitted facilities will be discovered, fined, closed, or compelled to obtain permits. In the interim, the focus of Mexico's efforts is to ensure that new facilities are properly permitted. As government officials describe their program. "Mexico is committed to growing clean." This means facilities now opening in Mexico will be subject to stricter standards than before.

Like its US counterpart (RCRA), Mexico's Ecology Law establishes a comprehensive scheme for regulating the treatment, storage, generation, disposal, and transportation of hazardous wastes "from cradle to grave." Moreover, Mexico's criteria for determining which wastes are "hazardous" are virtually identical to RCRA's. Even its standards for evaluating which chemicals are banned in Mexico are identical to those in the US.

As in the US, hazardous wastes in Mexico must be handled, contained, stored, and identified in compliance with specific environmental standards, including the manifesting of all wastes. Certain standards, however, are even more stringent than those imposed in the US. For example, waste generators must be listed in the Registry of Hazardous Waste Generators, and they are required to maintain a log of the volume of hazardous waste generated. This enables SEDESOL to keep a record on all facilities which treat, store, or dispose of hazardous wastes. In addition, waste generators must file monthly and biannual reports of waste generation with SEDESOL.

Last April, Mexico's Ministry of Communication and Transports published new regulations, modeled after RCRA, to regulate the land transportation of hazardous wastes and materials. The regulations are extensive and require detailed documentation of these wastes (as well as the transporting vehicle), special driver's licenses, logs of hours of service, vehicle inspections, and insurance policies. Rules also govern the design, condition, and labeling of transport containers; weather conditions under which wastes can be transported; and the routes and number of stops which the driver can make.

The Ecology Law is also fairly comprehensive with respect to water discharge and pollution. Mexico's water laws were modeled after the US Clean Water Act, although in many respects they are even broader than US laws. In addition to toxic substances and solid waste dumping, Mexico's water laws regulate effluents from industry and mining, municipalities, agriculture, livestock, pesticides, and fertilizers. Both point and non-point sources of pollution are regulated and discharge standards have been established that are virtually identical to those used in the US.

Mexico's air quality laws are modeled after the US Clean Air Act. Projects that fall under the nation's air laws must use systems and equipment designed to control, minimize, and measure emissions. They also must maintain logs of operations, maintenance, and emissions; register the results of all monitoring; monitor the perimeter of the site (in urban zones); and give notice of control equipment breakdown.

Because air regulation requires sophisticated testing equipment and trained inspectors, Mexico has made little progress in the area of air pollution abatement to date. However, increased EPA concern regarding air pollution in the border area already is leading to upgraded monitoring activities and binational enforcement.

The agency has been monitoring air pollution along the US–Mexico border for years. In fact, 1990 amendments to the Clean Air Act included a provision authorizing EPA to establish a program in cooperation with Mexico to monitor air quality along the border. In a similar vein, a recently proposed amendment to the 1983 La Paz Agreement between the US and Mexico will establish the first international air quality district, including the twin border cities of El Paso, Texas and Ciudad Juárez, Chihuahua. EPA's plan is to identify the major pollution sources in the air district for SEDESOL and seek cooperative efforts to take action against offenders.

Environmental Enforcement

Lack of enforcement is the most often cited reason for poor environmental compliance in Mexico. This is particularly true of the US–Mexico border region, where more than 2,000 foreign-owned *maquiladora* plants presently operate in towns with infrastructures (such as sewage systems) that are grossly inadequate to service the influx of workers, let alone the huge volume of industrial wastes now being generated by these *maquiladoras*.

In order to understand the environmental enforcement challenges in Mexico, one must first have a general understanding of the differences between the US and Mexican legal systems. The US has a common law tradition, while Mexico has a civil law tradition. In the US, the judicial system is the primary motivator to enforce laws and compel compliance. The mere possibility of a lawsuit over environmental problems probably does more to encourage compliance and improve environmental conditions than would even a hundredfold increase in the number of environmental agency inspectors.

Mexico does not have common law principles to induce compliance with its environmental standards. It is almost solely dependent on the ability of its inspectors to identify problems. There can never be enough inspectors in Mexico to achieve the level of compliance which the threat of a lawsuit for environmental violations accomplishes in a common law legal system.

Despite the difficulty of obtaining compliance in a civil law system, companies contemplating opening facilities in Mexico should recognize that Mexico recently developed an innovative enforcement program to achieve compliance, often with harsh results. For example, environmental enforcement in Mexico generally involves one or more of the following: plant closure (permanent or temporary, total or partial); negotiation of compliance agreements; posting of a surety bond to secure compliance; as well as the imposition of steep fines.

In Mexico, the strong sanction (facility shutdown) is imposed prior to the initiation of negotiations. The facility typically remains closed throughout the negotiation process and can stay closed until its problems are corrected. Mexico hopes that the threat of shutdown will be enough to induce compliance. Recent studies have shown that companies are now taking SEDESOL's threat of shutdown much more seriously.

SEDESOL's inspection program is organized into four sub-programs: (1) targeted inspections (industries commonly thought to pollute and users of large quantities of fuel—companies which deal with petroleum, petrochemicals, and recycling facilities); (2) public complaints (SEDESOL routinely investigates informal citizen complaints and is extremely vocal about the fact that it follows up on such complaints); (3) aerial surveillance (common in and around Mexico City; the searches typically are for air emission violations); (4) vehicle emissions (last year, 17,000 vehicles were stopped and inspected under this program).

Inspections for environmental violations have in-

ENVIRONMENTAL LAWS: NO LONGER A "POLLUTION HAVEN" (cont'd.)

creased dramatically in recent years and should be expected to continue to increase exponentially. Between 1992 and 1993, the number of inspections SEDESOL conducted each month increased fivefold over prior years. Between June 1992 and June 1993, the agency completed more than 16,000 inspections, resulting in the temporary partial closure of 1,161 companies and 216 temporary total closures. Last year more than 8,304 inspections were carried out in the Mexico City area alone, exceeding SEDESOL's target by more than 3,000 inspections.

As of several months ago, SEDESOL reported that it had 90 inspectors in Mexico City, 130 inspectors along the US–Mexico border, and a total of 400 inspectors countrywide. These numbers are expected to increase by 50 percent over the next few years as Mexico continues to receive millions in World Bank loans targeted for environmental problems. The loans are also slated to be used to obtain more and better equipment for sampling and analyzing pollutants. Over the short term, inspections (and shutdowns) will likely continue to be most prevalent in Mexico City (home to 40 percent of Mexico's industrial operations) and the US–Mexico border area (the location of most of the balance of industrial operations in Mexico).

NOTARIES PUBLIC

(Notarial Law of Jan. 9, 1932; Law of Dec. 30, 1947 as amended by Decrees of Dec. 21, 1950, Dec. 21, 1965 and Dec. 26, 1966).

A Mexican notary is a public official whose duties are much more important than those of the notaries under US system of law. Contracts and conveyances between private individuals, powers of attorney and wills which are required to be in the form of a public document (*see* Public Instruments) when entered into in Mexico, should be prepared by and executed before a notary public. Notaries are required to keep protocol, which comprises originals of all documents which are executed before them. General archives are kept to which protocols of notaries pass after certain length of time. Instruments executed before notaries must be prepared with certain formalities and drawn in Spanish language. If parties do not know Spanish they must appoint interpreter, who takes oath before notary that he will faithfully perform his duties. If parties are not known to notary, their identity must be certified to by two witnesses known to notary, who must also certify as to their legal capacity.

Contracts, powers of attorney, and other docu-

ments executed in foreign countries should be duly authenticated (*see* Acknowledgments) and translated and protocolized in the office of a notary by order of a competent court in order to receive full recognition in Mexico.

PARTNERSHIP

Governed by law of July 28, 1934 (General Law of Commercial Companies) which applies to whole nation.

All partnership agreements must be in form of public documents (*see* Public Instruments) which must be recorded in Public Registry of Commerce. All partnerships are regarded as legal entities.

General Partnership *(sociedad en nombre colectivo)* is a partnership in which all partners have unlimited and joint liability towards third persons. Between partners, liability of one or more may be limited to a certain amount.

Management of partnership may be entrusted to one or more administrators, who may or may not be partners; when administrators are not designated, all of partners have a voice in management.

Partnership agreement can be modified only by unanimous consent of all partners, unless it authorizes modification by a majority; in this case minority has right to withdraw. Partners may not assign partnership rights, nor may new partners be admitted without consent of all other partners, unless partnership agreement allows such assignment and admittance by majority vote.

Administrators may not sell or mortgage real property of partnership without consent of a majority of partners, unless such sale or encumbrance constitutes principal object of partnership or a natural consequence thereof. Administrators may grant powers of attorney for carrying on specified partnership business, but in order to delegate duties vote of a majority of partners is required; in this case dissenting minority has right to withdraw from partnership if delegate is a non-partner. Firm name may be used by all administrators unless partnership agreement limits said use to one or more. Partners not in administration may appoint an inspector and have right to examine books and accounts of partnership. Capital may not be distributed prior to dissolution and liquidation of partnership, unless otherwise agreed.

Capital of all kinds of partnerships may be variable; in this case expression *"de Capital Variable"* must be added to firm name. Capital may not be reduced to less than one-fifth of original capital.

Partnership agreement may be rescinded in respect of any of partners for: (a) use of firm name or capital for own business; (b) violation of partnership agreement; (c) violation of legal provisions governing partnership; (d) fraudulent and deceitful acts; (e) bankruptcy, interdiction, or incapacity to carry on commercial business.

Simple Limited Partnership *(sociedad en comandita simple)* is one in which one or more of partners are subject to unlimited and joint liability for partnership obligations and one or more of partners are responsible for debts and losses only to amount of capital which they have subscribed. Firm name must conclude with words *"Sociedad en Comandita"* or abbreviation "S. en C." Names of special partners must not appear in firm name. Special partners are also liable to same extent as general partners when expression S. en C. or words it represents are omitted. Special partners have no voice in management of company: if they intervene in any respect they are responsible to third persons together with general partners. Interests of special partners may be represented by shares in which case partnership is a *"sociedad en comandita por acciones"* (limited partnership with shares). Many of provisions regarding general partnerships are applicable to limited partnerships.

Sociedad en Comandita por Acciones (Limited Partnership with Shares) This is a legal entity which has aspects of both joint-stock company and partnership and is able to transact business, acquire real and personal property, and sue and be sued in its own name. It is composed of one or more general partners who have subsidiary, though unlimited, liability with company, and one or more limited partners responsible only to extent of their contributions.

Capital is divided into shares of stock; shares of general partners have to be registered and may not be transferred without consent of all of general partners and two-thirds of limited partners.

Name of firm may be composed of names of one or more of general partners [and] name must also be followed by the words *"Sociedad en Comandita por Acciones,"* abbreviated to "S. en C. por A."

Limited partners may not participate in administration of company. Organization, management, and liquidation are governed by company rules, with some exceptions.

Asociación en Participación This is contractual arrangement between two or more individuals or enterprises for realization of one or more business transactions. There is no legal entity, nor may association operate under name. Managing associate receives capital from contributing associates and underlying agreement provides how profits will be distributed. Managing associate operates in his own name and is liable for debts of business, whereas contributing associates are liable only up to amount of their respective contributions. Association is to be based on written contract, which may modify some of basic rules expressed above.

Sole Proprietorship Individual person, including foreign individual with proper immigration permit, can do business in his name as sole proprietor and is personally responsible for losses of enterprise. Business has no legal Personalty.

Business Associations In Mexico business enterprises are not only permitted, but are legally required to organize themselves into associations. Twenty firms in any particular industry may create national industrial association or chamber; for commercial chamber, minimum is 50.

Limited Liability Companies *(sociedades de responsabilidad limitada)* are formed by members who are liable only for amount subscribed by them. They have some characteristics of a corporation and some of a partnership. Firm name must include name of one or more members, and must conclude with words *"Sociedad de Responsabilidad Limitada"* or abbreviation "S. de R.L."

These companies cannot be constituted by public subscription, nor without total subscription of capital, nor without payment of at least 50 percent of each participation. Members cannot assign their interest and no new members may be admitted without consent of all others, unless company agreement provides for consent of a majority of members representing at least three-quarters of capital. No member may own more than one participation. When a member makes a further contribution or acquires all or part of interest of another associate, his participation is increased, unless participations are entitled to different rights, in which case they are held separately. Participations may not be divided unless in manner and cases provided by law.

Management is in hands of one or more managers, who need not be members, who may act temporarily or for an indefinite period, and whose appointment may be revoked any time. Resolutions of managers are adopted by majority, unless it is stipulated that they must act jointly, in which case vote must be unanimous. Members act through general meetings at which resolutions are approved by vote of a majority representing at least half the capital, unless company contract or instrument of organization agreement requires larger proportion. Meetings are held at least once a year at company domicile. Modification of company agreement must be approved by at least three quarters of capital; except any change of object of company or increase of obligations of members, which requires unanimous vote of all members.

Company agreement may provide that members shall have a right to receive interest not exceeding 9 percent per annum on contributions; this right is limited to period long enough to allow company to perform acts and works necessary to carrying on of business, and may not exceed three years. This interest is charged to general expenses.

Foreign Partnerships Requisites before qualifying to do business are same as those provided for foreign corporations.

PRESCRIPTION

(C.C. 1135-1180).

Acquisition of property or rights by virtue of possession or extinction of obligations by failure to require performance is called prescription.

Periods of prescription in commercial transactions are provided in Commercial Code and commercial laws, and consequently apply to whole nation. Prescription in commercial matters begins to run from date upon which an action might have been brought. It may be interrupted by any class of judicial proceedings for purpose of requiring debtor to recognize obligation or renew documents evidencing same. Prescriptive periods vary according to nature of action. More important are: (1) actions to reclaim ownership of vessels, ten years; (2) actions arising out of articles of incorporation and partnership and out of operations of corporations and partnerships as between them and their members and between members, actions against liquidators of companies and partnerships, actions to collect principal of corporate bonds, five years; (3) actions to collect bills of exchange, promissory notes, and coupons of corporate bonds, even though such documents were issued abroad, actions on warehouse certificates, actions based on maritime loans, three years; (4) actions by retail merchants on credit sales, except in case of accounts current, actions by commercial employees to recover salaries, actions arising out of contracts of transportation, actions against brokers for obligations arising out of their duties, actions against issuers of travelers' checks, actions derived from insurance contracts, many actions relating to admiralty matters, one year; (5) actions on checks, six months. In cases where shorter period is not established by Commercial Code, period is ten years. (Com. C. 1038-1048; Law of Aug. 26, 1932, arts. 165, 192, 207, 227, 250, 258).

Prescription already run can be waived, but not right to prescription in future. Government and municipalities are considered same as private individuals with respect to prescription of property, rights, or actions susceptible of private ownership.

PRINCIPAL AND AGENT

(C.C. 2546-2604, Com.C., arts. 273-308).

An agency may be oral, it may appear in private writing with two witnesses, and in public instrument, or in private instrument before two witnesses with all signatures acknowledged before notary or other authority, depending on amount involved and limit of power. Powers of attorney for appearing in court must be given by public instrument.

In order that the power of attorney may be un-

limited it need only state that it is given with general authority and with such special authority as must be specifically granted according to law; general powers of attorney for administration need only state that they are given for general administrative purposes; and general powers for acts of ownership may also be in general terms; in these three cases if the authority of the agent is to be limited, the limitations must be expressed. The document must transcribe the entire text of C.C., art. 2554. The agent cannot institute an action to enforce obligations contracted in the name of the principal, unless authority for this purpose is included in the power of attorney. Also agent needs express authority to subscribe for bills of exchange, promissory notes, and other exchangeable documents, to file *amparo* suits before courts, and to delegate powers to third persons.

The contract of agency is perfected by express or tacit acceptance on the part of the agent. If a power of attorney is given to a professional man for acts of

REAL ESTATE*

In general, outside of the restricted area (a strip 100 km wide along the borders and 50 km wide along the seashore), acquisition by foreigners of real estate is allowed.

In the restricted area, foreign-owned Mexican corporations may acquire real estate property so long as it is not residential property. In this case, registration of the acquisition with the Ministry of Foreign Affairs will be required.

In case of residential property or of foreign citizens or corporations, a trust will be required in the restricted area. In this case, a Mexican bank will act as trustee, the authorization from the Secretariat of Foreign Affairs must be obtained beforehand, and the trust will be good for 50 years which may be renewed.

The authorization (in the case of trusts) must be granted or denied within 30 days, and the registrations (in the case of acquisitions) shall be granted or denied within 15 days, or otherwise the authorization or registration will be deemed to have been granted.

The new benefits of the law will be applicable to existing foreign-owned Mexican corporations which have real estate trusts in the restricted area. The trust's term may now be of 50 years for residential property. Pre-existing trusts used to hold commercial or industrial property can be canceled to enable the beneficiaries to hold direct ownership title in fee simple in accord with the new law.

*Reprinted with permission of the author, Manuel F. Pasero, managing partner of Pasero, Martín-Sánchez y Sánchez, a business-oriented law firm in Tijuana, Baja California Norte. Copyright © 1994 by Pasero, Martín-Sánchez y Sánchez.

his profession, it is considered as accepted if not refused in three days. An agency is gratuitous only when expressly so agreed. The agent may delegate his powers if expressly authorized to do so. The principal must advance to the agent the funds required for the exercise of the agency.

An agency is terminated: (a) by revocation; (b) by renunciation on the part of the agent; (c) by death of principal or agent; (d) when either is declared incompetent; (e) by expiration of its term or conclusion of the business for which it was given; or (f) in certain cases when the principal has disappeared. The principal may freely revoke the agency, unless the same was stipulated as a condition in a bilateral contract or as a means to comply with an obligation contracted; in these cases the agent also cannot renounce the agency. The appointment of a new agent for the same matter implies revocation as to the former agent from the day he is notified of the new appointment. Although the agency is terminated by the death of the principal, the agent must continue his administration until the heirs can look after the business, if a different course might cause damage. If the agent renounces the agency he must continue acting until the principal can appoint another agent if damage might otherwise be caused.

RECORDS

Public Register of Property All contracts transferring or modifying ownership, possession, or enjoyment of real property or rights in rem must be registered in order to affect third persons. (C.C. 3002 et seq.). *See also* Deeds and Registration.

Commercial Register Corporate charter and its amendments, issuance of stock, and dissolution of commercial corporations must be registered. General and special powers of attorney must be registered. Individual merchants must register documents relating to their capacity to do business and family documents relating to their estate. Ship ownership must also be recorded in this register. (Com. C. 18 et seq.).

Technological Entities Registry (Decree of Nov. 26, 1980, art. 4). All persons devoted to research and development of technology must register.

There are various other registers such as Importers and Exporters Register and Taxpayers Register.

SALES (REALTY AND PERSONALTY)

(C.C. 2248-2326; Federal Law on Consumer Protection of Dec. 29, 1975 as amended).

In general a sale is perfected between the parties when they have agreed as to the object of the sale and the price, although neither has been delivered. Sales reserving the right to repurchase are prohibited; but it may be stipulated that the seller shall have

a preferential right to purchase at the same price offered by a third person, when the buyer wishes to sell the object; such right must be exercised within three days after notice of the third person's offer in the case of personal property, and within ten days after such notice in the case of real property.

It is legal to make installment sales with the condition that the sale shall be deemed rescinded if any installment is not paid. Such a condition is effective against third persons who may have acquired the object sold providing such object is real property or is some kind of personalty which can clearly be identified, and provided the condition is recorded in the public registry; but it is not effective against third persons acting in good faith, when the property is not susceptible of clear identification. In case of such rescision the buyer and seller must restore to each other the objects and amounts they have received, but the seller may demand rental for the object and an indemnity for its deterioration, both such rental and indemnity to be determined by experts, and the buyer may demand interest on the money paid to the seller.

It may also be stipulated that the seller retains the title until the price is paid and such a stipulation is effective as to third persons if it is recorded in the registry and the objects can be identified clearly. In such case the seller cannot sell the property to another until expiration of the period for paying the price and the buyer is meanwhile regarded as a lessee. If the property is retaken by the seller, the rules hereinbefore stated for retaking property sold on installments will be applied.

Mexico has enacted the Federal Law on Consumer Protection that regulates consumer sales. Moreover it has created a Public Office to deal with these matters.

TREATIES

Bilateral

Argentina Payments Agreement.

Belgo-Luxembourg Economic Union Commercial Convention.

Brazil Provisional Commercial Agreement.

Canada Commercial Convention.

Chile Commercial Modus Vivendi.

China Commercial Agreement.

Costa Rica Commercial Treaty.

Czechoslovakia [Czech Republic and Slovakia, status uncertain] Commercial Treaty.

Dominican Republic Treaty of Friendship, Commerce and Navigation.

El Salvador Treaty of Commerce.

France Commercial Agreement.

Indonesia Payments Agreement.

Israel Treaty of Commerce.

Italy Commercial Convention.

Japan Commercial Agreement.

Korea [South Korea] Commercial Agreement.

Netherlands Commercial Convention.

Spain Payments Agreement.

Switzerland Commercial Agreement.

United Arab Republic [Egypt] Commercial Agreement.

United States Agreement on documentation for non-immigrants traveling between US and Mexico. Agreement relating to allocation of television channels. Agreement relating to allocation of ultra high frequency channels for television along US–Mexican border. Agreement relating to radio broadcasting. Agreement relating to interchange of fiscal information. For complete list of US–Mexican Agreements, see Treaties in Force, publication compiled by the US Department of State annually as of Jan. 1.

Multilateral

Convention for the establishment of an Inter-American Tropical Tuna Commission.

International telecommunication convention.

Decree of Dec. 23, 1965, approving Organic Pact (*Pacto Constitutivo*) of American Coffee Growers' Federation (*Federación Cafetalera de America*).

Agreement establishing interim arrangements for global commercial communications satellite system.

International Coffee Agreement.

International Sugar Agreement.

Vienna Convention on Law of Treaties.

Universal Copyright Convention.

Convention on Recognition and Enforcement of Foreign Arbitral Awards.

Latin American Integration Association—LAIA.

Latin American Economic Systems—SELA.

Inter-American Conventions: On conflict of laws concerning bills of exchange, promissory notes, and invoices; On International Commercial Arbitration; On Letters Rogatory; On the Taking of Evidence Abroad; On legal regime of powers of attorney to be used abroad.

The Letter of Abidjan, establishing alliance of countries that are producers of cocoa.

Convention creating a Common Fund of basic products.

UN Convention on International Multimodal Transport of Goods.

Inter-American convention on general rules of private international law. On extraterritorial validity of foreign judgments and arbitral awards. On domicile of natural persons in private international law. On status and legal capacity of juridical persons in private international law; On international competence for extraterritorial validity of foreign judgments.

ONU Convention on Contracts for the International Sale of Goods.

MEXICO'S NEW INTELLECTUAL PROPERTY AND LICENSING REGIME*

Author's note: The passage of NAFTA was not assured at the time this article was originally published. Amendments to Mexico's Industrial Property Law (IPL) are expected shortly that will effect a number of changes, including those required by NAFTA. These amendments were to be submitted to the Mexican Congress in April 1994. Unfortunately, the focus on amendments has apparently resulted in further delay in the preparation of implementing regulations to the IPL.

Mexico's recent enactment in June 1991 of the *Ley de Fomento y Protección de La Propiedad Industrial* (Industrial Property Law, or IPL) completely revamps the Mexican industrial property regime and signals a significant step forward in Mexico's efforts to join the global economy. While the IPL increases the protection afforded most industrial property rights in Mexico to a level generally commensurate with that found in the industrialized nations, it still suffers from a number of flaws. Fortunately, the intellectual property provisions of the recently adopted North American Free Trade Agreement (NAFTA) address the most significant of these flaws, and once amendments to the IPL implementing the terms of NAFTA are passed, it is expected that Mexico's protection of industrial property rights will truly be first-rate. As a consequence, Mexico will have dramatically improved its business climate and removed another barrier to attracting foreign investment and advanced technology.

PROTECTION OF INTELLECTUAL PROPERTY RIGHTS

The IPL, which was published on June 27, 1991, and became effective the following day, replaced the Law of Inventions and Trademarks [or LIT]. The Regulations to the Law of Inventions and Trademarks, however, continue in effect, "insofar as they are not contradictory to the [IPL]," until new regulations are issued under the IPL. Originally these new regulations were to be issued in late 1991. After additional delays, the issuance of the new regulations [was] linked to progress on [NAFTA], and thus the regulations cannot be expected until at least [late-1994]. In the meantime a considerable amount of uncertainty will continue to exist over the proper interpretation of a number of provisions of the IPL.

Patents, Utility Models, and Industrial Designs

An invention is patentable under the IPL if it is novel, the result of inventive activity, and susceptible of industrial application. In particular the standard for novelty is high. An invention is no longer novel and will be deemed within the public domain if it is made public through oral or written description, by exploitation, or by other means in Mexico or abroad. However, exclusive rights will not be lost by disclosure for noncommercial purposes or at a Mexican or international exhibition, provided the patent application is filed within 12 months of the disclosure.

The IPL specifically broadens the class of inventions that are immediately patentable in Mexico, some of which were simply not previously patentable in Mexico or would not have been eligible for patent protection until 1997. The IPL specifically allows for immediate patent protection of certain chemicals, alloys, and living matter. The classes of living matter protected include:

(1) plant varieties;

(2) inventions related to microorganisms, such as those made by using them, inventions that are applied to microorganisms, or inventions that result therefrom. Included in this provision are all types of microorganisms, such as bacteria, fungi, algae, viruses, microplasms, protozoan, and cells that do not reproduce sexually; and

(3) biotechnological processes for obtaining pharmochemicals, medicines, foods and beverages for animal and human consumption, fertilizers, herbicides, fungicides, or products with a biological activity.

The following inventions relating to living matter are, however, expressly unpatentable:

(1) Essential biological processes for obtaining or reproducing plants, animals, or their varieties, including genetic processes or processes related to material capable of self-replication, by itself or by any other indirect manner, when the processes consist simply of selecting or isolating available biological material or leaving it to act under natural conditions;

(2) plant species and animal species and breeds;

(3) biological materials, as found in nature;

(4) genetic material; and

By John B. McKnight of the Dallas, Texas, law firm of Locke Purnell Rain Harrell (A Professional Corporation), and Carlos Müggenburg, R.V., of the Mexico City law firm of Creel, García-Cuéllar y Müggenburg. Reprinted substantially as it originally appeared in "Mexico's New Intellectual Property Regime: Improvements in the Protection of Industrial Property, Copyright, License and Franchise Rights in Mexico," The International Lawyer, Vol. 27:1, p. 27 (Spring 1993). Reprinted by permission of the authors and the American Bar Association. Copyright © 1993 American Bar Association.

(5) inventions relating to the living matter that composes the human body.

The extension of patent protection to the specified inventions involving living matter are especially noteworthy, as Mexico has for years suffered from a lack of many of the related pharmaceutical and agricultural chemical products that are commonplace in the industrial world. In recognition of this deficiency in its industrial property regime, the Mexican Congress in 1987 amended the LIT to provide that these types of inventions would become patentable in 1997. The IPL makes these inventions immediately patentable. It also provides that if a patent application for any such invention has been filed with a signatory to the Patent Cooperation Treaty and such invention has not been exploited in Mexico on a commercial scale, then a patent application filed with the Ministry of Commerce and Industrial Development (Ministry) within 12 months of the effective date of the IPL (June 28, 1992) would be given the priority date of the first application filed in any such country. This provision is specifically devised to immediately entice pharmaceutical and agricultural companies to Mexico, many of which have been hesitant to distribute their products in Mexico in the past.

The term of a patent granted under the IPL is changed from 14 years after the date of grant of the patent to 20 years after the date of filing the patent application with the Ministry. At first blush this may seem to be a substantial improvement in the area of patent protection. Due to the historically lengthy period between the filing and granting of a patent, however, this change does not significantly alter the period of protection extended patents under Mexican law. This change does nevertheless assure protection from infringement during the period from filing the patent application to the granting of the patent. The patent term of pharmochemical and pharmaceutical products and processes can be extended for an additional three years, provided the patentee grants a license to work the patent to a Mexican-controlled company.

As soon as possible after the expiration of an 18-month period following the date of filing of a patent application with the Ministry (or the date of priority given to an application), the IPL requires public disclosure of the invention described in the application. As the IPL does not provide procedures for third-party opposition to a pending patent application, the publication requirement appears designed to alert Mexican industry to new technological developments. Subsequent to publication of the patent application, the Ministry carries out an examination of the merits of the invention, which may involve obtaining technical advice from other specialized governmental agencies. In addition, the Ministry may accept or require information from foreign patent examining offices and may also seek additional information from the applicant. The applicant must comply with any such request within two months or such extended period as the Ministry may grant. After finally determining whether the invention is patentable, the Ministry will issue letters patent (upon payment of the appropriate fees) or reject the application. In the event of rejection the applicant may file a petition for reconsideration with the Ministry within 30 days. Should rejection of the patent application be confirmed, an *amparo* suit may be filed with a federal district court, the decisions of which are subject to final review by the federal circuit courts.

While the IPL significantly broadens the patent protection afforded inventions, it continues to suffer from provisions subjecting patentable inventions to compulsory licenses if the patent has not been worked in Mexico by the later of four years from the filing date of the patent application or three years from the date of granting the patent (unless failure to work the patent is justified for technical or economic reasons). A patentable invention is also subject to a compulsory license for public interest reasons where the production, supply, or distribution of basic commodities would otherwise be impeded. In addition, the IPL falls short of providing patent protection for the full array of inventions typically protected in industrialized countries. For example, it fails to offer patent protection for computer programs, many biological substances used in plant and animal reproduction, and surgical, therapeutic, and diagnostic methods. Software is, however, afforded some protection under the copyright laws.

The IPL introduces in Mexico the protection of utility models, which can be registered if (due to modifications to the structure, configuration, or form of goods, utensils, apparatus, or tools) new ways of using such items are developed or new functions are performable. This legal concept, which is recognized in a number of industrialized countries, is especially designed to induce industrial innovation among smaller companies and individuals that do not have the research and development resources that frequently are instrumental in developing patentable inventions. The stringency of the regulatory standards applicable to the registration of utility models are lower than those applicable to patents. Accordingly, the determination of novelty of a utility model is confined to Mexico, rather than the entire world. One effect of this provision is that Mexican pirates of utility models developed outside the country register and gain protection for such models in Mexico. The term of protection afforded registration of a utility model is 10 years from the application filing date.

Finally, the IPL extends enhanced protection to industrial designs. Industrial designs that are capable of being registered include industrial drawings (unique combinations of figures, lines, or colors that are incorporated into an industrial product) and distinctive forms of product trade dress (referred to in the IPL as three dimensional industrial models). The breadth of protection afforded industrial designs under the IPL is quantitatively increased by virtue of extending the registration term from seven to 15 years. It is qualitatively enhanced by providing for the rejection of registration of industrial designs that are confusingly similar, rather than identical, to previously registered industrial designs in Mexico.

Industrial or Trade Secrets

Prior to the enactment of the IPL, almost no legal protection existed in Mexico for general industrial or trade secrets. The IPL introduces protection of secrets having industrial applications relating to (1) the nature, characteristics, or purposes of products, (2) the processes and production methods of products, and (3) the means and methods of marketing and distributing products or rendering services. In order to qualify for protection under the IPL, a secret must (1) be identified as a secret (whether expressly under an agreement or otherwise in a confidential relationship), (2) provide a competitive or economic advantage over third parties in the marketplace, (3) be protected by the owner thereof through sufficient means or systems, and (4) be maintained and conveyed in documents, electronic or magnetic media, optical discs, microfilm, film, or other similar instruments. Of course an industrial or trade secret must not be within the public domain. A secret does not, however, fall into the public domain by virtue of its disclosure in connection with efforts to obtain licenses, permits, authorizations, registrations, or other official acts. This final provision underscores a significant concern about the confidentiality accorded certain governmental filings and is important in light of the potential breadth of the provisions in the IPL requiring recordation of license and franchise agreements.

The extension of legal protection to industrial or trade secrets is clearly one of the most important aspects of the IPL, as a very significant portion of the industrial property assets of most businesses may be classified as trade secrets. Nonetheless, this section of the IPL has a number of shortcomings. The chief concern is what constitutes an industrial or trade secret qualifying for protection (for example, what is the significance of the requirement that the secret have an industrial application, and are all secrets relating to rendering services protected or are only those relating to the marketing or distribution of services?). In addition, in light of the subjective nature of several of the elements of proof required to support a statutory claim (for example, proving that the secret provides a competitive or economic advantage over third parties) and the current absence of any injunctive relief for unauthorized disclosures or uses of secrets, concern remains over the effectiveness of the statutory remedies provided by the IPL.

Commercial Designations

Trademarks The IPL makes a number of notable improvements to the treatment of trademarks (and service marks) in Mexico. While these improvements are not monumental in their significance, when taken together they generally raise the substantive standards for handling marks in Mexico to a level commensurate with that in the industrialized world. Because trademarks can be used to designate products or services, tridimensional shapes and collective marks used by an association of producers, merchants, or purveyors of goods or services are now registrable. In addition, the IPL now permits variations of registered marks to be used in commerce so long as the essential features remain. The law also provides for greater flexibility in permitting the registration of marks that may have descriptive characteristics.

The actual procedure to register a mark under the IPL is notably simple. The registration application need only identify the applicant, the mark sought, the date of first use of the mark (if it has been used at all), and the classes of products or services to which the mark will relate. As Mexico is a party to the Paris Convention, if the registration application is filed in Mexico within six months of the date of filing a registration application in one's home country, the filing date in the home country will be deemed the priority date in Mexico. A Mexican attorney normally handles the registration application of a foreign company. To properly evidence the authority of the Mexican attorney to act on behalf of a foreign registrant, a power of attorney, carefully drawn to cover all necessary functions for trademark representation, is usually granted to the Mexican attorney. The IPL appears to indicate that a power of attorney granted in accordance with the laws of the applicant's country or according to international treaty is now acceptable. However, in the near future the applicant is advised to continue the more traditional practice of granting a power of attorney through preparation of a notary public deed that also references the corporate existence of the registrant and the corporate authority of the officer executing the deed under the registrant's governing documents. In the US the deed needs to be notarized by a US notary public and then submitted, along with governmental certification of the notary public's authority to act, to a Mexican consulate for legalization. While a registration application alone can be submitted to the Ministry in order to expediently secure a filing date for purposes of obtaining priority, eventually filing the aforementioned deed with samples of the mark and the applicable governmental fees will be necessary in order to complete the registrant's application package.

The IPL increases the term of the registration of a trademark from five to 10 years. In addition, the length of the term is now measured from the date of filing the registration application, rather than the legal date provided for under prior law. This change should help to eliminate some confusion in determining the commencement date of the term of registration.

The process of renewing a registered trademark and demonstrating use of the trademark is now considerably improved. Under the IPL, the renewal application must be submitted within the six-month period preceding or succeeding the expiration date of the registration term. To demonstrate use of the trademark during such term, only submission of an affidavit stating that the use of the mark has not been interrupted for any period of three or more years during such term is necessary. This simplified procedure of matching the date of renewal with the date upon which use must be proven contrasts with the confusion generated under the prior scheme wherein use was required to be demonstrated within three years of the date of registration and submission of the renewal application was required within five years of the legal date. In addition, by expressly requiring submission of an affidavit rather than labels, sales invoices, and other evidences of use previously required, the process [has been] streamlined and now relies upon an in-depth analysis of use only in the event the affidavit is later challenged by an interested party, instead of with each filing. Unfortunately, this change is likely to lead to increased litigation by unsuccessful applicants who seek to show that the mark has not actually been used. Due to the possibility that an affidavit may be so challenged, trademark owners are well advised to retain evidence of use of the trademark in the event of such a challenge.

Finally, the IPL contains several provisions designed to combat the piracy of foreign marks in Mexico. If marks are used and registered in a foreign country (having reciprocity with Mexico) prior to the filing in Mexico of an application to register such a mark by a party other than the foreign owner, the Mexican authorities are empowered under the IPL to reject such application. In addition, in the event such a mark is successfully registered in Mexico, the foreign owner may seek to nullify such registration within one year of the publication date of the registration. In the case of a registration that was improperly granted due to false information contained in the application, or if the trademark is identical or confusingly similar to a registered mark or an unregistered mark used on the same or similar products

or services, nullification may be sought within five years of the publication date of the registration. A nullification action may be brought at any time if a registered trademark was erroneously determined to meet the criteria for registration, or was wrongfully registered by the agent, representative, user, or distributor of the foreign holder of the mark.

Slogans Slogans, which are defined under the IPL as phrases or sentences whose purpose is to advertise to the public commercial, industrial, or service businesses, or products or services, can gain protection in Mexico only through registration with the Ministry. The protection afforded slogans under the IPL is strengthened from a 10-year nonrenewable term to successively renewable 10-year terms. In the absence of a contrary provision, the provisions of the IPL applicable to trademarks are also generally applicable to slogans. However, the IPL provides no specific sanctions for slogan infringement.

Trade Names The exclusive right to use a trade name identifying a company or industrial, commercial, or service establishment is provided for under the IPL, without the need to publish or register the trade name. This protection extends only to the geographic area of the actual clientele of such company or establishment, but can apply throughout Mexico if a massive and constant dissemination [of the trade name] at the national level occurs. The user of a trade name may also seek publication of the trade name in the Ministry's quarterly Gazette, effectively establishing for a 10-year renewable term from the publication filing date a strong presumption in the adoption and use of the trade name in the designated area. An application for publication of a trade name must be accompanied by evidence of use. Trade names are generally governed under the IPL in all applicable respects by the provisions applicable to trademarks.

Appellations of Origin An appellation of origin is the name of a geographic region used to designate a product originating there wherein the qualities or characteristics of such product are based exclusively on that geographic environment (which may be due to natural or human factors). A declaration of protection of an appellation of origin may be made ex officio by the Ministry or at the request of a party with a legal interest therein. In the event that a declaration of origin is sought for an appellation of origin, the Ministry will publish an abstract of the appellation of origin in the Official Federal Journal [*Diario Oficial*] and allow a public commentary period of two months. The Ministry thereafter determines whether to issue a declaration of protection for the appellation of origin. If the Ministry issues such a declaration, the Mexican federal government will be the holder thereof. The duration of declaration will continue so long as the conditions giving rise to the grant of the declaration of protection continue to exist.

The Ministry will grant an authorization to use an appellation of origin to anyone who (1) is directly engaged in the extraction, production, or preparation of products protected by the appellation of origin, (2) performs the foregoing activities within the territory set forth in the declaration, and (3) complies with the standards established by the Ministry with respect to the products in question. An authorization has a 10-year renewable term. In addition, an authorized user may permit distributors and retailers of its products to use the appellation of origin only if the related agreement with the distributor or retailer is approved and recorded with the Ministry.

Copyright Reforms

In a companion piece of legislation to the IPL, the Mexican Congress passed comprehensive reforms to its *Ley Federal de Derechos de Autor* (Copyright Law, or CL) on July 17, 1991.

The most important of these reforms extends copyright protection to software programs for a term of at least 50 years. Regardless of whether a software program is registered with the Copyright Bureau, a software owner is now entitled to identify itself as the sole legitimate source of the software and to take action against anyone effecting changes in the software or making total or partial unauthorized reproductions. In addition, sound recordings, which were not previously expressly protected under Mexican copyright law, are granted specific copyright protection for a term of at least 50 years. As a consequence, the producers of sound recordings will have greater legal control over the reproduction and distribution of their sound recordings in Mexico.

To support a copyright protection claim, registration of a copyrightable work is recommended. The CL sets forth general procedures for civil redress in the event of copyright infringement. A civil action may be initiated in a federal court or, if neither public policy issues are involved nor criminal sanctions sought, in state court. The CL contains provisions for injunctive relief (court precautionary measures) and also for damages. The minimum amount that may be awarded is equal to 40 percent of the revenues derived from the sale of the infringing products.

Unfortunately, while the Mexican Congress upgraded criminal sanctions for copyright infringement, the sanctions remain significantly flawed and may be of questionable practical value to the copyright owner. Criminal prosecution for copyright infringement requires proof that the infringer acted with the intent of obtaining profit from the illegal activities. While an unrelated provision of the CL defines "profit" as "direct or indirect economic benefit," the provisions setting forth criminal sanctions fail to define what constitutes "profitable intent." This lack of guidance in the CL may well create a substantial obstacle to prosecuting copyright infringement actions, particularly in light of provisions in the Mexican Constitution that prohibit the imposition of criminal sanctions where the legal standards for applying such sanctions are unclear.

LICENSING AND FRANCHISING

The IPL repeals the 1982 Transfer of Technology Law [or 1982 TTL] and the 1990 Transfer of Technology Regulations [or 1990 TTR]. The 1982 TTL, which built upon the restrictive policies embodied in the 1972 Transfer of Technology Law [or 1972 TTL], heavily regulated transfers of various technologies (or forms of industrial property) into Mexico, including patent licenses, industrial model or drawing licenses, trademark and trade name licenses, transfers of know-how, technical assistance, computer programs, certain copyright licenses, and the provision of operational, management, advisory, consulting, and supervisory services. Mexico's regulation of transfers of technology during the 1970s and 1980s, like the substandard protections afforded industrial property rights under the LIT, was philosophically based upon the premise that proprietary rights to ideas or concepts were illegitimate or overreaching and that technology was the heritage of all mankind. At a more practical level, however, the Mexican Government perceived a need to regulate transfers of technology into Mexico to (1) support the development of internally developed technologies and an export market, (2) decrease the amount of foreign exchange spent on importing technology, and (3) augment the bargaining position of the Mexican transferee who, it was believed, was forced to pay exorbitant royalties. To achieve these objectives, the 1982 TTL required the registration of technology transfer agreements and set forth a number of specific grounds for the denial of registration of such agreements. As a consequence, relatively few producers of technology chose to transfer their technologies to Mexico. Those that did so frequently found themselves renegotiating the terms of their private agreements with the Mexican Government.

The 1990 TTR substantially liberalized the procedures for transferring technology to Mexico and, as a consequence, the Ministry almost immediately experienced a flood of applications. (Within 12 months, the number of franchise agreements doubled, compared with the entire period before the 1990 TTR.) Nevertheless, the 1982 TTL remained in place and continued to have a chilling effect upon cautious investors and producers of technology who remained concerned about the permanence of regulatory change in Mexico. Based upon President Salinas' growing political influence, the passage of the IPL reveals the 1990

TTR to be only an interim measure in a continuing effort to obtain permanent change in the treatment of transfers of technology to Mexico. Its passage also reflects the recognition by the Mexican Government that Mexico's competitive position in the world is best enhanced through the removal of barriers to the free flow of technology.

Patent and Trademark Licensing

The IPL completely revamps the legal treatment of transfers of technology to Mexico, and while it does not eliminate all legal barriers to technology transfers, it appears to reduce these barriers to minimum levels. First, the regulatory scope of the IPL is limited to requiring the recordation of patent and trademark licenses and transfers (including licenses and transfers relating to the registration thereof) only, and does not extend to the other types of technology transfer agreements that were previously regulated. Also, while failure to register a technology transfer agreement under the 1982 TTL resulted in the imposition of fines and the agreement being deemed null and void, the primary purpose of recording a patent or trademark license or transfer agreement with the Ministry is to render the transfer of rights thereunder enforceable against third parties.

The application to record a license must be submitted to the Ministry in accordance with the regulations to the IPL. As previously noted, the transitional provisions of the IPL provide that until new regulations are prepared, the existing regulations relating to the LIT will apply. Since the LIT did not generally address the licensing of industrial property rights, no definitive regulatory criteria exist indicating what form of application must be submitted to the Ministry. Nor is it clear whether [to submit] a copy of the license agreement or [just] a simple writ setting forth certain basic information regarding the license agreement. In keeping with the economic policies underlying the IPL, it is hoped that the regulations will permit the filing of a writ so as to avoid public disclosure of the terms of the license agreement (which when recorded becomes available for public inspection).

In contrast to the numerous grounds for denial of registration of a technology transfer agreement under the 1982 TTL, the IPL provides that a license agreement will be recorded unless by its terms the applicability of the IPL is excluded. In addition, recordation of a patent license can be denied if the patent or registration has lapsed or if its duration is longer than the term of the patent or registration. The IPL also specifically provides that recordation of trademark licenses (and, as discussed below, franchise agreements) can be denied for reasons of the public interest. Obviously, the breadth of this provision is of great interest to all parties concerned with the permanence of change in Mexico and particu-

larly to those who have witnessed bureaucratic determinations based on political influence and other nonmeritorious factors. This concern is somewhat mitigated by the requirement that the Ministry state the reasons and legal grounds for rejection of an application to register a trademark license. However, this requirement seems oddly out of place in a law designed to foster the free flow of technology, and presumably reflects the need to make political concessions to isolationist factions within the Mexican Congress. In any event, the recordation of licenses is understood to be more a filing formality than a merit review. Assuming that this provision does not provide the basis for substantial regulatory interference in the transfer of technology to Mexico, the substitution of these recordation standards for those set forth in the 1982 TTL should return to the parties to a license agreement the freedom to contract unhindered by government intervention.

The remainder of the provisions relating to licenses in the IPL are fairly abbreviated, reflecting the expressed policy of deregulation. The working of a patent by a licensee and the use of a trademark by a licensee will constitute use by the patent or trademark owner, as the case may be, so long as the related license is recorded. In addition, if a patent or trademark license is recorded with the Ministry, the IPL empowers the licensee, absent an agreement to the contrary, to take legal action to protect such industrial property rights as if it were the owner thereof. The IPL requires that a trademark licensee produce products or render services of the same quality as are produced or rendered by the owner of the mark. Finally, the recordation of a license may in general be canceled only by a court order or at the joint request of the licensor and licensee. (As a terminated licensee may be less than wholly cooperative, the licensor is well advised to obtain agreement in advance with the licensee upon mechanisms to ensure the prompt cancellation of the license.) Of course, a patent license will terminate upon the nullity or lapsing of the related patent, and a trademark license will terminate in the event the trademark registration is canceled by virtue of the trademark becoming a generic designation for the related product or service.

Parallel Imports

The exponentially increasing volume of trade between the US and Mexico warrants an examination of the treatment of the problem of parallel imports under the IPL. The problem of parallel imports arises where the owner of a species of rights (for example, a patent or trademark) in one country grants a license to a party in another country for the use of such rights, and related products are subsequently transported from one country to the other. The IPL grants protection to any person who trades with, distributes, acquires, or uses the products in question, after such products have been legally introduced into trade. Thus, the foregoing specified persons are protected from legal action being taken against them under the IPL in connection with the importation and distribution of certain products, so long as such products were "legally introduced into trade." While the proper interpretation of this statutory phrase is admittedly open for discussion, the authors believe that the IPL provides the legal holder or licensee of rights in Mexico with the basis to take action against the illegitimate introduction into the Mexican market of products produced outside of Mexico, where legitimacy is based upon the legal authority of the manufacturer and distributor to handle such products. Thus, the legal holder or licensee of rights in Mexico would not, absent a provision to the contrary in a license agreement, be able to take action against the direct sales of products into Mexico by a foreign legal holder or licensee, or the indirect sale of products into Mexico by an authorized distributor. The Mexican holder or licensee of rights, however, should be able to take action under the IPL to prevent the importation of products produced or distributed by an unauthorized party.

Franchising

The sale of a franchise in Mexico has historically been treated as a transfer of technology and was therefore subject to the 1982 TTL. Franchising was first explicitly recognized as a method of doing business under Mexican law in the 1990 TTR, which introduced a number of provisions designed to encourage the development of franchising in Mexico. The IPL defines a franchise similarly to the definition set forth in the 1990 TTR: "A franchise will exist when, with the license of a mark, technical knowledge is transmitted or technical assistance is provided, allowing the person to whom it is granted to produce or sell products or render services uniformly and with the operational, commercial and administrative methods established by the holder of the mark, for the purpose of preserving the quality, prestige and image of the products or services distinguished by the mark."

Pursuant to the IPL, a franchise must be recorded with the Ministry pursuant to the same provisions, and with the same effect, as the recordation of a trademark license. Unfortunately, the ambiguities under the IPL regarding the method of recording trademark license agreements are further exacerbated in the case of franchise agreements. Whether it is necessary to submit a copy of the franchise agreement for recordation, submit a copy of the franchise agreement only if it contains a trademark license, or simply file a writ is not clear.

While the transitional provisions of the IPL do not address the treatment of license or franchise agreements that were registered or submitted for registration under the 1982 TTL (whether pursuant to Article 53 of the 1990 TTR or otherwise), the authors understand that any such agreement will be treated as recorded for purposes of the IPL. With respect to model franchise agreements submitted for registration pursuant to article 54 of the 1990 TTR, it will, however, be necessary to record any subsequently executed forms of franchise agreements under the IPL.

Of great concern to franchise legal practitioners is a passing reference in the IPL to the need to regulate the sale of franchises in Mexico through franchise disclosure requirements. The legislation requires that presale disclosure relating to the status of the franchisor's business be made to the prospective franchisee in accordance with the terms of the regulations to the IPL. Although some unofficial indications have surfaced that minimal disclosure requirements are contemplated, this matter will not be settled until such regulations are published. In the meantime, those selling franchises in Mexico have little guidance as to what disclosure, if any, need be made.

With the general deregulation of the licensing and franchising fields brought about by the repeal of the 1982 TTL and 1990 TTR, legal advisors must shift their attention from a regulatory analysis to more traditional business and legal issues. This role implies greater creativity on the legal advisor's part in handling tax, operational, industrial property, and dispute resolution issues. In addition, the applicability of civil and mercantile laws to the underlying transaction will need to be more carefully considered. Finally, attorneys representing franchisors must develop expertise in advising their clients regarding presale disclosure issues.

INFRINGEMENT AND ENFORCEMENT

Administrative Infringements

The IPL specifically sets forth numerous actionable administrative infringements that include, in general, (1) unfair competition matters, (2) most trademark matters (although actions for an infringing use of the exact trademark, rather than a similar trademark, are generally criminal offenses), (3) most slogan and trade name matters, and (4) all other violations of the IPL that do not constitute criminal offenses. For example, one of the most common causes of action that would be classified as an administrative infringement would be a proceeding brought in response to an unauthorized party's use of a trademark that is similar to, although not the same as, that registered by another for the same or similar goods or services.

An administrative infringement can be initiated ex officio or at the request of an interested party by submitting a petition to the Ministry. The Ministry may then conduct, if the nature of the alleged infringement so warrants, an inspection. If any bona fide infringing goods are found, the Ministry may seize and hold such goods as a precautionary measure. Seizure could be blocked by an *amparo* proceeding, but an alleged infringer is unlikely to have advance notice so as to be able to initiate a proceeding. The alleged infringer is then given an opportunity to respond to the petition, and the Ministry will issue its resolution of the matter based upon the evidence before it. If the Ministry finds an administrative infringement, it may (1) fine the infringer (up to approximately US$43,000, and up to approximately US$2,200 for each day that the infringement persists), (2) temporarily or permanently shut down the infringing business, or (3) imprison the infringer for up to 36 hours. However, the resolution of the Ministry may be appealed by means of an *amparo* proceeding to a federal district court, and from there to a federal circuit court. The implementation of the foregoing sanctions may be delayed until a final, unappealable resolution is entered.

Criminal Offenses

The IPL lists a multitude of criminal offenses, which may roughly be categorized to include (1) patent, utility model, and industrial design matters; (2) trade secret matters; (3) appellation of origin matters; and (4) trademark matters that are generally more egregious than those treated as administrative infringements (including the unauthorized use of a registered mark).

A criminal proceeding may be sought by filing a petition for indictment with the federal prosecutor, which may include a request for inspection and seizure of the allegedly infringing goods. Before the federal prosecutor can initiate a criminal proceeding, however, it is required to seek a technical opinion from the Ministry, which, while not further explained under the IPL, presumably addresses the merits of the petition under the IPL. This opinion is required so that the technical knowledge of the Ministry can be applied at an early date to assist the federal prosecutor in determining whether the alleged infringement justifies instituting criminal proceedings. In practice, attorneys in Mexico frequently seek to expedite this process by delivering directly to the Ministry the request for a technical opinion, and also the request for inspection and seizure of the allegedly infringing goods, as the Ministry is alone empowered to conduct such inspections and seizures.

If the federal prosecutor decides to instigate criminal proceedings, which will in all likelihood be largely determined by the technical opinion, the case will be submitted to a federal criminal court. That court will hear all evidence presented and render its resolution of the matter. The result can be a sentence of up to six years in prison and a fine of up to approximately US$43,000. The resolution of the federal criminal court is appealable to the federal circuit courts.

The foregoing actions for administrative infringements and criminal offenses are in addition to any civil action for damages that may be brought by an aggrieved party. Civil actions will, however, frequently be brought contemporaneously with the initiation of administrative or criminal proceedings, and such proceedings may provide the alleged infringer with the opportunity to raise procedural impediments to the continued prosecution of the related civil action. Given the slowness of the Mexican legal system and the fact that damage awards in Mexico are considerably smaller than in the United States, the incentives for seeking civil damages for an infringement may not be as attractive to holders of industrial property rights in Mexico as in other jurisdictions.

Nullity and Cancellation Proceedings

An interested party may seek a declaration of nullity of a patent (or a utility model or industrial design) or the related registration by filing a petition with the Ministry. A declaration of nullity may be sought on the basis that the patent was improperly granted, or that the pending registration should not be granted. In any event, it must be brought within five years of the date of publication of the patent or registration. Since Mexico provides patent protection to inventions on the basis of the "first to file" rule—rather than the US practice of the "first to invent"—the most common position advanced is that the patent should be annulled because it lacks novelty. Declarations of nullity are frequently submitted as a defense to a criminal proceeding instituted by a patent holder. This defense can be very effective because, under the Mexican legal system, the criminal proceedings may not be continued until the nullity proceedings are completed.

An interested party may seek the cancellation of a trademark (or a slogan or trade name) by filing a petition with the Ministry alleging (1) prior use in Mexico of the mark or a confusingly similar mark; (2) under certain circumstances, prior use and registration abroad; (3) bad faith on the part of the agent, representative, user, or distributor of the holder of a mark registered abroad; or (4) the improper granting of the registration. Proper documentation supporting the allegations must accompany a petition for nullity of a patent or cancellation of a trademark. The holder of the patent or trademark is given the opportunity to answer the allegations, and the Ministry then issues a resolution of the matter. This resolution can be appealed to the federal district courts, and then to the federal circuit courts.

Assessment of the Adequacy of Enforcement Measures

The foregoing enforcement measures reflect an increasing respect accorded to industrial property rights in Mexico. The underlying concern among foreign investors and holders of technology, however, is whether these enforcement measures will be efficiently and effectively implemented. Not only is there concern over whether the administrative infringements and criminal offenses outlined above will be handled expeditiously by the relevant tribunals, but also whether sufficient monies will be allocated to fund the efforts of the Ministry (and eventually the Mexican Industrial Property Institute) and federal prosecutor to carry out on-site inspections and prosecutions of infringements. (Notably, several high-profile enforcement actions have been taken against pirates of Levi's, Louis Vuitton, Bacardi, Reebok, and Pan Am.) Ultimately, Mexico's success in attracting foreign investment and technology may be determined by these types of enforcement issues. As noted below, the NAFTA provisions dealing with various enforcement measures provide further support for the hope that industrial property rights will be effectively protected in Mexico in the future.

NORTH AMERICAN FREE TRADE AGREEMENT (NAFTA)

The intellectual property chapter of NAFTA starts by stating that the basic objective of NAFTA shall be to require that each nation that is a party thereto ("Party") "shall provide in its territory to the nationals of another Party adequate and effective protection and enforcement of intellectual property rights, while ensuring that measures to enforce intellectual property rights do not themselves become barriers to legitimate trade." This laudable goal of removing the barriers to trade traditionally resulting from the territorial nature of intellectual property laws is achieved through a number of specific provisions designed to ensure that certain minimum standards relating to the treatment of intellectual property rights in Mexico, Canada, and the US are met. In fact, the intellectual property provisions of NAFTA [cure] a number of the flaws in Mexico's intellectual property regime that unintentionally, or by strategic design, [remained] after passage of the IPL and the recent reforms to the CL.

The most important improvements to the protection of intellectual property rights in Mexico that are provided for in NAFTA include the following:

- Software programs [obtain] much greater protection, as they [qualify] as "literary works"

under the Berne Convention for the Protection of Literary and Artistic Works (1971) (to which each of the Parties agreed to accede).

- The cable television industry [is] given greater protection, as it [is] a criminal offense to manufacture, import, sell, lease or otherwise make available a device or system used in decoding encrypted program-carrying satellite signals without the proper authorization. Additionally, it [is] a civil offense to receive or further distribute such signals that have been decoded without the proper authorization.

- In seeking cancellation of a trademark registration in Mexico on the basis that the trademark in question is already well known abroad, it [is only] necessary to prove that the trademark is well known in the sector of the public that normally deals with the relevant goods or services, rather than well known by the public at large.

- Where the subject matter of a patent is a process for manufacturing a product, in certain patent infringement proceedings the defendant [has] the burden of establishing that the allegedly infringing product was manufactured by a process other than the patented process.

- Mexico, which [previously provided] no intellectual property protection for semiconductor integrated circuits, will henceforth provide protection in accordance with certain provisions of the Treaty on Intellectual Property in Respect of Integrated Circuits (1989).

In addition to improvements in the protection of intellectual property rights, NAFTA also emphasizes the availability of enforcement measures, and specifically provides that "each Party shall ensure that enforcement procedures ... are available under its domestic law so as to permit effective action to be taken against any act of infringement of intellectual property rights ... including expeditious remedies to prevent infringements and remedies to deter further infringements." While NAFTA addresses a number of specific procedural and remedial aspects of civil and administrative proceedings that will benefit owners of intellectual property, the key thrust of NAFTA is to provide for equitable remedies similar to injunctions granted by US courts.

Mexican tribunals have historically refused to grant requests for pretrial equitable remedies due to their limited stated authority to do so, the imposition on the injured party of unrealistic conditions to the granting of such requests, and a general discomfort with equitable forms of relief. In recognition of the irreparable damage that can result from the infringement of intellectual property rights, NAFTA requires that "each Party shall provide that its judicial authorities shall have the authority to order prompt and effective provisional measures: (a) to prevent an infringement ... and (b) to preserve relevant evidence in regard to the alleged infringement." After determining that the complainant's rights are being infringed or that infringement is imminent, NAFTA provides that a judicial authority need only determine that "any delay in the issuance of [a provisional measure] is likely to cause irreparable harm to the [complainant], or there is a demonstrable risk of evidence being destroyed" in order to grant a provisional measure.

As noted above, Mexico's historic reluctance to grant interim equitable relief has been a matter of great concern to foreign owners of technology. The emphasis accorded such forms of relief in NAFTA is certainly a welcome development, and it is hoped that [now that] NAFTA [has been] adopted, the Mexican implementing legislation and courts will carry into effect its provisions. If [that comes] to pass, a critical step will have been taken to assure foreign owners of technology that their technologies will be effectively protected in Mexico.

Financial Institutions

Mexico's financial scene is in flux; it changes, if not daily or weekly, at least on a monthly basis. The commercial banking system has been in the process of reprivatization since 1990, following its abrupt nationalization in 1982. Some observers consider this reprivatization to be one of the signal achievements of the Salinas government. In an attempt to open up and modernize the system, new banking licenses have been granted to domestic firms, and for the first time in decades, foreign financial institutions are being allowed into Mexican markets, albeit as minority partners. Foreign participation will gradually increase, initially for US and Canadian institutions (which are guaranteed a share of the market under the terms of NAFTA), but also for financiers from other nations as internationalization and competition increases in future years. In a further attempt to demonstrate its commitment to modernization and professional management, in mid-1993 the government granted authority to its central bank, the *Banco de México* (Bank of Mexico, or BOM), to operate separately from the administration, allowing it greater latitude and independence in controlling monetary policy.

Mexican investment houses—brokerage firms, investment banks, mutual funds, venture capitalists, and similar entities, most of which are affiliated through financial groups with commercial banking interests—already play a major role in financial affairs. Mexican regulations do not draw exactly the same distinctions between commercial and merchant banking functions as those made in some other systems, and these entities are likely to play an even greater role as the system develops. Although Mexico wants to continue to shelter its commercial and retail banks from the full brunt of foreign interlopers, officials privately concede that Mexico will need to allow freer rein to outside securities practitioners in order to develop its capital markets operations. Such development is important to institutions such as the Mexican stock exchange—the *Bolsa de Valores*—which has been one of the best performing, most active, and most volatile in the world over the past

several years. The exchange is beginning to show some signs of maturing and gaining added sophistication, settling down to become a more stable, better controlled institution that will actually serve as a source of capital and funds management rather than just as a clubby casino.

Also of critical importance to Mexico's financial situation on a macro level is its foreign debt position. Although nominal debt has actually increased during the years since Mexico declared a moratorium on principal repayment in 1982, the country's ability to deal with its obligations has also grown so much that not only is Mexico no longer a pariah, but it is considered an acceptable credit risk in the international financial markets. Mexico's indebtedness still affects fiscal and monetary policy internally and the behavior of external actors to a huge extent, but Mexico now has considerably more leeway to manage its financial affairs now that it has been seen to be returning to economic and financial health.

For most of the 1980s, this international indebtedness cast a pall over domestic financial operations, leading to a rigorous tight money policy that was implemented by official and private financial institutions and induced the official sector to soak up virtually all credit and liquidity in an attempt to service its debt. This also led to massive capital flight among those who had funds to shelter. The United State's Morgan Guaranty Trust Co. estimated that between 1976 and 1985, US$53 billion left Mexico, US$17 billion of it within a matter of months following the nationalization of the banks in 1982. Although Mexican officials say that this overstates the actual figures and that many billions of dollars of flight capital have since returned, other sources argue that an estimated US$80 billion remains outside the country, nearly enough to cover Mexico's total 1982 foreign debt of US$85 billion.

Although conditions have changed and interest rates and maturities have been deregulated to attract funds into the system, credit is still scarce and extremely expensive in Mexico. In 1993 it was estimated that fewer than one-quarter of Mexico's roughly 1.3 million small- to medium-sized businesses could qualify for commercial bank credit. Credit is often not readily available to outsiders, either (although foreigners may well be able to obtain better access and terms than locals). Because of higher costs at home, most domestic Mexican borrowers large enough to obtain credit go abroad to secure more available and affordable funding. Rates are creeping down incrementally, but they remain suspiciously high. Smaller entities continue to complain that they can't get adequate credit on anything even vaguely approaching affordable terms.

Mexico is underbanked, underbranched, undermortgaged, underinsured, and lacking in corporate financial and securities services. Fewer than 1 percent of households hold mortgages, only about 8 percent have checking accounts, fewer than 2 percent have life insurance, and only about 1 percent have a brokerage account. The Mexican financial system at large does have pockets of sophistication and dynamism; however, it is generally acknowledged to be underdeveloped, inefficient, and lacking in technology, trained personnel, a service orientation, or adequate exposure to international operating standards. Nevertheless, observers are unanimous in saying that it has improved radically during the past several years and that it is virtually certain to improve to an even greater degree, and at an even faster pace, in the future.

THE BANKING SYSTEM

Mexico's banking system consists of the *Banco de México* (BOM), its central bank; commercial banks, including foreign banks; development banks; and auxiliary small institutions such as savings and loans and credit unions.

The Bank of Mexico

Even before 1982, when the banking system was nationalized and the BOM lost its nominal independence, the central bank was seen largely as a government tool, although it also had the reputation for employing honest and capable professionals. The 1993 constitutional amendment that sets the BOM on its own course removes it from the authority of the *Secretaría de Hacienda y Crédito Público* (the Finance Secretariat, generally referred to simply as *Hacienda*). The amendment also voids the authority of the government to borrow directly from the BOM that was granted under nationalization and adds provisions allowing directors to serve for staggered terms, which prevents any single president from packing the board of governors with his own appointees. Both measures are designed to ensure the political independence of the BOM by insulating it from the administration.

Created in 1925, the BOM is responsible for issuing currency, supervising foreign exchange activities, and regulating interest rates. It also functions as the primary clearing agency for the Mexican financial system. Under the terms of the 1993 constitutional amendment, it is explicitly charged with crafting and administering monetary and credit policy, although deregulation has removed several traditional levers from its grasp. In 1989 the government eliminated interest rate and maturity limits on deposit and other instruments which the BOM had previously used to manage interest rates. The administration also dropped burdensome reserve requirements, which had enabled central authorities to rein in credit and siphon off funds from the system to directly support policy initiatives. Absolute reserve requirements were replaced with less restrictive liquidity ratios, a move designed to add liquidity to the system and increase private lending. At the height of the crisis during the mid-1980s as much as 90 percent of available funds were channeled for direct government use, whereas now about 90 percent of funds go to the private sector. Nevertheless, credit has remained tight due to burgeoning demand and continued tight money policies. Finally, Mexico has also eliminated its foreign exchange controls and its two-tiered official and free market rate foreign exchange system that added red tape and expense to transactions. While this is a welcome development, it also leaves the BOM with even less direct control over foreign exchange operations. It now has to resort to such indirect methods of control as open market operations.

Commercial Banks

At the time of the nationalization of the banking system at the end of September 1982, Mexico had 60 private domestic banks of various types. The main ones were *bancas de primer plano* (first tier banks). These are also known as *multibancos*, indicating that they offer a comprehensive range of services. First tier banks are full license commercial banks that can operate in virtually all lines of business, either regionally or nationally. By the late 1980s, these had been consolidated into six national and 12 regional banks, operating more than 4,450 domestic branches, 23 foreign branches, and 21 foreign representative offices. Just the four largest banks—Banamex, Bancomer, Banca Serfin, and Multibanco Comermex—together operate more than 2,000 branches nationwide. They are also reported to be among the most experienced in dealing with multinational firms.

Prior to nationalization, many of these banks were primarily owned and operated by either individuals or closely held family groups. Following nationalization, they were run by executives named by federal authorities. These individuals were often

NOTES FOR FOREIGNERS DOING BUSINESS WITH MEXICAN BANKS

In general, foreign businesses have found that they need to spend more time with their Mexican bankers than with their home country bankers to establish and maintain relationships in hopes of getting needed financing and services. Many foreign observers report that it is necessary to establish multiple banking relationships, usually with as many as three separate banks, in order to be reasonably well assured of meeting all the various needs of a business. Although in theory, Mexican banks are full service banks, few in fact deliver all potential services, and shifting local variations in expertise, infrastructure, funding, and policy can require businesses—both foreign and domestic—to cobble together a correspondingly shifting package of services from different sources to meet their day-to-day as well as special or occasional needs.

Because of this situation, many foreign businesspeople say that they have to watch their cash flow and internal generation of funds far more carefully than they are used to doing at home just in order to avoid having to rely on difficult-to-obtain bank funding and services. As an aside to this cash flow problem, many note that Mexican federal, state, and local governments and official agencies are extremely slow payers, so many businesses have established relatively low caps on the level of official business that they will ac-

cept. (Some domestic firms have reportedly gone bankrupt over the failure of official agencies to pay, with politics reputedly being at the heart of some such disputes.)

Banks in Mexico expect to see a wide variety of documentation before granting a loan. The level of detail required often exceeds what the applicant may be used to providing in his or her home country. This documentation includes detailed, supported marketing information and multi-year business plans, as well as detailed financial information from a foreign parent firm—if one exists—and extensive references from home country banks. Most Mexican banks promise action within 15 days once the application is completed, but completion can be a lengthy procedure because the application itself often seems to be made up especially for the occasion rather than a standardized document. Banking operations are often idiosyncratic and extremely hierarchical, usually requiring successive approvals far up the chain of command before a loan can be authorized. Paperwork and documentary requirements vary from bank to bank, from agency to agency, and, apparently, from time to time—as well as at random. Difficulties in complying with the disclosures and formats required can further delay action for extended periods; some borrowers, finally, simply balk at disclosing the amount of data requested.

---

political appointees rather than banking professionals, operating under strict orders from the central authorities, and the banks were used mainly to collect funds and funnel them into official uses at low margins. In retrospect, most observers see the period as one during which the public was ill served (private credit dried up almost entirely) and the banking system fell even further behind, albeit more through errors of omission than through active mismanagement and malfeasance. The government did recognize the increased pressure of competition from the securities industry. It removed some of the barriers between commercial and investment banking in 1988 and also dropped its set reserve requirements to allow banks greater freedom to compete.

Reprivatization In 1985, as a first step toward reprivatization, the de la Madrid government allowed private ownership of up to 34 percent of banks. However, it remained for the Salinas government to push

through a constitutional amendment calling for the reprivatization of the financial system in May 1990. The banks were to be auctioned off to qualified bidders rather than returned to their previous owners (who had been indemnified following an acrimonious debate during the early part of the de la Madrid administration, his predecessor, López Portillo, having stated that he did not intend to reimburse the expropriated owners). In the first place, the government needed the revenues that would be generated, and in the second place, it wanted to diversify ownership rather than see it concentrated in a relatively few hands. As a practical matter, this diversification was relative because there existed only a small coterie of wealthy and connected individuals and interests capable of bidding for and operating banks. In fact, all the banks were bought by securities firms. Nevertheless, no single individual or institution was allowed to hold more than 5 percent of equity in a bank (10 percent with prior government approval). Foreign participation is allowed up to a maximum holding of 30 percent of equity, but again with a limit of no more than a 5 percent held by any single individual or institutional owner (this limit has subsequently been raised to as high as 20 percent with approval). Qualifying procedures were initiated in late 1990, and sales actually began in June 1991. Except for minority positions retained by the government, all 18 banks had been sold by June 1992, raising an estimated US$12.4 billion.

In late January 1994, the government announced plans to divest itself of its minority bank stock holdings: a 20.4 percent (worth about US$1.8 billion) share in Bancomer, a 6.2 percent (about US$220 million) share in Grupo Financiero Serfin, and a 21 percent (about US$400 million) share in Banco Internacional. The sale of these stakes—some of which consist of nontrading shares that were being held in reserve, to be issued out when conditions turned more favorable—was designed to provide funds to make good on some of the promises made in an attempt to settle social unrest. According to officials, the sale will completely remove the government as a private bank stockholder.

New Banking Licenses Having privatized the existing banks, the National Banking Commission (*Comisión Nacional Bancaria*), which directly regulates banking operations, began issuing new banking licenses, the first in decades. Official goals, both in the privatization of existing banks and the authorization of new ones, included: the encouragement of better regional coverage; the diversification and decentralization of ownership; and the encouragement of the growth of strong, balanced financial conglomerates, as well as the generation of revenue. As of January 1994, the commission had issued 14 new licenses, bringing the total number of authorized commercial banks to 33, including the Mexican subsidiary of Citibank, the only full license foreign bank to operate in Mexico. Three more were approved in early April 1994, nearly doubling the number of commercial bank licenses that had been issued since the reprivatization of the system. The commission announced its intention to issue 19 additional licenses by the end of 1994, bringing the total to 55, almost even with the pre-nationalization level.

Performance and Earnings The reprivatized commercial banks' earnings rose by 26.9 percent in real terms in 1993. As a group, they increased lending by 13.9 percent, again in real terms. The increased profitability resulted largely from the shift from public lending (at a 1 to 2 percent spread) to private lending (with its 10 to 12 percent or greater spread). The two largest banks, Banamex and Bancomer, accounted for 46 percent of the profits in absolute terms. However, their profits actually fell by 7 and

10 percent, respectively, due mainly to charges for investment in technology and restructuring as well as loan loss provisions. Smaller firms actually increased their profits and share by far greater percentage terms, led by BanCrecer (a former trouble spot) which reinforced its recovery with a nearly 345 percent jump in profits. However, these figures also hide huge loan loss provisions that, in some cases, could have resulted in reported losses at smaller banks were it not for creative accounting—such as charging loss provisions against capital instead of earnings (in the future, banks reportedly will be required to take such write-offs against earnings).

Observers expect much of this good news to fade in the future. In the first quarter of 1994, Banamex (Mexico's largest commercial bank), reported a 7.8 percent drop in profits over the prior year's first quarter, attributing the drop primarily to flat inflation-adjusted loan growth. During the 1980s, spreads were small, but government clients paid up, and nonperforming loans accounted for officially less than 1 percent of the dollar value of loans outstanding. Due primarily to rudimentary credit evaluation procedures and—according to the banks—dormant inherited bad loans, nonperforming loans were 7.5 percent of the portfolio at the end of the third quarter of 1993. These figures could rise if the economy continues to be weak. The situation could also deteriorate as the industry learns to cope with greater competition. Part of the reason for the issuance of the flurry of new licenses is the government's attempt to force banks to drop interest rates, which bankers argue have been kept high to cover the banks' high costs and bad loans.

Officials argue that they have done their part by bringing down inflation and deregulating markets, only to see banks keep their rates stubbornly high. Now they hope to bust what they see as a banking cartel, spurring the private sector to lower its rates by bringing to bear added competitive pressure as new bankers jump in droves into the market. Some observers worry that this tactic could backfire. Although the pool of new business is growing rapidly, the pool of lendable funds remains limited, as does the pool of trained personnel. Under the circumstances, having more minimally capitalized, minimally experienced banks, each running around trying to get a piece of the action, could well prove counterproductive. And everyone in Mexico is worried about the threat of the deep pockets, sharp practice foreign bankers hovering on the border, who under the terms of NAFTA must be given at least an 8 percent share of the domestic market by the end of 1994.

And despite its protestations to the contrary, many observers contend that the government continues to pressure the private banks to devote substantial portions of their funds and energies to supporting the existing structure on a favored basis. Although privatization was supposed to take the banks out of the policy-driven lending business, allowing them to conduct their affairs according to free market precepts of risk and reward, in fact they have been prevailed upon to devote portions of their lending to supporting threatened industries and to delaying foreclosure on some of their bad loans—most recently in the agricultural sector—at the behest of the government in order to maintain social peace. For instance, in March 1994 the government reportedly influenced the banks to restructure US$6 billion in loans to small- and medium-sized businesses to allow the entities to remain viable, stretching out repayment periods and reducing terms. The banks agreed only after being allowed by regulators to return some of the loans to performing status, thus reducing their loan loss provisions.

In spring 1994, the International Finance Institute (IFI) announced that it planned to extend membership invitations to some Mexican banks, along with banks from Argentina, Chile, and Venezuela. If accepted, they would become the first Third World members of the international association that represents primarily developed world financial institutions.

Foreign Banks

As of early 1994, Citibank was the only foreign private commercial bank allowed to operate in Mexico, a situation stemming from historical accident. Citibank began doing business in Mexico in 1928, at which time most foreign banks were withdrawing due to anti-foreign feeling and general unrest. By 1932 the government was entering an isolationist phase and banned foreign banks from setting up branches in the country. However, Citibank, the only remaining foreign bank operating in Mexico, was grandfathered and hung on in Mexico throughout the succeeding years. As an authorized wholly foreign-owned bank, it also escaped nationalization in 1982. Even so, it has operated under conditions that are somewhat more restrictive than those accorded to domestically owned banks. One of the advances of the new system, especially after NAFTA, is the requirement that Mexico accord foreign financial institutions the same treatment as national institutions. It has agreed to do so, but at the cost of requiring them to abide by all rules to which national entities are subject.

In the years following World War II, foreign banks were allowed to open representative offices that could engage in a variety of activities, as long as they did not generate income payable in Mexico. Representative offices can promote business or negotiate contracts and trade deals that are concluded and fulfilled overseas, and so have considerable freedom to operate as long as the revenue is not booked onshore. As of the end of 1993, there were more than 100 such representative offices operating in Mexico. Foreign banks are also allowed to operate offshore banking facilities physically located in Mexico but dealing exclusively in extraterritorial activities, although such operations receive no particular incentives and foreign institutions have been uninterested.

Provisions for Entry Because of the opening provided for in NAFTA, many foreign banks—especially US and Canadian banks—are expected to pour into Mexico. However, officials announced at the end of January 1994 that rules governing such foreign entry would be delayed until spring, after which they must go to US and Canadian officials for comment before they can be finalized and published. Even after the official publication of such regulations, there is usually a 90-day application period, and the authorities usually wait until the close of the application period to competitively evaluate the entire applicant pool at once before parceling out the limited number of licenses to be granted. The NAFTA accord itself provides a maximum of 120 days for national authorities to act on applications. Observers expect that it will be the end of the year before the first such foreign operating licenses are granted.

Mexico has announced that it plans to grant 10 foreign bank operating licenses between 1994 and 2004. Preliminary indications are that the minimum capital required will be in the neighborhood of US$20 million to US$25 million. The initial 1994 tranche for foreign banks will involve a total capitalization of about US$1.3 billion, with a maximum capitalization per unit of about US$250 million; no foreign entity will be allowed to hold more than a 1.5 percent share of the total Mexican market as determined by the total registered capital of the banking system. Observers estimate that between 20 and 30 foreign banks have already indicated interest by submitting applications to home country regulators for authorization to operate in Mexico.

Conversely, Mexican banks are also allowed to buy into US and Canadian banks. In April 1994, Grupo Financiero Interacciones bought 100 percent of the stock in the Laredo National Bank, a Texas bank involved in trade and retail operations.

Foreign banks seeking to operate in the country face another issue: Mexico places strict limitations on branching. Although the major Mexican banks have large networks of branches nationwide, long-time foreign operator Citibank has only five branch offices, in Mexico City and Monterrey. Citibank is seeking authorization to branch nationwide, although officials have indicated that they favor maintaining unitary banking rules for foreigners.

Many foreign banks have also expressed a particular interest in becoming involved in Mexican securities market operations. However, under the terms of NAFTA, no foreign bank engage in operations in Mexico that it does not pursue in its home country, and direct securities operations are still restricted for banks in the US and Canada (although banks in these countries are allowed to operate securities subsidiaries within certain limits). As a practical matter, foreign banks will probably need to establish a joint venture or some other type of formal strategic business alliance with Mexican national firms to engage in such businesses. However, it may ultimately prove to be easier for foreign banks to enter these businesses despite having to do so somewhat indirectly, because such activities are considered to be less sensitive than higher profile retail and commercial banking.

Although interested in doing business in Mexico, many foreign banks are wary of a direct commitment for a variety of reasons. Despite the opportunity to participate in a major opening in a rapidly developing economy, foreign bankers still worry that they will be treated as second class, alien corporate citizens. Few are willing to accept a subordinate minority position from which they feel they would be unable to exercise adequate control. Others are concerned that they would lose control over expensive technology and other information or be seen as a deep pockets source for special interest or otherwise speculative projects. Still others express fear that Mexican banks might not be willing to take on the larger deals that foreign banks are accustomed to doing because of lack of capital and experience; they fear also that the foreign partners could thus be restricted to doing marginal business. As an alternative to taking an official minority ownership position, many foreign institutions are considering project-specific joint ventures designed to enter particular areas of business on a stronger, more independent footing.

The goals of regulators involve the hope that a foreign presence will invigorate the national banking system by providing expertise, technology, capital, and healthy competition, resulting in a stronger domestic banking system and lower across-the-board interest rates. However, the limitations placed on foreign financial operations and the relatively small market share allotted to them under NAFTA—8 percent to begin with, rising to 15 percent by the year 2000, after which there are to be no limits—suggest that neither side is likely to be fully satisfied with the results for some time.

Bank Services, Operations, and Relationships

Lending Mexican first tier banks are allowed to offer virtually any financial service, including basic retail and commercial banking services and many investment and securities services. Commercial bank lending is relatively well developed, although funds are often scarce and costs are high. Mexican banks can finance land acquisition, plant construction, purchases of equipment—both domestic, which is preferred, or imported—and working capital loans. Under existing regulations, Mexican banks cannot finance imported used equipment unless it is of US origin. Most short-term financing is on a line-of-credit basis. Alternatively, it can be collateralized by inventory or customer receivables. Overdraft accounts and revolving credit facilities are not generally used. Parent company guarantees are often demanded, but have not usually resulted in lower rates or better conditions for borrowers. Borrowers are encouraged to do additional business with the lending bank and may be requested to maintain substantial compensating balances, although this may not legally be required as a condition of the loan.

The maximum loan amount to a single individual borrower was set at NP$198 million (about US$60 million) and NP$2.4 billion (about US$725 million) to a single corporate borrower as of mid-1993, amounts designed to limit lending to a percentage of the net capital of the lending bank and the commercial banking system as a whole. Most banks require a minimum total loan package amount—including ancillary fee-based services—of US$100,000. Lending can be in pesos or US dollars. Dollar working capital and trade financing loans are usually made for set terms of 30, 60, 90, 180, or 360 days. Term loans are usually for periods of seven to nine years, although Mexican banks will consider lengthier terms, usually if the project is approved by a government agency, especially if government agency guarantees are available. Lending is usually on a prime plus basis, with a spread of about 1.5 percent on short-term lending for top credits. Long-term lending has carried a spread of about 4 percent above prime, plus an additional 1 percent to cover withholding for taxes if land and buildings are financed.

Both public and private lenders will usually fund as much as 80 to 85 percent of the value of a project, but they expect to see the borrower put up the remainder using his or her own rather than borrowed funds. Commercial mortgages are usually made for up to 50 percent of the value of generalized facilities, although this is usually reduced to 30 percent of value for specialized plant. Payments are usually arranged on a quarterly, semiannual, or annual basis, and Mexican banks have usually expected a balloon payment at the end of the term rather than amortization over the life of the loan.

Peso financing is available to both foreign and domestic firms, but it is more expensive than dollar financing. Most banks require a package minimum of NP$1.5 million (about US$450,000). Peso credits of whatever maturity are usually offered on a floating rate basis tied to the rates of treasury bills plus a spread. At the end of the first quarter of 1994, treasury bills (*certificados de tesoreria*, known as CETEs) were running around 10 percent. Borrowers complain that the cost of such loans, which has reached levels as high as 40 percent and has recently stalled in the 20s, is a major drawback to successful operations. The situation is often even worse for consumers, who have been paying 30 percent on such big ticket long-term borrowings as auto loans and mortgages and 40 percent on revolving and credit card debt.

Services and Types of Accounts Other services offered by banks include basic transaction services, credits secured by receivables (some are even beginning to package and securitize such receivables for sale on international capital markets), trade financing, letters of credit, foreign exchange transactions, leasing, money market accounts and trading, and certificates of deposit. In addition to regular checking accounts, individual and commercial accounts offered include: *cuentas maestras* (master accounts, or asset management-type accounts that automatically transfer excess balances to an interest bearing investment account); passbook savings accounts; *pre-establecidos* (fixed rate savings accounts from which withdrawals can be made only on certain days of the month); nonnegotiable certificates of deposit with fixed rates and terms ranging from 30 to 725 days; and promissory notes (fixed rate discount notes with 7- or 30-day maturities). Banks also deal in banker's acceptances, commercial paper, *pagarés empresarial bursátil* (promissory notes issued by companies and backed by CETEs), and *pacobers* (promissory notes indexed to the foreign exchange rate). Most also offer a full range of securities services through other subsidiaries of their parent firms and may offer investment banking and management and other consulting services directly.

Real deposits grew by 27.5 percent in 1990 alone, and the character of deposits is also changing, with more going into specialized accounts such as *cuentas meastras* instead of to transaction accounts. However, the Mexican public is still underbanked, and the majority do not have the assets to make a basic transaction account worthwhile, much less support investment accounts, credit cards, or other services. Most Mexican banks require a minimum opening deposit of NP1,000 (about US$300, around 10 times the weekly minimum wage and beyond the means of the vast majority of Mexicans), and many require account holders to maintain a minimum balance. Consequently, an estimated 80 percent of Mexicans do not have any form of account or relationship with a formal financial institution. And despite the opening of tens of thousands of new individual retirement accounts, the total number of bank accounts fell by 60 percent from 21.5 million to 8.5 million between 1991 and 1993. The number of savings accounts fell by a comparable percentage, from 15.5 million to 5.9 million during the same period, and the total number of bank branch outlets shrank by about 5 percent, from 4,739 in 1991 to 4,493 in 1993, a further indication of the growing disparity in the distribution of wealth and incomes in Mexico.

Development Banks

The government of Mexico operates four development banks designed to support officially approved projects on a policy basis. These agencies include the *Nacional Financiera, S.A.* (Nafin, or sometimes Nafinsa), *Banco Nacional de Comercio Exterior, S.N.C.* (Bancomext), *Banco Nacional de Obras y Servicios Publicos* (Banobras), and *Banco Nacional de Crédito Rural, S.N.C.* (Banrural). Most international public, private, and agency funds to Mexico are administered by these national intermediaries, as are government funds. Access to funding through these agencies for firms with partial or major foreign ownership varies according to the specific funding programs, the particular project, and current policy dictates. However, at least some potential funding for firms with foreign participation is available, through Nafin and Bancomext in particular. (Because of the nature of the sectors in which they operate, Banobras and Banrural have not generally financed projects for foreign firms.)

Government development bank financing, when available for specific projects, is generally comparable to private financing for conditions, terms, and cost. The official development banks often offer their financing in cooperation with private banks or administratively channel their funds through such banks. Despite protestations from the government that it is focusing on market mechanisms, many of the programs supported by these official agencies involve the shoring up of threatened national industries, although generally the policy seems to be designed primarily to smooth the transition rather than impede it.

Nafin Founded in 1934, Nafin is the principle official source of industrial development funds. It has gradually shifted its development lending focus from large industrial firms (which are now able to borrow on their own in the private sector as well as internationally) to firms that range from the very small (also called microfirms) to those that are medium-sized. In decreasing the size of the clients it serves, Nafin has also increased the risk profile of the projects it funds. Nafin can also write guarantees on credits for government projects, as well as on private projects determined to be of importance for national development. Nafin is allowed to take minority positions in a variety of companies, usually for a maximum period of five years, after which it must sell its holdings to a third party. Because of this development role, which approaches operation as a venture capital firm, the agency also has had a hand in organizing the stock market, although it has largely been replaced in the capital markets by other institutions as those markets have grown. The agency also functions in a development promotion role.

Nafin focuses on supporting businesses that involve increased use of technology; the development of environmental industries; infrastructure improvement and industrial decentralization projects; very small- to medium-sized businesses; process upgrading; and support services. To underwrite the competitive position of its national industries in the wake of NAFTA, Nafin is targeting special support for such industries as textiles, apparel, leather, footwear, capital goods, pharmaceuticals, dairy products, plastics producers, and gas and oil distributors and retailers, all of which are under increased competitive pressure. (Many observers would put this focus under the heading of policy subsidies, although officials deny this characterization.) Other targeted projects include joint foreign-domestic ventures that will result in job creation, exports, or other foreign exchange generation. Tourism has been specifically targeted within this category.

Nafin is currently involved in projects with multinational firms designed to develop alternative crops and a marketing infrastructure for small farmers who currently grow staple crops and who are expected to lose their subsidies and economic viability.

Special rates exist for microbusinesses (with 15 or fewer employees), small businesses (15 to 100 employees), and medium-sized businesses (100 to 250 employees). Approved projects by such businesses can get up to 100 percent financing and special low interest rates for job creation and export generation. Nafin has also earmarked a US$20 million fund to finance joint ventures between Mexican nationals and US Hispanic-run businesses. Under the terms of this set-aside, Nafin will take up to 25 percent of the equity, with the Mexican partner taking 25 percent and the US partner 50 percent, for a period of up to seven years. The targeted areas are furniture, textiles, food processing, agriculture, generalized commerce, various services, and environmental industries.

Project lending has been for minimum packages of US$1.5 million, with no stated upper limits. Terms are five to seven years, although some preferred low-risk projects are eligible for financing for up to 20 years for fixed asset and long-term working capital uses. At the beginning of 1994, rates were typically between 10.5 and 12.75 percent.

In early 1994, Nafin announced that it expected to lower interest rates and increase lending during 1994 to as much as twice the level of 1992 (for a total of around US$20 billion). Two-thirds of this will be in peso credits, with the remainder in loans denominated in foreign currency. Nafin funds its lending through bonds placed in international capital markets. In January 1994, it placed US$150 million in floating rate Euronotes. It was also set to issue US$200 million in five-year notes as Dragon bonds in Far Eastern markets.

Bancomext Founded in 1937, Bancomext finances exports on a short- to long-term basis, writes guarantees on international trade transactions to ensure payment to domestic exporters, finances approved imports, and underwrites domestic development and production for export. It also promotes national exports and, to some extent, foreign investment in Mexico generally, operating a series of databases on products, prices, production, and bidding information. In its general role as the national entity in charge of trade, Bancomext seeks to serve small- and medium-sized exporters, trading intermediaries, and downstream producers supplying exporters. The primary focus is on export financing, but Bancomext also finances purchases of approved Mexican goods by foreign importers abroad and of approved foreign goods by domestic importers into Mexico. Credits are usually approved and funded by the agency, but delivered through existing correspondent financial institutions, either at home or abroad. Bancomext provides the discounted funds to the financial intermediary, which then passes them along to the borrower at a below-market rate. The agency also handles certain international financial negotiations and arrangements on behalf of the government of Mexico. Because it has this role, it maintains direct lines of credit and links with foreign banks, foreign government export-import agencies, and international agencies such as the World Bank. Headquartered in Mexico City, Bancomext operates 25 local offices nationwide and 40 international offices.

Bancomext provided US$13.5 billion in credits in 1990 and US$14.7 billion in 1991. Its 1990 operations included financing: non-oil exports (85 percent); imports (10 percent); trade-related infrastructure development (4 percent); and national export firms (1 percent). Bancomext relies primarily on international agency funding from the World Bank and the International Monetary Fund (IMF), as well as credits from overseas export-import banks. At the beginning of 1994, Bancomext was offering loans denominated in either US dollars or pesos for amounts up to US$10 million at rates of about prime plus 2.5 percent. Some preferred loans were going for a fixed rate of 7.5 percent. Most transaction-based financing was for periods ranging from 90 to 360 days. Long-term loans are available for a maximum of US$25 million to cover up to 75 percent of the value of a project for a maximum term of nine years. A three-year grace period can extend the effective life of the loan to 12 years. Some fixed asset loans were available at prime plus a 5 to 6 percent spread.

Specific programs include the successor to the Fund to Promote Exports of Manufactured Products, known as FOMEX. Bancomext took over responsibility for this program in 1989, which provides: working capital credits as pre-export financing; term financing to support general overseas export development; import substitution development financing; credit guarantees for associated risks not commercially insurable; financing of technical assistance programs designed to increase exports; financing of certain operations of trading companies (to provide improved access to their services for smaller exporters); and financing of downstream suppliers of components that go into export goods.

To promote Mexican exports, Bancomext offers a buyer's credit program to finance foreign importer's purchases of Mexican goods. The buyer opens a sight letter of credit (L/C) in favor of the Mexican supplier, and Bancomext offers financing issued through the buyer's home country bank, usually in US dollars. Terms can include financing of up to 100 percent of the total amount for up to one year for primary, intermediate, or noncapital manufactured goods; capital goods can receive multi-year loans at prime plus rates. Interest is payable in advance on loans of up to one year. A seller's credit plan allows sellers to get similar financing, which they can then extend to the buyer. In 1991 Bancomext began offering factoring services, discounting invoices from exporters seeking prompt payment, the first such organized official operation in Mexico.

Bancomext is also the agency charged with organizing countertrade. This type of exchange—in which commodities or other products are exchanged in self-canceling deals rather than as unrelated cash or credit transactions, usually on a government agency-to-agency basis—is uncommon. However, Bancomext has arranged some such transactions, usually with other members of ALADI (Latin American Integration Association). Bancomext has also been investigating countertrade as a means of encouraging trade with cash-poor countries such as those in Eastern Europe. In past deals, the exchange has been made on the basis of cash sales for which the participants arranged financing rather than through direct barter.

Banobras and Banrural Banobras provides financing for construction projects, usually officially approved housing and infrastructure projects that have been largely closed to foreign participation. Some of its operations are being replaced by private contractors operating under concessions—one of the Salinas administration's innovations designed to bring private capital into infrastructure development. Banrural provides financing for agricultural production and related rural development projects. Its primary focus has been on financing annual crop production, and it recently shifted from offering subsidized below-market rates on its lending to farmers to charging prime plus market rates, a move designed to discourage marginal production and one that has met with an outcry in the hinterlands.

The North American Development Bank One of the provisions inserted into NAFTA in response to concerns about environmental issues was the call for the creation of a North American Development Bank to fund environmental cleanup projects along the US–Mexico border. This bank, to be funded initially by contributions from the US and Mexico, is scheduled to begin operations October 1, 1994. The initial contribution of US$50 million has been appropriated by the US to fund start-up costs. Both the US and Mexico are to contribute US$225 million annually for four years to fund the operations of the bank, which is to be based in Houston, Texas. The bank is subsequently expected to issue its own bonds.

Financial Groups

The new face of the Mexican financial system is the financial group, or *grupo financiera*. The entities of this group are essentially holding companies for a series of interrelated financial and ancillary operations. These groups arose primarily to take over the reprivatized banks, but are in fact restructuring the financial system by making it more comprehensive. Individual investors were initially limited to a maximum of 5 percent of a bank's shares, although this limit has since been raised to as much as 20 percent with government approval. However, financial groups can now own 100 percent of not only a bank, but certain other financial institutions as well. In fact, all of the 18 reprivatized banks were bought by financial groups organized for the purpose and owned by brokerage houses. To date, all newly issued banking licenses have been granted to newly formed financial groups. Such groups are allowed to use the same group name for all their various subsidiary operations and share common administrative, clerical, and back office personnel—practices that are often discouraged or limited elsewhere.

The regulations governing financial groups allow holding company groups, bank groups, and brokerage groups. If a group is headed by a bank, it cannot have a brokerage member and vice versa. However, a holding company group can combine both a bank and a brokerage, as has been the case with all the major groups formed to date. As amended, the law allows financial groups to be formed by a minimum of two separate types of financial institutions (prior to 1994, it took a minimum of three types of institution). Such groups can consist of one of each type of financial institution: commercial bank, brokerage firm, financial warehousing operation, bonding company, leasing company, factoring company, mutual fund, and insurance company. More than one insurer can be included if the different firms operate in different areas, such as life as distinct from a separate property and casualty firm. Different mutual funds can be owned if they invest in different types of securities. A subsidiary of a financial group cannot acquire a partial interest in a similar firm, but it can merge or acquire all of another similar firm, thus increasing its coverage and clout.

The largest financial groups are GFB, Banacci, Invermexico, Inverlat, Probursa, OBSA, and Mexival. Each consists of a major bank and brokerage house as well as subsidiary institutions, and all were formed to privatize the major banks sold by the government in 1991.

NONBANK FINANCIAL INSTITUTIONS

Mexico has a variety of mostly medium-sized financial institutions that are designated as auxiliary credit institutions. These are designed to serve the specialized needs of particular clienteles. Although many of the basic types of institutions have existed in one form or another for some time, the system has been largely revamped by new legislation enacted since 1989. Many of these institutions represent spin-offs of banking operations. Others represent attempts to bring informal financial operations into the formal sector, both to improve control and to enhance coverage for previously underserved areas (which, as noted, include the 80 percent of the population that functions outside the banking system). Included among these specialized financial institutions are: new savings and loan companies, credit unions, leasing corporations, factoring companies, currency exchange houses, mortgage banks, chartered public merchandise warehouses, and bonding companies, as well as insurance companies and pension funds. NAFTA does not establish specific limits on foreign participation in many of these types of financial institution, although it does for larger, more formal, more heavily regulated institutions. This potentially allows foreigners greater freedom to operate in several of these areas.

Specialized Commercial Financial Institutions

These institutions include leasing companies, factoring companies, chartered public warehouses, bonding companies, and foreign exchange houses, as well as credit unions at the less formal end of the spectrum. Leasing companies (*arrendadoras financieras*) finance capital goods and equipment. Factoring companies deal in *factoraje*, the discounting of invoices

to enable firms to receive cash prior to the maturity of notes on sales—an activity pioneered by Bancomext, but now expanded as a service provided by various private companies. Financial warehouses (*almacenadoras*) cover a broad range of commercial applications, including: the bonded warehousing of imported goods; deposits of inventory; the holding of goods as security; the financing of goods held; and the writing of negotiable receipts on goods deposited that form the basis for the issue of derivative securities. Bonding companies issue *garantías*—guarantees or warranties—of performance to back up the primary parties in the contract. Exchange houses (*casas de cambio*) deal in foreign exchange. They may offer slightly less favorable exchange rates on primary transactions because they must make a profit on the bid–ask spread, although they are often as competitive as other outlets. They also offer additional, related services, such as providing a means to either hedge or speculate on Mexican currency, which is not heavily traded outside the country.

There are no formal limitations on foreign participation or individual firms' market share assignments for such auxiliary specialized financial institutions, although aggregate limits on market share exist for leasing and factoring firms. The Finance Secretariat has yet to issue specific rules and guidelines on many questions regarding these operations, and it retains discretionary authority to authorize foreign participation on a case-by-case basis. It has announced that foreign holdings in such institutions will be nontransferable to other parties, implying that foreign investors who sought to get out of such deals would have to liquidate the operations. However, it has indicated that it intends to be relatively amenable to approving applications by foreigners to operate in these areas.

A credit union is a semiformal cooperative financial institution organized to serve its member small enterprises, which operate in the same type of business and which are usually based in the same geographic area. Credit union members band together to improve their chances in applying for reduced rate credit from government development banks. In 1993 there were about 200 such unions, about half of them operating in the agricultural sector. In late 1993, in an effort to bring these institutions into the formal arena, the government authorized official credit union charters for virtually all existing entities. Because of the nature of credit unions, foreign businesses are not allowed to operate, participate in, or access financing through them.

Specialized Personal Financial Institutions

These institutions include savings and loan associations, mortgage companies, credit card com-

NAFTA: FINANCIAL SERVICES PROVISIONS

The North American Free Trade Agreement (NAFTA) extends the benefits of national treatment to US and Canadian financial service firms and bars Mexico from requiring that such firms establish Mexican incorporation or residency. The agreement allows for various limits on such foreign investment prior to the year 2000. Specific procedural rules remain to be worked out, and actual authorizations are expected to be delayed or modified. The limits included in the agreement are ceilings on foreign participation in a given year. However, there is no minimum requirement, or floor, established, and actual participation may not reach the maximum level.

Although NAFTA sets limits on the establishment of new financial services operations in the various member countries, it asserts the rights of residents to procure financial services from any source within the member nations. The member nations are also barred from instituting additional restrictions on cross-border provision of financial services, although existing restrictions will remain in place for the present. Each member country must also allow other signatory participants to offer within its territory any new services that it allows its own nationals to offer in the future.

Commercial Banks US and Canadian banks are to be allowed to establish commercial banking operations in Mexico equivalent to as much as 8 percent of the total domestic market (as determined by total bank capitalization) in 1994, the first year of the agreement. This percentage share is scheduled to rise incrementally to a maximum 15 percent market share in 1999. No individual foreign bank can exceed a maximum 1.5 percent of the total domestic banking market through 1999. These individual and cumulative share limits are scheduled to expire in the year 2000. However, even after the year 2000 arrives, foreign banks are prohibited from gaining cumulatively more than 4 percent of national market share in any one year through acquisition of existing domestic institutions.

Securities Firms US and Canadian securities firms can claim up to 10 percent of the domestic market as defined by securities firm capitalization in the first year of the agreement, 1994; this share allowance is scheduled to rise to a 20 percent maximum in 1999. Limits are scheduled to expire in the year 2000. No foreign securities firm can exceed a maximum 4 percent share of the market prior to the year 2000.

Finance Companies US and Canadian finance companies—leasing companies, factoring companies, chartered public warehouses, bonding companies, foreign exchange houses, mortgage companies, and credit card companies—can establish separate subsidiaries in Mexico. The size of such operations will be limited until the year 2000, but specific authorizations and limits are to be decided by the Secretariat of Finance *(Hacienda)* on a case-by-case basis. Foreign operators of these companies are not allowed to transfer their interests in the firms.

Insurance Companies A US or Canadian insurance firm that had an existing interest in a Mexican insurer as of July 1992 can acquire up to 100 percent of that Mexican firm by 1996. A US or Canadian firm that acquires a position in a Mexican insurer beginning in 1994 can acquire up to 100 percent ownership in that insurer by the year 2000. Such foreign investors can establish subsidiaries in Mexico taking up to 6 percent of the market (as defined by total insurance company capitalization) in 1994, rising to 12 percent in 1999, after which specific share limits will expire. They may also establish joint ventures with existing Mexican firms. Prior to the year 2000, no foreign firm can have more than a 1.5 percent share of the Mexican insurance market by sector. Preliminary interpretations suggest that a single firm could hold a 1.5 percent share in the life insurance sector as well as in the property and casualty sector.

Non-NAFTA Foreign Investors Under the terms of the 1993 Foreign Investment Law, foreigners are limited to a 30 percent ownership share in any Mexican financial group, commercial bank, insurance company (through a joint venture with an existing Mexican firm), securities firm, or stock market specialist operation. They are limited to a 49 percent stake in any Mexican insurance company, bonding company, bonded warehouse, leasing company, factoring company, and securities specialist. With prior Foreign Investment Committee approval, they may own between 49 and 100 percent of a Mexican credit information company, securities rating company, or insurance agency.

Many observers expect Mexico to extend the preferential treatment contained in the NAFTA agreement to other investors on a country-by-country basis via the signing of specific agreements that use NAFTA as a model.

panies, and the *Monte de Piedad* (a system of national pawn shops), all of which are designed to provide banking services and extend personal credit to individuals through the formal sector. Although personal financial services are readily available from established banks in urban areas (at least for those who are formally employed at reasonably high levels), rural and other lower-income individuals have not traditionally participated in the formal financial sector, which does not find it profitable to serve them. Much economic activity in Mexico occurs not merely informally and off the books, but as cash or noncash barter transactions—without the participation of financial intermediaries. This is partially due to a lack of information as well as a lack of available vehicles for participation in the formal system, compounded by the lack of interest of the financial institutions in small-scale business. Transactions and payment systems have never been primary focuses of the Mexican financial system as has been the case elsewhere. Even checks are still viewed—and distrusted—by many as somewhat exotic instruments, a perspective reinforced by years of high inflation and inefficient service that made payment by any means other than cash a risky venture.

Banks operate most of these ancillary personal finance institutions, such as mortgage and credit card companies, as subsidiary activities. However, savings and loan associations are organized as separate, not-for-profit independent entities, while the national pawn shop system is a quasi-official institution.

Mortgage companies make long-term (by Mexican standards) loans to finance the purchase of real estate. Most mortgage companies are owned and funded by banks. Although banks usually offer mortgage lending through their regular outlets, they seldom make much of an effort to get business, especially at the lower end of the retail market. Two new licenses were granted for mortgage companies in early 1994. Credit card companies are also a relatively new development in Mexico, where few qualify for or familiar with the concept of revolving credit, which has been further discouraged by hyperinflation, slow payment, and a high error rate. New regulations allow broader foreign participation in this area, primarily in hopes of upgrading relatively rudimentary existing national operations.

Mexico also operates a system of national pawn shops—the *Monte de Piedad* ("mountain of pity")—an institution dating back to colonial days. People can use this institution to obtain small, short-term loans using personal effects as collateral. In the mid-1980s the average loan was the peso equivalent of about US$10 (with most of the transactions made around the holidays), although loans in the US$50 to US$100 range can be arranged by entrepreneurs for purposes of small capital investments. *Monte de*

Piedad outlets were charging around 4 percent per month in late 1993.

Mexican savings and loan institutions are not-for-profit entities that offer basic transaction, savings, and lending services to provide short- to intermediate-term credit in relatively small amounts to individual consumers. These are the official successors to the *cajas populares* ("the people's strong boxes") founded in 1951 by a group of Catholic priests to provide credit and financial services for low-income people outside the banking system. These institutions, although quasi-religious in origin, are secularly administered. They operate as cooperatives, similar to credit unions elsewhere, in which someone becomes a member upon making a deposit—usually of around US$90 to US$150, still rather high for Mexico, but less than half the minimum required by a commercial bank—and then is eligible for services, including loans. In 1993 there were 147 *cajas*, serving roughly 320,000 members altogether, that were affiliated with the *Confederación Mexicano de Cajas Populares*, the national trade association. In late 1993, interest rates on loans from the *cajas* were as low as 15 percent on an annualized basis, well below market rates, although rates for many uses and amounts could run 35 percent or more—as high as those charged by commercial banks. Under a 1991 law, the semiformal *cajas* were allowed to register as not-for-profit recognized savings and loan institutions provided they met certain minimum requirements. There has been little rush to do so, although six savings and loans were licensed during the last half of 1993, plus four more in early 1994.

The savings and loan institution is being promoted as an alternative to the *tanda* ("turn" or "shift"), an informal (and at best only semi-legal) type of association common in much of Latin America. Such an operation is generally formed by a group of neighbors or associates and is often sponsored by a nonfinancial commercial business, with the purpose of selling its high-ticket goods (that require financing). In the classic *tanda*, a group of people—each interested in buying an item such as a refrigerator or automobile—band together and agree to put in a set amount on a weekly, monthly, or some other periodic basis for a specified period of time, generally long enough for each individual to save the price of one item. First, enough money is collected to purchase one in a timeframe that is based on the number of participants. Then the members either hold a lottery to decide who gets the first item, or award it based on an agreed-upon schedule (the organizer usually gets the first item so purchased). Members are obligated to continue to pay the periodic amount whether they get their item in the first period or the last period of the deal. Any excess funds are invested, with the earnings on the investment going either to reduce the cost to all members or paid out as dividends to them. Although the primary function has been to enable consumers to make purchases, some *tandas* are reportedly being used to provide venture capital to finance small businesses as well.

Although it is an ingenious and cooperative means of acquiring expensive items, the unregulated *tanda* can cause problems when early "winners" or other participants fail to make their subsequent payments, or when there is misuse of the collected proceeds by those managing the operation. However, because of social pressures on participants not to default, such occurrences are rare.

Insurance Companies

Mexico's insurance market was the 27th largest in the world, with premiums that reached US$3.5 billion in 1991. Premiums rose to US$5 billion in 1992, and observers predict that the market could grow to US$50 billion within the next 10 to 15 years. Mexico is considered to be one of the most underserved markets for its size and composition. Only about 1.5 million persons hold individual life policies; fewer than one-quarter of vehicles and only about 2 percent of homes are insured (insurance covered fewer than 15 percent of the buildings damaged in the 1985 earthquake); and the per capita expenditure on all insurance products was about US$31 in 1991 (as compared with US$1,929 in the US).

Insurers are allowed to invest the excess above their required reserves. Mexican insurers have primarily invested the higher risk portions of their portfolios in real estate, but because the industry is relatively underdeveloped, it has not been a ready source of investment funds in Mexico. This is expected to change as the industry grows and becomes more competitive as foreign companies begin to enter Mexico under the auspices of NAFTA.

The insurance industry is regulated by the National Insurance Commission (*Comisión Nacional de Seguros y Fianzas*) of the Finance Secretariat. Regulation has been highly restrictive, with all risks for which the insurable interest is located in Mexico required to be written by companies authorized to do business in Mexico—which has meant Mexican firms. Foreign firms can be authorized to have a maximum 49 percent minority interest in Mexican insurance firms. This overall stringent regulation, which began to ease in 1990, will loosen further under NAFTA.

Under NAFTA, US and Canadian firms with existing minority interests in Mexican firms as of July 1992 are eligible to acquire 100 percent ownership of those firms as early as 1996. New entrants can acquire as much as 30 percent ownership of operations beginning in 1994, a share that rises to 100 percent in the year 2000. However, foreigners may not acquire any firm holding more than a 1.5 percent market share

of a sector of the total Mexican insurance market (that is, of life, health, and property and casualty insurance). Foreign firms are initially limited to 6 percent of market share in 1994, rising to 12 percent in 1999, after which share limitations are to be dropped. Individual foreign agents and brokers will also be allowed to do business in the country as long as they meet Mexican licensing standards. There are no limits on what are termed intermediate and auxiliary insurance service companies.

There were 42 registered Mexican insurance companies in 1992, seven of which were members of financial groups. As of mid-1993 there were about a dozen foreign insurance firms operating in Mexico, primarily through joint ventures or as minority partners with existing Mexican firms. In early 1994 the government issued the first license for a foreign insurance company to operate in Mexico in more than 50 years, authorizing the US Principal Financial Group to conclude negotiations to offer individual and group insurance and pension plans through Servicios Especiales Profesionales of Mexico. Other foreign insurers have either purchased minority interests or increased existing holdings in Mexican insurers. In hopes of strengthening their positions in the increasingly competitive domestic market, several Mexican insurers have also merged.

Pension Funds

There are relatively few private pension plans in Mexico. On average, Mexican employees are generally young, and such benefits have neither been offered nor demanded in the past. Funded pension plans are eligible to receive favorable tax treatment under rather narrowly defined circumstances, but high interest rates have kept most firms from diverting much-needed internally generated funds to such uses. Some Mexican insurance companies have offered policies to cover pension obligations, but these are expensive and therefore not in common use. Because of these drawbacks, private pension funds have not provide a significant source of investment capital in the Mexican system.

Most pension activity occurs through the official Mexican social security system (*Instituto Mexicano del Seguro Social*, or IMSS), which was established in 1942. Participation in this comprehensive program, which covers most health care and pays some workmen's compensation, disability, and unemployment as well as retirement benefits, is mandatory for most entities (government employees participate through a separate system). The system is funded primarily by employer contributions based on a percentage of gross payroll adjusted for various risks.

Because retirement benefits were not being adequately funded, Mexico added a separate mandatory individual retirement savings system (*Sistema de Ahorro para el Retiro*, or SAR) in 1992 so that it could channel most existing payments into providing current services. This new system requires employers to set up a restricted long-term individual retirement account for each employee, to be funded directly by an employer contribution equal to 2 percent of pay and calculated on an amount capped at 25 times the minimum wage. Required employer housing contributions (5 percent of pay calculated on maximum amounts equal to 10 times the minimum wage) will also be vested in this account. An employee can borrow against the housing portion of the individual account for an approved housing expenditure, such as the purchase or remodeling of a home or the retirement of existing debt on a primary residence. Any unused housing sub-account funds accrue to the regular retirement sub-account, which is not available until formal retirement or—because few Mexicans formally retire—age 65; death and permanent disability also trigger payouts. Because of the large aggregate sums expected to accumulate rapidly under this auxiliary system, individual pension funds are expected to become a significant source of capital in the future.

In 1992, the year in which this provision went into effect, about 10 million such pension accounts were opened. In that year, funds could only be placed in interest-bearing bank accounts backed by and paying the rates of government securities. Such accounts represented more than 70 percent of all new bank accounts established during that year. In 1993 individual account holders were allowed to direct their own investments, which could be placed in mutual funds as well as in bank accounts backed by government securities. Beginning in 1993, brokerage houses and insurance companies were also allowed to offer pension management and investment services, and the bidding for such accounts is expected to heat up in future years. As noted, foreign insurers in particular have been drawn to Mexico with the express purpose of getting in on such pension funds management opportunities.

Underground Financial Operations

When Mexico abolished its two-tiered foreign exchange system, it eliminated one major area of underground financial manipulation. And with legal interest rates on loans approaching as much as 40 percent and averaging 25 percent or more, it would seem that the "legitimate" market has effectively usurped the role of the loan shark in the underground credit markets. Nevertheless, because the demand for credit even at such usurious rates is greater than the supply in the aboveground sector, unofficial financing is common.

Mexico continues to operate to a large extent using personal patron–client relationships. Otherwise unbankable supplicants often apply to locally known individuals, often shop owners or employers, for credit. These unofficial lenders often are offering such credit either out of noblesse oblige or as an aspect of business, or both. Although they are outside the formal system, these moneylenders are not considered to be operating illegally, even though they often charge 10 percent per month and have been known to charge double-digit daily rates. Small-scale wholesale suppliers often offer 30 to 60 days' grace on payment for goods—de facto short-term financing that enables the retailer to use the sale of the goods to pay off the wholesale purchase. However, most retailers prefer to pay cash up front because the delayed price they pay is often inflated by imputed financing charges, and a retailer who is unable to pay off the supplier on time can owe huge penalties.

Underground financing is common in local unofficial credit unions, or *tandas*, in which consumers informally pool their resources to invest or to obtain high-ticket goods for which they would not be able to obtain financing through regular channels. The government's new nonprofit savings and loan associations and the increased authorizations of credit unions are designed to replace such unregulated activity and bring more people within the official system. To date, government policy has been to entice such activity into the system rather than to punish it by cracking down on questionable informal practices. This is at least partially due to a recognition of the failure of the formal system to fill the same needs that the extralegal arrangements arise to satisfy. Mexico is still predominately a cash-based society, in which few people have accounts with financial institutions and formal payment systems are the exception rather than the norm.

Corruption has been endemic in Mexico for decades, and although much of it represents petty exactions at lower levels, it continues to play a role in higher level negotiations as well. The current administration has cracked down on some of the more blatant examples, but businesspeople must be aware of how deeply ingrained it is in the methods of doing business. One common tactic is for officials to suggest that foreign businesspeople retain special "consultants" who serve primarily as conduits, with funds paid as fees to the consultants ending up as bribes and kickbacks to officials. Many observers recommend that independent local talent be used to help navigate the system as cleanly as possible. Most of the larger agencies, such as the BOM and *Hacienda* in particular, are considered to be professional and generally "clean." However, some of the smaller agencies remain suspect when it comes to bribe solicitation. It is also worth noting that traditionally, the closer it is to the end of a presidential term, the more some people in authority will demand under-the-table considerations, seeking to cash in before the end of their tenure. The private sector is not immune to such activity, either, although it usually is more competitive and does not indulge in such practices to the same extent as has been found in the public sector. And although most of the funds derived from such questionable sources tend to be invested abroad, the large volumes of money from extensive drug operations in Mexico also serve to grease the wheels of the illicit, underground economy.

FINANCIAL MARKETS

The development of Mexico's financial markets has been one of the brightest spots in the country's overall economic reorganization during the past decade. Although such markets remain relatively small and volatile, with pockets of sophistication amid areas of nontransparent underdevelopment and yawning gaps, they have attracted a great deal of attention from international investors, propelling the overall trajectory upward. This in turn has meant that the markets have developed fairly rapidly, albeit unevenly, becoming increasingly more useful as a means of accessing capital or investing and managing funds. The main element of the financial markets is the Mexican stock exchange, known as the *Bolsa*. Futures and commodities transactions markets exist through informal market making by various entities, although only the bare beginnings of a formal commodities market exist. Officials have investigated options markets, but the stock market crash of 1987 imposed an effective moratorium on plans to set up markets formally to trade financial derivatives.

Equities Markets

The Mexican Stock Exchange The *Bolsa Mexicana de Valores*, or stock exchange (referred to simply as the *Bolsa*), has its origins in the late 19th century, when it served as a means of trading and speculating in issues, primarily mining stocks. After several intermediate steps, including operation as an over-the-counter market early in the 20th century and as a credit market collateralized through shareholdings during the 1930s, it was formally organized as a stock exchange in 1975. In that year, new legislation designed to promote investing—there were fewer than 5,000 active investors—led to the replacement of the previous system (of individual member stock agents) with one of more tightly organized and regulated incorporated securities houses (*casas de Bolsa*). In 1990 the exchange moved into a new, state-of-the-art facility; now it uses a fully computerized electronic auction system. In mid-1992, the *Bolsa* inaugurated a computerized automatic trading system, the *Sistema Automatisado de Transacciones Operativas* (SATO), to handle broker-placed orders.

The *Bolsa* is an incorporated, private, self-regulating entity that provides a trading forum to facilitate securities transactions. It is charged with: certifying and publishing real-time information and definitive summary information regarding trades; serving as a clearing house for data submitted by listed firms, including their quarterly and annual reports; and establishing and administering penalties for securities or trading violations committed by listed firms and others operating on the exchange.

Mexico also allows what are known as specialists to operate on the *Bolsa*. Specialists are brokers who operate as individuals rather than as part of a firm (and not as market makers, as is the case with specialists on the New York Stock Exchange). In early 1994, there was only one Mexican individual licensed to operate as a specialist. However, the 1993 foreign investment law allows outsiders to invest in such specialist operations, leaving open the possibility of foreign individual market operators in the future.

In 1993, the *Bolsa* became the ninth largest stock exchange in the world (it was 24th as recently as 1988). Its market value, US$3.2 billion in 1985, had grown to US$138.7 billion at the end of 1992 and to US$200.6 billion at the end of 1993. Foreign portfolio investment in the *Bolsa* was reported to be US$28.4 billion in 1993, with cumulative foreign portfolio investment rising to US$56.8 billion at the end of that year, representing an estimated 80 percent of total foreign investment. Foreign portfolio investment fell by US$6.5 billion in the first quarter of 1994, after having increased in each quarter during the preceding three years. Although the market and investment in it remained volatile in the second quarter of 1994, there were signs that foreigners had begun to invest again, albeit at a slower rate, following the disinvestment of the first quarter.

Common stocks of various categories, debt instruments, and warrants all trade on the *Bolsa*. Short selling has been allowed since 1991, although margin trading was suspended after the 1987 crash and has yet to be reinstated. Although the *Bolsa* listed 232 issues in early 1994—excluding mutual funds—only about 30 issues trade regularly and in any volume, and six of these account for about 60 percent of total market capitalization. The shares of just one, the recently privatized communications monopoly Telmex (*Teléfonos de México*), represent nearly 30 percent of equity market value. Mexican rating agencies assign a marketability rating to equities. At the end of January 1994, 9 percent of issues were listed as having high marketability, 19 percent as having medium marketability, 31 percent as having low marketability, and 41 percent as having only minimum marketability. In summary, the Mexican market is

MEXICO'S STOCK SHARE ALPHABET SOUP

Mexican equity shares (capital stock) are classified under a maze of different share types, each designated by a letter. The basic share type is the free subscription "B" share, which carries full proportional rights to corporate assets as well as full voting rights with regard to all issues of corporate governance. B shares can be held by anyone—individual or corporation, domestic or foreign. Ownership of "A" shares is restricted to Mexican nationals. Holders are entitled to proportional rights to all assets and participation in corporate governance, but they can dispose of their shares only to a qualified national individual or entity.

To facilitate foreign portfolio investment, the 1989 revision of foreign investment regulations created the concept of neutral investment. Such neutral investment can be effected through the purchase of certain categories of shares that have been created to satisfy legal requirements or through trust arrangements that allow certain ownership rights but withhold direct title to the underlying share. Such neutral investments are not counted toward the allowable percentage of foreign ownership—usually limited to 49 percent of the capital stock of a Mexican company.

"N" (neutral) shares represent specifically created share categories specifically created to allow foreigners proportional ownership of corporate assets, but N shares entail only limited (or no) rights regarding voting on issues of corporate governance. Actual traded shares include "C" and "L" shares, both of which provide for the right to a proportional share of corporate assets. "C" shares carry no voting rights at all, while "L" (*limitado*) shares are issued specifically to be held in trust accounts designed to allow foreign participation in areas in which direct foreign ownership is barred but for which indirect ownership is allowed. Such share categories can make up as much as 30 percent of total capitalization. "L" shares do imply voting rights with regard to major events such as mergers and liquidation, but not for lesser corporate governance and operational issues. As compensation for the loss of voting rights, "C" and "L" shares usually carry a higher dividend rate that is cumulative, making them similar to preferred shares issued in the US.

Although such shares are limited to a certain percentage of total capital stock and are not supposed to be counted in determining the percentage of a company's foreign ownership, the government reserves the right to require holders of such non-voting shares to dispose of some or all of their holdings if it determines that they result in improper diversification or concentration of ownership. The government can also require that improperly transferred shares—that is, shares sold to those who are not authorized to hold them—be sold, with the proceeds being confiscated.

Similar to ADRs (American Depository Receipts), Fiduciary Participation Certificates (*Certificados de Participación Ordinaria*, or CPOs) are designed to allow foreigners to hold a proxy share in a Mexican firm that is not traded directly in their home venue. In the case of CPOs, "A" shares—which are not normally available for purchase by foreigners—are bought and deposited with the sponsoring brokerage house, which then issues the CPO as a proxy for the underlying shares that are not—and in the case of A shares, cannot—themselves be transferred to the foreign buyers of the intermediate security created.

The 1993 Foreign Investment Law also creates "T" shares, which are not traded as equities, but which represent neutral investment proxy holdings in Mexican property involved in agriculture, ranching, and forestry operations. These are designed to get around legal limits on corporate and individual ownership of land that normally restrict ownership to plots that are considered too small to be developed economically.

extremely concentrated, top-heavy, and volatile. (It is not uncommon for Mexican stocks to gain or lose 5 percent of their value in a single trading session.)

To broaden this narrow market dominated by a few large issues, Mexican brokers received authorization in 1992 to form a small-capitalization, over-the-counter market. However, only a single company has registered to list its shares, and the market lies dormant. Regulations and tax rules hinder small firms from going public; entrepreneurs who manage to do so can be hit with capital gains taxes amounting to more than one-third of the value realized—a major disincentive. Taxes based on gross corporate assets also result in massive underreporting of such assets, reducing the ability to float shares. Observers hope that at some point a revision of the capital gains tax structure will enable more firms to offer shares to the public. However, because of concerns about loss of revenue and anti-business backlash, the government has so far refused to consider making any changes in the capital gains tax structure.

The primary index of stock market performance is the Price and Quotations Index (*Indice de Precios y Cotizaciones*, or IPC), a weighted composite index similar to other world market indices, such as New York's S&P 500 and London's FT 100. Its composition is reviewed every two months and additions and substitutions are far more common than elsewhere, although the core issues remain stable. Subsidiary sectoral indices are maintained for shares in mining, manufacturing, construction, retail, communications and transportation, services, and holding companies. In 1991 the decimal point was shifted and the last three digits were dropped, making the index less unwieldy—much as was done with Mexico's currency. All IPC figures have been restated to take this into account.

The IPC rose 754.4 percent between 1985 and 1991 in real peso terms, from 30.4 in 1985 to 465.2 in 1990. Since 1985, only in the crash year of 1987 did the IPC decline, and then by only 9.1 percent from year-end 1986 to year-end 1987, (although the market lost three-quarters of its value in the crash of October 1987 before recovering to the year-end position as measured by the index). Because of rampant inflation during the late 1980s and early 1990s, the real rate of return was much smaller than the nominal rate of return: 32 percent versus 100 percent in 1988, 66 percent versus 98 percent in 1989, 16 percent versus 50 percent in 1990, 92 percent versus 128 percent in 1991, and 10 percent versus 23 percent in 1992. In 1993 as inflation fell and the real and the nominal moved closer together, the real return was calculated at 37 percent versus a nominal return of 48 percent.

Turnover has also increased from 3 billion shares traded in 1985 to 28.3 billion shares in 1991, with the value of shares traded rising from US$2 billion to US$31.7 billion during the same period. The IPC closed 1992 at 1,759.44 and 1993 at 2,602.63. Because of concerns over the economy and political uncertainty at the end of the first quarter of 1994, the IPC stood at 2,410 after rising to an all-time high of 2,881 in early February. Thereafter IPC continued to weaken, reaching an interim low of 1,957 on April 20 before recovering to around 2,240 in mid-May.

Although the Mexican stock market as a whole has continued to rise in a noteworthy fashion, it remains a stock-picker's market rather than a sector or index investor's market: performance of individual issues varies widely. As of November 1993, foreign investment in the *Bolsa* amounted to US$43 billion, roughly 25.5 percent of total market value and a historic high. However, foreigners accounted for about 60 percent of turnover and activity.

International Operations Mexican stocks currently trade on foreign exchanges as American Depository Receipts, or ADRs. ADRs represent indirect proxy holdings of shares that are traded abroad, but kept on deposit (usually with a bank as trustee) in the home market. Mexican ADRs trade primarily on the New York Stock Exchange, which has 19 listed issues, and in the US over-the-counter market, which trades an additional 32 issues. As of the end of January 1994, ADRs represented 63 percent of all foreign portfolio investment in Mexican equities (about 60 percent of which was accounted for by a single issue—Telmex).

In addition, three closed-end Mexico funds and several open-ended Latin American and emerging markets funds trade in the US and in other developed markets, giving Mexican equities a fairly broad international exposure, although closed-end funds accounted for only about 2 percent of foreign portfolio investment as of early 1994.

Telmex, the largest and most active stock on the *Bolsa*, trades in greater volume in New York than it does in Mexico City, and there is a growing volume of arbitrage trading between the two venues. Several major Mexican brokerage houses now have operations in New York, primarily to facilitate such trading activity.

Mexican firms have also been active in issuing restricted shares in the US under the provisions of the US Securities and Exchange Commission Section 144-A, which requires limited disclosure as long as the shares are sold to institutional investors. Such restricted shares reached an apparent saturation point in 1992, leading to a fall-off in Mexican flotation of and foreign consumption of such shares. This oversold position triggered an 18 percent drop in the IPC in three weeks during 1992.

As of November, Mexican stock offerings during 1993 had reached US$3.8 billion: 38 percent on the *Bolsa* and 62 percent on international exchanges, mostly in the US.

Supervision, Regulation, and Operations Federal regulation of the securities markets falls under the National Securities Commission (*Comisión Nacional de Valores*, or CNV), the Mexican equivalent of the US Securities and Exchange Commission (SEC). Founded in 1946, the CNV is a unit of the Finance Secretariat. It is charged with regulating all aspects of the securities industry, and although its mandate and powers are broad—including authority to amend rules unilaterally or fine and suspend both dealers and securities—it has most often acted in concert with the industry. As is the case with most

Mexican regulatory bodies, the CNV has the power to act strongly and independently to control perceived problems or to advance policy, although it has seldom done so.

The CNV's main substantive activity is maintaining the national registry *(Registro Nacional de Valores e Intermedios)*—a roster of securities listed on the *Bolsa* (the securities section); of domestic firms listed abroad (the special section); as well as of all registered and authorized securities firms and dealers (in the intermediaries section). Only securities listed in the registry can be publicly offered in Mexico, and only enrolled firms can act as intermediaries in securities transactions. The CNV also maintains general supervisory control over the largely self-regulating self-registration system by which securities firms are readied for formal registration.

The Securities Market Law of 1975 provides the legal and regulatory framework for securities operations in Mexico. Although now somewhat dated, it has been amended with additional implementing regulations, primarily in the area of public offerings. These amendments have moved Mexico closer to prevailing international practice regarding types of securities and procedures for issue. Regulations now allow simultaneous issuance of shares in Mexico and the US, and procedures generally conform to US practice, with a registration period, an offering period, and a sales and aftermarket support and trading period.

The *Bolsa* capital markets operate from 8 am to 2:30 pm, and money market trading occurs between 10 am and 2 pm. Settlement is made for cash, with stock and bond transactions settling on the second business day while government securities settle on a next-day basis.

The Centralized Securities Depository, known as *Indeval*, was set up by the government in 1978. This quasi-public entity is charged with clearing, settlement, custody, transfer, and general recordkeeping for all registered securities transactions. All securities—stocks, bonds, and money market instruments, including commercial paper, but excluding some government securities—must be deposited with and cleared through *Indeval*.

The *Academia Mexicana de Derecho Bursátil* (Academy of Mexican Securities Law), founded in 1979, is a quasi-official body that studies securities regulation. The Mexican Capital Markets Institute *(Instituto Mexicano del Mercado de Capitales A.C.*, or IMMEC) is a nonprofit association founded by the *Bolsa* in 1980 to promote investment in and the understanding of capital markets. The *Asociación de Casas de Bolsa A.C.* (Mexican Brokers Association) was founded in 1980 to serve as a trade, promotion, and lobbying organ.

Listing and Registration Requirements The *Bolsa de Valores* is a private entity, and securities listings are technically a contractual agreement be-

tween it and the listing firm. However, no securities can be offered in Mexico unless they have been registered with the CNV, which requires additional information beyond what is required by the *Bolsa*, adding federal involvement to the process.

Basic *Bolsa* registration requires the submission of financial statements for the past five years—or since incorporation if less than five years—including the opinion of a Mexican certified public accountant *(contador público)*, the corporate charter, and the minutes of the meeting of the board of directors at which the motion to list was voted. The *Bolsa* acts as a preliminary screen for the CNV, which then performs an in-depth investigation. The CNV examines material such as would be contained in a US SEC 10-K filing, including most recent financial figures, descriptions of business operations, material events, and data regarding officers. Foreign firms or Mexican-incorporated firms with significant foreign ownership can expect to be required to submit even more documentation than is required of national firms. If the CNV approves the securities for listing, the *Bolsa* again becomes its semi-official agent, collecting quarterly and annual reports, all of which must be audited and completed within four months after the close of the period.

In theory, any security that meets the established requisites is eligible to list on the *Bolsa*. In practice, there is a bias toward domestic securities and against foreign-incorporated securities or those with substantial foreign ownership. The justification for this has been that because there is relatively limited capital available in Mexico, it should go to support national development rather than foreign-owned operations. Since mid-1993, the officially announced policy has been that foreign issues are to be encouraged to list on the *Bolsa* to enhance its development as an international as well as national securities venue. However, the authorities primarily have in mind the listing not of strong US, European, or Asian stocks, but of stocks from weaker, emerging markets in Latin America.

Brokerage Firms Mexican brokerage houses are structured much like the securities firms found in the financial markets of the developed world. Such an entity must register with the CNV, purchase a seat on the exchange, maintain minimum required capital levels, and contribute to the *Fondo de Contingencia* (an industry fund modeled after the US Security Investors' Protection Corporation—the SIPC—founded in 1980 to compensate clients in the event of a securities firm's default). Industry participants and foreigners generally cannot directly own shares in brokerage firms, which can only be held by approved national financial institutions, although these strictures are slated to ease under the terms of NAFTA and the new 1993 foreign investment law, which allow for greater foreign participation over time. Brokerage houses must also comply with both federal and association regulations that are designed to ensure open and appropriate fiduciary operations.

In 1993 there were 26 brokerage houses in Mexico. These firms were operating more than 200 branches nationwide, as well as six subsidiaries and one representative office in the US. Mexican securities houses are authorized to act as full service investment brokers and investment bankers, offering underwriting, corporate finance, and mergers and acquisition services in addition to securities trading. The largest brokerage operations are Accival, Obra-Serfin, Inversora, and InverMexico, which together control 21 percent of brokerage accounts, 28 percent of brokerage offices nationwide, 10 percent of brokerage employees, and 37 percent of securities in custody. The next six largest brokerage houses—Inverlat, Bancomer, Probursa, GBM, Vector, and Abaco—account for an additional 48 percent of brokerage accounts and 44 percent of securities in custody.

Brokerage commissions were deregulated in 1991, although transaction costs remain relatively high by the standards of developed international securities markets.

Although the role of banks in the securities markets has been expanded to allow the banks to compete for some securities business, restrictions remain. Banks are allowed to operate in money markets and government securities markets, both on behalf of clients and for their own accounts, but they are restricted from participating in the private capital markets as full-fledged securities firms. However, they can offer a full range of investment banking services, including advising on underwriting, corporate finance, and mergers and acquisition. Conversely, brokerage firms are generally barred from providing commercial banking services.

Foreign Participation Foreign individuals and companies are generally allowed to invest in Mexican securities, including government securities (although foreign governments or official agencies are barred from investing in Mexican government securities because of concern for potential issues of control and sovereignty). Open investment in equities (that is, investment open to any and all investors) is through "B" shares. Foreigners can cumulatively own up to 49 percent of the equity in a Mexican firm through investment in B shares, although individuals can own only up to 10 percent of the shares outstanding. The 49 percent limit can potentially be extended by application to the Foreign Investment Commission (FIC), which has authority to authorize higher levels of foreign investment in Mexican firms. The percentage allowance for foreign investment excludes any neutral investment held by foreigners (neutral investment being holdings that do not in-

clude rights to corporate governance). At the end of January 1994, foreign investors directly owned US$14.1 billion of "B" shares (accounting for 23 percent of total foreign portfolio investment) and US$7.2 billion of neutral shares (12 percent of total foreign portfolio investment). The remaining 65 percent of foreign portfolio investment consists of ADR and closed-end fund investment.

As part of the implementing regulations for NAFTA, US and Canadian brokerage houses are now allowed to open formal representative offices in Mexico (several already had unofficial presences), and, once regulations have been agreed upon, they are expected to be able to acquire minority positions in Mexican brokerages.

Debt and Money Markets

The debt market and the money market generally operate separately from each other. The money market consists primarily of short-term government paper dominated by treasury bills (*certificados de tesorería*, or CETEs), but also includes commercial paper, bankers' acceptances, bank promissory notes, collateral bonds, and *pagarés Pemex*. The capital markets include such private debt instruments as corporate bonds and silver certificates (*ceplatas*), and government and government agency debt, such as *tesobonos, bondes, ajustabonos*, and *bondis*, all of which have somewhat different characteristics. The greater availability of a variety of instruments, especially of the government-backed securities that dominate the markets, has brought greater participation, greater stability, increased liquidity, and lower interest rates through augmented supply.

Not only do government securities dominate the financial markets—for instance, during the first six months of 1992 trading in government securities accounted for 97 percent of all trading on the *Bolsa*—but short-term instruments dominate long-term securities as well. CETEs accounted for roughly 92 percent of all trading during the same period, while 4 percent of trading was in *ajustabonos*; 2 percent was in stocks; 1 percent was in private sector debt; and 1 percent was in long-term government debt. Part of this dominance reflects the development of the secondary trading market for government paper as distinct from other forms of investments, with essentially the same securities turning over (often in overnight repurchases) many times and with extreme velocity. This adds to the total value of transactions, which is far out of proportion to that of the underlying securities. This value nevertheless accounts for a huge proportion of the value of all securities in existence at any given point in time.

Given Mexico's high inflation rates in recent years, its international near-default, and the economic difficulties of the recent past, there has been no market either internally or externally for long-term securities. The government has only recently begun lengthening the maturity of not only individual instruments offered but also of its portfolio as a whole. In mid-1993, Banamex—the largest bank in Mexico—issued the first two-year peso-denominated private note in more than a decade. The bank has also announced plans to issue a five-year peso note.

Government and Agency Instruments The main instrument that pervades Mexican money and capital markets is the treasury bill, or CETE. The 28-day CETE forms the backbone of government financing and operations—including open-market operations to control liquidity in the system and implement monetary policy—and serves to set basic interest rates in the economy. CETEs account for the vast bulk of debt instruments in the economy. Since the abolition of reserve requirements and the substitution of liquidity ratios, banks have been required to maintain their liquidity reserves primarily in CETEs (they can also hold either *bondes* or cash positions, both in reserve accounts with the BOM). This gives the BOM leverage for its implementation of monetary policy.

CETEs, which are auctioned weekly by the BOM, are issued as discount instruments in maturities of 28, 91, 180, and 360 days. In mid-1993, the government authorized the BOM to issue CETEs with maturities of greater than one year that are to be priced at par and are to bear interest—that is, notes rather than discounted bills—designed to extend the overall maturity of government offerings. The BOM was also granted authority to issue such fixed-rate notes at a discount below par in order to manage monetary and financial affairs better, all with a view toward giving the central bank more leeway to manage the country's finances while extending its maturity profile.

Tesobonos (*Bonos de la Tesorería*, or treasury bonds) have been issued since 1989. Designed to dampen swings in the exchange rate, *tesobonos* are denominated in US dollars, although they are payable only in Mexican pesos converted at the current exchange rate. *Tesobonos* are auctioned at the government's discretion in minimum amounts of US$1,000. Maturities can vary from 28-days to several years, but 91- and 182- day terms have been most common. Short-term *tesobonos* are issued on a discount basis, while longer-term securities pay periodic interest. *Tesobonos* have replaced the *pagafé*, a short-term, fixed rate US dollar denominated government note.

Bondes (*Bonos de Desarrollo del Gobierno Federal*, or government development bonds) are somewhat longer-term government bonds designed to finance capital investment rather than to further monetary policy. The most common maturities have been one to two years, although longer-term bonds can be issued. *Bondes* are issued at the discretion

of the government in minimum values of NP100 (about US$30). The rate on these instruments is either the 28-day CETE bond equivalent yield or the rate on bank promissory notes (*pagarés bancarios*), whichever is higher. Banks can hold *bondes* as part of their liquidity reserves.

Ajustabonos (*Bonos Ajustables del Gobierno Federal*, or adjustable rate government bonds) are longer-term securities indexed to inflation. Issued since 1989, these instruments pay a fixed, guaranteed real interest rate above inflation on a quarterly coupon basis (payments are adjusted quarterly according to the consumer price index). Minimum values are NP100 (about US$30), with maturities of three to five years.

Bondis (*Bonos Bancarios de Desarrollo Industrial*, or development bank bonds) are issued by Nafin, the national industrial development bank, to finance bank projects and operations. *Bondis* are issued in minimum face values of NP10 (about US$3) with three- to 10-year maturities and pay either the 28-day CETEs rate plus a premium or the *bondes* rate, whichever is higher, on a quarterly basis. Half of the interest is paid in cash as due, with the remaining 50 percent being capitalized and added to the principal.

Pagarés Pemex (Pemex promissory notes) are issued by the state oil company—the largest Mexican firm—to finance its operations. The instruments have minimum values of NP100 (about US$30) and maturities of one year. Interest is paid monthly based on either the 28-day CETE yield or the bank promissory note yield, whichever is higher.

Private Instruments Commercial paper (*papel comercial*) is the short-term unsecured debt of private companies. Usually issued in minimum amounts of NP100 (about US$30), such paper has a maturity ranging from 15 to 360 days and is issued on a discount basis. Domestic firms with substantial international operations sometimes issue US dollar-indexed (or dollar-linked) commercial paper. Private firms also issue other short-term debt instruments known as *pagarés empresarial bursátil* (notes backed by deposits of CETEs) and *pacobers* (notes linked to foreign exchange rates). Commercial paper issues are rated by CAVAL (Calificadora de Valores), a quasi-official national credit rating agency. Other authorized rating agencies include Dictaminadora de Valores (DICTA), Duff & Phelps de Mexico, and Clasificadora de Riesgos, all of which rate commercial paper on a scale of A through E (these firms also operate the stock liquidity—but not safety—rating system). As is the case elsewhere, only the largest firms can float commercial paper, and the market is relatively limited.

Pagarés bancarios (bank promissory notes), equivalent in financial sector to commercial paper in the industrial and commercial sector, are issued by commercial banks to finance their operations. These short-term bank notes carry maturities of from one to 13 months. These instruments are relatively common and are used to set other interest rates as an alternative to the omnipresent CETE rate.

Aceptaciones bancarias (bankers' acceptances) are short-term notes issued by small- and medium-sized firms and backed by banks. Unlike bankers' acceptances elsewhere, which are simply discounted trade receipts, the Mexican instruments have been standardized and serve largely as substitutes for commercial paper for firms that are not large enough or creditworthy enough to issue rated commercial paper. Minimum value on these discount notes is NP100 (about US$30). Maturities are specified by the issuer, but are less than one year.

Bonos de Prenda (collateral bonds) are not secured by corporate assets as mortgage bonds are, but by a deposit of marketable commodities, held by a financial warehouse as security for the bonds. The standard contract calls for the deposit of goods valued at 40 percent above the value of the security to be issued. The warehouse then issues a negotiable deposit receipt that is securitized, usually in minimum units of NP100 (about US$30). *Bonos de prenda* are issued on a discount basis, with maturities of one year or less, usually for terms of less than 182 days.

Obligaciones (debentures) are something of a catchall corporate debt instrument. They can be secured, unsecured, or convertible securities and have no standardized minimum face value or maturity terms, although most maturities have been in the three- to 10 year range. Rates can follow market rates or the instruments can pay a premium over market, depending on the creditworthiness of the issuing entity. The bonds usually pay coupon interest quarterly.

Ceplatas (silver certificates) are issued by trusts that buy silver to be deposited and held as collateral for a standard period of 30 years. The basic unit of purchase for such certificates is 100 troy ounces. Certificates pay no interest, but they are negotiable based on the price of silver in the world commodities markets and are used as a hedge against inflation.

Derivative Instruments Mexican financial institutions are relatively limited, both in the amount of capital they can access in the domestic market (which is still dominated by government financing) and in types of securities they can offer in it. Some are pushing the envelope, gaining funds and experience by floating securities abroad. For instance, in late 1993, Banco Serfin and Citibank offered, in the US institutional market, participation certificates consisting of securitized future credit card receivables. Banamex is also negotiating agreements with Banc One of the US to expand its credit card operations and with Swiss Bank to provide liquidity and

expand its derivative operations.

International Operations Because of Mexico's effective default in 1982, the Mexican government, its agencies, and it national firms were absent from international debt markets for several years. With Mexico's reorganized and growing economy, this situation has been reversed in recent years, and some Mexican institutions have been able to return to the international markets. As of November 1993, Mexican companies had issued US$9.6 billion in debt in overseas markets during calendar 1993. Also in late 1993, Pemex floated the first 30-year bond issued by a Mexican entity since the early 1980s. The company issued a total of US$2.6 billion in debt in 1993, most of which was used to retire higher-interest debt from previous years. Pemex announced plans to issue more than US$3 billion in new debt during 1994, and expected to close a US$1.1 billion syndicated credit with an international banking consortium in the spring. Pemex' new money bank credits are the first accorded to a Mexican entity since 1982.

US rating agency Standard & Poor's has raised Mexico to a rating of B-plus, one notch below investment grade, and indicated that it would consider raising Mexico's rating to investment grade sometime in 1994. However, Moody's, another prominent US rating agency, has expressed skepticism over Mexico's recovery, arguing that its economy is likely to run into trouble, thus Moody's has reaffirmed its below investment grade rating of Ba-2. National firms cannot receive a rating higher than the one accorded to their home country, so continued below-investment-grade ratings will hamper private Mexican firms: most institutional investors are prohibited from or limited in investing in below investment grade debt.

Mutual Funds

Mutual funds are divided into three basic categories: fixed income mutual funds (*Sociedades de Inversión de Renta Fija*), common stock mutual funds (*Sociedades de Inversión Comunes*), and venture capital mutual funds (*Sociedades de Inversión de Capital*, or SINCAs).

Fixed income mutual funds invest in corporate and government debt instruments and have indefinite maturities, variable yields, and high liquidity. Because of their relatively short average maturities, many are functionally more similar to US money market mutual funds than they are to US bond funds, which deal in instruments having longer maturities. However, unlike money market mutual funds, they do not maintain constant share value.

Common stock mutual funds invest primarily in shares or convertible bonds (at least 30 percent), although they can hold any type of listed security. Maturity on open-ended stock funds is indefinite, and they are generally considered to be liquid.

Venture capital mutual funds invest in the long-term debt and equity of firms that are usually under contract with fund operators to receive consulting services designed to improve or turn around their operations. (In late 1993, all mutual funds were authorized to offer consulting, administrative, and accounting services in addition to investment in securities.) The assets of venture capital funds are generally considered to be less liquid.

Mutual funds are considered to be either diversified (that is, they can follow any investment strategy and change it virtually at will) or specialized (restricted to following the strategy specified in their offering prospectus, in which case they must maintain at least 60 percent of their assets in securities of a type appropriate to the stated strategy). Mutual funds are required to remain at least 96 percent invested in registered securities or cash, and can hold no more than 15 percent of their assets in the securities of a single company, no more than 40 percent of their assets in the securities of a single affiliated group, and no more than 30 percent of the securities of a single firm. All mutual funds are separately incorporated entities. Most are operated either as a direct subsidiary of a brokerage house or as part of a financial group. However, a mutual fund can also be operated as an independent unaffiliated entity, subject to compliance with applicable financial regulations and licensing by the authorities. In late 1993, the minimum paid-in capital necessary to open a mutual fund was set at NP322,000 (about US$98,000). Mexico does not have closed-end mutual funds.

There are no official limits on foreign participation via ownership of shares of fixed income and common stock funds. But, in keeping with limits for stock ownership in general, in the recent past, foreign ownership has been limited to a maximum 49 percent cumulative and a 10 percent individual holding. Because of their more direct and often concentrated ownership position in operating companies, venture capital funds have remained limited to 49 percent foreign ownership, although this is subject to change. And under the terms of NAFTA, Canadian and US investors will be allowed to actually own and operate Mexican mutual funds (through licensed Mexican personnel) without the limits on either individual or aggregate market share that apply to some other types of financial institutions. Financial groups are limited to one category of mutual fund per group, but because of different variations of potential mutual funds, such groups can, in effect, operate several mutual funds. The funds are licensed to be sold only in Mexico.

As of the first quarter of 1994, there were 148 listed fixed income (classified as general fixed income, corporate fixed income, or fixed income with exchange coverage funds) and 82 common stock mutual funds operating in Mexico. There are also about 37 separate venture capital mutual funds. Despite this impressive number of active funds, such entities play a relatively small role in Mexican financial markets. Participation is limited and generally restricted to a few sectors of the domestic investing public and foreign investors. This situation is expected to change as balances build up in SAR (individual retirement) accounts, which can be invested in mutual funds.

Futures and Commodity Markets

Mexico had planned to institute formal futures and options exchanges in the mid-1980s. However, the worldwide stock market crash in 1987 served to put those plans on hold indefinitely. The only formal such exchange in Mexico is the Sugar Market Fund, known as FORMA, which opened in March 1994. Officials report that the exchange is also interested in operating as a futures market, selling forward hedge contracts for sugar delivery. Currently spot and six-month forward contracts on lots of up to 10 tons of either refined industrial or coarse domestic-use sugar are offered. Additional commodities operations have been proposed for wheat, sorghum, and soybeans.

There are no markets in precious or other metals, even though Mexico is a major producer of silver and several other commodities. However, a fairly active wholesale and retail trade is carried on in gold and silver coins (*centenarios*—50 peso gold coins—and silver troy ounces minted by the government) through the securities markets. Such trades are made as a commodity hedge rather than out of numismatic interest. Securities markets also offer *ceplatas* (long-term silver certificates) as an investment.

Financial hedges such as interest rate and stock index futures and options are currently banned under Mexican regulations. However, in late 1993, brokerage houses were authorized to trade warrants designed to indirectly hedge the consumer price index. Such warrants were to be based on government securities that rise or fall in line with inflation, providing a form of index futures play.

Foreign Debt

Mexico's foreign debt overhangs the rest of its economy and has severely limited the ability of its financial system to function. Debt has been a perennial problem for Mexico, even leading to an attempted 19th century takeover of the country by European powers, and to the ostracizing of Mexico after it declared a moratorium on payments of principal on its roughly US$85 billion in foreign debt in 1982. The associated nationalization of the banking industry and exercise of rigid controls over the financial system as officials tried to maneuver their way out of the debt box nearly swamped the national economy. One of the most impressive accomplishments of the past two administrations has been the defusing of the debt situation.

Mexico still has a massive international public and private debt, estimated at the end of 1993 to be US$133.7 billion, two-thirds larger than the 1982 figure and one-third larger than the US$100.4 billion debt with which the Salinas presidency began in late 1988. The main reason for this continued growth in indebtedness is not new borrowing—few international entities would lend to Mexico until well into the 1990s—but the capitalization of unpaid interest. Mexico's international loans have called for long grace periods during which interest due was capitalized and for balloon payments at the end of the loan period, with little or no intervening amortization of principal.

Since the high point in the early and mid-1980s, debt and debt service have been reduced as a percentage of GDP, allowing greater domestic investment. This stabilization and reduction resulted from the negotiation of a comprehensive, long-term agreement that served to reduce overall debt and debt service, allowing Mexico access to new international credits and inducing some flight capital to return home.

Mexico's problem in the early and mid-1980s involved dealing with a multitude of international banks with different interests and needs. Mexico also needed to negotiate not only concessions on existing debt, but also needed new money to implement its reorganization—a need that ran counter to the interests of international lenders anxious to limit their existing positions rather than incur new liabilities. This situation largely stymied negotiations during the lame-duck López Portillo administration and during that of President de la Madrid. However, the Salinas government worked with the US on the so-called Brady Plan (named after US Treasury Secretary Nicholas Brady) in 1989 to restructure Mexico's debt. The situation was aided by International Monetary Fund and World Bank approval, resulting in commitments, respectively, of about US$4 billion and US$2 billion to underwrite the transition. The Paris Club, consisting of the top 10 national subscribers to the IMF, agreed to restructure US$2.6 billion in short- to intermediate-term debt held by its respective governments and to provide US$2 billion in import financing credits.

Under the auspices of the Brady Plan, Mexico was able to restructure US$48.1 billion in foreign commercial bank debt. This involved the exchange of 42.8 percent of the existing bank debt for discounted bonds paying LIBOR (the London Interbank Offering Rate) plus 13/16, which reduced the total face value of debt outstanding by 35 percent. Mexico also exchanged 46.6 percent of its debt for par bonds at the same face value as the existing debt but paying a fixed 6.25 percent in interest—a substantial interest concession. Some 9.1 percent of remaining existing debt was replaced with new loans at LIBOR plus 13/16 due in 15 years, with a seven-year grace period before interest is due. The remaining loans (1.5 percent) are subject to pre-existing agreements. The key provision of the deal was the purchase by Mexico of US Treasury zero coupon securities at deep discount to be held as a guarantee that Mexico would redeem its restructured debt in the future. Such maneuvers resulted in an 11.1 percent net reduction of official debt from US$95.1 to US$84 between 1989 and 1990, US$23 billion below the US$107 billion high point reached in 1987.

One additional point with which the refinancing package dealt was a clause linking payments to the price of oil, Mexico's chief export. The deal calls for payment adjustments—within limits—if oil prices drop below US$10 per barrel or rise above US$14 per barrel on a constant dollar basis.

FURTHER READING

This discussion has been provided as a basic guide to money, finances, financial institutions, and financial markets in Mexico. Because the situation is changing so rapidly in Mexico, no authoritative up-to-date sources are available on the structure and function of the financial sector. Those interested in current developments may wish to consult the *Wall Street Journal* and *El Financiero*, which cover economic and financial developments in Mexico from, respectively, an international and a domestic perspective. Other sources of interest include:

Handbook

Mexico Company Handbook, Mexico City: International Company Handbook, Ltd., IMF Edititora. Issued in cooperation with the Bolsa Mexicana de Valores and the Asociación Mexicana de Casas de Bolsa. Available in the US from: The Reference Press Inc., 6448 Highway 290 East, Suite E-104, Austin, TX 78723, USA; Tel: [1] (512) 454-7778 Fax: [1] (512) 454-9401. Available in Mexico from: Lic. Mario Valverde Garcés, Tonalá 62, México, DF, México; Tel: [52] (5) 514-7668 Fax: [52] (5) 514-3995.

Newspapers & Periodicals

Banca y Comercio
(Quarterly)
Escuela Bancaria y Comercial
Paseo de la Reforma 202
06600 México, DF
Fax: (5) 546-0326
Banking and commerce

El Economista
(Daily; Spanish)
Publicaciones Mercalba
Avda. Coyoacán No. 515
Col. del Valle
03100 México, DF
Tel: (5) 669-1742 Fax: (5) 687-3821, 523-6500
*National financial daily; competes with more
established* El Finaciero. *Circ: 35,000*

El Financiero
(Daily; Spanish)
Grupo Editorial SEFI
Lago Bolsena 176
11320 México, DF
Tel: (5) 254-6299 Fax: (5) 255-1881
*National financial paper for the business community.
Circ: 80,000*

El Financiero Internacional
(Weekly; English)
Lago Bolsena 176
Col. Anahuac
11320 México, DF
Tel: (5) 227-7600 Fax: (5) 227-7634
*Weekly English-language version of leading Mexican
financial daily. US Subscription address: 2300 S.
Broadway, Los Angeles, CA 90007; Tel: [1] (213)
747-7547 Fax: [1] (213) 747-2489.*

Expansión
(Fortnightly; Spanish)
Grupo Editorial Expansión, S.A.
Salamanca No. 35
Col. Roma
06700 México DF
Tel: (5) 208-9609 Fax: (5) 511-6351
Prominent general business publication

Mexican Stock Exchange Trading Report
(Quarterly; Spanish, English editions)
Bolsa Mexicana de Valores, S.A. de C.V.
Paseo de la Reforma 255
06500 México, DF
Tel: (5) 726-6791 Fax: (5) 591-0534
*Summary of the behavior of the securities market in
Mexico, general environment and trends*

Negocios y Bancos (Negobancos)
(24/yr.; Spanish)
Publicaciones Importantes, S.A.
Bolívar 8-601, Apdo. 1907
06000 México, DF
Tel: (5) 510-1884 Fax: (5) 512-9411
Important banking and finance journal

Revista Mexicana de Seguros y Finanzas
(Monthly; Spanish)
Apdo. 19-193
03910 México, DF
Fax: (5) 511-1133
Insurance and finance

Currency & Foreign Exchange

INTERNATIONAL PAYMENT INSTRUMENTS

Most standard internationally accepted methods of payment can be used in transactions with Mexico, which complies with International Chamber of Commerce (ICC) regulations. An international transaction with Mexico is usually accomplished using an irrevocable letter of credit (L/C) confirmed by an international bank. Documents Against Acceptance (D/A) or Documents Against Payment (D/P) may also be used, although such documentary payment arrangements are far less common in Mexico. Participants in these transactions can request sight or time drafts, with sight being more common and more desired. Other methods include consignment sales, open account sales, and direct cash payments via money order or wire transfer. Payments are usually made on an open account basis only where a long-term, relatively high-volume relationship already exists. Mechanisms exist for direct central bank settlement for transactions between members of the Latin American Integration Association (ALADI), mostly for countertrade—although countertrade is generally discouraged.

There are certain geographic and market preferences with regard to payment methods. Because of proximity, the relative ease of transfers, and because there are so many long-term trade relationships, many transactions between Mexican and US firms are accomplished using wire transfers or drafts or on an open account basis. European businesses prefer L/Cs or D/As and D/Ps using time or sight drafts. Asian firms almost invariably require L/Cs.

Because of Mexico's recent history of inflation and lack of available credit, many Mexican firms require foreign partners in both import and export transactions to offer some form of financing.

CURRENCY

The currency used in Mexico is the *nuevo peso* (new peso), which replaced the peso on January 1, 1993. This transition was accomplished without any added economic measures simply by dropping the last three zeros on the existing peso; thus 1,000 old pesos became 1 new peso. Within Mexico, the legal designation for new pesos (such as on checks) is N$. This will remain in effect until January 1, 1996, at which time the Bank of Mexico (BOM)—the central bank and the agency responsible for issuing currency—will officially withdraw the old peso from circulation. Although the BOM plans to continue to redeem old pesos after this date, it will no longer consider them to be legal tender. The BOM is also withdrawing old peso coins from circulation, but without a set schedule.

Despite the internal legal designation, many external sources refer to the currency as the NP, although various other conventions also exist. Moreover, after 1996 the Mexican domestic usage will revert to the old peso symbol—$—without additional qualification. Foreign businesspeople should make sure that the monetary unit under consideration is firmly established to avoid confusion between the peso and the US dollar (which uses the same symbol).

New pesos are divided into 100 *centavos*. Coins are issued in denominations of NP0.05 (which equals 5 centavos), NP0.10, NP0.20, NP0.50, NP1, NP2, NP5, and NP10. Paper currency is issued in denominations of NP2, NP5, NP10, NP20, NP50, and NP100. As of the end of 1993, NP100 was equal to about US$32.25; by the end of the first quarter of 1994 it had weakened to about US$30. While the new paper bills are the same colors as the old currency, none of them have as many zeros as the old bills, which came in 10,000, 20,000, 50,000, and 100,000 notes. The new coins replace the old 2,000, 5,000, and 10,000 peso notes. The old 1,000, 500, 200, 100, and 50 peso coins have been replaced with NP1, NP0.50, NP0.20, NP0.10, and NP0.05 coins—again recognizable as new pesos because of the smaller number of zeros. However, as of early 1994, both old and new coins and bills were being used indiscriminately. Some telephones and vending machines continued to accept only the old coins. Thus money is a potential source of confusion.

For cash payments, amounts are to be rounded to the nearest 5 centavos. However, for credit card and other purchases handled on account or for purchases requiring foreign exchange translation, actual figures are used. Small change is a chronic problem in Mexico, and some vendors attempt to effectively round up by saying that they have no change (*sencillo*). Travelers learn to hoard their coins and small bills for such occasions. Adding to the confusion is the fact that, in many areas, US dollars are widely accepted for transactions. Some retail merchants will specify "Dlrs" (or a variation thereof) or "M.N." (*moneda nacional*, or national money; *moneda* usually refers to coins, while money in general is *dinero* or *plata*) to clarify the units in question, just as some Mexican retail outlets continue to mark prices in both old and new pesos.

REMITTANCE AND EXCHANGE CONTROLS

In 1982 Mexico instituted exchange controls involving a two-tiered system with an official rate for specified approved transactions and a less favorable free market rate for all other transactions. The two rates crept closer together as the economy stabilized—the differential was 21.25 percent in 1985, but had eased to only 0.6 percent by 1988—and were unified, with all exchange controls being lifted in late 1991.

There are now no controls on either individuals or corporations, whether domestic or foreign, with regard to foreign exchange or national currency. There are no restrictions on the movement of investment capital into or out of Mexico, nor are there limits on repatriation of earnings or capital. No formalities, approvals, or registrations of flow of funds are required. Residents and nonresidents can borrow and hold accounts denominated in pesos, US dollars, or other currencies, either in Mexico or abroad (but use of currencies other than the peso or the US dollar is rare).

Under Mexican law, any obligations payable in Mexico can be canceled using pesos at the prevailing rate as of the date payment is due, regardless of the currency in which they were contracted, even if the contract specifies another currency. Mexico has no guarantees against inconvertibility, and all transactions depend on the availability of foreign exchange in the markets.

Observers note that although official policy calls for the maintenance of a stable currency and an open foreign exchange system, Mexico has had a tradition of manipulating its currency. The peso, which has traded at parity or even at a premium to the US dollar within living memory, was kept artificially overvalued during the 1970s. This policy kept imports cheap, enabling Mexicans to buy foreign consumer and capital goods, but made exports less competitive. Given the minor focus on exports, this was of little concern at first. However, it did result in a growing trade deficit and shortage of foreign exchange.

The Echeverría administration abruptly devalued the peso at the end of 1976 by about 57 percent, from 12.5 (where it had remained following a roughly 45 percent devaluation in 1954) to 29 to the dollar, sending shock waves through the Mexican economy and causing outsiders to distrust Mexico.

This rate was maintained by the succeeding López Portillo government until February 1982, when—after stating that he would "defend the peso like a dog,"—the president devalued the currency overnight from roughly 27 to 45 to the US dollar, causing it to lose about 40 percent of its value in the face of Mexico's deteriorating economic situation. López Portillo exacerbated the situation in August 1982, when he slapped on exchange controls, closed all foreign exchange markets, and froze all assets in US dollar accounts in Mexican banks (including those owned by foreigners), forcing their conversion to pesos at the official rate, which was substantially below the market rate. This shock was followed in September by the nationalization of the banking system.

Between year-end 1981 and year-end 1982, the peso lost 73 percent of its value. It lost 33 percent in 1983, 25 percent in 1984, 53 percent in 1985, 56 percent in 1986, and 58 percent in 1987 before it began to stabilize as the de la Madrid administration began to bring the slide in the economy under control. Between the end of 1988 and 1992, the peso's value dropped 33 percent overall. All in all, the cumulative loss in value between 1982 and 1993 was 97 percent. Between year-end 1992 and year-end 1993, the peso recovered marginally, actually gaining 0.3 percent against the US dollar. However, during the first quarter of 1994, the peso weakened, losing 7.5 percent of its value, before stabilizing in May.

Because there are currently no exchange controls, there is no black market, although exchange rates do vary depending on the outlet used. There is an active business among *casas de cambio* (foreign exchange houses) seeking to profit by trading and arbitrage of the currency. Businesses almost always operate through a bank or other financial institution and may be able to negotiate a wholesale rate, although the reduction in the spread will usually be marginal.

For smaller transactions by individuals, airport foreign exchange booths usually offer good rates and banks remain the primary outlets. Rates may vary from bank to bank, and some negate their favorable rates with minimum or sliding scale service and trans-

Mexico's Foreign Exchange Rates - Year End Actual
Mexican New Peso (NP) to United States Dollar (US$)

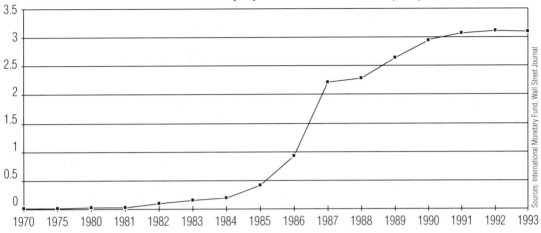

Sources: International Monetary Fund, Wall Street Journal

March 31, 1994 US$1 = NP3.3565

Note: The New Peso, equal to 1,000 Pesos, was introduced on January 1,1993

action fees. Traveler's checks usually get a slightly better rate than cash, although many outlets charge a percentage fee that more than offsets any advantage. In fact, in some areas, particularly along the US-Mexico border, cash might not be accepted because of recent exposure to counterfeit US dollars or, in more remote areas, due to lack of familiarity.

Hotels and some retail outlets can change US dollars, as can exchange houses, which actually prefer cash to other instruments. Most outlets won't conduct any transactions until after they receive the official daily rate, issued at 10 am. Receipts are given when money is changed, but because there are no exchange controls, it is not necessary to present them when reconverting pesos to other currencies.

Foreigners can often get money from home by using automated teller machines (ATMs). Some of these will accept foreign (usually US) ATM or debit cards; others may issue a cash advance on a recognized international credit card, as will most member banks. You will need to know the ATM networks (such as CIRRUS or STAR) to which your home bank belongs and, of course, your personal identification number (PIN). The ease of using these procedures is somewhat offset by the costs—interest and transfer fees—although the institutions backing the cards usually offer decent exchange rates on such transactions. Money transfers are available through the correspondent networks of larger banks. Funds can also be wired using American Express MoneyGram or Western Union, both of which have numerous outlets in Mexico. Although it is technically possible to cash a personal check, banks usually must wait for the check to clear before releasing the funds—which can take as long as two weeks, making this an ineffective means of getting funds.

International credit cards are readily accepted in larger cities and areas frequented by tourists, although smaller outlets and more remote areas will either reject them or ask for a hefty surcharge (or a reduced discount, if retail purchase bargaining is involved). Except for the largest outlets and those most accustomed to the tourist trade, most outlets prefer cash, although their insistence on cash (and surcharges) is waning somewhat as inflation and interest rates fall. VISA (locally branded as Bancomer), MasterCard (locally, Carnet), and American Express are the most commonly accepted cards.

FOREIGN EXCHANGE OPERATIONS

Because the peso is not an international transaction currency, foreign exchange trading is a relatively minor business in Mexico; foreign exchange (forex) trading focuses on exchange for use in actual transactions as needed. Historically, it has been a problem to attract enough foreign exchange to service the needs of the economy. Recently, as the economy has been restructured and opened up, foreign investment funds have flowed into Mexico, ameliorating the problem. Given its proximity to and the preponderance of trade and investment with the US, the US dollar is the main currency traded in Mexico.

As noted, the vast majority of foreign currency trading activity involves an exchange for specific use in a transaction for which the conversion is incidental. However, there is a growing market in exchange for hedging and speculative purposes, conducted primarily by exchange houses. In late 1993 and early 1994, this secondary activity began to have an effect on rates and policy.

The BOM is the agency responsible for managing foreign exchange, and its general policy has been to maintain the peso at a mildly to substantially overvalued level. An increasing number of foreign exchange houses (as well as many banks and brokerages) also deal in foreign exchange, offering spot and 30-, 60-, 90-, and 180-day forward contracts and speculating on small movements in the currency. The BOM has generally taken a relatively complacent hands-off posture toward foreign exchange trading, especially since the government dropped exchange controls. However, Mexico has a history of intervening in currency markets, mostly through devaluations of its currency (sometimes abruptly and sharply), when values have become too skewed to support broader policy goals. In early 1994, some observers were arguing that another devaluation of Mexico's somewhat overvalued (at the time) currency could be in the offing. However, most doubted that a devaluation would occur before the election in August 1994. The weakness of the peso in early 1994 may obviate the need for an official devaluation, especially if the BOM continues to allow it to slide relative to the US dollar.

Following the 1987 devaluation, the exchange rate was frozen. After negotiating the first Pact for Economic Stability and Growth (the PECE, or *pacto*) in 1989, the Salinas government instituted a creeping mini-devaluation of one peso per day. As the currency stabilized due to increased growth and foreign inflows, the mini-devaluation increment was eased from one peso per day in January 1989 to 0.2 per day in November 1991. The policy paid off, with the peso remaining remarkably stable against the dollar between late 1990 and late 1993. The latest *pacto*, negotiated in late 1993, continued the mini-devaluations at the level of about 0.04 new centavos per day, and allowed for a broad-band fluctuation of 10.27 percent in value against the US dollar. This wide band was designed to reduce short-term speculation that would provoke government overreaction if the allowable band were too narrow.

In late 1993, prior to the NAFTA vote, the peso came under considerable pressure. Inside observers indicate that the BOM attempted to defend the peso up to an agreed-upon level of intervention, which included spending about US$4 billion and jacking up overnight interest rates to attract inflows, after which it decided to let the market reach its own equilibrium level. This allowed the peso to fall from about 3.1 to the dollar to about 3.25 to the dollar.

A stable currency was considered highly appropriate before NAFTA because it helped attract foreign investment. However, in the immediate post-NAFTA period, the inflows of so-called "hot" money made the government nervous, mainly because most of it went into short-term speculative financial markets investments rather than into long-term productive investments. There was also an element of election year posturing in all this, as opposition parties trumpeted that the government was selling Mexico out. In short, the government was hoping to wring some of the excess out of the system by letting the speculative binge run its course before stepping in at what would hopefully be the correct time to restabilize the peso.

After stabilizing around 3.1 with the passage of NAFTA, the peso again came under pressure in March 1994, dropping to around 3.3 by mid-month. The apparent decision by the government not to intervene was designed to dampen speculation by allowing the speculators to have their way. The government hoped that the speculators would lose interest if it failed to respond. The assassination of presidential candidate Colosio in late March led to a further period of speculative pressure. However, the fact that the government had allowed the peso to drop to the apparent market level meant that there was relatively little premium in its price when the crisis hit. The US government also let it be known that it was making available up to US$6 billion to shore up the peso should it become necessary (this line of credit had been secretly negotiated prior to the passage of NAFTA to support the peso in case NAFTA did not receive multilateral approval). This vote of confidence did serve to calm edgy foreign exchange markets. On a practical level, it also deterred speculators from pressing the issue, because the relatively thin speculative float in peso trading meant that with the backing of such reserves, the BOM might well be able to support the peso at a level that would allow it to outspend the speculators in defending the currency should it decide to do so.

RATES OF EXCHANGE

The Mexican peso theoretically floats against a basket of currencies according to supply and demand. However, in reality, the BOM generally manages its exchange rate by pegging it to the US dollar and keeping it at least somewhat overvalued on the basis of relative purchasing power. This helps attract foreign investment and aids domestic importers, although it also hurts exporters to some extent. After being maintained at an artificially high level during much of the 1980s, the peso weakened to US$ = NP3.3565 at the end of March 1994. By mid-May it had stabilized at around 3.32.

FOREIGN RESERVES

In order to demonstrate its probity and stability Mexico has maintained somewhat artificially high international currency reserves in recent years. International reserves were US$568 million in 1970, rising steadily to US$2.96 billion in 1980, then jumping nearly 40 percent to US$4.1 billion in 1981. They plummeted almost 80 percent to US$834 million in the crisis year of 1982, before recovering to US$3.9 billion in 1983. These reserves reached US$8.2 billion in 1984, dropped back to US$5.8 billion in 1985, seesawed up to US$12.5 billion in 1987, fell again to US$5.3 billion in 1988, and rose to around US$9.9 billion in 1990. Reserves were US$17.7 billion in 1991, US$18.9 billion in 1992, and ended 1993—when foreign funds flooded into the country in the immediate post-NAFTA period—at about US$27 billion. In early 1994 such funds raised total foreign reserves to an outsized US$30 billion, although such reserves fell somewhat in the uncertainty following political turmoil in late March.

Some observers argue that Mexico would be better off applying its reserves to productive investments rather than keeping the economy in its tight money straitjacket. Yet others worry that Mexico's growing trade deficit will dispose of its excess reserves in the near future. And many fear that in their rush to embrace the "new" Mexico, investors will forget about the country's US$133.7 billion in foreign debt, which consumes around US$10 billion per year—3 percent of GDP—in servicing costs. And given its election year tradition of giveaways and the pressure from those who have been left out of the recovery (crystallizing around the Zapatista rebellion), there will be considerable impetus to raid the cookie jar to buy social peace.

FURTHER READING

This discussion has been provided as a basic guide to money, finances, financial institutions, and financial markets in Mexico. Those interested in current developments may wish to consult the *Wall Street Journal* and *El Financiero*, both of which cover economic and financial developments in Mexico, the first from an outside perspective and the second from a national perspective.

Exchange Rates NP/US$

	Jan	Feb	Mar	Apr	May	Jun	Jul	Aug	Sep	Oct	Nov	Dec
1980	.0228	.0228	.0228	.0228	.0229	.0229	.0230	.0230	.0231	.0231	.0232	.0233
1981	.0234	.0235	.0238	.0240	.0242	.0244	.0246	.0249	.0252	.0255	.0258	.0262
1982	.0266	.0446	.0455	.0463	.0471	.0480	.0489	.1040	.0700	.0700	.0700	.0965
1983	.1005	.1041	.1080	.1119	.1161	.1200	.1242	.1281	.1320	.1360	.1399	.1438
1984	.1480	.1517	.1556	.1600	.1637	.1675	.1716	.1756	.1793	.1836	.1875	.1926
1985	.2330	.2470	.2630	.2700	.2900	.3080	.3920	.3950	.3900	.5120	.5000	.4650
1986	.4760	.4850	.5000	.5260	.5880	.7150	.6900	.7400	.8150	.8690	.9260	.9800
1987	1.040	1.140	1.205	1.298	1.408	1.470	1.613	1.666	1.818	1.923	3.350	2.857
1988	2.860	2.875	2.890	2.880	2.940	2.950	2.630	2.650	2.640	2.635	2.625	2.630
1989	2.645	2.580	2.565	2.565	2.635	2.700	2.514	2.450	2.565	2.616	2.644	2.684
1990	2.710	2.754	2.764	2.800	2.833	2.849	2.865	2.882	2.892	2.921	2.933	2.944
1991	2.945	2.969	2.980	2.998	3.000	3.019	3.035	3.047	3.034	3.047	3.055	3.072
1992	3.065	3.089	3.062	3.058	3.067	3.075	3.114	3.122	3.108	3.076	3.107	3.107
1993	3.122	3.09	3.095	3.107	3.127	3.120	3.115	3.114	3.117	3.113	3.103	3.105
1/1/94		3.106										
3/31/94		3.356										

Note: converted to New Pesos (New Peso 1 = Old Peso 1,000) conversion January 1, 1993; end of period data
Sources: International Monetary Fund, New York Times, Wall Street Journal

International Payments

International transactions add an additional layer of risk for buyers and sellers that are familiar only with doing business domestically. Currency regulations, foreign exchange risk, political, economic, or social upheaval in the buyer's or seller's country, and different business customs may all contribute to uncertainty. Ultimately, however, the seller wants to make sure he gets paid and the buyer wants to get what he pays for. Choosing the right payment method can be the key to the transaction's feasibility and profitability.

There are four common methods of international payment, each providing the buyer and the seller with varying degrees of protection for getting paid and for guaranteeing shipment. Ranked in order of most security for the supplier to most security for the buyer, they are: Cash in Advance, Documentary Letters of Credit (L/C), Documentary Collections (D/P and D/A Terms), and Open Account (O/A).

Cash in Advance

In cash in advance terms the buyer simply prepays the supplier prior to shipment of goods. Cash in advance terms are generally used in new relationships where transactions are small and the buyer has no choice but to pre-pay. These terms give maximum security to the seller but leave the buyer at great risk. Since the buyer has no guarantee that the goods will be shipped, he must have a high degree of trust in the seller's ability and willingness to follow through. The buyer must also consider the economic, political and social stability of the seller's country, as these conditions may make it impossible for the seller to ship as promised.

Documentary Letters of Credit

A letter of credit is a bank's promise to pay a supplier on behalf of the buyer so long as the supplier meets the terms and conditions stated in the credit. Documents are the key issue in letter of credit transactions. Banks act as intermediaries, and have nothing to do with the goods themselves.

Letters of credit are the most common form of international payment because they provide a high degree of protection for both the seller and the buyer. The buyer specifies the documentation that he requires from the seller before the bank is to make payment, and the seller is given assurance that he will receive payment after shipping his goods so long as the documentation is in order.

Documentary Collections

A documentary collection is like an international cash on delivery (COD), but with a few twists. The exporter ships goods to the importer, but forwards shipping documents (including title document) to his bank for transmission to the buyer's bank. The buyer's bank is instructed not to transfer the documents to the buyer until payment is made (Documents against Payment, D/P) or upon guarantee that payment will be made within a specified period of time (Documents against Acceptance, D/A). Once the buyer has the documentation for the shipment he is able to take possession of the goods.

D/P and D/A terms are commonly used in ongoing business relationships and provide a measure of protection for both parties. The buyer and seller, however, both assume risk in the transaction, ranging from refusal on the part of the buyer to pay for the documents, to the seller's shipping of unacceptable goods.

Open Account

This is an agreement by the buyer to pay for goods within a designated time after their shipment, usually in 30, 60, or 90 days. Open account terms give maximum security to the buyer and greatest risk to the seller. This form of payment is used only when the seller has significant trust and faith in the buyer's ability and willingness to pay once the goods have been shipped. The seller must also consider the economic, political and social stability of the buyer's country as these conditions may make it impossible for the buyer to pay as promised.

DOCUMENTARY COLLECTIONS (D/P, D/A)

Documentary collections focus on the transfer of documents such as bills of lading for the transfer of ownership of goods rather than on the goods themselves. They are easier to use than letters of credit and bank service charges are generally lower.

This form of payment is excellent for buyers who wish to purchase goods without risking prepayment and without having to go through the more cumbersome letter of credit process.

Documentary collection procedures, however, entail risk for the supplier, because payment is not made until after goods are shipped. In addition, the supplier assumes the risk while the goods are in transit and storage until payment/acceptance take place. Banks involved in the transaction do not guarantee payments. A supplier should therefore only agree to a documentary collection procedure if the transaction includes the following characteristics:

- The supplier does not doubt the buyer's ability and willingness to pay for the goods;
- The buyer's country is politically, economically, and legally stable;
- There are no foreign exchange restrictions in the buyer's home country, or unless all necessary licenses for foreign exchange have already been obtained; and
- The goods to be shipped are easily marketable.

Types of Collections

The three types of documentary collections are:
1. Documents against Payment (D/P)
2. Documents against Acceptance (D/A)
3. Collection with Acceptance (Acceptance D/P)

All of these collection procedures follow the same general step-by-step process of exchanging documents proving title to goods for either cash or a contracted promise to pay at a later time. The documents are transferred from the supplier (called the remitter) to the buyer (called the drawee) via intermediary banks. When the supplier ships goods, he presents documents such as the bill of lading, invoices, and certificate of origin to his representative bank (the remitting bank), which then forwards them to the buyer's bank (the collecting bank). According to the type of documentary collection, the buyer may then do one of the following:

- With Documents against Payment (D/P), the buyer may only receive the title and other documents after paying for the goods;
- With Documents against Acceptance (D/A), the buyer may receive the title and other documents after signing a time draft promising to pay at a later date; or

- With Acceptance Documents against Payment, the buyer signs a time draft for payment at a latter date. However, he may only obtain the documents after the time draft reaches maturity. In essence, the goods remain in escrow until payment has been made.

In all cases the buyer may take possession of the goods only by presenting the bill of lading to customs or shipping authorities.

In the event that the prospective buyer cannot or will not pay for the goods shipped, they remain in legal possession of the supplier, but he may be stuck with them in an unfavorable situation. Also, the supplier has no legal basis to file claim against the prospective buyer. At this point the supplier may:

- Have the goods returned and sell them on his domestic market; or
- Sell the goods to another buyer near where the goods are currently held.

If the supplier takes no action the goods will be auctioned or otherwise disposed of by customs.

Documentary Collection Procedure

The documentary collection process has been standardized by a set of rules published by the International Chamber of Commerce (ICC). These rules are called the Uniform Rules for Collections (URC) and are contained in ICC Publication No. 322. (See the last page of this section for ICC addresses and list of available publications.)

The following is the basic set of steps used in a documentary collection. Refer to the illustration on the following page for a graphic representation of the procedure.

(1) The seller (remitter, exporter) ships the goods.
(2) and (3) The seller forwards the agreed upon documents to his bank, the remitting bank, which in turn forwards them to the collecting bank (buyer's bank).
(4) The collecting bank notifies the buyer (drawee, importer) and informs him of the conditions under which he can take possession of the documents.
(5) To take possession of the documents, the buyer makes payment or signs a time deposit.
(6) and (7) If the buyer draws the documents against payment, the collecting bank transfers payment to the remitting bank for credit to the supplier's account. If the buyer draws the documents against acceptance, the collecting bank sends the acceptance to the remitting bank or retains it up to maturity. On maturity, the collecting bank collects the bill and transfers it to the remitting bank for payment to the supplier.

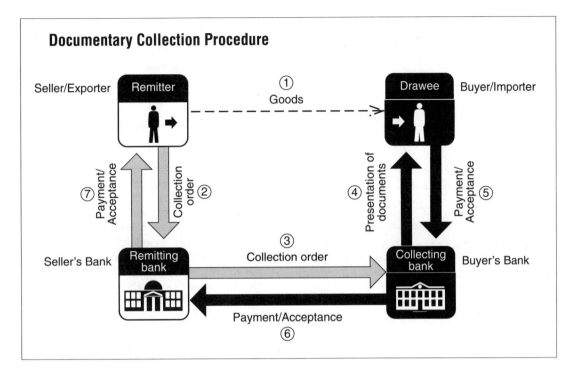

Documentary Collection Procedure

TIPS FOR BUYERS

1. The buyer is generally in a secure position because he does not assume ownership or responsibility for goods until he has paid for the documents or signed a time draft.
2. The buyer may not sample or inspect the goods before accepting and paying for the documents without authorization from the seller. However, the buyer may in advance specify a certificate of inspection as part of the required documentation package.
3. As a special favor, the collecting bank can allow the buyer to inspect the documents before payment. The collecting bank assumes responsibility for the documents until their redemption.
4. In the above case, the buyer should immediately return the entire set of documents to the collecting bank if he cannot meet the agreed payment procedure.
5. The buyer assumes no liability for goods if he refuses to take possession of the documents.
6. Partial payment in exchange for the documents is not allowed unless authorized in the collection order.
7. With documents against acceptance, the buyer may receive the goods and resell them for profit before the time draft matures, thereby using the proceeds of the sale to pay for the goods. The buyer remains responsible for payment, however, even if he cannot sell the goods.

TIPS FOR SUPPLIERS

1. The supplier assumes risk because he ships goods before receiving payment. The buyer is under no legal obligation to pay for or to accept the goods.
2. Before agreeing to a documentary collection, the supplier should check on the buyer's creditworthiness and business reputation.
3. The supplier should make sure the buyer's country is politically and financially stable.
4. The supplier should find out what documents are required for customs clearance in the buyer's country. Consulates may be of help.
5. The supplier should assemble the documents carefully and make sure they are in the required form and endorsed as necessary.
6. As a rule, the remitting bank will not review the documents before forwarding them to the collecting bank. This is the responsibility of the seller.
7. The goods travel and are stored at the risk of the supplier until payment or acceptance.
8. If the buyer refuses acceptance or payment for the documents, the supplier retains ownership. The supplier may have the goods shipped back or try to sell them to another buyer in the region.
9. If the buyer takes no action, customs authorities may seize the goods and auction them off or otherwise dispose of them.
10. Because goods may be refused, the supplier should only ship goods which are readily marketable to other sources.

LETTERS OF CREDIT (L/C)

A letter of credit is a document issued by a bank stating its commitment to pay someone (supplier/exporter/seller) a stated amount of money on behalf of a buyer (importer) so long as the seller meets very specific terms and conditions. Letters of credit are often called documentary letters of credit because the banks handling the transaction deal in documents as opposed to goods. Letters of credit are the most common method of making international payments, because the risks of the transaction are shared by both the buyer and the supplier.

STEPS IN USING AN L/C

The letter of credit process has been standardized by a set of rules published by the International Chamber of Commerce (ICC). These rules are called the Uniform Customs and Practice for Documentary Credits (UCP) and are contained in ICC Publication No. 400. (See the last page of this section for ICC addresses and list of available publications.) The following is the basic set of steps used in a letter of credit transaction. Specific letter of credit transactions follow somewhat different procedures.

- After the buyer and supplier agree on the terms of a sale, the buyer arranges for his bank to open a letter of credit in favor of the supplier.
- The buyer's bank (the issuing bank), prepares the letter of credit, including all of the buyer's instructions to the seller concerning shipment and required documentation.
- The buyer's bank sends the letter of credit to a correspondent bank (the advising bank), in the seller's country. The seller may request that a particular bank be the advising bank, or the domestic bank may select one of its correspondent banks in the seller's country.
- The advising bank forwards the letter of credit to the supplier.

- The supplier carefully reviews all conditions the buyer has stipulated in the letter of credit. If the supplier cannot comply with one or more of the provisions he immediately notifies the buyer and asks that an amendment be made to the letter of credit.
- After final terms are agreed upon, the supplier prepares the goods and arranges for their shipment to the appropriate port.
- The supplier ships the goods, and obtains a bill of lading and other documents as required by the buyer in the letter of credit. Some of these documents may need to be obtained prior to shipment.
- The supplier presents the required documents to the advising bank, indicating full compliance with the terms of the letter of credit. Required documents usually include a bill of lading, commercial invoice, certificate of origin, and possibly an inspection certificate if required by the buyer.
- The advising bank reviews the documents. If they are in order, the documents are forwarded to the issuing bank. If it is an irrevocable, confirmed letter of credit the supplier is guaranteed payment and may be paid immediately by the advising bank.
- Once the issuing bank receives the documents it notifies the buyer who then reviews the documents himself. If the documents are in order the buyer signs off, taking possession of the documents, including the bill of lading, which he uses to take possession of the shipment.
- The issuing bank initiates payment to the advising bank, which pays the supplier.

The transfer of funds from the buyer to his bank, from the buyer's bank to the supplier's bank, and from the supplier's bank to the supplier may be handled at the same time as the exchange of documents, or under terms agreed upon in advance.

Parties to a Letter of Credit Transaction

| Buyer/Importer | Buyer | Issuing bank | Buyer's bank |
| Seller/Supplier/Exporter | Seller | Advising bank | Seller's bank |

Issuance

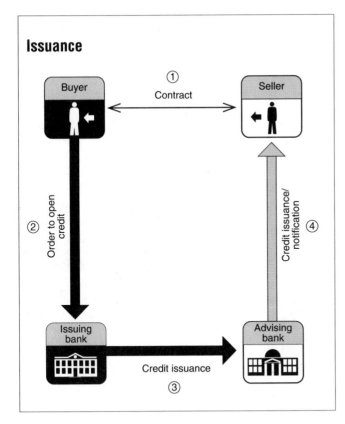

Issuance of a Letter of Credit

① Buyer and seller agree on purchase contract.
② Buyer applies for and opens a letter of credit with issuing ("buyer's") bank.
③ Issuing bank issues the letter of credit, forwarding it to advising ("seller's") bank.
④ Advising bank notifies seller of letter of credit.

Amendment

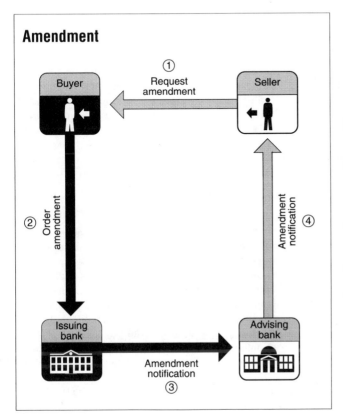

Amendment of a Letter of Credit

① Seller requests (of the buyer) a modification (amendment) of the terms of the letter of credit. Once the terms are agreed upon:
② Buyer issues order to issuing ("buyer's") bank to make an amendment to the terms of the letter of credit.
③ Issuing bank notifies advising ("seller's") bank of amendment.
④ Advising bank notifies seller of amendment.

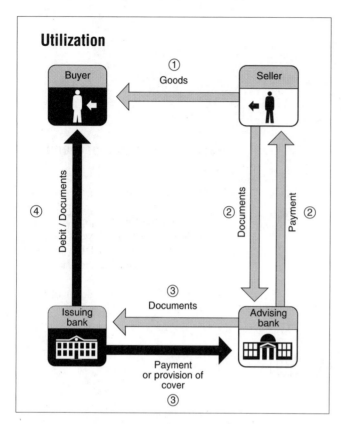

Utilization

① Goods — Buyer ← Seller
② Documents / Payment
③ Documents — Issuing bank ← Advising bank
④ Debit / Documents

Payment or provision of cover ③

Utilization of a Letter of Credit

(irrevocable, confirmed credit)

① Seller ships goods to buyer.
② Seller forwards all documents (as stipulated in the letter of credit) to advising bank. Once documents are reviewed and accepted, advising bank pays seller for the goods.
③ Advising bank forwards documents to issuing bank. Once documents are reviewed and accepted, issuing bank pays advising bank.
④ Issuing bank forwards documents to buyer. Seller's letter of credit, or account, is debited.

COMMON PROBLEMS IN LETTER OF CREDIT TRANSACTIONS

Most problems with letter of credit transactions have to do with the ability of the supplier to fulfill obligations the buyer establishes in the original letter of credit. The supplier may find the terms of the credit difficult or impossible to fulfill and either tries to do so and fails, or asks the buyer for an amendment to the letter of credit. Observers note that over half of all letters of credit involving parties in East Asia are amended or renegotiated entirely. Since most letters of credit are irrevocable, amendments to the original letter of credit can only be made after further negotiations and agreements between the buyer and the supplier. Suppliers may have one or more of the following problems:

• Shipment schedule stipulated in the letter of credit cannot be met.
• Stipulations concerning freight cost are deemed unacceptable.
• Price is insufficient due to changes in exchange rates.
• Quantity of product ordered is not the expected amount.
• Description of product to be shipped is either insufficient or too detailed.
• Documents stipulated in the letter of credit are difficult or impossible to obtain.

Even when suppliers accept the terms of a letter of credit, problems often arise at the stage where banks review, or negotiate, the documents provided by the supplier against the requirements specified in the letter of credit. If the documents are found not to be in accord with those specified in the letter of credit, the bank's commitment to pay is invalidated. In some cases the supplier can correct the documents and present them within the time specified in the letter of credit. Or, the advising bank may ask the issuing bank for authorization to accept the documents despite the discrepancies found.

Limits on Legal Obligations of Banks

It is important to note once again that banks *deal in documents and not in goods.* Only the wording of the credit is binding on the bank. Banks are not responsible for verifying the authenticity of the documents, nor for the quality or quantity of the goods being shipped. As long as the *documents* comply with the specified terms of the letter of credit, banks may accept them and initiate the payment process as stipulated in the letter of credit. Banks are free from liability for delays in sending messages caused by another party, consequences of Acts of God, or the acts of third parties whom they have instructed to carry out transactions.

TYPES OF LETTERS OF CREDIT

Basic Letters of Credit

There are two basic forms of letters of credit: the Revocable Credit and the Irrevocable Credit. There are also two types of irrevocable credit: the Irrevocable Credit not Confirmed, and the Irrevocable Confirmed Credit. Each type of credit has advantages and disadvantages for the buyer and for the seller. Also note that the more the banks assume risk by guaranteeing payment, the more they will charge for providing the service.

1. Revocable credit This credit can be changed or canceled by the buyer without prior notice to the supplier. Because it offers little security to the seller revocable credits are generally unacceptable to the seller and are rarely used.

2. Irrevocable credit The irrevocable credit is one which the issuing bank commits itself irrevocably to honor, provided the beneficiary complies with all stipulated conditions. This credit cannot be changed or canceled without the consent of both the buyer and the seller. As a result, this type of credit is the most widely used in international trade. Irrevocable credits are more expensive because of the issuing bank's added liability in guaranteeing the credit. There are two types of irrevocable credits:

a. The Irrevocable Credit not Confirmed by the Advising Bank (Unconfirmed Credit) This means that the buyer's bank which issues the credit is the only party responsible for payment to the supplier, and the supplier's bank is obliged to pay the supplier only after receiving payment from the buyer's bank. The supplier's bank merely acts on behalf of the issuing bank and therefore incurs no risk.

b. The Irrevocable, Confirmed Credit In a confirmed credit, the advising bank adds its guarantee to pay the supplier to that of the issuing bank. If the issuing bank fails to make payment the advising bank will pay. If a supplier is unfamiliar with the buyer's bank which issues the letter of credit, he may insist on an irrevocable confirmed credit. These credits may be used when trade is conducted in a high risk area where there are fears of outbreak of war or social, political, or financial instability. Confirmed credits may also be used by the supplier to enlist the aid of a local bank to extend financing to enable him to fill the order. A confirmed credit costs more because the bank has added liability.

Special Letters of Credit

There are numerous special letters of credit designed to meet specific needs of buyers, suppliers, and intermediaries. Special letters of credit usually involve increased participation by banks, so financing and service charges are higher than those for basic letters of credit. The following is a brief description of some special letters of credit.

1. Standby Letter of Credit This credit is primarily a payment or performance guarantee. It is used primarily in the United States because US banks are prevented by law from giving certain guarantees. Standby credits are often called non-performing letters of credit because they are only used as a backup payment method if the collection on a primary payment method is past due.

Standby letters of credit can be used, for example, to guarantee the following types of payment and performance:

- repayment of loans;
- fulfillment by subcontractors;
- securing the payment for goods delivered by third parties.

The beneficiary to a standby letter of credit can draw from it on demand, so the buyer assumes added risk.

2. Revolving Letter of Credit This credit is a commitment on the part of the issuing bank to restore the credit to the original amount after it has been used or drawn down. The number of times it can be utilized and the period of validity is stated in the credit. The credit can be cumulative or noncumulative. Cumulative means that unutilized sums can be added to the next installment whereas noncumulative means that partial amounts not utilized in time expire.

3. Deferred Payment Letter of Credit In this credit the buyer takes delivery of the shipped goods by accepting the documents and agreeing to pay his bank after a fixed period of time. This credit gives the buyer a grace period, and ensures that the seller gets payment on the due date.

4. Red Clause Letter of Credit This is used to provide the supplier with some funds prior to shipment to finance production of the goods. The credit may be advanced in part or in full, and the buyer's bank finances the advance payment. The buyer, in essence, extends financing to the seller and incurs ultimate risk for all advanced credits.

5. Transferable Letter of Credit This allows the supplier to transfer all or part of the proceeds of the letter of credit to a second beneficiary, usually the ultimate producer of the goods. This is a common financing tactic for middlemen and is used extensively in the Far East.

6. Back-to-Back Letter of Credit This is a new credit opened on the basis of an already existing, nontransferable credit. It is used by traders to make payment to the ultimate supplier. A trader receives a letter of credit from the buyer and then opens another letter of credit in favor of the supplier. The first letter of credit is used as collateral for the second credit. The second credit makes price adjustments from which come the trader's profit.

OPENING A LETTER OF CREDIT

The wording in a letter of credit should be simple but specific. The more detailed an L/C is, the more likely the supplier will reject it as too difficult to fulfill. At the same time, the buyer will wish to define in detail what he is paying for.

Although the L/C process is designed to ensure the satisfaction of all parties to the transaction, it cannot be considered a substitute for face-to-face agreements on doing business in good faith. It should therefore contain only those stipulations required from the banks involved in the documentary process.

L/Cs used in trade with East Asia are usually either irrevocable unconfirmed credits or irrevocable confirmed credits. In choosing the type of L/C to open in favor of the supplier, the buyer should take into consideration generally accepted payment processes in the supplier's country, the value and demand for the goods to be shipped, and the reputation of the supplier.

In specifying documents necessary from the supplier, it is very important to demand documents that are required for customs clearance and those that reflect the agreement reached between the buyer and the supplier. Required documents usually include the bill of lading, a commercial and/or consular invoice, the bill of exchange, the certificate of origin, and the insurance document. Other documents required may be copies of a cable sent to the buyer with shipping information, a confirmation from the shipping company of the state of its ship, and a confirmation from the forwarder that the goods are accompanied by a certificate of origin. Prices should be stated in the currency of the L/C, and documents should be supplied in the language of the L/C.

THE APPLICATION

The following information should be included on an application form for opening an L/C.

(1) **Beneficiary** The seller's company name and address should be written completely and correctly. Incomplete or incorrect information results in delays and unnecessary additional cost.

(2) **Amount** Is the figure a maximum amount or an approximate amount? If words like "circa," "ca.," "about," etc., are used in connection with the amount of the credit, it means that a difference as high as 10 percent upwards or downwards is permitted. In such a case, the same word should also be used in connection with the quantity.

(3) **Validity Period** The validity and period for presentation of the documents following shipment of the goods should be sufficiently long to allow the exporter time to prepare his documents and ship them to the bank. Under place of validity, state the domicile of either the advising bank or the issuing bank.

(4) **Beneficiary's Bank** If no bank is named, the issuing bank is free to select the correspondent bank.

(5) **Type of Payment Availability** Sight drafts, time drafts, or deferred payment may be used, as previously agreed to by the supplier and buyer.

(6) **Desired Documents** Here the buyer specifies precisely which documents he requires. To obtain effective protection against the supply of poor quality goods, for instance, he can demand the submission of analysis or quality certificates. These are generally issued by specialized inspection companies or laboratories.

(7) **Notify Address** An address is given for notification of the imminent arrival of goods at the port or airport of destination. Damage of goods in shipment is also cause for notification. An agent representing the buyer may be used.

(8) **Description of Goods** Here a short, precise description of the goods is given, along with quantity. If the credit amount carries the notation "ca.," the same notation should appear with the quantity.

(9) **Confirmation Order** It may happen that the foreign beneficiary insists on having the credit confirmed by the bank in his country.

Sample Letter of Credit Application

Sender American Import-Export Co., Inc. 123 Main Street San Francisco, California Our reference AB/02	**Instructions** **to open a Documentary Credit** San Francisco, 30th September 19.. Place / Date
Please open the following [X] irrevocable [ ] revocable documentary credit	**Domestic Bank Corporation** Documentary Credits P.O. Box 1040 San Francisco, California

Beneficiary ① Mexico Trading Corporation Paseo de la Reforma No 108, Piso 5 Col. Revolución 06030 Mexico, DF	Beneficiary's bank (if known) ④ Mexico Commercial Bank Mexico City Main Office 11570 Mexico, DF
Amount ② US$70,200.--	Please advise this bank [ ] by letter [X] by letter, cabling main details in advance [ ] by telex / telegram with full text of credit
Date and place of expiry ③ 25th November 19.. in San Francisco	

Partial shipments [X] allowed [ ] not allowed	Transhipment [ ] allowed [X] not allowed	Terms of shipment (FOB, C & F, CIF) CIF San Francisco
Despatch from / Taking in charge at Mexico, DF	For transportation to San Francisco	Latest date of shipment 10th Nov. 19.. ③ 15	Documents must be presented not later than days after date of despatch

Beneficiary may dispose of the credit amount as follows [X] at sight upon presentation of documents ⑤ [ ] after .... days, calculated from date of	[ ] by a draft due .... drawn on [ ] you [ ] your correspondents which you / your correspondents will please accept

against surrender of the following documents ⑥ [X] invoice (.....3.....copies) Shipping document [X] sea: bill of lading, to order, endorsed in blank [ ] rail: dublicate waybill [ ] air: air consignment note [ ]	[X] insurance policy, certificte (.................. copies) covering the following risks: "all risks" including war up to [ ] Additional documents final destination in the USA [X] Confirmation of the carrier that the ship is not more than 15 years old [X] packing list (3 copies)
Notify address in bill of lading / goods addressed to American Import-Export Co., Inc. ⑦ 123 Main Street San Francisco, California	Goods insured by [ ] us [X] seller

Goods ⑧ 1'000 "Record players ANC 83 as per pro forma invoice no. 74/1853 dd 10th September 19.." at US$70.20 per item

Your correspondents to advise beneficiary [ ] adding their confirmation [X] without adding their confirmation ⑨ Payments to be debited to our U.S. Dollars .... account no 10-32679150

NB. The applicable text is marked by [X]

American Import-Export Co., Inc.

E 6801 N 1/2 3.81 5000

Signature _____

For mailing please see overleaf

This credit is subject to the "Uniform customs and practice for documentary credits" fixed by the International Chamber of Commerce. It is understood that you do not assume any responsibility neither for the correctness, validity or genuineness of the documents which will be remitted to you nor for the description, quality, quantity and weight of the goods thereby represented.

TIPS FOR PARTIES TO A LETTER OF CREDIT

Buyer

1. Before opening a letter of credit, the buyer should reach agreement with the supplier on all particulars of payment procedures, schedules of shipment, type of goods to be sent, and documents to be supplied by the supplier.

2. When choosing the type of L/C to be used, the buyer should take into account standard payment methods in the country with which he is doing business.

3. When opening a letter of credit, the buyer should keep the details of the purchase short and concise.

4. The buyer should be prepared to amend or renegotiate terms of the L/C with the supplier. This is a common procedure in international trade. On irrevocable L/Cs, the most common type, amendments may be made only if all parties involved in the L/C agree.

5. The buyer can eliminate exchange risk involved with import credits in foreign currencies by purchasing foreign exchange on the forward markets.

6. The buyer should use a bank experienced in foreign trade as the L/C issuing bank.

7. The validation time stated on the L/C should give the supplier ample time to produce the goods or to pull them out of stock.

8. The buyer should be aware that an L/C is not fail-safe. Banks are only responsible for the documents exchanged and not the goods shipped. Documents in conformity with L/C specifications cannot be rejected on grounds that the goods were not delivered as specified in the contract. The goods shipped may not in fact be the goods ordered and paid for.

9. Purchase contracts and other agreements pertaining to the sale between the buyer and supplier are not the concern of the issuing bank. Only the terms of the L/C are binding on the bank.

10. Documents specified in the L/C should include those the buyer requires for customs clearance.

Supplier

1. Before signing a contract, the supplier should make inquiries about the buyer's creditworthiness and business practices. The supplier's bank will generally assist in this investigation.

2. The supplier should confirm the good standing of the buyer's bank if the credit is unconfirmed.

3. For confirmed credit, the supplier should determine that his local bank is willing to confirm credits from the buyer and his bank.

4. The supplier should carefully review the L/C to make sure he can meet the specified schedules of shipment, type of goods to be sent, packaging, and documentation. All aspects of the L/C must be in conformance with the terms agreed upon, including the supplier's address, the amount to be paid, and the prescribed transport route.

5. The supplier must comply with every detail of the L/C specifications, otherwise the security given by the credit is lost.

6. The supplier should ensure that the L/C is irrevocable.

7. If conditions of the credit have to be modified, the supplier should contact the buyer immediately so that he can instruct the issuing bank to make the necessary amendments.

8. The supplier should confirm with his insurance company that it can provide the coverage specified in the credit, and that insurance charges in the L/C are correct. Insurance coverage often is for CIF (cost, insurance, freight) value of the goods plus 10 percent.

9. The supplier must ensure that the details of goods being sent comply with the description in the L/C, and that the description on the invoice matches that on the L/C.

10. The supplier should be familiar with foreign exchange limitations in the buyer's country which may hinder payment procedures.

GLOSSARY OF DOCUMENTS IN INTERNATIONAL TRADE

The following is a list and description of some of the more common documents importers and exporters encounter in the course of international trade. For the importer/buyer this serves as a checklist of documents he may require of the seller/exporter in a letter of credit or documents against payment method.

Bill of Lading A document issued by a transportation company (such as a shipping line) to the shipper which serves as a receipt for goods shipped, a contract for delivery, and may serve as a title document. The major types are:

Straight (non-negotiable) Bill of Lading Indicates that the shipper will deliver the goods to the consignee. The document itself does not give title to the goods. The consignee need only identify himself to claim the goods. A straight bill of lading is often used when the goods have been paid for in advance.

Order (negotiable or "shippers order") Bill of Lading This is a title document which must be in the possession of the consignee (buyer/importer) in order for him to take possession of the shipped goods. Because this bill of lading is negotiable, it is usually made out "to the order of" the consignor (seller/exporter).

Air Waybill A bill of lading issued for air shipment of goods, which is always made out in straight non-negotiable form. It serves as a receipt for the shipper and needs to be made out to someone who can take possession of the goods upon arrival—without waiting for other documents to arrive.

Overland/Inland Bill of Lading Similar to an Air Waybill, except that it covers ground or water transport.

Certificate of Origin A document which certifies the country of origin of the goods. Because a certificate of origin is often required by customs for entry, a buyer will often stipulate in his letter of credit that a certificate of origin is a required document.

Certificate of Manufacture A document in which the producer of goods certifies that production has been completed and that the goods are at the disposal of the buyer.

Consular Invoice An invoice prepared on a special form supplied by the consul of an importing country, in the language of the importing country, and certified by a consular official of the foreign country.

Dock Receipt A document/receipt issued by an ocean carrier when the seller/exporter is not responsible for moving the goods to their final destination, but only to a dock in the exporting country. The document/receipt indicates that the goods were, in fact, delivered and received at the specified dock.

Export License A document, issued by a government agency, giving authorization to export certain commodities to specified countries.

Import License A document, issued by a government agency, giving authorization to import certain commodities.

Inspection Certificate An affidavit signed by the seller/exporter or an independent inspection firm (as required by the buyer/importer), confirming that merchandise meets certain specifications.

Insurance Document A document certifying that goods are insured for shipment.

Invoice/Commercial Invoice A document identifying the seller and buyer of goods or services, identifying numbers such as invoice number, date, shipping date, mode of transport, delivery and payment terms, and a complete listing and description of the goods or services being sold including prices, discounts, and quantities. The commercial invoice is usually used by customs to determine the true cost of goods when assessing duty.

Packing List A document listing the merchandise contained in a particular box, crate, or container, plus type, dimensions, and weight of the container.

Phytosanitary (plant health) Inspection Certificate A document certifying that an export shipment has been inspected and is free from pests and plant diseases considered harmful by the importing country.

Shipper's Export Declaration A form prepared by a shipper/exporter indicating the value, weight, destination, and other information about an export shipment.

GLOSSARY OF TERMS OF SALE

The following is a basic glossary of common terms of sale in international trade. Note that issues regarding responsibility for loss and insurance are complex and beyond the scope of this publication. The international standard of trade terms of sale are "Incoterms," published by the International Chamber of Commerce (ICC), 38, Cours Albert Ier, F-75008 Paris, France. Other offices of the ICC are British National Committee of the ICC, Centre Point, 103 New Oxford Street, London WC1A 1QB, UK and US Council of the ICC, 1212 Avenue of the Americas, New York, NY 10010, USA.

C&F (Cost and Freight) Named Point of Destination The seller's price includes the cost of the goods and transportation up to a named port of destination, but does not cover insurance. Under these terms insurance is the responsibility of the buyer/importer.

CIF (Cost, Insurance, and Freight) Named Point of Destination The seller's price includes the cost of the goods, insurance, and transportation up to a named port of destination.

Ex Dock—Named Port of Importation The seller's price includes the cost of the goods, and all additional charges necessary to put them on the dock at the named port of importation with import duty paid. The seller is obligated to pay for insurance and freight charges.

Ex Point of Origin ("Ex Works" "Ex Warehouse" etc.) The seller's price includes the cost of the goods and packing, but without any transport. The seller agrees to place the goods at the disposal of the buyer at a specified point of origin, on a specified date, and within a fixed period of time. The buyer is under obligation to take delivery of the goods at the agreed place and bear all costs of freight, transport and insurance.

FAS (Free Alongside Ship) The seller's price includes the cost of the goods and transportation up to the port of shipment alongside the vessel or on a designated dock. Insurance under these terms is usually the responsibility of the buyer.

FOB (Free On Board) The seller's price includes the cost of the goods, transportation to the port of shipment, and loading charges on a vessel. This might be on a ship, railway car, or truck at an inland point of departure. Loss or damage to the shipment is borne by the seller until loaded at the point named and by the buyer after loading at that point.

GLOSSARY OF INTERNATIONAL PAYMENT TERMS

Advice The forwarding of a letter of credit or an amendment to a letter of credit to the seller, or beneficiary of the letter of credit, by the advising bank (seller's bank).

Advising Bank The bank (usually the seller's bank) which receives a letter of credit from the issuing bank (the buyer's bank) and handles the transaction from the seller's side. This includes: validating the letter of credit, reviewing it for internal consistency, forwarding it to the seller, forwarding seller's documentation back to the issuing bank, and, in the case of a confirmed letter of credit, guaranteeing payment to the seller if his documents are in order and the terms of the credit are met.

Amendment A change in the terms and conditions of a letter of credit, usually to meet the needs of the seller. The seller requests an amendment of the buyer who, if he agrees, instructs his bank (the issuing bank) to issue the amendment. The issuing bank informs the seller's bank (the advising bank) who then notifies the seller of the amendment. In the case of irrevocable letters of credit, amendments may only be made with the agreement of all parties to the transaction.

Back-to-Back Letter of Credit A new letter of credit opened in favor of another beneficiary on the basis of an already existing, nontransferable letter of credit.

Beneficiary The entity to whom credits and payments are made, usually the seller/supplier of goods.

Bill of Exchange A written order from one person to another to pay a specified sum of money to a designated person. The following two versions are the most common:

Draft A financial/legal document where one individual (the drawer) instructs another individual (the drawee) to pay a certain amount of money to a named person, usually in payment for the transfer of goods or services. Sight Drafts are payable when presented. Time Drafts (also called usance drafts) are payable at a future fixed (specific) date or determinable (30, 60, 90 days etc.) date. Time drafts are used as a financing tool (as with Documents against Acceptance D/P terms) to give the buyer time to pay for his purchase.

Promissory Note A financial/legal document wherein one individual (the issuer) promises to pay another individual a certain amount.

Collecting Bank (also called the presenting bank) In a Documentary Collection, the bank (usually the buyer's bank) that collects payment or a time draft from the buyer to be forwarded to the remitting bank (usually the seller's bank) in exchange for shipping and other documents which enable the buyer to take possession of the goods.

Confirmed Letter of Credit A letter of credit which contains a guarantee on the part of both the issuing and advising bank of payment to the seller so long as the seller's documentation is in order and terms of the credit are met.

Deferred Payment Letter of Credit A letter of credit where the buyer takes possession of the title documents and the goods by agreeing to pay the issuing bank at a fixed time in the future.

Discrepancy The noncompliance with the terms and conditions of a letter of credit. A discrepancy may be as small as a misspelling, an inconsistency in dates or amounts, or a missing document. Some discrepancies can easily be fixed; others may lead to the eventual invalidation of the letter of credit.

D/A Abbreviation for "Documents against Acceptance."

D/P Abbreviation for "Documents against Payment."

Documents against Acceptance (D/A) *See* Documentary Collection

Documents against Payment (D/P) *See* Documentary Collection

Documentary Collection A method of effecting payment for goods whereby the seller/exporter instructs his bank to collect a certain sum from the buyer/importer in exchange for the transfer of shipping and other documentation enabling the buyer/importer to take possession of the goods. The two main types of Documentary Collection are:

Documents against Payment (D/P) Where the bank releases the documents to the buyer/importer only against a cash payment in a prescribed currency; and

Documents against Acceptance (D/A) Where the bank releases the documents to the buyer/importer against acceptance of a bill of exchange guaranteeing payment at a later date.

Draft *See* Bill of exchange.

Drawee The buyer in a documentary collection.

Forward Foreign Exchange An agreement to purchase foreign exchange (currency) at a future date at a predetermined rate of exchange. Forward foreign exchange contracts are often purchased by buyers of merchandise who wish to hedge against foreign exchange fluctuations between the time the contract is negotiated and the time payment is made.

Irrevocable Credit A letter of credit which cannot be revoked or amended without prior mutual consent of the supplier, the buyer, and all intermediaries.

Issuance The act of the issuing bank (buyer's bank) establishing a letter of credit based on the buyer's application.

Issuing Bank The buyer's bank which establishes a letter of credit in favor of the supplier, or beneficiary.

Letter of Credit A document stating commitment on the part of a bank to place an agreed upon sum of money at the disposal of a seller on behalf of a buyer under precisely defined conditions.

Negotiation In a letter of credit transaction, the examination of seller's documentation by the (negotiating) bank to determine if they comply with the terms and conditions of the letter of credit.

Open Account The shipping of goods by the supplier to the buyer prior to payment for the goods. The supplier will usually specify expected payment terms of 30, 60, or 90 days from date of shipment.

Red Clause Letter of Credit A letter of credit which makes funds available to the seller prior to shipment in order to provide him with funds for production of the goods.

Remitter In a documentary collection, an alternate name given to the seller who forwards documents to the buyer through banks.

Remitting Bank In a documentary collection, a bank which acts as an intermediary, forwarding the remitter's documents to, and payments from the collecting bank.

Revocable Letter of Credit A letter of credit which may be revoked or amended by the issuer (buyer) without prior notice to other parties in the letter of credit process. It is rarely used.

Revolving Letter of Credit A letter of credit which is automatically restored to its full amount after the completion of each documentary exchange. It is used when there are several shipments to be made over a specified period of time.

Sight Draft *See* Bill of Exchange.

Standby Letter of Credit A letter of credit used as a secondary payment method in the event that the primary payment method cannot be fulfilled.

Time Draft *See* Bill of Exchange.

Validity The time period for which a letter of credit is valid. After receiving notice of a letter of credit opened on his behalf, the seller/exporter must meet all the requirements of the letter of credit within the period of validity.

FURTHER READING

For more detailed information on international trade payments, refer to the following publications of the International Chamber of Commerce (ICC), Paris, France.

Uniform Rules for Collections This publication describes the conditions governing collections, including those for presentation, payment and acceptance terms. The Articles also specify the responsibility of the bank regarding protest, case of need and actions to protect the merchandise. An indispensable aid to everyday banking operations. (A revised, updated edition will be published in 1995.) ICC Publication No. 322.

Documentary Credits: UCP 500 and 400 Compared This publication was developed to train managers, supervisors, and practitioners of international trade in critical areas of the new UCP 500 Rules. It pays particular attention to those Articles that have been the source of litigation. ICC Publication No. 511.

The New ICC Standard Documentary Credit Forms Standard Documentary Credit Forms are a series of forms designed for bankers, attorneys, importers/exporters, and anyone involved in documentary credit transactions around the world. This comprehensive new edition, prepared by Charles del Busto, Chairman of the ICC Banking Commission, reflects the major changes instituted by the new "UCP 500." ICC Publication No. 516.

The New ICC Guide to Documentary Credit Operations This new Guide is a fully revised and expanded edition of the "Guide to Documentary Credits" (ICC publication No. 415, published in conjunction with the UCP No. 400). The new Guide uses a unique combination of graphs, charts, and sample documents to illustrate the Documentary Credit process. An indispensable tool for import/export traders, bankers, training services, and anyone involved in day-to-day Credit operations. ICC Publication No. 515.

Guide to Incoterms 1990 A companion to "Incoterms," the ICC "Guide to Incoterms 1990" gives detailed comments on the changes to the 1980 edition and indicates why it may be in the interest of a buyer or seller to use one or another trade term. This guide is indispensable for exporters/importers, bankers, insurers, and transporters. ICC Publication No. 461/90.

These and other relevant ICC publications may be obtained from the following sources:

ICC Publishing S.A.
International Chamber of Commerce
38, Cours Albert Ier
75008 Paris, France
Tel: [33] (1) 49-53-28-28 Fax: [33] (1) 49-53-28-62
Telex: 650770

International Chamber of Commerce
Borsenstrasse 26
P.O. Box 4138
8022 Zurich, Switzerland

British National Committee of the ICC
Centre Point, New Oxford Street
London WC1A QB, UK

ICC Publishing, Inc.
US Council of the ICC
156 Fifth Avenue, Suite 820
New York, NY 10010, USA
Tel: [1] (212) 206-1150 Fax: [1] (212) 633-6025

Corporate Taxation

AT A GLANCE

Corporate Income Tax Rate (%)	34
Capital Gains Tax Rate (%)	34
Branch Tax Rate (%)	34
Withholding Tax (%)	
Dividends	0(a)
Interest to Banks	4.9(b)
Interest to Machinery Suppliers	10(c)
Interest to Others	34(c)
Royalties from Patents, Know-how, etc.	15(c)
Branch Remittance Tax	0(a)
Net Operating Losses (Years)	
Carryback	0
Carryforward	5(d)

(a) See Taxes on Corporate Income and Gains.
(b) Final tax applicable to nonresident banks registered with the Mexican tax authorities.
(c) Final tax applicable to nonresidents.
(d) If also incurred for accounting purposes, the loss may be carried forward for an additional five years.

TAXES ON CORPORATE INCOME AND GAINS

Corporate Income Tax Corporations resident in Mexico are taxable on their worldwide income from all sources, including profits from business and property. A nonresident corporation in Mexico is also subject to profits tax on income earned from carrying on business in Mexico. Corporations are considered residents of Mexico if they are established under Mexican law.

Corporations are taxed in Mexico only by the federal government. Mexico has a general system for taxing corporate income, ensuring that all of a corporation's earnings are taxed only once, in the fiscal year in which the profits are obtained.

The income tax law recognizes the effects of inflation on the following items and transactions:

- Depreciation of fixed assets;
- Cost on sales of fixed assets;
- Sale of capital stock (shares);
- Monetary gain and loss; and
- Tax loss carryforward.

Investment in capital stock can be indexed at the time of capital stock reductions or liquidation.

Tax Rate For 1994, corporate taxable income is subject to federal corporate income tax of 34 percent.

Minimum Tax on Net Assets A tax of 2 percent is levied on net assets (TNA) of resident corporations and nonresident corporations that have a permanent establishment in Mexico. The tax also applies to nonresident corporations without a permanent establishment in Mexico if they maintain machinery or equipment and inventories for processing in Mexico. In principle *maquiladoras* are subject to this tax, but an exemption is generally applicable.

If a company has taxable earnings for the year and subsequently pays income tax, the income tax can be credited against the final TNA. TNA is levied on the average value of a company's assets after deducting investments in shares of Mexican companies and debts owed to resident corporate entities other than financial institutions. A company that pays TNA as a minimum tax may obtain a refund of TNA if its income tax liability for the next five tax years exceeds the TNA payable over that period. TNA is payable in advance in 12 monthly payments.

Capital Gains Mexican tax law treats capital gains as normal income and taxes them at regular corporate tax rates. However, to determine the deductible basis for sales of real estate, fixed assets and shares, the law allows for the indexation of the original cost for inflation.

Administration The tax period always ends on December 31 and cannot exceed 12 months. The tax return must be filed by the end of the third month following the tax year-end. Monthly tax installments

Note: This section is courtesy of and © Ernst & Young from their Worldwide Corporate Tax Guide, 1994 Edition. This material should not be regarded as offering a complete explanation of the taxation matters referred to. Ernst & Young is a leading international professional services firm with offices in 100 countries, including Mexico. Refer to "Important Addresses" chapter for addresses and telephone numbers of Ernst & Young offices in Mexico.

INVESTMENT MADE EASIER BY THE US–MEXICO TAX TREATY*

US and Mexican legislators have ratified the first US–Mexico income-tax treaty—an agreement that will have major implications for US companies operating south of the border.

Signed on September 18 last year, the treaty is designed to complement the North American Free Trade Agreement (NAFTA). It took effect January 1. Double taxation of those doing business in both countries will shrink. The treaty also aims to lower the overall tax on investment income flowing between the two signatories.

Here are the treaty's key provisions:

Exchange of Information The existing tax information-exchange agreement is incorporated into the treaty. It provides for much broader disclosure between the United States and Mexico than do most income-tax treaties entered into by the United States. The reason for this is to prevent tax evasion by those doing business in both countries.

Permanent Establishments In general, the profits of an enterprise of one country are taxable in the other country only if the company conducts business there through a "permanent establishment." The treaty defines a "permanent establishment" as a fixed place through which people conduct business, and it includes branches. A permanent establishment may be an office, factory, workshop, mine, quarry, or other site. But premises maintained solely for storage, display, or delivery of goods owned by the company are not considered permanent establishments. Similarly, an office used solely for purchasing goods or merchandise or for collecting information is not considered a permanent establishment.

Dividend Taxes Under existing law, dividends from US companies paid to a Mexican citizen or resident are subject to a 30 percent withholding tax. Under the treaty, that maximum tax rate goes down from 30 percent to 5 percent on dividends from a US corporation to a Mexican company, if the Mexican company owns more than 10 percent of the US corporation's voting stock. The withholding rate for other dividends is 15 percent for the first 5 years that the treaty is in force,

after which it goes to 10 percent. The protocol to the treaty also implements a most-favored-nation provision, in which the United States agrees to apply to Mexico the lowest dividend withholding rate that it grants to any other country.

Interest Taxes The treaty pins the maximum withholding tax on interest at 100 percent on bank loans and publicly traded bonds or securities and 15 percent on other types of interest. After five years, the 15 percent rate drops to 10 percent on interest paid by banks or by purchasers of machinery and equipment on credit. At the same time, the 10 percent rate goes down to 4.9 percent on interest paid on bank loans and publicly traded bonds or securities.

Both US and Mexican residents stand to benefit from these provisions. Consider that current Mexican withholding rates on interest run as high as 35 percent, and the current US withholding rate on interest paid to a nonresident is 30 percent. According to a Mexican official, agreeing to the 4.9 percent level represents an extraordinary concession by the Mexican government that will help US banks compete for business in Mexico. The treaty also provides that interest paid to pension funds will be exempt from withholding taxes.

Royalty Rates In the area of royalties, the US-Mexico tax treaty will reduce Mexico's statutory 35 percent and 15 percent withholding rates to 10 percent as soon as the treaty takes effect.

Mexico's Asset Tax According to the protocol accompanying the treaty, Mexico's asset tax generally will not be imposed on a US company unless it has a permanent establishment in Mexico. US companies that do have permanent establishments there cannot claim a credit on their US taxes for payment of Mexico's asset tax, since the tax is not considered an income tax under the treaty. However, in order to avoid offsetting the benefits of the tax treaty with the asset tax, Mexico may grant credits against taxes otherwise payable by US residents in Mexico.

Capital-Gains Exemptions Among other provisions, the treaty exempts companies from paying

By Neil P. Balmert, attorney, Gray Cary Ware & Freidenrich. Reprinted with permission from Global Production & Transportation magazine. Copyright © New Hope Communications, Inc.

capital-gains taxes for certain corporate reorganizations and restructurings that involve businesses filing a consolidated tax return. Under current law, corporate restructurings in Mexico generally are subject to taxation.

Charitable Contributions The treaty grants some reciprocity on the tax-exempt status of charities. A US charity operating in Mexico, for instance, generally will be tax exempt there if the income it earns there would have been tax exempt for a Mexican charity. Moreover, should Mexican law conform to certain US legal standards, a US taxpayer will be able to deduct charitable contributions to Mexican charities. Mexican citizens also will be permitted to deduct their contributions to US charities under the treaty.

Exceptions to the Rules The treaty does extend its benefits to those that do not satisfy all of its residency requirements. But these entities must be concerns that are wholly owned, either directly or indirectly, by residents of any NAFTA party (Canada, Mexico, or the United States).

must be paid during the corporation's tax year. An adjustment of the installments is required in the sixth month of the fiscal year.

Dividends Dividends received by resident and nonresident shareholders from a Mexican corporation are not subject to tax if the earnings were already subject to the corporate income tax and the distributing corporation has sufficient accumulation in its "net tax profit" or "basket" account to cover the dividend. If the accumulated amount is not sufficient, the dividends will be taxable at a rate of 34 percent. The following is an illustration of how to compute the net tax profit for the "basket" account:

Corporate taxable income	1,000
Income tax (34%)	(340)
Profit sharing to employees (estimated)	(150)
Nondeductible expenses	(30)
Net tax profit (not subject to dividend tax rates on distribution)	480

Similar rules apply to remittances abroad by branches of foreign corporations.

DETERMINATION OF TRADING INCOME

General Taxable profits are computed in accordance with generally accepted accounting principles, with the following exceptions:

- Nondeductibility of penalties and unauthorized donations;
- Nondeductibility of increases to reserves for bad debts, obsolescence, contingencies, indemnities and so forth; and
- Monetary gain on debts and monetary loss on credits to recognize the effect of inflation.

Employee profit sharing (*see* Other Significant Taxes) may be partially deductible in computing taxable profits.

Inventories Instead of deducting the normal cost of sales, inventory purchases, labor costs and overhead expenses are deductible each fiscal year.

Depreciation The straight-line method is used to depreciate tangible fixed assets and to amortize intangible assets. Depreciation must be computed using the annual percentages set by law. The depreciation of new assets must be computed on a proportional basis relating to the months in which the assets are used. Depreciation is computed on original cost of fixed assets, with the amount of depreciation indexed for inflation as measured by price indices.

The following are the maximum annual depreciation rates for certain types of assets.

Asset	Rate (%)
Buildings	5
Motor vehicles	25
Office equipment	10
Computers	
Mainframe equipment	25
Peripheral equipment	12
Plant and machinery	10
Environmental machinery and equipment	50

Taxpayers have the option of taking an immediate deduction for a percentage of their total original investment rather than calculating depreciation based on the useful lives of assets. However, this option is not available for certain assets.

Losses Business losses may be carried forward up to five years. Subject to certain limitations, the five-year period may be extended for an additional five years if a loss was also incurred for accounting purposes.

Consolidation As an option, a Mexican holding company can file a consolidated return including the tax results of its Mexican subsidiaries. This option is subject to several rules and limitations.

OTHER SIGNIFICANT TAXES

The table below summarizes other significant taxes.

Nature of Tax	Rate (%)
Value-added tax, on any supply of goods or service, excluding exports, and on imports	
General rate	10
Certain foods and medicines	0
Real estate acquisition tax, local or state tax on market value of real estate transferred	2
State tax on salaries	Various
Residence tax, on each employee's salary, up to 10 times the minimum salary of the region	5
Employee profit sharing, on taxable profits excluding the effect of inflation (loss carryforwards may not be deducted)	10
Social security contributions, on salaries paid up to a specified amount	
Employer (approximately)	18.55
Employee	5.15

MISCELLANEOUS MATTERS

Foreign-Exchange Controls Mexico has no foreign-exchange controls.

Transfer Pricing Mexico has transfer-pricing rules. Acceptable transfer-pricing methods include the resale price method, the cost-plus reasonable margin method, the market value method and the use of a specific appraisal. Transactions between related parties are subject to greater scrutiny. It is not possible to reach transfer-pricing agreements in advance with the tax authorities.

Debt-to-Equity Rules There are no debt-to-equity requirements in Mexico.

TREATY WITHHOLDING TAX RATES

The treaty rates reflect the lower of the treaty rate and the rate under domestic tax law.

	Dividends %	Interest %	Royalties %
Canada	10/15 (a)	15 (f)	15 (b)
France	5 (c)	15 (f)	15 (b)
Sweden	5/10 (d)	15 (f)	10 (e)
United States	5/15 (d)	10/15 (f)	10 (e)
Nontreaty countries	0 (g)	4.9/10/34 (h)	15

(a)   The 10 percent rate applies if the recipient is a corporation owning at least 25 percent of the shares of the payer. However, dividends are not subject to withholding tax under Mexican domestic law if they are paid from earnings that were already subject to corporate income tax (see Taxes on Corporate Income and Gains).

(b)   The effective beneficiary of royalties is subject to withholding tax on the gross payments. Royalties on cultural works (literature, music and artistic works other than films for movies or television) are not subject to withholding tax if they are taxed in the recipient's country.

(c)   The 5 percent rate applies if the recipient is a company resident in France and if at least 50 percent of such recipient is owned by residents of France.

(d)   The 5 percent rate applies if the recipient is a corporation owning at least 10 percent of the shares of the payer. However, dividends are not subject to withholding tax under Mexican domestic law if they are paid from earnings that were already subject to corporate income tax (see Taxes on Corporate Income and Gains).

(e)   The effective beneficiary of royalties is subject to withholding tax on the gross payments.

(f)   Under Mexican domestic law, interest paid to nonresident banks registered with the Mexican tax authorities is subject to withholding tax at a rate of 4.9 percent. The 10 percent rate under the United States treaty applies to interest paid on loans from banks and insurance companies, but, as indicated above, Mexican domestic law provides for a withholding rate of 4.9 percent for interest paid to registered banks.

(g)   See Taxes on Corporate Income and Gains.

(h)   See At a Glance.

Mexico has signed tax treaties with Belgium, Ecuador, Germany, Italy, Spain, and Switzerland, but these treaties are not yet in force.

Personal Taxation

AT A GLANCE—MAXIMUM RATES

Income Tax Rate (%)	35
Capital Gains Tax Rate (%)	35
Net Worth Tax Rate (%)	0
Estate and Gift Tax Rate (%)	0*

However gifts from persons other than direct relatives are included in the recipient's taxable income. See Estate and Gift Taxes.

INCOME TAX—EMPLOYMENT

Who is Liable

Resident individuals are taxed on worldwide income. Nonresidents are taxed only on Mexican-source income. *See* Nonresidents for nonresident information.

Individuals who establish their home in Mexico are considered resident. Status as a resident does not depend on the number of days an individual remains in the country during a calendar year. To be no longer regarded as a resident, the individual must remain in another country for more than 183 days in a calendar year (the days need not be consecutive) and acquire residency for tax purposes in the other country.

Taxable Income

Taxable employment income includes salaries, wages, directors' fees, bonuses, gratuities, allowances, certain fringe benefits, benefits in kind and employee profit-sharing distributions.

The following items are excluded from taxable income:

- Indemnities for accidents and illnesses;
- Retirement benefits and pensions;
- Reimbursement of medical, dental, hospital and funeral expenses;
- Social security benefits paid by public institutions;
- Savings funds;
- Living or travel expenses;
- Payments from insurance companies; and
- Social welfare payments.

Certain exemptions are subject to limitations and specific requirements.

INCOME TAX RATES

The income tax rates in the following table are in force from January 1, 1994, but are adjusted for inflation quarterly.

Taxable Income		Tax on Lower	Rate on
Exceeding	Not Exceeding	Amount	Excess
NP*	NP*	NP*	%
0	1,389.39	0	3
1,389.39	11,791.86	41.70	10
11,791.86	20,722.95	1,081.96	17
20,722.95	24,089.67	2,600.25	25
24,089.67	28,841.70	3,441.93	32
28,841.70	58,169.58	4,962.57	33
58,169.58	91,683.33	14,640.75	34
91,683.33	—	26,035.47	35

* Effective January 1, 1993, Mexico has changed its unit of currency from the Peso (Mex$) to the New Peso (NP). One New Peso equals 1,000 Pesos.

A fixed tax credit has replaced the credit equivalent to 10 percent of the legal annual minimum wage. The annual fixed credit amount varies based on the amount of the taxpayer's total income. The table on the next page presents the fixed credit amounts for 1994.

In 1994, an additional credit, or tax subsidy, of up to NP12,311.25 is available. The amount of the subsidy is determined under a sliding scale, which is affected by the nontaxable fringe benefits granted by the employer.

Note: This section is courtesy of and © Ernst & Young from their Worldwide Personal Tax Guide, 1994 Edition. This material should not be regarded as offering a complete explanation of the taxation matters referred to. Ernst & Young is a leading international professional services firm with offices in 100 countries, including Mexico. Refer to the "Important Addresses" chapter for addresses and telephone numbers of the Ernst & Young offices in Mexico.

| Total Income | | Amount of |
Exceeding NP	Not Exceeding NP	Fixed Credit NP
0	7,808.64	879.48
7,808.64	10,411.44	826.44
10,411.44	13,014.36	702.72
13,014.36	15,617.16	645.48
15,617.16	18,220.08	593.40
18,220.08	20,822.88	536.16
20,822.88	—	620.56

Married persons are taxed separately, not jointly, on all types of income.

Deductible Expenses

No deductions from employment income are permitted.

Personal Allowances and Deductions

Resident individuals are granted the following personal deductions:

- Medical, dental, and hospitalization services for a taxpayer and his or her dependents;
- Payments for the school bus transportation of dependent children if required by local law;
- Funeral expenses, limited to annual minimum salary; and
- Certain gifts to public works or utilities, charitable or welfare institutions, and promoters of arts or culture.

INCOME TAX—SELF-EMPLOYMENT/ BUSINESS INCOME

Who Is Liable

An individual who earns income as a self-employed person from business activities or professional services is liable for tax. This includes individuals deriving income from real estate rental activities.

Taxable Income

Taxable income is the net amount of gross revenue less normal expenses such as salaries, fees, rent, depreciation, interest and other general expenses. Instead of deducting actual expenses, individuals which rental income may elect to deduct as rental expenses an amount equal to 50 percent of rental income for residential property or 35 percent of other rental income.

Directors' Fees

Directors' fees received by Mexican residents from Mexican or foreign companies are subject to the income tax rates for employment income described in Income Tax—Employment—Income Tax Rates.

INVESTMENT INCOME

Dividends are not included in taxable income, but the distributing company is subject to a 34 percent final withholding tax to the extent it has not paid tax on the underlying income.

Interest on time deposits with Mexican banks and on publicly issued debentures is subject to a final 20 percent withholding tax on the first 10 percentage points of interest, but any excess interest is tax-exempt. Gains on the sale of those debentures are also subject to this tax. Other interest income is aggregated with other income and taxed at the rates set forth in Income Tax—Employment—Income Tax Rates.

For the taxation of real estate rental income, see Income Tax—Self-Employment/Business Income.

RELIEF FOR LOSSES

Losses incurred in a business activity may be carried forward for five years against future business earnings. Losses from self-employment activities of professional persons and insurance agents and brokers may not be carried forward.

CAPITAL GAINS AND LOSSES

In general, gains on the sale of shares and real estate are treated as capital gains. Gain on shares sold through the Mexican stock exchange, however, is tax exempt, and the gain on the sale of a personal residence is exempt if the seller used the residence as his or her personal residence for the preceding two years. Capital gains are not subject to a separate tax, but are included in income and taxed at the rates provided in Income Tax—Employment—Income Tax Rates. The gain is calculated by adjusting cost for inflation.

Capital gains on shares and real estate are taxed using an income-averaging concept. The taxable gain is calculated separately for each asset and then divided by the number of years the asset was held, up to a maximum of 20 years. The resulting amount is added to other taxable income. After the graduated marginal tax rates are applied to this total, the average rate is then applied to the balance of the capital gain. Income averaging does not apply to capital gains on real property used in a trade or business. These gains are added to business income.

Although computed in the same way, capital losses are treated differently. The tax benefit for the year in which a total loss is incurred is limited to the amount of tax on the total loss, divided by the number of years the underlying asset was held, up to a maximum of 10 years. That amount is deductible from the individual's gain on the sale of other assets or from the individual's other income. The remaining loss may be carried forward for three years, but only against capital gains on the sale of shares or real estate.

NET WORTH TAX

No tax is levied on an individual's net worth. However, a 2 percent minimum tax is imposed on business assets and real estate rented for business activities. This tax may be reduced or eliminated by crediting the income tax paid against the minimum tax.

ESTATE AND GIFT TAXES

No estate or inheritance tax is levied. Gifts from persons other than direct line (ascendant or descendant) family members are included in the recipient's taxable income.

Residents are subject to gift tax on assets received worldwide. Nonresidents are subject to gift tax on real estate located in Mexico and shares issued by Mexican companies.

PAYROLL TAXES

Social Security

The Social Security System provides

- Medical assistance in cases of illness, maternity care and accidents;
- Indemnities in case of temporary disability; and
- Pensions for disability, old age and death.
- Medical-assistance benefits extend to the members of an employee's family (that is, spouse, parents and children.)

For 1994, the employee's contribution is 5.15 percent, which is withheld by the employer, and the employer's contribution is approximately 16 percent. The contribution base is salaries, up to a specified amount.

Housing Fund

For 1994, an employer must contribute 5 percent of salaries (limited to 10 times the minimum wage) to the Housing Fund, which provides funds for the construction of housing for workers.

Mandatory Pension Plan Contribution

Effective May 1, 1992, employers must contribute 2 percent of an employee's compensation (limited to 25 times the minimum wage) to a pension trust, which is managed by a bank in the employee's name.

ADMINISTRATION

For individuals, the fiscal year is the calendar year. Tax returns must be filed no later than April 30 of the following year.

Personal income taxes of employed individuals and nonresidents are frequently withheld. An individual taxpayer has the option of paying the remaining tax due at the time the annual return is filed or in installments over a six-month period with interest.

Self-employed individuals must make estimated prepayments of tax in April, July, October, and January.

Employees of foreign companies who work in Mexico must make monthly estimated payments if their company does not have a permanent establishment in Mexico.

NONRESIDENTS

An individual who has established his or her home in Mexico is considered a resident of Mexico. Resident status is lost when the individual stays more than 183 days (during a calendar year) in another country and acquires residence for tax purposes in that country. To substantiate the establishment of residency in another country, individuals must provide Mexican authorities with proof of residency issued by the appropriate authorities in the other country.

Nonresident individuals pay Mexican income tax only on income from sources located in Mexico. For salaries paid by resident employers or by employers with a permanent establishment in Mexico, the following rates of withholding tax apply in 1994.

| Taxable Income | | Tax on Lower | Rate on |
| Exceeding | Not Exceeding | Amount | Excess |
NP	NP	NP	%
0	36,000	0	0
36,000	290,000	0	15
290,000	—	38,100	30

Salary income and income for personal services paid by a nonresident individual or company are exempt from the above withholding tax if the services are not related to the nonresident payer's permanent establishment in Mexico or the nonresident payer does not have a permanent establishment, and if the services are provided during fewer than 183 days in a 12-month period. If services are provided during more than 183 days, the above withholding rates apply.

Professional fees paid by a Mexican resident for services rendered in Mexico are subject to withholding tax at the rates described in the above table. If the services are rendered only partially in Mexico, income tax is payable on the portion of the income related to the services in Mexico.

A 34 percent tax is levied on dividends on which underlying corporate profits have not been taxed. Royalties for use of tradenames, trademarks, patents or certificates of invention are subject to a 35 percent withholding tax. Taxpayers with a capital gain from the disposal of shares or real estate may elect to pay a 20 percent tax on the gross amount or tax on the net amount at 30 percent for shares and 35 percent for real property. For 1994–1995, interest from Mexican banks is subject to 10 percent withholding tax. Income from the rental of real property is subject to a 21 percent withholding tax. Fees for technical assistance and expertise are subject to a 15 percent withholding tax.

DOUBLE TAX RELIEF/ DOUBLE TAX TREATIES

An individual with foreign-source income may take a credit for the foreign tax paid to the source country to the extent the foreign tax paid does not exceed the individual's Mexican tax liability on that income.

Mexico has concluded tax treaties with Canada, France, Sweden, and the United States to avoid double taxation and prevent tax evasion. In addition, Mexico has signed tax treaties with Belgium, Ecuador, Germany, Italy, and Spain, which await ratification.

Mexico is currently negotiating treaties with Korea, the Netherlands, Norway, Romania, Switzerland, and the United Kingdom.

Transportation

Transportation of goods into, out of, and within Mexico has traditionally been a major headache. A lack of facilities, outmoded equipment, customs delays, labor problems, and a poorly integrated infrastructure, compounded by the topography, climatic contrasts, and sheer distances involved, are just a few of the problems encountered by businesspeople trying to move goods around in Mexico. While many of these problems are a long way from being solved, there has been more forthright recognition of the existence and importance of such problems in recent years. And along with this seldom-seen willingness to acknowledge deficiencies, Mexico is also exhibiting a willingness to actually do something to strengthen its national transportation system. There is currently a genuine commitment to improve the situation, to come up with creative solutions to long-standing inefficiencies, and to construct new facilities.

Aside from the huge investment needed to make these changes the major obstacle is that the need is growing so rapidly. It is virtually impossible to fix everything at once, and the introduction of new, improved systems has been unable to keep pace with surging demand. The integration of existing and new services into a coherent, functioning system is also of major importance. For example, attempts have been made in the past few years to upgrade major Mexican port facilities, but as long as the rail and road networks linking the ports to the rest of the country remain below par, improved port facilities in and of themselves will make little difference. Although improvement is welcome, it will serve largely to shift the location of the bottleneck. Because Mexico's major economic centers—Mexico City, Monterrey, and Guadalajara—are all located inland, overland transport networks are particularly important. Many Asian shippers have long landed goods at the port of Long Beach in California and trans-shipped them overland from there to Mexico. Shippers maintain that despite the added distances and formalities, travel times are actually shorter (and customs clearance easier) for those using this route

than they are for those who go directly through Mexican Pacific Coast ports.

President Salinas' primary strategy for dealing with the simultaneous and staggering needs of the overland, air, and marine transportation infrastructure and the associated managerial systems has been to privatize many of the operations. Toll highways built with private funds are under construction across the country. The financial backers receive toll concessions for a specified period of time, after which the roads revert to the Mexican government. Most of the country's major ports are in the process of being privatized, and a number of airport operations are also going to private bidders. Air terminal improvements include construction and operation of passenger terminals, and parking, runway, and fueling facilities.

Customs delays for imports into Mexico have traditionally run from several days to as long as several weeks. A few new strategies are being used to speed up clearance of shipments. These range from a general cleanup of the notoriously corrupt Mexican customs service to turning over the operation of customs warehouses to private companies and setting up a new on-line system using bar codes to expedite the tracking and clearance of cargo. Only the Mexico City airport and the Nuevo Laredo customs offices had installed the system at press time. However, eventually all Mexican Customs offices are expected to have it. New Mexican Customs forms, in use since January, 1994, have already improved clearance time at the border. When everything is in order and documents have been pre-filed, trucks can get out of the import lot in as little as 15 minutes. Perhaps the most significant and far-reaching reform came in 1990, when President Salinas replaced 90 percent of all customs employees, transferring the responsibilities for operations to the treasury department. While the problem of bribery among low-paid customs officials may not have been eliminated entirely, the current situation represents a vast improvement. If anything, one is now likely to run into a customs official who causes delays by

CAN MEXICO'S ROADS CARRY THE LOAD?*

Mexico's own Communications and Transport Secretariat (SCT) admits it. Most of the country's 29,000 miles of federal highway were not built to withstand today's heavy trucking and traffic loads.

In fact, SCT reports, only 15 percent of those highways are in excellent condition; 57 percent are in average shape; and 28 percent are in poor condition. The agency estimates that annual maintenance of the federal highway network runs in the neighborhood of US$700 million. Mexico's inability to keep up with that maintenance, not to mention new construction, sends some manufacturers and truckers scrambling to protect products from transport damage.

Work-in-Progress

To take the load off the federal system, Mexican officials are planning a 7,240-mile network of superhighways that will crisscross the nation and connect most of Mexico's major ports with its principal commercial and industrial centers. Perhaps the most novel and challenging aspect of this program for Mexico is that the plan will be fully executed by concessions to the private sector.

Construction of the highway network is progressing under a BOT, or build-operate-transfer arrangement. Private contractors are building and operating toll roads for up to 20 years, after which the roads are slated to be transferred to the Mexican government.

So far, concessions for about a third of the roads have been awarded, and construction of approximately 1,000 miles has been completed, albeit in fragmented segments throughout the country. One of the highways near completion is the Mexico-Acapulco route, and the León-Lagos-Aguascalientes stretch is complete.

On the Drawing Board

Conceived in 1989, the network, when finished by the end of the decade (so planners hope), is supposed to look like this:

Four of the 10 projected turnpikes will stretch north from Mexico City toward principal border cities: Nogales in the northwest; Ciudad Juárez in north-central Mexico; and Nuevo Laredo and Matamoros in the northeast.

Two routes will reach south from Mexico City—one southwest to Ciudad Hidalgo and the other southeast to the Yucatán Peninsula. And four routes will extend from the Gulf Coast ports to the Pacific: Matamoros-Mazatlán, Tampico-Manzanillo, Veracruz-Acapulco, and Coatzacoalcos-Salina Cruz.

Where Are the Drivers?

Total concessions for roughly half of the road network are expected to be granted next year, by the end of the Salinas presidential term. But bidding on new concessions has stalled. Government officials are delaying the process while they try to figure out how to increase use of those toll roads already built while, at the same time, making concession terms easier to finance and more attractive to bidders.

Rising costs and lower-than-expected traffic volume on the new highways have forced the government to extend the life of some concessions and delay road completion, especially for highways that rely heavily on truck traffic.

Tolls are too high, say drivers, limiting highway use to "a privileged few." The estimated toll for a vehicle on the Mexico City-Guadalajara turnpike, for example, is more than NP340, compared to NP500 for an airplane ticket from Mexico City to Guadalajara. Indeed, there are times when flying that route is cheaper than driving it.

Concessionaires such as Emilio Gutiérrez Rodríguez, of the company AEC, admit that toll fees are costly. But, he counters, "you have to pay the price for a good turnpike" that reduces driving distances, limits vehicle wear and tear, and provides security.

Toll Discounts

To get truckers to use the new highways, government officials and contractors agreed to a three-month trial period at a 50 percent discount. The intent is for drivers to experience firsthand how savings in time and vehicle wear and tear offset turnpike fees. A case-in-point is the new León-Lagos-Aguascalientes turnpike, which is comparable in quality to the US interstate highway system and offers extras, such as emergency phones placed every mile or so.

"We are developing the business mentality of an

*By Baron F. Levin. Reprinted with permission from Global Production & Transportation magazine. Copyright © 1993 New Hope Communications, Inc.

operator who has to sell his services, instead of the mentality of a builder who wants to build and then sell off the concession," says Francisco Zurita of ICA, Mexico's largest construction company and winner of a large portion of the concessions.

Nonetheless, explains one cargo company executive, there are many small-scale truckers who drive and own their own vehicles, and "they think more about the money in their pockets than about how long the truck will last."

Victor Bravo, manager of financial analysis at ICA, calls the 1,000 highway miles built so far "a learning process" for both the public and private sectors. The projects suffered many change orders, he says, but initial specifications are now "more than 80 percent on target," resulting in fewer cost overruns and more realistic timetables.

insisting on a strict interpretation of the law, especially if the required paperwork is not in order. On the other hand, those who are in compliance are likely to be sped through.

The primary government authority for transportation issues is:

Secretaría de Comunicationes y Transportes
(Secretariat of Communications and Transport)
Avda. Universidad y Xola
Col. Navarte
03028 México, DF, México
Tel: [52] (5) 519-7456, 519-1319, 530-9203, 530-1074
Fax: [52] (5) 519-9748, 530-1074 Tlx: 017600

OVERLAND TRANSPORT

A staggering 86 percent of total trade comes and goes overland between Mexico and the US. Of that amount, 80 percent (69 percent of total trade) moves by truck, with the remaining 20 percent (17 percent of total trade) moving by rail. Despite the fact that new rail lines are either under construction or at least in the planning stages, trucking is expected to maintain its dominance in surface transportation well into the future. Under NAFTA, Mexican and US truckers will eventually be able to carry loads across the border (currently, all goods must transfer to domestic carriers at the border). However, the difference in rail gauges between the US and Mexico is expected to remain, preventing rail links from becoming a more important factor in cross-border transport.

Road Construction and Trucking

President Salinas' government has made the construction of new roads, or more specifically, of privately funded toll roads (*cuotas*), a major priority during his administration. At the time of the 1988 elections, there were approximately 2,800 km (1740 miles) of toll roads in Mexico. Between 1989 and 1991, the Salinas administration funneled an estimated US$10 billion into road development and improvements, of which three-quarters came from private concessions. The Secretariat of Communications and Transport estimates that 6,000 km (3725 miles) of new highway construction will have been completed by the year 2000, with an additional 6,000 km in the planning stage.

By all accounts, the new highways—like the newly opened *Autopista del Sol*, which stretches from Cuernevaca to Acapulco—are high-quality modern roads with four lanes, improved road shoulders, fences, and emergency telephones. However, they come with a higher-than-estimated price tag for builders, drivers, and the Mexican government. The *Autopista del Sol* cost US$2.1 billion to build, more than twice the original projections. The government is expected to extend the private concession period to compensate for the additional construction costs and for the fact that toll collections are still far below projections. One might think Mexican drivers would be eager to hop onto the new highways, but tolls run as high as US$75 one-way on the 163-mile stretch between Cuernevaca and Acapulco, making it reportedly the most expensive toll road in the world. Attempts are underway to lure truckers onto the toll roads (*see* "Can Mexico's Roads Carry the Load?" in this chapter), but so far most have kept to the crowded and potholed—but free—public road. In some areas, there are no free alternate routes, forcing drivers to take the expensive roads or go far out of their way.

The grand plan for the country's highway network is to have six routes radiating out of Mexico City. Three main routes are scheduled to link the capital with the north, ultimately reaching the US border centers of Nogales, Ciudad Juárez, and Matamoros, as well as with areas to the south. Four other arterial routes are to connect major ports on the Gulf of Mexico with those on the Pacific coast, serving Matamoros and Mazatlán, Tampico and Manzanillo, Veracruz and Acapulco, and Coatzacoalcos and Salina Cruz.

With few exceptions, Mexico's road system is in serious need of attention, and a large investment of federal funds must go to the less glamorous job of reconstructing and maintaining existing highways. At least 30,000 km (18,630 miles) of federal and state roads are in need of immediate repair—a substantial portion of the road network was damaged by heavy rains in 1993—and two-thirds of the country's

NAFTA EXPANDS TRUCKING ACCESS TO MEXICO*

US trucking companies started gearing up to handle increased volumes of Mexican business even before the recent ratification of the North American Free Trade Agreement (NAFTA). Partnerships and joint ventures with Mexican trucking companies, as well as with Mexican subsidiaries of US companies, have been springing up with one goal in mind: to provide US shippers with the same high-quality, seamless service south of the border that they have come to expect at home.

Their efforts are paying off in double-digit volume growth. In 1992, about 1.7 million truckloads of cargo crossed the Mexican border. By 2000, that's expected to increase to between six million and seven million truckloads a year.

With their business infrastructure in place, truckers say they are ready to capitalize on the new opportunities NAFTA will provide.

"What we had set up in Mexico worked quite well without NAFTA and will work even better with NAFTA," says John Hyer, manager of corporate communications for Roadway Express. Roadway has served Mexico since 1991 through a subsidiary, Roadway Bodegas y Consolidación. This past summer, it entered a joint venture with Transportes de Nuevo Laredo to form TNL Roadway, which will serve less-than-truckload (LTL) customers throughout North America.

NAFTA Provisions

"As a result of NAFTA, we will have expanded access to Mexico," says Linda Darr, vice president of international affairs at the American Trucking Association.

For the most part, NAFTA itself won't create dramatic changes for the trucking industry; the resulting trade volume will, insiders say.

"Business into Mexico has been strong the last four or five years," says Terry Matthews, vice president, international at J.B. Hunt. "This will ensure it will remain strong over the next five to 10 years."

Of the 20 transportation provisions NAFTA contains, trucking companies do consider a few significant.

First, three years after implementation of NAFTA, truckers will be allowed to cross the borders into contiguous states in their rigs. After six years, US trucks will be allowed to haul international freight through-

out Mexico, and Mexican trucks will be able to do the same throughout the US. Now, cargo can cross the border in a trailer, but must be picked up by a Mexican company's rig on the other side, a process known in the industry as "interlining."

Whether or not US operators take advantage of that provision depends to some extent on how Mexico improves its road infrastructure, however.

New Ownership Rules, Better Roads to Boost LTL Service

For full-truckload carriers, a provision allowing 53-foot trailers into Mexico will reduce extra handling now required at the border. A few months after NAFTA implementation, 53-footers will be allowed up to 26 km from the border; after 15 months, they'll be allowed on designated roads throughout the country.

Although 53-footers are standard on US highways, they have been outlawed on Mexican roads. That means that a 53-foot US truck arriving at the border with a full load has to devan the cargo and split it into a 48-foot trailer and a smaller shipment, a lengthy and damage-prone procedure.

Running a partially empty trailer whose cargo would fit into a 48-footer at the border is one alternative, but it costs shippers money in wasted space on the US side.

While the new provision will help, the NAFTA implementation schedule means it's going to be a slow process for 53-footers to gain access to all of Mexico, cautions Len Bennett, an adviser to the US and Mexican governments on NAFTA and CEO at Celadon, a US carrier that pioneered over-the-road service with through-trailer movements to Mexico.

Less-than-truckload carriers have been much more interested in the issue of ownership resolved by NAFTA. Under NAFTA, after three years, US truckers can own a 49 percent interest in Mexican trucking companies engaged in international business, a 51 percent interest after seven years, and a 100 percent interest after 10 years.

The issue is especially interesting to less-than-truckload carriers because of the virtual lack of such services in Mexico. The biggest inhibiting factor to LTL service in Mexico is a lack of road networks to support the operations, says Fritz Kromhout, director of marketing and

---

By Valerie Drogus. Reprinted with permission from Global Production & Transportation magazine. Copyright © 1994 New Hope Communications, Inc.

strategic planning for CF Motor Freight.

Most US truckers hope the increased business NAFTA brings will encourage the Mexican government to improve road conditions. Once that happens and the ownership provisions kick in, there will be a greater US and Canadian presence in Mexico, as well as a greater Mexican presence north of the border, predicts David Valdez, general manager of the Dallas terminal of Yellow Freight.

"You'll see some changes in ownership," he says.

NAFTA's Non-Treaty Effects

Truckers are counting as much on non-treaty effects of NAFTA to open Mexican business as on provisions of the treaty itself. Among them should be better customs service, Roadway's Hyer says.

"As NAFTA allows us to streamline, we will work with Mexican Customs much like we did in Canada (after the free-trade pact)," he says. For shippers, that means trucking companies will be able to offer more options, such as pre-clearance of customs, to make border crossings more efficient.

"NAFTA will create incentives to improve the border-crossing points," says CF Motor Freight's Kromhout, noting that crossing points have become bottlenecks. Increased volumes will motivate both governments to open additional gateways and make crossing physically easier, he says.

Highway Upgrade Expected

Better roads in Mexico are another hoped-for result of the NAFTA negotiations.

"Infrastructure will change," Celadon's Bennett predicts. The Mexican government already has taken steps in that direction by changing the way it finances new road construction, he adds. Longer-term paybacks on toll roads will reduce tolls and, consequently, increase usage of the new roads.

Many trucking companies are waiting for better roads before increasing service in Mexico, especially south of Mexico City and into Central America.

"We do have some requests for (service to Central America)," Kromhout says. "There is a highway, but, at this point, it's well maintained in some places but not in others." CF Motor Freight currently serves Central America with an NVOCC (non-vessel-operating common carrier) operation out of Miami.

Through to Central America

Demands for over-the-road service to Central America

may increase more rapidly as Mexican President Salinas de Gortari pursues negotiations on free-trade pacts similar to NAFTA with Central American nations.

"Mexico will become the springboard to a massive market," predicts Bennett, noting that Salinas has already negotiated free-trade pacts with three South American countries.

To get in on the ground floor, Celadon has been moving cargo overland from the US to Guatemala and Honduras for some time. If the impetus for hemispheric trade blocs continues, he foresees the day goods will move from Yucatán to Chile by truck.

With or without more trade pacts, there already are good reasons for US shippers to move goods overland to Central America, says Contract Freighters Inc.'s Peter Montaño.

Rail freight is nearly nonexistent, due to gauge differences between Mexican and US railways; ocean freight off the US West Coast is likewise difficult. Most US West Coast freight is trucked or flown to Miami before it goes by ship or plane to Central America, involving long transit times and several changes of hands before reaching its destination.

That's why CFI's over-the-road service to Central America, begun in February 1993, has met with success, says Gary Nichols, director of international development. Despite uncertain road conditions, CFI offers service from the West Coast to any point in Central America with a maximum eight-day transit time.

To prevent delays at the border, cargo moves in bond through Mexico, and then it is picked up at Puerto Hidalgo by the Guatemalan carrier Transfreyos, a CFI partner that provides the physical operation through Central America. The service is on a single bill of lading with CFI.

It's a turnaround service that so far has attracted mostly Fortune 500 textile manufacturers doing 807 business in Central America, Nichols says. (The 807 program provides offshore manufacturers with duty breaks on US content assembled abroad.) Textiles from the Far East are unloaded at the Port of Los Angeles, trucked to clothing factories in Central America, and brought back as manufactured goods to the US.

In the past year, 200 Korean textile subplants have moved from Asia to Central America, Nichols notes.

"We're totally committed to the (over-the-road) business. It's a growing business," he says.

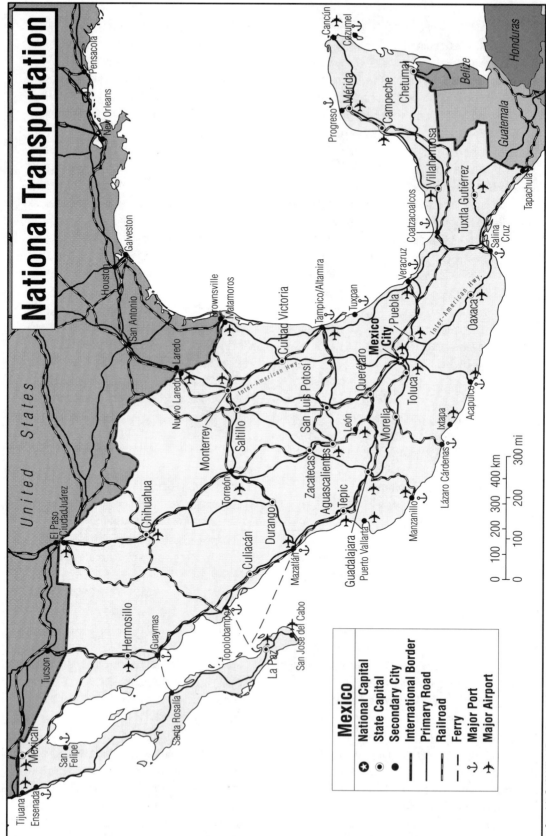

National Transportation

Mexico

- ⊛ National Capital
- ⊙ State Capital
- ● Secondary City
- ▬▬ International Border
- ─── Primary Road
- ─┼─ Railroad
- ─╎─ Ferry
- ⚓ Major Port
- ✈ Major Airport

roads remain unpaved. The following items were included in the 1993 federal budget for the road subsector:

- Reconstruction of 82 bridges and 2,077 km (1,290 miles) of federal roads;
- Improvement of 7,569 km (4,700 miles) of feeder roads;
- Maintenance of 46,590 km (28,937 miles) of federal and rural roads;
- Construction of 1200 km (745 miles) of new rural roads;
- Reconstruction of 750 km (466 miles) of rural roads and 450 km (280 miles) of secondary roads; and
- Improvement of 1,995 km (1,240 miles) of secondary roads and 360 km (224 miles) of rural roads.

Although more shipments will be arriving and departing via sea, rail, and air in coming years, the increasing pace of trade and the flexibility of over-the-road haulage means that trucking will certainly maintain its dominance in commercial transport. The country's truck fleet increased by 85 percent between 1989 and 1992, in large part due to the government's deregulation of the industry. Up until 1989, trucking companies had been licensed to operate only on certain routes or to carry only certain types of cargo, which led to a high degree of fragmentation and inefficiency within the industry. Companies may now carry any material other than dangerous goods or explosives on any route within the country. Mexico's trucking capacity has doubled since deregulation, and costs have fallen dramatically due to intensified competition. One remaining restriction is that companies must use a Mexican-registered vehicle with a Mexican driver. US trucking firms and Mexican companies are entering into partnerships in increasing numbers to offer door-to-door tracking and billing, although the cargo itself must be shifted from one vehicle to another at the border. Eventually, US trucks will be permitted on designated roads throughout Mexico—and Mexican trucks will be allowed throughout the US—although there are some logistical and safety concerns which remain to be worked out. (*See* NAFTA Expands Trucking Access to Mexico in this chapter.)

Railroads

A comparatively small amount of international cargo moves by rail, although with improvements in rail infrastructure, scheduling, and service, it is hoped that the *Ferrocarriles Nacionales de México* (National Railways of Mexico, or FNM) will soon be able to support intermodal transport. Although Mexico's outdated rail system has been simply dismissed by some, it should be remembered that the

FNM still carries more than 50 million metric tons of cargo a year, including approximately 15 percent of all US-Mexican trade. Some rail links in the planning stages include: a proposed line between Matamoros and the inland center of Ciudad Victoria; a system to connect Baja California's four major cities to each other and to the port of Ensenada; and a link between the Pacific port of Manzanillo and the Gulf Coast port of Altamira, with through connections to Laredo, Texas. The main office of the FNM is:

Ferrocarriles Nacional de México (FNM)
(National Railroads of Mexico)
Avda. Jesus García Corona 140
Piso 4, ALA B
06358 México, DF
Tel: [52] (5) 547-6583

Following the example of many trucking firms, FNM has reached agreements with a number of US railroads to develop through service. Southern Pacific (SP) has been particularly aggressive in pursuing the Mexican market. An unusual accord involving SP's Mexico Group, FNM, Sun Country Transportation, the US Department of Agriculture, and the Mexican *Secretaría de Agricultura y Recursos Hidráulicos* allows SP to haul refrigerated rail cars from locations within the US to Eagle Pass, Texas, where the cars are switched directly to Mexican passenger trains bound for Monterrey, where cargo inspection and customs clearance takes place. By avoiding the queue for regular customs clearance and inspection at the border, perishable goods can make it to market much more quickly. In 1993, SP established an office in Laredo to coordinate door-to-door delivery service through contracts with truckers and other carriers in the US and Mexico. Freight might travel by rail within the US, be taken to the border itself by a US trucker under contract to SP, and then travel into the interior of Mexico by a Mexican trucking firm also under contract to SP.

High-speed doublestack trains are making inroads, both for domestic and cross-border shipments. One of these trains, pre-cleared for customs, can cut rail travel time between Monterrey and Houston in half, making it competitive with trucks. A number of doublestack routes from Los Angeles, Chicago, and other major US cities to Mexico City are now in place, and doublestack service between Mexican ports and Guadalajara and Mexico City has gained in popularity. Southern Pacific now runs 11 doublestack trains a week into Mexico, moving cargo through six gateways: Calexico, Nogales, El Paso, Eagle Pass, Laredo, and Brownsville. Other US rail companies offering freight service to Mexico include the Texas Mexican Railway Company; Union Pacific Railroad; and the Atchison, Topeka, and Santa Fe Railway Company.

Examples of intermodal transport involving rail links include:

- The Port of Corpus Christi, Texas served by Union Pacific, Southern Pacific, and the Texas-Mexican Railway to link the port directly to Laredo, Texas.
- A rail-water service called "Gato Marino" (Nautical Cat) is scheduled to begin operations in 1994, linking US and Mexican Gulf Coast ports; candidate destinations include Mobile and New Orleans in the US and Veracruz and Altamira in Mexico.
- The Burlington Northern Railroad has joined with a construction and marine services company to launch a joint rail-barge service. Loaded rail cars in Galveston, Texas are rolled directly onto barges, which are then floated across the Gulf of Mexico to Coatzacoalcos and unloaded directly onto Mexican rail lines. Service to Altamira and Veracruz is expected to be inaugurated in the future.
- Plans call for developing the Salina Cruz-Coatzacoalcos rail line across the Isthmus of Tehuantepec as an alternative to the Panama Canal for containerized transshipments between Asia and Europe.

Overland Border Crossings

Three-quarters of the trade between the US and Mexico passes overland across the Texas border, with one-third of that (25 percent of total trade) crossing at Laredo-Nuevo Laredo. At the beginning of 1994, about 2,000 trucks per day were crossing and heading south at Laredo, Texas, up from 1,800 per day in early 1993. By the turn of the century, the total number of trucks crossing into Mexico from the US is expected to more than double.

El Paso–Ciudad Juárez and Brownsville–Matamoros are the other major Texas crossings, but there are currently a total of 27 international crossings linking the state with Mexico, including five railroad crossings and a hand-drawn ferry. Half of these are located along the Rio Grande between Laredo and Brownsville, a stretch of 200 miles. Population in this zone has doubled during the last 10 years, growing from 1.5 million to nearly three million. Currently, 16 new international crossings are actively under consideration along the entire 2,000 mile US-Mexico border. Of these, 11 are located along the Texas-Mexico border, and eight—half of all proposed new crossings—are located in the 200 miles between Laredo and Brownsville.

By definition, an international bridge serves as a port of entry, linking two countries and employing personnel from the federal agencies of the respective countries at each end. Texas' interest in becoming the site of such crossings is due in part to the congestion anticipated in coming years at existing crossings, and in part to the economic advantages to be gained. Aside from the financial impact of the millions of people passing through these cities and the new service industries which inevitably will spring up, there is a direct payoff from the money collected at the bridges, a portion of which goes directly to local entities. In 1993 the Laredo Bridge System collected over US$200 million, while Reynosa, Mexico collected more than US$150 million.

The Mexican border areas are administered by:

Dirección General de Asuntos Fronterizos
(Directorate General of Border Affairs)
Periférico Sur 3025, Piso 7
Col. Héroes de Padierna
Deleg. Magdalena Contreras
México, DF
Tel: [52] (5) 683-4394, 683-7055 x2706

PORTS

Historically, Mexican ports have not been up to international standards. Specialized equipment for containers has not been available, nor has equipment for handling specialized bulk cargo; storage facilities have been inadequate; customs clearance has been extremely slow; and the transit connections to rail and major roads have been poor. The overregulation of the ports has also contributed to high costs and a lack of competition. While the actual shipping time between US and Mexican Gulf ports is quite short—usually only two to three days—the delays and high costs often encountered at Mexican ports mean that a great deal of potential oceangoing traffic goes overland instead. Asian freight is often shipped to California ports and trucked overland into Mexico. By the same token, Mexican exporters often find it less expensive and more efficient to move merchandise overland to US ports for transshipment to non-US international destinations.

For many years, Mexico concentrated its infrastructure development inward on roads, neglecting its ports. However, Mexican port traffic has been growing in recent years and now involves more than 30 million tons of cargo a year, three-quarters of which represents international traffic. The anticipated increase in trade associated with the implementation of NAFTA could cause the level of oceangoing traffic to jump sharply and rapidly.

Eager to include seaports in its overhaul of the Mexican transport system, the Salinas government targeted the major ports of Veracruz, Tampico-Altamira, Manzanillo, and Lázaro Cárdenas for US$2 billion in major renovations during the late 1980s and enacted the sweeping Port Law in 1993. Under the

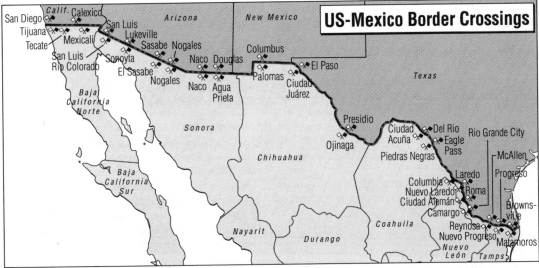

US-Mexico Border Crossings

new law, the country's 22 principal ports are now in the process of being privatized, with control scheduled to pass from the federal government to distinct local, public-private partnership port authorities. Tenders—in which foreigners are eligible to bid—have been issued to operate these new port authorities, and the winners will be permitted to collect rent from carriers and terminal operators. Suppliers will apply directly to the port authority at a specific location for operating permits to provide services. It is hoped that this transfer of operating authority will be complete by the end of 1995, providing more than US$400 million in investment funds and resulting in more efficient operations. Under the privatization plan, the government has also been granting private concessions (usually of 20 years' duration) for the construction and operation of new, modern terminals.

The improvements anticipated from the program can already be seen at the port of Veracruz, where restructuring began in 1991. Bidding on a range of port services was opened to several competing private companies; a corrupt stevedore union was replaced by three private unions; and, as elsewhere in Mexico, a new set of customs officials has been in place since 1990. Estimates of increased productivity run as high as 80 percent. Cargo that previously sat on the docks for weeks now moves through in two to three days. The time needed to unload a 600-container ship, that might have been 40 hours several years ago, has been cut nearly in half.

In order to allow Mexican ports to be outfitted for intermodal transport, particular emphasis has been placed on updating container facilities. In 1992, several major ports received 700-ton gantry cranes and new container terminals, greatly increasing the number of containers that can be handled. While container traffic at Mexican ports lags far behind that

found at Asian and European ports, it has been increasing by 12 percent or more annually in recent years. Veracruz, Altamira, Manzanillo, Tampico, Tuxpan, Salina Cruz, and Lázaro Cárdenas are the main container ports, although a few others also handle container traffic in small quantities. Construction of specialized terminals for bulk freight such as grains, minerals, and fluids is also receiving special emphasis in the port development plan.

US ports in particular are eager to promote port-to-port shipping in order to capture some of the traffic that has long been handled by overland carriers. Coastal shipping between US and Mexican Gulf ports can be faster and cheaper than land routes now that some of the logistical nightmares of the past have been ironed out at the ports. As the pace of trade picks up, congestion, handling costs, and inland freight charges for overland transportation are all expected to increase. The development of dedicated steamship services with roll-on, roll-off truck trailer capacity seems likely in the near future, which will make port-to-port traffic an even more attractive alternative.

The ports of New Orleans and Tampa (which now has a "sister port" arrangement with Veracruz) are positioning themselves for a major increase in shipments to and from Mexico by the end of the decade, while the ports at Brownsville and Corpus Christi expect even closer ties with a wider range of carriers dealing with Mexico. As it is, Brownsville already has the best transportation infrastructure on the border, with access for ships, barges, rail, truck, and air freight. Construction is currently underway for a rail bypass which will avoid the city and connect the port directly with Southern Pacific's rail lines.

Mexico's leading maritime shipping company, Transportación Maritima Mexicana (the Mexican Line, or TMM) predicts that its traffic will increase by 30 percent because of NAFTA. Mexico is seeking greater access to the international shipping market, in part through greater foreign participation by its merchant fleet, which numbered approximately 650 vessels in 1991, as well as through joint ventures. For example, TMM and American President Lines (APL) are teaming up to offer direct, all-water container service between Asia and the Mexican Pacific Coast. Cargo from Asia destined for Mexico will be collected by APL at its terminals in Japan and Korea, then loaded on TMM ships bound for Manzanillo and Lázaro Cárdenas.

The *Puertos Mexicanos* (the federal port authority) is part of the *Secretaría de Comunicaciones y Transportes:*

Puertos Mexicanos
(Mexican Port Authority)
Municipio Libre No. 377
Col. Santa Cruz Atoyac
03310 México, DF, México
Tel: [52] (5) 604-3070, 604-3829, 604-4249
Fax: [52] (5) 688-9368, 688-9243

Port Facilities

Coatzacoalos The principal oil shipping port of Mexico, Coatzacoalos is located about 275 km (171 miles) southeast of Veracruz, on the Gulf Coast. Coatzacoalos is linked by daily rail service to Salina Cruz on the Pacific Coast, and an effort is underway to promote the route as an alternative to the Panama Canal for shippers moving freight between Asia and Europe. A new rail-barge facility has been built by the US firm, Burlington Northern. Special handling and storage facilities are available for grain, cement, molasses, bulk sulfur, liquid sulfur, and fertilizer. Facilities and storage for container freight are available, but are not heavily used.

Puerto de Coatzacoalcos
Recinto Fiscal Autorizado, Apdo. 4
96400 Coatzacoalcos, Ver., México
Tel: [52] (921) 46-754 Fax: [52] (921) 46-758

Lázaro Cárdenas The port is located about halfway between Manzanillo and Acapulco on the Pacific Coast, about 460 km (286 miles) southwest of Mexico City. No major highways serve the port, but there is a rail link to the regional transport hub at Morelia. Several terminals have recently been reconditioned. A new 65,000-ton grain handling terminal with storage facilities makes Lázaro Cárdenas Mexico's premier grain terminal with a capacity of 80,000 tons and a discharging speed of 600 tons per hour. Two container terminals are available, although Lázaro Cárdenas is not a major container port; the completion of the second container terminal and additional handling facilities should help attract more traffic. However, the lack of developed road

links between Lázaro Cárdenas and the interior constitutes a major obstacle to growth.

Puerto de Lázaro Cárdenas
Río Tepalcatepec 29
60950 Lázaro Cárdenas, Mich., México
Tel: [52] (734) 22-130/1, 21-722/3
Fax: [52] (734) 22-786

Manzanillo The port is located approximately 300 km (185 miles) southwest of Guadalajara, on the Pacific coast. A new container terminal was constructed in 1992, while a liquid cargo terminal, grain terminal and warehouse, and fruit terminal are also available; one cement terminal is being expanded, while another is under construction with private funds. An automobile import-export facility is nearing completion to serve Nissan's Aguascalientes plant.

Puerto de Manzanillo
Av. Teniente Azueta 9
Fracc. Playa Azul
Manzanilla, Col., México
Tel: [52] (333) 21-254, 23-075, 23-054
Fax: [52] (333) 20-815

Tampico-Altamira Tampico and Altamira are adjacent to one another and administered as a single unit. They are located on the Gulf Coast approximately 500 km (310 miles) northeast of Mexico City, 575 km (357 miles) southeast of Monterrey, and halfway between the US border and Veracruz.

Altamira is the country's second-ranked container facility (after Veracruz). Three container berths with four gantry cranes are available. New petrochemical and steel and coal terminals were privately funded. There is an intermodal rail facility with two rail tracks at the wharf.

Tampico is Mexico's top bulk cargo port. In 1992, it handled 2.1 million tons of bulk cargo, although this was down 10 percent from 1991. Tampico is also the third largest Mexican container port in terms of total tonnage and annual TEUs (twenty foot equivalent units) handled. There are nine general cargo berths plus a metals and minerals quay, with bulk facilities for ore, manganese ore, gypsum, cement, and grain. Eight warehouses, two sheds, and open storage space are available. Available fixed cranes have a capacity up to 150 metric tons, and there are several mobile cranes with capacities ranging from 20 to 90 metric tons.

Puerto de Tampico
Recinto Fiscal Autorizado, Piso 1
89000 Tampico, Tamps., México
Tel: [52] (12) 12-5744, 12-4660, 12-4550, 16-2518
Fax: [52] (12) 14-3374, 16-2467

Veracruz Mexico's top container port handles more than 1 million metric tons annually. Veracruz is also Mexico's second-ranked bulk cargo port, with 1.5 million metric tons handled in 1992, up 6 percent from 1991. Located 350 km (217 miles) from Mexico City, the port has easy access to the capital via a new toll road or by doublestack rail service. There are 15 ship docking locations, and yard facilities were recently expanded to 20 acres, with both covered and open storage available. However, Veracruz lacks refrigerated storage. Container facilities include two specialized container terminals, and panamex-style gantry cranes, each capable of moving 40 containers. Special facilities are available for molasses, grain, and sugar. Rail lines serve all wharves.

Puerto de Veracruz
Plaza de la Republica 210
91700 Veracruz, Ver., México
Tel: [52] (29) 32-4612, 32-5232
Fax: [52] (29) 32-3040, 32-5232

AIRPORTS

Although Mexico's large size and the longtime importance of international tourism have led the authorities to develop and maintain airports throughout the country, air service has focused on passenger traffic, and air cargo has remained a relatively undeveloped mode of freight transport. Nonetheless, more than 60 airports provide regular commercial flights for passengers and cargo, and more than a dozen of these could be considered major airports. As is the case with other parts of its transportation system, Mexico is privatizing certain aspects of the air transport industry. A comprehensive plan for the privatization of airports is set to be completed in 1994. This plan is expected to allow private firms to provide such airport services as the operation of cargo and passenger terminals and fueling operations, and to construct parking facilities and new runways at many Mexican airports.

Private investment is already permitted in some areas of operations, primarily for the construction and operation of terminals. In 1993 the federal air transport budget was US$363 million, and estimates of private outlays during 1993–1994 run around US$392 million. Private funds are paying for new passenger facilities in Chihuahua, Culiacán, and Tijuana, and for new cargo terminals in Guadalajara, Mérida, and Puebla. Other plans call for the modernization of facilities and services in the tourist centers of Puerto Vallarta and Cancún and a nationwide upgrading of radar and air traffic control systems. The state is already selling the rights to operate air cargo handling services at major airports, in hopes that they will be improved.

Estimates of 1994 total air traffic predict at least 50.4 million passengers and 1.5 million flights in Mexico. As the country's international gateway, Mexico City is expected to handle 37 percent of those passengers and 18 percent of the flights through its Benito Juárez International Airport. Mexico City also handles the vast majority of international air cargo, with Guadalajara running a distant second, although a new cargo terminal is in the planning stages for the Guadalajara airport. Monterrey's cargo facilities are less well developed; shippers in Monterrey often send goods overland to Houston International or to other airports in Texas, where air cargo services are better and less expensive. San Jose del Cabo, Mazatlán, Cancún, Puerto Vallarta, and Acapulco handle some international air cargo as well. They have modern, well developed airports, but their facilities are designed primarily for tourism rather than for cargo. New cargo terminals are planned for the airports at Mérida and Guanajuato.

Customs warehouses at Mexico City's airport have been expanded, and private companies now operate sections of them, so the rate of customs clearance has improved greatly of late. Additional facilities are under construction at Mexico City, but officials are also studying the viability of a second international airport in the Mexico City metropolitan area to alleviate the congestion at Juárez International. The city of Pachuca, about 100 km (62 miles) northeast of Mexico City, has been mentioned as a possible alternative site, while the existing airport at Toluca, one hour west of the city, is already receiving a greater share of cargo traffic. Some of the larger air cargo carriers such as Federal Express and Airborne Express have opened offices at the Toluca Airport. The Puebla airport, 135 km (84 miles) southeast of Mexico City, has also seen an increase in air cargo traffic. Many observers have suggested that while a second major airport in Mexico City would be a welcome addition, improved infrastructure connecting the existing airport to highways and rail lines should be an even greater priority.

The largest Mexican airlines—Aeroméxico and Mexicana—provide more than 90 percent of the flights within Mexico, but air freight accounts for a small portion of their business and receives little emphasis. Mexicana took over Aeroméxico more than a year ago, but the two continue to operate as separate carriers. Aeromexpress acts as the general cargo sales agent for both. Total cargo shipments by Mexican airlines actually fell by 3.8 percent during the two-year period 1992–1993. During the same period, cargo service among foreign carriers grew by more than 30 percent. An estimated two-thirds of the air cargo market is now controlled by foreign carriers.

Neither domestic nor foreign airlines are prepared to handle a serious increase in air cargo traffic. Cargo capacity is minimal despite the growth of new private carriers and the increase in the number of international flights, and the majority of cargo is still carried on passenger flights. Aeroméxico and Mexicana operate most of the regular freight service, limited as it is, between the US and Mexico. The airlines have made little investment in their cargo handling capabilities.

While Mexicana and Aeroméxico provide the majority of flights in Mexico, there are several regional carriers, some of which also provide limited international service: Aero California, Aero Guadalajara, Aeromar, Aviacsa, Servicio Aereo Leo López, SARO, and TAESA. Major foreign carriers providing cargo service include: Aerolinas Argentinas, Alaska Airlines, American, Continental, Delta, Iberia, Japan Airlines, KLM, Northwest, United, and Varig. A number of international courier and air cargo carriers also provide service to and from Mexico, including Airborne Express, DHL, Emery Worldwide, Federal Express, TNT Express Worldwide, UPS, and the Mexican company, Zoom Internacional. For addresses, telephone and fax numbers of Mexico offices, refer to the "Important Addresses" chapter. The government agency directly involved in overseeing the air transport industry is:

Dirección General de Aeronautica Civil
(Directorate General of Civil Aviation)
Providencia 807, Piso 6
Col. del Valle
03100 México, DF, México
Tel: [52] (5) 687-7814, 687-7660

Business Dictionary

PRONUNCIATION GUIDE

Spanish is the language of Mexico, although a great number of ancient Indian languages are still spoken in different parts of the country. There are certain differences between the Spanish spoken in Mexico and the language as used in Spain. The Mexican pronunciation is softer, and the intonation more drawn out. Mexicans and Spaniards have no difficulty in understanding each other, but differences of accent and words and expressions used in each of these countries can immediately pinpoint the nationality of the speaker. Once you have listened for a while, you realize that Spanish is a phonetic language with fairly logical pronunciation and spelling.

Notes on pronunciation

The five vowels of the alphabet (a, e, i, o, u) are pronounced always in the same way, regardless of what consonants they appear with. 'a' is pronounced somewhere between the 'a' sound of back and that of father, 'e' as in get, 'i' as in police, 'o' as in hotel, 'u' as in rule.

In Mexico there is no 'lisping' sound on the 'z' as there is in Spain. Letters 'c' (only before 'e' and 'i') and 'z' are pronounced like an 's', as in sail. Note than when 'c' appears before an 'a', 'o' or 'u', it is pronounced like a 'k', as in kit.

'g'   before 'e' and 'i' it sounds like 'h'; when it appears before the other three vowels, it sounds like hard 'g', as in gate or hug.

'gue/gui'pronounced as hard 'g' but 'u' is silent as in guitar.

'h'   is always silent.

'j'   sounds like 'h', e.g., hide, hall.

'll'   sounds like 'y', e.g., yoyo.

'ñ'   sounds like 'ny', e.g., canyon.

'qu'   sounds like 'k', e.g., duck.

'r'   is rolled, 'rr' doubly so.

'v'   sounds more like 'b', e.g., vino sounds somewhat like beano.

Some old Indian names have an 'x' in them and the pronunciation can vary. It can sound like an 'h' (e.g., Oaxaca is pronounced wah-<u>ha</u>-kah) but it can also sound like 'z' as in Xochimilco (zo-chee-m<u>ee</u>l-co). For names like Ixtapa, pronounce the 'x' as 'sh' as in 'dish' (ish-t<u>ah</u>-pah).

Stress

In general, if a word has a letter with an accent marked over it, that letter should be pronounced with greater stress. Unless otherwise accented, the stress falls on the next to the last vowel. For pronunciation purposes, in this dictionary the letters underlined in a word are the ones that carry the stress of the word, e.g., <u>oh</u>-la for hola (hello).

Forms of address

In Spanish there are two forms of address: one formal (singular—usted, plural—ustedes) and one informal (singular—tú, plural—ustedes, the same as in the formal), each to be used where appropriate. As a general rule, the formal address should be used when talking with someone you've never met before, with an older person, with someone of higher rank, etc., unless the person addressed expresses his or her wish to the contrary. (Note that expressions in this mini-dictionary are suited for formal address, giving priority to the business context.)

Gender

Nouns in Spanish are either masculine or feminine. Nouns ending in 'o', 'e' or 'ma' are usually masculine. Nouns ending in 'a', 'ión' or 'dad' are usually feminine. Some nouns have both a masculine and a feminine form, depending on the ending, as in viajero (male traveler), viajera (female traveler). An adjective usually comes after the noun it describes, and must take the same gender form.

English	*Spanish*	*Pronunciation*

GREETINGS AND POLITE EXPRESSIONS

Hello	Hola	<u>Oh</u>-lah
Good morning	Buenos días	Bw<u>eh</u>n-ohss d<u>ee</u>-yahss
Good afternoon	Buenas tardes	Bw<u>eh</u>n-ahss t<u>ah</u>r-dehs
Good evening	Buenas noches	Bw<u>eh</u>n-ahss n<u>oh</u>-chehss
Good night	Buenas noches	Bw<u>eh</u>n-ahss n<u>oh</u>-chehss
Hello (on the telephone)	¿Sí, diga?	Ss<u>ee</u>, d<u>ee</u>-gah?
	¿Mande?	M<u>ah</u>n-deh?
Goodbye		
(more final)	Adiós	Ah-dee-y<u>oh</u>ss
(less definite)	Hasta pronto	<u>Ah</u>ss-tah pr<u>oh</u>n-toh
See you tomorrow	Hasta mañana	<u>Ah</u>ss-tah mahn-y<u>ah</u>-nah
How do you do?	¿Cómo está usted?	K<u>oh</u>-moh eh-st<u>ah</u> oo-st<u>eh</u>d?
Please	Por favor	Pohrr fah-v<u>oh</u>rr
Pleased to meet you	Mucho gusto en conocerle	M<u>oo</u>-choh g<u>oo</u>-stoh en koh-noh-ss<u>eh</u>rr-leh
Please excuse me	Con permiso	Kon perr-m<u>ee</u>-ssoh
Congratulations	¡Felicidades!	Feh-lee-ssee-d<u>ah</u>-dehss
Thank you	Gracias	Gr<u>ah</u>-ssee-yahss
Thank you very much	Muchas gracias	M<u>oo</u>-chas gr<u>ah</u>-ssee-yahss
Thank you for your gift	Gracias por el regalo	Gr<u>ah</u>-ssee-yahss pohrr el rreh-g<u>ah</u>-loh
You are welcome	De nada	Deh n<u>ah</u>-dah
I don't speak Spanish	No hablo español	Noh <u>ah</u>b-loh eh-spahn-y<u>oh</u>l
I don't understand	No entiendo	N<u>oh</u> ehn-tee-<u>eh</u>n-doh
I understand	Entiendo	Ehn-tee-<u>eh</u>n-doh
Do you speak English?	¿Habla usted inglés?	<u>Ah</u>-blah oo-st<u>eh</u>d in-gl<u>eh</u>ss?
My name is John Smith	Mi nombre es John Smith	Mee n<u>oh</u>m-breh ehss John Smith
I am John Smith	Yo soy John Smith	Yoh ssoy John Smith
I am called John Smith	Me llamo John Smith	Mee y<u>ah</u>-moh John Smith
Is Mr./Miss Smith there? (on the telephone)	¿Me puede comunicar con el Señor/la Señorita Smith?	Meh pw<u>eh</u>-deh ko-moo-nee-k<u>ah</u>rr kohn el Ssehn-y<u>oh</u>rr/la Ssehn-yohrr-<u>ee</u>-tah Smith?
Is Mr./Miss Smith there?	¿Está el Señor/la Señorita Smith?	<u>Eh</u>-stah el Ssehn-y<u>oh</u>rr/la Ssehn-yohrr-<u>ee</u>-tah Smith
Who may I say is calling?	¿De parte de quien?	Day p<u>ah</u>rr-tay day k<u>ee</u>-in?
Can we meet tomorrow	¿Nos podemos ver mañana?	Nohss poh-d<u>eh</u>-mohss ver mahn-y<u>ah</u>-nah?
Would you like to have dinner together?	¿Podríamos cenar juntos/as?	Poh-dr<u>ee</u>-yah-mohs seh-n<u>ah</u>r h<u>oo</u>n-tohs/tahs?
Yes	Sí	Ss<u>ee</u>
No	No	N<u>oh</u>
Could you please (get me a taxi?)	¿Sería tan amable de (llamarme un taxi)?	Sseh-rr<u>ee</u>-yah tahn ah-m<u>ah</u>-bleh deh (yah-m<u>ah</u>rr-meh oon t<u>ah</u>k-ssee?

English	Spanish	Pronunciation
I'm sorry (I feel it)	Lo siento	Loh ssee-yehn-toh
I'm sorry (how sad)	Que lástima	Kay lahss-tee-mah
At your service	A sus ordenes	Ah soos or-dehn-ayss
Of course	Por supuesto	Pohrr soo-pwehs-toh
It is not important	No importa	Noh eem-pohrr-tah
How do you say?	¿Como se dice?	Koh-moh say dee-say?
Slower, please	Más lento por favor	Mahs len-toh pohrr fah-vohrr
Again	Otra vez	Oh-trah vayss
At what time?	¿A qué hora?	Ah kay oh-rrah?
Who	Quien	Kee-ehn
Where	Donde	Dohn-day
Which	Cual	Kwahl
When	Cuando	Kwahn-doh
How many	Cuanto	Kwahn-toh
What	Qué	Kay
Why	Por qué	Pohrr kay
Because	Porqué	Pohrr-kay

DAY/TIME OF DAY

morning	mañana	mahn-yah-nah
noon	mediodía	meh-dee-yoh-dee-yah
afternoon	tarde	tahrr-deh
evening	tarde	tahrr-deh
night	noche	noh-cheh
today	hoy	oy
yesterday	ayer	ah-yehrr
tomorrow	mañana	mahn-yah-nah
Monday	lunes	loo-nehss
Tuesday	martes	mahrr-tehss
Wednesday	miércoles	mee-yehrr-koh-lehss
Thursday	jueves	hoo-eh-vehss
Friday	viernes	vee-yehrr-nehss
Saturday	sábado	ssah-bah-doh
Sunday	domingo	doh-meen-goh
holiday	día feriado	dee-ah fehrr-ee-yah-doh
New Year's Day	día del año nuevo	dee-ah dell ahn-nyoh nweh-voh
time (hour)	hora	oh-rrah
place	lugar	loo-gahrr
early	temprano	teem-prah-noh
late	tarde	tahrr-deh

English	*Spanish*	*Pronunciation*

GETTING AROUND TOWN

Where is (the railway station)?	¿Dónde está (la estación del tren)?	D<u>oh</u>n-deh eh-st<u>ah</u> (lah eh-stah-ssee-y<u>oh</u>n de trehn)?
Does this train go to Mexico City?	¿Este tren va a la Ciudad de México?	<u>Eh</u>-steh trehn vah ah lah See-<u>oo</u>-dahd M<u>eh</u>-hee-koh?
Please take me to Mexico City	Por favor, lléveme a la Ciudad de México	Pohr fah-v<u>oh</u>r, y<u>eh</u>-veh-meh ah lah See-<u>oo</u>-dahd deh M<u>eh</u>-hee-koh
Where am I?	¿Dónde estoy?	D<u>oh</u>n-deh eh-st<u>oy</u>?
airplane	avión	ah-vee-y<u>oh</u>n
airport	aeropuerto	ay-eh-rroh-pw<u>eh</u>r-toh
bus (public)	autobús	ow-toh-<u>boo</u>s
taxi	taxi	t<u>ah</u>k-ssee
train	tren	trehn
train station	estación del tren	eh-stah-ssee-y<u>oh</u>n deh trehn
ticket	boleto	boh-l<u>eh</u>-toh
one-way (single) ticket	boleto sencillo	boh-l<u>eh</u>-toh ssehn-ss<u>ee</u>-yoh
round trip (return) ticket	boleto ida y vuelta	boh-l<u>eh</u>-toh <u>ee</u>-dah ee vw<u>eh</u>l-tah

NUMBERS

one	uno	<u>oo</u>-noh
two	dos	dohss
three	tres	trehss
four	cuatro	kw<u>ah</u>-troh
five	cinco	ss<u>ee</u>n-koh
six	seis	s<u>eh</u>-eess
seven	siete	see-y<u>eh</u>-teh
eight	ocho	<u>oh</u>-choh
nine	nueve	noo-w<u>eh</u>-veh
ten	diez	d<u>ee</u>-yehss
eleven	once	<u>oh</u>n-sseh
twelve	doce	d<u>oh</u>-sseh
thirteen	trece	treh-sseh
fourteen	catorce	ka-t<u>oh</u>rr-sseh
fifteen	quince	k<u>ee</u>n-sseh
sixteen	dieciseis	dee-yehs-ee-s<u>eh</u>ss
seventeen	diecisiete	dee-yehss-ee-ssee-y<u>eh</u>-teh
eighteen	dieciocho	dee-yehss-ee-<u>oh</u>-choh
nineteen	diecinueve	dee-yehss-ee-noo-w<u>eh</u>-veh
twenty	veinte	v<u>eh</u>-yeen-teh
twenty-one	veintiuno	veh-yeen-tee-y<u>oo</u>-noh
thirty	treinta	tr<u>eh</u>-yeen-teh
forty	cuarenta	kwah-r<u>eh</u>n-tah

English	Spanish	Pronunciation
fifty	cincuenta	sseen-kw<u>eh</u>n-tah
sixty	sesenta	sseh-ss<u>eh</u>n-tah
seventy	setenta	sseh-t<u>eh</u>n-tah
eighty	ochenta	oh-ch<u>eh</u>n-tah
ninety	noventa	noh-v<u>eh</u>n-tah
one hundred	cien	ss<u>ee</u>-ehn
two hundred	doscientos	doh-ssee-y<u>eh</u>n-tohs
three hundred	trescientos	treh-ssee-y<u>eh</u>n-tohs
one thousand	mil	meel
one million	un millón	oon mee-y<u>oh</u>n
first	primero	pree-m<u>eh</u>-rroh
second	segundo	seh-g<u>oo</u>n-doh
third	tercero	tehr-s<u>eh</u>-rroh

PLACES

English	Spanish	Pronunciation
airport	aeropuerto	ay-eh-roh-pw<u>eh</u>rr-toh
bank	banco	b<u>ah</u>n-koh
barber shop	peluquería	peh-loo-keh-rr<u>ee</u>-ya
beauty parlor	salón de belleza	sah-l<u>oh</u>n deh beh-y<u>eh</u>ss-ah
business district	distrito comercial	dee-str<u>ee</u>-toh ko-mehrr-ssee-y<u>ah</u>l
clothes store	tienda de ropa	tee-<u>eh</u>n-dah deh rr<u>oh</u>-pah
exhibition	exposición	eks-poh-ssee-ssee-y<u>oh</u>n
factory	fábrica	f<u>ah</u>-bree-kah
hotel	hotel	oh-t<u>eh</u>l
hospital	hospital	oh-spee-t<u>ah</u>l
market	mercado	mehr-k<u>ah</u>-doh
post office	oficina de correos	oh-fee-ss<u>ee</u>-nah deh koh-rr<u>ay</u>-ohss
restaurant	restaurante	rreh-sta-oo-rr<u>ah</u>n-teh
restroom/toilet		
women's	tocador	toh-kah-d<u>oh</u>rr
men's	baño	b<u>ah</u>-nyoh
seaport	puerto	pw<u>eh</u>rr-toh
train station	estación de tren	eh-stah-ssee-y<u>oh</u>n deh trehn
town square	zócalo	ss<u>oh</u>-k<u>ah</u>-loh

At the bank

English	Spanish	Pronunciation
What is the exchange rate?	¿Cuál es el tipo de cambio?	Kwal ehss ehl t<u>ee</u>-poh deh k<u>ah</u>m-bee-oh?
I want to exchange (dollars)	quisiera cambiar (dólares)	kee-ssee-y<u>eh</u>rr-ah kahm-bee-<u>ah</u>rr (d<u>oh</u>-lah-rehss)
new Mexican peso	nuevo peso mexicano	nw<u>eh</u>-voh p<u>eh</u>-ssoh meh-hee-k<u>ah</u>-noh
Guatemalan quetzal	quetzal de Guatemala	keht-ss<u>ah</u>l deh Gwah-teh-m<u>ah</u>-lah
Venezuelan bolivar	bolívar venezolano	boh-l<u>ee</u>-vahrr veh-neh-ssoh-l<u>ah</u>-noh

English	*Spanish*	*Pronunciation*
Brazilian cruzeiro	cruzeiro brasileño	kroo-s<u>eh</u>-rroh brah-ssee-l<u>eh</u>n-yoh
Nicaraguan cordoba	córdoba nicaragüense	k<u>oh</u>rr-doh-bah nee-kah-rrah-w<u>eh</u>n-sseh
Colombian peso	peso colombiano	p<u>eh</u>-ssoh koh-lohm-bee-<u>ah</u>-noh
Argentinian peso	peso argentino	p<u>eh</u>-ssoh ahrr-hehn-t<u>ee</u>-noh
Canadian dollar	dólar canadiense	d<u>oh</u>-lahrr kah-nah-dee-<u>eh</u>n-seh
U.S. dollar	dólar americano	d<u>oh</u>-lahrr ah-meh-ree-k<u>ah</u>-noh
Can you cash a personal check?	¿Puede cambiarme un cheque personal?	Pw<u>eh</u>-deh kahm-bee-y<u>ah</u>rr-meh oon ch<u>eh</u>-keh pehr-sso-n<u>ah</u>l?
Where should I sign?	¿Dónde debo firmar?	D<u>oh</u>n-deh d<u>eh</u>-bo feer-m<u>ah</u>rr?
traveler's check	cheque de viajero	ch<u>eh</u>-keh deh vee-yah-h<u>eh</u>-roh
bank draft	giro bancario	h<u>ee</u>-roh bahn-k<u>ah</u>-rree-oh

At the hotel

I have a reservation	Tengo una reservación	T<u>eh</u>n-goh <u>oo</u>-nah rreh-ssehr-vah-ssee-y<u>oh</u>n
Could you give me a single (double) room?	¿Tiene una habitación sencilla (doble) libre?	Ty<u>eh</u>-neh <u>oo</u>-nah ah-bee-tah-ssee-y<u>oh</u>n sehn-ss<u>ee</u>-yah (d<u>oh</u>-bleh) l<u>ee</u>-breh?
Is there...	¿Hay...	<u>ah</u>-ee...
air conditioning?	aire acondicionado?	<u>a</u>-ee-rreh ah-kohn-dee-ssee-oh-n<u>ah</u>-doh?
heating?	calefacción?	kah-leh-fahk-sy<u>oh</u>n?
private toilet?	baño privado?	b<u>ah</u>n-yoh pree-v<u>ah</u>-doh?
hot water?	agua caliente?	ah-wa kah-lee-y<u>eh</u>n-teh?
May I see the room?	¿Puedo ver la habitación?	Pw<u>eh</u>-doh vehr lah ah-bee-tah-ssee-y<u>oh</u>n?
Would you mail this for me please?	Por favor, ¿puede mandarme esto por correspondencia?	Pohr fah-v<u>oh</u>rr, pw<u>eh</u>-deh mahn-d<u>ah</u>rr-meh <u>eh</u>-sstoh pohrr koh-rrehss-pohn-d<u>eh</u>n-ssee-yah?
Would you mail this for me?	¿Puede mandarme esto por correo?	Pw<u>eh</u>-deh mahn-d<u>ah</u>r-meh <u>eh</u>-sstow pohrr koh-rr<u>ay</u>-oh?
Do you have any stamps?	¿Tiene estampillas por favor?	Ty<u>eh</u>-neh eh-stahm-p<u>ee</u>-yass pohrr fah-v<u>oh</u>rr?
May I have my bill?	¿Me puede dar la cuenta por favor?	Meh pw<u>eh</u>-deh dahr lah koo-<u>eh</u>n-tah pohr fah-v<u>oh</u>r?
Do you accept credit cards?	¿Aceptan tarjetas de crédito?	Ah-ss<u>eh</u>p-tahn tar-h<u>eh</u>-tahss deh kr<u>eh</u>-dee-toh

In the shop

Do you sell (books)?	¿Vende (libros)?	V<u>eh</u>n-deh (l<u>ee</u>-brohss)?
Do you have anything cheaper?	¿Tiene algo más barato?	Tee-y<u>eh</u>-neh <u>ah</u>l-goh mahss bah-rr<u>ah</u>-toh?
Do you have anything less expensive?	¿Tiene algo menos costoso?	Tee-y<u>eh</u>-neh <u>ah</u>l-goh m<u>eh</u>-nohs kos-t<u>oh</u>-sow
I would like (three books)	Desearía (tres libros) por favoı	Deh-sseh-ah-rr<u>ee</u>-ah (trehss l<u>ee</u>-brohss) pohrr fah-v<u>oh</u>rr

English	Spanish	Pronunciation
Give me three	Dame tres	Dah-meh trayhs
I'll take it	Me lo llevo	Meh loh yeh-voh
I'll take it	Me lo traigo	Meh loh try-goh
I want this one	Quiero ésto por favor	Kee-yehrr-oh eh-stoh pohrr fah-vohrr
When does it open?	¿A qué hora abren?	Ah keh oh-rrah ah-brehn?
When does it close?	¿A qué hora cierran?	Ah keh oh-rrah see-yehr-rahn?
How much?	¿Cuanto cuesta?	Kwahn-toh kwayss-tah?

COUNTRIES

America (USA)	Norteamerica (los Estados Unidos)	Norr-teh ah-meh-rree-kah (lohs Ay-stah-dohss Oo-nee-dohss)
France	Francia	Frahn-ssee-yah
Germany	Alemania	Ah-leh-mahn-yah
Great Britain	Gran Bretaña	Grahn Bray-tahn-yah
Mexico	México	Meh-hee-koh
Guatemala	Guatemala	Gwah-teh-mah-lah
Nicaragua	Nicaragua	Nee-kah-rrah-wah
Venezuela	Venezuela	Veh-neh-sweh-lah
Argentina	Argentina	Ahrr-hehn-tee-nah
Colombia	Colombia	Koh-lohm-bee-ah
Brazil	Brasil	Brah-sseel
Costa Rica	Costa Rica	Koh-sstah Rree-kah
Panama	Panamá	Pah-nah-mah
El Salvador	El Salvador	Ayl Sahl-vah-dohrr
Peru	el Perú	ell Peh-rroo

EXPRESSIONS IN BUSINESS

1) General business-related terms

accounting	contabilidad	kohn-tah-bee-lee-dahd
additional charge	cargo adicional	kahrr-goh ah-dee-ssee-yoh-nahl
advertise	anunciar	ah-noon-ssee-yahrr
application	solicitud	soh-lee-ssee-tood
appointment	cita	ssee-tah
bankrupt	insolvente	een-sohl-vehn-teh
brand name	nombre de marca	nohm-breh deh mahrr-kah
business	negocio	neh-goh-ssee-yoh
buyer	comprador	kohm-prah-dohrr
commercial affairs (business)	asuntos comerciales	ah-soon-tohs koh-mehrr-ssee-yahl-ehss
capital	capital	kah-pee-tahl
cash	efectivo	eh-fehk-tee-voh

English	Spanish	Pronunciation
change (from a purchase)	sencillo	sehn-ss<u>ee</u>-yoh
charge	cargo	k<u>a</u>hrr-goh
check (draft)	cheque	ch<u>eh</u>-keh
check (examine)	revisar	rray-v<u>ee</u>-ssahrr
claim	reclamación	rreh-klah-mah-ssee-y<u>oh</u>n
collect (payment)	recaudar	rreh-ka-oo-d<u>a</u>hrr
collect (payment)	cobrar	koh-br<u>a</u>hrr
collect (items)	recoger	rreh-k<u>oh</u>-hehrr
commission	comisión	koh-mee-ssee-y<u>oh</u>n
company	compania	kohm-pah-<u>nee</u>-yah
complain/inquire	reclamar	rreh-kl<u>ah</u>-mahr
complaint/inquiry	reclamo	rreh-kl<u>ah</u>-moh
copyright	derechos de autor	deh-rr<u>eh</u>-chohss deh ah-oo-t<u>oh</u>r
corporation	sociedad	soh-see-yeh-d<u>ah</u>d
cost	costo	k<u>oh</u>-stoh
credit	crédito	krr<u>eh</u>-dih-toh
on credit	al fiado	ahl fee-<u>ah</u>-doh
credit card	tarjeta de crédito	tahrr-h<u>ay</u>-tah deh krr<u>eh</u>-dih-toh
currency	moneda	moh-n<u>eh</u>-dah
customer	cliente	klee-y<u>eh</u>n-teh
customs duties	aranceles de aduana	ahrr-ahn-s<u>eh</u>-lehss deh ah-dw<u>ah</u>-na
D/A (documents against acceptance)	documentos contra aceptación	doh-koo-m<u>eh</u>n-tohss k<u>oh</u>n-trah ahk-sehp-tah-ssee-y<u>oh</u>n
D/P (documents against payment)	documentos contra pago	doh-koo-m<u>eh</u>n-tohss k<u>oh</u>n-trah p<u>ah</u>-goh
deferred payment	pago aplazado	p<u>ah</u>-goh ah-plah-ss<u>ah</u>-doh
deposit (n)	depósito	deh-p<u>oh</u>-ssee-toh
design	diseño	dee-ss<u>eh</u>n-yoh
discount	descuento	dehss-kw<u>eh</u>n-toh
distribution	distribución	dee-stree-boo-ssee-y<u>oh</u>n
dividends	dividendos	dee-vee-d<u>eh</u>n-dohss
documents	documentos	doh-koo-m<u>eh</u>n-tohss
due date	fecha de vencimiento	f<u>eh</u>-chah deh vehn-ssee-mee-y<u>eh</u>n-toh
exhibit	exhibir (v), exhibición (n)	ehk-ssee-b<u>ee</u>rr (v), ehk-see-bee-ssee-y<u>oh</u>n (n)
facsimile (fax)	facsímile (fax)	fahk-ss<u>ee</u>-mee-leh (fahks)
finance	finanzas	fee-n<u>ah</u>n-ssass
firm	empresa	ehm-pr<u>eh</u>-ssah
foreign businessman	hombre de negocios extranjero	<u>oh</u>m-breh deh neh-g<u>oh</u>-ssee-yoss ehk-strahn-h<u>eh</u>-rroh
foreign capital	capital extranjero	kah-pee-t<u>ah</u>l ehk-strahn-h<u>eh</u>-rroh
foreign currency	moneda extranjera	moh-n<u>eh</u>-dah ehk-strahn-h<u>eh</u>-rrah
foreign exchange	cambio de divisas	kahm-b<u>ee</u>-yoh deh dee-v<u>ee</u>-sahs

English	Spanish	Pronunciation
foreign trade	comercio exterior	koh-m<u>e</u>hrr-ssee-yoh ehk-steh-rree-y<u>oh</u>rr
goods	bienes	bee-<u>e</u>hn-ehs
government	gobierno	goh-bee-y<u>e</u>hrr-noh
industry	industria	een-d<u>oo</u>ss-tree-yah
inspection	inspección	een-spehk-ssee-y<u>oh</u>n
insurance	seguro	seh-g<u>oo</u>-rroh
interest	interés	een-teh-rr<u>e</u>hss
international	internacional	een-tehr-nah-ssee-yoh-n<u>ah</u>l
investment	inversión	een-vehr-ssee-y<u>oh</u>n
invoice	factura	fahk-t<u>oo</u>-rrah
joint venture	coinversión	koh-ihn-vehr-ssee-y<u>oh</u>n
label	marca	m<u>a</u>hrr-kah
letter of credit	carta de crédito	k<u>a</u>hrr-tah deh kr<u>e</u>h-dee-toh
license	licencia (n), autorizar (v)	lee-ss<u>e</u>hn-ssee-yah (n), a-oo-toh-rree-ss<u>a</u>hr (v)
loan	préstamo	pr<u>e</u>h-stah-moh
mergers and acquisitions	fusiónes y adquisiciónes	foo-ssee-y<u>oh</u>n-ayss ee ahd-kee-ssee-ssee-y<u>oh</u>n-ehss
model (of a product)	modelo	moh-d<u>e</u>h-loh
money	dinero	dee-n<u>e</u>hr-oh
monopoly	monopolio	moh-noh-poh-l<u>ee</u>-yoh
office	oficina	oh-fee-ss<u>ee</u>-nah
owner	dueño	dwayn-y<u>oh</u>
patent	patente	pah-t<u>e</u>hn-teh
pay (v)	pagar	pah-g<u>a</u>hrr
payment of goods	pago de mercancías	p<u>a</u>h-goh deh mehrr-kan-ss<u>ee</u>-yahss
payment by installment	pago a plazos	p<u>a</u>h-goh ah pl<u>a</u>h-ssohss
payment in cash	pago al contado	p<u>a</u>h-goh ahl kohn-t<u>a</u>h-doh
payment in advance	pago en avance	p<u>a</u>h-goh ehn ah-v<u>a</u>hn-ssay
permit	permiso	pehrr-m<u>ee</u>-ssoh
principal	capital principal	kah-pee-t<u>a</u>hl preen-ssee-p<u>a</u>hl
private (not government)	privado	pree-v<u>a</u>h-doh
product	producto	proh-d<u>oo</u>k-toh
profit margin	margen de utilidad	m<u>a</u>hrr-hehn deh oo-tee-lee-d<u>a</u>hd
range of goods	inventario de mercancías	een-vehn-t<u>a</u>h-ree-oh deh mehrr-kahn-ss<u>ee</u>-yahss
receipt	recibo	rray-ss<u>ee</u>-boh
register	registro(n), registrar (v)	rreh-h<u>ee</u>ss-troh (n), rreh-h<u>ee</u>s-trahrr (v)
report	informe (n), informar (v)	een-f<u>oh</u>r-meh (n), een-fohr-m<u>a</u>hrr (v)
research and development (R&D)	investigación y desarrollo	een-veh-stee-gah-ssee-y<u>oh</u>n ee deh-ssah-r<u>oh</u>-yoh
return on investment/yield	rendimiento	rrehn-dee-mee-y<u>e</u>hn-toh

English	*Spanish*	*Pronunciation*
sample	muestra	mweh-strah
sale	venta	vehn-tah
savings	ahorros	ah-ohrr-rrohss
seller	vendedor	vehn-deh-dohrr
settle accounts	liquidar cuentas	lee-kwee-dahrr kwehn-tahss
service charge	cargo por servicio	kahrr-goh pohrr sehrr-vee-ssee-yoh
sight draft	giro a la vista	hee-rroh ah lah vee-stah
tariffs	tarifas	tah-rreef-ahss
tax	impuestos	eem-pwehs-tohss
telephone	teléfono	teh-leh-foh-noh
telex	telex	teh-lehks
trademark	marca registrada	mahrr-kah reh-hee-strah-dah
visa	visa	vee-ssah

2) Labor

compensation	compensación	kohm-pehn-sah-ssee-yohn
employee	empleado	ehm-pleh-ah-doh
employer	patrón	pah-trohn
employment	empleo	eem-play-yoh
fire, dismiss (v)	despedir	deh-sspeh-deerr
foreign worker	trabajador extranjero	trah-bah-hah-dohrr ehk-strahn-heh-rroh
hire (v)	emplear	ehm-pleh-ahrr
immigration	inmigración	een-mee-grah-ssee-yohn
interview	entrevista	ehn-treh-vee-stah
job	puesto	pwehss-toh
laborer	obrero	oh-breh-rroh
skilled	obreros especializados	oh-breh-rrohss eh-speh-ssee-yah-lee-ssah-dohss
unskilled	obreros no especializados	oh-breh-rrohss noh eh-speh-ssee-yah-lee-ssah-dohs
labor force	mano de obra	mah-noh deh oh-brah
labor shortage	falta de mano de obra	fahl-tah deh mah-noh deh oh-brah
labor stoppage	paro en la mano de obra	pah-roh ehn lah mah-noh deh oh-brah
labor surplus	excedente de mano de obra	ehk-sseh-dehn-teh deh mah-noh deh oh-brah
minimun wage	sueldo mínimo	swehl-doh mee-nee-moh
profession/ occupation	profesión/ocupación	proh-feh-ssee-yohn/ oh-kuh-pah-ssee-yohn
salary	salario	sah-lah-rree-oh
strike	huelga	wehl-gah
training	entrenamiento	ehn-tray-nah-mee-ehn-toh
union	sindicato	seen-dee-kah-toh
wage	sueldo	swehl-doh

English	Spanish	Pronunciation
work	trabajo (n), trabajar (v)	trah-b<u>ah</u>-hoh (n), trah-b<u>ah</u>-hahrr (v)

3) Negotiations (Buying/Selling)

English	Spanish	Pronunciation
agreement	acuerdo	ah-kw<u>eh</u>rr-doh
arbitrate	arbitrar	ahr-bee-tr<u>a</u>hrr
brochure, pamphlet	folleto	foh-y<u>eh</u>-toh
buy (v)	comprar	kohm-pr<u>a</u>hrr
confirm (v)	confirmar	kohn-feer-m<u>a</u>hrr
contract	contrato (n), contratar (v)	kohn-tr<u>ah</u>-toh (n), kohn-trah-t<u>a</u>hrr(v)
cooperator	cooperador	koh-oh-peh-rah-d<u>o</u>hrr
cost	costo	k<u>oh</u>-stoh
counteroffer	contraoferta	kohn-trah-oh-f<u>eh</u>rr-tah
countersign	contraseñar	kohn-trah-sehn-y<u>a</u>hrr
deadline	plazo límite	pl<u>ah</u>-ssoh l<u>ee</u>-mee-teh
demand	exigencia (n), exigir (v)	ehk-ssee-h<u>eh</u>n-ssee-yah (n), ehk-ssee-h<u>ee</u>rr (v)
estimate (v)	estimar	eh-stee-m<u>a</u>hrr
guarantee (v)	garantizar	gah-rrahn-tee-ss<u>a</u>hrr
label	marca	m<u>a</u>hrr-kah
license (n)	licencia	lee-ss<u>eh</u>n-ssee-yah
market	mercado	mehrr-k<u>ah</u>-doh
market price	precio de mercado	pr<u>eh</u>-ssee-yoh deh mehrr-k<u>ah</u>-doh
minimum quantity	cantidad mínima	kahn-tee-d<u>ah</u>d m<u>ee</u>-nee-mah
negotiate	negociar	neh-goh-ssee-y<u>a</u>hrr
negotiate payment	negociar el pago	neh-goh-ssee-y<u>a</u>hrr ehl p<u>ah</u>-goh
order	pedido	peh-d<u>ee</u>-doh
packaging	envasado	ehn-vah-ss<u>ah</u>-doh
place an order	hacer un pedido	ah-ss<u>eh</u>r oon peh-d<u>ee</u>-doh
price	precio	pr<u>eh</u>-ssee-yoh
price list	lista de precios	l<u>ee</u>-stah deh pr<u>eh</u>-ssee-yohss
product features	características del producto	kah-rrahk-teh-rr<u>ee</u>-stee-kahss dehl proh-d<u>oo</u>k-toh
product line	una línea de productos	<u>oo</u>-nah l<u>ee</u>-neh-ah deh proh-d<u>oo</u>k-tohss
quality	calidad	kah-lee-d<u>ah</u>d
quantity	cantidad	kahn-tee-d<u>ah</u>d
quota	cuota	kw<u>oh</u>-tah
quote (offer)/proposal	presupuesto	preh-ssoo-pw<u>eh</u>-stoh
sale	venta	v<u>eh</u>n-tah
sales confirmation	confirmación de venta	kohn-feer-mah-ssee-y<u>oh</u>n deh v<u>eh</u>n-tah
sell	vender	vehn-d<u>eh</u>rr
sign	firmar	feer-m<u>a</u>hrr
specifications	especificaciones	eh-speh-see-fee-kah-ssee-y<u>oh</u>n-ehss

English	*Spanish*	*Pronunciation*
standard (quality)	(calidad) estándar	(kah-lee-d<u>ah</u>d) eh-st<u>ah</u>n-dahr
superior (quality)	(calidad) superior	(kah-lee-d<u>ah</u>d) soo-peh-ree-<u>ohr</u>
trade	comercio (n) comerciar (v)	koh-m<u>eh</u>rr-ssee-yoh (n) koh-mehrr-ssee-y<u>ah</u>r (v)
unit price	precio unitario	pr<u>eh</u>-ssee-yoh oo-nee-t<u>ah</u>-ree-yoh
value	valor	vah-l<u>oh</u>rr
value added	valor agregado	vah-l<u>oh</u>rr ah-gray-g<u>ah</u>-doh
warranty (and services)	garantía y servicios	gah-rrahn-t<u>ee</u>-ah ee ssehr-v<u>ee</u>-ssee-yohss
The price is very high	El precio es muy elevado	Ayl pr<u>eh</u>-ssee-yoh ehss m<u>oo</u>-ee eh-leh-v<u>ah</u>-doh
The price is too high	El precio es demasiado elevado	Ayl pr<u>eh</u>-ssee-yoh ehss deh-mah-see-y<u>ah</u>-doh eh-leh-v<u>ah</u>-doh
We need a faster delivery	Necesitamos una entrega	Neh-sseh-ssee-t<u>ah</u>-mohss <u>oo</u>-nah más rápida ehn-tr<u>eh</u>-gah mahss rr<u>ah</u>-pee-dah
We need it by (tomorrow)	Lo necesitamos (para mañana)	Loh neh-sseh-ssee-t<u>ah</u>-mohss (p<u>ah</u>-rrah mahn-y<u>ah</u>-nah)
We need a better quality	Necesitamos una mejor calidad	Neh-sseh-see-t<u>ah</u>-mohss <u>oo</u>-na meh-h<u>oh</u>rr kah-lee-d<u>ah</u>d
We need it to these specifications	Lo necesitamos con estas especificaciones	Loh neh-sseh-see-t<u>ah</u>-mohss kohn <u>eh</u>-stah-speh-ssee-fee-kah-ssee-y<u>oh</u>n-ehss
I want to pay less	Quisiera pagar menos	Kee-ssee-yehrr rah pah-g<u>ah</u>rr m<u>eh</u>-nohss
I want the price to include...	Quiero que el precio incluya...	Kee-y<u>eh</u>rr oh keh ehl pr<u>eh</u>-ssee-yoh een-kl<u>oo</u>-yah...
Can you guarantee delivery?	¿Puede garantizarme la entrega?	Pw<u>eh</u>-deh gah-rrahn-tee-ss<u>ah</u>rr-meh lah ehn-tr<u>eh</u>-gah?
Can you guarantee the delivery date?	¿Puede guarantizarme la fecha de la entrega?	Pw<u>eh</u>-deh gah-rrahn-tee-ss<u>ah</u>r-meh lah f<u>ay</u>-chah deh lah ehn-tr<u>eh</u>-gah?

4) Products/Industries

aluminium	aluminio	ah-loo-m<u>ee</u>-nee-yoh
automobile	automóvil	ah-oo-toh-m<u>oh</u>-veel
automotive accessories	accesorios de automóvil	ahk-sseh-ss<u>oh</u>-rree-ohs deh ah-oo-toh-m<u>oh</u>-veel
biotechnology	biotecnología	bee-oh-tehk-noh-loh-h<u>ee</u>-ah
brick	ladrillo	lah-dr<u>ee</u>-yoh
carpets	alfombras	ahl-f<u>ohm</u>-brahss
cement	cemento	sseh-m<u>eh</u>n-toh
ceramics	cerámica	sseh-rr<u>ah</u>-mee-kah
chemicals	productos químicos	proh-d<u>oo</u>k-tohss k<u>ee</u>-mee-kohss
clothing...	ropa ...	rr<u>oh</u>-pah...
for women	de mujer	deh moo-h<u>eh</u>r

English	Spanish	Pronunciation
for men	de hombre	deh <u>oh</u>m-breh
for children	de niños	deh n<u>ee</u>n-yohss
coal	carbón	kahr-b<u>oh</u>n
computer	computadora	kohm-poo-tah-d<u>oh</u>-rrah
computer hardware	hardware de computadora	hardware deh kohm-poo-tah-d<u>oh</u>-rrah
computer software	software de computadora	software deh kohm-poo-tah-d<u>oh</u>-rrah
concrete	concreto	kohn-kr<u>eh</u>-toh
construction	construcción	kohn-strook-ssee-y<u>oh</u>n
electrical equipment	maquinaria eléctrica	mah-kee-n<u>ah</u>-ree-yah eh-l<u>eh</u>k-tree-kah
glass	vidrio	v<u>ee</u>-dee-yoh
gold	oro	<u>oh</u>-rroh
handicrafts	artesanía	ahrr-teh-sah-n<u>ee</u>-ah
minerals	minerales	mee-neh-rr<u>ah</u>-lehss
mining industry	industria minera	een-d<u>oo</u>-stree-yah mee-n<u>eh</u>-rrah
musical instruments	instrumentos musicales	een-stroo-m<u>eh</u>n-tohss moo-ssee-k<u>ah</u>-lehss
paper	papel	pah-p<u>eh</u>l
petroleum	petróleo	peh-tr<u>oh</u>-leh-oh
pharmaceuticals	productos farmacéuticos	proh-d<u>oo</u>k-tohss fahrr-mah-seh-<u>oo</u>-tee-kohss
plastics	plásticos	pl<u>ah</u>ss-tee-kohss
pottery	cerámica	seh-rr<u>ah</u>-mee-kah
rugs	tapetes	tah-p<u>eh</u>-tehss
silver	plata	pl<u>ah</u>-tah
spare parts	piezas de repuesto	pee-y<u>eh</u>-ssass deh rreh-pw<u>eh</u>-stoh
sporting goods	artículos para deporte	arr-t<u>ee</u>-koo-lohss pah-rrah deh-p<u>oh</u>r-teh
steel	acero	ah-ss<u>eh</u>-roh
telecommunications	equipo de telecomunicaciones	eh-k<u>ey</u>-poh deh teh-leh-koh-moo-nee-kah-ssee-y<u>oh</u>n-nehss
television	televisión	teh-leh-vee-ssee<u>e</u>-yohn
television set	televisor	teh-leh-vee-s<u>ee</u>-sohrr
textiles	textiles	tehk-st<u>ee</u>-lehss
tobacco	tabaco	tah-b<u>ah</u>-koh
tools	herramientas	eh-rrah-mee-y<u>eh</u>n-tahss
hand tool	herramienta manual	eh-rrah-mee-y<u>eh</u>n-tah mah-noo-<u>ah</u>l
power tool	herramienta mecánica	eh-rrah-mee-y<u>eh</u>n-tah meh-k<u>ah</u>-nee-kah
tourism	turismo	too-rr<u>ee</u>ss-moh
toys	juguetes	hoo-g<u>eh</u>-tehss
watches/clocks	relojes	rreh-l<u>oh</u>-hehss

English	Spanish	Pronunciation
wood	madera	mah-d<u>eh</u>-rrah

5) Services

English	Spanish	Pronunciation
accounting service	servicio de contabilidad	sehr-v<u>ee</u>-ssee-yoh deh kohn-tah-bee-lee-d<u>ah</u>d
advertising agency	agencia de publicidad	ah-h<u>eh</u>n-ssee-yah deh poob-lee-ssee-d<u>ah</u>d
agent	agente	ah-h<u>eh</u>n-teh
customs broker	agente de aduanas	ah-h<u>eh</u>n-teh deh ah-dw<u>ah</u>-nahss
distributor	distribuidor	dee-stree-bwee-d<u>oh</u>rr
employment agency	agencia de empleo	aa-h<u>eh</u>n-see-yah deh ehm-pl<u>eh</u>-oh
exporter	exportador	ehkss-pohrr-tah-d<u>oh</u>rr
freight forwarder	corredor	koh-rr<u>ay</u>-dohrr
importer	importador	eem-porr-tah-d<u>oh</u>rr
manufacturer	fabricante	fah-bree-k<u>ah</u>n-teh
packing services	servicios de empaque	sehr-v<u>ee</u>-ssee-yohss deh ehm-p<u>ah</u>-kay
printing company	empresa imprenta	ehm-pr<u>eh</u>-ssah eem-pr<u>eh</u>n-tah
retailer	minorista	mee-noh-rr<u>ee</u>-stah
service(s)	servicio(s)	sehr-v<u>ee</u>-ssee-yoh(ss)
supplier	proveedor	proh-veh-eh-d<u>oh</u>rr
translation services	servicios de traducción	sehr-v<u>ee</u>-ssee-yohss deh trah-dook-ssee-y<u>oh</u>n
wholesaler	mayorista	mah-yoh-rr<u>ee</u>-stah

6) Shipping/Transportation

English	Spanish	Pronunciation
bill of lading	conocimiento de embarque	koh-noh-see-mee-y<u>eh</u>n-toh deh ehm-b<u>ah</u>rr-keh
carriage and insurance paid to	flete y seguro pagado a	fl<u>ay</u>-teh ee say-g<u>uh</u>-roh pah-g<u>ah</u>-doh ah
carriage paid to	flete pagado a	fl<u>ay</u>-teh pah-g<u>ah</u>-doh ah
cost and freight	costo y flete	k<u>oh</u>-stoh ee fl<u>ay</u>-teh
cost, insurance, freight (CIF)	Costo, seguro y flete	k<u>oh</u>-stoh, seh-g<u>oo</u>-rroh ee fl<u>ay</u>-teh
customs	aduanas	ah-dw<u>ah</u>-nahs
customs duty	derechos aduaneros	deh-rr<u>eh</u>-choss ah-dwah-n<u>eh</u>-rrohs
date of delivery	fecha de entrega	f<u>eh</u>-chah deh ehn-tr<u>eh</u>-gah
deliver (delivery)	entregar (entrega)	ehn-treh-g<u>ah</u>r (ehn-tr<u>eh</u>-gah)
delivered at frontier	entregada en frontera	ehn-tray-g<u>ah</u>-dah ehn fron-t<u>eh</u>r-ah
delivered duty paid	entregada con impuestos pagados	ehn-tray-g<u>ah</u>-dah kohn eem-pw<u>eh</u>s-tohs pah-g<u>ah</u>-dohs
delivered duty unpaid	entregada sin impuestos pagados	ehn-tray-g<u>ah</u>-dah seehn eem-pw<u>eh</u>s-tohs pah-g<u>ah</u>-dohs
delivered ex quay	entregada al desembarcadero	ehn-tray-g<u>ah</u>-dah ahl dehss-ehm-barr-kah-d<u>eh</u>-rroh
delivered ex ship	entregada al barco	ehn-tray-g<u>ah</u>-dah ahl b<u>ah</u>r-koh

English	Spanish	Pronunciation
export	exportación (n), exportar (v)	ehkss-pohrr-tah-ssee-y<u>oh</u>n (n) ehkss-pohrr-t<u>ah</u>rr (v)
ex works	ex works	ex works
free alongside ship (FAS)	free alongside ship	free alongside ship
free carrier	franco transportador	fr<u>ah</u>n-koh trahns-pohrr-t<u>ah</u>-dohrr
free on board (FOB)	free on board	free on board
import	importación (n), importar (v)	eem-pohrr-tah-ssee-y<u>oh</u>n (n), eem-pohrr-t<u>ah</u>rr (v)
in bulk	a granel	ah grah-n<u>eh</u>l
mail (post) (n)	correo postal	k<u>oh</u>-rray-oh poh-st<u>ah</u>l
country of origin	país de origen	pah-<u>ee</u>s deh oh-rr<u>ee</u>-hehn
packing	empacado	ehm-pah-k<u>ah</u>-doh
packing list	lista de empaque	l<u>ee</u>-stah deh ehm-p<u>ah</u>-kay
port	puerto	pw<u>eh</u>rr-toh
ship (to send)…	enviar…	ehn-vee-y<u>ah</u>rr…
by air	por avión	pohrr ah-vy<u>oh</u>n
by sea	por barco	pohrr b<u>ah</u>rr-koh
by train	por tren	pohrr trehn
by truck	por camión	pohrr kah-mee-y<u>oh</u>n

WEIGHTS, MEASURES, AMOUNTS

barrel	barril	bah-rr<u>ee</u>l
centimeter	centímetro	sehn-t<u>ee</u>-meh-troh
dozen	docena	doh-ss<u>eh</u>-nah
foot	pie	pyeh
gallon	galón	gah-l<u>oh</u>n
gram	gramo	gr<u>ah</u>-moh
gross (144 pieces)	gruesa (144 piezas)	grw<u>eh</u>-ssah (ssy<u>eh</u>n-toh kwah-rrehn- tah ee kw<u>ah</u>-troh py<u>eh</u>-ssahss)
gross weight	peso bruto	p<u>eh</u>-ssoh br<u>oo</u>-toh
hectare	hectárea	ehk-t<u>ah</u>-rreh-ah
hundred (100)	cien	ssee-y<u>eh</u>n
inch	pulgada	p<u>oo</u>l-gah-da
kilogram	kilogramo	kee-loh-gr<u>ah</u>-moh
meter	metro	m<u>eh</u>-troh
net weight	peso neto	p<u>eh</u>-ssoh n<u>eh</u>-toh
mile (English)	milla	m<u>ee</u>-yah
liter	litro	l<u>ee</u>-troh
ounce	onza	<u>oh</u>n-ssah
pint	pinta	p<u>ee</u>n-tah
pound (weight–measure avoirdupois)	libra	l<u>ee</u>-brah
quart (avoirdupois)	cuarto de galón	kw<u>ah</u>r-toh deh gah-l<u>oh</u>n

English	Spanish	Pronunciation
square meter	metro cuadrado	m<u>eh</u>-troh kwah-dr<u>ah</u>-doh
cubic meter	metro cúbico	m<u>eh</u>-troh k<u>oo</u>-bee-koh
square yard	yarda cuadrada	y<u>ah</u>rr-dah kwah-dr<u>ah</u>-dah
size	tamaño	tah-m<u>ah</u>-nee-yoh
ton (metric)	tonelada	toh-neh-l<u>ah</u>-dah
yard	yarda	y<u>ah</u>rr-dah

MEXICO-SPECIFIC ORGANIZATIONAL TITLES

board of directors	consejo de administración	kohn-s<u>eh</u>-ho deh ahd-meen-eess-trah-ssee-y<u>oh</u>n
chairman	chairman	chairman
deputy director	subdirector	ssoob-dee-rrehk-t<u>oh</u>rr
manager	gerente	hehr-rr<u>eh</u>n-teh
assistant manager	subgerente	ssoob-heh-rr<u>eh</u>n-teh
president	presidente	preh-ssee-d<u>eh</u>n-teh
vice president	vicepresidente	veess-preh-ssee-d<u>eh</u>n-teh
company secretary	secretario	sseh-kreh-t<u>ah</u>-rree-yoh
supervisor	supervisor	ssoo-pehr-vee-ss<u>oh</u>rr
marketing director	director de mercadotecnia	dee-rrehk-t<u>oh</u>rr deh mehrr-kah-doh-t<u>eh</u>k-nee-yah
sales manager	jefe de ventas	h<u>eh</u>-feh deh v<u>eh</u>n-tahss
accountant	contador	kohn-tah-d<u>oh</u>r
attorney	abogado	ah-boh-g<u>ah</u>-doh

COMMON SIGNS

Entrance	Entrada	ehn-tr<u>ah</u>-dah
Exit	Salida	ssah-l<u>ee</u>-dah
Men (restroom)	Caballeros	kah-bah-y<u>eh</u>-rrohss
Women (restroom)	Damas	d<u>ah</u>-mahss
Up	Arriba	ah-rr<u>ee</u>-bah
Down	Abajo	ah-b<u>ah</u>-ho

MEXICO-SPECIFIC EXPRESSIONS AND TERMS

Greetings

Hello (on the phone)	¿Mande?	M<u>ah</u>n-deh?
How do you do?	¿Cómo está usted?	K<u>oh</u>-moh eh-st<u>ah</u> oo-st<u>eh</u>d?
See you later	Nos vemos	Nohss v<u>eh</u>-mohss
Are you ill?	¿Está enfermo?	Eh-st<u>ah</u> ehn-f<u>eh</u>rr-moh?
How are you doing?	¿Cómo te va?	K<u>oh</u>-moh teh vah?
How is your business going?	¿Cómo van los negocios?	K<u>oh</u>-mo vahn lohss neh-g<u>oh</u>-ssee-ohss
Is your family well?	¿Qué tal la familia?	Keh tahl lah fah-m<u>ee</u>-lee-yah?
Did you sleep well?	¿Cómo amaneció?	K<u>oh</u>-moh ah-mah-neh-ssee-y<u>oh</u>?

English	Spanish	Pronunciation
What did you say (pardon)?	¿Mande?	M<u>ah</u>n-deh?
It's very hot (weather)	Hace mucho calor	<u>Ah</u>-sseh m<u>oo</u>-cho kah-l<u>oh</u>r
It's very cold (weather)	Hace mucho frío	<u>Ah</u>-sseh m<u>oo</u>-cho fr<u>ee</u>-oh
Would you like a drink?	¿Le gustaría tomar algo?	Ley goo-stah-rr<u>ee</u>-yah toh-m<u>ah</u>rr <u>ah</u>l-goh?
Welcome to Mexico	Bienvenido a México (man)	Byehn-veh-n<u>ee</u>-doh ah m<u>eh</u>-hee-koh
	Bienvenida a México (woman)	Byehn-veh-n<u>ee</u>-dah ah m<u>eh</u>-hee-koh
It's a beautiful country	Es un país muy hermoso	Ays oon pah-<u>ee</u>ss m<u>oo</u>-ee ehr-m<u>oh</u>-ssoh
It's a very interesting country	Es un país muy interesante	Ays oon pah-<u>ee</u>ss m<u>oo</u>-ee een-tehrr-ay-s<u>ah</u>n-teh

At the restaurant

English	Spanish	Pronunciation
Waiter	Mesero/mesera	Meh-s<u>eh</u>-rroh, meh-s<u>eh</u>-rrah
Please bring me a menu	Tráigame el menú, por favor	Tr<u>ah</u>-ee-gah-meh ehl meh-n<u>oo</u>, pohrr fah-v<u>oh</u>rr
We want to order	Queremos pedir, por favor	Keh-rr<u>eh</u>-mohs peh-d<u>ee</u>rr, pohrr fah-v<u>oh</u>rr
The check	La cuenta, por favor	Lah kw<u>eh</u>n-tah, pohrr fah-v<u>oh</u>rr
Is it spicy?	¿Es picante?	Ehss pee-k<u>ah</u>n-teh?
meal (main meal)	comida	koh-m<u>ee</u>-dah
breakfast	desayuno	deh-ssah-y<u>oo</u>-noh
lunch	almuerzo	ahl-mw<u>eh</u>r-ssoh
supper	cena	ss<u>eh</u>-nah
appetizer	aperitivo	ah-peh-rree-t<u>ee</u>-voh
dessert	postre	p<u>oh</u>-streh
a bottle of white wine	una botella de vino blanco	<u>oo</u>-nah boh-t<u>eh</u>-yah deh v<u>ee</u>-noh bl<u>ah</u>n-koh
a glass of red wine	una copa de vino tinto	<u>oo</u>-nah k<u>oh</u>-pah deh v<u>ee</u>-noh t<u>ee</u>n-toh
beer	cerveza	sehrr-v<u>eh</u>-ssah
mineral water...	agua mineral...	<u>ah</u>-wah mee-neh-rr<u>ah</u>l...
with ice	con hielo	kohn y<u>ay</u>-loh
without ice	sin hielo	sseen y<u>ay</u>-loh
carbonated	con gas	kohn gahss
uncarbonated	sin gas	sseen gahss
soft drink	refresco	reh-fr<u>eh</u>ss-koh
fruit juice	jugo	h<u>oo</u>-goh
coffee...	café...	kah-f<u>eh</u>...
black	solo	s<u>oh</u>-lo
with milk	con leche	kohn l<u>eh</u>-cheh
tea	té	teh
bread	pan	pahn
salad	ensalada	ehn-sah-l<u>ah</u>-dah

English	*Spanish*	*Pronunciation*
fruit	fruta	froo-tah
I need	necesito…	neh-sseh-ssee-toh…
a knife	un cuchillo	oon koo-chee-yoh
a fork	un tenedor	oon teh-neh-dohrr
a spoon	una cuchara	oo-nah koo-chah-rrah
napkin	servilleta	sehrr-vee-yeh-tah
cover charge	cubierta	koo-bee-ehrr-tah
tortilla	tortilla	tohrr-tee-yah
beans	frijoles	free-hoh-lehss
fish	pescado	pess-kah-doh
meat	carne	kahrr-nay
vegetables	verduras	vehrr-doo-rrahss
vegetarian	vegetariano	veh-heh-tahrr-ee-ah-no
seafood	mariscos	mahrr-eess-kohss
chicken (poultry)	pollo	poh-yoh
bon appetit	buen provecho	bwehn proh-veh-choh

Important Addresses

The following addresses have been gathered from a wide range of sources. We have attempted to verify each address at press time; however, it is likely that some of the information has already changed. Inclusion of an organization, product, or service does not imply a recommendation or endorsement. In many cases we have provided English translations of the names of the organizations. Other translations of the names may be used as well; those included here are given primarily to assist you in deciding which may be the most appropriate for you to contact.

Unless otherwise noted, all addresses are in Mexico; the international country code for calling Mexico is [52] and is not shown in the Mexican listings. City codes are given in parentheses, while non-Mexican country codes are in square brackets. For a listing of Mexican city codes and state abbreviations, see the list on the following page. Refer to the chapter "Business Travel" for details on making telephone calls in Mexico.

A few common elements and abbreviations in Mexican addresses are:

Apartado Postal (Apdo.)	Post office box
Avenida (Av., Avda.)	Avenue
Calle	Street
Calzada (Calz.)	Avenue
Carretera	Highway
Code Postal (C.P.)	Postal code
Colonia (Col.)	District (neighborhood)
Delegación (Deleg.)	Delegation (neighborhood)
Despacho (Desp.)	Suite or Office
Edificio (Edif.)	Building
Esquina (esq.)	At the corner of
Norte (N.)	North
Número (No.)	Street number
Oriente (Ote.)	East
Piso	Floor, Story
Planta Baja (P.B.)	Ground Floor
Poniente (Pte.)	West
Sur (S.)	South
Torre	Tower or Building

CITY CODES IN MEXICO

Cities with * appearing after their name are state capitals. There are 31 states plus the Distrito Federal, where the national capital, Mexico City (usually written simply as México), is located.

State name	Abbreviation	City name	City code
Aguascalientes	Ags.	Aguascalientes*	49
Baja California (Norte)	BC (or BCN)	Ensenada	667
		Mexicali*	65
		Tijuana	66
Baja California Sur	BCS	La Paz*	682
Campeche	Camp.	Campeche*	981
Chiapas	Chis.	Tuxtla Gutiérrez*	961
Chihuahua	Chih.	Chihuahua*	14
		Ciudad Juárez	16
Coahuila	Coah.	Ciudad Acuña	877
		Piedras Negras	878
		Saltillo*	84
		Torreón	17
Colima	Col.	Colima*	331
Distrito Federal	DF	México	5
Durango	Dgo.	Durango*	181
Guanajuato	Gto.	Guanajuato*	473
		León	47
Guerrero	Gro.	Chilpancingo*	747
		Acapulco	74
Hidalgo	Hgo.	Pachuca*	771
Jalisco	Jal.	Guadalajara*	3
		Puerto Vallarta	322
México (Estado de)	Méx (or Edo. de Méx.)	Toluca*	72
Michoacan	Mich.	Morelia*	451
Morelos	Mor.	Cuernavaca*	73
Nayarit	Nay.	Tepic*	321
Nuevo León	NL	Monterrey*	83
Oaxaca	Oax.	Oaxaca*	951
Puebla	Pue.	Puebla*	22
Querétaro	Qro.	Querétaro*	42
Quintana Roo	QR	Chetumal*	983
		Cancún	98
San Luis Potosí	SLP	San Luis Potosí*	48
Sinaloa	Sin.	Culiacán*	67
		Mazatlán	69
Sonora	Son.	Hermosillo*	62
		Nogales	631
		Ciudad Obregón	641
Tabasco	Tab.	Villahermosa*	93
Tamaulipas	Tamps.	Ciudad Victoria*	131
		Tampico	12
		Matamoros	891
		Nuevo Laredo	87
		Reynosa	89
		Río Bravo	893
Tlaxcala	Tlax.	Tlaxcala*	246
Veracruz	Ver.	Jalapa*	281
		Veracruz	29
Yucatán	Yuc.	Mérida*	99
Zacatecas	Zac.	Zacatecas*	492

GOVERNMENT

MEXICAN GOVERNMENT AGENCIES AND ENTITIES

Azúcar, S.A.
Insurgentes Sur No. 1079
Col. Nochebuena
03910 México, DF
Tel: (5) 563-7100 Tlx: 1772554

Banco de México (BANXICO)
Bank of Mexico
Avda. 5 de Mayo 2, Apdo. 98 bis
Col. Centro
06059 México, DF
Tel: (5) 237-2000, 709-0140, 709-0440
Fax: (5) 510-9337, 512-4813 Tlx: 1773050

Comisión del Cuadro Básico de Medicamentos
y Equipo
National Commission for Medicines and Equipment
Durango No. 289-11
Roma
06700 México, DF, México
Tel: (5) 553-8523, 553-2666

Comisión Federal de Electricidad (CFE)
Federal Electricity Commission
León Tolstoi 29, Piso 7, esq. Mariano Escobedo
Col. Anzures
11500 México, DF
Tel: (5) 731-7567

Comisión Nacional Bancaria
National Banking Commission
República del Salvador 47
Col. Centro
06080 México, DF
Tel: (5) 709-7311 Fax: (5) 709-7327

Comisión Nacional Coordinadora de Puertos
National Coordination Commission of Ports
Edif. Zona Franca, Antiguo Puerto Libre
Coatzacoalcos, Ver.
Tel: (921) 25-077 Tlx: 78842

Comisión Nacional del Agua (CNA)
National Water Commission
Infr. Hica Urbana E. Ind.
Cda. J. Sánchez Azcona 1723, Piso 4
Col. del Valle
03100 México, DF
Tel: (5) 524-6985, 524-2650

Comisión Nacional del Cacao
National Cocoa Commission
Tlaxcala No. 208, Piso 5
Hipódromo Condesa
06170 México, DF
Tel: (5) 282-9376

Comisión Nacional de Precios
National Prices Commission
Avda. Juárez 101, Piso 17
México, DF
Tel: (5) 510-0436

Comisión Nacional de Salarios Mínimos
National Commission on Minimum Salaries
Avda. Cuauhtémoc 14
Col. Doctores
06720 México, DF
Tel: (5) 578-9021 Fax: (5) 578-5775

Comisión Nacional de Valores
National Securities Commission
Barranca del Muerto 275
Col. San José Insurgentes
03900 México, DF
Tel: (5) 651-0129

Consejo Nacional de Turismo
National Council of Tourism
Mariano Escobedo No. 726
México, DF
Tel: (5) 531-0949

Departmento del Distrito Federal
Department of the Federal District
Plaza de la Constitución y Pino Suárez, Piso 1
Col. Centro
06068 México, DF
Tel: (5) 585-0187, 510-0349
Fax: (5) 518-2998 Tlx: 1774460

Dirección de Normas de Radiodifusión
Directorate of Radio Broadcasting Standards
Eugenia 197, Piso 1
Col. Vértiz Navarte
03020 México, DF
Tel: (5) 590-4372

Dirección de la Procuraduría General
Directorate of the Attorney General
Eje Lázaro Cárdenas 9
06058 México, DF
Tel: (5) 521-3725 Tlx: 1772701

Dirección General de Aduanas
Directorate General of Customs
20 de Noviembre 195, Piso 6
Col. Centro
06090 México, DF
Tel: (5) 709-6365, 709-2900, 709-2185, 709-6287
Fax: (5) 709-6038, 709-6360 Tlx: 1774303

Dirección General de Aeronáutica Civil
Directorate General of Civil Aviation
Providencia 807, Piso 6
Col. del Valle
03100 México, DF
Tel: (5) 687-7814, 687-7660

Dirección General de Asuntos Fronterizos
Directorate General of Border Affairs
Periférico Sur 3025, Piso 7
Col. Héroes de Padierna
Deleg. Magdalena Contreras
México, DF
Tel: (5) 683-4394, 683-7055 x2706

Dirección General de Bibliotecas
Directorate General of Libraries
Universidad Nacional Autónoma de México
Circuito Interior, Ciudad Universitaria
Apdo. 70-308
04510 México, DF
Tel: (5) 548-9780, 550-5212 Fax: (5) 550-1398

Dirección General de Control de Insumos Para la
Salud, SS
Directorate General of Control of Medical Products
Insurgentes Sur 1397, Piso 3
Col. Guadalupe Inn
01020 México, DF
Tel: (5) 598-9029

Dirección General de Control Sanitario de Bienes y
Servicios, SS
Directorate General of Sanitary Control of Works and
Services
Donceles 39
Col. Centro
06000 México, DF
Tel: (5) 521-3050, 512-9994

Dirección General de Desarrollo Tecnológico, SECOFI
Technology Development General Directorate
Azafran No. 18, Piso 3
Granjas México
08400 México, DF
Tel: (5) 654-0781, 650-1333 Fax: (5) 654-0771

Dirección General de Normas (DGN)
Directorate General of Standards
Avda. Puente de Tecamachalco 6, Piso 3
Lomas de Tecamachalco
53950 Naucalpan, Edo. de Méx.
Tel: (5) 520-8493/4, 540-2620, 589-9877
Fax: (5) 606-0386

Dirección General de Normas (DGN)
Departmento de Información Comercial
Department of Commercial Information
Avda. Puente de Tecamachalco 6, Piso 3
Lomas de Tecamachalco
53950 Naucalpan, Edo. de Méx.
Tel: (5) 589-9592 Fax: (5) 540-5153

Dirección General de Prevención y Control de la
Contaminación Ambiental
Directorate General of Environmental Contamination,
Prevention and Control
Río Elba 20
Col. Cuauhtémoc
06500 México, DF
Tel: (5) 553-2977, 553-9481
Fax: (5) 658-6059, 286-8559

Dirección General de Radio, Televisión y Cine (RTC)
Directorate General of Radio, Television and Film
Atletas 2
Col. Country Club
04220 México, DF
Tel: (5) 544-9692, 544-3768 Tlx: 1760298

Dirección General de Sanidad Forestal
Directorate General of Forestry Protection
Progreso 5, Piso 2
Col. Viveros de Coyoacán
México, DF
Tel: (5) 658-8974, 658-8438

Dirección General de Sanidad Vegetal
Directorate General of Plant Protection
Guillermo Pérez Valenzuela No. 127
México, DF
Tel: (5) 554-0512, 658-1671 Fax: (5) 554-0529

Dirección General de Servicios del Comercio Exterior
Directorate General of Foreign Trade Services
Blvd. Adolfo López Mateos No. 3025
Col. Héroes de Padierna
00700 México, DF
Tel: (5) 683-5066, 683-4344 Fax: (5) 595-5881/3

Dirección General de Telecomunicaciones
Directorate General of Telecommunications
Lázaro Cárdenas 567, Piso 11
Ala Norte, Navarte
03020 México, DF
Tel: (5) 519-9161

Ejército Mexicano
Mexican Army
Avila Camacho e Industria Militar
Lomas de Sotelo
11640 México, DF
Tel: (5) 557-4500, 557-1932

Ferrocarriles Nacional de México (FNM)
National Railroads of Mexico
Avda. Jesús García Corona 140, Piso 4, Ala B
06358 México, DF
Tel: (5) 547-6583

Fuerza Aérea Mexicana
Mexican Air Force
Avila Camacho e Industria Militar
Lomas de Sotelo
11640 México, DF
Tel: (5) 557-3310, 557-4500

Información Tecnologiá y Consultoría (INFOTEC)
Office of Information Technology
Apdo. 22-860
Tlalpan
14060 México, DF
Tel: (5) 606-0011, 606-1620 Fax: (5) 606-0386

Instituto de Seguridad y Servicios Sociales de los
Trabajadores del Estado (ISSTE)
Institute of Federal Employees' Insurance and Social
Services
Callejón Vía San Fernando 12, Piso 4
Col. Barrio San Fernando Tlalpan
01407 México, DF
Tel: (5) 606-2121, 606-7000

Instituto Mexicano de Control de Calidad (IMECCA)
Mexican Institute of Quality Control
Mariano Escobedo 396, Piso 1
Anzures
11590 México, DF
Tel: (5) 250-1099 Fax: (5) 254-1047

Instituto Mexicano de la Radio (IMER)
Mexican Radio Institute
Mayorazgo 83
Col. Xoco
03330 México, DF
Tel: (5) 604-8532, 604-7741

Instituto Mexicano del Café
Mexican Coffee Institute
Carretera Jalapa-Veracruz KM4
Campo Experimental Garnica
Jalapa, Lago Merú 32, Col. Granada
México, DF
Tel: (5) 250-5543 Tlx: 15536

Instituto Mexicano del Plástico Industrial (IMPI)
Mexican Institute of Industrial Plastics
General Juan Carlos Cano 25
11850 México, DF
Tel: (5) 515-6356, 515-6152 Fax: (5) 578-1571

Instituto Mexicano de Seguro Social (IMSS)
Mexican Institute of Social Security
Shakespeare 157
Col. Anzures
11590 México, DF
Tel: (5) 545-5683

Instituto Mexicano de Televisión (IMEVISION)
Mexican Television Institute
Avda. Periférico Sur 4121
Col. Fuentes del Pedregal
14141 México, DF
Tel: (5) 568-5684, 568-1313 Tlx: 1773878

Instituto Nacional de Estadística, Geografía e
Informática (INEGI)
National Institute of Statistics, Geography and
Informatics
Avda. Héroe de Nacozari Sur 2301
Edificio Sede, Puerta 11, Primer Nivel
Fracc. Jardines del Parque
20270 Aguascalientes, Ags.
Tel: (49) 18-2232 Fax: (49) 18-0739

Instituto Nacional del Consumidor
National Institute for Consumer Protection
Insurgentes Sur 1228, Piso 10
Col. del Valle Tlacoquemecatl
03210 México, DF
Tel: (5) 559-2478 Fax: (5) 559-0123

Laboratorios Nacionales de Fomento Industrial
(LANFI)
National Laboratories of Industrial Development
Avda. Industria Militar 261
Lomas de Sotelo
11200 México, DF
Tel: (5) 589-0199 Fax: (5) 589-9103

Petróleos Mexicanos (PEMEX)
Mexican National Oil Company
Oficinas Generales
Marina Nacional 329, Edificio B-2, Piso 11
Col. Huasteca
11311 México, DF
Tel: (5) 531-6238, 250-2611 Tlx: 1774286

Procuraduría Federal del Consumidor
Federal Attorney of the Consumer
Dr. Carmona y Valle 11
Col. Doctores
06720 México, DF
Tel: (5) 761-3021

Puertos Mexicanos
Mexican Port Authority
Municipio Libre No. 377
Col. Santa Cruz Atoyac
03310 México, DF
Tel: (5) 604-3070, 604-3829, 604-4249
Fax: (5) 688-9243, 688-9368

Secretaría de Agricultura y Recursos Hidráulicos
(SARH)
Secretariat of Agriculture and Water Resources
Avda. Insurgentes Sur No. 476, Piso 13
Col. Roma Sur
06038 México, DF
Tel: (5) 584-0066, 584-0096, 584-0271 Tlx: 1775890

Secretaría de Agricultura y Recursos Hidráulicos
(SARH)
Department of Agricultural Machinery
Lope de Vega 125, 9
Chapultepec Morales
11570 México, DF
Tel: (5) 250-6649, 250-9535   Fax: (5) 250-9960

Secretaría de Agricultura y Recursos Hidraulicos
(SARH)
Departamento de Autorizaciones Zoosanitarias
Department of Animal Health Authorization
Recreo 51
México, DF
Tel: (5) 534-1131/8 Fax: (5) 534-3985

Secretaría de Agricultura y Recursos Hidráulicos
(SARH)
Department of Science and Technology
Av. Nuevo León 210, 18
Hipódromo Condesa
06100 México, DF
Tel: (5) 584-7980, 564-9859   Fax: (5) 574-3160

Secretaría de Comercio y Fomento Industrial (SECOFI)
Secretariat of Commerce and Industrial Development
Alfonso Reyes No. 30
Col. Condesa
06140 México, DF
Tel: (5) 211-0036, 286-1757, 286-1823, 286-1461
Fax: (5) 224-3000, 286-0804, 286-1551, 286-1543
Tlx: 1775840, 1775833, 1775718

Secretaría de Comunicaciones y Transportes
Secretariat of Communications and Transport
Avda. Universidad y Xola
Col. Navarte
03028 México, DF
Tel: (5) 519-7456, 519-1319, 530-9203, 530-1074
Fax: (5) 519-9748, 530-1074 Tlx: 017600

Secretaría de Desarrollo Social (SEDESOL)
Secretariat of Social Development
Avda. Constituyentes No. 947
Col. Belén de las Flores
01110 México, DF
Tel: (5) 271-0355, 271-8521, 271-1616, 271-8481
Fax: (5) 271-6614, 271-8217 Tlx: 1771198

Secretaría de Desarrollo Urbano y Ecología (SEDUE)
Secretariat of Urban Development and Ecology
Constituyentes No. 947
Col. Belén de las Flores
01110 México, DF
Tel: (5) 271-1616

Secretaría de Educación Pública (SEP)
Secretariat of Public Education
Argentina No. 28, Desp. 310
Col. Centro
06029 México, DF
Tel: (5) 510-3029, 521-9574 Fax: (5) 510-4766

Secretaría de Energía, Minas y Industria Paraestatal
Secretariat of Energy, Mine and Parastatal Industry
Avda. Insurgentes Sur No. 552, Piso 3
Col. Roma Sur
06769 México, DF
Tel: (5) 564-9789, 564-9790, 584-4304
Fax: (5) 574-3396 Tlx: 1775690

Secretaría de Gobernación (SG)
Secretariat of Internal Affairs
Bucareli No. 99, Piso 1
Col. Juárez
06699 México, DF
Tel: (5) 535-1513, 566-0245
Fax: (5) 546-8120 Tlx: 1774375

Secretaría de Hacienda y Crédito Público (SHCP)
Secretariat of Finance and Public Credit
Palacio Nacional, 1 Patio Mariano
Col. Centro
06066 México, DF
Tel: (5) 518-2060, 518-2711, 518-1060, 518-5420/9
Fax: (5) 542-2821, 510-3796 Tlx: 1776397

Secretaría de la Contraloría General de la Federación
Secretariat of the Comptroller General
Avda. Insurgentes Sur 1735, Piso 10
Col. Guadalupe Insurgentes
01020 México, DF
Tel: (5) 559-2690, 575-3983, 575-8088, 682-4580
Fax: (5) 524-8306 Tlx: 1764014

Secretaría de la Defensa Nacional (SDN)
Secretariat of National Defense
Avila Camacho e Industria Militar
Col. Lomas do Sotelo
11640 México, DF
Tel: (5) 557-4500, 557-1932, 395-6766
Fax: (5) 557-1370 Tlx: 1776312

Secretaría de la Reforma Agraria (SPA)
Secretariat of Agrarian Reform
Bolívar 145, Piso 6
06088 México, DF
Tel: (5) 761-0266 Tlx: 1772505

Secretaría de Marina (SH)
Secretariat of the Navy
Eje 2 Oriente, Tramo H
Escuela Naval Militar 861
Col. Los Cipreses
04830 México, DF
Tel: (5) 679-6411, 684-8188, 679-8290, 684-4188
Fax: (5) 684-4266, 679-6411

Secretaría de Pesca
Secretariat of Fisheries
Avda. Alvaro Obregón No. 269, Piso 6
Col. Roma Sur
06700 México, DF
Tel: (5) 511-9870, 525-6662, 511-9278, 208-1291
Fax: (5) 208-1834 Tlx: 1777483

Secretaría de Programación y Presupuesto (SPP)
Secretariat of Programming and the Budget
Palacio Nacional
Patio de Honor
Col. Centro
06060 México, DF
Tel: (5) 782-1019

Secretaría de Relaciones Exteriores
Secretariat of Foreign Affairs
Ricardo Flores Magón No. 1, Piso 19
Col. Guerrero
06995 México, DF
Tel: (5) 277-5470, 782-3312, 782-3660, 782-4144
Fax: (5) 254-5549, 254-7285, 782-3511
Tlx: 1762479, 1763478

Secretaría de Salud
Secretariat of Health
Lieja No. 7, Piso 1
Col. Juárez
06696 México, DF
Tel: (5) 533-6967, 533-1353, 553-7017, 553-7670
Fax: (5) 286-5497 Tlx: 1776519, 1773429

Secretaría de Trabajo y Previsión Social (STPS)
Secretariat of Labor and Social Welfare
Anillo Periférico No. 4271
Edificio A, Piso 9
Col. Fuentes de Pedregal
14140 México, DF
Tel: (5) 652-0636, 568-1720, 645-3969
Fax: (5) 568-3470, 568-2928 Tlx: 1760097

Secretaría de Turismo (SECTUR)
Secretariat of Tourism
Avda. Presidente Masaryk No. 172
Col. Polanco
11587 México, DF
Tel: (5) 250-8204/6, 250-8228, 250-8555, 250-0123
Fax: (5) 254-0014 Tlx: 1777566

Servicio Postal Mexicano
Mexican Postal Service
Netzahualcóyotl 109
06000 México, DF
Tel: (5) 709-9502, 709-9600, 709-1566

Siderúrgica Nacional
National Iron and Steel Company
Miguel Angel de Quevedo No. 980, Piso 4
04040 México, DF
Tel: (5) 544-7017, 549-0124 Tlx: 1772883

Subsecretaría de Negociaciones Comerciales
Internacionales, SECOFI
Undersecretary of International Commercial
Negotiations
Alfonso Reyes 30
Col. Hipódromo Condesa
06140 México, DF
Tel: (5) 211-3545, 211-3405, 211-0872, 211-3050
Fax: (5) 224-3000

Subsecretaría de Industria e Inversión Extranjera,
SECOFI
Undersecretary of Industry and Foreign Investment
Alfonso Reyes 30, Piso 13
Col. Hipódromo Condesa
06140 México, DF
Tel: (5) 286-1471 Fax: (5) 553-5690

Subsecretaría de Ingresos, SHCP
Undersecretary of Revenues
Avda. Hidalgo No. 77, Módulo 1, P.B.
Col. Guerrero, Deleg. Cuauhtémoc
06300 México, DF

STATE OFFICES OF SECRETARÍA DE COMERCIO Y FOMENTO INDUSTRIAL

SECOFI Aguascalientes
Aguascalientes, Ags.
Tel: (49) 15-2024 Fax: (49) 69-615

SECOFI Baja California
Mexicali, BC
Tel: (65) 57-4273 Fax: (65) 57-1559

SECOFI Baja California
Tijuana, BC
Tel: (66) 34-0203 Fax: (66) 34-0201

SECOFI Baja California Sur
La Paz, BCS
Tel: (682) 28-056 Fax: (682) 20-260

SECOFI Campeche
Campeche, Camp.
Tel: (981) 63-365 Fax: (981) 62-130

SECOFI Chiapas
Tuxtla Gutiérrez, Chis.
Tel: (961) 26-298 Fax: (961) 20-398

SECOFI Chihuahua
Chihuahua, Chih.
Tel: (14) 13-6641 Fax: (14) 13-6218

SECOFI Coahuila
Saltillo, Coah.
Tel: (84) 16-7212 Fax: (84) 16-7152

SECOFI Colima
Colima, Col.
Tel: (331) 23-766 Fax: (331) 22-567

SECOFI Durango
Durango, Dgo.
Tel: (181) 20-905 Fax: (181) 28-580

SECOFI Guanajuato
Guanajuato, Gto.
Tel: (473) 27-407 Fax: (473) 27-350

SECOFI Guererro
Chilpancingo, Gro.
Tel: (747) 26-321 Fax: (747) 75-497

SECOFI Hidalgo
Pachuca, Hgo.
Tel: (771) 52-303 Fax: (771) 55-010

SECOFI Jalisco
Avda. Mariano Otero 3431
Col. Valle Verde
Guadalajara, Jal.
Tel: (3) 621-0694, 621-1642, 621-1115
Fax: (3) 621-6534, 621-1360, 621-0534

SECOFI México (Estado de)
Toluca, Edo. de Méx.
Tel: (72) 19-5152 Fax: (72) 19-5701

SECOFI Michoacán
Morelia, Mich.
Tel: (451) 56-601 Fax: (451) 56-832

SECOFI Morelos
Cuernavaca, Mor.
Tel: (73) 17-0741 Fax: (73) 17-0761

SECOFI Nayarit
Tepic, Nay.
Tel: (321) 25-082 Fax: (321) 23-054

SECOFI Nuevo León
Edif. Cintermex, Local 88
Avda. Fundidora y Adolfo P.
Monterrey, NL
Tel: (83) 69-6480/2 Fax: (83) 69-6487/9

SECOFI Oaxaca
Oaxaca, Oax.
Tel: (951) 55-002 Fax: (951) 59-663

SECOFI Puebla
Puebla, Pue.
Tel: (22) 40-4509 Fax: (22) 37-9374

SECOFI Querétaro
Querétaro, Qro.
Tel: (42) 12-0399 Fax: (42) 12-5101

SECOFI Quintana Roo
Chetumal, QR
Tel: (983) 23-056 Fax: (983) 20-729

SECOFI San Luis Potosí
San Luis Potosí, SLP
Tel: (48) 15-2114 Fax: (48) 15-7150

SECOFI Sinaloa
Culicán, Sin.
Tel: (67) 13-9200 Fax: (67) 13-9377

SECOFI Sonora
Hermosillo, Son.
Tel: (62) 16-7633 Fax: (62) 16-1990

SECOFI Tabasco
Villahermosa, Tab.
Tel: (931) 59-077 Fax: (931) 59-079

SECOFI Tamaulipas
Ciudad Victoria, Tamps.
Tel: (131) 29-133 Fax: (131) 29-018

SECOFI Tlaxcala
Tlaxcala, Tlax.
Tel: (246) 25-726 Fax: (246) 26-976

SECOFI Veracruz
Jalapa, Ver.
Tel: (281) 72-030 Fax: (281) 78-759

SECOFI Yucatán
Mérida, Yuc.
Tel: (99) 25-6822 Fax: (99) 25-6933

SECOFI Zacatecas
Zacatecas, Zac.
Tel: (492) 21-214 Fax: (492) 26-889

OVERSEAS DIPLOMATIC MISSIONS OF MEXICO

Argentina
Embassy
Calle Larrea 1230
1117 Buenos Aires, Argentina
Tel: [54] (1) 824-7161, 826-2161

Australia
Embassy
14 Perth Ave.
Yarralumla
Canberra, ACT 2600, Australia
Tel: [61] (62) 73-3905, 73-3947 Fax: [61] (62) 73-3488

Austria
Embassy
Turkenstrasse 15
1090 Vienna, Austria
Tel: [43] (222) 310-7383/6 Fax: [43] (222) 310-7387

Belgium
Embassy
Chaussée de la Hulpe 164, 1er étage
1170 Brussels, Belgium
Tel: [32] (2) 676-0711, 676-0700/3

Bolivia
Embassy
Avda. 6 de Agosto 2652
Col. San Jorge
La Paz, Bolivia
Tel: [591] (2) 32-2592, 32-7109

Brazil
Embassy
SES Av. das Nacoes Lote 18
70359 Brasilia, DF, Brazil
Tel: [55] (61) 243-8624, 244-1011
Fax: [55] (61) 244-1755

Canada
Embassy
130 Albert St., Suite 1800
Ottawa, ON K1P 5G4, Canada
Tel: [1] (613) 233-6665, 233-8988, 233-9917
Fax: [1] (613) 235-9123, 235-7765 Tlx: 0534520

Consulates:

2000 Rue Mansfield, Suite 1015
Montreal, PQ H3A 2Z7, Canada
Tel: [1] (514) 288-2502, 288-4916
Fax: [1] (514) 288-8287

60 Bloor St. W., Suite 203
Toronto, ON M4W 3B8, Canada
Tel: [1] (416) 922-2718, 922-3196
Fax: [1] (416) 922-8867

810-1130 W. Pender St.
Vancouver, BC V6E 4E4, Canada
Tel: [1] (416) 684-3547, 684-5725
Fax: [1] (416) 684-2485

Chile
Embassy
San Sebastián No. 2839-605, 606 y 607
Las Condes
Santiago, Chile
Tel: [56] (2) 246-0941, 246-7835

China (People's Republic of)
Embassy
San Li Tun Dong Wu Jie 5
Chao Yang
100600 Beijing, PRC
Tel: [86] (1) 532-2551, 532-3951, 532-2574
Fax: [86] (1) 532-3744

Colombia
Embassy
Calle 99 No. 12-08
Bogotá, Colombia
Tel: [57] (1) 256-6121, 236-4957

Costa Rica
Embassy
Avda. 7a. No. 1371
San José, Costa Rica
Tel: [506] 22-5528, 22-4448 Fax: [506] 22-5485

Denmark
Embassy
Gammel Vartov Vej 18
Hellerup
2900 Copenhagen, Denmark
Tel: [45] 31-20-80-81 Fax: [45] 31-20-82-48

Dominican Republic
Embassy
Rafael Hernández No. 11
Ensanche Naco
Santo Domingo, Dominican Republic
Tel: [1] (809) 565-2565, 565-2744
Fax: [1] (809) 346-4187

Ecuador
Embassy
Avda. 6 de Diciembre 4843 y Naciones Unidas
Quito, Ecuador
Tel: [593] (2) 45-7931, 45-7820

El Salvador
Embassy
Paseo General Escalón 3832
Col. Escalón
San Salvador, El Salvador
Tel: [503] 98-1084, 98-1079 Fax: [503] 23-0464

Finland
Embassy
Fredrickinukatu 51-53, A 3rd Fl.
00100 Helsinki, Finland
Tel: [358] (0) 64-0637 Fax: [358] (0) 680-1227

France
Embassy
9, rue de Longchamp
75116 Paris, France
Tel: [33] (1) 47-04-47-09, 45-53-76-43

Germany
Embassy
Adenauerallee 100
5300 Bonn, Germany
Tel: [49] (228) 21-8043, 21-8046
Fax: [49] (228) 211-1118

Greece
Embassy
Diamandidou 73A
Paleo Psychico
15452 Athens, Greece
Tel: [30] (1) 647-0852, 647-5908 Fax: [30] (1) 647-1506

Guatemala
Embassy
16 Calle 1-45
Zona 10 Guatemala, Guatemala
Tel: [502] (2) 68-0202, 68-2867

Hungary
Embassy
Budakeszi ut 55/D, P/5 1.2 y IX.1
1021 Budapest, Hungary
Tel: [36] (1) 176-7598, 176-7793 Fax: [36] (1) 176-7906

India
Embassy
10 Jor Bagh
New Delhi 110-003, India
Tel: [91] (11) 69-7991, 61-1145 Fax: [91] (11) 69-2360

Indonesia
Embassy
Nusantara Building, 4th Fl.
Jakarta, Indonesia
Tel: [62] (21) 33-7974, 33-3909

Israel
Embassy
Bograshov 3
63808 Tel Aviv, Israel
Tel: [972] (2) 523-0367, 523-0368
Fax: [972] (2) 523-7399

Italy
Embassy
Vía Lazzaro, Spalianzani 16
00161 Rome, Italy
Tel: [39] (6) 440-2319, 440-2323

Japan
Embassy
2-15-1 Nagata-cho
Chiyoda-ku
Tokyo 100, Japan
Tel: [81] (3) 3581-1131, 3580-0811
Fax: [81] (3) 3581-4058

Korea (South)
Embassy
Hwang Kyung Group Bldg., 3rd Fl.
Changchung-dong 1-ga
Chung-gu
100-391 Seoul, Korea
Tel: [82] (2) 269-4011, 269-4012
Fax: [82] (2) 742-2682

Netherlands
Embassy
Nassauplein 17
2585-EB The Hague, Netherlands
Tel: [31] (70) 60-2900, 60-6857

Norway
Embassy
Drammensveien 108-B
0244 Oslo 2, Norway
Tel: [47] 22-43-11-65, 22-43-14-77
Fax: [47] 22-44-43-52

Panama
Embassy
Calle 50 y Calle San José
Edif. Bank of America, Piso 5
7 Panamá, Panamá
Tel: [507] 63-5021, 63-8990 Fax: [507] 64-2022

Paraguay
Embassy
Juan E. O'Leary 499
Edif. "Parapiti" - 511 al 515, Piso 5
Estrella
Asunción, Paraguay
Tel: [595] (21) 44-4421, 44-1877 Fax: [595] (21) 44-1877

Philippines
Embassy
Adamson Center Bldg., 2nd Fl.
121 Alfarro St., Salcedo Village
Makati, Metro Manila, Philippines
Tel: [63] (2) 815-2566 Fax: [63] (2) 817-4684

Poland
Embassy
Staroscinka 18-4-5
00683 Warsaw, Poland
Tel: [48] (22) 49-5250, 49-5258

Portugal
Embassy
Rua Castilho 50, 4 Izquierdo
1200 Lisbon, Portugal
Tel: [351] (1) 57-0683, 57-0792 Fax: [351] (1) 57-0563

Puerto Rico
Consulate General
623 Ave. Ponce de León, Suite 305
San Juan 00918, Puerto Rico
Tel: [1] (809) 764-0254

Russian Federation
Embassy
Ul. Schukina 4
Moscow, Russia
Tel: [7] (095) 201-2553, 201-4848

Saudi Arabia
Embassy
PO Box 94391
11693 Riyadh, Saudi Arabia
Tel: [966] (1) 478-1900, 476-1200
Fax: [966] (1) 478-1900

Singapore
Embassy
152 Beach Rd. No. 06-07/08
Gateway East
0718 Singapore, Rep. of Singapore
Tel: [65] 298-2678, 298-5015 Fax: [65] 293-3484

Spain
Embassy
Avda. Paseo de la Castellana No. 93, Piso 7
28046 Madrid, Spain
Tel: [34] (1) 456-1349, 456-1496

Sweden
Embassy
Grevgatan 3
11453 Stockholm, Sweden
Tel: [46] (8) 661-6175, 660-3970

Switzerland
Embassy
Bernastrasse 57
3005 Berne, Switzerland
Tel: [41] (31) 43-1814, 43-1875

Thailand
Embassy
44/7-8 Convent Road
Bangkok 10120, Thailand
Tel: [66] (2) 235-6367, 234-0935

Turkey
Embassy
Iran Caddesi 45/2
Cankaya
06700 Ankara, Turkey
Tel: [90] (312) 167-5056/7 Fax: [90] (312) 167-3566

United Kingdom
Embassy
8 Halkin St.
London SW1X 7DW, UK
Tel: [44] (71) 235-6393, 235-6351

United Nations
Permanent Mission
Two United Nations Plaza, 28th Floor
New York, NY 10017, USA
Tel: [1] (212) 752-0220 Fax: [1] (212) 688-8862

United States of America
Embassy
1911 Pennsylvania Ave. NW
Washington, DC 20006, USA
Tel: [1] (202) 728-1600 Fax: [1] (202) 728-1698

Consulates General in the USA:

3220 Peachtree Rd. NE
Atlanta, GA 30305, USA
Tel: [1] (404) 266-2233 Fax: [1] (404) 266-2302

300 N. Michigan Ave., 2nd Fl.
Chicago, IL 60601, USA
Tel: [1] (312) 855-1380
Fax: [1] (312) 855-9257 Tlx: 21019

1349 Empire Central, Suite 100
Dallas, TX 75247, USA
Tel: [1] (214) 630-7341/3
Fax: [1] (214) 630-3511 Tlx: 0791596

707 Washington St., Suite A
Denver, CO 80203, USA
Tel: [1] (303) 830-0601/7 Tlx: 216162

910 E. San Antonio St.
Box 812
El Paso, TX 79901, USA
Tel: [1] (915) 533-3644/5
Fax: [1] (915) 532-7163 Tlx: 0763152

4200 Montrose Blvd., Suite 120
Houston, TX 77006, USA
Tel: [1] (713) 524-2300/3
Fax: [1] (713) 533-5238 Tlx: 762142

125 Paseo de la Plaza
Los Angeles, CA 90012, USA
Tel: [1] (213) 624-3261
Fax: [1] (213) 624-8995 Tlx: 673566

World Trade Center Bldg.
2 Canal St., Suite 840
New Orleans, LA 70130, USA
Tel: [1] (504) 522-3596 Fax: [1] (504) 525-2332

8 E. 41st St.
New York, NY 10017, USA
Tel: [1] (212) 689-0456/9
Fax: [1] (212) 545-8197 Tlx: 147234

127 Navarro St.
San Antonio, TX 78205, USA
Tel: [1] (210) 227-9145/7
Fax: [1] (210) 227-1817 Tlx: 767334

610 A St., Suite 100
San Diego, CA 92101, USA
Tel: [1] (619) 231-8414
Fax: [1] (619) 231-4802 Tlx: 182782

870 Market St., Suite 528
San Francisco, CA 94102, USA
Tel: [1] (312) 392-5554/6
Fax: [1] (312) 392-3233 Tlx: 340613

Consulates in the USA:

Western Bank Bldg.
401 5th St. NW
Albuquerque, NM 87102, USA
Tel: [1] (505) 247-2139
Fax: [1] (505) 842-9240 Tlx: 169031

200 E. Sixth St., Suite 200
Austin, TX 78701, USA
Tel: [1] (512) 478-2866
Fax: [1] (512) 478-8008 Tlx: 763542

20 Park Plaza, Suite 321
Boston, MA 02116, USA
Tel: [1] (617) 426-8782
Fax: [1] (617) 426-4942 Tlx: 200220

724 Elizabeth and Seventh St.
Box 1711
Brownsville, TX 78520, USA
Tel: [1] (210) 541-7061 Tlx: 0361445

331 W. Second St.
Calexico, CA 92231, USA
Tel: [1] (619) 357-3863 Tlx: 9103507447

410 North Tower
800 N. Shoreline
Corpus Christi, TX 78401, USA
Tel: [1] (512) 882-3375 Fax: [1] (512) 882-9324

1010 S. Main St.
Box 1275
Del Rio, TX 78840, USA
Tel: [1] (210) 774-5031 Tlx: 735371

1515 Book Blvd. at W. Grand River
Detroit, MI 48226, USA
Tel: [1] (313) 965-1868/9 Tlx: 211859

140 Adams St.
Box 4230
Eagle Pass, TX 78852, USA
Tel: [1] (210) 773-9255 Fax: [1] (210) 773-9397

905 N. Fulton St.
Fresno, CA 93721, USA
Tel: [1] (209) 233-3065 Tlx: 279389

1612 Farragut St.
Box 659
Laredo, TX 78040, USA
Tel: [1] (210) 723-6360/9
Fax: [1] (210) 723-1741 Tlx: 767035

1418 Beech St., Suite 102-104
Box 603
McAllen, TX 78501, USA
Tel: [1] (210) 686-0243/4 Tlx: 5106003595

All addresses and telephone numbers arc in Mexico unless otherwise noted. The country code for Mexico is [52].

Consulates in the USA (cont.):

780 N. LeJeune Rd., Suite 525
Miami, FL 33145, USA
Tel: [1] (305) 441-8780/3
Fax: [1] (305) 441-7180 Tlx: 264025

511 W. Ohio, Suite 121
Midland, TX 79701, USA
Tel: [1] (915) 687-2334/5 Tlx: 415265

135 Terrace Ave.
Nogales, AZ 85621, USA
Tel: [1] (602) 287-2521 Tlx: 165162

Transportation Center
201 E. Fourth St.
Oxnard, CA 93030, USA
Tel: [1] (805) 483-4684

575 Philadelphia Bourse Bldg.
21 S. Fifth St.
Philadelphia, PA 19106, USA
Tel: [1] (215) 922-4262
Fax: [1] (215) 244407 Tlx: 923-7281

Saguaro Savings Bldg.
700 E. Jefferson, Suite 150
Phoenix, AZ 85034, USA
Tel: [1] (602) 242-7398/9 Tlx: 249977

9812 Old Winery Place, Suite 10
Sacramento, CA 95814, USA
Tel: [1] (916) 363-3885

182 South 600 E., Suite 202
Salt Lake City, UT 84102, USA
Tel: [1] (801) 521-8502/3
Fax: [1] (801) 521-0534 Tlx: 388875

588 W. Sixth St.
San Bernadino, CA 92401, USA
Tel: [1] (714) 889-9836/7 Tlx: 9102502042

380 N. First St., Suite 102
San Jose, CA 95113, USA
Tel: [1] (408) 294-3414/5
Fax: [1] (408) 294-4506 Tlx: 278829

406 W. Fourth St.
Santa Ana, CA 92701, USA
Tel: [1] (714) 835-3069

2132 Third Avenue
Seattle, WA 98121, USA
Tel: [1] (206) 448-3526 Tlx: 27716

1015 Locust St., Suite 922
St. Louis, MO 63101, USA
Tel: [1] (314) 436-3233, 436-3065 Tlx: 209922

Uruguay
Embassy
Andes 1365, Piso 7
Edif. Torre Independencia
Montevideo, Uruguay
Tel: [598] (2) 92-0791, 98-5677

Venezuela
Embassy
Avda. F. Miranda y A. Bello
Edif. Centro Plaza, Torre A, Piso 11
Los Palos Grandes
Caracas, Venezuela
Tel: [58] (2) 283-6622, 283-6843

FOREIGN DIPLOMATIC MISSIONS IN MEXICO

Argentina
Embassy
M. Avila Camacho 1, Piso 7
Col. Lomas de Chapultepec
11000 México, DF
Tel: (5) 540-4867, 520-9431 Tlx: 1774214

Australia
Embassy
Plaza Polanco Torre 8
Jaime Balmes 11, Piso 10
Col. Los Morales
11510 México, DF
Tel: (5) 395-9988, 566-3053
Fax: (5) 395-7153 Tlx: 1773920

Austria
Embassy
Campos Elíseos 305
Col. Polanco
11560 México, DF
Tel: (5) 540-3651, 540-3415
Fax: (5) 262-9284 Tlx: 1774448

Belgium
Embassy
Musset 41
Col. Polanco
11550 México, DF
Tel: (5) 254-3276, 254-3800 Tlx: 1771030

Bolivia
Embassy
Campos Elíseos 169, Piso 3
Col. Polanco
11560 México, DF
Tel: (5) 254-1998

Brazil
Embassy
Lope de Armendáriz 130
Col. Lomas Virreyes
11000 México, DF
Tel: (5) 202-7500, 202-6907
Fax: (5) 520-4929 Tlx: 1771334

Canada
Embassy
Schiller 529
Col. Polanco
11000 México, DF
Tel: (5) 254-3288
Fax: (5) 545-1764/9 Tlx: 1771191

Consulates:

Hotel Fiesta Americana, Local 30
Aurelio Aceves 225
44100 Guadalajara, Jal.
Tel: (3) 625-3434, 615-8665
Fax: (3) 630-3725

German Gedovius 5-201
Condomino del Parque
Desarrollo Urbano Río Tijuana
22320 Tijuana, BC
Tel: (66) 84-0461

China (People's Republic of)
Embassy
Avda. Río Magdalena 172
Col. Tizapán
01090 México, DF
Tel: (5) 250-8577, 548-0898 Tlx: 1773907

Colombia
Embassy
Génova 2-105
Col. Juárez
06600 México, DF
Tel: (5) 528-9290, 207-0930 Tlx: 1772951

Costa Rica
Embassy
Sierra Gorda
Col. Lomas Barrilaco
11010 México, DF
Tel: (5) 520-1718, 525-7764 Tlx: 1763134

Denmark
Embassy
Tres Picos 43, Apdo. 105
Col. Polanco
11560 México, DF
Tel: (5) 545-9504, 255-3405
Fax: (5) 545-5797 Tlx: 1773049

Dominican Republic
Embassy
Avda. Insurgentes Sur 216-301
06170 México, DF
Tel: (5) 533-0215, 520-9692

Ecuador
Embassy
Tennyson 217
Col. Polanco
11550 México, DF
Tel: (5) 545-7041, 545-7944

El Salvador
Embassy
Aristóteles 153
Col. Polanco
11550 México, DF
Tel: (5) 250-1391 Tlx: 1777399

Finland
Embassy
Monte Pelvoux No. 111, Piso 4
Col. Lomas de Chapultepec
11000 México, DF
Tel: (5) 540-6036/7, 533-1360, 202-0495
Fax: (5) 540-0114 Tlx: 1771187

France
Embassy
Havre 15
Col. Juárez
06600 México, DF
Tel: (5) 207-2149, 533-1360, 533-1657
Fax: (5) 514-7311 Tlx: 1771302

Germany
Embassy
Lord Byron 737
Col. Bosque de Chapultepec
11580 México, DF
Tcl: (5) 545-6655
Fax: (5) 255-3180 Tlx: 1773089

Consulates:

Casa Wagner de Guadalajara
Avda. Ramón Corona 202
44100 Guadalajara, Jal.
Tel: (3) 613-9623

Troa Consultores, SC
Calazada del Valle 400, Local 77
Col. del Valle
66220 Monterrey, NL
Tel: (83) 35-1784

Avda. Mérida 221
Col. Hipódromo
22420 Tijuana, BC
Tel: (66) 81-8274

Greece
Embassy
Paseo de las Palmas 2060
Col. Lomas Reforma
11000 México, DF
Tel: (5) 596-6333, 540-7520 Tlx: 1777319

Guatemala
Embassy
Avda. Esplanada 1025
Col. Lomas de Chapultepec
11000 México, DF
Tel: (5) 520-2794, 540-7520, 250-7918

Hungary
Embassy
Paseo de Las Palmas 2005
Col. Lomas Reforma
11020 México, DF
Tel: (5) 596-0523, 531-1050
Fax: (5) 596-2378 Tlx: 1774503

India
Embassy
Musset 325
Col. Polanco
11560 México, DF
Tel: (5) 531-1050, 520-4167
Fax: (5) 254-2349 Tlx: 1775864

Indonesia
Embassy
Julio Verne 27
Col. Polanco
11560 México, DF
Tel: (5) 540-4167, 596-5399 Tlx: 1772712

Israel
Embassy
Sierra Madre 215
Deleg. Miguel Hidalgo
11000 México, DF
Tel: (5) 540-6340, 202-7939, 596-3655
Tlx: 1773094

Italy
Embassy
Paseo de las Palmas 1994
Col. Lomas de Chapultepec
11020 México, DF
Tel: (5) 596-3655, 250-0011 Tlx: 1772717

Japan
Embassy
Paseo de la Reforma 395
Col. Cuauhtémoc
06500 México, DF
Tel: (5) 211-0028, 540-3295
Fax: (5) 207-7743 Tlx: 1772420

Korea (South)
Embassy
Lope de Armendáriz 110
Col. Lomas Virreyes
11000 México, DF
Tel: (5) 596-7131, 254-4398 Tlx: 1773102

Lebanon
Embassy
Julio Verne 8
Col. Polanco
11560 México, DF
Tel: (5) 540-3295, 540-5625 Tlx: 1763169

Netherlands
Embassy
Montes Urales Sur 635, Piso 2
Col. Lomas de Chapultepec
11000 México, DF
Tel: (5) 540-7788, 545-2129
Fax: (5) 202-6148 Tlx: 1774366

New Zealand
Embassy
Homero 229, Piso 8
Col. Chapultepec Morales
11570 México, DF
Tel: (5) 250-5999, 250-5914, 540-7788
Fax: (5) 255-4142 Tlx: 1763154

All addresses and telephone numbers are in Mexico unless otherwise noted. The country code for Mexico is [52].

Nicaragua
Embassy
Ahumada Villagrán 36
Col. Lomas de Chapultepec
11000 México, DF
Tel: (5) 540-5625, 520-2270, 540-3486
Tlx: 1772381

Norway
Embassy
Avda. Virreyes 1460
Col. Lomas de Chapultepec
11000 México, DF
Tel: (5) 540-3486, 540-5220, 250-5999
Fax: (5) 202-3019 Tlx: 1772996

Panama
Embassy
Campos Elíseos 111
Col. Bosque de Chapultepec
11580 México, DF
Tel: (5) 250-4045, 250-4229, 395-3036

Paraguay
Embassy
Avda. Taine 713
Col. Bosque de Chapultepec
11580 México, DF
Tel: (5) 545-8155

Peru
Embassy
Paseo de las Palmas 2030
Col. Lomas Reforma
11020 México, DF
Tel: (5) 596-0521, 550-4700 Tlx: 1773087

Philippines
Embassy
Calderón de la Barca 240
Col. Reforma Polanco
11550 México, DF
Tel: (5) 254-8055, 540-6036
Fax: (5) 545-8631 Tlx: 1772058

Poland
Embassy
Cracovia 40
Col. San Angel
01000 México, DF
Tel: (5) 550-4700, 545-6213
Fax: (5) 548-0532 Tlx: 1773090

Portugal
Embassy
Alejandro Dumas 311
Col. Polanco
11550 México, DF
Tel: (5) 545-6213, 203-0790, 533-0215
Fax: (5) 203-0790 Tlx: 1772533

Russian Federation
Embassy
José Vasoncelos 204
Col. Condesa
06170 México, DF
Tel: (5) 515-6055, 202-9866 Tlx: 1777570

Saudi Arabia
Embassy
Paseo de la Reforma 607
Col. Lomas de Chapultepec
11000 México, DF
Tel: (5) 540-0240, 520-1531 Tlx: 1775714

Spain
Embassy
Parque Vía Reforma 2105
Col. Lomas de Chapultepec
11000 México, DF
Tel: (5) 596-1833, 211-0042
Fax: (5) 596-0646 Tlx: 1776295

Sweden
Embassy
Edif. Plaza Comermex, Piso 6
Blvd. Manuel Avila Camacho 1
Col. Lomas de Chapultepec
11000 México, DF
Tel: (5) 540-6393, 540-4090, 533-0735
Fax: (5) 540-6583 Tlx: 1771115

Switzerland
Embassy
Hamburgo 66, Piso 4
Col. Juárez, Apdo. 1027
06600 México, DF
Tel: (5) 533-0735, 514-1727, 596-1290
Fax: (5) 514-7083 Tlx: 1774396

Thailand
Embassy
Sierra Vertientes 1030
Col. Lomas de Chapultepec
11000 México, DF
Tel: (5) 596-1290, 520-2344
Fax: (5) 596-8236 Tlx: 1772910

Turkey
Embassy
Paseo de las Palmas 1525
Col. Lomas de Barrilaco
11000 México, DF
Tel: (5) 520-2344, 516-6055
Fax: (5) 540-3185 Tlx: 1774495

United Kingdom
Embassy
Río Lerma 71
Col. Cuauhtémoc
06500 México, DF
Tel: (5) 207-2089, 207-2186
Fax: (5) 207-7672 Tlx: 1773093

Consulates:

Río Usumacinta 30
Col. Cuauhtémoc
06500 México, DF
Tel: (5) 596-6333

Hotel Las Brisas
Carretera Escénica, Apdo. 281
Aculpulco, Gro.
Tel: (74) 84-6605
Fax: (74) 84-2269 Tlx: 16837

Calzada González Gallo 1897
Guadalajara, Jal.
Tel: (3) 635-8927, 635-8295
Fax: (3) 639-1616

Calle 58 y 53, No. 450, Apdo. 89
Mérida, Yuc.
Tel: (99) 16-799 Tlx: 753610

Privada de Tamazunchale 104
Col. del Valle
Garza García
Monterrey, NL
Tel: (83) 56-9114 Fax: (83) 35-5438

2 de Enero 102 Sur-A
Tampico, Tamps.
Tel: (12) 12-9784
Fax: (12) 14-1147

Lloyd's Register of Shipping
Emparan 200, P.B.
Apdo. 724
Veracruz, Ver.
Tel: (29) 31-0955 Tlx: 151681

United States of America
Embassy
Paseo de la Reforma 305
06500 México, DF
Tel: (5) 211-0042, 557-2238
Fax: (5) 511-9980 Tlx: 1773091

US Trade Center
Liverpool 31
06600 México, DF
Tel: (5) 591-0155
Fax: (5) 566-1115

Consulates General:

Avenue López Mateos 924N
Cuidad Juárez, Chih.
Tel: (16) 13-4048
Fax: (16) 16-9056 Tlx: 033840

Progreso 175
44100 Guadalajara, Jal.
Tel: (3) 625-2770, 625-2998
Fax: (3) 626-3576, 626-6549 Tlx: 0682860

Avda. Constitución 411 Pte.
64000 Monterrey, NL
Tel: (83) 45-2120, 42-5172
Fax: (83) 45-7748, 45-0177 Tlx: 0382853

Tapachula 96
Tijuana, BC
Tel: (66) 81-7400, 81-7700
Fax: (66) 81-8016 Tlx: 0566836

Consulates:

Monterrey 141
Hermosillo, Son.
Tel: (62) 17-2375
Fax: (62) 17-2578, 17-2758 Tlx: 058829

Avda. Primera No. 2002
Matamoros, Tamps.
Tel: (891) 67-270/2, 25-250
Fax: (891) 38-048 Tlx: 78520-0633

6 Circunvalación 120
Centro
Mazatlán, Sin.
Tel: (69) 85-2205 Fax: (69) 82-1454 Tlx: 066883

Paseo Montejo 453
Mérida, Yuc.
Tel: (99) 25-5011 Fax: (99) 25-6219 Tlx: 0753885

Calle Allende 3330
Col. Jardín
88260 Nuevo Laredo, Tamps.
Tel: (87) 14-0512
Fax: (87) 14-0696 x128 Tlx: 036849

Uruguay
Embassy
Hegel 149, Piso 1
Col. Chapultepec Morales
11570 México, DF
Tel: (5) 531-0880, 254-1163
Fax: (5) 531-4029 Tlx: 1771396

Venezuela
Embassy
Schiller 326
Col. Chaptultepec Morales
11550 México, DF
Tel: (5) 203-4233
Fax: (5) 203-8614 Tlx: 1775813

CANADIAN GOVERNMENT RESOURCES FOR TRADE WITH MEXICO

Info Export
External Affairs and International Trade Canada
125 Sussex Drive
Ottawa, ON K1A 0G2, Canada
Tel: [1] (613) 944-4000 Fax: [1] (613) 996-9709
Provides publications on NAFTA and information on export programs and services.

Divisional Secretary
Foreign Affairs and International Trade Development
Latin America and Carribean Trade Division
125 Sussex Drive
Ottawa, ON K1A OG2, Canada
Tel: [1] (613) 996-5547 Fax: [1] (613) 943-8806
Trade office specializing in Mexico

NAFTA Information Desk
Revenue Canada Customs, Excise and Tax
555 MacKenzie Avenue
Ottawa, ON K1A 0L5, Canada
Tel: [1] (613) 941-0965 Fax: [1] (613) 941-8138

NAFTA Secretariat, Canadian Section
90 Sparks Street, Suite 705
Ottawa, ON K1P 5B4, Canada
Tel: [1] (613) 992-9380 Fax: [1] (613) 992-9392

US GOVERNMENT RESOURCES FOR TRADE WITH MEXICO

Export-Import Bank of the United States (Eximbank)
Loan Office, Mexico
811 Vermont Ave. NW
Washington, DC 20571, USA
Tel: [1] 566-8234

NAFTA Facts Flash Facts System
US Department of Commerce
Tel: [1] (202) 482-4464
Automated system available 24 hours a day; transmits wide range of documents via fax. Available only to fax machines in the US.

NAFTA Help Desk
US Customs Service
1301 Constitution Ave. NW, Room 1325
Washington, DC 20229, USA
Tel: [1] (202) 927-0066 Fax: [1] (202) 927-0097

Overseas Private Investment Corporation (OPIC)
Latin America Office
1100 New York Ave. NW
Washington, DC 20527, USA
Tel: [1] (202) 336-8488

US Department of Agriculture
Mexico Desk
14th St. and Independence Ave. SW
Washington, DC 20250, USA
Tel: [1] (202) 720-1340, 720-8631

US Department of Commerce
Office of Mexico, Room 3022
14th St. and Constitution Ave. NW
Washington, DC 20229, USA
Tel: [1] (202) 482-0300

US Department of the Treasury
Mexico Desk
15th St. and Pennsylvania Ave. NW
Washington, DC 20220, USA
Tel: [1] (202) 622-1270

US Department of Transportation
Mexico Desk
400 7th St. SW
Washington, DC 20590, USA
Tel: [1] (202) 366-2892

All addresses and telephone numbers are in Mexico unless otherwise noted. The country code for Mexico is [52].

TRADE PROMOTION ORGANIZATIONS

WORLD TRADE CENTERS

World Trade Center Guadalajara
Avda. de las Rosas No. 2965
Col. Miraville
Guadalajara, Jal.
Tel: (3) 671-0000 Fax: (3) 671-0017

World Trade Center Mexico City
Montecito 38, Piso 34
Col. Nápoles
México, DF
Tel: (5) 682-9822, 682-9581 Fax: (5) 682-1067

World Trade Center Monterrey
Filadelfia No. 42
Col. Nápoles
México, DF
Tel: (5) 682-9666, 682-5990 Fax: (5) 682-5990
This is an administrative office only; the actual World Trade Center in Monterrey is not yet open.

GENERAL TRADE ORGANIZATIONS

† Membership in these umbrella organizations is mandatory for qualifying businesses.

Asociación Nacional de la Micro, Pequeña y Mediana Industria
National Association of Micro, Small and Medium Industry
Bajío No. 107
Col. Roma Sur
México, DF
Tel: (5) 584-0494, 564-0694 Fax: (5) 564-5398

Asociación Nacional de Importadores y Exportadores de la República Mexicana (ANIERM)†
National Association of Importers and Exporters
Monterrey 130
Col. Roma
México, DF
Tel: (5) 564-9379, 584-9522
Fax: (5) 584-5137 Tlx: 1772443

ANIERM Guadalajara
Avda. de la Paz No. 2530
Sector Juárez
Guadalajara, Jal.
Tel: (3) 615-0295

ANIERM Hermosillo
Avda. Serdán No. 20-1
Edif. Seguros del Pacífico
Hermosillo, Son.
Tel: (62) 13-3839, 14-3671

ANIERM Mérida
Calle 21 No. 151-6
Buenavista
Mérida, Yuc.
Tel: (99) 64-656, 60-589

ANIERM Monterrey
San Patricio No. 102
San Francisco
Garza García, NL
Tel: (83) 38-1010

ANIERM Oaxaca
José M. Bocanegra No. 111
Alemán
Oaxaca, Oax.
Tel: (951) 62-622, 63-738

ANIERM Querétaro
Acueducto No. 113
Caleza
Querétaro, Qro.
Tel: (42) 32-0225

ANIERM San Luis Potosí
Avda. Carranza No. 707-2021
San Luis Potosí, SLP
Tel: (48) 143-363, 146-371

ANIERM Toluca
Avda. Juárez Sur No. 204-305
Toluca, Edo. de Méx.
Tel: (72) 14-6744, 15-9088

ANIERM Veracruz
Constitución No. 288
Veracruz, Ver.
Tel: (29) 34-1641, 34-1574

ANIERM Zacatecas
Tacuba No. 123
Zacatecas, Zac.
Tel: (492) 20-032

Cámara Nacional de Comercio de Guadalajara
National Chamber of Commerce of Guadalajara
Avda. Vallarta No. 4095
Fracc. Camino Real
Guadalajara, Jal.
Tel: (3) 647-1100, 647-3300 Fax: (3) 647-8411

Cámara Nacional de Comercio de la Ciudad de México†
National Chamber of Commerce of Mexico City
Paseo de la Reforma 42, Piso 3
México, DF
Tel: (5) 705-0549, 593-5867
Fax: (5) 592-3402, 664-3039

Cámara Nacional de Comercio de Monterrey
National Chamber of Commerce of Monterrey
Ocampo Pte. No. 250, Piso 1
Edif. de la Instituciones
Monterrey, NL
Tel: (83) 42-2166, 42-2168 Fax: (83) 45-6700

Cámara Nacional de Comercio en Pequeño
Small Business National Chamber
Paseo de la Reforma No. 42
06048 México, DF
Tel: (5) 705-0549, 705-0424 Fax: (5) 592-2677

Cámara Nacional de la Industria de la Transformación (CANACINTRA)†
National Chamber of the Manufacturing Industry
Avda. San Antonio 256
Col. Ampliación Nápoles, Deleg. Benito Juárez
03849 México, DF
Tel: (5) 563-3400, 611-6238 Fax: (5) 598-9467

Comité Empresarial Mexicano para Asuntos Internacionales (CEMAI)
Mexican Business Committee for International Affairs
Homero 527, Piso 7
Col. Polanco
México, DF
Tel: (5) 531-7319, 531-7036

Confederación de Cámaras Industriales de los Estados Unidos Mexicanos (CONCAMIN)†
Confederation of the National Chambers of Industry
Manuel María Contreras 133, Piso 8
México, DF
Tel: (5) 546-9053, 566-7822 Fax: (5) 535-6871

Confederación de Cámaras Nacionales de Comercio
(CONCANACO)†
Confederation of National Chambers of Commerce
Balderas No. 144, Piso 3
Col. Centro
06078 México, DF
Tel: (5) 709-1146, 709-1132/8
Fax: (5) 709-1152 Tlx: 1777318

Confederación Patronal de la República Mexicana
(COPARMEX)
Employers Confederation of Mexico
Insurgentes Sur 950
Col. del Valle
México, DF
Tel: (5) 687-2821, 687-6493 Fax: (5) 536-2160

Consejo Coordinador Empresarial (CCE)†
Businessmen's Coordinating Council
Homero 527, Piso 6
Col. Polanco
México, DF
Tel: (5) 531-7636, 531-1146 Fax: (5) 250-6996

Consejo Nacional de Comercio Exterior (CONACEX)
National Council of Foreign Trade
Tlaxcala 177, Desp. 803
Col. Hipódromo Condesa
México, DF
Tel: (5) 286-8744, 286-8798 Fax: (5) 211-8465

CONACEX Chihuahua
National Council of Foreign Trade
Altamirano No. 2306
Alta Vista
Chihuahua, Chih.
Tel: (14) 13-9098 Fax: (14) 13-3130 Tlx: 349892

CONACEX Jalisco
National Council of Foreign Trade
Calz. Lázaro Cárdenas No. 3294, Piso 2
Chapalita
Guadalajara, Jal.
Tel: (3) 622-1090/1 Fax: (3) 622-0460 Tlx: 682050

CONACEX Nuevo Laredo
National Council of Foreign Trade
Ocampo No. 250-702 Pte., Piso 7
Edif. de Instituciones
Centro
Monterrey, NL
Tel: (83) 42-8010, 42-2143 Fax: (83) 42-8207

CONACEX Puebla
National Council of Foreign Trade
24B Poniente No. 3122-1
Fracc. Valle Dorado
Puebla, Pue.
Tel: (22) 48-9191 Fax: (22) 49-9155

Institute for International Research
Shakespeare 15, Piso 6
Col. Anzures
México, DF
Tel: (5) 211-1194, 211-0837 Fax: (5) 211-1568

Mexican Investment Board (MIB)
Paseo de la Reforma 915
Lomas de Chapultepec
México, DF
Tel: (5) 328-9929, 202-7804
Fax: (5) 328-9930, 202-7925
*Offers an automated fax information line in the USA.
Call [1] (602) 930-4802 on your fax machine, or [1]
(602) 569-1125 for assistance.*

World Trade Information Center
Lope de Vega No. 316
Col. Polanco
México, DF
Tel: (5) 254-4900, 250-3014 Fax: (5) 203-5292

LOCAL CHAMBERS OF COMMERCE

Ciudad Juárez Chamber of Commerce
Abraham González y Pino Suárez #311
32000 Cuidad Juárez, Chih.
Tel: (16) 14-1904 Fax: (16) 14-9887

Ciudad Victoria Chamber of Commerce
Juárez 14 y 15 N. 324
87000 Ciudad Victoria, Tamps.
Tel: (131) 20-031, 25-131 Fax: (131) 23-747

Cuernavaca Chamber of Commerce
Morelos Sur 609
62050 Cuernavaca, Mor.
Tel: (73) 12-0031, 18-5701 Fax: (73) 18-5005

Guadalajara Chamber of Commerce
Avda. Vallarta No. 4095
44490 Guadalajara, Jal.
Tel: (3) 647-8331, 647-8081 Fax: (3) 647-9131

Hermosillo Chamber of Commerce
Gastón Madrid 31
83000 Hermosillo, Son.
Tel: (62) 17-3673 Fax: (62) 17-3708

León Chamber of Commerce
Edif. Ciel, Piso 3
Blvd. López Mateos y Iguel
37000 León, Gto.
Tel: (417) 42-800, 32-728, 41-467
Fax: (417) 40-397

Mexicali Chamber of Commerce
Calle del Comercio No. 254
21100 Mexicali, BC
Tel: (65) 53-4660 Fax: (65) 54-0372

México, Distrito Federal Chamber of Commerce
Paseo de la Reforma No. 42
06048 México, DF
Tel: (5) 592-2677 Fax: (5) 592-3403

Monterrey Chamber of Commerce
Ocampo Pte. 250-1P
Edif. de Las Instituciones
64000 Monterrey, NL
Tel: (83) 42-2166, 44-3769, 44-0333
Fax: (83) 45-6700

Puebla Chamber of Commerce
Diag. Def. de la Rep. y Avda. Reforma, Piso 7
72160 Puebla, Pue.
Tel: (22) 48-6435, 48-0998 Fax: (22) 48-3723

San Luis Potosí Chamber of Commerce
Avda. Venustiano Carranza No. 1325
78250 San Luis Potosí, SLP
Tel: (481) 34-966, 34-968 Fax: (481) 34-228

Tijuana Chamber of Commerce
Javier Urrutia entre Villa Juventud y Paseo Tijuana
20200 Tijuana, BC
Tel: (66) 82-8488 Fax: (66) 82-8486

Tlaxcala Chamber of Commerce
Calle Uno Lado Sur
Central Camionera
90000 Tlaxcala, Tlax.
Tel: (246) 21-234, 22-226 Fax: (246) 24-860

FOREIGN CHAMBERS OF COMMERCE
AND BUSINESS ASSOCIATIONS

American Chamber of Commerce of Mexico
Avda. 16 de Septiembre 730-1209
Guadalajara, Jal.
Tel: (3) 614-6300, 614-8068 Tlx: 0684241

American Chamber of Commerce of Mexico
Lucerna 78-4
Col. Juárez, Deleg. Cuauhtémoc
06600 México, DF
Tel: (5) 705-0995, 724-3800, 703-3908
Fax: (5) 703-2911 Tlx: 1777609
US mailing address: PO Box 60326, Apdo. 113, Houston, TX 77205-1794, USA

American Chamber of Commerce of Mexico
Picachos 760, Desp. 4 y 6
Col. Obispado
64060 Monterrey, NL
Tel: (83) 48-7141, 48-4749
Fax: (83) 48-5574 Tlx: 383087

Belgian-Luxembourgese-Mexican Chamber
Avda. de los Andes No. 115
Lomas de Chapultepec
11000 México, DF
Tel: (5) 202-5345 Fax: (5) 202-5417 Tlx: 1774382

British Chamber of Commerce
Río de la Plata 30
06500 México, DF
Tel: (5) 286-2526, 286-2705, 533-2453

Canadian-Latin American Association
Paseo de la Reforma 107, Piso 14
06430 México, DF
Tel: (5) 705-2948

Franco-Mexican Chamber of Commerce
and Industry
Río Nilo 80, Piso 6
06500 México, DF
Tel: (5) 511-9963

Italian Chamber of Commerce
Garibaldi No. 1849
44260 Guadalajara, Jal.
Tel: (3) 652-0716

Italian Chamber of Commerce
Marsella No. 39, Piso 1
Col. Juárez
06600 México, DF
Tel: (5) 511-5257, 511-5286 Fax: (5) 207-5637

Italian Chamber of Commerce
Dr. Coss Sur No. 465
64000 Monterrey, NL
Tel: (83) 44-3250

Japanese Chamber of Commerce and Industry
Sevilla No. 9, Piso 2
Col. Juárez
06600 México, DF
Tel: (5) 207-5110 Fax: (5) 207-7116

Mexican-German Chamber of Commerce
and Industry
Apdo. 1-107
44100 Guadalajara, Jal.
Tel: (3) 613-1414, 613-9623 Fax: (3) 613-2609

Mexican-German Chamber of Commerce and Industry
Bosque de Ciruelos 130 PH
México, DF
Tel: (5) 251-4501, 251-4022

Mexican-Japanese Association
Fujiyama 144
01710 México, DF
Tel: (5) 593-1333, 664-1500

Mexico-Argentina Chamber of Commerce
Temistocles 103
11550 México, DF
Tel: (5) 203-4192

Scandinavian Association of Mexico
Presa Salinillas 178
México, DF
Tel: (5) 557-1625

Spanish Chamber of Commerce
Homero 1430
11510 México, DF
Tel: (5) 395-7066

United States-Mexico Chamber of Commerce
Mexico City Office
Homero 527, Piso 7
11570 México, DF
Tel: (5) 250-7033 Fax: (5) 531-1590

United States-Mexico Chamber of Commerce
National Office (US)
1730 Rhode Island Ave. NW, Suite 1112
Washington, DC 20036, USA
Tel: [1] (202) 296-5198 Fax: [1] (202) 728-0768

United States-Mexico Chamber of Commerce
Southwest Chapter (US)
3000 Carlisle St., Suite 210
Dallas, TX 75204, USA
Tel: [1] (214) 754-8060 Fax: [1] (214) 871-9533

United States-Mexico Chamber of Commerce
Rocky Mountain Chapter (US)
720 Kipling, Suite 201
Lakewood, CO 80215, USA
Tel: [1] (303) 237-7080 Fax: [1] (303) 237-5568

United States-Mexico Chamber of Commerce
Pacific Chapter (US)
555 S. Flower St., 25th Fl.
Los Angeles, CA 90071-2236, USA
Tel: [1] (213) 623-7725 Fax: [1] (213) 623-0032

United States-Mexico Chamber of Commerce
Northeast Chapter (US)
400 East 59th St., Suite 8B
New York, NY 10022, USA
Tel: [1] (212) 750-2638 Fax: [1] (212) 750-2149

United States-Mexico Chamber of Commerce
Mid-America Chapter (US)
150 N. Michigan Ave.
Chicago, IL 60601, USA
Tel: [1] (312) 236-8745 Fax: [1] (312) 781-5925

TRADE COMMISSION OF MEXICO OVERSEAS OFFICES

Argentina
Esmeralda 715, Piso 4B
1007 Buenos Aires, Argentina
Tel: [54] (1) 394-3602, 394-3571
Fax: [54] (1) 322-5619 Tlx: 24428

Brazil
Rua Paes de Arajuo 29
Conj. 94, 95 y 96
ITAIM-BIBI
04531 Sao Paulo, SP, Brazil
Tel: [55] (11) 820-7672, 820-9870
Fax: [55] (11) 820-7717 Tlx: 1130980

Canada
1501 McGill College, Suite 1540
Montreal, PQ H3A 3M8, Canada
Tel: [1] (514) 287-1669 Fax: [1] (514) 287-1844

66 Wellington St. West, Suite 2712
Toronto-Dominion Bank Tower
Toronto, ON M5K 1A1, Canada
Tel: [1] (416) 867-9292 Fax: [1] (416) 867-1847

Granville St. 1356-200
Vancouver, BC V6C 1S4, Canada
Tel: [1] (604) 682-3648 Fax: [1] (604) 682-1355

Chile
San Sebastián 2807, Piso 4
413-414 Comuna de los Condes
Santiago, Chile
Tel: [56] (2) 233-5600, 233-5472 Fax: [56] (2) 231-6302

Colombia
Calle 100 8A-55
World Trade Center
Bogotá, Colombia
Tel: [57] (1) 226-8033, 219-1448
Fax: [57] (1) 610-5303 Tlx: 413125

Costa Rica
San José, Barrio de las Yoses
de la 3a. Entrada 310 mts. Sur
San José, Costa Rica
Tel: [506] 34-2466, 34-9637
Fax: [506] 34-9613 Tlx: 2489

France
4 rue Notre Dame Des Victoires
75002 Paris, France
Tel: [33] (1) 40-20-07-31, 42-61-51-80
Fax: [33] (1) 42-61-52-95

Germany
Adenauerallee 100
D-5300 Bonn 1, Germany
Tel: [49] (228) 22-3021
Fax: [49] (228) 26-1004 Tlx: 885286

Guatemala
Edificio Géminis 10
12 Calle 1-25, Zona 10
Piso 11 (1111-1112)
01010 Guatemala, C.A., Guatemala
Tel: [502] (2) 35-3031, 35-3205
Fax: [502] (2) 35-2724

Hong Kong
St. 1809, World Wide House
19 Des Voeux Road Central
Hong Kong
Tel: [852] 877-3434 Fax: [852] 877-6607

Italy
Foro Buonaparte 12
20121 Milan, Italy
Tel: [39] (2) 7200-4840 Fax: [39] (2) 7200-4000

Japan
2-15-2 Nagata-cho
Chiyoda-ku
Tokyo 100, Japan
Tel: [81] (3) 3580-0811/2
Fax: [81] (3) 3580-9204 Tlx: 28476

Korea
KCCI Bldg., 642-6F1
45, 4-ka, Namdaemun-ro
Chung-ku
Seoul, Rep. of Korea
Tel: [82] (2) 775-5613 Fax: [82] (2) 775-5615 Tlx: 23553

Netherlands
Rotterdam Building
45 Aert Van Neestraat, 10th Fl.
3012 Ca Rotterdam, Netherlands
Tel: [31] (10) 213-0992, 213-0995
Fax: [31] (10) 213-0997

Spain
Basílica 19, Piso 6
28020 Madrid, Spain
Tel: [34] (1) 597-4767, 597-3033, 597-4033
Fax: [34] (1) 597-0039 Tlx: 23863

Taiwan
International Trade Bldg., Suite 2602
333 Keelung Road, Sec. 1
Taipei, Taiwan
Tel: [886] (2) 757-6526/8 Fax: [886] (2) 757-6180

United Kingdom
60/61 Trafalgar Square, 2nd Fl.
London WC2N 5DS, UK
Tel: [44] (71) 839-6586/7, 839-7860
Fax: [44] (71) 839-4425

United States of America
Cain Tower
229 Peachtree St. NE, Suite 917
Atlanta, GA 30303, USA
Tel: [1] (404) 522-5373/4 Fax: [1] (404) 681-3361

225 N. Michigan Ave., Suite 708
Chicago, IL 60601, USA
Tel: [1] (312) 856-0316/9 Fax: [1] (312) 856-1834

2777 Stemmons Freeway, Suite 1622
Dallas, TX 75207, USA
Tel: [1] (214) 688-4096/7, 637-0233
Fax: [1] (214) 905-3831

350 South Figueroa St.
World Trade Center, Suite 296
Los Angeles, CA 90071, USA
Tel: [1] (213) 628-1220 Fax: [1] (213) 628-8466

New World Tower
100 N. Biscayne Blvd., Suite 1601
Miami, FL 33132, USA
Tel: [1] (305) 372-9929 Fax: [1] (305) 374-1238

150 East 58th St., 17th Fl.
New York, NY 10155, USA
Tel: [1] (212) 826-2916/9, 826-2921
Fax: [1] (212) 826-2979

1100 NW Loop 410, Suite 409
San Antonio, TX 78213, USA
Tel: [1] (512) 525-9748 Fax: [1] (512) 525-8355

INDUSTRY-SPECIFIC TRADE AND PROFESSIONAL ORGANIZATIONS

*Note: English translations are not necessarily exact, and are ordered to create a keyword first method of alphabetization. Some organizations have offices in several states, although only the Mexico City office may be listed here. Membership in organizations marked †
is mandatory.*

Advertising Agency Association
Asociación Mexicana de Agencias de Publicidad†
Plaza Carlos J. Finlay 6, Piso 4
06500 México, DF
Tel: (5) 535-0439 Fax: (5) 592-7139

Air Transport National Chamber
Cámara Nacional del Aerotransporte†
Paseo de la Reforma No. 76, Piso 17
Col. Juárez
06600 México, DF
Tel: (5) 592-4472, 535-1458 Fax: (5) 535-1458

Aluminum Institute
Instituto del Aluminio†
Francisco Petrarca 133, Piso 9
11560 México, DF
Tel: (5) 531-2614, 531-1892

Automatic Meter and Control Equipment
Manufacturers Association
Asociación Mexicana de Fabricantes de Equipo de
Medición y Control Automático (AMFEMCA)
San Antonio No. 256, Piso 4
Col. Amp. Nápoles
03849 México, DF
Tel: (5) 563-3400, 663-0511 Fax: (5) 598-6666

Automobile Repair and Reconstruction Association
Asociación de Rectificadores y Reconstructores
Automotrices (ARRA)
J. Hernández y Davalos No. 7
Algarin
06880 México, DF
Tel: (5) 519-6448, 519-4892

Automobile Repair Shops Association
Asociación de Talleres Automotrices (ATA)
Avda. Oaxaca No. 23, Piso 2
Col. Roma
06700 México, DF
Tel: (5) 514-9127

Automotive Industry Association
Asociación Mexicana de la Industria Automotriz
Ensenada No. 90
Col. Condesa
06100 México, DF
Tel: (5) 515-2542, 272-1144 Fax: (5) 272-7139

Auto Parts Industry National Association
Asociación de la Industria Nacional de Autopartes
Sor Juana Inés de la Cruz No. 344
Col. Centro
04030 Tlalnepantla, Edo. de Méx.
Tel: (5) 390-5619, 390-5331 Fax: (5) 390-7303

Auto Parts Wholesalers National Association
Asociación Nacional de Mayoristas de Partes
para Automóviles
Dr. Lucio No. 127-202
Col. Doctores
06720 México, DF
Tel: (5) 578-3527, 578-8841 Fax: (5) 578-8841

Bakery Industry National Chamber
Cámara Nacional de la Industria Panificadora†
Dr. Liceaga 96
Doctores
06620 México, DF
Tel: (5) 578-9277 Fax: (5) 761-8924

Bank Association
Asociación Mexicana de Bancos†
Torre Latinoamericana
Lázaro Cárdenas 2, Piso 9
06079 México, DF
Tel: (5) 521-4150, 521-4080
Fax: (5) 521-5229 Tlx: 1774510

Battery Manufacturers National Association
Asociación Nacional de Fabricantes
de Acumuladores
Paseo de la Reforma No. 107, Piso 7
Col. Revolución
06030 México, DF
Tel: (5) 535-0553, 535-3685 Fax: (5) 535-7102

Beer Manufacturing National Chamber
Asociación de Fabricantes de la Cerveza†
Avda. Horacio 1556
Col. Chapultepec Moreles
11570 México, DF
Tel: (5) 520-6283 Fax: (5) 202-1124

Beverage and Carbonated Water Producers National
Association
Asociación Nacional de Productores de Refrescos y
Aguas Carbonadas
Moliere No. 39, Piso 3
Col. Polanco
11560 México, DF
Tel: (5) 281-2496 Fax: (5) 280-0652

Bottled Water Producers National Chamber
Asociación Nacional de Productores de Aguas
Envasades
Paseo de la Reforma 195-301
06500 México, DF
Tel: (5) 566-2244 Fax: (5) 535-0374

Cable Television Industry National Chamber
Cámara Nacional de la Industria de Televisión
por Cable
Monte Albán No. 281
Navarte
03020 México, DF
Tel: (5) 682-0173, 682-0298 Fax: (5) 682-0881

Canned Goods Industry National Chamber
Cámara Nacional de la Industria de
Conservas Alimenticias
Calderón de la Barca 359, Desp. 200
Col. Polanco
11560 México, DF
Tel: (5) 531-5939, 250-0507 Fax: (5) 203-6798

Cardboard Box and Packaging Manufacturers National
Association
Asociación Nacional de Fabricantes de Cajas y
Empaques de Cartón
Paseo de las Palmas No. 765-401
Col. Lomas de Chapultepec
11000 México, DF
Tel: (5) 520-0835, 540-2724

Cement National Chamber
Cámara Nacional del Cemento†
Leibnitz No. 77, Piso 1
Col. Anzures
11590 México, DF
Tel: (5) 533-2400, 533-0134 Fax: (5) 203-4102

Chemical and Pharmaceutical Industry National
Chamber
Cámara Nacional de la Industria Química y
Farmacéutica†
Avda. Cuauhtémoc No. 1481
Santa Cruz Atoyac
03310 México, DF
Tel: (5) 688-9477, 688-9817 Fax: (5) 604-9808

Chemical Industry National Association
Asociación Nacional de la Industria Química
Avda. Providencia 1118
Col. del Valle
03100 México, DF
Tel: (5) 559-7833, 559-1979 Fax: (5) 575-5589

Chocolate and Candy Manufacturers National
Association
Asociación Nacional de Fabricantes de Chocolate,
Dulces y Similares
Manuel María Contreras No. 133-301
Col. Cuauhtémoc
06500 México, DF
Tel: (5) 546-1259, 546-0974 Fax: (5) 546-0974

Cinematic Industry National Chamber
Cámara Nacional de la Industria Cinematográfica†
General Anaya 198
04210 México, DF
Tel: (5) 688-0442

Coconut Product Manufacturers National
Confederation
Confederación Nacional de Productores de Coco y Sus
Derivados
Paseo de la Reforma No. 122-F, Piso 4
Col. Juárez
06600 México, DF
Tel: (5) 546-4831/2 Fax: (5) 546-4830

Coffee Exporters Association
Asociación Mexicana de Exportadores de Café
Avda. Insurgentes Sur No. 682, Piso 8
Col. del Valle
03100 México, DF
Tel: (5) 536-7767/8

Coffee Industry National Chamber
Asociación Nacional de la Industria del Café
Avda. Insurgentes Sur 682
03100 México, DF
Tel: (5) 536-7767 Fax: (5) 536-7768

Communications and Transportation National
Chamber
Cámara Nacional de Transportes
y Comunicaciones†
Pachuca 158 Bis
06140 México, DF
Tel: (5) 288-1651, 286-4512

Construction Industry National Chamber
Cámara Nacional de la Industria
de la Construcción†
Periférico Sur 4839
Col. del Pedregal
14010 México, DF
Tel: (5) 665-2167, 665-1500, 665-2167
Fax: (5) 606-6720, 606-8329

Consulting Firms National Chamber
Cámara Nacional de Empresas de Consultoria
Miguel Laurent 70, Pisos 3 y 4
Col. del Valle
03100 México, DF
Tel: (5) 559-4914, 559-9888

Copper Association
Asociación Mexicana del Cobre
Avda. Sonora No. 166, Piso 1
Col. Hipódromo Condesa
06100 México, DF
Tel: (5) 207-2254, 533-4441
Fax: (5) 286-7723 Tlx: 1771673

Corn Industry National Chamber
Cámara Nacional de Maíz Industrializado
Varsovia No. 44-504
Col. Juárez
06600 México, DF
Tel: (5) 525-3000, 514-1220

Cotton Growers Associations Confederation
Confederación de Asociaciones Algodoneras
Calle de López No. 15-301 y 302
Col. Centro
06050 México, DF
Tel: (5) 518-6189, 518-6756 Fax: (5) 518-6756

Customs Brokers Association
Asociación de Agentes Aduanales
Xola 1707-A
México, DF
Tel: (5) 530-6804

Customs Brokers Association Confederation
Confederación de Asoc. de Agentes Aduanales
de la República de México
Hamburgo No. 225
Juárez
06600 México, DF
Tel: (5) 533-0075/7 Fax: (5) 525-8070

Detergent Manufacturers Association
Asociación de Fabricantes de Detergentes de la
República Mexicana
Melchor Ocampo 193, Torre A, Piso 8
11300 México, DF
Tel: (5) 203-1567 Fax: (5) 254-0325

Electric Manufacturers National Chamber
Cámara Nacional de las Manufacturas Eléctricas
(CANAME)†
Ibsen No. 13
Col. Chapultepec Polanco
11560 México, DF
Tel: (5) 202-1440 Fax: (5) 202-2020

Electronics and Communications Industry National
Chamber
Cámara Nacional de la Industria Electronica y de
Comunicaciones Eléctricas†
Guanajuato No. 65
Col. Roma
06700 México, DF
Tel: (5) 574-7411, 574-7700 Fax: (5) 584-5083

Fair, Exposition and Conference Professionals
Association
Asociación Mexicana de Profesionales en Ferias,
Exposiciones y Convenciones
Atenas 21, Desp. 302
Col. Juárez
06600 México, DF
Tel: (5) 592-5785

Fishing Industry National Chamber
Cámara Nacional de la Industria de la Pesca†
Manuel María Contreras No. 133
Col. Cuauhtémoc
06500 México, DF
Tel: (5) 566-9411 Fax: (5) 546-0828

Floriculturist and Nursery National Confederation
Confederación Nacional de Floricultores
y Viveristas
Dr. Vértiz No. 652
Navarte
03020 México, DF
Tel: (5) 530-3929, 519-0796

Food and Restaurant Industry National Chamber
Cámara Nacional de la Industria de Restaurantes
y Alimentos Condimentados (CANIRAC)
Aniceto Ortega 1009
Col. del Valle
03100 México, DF
Tel: (5) 604-0418 Fax: (5) 604-4086

Food Processors Industry of Jalisco Chamber
Cámara de la Industria Alimenticia de Jalisco
Washington No. 1920, Pisos 1 y 2
Moderna
44100 Guadalajara, Jal.
Tel: (3) 610-4177, 612-4065 Fax: (3) 610-4179

Forest Industry National Chamber
Cámara Nacional de la Industria Forestal
Viaducto Miguel Alemán No. 277
Col. Escandón
11800 México, DF
Tel: (5) 516-2545/7 Fax: (5) 273-0933

Forest Products and Derivatives Industries National
Chamber
Cámara Nacional de las Industrias
de la Silvicultura†
Baja California 225
Edif. "A", Piso 12
06170 México, DF
Tel: (5) 584-4044 Fax: (5) 574-5936

Freight Transportation National Chamber
Cámara Nacional de Autotransportes de Carga
Pachuca No. 158 bis
06140 México, DF
Tel: (5) 553-9809, 553-2682 Fax: (5) 211-5568

Furniture Makers of Jalisco Association
Asociación de Fabricantes de Muebles de Jalisco
Avda. Niños Héroes No. 2663
Jardines del Bosque
44520 Guadalajara, Jal.
Tel: (3) 622-7178, 621-5035 Fax: (3) 622-7103

Garment Industry National Chamber
Cámara Nacional de la Industria del Vestido†
Tolsá 54
Col. Centro
06040 México, DF
Tel: (5) 588-7822, 588-7664
Fax: (5) 578-6210 Tlx: 1762407

Gas Distributors Association
Asociación Mexicana de Distribuidores de Gas
Licuado y Empresas Conexas
Filadelfia No. 119, Piso 1
Col. Nápoles
México, DF
Tel: (5) 543-7575, 543-6591

General Counsel National Association
Asociación Nacional de Abogados de Empresas
Torcuato Tasso No. 325, Mezzanine
Col. Chapultepec Morales
11570 México, DF
Tel: (5) 250-6780, 531-4101 Fax: (5) 531-4101

Gift, Decoration, and Craft Manufactures Association
of Mexico
Asociación Mexicana de Fabricantes de Artículos para
Regalo, Decoración y Artesanías
Monterrey No. 149
Col. Roma
06700 México, DF
Tel: (5) 564-8961, 564-3668 Fax: (5) 574-9709

Grape Growers and Wine Producers National
Association
Asociación Nacional de Vitivinicultores
Calz. de Tlalpan 3515
04650 México, DF
Tel: (5) 573-6215, 573-8748

Graphic Arts Industry National Chamber
Cámara Nacional de la Industria de Artes Gráficas†
Avda. Río Churubusco 428, Piso 2
Col. del Carmen Coyoacán
04100 México, DF
Tel: (5) 554-0255, 554-3500 Fax: (5) 554-3545

Guarantee Companies of Mexico Association
Asociación de Compañías Afianzadoras de México
(ACAM)
Adolfo Prieto No. 1012, Piso 4
Col. del Valle
03100 México, DF
Tel: (5) 523-6855, 523-6835 Fax: (5) 523-8939

Hospital National Chamber
Cámara Nacional de Hospitales†
Vito Alessio Robles 23, Piso 6
01030 México, DF
Tel: (5) 548-5430, 548-3003

Hotel and Motel Association
Asociación Mexicana de Hoteles y Moteles
de la República
Hamburgo 108-104
06600 México, DF
Tel: (5) 525-0023 Fax: (5) 523-0303

Hotel Association
Asociación Nacional Hotelera
Edison 84, Piso 2
Col. Tabacalera
México, DF
Tel: (5) 535-9341

Household Appliance Manufacturers National
Association
Asociación Nacional de Fabricantes de
Aparatos Domésticos
Zacatecas 155
Col. Roma
06067 México, DF
Tel: (5) 584-1426, 584-8844

Household Appliance Suppliers National Association
Asociación Nacional de Distribuidores de
Aparatos Domésticos
Zacatecas 155
Col. Roma
06067 México, DF
Tel: (5) 584-1426, 584-8844

Household Electric Appliance Manufacturers National
Association
Asociación Nacional de Fabricantes de
Aparatos Electrodomésticos
Bahía de Ballenas No. 88, Piso 2
Col. Verónica Anzures
11300 México, DF
Tel: (5) 531-2375 Fax: (5) 545-1584

Hygiene and Safety Association
Asociación Mexicana de Higiene y Seguridad
Lirio No. 7
Santa María la Rivera
06400 México, DF
Tel: (5) 547-8587, 547-8608
Fax: (525) 541-1566, 547-8782, 547-0938

Insurance and Guarantee Agents Association
Asociación Mexicana de Agentes de Seguros
y Fianzas
Florencia No. 18, Piso 1
Col. Juárez
06600 México, DF
Tel: (5) 511-3118, 511-5937 Fax: (5) 533-4983

Insurance Institutions Association
Asociación Mexicana de Instituciones de Seguros
Madero 21
01049 México, DF
Tel: (5) 662-0253

International Transport and Commerce Industries
Association
Asociación de Industriales de Transporte y Comercio
Internacional
Presidente Masaryk No. 134-204
Col. Polanco
11560 México, DF
Tel: (5) 254-1863, 250-9842

Iron and Steel Industry National Chamber
Cámara Nacional de la Industria del Hierro
y del Acero†
Amores 338
Col. del Valle
03199 México, DF
Tel: (5) 543-4443/5, 536-1287 Fax: (5) 687-0517

Laundry Industry National Chamber
Cámara Nacional de la Industria de Lavanderías
Río Danubio No. 38
Col. Cuauhtémoc
06500 México, DF
Tel: (5) 511-6978, 511-7442

Lawyers National Association
Asociación Nacional de Abogados de México
Brasil 31
México, DF
Tel: (5) 510-3831

Lumber Industry National Chamber
Cámara Nacional de la Industria Maderera y Similares†
Santander No. 15-301
Insurgentes Mixcoac
03920 México, DF
Tel: (5) 598-6725 Fax: (5) 598-6932

Lumber Manufacturers National Association
Asociación Nacional de Fabricantes de Tableros
de Madera
Acapulco 35-501
06700 México, DF
Tel: (5) 553-4133, 553-4187

Machinery Distributors Association
Asociación Mexicana de Distribuidores de Maquinaria
Tenayuca No. 107
Vértiz Navarte
03900 México, DF
Tel: (5) 604-8807, 604-8654
Fax: (5) 604-6328, 605-2877

Maritime Agents National Association
Asociación Nacional de Agentes Navieros
Homero No. 1425-302
Col. Los Morales
11510 México, DF
Tel: (5) 395-8931, 395-8079
Fax: (5) 520-7165 Tlx: 1172690

Match Industry National Chamber
Cámara Nacional de la Industria Cerillera
Viena 36, Piso 5
Col. Juárez
06600 México, DF
Tel: (5) 535-8877, 535-6106

Medicine Distributors National Association
Asociación Nacional de Distribuidores
de Medicinas
Tuxpan No. 39-104
Col. Roma
06700 México, DF
Tel: (5) 584-0088 Fax: (5) 264-0408

Milk Products Industry National Chamber
Cámara Nacional de Industriales de la Leche†
B. Franklin 134
Col. Escandón
11800 México, DF
Tel: (5) 271-3848 Fax: (5) 271-3798

Mining Chamber of Mexico
Cámara Minera de México†
Sierra Vertientes 369
Col. Lomas de Chapultepec
11000 México, DF
Tel: (5) 540-6788/9 Fax: (5) 540-6061

Mining Engineers, Metallurgists and Geologists
Association
Asociación de Ingenieros de Minas, Metalurgistas y
Geólogos de México
Tacuba 5-19B
Apdo. 1260
06000 México, DF
Tel: (5) 521-3982

Naval Industry National Chamber
Cámara Nacional de la Industria Naval
Acapulco No. 35-702
06700 México, DF
Tel: (5) 211-5506 Fax: (5) 286-7664

Oil, Grease and Soap Industry National Chamber
Cámara Nacional de la Industria de Aceites, Grasa y
Jabones†
Mechor Ocampo 193
Torre A, Nivel 8
Col. Verónica Anzures
11300 México, DF
Tel: (5) 203-1640 Fax: (5) 254-0325

Oils and Foodstuffs Industries National Association
Asociación Nacional de Industriales de Aceites
y Comestibles
Praga No. 39, 3er Piso 1
Col. Juárez
06600 México, DF
Tel: (5) 533-2859, 533-2847
Fax: (5) 525-5124 Tlx: 1777371

Packing Association
Asociación Mexicana de Envase y Embalaje
Avda. de las Palmas 731-203B
Col. Lomas de Chapultepec
11000 México, DF
Tel: (5) 520-8452, 520-8389

Paint and Ink Manufacturers National Association
Asociación Nacional de Fabricantes de Pinturas
y Tintas
Gabriel Mancera 309
Col. del Valle
03100 México, DF
Tel: (5) 543-6488 Fax: (5) 682-7975

Paper and Cellulose Industries National Chamber
Cámara Nacional de las Industrias de la Celulosa y el
Papel†
Priv. de San Isidro 30
Col. Reforma Social
11650 México, DF
Tel: (5) 202-8603 Fax: (5) 202-1349

Paper Bag Manufacturers National Association
Asociación Nacional de Fabricantes de Sacos de Papel
Rey Maxtla No. 187
Industrial de San Antonio
02760 México, DF
Tel: (5) 561-3200, 561-1879
Fax: (5) 561-4509

Perfumery and Cosmetics Industry National Chamber
Cámara Nacional de la Industria de Perfumería
y Cosméticos
Gabriel Mancera 1134
Col. del Valle
03100 México, DF
Tel: (5) 575-3108, 559-9018, 575-0507
Fax: (5) 575-2121

Pesticides and Fertilizer Industry Association
Asociación Mexicana de la Industria de Plaguicidas
y Fertilizantes
San Antonio 256-8
03849 México, DF
Tel: (5) 563-3400, 663-0511 Fax: (5) 598-6666

Pharmaceutical Association
Asociación Farmacéutica Mexicana
Adolfo Prieto No. 1649-203
Col. del Valle
03100 México, DF
Tel: (5) 524-5685, 524-0993 Fax: (5) 534-5098

Pharmaceutical Manufacturers National Association
Asociación Nacional de Fabricantes
de Medicamentos
Eugenia 13-601
Col. Nápoles
03810 México, DF
Tel: (5) 536-1405 Fax: (5) 536-1406

Physical Fitness Industry National Chamber
Cámara Nacional de la Industria del Embellecimiento
Físico†
Salamanca No. 5
Col. Roma
06700 México, DF
Tel: (5) 533-2707 Fax: (3) 208-7828

Plastic Industries National Association
Asociación Nacional de Industrias del Plástico
Doctor Vértiz 546
Vértiz Navarte
03500 México, DF
Tel: (5) 566-7466, 535-2223 Fax: (5) 566-5017

Plastic Pipes National Institute
Instituto Nacional de Tuberías Plásticas
Alambama No. 35
Col. Nápoles
03810 México, DF
Tel: (5) 687-3702, 669-0510 Fax: (5) 669-0496

Publishing Industry National Chamber
Cámara Nacional de Industria Editorial Mexicana†
Holanda No. 13
04120 México, DF
Tel: (5) 688-2221, 688-2011 Fax: (5) 604-4347

Radio and Television National Chamber
Cámara Nacional de la Industria de Radio y Televisión
Horacio No. 1013
Col. Polanco
11550 México, DF
Tel: (5) 250-2577, 250-2896, 254-1809
Fax: (5) 545-6767, 250-2577

Restaurant Association of Mexico
Asociación Mexicana de Restaurantes
Torcuato Tasso 325-103
11560 México, DF
Tel: (5) 250-1146, 531-3047

Roads Association
Asociación Mexicana de Caminos
Río Tíber 103, Piso 2
06500 México, DF
Tel: (5) 528-6676, 207-4660

Rubber Industry National Chamber
Cámara Nacional de la Industria Hulera†
Manuel María Contreras 133-115
06500 México, DF
Tel: (5) 535-2266, 535-8917

Salt Producers Association
Asociación Mexicana de Productores de Sal
Tacuba No. 37-332
Col. Centro
0600 México, DF
Tel: (5) 518-3653

Shoe Industry National Chamber
Cámara Nacional de la Industria del Calzado†
Durango 245, Piso 12
Col. Roma
06700 México, DF
Tel: (5) 533-6255, 525-4960 Fax: (5) 511-5054

Silver and Jewelry Exporters and Importers
Association
Asociación Nacional de Exportadores e Importadores
de Platería y Joyería
Madero No. 47-702
Col. Centro
06000 México, DF
Tel: (5) 512-2016, 510-3200 Fax: (5) 510-3554

Silver and Jewelry Industry National Chamber
Cámara Nacional de la Industria de la Platería
y la Joyería†
Reynosa 13
Condesa
06100 México, DF
Tel: (5) 516-1771 Fax: (5) 516-8481

Stock Brokers Association
Asociación Mexicana de Casas de Bolsa
Paseo de la Reforma 225, Piso 1
Cuauhtémoc
06500 México, DF
Tel: (5) 531-5272, 545-5728

Sugar and Alcohol Industry National Chamber
Cámara Nacional de la Industria Azucarera
y Alcoholera†
Río Niágara 11
Cuauhtémoc
06500 México, DF
Tel: (5) 533-3040/1 Fax: (5) 511-7803

Swiss Registered Cattle Breeders Association
Asociación Mexicana de Criadores de Ganado Suizo
Andalucía 162
03400 México, DF
Tel: (5) 768-0544

Tannery Industry National Chamber
Cámara Nacional de la Industria de la Curtiduría†
Tehuantepec 255, Piso 1
Col. Roma Sur
06760 México, DF
Tel: (5) 564-6600, 564-4866 Fax: (5) 574-2552/5

Tequila Industry Regional Chamber
Cámara Regional de la Industria Tequilera
Lázaro Cárdenas No. 3289, Piso 5
Chapalita
45000 Guadalajara, Jal.
Tel: (3) 621-5021 Fax: (3) 647-2031

Textile Industry National Chamber
Cámara Nacional de la Industria Textil†
Plionio 20, esq. Horacio
Los Morales Polanco
11560 México, DF
Tel: (5) 202-2567 Fax: (5) 540-1946

Tourist Transportation National Chamber
Cámara Nacional de Autotransporte de Pasaje
y Turismo
Versalles No. 16
Col. Juárez
06600 México, DF
Tel: (5) 566-5421, 566-5414 Fax: (5) 566-5636

Touristic Development Association
Asociación Mexicana de Desarrolladores Turísticos
Río Becerra No. 11
Col. Nápoles
03810 México, DF
Tel: (5) 687-7196, 669-4630 Fax: (5) 687-7196

Travel Agents of Mexico Association
Asociación Mexicana de Agencias de Viajes
Ameyalco No. 10-646
Col. del Valle
03100 México, DF
Tel: (5) 660-4403, 536-7008
Fax: (5) 543-9092 Tlx: 1764103

Tuna Producers National Association
Asociación Nacional de Productores de Atún
Manuel Ma. Contreras No. 133-507
Col. Cuauhtémoc
06500 México, DF
Tel: (5) 566-1066, 546-8750 Fax: (5) 546-8750

Valves Manufacturers National Association
Asociación Mexicana de Fabricantes de Valvulas
Copérnico 47
Col. Anzures
11590 México, DF
Tel: (5) 203-8229 Fax: (5) 203-0290

Zinc and Lead Institute
Instituto Mexicano del Zinc, Plomo y Coproductos†
Sonora 166, Piso 1
06100 México, DF
Tel: (5) 553-4191

FINANCIAL INSTITUTIONS

BANKING

Bank Association

Asociación Mexicana de Bancos
Torre Latinoamericana
Lázaro Cárdenas 2, Piso 9
06079 México, DF
Tel: (5) 521-4150, 521-4080
Fax: (5) 521-5229 Tlx: 1774510

Regulatory Agencies

Banco de México (BANXICO)
Avda. 5 de Mayo 2, Apdo. 98 bis
Col. Centro
06059 México, DF
Tel: (5) 237-2000, 709-0140, 709-0440
Fax: (5) 510-9337, 512-4813 Tlx: 1773050
Central bank; issues currency, controls monetary policy,
including bank reserve requirements and interest rates.

Comisión Nacional Bancaria
República del Salvador 47
Col. Centro
06080 México, DF
Tel: (5) 709-7311 Fax: (5) 709-7327
Controls all credit institutions in Mexico.

Domestic Banks

Banca Confía
Paseo de la Reforma 450, PH
06500 México, DF
Tel: (5) 514-6945, 514-6785
Fax: (5) 208-5821, 208-5881

Banca Cremi
Paseo de la Reforma 93, Piso 9
06030 México, DF
Tel: (5) 703-0333 x4043 Fax: (5) 227-7099

Banca Promex
Avda. La Paz 875
44100 Guadalajara, Jal.
Tel: (3) 613-4916, 679-5000
Fax: (3) 613-0937, 679-5007

Banca Promex
Paseo de la Reforma 199, Piso 1
México, DF
Tel: (5) 592-4007 Fax: (5) 592-1804

Banca Serfin
Padre Mier Oriente 134, Piso 9
Monterrey, NL
Tel: (83) 42-7944, 40-1760 Fax: (83) 43-4844

Banca Serfin
16 de Septiembre 38, Piso 1, esq. Bolívar
06000 México, DF
Tel: (5) 709-7644 Fax: (5) 512-1173

Banco de Cédulas Hipotecarias (BCH)
Paseo de la Reforma 364, Piso 2
06600 México, DF
Tel: (5) 625-6000 Fax: (5) 207-0708

Banco de Crédito y Servico (Bancreser)
Paseo de la Reforma 116, Piso 18
México, DF
Tel: (5) 535-2685, 535-4699 Fax: (5) 703-0605

Banco del Atlántico
Florencia 39, Piso 5
06600 México, DF
Tel: (5) 514-6126, 721-2393 Fax: (5) 533-5211

Banco del Centro (Bancén)
Paseo de la Reforma 195, Piso 1
06500 México, DF
Tel: (5) 566-7259, 703-3455 Fax: (5) 703-3502

Banco de Oriente (Banorie)
Paseo de la Reforma 506, Piso 20
México, DF
Tel: (5) 286-86-25, 286-8176 Fax: (5) 286-8354

Banco de Oriente (Banorie)
Avda. Dos Oriente 10
Puebla, Pue.
Tel: (22) 41-6752, 41-4251 Fax: (22) 42-0413

Banco Internacional S.A.
Paseo de la Reforma 156
06600 México, DF
Tel: (5) 721-2222, 721-2630/2 Fax: (5) 566-2404

Banco Mercantil del Norte (Banorte)
Madero 22, Mezzanine
06000 México, DF
Tel: (5) 510-1877, 512-7440 Fax: (5) 512-3685

Banco Mercantil del Norte (Banorte)
Zaragoza Sur 920
Monterrey, NL
Tel: (83) 40-5670, 45-1030 Fax: (83) 44-8322

Banco Mexicano Somex
Paseo de la Reforma 211
Col. Cuauhtémoc
06500 México, DF
Tel: (5) 591-1611 Fax: (5) 705-1514

Banco Nacional de Comercio Exterior S.N.C.
(Bancomext)
Camino Santa Teresa No. 1679, Piso 12 Ala Norte
Col. Jardines del Pedregal
01900 México, DF
Tel: (5) 652-4022, 227-9000 x3394, 568-2122
Fax: (5) 652-7255, 652-4235

Bancomext Chihuahua
Antonio de Montes No. 1103
San Felipe
31240 Chihuahua, Chih.
Tel: (14) 13-9601, 14-5155, 14-5232, 14-5337
Fax: (14) 13-9522, 13-9878

Bancomext Guadalajara
Miguel Blanco No. 883
Sector Juárez
44100 Guadalajara, Jal.
Tel: (3) 658-0855, 658-0852, 658-1764, 658-0812
Fax: (3) 658-2388, 658-4301 Tlx: 681824

Bancomext Mérida
Paseo de Montejo No. 475-A (37 y 39)
97000 Mérida, Yuc.
Tel: (99) 27-6169, 27-6265, 27-6309, 27-6390
Fax: (99) 27-6955

Bancomext Monterrey
Avda. Lázaro Cárdenas 2499, Pte. Local 1
San Pedro
66260 Garza García, NL
Tel: (83) 63-0594, 63-0741, 63-0485, 63-0300
Fax: (83) 63-0858 Tlx: 382578

Bancomext Puebla
Teziutlán Sur No. 5
La Paz
72160 Puebla, Pue.
Tel: (22) 49-9922, 49-9806, 49-9692, 49-9554
Fax: (22) 49-9526, 49-9327 Tlx: 178334

Bancomext Querétaro
Avda. Pasteur Sur No. 263
Mercurio
76040 Querétaro, Qro.
Tel: (42) 12-6149, 12-1454, 14-4472, 14-4752
Fax: (42) 14-5022 Tlx: 121619

Bancomext Tijuana
Blvd. Gral. Abelardo L. Rdgz. 1405, esq. con Frida
Kahlo
Zona del Río
22320 Tijuana, BC
Tel: (66) 34-2623, 34-2635, 34-2643, 34-2650
Fax: (66) 34-2654

Banco Nacional de México (Banamex)
Isabel la Católica 40
Col. Centro
06089 México, DF
Tel: (5) 225-5178 Fax: (5) 709-9446

Banco Unión
Paseo de la Reforma 364
06694 México, DF
Tel: (5) 625-6000 Fax: (5) 207-0214

Bancomer
Avda. Universidad 1200
Col. Xoco, Deleg. Benito Juárez
03339 México, DF
Tel: (5) 621-5727 Fax: (5) 621-3265

Banoro
Obregón y Angel Flores
Culiacán, Sin.
Tel: (671) 34-062, 38-030 Fax: (671) 53-871

Banoro
Insurgentes Sur 819, Piso 5
03810 México, DF
Tel: (5) 543-2134, 543-3467 Fax: (5) 543-0473

Banpaís
Insurgentes Sur 1443, Piso 1
03900 México, DF
Tel: (5) 563-4438, 563-7459, 598-6649
Fax: (5) 563-3312

Banpaís
Hidalgo 250 Pte.
Monterrey, NL
Tel: (83) 42-8383, 43-6030 Fax: (83) 44-3978

Multibanco Comermex
Plaza Comermex
Blvd. M. Avila Camacho 1-17
11000 México, DF
Tel: (5) 520-5939 Fax: (5) 202-5264

Multibanco Mercantil de México
Montes Urales 620, Piso 3
Lomas de Chapultepec
11000 México, DF
Tel: (5) 596-6805, 520-3643 Fax: (5) 259-1514

Nacional Financiera (Nafin)
Insurgentes Sur No. 1971, Torre IV, Piso 8
Col. Guadalupe Inn
Deleg. Alvaro Obregón
01020 México, DF
Tel: (5) 325-7050, 325-7051 Fax: (5) 325-7249

Foreign Banks

American Express
Campos Elíseos 345, Pisos 9 y 12
Col. Polanco Chapultepec
11560 México, DF
Tel: (5) 596-8133 Fax: (5) 202-0574

Banco Español de Crédito
Eugenio Sue No. 94
Col. Polanco
11560 México, DF
Tel: (5) 545-3926, 281-1825
Fax: (5) 255-1726 Tlx: 1762008

Bankers Trust
Blvd. Manuel Avila Camacho 1
Desp. 806, Piso 8
Col. Chapultepec
01560 México, DF
Tel: (5) 540-4855 Fax: (5) 520-5740

Bank of America
Paseo de la Reforma 116, Piso 12
Col. Juárez
06600 México, DF
Tel: (5) 591-0011 Fax: (5) 546-1525

Bank of Tokyo
Paseo de la Reforma 390
06600 México, DF
Tel: (5) 207-8077

Banque Paribas
Paseo de la Reforma 359, Piso 6
Col. Juárez
06500 México, DF
Tel: (5) 533-4474, 208-3788 Fax: (5) 533-4811

Barclays Bank
Paseo de la Reforma 390-1203
06695 México, DF
Tel: (5) 525-1870 Fax: (5) 533-2363

Chase Manhattan Bank
Hamburgo 213, Piso 7
Col. Juárez
06600 México, DF
Tel: (5) 208-5666 Fax: (5) 208-6566

Chemical Bank
Campos Elíseos No. 345, Piso 11
Col. Polanco
11560 México, DF
Tel: (5) 202-2306 Fax: (5) 202-7422

Citibank
Paseo de la Reforma 390, Piso 18
Col. Juárez
06600 México, DF
Tel: (5) 211-3030 Fax: (5) 208-0250

Commerzbank
Paseo de la Reforma 390-1304
Col. Juárez
06600 México, DF
Tel: (5) 525-0095 Fax: (5) 525-4587 Tlx: 1772334

Credit Lyonnais
Londres 164-166
06600 México, DF
Tel: (5) 207-3220, 207-3296

Credit Suisse
Campos Elíseos 345, Piso 9
11560 México, DF
Tel: (5) 202-3923, 202-4223

Morgan Guaranty Trust Company
Blvd. M. Avila Camacho 1, Desp. 802
11580 México, DF
Tel: (5) 540-6765 Fax: (5) 540-6774

NationsBank International
Paseo de la Reforma 509, Piso 3
México, DF
Tel: (5) 553-3355 Fax: (5) 553-3366

Royal Bank of Canada
Representación en México
Apdo. 6-1020
Hamburgo 172, Piso 5
06600 México, DF
Tel: (5) 533-6958 Fax: (5) 533-6970

INSURANCE

Insurance Associations

Asociación Mexicana de Agentes de Seguros
y Fianzas
Insurance and Guarantee Agents of Mexico
Association
Florencia No. 18, Piso 1
Col. Juárez
06600 México, DF
Tel: (5) 511-3118, 511-5937 Fax: (5) 533-4983

Asociación Mexicana de Instituciones de Seguros
Madero 21
01049 México, DF
Tel: (5) 662-0153

Regulatory Commission

Comisión Nacional de Seguros y Fianzas
Avda. de los Insurgentes Sur 1971
Plaza Inn, Torre 2 N., Piso 2
01020 México, DF

Insurance Companies

Aseguradora Banpaís
Insurgentes Sur 1443, Piso 7
México, DF
Tel: (5) 563-0910, 598-5311

Aseguradora Cuauhtémoc, S.A.
Blvd. Manuel Avila Camacho 164
Col. Chapultepec Morales
11570 México, DF
Tel: (5) 250-9800 Fax: (5) 540-3204 Tlx: 1772617

Aseguradora Hidalgo, S.A.
Avda. Presidente Masaryk 111
Col. Polanco, Deleg. Miguel Hidalgo
11570 México, DF
Tel: (5) 531-2942

Aseguradora Mexicana (Asemex)
Paseo de la Reforma 175
06500 México, DF
Tel: (5) 703-1312 Fax: (5) 705-4418 Tlx: 1775817

La Continental Seguros, S.A.
Torre Latinoamericano, Pisos 10 y 11
Col. Centro
06007 México, DF
Tel: (5) 518-1670 Fax: (5) 510-3259 Tlx: 1771210

La Nacional, Cía. de Seguros, S.A.
Dom. Miguel Angel de Quevedo 915
04339 México, DF
Tel: (5) 549-0772, 549-6039 Tlx: 17760006

Pan Américan de México, Cía. de Seguros, S.A.
Paseo de la Reforma 355
06500 México, DF
Tel: (5) 525-7024, 533-4830

Seguros América Banamex, S.A.
Avda. Revolución 1508
Col. Guadalupe Inn
01020 México, DF
Tel: (5) 660-7033, 664-0055

Seguros Atlántica Multiba, S.A.
Independencia 37, Piso 2
06050 México, DF
Tel: (5) 510-8810 Fax: (5) 512-4091 Tlx: 1771125

Seguros Azteca, S.A.
Avda. 20 de Noviembre 700
Xochimilco
México, DF
Tel: (5) 653-4411, 653-4444

Seguros Constitución
Avda. Revolución 2042
Col. La Otra Banda
01090 México, DF
Tel: (5) 550-7910 Tlx: 1764504

Seguros de México, S.A.
Insurgentes Sur 3500
Col. Peña Pobre
14060 México, DF
Tel: (5) 679-3855, 679-9979 Tlx: 1771936

Seguros la Comercial, S.A.
Insurgentes Sur 3900
Deleg. Tlalpan
14000 México, DF
Tel: (5) 573-1100

Seguros la Provincial, S.A.
Miguel Angel de Quevedo 915
04339 México, DF
Tel: (5) 549-2458 Tlx: 1760006

Seguros la República, S.A.
Paseo de la Reforma 383
Col. Cuauhtémoc
06500 México, DF
Tel: (5) 533-5080, 211-0054
Fax: (5) 533-5721 Tlx: 1772703

Seguros Protección Mutual, S.A.
Constituyentes 357
11830 México, DF
Tel: (5) 277-7100 Tlx: 1761933

Seguros Tepeyac, S.A.
Humboldt 56, esq. Artículo 123
Col. Centro
06040 México, DF
Tel: (5) 325-9595, 521-8684
Fax: (5) 510-1347 Tlx: 1771289

SECURITIES

Stock Exchange Association

Asociación Mexicana de Casas de Bolsa
Mexican Association of Stock Brokerage Houses
Paseo de la Reforma 255, Piso 1
06500 México, DF
Tel: (5) 705-0277 Fax: (5) 703-0417

Asociación Mexicana de Casas de Bolsa
Mexican Association of Stock Brokerage Houses
Calz. del Valle No. 366
Del Valle
66220 Garza García, NL
Tel: (83) 35-4254, 35-1352

Regulatory Commission

Comisión Nacional de Valores
National Securities Commission
Barranca del Muerto 275
Col. San José Insurgentes
03900 México, DF
Tel: (5) 651-0129

Mexican Stock Exchange

Bolsa Mexicana de Valores, S.A. de C.V.
Paseo de la Reforma 255
Col. Cuauhtémoc
06500 México, DF
Tel: (5) 208-3131 Fax: (5) 703-3776, 591-0534
Tlx: 1773032

All addresses and telephone numbers are in Mexico unless otherwise noted. The country code for Mexico is [52].

Stock Brokerage Houses

Abaco Casa de Bolsa, S.A. de C.V.
Londres No. 32, esq. Dinamarca
Col. Juárez
06600 México, DF
Tel: (5) 511-9298

Abaco Casa de Bolsa, S.A. de C.V.
Montes Rocallosos No. 505 Sur
Col. Residencial San Agustín, GG
66260 Monterrey, NL
Tel: (83) 35-2911, 35-3586 Fax: (83) 35-0451

Acciones y Valores de México, S.A. de C.V.
Paseo de la Reforma No. 398
Col. Juárez, Deleg. Cuauhtémoc
06600 México, DF
Tel: (5) 584-2977 Fax: (5) 208-5048, 584-2977 x1552

AFIN, Casa de Bolsa, S.A. de C.V.
Periférico Sur No. 4355
Col. Jardines de la Montaña
01900 México, DF
Tel: (5) 645-0614, 645-6739 Fax: (5) 645-0864

Bursamex, S.A. de C.V.
Fuente de Piramides No. 1, Pisos 6 y 7
Col. Lomas de Tecamachalco
53950 Naucalpan, Edo. de Méx.
Tel: (5) 294-6344, 294-6158 Fax: (5) 203-5287

Casa de Bolsa Arka, S.A. de C.V.
Emilio Castelar No. 75
Col. Chapultepec Polanco
11560 México, DF
Tel: (5) 255-2155, 203-4034 Fax: (5) 203-5287

Casa de Bolsa Bancomer, S.A. de C.V.
Grupo Financiero Bancomer
Hamburgo No. 190
Col. Chapultepec Polanco
11560 México, DF
Tel: (5) 207-0247 Fax: (5) 514-1941

Casa de Bolsa Cremi, S.A. de C.V.
Paseo de la Reforma No. 144, Piso 1
Col. Juárez, Deleg. Cuauhtémoc
06600 México, DF
Tel: (5) 566-6211 Fax: (5) 566-6211 x1525

Casa de Bolsa Inverlat, S.A. de C.V.
Bosques de Ciruelos No. 120
Col. Bosques de la Lomas, Deleg. Miguel Hidalgo
11700 México, DF
Tel: (5) 596-6222, 596-2555 Fax: (5) 596-2555 x1051

Casa de Bolsa México, S.A. de C.V.
Paseo de la Reforma No. 231
Col. Cuauhtémoc
06500 México, DF
Tel: (5) 584-9922 Fax: (5) 511-2746

Casa de Bolsa Prime, S.A. de C.V.
Paseo de la Reforma No. 243
Piso 3, Torre B
Col. Cuauhtémoc
06500 México, DF
Tel: (5) 533-5970 Fax: (5) 207-0181

CBI Casa de Bolsa, S.A. de C.V.
Insurgentes Sur No. 1886
Col. Florida, Deleg. Alvaro Obregón
01030 México, DF
Tel: (5) 575-3133 Fax: (5) 534-9667, 534-8846

Estrategia Bursátil, S.A. de C.V.
Camino al Desierto de los Leones No. 19
Col. Guadalupe Inn, Deleg. A. Obregón
01030 México, DF
Tel: (5) 550-7100 Fax: (5) 550-7100 x4018

Fimsa Casa de Bolsa, S.A. de C.V.
Jaime Balmes No. 11, Edif. B, Piso 6
Col. Polanco, Deleg. Miguel Hidalgo
11510 México, DF
Tel: (5) 395-7333, 395-7605 Fax: (5) 395-7018

Grupo Bursátil Mexicano, S.A. de C.V.
Paseo de la Reforma No. 382-2, esq. Oxford
Col. Cuauhtémoc, Deleg. Cuauhtémoc
06600 México, DF
Tel: (5) 207-0202 Fax: (5) 208-4911

Interacciones Casa de Bolsa, S.A. de C.V.
Paseo de la Reforma No. 383 PB
Col. Cuauhtémoc, Deleg. Cuauhtémoc
06500 México, DF
Tel: (5) 264-1800, 208-0066 Fax: (5) 525-3942

Invermexico, S.A. de C.V.
Blvd. Manuel Avila Camacho No. 170
Col. Lomas San Isidro, Deleg. M. Hidalgo
11620 México, DF
Tel: (5) 570-7000, 570-5022 Fax: (5) 202-1070

Inversora Bursátil, S.A. de C.V.
Paseo de las Palmas No. 736 PB
Col. Lomas de Chapultepec
Deleg. Miguel Hidalgo
11000 México, DF
Tel: (5) 259-1542, 202-1122 Fax: (5) 540-7492

Invex Casa de Bolsa, S.A. de C.V.
Paseo de la Reforma No. 10, Pisos 21 y 22
Col. Centro
06500 México, DF
Tel: (5) 327-3333 Fax: (5) 327-3399

Mexival, S.A. de C.V.
Paseo de la Reforma No. 359, Piso 1
Col. Cuauhtémoc, Deleg. Cuauhtémoc
06560 México, DF
Tel: (5) 208-2044 Fax: (5) 208-5215, 202-2107

Multivalores, S.A. de C.V.
Blas Pascal No. 105, esq. Ejército Nacional
Col. Morales Polanco, Deleg. M. Hidalgo
11510 México, DF
Tel: (5) 557-6255, 557-2833 Fax: (5) 557-6255 x3720

Operadora de Bolsa, S.A. de C.V.
Río Amazonas No. 62
Col. Cuauhtémoc, Deleg. Cuauhtémoc
06500 México, DF
Tel: (5) 592-6988 Fax: (5) 592-6988 x2821

Probursa, S.A. de C.V.
Blvd. Adolfo López Mateos No. 2448
Col. Altavista, Deleg. Alvaro Obregón
01060 México, DF
Tel: (5) 660-1111, 660-1335 Fax: (5) 660-1111 x2235

Valores Bursátiles de México, S.A. de C.V.
Insurgentes Sur No. 670, Piso 6
Col. del Valle, Deleg. Benito Juárez
03100 México, DF
Tel: (5) 536-3060, 687-9011 Fax: (5) 510-8980

Valores Finamex, S.A. de C.V.
Río Amazonas No. 91
Col. Cuauhtémoc, Deleg. Cuauhtémoc
06500 México, DF
Tel: (5) 525-9020, 208-0033 Fax: (5) 208-1756

Value Casa de Bolsa, S.A. de C.V.
Liverpool No. 54, esq. Dinamarca
Col. Juárez, Deleg. Cuauhtémoc
06600 México, DF
Tel: (5) 207-2726, 525-4600 Fax: (5) 207-2726 x3323

Vector Casa de Bolsa, S.A. de C.V.
Avda. Roble No. 565 Ote.
Col. Valle del Campestre
66265 Garza García, NL
Tel: (83) 35-6777, 35-7777 Fax: (83) 35-7897

SERVICES

ACCOUNTING & CONSULTING FIRMS

Coopers & Lybrand México
Avda. Américas 176
Col. Ladrón de Guevara
44600 Guadalajara, Jal.
Tel: (3) 615-3676 Fax: (3) 615-2550

Coopers & Lybrand México
Durango 81
Col. Roma
06700 México, DF
Tel: (5) 229-8100 Fax: (5) 229-8101

Coopers & Lybrand México
Matamoros Pte. 1441
Col. María Luisa
64040 Monterrey, NL
Tel: (83) 44-9047 Fax: (83) 44-1754

Coopers & Lybrand México
Cond. Plaza Agua Caliente
Blvd. Agua Caliente 4558-807
Col. Aviación
22420 Tijuana, BC
Tel: (66) 81-7769, 81-8233 Fax: (66) 81-8040

Galaz, Gómez Morfin, Chavero, Yamazaki
(Deloitte & Touche)
Jaime Balmes No. 11, Edif. B
Col. Polanco
11510 México, DF
Tel: (5) 280-9255 Fax: (5) 280-9422

Galaz, Gómez Morfin, Chavero, Yamazaki
(Deloitte & Touche)
Àvda. López Mateos Sur 2220, Piso 10
Col. Ciudad del Sol
45050 Guadalajara, Jal.
Tel: (3) 682-8068, 622-8271, 622-8284 Fax: (3) 687-8083

Galaz, Gómez Morfin, Chavero, Yamazaki
(Deloitte & Touche)
Vicente Farrara 114
Col. Parque Obispado
64060 Monterrey, NL
Tel: (83) 33-1033, 48-6892 Fax: (83) 33-3972

Galaz, Gómez Morfin, Chavero, Yamazaki
(Deloitte & Touche)
Blvd. Agua Caliente No. 4558
Col. Aviación
22420, Tijuana, BC
Tel: (66) 81-7812 Fax: (66) 81-7813
*US mailing address: 4492 Camino de la Plaza, Suite 373,
San Ysidro, CA 92073, USA*

KMPG Cárdenas Dosal
Prol. Américas No. 1297, Piso 1
Fracc. Country Club
44610 Guadalajara, Jal.
Tel: (3) 642-3142, 642-3246 Fax: (3) 642-1018

KMPG Cárdenas Dosal
Bosque de Duraznos 55, Piso 1
Bosques de las Lomas
11700 México, DF
Tel: (5) 726-4343 Fax: (5) 596-8060

KMPG Cárdenas Dosal
Apartado Postal 904
Col. del Valle
66250 Monterrey, NL

KPMG Cárdenas Dosal
Blvd. Agua Caliente No. 3401-601
22000 Tijuana, BC
Tel: (66) 81-5130/3 Fax: (66) 81-7221

Mancera, SC (Ernst & Young)
Avda. Vallarta 1540, Desp. 108
44140 Guadalajara, Jal.
Tel: (3) 616-8194, 616-5077, 652-1794, 652-1266
Fax: (3) 630-2679

Mancera (Ernst & Young)
Plaza Polanco
Jaime Balmes No. 11, Torre D, Pisos 4, 5 y 6
Col. Los Morales Polanco
11510 México, DF
Tel: (5) 557-5555, 557-9322, 557-9753
Fax: (5) 255-0719, 255-1199, 255-0999

Mancera (Ernst & Young)
José Luis Lagrange 103, Pisos 8, 10 y 11
Col. Los Morales Polanco
11510 México, DF
Tel: (5) 557-9167, 557-9418, 395-8769
Fax: (5) 557-9759, 557-9369

Mancera (Ernst & Young)
Río de la Plata 449 Oriente
Col. del Valle
66220 Garza García, NL
Tel: (83) 35-3560, 35-4515, 35-4635

Mancera (Ernst & Young)
Blvd. Agua Caliente 4558, Desp. 706-708
Plaza Torres
22420 Tijuana, BC
Tel: (66) 81-7844 Fax: (66) 81-7876

Price Waterhouse
Prol. Américas 1592, Piso 4
Col. Country Club
44620 Guadalajara, Jal.
Tel: (3) 640-1080 Fax: (3) 640-0696

Price Waterhouse
Río de la Plata No. 48
Col. Cuauhtémoc
06500 México, DF
Tel: (5) 211-7883
Fax: (5) 286-6248, 256-1133 Tlx: 1772579

Price Waterhouse
Condominio Losoles D-21 y D-16
Avda. Lázaro Cárdenas Pte. 2400
66270 Garza García, NL
Tel: (83) 63-3500 Fax: (83) 63-3483

Price Waterhouse
Plaza Agua Caliente
Blvd. Agua Caliente 4558-505
22420 Tijuana, BC
Tel: (66) 81-7728, 81-7588 Fax: (66) 81-8282

Ruiz, Urquiza y Cía. (Arthur Andersen)
Avda. de la Américas 1685, Piso 10
Torre Inverlat
44638 Guadalajara, Jal.
Tel: (3) 669-0404 Fax: (3) 669-0468/9

Ruiz, Urquiza y Cía. (Arthur Andersen)
Bosque de Duraznos 127
Bosques de las Lomas
11700 México, DF
Tel: (5) 326-8800, 251-9457, 596-4662
Fax: (5) 596-4692, 326-6468

Ruiz, Urquiza y Cía. (Arthur Andersen)
Avda. San Pedro 100 Norte
Col. del Valle
66220 San Pedro Garza García, NL
Tel: (83) 35-8484, 35-8635
Fax: (83) 35-6268, 35-8911

Ruiz, Urquiza y Cía. (Arthur Andersen)
Paseo de los Héroes 9288, Piso 4
Zona Río Tijuana
22320 Tijuana, BC
Tel: (66) 84-3105 Fax: (66) 84-2721

All addresses and telephone numbers are in Mexico unless otherwise noted. The country code for Mexico is [52].

ADVERTISING

Advertising Agency Association

Asociación Mexicana de Agencias de Publicidad
Plaza Carlos J. Finlay 6, Piso 4
06500 México, DF
Tel: (5) 535-0439 Fax: (5) 592-7139

Advertising Agencies

Arellano/BSB Publicidad
Goldsmith No. 225
11550 México, DF
Tel: (5) 250-1000, 255-2424
Fax: (5) 203-1511 Tlx: 1763464

BBDO México, S.A. de C.V.
Bosques de Ciruelos, Piso 5
Bosques de las Lomas
11700 México, DF
Tel: (5) 251-0175 Fax: (5) 596-5957 Tlx: 1773839

BMB Publicidad
Bosque de Duraznos 65-6
Bosques de las Lomas
11700 México, DF
Tel: (5) 596-7979 Fax: (5) 596-8353

Bozell, S.A. de C.V.
Paseo de la Reforma 106
Col. Lomas de Chapultepec
11000 México, DF
Tel: (5) 724-3500 Fax: (5) 202-7260 Tlx: 1761371

FCB México
Presidente Masaryk 61
Col. Polanco
11560 México, DF
Tel: (5) 250-1600 Fax: (5) 250-9510

Grey México
Horacio No. 1844, Pisos 2 y 6, esq. Con Periférico
Col. Polanco Reforma
11550 México, DF
Tel: (5) 202-0108 Fax: (5) 202-2360

Griffin Bacal Publicidad
Reyna No. 6
Col. San Angel
01000 México, DF
Tel: (5) 550-7007, 550-4874, 548-0232
Fax: (5) 550-2539, 550-9958

J. Walter Thompson de México S.A.
Ejército Nacional No. 519
Col. Granada
11520 México, DF
Tel: (5) 531-3400 Fax: (5) 545-4048, 254-3416

JWG Asociados México
Artimio del Valle Arispe 16
Col. de Valle
03100 México, DF
Tel: (5) 682-8889

Lebrija Rubio Publicidad S.A.
Sierra Santa Rosa 99-30
Col. Lomas de Barrilaco
Sec. Vertientes
11010 México, DF
Tel: (5) 259-2323 Fax: (5) 202-4507 Tlx: 1763436

Leo Burnett S.A. de C.V.
Bosque de Duraznos 65-8P
Bosques de las Lomas
11700 México, DF
Tel: (5) 596-6188 Fax: (5) 596-6248 Tlx: 1774278

Lintas México
J.L. Lagrange 103-12
11510 México, DF
Tel: (5) 580-1622 Fax: (5) 395-0766

Marketing Mercadeo International Co., Inc.
Puebla 151
Col. Roma
06700 México, DF
Tel: (5) 208-8068

McCann Universal
Londres 259, esq. Sevilla
Col. Juárez
06600 México, DF
Tel: (5) 511-8767 Fax: (5) 533-0957

McCann-Erickson
Londres 259, esq. Sevilla
Col. Juárez
06600 México, DF
Tel: (5) 207-0600, 533-0320
Fax: (5) 525-3199 Tlx: 1771569

Noble/DMB&B S.A. de C.V.
Avda. Constituyentes 908
11950 México, DF
Tel: (5) 327-2600 Fax: (5) 327-2601

Ogilvy & Mather Direct
Bahía de Santa Barbara 143
Col. Verónica Anzures
11300 México, DF
Tel: (5) 260-4690 Fax: (5) 260-2924 Tlx: 1774285

Panamericana Ogilvy & Mather
Bahía Santa Bárbara 143
Col. Verónica Anzures
11300 México, DF
Tel: (5) 260-3690 Fax: (5) 260-2924 Tlx: 1774285

Poppe Tyson/CPV, S.A. de C.V.
Monte Pelvoux No. 130
Lomas de Chapultepec
11000 México, DF
Tel: (5) 724-3600 Fax: (5) 282-4836

Publicidad Saiffe
Calle Día 2750
Col. Jardines del Bosque
44520 Guadalajara, Jal.
Tel: (3) 621-6502

Saatchi & Saatchi Advertising
Bosque de Ciruelos 194, Piso 3
Col. Bosques de las Lomas
11700 México, DF
Tel: (5) 596-8596, 596-2615 Fax: (5) 596-8450

Scali, McCabe, Sloves de México, S.A. de C.V.
Lafayette 88
Col. Anzures
11590 México, DF
Tel: (5) 628-0201 Fax: (5) 255-3326

Sevicios, S.A.
Ejército Nacional No. 519
Col. Granada
11560 México, DF
Tel: (5) 531-3400 Tlx: 1772681

Wunderman Cato Johnson
Leibnitz No. 13, Piso 4
Col. Polanco
México, DF
Tel: (5) 250-8879, 250-8958 Fax: (5) 250-8838

Young & Rubicam, S.A. de C.V.
Leibnitz No. 13
Col. Anzures
11590 México, DF
Tel: (5) 250-3200 Fax: (5) 250-0862

LEGAL

Legal Association

Asociación Nacional de Abodados de México
Brasil 31
México, DF
Tel: (5) 510-3831

Law Firms

Baker & McKenzie
P.T. de la República 3304, Piso 2
32330 Ciudad Juárez, Chih.
Tel: (16) 29-1300 Fax: (16) 29-1399

Baker & McKenzie
Edificio Losoles B-16
Avda. Lázaro Cárdenas 2400
66220 Garza García, NL
Tel: (83) 63-5023 Fax: (83) 63-5024

Baker & McKenzie
Plaza Comermex, Piso 9
Blvd. M. Avila Camacho No. 1
11000 México, DF
Tel: (5) 557-8844 Fax: (5) 557-8829, 557-8841

Baker & McKenzie
Blvd. Agua Caliente No. 4558-1005
22420 Tijuana, BC
Tel: (66) 81-7740 Fax: (66) 81-7745

Brennan Winum John W.
Placeres No. 1220
Col. Chapalita
Guadalajara, Jal.
Tel: (3) 647-7522 Fax: (3) 647-7523

Bryan González Vargas y González Baz
Paseo Bolívar 421 Centro
31000 Chihuahua, Chih.
Tel: (14) 16-6310 Fax: (14) 16-9900

Bryan González Vargas y González Baz
Avda. 16 de Septiembre 2026 Ote.
32030 Cuidad Juárez, Chih.
Tel: (16) 15-1515 Fax: (16) 14-2910

Bryan González Vargas y González Baz
Calle Azucenas 44
Col. Jardín
87330 Matamoros, Tamps.
Tel: (891) 36-806 Fax: (891) 64-285

Bryan González Vargas y González Baz
Avda. Justo Sierra 377-1
21200 Mexicali, BC
Tel: (65) 68-1318 Fax: (65) 68-1325

Bryan González Vargas y González Baz
Torre Chapultepec
Ruben Darío 281, Piso 10
Bosque de Chapultepec
11580 México, DF
Tel: (5) 282-1155 Fax: (5) 282-0450

Bryan González Vargas y González Baz
Blvd. Agua Caliente 3401, Desp. 205
22420 Tijuana, BC
Tel: (66) 86-4924 Fax: (66) 86-1984

Bufete Sepulveda
Blvd. Avila Camacho No. 1, Piso 9
Col. Lomas de Chapultepec
11000 México, DF
Tel: (5) 557-8844 Fax: (5) 557-8829

Cantu y Asociados Bufete Juridico
Gregorio Dávila No. 42, Desp. 13
Guadalajara, Jal.
Tel: (3) 626-2720/2 Fax: (3) 626-9607

Carlsmith Ball García Cacho y Asociados
Campos Elíseos 385, Torre "B", Piso 6
Col. Chapultepec Polanco
11560 México, DF
Tel: (5) 281-2553 Fax: (5) 281-2196

Carlsmith Ball Wichman Murray Case & Ichiki
Campos Elíseos 385, Torre "B", Piso 6
Col. Chapultepec Polanco
11560 México, DF
Tel: (5) 281-2428 Fax: (5) 281-2196

Cervantes Quijana y Bustamante
Calle Misión de San Diego No. 1511-3011
Zona del Río
Tijuana, BC
Tel: (66) 84-0562 Fax: (66) 84-0436

Creel García-Cuellar y Muggenburg
Blvd. Agua Caliente No. 4558-1407
Tijuana, BC
Tel: (66) 86-5372 Fax: (66) 86-5880

Creel y García Cuellar
Bosques de Ciruelos No. 304, Piso 2
Col. Bosques de Las Lomas
11700 México, DF
Tel: (5) 596-2177 Fax: (5) 596-3309

Cruz González y Asociados
Simón Bolívar 456, esq. Mexicaltzingo
Desp. 13
Col. América, Sector Juárez
Guadalajara, Jal.
Tel: (3) 616-5339, 615-8045, 615-8043
Fax: (3) 615-8043

Davis & Associates
Avda. de Las Palmas No. 735-104
Col. Lomas de Chapultepec
11000 México, DF
Tel: (5) 520-8263, 202-7782 Fax: (5) 520-2802

Dun & Bradstreet
López Cotilla No. 1713, Desp. 203
44100 Guadalajara, Jal.
Tel: (3) 623-9797, 626-3208 Fax: (3) 626-9798

Gallastegui y Lozano
Bosque Duraznos 69-503
11700 México, DF
Tel: (5) 251-0104, 251-0354, 251-2104

Gardere & Wynne
Séneca 425
Col. Chapultepec Polanco
11560 México, DF
Tel: (5) 282-0031 Fax: (5) 282-1821

Hardin Hess Santons Galindo & Hanhausen
Jorge Elliot No. 12, Piso 7
Col. Polanco
11560 México, DF
Tel: (5) 250-9977 Fax: (5) 250-7748

Jaurigui Navarette y Nader
Paseo de la Reforma 199, Pisos 15 y 16
06500 México, DF
Tel: (5) 591-1655

Krasovsky Gallardo y Zorrivas
Blvd. Agua Caliente No. 4558-802
Tijuana, BC
Tel: (66) 82-5266, 86-5267 Fax: (66) 81-8139

Paseo y Martín-Sánchez
Blvd. Agua Caliente 4558, Desp. 403
22420 Tijuana, BC
Tel: (66) 86-5557 Fax: (66) 86-5558
US mailing address: PO Box 767, Bonita, CA 91908, USA

All addresses and telephone numbers are in Mexico unless otherwise noted. The country code for Mexico is [52].

Roberto Paryeon Castillo
Blvd. Agua Caliente No. 3401-904-B
Tijuana, BC
Tel: (66) 20-5283, 86-2503

Thompson & Knight
Edificio Losoles TD-4
Avda. Lázaro Cárdenas No. 2400
66220 Garza García, NL
Tel: (83) 63-0096 Fax: (83) 63-3067

White & Case
Paseo de la Reforma 390, Piso 17
Col. Juárez
06600 México, DF
Tel: (5) 207-9717 Fax: (5) 208-3628

TRANSLATORS & INTERPRETERS

Asociación de Personal Técnico para Conferencias
Internacionales AC
Universidad 1855-502
México, DF
Tel: (5) 548-1119, 548-0210

Berlitz
E. Nacional 530 P.B.
Col. Polanco
México, DF
Tel: (5) 255-3341 Fax: (5) 255-3817

Centro Integral de Traducción (CITI)
Avda. Chapultepec 471
Desp. 403
Col. Juárez
México, DF
Tel: (5) 286-9192, 286-8832 Fax: (5) 538-0421

Corporación Internacional Eisco
Lanz Duret 51
11220 México, DF
Tel: (5) 395-5995 Fax: (5) 395-1435

Instituto de Intérpretes y Traductores
Río Rhin 40
06500 México, DF
Tel: (5) 566-7722

Intredec
Goethe No. 32, Piso 1
México, DF
Tel: (5) 511-0368, 511-6507 Fax: (5) 511-8978

Intredec
Monterrey, NL
Tel: (83) 43-8034 Fax: (83) 42-8011

Lanser de México
Durango 247, Piso 4
06700 México, DF
Tel: (5) 208-5735, 514-0605

Multilingua
Bajío 335-104
Col. Roma
México, DF
Tel: (5) 584-6993, 564-5256 Fax: (5) 264-6787

Promociones Anahi
Paseo de la Reforma 36-6
México, DF
Tel: (5) 546-3352

Servicios Integrales de Comunicación (Sittco)
Melchor Ocampo No. 193
Torre A, Piso 5, Desp. A
Plaza Galerías
México, DF
Tel: (5) 260-0676

TRANSPORTATION

TRANSPORTATION ASSOCIATIONS

Asociación de Agentes Aduanales
Customs Brokers Association
Xola 1707-A
México, DF
Tel: (5) 530-6804

Asociación de Industriales de Transporte
y Comercio Internacional
International Transport and Commerce Industries
Association
Presidente Marsaryk No. 134-204
Col. Polanco
11560 México, DF
Tel: (5) 254-1863, 250-9842

Asociación Nacional de Agentes Navieros
Maritime Agents National Association
Homero No. 1425-302
Col. Los Morales
11510 México, DF
Tel: (5) 395-8931, 395-8079
Fax: (5) 520-7165 Tlx: 1172690

Cámara Nacional de Autotransporte de Pasaje
y Turismo
Versalles No. 16
Col. Juárez
06600 México, DF
Tel: (5) 566-5421, 566-5414 Fax: (5) 566-5636

Cámara Nacional de Autotransportes de Carga
Pachuca No. 158-bis
06140 México, DF
Tel: (5) 553-9809, 553-2682 Fax: (5) 211-5568

Cámara Nacional del Aerotransporte
Air Transport National Chamber
Paseo de la Reforma No. 76, Piso 17
Col. Juárez
06600 México, DF
Tel: (5) 592-4472, 535-1458 Fax: (5) 535-1458

Cámara Nacional de Transportes y Comunicaciones
Communications and Transportation National
Chamber
Pachuca 158 Bis
06140 México, DF
Tel: (5) 288-1651, 286-4512

REGULATORY AGENCIES

Dirección General de Aeronáutica Civil
Directorate General of Civil Aviation
Providencia 807, Piso 6
Col. del Valle
03100 México, DF
Tel: (5) 687-7814, 687-7660

Ferrocarriles Nacional de México (FNM)
National Railroads of Mexico
Avda. Jesús García Corona 140, Piso 4, Ala B
06358 México, DF
Tel: (5) 547-6583

Secretaría de Comunicaciones y Transportes
Secretariat of Communications and Transport
Avda. Universidad y Xola
Col. Navarte
03028 México, DF
Tel: (5) 519-7456, 519-1319, 530-9203, 530-1074
Fax: (5) 519-9748, 530-1074 Tlx: 017600

PORT AUTHORITIES

Puertos Mexicanos
Mexican Port Authority
Municipio Libre No. 377
Col. Santa Cruz Atoyac
03310 México, DF
Tel: (5) 604-3070, 604-3829, 604-4249
Fax: (5) 688-9243, 688-9368

Puerto de Acapulco
Port Authority of Acapulco
Malecón Fiscal s/n
Acapulco, Gro.
Tel: (74) 82-2067 Fax: (74) 83-1648 Tlx: 16925

Puerto de Coatzacoalcos
Port Authority of Coatzacoalcos
Recinto Fiscal Autorizado, Apdo. 4
96400 Coatzacoalcos, Ver.
Tel: (921) 46-754 Fax: (921) 46-758

Puerto de Ensenada
Port Authority of Ensenada
Blvd. Teniente
Azueta No. 224
Ensenada, BC
Tel: (667) 40-846, 40-540 Fax: (667) 52-667

Puerto de Lázaro Cárdenas
Port Authority of Lázaro Cárdenas
Río Tepalcatepec 29
60950 Lázaro Cárdenas, Mich.
Tel: (734) 22-130/1, 22-786, 21-723 Fax: (734) 22-786

Puerto de Manzanillo
Port Authority of Manzanillo
Avda. Teniente Azueta 9
Fracc. Playa Azul
Manzanilla, Col.
Tel: (333) 21-254, 23-075, 23-054 Fax: (333) 20-815

Puerto de Mazatlán
Port Authority of Mazatlán
Avda. Emilio Barragán No. 127
Mazatlán, Sin.
Tel: (69) 82-0278, 23-611 Fax: (69) 82-1822

Puerto de Progreso
Port Authority of Progreso
Edificio Muelle Nuevo, Piso 3
Progreso, Yuc.
Tel: (993) 46-754/8 Fax: (993) 51-567

Puerto de Puerto Vallarta
Port Authority of Puerto Vallarta
Recinto Portuario No. 359
Puerto Vallarta, Jal.
Tel: (322) 20-100, 20-839 Fax: (322) 21-350

Puerto de Tampico
Port Authority of Tampico
Recinto Fiscal Autorizado, Piso 1
Tampico, Tamps.
Tel: (12) 12-5744, 12-4660, 12-4550 Fax: (12) 14-3374

Puerto de Tuxpan
Port Authority of Tuxpan
Carretera la Barra Km. 6.5
Tuxpan, Ver.
Tel: (783) 43-374, 45-395 Fax: (783) 43-374

Puerto de Veracruz
Port Authority of Veracruz
Plaza de la República 210
Veracruz, Ver.
Tel: (29) 32-5232, 32-4612 Fax: (29) 32-5232

AIRLINES

Aero California
Guadalajara, Jal.
Tel: (3) 626-1901, 626-1064, 689-0924 (airport)

Aero California
Paseo de la Reforma No. 332
06600 México, DF
Tel: (5) 207-1392

Aero California
Corporate Offices
Hidalgo 400-A, Apdo. 555
La Paz, BCS
Tel: (682) 22-109 Tlx: 52237

Aero Guadalajara
Niños Héroes 2828
Jardines del Bosque
Guadalajara, Jal.
Tel: (3) 647-2776, 616-1421 Fax: (3) 621-5486

Aero Guadalajara
Avda. de las Torres 489
Nva. Industrial Vallejo
México, DF
Tel: (5) 752-6237

Aeroflot
Insurgentes Sur 569
03810 México, DF
Tel: (5) 523-7139, 523-8729

Aerolíneas Argentinas
Estocolmo 8
Col. Juárez
México, DF
Tel: (5) 208-1050 (reservations), 762-2636 (airport)
Fax: (5) 514-6321

Aeromar
Guadalajara, Jal.
Tel: (3) 626-4656/8

Aeromar
Sevilla No. 4, PB
Col. Juárez
06600 México, DF
Tel: (5) 207-6666 (office), 784-1139 (airport)
Fax: (5) 207-5766 (office), 784-1145 (airport)

Aeromar
Escobedo Sur 1011-15
Monterrey, NL
Tel: (83) 45-3141, 45-3201

Aeroméxico
Guadalajara, Jal.
Tel: (3) 669-0202, 689-0028 (airport)

Aeroméxico
Oficinas Generales
Paseo de la Reforma No. 445
Col. Cuauhtémoc
06500 México, DF
Tel: (5) 207-8233 (reservations), 207-6311 (office)

Aeroméxico
Avda. Cuauhtémoc y Padre Mier
Monterrey, NL
Tel: (83) 40-8760, 40-0617, 44-7730 (airport)

Aerónica Aerolíneas Nicaraguenses
Paseo de la Reforma 322-A
06600 México, DF
Tel: (5) 207-4814, 207-4887

Air France
Paseo de la Reforma 404, Piso 15
06400 México, DF
Tel: (5) 566-0066

All addresses and telephone numbers are in Mexico unless otherwise noted. The country code for Mexico is [52].

American Airlines
Guadalajara, Jal.
Tel: (3) 689-0304, 689-0480 (airport)

American Airlines
Paseo de la Reforma No. 300
06600 México, DF
Tel: (5) 399-9222 (reservations), 208-6396 (office)

American Airlines
Kalos Bldg.
Zaragoza 1300 Sur
Monterrey, NL
Tel: (83) 40-3031, 45-5809 (airport)

Avensa Aerovías Venezolanas
Paseo de la Reforma No. 325, Locs. 2 y 3
Hotel María Isabel Sheraton
México, DF
Tel: (5) 660-4444, 208-3018

Aviacsa
Insurgentes Sur 1261, Piso 6
Col. Insurgentes Extremadura
03740 México, DF
Tel: (5) 590-9522 (reservations), 563-4400 (office)
Fax: (5) 590-2706 (reservations), 563-4833 (office)

Avianca
Paseo de la Reforma 195, PB y 301
06500 México, DF
Tel: (5) 566-8550

Aviateca
Paseo de la Reforma No. 56
06600 México, DF
Tel: (5) 592-5289, 566-5966

Canadian Airlines International
Paseo de la Reforma 325
06500 México, DF
Tel: (5) 208-1654, 208-1691 (reservations)

Continental Airlines
Guadalajara, Jal.
Tel: (3) 689-0433, 689-0261

Continental Airlines
Oficina de Boletas
Paseo de la Reforma No. 325, Local 11
06600 México, DF
Tel: (5) 203-1148 (reservations office)

Continental Airlines
Insurgentes 2500
Galerías Monterrey, Local 613
Monterrey, NL
Tel: (83) 33-2622, 44-7505, 45-7734 (airport)

Delta Airlines
Guadalajara, Jal.
Tel: (3) 630-3530, 630-3226

Delta Airlines
Paseo de la Reforma 381
06500 México, DF
Tel: (5) 202-1608 (reservations), 511-0565 (office)

Iberia
Paseo de la Reforma No. 24
06040 México, DF
Tel: (5) 705-0716 (reservations)
Fax: (5) 546-6366 (reservations)

JAL Japan Airlines
Paseo de la Reforma 295
México, DF
Tel: (5) 533-5515/9 Fax: (5) 207-6678

KLM Airlines
Avda. Paseo de las Palmas 735, Piso 7
México, DF
Tel: (5) 202-4444 (reservations) Fax: (5) 202-4476

LAB (Lloyd Aéreo Boliviano) Airlines
Campos Elíseos No. 169, Piso 3
Col. Polanco
11560 México, DF
Tel: (5) 250-8556, 250-8543

LanChile
Paseo de la Reforma No. 87, Local 201
México, DF
Tel: (5) 566-5211 (reservations), 571-9028 (airport)
Fax: (5) 566-0665 (reservations), 571-5734 (airport)

Lufthansa
Avda. Paseo de las Palmas 239
Col. Lomas de Chapultepec
11000 México, DF
Tel: (5) 202-8866 Fax: (5) 202-9752 (reservations)

Mexicana
Guadalajara, Jal.
Tel: (3) 647-2222, 689-0119 (airport)

Mexicana
Insurgentes Sur 753
México, DF
Tel: (5) 325-0990 (reservations), 523-3090 (office)

Mexicana
Stouffer Presidente Hotel
Campos Elíseos 218
11560 México, DF
Tel: (5) 325-0990 (reservations), 282-2697 (office)

Mexicana
Hidalgo 922 Pte.
Monterrey, NL
Tel: (83) 40-5511, 45-0811 (airport)

SARO (Servicios Aéreos Rutas Oriente)
Corporate Offices
Plaza Dorada Local No. 9
Apdo. 803
6400 Monterrey, NL
Tel: (83) 42-3597 Fax: (83) 42-5393

SAS Scandinavian Airlines
Hamburgo No. 61 y Havre
06600 México, DF
Tel: (5) 208-8533 Fax: (5) 525-0667

Servicio Aéreo Leo López
Aéreoporto Internacional
Apdo. 586
Chihuahua, Chih.
Tel: (14) 20-0678 Fax: (14) 15-4454

Swissair
Hamburgo 66, Piso 3
06600 México, DF
Tel: (5) 533-6463

TACA International Airlines
Paseo de la Reforma 87
06030 México, DF
Tel: (5) 546-8807/9, 566-1850

TAESA (Transportes Aéreos Ejecutivos)
Corporate Offices
Terminal de Aviación General, Hangar 27
International Airport, Mexico City
15620 México, DF
Tel: (5) 758-5586

United Airlines
Hamburgo 213, Piso 15
Col. Juárez
06600 México, DF
Tel: (5) 627-0202, 762-8485 (airport)

Varig Líneas Aéreas Brasileñas
Paseo de la Reforma No. 80, Local 12
México, DF
Tel: (5) 591-1744 (reservations), 280-9027 (sales)

TRANSPORTATION AND CUSTOMS BROKERAGE FIRMS

Companies here may offer more services in addition to those listed here. Service information is provided as a guideline and is not intended to be comprehensive. Some companies have several offices, although only one may be listed.

Aereotráfico
Amores No. 1110-A
Del Valle
03100 México, DF
Tel: (5) 559-9762, 559-9131 Fax: (5) 575-1655
Air cargo agent, freight forwarder

Aero Despachos Iturbide
Plaza de la Repúblic No. 48, P.B.
06030 México, DF
Tel: (5) 566-2343, 566-6379 Fax: (5) 535-9391
Customs broker, freight forwarder

Aerodocumentador Aduanal
Asturias No. 94-B
Alamos
03400 México, DF
Tel: (5) 530-4366, 530-4796 Fax: (5) 530-7664
Customs broker, freight forwarder

Aerofletes Internacionales
Edif. Agentes Aduanales L-4
Aeropuerto Internacional
Moctezuma
15620 México, DF
Tel: (5) 762-1522, 762-6251, 762-0455
Fax: (5) 762-9034 Tlx: 1776216
Customs broker

Aeroméxico
Oficinas Generales
Paseo de la Reforma No. 445
Col. Cuauhtémoc
06500 México, DF
Tel: (5) 286-4422
Air cargo carrier

Aeromexpress
Avda. Texcoco s/n, esq. Avda. Tahel
Col. Peñon de los Baños
15620 México, DF
Tel: (5) 237-0220, 752-6334, 752-6394
Fax: (5) 237-0226, 752-6472
Air cargo carrier, international and national courier service

Aeroservicio Aduanal
Matilde Márquez No. 40
15520 México, DF
Tel: (5) 571-5636, 762-6437
Customs broker, freight forwarder

Agencia Aduanal Mexicana
Avda. Insurgentes Sur No. 1180-602
Col. del Valle
03100 México, DF
Tel: (5) 575-1686, 559-3785
Fax: (5) 575-6517 Tlx: 1771615
Customs broker

Agencia de Buques Internacional
Barranca del Muerto 525
01600 México, DF
Tel: (5) 664-2242
Ship agents

Agencia Guillermo Woodward Rojas
Tula No. 53
06140 México, DF
Tel: (5) 211-7756 Fax: (5) 286-6465 Tlx: 1761314
Customs broker

Agencia Mexicana de Carga
Genaro García No. 52
Col. Jardín Balbuena
15900 México, DF
Tel: (5) 785-6367, 785-6631
Air cargo agent

Agencia Naviera de México
Avda. Periférico Sur 3190 PB
01900 México, DF
Tel: (5) 652-2218, 652-2239
Ship agents

Agencias Marítimas del Pacífico
Ruben Darío No. 13, Mezzanine
11560 México, DF
Tel: (5) 250-4300
Ship agents

Agencias Marítimas Latinoamericanas
Paseo de la Reforma No. 51, Piso 19
06600 México, DF
Tel: (5) 566-1600, 546-9820 Tlx: 1773915
Ship agents

Air Carga de México
Aeropuerto Internacional
Sec. Agentes Aduanales Loc. 19
07470 México, DF
Tel: (5) 571-7019, 762-8211
Air cargo, customs broker, freight forwarder

American Airlines
Paseo de la Reforma No. 300
06600 México, DF
Tel: (5) 785-2433
Air cargo carrier

Auto Líneas Regiomontanas
Oficinas Generales
Prolg. Díaz Ordaz No. 205
San Nicolás de los Garza, NL
Tel: (83) 53-3050, 53-8834, 53-8887 Fax: (83) 53-8727
National trucking company

Autotransportes de Carga Tresguerras
Vallejo 1830 Nave 2-23
02340 México, DF
Tel: (5) 389-5052, 389-3615 Fax: (5) 389-3750
National trucking company

Aviacsa
Corporate Offices
Insurgentes Sur 1228, Piso 3
Col. del Valle
03100 México, DF
Tel: (5) 579-1515, 785-0735 (airport)
Fax: (5) 579-7261, 785-5657 (airport)
Air cargo carrier

Buró Aduanal Internacional
Baja California No. 278-202
Col. Hipódromo Condesa
06170 México, DF
Tel: (5) 273-1484, 516-7750 Fax: (5) 272-1340
Customs broker

Carga Aerotransportada de México
Río Panuco No. 55-702
Cuauhtémoc
06500 México, DF
Tel: (5) 703-2411, 535-0111
Fax: (5) 703-3994 Tlx: 1762456
Air cargo agent, freight forwarder

Central de Aduanas de México
Sinaloa 14
Peñon de los Baños
15520 México, DF
Tel: (5) 785-4755, 571-3400, 571-7080
Fax: (5) 571-2405, 571-2386 Tlx: 1772602
Customs broker; air, ground, and maritime service, freight consolidation

Central de Aerocarga Internacional
Avda. Insurgentes Centro No. 86, Loc. C, D y E
San Rafael Revolución
06030 México, DF
Tel: (5) 566-4388, 566-7539, 566-7540
Customs broker, freight forwarder, air cargo

Compañía Naviera Minera del Golfo (NAVIMIN)
Mercaderes 15
San José Insurgentes
03900 México, DF
Tel: (5) 660-1313, 598-6088
Fax: (5) 660-1386, 598-0765 Tlx: 1773462
Ship owners

Concorde de Carga
San Francisco No. 1626-405
Del Valle
03100 México, DF
Tel: (5) 524-6045, 524-7664
Fax: (5) 524-9334 Tlx: 1764301
Customs broker

Condor Air
Matamoros No. 50
Col. Roma
15520 México, DF
Tel: (5) 762-8843, 785-4550 Fax: (5) 785-4800
Customs broker, freight forwarder

Consolidadora de Carga Aérea Apolo
Morelos No. 176
Col. Peñon de los Baños
15520 México, DF
Tel: (5) 571-7037, 784-4656, 762-8055
Customs broker, freight forwarder, air cargo

Continental Airlines
Aeropuerto Internacional, Loc. 3
15620 México, DF
Tel: (5) 785-2272, 785-2405
Air cargo carrier

Corporación Marítima Delmex
Homero No. 1425, Desp. 501
Col. Polanco
11510 México, DF
Tel: (5) 395-9550, 395-9716
Fax: (5) 395-7197 Tlx: 01763066
Ship owners

Delfín & Compañía
Homero No. 1425-505
11510 México, DF
Tel: (5) 395-4042, 395-4955
Ship agents

Delta Airlines
Paseo de la Reforma 381
06500 México, DF
Tel: (5) 762-8523
Air cargo carrier

Despachos Aduanales
Blvd. Aeropuerto No. 81
Industrial Puerto Aéreo
15700 México, DF
Tel: (5) 784-4188, 762-2640
Fax: (5) 571-9924 Tlx: 1777446
Customs broker, air cargo, freight forwarder

Despachos del Centro
Oaxaca No. 96-C
Col. Roma
06700 México, DF
Tel: (5) 533-5864, 207-9106
Fax: (5) 514-0507 Tlx: 1774318
Customs broker, freight forwarder

DHL
Lázaro Cárdenas 1299
Fracc. Industrial Alamo
44900 Guadalajara, Jal.
Tel: (3) 670-1885 Fax: (3) 670-2141
*International courier, air cargo, package delivery,
freight forwarder, customs broker*

DHL
Carretera Miguel Alemán Valdez No. 205
Col. Lindavista
67130 Guadalupe, NL
Tel: (83) 77-1672 Fax: (83) 34-4624

DHL
Paseo de la Reforma 76
Col. Juárez
06600 México, DF
Tel: (5) 546-5302, 566-8088 Fax: (5) 546-5939

Doal
Asistencia Pública No. 596
Federal
15700 México, DF
Tel: (5) 571-6864, 571-8717
Fax: (5) 571-2406 Tlx: 01762424
Air cargo agent, freight forwarder

Emery Worldwide
Irapuato 188, Piso 1
Col. Peñon de los Baños
15520 México, DF
Tel: (5) 784-1422, 571-7577 Fax: (5) 571-7614
*National and international courier, air freight, package
delivery, freight forwarder*

Estrella Blanca Paquetería y Envíos
José Gpe. López Velarde s/n
Col. Magdalena de las Salinas
México, DF
Tel: (5) 368-6577, 368-4597
*National and international courier and package
delivery service*

Federal Express
Calle B No. 506
64860 Apodaca, NL
Tel: (83) 69-3659 Fax: (83) 69-3654
International courier, air cargo, package delivery

Federal Express
Calzada Independencia Sur 1065
Col. Moderna, Sec. Reforma XP
44100 Guadalajara, Jal.
Tel: (3) 619-6441, 619-0071 Fax: (3) 619-0100

Federal Express
Enrique Jacob 16
Col. San Adress Atoto
Naucalpan, Edo. de Méx.
Tel: (5) 228-8000

Federal Express
Oficina Matriz
Insurgentes Sur 899
Col. Ampliación Nápoles
03810 México, DF
Tel: (5) 255-4140 Fax: (5) 254-5340, 203-4066

Fletes Magos
Rosario Bustamante
Col. Sta. Martha Acatitla
09510 México, DF
Tel: (5) 745-5722, 744-0990 Fax: (5) 744-3482
Trucking company with connections to Central America

Francisco Rodríguez Pérez Agente Aduanal
Chichen Itza 217, Letra B
Col. Letran Valle, Deleg. Benito Juárez
03650 México, DF
Tel: (5) 604-9042, 604-7723
Fax: (5) 604-9075 Tlx: 1764456
Customs broker

Genmar
Paseo de la Reforma 51, Piso 12
06030 México, DF
Tel: (5) 546-9820, 566-1600
Fax: (5) 591-0856, 546-9829
Ship agents

Gloria G. Hernández Cota Agencia Aduanal
Avda. 602 Edif. Aduanales Local No. 18
Peñon de los Baños
15520 México, DF
Tel: (5) 785-3266, 784-8238
Fax: (5) 784-8552
Customs broker

Hercel, Oficinas Generales
Paseo de la Reforma No. 383, Piso 10
Col. Cuauhtémoc
06500 México, DF
Tel: (5) 533-4874/6, 514-6767 Fax: (5) 533-3203
*International and national ground, air, maritime
transport company*

Imex
Irapuato No. 188, esq. Mérida
Col. Peñon de los Baños
México, DF
Tel: (5) 762-0893, 762-2346
Freight forwarder, customs broker

Importaciones y Exportaciones Mexicanas
Génova No. 33, Desp. 401
Col. Juárez
06600 México, DF
Tel: (5) 514-7979, 208-4325
Fax: (5) 514-7212 Tlx: 01771290
Customs broker

Incotrans Norsemex
Insurgentes Sur No. 421
Edif. "A", Desp. 601-602
Col. Hipódromo Condesa
06100 México, DF
Tel: (5) 564-5700, 574-6467
Fax: (5) 574-6469 Tlx: 01771086
Ship agents

Internacional de Aduanas
Lago Merú No. 45
Granada
11520 México, DF
Tel: (5) 531-9500, 203-5731
Customs broker

International Bonded Couriers de México
B. Franklin No. 234-1
Escandón
11800 México, DF
Tel: (5) 271-6522, 272-3982
Fax: (5) 272-3043 Tlx: 1764302
Freight forwarder, international courier service

Japan Airlines
Aeropuerto Internacional
México, DF
Tel: (5) 571-2547, 784-2642 Fax: (5) 785-6357
Air cargo carrier

Jorge M. Ocampo y Cía.
Insurgentes Sur 421
Conjunto Aristos Edificio B, Piso 8
Col. Hipódromo Condesa
06170 México, DF
Tel: (5) 584-3911, 574-7166
Fax: (5) 574-4403 Tlx: 1774282
Customs broker, air cargo

KLM Airlines
Aeropuerto Internacional
15620 México, DF
Tel: (5) 571-8511
Air cargo carrier

Líneas Internacionales Tijuana
Insurgentes Norte 1275
07800 México, DF
Tel: (5) 517-0100/2, 392-9718 Fax: (5) 392-9225
North American trucking company

Mensajeria Pegaso (Airborne Express)
Lago Banjueolo 64
11520 México, DF
Tel: (5) 203-6811
International courier, air cargo carrier

Martínez Oñate y Cía.
Aeropuerto Internacional
Lote 5 Zona Agentes Aduanales
15620 México, DF
Tel: (5) 571-3235, 762-0100 Fax: (5) 571-3235
Customs broker, air cargo agents, freight forwarder

Mexicana
Avda. Xola 535
Col. del Valle
03100 México, DF
Tel: (5) 660-4433, 325-0922 Fax: (5) 523-2016
Air cargo carrier

Mexpost
Avda. Tahel s/n, esq. Avda. Norte No. 202
Col. Pensador Mexicano
15620 México, DF
Tel: (5) 785-3221, 785-3033 Fax: (5) 571-3045
*Mexican Postal Service national and international
courier service*

Naviera Armamex
Lope de Vega 111
Col. Chapultepec Morales
11570 México, DF
Tel: (5) 545-8206 Fax: (5) 203-2151 Tlx: 1763574
Ship managers and agents

OCS de México
Río de la Planta No. 56-203
Col. Cuauhtémoc
06500 México, DF
Tel: (5) 211-1400, 211-8340
Fax: (5) 286-9698 Tlx: 1761307
*National and international courier and package
delivery service*

Palazuelos Hermanos
Colima No. 114, P.B.
06700 México, DF
Tel: (5) 514-7136
*Customs broker, freight forwarder, air cargo, freight
forwarder*

Ramón Barrios y Cía.
Petrarca 223-101
11570 México, DF
Tel: (5) 531-3928, 531-5851
Customs broker

Roberto Zuñiga y Cía.
Avda. Paseo de la Reforma No. 444, Piso 2
06600 México, DF
Tel: (5) 533-2160, 525-2680
Customs broker

Romane Aeroexim
Irapuato No. 188, Piso 2, esq. Mérida
Col. Peñon de los Baños
15520 México, DF
Tel: (5) 762-2733/4 Fax: (5) 784-4314 Tlx: 0177384
*Customs broker; air, ground, and maritime cargo
consolidator; freight forwarder*

Setexim
Avda. Insurgentes Sur No. 421, Local B-3
06140 México, DF
Tel: (5) 564-7181, 564-0035
Customs broker

All addresses and telephone numbers are in Mexico unless otherwise noted. The country code for Mexico is [52].

Skypak Internacional de México
Cuernavaca No. 57
Col. Condesa
06140 México, DF
Tel: (5) 286-4419, 286-4632
International courier service

TAESA (Transportes Aéreos Ejecutivos)
Terminal de Aviación General, Hangar 27
International Airport, Mexico City
15620 México, DF
Tel: (5) 758-5586
Air cargo carrier

Tecomar
B. Franklin 232
Col. Escandón
11800 México, DF
Tel: (5) 272-8010 Fax: (5) 271-4010 Tlx: 1772690
Ship owners

TNT Worldwide Express
Mex Courier America
San Lucas No. 181
Coyoacan
04030 México, DF
Tel: (5) 689-4184 Fax: (5) 689-7198
International courier, air cargo carrier

Tráfico Aéreo Internacional
Sinaloa No. 72
15520 México, DF
Tel: (5) 762-3217, 784-3012
Customs broker, freight forwarder

Tráfico Universal de Carga
Juan Escutia No. 45, Piso 4
06140 México, DF
Tel: (5) 286-1972, 256-4556
Customs broker

Tramitadores Asociados de Aerocarga
Texcoco No. 14
Col. Peñon de los Baños
15520 México, DF
Tel: (5) 571-4533, 571-0748
Customs broker, freight forwarder, air cargo

Transcarga Internacional
Norte 196 No. 694
Pensador Mexicano
15510 México, DF
Tel: (5) 760-1422 Fax: (5) 760-0114 Tlx: 1773269
Customs broker, freight forwarder

Transportación Aérea Internacional
Río Mixcoac No. 158
Col. Acacias
03100 México, DF
Tel: (5) 524-4313, 534-9879 Fax: (5) 524-6197
Customs broker, air cargo agent

Transportación Marítima Mexicana
Avda. de la Cúspide No. 4755
Col. Parques de Pedregal
Deleg. Tlalpan
14010 México, DF
Tel: (5) 606-0444, 652-4111
Fax: (5) 652-7040 Tlx: 01773949
Ship owners

Transportadora Nacional
Salonica 219-A
Col. Sector Naval, Azcapotzalco
02080 México, DF
Tel: (5) 396-1045, 396-1771 Fax: (5) 396-5366
National trucking company

Transportes Arwest
Avda. Central No. 34
Col. Melchor Múzquiz
Valle de Aragón
Ecatepec, Edo. de Méx.
Tel: (5) 710-7255, 710-7309 Fax: (5) 710-7062
*International trucking company, including service to
Central America*

Transportes Terrestres Aduanales
Pirules No. 16
Col. Sta. Ma. Tomatlan
09870 Iztapalapa, DF
Tel: (5) 656-4716 Fax: (5) 656-3570
*Door-to-door trucking service to Canada and the US
without transfers*

Transportes Universales
Guadalajara No. 32
16700 México, DF
Tel: (5) 533-0044, 687-4478
Customs broker, ship agent

Tricarga Internacional
Tahel No. 435
Col. Pensador Mexicano
15510 México, DF
Tel: (5) 760-1191, 751-3151
Customs broker, freight forwarder

United Airlines
Aeropuerto Internacional, Sala C-64
15620 México, DF
Tel: (5) 762-8485
Air cargo carrier

United Parcel Service
Río Obi No. 1781
Col. Alamo Industrial
44910 Guadalajara, Jal.
Tel: (3) 657-2390, 657-2490
International courier, air cargo, package delivery

United Parcel Service
Calle 2 No. 284, esq. Calle Unión
Col. Pantitlan
08100 México, DF
Tel: (5) 756-6590, 756-8122 Fax: (5) 758-5104

United Parcel Service
Carretera Miguel Alemán
Km. 16.5 Apodaca Bodega No. 15
Monterrey, NL
Tel: (83) 69-3548/9 Fax: (83) 86-2217

Varig Líneas Aéreas Brasileñas
Paseo de la Reforma No. 80, Local 12
México, DF
Tel: (5) 784-8689, 784-8790, 785-1513
Air cargo carrier

Zamudio y Asociados
Presidente Masaryk No. 61-401
Col. Chapultepec Morales
11560 México, DF
Tel: (5) 254-6134, 254-6019 Fax: (5) 254-8604
Customs broker

Zoom Internacional de México
Tuxpan 2, Piso 1
06760 México, DF
Tel: (5) 574-6348, 584-0984
Air cargo, national and international courier service

PUBLICATIONS, MEDIA & INFORMATION SOURCES

DIRECTORIES, ANNUALS & SURVEYS

Access Mexico: Emerging Market Handbook
& Directory
(English)
Cambridge Data & Development Ltd.
307 N. Bryan St.
Arlington, VA 22201, USA
Tel: [1] (703) 525-3282 Fax: [1] (703) 525-3282

Anuario Latinoamericano de los Plásticos
(Annual)
Anuarios Latinoamericanos, S.A. de C.V.
Colima 436, Piso 2
06700 México, DF
Tel: (5) 286-3113
Plastics industry

Apparel: Latin American Industrial Report
(Annual; English)
Aquino Productions
Box 15760
Stamford, CT 06901, USA
Tel: [1] (203) 325-3138
Available for each of 22 Latin American countries

Arthur Andersen North American Business
Sourcebook
(English)
Triumph Books
644 S. Clark St.
Chicago, IL 60605, USA
Tel: [1] (312) 939-3330 Fax: [1] (312) 663-3557

Bancomext Trade Directory of Mexico
(Annual; English, Spanish)
Periférico Sur 4333
Col. Jardines de la Montaña
01900 México, DF
Tel: (5) 227-9000
*Available in the USA from: Market Entry Inc., 2651 N.
Harwood, Suite 400, Dallas, TX 75201, USA; Tel: [1]
(214) 871-3184 Fax: [1] (214) 220-2112*

Benefits Survey and Survey of Salaries
(Annual; English, Spanish)
American Chamber of Commerce of Mexico
Lucerna 78-4
Col. Juárez, Deleg. Cuauhtémoc
06600 México, DF
Tel: (5) 705-0995, 724-3800
Fax: (5) 703-2911, 703-3908 Tlx: 1777609
*Fringe benefits and salary rate received by executives,
other high-level personnel and salespeople by company
size, location, and industrial sector within Mexico*

Cámara Nacional de la Industria del Hierro y del
Acero: Informe del Presidente
(Annual)
Cámara Nacional de la Industria del Hierro y del Acero
Amores 338
Col. del Valle
03199 México, DF
Tel: (5) 543-4443/5, 536-1287 Fax: (5) 687-0517
Iron and steel industry

Compensation and Benefits Survey for Executive
Levels—Mexico
(Annual; English)
Wyatt Data Services
Two Executive Dr.
Fort Lee, NJ 07024, USA
Tel: [1] (201) 585-9808 Fax: [1] (201) 585-0127
*Compensation information on more than 60 executive
positions in Mexico*

Complete Twin Plant Guide
(Annual; English)
Solunet
4416 North Mesa
El Paso, TX 79902, USA
Tel: [1] (916) 532-1166
Directory of maquiladoras

Comportamiento Del Sistema Asegurador Mexicano
(Annual with monthly cumulative supplements)
Comisión Nacional de Seguros y Fianzas
Avda. de los Insurgentes Sur 1971
Plaza Inn, Torre 2 N., Piso 2
01020 México, DF
*Financial information about groups of companies in the
insurance sector.*

Davison's Textile Blue Book
(Annual; English)
Davison Publishing Co., Inc.
Box 477
Ridgewood, NJ 07451, USA
Tel: [1] (201) 445-3135 Fax: [1] (201) 445-4397
*Mills, dyers, and finishers in the US, Canada, and
Mexico, plus sales offices, yarn dealers, cotton dealers*

Directorio del Gobierno
(Irregular; Spanish)
Ibcon S.A.
Gutemberg 224
Col. Anzures
11590 México, DF
Tel: (5) 255-4577
*Federal, state, and municipal government personnel and
executive, legislative, and judicial branch personnel*

Directorio MPM—Agencias y Anunciantes
(MPM—Mexican Advertising Agencies Directory)
(Semiannual; Spanish)
Directorio MPM—Medios Audiovisuales
(MPM—Mexican Audiovisual Media Rates & Data)
(Quarterly; Spanish)
Directorio MPM—Medios Impresos Tarifas y Datos
(MPM—Mexican Print Media Rates & Data)
(Quarterly; Spanish)
Medios Publicitarios Mexicanos, S.A.
Avda. México No. 99-303
Col. Hipódromo Condesa
06170 México, DF
Tel: (5) 573-3118 Fax: (5) 574-2668
*Available in USA from: Standard Rate and Data Service,
3004 Glenview Rd., Wilmette, IL 60091, USA; Tel: [1]
(312) 256-1200*

Directory of American Companies
(Irregular; English, Spanish)
American Chamber of Commerce of Mexico
Lucerna 78-4
Col. Juárez, Deleg. Cuauhtémoc
06600 México, DF
Tel: (5) 705-0995, 724-3800
Fax: (5) 703-2911, 703-3908 Tlx: 1777609
*Details on 2900 US firms operating in Mexico, Mexican
companies, products, and services manufactured, sold,
or offered by representative firms, and US locations*

Directory of Executive Recruiters
(Annual)
Kennedy Publications
Templeton Rd.
Fitzwilliam, NH 03447, USA
Tel: [1] (603) 585-6544 Fax: [1] (603) 585-9555
*Over 2,700 executive recruiting offices in the US,
Canada and Mexico*

Directory of In-Bond Plants (Maquiladoras) in Mexico
(Annual)
Mexico Communications
Box 1707
El Paso, TX 79949-1707, USA
Tel: [1] (915) 533-5251

All addresses and telephone numbers are in Mexico unless otherwise noted. The country code for Mexico is [52].

Directory of Steel Foundries in the United States, Canada And Mexico
(Biennial)
Steel Founders' Society of America
455 State St.
Des Plaines, IL 60016, USA
Tel: [1] (708) 299-9160, 299-3105

Directorio Telefónico Sección Amarilla Ciudad de México
(Annual; Spanish)
Anuncios en Directorios
Río Pánuco 38
06500 México, DF
Yellow pages telephone directory for Mexico City; available in the US from Worldwide Directory Products Sales, 44 Kimler, Suite 100, St. Louis, MO 63043, USA; Tel: [1] (800) 792-2665 Fax: [1] (800) 848-9012

Glass Factory Directory; and U.S. Industry Factbook
(Annual)
National Glass Budget
LJV, Inc.
Box 2267
Hempstead, NY 11551-2267, USA
Tel: [1] (516) 481-2188
Glass factories in the US, Canada, and Mexico

Guía de la Industria Alimentaria
Food industry
Guía de la Industria: Automotriz
Automotive industry
Guía de la Industria: Equipo y Aparatos (Para Laboratorios y Plantas)
Machinery for laboratories and plants
Guía de la Industria: Equipo y Materiales
Machinery and materials
Guía de la Industria: Hule, Plásticos y Resinas
Plastics, rubber and resins
Guía de la Industria: Laboratorios De Especialades Y Control
Laboratory instruments
Guía de la Industria Química: Productos Químicos
Chemical engineering
Guía Del Envase Y Embalaje
Packaging industry
(Annual; Spanish)
Informática Cosmos, S.A. de C.V.
Fernández Arrieta 5-101
Col. Los Cipreses
04830 México, DF
Tel: (5) 677-4868 Fax: (5) 679-3575

Guía Industrial Mexicana
(Semiannual)
Augustan Melgar, No. 44-5
Col. Condesa
06140 México, DF
Industrial directory

How to Sell Your Product in Mexico
(Annual; English)
American Chamber of Commerce of Mexico
Lucerna 78-4
Col. Juárez, Deleg. Cuauhtémoc
06600 México, DF
Tel: (5) 705-0995, 724-3800
Fax: (5) 703-2911, 703-3908 Tlx: 1777609

Informe Anual: Instituto de Investigaciones Eléctricas
(Annual; English and Spanish editions)
Instituto de Investigaciones Eléctricas, Interior
Internado Palmira
Apdo. 475
62000 Cuernavaca, Mor.
Tel: (73) 18-2527
Electric industry

International Directory of Importers: South-Central America
(Irregular; English)
Interdata
1480 Grove St.
Healdsburg, CA 95448, USA
Tel: [1] (707) 433-3900 Fax: [1] (707) 433-8920
14,000 importers in South and Central America, including Mexico

International Green Book Directory
(Annual; English)
Haughton Publishing Co. of Texas
Box 180218
Dallas, TX 75218, USA
Tel: [1] (214) 288-7511
US and Latin American processors of cottonseed, soybean, linseed, and peanuts

Kompass México
(Annual; English, Spanish)
Avda. San Fernando 37
Col. Tlalpan
14050 México, DF
Tel: (5) 606-1097 Fax: (5) 665-7988 Tlx: 1777569
General business and industry directory

La Minería en México
(Biennial)
Instituto Nacional de Estadística, Geografía e Informática
Secretaría de Programación y Presupuesto
Prol. Héroe de Nacozari 2301 Sur
Puerta 10, P.B.
20290 Aguascalientes, Ags.
Tel: (49) 18-1477 Fax: (49) 18-0739
Mining

Latin America Market Guide
(Semiannual)
Dun & Bradstreet International
International Marketing Services
One World Trade Center, Suite 9069
New York, NY 10048, USA
Tel: [1] (212) 524-8840
Business firms in 43 countries in Central and South America.

Latin American Import-Export Directory
(Annual; English, Spanish)
International Trade Council
Box 73
1007 San Jose, Costa Rica
Tel: [506] 33-8697

LAWG Letter
(Irregular)
Latin American Working Group
Box 2207, Sta. P
Toronto, ON M5S 2T2, Canada
Tel: [1] (416) 533-4221 Fax: [1] (416) 533-4579
Focuses on Canada's trade, aid, and investment links to South and Central America.

Mexico Data Bank
(Annual; English, Spanish)
El Inversionista Mexicana
Mexican Financial Advisory Service, S.A.
Félix Cuevas 301-204
Col. del Valle, Deleg. Benito Juárez
03100 México, DF
Tel: (5) 534-9297 Fax: (5) 524-3756
Available in the USA from: ICQ Network, 1675 Broadway, Suite 2325, Denver, CO 80202, USA; Tel: [1] (303) 592-8990 Fax: [1] (303) 592-8995.

Mexican Economy
(Annual)
Banco de México, Subdirección de Investigación
Económica y Bancaria
Avda. Juárez 90
Col. Centro, Deleg. Cuauhtemoc
06059 México, DF
Tel: (5) 761-85-88

Mexico Country Profile: Survey of Political and
Economic Background
(Annual; English)
Economist Intelligence Unit
111 West 57th St.
New York, NY 10019-2211
Tel: [1] (212) 554-0600 Fax: [1] (212) 586-1181/2

Mexico: Financing Foreign Operations
(Annual)
Economist Intelligence Unit
111 West 57th St.
New York, NY 10019-2211, USA
Tel: [1] (212) 554-0600 Fax: [1] (212) 586-1181/2
*Provides details on critical areas such as exchange
controls, sources of funding, financial markets, cash
management, and trade credit facilities for Mexico.*

Mexico: Investing, Licensing and Trading Conditions
Abroad
(Annual)
Economist Intelligence Unit
111 West 57th St.
New York, NY 10019-2211
Tel: [1] (212) 554-0600 Fax: [1] (212) 586-1181/2
*Provides information on corporate tax rules, exchange
and price controls, trade and licensing restrictions, labor
conditions, and investment rules for Mexico.*

Mexico: Political Risk Services
(Annual)
Political Risk Services
Box 6482, Syracuse, NY 13217-6482, USA
Tel: [1] (315) 472-1224 Fax: [1] (315) 472-1235
*In-depth analysis and forecasts of political and
economic conditions.*

Nacional Financiera Annual Report
(Annual)
Nacional Financiera, SNC
Subdirección de Información Técnica y Publicaciones
Venustiano Carranza 25, Del. Cuauhtemoc
06008 México, DF

National Customs Tariff Guidebook—Mexico
(Annual; English)
Worldtariff
220 Montgomery St., Suite 432
San Francisco, CA 94104-3410, USA
Tel: [1] (415) 391-7501 Fax: [1] (415) 391-7537

Official International Business Directory of the Latin
American World
(Annual; English, Portuguese, Spanish)
Aquino Productions
Box 15760
Stamford, CT 06901, USA
Tel: [1] (203) 325-3138

Pan Directorio de Proveedores/Bread Caterers'
Directory
(Annual)
Bravo Grupo Editorial, S.A.
Jose María Bustillos 49
Col. Algarin
06880 México, DF
*Wheat, flour, bread, bakery, crackers, and pasta
industries*

Printing & Publishing: Latin American Industrial
Report
(Annual)
Aquino Productions
Box 15760
Stamford, CT 06901, USA
Tel: [1] (203) 325-3138
*Reports available for each of 22 Latin American
countries*

Producción Química Mexicana
(Annual)
Informática Cosmos, S.A. de C.V.
Fernando Arrieta 5-101
Col. Los Cipreses
04830 México, DF
Tel: (5) 677-4868 Fax: (5) 679-3575
Chemical engineering

Registro Industrial Mexicano
(Annual)
Reportero Industrial Mexicano, S.A.
Goldsmith 38-301
11560 México, DF
Tel: (5) 280-6122 Fax: (5) 280-8697
Industrial directory

Revista Mexicana de Fianzas
(Annual)
Mexican Bond Companies and Bancomer, S.N.C.
Puebla 383
Col. Roma, Deleg. Cuauhtemoc
06700 México, DF

Strategic Planning
(Annual; English, Spanish)
American Chamber of Commerce of Mexico
Lucerna 78-4
Col. Juárez, Deleg. Cuauhtémoc
06600 México, DF
Tel: (5) 705-0995, 724-3800
Fax: (5) 703-2911, 703-3908 Tlx: 1777609
*Macroeconomic overview, alternative economic
scenarios, survey of business perspectives, analysis,
historic data.*

US-Mexico Trade Pages
(Annual; English, Spanish)
Global Source, Inc.
1511 K St. NW, Suite 927
Washington, DC 20005, USA
Tel: [1] (202) 429-5582 Fax: [1] (202) 638-1284
*Trade statistics, detailed export information,contacts in
US and Mexico.*

ONLINE RESOURCES

MEXIS On-Line Data Service
Mexico Information Services
PO Box 11770
Forth Worth, TX 76110, USA
Tel: [1] (817) 924-0746, (800) 446-0746 (toll-free in the
US only)
Fax: [1] (817) 924-9687
*Access to international e-mail, legal information, books,
magazines, NAFTA text, financial reports on Mexican
companies, articles, research reports, Diario Oficial.*

MexNET Online (US office)
2810 South 400 West
Salt Lake City, UT 84115, USA
Tel: [1] (801) 486-8181 Fax: [1] (801) 486-6969
MexNET Online (Mexico office)
Calz. de Tlalpan 2250
Col. Avante
04460 México, DF
Tel: (5) 549-9267 Fax: (5) 544-7724
*Provides online access to trade leads, e-mail
communications with Mexican companies, NAFTA
schedules, regulations, event calendar, business card
directory, and classified advertisements.*

All addresses and telephone numbers are in Mexico unless otherwise noted. The country code for Mexico is [52].

NEWSPAPERS

ABC
(Daily; Spanish)
Editorial Monterrey
Platón Sánchez 411 Sur
64000 Monterrey, NL
Tel: (83) 44-2510, 44-4480, 44-5990
Tlx: 382056
Circ: 75,000

El Día
(Daily; Spanish)
Avda. Insurgentes Norete 1210
Capukiklan
070370 México, DF
Tel: (5) 546-0456 Fax: (5) 537-6629 Tlx: 1771029
National. Relatively small but serious newspaper.
Published by the left wing of the PRI. Circ: 75,000

El Diario de Guadalajara
(Daily; Spanish)
Editorial Hispano Mexicana
Calle 14, No. 2550
Zona Industrial
44940 Guadalajara, Jal.
Tel: (3) 612-0043 Fax: (3) 612-0818 Tlx: 1774579
Circ: 78,000

El Diario de Monterrey
(Daily; Spanish)
Periódico El Diario de Monterrey
Eugenio Garza Sada 2245
Col. Roma Sur
64700 Monterrey, NL
Tel: (83) 59-2525, 58-2519
Fax: (83) 59-7380 Tlx: 382605
Circ: 75,000

El Economista
(Daily; Spanish)
Publicaciones Mercalba
Avda. Coyoacán No. 515
Col. del Valle
03100 México, DF
Tel: (5) 669-1742 Fax: 687-3821, 523-6500
National financial daily; competes with more
established El Finaciero. Circ: 35,000

El Financiero
(Daily; Spanish)
Grupo Editorial SEFI
Lago Bolsena 176
11320 México, DF
Tel: (5) 254-6299 Fax: (5) 255-1881
National financial paper for the business community.
Circ: 80,000

El Financiero Internacional
(Weekly; English)
Lago Bolsena 176
Col. Anahuac
11320 México, DF
Tel: (5) 227-7600 Fax: (5) 227-7634
Weekly English-language version of leading Mexican
financial daily. US Subscription address: 2300 S.
Broadway, Los Angeles, CA 90007; Tel: [1] (213) 747-
7547 Fax: [1] (213) 747-2489.

El Heraldo
(Daily; Spanish)
Grupo Editorial SEFI
Lago Bolsena 176
11320 México, DF
Tel: (5) 578-3632 Fax: (5) 578-9824 Tlx: 1771219
Lively, colorful right-wing paper. Circ: 209,000.

El Informador
(Daily; Spanish)
Unión Editorial
Calle Independencia 300
Apdo. 3 bis
44100 Guadalajara, Jal.
Tel: (3) 614-6340 Fax: (3) 614-4653 Tlx: 683241
Circ: 60,000

El Nacional
(Daily; Spanish)
Ignacio Mariscal 25, Piso 3
Col. Tabacalera
Apdo. 446
06030 México, DF
Tel: (5) 535-3074 Fax: (5) 705-5615
Government newspaper. Circ: 120,000

El Norte
(Daily; Spanish)
Editora El Sol
Washington Ote. 629
Apdo. 186
64000 Monterrey, NL
Tel: (83) 45-5100, 40-1040
Fax: (83) 45-0264 Tlx: 382642
National paper with international coverage; includes
business and financial sections. Circ: 165,000

El Occidental
(Daily; Spanish)
Cía. Periodista del Sol de Guadalajara
Calzada Independencia Sur 324, Apdo. 1-699
44100 Guadalajara, Jal.
Tel: (3) 613-0690 Fax: (3) 613-6796 Tlx: 681799
Circ: 85,000

El Porvenir
(Daily; Spanish)
Galeana Sur 344
Apdo. 218
64000 Monterrey, NL
Tel: (83) 45-4080, 43-4605
Fax: (83) 45-7795 Tlx: 382739
Local, national, and international news. Circ: 75,000

El Sol
(Daily; Spanish)
Editora El Sol
Washington 629 Ote.
Apdo. 186
64000 Monterrey, NL
Tel: (83) 45-3388, 40-1040
Fax: (83) 45-0264 Tlx: 382642
Circ: 80,000

El Sol de México
(Daily; Spanish)
Organización Editoria Mexicana
Guillermo Prieto 7, Piso 20
Col. San Rafael
06470 México, DF
Tel: (5) 566-1511, 566-2866
National circulation. Circ: 110,000

El Universal
(Daily; Spanish)
El Universal Compañía Periodistical Nacional
Iturbide 7, Bucareli 8
Apdo. 909
06040 México, DF
Tel: (5) 709-1313
Oldest established Mexican newspaper; influential,
moderate. Important for classified ads. Publishes
afternoon paper, El Universal Grafico. *Circ: 180,000.*

Excelsior
(Daily; Spanish)
Cía. Editorial SCL
Paseo de la Reforma No. 18
Talleres
06600 México, DF
Tel: (5) 546-6262 Fax: (5) 566-0223 Tlx: 01772616
Pro-government, prestigious paper, leading daily. Best-known internationally. Also publishes afternoon paper, Ultimas Noticias, in two editions. Circ: 200,000

La Jornada
(Daily; Spanish)
DEMOS Desarrollo de Medios
Balderas 68
Col. Centro
06050 México, DF
Tel: (5) 518-1764 Fax: (5) 521-2763 Tlx: 1762334
Left-wing, independent, high-quality tabloid-size paper. Circ: 50,000

La Prensa
(Daily; Spanish)
Prensa Editora de Periódicos
Basilo Badillo 40
06030 México, DF
Tel: (5) 512-0799, 510-3434 Tlx: 01774253
Popular tabloid. Circ: 300,000.

Mexico City Daily Bulletin
(Daily; English)
Edit, S.A.
Gómez Farías 41
Col. San Rafael
06470 México, DF
Tel: (5) 546-5115 Fax: (5) 535-6060
Provides English-speaking visitors with information of major international happenings as well as information on sites of interest in their own language; includes local news.

Novedades
(Daily; Spanish)
Balderas 87, esq. Morelas
06040 México, DF
Tel: (5) 510-9707 Fax: (5) 521-4505 Tlx: 1773031
Good coverage of national events; color paper. Circ: 210,000.

Prontuario Internacional
(Daily)
Banco de México
Subdirección de Investigación Económica y Bancaria
Avda. Juárez 90
Col. Centro, Deleg. Cuauhtémoc
06059 México, DF
Tel: (5) 761-8588
Banking and finance

Siglo 21
(Daily; Spanish)
Alda Editores
Avda. Washington 250
Col. Ferrocaril
44440 Guadalajara, Jal.
Tel: (3) 650-3121 Fax: (3) 650-0419
Tabloid size with national and international focus, pictorial emphasis.

Uno Más Uno
(Daily; Spanish)
Editorial Uno
Primer Retorno de Correggio 12
03720 México, DF
Tel: (5) 563-9911 Tlx: 177255
Small circulation, but an influential, compact newspaper. Left-wing, aimed at political and intellectual circles. Circ: 75,000

GENERAL BUSINESS & TRADE PERIODICALS

Americas Trade & Finance: Report on the Emerging Common Markets of the Americas
(Monthly; English)
Latin American Information Services, Inc.
159 W. 53rd St., 28th Fl.
New York, NY 10019, USA
Tel: [1] (212) 765-5520 Fax: [1] (212) 765-2927

Avance
(Monthly)
American Chamber of Commerce of Mexico
Lucerna 78-4
Col. Juárez, Deleg. Cuauhtémoc
06600 México, DF
Tel: (5) 705-0995, 724-3800
Fax: (5) 703-2911, 703-3908 Tlx: 1777609
Activities of the chamber, trade fairs, offers and demands, and government decrees.

Bancomer Economic Report on Mexico
(English and Spanish eds. available)
Economic Studies, Bancomer S.A.
Avda. Universidad 1200
Deleg. Benito Juárez
03339 México, DF
Tel: (5) 534-0034 x5245 Fax: (5) 621-3297
Newsletter; comments on growth, domestic savings, trade balance, inflation, inter-bank rates, NAFTA

Boletín Comercial
(Quarterly; Spanish)
US Embassy, Commercial Section
Paseo de la Reforma 305
06500 México, DF
Tel: (5) 211-0042 x3739 Fax: (5) 511-9980
Targeted at Mexican CEOs who represent or want to represent US firms.

Buen Viaje!
(Bimonthly; English, Spanish)
Grupo Editoriale Aviare
Querétaro 229, Desp. 407, Apdo. 71339
06700 México, DF
Tel: (5) 584-3194 Fax: (5) 584-4821
Travel information for business travelers.

Business Latin America
(50/yr.; English)
Economist Intelligence Unit
111 West 57th St.
New York, NY 10019-2211
Tel: [1] (212) 554-0600 Fax: [1] (212) 586-1181/2

Business Mexico
(11/yr.; English)
American Chamber of Commerce of Mexico
Lucerna 78-4
Col. Juárez, Deleg. Cuauhtémoc
06600 México, DF
Tel: (5) 705-0995, 724-3800
Fax: (5) 703-2911, 703-3908 Tlx: 1777609
Comprehensive view of Mexico's economics, investment, trade, environment, and industries.

Canadian Free Trader
(Monthly; English)
Intratech
Minto Place Postal Outlet
Box 56067
Ottawa, ON K1R 7Z1, Canada
Tel: [1] (613) 235-9183
Covers Canada, the US, and Mexico.

Chronicle of Latin American Economic Affairs
(Weekly; English)
Latin American Institute
801 Yale NE
Albuquerque, NM 87131-1016, USA
Tel: [1] (505) 277-6839 Fax: [1] (505) 277-5989
Economic and political climates of Latin America

All addresses and telephone numbers are in Mexico unless otherwise noted. The country code for Mexico is [52].

Comercio
(Monthly; Spanish)
Río Tíber 8-70
06500 México, DF
Tel: (5) 514-0873 Fax: (5) 514-1169
International commerce

Comercio Exterior
(Monthly; Spanish)
Banco Nacional de Comercio Exterior, S.A.
Gerencia de la Revista Comercio Exterior
Periférico Sur 4333, Piso 4 Pte.
Tlalpan
14210 México, DF
Tel: (5) 227-9000 Fax: (5) 227-9318
International commerce

Decisión
(Monthly; Spanish)
Confederación de Cámaras Nacionales de Comercio,
Servicios y Turismo
Balderas 144, Piso 2, Apdo. 113
06079 México, DF
Tel: (5) 709-1679 Fax: (5) 709-1152
Business and economics

Diario Oficial (Mexican Government Official Daily)
(Daily; Spanish)
Secretaría de Gobernación
Bucareli No. 99, Piso 1
Col. Juárez
06699 México, DF
Tel: (5) 532-5630, 672-1654
Mexican procurement announcements and requests for
bids are in this publication. Contracts covered by NAFTA
will be indicated.

Ejecutivos de Finanzas
(Monthly; Spanish)
Instituto Mexicano de Ejecutivos de Finanzas
Patricio Sanz 1516
03100, México, DF
Fax: (5) 575-4410 Tlx: 1764183
Executive management

Examen de la Situación Económica de México
English ed.: Review of the Economic Situation of
Mexico
(Monthly; Spanish and English eds.)
Banco Nacional de México, Dept. of Economic
Research
Madero 21, Piso 2
00600 México, DF
Fax: (5) 761-9044

Expansión
(Fortnightly; Spanish)
Grupo Editorial Expansión, S.A.
Salamanca No. 35
Col. Roma
06700 México DF
Tel: (5) 208-9609 Fax: (5) 511-6351
Prominent general business publication

Foreign Broadcasting Information Service Daily
Reports: Latin America
(Daily; English)
National Technical Information Service
5285 Port Royal Road
Springfield, VA 22161, USA
Tel: [1] (703) 487-4630
Information from foreign radio and television
broadcasts, news agency transmissions, etc.

Global Production & Transportation: Manufacturing &
Sourcing in the Americas
(Bimonthly; English)
1319 Spruce St.
Boulder, CO 80302, USA
Tel: [1] (303) 939-8440 Fax: [1] (303) 939-0069

Industria
(Monthly; Spanish)
Confederación de Cámaras Industriales de los Estados
Unidos Mexicanos
Manuel Ma. Contreras No. 133, Piso 1
Col. Cuauhtémoc, Deleg. Cuauhtémoc
06597 México, DF
Tel: (5) 592-0529 Fax: (5) 535-6871 Tlx: 1772789
Domestic commerce

Inter-Cambio
(3/yr.; English; Spanish)
Cámara de Comercio Británica, A.C.
Río de la Plata 30
Col. Cuauhtémoc
06500 México, DF
Tel: (5) 256-0901 Fax: (5) 211-5451
Anglo-Mexican business

Intercambio Internacional
(Semiannual; Spanish)
Grupo Internacional Editores, S.A.
Nicolás San Juan No. 1154
México, DF
International trade

Inversionista Mexicano
(Monthly; English, Spanish)
Mexican Financial Advisory Service, S.A.
Félix Cuevas 301-204
Col. del Valle, Deleg. Benito Juárez
03100 México, DF
Tel: (5) 534-9297 Fax: (5) 524-3756
Investment business newsletter

Lagniappe Letter
(Biweekly; English)
Latin American Information Services, Inc.
159 W. 53rd St., 28th Fl.
New York, NY 10019, USA
Tel: [1] (212) 765-5520 Fax: [1] (212) 765-2927
Issues affecting business in Latin America

Latin American Law and Business Report
(Monthly; English)
WorldTrade Executive
PO Box 761
Concord, MA 01742, USA
Tel: [1] (508) 287-0302 Fax: [1] (508) 287-0301

Laws of Mexico in English
Foreign Tax Law Publishers, Inc.
PO Box 2189
Orlando Beach, FL 32175-2189, USA
Tel: [1] (904) 253-5785 Fax: [1] (904) 257-3003

Made in Mexico: The International Business Magazine
(Quarterly; English, Spanish)
2865 S. Colorado Blvd.
Suite 321, Denver, CO 80222, USA
Tel: [1] (303) 934-8694

Management Today: En Español
(Every 45 days; Spanish)
Comunicación Profesional Impresa, S.A.
Sinaloa No. 222, Primer Piso
06700 México, DF
Tel: (5) 286-3632 Fax: (5) 553-4107

Marynka: Mercados de México en Accion
(Annual; Spanish)
Publicaciones Marynka S.A.
Salaverry 1204
Col. Zacatenco
07360 México, DF
Tel: (5) 574-1381
Domestic commerce

Mercado de Valores
(Weekly; Spanish)
Nacional Financiera, Subdirección de Información
Técnica y Publicaciones
Venustiano Carranza 25
Deleg. Cuauhtémoc
06008 México, DF
Investments

Mexican Business & Investment
(Every 15 days; English)
El Inversionista Mexicano
Félix Cuevas 301-204
Col. del Valle
03100 México, DF
Tel: (5) 534-9297, 524-5396 Fax: (5) 524-3794
English language version of El Inversionista Mexicano.
Updates on consumer prices, foreign investment,
economic indicators; many tables and graphs.

Mexican Business Review
(Monthly; English)
Mexican Information Services
PO Box 11770
Fort Worth, TX 76110, USA
Tel: [1] (817) 924-0746 Fax: [1] (817) 924-9687

Mexican Forecast: Fortnightly Forecast for
Management and Investors on Mexican Business and
Investment Trends
(Fortnightly; English)
Grupo Editorial Espansion, S.A.
Salamanca No. 35
Col. Roma
06700 México, DF
Tel: (5) 208-9609

Mexican Stock Exchange Trading Report
(Quarterly; Spanish, English editions)
Bolsa Mexicana de Valores, S.A. de C.V.
Paseo de la Reforma 255
06500 México, DF
Tel: (5) 726-6791 Fax: (5) 591-0534
Summary of the behavior of the securities market in
Mexico, general environment, and trends

Mexico Business Monthly
(Monthly; English)
52 Maple Ave.
Maplewood, NJ 07040, USA
Tel: [1] (201) 762-1565 Fax: [1] (201) 762-9585
Business, economic, and political news

Mexico Country Forecast
(Quarterly; English)
Economist Intelligence Unit
111 West 57th St.
New York, NY 10019-2211, USA
Tel: [1] (212) 554-0600 Fax: [1] (212) 586-1181/2
Key factors affecting Mexico's political and economic
outlook and its business environment over next five
years

Mexico Country Report
(Quarterly; English)
Economist Intelligence Unit
111 West 57th St.
New York, NY 10019-2211, USA
Tel: [1] (212) 554-0600 Fax: [1] (212) 586-1181/2
Analysis of Mexico's current political and economic
climate and short-term economic projections.

Mexico Country Risk Service
(Quarterly; English)
Economist Intelligence Unit
111 West 57th St.
New York, NY 10019-2211, USA
Tel: [1] (212) 554-0600 Fax: [1] (212) 586-1181/2
Focuses on predicting growth, budget deficits, trade and
current accounts, foreign financing requirements and
sources, and debt service for Mexico.

Mexico Insight
(Biweekly; English)
Bucareli No. 1, Piso 5
Col. Centro
06600 México, DF
Tel: (5) 705-4444 Fax: (5) 705-2631
English-language news magazine with business
emphasis published by the national newspaper
Excelsior. Available in the US from: PO Box 302,
Somers, WI 53144, USA; Tel: (800) 552-1262 (toll-free in
the US only) Fax: [1] (414) 551-8310.

Mexico Service
(Fortnightly; English)
International Reports, Inc.
11300 Rockville Pike, Suite 1100
Rockville, MD 20852-3035, USA
Tel: [1] (212) 685-6900
Economic, financial, and political developments in
Mexico

Mexico Today
(Quarterly; English, Spanish)
Diplomatist Associates, Ltd.
58 Theobalds Rd.
London WC1, UK
From the Embassy of Mexico in London

Mexico Watch
(Monthly; English)
Heritage Foundation
214 Massachusetts Ave., NE
Washington, DC 20002, USA
Tel: [1] (202) 546-4400 Fax: [1] (202) 546-8328
Tracks changes in US-Mexican ties, Mexican foreign
policy, Mexican domestic affairs, and NAFTA.

Negocios y Bancos (Negobancos)
(24/yr.; Spanish)
Publicaciones Importantes, S.A.
Bolívar 8-601, Apdo. 1907
06000 México, DF
Tel: (5) 510-1884 Fax: (5) 512-9411
Important banking and finance journal

Panorama Económico/Economic Panorama
(Bimonthly; English and Spanish eds.)
Bancomer, Sociedad Nacional Crédito
Grupo Investigaciones Economicas
Universidad Avenue 1200
03339 México, DF
Tel: (5) 534-0034 x5245
Covers Mexican economy with emphasis on the
automotive and textile industries

Progreso: Comercio-Industria-Finanzas-Desarrollo
(9/yr.; Spanish)
Editorial Visión, S.A.
Gutemberg 143
11590 México, DF

Puertos: Toward World Commerce
(Monthly)
Balderas No. 44, Desp. 402-403
Apdo. 1281
06050 México, DF
Tel: (5) 510-9953, 510-8808 Tlx: 5128280
International commerce

Reportero Industrial Mexicano
(Monthly; Spanish)
Keller International Publishing Corporation
150 Great Neck Rd.
Great Neck, NY 11021, USA
Tel: [1] (516) 829-9210
Fax: [1] (516) 829-5414 Tlx: 221574

Review of Trade and Industry in Mexico
(Quarterly, English)
American Chamber of Commerce of Mexico
Lucerna 78-4
Col. Juárez, Deleg. Cuauhtémoc
06600 México, DF
Tel: (5) 705-0995, 724-3800
Fax: (5) 703-2911, 703-3908 Tlx: 1777609

Sourcemex: Economic News and Analysis on Mexico
(Weekly)
University of New Mexico
Latin American Institute
801 Yale NE
Albuquerque, NM 87131-1016, USA
Tel: [1] (505) 277-6839 Fax: [1] (505) 277-5989
Economic environment, including private investment,
public policy, petroleum, agriculture, trade,
environment, and social welfare

TribunAMCHAM
(Bimonthly; English)
American Chamber of Commerce of Mexico
Lucerna 78-4
Col. Juárez, Deleg. Cuauhtémoc
06600 México, DF
Tel: (5) 705-0995, 724-3800
Fax: (5) 703-2911, 703-3908 Tlx: 1777609

Tricontinental Trade Connection
(Quarterly)
Cross International Infotransfer Systems
194 S. Franklin
Nyack, NY 10960, USA
Tel: [1] (501) 367-7309
Joint ventures in developing countries of Africa, Asia,
Latin America with moderate risk and high yield
potential

Twin Plant News: The Magazine of the Maquiladora
Industry
(Monthly)
Nibbe, Hernández & Associates, Inc.
4110 Río Bravo Dr., No. 108
El Paso, TX 79902, USA
Tel: [1] (915) 532-1567 Fax: [1] (915) 544-7556

US/Latin Trade
(Monthly; English)
New World Communications
One Biscayne Tower
2 South Biscayne Blvd., Suite 2950
Miami, FL 33131, USA
Tel: [1] (305) 358-8373 Fax: [1] (305) 358-9166

US-Mexico Free Trade Reporter
(Biweekly; English)
WorldTrade Executive Inc.
Box 761, Concord, MA 01742, USA
Tel: [1] (508) 287-0301 Fax: [1] (508) 287-0302
News on trade, investment, and related trans-border
issues

Visión: La Revista Interamericana
(Fortnightly; Spanish)
Arquémedies 199, Pisos 6 y 7
Col. Polanco
11570 México, DF
Tel: (5) 203-6091 Tlx: 1763168
Latin American news. US office: 310 Madison Ave., Suite
1412, New York, NY 10017; Tel: [1] (212) 953-1308 Fax:
[1] (212) 953-1619.

INDUSTRY-SPECIFIC PERIODICALS

Actualidad en Seguros y Fianzas
(Quarterly; Spanish)
Comisión Nacional de Seguros y Fianzas
Avda. de los Insurgentes Sur 1971
Plaza Inn, Torre 2 N., Piso 2
01020 México, DF
Insurance and surety bonds sector

ADM
(Bimonthly)
Asociación Dental Mexicana, A.C.
Ezequiel Montes No. 92
Col. Revolución, Deleg. Cuauhtémoc
06030 México, DF
Tel: (5) 566-6133 Fax: (5) 705-4629
Dentistry

Agricultura Técnica en México
(Semiannual; Spanish with English summaries)
Instituto Nacional de Investigaciones Forestales y
Agropecuarias
Subdirección de Difusión Científica y Tecnológica
Apdo. 6-882
06600 México, DF
Agricultural technology

Agro-Cultura
(Spanish)
Grupo Editorial Eikon
Apdo. 328
45101 Zapopan, Jal.
Tel: (3) 660-5641
Agriculture

Agro-Síntesis: Agricultura-Ganadería-Avicultura
(Monthly; Spanish)
Editorial Año Dos Mil, S.A.
Indianápolis 70
03810 México, DF
Tel: (5) 523-9912 Fax: (5) 523-3007
Agriculture, livestock, and poultry

Agromundo
(Spanish)
Editorial Agromundo
Guadalajara 809
89120 Tampico, Tamps.
Tel: (12) 17-0005, 13-4611 Fax: (12) 13-4639

Agronegocios en México
(Monthly; Spanish)
3A Coa. Bahamas 31
Col. Lomas Estrella, Iztapalapa
09890 México, DF
Tel: (5) 656-5918
Cattle, finance, forestry, poultry, and industry

Alto Peinado
(Monthly; Spanish)
Editorial Famari
Norte 72-A, No. 6120
Col. Gertrúdiz Sánchez
07820 México, DF
Tel: (5) 760-9391 Fax: (5) 751-5918
Beauty industry

Apparel Industry Internacional
(Bimonthly)
Shore Communications, Inc.
6255 Barfield Rd., NE, Suite 200
Atlanta, GA 30328-4300, USA
Tel: [1] (404) 252-8831 Fax: [1] (404) 252-4436
Factory management for apparel companies in Latin
America

Apparel Industry Magazine
(Monthly; English)
Shore Communications, Inc.
180 Allen Rd., NE, Suite 300 N.
Atlanta, GA 30328, USA
Tel: [1] (404) 252-8831 Fax: [1] (404) 252-4436
Apparel manufacturing in the US, Canada, and Latin America

ATCP Revista
(Bimonthly; Spanish with English summaries)
Asociación Mexicana de Técnicos de las Industrias de la Celulosa y del Papel, A.C.
GSA Publicidad
Avda. Insurgentes No. 3493, Poseidon No. 504
14020 México, DF
Tel: (5) 665-0368 Tlx: 1773608
Worldwide pulp and paper trade industry

Atención Médica
(Monthly; Spanish)
Intersistemas
Fernando Alencastre No. 110
Lomas de Chapultepec
11000 México, DF
Tel: (5) 540-5600, 540-0798
Directed at the doctor in general practice

Autoindustria
(Monthly; English)
Grupo Editorial Aviare
Querétaro 229, Desp. 402, Apdo. 71339
06700 México, DF
Tel: (5) 584-3194 Fax: (5) 584-4821
Automotive industry

Banca y Comercio
(Quarterly)
Escuela Bancaria y Comercial
Paseo de la Reforma 202
06600 México, DF
Fax: (5) 546-0326
Banking and commerce

Cámara Nacional de la Industria de Transformación: Boletín Informativo
(Monthly)
CANACINTRA
Avda. San Antonio 256
Col. Amp. Nápoles
03849 México, DF
Tel: (5) 563-3400, 611-6238 Fax: (5) 598-9464
Manufacturing industry

Ciencia y Desarrollo
(Bimonthly; Spanish)
Consejo Nacional de Ciencia y Tecnología
Avda. Constituyentes 1046
Col. Lomas Altas
11950 México, DF
Tel: (5) 655-6366 Fax: (5) 655-3906 Tlx: 01774521
Science and technology

Communicator
(Monthly; English)
Associated Credit Bureaus, Inc.
1090 Vermont Ave. NW, Suite 200
Washington, DC 20005-4905, USA
Tel: [1] (202) 371-0910 Fax: [1] (202) 371-0134
For owners and managers of credit bureaus, collection agencies, and related services throughout the US, Canada, and Mexico

Comunicaciones
(Spanish)
Latcom de México
Cuernavaca No. 106
Col. Condesa
06140 México, DF
Tel: (5) 553-0922
Telecommunications

Confección
(Spanish)
Talleres de Ediciones Comerciales
Norte 17 No. 5258
Nueva Vallejo
07750 México, DF
Tel/Fax: (5) 368-0550

Constru-Noticias
(Monthly; Spanish)
Publi-News Latinoamericana, S.A.C.V.
Colima 436, Piso 2
06700 México, DF
Tel: (5) 286-3113
Building and construction

Construcción y Tecnología
(Monthly; Spanish)
Instituto Mexicano del Cemento y del Concreto, A.C.
Insurgentes sur No. 1846
01030 México, DF
Fax: (5) 534-8806
Technological reports on cement and concrete for application to work done in Mexico

Desarrollo Tecnológico
(2-3/yr.; Spanish with summaries in English)
Universidad Nacional Autónoma de México
Instituto de Investigaciones en Matemáticas Aplicadas y en Sistemas
Apdo. 20-726, Deleg. V.A. Obregón
01000 México, DF
Tel: (5) 622-3562 Fax: (5) 550-0047
Electronics and computer sciences

Dulcelandia: Industrias Alimenticias
(Monthly)
Editorial Manila
Milán 38-202 B
Col. Juárez, Deleg. Cuauhtémoc
06600 México, DF
Tel: (5) 592-3124 Fax: (5) 592-3858
Baking and confection indutries

El Campo: Revista Mensual Agrícola y Ganadera
(Monthly)
Publicaciones Armol, S.A.
Mar Negro No. 147, Apdo. 17-506
11410 México, DF
Tel: (5) 527-4554
Agriculture and livestock

En Concreto
(6/yr.)
Instituto Nacional de Planificación Integral
D'Pastrana Editores, S.A.
Kepler No. 147-A
Col. Anzures
México, DF
Housing and urban planning

Energía y Movimiento
(Spanish)
Editorial Mundo Color Gráfico
Retorno 32 No. 24
Avante
04460 México, DF
Tel: (5) 544-0250 Fax: (5) 689-5238
Electric toys

Environment Watch Latin America: News and Analysis for Business and Policy Professionals
(Monthly; English)
Cutter Information Corp.
37 Broadway
Arlington, MA 02174-5539, USA
Tel: [1] (800) 888-8939 (Toll-free in the US only)
Fax: [1] (617) 648-8707 Tlx: 6501009891
Covers the business implications of policy developments in the environmental arena. Focus includes Mexico.

All addresses and telephone numbers are in Mexico unless otherwise noted. The country code for Mexico is [52].

Farmacia Actual
(Monthly; Spanish)
Galo Editores
Alfonso Esparza Oteo 153
Col. Guadalupe Inn
01020 México, DF
Tel: (5) 548-1844, 548-6774
Pharmaceuticals

Ferretecnic—FYT: La Revista de la Industria Ferretera
(Monthly)
Publitecnic S.A.
Calle 4, no. 188, Apdo. 74-290
09070 México, DF
Tel: (5) 685-2819 Fax: (5) 670-6318
Metallurgy

Gaceta Agrícola
(Every 10 days; Spanish)
Àvda. La Paz 1522, Apdo. 5-225
45000 Guadalajara, Jal.
Agriculture

Gaceta Médica de México
(Bimonthly; Spanish with summaries in English)
Academia Nacional de Medicina
Unidad de Congresos del Centro Médico Nacional
Avda. Cuauhtémoc 330
06725 México, DF
Tel: (5) 578-2044 Fax: (5) 578-4271
Medical sciences

Ganadero/Rancher
(Bimonthly)
Editorial Ocampo S.A. de C.V.
Zaragoza No. 11
San Juan Tepepan
16020 México, DF
Tel: (5) 676-0515
Livestock

Geomimet
(Bimonthly; Spanish)
Asociación de Ingenieros de Minas, Metalurgistas y
Geólogos de México
Paseo de la Reforma 51, Piso 18-801
Col. Revolución, Deleg. Cuauhtémoc
06030 México, DF
Energy resources sector of Mexico.

Guía Automotriz
(Monthly)
J. Rodríguez & Cía., S.A.
Sur 51 No. 118
Col. Ermita
México, DF
Transportation industry

Hair Fashion de México: Sólo Moda en Peinados y
Belleza
(Bimonthly)
Editorial Famari
Norte 72-A No. 6120
Col. Gertrudis Sánchez
07830 México, DF
Tel: (5) 760-9391 Fax: (5) 751-5918
Beauty industry

Hélice
(Bimonthly)
Mexican Air Line Pilots Association
Avda. Palomas 110
Lomas de Sotelo
México, DF
Fax: (5) 202-2573 Tlx: 1763468
Aeronautics and aviation

Hombre y Trabajo: Boletín de Medicina, Seguridad e
Higiene
(Monthly; Spanish)
Dirección General de Medicina y Seguridad en el
Trabajo
Calzada Azcapotzalco-La Villa No. 209
Junto Metro Ferrería
02020 México, DF
Tel: (5) 394-3344
Occupational health and general medicine

Hule Mexicano y Plásticos: Revista Técnica Industrial
(Monthly; Spanish)
Filomeno Mata 13-11
Col. Centro, Deleg. Cuauhtémoc,
06000 México, DF
Tel: (5) 521-5751
Rubber and plastics

Hulequipo
(Monthly; Spanish)
Querétaro No. 229-402
06700 México, DF
Rubber

Impresor: Al Servicio de las Artes Gráficas
(Monthly; English, Spanish)
Imprentas Menra, S.A.
Sta. Ma. la Rivera 9-103
06400 México, DF
Tel: (5) 546-8725 Fax: (5) 566-1038
Graphic arts industry

Industria Alimentaria
(Bimonthly)
Alfa Editores Técnicos S.A.
Libertad No. 107-402
03660 México, DF
Fax: (5) 532-9504, 539-5737
Food industry

Información: Imagen Nacional e Internacional de
Comunicaciones y Transportes
(Bimonthly)
Secretaría de Comunicaciones y Transportes
Avda. Universidad y Xola
Col. Navarte
03028 México, DF
Tel: (5) 519-7456, 519-1319, 530-9203, 530-1074
Fax: (5) 519-9748, 530-1074 Tlx: 017600
Communications and transportation

Informador: Noticias y Comentarios de la Industria
Mueblera y Maderera
(Semi-monthly; Spanish)
Playa Caleta No. 359
Col. Reforma Iztaccihuatl
08810 México, DF
Lumber and furniture

Ingenieria Civil/Civil Engineering
(Bimonthly)
Camino de Santa Teresa No. 187
México 22, DF
Civil engineering

Ingenieria Mecánica y Eléctrica
(Monthly; Spanish)
Asociación Mexicana de Ingenieros Mecanicos y
Electricistas
Culiacán 115
Col. Roma Sur
México, DF
Mechanical and electrical engineering

Ingenieria Petrolera
(Monthly)
Asociación de Ingenieros Petroleros de México
Apdo. 53-013
11490 México, DF
Petroleum engineering

Instituto Mexicano del Petróleo: Revista
(Quarterly; Spanish with summaries in English)
Instituto Mexicano del Petróleo
Eje Central Lázaro Cárdenas Norte 152
Col. San Bartolo Atepehuacan
07730 México, DF
Tel: (5) 398-17-99
Petroleum and gas

Intermueble
(Spanish)
Avda. Guadalupe No. 5511-42
Residencial Plaza Guadalupe
45030 Zapopan, Jal.
Tel: (3) 628-0146, 628-0905 Fax: (3) 628-0146
Furniture

La Bobina—Notivest
(Monthly; Spanish)
Bobbin Blenheim Media Corp.
1110 Shop Rd., Box 1986
Columbia, SC 29202, USA
Tel: [1] (803) 771-7500 Fax: [1] (803) 799-1461
*Serves executives in Latin-American apparel-sewn
products industry.*

Lector
(Semiannual)
Floricanto Press
16161 Ventura Blvd., Suite 830
Encino, CA 91436-2504, USA
Tel: [1] (818) 990-1885
*Information about Spanish language books published in
Spain, Latin America, and the US of interest to
Hispanics in America.*

Libros de México
(Quarterly; Spanish)
Cámara Nacional de la Industria Editorial Mexicana
Holanda 13
Col. San Diego Churubusco
04120 Coyoacán, Edo. de Méx.
Tel: (5) 688-7122 Fax: (5) 604-3147
Publishing and book trade

Madera y Su Uso en la Construcción
(Irregular; Spanish)
Instituto de Ecologia
Apdo. 63, 9100 Xalapa
Veracruz
México, DF
Fax: (5) 281-6910
Building and construction

Más Caminos: Por un Sistema Integral de Transportes
(Monthly; Spanish)
Asociación Mexicana de Caminos
Río Tíber 103, Piso 2
06500 México, DF
Tel: (5) 528-6676, 207-4660
Transportation

Mayoreo y Distribución
(Monthly; Spanish)
Editorial Manila
Milán 38-202
Col. Juárez, Deleg. Cuauhtémoc
06600 México, DF
Tel: (5) 592-3124 Fax: (5) 592-3858
Grocery industry

Mercado de las Artes Gráficas
(6/yr.; Spanish)
Publi-Representaciones
Tlacotalpan No. 109-204
México 7, DF
Graphic arts and printing

Mexico & NAFTA Report
(Monthly; English)
Latin American Newsletters
61 Old St.
London EC1V 9HX, UK
Tel: [44] (71) 251-0012 Fax: [44] (71) 253-8193

Mexico Holstein
(Monthly)
Mexican Holstein Breeders Association
Editorial Año Dos Mil, S.A.
Indianápolis 70
Col. Nápoles
03810 México, DF
Tel: (5) 543-0710
Dairy industry

Minero-Noticias
(Monthly; Spanish)
Publi-News Latinoamericana, S.A. de C.V.
Colima 436, Piso 2
06700 México, DF
Tel: (5) 514-4503
Mining

Mueble Equipo
(Spanish)
Notimueble
28 de Enero No. 337
Sec. Reforma
44400 Guadalajara, Jal.
Tel: (3) 617-4455, 617-6076 Fax: (3) 654-0732
Furniture manufacturing equipment

Mundo Médico
(Monthly; Spanish)
Matias Romero 116
Col. del Valle
03100 México, DF
Tel: (5) 559-2755 Fax: (5) 559-2821
Medical science

NAFTA Law Reporter
(Looseleaf service; English)
WorldTrade Executive
PO Box 761
Concord, MA 01742, USA
Tel: [1] (508) 287-0302
Fax: [1] (508) 287-0301

Obras
(Monthly; Spanish)
Grupo Editorial Expansión, S.A.
Salamanca No. 35
06700 México, DF
Tel: (5) 208-9609 Fax: (5) 511-6351
Housing and urban planning

Pan
(Monthly; Spanish)
Bravo Grupo Editorial, S.A.
J. Ma. Bustillos 49
Col. Algarin
06880 México, DF
Tel: (5) 530-6062 Fax: (5) 538-8679
Baking industry

Panorama Plástico: La Revista Mexicana del Plástico
(Monthly; Spanish)
Editorial Corso, S.A. de C.V.
Insurgentes Sur No. 594-502
Col. del Valle
03100 México, DF
Tel: (5) 669-3087, 669-3087
Fax: (5) 523-2203, 523-2203
Technical information on plastics industry

Pastizales
(Semiannual; Spanish with summaries in English)
Instituto Nacional de Investigaciones Forestales y
Agropecuarias
Campo Experimental "La Campana"
Apdo. 1204
Chihuahua, Chih.
Tel: (14) 81-0769 Fax: (14) 81-0257
*Research in range management, cattle production, and
other topics*

PC-TIPS: Ideas y Recomendaciones Para Optimizar el
Uso de Su Computadora Personal
(Monthly; Spanish)
Editora y Comercializadora de Bienes de Informática
Goldsmith No. 38, Piso 3
Col. Polanco
11560 México, DF
Tel: (5) 259-1448 Fax: (5) 202-6970 Tlx: 1763259
Personal computers

PEMEX: Boletín Bibliográfico
(Monthly; English)
Petróleos Mexicanos
Unidad de Servicios Sociales y Culturales, Biblioteca
Central
Marina Nacional 329, Edif. A, Mezzanine
11300 México, DF
Abstracts from scientific and technical journals.

Pequeña Diana
(Monthly; Spanish)
Lucio Blanco 435
Col. Juan Tlihuaca
02400 México, DF
Tel: (5) 352-6056
Arts and handicrafts

Perfumería Moderna/Modern Perfuming
(Monthly)
Bravo Grupo Editorial, S.A.
J. Ma. Bustillos 49
Col. Algarin
06880 México, DF
Tel: (5) 530-6062 Fax: (5) 538-8679
*Suppliers' guide to perfumes, cosmetics, aerosols,
detergents, insecticides, pharmaceuticals, and chemical
products*

Plasti-Noticias
(Monthly; Spanish)
Publi-News Latinoamericana, S.A. de C.V.
Colima 436, Piso 2
06700 México, DF
Tel: (5) 514-4503
Plastics

Promacasa
(Monthly; Spanish)
Avda. Cuauhtémoc, No. 1486-401C
México, DF
Building and construction

Prontuario Agroquímico
(Annual; Spanish)
Ediciones PLM
San Bernardino 17
Col. del Valle, Deleg. Benito Juárez
03100 México, DF
Tel: (5) 684-1311 Tlx: 01772912
Agricultural chemicals

Revista Mexicana de Comunicación
(Bimonthly; Spanish)
Funación Manuel Buendía
Avda. Cuauhtémoc 16, Mezzanine 2
Col. Doctores
06720 México, DF
Tel: (5) 578-1943, 761-4863
Fax: (5) 578-1943 Tlx: 1775646
Communications

Revista Mexicana de Seguros y Finanzas
(Monthly; Spanish)
Apdo. 19-193
03910 México, DF
Fax: (5) 511-1133
Insurance and finance

Revista Mexicana del Petróleo
(Bimonthly; English and Spanish)
Ediciones y Publicaciones Petroleras
Morelos 31, Desp. 303
06040 México, DF
Tel: (5) 510-9950, 521-0080
Fax: (5) 521-4630
Oil, gas, and petrochemical industries

Tecno Industria
(Spanish)
Consejo Nacional de Ciencia y Tecnología
Avda. Constituyentes 1046
Col. Lomas Altas
11950 México, DF
Tel: (5) 627-7400
Technology and industry

Tecnología de Alimentos
(Bimonthly: Spanish with summaries in English)
Asociación de Tecnologos Alimentos de México
Indianápolis No. 63-2
03810 México, DF
Food industry

Textil Vestido
(Monthly; Spanish)
Melchor Ocampo 156
México, DF
Apparel industry

Transpor
(Monthly; Spanish)
San Francisco 224, Piso 5
Col. del Valle, Apdo. 12879
México, DF
Transportation industry

Transportes y Turismo
(Monthly; Spanish)
Insurgentes Norte No. 696
México, DF
Tel: (5) 782-2140 Fax: (5) 583-3318
Transportation and tourism industries

Ultima Moda
(Fortnightly)
Publicaciones Herrerias, S.A.
Balderas 87, Piso 2
06040 México, DF
Tel: (5) 518-5481
Apparel and fashion industry

US-Mexico Law Journal
University of New Mexico, School of Law
1117 Stanford NE
Albuquerque, NM 87131
Tel: [1] (505) 277-2146

Vesti-Noticias
(Spanish)
Publi-News Latinoamericana
Colima 436, Piso 2
06700 México, DF
Tel: (5) 211-0729 Fax: (5) 211-0692

RADIO & TELEVISION

Cablevisión
Dr. Río de la Loza 182
06720 México, DF
Tel: (5) 588-1481 Fax: (5) 588-1546
Cable television network

Cadena Crystal Radio y TV
Montecito 59
Col. Nápoles
03810 México, DF
Tel: (5) 687-8495, 687-8445 Fax: (5) 543-3242
Radio network providing news and music programs

Cámara Nacional de la Industria de Radio y Televisión
(CIRT)
Avda. Horacio 1013
Col. Polanco
11550 México, DF
Tel: (5) 545-4165, 726-9909
Fax: (5) 545-6767 Tlx: 1777272
Government regulatory body, national radio and TV broadcasting company

Corporación Mexicana de Radiodifusión
Paseo de la Reforma 403, Piso 20
06500 México, DF
Tel: (5) 528-6532, 525-2466 Fax: (5) 207-6503
Represents commercial radio stations

Dirección de Normas de Radiodifusión
Eugenia 197, Piso 1
Col. Vértiz Narvarte
03020 México, DF
Tel: (5) 590-4372
License issuing authority

Dirección General de Radio, Televisión y Cine (RTC)
Atletas 2
Col. Country Club
04220 México, DF
Tel: (5) 544-9692, 544-3768
Government body that directs the transmission of broadcasting and films in Mexico

FM Globo Stereo—Stereorey
Frecuencia Modulada Mexicana
Mariano Escobedo No. 532
Col. Anzures
11590 México, DF
Tel: (5) 203-4120, 203-4520 Fax: (5) 203-4574
Radio network providing news programs, commercials, and music

Grupo ACIR
Monte Pirineos
Col. Lomas de Chapultepec
11000 México, DF
Tel: (5) 540-4291 Fax: (5) 540-4106
Radio network, broadcasts 24 hours a day throughout Mexico

Instituto Mexicano de la Radio (IMER)
Mexican Radio Institute
Mayorazgo 83
Col. Xoco
03330 México, DF
Tel: (5) 604-8532, 604-7741

Instituto Mexicano de Televisión (IMEVISION)
Avda. Periférico Sur 4121
Col. Fuentes del Pedregal
14141 México, DF
Tel: (5) 568-5684, 568-1313 Tlx: 1773878
Government TV institute; controls several channels and produces educational and cultural programs

MVS (Multivision)
Blvd. Puerto Aéreo 486
Col. Moctezuma
15500 México, DF
Tel: (5) 254-4446, 254-2856, 254-8378
Commercial TV channel offering a wide variety of programs

Organización Impulsora de Radio
Avda. Nuevo León 16, Piso 2
Col. Hipódromo Condesa, Deleg. Cuauhtémoc
06170 México, DF
Tel: (5) 286-5844 Fax: (5) 207-5778
Radio organization which produces programs and represents a variety of stations

Radio Cadena Nacional (RCN)
Avda. Coyoacán 1899
Col. Acacias
03240 México, DF
Tel: (5) 534-2300/3 Fax: (5) 524-2753
National radio network

Radio Comerciales
Avda. México y López Mateos
44680 Guadalajara, Jal.
Tel: (3) 615-0852, 616-0327 Fax: (3) 630-3487
Radio network of seven major commercial stations in the Jalisco region

Radiodifusoras y Televisoras de Occidente
Vallarta 1393, Desp. 102
Guadalajara, Jal.
Tel: (3) 625-2206, 622-1922 Fax: (3) 622-1903
Private organization holding information about TV and radio broadcasting in Mexico, including advertising rates

Radio Educación
Angel Urraza 622
Col. del Valle
03100 México, DF
Tel: (5) 575-9886, 559-3251 Tlx: 1764075
Independent radio station broadcasting cultural programs nationally

Radio Programas de México (RPM)
La Presa 212
San Jerónimo Lidice
10200 México, DF
Tel: (5) 683-1849, 683-2662 Fax: (5) 683-5044
Offices for Radio VIP (88.1 FM), which broadcasts English-language programming

Sistema Radio Juventud
Pablo Casals No. 567
Prados Providencia
Guadalajara, Jal.
Tel: (3) 641-6096, 641-6677
Radio network

Sociedad Mexicana de Radio (SOMER)
Gutemberg 89
Col. Anzures
11590 México, DF
Tel: (5) 255-5297, 255-5871 Fax: (5) 545-0310
Owns radio stations and represents them for advertising purposes

Televisa
Edif. Televicentro
Avda. Chapultepec 28
Col. Doctores
06724 México, DF
Tel: (5) 709-3333, 709-2314 Fax: (5) 709-2136
Controls majority of TV channels; also produces programs, films, and merchandise.

LIBRARIES

American Chamber of Commerce Library
Lucerna 78-4
Col. Juárez, Deleg. Cuauhtémoc
06600 México, DF
Tel: (5) 546-7154, 705-0995

Benjamin Franklin Library
Calle Londres 16
06600 México, DF
Tel: (5) 591-0244, 211-0042 x3482
Library of the US Information Agency; includes Department of Commerce publications, US and Mexican books and periodicals.

Canadian Embassy Library
Schiller 529
Col. Polanco
11020 México, DF
Tel: (5) 254-3288
Wide selection of Canadian books and periodicals in English and French.

Center for Latin American Monetary Studies
Durango 54
Deleg. Cuauhtémoc
06700 México, DF
Tel: (5) 533-0300

Centro Universitario de Investigaciones
Bibliotecológicas
Universidad Nacional Autónoma de México
Torre II de Humanidades, Piso 12
Cuidad Universitaria
04510 México, DF
Tel: (5) 550-5215
Concerned with dissemination of information to researchers and libraries throughout Mexico. Publishes many books and pamphlets.

Dirección General de Bibliotecas
General Library Administration
Universidad Nacional Autónoma de México
Circuito Interior, Ciudad Universitaria
Apdo. 70-308
04510 México, DF
Tel: (5) 548-9780, 550-5212 Fax: (5) 550-1398
Coordinating body for library activities, provides internal and interlibrary searches, including online and CD-ROM databases.

Instituto de Investigaciones Electricas
Apdo. 5-849
11590 México, DF
Tel: (5) 208-5949 Fax: (5) 271-6172

Instituto Tecnológico y de Estudios Superiores de Monterrey Biblioteca
Surcursal de Corresos J
64849 Monterrey, NL
Tel: (83) 58-2000 Fax: (83) 58-8931

National Institute of Nuclear Research
Nuclear Information and Documentation Center
Apdo. 18-1027
11800 México, DF
Tel: (5) 521-9402

United Nations Environment Program Library
Regional Office for Latin America
Presidente Masaryk 29, Piso 5
11570 México, DF

BOOKSTORES

American Bookstore
Avda. Madero 25
06000 México, DF
Tel: (5) 512-7279, 512-7284, 512-0306
Fax: (5) 518-6931

American Bookstore
Avda. Revolución 1570
01020 México, DF
Tel: (5) 550-0162, 548-8901 Fax: (5) 548-6628

Biblos Librería y Papelería
Insurgentes Sur 27
06600 México, DF
Tel: (5) 592-6610, 535-9648 Fax: (5) 546-0326
Specializes in business books.

Central de Publicaciones—Librería Mizrachi
Avda. Juárez 4-B
06050 México, DF
Tel: (5) 512-4380, 510-4231

Gonvill
8 de Julio No. 825
44190 Guadalajara, Jal.
Tel: (3) 614-1946 Fax: (3) 613-2379

Librería Británica
Serapio Rendón 125
Col. San Rafael
06470 México, DF
Tel: (5) 705-0585 Fax: (5) 535-2009

Librería Británica
Coyoacán 1995-A
03330 México, DF
Tel: (5) 604-7443

Librería Ciencias
Avda. Cerro del Agua 274
Col. Copilco Universidad
04360 México, DF
Tel: (5) 658-0714, 554-2555, 658-9005
Specializes in technical and business books, both in Spanish and English

Librería de Porrúa Hermanos y Cía.
Argentina 15
06020 México, DF
Tel: (5) 702-4934 Fax: (5) 702-6529 Tlx: 1762040

Librería de Porrúa Hermanos y Cía.
Wholesale Department
Justo Sierra 36
06020 México, DF
Tel: (5) 702-4574
Specializes in French and English books and magazines

Librería Interacadémica
Avda. Sonora 206
Col. Hipódromo
06100 México, DF
Tel: (5) 584-2511, 264-0871 Fax: (5) 264-1701

Libros Internacionales
San Luis Potosí 5
06700 México, DF
Tel: (5) 264-1350

Index

F

U